Praise for *MySQL Cookbook, 4th Edition*

Whether you are struggling to simply log in to your MySQL server, or trying to architect the right replication topology, *MySQL Cookbook* has your back. Sveta and Alkin share their decades of experience helping hundreds of MySQL users complete their everyday tasks.

—*Henrik Ingo, Chief of Staff,*
Engineering, DataStax

MySQL gets better with each release. This update by long-time MySQL experts makes it easier to keep up with the improvements. A valuable resource whether you are a beginner or an experienced user like me.

—*Mark Callaghan, ProUnlimited,*
long-time MySQL contributor

A great learning resource for all MySQL users. Sveta and Alkin have curated a comprehensive list of solutions to problems spanning all aspects of MySQL.

—*Shlomi Noach, database engineer,*
PlanetScale

I recommend this comprehensive book for all MySQL users. Its examples will help both beginners and advanced users of MySQL, and it features excellent chapters about MySQL Shell and JSON.

—*Frederic Descamps, MySQL*
Community Manager, Oracle

Sveta and Alkin walk you through practical examples of things you will need to do as a MySQL developer, operator, or DBA. This wealth of knowledge, distilled and condensed, is a next level "how to" guide for mastering MySQL.

—*Matt Lord, Vitess Maintainer,*
PlanetScale

FOURTH EDITION

MySQL Cookbook

Solutions for Database Developers and Administrators

Sveta Smirnova and Alkin Tezuysal

Beijing · Boston · Farnham · Sebastopol · Tokyo

MySQL Cookbook

by Sveta Smirnova and Alkin Tezuysal

Printed in the United States of America.

Published by O'Reilly Media, Inc., 1005 Gravenstein Highway North, Sebastopol, CA 95472.

O'Reilly books may be purchased for educational, business, or sales promotional use. Online editions are also available for most titles (*http://oreilly.com*). For more information, contact our corporate/institutional sales department: 800-998-9938 or *corporate@oreilly.com*.

Acquisitions Editor: Andy Kwan
Development Editors: Amelia Blevins and Jeff Bleiel
Production Editor: Ashley Stussy
Copyeditor: Piper Editorial Consulting, LLC
Proofreader: Liz Wheeler

Indexer: Sue Klefstad
Interior Designer: David Futato
Cover Designer: Karen Montgomery
Illustrator: Kate Dullea

October 2002:   First Edition
November 2006:   Second Edition
August 2014:   Third Edition
August 2022:   Fourth Edition

Revision History for the Fourth Edition
2022-08-02:   First Release

See *http://oreilly.com/catalog/errata.csp?isbn=9781492093169* for release details.

978-1-492-09316-9

[LSI]

Table of Contents

Foreword... xv

Preface... xvii

1. Using the mysql Client Program... 1
  1.0 Introduction   1
  1.1 Setting Up a MySQL User Account   2
  1.2 Creating a Database and a Sample Table   5
  1.3 Finding mysql Client   7
  1.4 Specifying mysql Command Options   8
  1.5 Executing SQL Statements Interactively   14
  1.6 Executing SQL Statements Read from a File or Program   16
  1.7 Controlling mysql Output Destination and Format   18
  1.8 Using User-Defined Variables in SQL Statements   23
  1.9 Customizing a mysql Prompt   26
  1.10 Using External Programs   28
  1.11 Filtering and Processing Output   29

2. Using MySQL Shell.. 33
  2.0 Introduction   33
  2.1 Connecting to MySQL Server with MySQL Shell   34
  2.2 Selecting the Protocol   37
  2.3 Selecting SQL, JavaScript, or Python Mode   40
  2.4 Running SQL Session   41
  2.5 Running SQL in JavaScript Mode   42
  2.6 Running SQL in Python Mode   44
  2.7 Working with Tables in JavaScript Mode   46
  2.8 Working with Tables in Python Mode   49

2.9 Working with Collections in JavaScript Mode   51
2.10 Working with Collections in Python Mode   54
2.11 Controlling the Output Format   56
2.12 Running Reports with MySQL Shell   60
2.13 Using MySQL Shell Utilities   63
2.14 Using the Admin API to Automate Replication Management   67
2.15 Working with JavaScript Objects   69
2.16 Filling Test Data Using Python's Data Science Modules   73
2.17 Reusing Your Scripts for MySQL Shell   82

3. **MySQL Replication**. **87**
3.0 Introduction   87
3.1 Configuring Basic Replication Between One Source and One Replica   89
3.2 Position-Based Replication in the New Installation Environment   91
3.3 Setting Up a Position-Based Replica of a MySQL Installation that Is
    Already in Use   92
3.4 Setting Up GTID-Based Replication   94
3.5 Configuring a Binary Log Format   98
3.6 Using Replication Filters   100
3.7 Rewriting a Database on the Replica   105
3.8 Using a Multithreaded Replica   107
3.9 Setting Up Circular Replication   109
3.10 Using Multisource Replication   111
3.11 Using a Semisynchronous Replication Plug-In   115
3.12 Using Group Replication   118
3.13 Storing Replication Credentials Securely   123
3.14 Using TLS (SSL) for Replication   124
3.15 Replication Troubleshooting   126
3.16 Using Processlist to Understand Replication Performance   140
3.17 Setting Up Automated Replication   144

4. **Writing MySQL-Based Programs**. **153**
4.0 Introduction   153
4.1 Connecting, Selecting a Database, and Disconnecting   157
4.2 Checking for Errors   172
4.3 Writing Library Files   181
4.4 Executing Statements and Retrieving Results   196
4.5 Handling Special Characters and NULL Values in Statements   210
4.6 Handling Special Characters in Identifiers   220
4.7 Identifying NULL Values in Result Sets   221
4.8 Obtaining Connection Parameters   227
4.9 Resetting the profile Table   237

5. Selecting Data from Tables.................................... **239**

5.0 Introduction   239
5.1 Specifying Which Columns and Rows to Select   240
5.2 Naming Query Result Columns   242
5.3 Sorting Query Results   246
5.4 Removing Duplicate Rows   247
5.5 Working with NULL Values   248
5.6 Writing Comparisons Involving NULL in Programs   251
5.7 Using Views to Simplify Table Access   252
5.8 Selecting Data from Multiple Tables   253
5.9 Selecting Rows from the Beginning, End, or Middle of Query Results   255
5.10 What to Do When LIMIT and the Final Result Require a Different
   Sort Order   258
5.11 Calculating LIMIT Values from Expressions   259
5.12 Combining Two or More SELECT Results   260
5.13 Selecting Results of Subqueries   262

6. Table Management.................................... **265**

6.0 Introduction   265
6.1 Cloning a Table   265
6.2 Saving a Query Result in a Table   266
6.3 Creating Temporary Tables   269
6.4 Generating Unique Table Names   271
6.5 Checking or Changing a Table Storage Engine   272
6.6 Copying a Table Using mysqldump   273
6.7 Copying an InnoDB Table Using Transportable Tablespaces   276
6.8 Copying a MyISAM Table Using an sdi File   278

7. Working with Strings.................................... **281**

7.0 Introduction   281
7.1 String Properties   282
7.2 Choosing a String Data Type   286
7.3 Setting the Client Connection Character Set   288
7.4 Writing String Literals   291
7.5 Checking or Changing a String's Character Set or Collation   294
7.6 Converting the Lettercase of a String   296
7.7 Comparing String Values   298
7.8 Converting Between Decimal, Octal, and Hexadecimal Formats   301
7.9 Converting Between ASCII, BIT, and Hexadecimal Formats   302
7.10 Pattern Matching with SQL Patterns   305
7.11 Pattern Matching with Regular Expressions   308
7.12 Reversing the String Content   313

7.13 Searching for Substrings   314
7.14 Breaking Apart or Combining Strings   315
7.15 Using Full-Text Searches   318
7.16 Using a Full-Text Search with Short Words   323
7.17 Requiring or Prohibiting Full-Text Search Words   325
7.18 Performing Full-Text Phrase Searches   327

8. Working with Dates and Times. **329**
8.0 Introduction   329
8.1 Choosing a Temporal Data Type   330
8.2 Using Fractional Seconds Support   332
8.3 Changing MySQL's Date Format   335
8.4 Setting the Client Time Zone   339
8.5 Setting the Server Time Zone   341
8.6 Shifting Temporal Values Between Time Zones   342
8.7 Determining the Current Date or Time   344
8.8 Using TIMESTAMP or DATETIME to Track Row-Modification Times   345
8.9 Extracting Parts of Dates or Times   348
8.10 Synthesizing Dates or Times from Component Values   352
8.11 Converting Between Temporal Values and Basic Units   354
8.12 Calculating Intervals Between Dates or Times   358
8.13 Adding Date or Time Values   362
8.14 Calculating Ages   368
8.15 Finding the First Day, Last Day, or Length of a Month   369
8.16 Finding the Day of the Week for a Date   371
8.17 Finding Dates for Any Weekday of a Given Week   372
8.18 Canonizing Not-Quite-ISO Date Strings   375
8.19 Selecting Rows Based on Temporal Characteristics   376

9. Sorting Query Results. **381**
9.0 Introduction   381
9.1 Using ORDER BY to Sort Query Results   382
9.2 Using Expressions for Sorting   385
9.3 Displaying One Set of Values While Sorting by Another   387
9.4 Controlling Case Sensitivity of String Sorts   390
9.5 Sorting in Temporal Order   394
9.6 Sorting by Substrings of Column Values   397
9.7 Sorting by Fixed-Length Substrings   398
9.8 Sorting by Variable-Length Substrings   401
9.9 Sorting Hostnames in Domain Order   405
9.10 Sorting Dotted-Quad IP Values in Numeric Order   408
9.11 Floating Values to the Head or Tail of the Sort Order   410

9.12 Defining a Custom Sort Order   412
9.13 Sorting ENUM Values   413

10. Generating Summaries. 417
10.0 Introduction   417
10.1 Summarizing with COUNT()   419
10.2 Summarizing with MIN() and MAX()   421
10.3 Summarizing with SUM() and AVG()   422
10.4 Using DISTINCT to Eliminate Duplicates   424
10.5 Creating a View to Simplify Using a Summary   426
10.6 Finding Values Associated with Minimum and Maximum Values   426
10.7 Controlling String Case Sensitivity for MIN() and MAX()   429
10.8 Dividing a Summary into Subgroups   430
10.9 Handling NULL Values with Aggregate Functions   434
10.10 Selecting Only Groups with Certain Characteristics   437
10.11 Using Counts to Determine Whether Values Are Unique   438
10.12 Grouping by Expression Results   439
10.13 Summarizing Noncategorical Data   440
10.14 Finding Smallest or Largest Summary Values   443
10.15 Producing Date-Based Summaries   445
10.16 Working with Per-Group and Overall Summary Values Simultaneously   446
10.17 Generating a Report that Includes a Summary and a List   449
10.18 Generating Summaries from Temporary Result Sets   452

11. Using Stored Routines, Triggers, and Scheduled Events. 455
11.0 Introduction   455
11.1 Creating Compound-Statement Objects   458
11.2 Using Stored Functions to Simplify Calculations   460
11.3 Using Stored Procedures to Produce Multiple Values   462
11.4 Using Triggers to Log Changes to a Table   463
11.5 Using Events to Schedule Database Actions   466
11.6 Writing Helper Routines for Executing Dynamic SQL   468
11.7 Detecting "No More Rows" Conditions Using Condition Handlers   470
11.8 Catching and Ignoring Errors with Condition Handlers   472
11.9 Raising Errors and Warnings   473
11.10 Logging Errors by Accessing the Diagnostic Area   474
11.11 Using Triggers to Preprocess or Reject Data   478

12. Working with Metadata. 481
12.0 Introduction   481
12.1 Determining the Number of Rows Affected by a Statement   483
12.2 Obtaining Result Set Metadata   486

12.3 Listing or Checking the Existence of Databases or Tables   496
12.4 Listing or Checking the Existence of Views   497
12.5 Accessing Table Column Definitions   498
12.6 Getting ENUM and SET Column Information   503
12.7 Getting Server Metadata   505
12.8 Writing Applications That Adapt to the MySQL Server Version   507
12.9 Getting Child Tables That Reference a Specific Table via Foreign Key
     Constraints   509
12.10 Listing Triggers   510
12.11 Listing Stored Routines and Scheduled Events   511
12.12 Listing Installed Plug-Ins   513
12.13 Listing Character Sets and Collations   514
12.14 Listing CHECK Constraints   517

13. Importing and Exporting Data. **519**
13.0 Introduction   519
13.1 Importing Data with LOAD DATA and mysqlimport   523
13.2 Specifying Column and Line Delimiters   527
13.3 Dealing with Quotes and Special Characters   529
13.4 Handling Duplicate Key Values   530
13.5 Obtaining Diagnostics About Bad Input Data   531
13.6 Skipping Datafile Lines   533
13.7 Specifying Input Column Order   534
13.8 Preprocessing Input Values Before Inserting Them   534
13.9 Ignoring Datafile Columns   536
13.10 Importing CSV Files   537
13.11 Exporting Query Results from MySQL   538
13.12 Importing and Exporting NULL Values   540
13.13 Exporting Data in SQL Format   542
13.14 Importing SQL Data   544
13.15 Exporting Query Results as XML   545
13.16 Importing XML into MySQL   546
13.17 Importing Data in JSON Format   547
13.18 Importing Data from MongoDB   549
13.19 Exporting Data in JSON Format   550
13.20 Guessing Table Structure from a Datafile   551

14. Validating and Reformatting Data. **555**
14.0 Introduction   555
14.1 Using the SQL Mode to Reject Bad Input Values   556
14.2 Using CHECK Constraints to Reject Invalid Values   558
14.3 Using Triggers to Reject Input Values   560

14.4 Writing an Input-Processing Loop   562
14.5 Putting Common Tests in Libraries   563
14.6 Using Pattern Matching to Validate Data   565
14.7 Using Patterns to Match Broad Content Types   568
14.8 Using Patterns to Match Numeric Values   568
14.9 Using Patterns to Match Dates or Times   570
14.10 Using Patterns to Match Email Addresses or URLs   574
14.11 Using Table Metadata to Validate Data   575
14.12 Using a Lookup Table to Validate Data   578
14.13 Converting Two-Digit Year Values to Four-Digit Form   581
14.14 Performing Validity Checking on Date or Time Subparts   582
14.15 Writing Date-Processing Utilities   584
14.16 Importing Non-ISO Date Values   589
14.17 Exporting Dates Using Non-ISO Formats   590
14.18 Preprocessing and Importing a File   592

15. Generating and Using Sequences.   595
15.0 Introduction   595
15.1 Generating a Sequence with AUTO_INCREMENT Columns   596
15.2 Choosing the Data Type for a Sequence Column   599
15.3 Deleting Rows Without Changing a Sequence   601
15.4 Retrieving Sequence Values   603
15.5 Renumbering an Existing Sequence   607
15.6 Extending the Range of a Sequence Column   610
15.7 Reusing Values at the Top of a Sequence   610
15.8 Ensuring That Rows Are Renumbered in a Particular Order   611
15.9 Sequencing an Unsequenced Table   612
15.10 Managing Multiple Auto-Increment Values Simultaneously   614
15.11 Using Auto-Increment Values to Associate Tables   615
15.12 Using Sequence Generators as Counters   617
15.13 Generating Repeating Sequences   621
15.14 Using Custom Increment Values   622
15.15 Using Window Functions to Number Rows in the Result Set   624
15.16 Generating Series with Recursive CTEs   626
15.17 Creating and Storing Custom Sequences   629

16. Using Joins and Subqueries.   635
16.0 Introduction   635
16.1 Finding Matches Between Tables   636
16.2 Finding Mismatches Between Tables   644
16.3 Identifying and Removing Mismatched or Unattached Rows   649
16.4 Comparing a Table to Itself   652

16.5 Producing Candidate-Detail Lists and Summaries   656
16.6 Enumerating a Many-to-Many Relationship   660
16.7 Finding Per-Group Minimum or Maximum Values   663
16.8 Using a Join to Fill or Identify Holes in a List   666
16.9 Using a Join to Control Query Sort Order   669
16.10 Joining Results of Multiple Queries   671
16.11 Referring to Join Output Column Names in Programs   673

17. Statistical Techniques. 675
17.0 Introduction   675
17.1 Calculating Descriptive Statistics   676
17.2 Calculating Descriptive Statistics for Groups   679
17.3 Generating Frequency Distributions   681
17.4 Counting Missing Values   684
17.5 Calculating Linear Regressions or Correlation Coefficients 686
17.6 Generating Random Numbers   688
17.7 Randomizing a Set of Rows   690
17.8 Selecting Random Items from a Set of Rows   693
17.9 Calculating Successive-Row Differences   694
17.10 Finding Cumulative Sums and Running Averages   696
17.11 Assigning Ranks   701
17.12 Computing Team Standings   704

18. Handling Duplicates. 711
18.0 Introduction   711
18.1 Preventing Duplicates from Occurring in a Table   712
18.2 Having More Than One Unique Key in the Table   714
18.3 Dealing with Duplicates When Loading Rows into a Table 715
18.4 Counting and Identifying Duplicates   720
18.5 Eliminating Duplicates from a Table   724

19. Working with JSON. 729
19.0 Introduction   729
19.1 Choosing the Right Data Type   730
19.2 Inserting JSON Values   731
19.3 Validating JSON   732
19.4 Formatting JSON Values   735
19.5 Extracting Values from JSON   736
19.6 Searching Inside JSON   738
19.7 Inserting New Elements into a JSON Document   739
19.8 Updating JSON   741
19.9 Removing Elements from JSON   742

19.10 Merging Two or More JSON Documents into One   742
19.11 Creating JSON from Relational Data   746
19.12 Converting JSON into Relational Format   748
19.13 Investigating JSON   750
19.14 Working with JSON in MySQL as a Document Store   752

20. Performing Transactions...................................... **761**
20.0 Introduction   761
20.1 Choosing a Transactional Storage Engine   762
20.2 Performing Transactions Using SQL   763
20.3 Performing Transactions from Within Programs   765
20.4 Performing Transactions in Perl Programs   767
20.5 Performing Transactions in Ruby Programs   769
20.6 Performing Transactions in PHP Programs   770
20.7 Performing Transactions in Python Programs   771
20.8 Performing Transactions in Go Programs   771
20.9 Using Context-Aware Functions to Handle Transactions in Go   772
20.10 Performing Transactions in Java Programs   776

21. Query Performance.. **779**
21.0 Introduction   779
21.1 Creating Indexes   781
21.2 Creating a Surrogate Primary Key   783
21.3 Maintaining Indexes   784
21.4 Deciding When a Query Can Use an Index   786
21.5 Deciding the Order for Multiple Column Indexes   787
21.6 Using Ascending and Descending Indexes   789
21.7 Using Function-Based Indexes   792
21.8 Using Indexes on Generated Columns with JSON Data   794
21.9 Using Full Text Indexes   797
21.10 Utilizing Spatial Indexes and Geographical Data   799
21.11 Creating and Using Histograms   803
21.12 Writing Performant Queries   809

22. Server Administration.. **817**
22.0 Introduction   817
22.1 Configuring the Server   817
22.2 Managing the Plug-In Interface   820
22.3 Controlling Server Logging   822
22.4 Rotating or Expiring Logfiles   826
22.5 Rotating Log Tables or Expiring Log Table Rows   828
22.6 Configuring Storage Engines   829

23. Monitoring the MySQL Server... 833
    23.0 Introduction   833
    23.1 Why Monitor the MySQL Server?   834
    23.2 Discovering Sources of MySQL Monitoring Information   840
    23.3 Checking Server Uptime and Progress   844
    23.4 Troubleshooting Server Start Problems   845
    23.5 Determining the IO Utilization of the MySQL Server   846
    23.6 Determining MySQL Thread's CPU Utilization   849
    23.7 Determining if MySQL Has Reached Its Connection Limits   851
    23.8 Verifying That the Buffer Pool Is Sized Properly   853
    23.9 Finding Information About the Storage Engine   856
    23.10 Using the Error Log File to Troubleshoot MySQL Server Crashes   859
    23.11 Slow Query Log File   861
    23.12 Monitoring with the General Query Log   863
    23.13 Using the Binary Log to Identify Changes   865

24. Security... 867
    24.0 Introduction   867
    24.1 Understanding the mysql.user Table   868
    24.2 Managing User Accounts   869
    24.3 Implementing a Password Policy   872
    24.4 Checking Password Strength   874
    24.5 Expiring Passwords   875
    24.6 Assigning Yourself a New Password   876
    24.7 Resetting an Expired Password   877
    24.8 Finding and Removing Anonymous Accounts   878
    24.9 Modifying "Any Host" and "Many Host" Accounts   879
    24.10 Using TLS (SSL)   880
    24.11 Using Roles   883
    24.12 Using Views to Secure Data Access   885
    24.13 Using Stored Routines to Secure Data Modifications   887

Index.. 891

Foreword

MySQL is one of the most pragmatic relational databases that I have come across. It is fast, reliable, and easy to use. You can start off fairly easily with a very small footprint. Yet, it can be deployed at a massive scale. Some of the largest companies in the world run on MySQL. What makes MySQL attractive is that it makes the bread-and-butter features of a relational database work extremely well: these are indexes, joins and transactions. To top it off, it provides all the benefits of being open source.

The recent trend to migrate software to cloud providers has brought a unique momentum to MySQL. This is because some of the complexities associated with managing a relational database are being taken on by the cloud providers. This lets you enjoy all that is good about MySQL without incurring the overhead of having to manage it.

I have known Alkin and Sveta for many years. We have been meeting at various conferences, I have attended many of their sessions, and we have spent time together at many social events. Alkin was also a colleague at PlanetScale where he made substantial contributions to the Vitess project. What is best about Alkin and Sveta? They are both genuine individuals who like to work hard and want to help the community. Also, they have a vast amount of experience and possess a deep knowledge of how to get the best out of MySQL.

You can see their diligence in this book. They spend time making sure that every subject is well introduced. Each chapter reads like a story. But then, at the end, you have learned something extremely valuable. If you are getting started with MySQL, this is a great book. If you come back to this after using MySQL for a bit, you'll discover hidden gems that you've missed before. And finally, the Problem-Solution-Discussion format allows you to quickly find a solution if you run into a specific problem while using MySQL.

If you intend to learn and use MySQL, this is the book for you.

—Sugu Sougoumarane
CTO, PlanetScale
Co-creator, Vitess

Preface

The MySQL database management system is popular for many reasons. It's fast, and it's easy to set up, use, and administer. It runs under many varieties of Unix and Windows, and MySQL-based programs can be written in many languages.

MySQL's popularity raises the need to address questions its users have about how to solve specific problems. That is the purpose of *MySQL Cookbook*: to serve as a handy resource to which you can turn for quick solutions or techniques for attacking particular types of questions that come up when you use MySQL. Naturally, because it's a cookbook, it contains recipes: straightforward instructions you can follow, rather than how to develop your own code from scratch. It's written using a problem-and-solution format designed to be extremely practical and to make the contents easy to read and assimilate. It contains many short sections, each describing how to write a query, apply a technique, or develop a script to solve a problem of limited and specific scope. This book doesn't develop full-fledged, complex applications. Instead, it assists you in developing such applications yourself by helping you get past problems that have you stumped.

For example, a common question is "How can I deal with quotes and special characters in data values when I'm writing queries?" That's not difficult, but figuring out how to do it is frustrating when you're not sure where to start. This book demonstrates what to do; it shows you where to begin and how to proceed from there. This knowledge will serve you repeatedly because after you see what's involved, you'll be able to apply the technique to any kind of data, such as text, images, sound or video clips, news articles, compressed files, or PDF documents. Another common question is "Can I access data from multiple tables at the same time?" The answer is "Yes," and it's easy to do because it's just a matter of knowing the proper SQL syntax. But it's not always clear how until you see examples, which this book gives you. Other techniques that you'll learn from this book include how to do the following:

- Use SQL to select, sort, and summarize rows
- Find matches or mismatches between tables
- Perform transactions
- Determine intervals between dates or times, including age calculations
- Identify or remove duplicate rows
- Use LOAD DATA to read your datafiles properly or find which values in the file are invalid
- Use CHECK constraints to prevent entry of bad data into your database
- Generate sequence numbers to use as unique row identifiers
- Use a view as a "virtual table"
- Write stored procedures and functions, set up triggers that activate to perform specific data-handling operations when you insert or update table rows, and use the Event Scheduler to run queries on a schedule
- Set up replication
- Manage user accounts
- Control server logging

One part of using MySQL is understanding how to communicate with the server—that is, how to use Structured Query Language (SQL; pronounced "sequel"), the language in which queries are formulated. Therefore, one major emphasis of this book is using SQL to formulate queries that answer particular kinds of questions. One helpful tool for learning and using SQL is the mysql client program that is included in MySQL distributions. You can use client interactively to send SQL statements to the server and see the results. This is extremely useful because it provides a direct interface to SQL—so useful, in fact, that the first chapter is devoted to mysql.

But the ability to issue SQL queries alone is not enough. Information extracted from a database often requires further processing or presentation in a particular way. What if you have queries with complex interrelationships, such as when you need to use the results of one query as the basis for others? What if you need to generate a specialized report with very specific formatting requirements? These problems bring us to the other major emphasis of the book—how to write programs that interact with the MySQL server through an application programming interface (API). When you know how to use MySQL from within the context of a programming language, you gain other ways to exploit MySQL's capabilities:

- You can save query results and reuse them later.

- You have full access to the expressive power of a general-purpose programming language. This enables you to make decisions based on the success or failure of a query, or on the content of the rows that are returned, and then tailor the actions taken accordingly.

- You can format and display query results however you like. If you're writing a command-line script, you can generate plain text. If it's a web-based script, you can generate an HTML table. If it's an application that extracts information for transfer to some other system, you might generate a datafile expressed in XML or JSON.

Combining SQL with a general-purpose programming language gives you an extremely flexible framework for issuing queries and processing their results. Programming languages increase your capability to perform complex database operations. But that doesn't mean this book is complex. It keeps things simple, showing how to construct small building blocks using techniques that are easy to understand and easily mastered.

We'll leave it to you to combine these techniques in your own programs, which you can do to produce arbitrarily complex applications. After all, the genetic code is based on only four nucleic acids, but these basic elements have been combined to produce the astonishing array of biological life we see all around us. Similarly, there are only 12 notes in the scale, but in the hands of skilled composers, they are interwoven to produce a rich and endless variety of music. In the same way, when you take a set of simple recipes, add your imagination, and apply them to the database programming problems you want to solve, you can produce applications that perhaps are not works of art but are certainly useful and will help you and others be more productive.

Who This Book Is For

This book will be useful for anybody who uses MySQL, ranging from individuals who want to use a database for personal projects such as a blog or wiki, to professional database and web developers. The book is also intended for people who do not know how to use MySQL but would like to.

If you're new to MySQL, you'll find lots of ways to use it here. If you're more experienced, you're probably already familiar with many of the problems addressed here but may not have had to solve them before and should find the book a great time-saver. Take advantage of the recipes given in the book, and use them in your own programs rather than writing the code from scratch.

The material ranges from introductory to advanced, so if a recipe describes techniques that seem obvious to you, skip it. Conversely, if you don't understand a recipe, set it aside and come back to it later, perhaps after reading some of the other recipes.

What's in This Book

It's very likely when you use this book that you're trying to develop an application but are not sure how to implement certain pieces of it. In this case, you already know what type of problem you want to solve; check the table of contents or the index for a recipe that shows how to do what you want. Ideally, the recipe will be just what you had in mind. Alternatively, you may be able to adapt a recipe for a similar problem to suit the issue at hand. We explain the principles involved in developing each technique so that you can modify it to fit the particular requirements of your own applications.

Another way to approach this book is to just read through it with no specific problem in mind. This can give you a broader understanding of the things MySQL can do, so we recommend that you page through the book occasionally. It's a more effective tool if you know the kinds of problems it addresses.

As you get into later chapters, you'll find recipes that assume a knowledge of topics covered in earlier chapters. This also applies within a chapter, where later sections often use techniques discussed earlier in the chapter. If you jump into a chapter and find a recipe that uses a technique with which you're not familiar, check the table of contents or the index to find where the technique is explained earlier. For example, if a recipe sorts a query result using an ORDER BY clause that you don't understand, turn to Chapter 9, which discusses various sorting methods and explains how they work.

Here's a summary of each chapter to give you an overview of the book's contents.

Chapter 1, "Using the mysql Client Program", describes how to use the standard MySQL command-line client. mysql is often the first or primary interface to MySQL that people use, and it's important to know how to exploit its capabilities. This program enables you to issue queries and see their results interactively, so it's good for quick experimentation. You can also use it in batch mode to execute canned SQL scripts or send its output into other programs. In addition, the chapter discusses other ways to use mysql, such as how to make long lines more readable or generate output in various formats.

Chapter 2, "Using MySQL Shell", introduces the new MySQL command-line client, developed by the MySQL Team for versions 5.7 and newer. mysqlsh is compatible with mysql when it is running in SQL mode but also supports NoSQL in JavaScript and Python programming interfaces. With MySQL Shell, you can run SQL and NoSQL queries and automate many administrative tasks easily.

Chapter 3, "MySQL Replication", describes how to set up and use replication. Some of the content in this chapter is advanced. However, we decided to place it in the beginning of the book, because the replication is necessary for stable MySQL installations that can survive such disasters as corruptions or hardware failures. Practically, any production MySQL installation should use one of the replication setups. While setting up a replication is an administrative task, we believe that all MySQL users need to have knowledge of how the replication works and, as a result, write effective queries that would be performant on both source and replica servers.

Chapter 4, "Writing MySQL-Based Programs", demonstrates the essential elements of MySQL programming: how to connect to the server, issue queries, retrieve the results, and handle errors. It also discusses how to handle special characters and NULL values in queries, how to write library files to encapsulate code for commonly used operations, and various ways to gather the parameters needed for making connections to the server.

Chapter 5, "Selecting Data from Tables", covers several aspects of the SELECT statement, which is the primary vehicle for retrieving data from the MySQL server: specifying which columns and rows you want to retrieve, dealing with NULL values, and selecting one section of a query result. Later chapters cover some of these topics in more detail, but this chapter provides an overview of the concepts on which they depend if you need some introductory background on row selection or don't yet know a lot about SQL.

Chapter 6, "Table Management", covers table cloning, copying results into other tables, using temporary tables, and checking or changing a table's storage engine.

Chapter 7, "Working with Strings", describes how to deal with string data. It covers character sets and collations, string comparisons, dealing with case-sensitivity issues, pattern matching, breaking apart and combining strings, and performing FULLTEXT searches.

Chapter 8, "Working with Dates and Times", shows how to work with temporal data. It describes MySQL's date format and how to display date values in other formats. It also covers how to use MySQL's special TIMESTAMP data type, how to set the time zone, how to convert between different temporal units, how to perform date arithmetic to compute intervals or generate one date from another, and how to perform leap-year calculations.

Chapter 9, "Sorting Query Results", describes how to put the rows of a query result in the order you want. This includes specifying the sort direction, dealing with NULL values, accounting for string case sensitivity, and sorting by dates or partial column values. It also provides examples that show how to sort special kinds of values, such as domain names, IP numbers, and ENUM values.

Chapter 10, "Generating Summaries", shows techniques for assessing the general characteristics of a set of data, such as how many values it contains or its minimum, maximum, and average values.

Chapter 11, "Using Stored Routines, Triggers, and Scheduled Events", describes how to write functions and procedures that are stored on the server side, triggers that activate when tables are modified, and events that execute on a scheduled basis.

Chapter 12, "Working with Metadata", discusses how to get information *about* the data that a query returns, such as the number of rows or columns in the result, or the name and data type of each column. It also shows how to ask MySQL what databases and tables are available or how to determine the structure of a table.

Chapter 13, "Importing and Exporting Data", describes how to transfer information between MySQL and other programs. This includes how to use LOAD DATA, convert files from one format to another, and determine table structure appropriate for a dataset.

Chapter 14, "Validating and Reformatting Data", describes how to extract or rearrange columns in datafiles, check and validate data, and rewrite values such as dates that often come in a variety of formats.

Chapter 15, "Generating and Using Sequences", discusses AUTO_INCREMENT columns, MySQL's mechanism for producing sequence numbers. It shows how to generate new sequence values or determine the most recent value, how to resequence a column, and how to use sequences to generate counters. It also shows how to use AUTO_INCRE MENT values to maintain a master-detail relationship between tables, including pitfalls to avoid.

Chapter 16, "Using Joins and Subqueries", shows how to perform operations that select rows from multiple tables. It demonstrates how to compare tables to find matches or mismatches, produce master-detail lists and summaries, and enumerate many-to-many relationships.

Chapter 17, "Statistical Techniques", illustrates how to produce descriptive statistics, frequency distributions, regressions, and correlations. It also covers how to randomize a set of rows or pick rows at random from the set.

Chapter 18, "Handling Duplicates", discusses how to identify, count, and remove duplicate rows—and how to prevent them from occurring in the first place.

Chapter 19, "Working with JSON", illustrates how to use JSON in MySQL. It covers such topics as validation, searching, and manipulation of JSON data. The chapter also discusses how to use MySQL as a Document Store.

Chapter 20, "Performing Transactions", shows how to handle multiple SQL statements that must execute together as a unit. It discusses how to control MySQL's auto-commit mode and how to commit or roll back transactions.

Chapter 22, "Server Administration", is written for database administrators. It covers server configuration, the plug-in interface, and log management.

Chapter 23, "Monitoring the MySQL Server", illustrates how to monitor and troubleshoot MySQL issues, such as startup or connection failures. It shows how to use MySQL log files, built-in instruments, and standard operating system utilities to get information about the performance of MySQL queries and internal structures.

Chapter 24, "Security", is another administrative chapter. It discusses user account management, including creating accounts, setting passwords, and assigning privileges. It also describes how to implement password policy, find and fix insecure accounts, and expire or unexpire passwords.

MySQL APIs Used in This Book

MySQL programming interfaces exist for many languages, including C, C++, Eiffel, Go, Java, Perl, PHP, Python, Ruby, and Tcl. Given this fact, writing a MySQL cookbook presents authors with a challenge. The book should provide recipes for doing many interesting and useful things with MySQL, but which API or APIs should the book use? Showing an implementation of every recipe in every language results either in covering very few recipes or in a very, very large book! It also results in redundancies when implementations in different languages bear a strong resemblance to one another. On the other hand, it's worthwhile taking advantage of multiple languages, because one is often more suitable than another for solving a particular problem.

To resolve this dilemma, we've chosen a small number of APIs to write the recipes in this book. This makes its scope manageable while permitting latitude to choose from multiple APIs:

- The Perl DBI module
- Ruby, using the Mysql2 gem
- PHP, using the PDO extension
- Python, using the MySQL Connector/Python driver for the DB API
- Go, using the Go-MySQL-Driver for the sql interface
- Java, using the MySQL Connector/J driver for the JDBC interface

Why these languages? Perl is a widely used language that was very popular for writing MySQL programs when the first edition of this book was published and is still used in many applications today. Ruby has an easy-to-use database-access module. PHP is widely deployed, especially on the web. Go is getting very popular lately and replaces other languages, especially Perl, in many MySQL applications. Python and Java each has a significant number of followers.

We believe these languages taken together reflect pretty well the majority of the existing user base of MySQL programmers. If you prefer some language not shown here, be sure to pay careful attention to Chapter 4, to familiarize yourself with the book's primary APIs. Knowing how to perform database operations with the programming interfaces used here will help you translate recipes for other languages.

Version and Platform Notes

Development of the code in this book took place under MySQL 5.7 and 8.0. Because new features are added to MySQL on a regular basis, some examples will not work under older versions. For example, MySQL 5.7 introduces group replication, and MySQL 8.0 introduces CHECK constraints and common table expressions.

We do not assume that you are using Unix, although that is our own preferred development platform. (In this book, *Unix* also refers to Unix-like systems such as Linux and macOS X.) Most of the material here is applicable both to Unix and Windows.

Conventions Used in This Book

This book uses the following font conventions:

Constant width
> Used for program listings, as well as within paragraphs to refer to program elements such as variable or function names, databases, data types, environment variables, statements, and keywords.

Constant width bold
> Used to indicate text that you type when running commands.

Constant width italic
> Used to indicate variable input; you should substitute a value of your own choosing.

Italic
> Used for URLs, hostnames, names of directories and files, Unix commands and options, programs, and occasionally for emphasis.

This element signifies a tip or suggestion.

 This element indicates a warning or caution.

 This element signifies a general note.

Commands often are shown with a prompt to illustrate the context in which they are used. Commands issued from the command line are shown with a $ prompt:

```
$ chmod 600 my.cnf
```

That prompt is one that Unix users are used to seeing, but it doesn't necessarily signify that a command works only under Unix. Unless indicated otherwise, commands shown with a $ prompt generally should work under Windows, too.

If you should run a command under Unix as the root user, the prompt is # instead:

```
# perl -MCPAN -e shell
```

Commands that are specific to Windows use the C:\> prompt:

```
C:\> "C:\Program Files\MySQL\MySQL Server 5.6\bin\mysql"
```

SQL statements that are issued from within the mysql client program are shown with a mysql> prompt and terminated with a semicolon:

```
mysql> SELECT * FROM my_table;
```

For examples that show a query result as you would see it when using mysql, we sometimes truncate the output, using an ellipsis (...) to indicate that the result consists of more rows than are shown. The following query produces many rows of output, from which those in the middle have been omitted:

```
mysql> SELECT name, abbrev FROM states ORDER BY name;
+-----------------+--------+
| name            | abbrev |
+-----------------+--------+
| Alabama         | AL     |
| Alaska          | AK     |
| Arizona         | AZ     |
...
```

```
| West Virginia | WV    |
| Wisconsin     | WI    |
| Wyoming       | WY    |
+---------------+-------+
```

Examples that show only the syntax for SQL statements do not include the mysql> prompt, but they do include semicolons as necessary to make it clearer where statements end. For example, this is a single statement:

```
CREATE TABLE t1 (i INT)
SELECT * FROM t2;
```

But this example represents two statements:

```
CREATE TABLE t1 (i INT);
SELECT * FROM t2;
```

The semicolon is a notational convenience used within mysql as a statement terminator. But it is not part of SQL itself, so when you issue SQL statements from within programs that you write (for example, using Perl or Java), don't include terminating semicolons.

If a statement or a command output is too long and does not fit the book page, we use the symbol ↵ to show that the line was indented to fit:

```
mysql> SELECT 'Mysql: The Definitive Guide to Using, Programming,↵
    -> and Administering Mysql 4 (Developer\'s Library)' AS book;
+--------------------------------------------------------+
| book                                                   |
+--------------------------------------------------------+
| Mysql: The Definitive Guide to Using, Programming,↵
  and Administering Mysql 4 (Developer's Library)        |
+--------------------------------------------------------+
1 row in set (0,00 sec)
```

The MySQL Cookbook Companion GitHub Repository

MySQL Cookbook has a companion GitHub repository (*https://github.com/svetasmir nova/mysqlcookbook*) where you can obtain source code and sample data for examples developed throughout this book, and auxiliary documentation.

Recipe Source Code and Data

The examples in this book are based on source code and sample data from a distribution named recipes available at the companion GitHub repository.

The recipes distribution is the primary source of examples, and references to it occur throughout the book. The distribution is also available as a compressed TAR file (*recipes.tar.gz*) or as a ZIP file (*recipes.zip*). Either distribution format when unpacked creates a directory named *mysqlcookbook-VERSION/recipes*.

Use the `recipes` distribution to save yourself a lot of typing. For example, when you see a CREATE TABLE statement in the book that describes what a database table looks like, you'll usually find a SQL batch file in the *tables* directory that you can use to create the table instead of entering the definition manually. Change location into the *tables* directory and execute the following command, where `filename` is the name of the file containing the CREATE TABLE statement:

```
$ mysql cookbook < filename
```

If you need to specify MySQL username or password options, add them to the command line.

To import all the tables from the `recipes` distribution, use the command:

```
$ mysql cookbook < cookbook.sql
```

The `recipes` distribution contains programs as shown in the book, but in many cases it also includes implementations in additional languages. For example, a script shown in the book using Python may be available in the `recipes` distribution in Perl, Ruby, PHP, Go, or Java as well. This may save you translation effort should you wish to convert a program shown in the book to a different language.

Amazon Review Data (2018)

Amazon-related review data used in Chapter 7, "Working with Strings", can be found at *http://deepyeti.ucsd.edu/jianmo/amazon/index.html* and can be downloaded using this form (*https://forms.gle/A8hBfPxKkKGFCP238*). Justifying recommendations using distantly labeled reviews and fined-grained aspects. Jianmo Ni, Jiacheng Li, Julian McAuley Empirical Methods in Natural Language Processing (EMNLP), 2019.

MySQL Cookbook Companion Documents

Some appendices included in previous *MySQL Cookbook* editions are now available in standalone form at the companion GitHub repository. They provide background information for topics covered in the book.

"Executing Programs from the Command Line" (*https://github.com/svetasmir nova/mysqlcookbook/blob/master/cmdline.md*) provides instructions for executing commands at the command prompt and setting environment variables such as PATH.

Obtaining MySQL and Related Software

To run the examples in this book, you need access to MySQL, as well as the appropriate MySQL-specific interfaces for the programming languages that you want to use. The following notes describe what software is required and where to get it.

If you access a MySQL server run by somebody else, you need only the MySQL client software on your own machine. To run your own server, you need a full MySQL distribution.

To write your own MySQL-based programs, you communicate with the server through a language-specific API. The Perl and Ruby interfaces rely on the MySQL C API client library to handle the low-level client-server protocol. This is also true for the PHP interface, unless PHP is configured to use mysqlnd, the native protocol driver. For Perl and Ruby, you must install the C client library and header files first. PHP includes the required MySQL client support files but must be compiled with MySQL support enabled or you won't be able to use it. The Python, Go, and Java drivers for MySQL implement the client-server protocol directly, so they do not require the MySQL C client library.

You may not need to install the client software yourself—it might already be present on your system. This is a common situation if you have an account with an Internet service provider (ISP) that provides services such as a web server already enabled for access to MySQL.

MySQL

MySQL distributions (*http://dev.mysql.com/downloads*) and documentation (*http:// dev.mysql.com/doc*), including the *MySQL Reference Manual* and *MySQL Shell*, are available online.

If you need to install the MySQL C client library and header files, they're included when you install MySQL from a source distribution, or when you install MySQL using a binary (precompiled) distribution other than an RPM or a DEB binary distribution. Under Linux, you have the option of installing MySQL using RPM or DEB files, but the client library and header files are not installed unless you install the development RPM or DEB. (There are separate RPM or DEB files for the server, the standard client programs, and the development libraries and header files.)

Perl Support

General Perl information is available on the Perl Programming Language website (*http://www.perl.org*).

You can obtain Perl software from the Comprehensive Perl Archive Network (CPAN) (*http://cpan.perl.org*).

To write MySQL-based Perl programs, you need the DBI module and the MySQL-specific DBD module, DBD::mysql.

To install these modules under Unix, let Perl itself help you. For example, to install DBI and DBD::mysql, run the following commands (you'll probably need to do this as root):

```
# perl -MCPAN -e shell
cpan> install DBI
cpan> install DBD::mysql
```

If the last command complains about failed tests, use force install DBD::mysql instead. Under ActiveState Perl for Windows, use the ppm utility:

```
C:\> ppm
ppm> install DBI
ppm> install DBD-mysql
```

You can also use the CPAN shell or ppm to install other Perl modules mentioned in this book.

Once the DBI and DBD::mysql modules are installed, documentation is available from the command line:

```
$ perldoc DBI
$ perldoc DBI::FAQ
$ perldoc DBD::mysql
```

Documentation is also available from the Perl website (*http://dbi.perl.org*).

Ruby Support

The primary Ruby website (*http://www.ruby-lang.org*) provides access to Ruby distributions and documentation.

The Ruby MySQL2 gem is available from RubyGems (*http://www.rubygems.org*).

PHP Support

The primary PHP website (*http://www.php.net*) provides access to PHP distributions and documentation, including PDO documentation.

PHP source distributions include PDO support, so you need not obtain it separately. However, you must enable PDO support for MySQL when you configure the distribution. If you use a binary distribution, be sure that it includes PDO MySQL support.

Python Support

The primary Python website (*http://www.python.org*) provides access to Python distributions and documentation. General documentation for the DB API database access interface is on the Python Wiki (*http://bit.ly/py-wiki*).

For MySQL Connector/Python, the driver module that provides MySQL connectivity for the DB API, distributions, and documentation are available from MySQL

Community Downloads (*http://bit.ly/py-connect*) and MySQL Connector/Python Developer Guide (*http://bit.ly/py-dev-guide*).

Go Support

The primary Go website (*https://go.dev*) provides access to Go distributions and documentation, including the sql package and documentation.

The Go-MySQL-Driver and its documentation are available from the GitHub go-sql-driver/mysql repository (*https://github.com/go-sql-driver/mysql*).

Java Support

You need a Java compiler to build and run Java programs. The `javac` compiler is a part of the Java Development Kit (JDK). If no JDK is installed on your system, versions are available for macOS, Linux, and Windows at Oracle's Java site (*http://www.oracle.com/technetwork/java*). The same site provides access to documentation (including the specifications) for JDBC, servlets, JavaServer Pages (JSP), and the JSP Standard Tag Library (JSTL).

For MySQL Connector/J, the driver that provides MySQL connectivity for the JDBC interface, distributions and documentation are available from MySQL Community Downloads (*http://bit.ly/jconn-dl*) and MySQL Connector/J 8.0 Developer Guide (*http://bit.ly/j-dev-guide*).

Using Code Examples

Supplemental material (code examples, exercises, etc.) is available for download at *https://github.com/svetasmirnova/mysqlcookbook*.

If you have a technical question or a problem using the code examples, please email *bookquestions@oreilly.com*.

This book is here to help you get your job done. In general, if example code is offered with this book, you may use it in your programs and documentation. You do not need to contact us for permission unless you're reproducing a significant portion of the code. For example, writing a program that uses several chunks of code from this book does not require permission. Selling or distributing examples from O'Reilly books does require permission. Answering a question by citing this book and quoting example code does not require permission. Incorporating a significant amount of example code from this book into your product's documentation does require permission.

We appreciate, but do not require, attribution. An attribution usually includes the title, author, publisher, and ISBN. For example: "*MySQL Cookbook, Fourth Edition* by

Sveta Smirnova and Alkin Tezuysal (O'Reilly). Copyright 2022 Sveta Smirnova and Alkin Tezuysal, 978-1-492-09316-9."

If you feel your use of code examples falls outside fair use or the permission given above, feel free to contact us at *permissions@oreilly.com*.

O'Reilly Online Learning

 For more than 40 years, O'Reilly Media has provided technology and business training, knowledge, and insight to help companies succeed.

Our unique network of experts and innovators share their knowledge and expertise through books, articles, and our online learning platform. O'Reilly's online learning platform gives you on-demand access to live training courses, in-depth learning paths, interactive coding environments, and a vast collection of text and video from O'Reilly and 200+ other publishers. For more information, visit *http://oreilly.com*.

How to Contact Us

Please address comments and questions concerning this book to the publisher:

O'Reilly Media, Inc.
1005 Gravenstein Highway North
Sebastopol, CA 95472
800-998-9938 (in the United States or Canada)
707-829-0515 (international or local)
707-829-0104 (fax)

We have a web page for this book, where we list errata, examples, and any additional information. You can access this page at *https://oreil.ly/oreillymysql-ckbk4e*.

Email *bookquestions@oreilly.com* to comment or ask technical questions about this book.

For more information about our books, courses, conferences, and news, see our website at *https://www.oreilly.com*.

Find us on LinkedIn: *https://linkedin.com/company/oreilly-media*

Follow us on Twitter: *https://twitter.com/oreillymedia*

Watch us on YouTube: *https://www.youtube.com/oreillymedia*

Acknowledgments

To each reader, thank you for reading our book. We hope that it serves you well and that you find it useful.

From Paul DuBois, for the Third Edition

Thanks to my technical reviewers, Johannes Schlüter, Geert Vanderkelen, and Ulf Wendel. They made several corrections and suggestions that improved the text in many ways, and I appreciate their help.

Andy Oram prodded me to begin the third edition and served as its editor, Nicole Shelby guided the book through production, and Kim Cofer and Lucie Haskins provided proofreading and indexing.

Thanks to my wife, Karen, whose encouragement and support throughout the writing process means more than I can say.

From Sveta Smirnova and Alkin Tezuysal

Many thanks to our technical reviewers for their invaluable contributions for this book.

Gillian Gunson not only provided comprehensive technical feedback but also showed how our text could be read by people with different backgrounds. Her language suggestions helped us make the recipes easier to read. Her attentiveness to details helped us identify inaccuracies and even potential risk areas that may show up when your database load grows. Gillian also reviewed all code examples and suggested how to make Ruby and Java code more aligned to current standards.

Ege Gunes reviewed all Go language examples to ensure they were aligned with Go's standard style.

Karthik Appigatla, Timur Solodovnikov, Daniel Guzman Burgos, and Vladimir Fedorkov reviewed selected chapters of the book. Their suggested corrections helped us improve the book a great deal.

Andy Kwan invited us to write the fourth edition of this book. Amelia Blevins and Jeff Bleiel were our editors and helped make the book easier to read. Rita Fernando reviewed a few chapters and provided feedback that allowed us to make the book easier to read and be more aligned with O'Reilly standards.

From Sveta Smirnova

I want to thank my colleagues at Percona Support who understood that I needed to work a second shift on the book and allowed me to take time off when needed.

Many thanks to my husband, Serguei Lassounov, who always supports me in all of my professional endeavors.

From Alkin Tezuysal

I want to thank my wife, Aslihan, and my daughters, Ilayda and Lara, for their patience and support when I needed to focus and use family time to write this book.

Many thanks to my colleagues and team at PlanetScale, especially Deepthi Sigireddi, for her extra care and support. Special thanks go to the MySQL community and my friends, and family members as well.

I also want to take a moment to thank Sveta Smirnova for her endless support while coaching me throughout my first book journey.

## CHAPTER 1

Using the mysql Client Program

1.0 Introduction

The MySQL database system uses a client-server architecture. The server, mysqld, is the program that actually manipulates databases. To tell the server what to do, use a client program that communicates your intent by means of statements written in SQL. Client programs are written for diverse purposes, but each interacts with the server by connecting to it, sending SQL statements to have database operations performed, and receiving the results.

Clients are installed locally on the machine from which you want to access MySQL, but the server can be installed anywhere, as long as clients can connect to it. Because MySQL is an inherently networked database system, clients can communicate with a server running locally on your own machine or somewhere on the other side of the planet.

The mysql program is one of the clients included in MySQL distributions. When used interactively, mysql prompts you for a statement, sends it to the MySQL server for execution, and displays the results. mysql can also be used noninteractively in batch mode to read statements stored in files or produced by programs. This enables the use of mysql from within scripts or cron jobs or in conjunction with other applications.

This chapter describes mysql's capabilities so that you can use it more effectively:

- Setting up a MySQL account using the cookbook database
- Specifying connection parameters and using option files
- Executing SQL statements interactively and in batch mode

- Controlling `mysql` output format
- Using user-defined variables to save information

To try the examples shown in this book, you need a MySQL user account and a database. The first two recipes in this chapter describe how to use `mysql` to set those up, based on these assumptions:

- The MySQL server is running locally on your own system
- Your MySQL username and password are `cbuser` and `cbpass`
- Your database is named `cookbook`

If you like, you can violate any of the assumptions. Your server need not be running locally, and you need not use the username, password, or database name that are used in this book. Naturally, in such cases, you must modify the examples accordingly.

Even if you choose not to use `cookbook` as your database name, we recommend that you use a database dedicated to the examples shown here, not one that you also use for other purposes. Otherwise, the names of existing tables may conflict with those used in the examples, and you'll have to make modifications that would be unnecessary with a dedicated database.

Scripts that create the tables used in this chapter are located in the *tables* directory of the `recipes` distribution that accompanies *MySQL Cookbook*. Other scripts are located in the *mysql* directory. To get the `recipes` distribution, see the Preface.

Alternatives to the mysql Program

The `mysql` client is not the only program you can use for executing queries. For example, you might prefer the graphical MySQL Workbench program, which provides a point-and-click interface to MySQL servers. Another popular interface is phpMyAdmin, which enables you to access MySQL through your web browser. Chapter 2 covers MySQL Shell, a powerful command line client that supports SQL, JavaScript, and Python modes for running your queries using both SQL and NoSQL syntaxes. However, please note that if you execute queries other than by using `mysql`, some concepts covered in this chapter may not apply.

1.1 Setting Up a MySQL User Account

Problem

You need an account for connecting to your MySQL server.

Solution

Use CREATE USER and GRANT statements to set up the account. Then use the account name and password to make connections to the server.

Discussion

Connecting to a MySQL server requires a username and password. You may also need to specify the name of the host on which the server is running. If you don't specify connection parameters explicitly, mysql assumes default values. For example, given no explicit hostname, mysql assumes that the server is running on the local host.

If someone else has already set up an account for you and granted you privileges to create and modify the cookbook database, use that account. Otherwise, the following example shows how to use the mysql program to connect to the server and issue the statements that set up a user account with privileges for accessing a database named cookbook. The arguments to mysql include -h localhost to connect to the MySQL server running on the local host, -u root to connect as the MySQL root user, and -p to tell mysql to prompt for a password:

```
$ mysql -h localhost -u root -p
Enter password: ******
Welcome to the MySQL monitor.  Commands end with ; or \g.
Your MySQL connection id is 54117
Server version: 8.0.27 MySQL Community Server - GPL

Copyright (c) 2000, 2021, Oracle and/or its affiliates.

Oracle is a registered trademark of Oracle Corporation and/or its
affiliates. Other names may be trademarks of their respective
owners.

Type 'help;' or '\h' for help. Type '\c' to clear the current input statement.

mysql> CREATE USER 'cbuser'@'localhost' IDENTIFIED BY 'cbpass';
mysql> GRANT ALL ON cookbook.* TO 'cbuser'@'localhost';
Query OK, 0 rows affected (0.09 sec)
mysql> GRANT PROCESS ON *.* to `cbuser`@`localhost` ;
Query OK, 0 rows affected (0,01 sec)
mysql> quit
Bye
```

The PROCESS privilege is required if you need to generate a dump file of your MySQL data. See also Recipe 1.4.

If you attempt to invoke `mysql` and receive an error message that it cannot be found or is an invalid command, that means your command interpreter doesn't know where `mysql` is installed. See Recipe 1.3 for information about setting the PATH environment variable that the interpreter uses to find commands.

In the commands shown, the $ represents the prompt displayed by your shell or command interpreter, and `mysql>` is the prompt displayed by `mysql`. Text that you type is shown in bold. Nonbold text (including the prompts) is program output; don't type any of that.

When `mysql` prints the password prompt, enter the MySQL `root` password where you see the ******; if the MySQL `root` user has no password, just press the Enter (or Return) key at the password prompt. You will see the MySQL welcome prompt, which could be slightly different for the MySQL version you use. Then enter the CREATE USER and GRANT statements as shown.

The `quit` command terminates your `mysql` session. You can also terminate a session by using an `exit` command or (under Unix) by typing Ctrl-D.

To grant the `cbuser` account access to a database other than cookbook, substitute the database name where you see cookbook in the GRANT statement. To grant access for the cookbook database to an existing account, omit the CREATE USER statement and substitute that account for `'cbuser'@'localhost'` in the GRANT statement.

> The MySQL user account record contains two parts: the username and the host. The username is an identifier or the user who is accessing the MySQL server. You can specify anything for this part. The hostname is the IP address or name of the host from which this user will connect to the MySQL server. We discuss the MySQL security model and user accounts in Recipe 24.0.

The hostname part of `'cbuser'@'localhost'` indicates the host *from which* you'll connect to the MySQL server. To set up an account that will connect to a server running on the local host, use `localhost`, as shown. If you plan to connect to the server from another host, substitute that host in the CREATE USER and GRANT statements. For example, if you'll connect to the server from a host named *myhost.example.com*, the statements look like this:

```
mysql> CREATE USER 'cbuser'@'myhost.example.com' IDENTIFIED BY 'cbpass';
mysql> GRANT ALL ON cookbook.* TO 'cbuser'@'myhost.example.com';
```

It may have occurred to you that there's a paradox in the procedure just described: to set up a `cbuser` account that can connect to the MySQL server, you must first connect to the server so that you can execute the CREATE USER and GRANT statements. I'm assuming that you can already connect as the MySQL `root` user because CREATE

USER and GRANT can be used only by a user such as root that has the administrative privileges needed to set up other user accounts. If you can't connect to the server as root, ask your MySQL administrator to create the cbuser account for you.

MySQL Accounts and Login Accounts

MySQL accounts differ from login accounts for your operating system. For example, the MySQL root user and the Unix root user are separate and have nothing to do with each other, even though the username is the same in each case. This means you don't create new MySQL accounts by creating login accounts for your operating system; use CREATE USER and GRANT instead.

After creating the cbuser account, verify that you can use it to connect to the MySQL server. From the host that was named in the CREATE USER statement, run the following command to do this (the host named after -h should be the host where the MySQL server is running):

```
$ mysql -h localhost -u cbuser -p
Enter password: cbpass
```

Now you can proceed to create the cookbook database and tables within it, as described in Recipe 1.2. To make it easier to invoke mysql without specifying connection parameters each time, put them in an option file (see Recipe 1.4).

See Also

For additional information about administering MySQL accounts, see Chapter 24.

1.2 Creating a Database and a Sample Table

Problem

You want to create a database and set up tables within it.

Solution

Use a CREATE DATABASE statement to create the database, a CREATE TABLE statement for each table, and INSERT statements to add rows to the tables.

Discussion

The GRANT statement shown in Recipe 1.1 sets up privileges for accessing the cookbook database but does not create the database. This section shows how to do that and also how to create a table and load it with the sample data used for examples in the following sections. Similar instructions apply for creating other tables used elsewhere in this book.

Connect to the MySQL server as shown at the end of Recipe 1.1, then create the database like this:

```
mysql> CREATE DATABASE cookbook;
```

Now that you have a database, you can create tables in it. First, select cookbook as the default database:

```
mysql> USE cookbook;
```

Then create a simple table:

```
mysql> CREATE TABLE limbs (thing VARCHAR(20), legs INT, arms INT, PRIMARY KEY(thing));
```

And populate it with a few rows:

```
mysql> INSERT INTO limbs (thing,legs,arms) VALUES('human',2,2);
mysql> INSERT INTO limbs (thing,legs,arms) VALUES('insect',6,0);
mysql> INSERT INTO limbs (thing,legs,arms) VALUES('squid',0,10);
mysql> INSERT INTO limbs (thing,legs,arms) VALUES('fish',0,0);
mysql> INSERT INTO limbs (thing,legs,arms) VALUES('centipede',99,0);
mysql> INSERT INTO limbs (thing,legs,arms) VALUES('table',4,0);
mysql> INSERT INTO limbs (thing,legs,arms) VALUES('armchair',4,2);
mysql> INSERT INTO limbs (thing,legs,arms) VALUES('phonograph',0,1);
mysql> INSERT INTO limbs (thing,legs,arms) VALUES('tripod',3,0);
mysql> INSERT INTO limbs (thing,legs,arms) VALUES('Peg Leg Pete',1,2);
mysql> INSERT INTO limbs (thing,legs,arms) VALUES('space alien',NULL,NULL);
```

To enter the INSERT statements more easily, after entering the first one, press the up arrow to recall it, press Backspace (or Delete) a few times to erase characters back to the last open parenthesis, then type the data values for the next statement. Or, to avoid typing the INSERT statements altogether, skip ahead to Recipe 1.6.

The table you just created is named limbs and contains three columns to record the number of legs and arms possessed by various life forms and objects. The physiology of the alien in the last row is such that the proper values for the arms and legs columns cannot be determined; NULL indicates "unknown value."

The PRIMARY KEY clause defines the primary key that uniquely identifies the table row. This prevents inserting ambiguous data into the table and also helps MySQL to perform queries faster. We discuss ambiguous data in Chapter 18 and performance issues in Chapter 21.

Verify that the rows were added to the `limbs` table by executing a `SELECT` statement:

```
mysql> SELECT * FROM limbs;
+--------------+------+------+
| thing        | legs | arms |
+--------------+------+------+
| human        |    2 |    2 |
| insect       |    6 |    0 |
| squid        |    0 |   10 |
| fish         |    0 |    0 |
| centipede    |   99 |    0 |
| table        |    4 |    0 |
| armchair     |    4 |    2 |
| phonograph   |    0 |    1 |
| tripod       |    3 |    0 |
| Peg Leg Pete |    1 |    2 |
| space alien  | NULL | NULL |
+--------------+------+------+
11 rows in set (0,01 sec)
```

At this point, you're all set up with a database and a table. For additional information about executing SQL statements, see Recipes 1.5 and 1.6.

In this book, statements show SQL keywords such as `SELECT` or `INSERT` in uppercase for distinctiveness. That's only a typographical convention; keywords can be any letter case.

1.3 Finding mysql Client

Problem

When you invoke `mysql` client from the command line, your command interpreter can't find it.

Solution

Add the directory where `mysql` is installed to your `PATH` setting. Then you can run `mysql` from any directory easily.

Discussion

If your shell or command interpreter can't find `mysql` when you invoke it, you'll see some sort of error message. It might look like this under Unix:

```
$ mysql
mysql: Command not found.
```

Or like this under Windows:

```
C:\> mysql.exe
'mysql.exe' is not recognized as an internal or external command,↵
operable program or batch file.
```

One way to tell your command interpreter where to find mysql is to type its full pathname each time you run it. The command might look like this under Unix:

```
$ /usr/local/mysql/bin/mysql
```

Or like this under Windows:

```
C:\> "C:\Program Files\MySQL\MySQL Server 8.0\bin\mysql"
```

Typing long pathnames gets tiresome pretty quickly. You can avoid doing so by changing location into the directory where mysql is installed before you run it. But if you do that, you may be tempted to put all your datafiles and SQL batch files in the same directory as mysql, thus unnecessarily cluttering up a location intended only for programs.

A better solution is to modify your PATH search-path environment variable, which specifies directories where the command interpreter looks for commands. Add to the PATH value the directory where mysql is installed. Then you can invoke mysql from any location by entering only its name, which eliminates pathname typing. For instructions on setting your PATH variable, read "Executing Programs from the Command Line" (*https://github.com/svetasmirnova/mysqlcookbook/blob/master/cmdline.md*) on the companion GitHub repository (see the Preface).

On Windows, another way to avoid typing the pathname or changing into the mysql directory is to create a shortcut and place it in a more convenient location, such as the desktop. This makes it easy to start mysql simply by opening the shortcut. To specify command options or the startup directory, edit the shortcut's properties. If you don't always invoke mysql with the same options, it might be useful to create one shortcut for each set of options you need. For example, create one shortcut to connect as an ordinary user for general work and another to connect as the MySQL root user for administrative purposes.

1.4 Specifying mysql Command Options

Problem

When you invoke the mysql program without command options, it exits immediately with an error message.

Solution

You must specify connection parameters. Do this on the command line, in an option file, or using a mix of the two.

Discussion

If you invoke mysql with no command options, the result may be an "access denied" error. To avoid that, connect to the MySQL server as shown in Recipe 1.1, using mysql like this:

```
$ mysql -h localhost -u cbuser -p
Enter password: cbpass
```

Each option is the single-dash "short" form: -h and -u to specify the hostname and username, and -p to be prompted for the password. There are also corresponding double-dash "long" forms: --host, --user, and --password. Use them like this:

```
$ mysql --host=localhost --user=cbuser --password
Enter password: cbpass
```

To see all options that mysql supports, use this command:

```
$ mysql --help
```

The way you specify command options for mysql also applies to other MySQL programs such as mysqldump and mysqladmin. For example, to generate a dump file named *cookbook.sql* that contains a backup of the tables in the cookbook database, execute mysqldump like this:

```
$ mysqldump -h localhost -u cbuser -p cookbook > cookbook.sql
Enter password: cbpass
```

Some operations require an administrative MySQL account. The mysqladmin program can perform operations that are available only to the MySQL root account. For example, to stop the server, invoke mysqladmin as follows:

```
$ mysqladmin -h localhost -u root -p shutdown
Enter password:          ← enter MySQL root account password here
```

If the value that you use for an option is the same as its default value, you can omit the option. However, there is no default password. If you like, you can specify the password directly on the command line by using -p*password* (with *no space* between the option and the password) or --password=*password*.

> We don't recommend this because the password is visible to onlookers and, on multiple-user systems, may be discoverable to other users who run tools such as ps that report process information or can read content of your shell history file.

Because the default host is localhost, the same value we've been specifying explicitly, you can omit the -h (or --host) option from the command line:

```
$ mysql -u cbuser -p
```

But suppose that you'd really rather not specify *any* options. How can you get `mysql` to "just know" what values to use? That's easy because MySQL programs support option files:

- If you put an option in an option file, you need not specify it on the command line each time you invoke a given program.
- You can mix command-line and option-file options. This enables you to store the most commonly used option values in a file but override them as desired on the command line.

The rest of this section describes these capabilities.

The Meaning of Localhost in MySQL

One of the parameters you specify when connecting to a MySQL server is the host where the server is running. Most programs treat the hostname *localhost* and the IP address `127.0.0.1` as synonyms for "the local host." Under Unix, MySQL programs behave differently: by convention, they treat the hostname *localhost* specially and attempt to connect to the local server using a Unix domain socket file. To force a TCP/IP connection to the local server, use the IP address `127.0.0.1` (or `::1` if your system is configured to support IPv6) rather than the hostname *localhost*. Alternatively, you can specify a `--protocol=tcp` option to force use of TCP/IP for connecting.

The default port number is 3306 for TCP/IP connections. The pathname for the Unix domain socket varies, although it's often */tmp/mysql.sock*. To name the socket file pathname explicitly for the `mysql` client in the connection string, use `-S file_name` or `--socket=file_name`.

Specifying connection parameters using option files

To avoid entering options on the command line each time you invoke `mysql`, put them in an option file for `mysql` to read automatically. Option files are plain-text files:

- Under Unix, your personal option file is named *.my.cnf* in your home directory. There are also site-wide option files that administrators can use to specify parameters that apply globally to all users. You can use the *my.cnf* file in the */etc* or */etc/mysql* directory, or in the *etc* directory under the MySQL installation directory.
- Under Windows, files you can use include the *my.ini* or *my.cnf* file in your MySQL installation directory (for example, *C:\Program Files\MySQL\MySQL Server 8.0*), your Windows directory (likely *C:\WINDOWS*), or the *C:* directory.

To see the exact list of permitted option-file locations, invoke `mysql --help`.

The following example illustrates the format used in MySQL option files:

```
# general client program connection options
[client]
host     = localhost
user     = cbuser
password = cbpass

# options specific to the mysql program
[mysql]
skip-auto-rehash
pager="/usr/bin/less -i" # specify pager for interactive mode
```

With connection parameters listed in the [client] group as just shown, you can connect as cbuser by invoking mysql with no options on the command line:

```
$ mysql
```

The same holds for other MySQL client programs, such as mysqldump.

The password option is stored in the configuration file in plain text format, and any user who has access to this file can read it. If you want to secure the connection credentials, you should use mysql_config_editor to store them securely.

mysql_config_editor stores connection credentials in a file, named *.mylogin.cnf*, located in your home directory under Unix and in the *%APPDATA%\MySQL* directory under Windows. It supports only the connection parameters host, user, password, and socket. The --login-path option specifies a group under which credentials are stored. The default is [client].

Following is an example of using mysql_config_editor to create an encrypted login file:

```
$ mysql_config_editor set --login-path=client \
> --host=localhost --user=cbuser --password
Enter password: cbpass

# print stored credentials
$ mysql_config_editor print --all
[client]
user = cbuser
password = *****
host = localhost
```

MySQL option files have these characteristics:

- Lines are written in groups (or sections). The first line of a group specifies the group name within square brackets, and the remaining lines specify options associated with the group. The example file just shown has a [client] group and a [mysql] group. To specify options for the server, mysqld, put them in a [mysqld] group.

- The usual option group for specifying client connection parameters is [client]. This group is actually used by all the standard MySQL clients. By listing an option in this group, you make it easier to invoke not only mysql but also other programs such as mysqldump and mysqladmin. Just make sure that any option you put in this group is understood by *all* client programs. Otherwise, invoking any client that does not understand it results in an "unknown option" error.

- You can define multiple groups in an option file. By convention, MySQL clients look for parameters in the [client] group and in the group named for the program itself. This provides a convenient way to list general client parameters that you want all client programs to use, but you can still specify options that apply only to a particular program. The preceding sample option file illustrates this convention for the mysql program, which gets general connection parameters from the [client] group and also picks up the skip-auto-rehash and pager options from the [mysql] group.

- Within a group, write option lines in *name=value* format, where *name* corresponds to an option name (without leading dashes) and *value* is the option's value. If an option takes no value (such as skip-auto-rehash), list the name by itself with no trailing *=value* part.

- In option files, only the long form of an option is permitted, not the short form. For example, on the command line, the hostname can be given using either -h *host_name* or --host=*host_name*. In an option file, only host=*host_name* is permitted.

- Many programs, mysql and mysqld included, have program variables in addition to command options. (For the server, these are called *system variables*; see Recipe 22.1.) Program variables can be specified in option files, just like options. Internally, program variable names use underscores, but in option files, you can write options and variables using dashes or underscores interchangeably. For example, skip-auto-rehash and skip_auto_rehash are equivalent. To set the server's sql_mode system variable in a [mysqld] option group, sql_mode=*value* and sql-mode=*value* are equivalent. (The interchangeability of the dash and underscore also applies for options or variables specified on the command line.)

- In option files, spaces are permitted around the = that separates an option name and value. This contrasts with command lines, where no spaces around = are permitted. If an option value contains spaces or other special characters, you can quote it using single or double quotes. The pager option illustrates this.

- It's common to use an option file to specify options for connection parameters (such as host, user, and password). However, the file can list options that have other purposes. The pager option shown for the [mysql] group specifies the paging program that mysql should use for displaying output in interactive mode.

It has nothing to do with how the program connects to the server. We do not recommend putting `password` into the option file, because it is stored as plain text and could be discovered by users who have filesystem access to the configuration file while not necessary having access to the MySQL installation.

- If a parameter appears multiple times in an option file, the last value found takes precedence. Normally, you should list any program-specific groups following the `[client]` group so that if there is any overlap in the options set by the two groups, the more general options are overridden by the program-specific values.

- Lines beginning with # or ; characters are ignored as comments. Blank lines are ignored, too. # can be used to write comments at the end of option lines, as shown for the `pager` option.

- Options that specify file or directory pathnames should be written using / as the pathname separator character, even under Windows, which uses \ as the pathname separator. Alternatively, write \ by doubling it as \\ (this is necessary because \ is the MySQL escape character in strings).

To find out which options the `mysql` program will read from option files, use this command:

```
$ mysql --print-defaults
```

You can also use the `my_print_defaults` utility, which takes as arguments the names of the option-file groups that it should read. For example, `mysqldump` looks in both the `[client]` and `[mysqldump]` groups for options. To check which option-file settings are in those groups, use this command:

```
$ my_print_defaults client mysqldump
```

Mixing command-line and option-file parameters

It's possible to mix command-line options and options in option files. Perhaps you want to list your username and server host in an option file but would rather not store your password there. That's okay; MySQL programs first read your option file to see what connection parameters are listed there, then check the command line for additional parameters. This means you can specify some options one way and some the other way. For example, you can list your username and hostname in an option file but use a password option on the command line:

```
$ mysql -p
Enter password:        ← enter your password here
```

Command-line parameters take precedence over parameters found in your option file, so to override an option file parameter, just specify it on the command line. For example, you can list your regular MySQL username and password in the option-file for general-purpose use. Then, if you must connect on occasion as the MySQL root user, specify the user and password options on the command line to override the option-file values:

```
$ mysql -u root -p
Enter password:          ← enter MySQL root account password here
```

To explicitly specify "no password" when there is a nonempty password in the option file, use `--skip-password` on the command line:

```
$ mysql --skip-password
```

 From this point on, we'll usually show commands for MySQL programs with no connection-parameter options. We assume that you'll supply any parameters you need, either on the command line or in an option file.

Protecting option files from other users

On a multiple-user operating system such as Unix, protect the option file located in your home directory to prevent other users from reading it and finding out how to connect to MySQL using your account. Use chmod to make the file private by setting its mode to enable access only by yourself. Either of the following commands do this:

```
$ chmod 600 .my.cnf
$ chmod go-rwx .my.cnf
```

On Windows, you can use Windows Explorer to set file permissions.

1.5 Executing SQL Statements Interactively

Problem

You've started mysql. Now you want to send SQL statements to the MySQL server to be executed.

Solution

Just type them in, letting mysql know where each one ends. Alternatively, specify "one-liners" directly on the command line.

Discussion

When you invoke mysql, by default, it displays a mysql> prompt to tell you that it's ready for input. To execute a SQL statement at the mysql> prompt, type it in, add a semicolon (;) at the end to signify the end of the statement, and press Enter. An explicit statement terminator is necessary; mysql doesn't interpret Enter as a terminator because you can enter a statement using multiple input lines. The semicolon is the most common terminator, but you can also use \g ("go") as a synonym for the semicolon. Thus, the following examples are equivalent ways of issuing the same statement, even though they are entered differently and terminated differently:

```
mysql> SELECT NOW();
+---------------------+
| NOW()               |
+---------------------+
| 2014-04-06 17:43:52 |
+---------------------+
mysql> SELECT
    -> NOW()\g
+---------------------+
| NOW()               |
+---------------------+
| 2014-04-06 17:43:57 |
+---------------------+
```

For the second statement, mysql changes the prompt from mysql> to -> to let you know that it's still waiting to see the statement terminator.

The ; and \g statement terminators are not part of the statement itself. They're conventions used by the mysql program, which recognizes these terminators and strips them from the input before sending the statement to the MySQL server.

Some statements generate output lines that are so long they take up more than one line on your terminal, which can make query results difficult to read. To avoid this problem, generate "vertical" output by terminating the statement with \G rather than with ; or \g. The output shows column values on separate lines:

```
mysql> USE cookbook
mysql> SHOW FULL COLUMNS FROM limbs LIKE 'thing'\G
*************************** 1. row ***************************
    Field: thing
     Type: varchar(20)
Collation: utf8mb4_0900_ai_ci
     Null: YES
      Key:
  Default: NULL
    Extra:
Privileges: select,insert,update,references
  Comment:
```

To produce vertical output for all statements executed within a session, invoke mysql with the -E (or --vertical) option. To produce vertical output only for those results that exceed your terminal width, use --auto-vertical-output.

To execute a statement directly from the command line, specify it using the -e (or --execute) option. This is useful for "one-liners." For example, to count the rows in the limbs table, use this command:

```
$ mysql -e "SELECT COUNT(*) FROM limbs" cookbook
+----------+
| COUNT(*) |
+----------+
|       11 |
+----------+
```

To execute multiple statements, separate them with semicolons:

```
$ mysql -e "SELECT COUNT(*) FROM limbs;SELECT NOW()" cookbook
+----------+
| COUNT(*) |
+----------+
|       11 |
+----------+
+---------------------+
| NOW()               |
+---------------------+
| 2014-04-06 17:43:57 |
+---------------------+
```

mysql can also read statements from a file or from another program (see Recipe 1.6).

1.6 Executing SQL Statements Read from a File or Program

Problem

You want mysql to read statements stored in a file so you don't have to enter them manually. Or you want mysql to read the output from another program.

Solution

To read a file, redirect mysql's input, or use the source command. To read from a program, use a pipe.

Discussion

By default, the mysql program reads input interactively from the terminal, but you can feed it statements using other input sources such as a file or program.

For this purpose, MySQL supports batch mode, which is convenient for executing a set of statements on repeated occasions without entering them manually each time. Batch mode makes it easy to set up cron jobs that run with no user intervention.

To create a SQL script for mysql to execute in batch mode, put your statements in a text file. Then invoke mysql and redirect its input to read from that file:

```
$ mysql cookbook < file_name
```

Statements read from an input file substitute for what you'd normally enter interactively by hand, so they must be terminated with ;, \g, or \G, just as if you were entering them manually. Interactive and batch modes do differ in default output format. For interactive mode, the default is the tabular (boxed) format. For batch mode, the default is the tab-delimited format. To override the default, use the appropriate command option (see Recipe 1.7).

SQL scripts also are useful for distributing sets of SQL statements to other people. That is, in fact, how we distribute SQL examples for this book. Many of the examples shown here can be run using script files available in the accompanying recipes distribution (see the Preface). Feed these files to mysql in batch mode to avoid typing statements yourself. For example, when a recipe shows a CREATE TABLE statement that defines a table, you'll usually find a SQL batch file in the recipes distribution that you can use to create (and perhaps load data into) the table. Recall that Recipe 1.2 shows the statements for creating and populating the limbs table. Those statements were shown as you would enter them manually, but the *tables* directory of the recipes distribution includes a *limbs.sql* file that contains statements to do the same thing. The file looks like this:

```
DROP TABLE IF EXISTS limbs;
CREATE TABLE limbs
(
  thing VARCHAR(20),  # what the thing is
  legs  INT,          # number of legs it has
  arms  INT,          # number of arms it has
  PRIMARY KEY(thing)
);

INSERT INTO limbs (thing,legs,arms) VALUES('human',2,2);
INSERT INTO limbs (thing,legs,arms) VALUES('insect',6,0);
INSERT INTO limbs (thing,legs,arms) VALUES('squid',0,10);
INSERT INTO limbs (thing,legs,arms) VALUES('fish',0,0);
INSERT INTO limbs (thing,legs,arms) VALUES('centipede',99,0);
INSERT INTO limbs (thing,legs,arms) VALUES('table',4,0);
INSERT INTO limbs (thing,legs,arms) VALUES('armchair',4,2);
INSERT INTO limbs (thing,legs,arms) VALUES('phonograph',0,1);
INSERT INTO limbs (thing,legs,arms) VALUES('tripod',3,0);
INSERT INTO limbs (thing,legs,arms) VALUES('Peg Leg Pete',1,2);
INSERT INTO limbs (thing,legs,arms) VALUES('space alien',NULL,NULL);
```

To execute the statements in this SQL script file, change location into the *tables* directory of the recipes distribution and run this command:

```
$ mysql cookbook < limbs.sql
```

You'll note that the script contains a statement to drop the table if it exists before creating the table anew and loading it with data. That enables you to experiment with the table, perhaps making changes to it, confident that you can easily restore it to its baseline state any time by running the script again.

The command just shown illustrates how to specify an input file for mysql on the command line. Alternatively, to read a file of SQL statements from within a mysql session, use a source *filename* command (or \. *filename*, which is synonymous):

```
mysql> source limbs.sql
mysql> \. limbs.sql
```

SQL scripts can themselves include source or \. commands to include other scripts. This gives you additional flexibility, but take care to avoid loops.

A file to be read by mysql need not be written by hand; it could be program generated. For example, the mysqldump utility generates database backups by writing a set of SQL statements that re-create the database. To reload mysqldump output, feed it to mysql. For example, you can copy a database over the network to another MySQL server like this:

```
$ mysqldump cookbook > dump.sql
$ mysql -h other-host.example.com cookbook < dump.sql
```

mysql can also read a pipe, so it can take output from other programs as its input. *Any* command that produces output consisting of properly terminated SQL statements can be used as an input source for mysql. The dump-and-reload example can be rewritten to connect the two programs directly with a pipe, avoiding the need for an intermediary file:

```
$ mysqldump cookbook | mysql -h other-host.example.com cookbook
```

Program-generated SQL can also be useful for populating a table with test data without writing the INSERT statements by hand. Create a program that generates the statements, then send its output to mysql using a pipe:

```
$ generate-test-data | mysql cookbook
```

Recipe 6.6 discusses mysqldump further.

1.7 Controlling mysql Output Destination and Format

Problem

You want mysql output to go somewhere other than your screen. And you don't necessarily want the default output format.

Solution

Redirect the output to a file, or use a pipe to send the output to a program. You can also control other aspects of mysql output to produce tabular, tab-delimited, HTML, or XML output; suppress column headers; or make mysql more or less verbose.

Discussion

Unless you send mysql output elsewhere, it goes to your screen. To save output from mysql in a file, use your shell's redirection capability:

```
$ mysql cookbook > outputfile
```

If you run mysql interactively with the output redirected, you can't see what you type, so in this case you usually also read the input from a file (or another program):

```
$ mysql cookbook < inputfile > outputfile
```

To send the output to another program (for example, to parse the output of the query), use a pipe:

```
$ mysql cookbook < inputfile | sed -e "s/\t/:/g" > outputfile
```

The rest of this section shows how to control the mysql output format.

Producing tabular or tab-delimited output

mysql chooses its default output format by whether it runs interactively or noninteractively. For interactive use, mysql writes output to the terminal using the tabular (boxed) format:

```
$ mysql cookbook
mysql> SELECT * FROM limbs WHERE legs=0;
+------------+------+------+
| thing      | legs | arms |
+------------+------+------+
| squid      |    0 |   10 |
| fish       |    0 |    0 |
| phonograph |    0 |    1 |
+------------+------+------+
3 rows in set (0.00 sec)
```

For noninteractive use (when the input or output is redirected), mysql writes tab-delimited output:

```
$ echo "SELECT * FROM limbs WHERE legs=0" | mysql cookbook
thing      legs    arms
squid      0       10
fish       0       0
phonograph 0       1
```

To override the default output format, use the appropriate command option. Consider a sed command, shown earlier, and change its parameters to obfuscate the output:

```
$ mysql cookbook < inputfile | sed -e "s/table/XXXXX/g"

$ mysql cookbook -e "SELECT * FROM limbs where legs=4" | ↵
        sed -e "s/table/XXXXX/g"
 thing legs arms
 XXXXX 4 0
 armchair 4 2
```

Because `mysql` runs noninteractively in that context, it produces tab-delimited output, which could be more difficult to read than tabular output. Use the `-t` (or `--table`) option to produce more readable tabular output:

```
$ mysql cookbook -t -e "SELECT * FROM limbs where legs=4" | ↵
        sed -e "s/table/XXXXX/g"

+----------+------+------+
| thing    | legs | arms |
+----------+------+------+
| XXXXX    |    4 |    0 |
| armchair |    4 |    2 |
+----------+------+------+
```

The inverse operation is to produce batch (tab-delimited) output in interactive mode. To do this, use `-B` (or `--batch`).

Producing HTML or XML output

`mysql` generates an HTML table from each query result set if you use the `-H` (or `--html`) option. This enables you to easily produce output for inclusion in a web page that shows a query result. Here's an example (with line breaks added to make the output easier to read):

```
$ mysql -H -e "SELECT * FROM limbs WHERE legs=0" cookbook
<TABLE BORDER=1>
<TR><TH>thing</TH><TH>legs</TH><TH>arms</TH></TR>
<TR><TD>squid</TD><TD>0</TD><TD>10</TD></TR>
<TR><TD>fish</TD><TD>0</TD><TD>0</TD></TR>
<TR><TD>phonograph</TD><TD>0</TD><TD>1</TD></TR>
</TABLE>
```

The first row of the table contains column headings. If you don't want a header row, see the next section for instructions.

You can save the output in a file, then view it with a web browser. For example, on Mac OS X, do this:

```
$ mysql -H -e "SELECT * FROM limbs WHERE legs=0" cookbook > limbs.html
$ open -a safari limbs.html
```

To generate an XML document instead of HTML, use the `-X` (or `--xml`) option:

```
$ mysql -X -e "SELECT * FROM limbs WHERE legs=0" cookbook
<?xml version="1.0"?>

<resultset statement="select * from limbs where legs=0
">
  <row>
    <field name="thing">squid</field>
    <field name="legs">0</field>
    <field name="arms">10</field>
  </row>

  <row>
    <field name="thing">fish</field>
```

```
    <field name="legs">0</field>
    <field name="arms">0</field>
  </row>

  <row>
    <field name="thing">phonograph</field>
    <field name="legs">0</field>
    <field name="arms">1</field>
  </row>
</resultset>
```

You can reformat XML to suit a variety of purposes by running it through XSLT transforms. This enables you to use the same input to produce many output formats.

The -H, --html -X, and --xml options produce output only for statements that generate a result set, not for statements such as INSERT or UPDATE.

To write your own programs that generate XML from query results, see Recipe 13.15.

Suppressing column headings in query output

The tab-delimited format is convenient for generating datafiles for import into other programs. However, the first row of output for each query lists the column headings by default, which may not always be what you want. Suppose that a program named summarize produces descriptive statistics for a column of numbers. If you produce output from mysql to be used with this program, a column header row would throw off the results because summarize would treat it as data. To create output that contains only data values, suppress the header row with the --skip-column-names option:

```
$ mysql --skip-column-names -e "SELECT arms FROM limbs" cookbook | summarize
```

Specifying the "silent" option (-s or --silent) twice achieves the same effect:

```
$ mysql -ss -e "SELECT arms FROM limbs" cookbook | summarize
```

Specifying the output column delimiter

In noninteractive mode, mysql separates output columns by tabs, and there is no option for specifying the output delimiter. To produce output that uses a different delimiter, postprocess mysql output. Suppose that you want to create an output file for use by a program that expects values to be separated by colon characters (:) rather than tabs. Under Unix, you can convert tabs to arbitrary delimiters by using a utility such as tr or sed. Any of the following commands change tabs to colons (*TAB* indicates where you type a tab character):

```
$ mysql cookbook < inputfile  | sed -e "s/TAB/:/g" > outputfile
$ mysql cookbook < inputfile  | tr "TAB" ":" > outputfile
$ mysql cookbook < inputfile  | tr "\011" ":" > outputfile
```

The syntax differs among versions of tr; consult your local documentation. Also, some shells use the tab character for special purposes such as filename completion. For such shells, type a literal tab into the command by preceding it with Ctrl-V.

sed is more powerful than tr because it understands regular expressions and permits multiple substitutions. This is useful for producing output in something like the comma-separated values (CSV) format, which requires three substitutions:

1. Escape any quote characters that appear in the data by doubling them so that when you use the resulting CSV file, they won't be interpreted as column delimiters.

2. Change the tabs to commas.

3. Surround column values with quotes.

sed permits all three substitutions to be performed in a single command line:

```
$ mysql cookbook < inputfile \
    | sed -e 's/"/""/g' -e 's/TAB/","/g' -e 's/^/"/' -e 's/$/"/' > outputfile
```

That's cryptic, to say the least. You can achieve the same result with other languages that may be easier to read. Here's a short Perl script that does the same thing as the sed command (it converts tab-delimited input to CSV output) and includes comments to document how it works:

```perl
#!/usr/bin/perl
# csv.pl: convert tab-delimited input to comma-separated values output
while (<>)          # read next input line
{
  s/"/""/g;         # double quotes within column values
  s/\t/","/g;       # put "," between column values
  s/^/"/;           # add " before the first value
  s/$/"/;           # add " after the last value
  print;            # print the result
}
```

If you name the script csv.pl, use it like this:

```
$ mysql cookbook < inputfile  | perl csv.pl > outputfile
```

tr and sed normally are unavailable under Windows. Perl may be more suitable as a cross-platform solution because it runs under both Unix and Windows. (On Unix systems, Perl is usually preinstalled. On Windows, it is freely available for you to install.)

Another way to produce CSV output is to use the Perl Text::CSV_XS module, which was designed for that purpose. The cvt_file.pl utility, available in the recipes distribution, uses this module to construct a general-purpose file reformatter.

Controlling mysql's verbosity level

When you run `mysql` noninteractively, not only does the default output format change, but it becomes more terse. For example, `mysql` doesn't print row counts or indicate how long statements took to execute. To tell `mysql` to be more verbose, use `-v` (or `--verbose`), specifying the option multiple times for increasing verbosity. Try the following commands to see how the output differs:

```
$ echo "SELECT NOW()" | mysql
$ echo "SELECT NOW()" | mysql -v
$ echo "SELECT NOW()" | mysql -vv
$ echo "SELECT NOW()" | mysql -vvv
```

The counterparts of `-v` and `--verbose` are `-s` and `--silent`, which also can be used multiple times for increased effect.

1.8 Using User-Defined Variables in SQL Statements

Problem

You want to use a value in one statement that is produced by an earlier statement.

Solution

Save the value in a user-defined variable to store it for later use.

Discussion

To save a value returned by a `SELECT` statement, assign it to a user-defined variable. This enables you to refer to it in other statements later in the same session (but not *across* sessions). User variables are a MySQL-specific extension to standard SQL. They will not work with other database engines.

To assign a value to a user variable within a `SELECT` statement, use `@var_name :=` *value* syntax. The variable can be used in subsequent statements wherever an expression is permitted, such as in a `WHERE` clause or in an `INSERT` statement.

Here is an example that assigns a value to a user variable, then refers to that variable later. This is a simple way to determine a value that characterizes some row in a table, then select that particular row:

```
mysql> SELECT MAX(arms+legs) INTO @max_limbs FROM limbs;
Query OK, 1 row affected (0,01 sec)
mysql> SELECT * FROM limbs WHERE arms+legs = @max_limbs;
+-----------+------+------+
| thing     | legs | arms |
+-----------+------+------+
| centipede |   99 |    0 |
+-----------+------+------+
```

Another use for a variable is to save the result from LAST_INSERT_ID() after creating a new row in a table that has an AUTO_INCREMENT column:

```
mysql> SELECT @last_id := LAST_INSERT_ID();
```

LAST_INSERT_ID() returns the most recent AUTO_INCREMENT value. By saving it in a variable, you can refer to the value several times in subsequent statements, even if you issue other statements that create their own AUTO_INCREMENT values and thus change the value returned by LAST_INSERT_ID(). Recipe 15.10 discusses this technique further.

User variables hold single values. If a statement returns multiple rows, the statement will fail with an error, but the value from the first row is assigned:

```
mysql> SELECT thing FROM limbs WHERE legs = 0;
+------------+
| thing      |
+------------+
| squid      |
| fish       |
| phonograph |
+------------+
3 rows in set (0,00 sec)

mysql> SELECT thing INTO @name FROM limbs WHERE legs = 0;
ERROR 1172 (42000): Result consisted of more than one row
mysql> SELECT @name;
+-------+
| @name |
+-------+
| squid |
+-------+
```

If the statement returns no rows, no assignment takes place, and the variable retains its previous value. If the variable has not been used previously, its value is NULL:

```
mysql> SELECT thing INTO @name2 FROM limbs WHERE legs < 0;
Query OK, 0 rows affected, 1 warning (0,00 sec)

mysql> SHOW WARNINGS;
+---------+------+-------------------------------------------------------+
| Level   | Code | Message                                               |
+---------+------+-------------------------------------------------------+
| Warning | 1329 | No data - zero rows fetched, selected, or processed   |
+---------+------+-------------------------------------------------------+
1 row in set (0,00 sec)

mysql> select @name2;
+--------+
| @name2 |
+--------+
| NULL   |
+--------+
1 row in set (0,00 sec)
```

The SQL SHOW WARNINGS command returns informational messages about recoverable errors, such as assigning an empty result to a variable or the use of a deprecated feature.

To set a variable explicitly to a particular value, use a SET statement. SET syntax can use either := or = as the assignment operator:

```
mysql> SET @sum = 4 + 7;
mysql> SELECT @sum;
+------+
| @sum |
+------+
|   11 |
+------+
```

You can assign a SELECT result to a variable, provided that you write it as a scalar subquery (a query within parentheses that returns a single value):

```
mysql> SET @max_limbs = (SELECT MAX(arms+legs) FROM limbs);
```

User variable names are not case sensitive:

```
mysql> SET @x = 1, @X = 2; SELECT @x, @X;
+------+------+
| @x   | @X   |
+------+------+
| 2    | 2    |
+------+------+
```

User variables can appear only where expressions are permitted, not where constants or literal identifiers must be provided. It's tempting to attempt to use variables for such things as table names, but it doesn't work. For example, if you try to generate a temporary table name using a variable as follows, it fails:

```
mysql> SET @tbl_name = CONCAT('tmp_tbl_', CONNECTION_ID());
mysql> CREATE TABLE @tbl_name (int_col INT);
ERROR 1064 (42000): You have an error in your SQL syntax; ↵
check the manual that corresponds to your MySQL server version for ↵
the right syntax to use near '@tbl_name (int_col INT)' at line 1
```

However, you *can* generate a prepared SQL statement that incorporates @tbl_name, then execute the result. Recipe 6.4 shows how.

SET is also used to assign values to stored program parameters, local variables, and system variables. For examples, see Chapter 11 and Recipe 22.1.

1.9 Customizing a mysql Prompt

Problem

You opened several connections in different terminal windows and want to visually distinguish them.

Solution

Set a mysql prompt to a custom value.

Discussion

You can customize a mysql prompt by providing the --prompt option on start:

```
$ mysql --prompt="MySQL Cookbook> "
MySQL Cookbook>
```

If the client has already been started, you can use the prompt command to change it interactively:

```
mysql> prompt MySQL Cookbook>
PROMPT set to 'MySQL Cookbook> '
MySQL Cookbook>
```

The command prompt, like other mysql commands, supports a short version: \R:

```
mysql> \R MySQL Cookbook>
PROMPT set to 'MySQL Cookbook> '
MySQL Cookbook>
```

To specify the prompt value in the configuration file, put the prompt option under the [mysql] section:

```
[mysql]
prompt="MySQL Cookbook> "
```

Quotes are optional and required only when you want to have special characters, such as a space at the end of the prompt string.

Finally, you can specify a prompt using the environment variable MYSQL_PS1:

```
$ export MYSQL_PS1="MySQL Cookbook> "
$ mysql
MySQL Cookbook>
```

To reset a prompt to its default value, run the prompt command without arguments:

```
MySQL Cookbook> prompt
Returning to default PROMPT of mysql>
mysql>
```

If you used the MYSQL_PS1 environment variable, the prompt default will be the value of the MYSQL_PS1 variable instead of mysql.

The mysql prompt is highly customizable. You can set it to show the current date, time, user account, default database, server host, and other information about your database connection. You will find the full list of supported options in the MySQL User Reference Manual (*https://oreil.ly/e76Zj*).

To have a user account in the prompt, use either the special sequence \u to display just a user name or \U to show the full user account:

```
mysql> prompt \U>
PROMPT set to '\U> '
cbuser@localhost>
```

If you connect to MySQL servers on different machines, you may want to see the MySQL server host name in the prompt. A special sequence, \h, exists just for this:

```
mysql> \R \h>
PROMPT set to '\h> '
Delly-7390>
```

To have the current default database in the prompt, use the special sequence \d:

```
mysql> \R \d>
PROMPT set to '\d> '
(none)> use cookbook
Database changed
cookbook>
```

mysql supports multiple options to include time into the prompt. You can have full date and time information or just part of it:

```
mysql> prompt \R:\m:\s>
PROMPT set to '\R:\m:\s> '
15:30:10>
15:30:10> prompt \D>
PROMPT set to '\D> '
Sat Sep 19 15:31:19 2020>
```

You cannot specify the current day of the month unless you use the full current date. This was reported at MySQL Bug #72071 (*https://oreil.ly/oHJbO*) and is still not fixed.

Special sequences can be combined together and with any other text, mysql uses the UTF-8 character set, and, if your terminal supports UTF-8 too, you can use smiley characters to make your prompt more impressive. For example, to have on hand information about the connected user account, MySQL host, default database, and current time, you can set the prompt to \u@\h [♥\d] (⊘\R:\m:\s)> :

```
mysql> prompt \u@\h [♥\d] (⊘\R:\m:\s)>
PROMPT set to '\u@\h [♥\d] (⊘\R:\m:\s)> '
cbuser@Delly-7390 [♥ cookbook] (⊘ 16:15:41)>
```

1.10 Using External Programs

Problem

You want to use an external program without leaving the mysql client command prompt.

Solution

Use the system command to call a program.

Discussion

While MySQL allows you to generate random passwords for its own internal user accounts, it still does not have an internal function for generating a safe user password for all other cases. Run the system command to use one of the Operating System tools:

```
mysql> system openssl rand -base64 16
p1+iSG9rveeKc6v0+lFUHA==
```

\! is a short version of the system command:

```
mysql> \! pwgen -synBC 16 1
Nu=3dWvrH7o_tWiE
```

pwgen may not be installed on your operating system. You need to install the pwgen package before running this example.

system is a command of the mysql client and is executed locally, using permissions belonging to the client. By default, the MySQL server is running as user mysql, though you can connect using any user account. In this case, you'll be able to access only those programs and files that are permitted for your operating system account. Thus, regular users cannot access the data directory, which belongs to the special user mysqld process is running as:

```
mysql> select @@datadir;
+-----------------+
| @@datadir       |
+-----------------+
| /var/lib/mysql/ |
+-----------------+
1 row in set (0,00 sec)
```

```
mysql> system ls /var/lib/mysql/
ls: cannot open directory '/var/lib/mysql/': Permission denied
mysql> \! id
uid=1000(sveta) gid=1000(sveta) groups=1000(sveta)
```

For the same reason, `system` does not execute any command on the remote server.

You can use any program, specify options, redirect output, and pipe it to other commands. One useful insight the operating system can give you is how much physical resources are occupied by the `mysqld` process and compare it with data collected internally by the MySQL server itself.

MySQL stores information about memory usage in the `Performance Schema` (*https://oreil.ly/BBMN8*). Its companion *sys* schema (*https://oreil.ly/BBMN8*) contains views, allowing you to access this information easily. Particularly, you can find the total amount of allocated memory in human-readable format by querying the `sys.memory_global_total` view:

```
mysql> SELECT * FROM sys.memory_global_total;
+-----------------+
| total_allocated |
+-----------------+
| 253.90 MiB      |
+-----------------+
1 row in set (0.00 sec)

mysql> \! ps -o rss hp `pidof mysqld` | awk '{print $1/1024}'
298.66
```

The chain of the operating system requests statistics about physical memory usage from the operating system and converts it into human-readable format. This example shows that not all allocated memory is instrumented inside the MySQL server.

Note that you need to run `mysql` client on the same machine with your MySQL server for this to work.

1.11 Filtering and Processing Output

 This recipe works only on Unix platforms!

Problem

You want to change the output format of the MySQL client beyond its built-in capabilities.

Solution

Set pager to a chain of commands, filtering output the way you want.

Discussion

Sometimes the formatting capabilities of the mysql client do not allow you to work with the result set easily. For example, the number of returned rows could be too big to fit the screen. Or the number of columns may make the result too wide to comfortably read it on the screen. Standard operating system pagers, such as less or more, allow you to work with long and wide texts more comfortably.

You can specify which pager to use either by providing the --pager option when you start mysql client or by using the pager command and its shorter version, \P. You can specify any argument for the pager.

To tell mysql to use less as a pager, specify the --pager=less option or assign this value interactively. Provide configuration parameters for the command the same way you do when you're working in your favorite shell. In the following example, we specified options -F and -X, so less exits if the result set is small enough to fit the screen and works normally when needed:

```
mysql> pager less -F -X
PAGER set to 'less -F -X'
mysql> SELECT * FROM city;
+----------------+----------------+----------------+
| state          | capital        | largest        |
+----------------+----------------+----------------+
| Alabama        | Montgomery     | Birmingham     |
| Alaska         | Juneau         | Anchorage      |
| Arizona        | Phoenix        | Phoenix        |
| Arkansas       | Little Rock    | Little Rock    |
| California     | Sacramento     | Los Angeles    |
| Colorado       | Denver         | Denver         |
| Connecticut    | Hartford       | Bridgeport     |
| Delaware       | Dover          | Wilmington     |
| Florida        | Tallahassee    | Jacksonville   |
| Georgia        | Atlanta        | Atlanta        |
| Hawaii         | Honolulu       | Honolulu       |
| Idaho          | Boise          | Boise          |
| Illinois       | Springfield    | Chicago        |
| Indiana        | Indianapolis   | Indianapolis   |
| Iowa           | Des Moines     | Des Moines     |
| Kansas         | Topeka         | Wichita        |
| Kentucky       | Frankfort      | Louisville     |
:
mysql> SELECT * FROM movies;
+----+------+---------------------------+
| id | year | movie                     |
+----+------+---------------------------+
|  1 | 1997 | The Fifth Element         |
|  2 | 1999 | The Phantom Menace        |
|  3 | 2001 | The Fellowship of the Ring |
```

```
|  4 | 2005 | Kingdom of Heaven      |
|  5 | 2010 | Red                   |
|  6 | 2011 | Unknown               |
+----+------+-----------------------+
6 rows in set (0,00 sec)
```

You can use pager not only to beautify output but also to run any command that can process text. One common use is to search for a pattern in the data, printed by the diagnostic statement, using grep. For example, to watch only History list length in the long SHOW ENGINE INNODB STATUS output, use \P grep "History list length." Once you are done with the search, reset the pager with the empty pager command or instruct mysql to disable pager and print to STDOUT using nopager or \n:

```
mysql> \P grep "History list length"
PAGER set to 'grep "History list length"'
mysql> SHOW ENGINE INNODB STATUS\G
History list length 30
1 row in set (0,00 sec)

mysql> SELECT SLEEP(60);
1 row in set (1 min 0,00 sec)

mysql> SHOW ENGINE INNODB STATUS\G
History list length 37
1 row in set (0,00 sec)

mysql> nopager
PAGER set to stdout
```

Another useful option during diagnostics is sending output nowhere. For example, to measure the effectiveness of a query, you may want to examine session status variable Handler_*. In this case, you're not interested in the result of the query but only in the output of the following diagnostic command. Even more, you may want to send diagnostic data to professional database consultants but do not want them to see actual query output due to security considerations.

In this case, instruct pager to use a hashing function or to send output to nowhere:

```
mysql> pager md5sum
PAGER set to 'md5sum'
mysql> SELECT 'Output of this statement is a hash';
8d83fa642dbf6a2b7922bcf83bc1d861  -
1 row in set (0,00 sec)

mysql> pager cat > /dev/null
PAGER set to 'cat > /dev/null'
mysql> SELECT 'Output of this statement goes to nowhere';
1 row in set (0,00 sec)

mysql> pager
Default pager wasn't set, using stdout.
mysql> SELECT 'Output of this statement is visible';
```

```
+------------------------------------+
| Output of this statement is visible |
+------------------------------------+
| Output of this statement is visible |
+------------------------------------+
1 row in set (0,00 sec)
```

 To redirect the output of a query, information messages, and all commands you type into a file, use `pager cat > FILENAME`. To redirect to a file and still see the output, use the `tee` command and its short version, `\T`. The built-in `tee` command works on both UNIX and Windows platforms.

You can chain together `pager` commands using pipes. For example, to print the content of the `limbs` table in different font styles, set `pager` to a chain of calls as in the following list:

1. `tr -d ' '` to remove extra spaces
2. `awk -F'|' '{print "+"$2"+\033[3m"$3"\033[0m+\033[1m"$4"\033[0m"$5"+"}'` to add styles to the text
3. `column -s '+' -t'` for nicely formatted output

```
mysql> \P tr -d ' ' | ↵
awk -F'|' '{print "+"$2"+\033[3m"$3"\033[0m+\033[1m"$4"\033[0m"$5"+"}' | ↵
column -s '+' -t
PAGER set to 'tr -d ' ' | ↵
awk -F'|' '{print "+"$2"+\033[3m"$3"\033[0m+\033[1m"$4"\033[0m"$5"+"}' | ↵
column -s '+' -t'
mysql> select * from limbs;

thing        legs  arms

human        2     2
insect       6     0
squid        0     10
fish         0     0
centipede    99    0
table        4     0
armchair     4     2
phonograph   0     1
tripod       3     0
PegLegPete   1     2
spacealien   NULL  NULL

11 rows in set (0,00 sec)
```

## CHAPTER 2

Using MySQL Shell

2.0 Introduction

We discussed the mysql Client Program in Chapter 1. MySQL Shell is the modern alternative client. In addition to SQL, it supports nonrelational syntax for the database queries, also known as NoSQL, via the JavaScript or Python programming interface and provides a set of features to automate routine tasks.

In this chapter, we will discuss how to do the following:

- Connect to MySQL Shell and select the right protocol
- Select the SQL, JavaScript, or Python interface
- Use both SQL and NoSQL syntax
- Control the output format
- Use MySQL Shell's built-in utilities
- Write a script to automate your custom needs
- Use the Admin API
- Reuse your scripts

Although MySQL Shell is a standard tool for certain tasks, it is not included in MySQL packages and needs to be installed separately. You can download it from the MySQL Shell download page (*https://oreil.ly/nz43Q*) or using the standard package manager of your operating system. We won't cover MySQL Shell installation in this book, because it is straightforward.

The MySQL Shell's command name is `mysqlsh`. You can invoke it by typing `mysqlsh` in the terminal.

MySQL Shell supports two protocols: the Classic MySQL protocol (similar to the one the `mysql` client uses) and the new X protocol. The X protocol is a modern protocol that communicates with the MySQL server on a separate port (the default is 33060). It supports both SQL and NoSQL APIs and provides an asynchronous API, allowing clients to send multiple queries to the server without waiting for the result from the previous ones. The X protocol is the preferred way to work with MySQL Shell. It's especially important if you want to use NoSQL features.

2.1 Connecting to MySQL Server with MySQL Shell

Problem

When you invoke `mysqlsh`, it opens a new session but does not connect to any MySQL server.

Solution

Use the `\connect` command inside MySQL Shell, or provide your MySQL server uniform resource identifier (URI) at startup.

Discussion

MySQL Shell allows you to connect to the MySQL server after you start the tool by providing connections options as a command-line parameter. You can also put default connection parameters in a startup script.

MySQL Shell is flexible regarding connection options. You can supply them as a URI or name-value pairs, similar to one that `mysql` client accepts.

URI uses this format:

```
[scheme://][user[:password]@]<host[:port]|socket>[/schema]↵
[?option=value&option=value...]
```

Explanations of the parameters are explained in Table 2-1.

Table 2-1. Connection options in URI

Parameter	Explanation	Default
scheme	A protocol to use. Could be one of `mysql` if you want to use the Classic protocol or `mysqlx` for the X protocol.	`mysqlx`
user	User name to connect as.	Your operating system account.
password	Password	Asks for a password.

Parameter	Explanation	Default
host	Host to connect to.	No default. This is the only *required* parameter unless the socket option is specified.
port	Port to connect to.	3306 for the Classic protocol, and 33060 for the X protocol.
socket	Socket, used for the localhost connection.	You must provide this or the host parameter.
schema	Database schema to connect to.	No value. Do not select any schema.
option	Any additional option you want to use.	No value. Choose any or no option.

So, to connect to the MySQL server on your local machine via an interactive interface, type \connect 127.0.0.1:

```
MySQL  localhost  JS > \connect 127.0.0.1
Creating a session to 'sveta@127.0.0.1'
Please provide the password for 'sveta@127.0.0.1':
Save password for 'sveta@127.0.0.1'? [Y]es/[N]o/Ne[v]er (default No):
Fetching schema names for autocompletion... Press ^C to stop.
Your MySQL connection id is 1066144 (X protocol)
Server version: 8.0.27 MySQL Community Server - GPL
No default schema selected; type \use <schema> to set one.
```

This will create a connection using the X protocol.

 When connecting without specifying a user name, MySQL Shell uses the operating system login. This is why a connection is created for the user sveta and not for the user cbuser that we used everywhere else in the book. We'll cover how to specify the MySQL user account when connecting later.

To exit from the MySQL Shell session, use the \exit or \quit command and its short form, \q:

```
MySQL  JS > \exit
Bye!
```

To connect interactively using a socket, type \c (/var/run/mysqld/mysqld.sock):

```
MySQL  127.0.0.1:33060+ ssl  JS > \c (/var/run/mysqld/mysqld.sock)
Creating a session to 'sveta@/var%2Frun%2Fmysqld%2Fmysqld.sock'
Fetching schema names for autocompletion... Press ^C to stop.
Your MySQL connection id is 1067565
Server version: 8.0.27 MySQL Community Server - GPL
No default schema selected; type \use <schema> to set one.
```

This will create a connection using the Classic protocol. If you want to connect via the socket with the X protocol, use mysqlx_socket. You'll find the value of the mysqlx_socket if you run the following query:

```
mysql> SELECT @@mysqlx_socket;

+-----------------------------+
| @@mysqlx_socket             |
```

```
+-----------------------------+
| /var/run/mysqld/mysqlx.sock |
+-----------------------------+
1 row in set (0,00 sec)
```

The \connect command has a shorter version, \c, that we used in the connection via the socket example. Note the parentheses in the command argument. Without parentheses, the command will fail with a syntax error. Alternatively, you can replace all of the following slash symbols with their URI-encoded value, %2F:

```
MySQL  localhost  JS > \connect /var%2Frun%2Fmysqld%2Fmysqld.sock
Creating a session to 'sveta@/var%2Frun%2Fmysqld%2Fmysqld.sock'
Fetching schema names for autocompletion... Press ^C to stop.
Your MySQL connection id is 1073606
Server version: 8.0.27 MySQL Community Server - GPL
No default schema selected; type \use <schema> to set one.
```

To connect using URI when opening a MySQL Shell session, use the following command:

```
$ mysqlsh mysqlx://cbuser:cbpass@127.0.0.1/cookbook
Please provide the password for 'cbuser@127.0.0.1:33060': ******
Save password for 'cbuser@127.0.0.1:33060'? [Y]es/[N]o/Ne[v]er (default No):
MySQL Shell 8.0.27

Copyright (c) 2016, 2021, Oracle and/or its affiliates.
Oracle is a registered trademark of Oracle Corporation and/or its affiliates.
Other names may be trademarks of their respective owners.

Type '\help' or '\?' for help; '\quit' to exit.
Creating a session to 'cbuser@127.0.0.1:33060/cookbook'
Fetching schema names for autocompletion... Press ^C to stop.
Your MySQL connection id is 1076096 (X protocol)
Server version: 8.0.27 MySQL Community Server - GPL
Default schema `cookbook` accessible through db.
 MySQL  127.0.0.1:33060+ ssl  cookbook  JS >
```

In this case, we specified a user name and a password via the command line and selected cookbook as the default database.

When connecting while invoking the mysqlsh command, you can also specify connection credentials separately, similar to when you connected with the mysql client:

```
$ mysqlsh --host=127.0.0.1 --port=33060 --user=cbuser --schema=cookbook
Please provide the password for 'cbuser@127.0.0.1:33060': ******
MySQL Shell 8.0.22

Copyright (c) 2016, 2020, Oracle and/or its affiliates.
Oracle is a registered trademark of Oracle Corporation and/or its affiliates.
Other names may be trademarks of their respective owners.

Type '\help' or '\?' for help; '\quit' to exit.
Creating a session to 'cbuser@127.0.0.1:33060/cookbook'
Fetching schema names for autocompletion... Press ^C to stop.
Your MySQL connection id is 8738 (X protocol)
Server version: 8.0.22-13 Percona Server (GPL), Release '13', Revision '6f7822f'
```

```
Default schema `cookbook` accessible through db.
 MySQL  127.0.0.1:33060+ ssl  cookbook  JS >
```

If you want to specify the default schema, you need to pass it as a parameter to the configuration option `schema`. Otherwise, `mysqlsh` will treat it as a host name and fail with an error.

Inside MySQL Shell, you can also specify options via named parameters. First, you need to create a dictionary with connection parameters, then pass it as an option to the `connect()` method of the built-in automatically created `shell` object:

```
MySQL  127.0.0.1:33060+ ssl  JS > connectionData={
                            -> "host": "127.0.0.1",
                            -> "user": "cbuser",
                            -> "schema": "cookbook"
                            -> }
                            ->
{
    "host": "127.0.0.1",
    "schema": "cookbook",
    "user": "cbuser"
}
 MySQL  127.0.0.1:33060+ ssl  JS > shell.connect(connectionData)
Creating a session to 'cbuser@127.0.0.1/cookbook'
Please provide the password for 'cbuser@127.0.0.1': ******
Save password for 'cbuser@127.0.0.1'? [Y]es/[N]o/Ne[v]er (default No):
Fetching schema names for autocompletion... Press ^C to stop.
Your MySQL connection id is 1077318 (X protocol)
Server version: 8.0.27 MySQL Community Server - GPL
Default schema `cookbook` accessible through db.
<Session:cbuser@127.0.0.1:33060>
 MySQL  127.0.0.1:33060+ ssl  cookbook  JS >
```

See Also

For additional information about how to connect to the MySQL server via MySQL Shell, see "MySQL Shell Connections" (*https://oreil.ly/A1E1w*).

2.2 Selecting the Protocol

Problem

You don't want to use MySQL Shell's default, and you want to select either the X protocol or the Classic protocol yourself.

Solution

To select the X protocol, use the `mysqlx`, `mx`, or `sqlx` option. To select the Classic protocol, use the `mysql`, `mc`, and `sqlc` options.

Discussion

MySQL Shell selects the protocol automatically using connection options and server response. If a port or socket option is not used, it tries to connect using a default port or socket for the X protocol. If that's not available, it defaults to the Classic protocol. If you want to avoid this, or if you simply want to control which protocol to use explicitly, you can specify it by passing the mysqlx, mx, and sqlx options when starting the mysqlsh client to select the X protocol, and the mysql, mc, and sqlc options to select the Classic protocol:

```
$ mysqlsh --host=127.0.0.1 --user=cbuser --schema=cookbook --mysqlx
Please provide the password for 'cbuser@127.0.0.1': ******
MySQL Shell 8.0.22
...
Your MySQL connection id is 9143 (X protocol)

$ mysqlsh --host=127.0.0.1 --user=cbuser --schema=cookbook --mysql
Please provide the password for 'cbuser@127.0.0.1': ******
MySQL Shell 8.0.22
...
Creating a Classic session to 'cbuser@127.0.0.1/cookbook'
```

Inside MySQL Shell, when opening a new connection, specify the value for the scheme key when passing options to the connectionData dictionary:

```
MySQL  127.0.0.1:3306 ssl  cookbook  JS > connectionData={
                            ->     "scheme": "mysql", "host": "127.0.0.1",
                            ->     "user": "cbuser", "schema": "cookbook"
                            -> }
{
    "host": "127.0.0.1",
    "schema": "cookbook",
    "scheme": "mysql",
    "user": "cbuser"
}
 MySQL  127.0.0.1:3306 ssl  cookbook  JS > shell.connect(connectionData, "cbpass")
Creating a Classic session to 'cbuser@127.0.0.1/cookbook'
```

In both cases, when specifying a URI, you can prefix connection options by the scheme:

```
mysqlsh mysqlx://cbuser:cbpass@127.0.0.1/cookbook
```

```
\c mysql://cbuser:cbpass@127.0.0.1/cookbook
```

If the specified protocol could not be used, MySQL Shell will fail with an error:

```
 MySQL  JS > \c mysql://cbuser:cbpass@127.0.0.1:33060/cookbook
Creating a Classic session to 'cbuser@127.0.0.1:33060/cookbook'
MySQL Error 2007 (HY000): Protocol mismatch; server version = 11, client version = 10

$ mysqlsh --host=127.0.0.1 --port=3306 --user=cbuser --schema=cookbook --mx
Please provide the password for 'cbuser@127.0.0.1:3306': ******
MySQL Shell 8.0.22

Copyright (c) 2016, 2020, Oracle and/or its affiliates.
Oracle is a registered trademark of Oracle Corporation and/or its affiliates.
```

```
Other names may be trademarks of their respective owners.

Type '\help' or '\?' for help; '\quit' to exit.
Creating an X protocol session to 'cbuser@127.0.0.1:3306/cookbook' ↵
MySQL Error 2027: Requested session assumes MySQL X Protocol but '127.0.0.1:3306' ↵
seems to speak the classic MySQL protocol
(Unexpected response received from server, msg-id:10)
```

You can find details of your current MySQL Shell connection by running the
shell.status() command:

```
 MySQL  127.0.0.1:33060+ ssl  cookbook  JS > shell.status()
MySQL Shell version 8.0.22

Connection Id:            61
Default schema:           cookbook
Current schema:           cookbook
Current user:             cbuser@localhost
SSL:                      Cipher in use: TLS_AES_256_GCM_SHA384 TLSv1.3
Using delimiter:          ;
Server version:           8.0.22-13 Percona Server (GPL), Release '13', ↵
                          Revision '6f7822f'
Protocol version:         X protocol
Client library:           8.0.22
Connection:               127.0.0.1 via TCP/IP
TCP port:                 33060
Server characterset:      utf8mb4
Schema characterset:      utf8mb4
Client characterset:      utf8mb4
Conn. characterset:       utf8mb4
Result characterset:      utf8mb4
Compression:              Enabled (DEFLATE_STREAM)
Uptime:                   4 min 57.0000 sec
```

MySQL Shell, like MySQL CLI, allows you to customize its prompt.
To do it, you need to edit the prompt.json file, located in the
configuration home of MySQL Shell. This file is in JSON format.
MySQL Shell comes with a good number of custom prompt tem-
plates and the README.prompt file, explaining how to modify the
prompt.

We won't cover in detail how to customize the MySQL Shell user
prompt, but we will remove the host, port, and protocol information from the default prompt, so our examples will take less space
in the book.

The configuration home of the MySQL Shell is either ~/.mysqlsh/
on Unix or %AppData%\MySQL\mysqlsh\ on Windows. You can
overwrite this location if you set the MYSQLSH_USER_CONFIG_HOME
variable. README.prompt and examples are located in the share/
mysqlsh/prompt/ directory under the MySQL Shell installation
root.

See Also

For additional information about `mysqlsh` command options, see "A.1 mysqlsh—The MySQL Shell" (*https://oreil.ly/w01Fg*).

2.3 Selecting SQL, JavaScript, or Python Mode

Problem

MySQL Shell starts in the wrong mode, and you want to select a different mode than the default.

Solution

Use the `sql`, `js`, or `py` options, or switch the mode after starting `mysqlsh`.

Discussion

By default, MySQL Shell starts in JavaScript mode. You can see it by looking at the prompt string:

```
MySQL  cookbook  JS >
```

You can change the default mode by starting with the `--sql` option to select SQL mode or the `--py` option to select Python mode. To select JavaScript mode explicitly at startup, use the `--js` option. You will see that the MySQL Shell client's prompt message will change to the selected mode. Here, we select the Python mode:

```
$ mysqlsh cbuser:cbpass@127.0.0.1/cookbook --py
...
Default schema `cookbook` accessible through db.
 MySQL  cookbook  Py >
```

 For SQL mode, you can explicitly instruct the tool to use not only the desired mode but also the desired protocol with the `sqlx` option to select the X protocol and the `sqlc` option to select the Classic protocol. This could be handy when you connect via the default TCP/IP port.

Inside `mysqlsh`, you can change the processing mode with the `\js`, `\py`, and `\sql` commands to switch to JavaScript, Python, and SQL modes:

```
 MySQL  cookbook  SQL > \js
Switching to JavaScript mode...
 MySQL  cookbook  JS > \py
Switching to Python mode...
 MySQL  cookbook  Py > \sql
Switching to SQL mode... Commands end with ;
 MySQL  cookbook  SQL >
```

2.4 Running SQL Session

Problem

You want to have the functionality of a mysql client, but you don't want to leave MySQL Shell.

Solution

Use SQL mode.

Discussion

With SQL mode, MySQL Shell behaves exactly the same as the mysql client that we described in Chapter 1. You can run queries, control output using the \pager command, edit SQL in the system editor with the \edit command, execute SQL from a file with the \source command, and execute a system shell command with \system. You can view and edit the command-line history.

There is no shortcut, \d, for the delimiter command, but the command itself works:

```
MySQL  cookbook  SQL > delimiter |
MySQL  cookbook  SQL > CREATE PROCEDURE get_client_info()
                   -> BEGIN
                   -> SELECT GROUP_CONCAT(ATTR_NAME, '=', ATTR_VALUE)
                   -> FROM performance_schema.session_account_connect_attrs
                   -> WHERE ATTR_NAME IN ('_client_name', '_client_version');
                   -> END
                   -> |
Query OK, 0 rows affected (0.0163 sec)
 MySQL  cookbook  SQL > delimiter ;
 MySQL  cookbook  SQL > CALL get_client_info();
+-----------------------------------------------+
| GROUP_CONCAT(ATTR_NAME, '=', ATTR_VALUE)      |
+-----------------------------------------------+
| _client_name=libmysql,_client_version=8.0.22  |
+-----------------------------------------------+
1 row in set (0.0017 sec)

Query OK, 0 rows affected (0.0017 sec)
```

There is no tee command. If you want to log query results into a file, set the pager to tee -a <DESIRED LOG FILE LOCATION>. However, it will not log SQL statements. They're available only in the history file.

By default, MySQL Shell does not save history between client sessions. This means that you cannot access your previous commands once you exit the shell. You can overwrite this behavior if you enable the history.autoSave option:

```
MySQL  JS > \option --persist history.autoSave=1
```

2.5 Running SQL in JavaScript Mode

Problem

You're in JavaScript mode but want to execute traditional SQL.

Solution

Use the \sql command, or use the sql() and runSQL() methods that belong to the Session class.

Discussion

JavaScript mode supports the object-oriented style of querying your database. Or, you can run plain SQL.

If you want to run a single SQL statement and get results like you can in the MySQL client without leaving JavaScript mode, use the \sql command. In the following example, we run a plain SQL statement, selecting data from the table limbs for things that have two or more arms:

```
MySQL  cookbook  JS > \sql SELECT * FROM limbs WHERE arms >=2 ORDER BY arms;
Fetching table and column names from `cookbook` for auto-completion...↵
Press ^C to stop.
+--------------+------+------+
| thing        | legs | arms |
+--------------+------+------+
| human        |    2 |    2 |
| armchair     |    4 |    2 |
| Peg Leg Pete |    1 |    2 |
| squid        |    0 |   10 |
+--------------+------+------+
4 rows in set (0.0002 sec)
```

The object-oriented style of running SQL is more flexible and provides more options. To run a single statement, use the runSQL method of the Session class:

```
MySQL  cookbook  JS > session.runSql(
                   > "SELECT * FROM limbs WHERE arms >=2 ORDER BY arms")
+--------------+------+------+
| thing        | legs | arms |
+--------------+------+------+
| human        |    2 |    2 |
| armchair     |    4 |    2 |
```

```
| Peg Leg Pete |      1 |    2 |
| squid        |      0 |   10 |
+--------------+------+------+
4 rows in set (0.0014 sec)
```

 When you connect to MySQL Shell, it creates a default instance of the Session class. It's accessible via the global session object.

The runSQL method supports placeholders: just replace the variable values with the ? sign and pass parameters as an array:

```
MySQL  cookbook  JS > session.runSql("SELECT * FROM limbs ↵
       WHERE arms >= ? AND legs != ? ↵
       ORDER BY arms", [2, 0])
+--------------+------+------+
| thing        | legs | arms |
+--------------+------+------+
| human        |    2 |    2 |
| armchair     |    4 |    2 |
| Peg Leg Pete |    1 |    2 |
+--------------+------+------+
3 rows in set (0.0005 sec)
```

You can combine this method with standard JavaScript syntax and create a script that can do more than just run SQL queries:

```
MySQL  cookbook  JS > for (i = 1;
              ->    i <= session.sql("SELECT MAX(arms) AS maxarms FROM limbs"). ❶
              ->       execute().fetchOne(). ❷
              ->       getField('maxarms'); ❸
              ->    i++) ❹
              -> {
              ->    species=session.sql("SELECT COUNT(*) AS countarms \
              ->                      FROM limbs WHERE arms =?").
              ->                      bind(i).execute(); ❺
              ->    if (species.hasData() && (armscount = species.fetchOne().
              ->       getField('countarms')) > 0 ) ❻
              ->    {
              ->       print("We have " + armscount + " species with " + i + ❼
              ->       (i == 1 ? " arm\n" : " arms\n"));
              ->    }
              -> }
              ->
We have 1 species with 1 arm
We have 3 species with 2 arms
We have 1 species with 10 arms
```

❶ Select the maximum number of arms in the limbs table.

❷ The session.sql.execute() method returns a SqlResult object that has a method, called fetchOne, that returns the first row of the result set.

❸ Since our query is supposed to return one row, we didn't traverse the result set but simply called the getField method, which takes a column name or its alias as a parameter to get the maximum number of arms, stored in the table limbs.

❹ We used this number as a stopping condition for the for loop.

❺ In the loop, we executed queries to get the number of the species with the specified number of arms. We used the sql method and its bind method to bind the value of the loop iterator i to the query.

❻ Check if we received a result and if the number of arms is greater than 0.

❼ If both conditions are true, print the result.

 When you execute the sql or runSQL methods separately, MySQL Shell calls the execute method for them automatically. But if using these methods in more complicated code, like in the loops or multiple-statements blocks, you need to call the execute method explicitly. Otherwise, only the last statement will be executed, and all previous invocations will be ignored.

See Also

For additional information about the MySQL Shell API, see "Shell API" in the advanced MySQL User Reference Manual (*https://oreil.ly/4Sauh*).

2.6 Running SQL in Python Mode

Problem

You're in Python mode but want to execute traditional SQL.

Solution

Use the \sql command or the sql or run_sql methods of the Session class.

Discussion

Just as we saw with JavaScript mode, Python mode also supports the \sql command. You can use it if you want to execute a SQL statement and don't want to do anything with its result.

The following code selects all rows from the table movies:

```
MySQL cookbook Py > \sql SELECT * FROM movies;
+----+------+---------------------------+
| id | year | movie                     |
+----+------+---------------------------+
|  1 | 1997 | The Fifth Element         |
|  2 | 1999 | The Phantom Menace         |
|  3 | 2001 | The Fellowship of the Ring |
|  4 | 2005 | Kingdom of Heaven         |
|  5 | 2010 | Red                       |
|  6 | 2011 | Unknown                   |
+----+------+---------------------------+
6 rows in set (0.0008 sec)
```

Method names in Python mode are slightly different from those in JavaScript mode. Thus, to run a SQL statement, using the `Session` object and binding parameters to it as an array, use the `run_sql` method:

```
MySQL cookbook Py > session.run_sql("SELECT * FROM movies WHERE year < ?",[2000])
+----+------+--------------------+
| id | year | movie              |
+----+------+--------------------+
|  1 | 1997 | The Fifth Element  |
|  2 | 1999 | The Phantom Menace |
+----+------+--------------------+
2 rows in set (0.0009 sec)
```

This example selects all movies created before the year 2000.

You can program in Python as well as in JavaScript. For example, if you want to know the number of movies each actor was featured in as well as years when they starred, join the `movies` table with the `movies_actors` table, then print the result using Python code:

```
MySQL cookbook Py > myres=session.sql("SELECT actor, COUNT(movie) as movies,↵  ❶
                       GROUP_CONCAT(year SEPARATOR ', ') AS years_string,↵
                       COUNT(year) AS years FROM movies_actors ↵
                       GROUP BY actor ORDER BY movies DESC").↵
                       execute().fetch_all()
MySQL cookbook Py > for myrow in myres:  ❷
                 -> print(myrow[0] + " was featured in " + str(myrow[1]) +↵  ❸
                    (" movies" if (myrow[1] > 1) else " movie") + ↵
                    " in " + ("years " if (myrow[3] > 1) else "the year ") +↵
                    myrow[2] + ".")
                 ->
Liam Neeson was featured in 3 movies in the years 2005, 1999, 2011.
Bruce Willis was featured in 2 movies in the years 1997, 2010.
Ian Holm was featured in 2 movies in the years 1997, 2001.
Orlando Bloom was featured in 2 movies in the years 2005, 2001.
Diane Kruger was featured in 1 movie in the year 2011.
Elijah Wood was featured in 1 movie in the year 2001.
Ewan McGregor was featured in 1 movie in the year 1999.
Gary Oldman was featured in 1 movie in the year 1997.
Helen Mirren was featured in 1 movie in the year 2010.
Ian McKellen was featured in 1 movie in the year 2001.
```

❶ Run the query, and fetch all the rows that it returns into a variable, `myres`.

❷ Traverse this variable in a `for...in` loop.

❸ Print the result.

 If you're not familiar with the query syntax yet, don't worry: we'll discuss ways of querying data in Chapter 5 and how to join two or more tables in Recipe 16.0.

See Also

For additional information about the Python MySQL Shell API, use the `\? mysqlx` command inside the Python shell session.

2.7 Working with Tables in JavaScript Mode

Problem

You want to query your tables using the object-oriented style in JavaScript mode.

Solution

Use the `getTable` method to select a table, then the `select`, `count`, `insert`, `update`, and `delete` methods to select, retrieve number of rows, insert, update, or delete from the table.

Discussion

MySQL Shell supports object-oriented syntax for querying and modifying database objects. Thus, to select all rows from the table `limbs`, we can use the `select` method:

```
MySQL  cookbook  JS > session.getDefaultSchema().getTable('limbs').select()
+--------------+------+------+
| thing        | legs | arms |
+--------------+------+------+
| human        |    2 |    2 |
| insect       |    6 |    0 |
| squid        |    0 |   10 |
| fish         |    0 |    0 |
| centipede    |   99 |    0 |
| table        |    4 |    0 |
| armchair     |    4 |    2 |
| phonograph   |    0 |    1 |
| tripod       |    3 |    0 |
| Peg Leg Pete |    1 |    2 |
| space alien  | NULL | NULL |
+--------------+------+------+
11 rows in set (0.0003 sec)
```

In the preceding listing, we first selected the schema using the `getDefaultSchema` method, then selected a table with the `getTable` method, and finally retrieved all rows with `select`.

The `select` method returns the `TableSelect` object that supports methods allowing you to specify the `WHERE` condition, `ORDER BY` and `GROUP BY` clauses, and other features that SQL `SELECT` has. It also supports prepared statements and parameters binding. Thus, to select only those species from the `limbs` table that have four or more legs and order them by number of legs, try the following code:

```
MySQL  cookbook  JS > session.getDefaultSchema().getTable('limbs').select().
                   -> where('legs >= :legs').orderBy('legs').bind('legs', 4)
+-----------+------+------+
| thing     | legs | arms |
+-----------+------+------+
| table     |    4 |    0 |
| armchair  |    4 |    2 |
| insect    |    6 |    0 |
| centipede |   99 |    0 |
+-----------+------+------+
4 rows in set (0.0004 sec)
```

Notice that here we're using named parameters for placeholders instead of question marks like we did when we queried the database with SQL.

The MySQL Shell API also supports methods to insert, update, and delete data in the object-oriented style as well as to start and finish transactions. For instance, if we want to experiment with the `cookbook` database without actually modifying data, we can do so inside a transaction:

```
MySQL  cookbook  JS > limbs = session.getDefaultSchema().getTable('limbs') ❶
<Table:limbs>
MySQL  cookbook  JS > session.startTransaction() ❷
Query OK, 0 rows affected (0.0006 sec)
MySQL  cookbook  JS > limbs.insert('thing', 'legs', 'arms'). ❸
                  -> values('cat', 4, 0).
                  -> values('dog', 2, 2)
                  ->
Query OK, 2 items affected (0.0012 sec)

Records: 2  Duplicates: 0  Warnings: 0
MySQL  cookbook  JS > limbs.count() ❹
13
MySQL  cookbook  JS > limbs.update().set('legs', 4).set('arms', 0).
                  -> where("thing='dog'") ❺
Query OK, 1 item affected (0.0012 sec)

Rows matched: 1  Changed: 1  Warnings: 0
MySQL  cookbook  JS > limbs.select().where("thing='dog'") ❻
```

```
+-------+------+------+
| thing | legs | arms |
+-------+------+------+
| dog   |    4 |    0 |
+-------+------+------+
1 row in set (0.0004 sec)
 MySQL  cookbook  JS > limbs.delete().where("thing='cat'") ➐
Query OK, 1 item affected (0.0010 sec)
 MySQL  cookbook  JS > limbs.count() ➑
12
 MySQL  cookbook  JS > session.rollback() ➒
Query OK, 0 rows affected (0.0054 sec)
 MySQL  cookbook  JS > limbs.count() ➓
11
 MySQL  cookbook  JS > limbs.select().where("thing='dog' or thing='cat'")
Empty set (0.0010 sec)
```

➊ Save the table object for the limbs table into a limbs variable.

➋ Start a transaction, so we can roll back our experiments.

➌ Insert two rows into the limbs table using the insert method, which takes a list
    of columns as a parameter, and the values method, that takes a list of values to
    be inserted as a parameter.

➍ Check the number of rows that now exist in the table.

➎ If you look back to the rows that we inserted, you may notice an error. A dog
    actually has four legs and not two legs and two arms. To fix this mistake, call the
    update method.

➏ The select command confirmed that our changes were applied to the limbs
    table.

➐ Then we figured out that cats and dogs are not always friends with one another,
    and we removed a cat from the table with the delete method.

➑ Confirm that the cat was successfully removed.

➒ Roll back the transaction to restore the table to its initial state.

➓ The count and select methods confirm that the table is in its initial state.

 Since we executed all statements one by one in the interactive
session, we omitted the execute method. This method is required
if you're executing SQL commands in loops or program scripts.

See Also

For additional information about how to work with tables in JavaScript mode, see "Table Class Reference" in the Reference Manual (*https://oreil.ly/l43WN*).

2.8 Working with Tables in Python Mode

Problem

You have tables in your database and want to work with them in Python mode.

Solution

Use the `get_table` method to get the `table` object, then the `select`, `count`, `insert`, `update`, and `delete` methods to select, retrieve number of rows, insert, update, or delete from the table.

Discussion

Like JavaScript, Python supports working with tables in the object-oriented style. Thus, to select all rows from the `movies` table, try the `select` method of the `Table` class:

```
MySQL  cookbook  Py > session.get_schema('cookbook').get_table('movies').select()
+----+------+-----------------------------+
| id | year | movie                       |
+----+------+-----------------------------+
|  1 | 1997 | The Fifth Element           |
|  2 | 1999 | The Phantom Menace          |
|  3 | 2001 | The Fellowship of the Ring  |
|  4 | 2005 | Kingdom of Heaven           |
|  5 | 2010 | Red                         |
|  6 | 2011 | Unknown                     |
+----+------+-----------------------------+
6 rows in set (0.0003 sec)
```

In this example, we used the `get_schema` method, which allows us to select any schema stored in the database to which the session user has been granted access.

Python mode supports methods, allowing you to modify data in the tables as well as transaction statements.

For our examples, we'll save the tables `movies` and `movies_actors` into the variables first:

```
MySQL  cookbook  Py > movies=session.get_schema('cookbook').get_table('movies')
MySQL  cookbook  Py > movies_actors=session.get_schema('cookbook').↵
                      get_table('movies_actors')
```

Then, we'll open a transaction, so our changes will apply either to both tables or to none at all, and we'll insert a movie, *Darkest Hour*, starring Gary Oldman. Finally, we'll commit the transaction:

```
 MySQL  cookbook  Py > session.start_transaction()
Query OK, 0 rows affected (0.0003 sec)
 MySQL  cookbook  Py > movies.insert('year', 'movie').↵
                       values(2017, 'Darkest Hour')
Query OK, 1 item affected (0.0013 sec)
 MySQL  cookbook  Py > movies_actors.insert().↵
                       values(1997, 'Darkest Hour', 'Gary Oldman')
Query OK, 1 item affected (0.0011 sec)
 MySQL  cookbook  Py > session.commit()
Query OK, 0 rows affected (0.0075 sec)
```

To find all movies starring Gary Oldman we'll use a SQL query, because the X API does not support joins:

```
 MySQL  cookbook  Py > session.sql("SELECT * FROM movies ↵
                       JOIN movies_actors USING(movie) WHERE actor = 'Gary Oldman'")
+-------------------+----+------+------+-------------+
| movie             | id | year | year | actor       |
+-------------------+----+------+------+-------------+
| The Fifth Element |  1 | 1997 | 1997 | Gary Oldman |
| Darkest Hour      |  7 | 2017 | 1997 | Gary Oldman |
+-------------------+----+------+------+-------------+
2 rows in set (0.0012 sec)
```

Oops! The year for the movie *Darkest Hour* is not correct in one of the tables. Let's update it:

```
 MySQL  cookbook  Py > session.start_transaction() ❶
Query OK, 0 rows affected (0.0007 sec)
 MySQL  cookbook  Py > movies.update().set('year', 2017).where("movie='Darkest Hour'") ❷
Query OK, 0 items affected (0.0013 sec)

Rows matched: 1  Changed: 0  Warnings: 0
 MySQL  cookbook  Py > movies_actors.update().set('year', 2017).↵ ❸
 where("movie='Darkest Hour'")
Query OK, 1 item affected (0.0012 sec)

Rows matched: 1  Changed: 1  Warnings: 0
 MySQL  cookbook  Py > session.commit() ❹
Query OK, 0 rows affected (0.0073 sec)
 MySQL  cookbook  Py > session.run_sql("SELECT * FROM movies JOIN movies_actors↵ ❺
                       USING(movie) WHERE actor = 'Gary Oldman'")
+-------------------+----+------+------+-------------+
| movie             | id | year | year | actor       |
+-------------------+----+------+------+-------------+
| The Fifth Element |  1 | 1997 | 1997 | Gary Oldman |
| Darkest Hour      |  7 | 2017 | 2017 | Gary Oldman |
+-------------------+----+------+------+-------------+
2 rows in set (0.0005 sec)
```

❶ Start a transaction, so we update either all tables or no tables.

❷ Update the `movies` table.

❸ Update the `movies_actors` table.

❹ Commit the changes.

❺ Confirm that the changes were applied to the table.

If we want to remove our newly inserted movie, we can use the `delete` method:

```
 MySQL  cookbook  Py > session.start_transaction()
Query OK, 0 rows affected (0.0006 sec)
 MySQL  cookbook  Py > movies.delete().where("movie='Darkest Hour'")
Query OK, 1 item affected (0.0012 sec)
 MySQL  cookbook  Py > movies_actors.delete().where("movie='Darkest Hour'")
Query OK, 1 item affected (0.0004 sec)
 MySQL  cookbook  Py > session.commit()
Query OK, 0 rows affected (0.0061 sec)
```

In this example, we also started the transaction first, then called the `delete` method on two tables, and finally committed the transaction.

See Also

For additional information about accessing tables in the object-oriented style while in Python mode, see MySQL Shell's interactive help using the `\?` command.

2.9 Working with Collections in JavaScript Mode

Problem

You have semistructured data and want to use MySQL as a Document Store. You also want to query your data with NoSQL, without leaving the programming style of your preferred language.

Solution

Use the `Collection` object and its methods.

Discussion

MySQL supports not only SQL syntax but also NoSQL. When you use SQL, you query tables, and when you use NoSQL, you query collections. Physically, such collections are stored in tables that have three columns: a generated unique identifier column that is also a primary key, a JSON column that stores the document, and an internal column that stores the JSON schema. You can create a collection by using the `createCollection` method of the Schema class:

```
MySQL cookbook JS > collectionLimbs=session.getCurrentSchema().
                -> createCollection('CollectionLimbs')
<Collection:CollectionLimbs>
```

The preceding code creates the NoSQL `CollectionLimbs` collection.

Collections support schema validation. There is no method to add a schema validation for the existent collection, but we can add the schema when creating the collection:

```
MySQL cookbook JS > session.getCurrentSchema().
                -> dropCollection('collectionLimbs')
                ->
MySQL cookbook JS > schema={
                ->    "$schema": "http://json-schema.org/draft-07/schema",
                ->    "id": "http://example.com/cookbook.json",
                ->    "type": "object",
                ->    "description": "Table limbs as a collection",
                ->    "properties": {
                ->        "thing": {"type": "string"},
                ->        "legs": {
                ->            "anyOf": [{"type": "number"},{"type": "null"}],
                ->            "default": 0
                ->        },
                ->        "arms": {
                ->            "anyOf": [{"type": "number"},{"type": "null"}],
                ->            "default": 0
                ->        }
                ->    },
                ->    "required": ["thing","legs","arms"]
                -> }
                ->
{
    "$schema": "http://json-schema.org/draft-07/schema",
    "description": "Table limbs as a collection",
    "id": "http://example.com/cookbook.json",
    "properties": {
        "arms": {
            "anyOf": [
                {
                    "type": "number"
                },
                {
                    "type": "null"
                }
            ],
            "default": 0
        },
        "legs": {
            "anyOf": [
                {
                    "type": "number"
                },
                {
                    "type": "null"
                }
            ],
            "default": 0
        },
```

```
            "thing": {
                "type": "string"
            }
        },
        "required": [
            "thing",
            "legs",
            "arms"
        ],
        "type": "object"
}
MySQL  cookbook  JS > collectionLimbs=session.getCurrentSchema().
                  -> createCollection('collectionLimbs',
                  -> {"validation": {"level": "strict", "schema": schema}})
                  ->
<Collection:CollectionLimbs>
```

Once the NoSQL collection is created, you can insert, update, delete, and search documents.

For example, to insert documents from the `limbs` table into the `CollectionLimbs` collection, we can use the following code:

```
MySQL  cookbook  JS > {
                  ->    limbs=session.getCurrentSchema().
                  ->       getTable('limbs').select().execute(); ❶
                  ->    while (limb = limbs.fetchOneObject()) { ❷
                  ->      collectionLimbs.add( ❸
                  ->        mysqlx.expr(JSON.stringify(limb)) ❹
                  ->        ).execute(); ❺
                  ->    }
                  -> }
                  ->
Query OK, 1 item affected (0.0049 sec)
```

❶ Select all rows from the `limbs` table.

❷ The `fetchOneObject` method returns a dictionary object.

❸ A dictionary object method cannot be saved in the collection without converting it to the proper JSON object. Therefore, we converted it into a JSON string first, then created an expression out of this string that could be inserted into the collection.

❹ The `add` method inserts a document into the collection.

❺ The `execute` method is required every time we update a database inside script blocks.

We enclosed the code in curly braces because otherwise, if the code is put on multiple lines, MySQL Shell will output the result of `session.getCurrentSchema().getTable('limbs').select().execute()`, and the `limbs` variable will contain only diagnostic messages about the number of rows affected.

Finally, we can examine data just inserted into the `CollectionLimbs` collection:

```
MySQL  cookbook  JS > collectionLimbs.count()
11
MySQL  cookbook  JS > collectionLimbs.find().limit(3)
{
    "_id": "00006002f0650000000000000060",
    "arms": 2,
    "legs": 2,
    "thing": "human"
}
{
    "_id": "00006002f0650000000000000061",
    "arms": 0,
    "legs": 6,
    "thing": "insect"
}
{
    "_id": "00006002f0650000000000000062",
    "arms": 10,
    "legs": 0,
    "thing": "squid"
}
3 documents in set (0.0010 sec)
```

You can also modify and remove documents from your collections. We'll show examples of this in Recipe 2.10.

See Also

For additional information about how to use MySQL with JSON documents and NoSQL, see Chapter 19.

2.10 Working with Collections in Python Mode

Problem

You want to use Document Store and NoSQL in Python mode.

Solution

Use the `Collection` object and its methods.

Discussion

Just as you can in JavaScript mode, you can work with NoSQL in Python mode. The syntax is also similar to JavaScript mode. However, method names follow the naming style recommended for programs written in Python.

Thus, to assign a collection to a variable, use the `get_collection` method of the Schema class:

```
MySQL  cookbook  Py > collectionLimbs=session.get_current_schema().↵
                         get_collection('collectionLimbs')
```

To select documents, use the `find` method:

```
MySQL  cookbook  Py > collectionLimbs.find('legs > 3 and arms > 1')
{
    "_id": "00006002f0650000000000000066",
    "arms": 2,
    "legs": 4,
    "thing": "armchair"
}
1 document in set (0.0010 sec)
```

The `find` method supports arguments that allow you to search for specific documents similar to the syntax of the WHERE clause in SQL. It also allows you to aggregate results and sort them and select specific fields. It does not support joining the collections.

To insert a new document, use the `add` method:

```
MySQL  cookbook  Py > collectionLimbs.add(mysqlx.expr(↵
                         '{"thing": "cat", "legs": 2, "arms": 2}'))
Query OK, 1 item affected (0.0093 sec)
MySQL  cookbook  Py > collectionLimbs.find('thing="cat"')
{
    "_id": "00006002f065000000000000006b",
    "arms": 2,
    "legs": 2,
    "thing": "cat"
}
1 document in set (0.0012 sec)
MySQL  cookbook  Py > collectionLimbs.add(mysqlx.expr(↵
                         '{"thing": "dog", "legs": 2, "arms": 2}'))
Query OK, 1 item affected (0.0086 sec)
```

To modify an existing row, use either the `add_or_replace_one` method or the `modify` method:

```
MySQL  cookbook  Py > collectionLimbs.add_or_replace_one(↵
                         '00006002f065000000000000006b',↵
                         {"thing": "cat", "legs": 4, "arms": 0})
Query OK, 2 items affected (0.0056 sec)
```

The `add_or_replace_one` method takes the document `_id` as the first parameter and a JSON document as the second one. If a document with the specified `_id` is not found, it inserts a new document. If a document with the specified _id is found, it replaces the existing one.

The modify method takes a search condition as an argument and returns an object of the CollectionModify class that supports methods, allowing you to modify parameters such as set. You can chain calls to the set method as many times as needed:

```
MySQL  cookbook  Py > collectionLimbs.modify('thing = "dog"').set("legs", 4).set("arms", 0)
Query OK, 1 item affected (0.0077 sec)

Rows matched: 1  Changed: 1  Warnings: 0
```

To check if we successfully changed the quantity of arms and legs for the newly inserted cat and dog documents, we can use the find method:

```
MySQL  cookbook  Py > collectionLimbs.find('thing in ("dog", "cat")')
{
    "_id": "00006002f0650000000000000006b",
    "arms": 0,
    "legs": 4,
    "thing": "cat"
}
{
    "_id": "00006002f0650000000000000006c",
    "arms": 0,
    "legs": 4,
    "thing": "dog"
}
2 documents in set (0.0013 sec)
```

The remove method deletes documents from the collection:

```
MySQL  cookbook  Py > collectionLimbs.remove('thing in ("dog", "cat")')
Query OK, 2 items affected (0.0119 sec)
MySQL  cookbook  Py > collectionLimbs.find('thing in ("dog", "cat")')
Empty set (0.0011 sec)
MySQL  cookbook  Py > collectionLimbs.count()
11
```

The remove method supports searching conditions similar to the modify and find methods.

See Also

For additional information about using MySQL with JSON documents and NoSQL, see Chapter 19.

2.11 Controlling the Output Format

Problem

You want to print results in a format different from the default.

Solution

Use the configuration option `resultFormat` or the command-line parameters `--result-format`, `--table`, `--tabbed`, `--vertical`, or `--json`.

Discussion

By default, MySQL Shell prints results in a table format, similar to the default format of the `mysql` client. However, this format can be customized.

Inside MySQL Shell, you can customize the format with the help of the `\option` command or the `set` method of the `shell.options` member of the `Shell` class.

Thus, to print the content of the `artist` table in a tabbed format, run the following:

```
MySQL  cookbook  JS > \option resultFormat=tabbed
MySQL  cookbook  JS > artist=session.getCurrentSchema().getTable('artist')
<Table:artist>
MySQL  cookbook  JS > artist.select()
a_id    name
1       Da Vinci
2       Monet
4       Renoir
3       Van Gogh
4 rows in set (0.0009 sec)
```

To switch to the vertical format, run the following:

```
MySQL  cookbook  JS > shell.options.set('resultFormat', 'vertical')
MySQL  cookbook  JS > artist.select()
*************************** 1. row ***************************
a_id: 1
name: Da Vinci
*************************** 2. row ***************************
a_id: 2
name: Monet
*************************** 3. row ***************************
a_id: 4
name: Renoir
*************************** 4. row ***************************
a_id: 3
name: Van Gogh
4 rows in set (0.0009 sec)
```

The JSON format supports few options. By default, if the value of the `resultFormat` option is set to `json` or MySQL Shell started with the `--json` option, it is same as `json/pretty`, or `--json=pretty`, which means that the result is printed as a JSON, formatted for better readability:

```
MySQL  cookbook  JS > shell.options.set('resultFormat', 'json')
MySQL  cookbook  JS > artist.select()
{
    "a_id": 1,
    "name": "Da Vinci"
}
```

```
{
    "a_id": 2,
    "name": "Monet"
}
{
    "a_id": 4,
    "name": "Renoir"
}
{
    "a_id": 3,
    "name": "Van Gogh"
}
4 rows in set (0.0008 sec)
```

The ndjson, json/raw, and --json=raw options produce more compact raw JSON output:

```
MySQL  cookbook  JS > shell.options.set('resultFormat', 'json/raw')
MySQL  cookbook  JS > artist.select()
{"a_id":1,"name":"Da Vinci"}
{"a_id":2,"name":"Monet"}
{"a_id":4,"name":"Renoir"}
{"a_id":3,"name":"Van Gogh"}
4 rows in set (0.0003 sec)
```

The json/array option represents the result as an array of JSON documents:

```
MySQL  cookbook  JS > shell.options.set('resultFormat', 'json/array')
MySQL  cookbook  JS > artist.select()
[
{"a_id":1,"name":"Da Vinci"},
{"a_id":2,"name":"Monet"},
{"a_id":4,"name":"Renoir"},
{"a_id":3,"name":"Van Gogh"}
]
4 rows in set (0.0010 sec)
```

This could be especially useful if you're selecting the data from the command line and later passing it to another program:

```
$ mysqlsh cbuser:cbpass@127.0.0.1:33060/cookbook \
> -i --execute="session.getSchema('cookbook').\
> getTable('artist').select().execute()" \
> --result-format=json/array --quiet-start=2 \
> | head -n -1 \
> | jq '.[] | .name'
"Da Vinci"
"Monet"
"Renoir"
"Van Gogh"
```

In the preceding code, we started mysqlsh with the -i option, which enables interactive mode, so MySQL Shell behaves as if it were run interactively, and with the --quiet-start=2 option, which disables all welcome messages. Then we set the --result-format option to json/array to enable JSON array output, used the --execute option to select from the table artist, and passed output to the jq command, which removed all metadata information and printed only names of artists.

 The `head -n -1` command removes the last line from the result that shows the number of rows returned by the `select` method. Note that specifying a negative number as a command `head -n` parameter may not work everywhere. If you're on such a system, you can ignore the error message that the command `jq` will print or redirect it somewhere else:

```
$ mysqlsh cbuser:cbpass@127.0.0.1:33060/cookbook \
> -i --execute="session.getSchema('cookbook').\
> getTable('artist').select().execute()" \
> --result-format=json/array --quiet-start=2 \
> | jq '.[] | .name' 2>/dev/null
"Da Vinci"
"Monet"
"Renoir"
"Van Gogh"
```

When JSON wrapping is enabled at the MySQL Shell startup with `--json[=pretty|raw]` option, it will also print diagnostic information in the resulting JSON output:

```
MySQL cookbook JS > session.getCurrentSchema().getTable('artist').select()
{
    "hasData": true,
    "rows": [
        {
            "a_id": 1,
            "name": "Da Vinci"
        },
        {
            "a_id": 2,
            "name": "Monet"
        },
        {
            "a_id": 4,
            "name": "Renoir"
        },
        {
            "a_id": 3,
            "name": "Van Gogh"
        }
    ],
    "executionTime": "0.0007 sec",
    "affectedRowCount": 0,
    "affectedItemsCount": 0,
    "warningCount": 0,
    "warningsCount": 0,
    "warnings": [],
    "info": "",
    "autoIncrementValue": 0
}
```

If you enabled JSON output using the `--result-format=json[/pretty|/raw|/array]` command-line option, this additional information is not printed.

All output formats are independent from how you select data and are available in all modes.

See Also

For additional information about MySQL Shell output formats, see "Output Formats" in the MySQL User Reference Manual (*https://oreil.ly/A3KUt*).

2.12 Running Reports with MySQL Shell

Problem

You want to run periodic reports.

Solution

Use the `\show` and `\watch` commands.

Discussion

The MySQL Shell `\show` and `\watch` commands execute reports, both built-in and user-defined. `\show` executes a report once, whereas `\watch` runs the report continuously until interrupted.

A report is a predefined sequence of commands. Reports may support arguments. For example, the built-in report `query` takes a SQL query as an argument. The built-in report `thread` reports details about a specific thread. By default, it reports details about the current thread:

```
 MySQL  cookbook  SQL > \show thread
GENERAL
Thread ID:              1434
Connection ID:          1382
Thread type:            FOREGROUND
Program name:           mysqlsh
User:                   sveta
Host:                   localhost
Database:               cookbook
Command:                Query
Time:                   00:00:00
State:                  executing
Transaction state:      NULL
Prepared statements:    0
Bytes received:         20280
Bytes sent:             40227
Info:                   SELECT json_object('tid',t.THR ... ↵
```

```
                           JOIN information_schema.innodb
Previous statement:        NULL
```

 The built-in report thread queries tables in performance_schema and *sys*; therefore, you should connect as a user that has SELECT privilege on performance_schema and *sys* schemas and EXECUTE privilege on *sys* schema. Otherwise, the report will fail with an "access denied" error.

But the report thread supports arguments, so you can specify, for example, Connection ID of the thread and output information about the specific one:

```
MySQL  cookbook  SQL > \show thread -c 1386
GENERAL
Thread ID:                 1438
Connection ID:             1386
Thread type:               FOREGROUND
Program name:              mysql
User:                      sveta
Host:                      localhost
Database:                  cookbook
Command:                   Sleep
Time:                      00:05:44
State:                     NULL
Transaction state:         RUNNING
Prepared statements:       0
Bytes received:            1720
Bytes sent:                29733
Info:                      NULL
Previous statement:        select * from adcount for update
```

The output of the thread report is similar to the standard PROCESSLIST output but contains additional information, such as Transaction state and Previous statement. The latter could be especially useful when you're trying to figure out what is preventing your transaction from finishing. For example, if one of the transactions runs in multiple statements and locks a record, it may cause other transactions to wait until the lock is released. But since the statement was already executed, it would not be visible in the regular PROCESSLIST output.

Even more useful information could be found in the threads report that by default outputs information about all threads that belong to the current user. It runs the MySQL Shell session but can print information about all the threads running on the server and also filter them and define the output format.

For example, to find all blocked and blocking transactions, you can define the --where "nblocked > 0 or nblocking > 0" option:

```
MySQL  cookbook  SQL > \show threads --foreground ↵
                       --where "nblocked > 0 or nblocking > 0" ↵
                       -o tid,cid,txid,txstate,nblocked,nblocking,info,pinfo↵
                       --vertical
*************************** 1. row ***************************
```

```
        tid: 1438
        cid: 1386
       txid: 292253
    txstate: RUNNING
   nblocked: 1
  nblocking: 0
       info: NULL
      pinfo: select * from adcount for update
*************************** 2. row ***************************
        tid: 3320
        cid: 3268
       txid: 292254
    txstate: LOCK WAIT
   nblocked: 0
  nblocking: 1
       info: update adcount set impressions = impressions + 1 where id=3
      pinfo: NULL
```

Thus, in the preceding example, the thread with `Connection ID 3268` is trying to execute an update:

```
UPDATE adcount SET impressions = impressions + 1 WHERE id=3;
```

but is blocked by another transaction. Otherwise, the thread with `Connection ID 1386` is not executing anything but blocks a thread. Its previous statement was:

```
SELECT * FROM adcount FOR UPDATE;
```

which blocks all rows in the `adcount` table for writing. With this, we easily found why the `UPDATE` in the connection 3268 couldn't finish.

The `threads` report has more options. You can find all of them by running the `\show` command with the report name followed by the `--help` option:

```
MySQL  cookbook  SQL > \show threads --help
NAME
      threads - Lists threads that belong to the user who owns the current
      session.

SYNTAX
      \show threads [OPTIONS]
      \watch threads [OPTIONS]

DESCRIPTION
      This report may contain the following columns:
...
```

 All MySQL Shell commands support help options. For built-in commands, run `\?` `COMMAND`, `\help` `COMMAND`, or `\h` `COMMAND`. For commands with parameters, try the `--help` option.

The `\watch` command not only executes the report but does so repeatedly, at certain intervals. This could be very useful when you want to watch changes of a certain parameter. For example, to watch the number of internal temporary tables created to resolve queries, run the following command:

```
MySQL  cookbook  SQL > \watch query --nocls ↵
                        SHOW GLOBAL STATUS LIKE 'Created\_tmp\_%tables'
+-------------------------+-------+
| Variable_name           | Value |
+-------------------------+-------+
| Created_tmp_disk_tables | 4758  |
| Created_tmp_tables      | 25306 |
+-------------------------+-------+
+-------------------------+-------+
| Variable_name           | Value |
+-------------------------+-------+
| Created_tmp_disk_tables | 4758  |
| Created_tmp_tables      | 25309 |
+-------------------------+-------+
+-------------------------+-------+
| Variable_name           | Value |
+-------------------------+-------+
| Created_tmp_disk_tables | 4758  |
| Created_tmp_tables      | 25310 |
+-------------------------+-------+
+-------------------------+-------+
| Variable_name           | Value |
+-------------------------+-------+
| Created_tmp_disk_tables | 4760  |
| Created_tmp_tables      | 25318 |
+-------------------------+-------+
+-------------------------+-------+
| Variable_name           | Value |
+-------------------------+-------+
| Created_tmp_disk_tables | 4760  |
| Created_tmp_tables      | 25319 |
+-------------------------+-------+
...
```

The query uses the LIKE operator and patterns to match the names of two system variables. We discuss how the LIKE operator works and matches patterns in Recipe 7.10.

The query runs with a default interval of 2 seconds. The --nocls parameter instructs the command to not clear the screen before printing the latest result. To stop watching, issue the termination command Ctrl+C.

2.13 Using MySQL Shell Utilities

Problem

You want to use MySQL Shell utilities.

Solution

In JavaScript or Python modes, use the methods of the global util object interactively or pass the method via the command line.

Discussion

MySQL Shell comes with a number of built-in utilities that allow you to perform common administrative tasks, such as checking if your MySQL server can be safely updated to the new version or making a reserve copy of the data. These utilities could be called as methods of the global util object in JavaScript and Python modes or specified as a command-line option.

To find out which utilities MySQL Shell supports, run the \? util command. The names of methods are different in JavaScript and Python modes and follow naming best practices for each of the languages. The global util object isn't available in the SQL mode, nor are utilities.

To figure out how a utility works, use the help command with the name of the utility as an argument. For example, \? checkForServerUpgrade will print comprehensive help for the upgrade checker utility in JavaScript mode. \? dump_instance will print detailed usage instructions for the utility that dumps the instance in Python mode.

Calling utility methods is no different than calling any other method. For example, the following code exports the limbs table into the limbs.csv file in fully quoted CSV format:

```
MySQL  cookbook  JS > util.exportTable(
                  -> 'limbs', 'BACKUP/cookbook/limbs.csv',
                  -> {dialect: "csv-unix"})
Preparing data dump for table `cookbook`.`limbs`
Data dump for table `cookbook`.`limbs` will not use an index
Running data dump using 1 thread.
NOTE: Progress information uses estimated values and may not be accurate.
Data dump for table `cookbook`.`limbs` will be written to 1 file
91% (11 rows / ~12 rows), 0.00 rows/s, 0.00 B/s
Duration: 00:00:00s
Data size: 203 bytes
Rows written: 11
Bytes written: 203 bytes
Average throughput: 203.00 B/s

The dump can be loaded using:
util.importTable("BACKUP/cookbook/limbs.csv", {
    "characterSet": "utf8mb4",
    "dialect": "csv-unix",
    "schema": "cookbook",
    "table": "limbs"
})
```

You need to create the BACKUP/cookbook directory before running this command or use a different location.

This Python code restores the table into the limbs table in the database test:

```
MySQL  cookbook  Py > \sql CREATE TABLE test.limbs LIKE limbs;
Fetching table and column names from `cookbook` for auto-completion... ↵
Press ^C to stop.
Query OK, 0 rows affected (0.0264 sec)
MySQL  cookbook  Py > util.import_table("BACKUP/cookbook/limbs.csv", ↵
                        {"dialect": "csv-unix", "schema": "test"})
Importing from file '/home/sveta/BACKUP/cookbook/limbs.csv' to table `test`.`limbs` ↵
in MySQL Server at 127.0.0.1:3306 using 1 thread
[Worker000] limbs.csv: Records: 11  Deleted: 0  Skipped: 0  Warnings: 0
100% (203 bytes / 203 bytes), 0.00 B/s
File '/home/sveta/BACKUP/cookbook/limbs.csv' (203 bytes) ↵
was imported in 0.0109 sec at 203.00 B/s
Total rows affected in test.limbs: Records: 11  Deleted: 0  Skipped: 0 Warnings: 0
```

We omitted all but the necessary options for the import example to make it shorter.

To use import_table, you need to be in the Classic protocol session. Otherwise, the command will fail with an error:

```
MySQL  cookbook  Py > util.import_table("BACKUP/cookbook/limbs.csv", ↵
                        {"dialect": "csv-unix", "schema": "test"})
Traceback (most recent call last):
  File "<string>", line 1, in <module>
SystemError: RuntimeError: Util.import_table: ↵
A classic protocol session is required to perform this operation.
```

It's always a good idea to read error messages, because they clearly show what is wrong and often contain instructions on how to fix the failure.

Following is another error you can hit:

```
ERROR: The 'local_infile' global system variable must be set to ON ↵
in the target server, after the server is verified to be trusted:
```

To bypass this error, enable the local_infile option with the following command:

```
SET GLOBAL local_infile=1;
```

Or leave this example until you get to the Chapter 13, which covers exporting and importing MySQL database objects.

If you don't understand what the utility is doing in these examples, don't worry. We'll cover exporting and importing MySQL database objects in Chapter 13.

If you want to run utilities without entering interactive mode, you can specify them after the two dashes, following standard `mysqlsh` options:

```
$ mysqlsh -- util check-for-server-upgrade root@127.0.0.1:13000 --output-format=JSON
Please provide the password for 'root@127.0.0.1:13000':
Save password for 'root@127.0.0.1:13000'? [Y]es/[N]o/Ne[v]er (default No):
{
    "serverAddress": "127.0.0.1:13000",
    "serverVersion": "8.0.23-debug - Source distribution",
    "targetVersion": "8.0.27",
    "errorCount": 0,
    "warningCount": 0,
    "noticeCount": 0,
    "summary": "No known compatibility errors or issues were found.",
...
```

In this example, we first specified the command name, then added two dashes, followed by the global object name, the method we wanted to use, the connection string, and, finally, the method arguments.

The command line uses the method names of JavaScript mode Camel-case syntax, `checkForServerUpgrade`; Kebab-case syntax, `check-for-server-upgrade`; or Snake-case syntax: `check_for_server_upgrade`. For more information about using global objects without entering interactive mode, use the `\?` command interactively.

You can use `--` syntax to call methods of other global objects on the command line:

```
$ mysqlsh cbuser:cbpass@127.0.0.1:33060/cookbook
          > -- shell status
WARNING: Using a password on the command-line interface ↵
can be insecure.
MySQL Shell version 8.0.22

Connection Id:              23563
Default schema:             cookbook
Current schema:             cookbook
Current user:               cbuser@localhost
SSL:                        Cipher in use: ↵
                            TLS_AES_256_GCM_SHA384 ↵
                            TLSv1.3
...
```

However, not all global objects are supported. Check `\?` `cmdline` for the list of supported objects.

See Also

For additional information about MySQL Shell utilities, see "MySQL Shell Utilities" in the Reference Manual (*https://oreil.ly/vuAGM*).

2.14 Using the Admin API to Automate Replication Management

Problem

You want to automate routine database administrator (DBA) tasks, such as deploying MySQL servers.

Solution

Use the Admin API.

Discussion

MySQL Shell supports not only the X DevAPI for querying the database but also the Admin API that allows you to manage the InnoDB ReplicaSet and InnoDB Cluster. The Admin API consists of three classes: `Dba`, `Cluster`, and `ReplicaSet`.

Admin API is accessible from the global `dba` object of the `DBA` class. It allows you to configure MySQL instances and start either a standalone sandbox, ReplicaSet, or Cluster.

To configure a standalone sandbox, use the `deploySandboxInstance` method in JavaScript mode or `deploy_sandbox_instance` in Python mode. This method takes a port number and a dictionary of parameters as arguments:

```
MySQL  cookbook  JS > dba.deploySandboxInstance(13000,
                    -> {"portx": 13010, "mysqldOptions": ["log-bin=cookbook"]})
A new MySQL sandbox instance will be created on this host in
/home/sveta/mysql-sandboxes/13000

Warning: Sandbox instances are only suitable for deploying and
running on your local machine for testing purposes and are not
accessible from external networks.

Please enter a MySQL root password for the new instance:

Deploying new MySQL instance...

Instance localhost:13000 successfully deployed and started.
Use shell.connect('root@localhost:13000') to connect to the instance.
```

This will create a sandbox instance with X port 13010 and an enabled binary log with a name, starting from *cookbook*:

```
MySQL  localhost:13000 ssl  JS > shell.connect('root@localhost:13000')
Creating a session to 'root@localhost:13000'
Please provide the password for 'root@localhost:13000':
Fetching schema names for autocompletion... Press ^C to stop.
Closing old connection...
Your MySQL connection id is 13
```

```
Server version: 8.0.22-13 Percona Server (GPL), Release '13', Revision '6f7822f'
No default schema selected; type \use <schema> to set one.
 MySQL  localhost:13000 ssl  JS > \sql show variables like 'log_bin_basename';
+------------------+----------------------------------------------------------+
| Variable_name    | Value                                                    |
+------------------+----------------------------------------------------------+
| log_bin_basename | /home/sveta/mysql-sandboxes/13000/sandboxdata/cookbook   |
+------------------+----------------------------------------------------------+
1 row in set (0.0027 sec)
```

To stop the instance, use the `stopSandboxInstance` method in JavaScript mode or `stop_sandbox_instance` in Python mode:

```
 MySQL  localhost:13000 ssl  JS > dba.stopSandboxInstance(13000)
The MySQL sandbox instance on this host in
/home/sveta/mysql-sandboxes/13000 will be stopped

Please enter the MySQL root password for the instance 'localhost:13000':

Stopping MySQL instance...

Instance localhost:13000 successfully stopped.
```

To destroy the instance, use the `deleteSandboxInstance` method in JavaScript mode or `delete_sandbox_instance` in Python mode:

```
 MySQL  cookbook  Py > dba.delete_sandbox_instance(13000)

Deleting MySQL instance...

Instance localhost:13000 successfully deleted.
```

The global dba object is accessible from the command line:

```
$ mysqlsh cbuser:cbpass@127.0.0.1:33060/cookbook -- dba kill-sandbox-instance 13000
WARNING: Using a password on the command-line interface can be insecure.

Killing MySQL instance...

Instance localhost:1300 successfully killed.
```

The global dba object is not available in SQL mode.

See Also

For additional information about using Admin API to create and manage a Replica-Set, see Recipe 3.17. For additional information about using Admin API to create and manage InnoDB Cluster, see "InnoDB Cluster" on page 148.

2.15 Working with JavaScript Objects

Problem

You want to work with your documents as objects, and you want to modify them and store them in the database using your own methods and properties.

Solution

Create an object that will have all the necessary methods to communicate with the database, and use it as a prototype of your data objects.

Discussion

JavaScript is an object-oriented programming language, and it's easy to create objects, modify them, and store them in the database. Sometimes it may be easier to simply write `myObject.save()` instead of calling the full chain of methods of the X DevAPI Collection class. For example, you may want to replace the following code:

```
session.getCurrentSchema().getCollection('CollectionLimbs').
        addOrReplaceOne(myObject).execute()
```

with the following single call:

```
CollectionLimbs.save()
```

JavaScript supports inheritance; therefore, you can create an object that will have all the necessary methods, working with the `Collection` class methods, and use it as a prototype of the object, containing your business logic.

As an example, let's create a `CookbookCollection` object that will have the `find`, `save` and `remove` methods. They will search for an object in the collection, save it after modification, and remove it from the database if necessary. The `CookbookCollection` object will also have a `collection` property that will store an object, representing the collection where our object is stored.

To make our methods clear, we won't add error handling. You can add this functionality yourself. For example, if a user forgets to set a collection property, you can throw a custom exception or have a default collection that will be used instead. We're relying on JavaScript built-in exceptions.

Let's get started and create our object:

```
mysql-js [cookbook]> var CookbookCollection = {
                  ->    // Collection where the object is stored
                  ->    collection: null,
```

First, we define the property collection where the object is stored. We don't set the name of the collection here, because we want our prototype to work with any collection:

```
->    // Searches collection and returns first
->    // object that satisfies search condition.
->    find: function(searchCondition) {
->      return this.collection.find(searchCondition).
->              execute().fetchOne();
->    },
```

The find function searches the collection using any search condition. It could be '_id = "00006002f0650000000000000061"' or 'thing="human"'. In other words, it can be any condition the Collection.find method accepts. Then we fetch one document and return it as a result. We intentionally didn't add any unique check code or any other way to ensure that there is only one document satisfying our condition because we wanted to make the example as simple as possible and have it work with any collection:

```
->    // Saves the object in the database
->    save: function() {
->      // If we know _id of the object we are
->      // updating the existing one
->      // We use the less-effective method addOrReplaceOne
->      // instead of modify for simplicity.
->      if ('_id' in this) {
->        this.collection.addOrReplaceOne(this._id,
->          // We use double conversion, because we cannot
->          // store an object with methods in the database
->          JSON.parse(
->            JSON.stringify(
->              this, Object.getOwnPropertyNames(
->                    Object.getPrototypeOf(this))
->            )
->          )
->        )
->      } else {
->        // In case the object does not exist in the
->        //  database yet, we add it and assign
->        // generated _id to its own property.
->        // This _id could be used later if we want to update
->        // or remove the database entry.
->        this._id = this.collection.add(
->          JSON.parse(
->            JSON.stringify(
->              this, Object.getOwnPropertyNames(
->                    Object.getPrototypeOf(this))
->            )
->          )
->        ).execute().getGeneratedIds()[0]
->      }
->    },
```

The save method stores the object in the database. If there is no _id field in the object, that usually means there is no such object in the database yet. So, we use the add method to insert it into the database and set the `_id` property of the object to the value, generated by MySQL. If such a property already exists, that either means that the object is already in the database or we want to set `_id` explicitly. In this case, we use the `addOrReplaceOne` method that either adds a new object with the specified unique identifier or replaces the existing one:

```
-> // Removes the entry from the database.
-> // Once removed we unset property _id of the object.
-> remove: function() {
->    this.collection.remove("_id = '" + this._id + "'").
->      execute()
->    delete Object.getPrototypeOf(this)._id
->    delete this._id
->  }
-> }
```

The `remove` method deletes the record from the database and also deletes the `_id` property of our object so that, in case we want to store it in the database again, it will be considered a new record, and a new unique identifier will be generated. We remove the `_id` property from both the prototype and the object.

Let's take the `CollectionLimbs` collection that we created in Recipe 2.9 as an example. First, we retrieve it from the current `session` and set as a `collection` property of the `CookbookCollection` object:

```
mysql-js [cookbook]> CookbookCollection.collection=session.getCurrentSchema().
                  -> getCollection('CollectionLimbs')
                  ->
<Collection:CollectionLimbs>
```

In Recipe 2.9, we rolled back all our modifications to the `Collec tionLimbs`. If you continued your own experiments further before running the examples in this recipe, execute the following:

```
CookbookCollection.collection ↵
.remove("thing='cat' or thing='dog'")
```

Then let's create an object, `cat`, with two arms and two legs:

```
mysql-js [cookbook]> var cat = {
                  ->    thing: "cat",
                  ->    arms: 2,
                  ->    legs: 2
                  -> }
                  ->
```

To be able to store our cat in the database, we need to assign the `CookbookCollection` object as a prototype of the `cat` object:

```
mysql-js [cookbook]> cat = Object.setPrototypeOf(CookbookCollection, cat)
{
    "arms": 2,
    "collection": <Collection:CollectionLimbs>,
```

```
    "find": <Function:find>,
    "legs": 2,
    "remove": <Function:remove>,
    "save": <Function:save>,
    "thing": "cat"
}
```

Now we can save our object in the database:

```
mysql-js [cookbook]> cat.save()
```

We can check if we can retrieve the object with the `find` method:

```
mysql-js [cookbook]> CookbookCollection.find('thing = "cat"')
{
    "_id": "000060140a2d0000000000000007",
    "arms": 2,
    "legs": 2,
    "thing": "cat"
}
```

We can also confirm that our object now has `_id` property:

```
mysql-js [cookbook]> cat._id
000060140a2d0000000000000007
```

Do you see anything wrong here? Yes! The cat has two arms and two legs, but cats usually have no arms and four legs. Let's fix it:

```
mysql-js [cookbook]> cat.arms=0
0
mysql-js [cookbook]> cat.legs=4
4
mysql-js [cookbook]> cat.save()
mysql-js [cookbook]> CookbookCollection.find('thing = "cat"')
{
    "_id": "000060140a2d0000000000000007",
    "arms": 0,
    "legs": 4,
    "thing": "cat"
}
```

Now our cat is in good shape.

If we want to clean up the collection and leave it in the state it was in before our experiments, we can remove the `cat` document from the database:

```
mysql-js [cookbook]>  cat.remove()
```

We may also notice that the `cat._id` property does not exist in our object anymore:

```
mysql-js [cookbook]> cat._id
mysql-js [cookbook]>
```

If we decide to store the object in the database again, a new unique identifier will be generated.

You'll find the `CookbookCollection` code in the file *mysql_shell/CookbookCollection.js* of the `recipes` distribution.

2.16 Filling Test Data Using Python's Data Science Modules

Problem

You want to fill a test table with partially random data. For example, you need IDs to follow a sequence. You also want them to have realistic names and surnames. The rest of the values in the table can be random, but the index should have certain a cardinality. More about indexes in Chapter 21.

Solution

Script data population using Python and its specific data science modules.

Discussion

We're often in the situation where we need to fill a table with fake data that mimics real-world data for testing purposes. For example, perhaps you've developed an application and want to check what happens if the volume of data stored in it increases. Or you've hit a situation where a particular query works slowly in production, and you want to experiment on the test server but do not want to copy production data due to security or performance reasons. This task may also be required when you want to ask third-party consultants for help.

One such example is the `patients` table that we used in Recipe 24.12. This table contains records of patients who spent more than one day in a hospital. It stores this data as national ID, name, surname, gender, diagnosis, and outcome, such as dates a patient spent in the hospital and if they recovered, checked out of the hospital with the same symptoms, or even died. You can find these details by running the SHOW CREATE TABLE command:

```
MySQL  cookbook  Py > session.sql('SHOW CREATE TABLE patients')
*************************** 1. row ***************************
       Table: patients
Create Table: CREATE TABLE `patients` (
  `id` int NOT NULL AUTO_INCREMENT,
  `national_id` char(32) DEFAULT NULL,
  `name` varchar(255) DEFAULT NULL,
  `surname` varchar(255) DEFAULT NULL,
  `gender` enum('F','M') DEFAULT NULL,
  `age` tinyint unsigned DEFAULT NULL,
  `additional_data` json DEFAULT NULL,
  `diagnosis` varchar(255) DEFAULT NULL,
  `result` enum('R','N','D') DEFAULT NULL↵
   COMMENT 'R=Recovered, N=Not Recovered, D=Dead',
  `date_arrived` date NOT NULL,
  `date_departed` date DEFAULT NULL,
  PRIMARY KEY (`id`)
) ENGINE=InnoDB AUTO_INCREMENT=1101 ↵
```

```
DEFAULT CHARSET=utf8mb4 COLLATE=utf8mb4_0900_ai_ci
1 row in set (0.0009 sec)
```

Of course, we wouldn't even think about using real data for examples in this table. However, we still want to pretend that the data is real. For example, names and surnames should be ones that are popular, and genders should correspond to the right names. For example, John is likely a male and Ann is likely a female. Ages should fall in realistic ranges, and departure dates should be greater than the date when the patient arrived to the hospital. It is also unlikely that a patient would spend 10 years in the hospital.

Python is often used for data analysis and statistics. It has libraries, such as `pandas`, that help to manipulate large datasets and has convenient methods to read and generate data. All of these make Python ideal for performing our task.

To use the `pandas` module in MySQL Shell, you need to have it installed on your machine and add the path where the library is located, in MySQL Shell's `sys.path`. Here are the steps that will help you perform this task:

1. First, check which version of Python MySQL Shell is running. In our case, it's version 3.7.7:
   ```
   MySQL  cookbook  Py > import sys
   MySQL  cookbook  Py > sys.version
   3.7.7 (default, Aug 12 2020, 09:13:48)
   [GCC 4.4.7 20120313 (Red Hat 4.4.7-23.0.1)]
   ```

2. MySQL Shell does not come with the python executable and `pip` that you can run from outside MySQL Shell. Therefore, you need to install the same version as MySQL Shell's Python. We preferred to keep the system-wide installed version 3.8.5 untouched and install the same version that our MySQL Shell instance used: 3.7.7 into a local directory from the source code. You can decide to have the same version system-wide.

3. Once the correct version of Python is installed, check where it stores its modules, and add this directory to the `sys.path` of the MySQL Shell:
   ```
   MySQL  cookbook  Py > sys.path.append(↵
   "/home/sveta/bin/python-3.7.7/lib/python3.7/site-packages")
   ```

    To avoid typing this command each time you want to use modules that are not part of the MySQL Shell distribution, add this command to the Python mode configuration file. This file, by default, is located at `~/.mysqlsh/mysqlshrc.py`.

4. Install the necessary packages. For our example, we used `numpy`, `pandas`, `random`, `string`, and `datetime`.

Once these prerequisites are met, we're ready to fill our table with example data.

Data filling step-by-step

First, we need to import all of the necessary packages. Type the following in the MySQL Shell Python protocol session:

```
import numpy
from pandas import pandas
import random
import string
from datetime import datetime
from datetime import timedelta
```

Now we're ready to generate the data.

For names and surnames, we decided to use real names found in the datasets, available on the internet. You'll find the datasets we used and their licenses and distribution rights in the *datasets* directory of the `recipes` distribution. For diagnoses, we also used publicly available data of the top 8 diagnoses and their frequencies, and the fake diagnosis "Data Phobia" with an even higher frequency. Data for genders is stored with the names. All other values are generated. The data doesn't need to look real. For example, a 16-year-old patient may end up dying from alcoholic liver disease, which would be unlikely to happen in real life but is sufficient for demonstration purposes. However, Python allows to solve such collisions. You can change our example to have even more realistic data.

It's convenient to have a variable defining the final number of rows in the table:

```
MySQL  cookbook  Py > num_rows=1000
```

Now let's discuss how we'll process each column in the `patients` table.

Names and genders.   Names and genders are stored in the `top-350-male-and-female-names-since-1848-2019-02-26.csv` file in the following format:

```
$ head datasets/top-350-male-and-female-names-since-1848-2019-02-26.csv
Rank,Female Name,Count,Male Name,Count_
1,Mary,54276,John,108533
2,Margaret,49170,William,87239
3,Elizabeth,36556,James,69987
4,Sarah,28230,David,62774
5,Patricia,20689,Robert,56511
6,Catherine,19713,Michael,51768
7,Susan,19165,Peter,44758
8,Helen,18881,Thomas,42467
9,Emma,18192,George,39195
```

This means that each row contains a rank from 1 to 350, one name that is traditionally female and one name that is traditionally male of this rank and count of such names. We're not interested in the rank and count. We just need female and male names with gender information. Therefore, we need to perform slight manipulation on this dataset after reading.

First, we read the file using the `read_csv` pandas method. We'll read the file twice: once for traditional female names and once for traditional male names. We'll use only the `Female Name` column in the first attempt and only the `Male Name` column in the second attempt. We'll also rename this column so it corresponds with the name of the column in our database:

```
MySQL  cookbook  Py > female_names=pandas.\
                 -> read_csv(
                 ->   "top-350-male-and-female-names-since-1848-2019-02-26.csv",
                 ->   usecols=["Female Name"]
                 -> ).rename(columns={'Female Name': 'name'})
                 ->
MySQL  cookbook  Py > male_names=pandas.\
                 -> read_csv(
                 ->   "top-350-male-and-female-names-since-1848-2019-02-26.csv",
                 ->   usecols=["Male Name"]
                 -> ).rename(columns={'Male Name': 'name'})
                 ->
```

Once done, we'll add a gender column to our datasets:

```
MySQL  cookbook  Py > female_names['gender']=(['F']*↵
                       female_names.count()['name'])
MySQL  cookbook  Py > male_names['gender']=(['M']*↵
                       male_names.count()['name'])
```

And, finally, we'll concatenate the two datasets into one:

```
MySQL  cookbook  Py > names=pandas.\
                 -> concat([female_names, male_names],
                 ->   ignore_index=True)
                 ->
```

In order to read the `top-350-male-and-female-names-since-1848-2019-02-26.csv` file, it needs to be in the current working directory, or you need to provide the absolute path to the file. To find your current working directory, run the following:

```
os.getcwd()
```

To change the working directory, run the following:

```
os.chdir('/mysqlcookbook/recipes/datasets')
```

This will allow you to read files located in `/mysqlcookbook/recipes/datasets`. Adjust the directory path to reflect your environment.

 The `concat` method of the Python pandas module works similarly to the SQL `UNION` clause.

We can examine the content of our dataset that uses the pandas `DataFrame` data structure by typing its name:

```
MySQL cookbook Py > names
           name gender
0          Mary      F
1      Margaret      F
2     Elizabeth      F
3         Sarah      F
4      Patricia      F
..          ...    ...
695      Quentin      M
696       Henare      M
697          Joe      M
698        Darcy      M
699         Wade      M

[700 rows x 2 columns]
```

The number of rows in the DataFrame is smaller than the number of rows we want to have in our table, so we need to generate more. We also want to shuffle the data so we have a random distribution of names. We'll use the `sample` method for this purpose. Since we're creating a larger set than the initial one, we need to specify the `replace=True` option. We'll also re-create the index for the new DataFrame using the `pandas.Series` method, so it will be ordered:

```
MySQL cookbook Py > names=names.sample(num_rows, replace=True).\
                 -> set_index(pandas.Series(range(num_rows)))
                 ->
```

Surnames. For surnames, we'll use a dataset stored in the `Names_2010Census.csv` file. It has multiple columns, such as a rank, the number of surnames, and so on, but we're interested only in the first column: `name`. We also don't need the last row of this file, containing a record for ALL OTHER NAMES. Surnames in this file are stored in uppercase. We could format them differently, but we'll leave them as is. We'll also rename the `name` column to `surname` so it matches our table definition:

```
MySQL cookbook Py > surnames=pandas.read_csv("Names_2010Census.csv",
                 -> usecols=['name'], skipfooter=1, engine='python').\
                 -> rename(columns={'name': 'surname'})
                 ->
```

pandas prints a warning that it will use a slower but more powerful `python` engine to process the file, but this warning can be ignored.

We'll shuffle the surnames using the same method that we used for the names:

```
MySQL cookbook Py > surnames=surnames.sample(num_rows, replace=True).\
                 -> set_index(pandas.Series(range(num_rows)))
                 ->
```

Diagnoses. We manually prepared the `diagnosis.csv` file that has just 9 diagnoses; therefore, we only need to read it and don't need to specify any option:

```
MySQL  cookbook  Py > diagnoses=pandas.read_csv('diagnosis.csv')
MySQL  cookbook  Py > diagnoses
                           diagnosis  frequency
0            Acute coronary syndrome        2.1
1             Alcoholic liver disease        0.3
2                          Pneumonia        3.6
3  Chronic obstructive pulmonary disease    2.1
4               Gastro-intestinal bleed       0.8
5                       Heart failure        0.8
6                              Sepsis        0.8
7              Urinary tract infection        2.4
8                         Data Phobia        6.2
```

Diagnoses are different from the names and surnames, because they have different frequencies and we want them distributed in our final dataset according to those frequencies. Therefore, we'll pass the `weights` parameter to the `sample` method:

```
MySQL  cookbook  Py > diagnoses=diagnoses.sample(
               ->    num_rows, replace=True,
               ->    weights=diagnoses['frequency']
               -> ).set_index(pandas.Series(range(num_rows)))
               ->
```

Results. The data type for the results is an `ENUM` that can contain only three possible values: `R` for recovered, `N` for not recovered, and `D` for dead. We would not use any source for such results but generate a DataFrame interactively:

```
MySQL  cookbook  Py > results = pandas.DataFrame({
               ->    "result": ["R", "N", "D"],
               ->    "frequency": [6,3,1]
               -> })
               ->
```

We added a frequency to our results. These frequencies have nothing to do with reality: we need them only to distribute our results differently.

Since we have a frequency for our results, we'll generate the dataset the same way we did for diagnoses:

```
MySQL  cookbook  Py > results=results.sample(
               ->    num_rows, replace=True,
               ->    weights=results['frequency']
               -> ).set_index(pandas.Series(range(num_rows)))
               ->
```

The table. Our main datasets are prepared. Now we can start inserting rows into the table one by one.

First, let's retrieve a `Table` object so we can query it comfortably:

```
MySQL  cookbook  Py > patients=session.get_schema('cookbook').↵
                            get_table('patients')
```

Then we'll start the loop:

```
MySQL  cookbook  Py > for i in range(num_rows):
```

All subsequent generations will be proceeded in this loop.

National ID. The format of the national ID can vary between countries, and we simply need something unique that follows some pattern. We decided to use two digits, followed by two uppercase letters, followed by six digits. To generate random digits we'll use the `randrange` method of the `random` module, and to generate letters, we'll use the `sample` method from the `random` module. We'll use the predefined set `string.ascii_uppercase` as a dataset to sample. Then we'll join the generated array to an empty string so it will create a string:

```
MySQL cookbook Py > national_id=str(random.randrange(10,99)) +\
               -> ''.join(random.sample(string.ascii_uppercase, 2)) + \
               -> str(random.randrange(100000, 999999))
               ->
```

Age. For the age we'll simply choose a number between 15 and 99. We don't care about the frequency of ages or about how many patients of certain ages have a certain disease:

```
MySQL cookbook Py > age=random.randrange(15, 99)
```

Dates a patient spent in the hospital. For the `date_arrived` column, we decided to just use any date in the year 2020. We can generate this date by specifying the start date as January 1, 2020, and using the `timedelta` method:

```
MySQL cookbook Py > date_arrived=datetime.\
               -> strptime('2020-01-01', '%Y-%m-%d') +\
               -> timedelta(days=random.randrange(365))
               ->
```

For the `date_departed` column, we'll use the same idea, but we'll use `date_arrived` as the starting date and an interval of two months:

```
MySQL cookbook Py > date_departed=date_arrived +\
               -> timedelta(days=random.randrange(60))
               ->
```

This code creates values for `date_arrived` and `date_departed` as `datetime` Python objects that could not be inserted into the MySQL table, so we need to convert them into the string format:

```
MySQL cookbook Py > date_arrived=date_arrived.strftime('%Y-%m-%d')
MySQL cookbook Py > date_departed=date_departed.strftime('%Y-%m-%d')
```

Preparing the row. We have values to be inserted into the `i`-th row of our table into the columns `national_id`, `age`, `date_arrived`, and `date_departed`. But the rest of the values are stored in `DataFrame`s of exactly the desired number of rows. We need to retrieve only a specific row from the `DataFrame`:

```
MySQL cookbook Py > name=names['name'][i]
MySQL cookbook Py > gender=names['gender'][i]
```

```
MySQL  cookbook  Py > surname=surnames['surname'][i]
MySQL  cookbook  Py > result=results['result'][i]
MySQL  cookbook  Py > diagnosis=diagnoses['diagnosis'][i]
```

Inserting a row into a table. Now we're ready to insert a row into our table. We'll use the insert method of the Table class that we discussed in detail in Recipe 2.8:

```
MySQL  cookbook  Py > patients.insert(
                  ->    'national_id', 'name', 'surname',
                  ->    'gender', 'age', 'diagnosis',
                  ->    'result', 'date_arrived', 'date_departed'
                  -> ).values(
                  ->    national_id, name, surname,
                  ->    gender, age, diagnosis,
                  ->    result, date_arrived, date_departed
                  -> ).execute()
```

Putting it all together. It may be convenient to define the code we just wrote as a function so we can reuse it. Let's create one, called generate_patients_data:

```
def generate_patients_data(num_rows):
    # read datasets
    # names and genders
    female_names = pandas.read_csv(
        "top-350-male-and-female-names-since-1848-2019-02-26.csv",
        usecols = ["Female Name"]
    ).rename(columns = {'Female Name': 'name'})
    female_names['gender'] = (['F']*female_names.count()['name'])
    male_names = pandas.read_csv(
        "top-350-male-and-female-names-since-1848-2019-02-26.csv",
        usecols = ["Male Name"]
    ).rename(columns = {'Male Name': 'name'})
    male_names['gender'] = (['M']*male_names.count()['name'])
    names = pandas.concat([female_names, male_names], ignore_index=True)
    surnames = pandas.read_csv(
        "Names_2010Census.csv",
        usecols=['name'], skipfooter=1
    ).rename(columns={'name': 'surname'})
    # diagnoses
    diagnoses = pandas.read_csv('diagnosis.csv')
    # Possible results
    results = pandas.DataFrame({
        "result": ["R", "N", "D"],
        "frequency": [6,3,1]
    })
    # Start building data
    diagnoses = diagnoses.sample(
        num_rows, replace=True,
        weights=diagnoses['frequency']
    ).set_index(pandas.Series(range(num_rows)))
    results = results.sample(
        num_rows, replace=True,
        weights=results['frequency']
    ).set_index(pandas.Series(range(num_rows)))
    names=names.sample(
        num_rows, replace=True
    ).set_index(pandas.Series(range(num_rows)))
    surnames=surnames.sample(
```

```
        num_rows, replace=True
    ).set_index(pandas.Series(range(num_rows)))
    # Get table object
    patients=session.get_schema('cookbook').get_table('patients')
    # Loop, inserting rows
    for i in range(num_rows):
        national_id = str(random.randrange(10,99)) + \
            ''.join(random.sample(string.ascii_uppercase, 2)) + \
            str(random.randrange(100000, 999999))
        age = random.randrange(15, 99)
        date_arrived = datetime.strptime('2020-01-01', '%Y-%m-%d') + \
            timedelta(days=random.randrange(365))
        date_departed = date_arrived + timedelta(days=random.randrange(60))
        date_arrived = date_arrived.strftime('%Y-%m-%d')
        date_departed = date_departed.strftime('%Y-%m-%d')
        name = names['name'][i]
        gender = names['gender'][i]
        surname = surnames['surname'][i]
        result = results['result'][i]
        diagnosis = diagnoses['diagnosis'][i]
        patients.insert(
            'national_id', 'name', 'surname',
            'gender', 'age', 'diagnosis',
            'result', 'date_arrived', 'date_departed'
        ).values(
            national_id, name, surname,
            gender, age, diagnosis,
            result, date_arrived, date_departed
        ).execute()
```

We can check how it works by truncating the patients table and then calling the function:

```
 MySQL  cookbook  Py > \sql truncate table patients
Query OK, 0 rows affected (0.0477 sec)
 MySQL  cookbook  Py > session.get_schema('cookbook').get_table('patients').count()
0
 MySQL  cookbook  Py > generate_patients_data(1000)
__main__:17: ParserWarning: Falling back to the 'python' engine ↵
because the 'c' engine does not support skipfooter; ↵
you can avoid this warning by specifying engine='python'.
 MySQL  cookbook  Py > session.get_schema('cookbook'). ↵
get_table('patients').count()
1000
 MySQL  cookbook  Py > session.get_schema('cookbook'). ↵
get_table('patients').select().limit(10)
+----+-------------+----------+------------+--------+-----+-----------------+....
| id | national_id | name     | surname    | gender | age | additional_data | ...
+----+-------------+----------+------------+--------+-----+-----------------+....
|  1 | 74LM282144  | May      | NESSELRODE | F      |  83 | NULL            | ...
|  2 | 44PR883357  | Kathryn  | DAKROUB    | F      |  44 | NULL            | ...
|  3 | 60JP130066  | Owen     | CIELINSKI  | M      |  47 | NULL            | ...
|  4 | 28ST588095  | Diana    | KILAR      | F      |  35 | NULL            | ...
|  5 | 77RP202627  | Beryl    | ANGIONE    | F      |  43 | NULL            | ...
|  6 | 27MU569536  | Brian    | HOUDEK     | M      |  84 | NULL            | ...
|  7 | 94AG787006  | Fredrick | WOHLMAN    | M      |  20 | NULL            | ...
|  8 | 42BX974594  | Jarrod   | DECAPUA    | M      |  64 | NULL            | ...
|  9 | 63XJ322387  | Ruth     | PAHUJA     | F      |  16 | NULL            | ...
| 10 | 91AT797455  | Frances  | VANBRUGGEN | F      |  63 | NULL            | ...
```

```
+----+---------------+---------------------+--------+-------------+---------------+....
+----+.....+---------------------------+--------+-------------+---------------+
| id | ... | diagnosis                 | result | date_arrived | date_departed |
+----+.....+---------------------------+--------+-------------+---------------+
|  1 | ... | Data Phobia               | D      | 2020-03-20  | 2020-04-26    |
|  2 | ... | Data Phobia               | R      | 2020-03-20  | 2020-05-09    |
|  3 | ... | Pneumonia                 | R      | 2020-04-05  | 2020-04-23    |
|  4 | ... | Acute coronary syndrome   | R      | 2020-04-18  | 2020-05-01    |
|  5 | ... | Pneumonia                 | R      | 2020-01-31  | 2020-02-07    |
|  6 | ... | Acute coronary syndrome   | D      | 2020-01-25  | 2020-03-06    |
|  7 | ... | Data Phobia               | R      | 2020-08-10  | 2020-09-04    |
|  8 | ... | Pneumonia                 | R      | 2020-02-12  | 2020-03-31    |
|  9 | ... | Pneumonia                 | N      | 2020-11-17  | 2020-12-19    |
| 10 | ... | Sepsis                    | R      | 2020-12-11  | 2020-12-29    |
+----+.....+---------------------------+--------+-------------+---------------+
10 rows in set (0.0004 sec)
```

We can also store this function in a file and reuse it later. We'll discuss reusing user code in Recipe 2.17.

You'll find the code for the generate_patients_data function in the *mysql_shell/ generate_patients_data.py* file of the recipes distribution.

See Also

For additional information about the Python pandas module, see the pandas documentation (*https://oreil.ly/qUwgV*).

2.17 Reusing Your Scripts for MySQL Shell

Problem

You wrote code for MySQL Shell and want to reuse it later.

Solution

Store your work, and later load the files using the \source command. Or, set up the files as startup scripts.

Discussion

MySQL Shell allows you to reuse your code. You can do it either by using the \source command or by setting your scripts to be executed at startup. Let's examine each of these possibilities in detail.

The \source command is available for each of the modes and works similarly to the \source of mysql command client. The only difference is that your source files should be written in the same language as the selected mode.

For example, to load the `CookbookCollection` object that we discussed in Recipe 2.15, we can type this command:

```
MySQL  cookbook  JS > \source /cookbook/recipes/mysql_shell/CookbookCollection.js
MySQL  cookbook  JS > CookbookCollection
{
    "collection": null,
    "find": <Function:find>,
    "remove": <Function:remove>,
    "save": <Function:save>
}
```

As you see, it immediately becomes available for use.

Similarly, you can import the definition of the `generate_patients_data` function that we discussed in Recipe 2.16:

```
MySQL  cookbook  Py > \source /cookbook/recipes/mysql_shell/generate_patients_data.py
```

Or, in SQL mode, you can load any SQL file:

```
MySQL  cookbook  SQL > \source /cookbook/recipes/tables/patients.sql
Query OK, 0 rows affected (0.0003 sec)
Query OK, 0 rows affected (0.0202 sec)
Query OK, 0 rows affected (0.0001 sec)
Query OK, 0 rows affected (0.0334 sec)
Query OK, 0 rows affected (0.0001 sec)
Query OK, 20 rows affected (0.0083 sec)

Records: 20  Duplicates: 0  Warnings: 0
```

If you want to execute scripts at startup, you need to edit the `mysqlshrc.js` file for JavaScript mode and `mysqlshrc.py` for Python mode, located in one of the locations that MySQL Shell uses to search for the startup scripts. These can be located in any of the following:

- The global configuration file, located in `/etc/mysql/mysqlsh/mysqlshrc.[js|py]` on Unix or `%PROGRAMDATA%\MySQL\mysqlsh\mysqlshrc.[js|py]` on Windows.

- Your personal configuration file, located either under `$HOME/.mysqlsh/mysqlshrc.[js|py]` on Unix or under `%APPDATA%\MySQL\mysqlsh\mysqlshrc.[js|py]` on Windows. Alternatively, you can specify the `MYSQLSH_USER_CONFIG_HOME` variable and store the `mysqlshrc.[js|py]` file under it.

- The `share/mysqlsh` directory, located under the MySQL Shell installation root or specified by the `MYSQLSH_HOME` variable.

The `mysqlshrc.[js|py]` format is the same as for the corresponding modes. Thus, to preload the `CookbookCollection` object, you need to convert `CookbookCollection.js` into a module by exporting our `CookbookCollection` object:

```
exports.CookbookCollection = {
// Collection where the object is stored
collection: null,
...
```

Then you need to put two lines in the `mysqlshrc.js` file:

```
sys.path = [...sys.path, '/cookbook/recipes/mysql_shell'];
const cookbook=require('CookbookCollectionModule.js')
```

In the first line, we added a directory where our modules are located in the modules' search path. On the second line, we imported the module itself. The `CookbookCollection` object is available as a property of the global `cookbook` object:

```
MySQL  cookbook  JS > cookbook
{
    "CookbookCollection": {
        "collection": null,
        "find": <Function:find>,
        "remove": <Function:remove>,
        "save": <Function:save>
    }
}
```

 MySQL Shell uses Node.js modules. Read the Node.js documentation (*https://oreil.ly/FmGCN*) to explain how to write and use JavaScript modules in MySQL Shell.

CookbookCollectionModule.js is located in the *mysql_shell* directory of the `recipes` distribution.

To import the Python `generate_patients_data` function in the startup script, we need to add the `import mysqlsh` instruction to our Python file, because when the module is loaded, global objects of the MySQL Shell are not yet available. We'll also change the following line:

```
patients=session.get_schema('cookbook').get_table('patients')
```

to:

```
patients=mysqlsh.globals.session.get_schema('cookbook').get_table('patients')
```

Otherwise, Python will fail with an error that the `session` name is not yet defined.

We'll name our module `cookbook.py` for brevity.

In our function, we use local paths from the current directory to the files; therefore, we'll change the default search path to the directory that has all the datasets in it. To do this, we'll import the os module and use its chdir method. Then we simply import the cookbook module. The resulting mysqlshrc.py will have the following code:

```
sys.path.append("/home/sveta/bin/python-3.7.7/lib/python3.7/site-packages")
sys.path.append("/cookbook/recipes/mysql_shell")

import os
os.chdir('/cookbook/recipes/datasets')
import cookbook
```

The *cookbook.py* module is located in the *mysql_shell* directory of the recipes distribution.

See Also

For additional information about customizing MySQL Shell with external scripts, see "Customizing MySQL Shell" (*https://oreil.ly/fZH38*) in the MySQL User Reference Manual.

## CHAPTER 3

MySQL Replication

3.0 Introduction

MySQL replication provides a way to set up a copy (replica) server of the active (source) database, then automatically continuously update such a copy applying all of the changes the source server receives.

Replica is useful in many situations, particularly the following:

Hot Standby
    A server, normally idle, will replace an active one in case of a failure.

Read scale
    Multiple servers, replicating from the same source, can process more parallel read requests than a single machine.

Geographical distribution
    When an application serves users in different regions, having a local database server can help users retrieve data faster.

Analytics server
    Complicated analytics queries may take hours to run, set plenty of locks, and use a lot of resources. Running them on the replica minimizes the impact on other parts of the application.

Backup server
    Taking backups from a live database involves high-IO resource usage and locking, which is necessary to avoid data inconsistencies between the backup and active dataset. Taking backups from the dedicated replica reduces the impact on production.

Delayed copy

A replica, applying updates with a delay, configured by the SOURCE_DELAY (MASTER_DELAY) option, allows for rolling back human errors, such as the removal of an important table.

 Historically, the source server was called a "master," and the replica server was called a "slave." Recently, it was discovered that the terminology *master* and *slave* do not correctly reflect how replication works, and further, the words themselves are very problematic. In the last few years, most software vendors are switching from the old to the new terminology. For MySQL, this change was implemented in version 8.0.22 and is still in progress. Not all option names and commands support the new syntax. There's also a good chance that even if your MySQL version fully supports the new syntax, you may still find legacy terminology on public forums and in previously printed books. Therefore, in this book we use the terms *source* and *replica* when discussing replication roles. For the commands and variable names that support the new syntax, we provide both syntaxes the first time, then use the new syntax. We use the legacy syntax if the change is still in progress.

MySQL replication requires special activities on both servers.

The source server stores all updates in binary log files. These files contain encoded update events. The source server writes to a single binary log file. Once it reaches max_binlog_size, the binary log is rotated and a new file is created.

The binary log file supports two formats: STATEMENT and ROW. In the STATEMENT format, SQL statements are written as they are and then encoded into binary format. In the ROW format, SQL statements are not recorded. Instead, actual updates to the table rows are stored. The ROW binary log format is preferred.

 When using the ROW binary log format it could be useful, when troubleshooting replication errors, to know the actual statement received by the source server. Use the binlog_rows_query_log_events option to store the information log event with the original query. Such an event is not participating in replication and can be retrieved for informational purposes only.

The replica server continuously requests binary log events from the source server, then stores them in special files called *relay log files*. It has a separate thread, called *IO*, or the *connection thread*, which does only this job. Another thread, or threads, called *SQL*, or the *applier thread*, reads events from the relay logs and applies them to the tables.

Each event in the binary log has its own unique identifier: its position. The position is unique to each file and resets when a new one is created. The replica may use the binary log file name and position as a unique identifier of the event.

While the binary log position uniquely identifies an event in a particular file, it cannot be used to identify whether a particular event was applied on the replica or not. To resolve this problem, *Global Transaction Identifiers (GTIDs)* were introduced. GTIDS are assigned to each transaction. They are unique across the life of a MySQL installation. They also use a mechanism to uniquely identify the server; therefore, they're safe to use even if replication is possible from multiple sources.

The replica stores information about source binary log coordinates in the special repository, defined by the `master_info_repository` variable. Such a repository can be stored either in a table or in a file.

This chapter describes how to set up and use MySQL replication. It covers all typical replication scenarios, including the following:

- One-way source-replica setup for two servers
- Circular replication
- Multisource replication
- Semisynchronous replication
- Group replication

3.1 Configuring Basic Replication Between One Source and One Replica

Problem

You want to prepare two servers for the replication.

Solution

Add the configuration `log-bin` option to the source configuration file, specify a unique `server_id` for both servers, add options to support GTIDs and/or the nondefault binary log format, and create a user with the `REPLICATION SLAVE` privilege on the source.

Discussion

First, you need to prepare both servers to be able to handle replication events.

On the source server, do the following:

- Enable the binary log by adding the log-bin option into the configuration file. Changing this option requires a restart. The binary log is enabled by default since version 8.0.

- Set the unique server_id. server_id is a dynamic variable and can be changed without taking the server offline, but we strongly recommend setting it in the configuration file too, so it won't be overridden after restart.

- Create a replication user, and grant REPLICATION SLAVE to it:

```
mysql> CREATE USER repl@'%' IDENTIFIED BY 'replrepl';
Query OK, 0 rows affected (0,01 sec)

mysql> GRANT REPLICATION SLAVE ON *.* TO repl@'%';
Query OK, 0 rows affected (0,03 sec)
```

 In MySQL 8.0, the default authentication plug-in is cach ing_sha2_password, which requires TLS connection or the source public key. Therefore, if you want to use this plug-in, you need to enable TLS connection for the replica as described in Recipe 3.14 or use the SOURCE_PUBLIC_KEY_PATH=1 (GET_MAS TER_PUBLIC_KEY=1) option of the CHANGE REPLICATION SOURCE (CHANGE MASTER) command.

Alternatively, you can use the authentication plug-in, allowing insecure connections:

```
mysql> CREATE USER repl@'%' IDENTIFIED WITH mysql_native_password BY 'replrepl';
Query OK, 0 rows affected (0,01 sec)

mysql> GRANT REPLICATION SLAVE ON *.* TO repl@'%';
Query OK, 0 rows affected (0,03 sec)
```

On the replica, just set the unique server_id.

 Since version 8.0, you can use SET PERSIST to save a dynamically changed variable permanently:

```
mysql> SET PERSIST server_id=200;
Query OK, 0 rows affected (0,01 sec)
```

See "Persisted System Variables" in the MySQL User Reference Manual (*https://oreil.ly/3ImnL*) for details.

At this stage, you can tune other options that affect replication safety and performance, particularly the following:

binlog_format
Binary log format

GTID support
    Support for global transaction identifiers

`replica_parallel_type` *(slave_parallel_type) and* `replica_parallel_workers`
`(slave_parallel_workers)`
    Multithreaded replica support

Binary log on the replica
    Define if and how the replica will use the binary log

We'll cover these options in the following recipes.

3.2 Position-Based Replication in the New Installation Environment

Problem

You want to set up a replica of the just-installed MySQL server using position-based configuration.

Solution

Prepare the source and replica servers as described in Recipe 3.1. Obtain the current binary log position using the `SHOW MASTER STATUS` command on the source server, and point the replica to the appropriate position using the `CHANGE REPLICATION SOURCE...source_log_file='BINARY LOG FILE NAME'`, `source_log_pos=POSITION;` (`CHANGE MASTER...master_log_file='BINARY LOG FILE NAME'`, `master_log_pos=POSITION;`) command.

Discussion

For this recipe, we assume that you have two freshly installed servers with no user data in them. There is no write activity on any of the servers.

First, prepare them for replication as described in Recipe 3.1. Then, on the source, run the `SHOW MASTER STATUS` command:

```
mysql> SHOW MASTER STATUS;
+------------------+----------+--------------+------------------+-------------------+
| File             | Position | Binlog_Do_DB | Binlog_Ignore_DB | Executed_Gtid_Set |
+------------------+----------+--------------+------------------+-------------------+
| master-bin.000001|     156  |              |                  |                   |
+------------------+----------+--------------+------------------+-------------------+
1 row in set (0.00 sec)
```

The field `File` contains the name of the current binary log, and the `Position` field contains the current position. Record the values of these fields.

On the replica, run the CHANGE REPLICATION SOURCE (CHANGE MASTER) command (*https://oreil.ly/ZDeOm*):

```
mysql> CHANGE REPLICATION SOURCE
    -> TO SOURCE_HOST='sourcehost',        -- Host of the source server
    -> SOURCE_PORT=3306,                   -- Port of the source server
    -> SOURCE_USER='repl',                 -- Replication user
    -> SOURCE_PASSWORD='replrepl',         -- Password
    -> SOURCE_LOG_FILE='source-bin.000001', -- Binary log file
    -> SOURCE_LOG_POS=156,                 -- Start position
    -> GET_SOURCE_PUBLIC_KEY=1;
Query OK, 0 rows affected, 1 warning (0.06 sec)
```

To start the replica, use the START REPLICA (START SLAVE) command:

```
mysql> START REPLICA;
Query OK, 0 rows affected (0.01 sec)
```

To check if the replica is running, use SHOW REPLICA STATUS (SHOW SLAVE STATUS):

```
mysql> \P grep Running
PAGER set to 'grep Running'
mysql> SHOW REPLICA STATUS\G
            Replica_IO_Running: Yes
           Replica_SQL_Running: Yes
     Replica_SQL_Running_State: Slave has read all relay log;↵
                                waiting for more updates
1 row in set (0.00 sec)
```

The preceding listing confirms that both the IO (connection) and SQL (applier) replica threads are running and that the replication state is fine. We'll discuss the full output of the SHOW REPLICA STATUS command in Recipe 3.15.

Now you can enable writes on the source server.

3.3 Setting Up a Position-Based Replica of a MySQL Installation that Is Already in Use

Problem

Setting up a replica for the newly installed server is different from the case in which the future source already has data. In the latter case, you need to be especially careful to not introduce data inconsistency by specifying the wrong starting position. In this recipe, we provide instructions on how to set up a replica of the MySQL installation in use.

Solution

Prepare the source and replica servers as described in Recipe 3.1, stop all writes on the source server, back it up, then obtain the current binary log position using the SHOW MASTER STATUS command, which will be used for pointing the replica to the appropriate position using the CHANGE REPLICATION SOURCE...source_log_file='BINARY LOG FILE NAME', source_log_pos=POSITION command.

Discussion

As in the case of installing a new replica, both servers need to be configured for replication use, as described in Recipe 3.1. Before initiating setup, you need to ensure that both servers have the unique server_id and that the source server has binary logging enabled. You can create a replication user now, or you can do it before setting up a replica.

If you have a server that has already been running for a while and want to set up a replica of it, you need to make a backup first, restore it on the replica, then point the replica to the source server. The challenge for this setup is using the correct binary log position: if the server is accepting writes while backup is running, the position will be consistently changing. As a result, the SHOW MASTER STATUS command will return the wrong result unless you stop all writes while making the backup.

Standard backup tools support special options when making a backup of the future source server for a replica to bypass this issue.

mysqldump, described in Recipe 6.6, has the --source-data (--master-data) option. If the --source-data option is set to 1, the CHANGE REPLICATION SOURCE statement, with the binary log coordinates at the time of the backup start, will be written into the resulting dump file and executed when the dump file is loaded:

```
$ mysqldump --host=127.0.0.1 --user=root \
>    --source-data=1 --all-databases > mydump.sql
$ grep -b5 "CHANGE REPLICATION SOURCE" -m1 mydump.sql
906-
907---
910--- Position to start replication or point-in-time recovery from
974---
977-
978:CHANGE REPLICATION SOURCE TO SOURCE_LOG_FILE='source-bin.000002',↵
    SOURCE_LOG_POS=156;
1052-
1053---
1056--- Current Database: `mtr`
1083---
1086-
```

If you want the replication position to be in the resulting dump file, but do not want the CHANGE REPLICATION SOURCE command to be automatically executed, set the --source-data option to 2: in this case, the statement will be written as a comment. You can execute it manually later.

Tools that make online binary backups, such as Percona XtraBackup (*https://oreil.ly/bpPMg*) or MySQL Enterprise Backup (*https://oreil.ly/hzrV5*), store binary log coordinates in special metadata files. Consult the documentation of your backup tool to find out how to safely back up the source server.

There are several kinds of backups for MySQL. Tools that perform online backups don't require you to stop the MySQL server. Logical backups result in a file with a set of commands that allow you to restore data. Binary backups copy physical database files. Binary backups are usually much faster than logical backups. Restoring binary backups is dramatically faster compared to restoring logical backups.

The simplest and fastest binary backup utility is `cp`, which requires MySQL server to be stopped. Online backup tools allow you to copy binary data while the server is running and are the preferable solution for large datasets.

Logical backup solutions, however, are compatible with higher differences between versions and can be used to recover data. They are also handy when you need to migrate a small part of your data, such as a table or even part of the table.

Once you have a backup, restore it on the replica. For `mysqldump`, use `mysql` client to load the dump:

```
$ mysql < mydump.sql
```

Once the backup is restored, start replication using the START REPLICA command.

3.4 Setting Up GTID-Based Replication

Problem

You want to set up a replica using global transaction identifiers (GTIDs).

Solution

Add the `gtid_mode=ON` and `enforce_gtid_consistency=ON` option in both the source and replica configuration files, then point the replica to the source server using the CHANGE REPLICATION SOURCE...SOURCE_AUTO_POSITION=1 command.

Discussion

Position-based replication is easy to set up but is error-prone. What if you mix up and specify a position in the future? In this case, some transactions will be missed. Or, what happens if you specify a position in the past? In this case, the same transaction will be applied twice, and you'll end up with duplicated, missed, or corrupted rows.

To solve this issue, GTIDs were introduced to uniquely identify each transaction on the server. A GTID consists of two parts: the unique ID of the server where this transaction as executed the first time, and the unique ID of the transaction on this server. The source server ID is usually the value of the server_uuid global variable, and the transaction ID is a number starting with 1:

```
mysql> SHOW MASTER STATUS\G
*************************** 1. row ***************************
             File: binlog.000001
         Position: 358
     Binlog_Do_DB:
 Binlog_Ignore_DB:
Executed_Gtid_Set: 467ccf91-0341-11eb-a2ae-0242dc638c6c:1
1 row in set (0.00 sec)

mysql> select @@gtid_executed;
+----------------------------------------+
| @@gtid_executed                        |
+----------------------------------------+
| 467ccf91-0341-11eb-a2ae-0242dc638c6c:1 |
+----------------------------------------+
1 row in set (0.00 sec)
```

Transactions, executed by the server, are stored in GTID sets, and their GTIDs are visible in the SHOW MASTER STATUS output. You will also find them in the gtid_exe cuted variable. The set contains the unique ID of the originating server and the range of transaction numbers.

In the following example, 467ccf91-0341-11eb-a2ae-0242dc638c6c is the source server's unique ID, and 1-299 is the range of transaction numbers that were executed on this server:

```
mysql> select @@gtid_executed;
+--------------------------------------------+
| @@gtid_executed                            |
+--------------------------------------------+
| 467ccf91-0341-11eb-a2ae-0242dc638c6c:1-299 |
+--------------------------------------------+
1 row in set (0.00 sec)
```

GTID sets can contain ranges, individual transactions, and groups of them, separated by a colon symbol. GTIDs with different source IDs are separated by a comma:

```
mysql> select @@gtid_executed\G
*************************** 1. row ***************************
@@gtid_executed: 000bbf91-0341-11eb-a2ae-0242dc638c6c:1,
467ccf91-0341-11eb-a2ae-0242dc638c6c:1-310:400
1 row in set (0.00 sec)
```

Normally, GTIDs are automatically assigned, and you don't need to worry about their values.

However, in order to use GTIDs, there are additional steps to prepare your servers.

Two configuration options are required to enable GTIDs: `gtid_mode=ON` and `enforce-gtid-consistency=ON`. They must be enabled on both servers before starting replication.

If you're setting up a new replica of a source that is running with GTIDs enabled, just adding these options into the configuration file and restarting the servers is enough. Once you've done that, you can enable replication using the CHANGE REPLICATION SOURCE...SOURCE_AUTO_POSITION=1 command and start it, as follows:

```
mysql> CHANGE REPLICATION SOURCE TO
    -> SOURCE_HOST='sourcehost',      -- Host of the source server
    -> SOURCE_PORT=3306,              -- Port of the source server
    -> SOURCE_USER='repl',            -- Replication user
    -> SOURCE_PASSWORD='replrepl',    -- Password
    -> GET_SOURCE_PUBLIC_KEY=1,
    -> SOURCE_AUTO_POSITION=1;
Query OK, 0 rows affected, 1 warning (0.06 sec)

mysql> START REPLICA;
Query OK, 0 rows affected (0.01 sec)
```

However, if replication was already running using position-based setup, you need to perform additional steps:

1. Stop all updates, making both servers read only:
   ```
   mysql> SET GLOBAL super_read_only=1;
   Query OK, 0 rows affected (0.01 sec)
   ```

2. Wait until the replica catches up with all updates from the source server: the `File` and `Position` values from the `SHOW MASTER STATUS` output on the source server should match the `Relay_Source_Log_File` and `Exec_Source_Log_Pos` values of the `SHOW REPLICA STATUS`, taken on the replica.

Inaccuracy of Seconds_Behind_Source

Don't rely on the `Seconds_Behind_Source` value, because it's inaccurate.

For example, in the following output on the source server:
```
mysql> SHOW MASTER STATUS\G
*************************** 1. row ***************************
             File: master-bin.000001
         Position: 9614
     Binlog_Do_DB:
 Binlog_Ignore_DB:
Executed_Gtid_Set:
1 row in set (0.00 sec)
```

the binary log position is 7090:
```
mysql> \P grep -E "Source_Log_Pos|Seconds_Behind_Source"
PAGER set to 'grep -E "Source_Log_Pos|Seconds_Behind_Source"'
mysql> SHOW REPLICA STATUS\G
```

```
            Read_Source_Log_Pos: 9614
            Exec_Source_Log_Pos: 7308
          Seconds_Behind_Source: 0
    1 row in set (0.00 sec)
```

On the replica, instead, the `Read_Source_Log_Pos` position that was read by the IO thread is same as on the source server, while the value position of the latest executed event, `Exec_Source_Log_Pos`, is 7308: somewhere earlier in the binary log file. The `Seconds_Behind_Source` value of 0 is normal because the MySQL server can execute thousands of updates per second. Still, this doesn't mean that the replica fully catches up with the source server.

3. Once the replica has caught up, stop both servers, enable the `gtid_mode=ON` and `enforce-gtid-consistency=ON` options, start them, and enable replication:

```
mysql> CHANGE REPLICATION SOURCE TO
    -> SOURCE_HOST='sourcehost',    -- Host of the source server
    -> SOURCE_PORT=3306,            -- Port of the source server
    -> SOURCE_USER='repl',          -- Replication user
    -> SOURCE_PASSWORD='replrepl',  -- Password
    -> GET_SOURCE_PUBLIC_KEY=1,
    -> SOURCE_AUTO_POSITION=1;
Query OK, 0 rows affected, 1 warning (0.06 sec)

mysql> START REPLICA;
Query OK, 0 rows affected (0.01 sec)
```

You can omit replication source connection options if they were already known to the replica before you started switching the replication from position-based to GTID-based.

You're not required to enable binary logging on the replica in order to use GTIDs. But if you're going to write to the replica outside of the replication, its transactions wouldn't have their own GTID assigned. GTIDs will be used only for the replicated events.

See Also

For additional information about setting up MySQL replication with GTIDs, see the MySQL User Reference Manual (*https://oreil.ly/JHoGF*).

3.5 Configuring a Binary Log Format

Problem

You want to use the most suitable binary log format that is the most suitable for your application.

Solution

Decide which format best suits your needs, and set it up using the `binlog_format` configuration option.

Discussion

`ROW` has been the default MySQL binary log format since version 5.7.7. This is the safest possible format, fitting most applications. It stores encoded table rows, modified by the binary log event.

However, the `ROW` binary log format may generate more disk and network traffic than the `STATEMENT` format. This happens because it stores two copies of the modified row in the binary log file: before the changes and after the changes. If a table has several columns, the values for all of them will be logged two times even if only one column was modified.

If you want the binary log to store only the changed column and the column that can be used to identify the changed rows (normally the primary key), you can use the `binlog_row_image=minimal` configuration option. This will work perfectly if the tables on the source server and its replica are identical but may cause issues if the number of columns, their data types, or the primary key definitions do not match.

To store a full row, except `TEXT` or `BLOB` columns that weren't changed by the statement and are not required to uniquely identify the modified row, use the `bin log_row_image=noblob` option.

If the row format still generates too much traffic, you can switch it to the `STATEMENT`. In this case, statements, modifying rows, will be recorded, then executed by the replica. To use the `STATEMENT` binary log format, set the `binlog_format=STATEMENT` option.

The `STATEMENT` format is not recommended because some statements can produce different updates on different servers, even if the data was originally identical. These statements are called *nondeterministic statements*. To deal with this downside, MySQL has a special binary log format, `MIXED`, that normally logs events in the `STATEMENT` format and automatically switches to `ROW` if a statement is nondeterministic.

If the binary log is enabled on the replica, it should use either the same binary log format as its source server or the MIXED format, unless you disabled binary logging of the replicated events using the `log_replica_updates=OFF` (`log_slave_updates=OFF`) option. This is required because the replica doesn't convert the binary log format and simply copies received events into its own binary log file. If the formats don't match, replication will stop with an error.

The binary log format can be changed dynamically on the global or session level. To change the format on the global level, run the following:

```
mysql> set global binlog_format='statement';
Query OK, 0 rows affected (0,00 sec)
```

To change the format on the global level and store it permanently, use the following:

```
mysql> set persist binlog_format='row';
Query OK, 0 rows affected (0,00 sec)
```

Note that this will not change the binary logging format for the existing connections. To change the format on the session level, execute the following:

```
mysql> set session binlog_format='mixed';
Query OK, 0 rows affected (0,00 sec)
```

While the STATEMENT format usually generates less traffic than ROW, this is not always the case. For example, complicated statements with long WHERE or IN clauses that modify just a few rows generate a bigger binary log event with the STATEMENT format.

Another issue with the STATEMENT format is that the replica executes received events the same way they were running on the source server. Therefore, if a statement isn't effective, it will run slow on the replica too. For example, statements on large tables that have a WHERE clause that cannot be resolved using indexes are usually slow. In this case, switching to the ROW format may improve performance.

 Normally, ROW events use a primary key to find the row on the replica that needs to be updated. If a table has no primary key, the ROW format can work extremely slowly. Older versions of MySQL could even update the wrong row because of (now-fixed) bugs. An auto-generated primary key that is used by the InnoDB storage engine is no help here, because it may generate different values on the source and replica servers for the same row. Therefore, it's mandatory to define a primary key for tables when using the ROW binary log format.

3.6 Using Replication Filters

Problem

You want to replicate only events for specific databases or tables.

Solution

Use replication filters on the source, replica, or on both.

Discussion

MySQL can filter updates to the specific databases or tables. You can set up such filters on the source server to prevent them from being recorded in the binary log, or on the replica server so replication won't execute them.

Filtering on the source server

 Replication filters can cause data loss if set up incorrectly. Study this recipe very carefully, and always test how they work for your setup before deploying on production.

To log only updates to a specific database, use the `binlog-do-db=db_name` configuration option. There is no corresponding variable for this option; therefore, changing the binary log filter requires a restart. To log updates for two or more specific databases, specify the `binlog-do-db` option as many times as needed:

```
[mysqld]
binlog-do-db=cookbook
binlog-do-db=test
```

Binary log filters behave differently for `ROW` and `STATEMENT` binary log formats. For statement-based logging, only the default database is taken into account. If you are using fully qualified table names, such as `mydatabase.mytable`, they'll be logged based on the default database value and not on the database part of the update.

Thus, for the preceding configuration file snippet, the following three updates will be logged in the binary log:

- ```
  $ mysql cookbook
  mysql> INSERT INTO limbs (thing, legs, arms) VALUES('horse', 4, 0);
  Query OK, 1 row affected (0,01 sec)
  ```

- ```
  mysql> USE cookbook
  Database changed
  mysql> DELETE FROM limbs WHERE thing='horse';
  Query OK, 1 row affected (0,00 sec)
  ```

```
•   mysql> USE cookbook
    Database changed
    mysql> INSERT INTO donotlog.onlylocal (mysecret)
        -> values('I do not want to replicate it!');
    Query OK, 1 row affected (0,01 sec)
```

However, this update on the cookbook database would not be logged:

```
mysql> use donotlog
Database changed
mysql> UPDATE cookbook.limbs set arms=8 WHERE thing='squid';
Query OK, 1 row affected (0,01 sec)
Rows matched: 1  Changed: 1  Warnings: 0
```

When the ROW binary log format is used, the default database is ignored for fully qualified table names. Thus, all these updates will be logged:

```
$ mysql cookbook
mysql> INSERT INTO limbs (thing, legs, arms) VALUES('horse', 4, 0);
Query OK, 1 row affected (0,01 sec)
mysql> USE cookbook
Database changed
mysql> DELETE FROM limbs WHERE thing='horse';
Query OK, 1 row affected (0,00 sec)
mysql> USE donotlog
Database changed
mysql> UPDATE cookbook.limbs SET arms=10 WHERE thing='squid';
Query OK, 1 row affected (0,01 sec)
Rows matched: 1  Changed: 1  Warnings: 0
```

However, this statement will not be logged:

```
mysql> USE cookbook
Database changed
mysql> INSERT INTO donotlog.onlylocal (mysecret)
    -> VALUES('I do not want to replicate it!');
Query OK, 1 row affected (0,01 sec)
```

For multiple table updates, only updates to tables belonging to databases specified by filters are logged. In the following examples, only updates to the cookbook.limbs table are logged:

```
mysql> use donotlog
Database changed
mysql> UPDATE cookbook.limbs, donotlog.onlylocal SET arms=1,
    -> mysecret='I do not want to log it!';
Query OK, 12 rows affected (0,01 sec)
Rows matched: 12  Changed: 12  Warnings: 0
mysql> USE cookbook
Database changed
mysql> UPDATE cookbook.limbs, donotlog.onlylocal SET arms=0,
    -> mysecret='I do not want to log and replicate this!'
    -> WHERE cookbook.limbs.thing='table';
Query OK, 2 rows affected (0,00 sec)
Rows matched: 2  Changed: 2  Warnings: 0
```

Data Definition Language (DDL) statements, such as ALTER TABLE, are always replicated in the STATEMENT format. Therefore, filtering rules for this format apply to them no matter the value of the binlog_format variable.

If you want to log updates to all databases on your server and skip only a few of them, use binlog-ignore-db filters. Specify the filter multiple times to ignore multiple databases:

```
[mysqld]
binlog-ignore-db=donotlog
binlog-ignore-db=mysql
```

binlog-ignore-db filters work similarly to binlog-do-db filters. In the case of STATE MENT binary logging, they honor the default database and ignore it if the ROW binary log format is used. If you didn't specify a default database and use the STATEMENT binary log format, all updates will be logged.

If you use the MIXED binary log format, filtering rules will be applied depending on whether the update is stored in the STATEMENT or ROW format.

To find out which binary log filters are currently in use, run the SHOW MASTER STATUS command:

```
mysql> SHOW MASTER STATUS\G
*************************** 1. row ***************************
             File: binlog.000008
         Position: 1202
     Binlog_Do_DB: cookbook,test
 Binlog_Ignore_DB: donotlog,mysql
Executed_Gtid_Set:
1 row in set (0,00 sec)
```

 Binary log files are often used not only for replication but also for point-in-time recovery (PITR) from failure. In this case, filtered updates cannot be restored, because they're not stored anywhere. If you want to use binary logs for PITR and still filter some databases, log everything on the source server and filter on the replica.

Filtering on the replica

The replica has more options to filter events. You can filter either specific databases or tables. You can also use wildcards.

Filtering on the database level works in the same fashion as on the source server. It's controlled by the replicate-do-db and replicate-ignore-db options. If you want to filter multiple databases, specify these options as many times as you need.

To filter specific tables, use the `replicate-do-table` and `replicate-ignore-table` options. They take the fully qualified table name as an argument:

```
[mysqld]
replicate-do-db=cookbook
replicate-ignore-db=donotlog
replicate-do-table=donotlog.dataforeveryone
replicate-ignore-table=cookbook.limbs
```

But the most flexible and safe syntax for replication filters is `replicate-wild-do-table` and `replicate-wild-ignore-table`. As the names suggest, they accept wildcards in the arguments. Wildcard syntax is the same as used for the `LIKE` clause. Refer to Recipe 7.10 for details on the `LIKE` clause syntax.

The `_` symbol replaces exactly one character. Thus, `replicate-wild-ignore-table=cookbook.standings_` filters the `cookbook.standings1` and `cookbook.standings2` tables, but doesn't filter `cookbook.standings12` and `cookbook.standings`.

The `%` symbol replaces zero or more characters. Thus, `replicate-wild-do-table=cookbook.movies%` instructs the replica to apply updates to the `cookbook.movies`, `cookbook.movies_actors`, and `cookbook.movies_actors_link` tables.

If a table name itself contains a wildcard character that you don't want to replace, you need to escape it. Thus, the `replicate-wild-ignore-table=cookbook.trip_l_g` option will filter the `cookbook.trip_leg` and `cookbook.trip_log` tables but also `cookbook.tripslag`, while `replicate-wild-ignore-table=cookbook.trip\_l_g` will filter updates only to the `cookbook.trip_leg` and `cookbook.trip_log` tables. Note that if you specify this option on the command line, you may need to double escape wildcard characters depending on the `SHELL` version you use.

Table-level filters are independent from the default database regardless of the binary log format. Therefore, it is safer to use them. If you want to filter all tables in the specific database or databases, use wildcards:

```
[mysqld]
replicate-wild-do-table=cookbook.%
replicate-wild-ignore-table=donotlog.%
```

However, unlike database filters, `replicate-wild-do-table` and `replicate-wild-ignore-table` cannot filter stored routines or events. If you need to filter them, you have to use database-level filters.

Replication filters can be set for the specific replication channel (Recipe 3.10). To specify the per-channel filter prefix database, table name, or wildcard expression with the channel name, followed by a colon, run the following:

```
[mysqld]
replicate-do-db=first:cookbook
replicate-ignore-db=second:donotlog
replicate-do-table=first:donotlog.dataforeveryone
replicate-ignore-table=second:cookbook.hitlog
replicate-wild-do-table=first:cookbook.movies%
replicate-wild-ignore-table=second:cookbook.movies%
```

You can specify replication filters not only via configuration options but also using the CHANGE REPLICATION FILTER command:

```
mysql> CHANGE REPLICATION FILTER
    -> REPLICATE_DO_DB = (cookbook),
    -> REPLICATE_IGNORE_DB = (donotlog),
    -> REPLICATE_DO_TABLE = (donotlog.dataforeveryone),
    -> REPLICATE_IGNORE_TABLE = (cookbook.limbs),
    -> REPLICATE_WILD_DO_TABLE = ('cookbook.%'),
    -> REPLICATE_WILD_IGNORE_TABLE = ('cookbook.trip\_l_g');
Query OK, 0 rows affected (0.00 sec)
```

 You need to stop replication using the STOP REPLICA (STOP SLAVE) command each time you change the replication parameters.

To find out which replication filters are currently applied, use the SHOW REPLICA STATUS\G command or query tables replication_applier_filters and replication_applier_global_filters in the Performance Schema:

```
mysql> SHOW REPLICA STATUS\G
*************************** 1. row ***************************
              Replica_IO_State:
                   Source_Host: 127.0.0.1
                   Source_User: root
                   Source_Port: 13000
                 Connect_Retry: 60
               Source_Log_File: binlog.000001
           Read_Source_Log_Pos: 156
                Relay_Log_File: Delly-7390-relay-bin.000002
                 Relay_Log_Pos: 365
         Relay_Source_Log_File: binlog.000001
            Replica_IO_Running: No
           Replica_SQL_Running: No
               Replicate_Do_DB: cookbook
           Replicate_Ignore_DB: donotlog
            Replicate_Do_Table: donotlog.dataforeveryone
        Replicate_Ignore_Table: cookbook.limbs
       Replicate_Wild_Do_Table: cookbook.%
   Replicate_Wild_Ignore_Table: cookbook.trip\_l_g
...

mysql> SELECT * FROM performance_schema.replication_applier_filters\G
*************************** 1. row ***************************
  CHANNEL_NAME:
   FILTER_NAME: REPLICATE_DO_DB
```

```
        FILTER_RULE: cookbook
      CONFIGURED_BY: CHANGE_REPLICATION_FILTER
       ACTIVE_SINCE: 2020-10-04 13:43:21.183768
            COUNTER: 0
*************************** 2. row ***************************
       CHANNEL_NAME:
        FILTER_NAME: REPLICATE_IGNORE_DB
        FILTER_RULE: donotlog
      CONFIGURED_BY: CHANGE_REPLICATION_FILTER
       ACTIVE_SINCE: 2020-10-04 13:43:21.183768
            COUNTER: 0
*************************** 3. row ***************************
       CHANNEL_NAME:
        FILTER_NAME: REPLICATE_DO_TABLE
        FILTER_RULE: donotlog.dataforeveryone
      CONFIGURED_BY: CHANGE_REPLICATION_FILTER
       ACTIVE_SINCE: 2020-10-04 13:43:21.183768
            COUNTER: 0
*************************** 4. row ***************************
       CHANNEL_NAME:
        FILTER_NAME: REPLICATE_IGNORE_TABLE
        FILTER_RULE: cookbook.limbs
      CONFIGURED_BY: CHANGE_REPLICATION_FILTER
       ACTIVE_SINCE: 2020-10-04 13:43:21.183768
            COUNTER: 0
*************************** 5. row ***************************
       CHANNEL_NAME:
        FILTER_NAME: REPLICATE_WILD_DO_TABLE
        FILTER_RULE: cookbook.%
      CONFIGURED_BY: CHANGE_REPLICATION_FILTER
       ACTIVE_SINCE: 2020-10-04 13:43:21.183768
            COUNTER: 0
*************************** 6. row ***************************
       CHANNEL_NAME:
        FILTER_NAME: REPLICATE_WILD_IGNORE_TABLE
        FILTER_RULE: cookbook.trip\_l_g
      CONFIGURED_BY: CHANGE_REPLICATION_FILTER
       ACTIVE_SINCE: 2020-10-04 13:43:21.183768
            COUNTER: 0
6 rows in set (0.00 sec)
```

See Also

For additional information about replication filters, see "How Servers Evaluate Replication Filtering Rules" (*https://oreil.ly/1kmxC*).

3.7 Rewriting a Database on the Replica

Problem

You want to replicate to a database on a replica that has a different name from the one used on the source server.

Solution

Use the `replicate-rewrite-db` option on the replica server.

Discussion

MySQL allows rewriting a database name on the fly using the replication filter `replicate-rewrite-db`.

You can set this filter in the configuration file command line:

```
[mysqld]
replicate-rewrite-db=cookbook->recipes
```

or via the CHANGE REPLICATION FILTER command:

```
mysql> CHANGE REPLICATION FILTER
    -> REPLICATE_REWRITE_DB=((cookbook,recipes));
```

Or, for the multiple-channel replica:

```
[mysqld]
replicate-rewrite-db=channel_id:cookbook->recipes
```

or via the CHANGE REPLICATION FILTER command:

```
mysql> CHANGE REPLICATION FILTER
    -> REPLICATE_REWRITE_DB=((cookbook,recipes))
    -> FOR CHANNEL 'channel_id';
```

 Be sure to use double brackets for the filter value and quotes for the channel name.

MySQL does not support RENAME DATABASE operation. Therefore, to rename the database, you need to first create a database with the new name, then restore the data from the original database into the new database:

```
mysql> CREATE DATABASE recipes;
$ mysql recipes < cookbook.sql
```

You need to take a dump with the `mysqldump` command of the single database. If you are dumping with the `--databases` option, also specify the `--no-create-db` option, so the resulting file will not contain the CREATE DATABASE statement.

3.8 Using a Multithreaded Replica

Problem

The replica is installed on better hardware than the source, and the network connection between servers is good, but replication lag is increasing.

Solution

Use multiple replication applier threads.

Discussion

The MySQL server is multithreaded. It applies incoming updates in a highly concurrent manner. By default, it uses all hardware CPU cores when processing application requests. However, the replica by default uses a single thread to apply incoming events from the source server. As a result, it uses fewer resources to process replicated events and may lag even on decent hardware.

To resolve this issue, use multiple applier threads. To do so, set the `replica_paral lel_workers` variable to a value greater than 1. This specifies the number of parallel threads the replica will use to apply events. It makes sense to set the value of this variable up to or below the number of virtual CPU cores. Variable has no immediate effect; you have to restart replication to apply the change:

```
mysql> SET GLOBAL replica_parallel_workers=8;
Query OK, 0 rows affected (0.01 sec)

mysql> STOP REPLICA SQL_THREAD;
Query OK, 0 rows affected (0.01 sec)

mysql> START REPLICA;
Query OK, 0 rows affected (0.04 sec)
```

Not all replication events can be applied in parallel. What if the binary log contains two statements updating the same row?

```
update limbs set arms=8 where thing='squid';
update limbs set arms=10 where thing='squid';
```

Depending on the order of events, the `limbs` table will have either 8 or 10 arms for the squid. If these two statements are executed in different order on the source and replica, they will end up with different data.

MySQL uses a special algorithm for dependency tracking. The current algorithm is set by the `replica_parallel_type` variable on the replica and the `binlog_transac tion_dependency_tracking` variable on the source.

The default value of the `replica_parallel_type` variable was DATABASE before 8.0.27 and is LOGICAL_CLOCK since this version. With this value, updates belonging to different databases can be applied in parallel, while updates to the same database are applied sequentially. This value does not correlate with `binlog_transaction_depend ency_tracking` on the source.

Parallelization on the database level does not perform much better for setups that update fewer databases than the number of CPU cores on the replica. To resolve this issue, `replica_parallel_type=LOGICAL_CLOCK` has been introduced. For this type, transactions belonging to the same binary log group commit on the source are applied in parallel.

After changing the `replica_parallel_type` variable, you need to restart the replica.

The value of the `binlog_transaction_dependency_tracking` variable on the *source* server defines which transactions belong to the same commit group. Default is COMMIT_ORDER, which is generated from the source's timestamps. With this value, transactions committed nearly at the same time on the source server will be executed in parallel on the replica. This mode works perfectly if the source actively executes many small transactions. However, if the source server does not commit often, the replica will execute sequentially those transactions that were committed in different times even if they cannot interfere with each other and were executed on the source in parallel.

To resolve this issue, the `binlog_transaction_dependency_tracking` modes WRITE SET and WRITESET_SESSION were introduced. In these modes, MySQL decides if transactions are dependent on each other using a hashing algorithm, specified by the `transaction_write_set_extraction` variable and can be either XXHASH64 (default) or MURMUR32. This means that if the transactions modify a set of rows independent from one another, they can be executed in parallel, no matter how much time has passed between commits on each of them.

With the `binlog_transaction_dependency_tracking` mode set to WRITESET, even transactions originally executed within the same session can be applied in parallel. This may cause issues when the replica sees changes in a different order from the source in some periods of time. It may or may not be acceptable depending on your application needs. To avoid such a situation, you can enable the `replica_pre serve_commit_order` (`slave_preserve_commit_order`) option, which instructs the replica to apply binary log events in the same order as they were originally executed on the source server. Another solutions is to set `binlog_transaction_depend ency_tracking` to WRITESET_SESSION. This mode ensures that transactions that originated from the same session are never applied in parallel.

The `binlog_transaction_dependency_tracking` variable is dynamic, and you can modify it without stopping the server. You can also set it on the session level for the specific session only.

See Also

For additional information about multithreaded replicas, see "Improving the Parallel Applier with Writeset-based Dependency Tracking" (*https://oreil.ly/TQi7f*).

3.9 Setting Up Circular Replication

Problem

You want to set up a chain of servers that replicate from one another.

Solution

Make each server in the chain a source and a replica of its peers.

Discussion

Sometimes you may need to write to several MySQL servers and want updates to be visible on each of them. With MySQL replication, this is possible. It supports such popular setups as two-server, a chain of servers (A -> B -> C -> D ->...), circular, and star (*https://oreil.ly/G5MGQ*), as well as any creative setup you can imagine. For our circular replication example, you just need to set up every server as a source and replica of one another.

You need to be very careful when using such a replication. Because updates are incoming from any server, they can conflict with one another. Imagine two nodes inserting a row with id=42 at the same time. First, each node inserts a row, then receives the exact same event from the binary log. The replication will stop with a duplicate key error.

If you then try to delete a row with id=42 on both nodes, you will receive an error again! Because when the DELETE statement is received by the replication, the channel row will already have been deleted.

But the worst can happen if you update a row with the same ID. Imagine if node1 sets the value to 42, and node2 sets the value to 25. After the replication events are applied, node1 will have a row with the value 25 and node2 with the value 42. This is different from what they initially had after the local update!

Still, there can be very valid reasons to use circular replication. For example, you may want to use one of the nodes mostly for the purposes of one application and another for another application. You can have options and hardware that is suitable for both. Or you may have servers in different geographical locations (e.g., countries) and want to store local data closer to users. Or you can use your servers mostly for reads but still need to update them. And, finally, you may set up a hot standby server that technically allows writes but practically receives them only when the main source server dies.

In this recipe, we'll discuss how to set up a chain of three servers. You can modify this recipe for two or more servers. Then we'll discuss safety considerations concerning the use of replication chains.

Setting up circle replication with three servers

Prepare servers to use in the circular replication
Here are the steps:

- Follow the instructions in Recipe 3.1 for the source server.

- Make sure the `log_replica_updates` option is enabled. Otherwise, if your replication chain includes more than two servers, updates would apply only on the neighboring ones.

- Ensure that the `replicate-same-server-id` option is disabled. Otherwise, you may end up in a situation where the same update will be applying in loops forever.

Point nodes to each other
Run the `CHANGE REPLICATION SOURCE` command on each server, as described in Recipe 3.2 or in Recipe 3.4. Specify the correct connection values. For example, if you want to have a circle of servers `hostA -> hostB -> hostC -> hostA`, you need to point `hostB` to `hostA`, `hostA` to `hostC`, and `hostC` to `hostB`:

```
hostA> CHANGE REPLICATION SOURCE TO SOURCE_HOST='hostC', ...
hostB> CHANGE REPLICATION SOURCE TO SOURCE_HOST='hostA', ...
hostC> CHANGE REPLICATION SOURCE TO SOURCE_HOST='hostB', ...
```

Start replication
Start replication using the `START REPLICA` command.

Safety considerations when using replication chains

When writing to multiple servers which are replicating to one another, you need to logically separate objects to which you are going to write. You can do so on different levels.

Business Logic
Make sure at the application level that you do not update the same rows on multiple servers at the same time.

Server

> Write to only one server at a time. This is a good solution for creating hot standby servers.

Databases and Tables

> In your application, assign a specific set of tables to each server. For example, write only to the movies, movies_actors, and movies_actors_link tables on nodeA; to the trip_leg and trip_log tables on nodeB; and to the weatherdata and weekday tables on nodeC.

Rows

> If you still need to write to the same table on all the servers, separate the rows that each node can update. If you use an integer primary key with the AUTO_INCREMENT option, you can do it by setting the auto_increment_increment option to the number of servers and setting auto_increment_offset to the number of the server in the chain, starting from 1. For example, on our three-servers setup, we set auto_increment_increment to 3 and auto_increment_offset to 1 on nodeA, to 2 on nodeB, and to 3 on nodeC. We discuss how to tune auto_incre ment_increment and auto_increment_offset in Recipe 15.14.

> If you do not use AUTO_INCREMENT, you need to create a rule at the application level so the identifier will follow its own unique pattern on each node.

3.10 Using Multisource Replication

Problem

You want a replica to apply events from two or more source servers that are independent from one another.

Solution

Create multiple replication channels by running the CHANGE REPLICATION SOURCE...FOR CHANNEL 'my source'; command for each of the source servers.

Discussion

You may want to replicate from multiple servers to one, for example, if separate source servers are updated by different applications and you want to use a replica for backups or for analytics. To achieve this, you need to use multisource replica.

Prepare servers for the replication

Prepare source and replica servers as described in Recipe 3.1. For the replica server, add an additional step: configure `master_info_repository` and `relay_log_info_repository` to use tables:

```
mysql> SET PERSIST master_info_repository = 'TABLE';
mysql> SET PERSIST relay_log_info_repository = 'TABLE';
```

Replication Coordinates Storage

MySQL stores information about source server coordinates, credentials, binary log, its position, and about current relay log status in the repositories, called `master_info_repository` and `relay_log_info_repository`, respectively. These repositories are physically stored either in a file or in a table inside the database `mysql`.

File storage for the replication metadata existed since the very beginning. But it has a durability issue: when a transaction commits, MySQL has to perform synchronization between the storage engine and the filesystem. They are two completely independent systems; therefore, additional safety measures are performed to provide such a synchronization. The storage engine and filesystem affect performance and are not atomic; therefore, durability cannot be guaranteed in case of failure.

Since version 5.6, table storage for the replication information repositories was introduced. It stores metadata in the InnoDB table, which supports transactions and does not require additional checks to ensure that the replication position update is written to the disk. Since then, synchronizing changes has become safe and fast.

For multisource replication, table storage has a unique row for each channel, storing replication coordinates for each of the source servers.

In version 8.0, file storage for the replication information repositories is deprecated, and table storage is the default. In version 5.7 and earlier, the default storage for the replication metadata was a file.

Backup data on the source servers

Make a full backup, or back up only the databases you want to replicate. For example, if you want to replicate the database `cookbook` from one server and the database `production` from another server, back up only these databases.

If you're going to use position-based replication, use `mysqldump` with the `--source-data=2` option, which instructs the tool to log the `CHANGE REPLICA TION SOURCE` command but comment it out:

```
$ mysqldump --host=source_cookbook --single-transaction --triggers --routines \
> --source-data=2 --databases cookbook > cookbook.sql
```

For the GTID-based replication, use the `--set-gtid-purged=COMMENTED` option instead:

```
$ mysqldump --host=source_production --single-transaction --triggers --routines \
> --set-gtid-purged=COMMENTED --databases production > production.sql
```

 You can use position-based and GTID-based replication for different channels. You can use different binary log formats on the source servers as well, but in this case you need to set the binary log format on the replica to MIXED so it can store updates in any format.

Restore data on the replica

Restore the data collected from the source servers:

```
$ mysql < cookbook.sql
$ mysql < production.sql
```

 Ensure the data on the source servers do not have databases with the same name. If they have the same name, you'll need to rename one of the databases and use the `replicate-rewrite-db` filter, which will rewrite the database name while applying the replication events. See Recipe 3.7 for details.

Configure replication channels

For the position-based replication, locate in the CHANGE REPLICATION SOURCE command in the dump file:

```
$ cat cookbook.sql | grep "CHANGE REPLICATION SOURCE"
-- CHANGE REPLICATION SOURCE TO SOURCE_LOG_FILE='binlog.000008', ↵
   SOURCE_LOG_POS=2603;
```

Use the resulting coordinates to set up replication. Use the FOR CHANNEL clause of the CHANGE REPLICATION SOURCE command to specify which channel to use:

```
mysql> CHANGE REPLICATION SOURCE TO
    -> SOURCE_HOST='source_cookbook',
    -> SOURCE_LOG_FILE='binlog.000008',
    -> SOURCE_LOG_POS=2603
    -> FOR CHANNEL 'cookbook_channel';
```

For the GTID-based replication, first locate the SET @@GLOBAL.GTID_PURGED statement:

```
$ grep GTID_PURGED production.sql
/* SET @@GLOBAL.GTID_PURGED='+9113f6b1-0751-11eb-9e7d-0242dc638c6c:1-385';*/
```

Do this for all channels that will use GTID-based replication:

```
$ grep GTID_PURGED recipes.sql
/* SET @@GLOBAL.GTID_PURGED='+910c760a-0751-11eb-9da8-0242dc638c6c:1-385';*/
```

Then combine them into a single set:

```
'9113f6b1-0751-11eb-9e7d-0242dc638c6c:1-385,910c760a-0751-11eb-9da8-0242dc638c6c:1-385'
```

run RESET MASTER to reset the GTID execution history, and set GTID_PURGED to the set you just compiled:

```
mysql> RESET MASTER;
Query OK, 0 rows affected (0,03 sec)

mysql> SET @@GLOBAL.gtid_purged = '9113f6b1-0751-11eb-9e7d-0242dc638c6c:1-385,
    '> 910c760a-0751-11eb-9da8-0242dc638c6c:1-385';
Query OK, 0 rows affected (0,00 sec)
```

Then use the CHANGE REPLICATION SOURCE command to set up the new channel:

```
mysql> CHANGE REPLICATION SOURCE TO
    -> SOURCE_HOST='source_production',
    -> SOURCE_AUTO_POSITION=1
    -> FOR CHANNEL 'production_channel';
```

Start replication

Start replication using the START REPLICA command:

```
mysql> START REPLICA FOR CHANNEL'cookbook_channel';
Query OK, 0 rows affected (0,00 sec)

mysql> START REPLICA FOR CHANNEL 'production_channel';
Query OK, 0 rows affected (0,00 sec)
```

Confirm replication is running

Run SHOW REPLICA STATUS and check the records for all channels:

```
mysql> SHOW REPLICA STATUS\G
...
              Replica_IO_Running: Yes
             Replica_SQL_Running: Yes
              ...
                    Channel_Name: cookbook_channel
              Source_TLS_Version:
           Source_public_key_path:
           Get_source_public_key: 0
               Network_Namespace:
*************************** 2. row ***************************
...
              Replica_IO_Running: Yes
             Replica_SQL_Running: Yes
              ...
                    Channel_Name: production_channel
              Source_TLS_Version:
           Source_public_key_path:
           Get_source_public_key: 0
               Network_Namespace:
2 rows in set (0.00 sec)
```

Or query the Performance Schema:

```
mysql> SELECT CHANNEL_NAME, io.SERVICE_STATE as io_status,
    -> sqlt.SERVICE_STATE as sql_status,
    -> COUNT_RECEIVED_HEARTBEATS, RECEIVED_TRANSACTION_SET
    -> FROM performance_schema.replication_connection_status AS io
    -> JOIN performance_schema.replication_applier_status AS sqlt USING(channel_name)\G
*************************** 1. row ***************************
            CHANNEL_NAME: cookbook_channel
               io_status: ON
              sql_status: ON
COUNT_RECEIVED_HEARTBEATS: 11
 RECEIVED_TRANSACTION_SET: 9113f6b1-0751-11eb-9e7d-0242dc638c6c:1-387
*************************** 2. row ***************************
            CHANNEL_NAME: production_channel
               io_status: ON
              sql_status: ON
COUNT_RECEIVED_HEARTBEATS: 11
 RECEIVED_TRANSACTION_SET: 910c760a-0751-11eb-9da8-0242dc638c6c:1-385
2 rows in set (0.00 sec)
```

3.11 Using a Semisynchronous Replication Plug-In

Problem

You want to ensure that at least one replica has the update before the client receives confirmation from the server that its COMMIT operation succeeded.

Solution

Use a semisynchronous replication plug-in.

Discussion

MySQL replication is asynchronous. This means that the source server can accept writes very fast. All it needs is to store data in the tables and write information about changes into the binary log file. However, it does not have any idea if any of the replicas received updates and if the updates they received were applied.

We cannot guarantee that the asynchronous replica applies updates, but we can set it up to ensure that updates are received and stored in the relay log file. This does not guarantee that the update will be applied or, if applied, that it will result in the same values as on the source server, but it does guarantee that at least two servers will have a record of the update, which could be applied, say, in case of a disaster recovery. To achieve this, you'll need to use a semisynchronous replication plug-in.

The semisynchronous replication plug-in should be installed on both the source and replica servers.

On the source server, run:

```
mysql> INSTALL PLUGIN rpl_semi_sync_source SONAME 'semisync_source.so';
Query OK, 0 rows affected (0.03 sec)
```

On the replica, run:

```
mysql> INSTALL PLUGIN rpl_semi_sync_replica SONAME 'semisync_replica.so';
Query OK, 0 rows affected (0.00 sec)
```

Once installed, you can enable semisynchronous replication. On the source, set the global `rpl_semi_sync_source_enabled` variable to 1. On the replica, use the `rpl_semi_sync_replica_enabled` variable.

 Semisynchronous replication works only with the default replication channel. You cannot use it with multisource replication.

You can control semisynchronous replication behavior with help of variables, as seen in Table 3-1.

Table 3-1. Variables that control the behavior of the semisynchronous replication plug-in

Variable	What it controls	Default value
`rpl_semi_sync_source_timeout`	How many milliseconds to wait for a response from the replica. If this value is exceeded, replication silently converts to the asynchronous.	10000
`rpl_semi_sync_source_wait_for_replica_count`	The number of replicas the source server needs to receive acknowledgment from before committing a transaction.	1
`rpl_semi_sync_source_wait_no_replica`	What happens if the number of connected replicas falls below `rpl_semi_sync_source_wait_for_replica_count`. As long as these servers later reconnect and acknowledge the transaction, semisynchronous replication remains functional. If this variable is `OFF`, replication is converted to asynchronous as soon as the number of replicas drops below `rpl_semi_sync_source_wait_for_replica_count`.	ON
`rpl_semi_sync_source_wait_point`	When to expect acknowledgment from the replica that it received the transaction. This variable supports two possible values. In the case of `AFTER_SYNC`, the source writes each transaction into the binary log, then syncs it to the disk. The source waits for acknowledgment from the replica about the received changes, then commits the transaction. In the case of `AFTER_COMMIT`, the source commits the transaction, then waits for acknowledgment from the replica and upon success returns to the client.	AFTER_SYNC

To find out the status of the semisynchronous replication, use the `Rpl_semi_sync_*` variable. The source server has plenty of them:

```
mysql> SHOW GLOBAL STATUS LIKE 'Rpl_semi_sync%';
+--------------------------------------------+-------+
| Variable_name                              | Value |
+--------------------------------------------+-------+
| Rpl_semi_sync_source_clients               | 1     |
| Rpl_semi_sync_source_net_avg_wait_time     | 0     |
| Rpl_semi_sync_source_net_wait_time         | 0     |
| Rpl_semi_sync_source_net_waits             | 9     |
| Rpl_semi_sync_source_no_times              | 3     |
| Rpl_semi_sync_source_no_tx                 | 6     |
| Rpl_semi_sync_source_status                | ON    |
| Rpl_semi_sync_source_timefunc_failures     | 0     |
| Rpl_semi_sync_source_tx_avg_wait_time      | 1021  |
| Rpl_semi_sync_source_tx_wait_time          | 4087  |
| Rpl_semi_sync_source_tx_waits              | 4     |
| Rpl_semi_sync_source_wait_pos_backtraverse | 0     |
| Rpl_semi_sync_source_wait_sessions         | 0     |
| Rpl_semi_sync_source_yes_tx                | 4     |
+--------------------------------------------+-------+
14 rows in set (0.00 sec)
```

The most important variable is `Rpl_semi_sync_source_clients`, which shows if semisynchronous replication is currently in use and how many semisynchronous replicas are connected. If `Rpl_semi_sync_source_clients` is zero, no semisynchronous replica is connected, and asynchronous replication is used.

On the replica server, only the `Rpl_semi_sync_replica_status` (`Rpl_semi_sync_slave_status`) variable is available and can have values either ON or OFF.

Failing Back to the Asynchronous Replication

If no replica accepts the write in `rpl_semi_sync_source_timeout` milliseconds, replication will switch to the asynchronous without any message or warning for the client. The only way to figure out that the replication mode switched to asynchronous is to examine the value of the `Rpl_semi_sync_source_clients` variable or to check the error log file for messages like:

```
2020-10-12T22:25:17.654563Z 0 [ERROR] [MY-013129] [Server] ↵
A message intended for a client cannot be sent there as ↵
no client-session is attached. Therefore, ↵
we're sending the information to the error-log instead: ↵

MY-001158 - Got an error reading communication packets

2020-10-12T22:25:20.083796Z 198 [Note] [MY-010014] [Repl] ↵
While initializing dump thread for slave with UUID ↵
<09bf4498-0cd2-11eb-9161-98af65266957>, ↵
found a zombie dump thread with the same UUID. ↵
Master is killing the zombie dump thread(180).
```

```
2020-10-12T22:25:20.084088Z 180 [Note] [MY-011171] [Server] ↵
Stop semi-sync binlog_dump to slave (server_id: 2).

2020-10-12T22:25:20.084204Z 198 [Note] [MY-010462] [Repl] ↵
Start binlog_dump to master_thread_id(198) slave_server(2), ↵
pos(, 4)

2020-10-12T22:25:20.084248Z 198 [Note] [MY-011170] [Server] ↵
Start asynchronous binlog_dump to slave (server_id: 2), pos(, 4).

2020-10-12T22:25:20.657800Z 180 [Note] [MY-011155] [Server] ↵
Semi-sync replication switched OFF.
```

We discuss error log files in Recipe 23.2.

3.12 Using Group Replication

Problem

You want to apply updates either on all the nodes or nowhere.

Solution

Use Group Replication.

Discussion

Starting from version 5.7.17, MySQL supports fully synchronous replication with help of the Group Replication plug-in. If the plug-in is in use, MySQL servers, called *nodes*, create a group that commits a transaction together or, if one of the members fails to apply the transaction, rolls it back. This way the update is either replicated to all group members or nowhere. High availability is ensured.

You can have up to nine servers in the group. More than nine is not supported. There is a very good reason for this limitation: a higher number of servers implies higher replication delay. In the case of synchronous replication, all updates are applied to all the nodes before the transaction completes. Each update transferred to each node waits to be applied and only then commits. Thus, replication delay corresponds to the speed of the slowest member and the network transfer rate.

While it is technically possible to have fewer than three servers in the Group Replication setup, a smaller number does not provide high availability. This is because the Paxos algorithm (*https://oreil.ly/nNxTr*), used by the Group Communication Engine (*https://oreil.ly/H0Np7*), requires $2F + 1$ nodes to create a quorum, where F is any natural number. In other words, in case of a disaster, the number of active nodes should be greater than the number of disconnected nodes.

Group Replication has limitations. First, and most importantly, it supports only the InnoDB storage engine. You need to disable other storage engines before enabling the plug-in. Each replicated table must have a primary key. You should put servers into the local network. While having Group Replication across the internet is possible, it may lead to longer times for applying transactions and disconnecting nodes from the group due to network timeouts. The LOCK TABLE and GET_LOCK statements are not taken into account in the certification process that determines whether the transaction should be applied or rolled back on all nodes, which means they are local to the node and error prone. The full list of limitations is available in the "Group Replication Limitations" user reference manual (*https://oreil.ly/bkgV2*).

To enable Group Replication, you need to prepare all the participating servers as described in Recipe 3.1, as they're going to act as both source and replica, and perform additional preparations:

1. Prepare the configuration file:

```
[mysqld]
# Disable unsupported storage engines
disabled_storage_engines="MyISAM,BLACKHOLE,FEDERATED,ARCHIVE,MEMORY"

# Set unique server ID. Each server in the group should have its own ID
server_id=1

# Enable GTIDs
gtid_mode=ON
enforce_gtid_consistency=ON

# Enable replica updates
log_replica_updates=ON

# Only ROW binary log format supported
binlog_format=ROW

# For versions before 8.0.21
binlog_checksum=NONE

# Ensure that replication repository is TABLE
master_info_repository=TABLE
relay_log_info_repository=TABLE

# Ensure that transaction_write_set_extraction is enabled
# This option is deprecated starting from version 8.0.26
transaction_write_set_extraction=XXHASH64

# Add Group Replication options
plugin_load_add='group_replication.so'

# Any valid UUID should be the same for all group members
# Use SELECT UUID() to generate a UUID
group_replication_group_name="dc527338-13d1-11eb-abf7-98af65266957"

# Host of the local node and port that will be used
# for communication between members
# Put either hostname (in our case node1) or IP address here
```

```
# Port number should be different from the one used for serving clients
# E.g., if default MySQL port is 3306, specify any different number here
group_replication_local_address= "node1:33061"

# Ports and addresses of all nodes in the group
# Should be same on all nodes
group_replication_group_seeds= "node1:33061,node2:33061,node3:33061"

# Since we did not set up Group replication at this stage,
# it should not be started on boot
# You may set this option ON after bootstrapping the group
group_replication_start_on_boot=off
group_replication_bootstrap_group=off

# Request source server public key for
#the authentication plug-in caching_sha2_password
group_replication_recovery_get_public_key=1
```

2. Start the servers. Do not enable replication yet.

3. Choose a node to be the first node in the group.

4. Create a replication user only on the first member, as described in Recipe 3.1, and additionally grant BACKUP_ADMIN to it:

```
node1> CREATE USER repl@'%' IDENTIFIED BY 'replrepl';
Query OK, 0 rows affected (0,01 sec)

node1> GRANT REPLICATION SLAVE, BACKUP_ADMIN ON *.* TO repl@'%';
Query OK, 0 rows affected (0,03 sec)
```

You do not need to create a replication user on other group members, because the CREATE USER statement will be replicated.

5. Set up replication on the first member to use this user:

```
node1> CHANGE REPLICATION SOURCE TO SOURCE_USER='repl',
    -> SOURCE_PASSWORD='replrepl'
    -> FOR CHANNEL 'group_replication_recovery';
Query OK, 0 rows affected (0,01 sec)
```

group_replication_recovery is the special built-in name of the Group Replication channel.

> If you do not want replication credentials to be stored as plain text in the replication repository, skip this step and provide the credentials later when you run START GROUP_REPLICATION. See also Recipe 3.13.

6. Bootstrap the node:

```
node1> SET GLOBAL group_replication_bootstrap_group=ON;
Query OK, 0 rows affected (0,00 sec)

node1> START GROUP_REPLICATION;
Query OK, 0 rows affected (0,00 sec)
```

```
node1> SET GLOBAL group_replication_bootstrap_group=OFF;
Query OK, 0 rows affected (0,00 sec)
```

7. Check the Group Replication status by selecting from performance_schema.rep
   lication_group_members:

```
node1> SELECT * FROM performance_schema.replication_group_members\G
*************************** 1. row ***************************
  CHANNEL_NAME: group_replication_applier
     MEMBER_ID: d8a706aa-16ee-11eb-ba5a-98af65266957
   MEMBER_HOST: node1
   MEMBER_PORT: 33361
  MEMBER_STATE: ONLINE
   MEMBER_ROLE: PRIMARY
MEMBER_VERSION: 8.0.21
1 row in set (0.00 sec)
```

And wait when the first member state becomes ONLINE.

8. Start replication on the second and third nodes:

```
node2> CHANGE REPLICATION SOURCE TO SOURCE_USER='repl',
    -> SOURCE_PASSWORD='replrepl'
    -> FOR CHANNEL 'group_replication_recovery';
Query OK, 0 rows affected (0,01 sec)

node2> START GROUP_REPLICATION;
Query OK, 0 rows affected (0,00 sec)
```

Once you confirm that all members are in the ONLINE state, you can use Group
Replication. Query the performance_schema.replication_group_members table to
get this information. A healthy setup will output something like this:

```
node1> SELECT * FROM performance_schema.replication_group_members\G
*************************** 1. row ***************************
  CHANNEL_NAME: group_replication_applier
     MEMBER_ID: d8a706aa-16ee-11eb-ba5a-98af65266957
   MEMBER_HOST: node1
   MEMBER_PORT: 33061
  MEMBER_STATE: ONLINE
   MEMBER_ROLE: PRIMARY
MEMBER_VERSION: 8.0.21
*************************** 2. row ***************************
  CHANNEL_NAME: group_replication_applier
     MEMBER_ID: e14043d7-16ee-11eb-b77a-98af65266957
   MEMBER_HOST: node2
   MEMBER_PORT: 33061
  MEMBER_STATE: ONLINE
   MEMBER_ROLE: SECONDARY
MEMBER_VERSION: 8.0.21
*************************** 3. row ***************************
  CHANNEL_NAME: group_replication_applier
     MEMBER_ID: ea775284-16ee-11eb-8762-98af65266957
   MEMBER_HOST: node3
   MEMBER_PORT: 33061
  MEMBER_STATE: ONLINE
   MEMBER_ROLE: SECONDARY
MEMBER_VERSION: 8.0.21
3 rows in set (0.00 sec)
```

The `SHOW REPLICA STATUS` command does not work with Group Replication.

If you want to start Group Replication with existent data, restore it on the first node before bootstrapping it. The data will be copied when the other nodes join the group.

Finally, enable the `group_replication_start_on_boot=on` option in the node configuration files, so replication will be enabled after the node restart.

Writing on Multiple Nodes in the Group Replication Setup

In this recipe, we started Group Replication in the single-primary mode. This mode allows writes on only one member of the group. This is the safest and recommended option. However, if you want to write on multiple nodes, you can switch to the multiprimary node by using the `group_replication_switch_to_multi_pri mary_mode` function:

```
mysql> SELECT group_replication_switch_to_multi_primary_mode();
+--------------------------------------------------+
| group_replication_switch_to_multi_primary_mode() |
+--------------------------------------------------+
| Mode switched to multi-primary successfully.     |
+--------------------------------------------------+
1 row in set (1.01 sec)

mysql> SELECT * FROM performance_schema.replication_group ↵
_members\G
*************************** 1. row ***************************
  CHANNEL_NAME: group_replication_applier
     MEMBER_ID: d8a706aa-16ee-11eb-ba5a-98af65266957
   MEMBER_HOST: node1
   MEMBER_PORT: 33061
  MEMBER_STATE: ONLINE
   MEMBER_ROLE: PRIMARY
MEMBER_VERSION: 8.0.21
*************************** 2. row ***************************
  CHANNEL_NAME: group_replication_applier
     MEMBER_ID: e14043d7-16ee-11eb-b77a-98af65266957
   MEMBER_HOST: node2
   MEMBER_PORT: 33061
  MEMBER_STATE: ONLINE
   MEMBER_ROLE: PRIMARY
MEMBER_VERSION: 8.0.21
*************************** 3. row ***************************
  CHANNEL_NAME: group_replication_applier
     MEMBER_ID: ea775284-16ee-11eb-8762-98af65266957
   MEMBER_HOST: node3
   MEMBER_PORT: 33061
  MEMBER_STATE: ONLINE
```

```
       MEMBER_ROLE: PRIMARY
    MEMBER_VERSION: 8.0.21
    3 rows in set (0.00 sec)
```

For more details, check "Changing a Group's Mode" in the MySQL Reference Manual (*https://oreil.ly/tRX9P*).

See Also

For additional information about Group Replication, see "Group Replication" in the Reference Manual (*https://oreil.ly/Hgibr*).

3.13 Storing Replication Credentials Securely

Problem

By default, replication credentials are visible in the replication information repository if specified as part of the CHANGE REPLICATION SOURCE command. You want to hide them from occasional access by unauthorized users.

Solution

Use the USER and PASSWORD options in the START REPLICA command.

Discussion

When you specify replication user credentials using the CHANGE REPLICATION SOURCE command, they are stored in plain text, unencrypted, regardless of the master_info_repository option.

Thus, if master_info_repository is set to TABLE, which is the default since version 8.0, any user with read access to the mysql database can query the slave_master_info table and read the password:

```
mysql> SELECT User_name, User_password FROM slave_master_info;
+-----------+---------------+
| User_name | User_password |
+-----------+---------------+
| repl      | replrepl      |
+-----------+---------------+
1 row in set (0.00 sec)
```

Or, if master_info_repository is set to FILE, any operating system user who can access the file, by default located in the MySQL data directory, can get replication credentials:

```
$ head -n6 var/mysqld.3/data/master.info
31
binlog.000001
```

```
688
127.0.0.1
repl
replrepl
```

If having replication credentials visible in the source information repository is not desirable, you can specify replication credentials as part of the START REPLICA or START GROUP_REPLICATION command:

```
mysql> START REPLICA USER='repl' PASSWORD='replrepl';
Query OK, 0 rows affected (0.01 sec)
```

However, if you previously specified replication credentials as part of the CHANGE MASTER command, they will remain visible in the master information repository. To clear a previously entered user and password, run the CHANGE MASTER command with empty arguments for MASTER_USER and MASTER_PASSWORD:

```
mysql> SELECT User_name, User_password FROM slave_master_info;
+-----------+---------------+
| User_name | User_password |
+-----------+---------------+
| repl      | replrepl      |
+-----------+---------------+
1 row in set (0.00 sec)

mysql> CHANGE REPLICATION SOURCE TO SOURCE_USER='', SOURCE_PASSWORD='';
Query OK, 0 rows affected, 1 warning (0.01 sec)

mysql> START REPLICA USER='repl' PASSWORD='replrepl';
Query OK, 0 rows affected (0.01 sec)

mysql> SELECT User_name, User_password FROM slave_master_info;
+-----------+---------------+
| User_name | User_password |
+-----------+---------------+
|           |               |
+-----------+---------------+
1 row in set (0.00 sec)
```

 Once you've cleared the replication credentials from the source information repository, they won't be stored anywhere, and you will need to provide them each time you restart replication.

3.14 Using TLS (SSL) for Replication

Problem

You want to transfer data between the source and replica securely.

Solution

Set up TLS (Transport Layer Security (*https://oreil.ly/f9XBK*)) connections for the replication channel.

Discussion

The connection between source and replica servers is technically similar to any other client connections to the MySQL server. Therefore, encrypting the connection between source and replica servers via TLS requires preparations similar to encrypting client connections, as described in Recipe 24.10.

To create an encrypted replication setup, follow these steps:

1. Obtain or create TLS keys and certificates as described in Recipe 24.10.

2. Ensure that the source server has TLS configuration parameters under the `[mysqld]` section:

   ```
   [mysqld]
   ssl_ca=ca.pem
   ssl_cert=server-cert.pem
   ssl_key=server-key.pem
   ```

    While MySQL uses the modern and safer TLS protocol in the latest versions, its configuration options still use the abbreviation SSL. The MySQL User Reference Manual also often refers to TLS as SSL.

   You can figure out if TLS is enabled by checking the value of the `have_ssl` system variable:

   ```
   mysql> SHOW VARIABLES LIKE 'have_ssl';
   +---------------+-------+
   | Variable_name | Value |
   +---------------+-------+
   | have_ssl      | YES   |
   +---------------+-------+
   1 row in set (0,01 sec)
   ```

3. If insecure replication is running, stop the replica IO thread:

   ```
   mysql> STOP REPLICA IO_THREAD; -- (STOP SLAVE IO_THREAD;)
   Query OK, 0 rows affected (0.00 sec)
   ```

4. On the replica server, put paths to the TLS client key and certificate under `[client]` of the configuration file:

   ```
   [client]
   ssl-ca=ca.pem
   ssl-cert=client-cert.pem
   ssl-key=client-key.pem
   ```

and specify the SOURCE_SSL=1 option for the CHANGE REPLICATION SOURCE command:

```
mysql> CHANGE REPLICATION SOURCE TO SOURCE_SSL=1;
Query OK, 0 rows affected (0.03 sec)
```

Alternatively, you can specify paths to the client key and certificate as part of the CHANGE REPLICATION SOURCE command:

```
mysql> CHANGE REPLICATION SOURCE TO
    -> SOURCE_SSL_CA='ca.pem',
    -> SOURCE_SSL_CERT='client-cert.pem',
    -> SOURCE_SSL_KEY='client-key.pem',
    -> SOURCE_SSL=1;
Query OK, 0 rows affected (0.02 sec)
```

 We intentionally omitted other parameters of the CHANGE REPLICATION SOURCE command, such as SOURCE_HOST, for brevity. But you need to use them as described in Recipes 3.2 or 3.4.

5. Start replication:

```
mysql> START REPLICA;
Query OK, 0 rows affected (0.00 sec)
```

The CHANGE REPLICATION SOURCE command supports other TLS modifiers that are compatible with regular client connection encryption options. For example, you can specify a cipher to use with the SOURCE_SSL_CIPHER clause or enforce source server certificate verification with the SOURCE_SSL_VERIFY_SERVER_CERT clause.

See Also

For additional information about securing connections between the source and replica servers, see "Setting Up Replication to Use Encrypted Connections" (*https://oreil.ly/ZUAAg*).

3.15 Replication Troubleshooting

Problem

Replication is not working, and you want to fix it.

Solution

Use the SHOW REPLICA STATUS command, query the replication tables in the Performance Schema, and check the error log file to understand why the replication failed, then fix it.

Discussion

Replication is managed by two kinds of threads: IO and SQL (or connection and applier). The IO, or connection, thread is responsible for connecting to the source server, retrieving updates and storing them in the relay log file. There is always one IO thread per replication channel. The SQL, or applier, thread reads data from the relay log file and applies changes to the tables. One replication channel may have multiple SQL threads. Connection and applier threads are totally independent, and their errors are reported by different replication diagnostic instruments.

There are two main instruments to diagnose replication errors: the SHOW REPLICA STATUS command and replication tables in the Performance Schema. SHOW REPLICA STATUS has existed since the very beginning, while replication tables in the Performance Schema were added in version 5.7. You'll get very similar information by using these two instruments, and which to use depends on your preferences. In our opinion, SHOW REPLICA STATUS is good for manual review in the command line, while it is much easier to write monitoring alerts, querying the Performance Schema, rather than to parse SHOW REPLICA STATUS output.

SHOW REPLICA STATUS

SHOW REPLICA STATUS contains all the information about IO and SQL thread configuration, status, and errors. All data is printed in a single row. However, this row is formatted with spaces and newlines. You can examine it comfortably by using the \G modifier of the mysql client. For a multisource replica, SHOW REPLICA STATUS prints information about each channel in a separate row:

```
mysql> SHOW REPLICA STATUS\G
*************************** 1. row ***************************
             Replica_IO_State: Waiting for master to send event
                  Source_Host: 127.0.0.1
                  Source_User: root
                  Source_Port: 13000
                Connect_Retry: 60
              Source_Log_File: binlog.000001
          Read_Source_Log_Pos: 156
               Relay_Log_File: Delly-7390-relay-bin-cookbook.000002
                Relay_Log_Pos: 365
        Relay_Source_Log_File: binlog.000001
           Replica_IO_Running: Yes
          Replica_SQL_Running: Yes
           ...
                 Channel_Name: cookbook
           Source_TLS_Version:
        Source_public_key_path:
         Get_source_public_key: 0
            Network_Namespace:
*************************** 2. row ***************************
             Replica_IO_State: Waiting for master to send event
                  Source_Host: 127.0.0.1
                  Source_User: root
```

```
            Source_Port: 13004
           Connect_Retry: 60
         Source_Log_File: binlog.000001
     Read_Source_Log_Pos: 156
          Relay_Log_File: Delly-7390-relay-bin-test.000002
           Relay_Log_Pos: 365
   Relay_Source_Log_File: binlog.000001
       Replica_IO_Running: Yes
      Replica_SQL_Running: Yes
            ...
            Channel_Name: test
      Source_TLS_Version:
   Source_public_key_path:
    Get_source_public_key: 0
       Network_Namespace:
2 rows in set (0.00 sec)
```

We intentionally skipped part of the output for brevity. We don't describe each field–only those required for handling stopped replication (see Table 3-2). If you are curious what other fields mean, consult "SHOW REPLICA STATUS Statement" (*https://oreil.ly/eJhiK*) in the Reference Manual.

Table 3-2. Explanation of the SHOW REPLICA STATUS *fields for understanding and fixing errors*

Field	Description	Subsystem
Replica_IO_State (Slave_IO_State)	Status of the IO thread. Contains information on what the connection thread is doing when running: empty if IO thread is stopped and Connecting if connection is not yet established.	IO thread status
Source_Host (Master_Host)	Host of the source server.	IO thread configuration
Source_User (Master_User)	Replication user.	IO thread configuration
Source_Port (Master_Port)	Port of the source server.	IO thread configuration
Source_Log_File (Master_Log_File)	Binary log on the source server from which IO thread is currently reading.	IO thread status
Read_Source_Log_Pos (Read_Master_Log_Pos)	Position in the binary log file on the source server from which IO thread is reading.	IO thread status
Relay_Log_File	Current relay log file: the file the SQL thread is currently executing from.	IO thread status
Relay_Log_Pos	The position in the relay log file the SQL thread has executed up to.	IO thread status
Relay_Source_Log_File (Relay_Master_Log_File)	Binary log on the source server from which SQL thread is executing events.	SQL thread status
Replica_IO_Running (Slave_IO_Running)	If IO thread is running. Use this field to quickly identify health of the connection thread.	IO thread status
Replica_SQL_Running (Slave_SQL_Running)	If SQL thread is running. Use to quickly identify health of the applier thread.	SQL thread status
Replicate_*	Replication filters.	SQL thread configuration
Exec_Source_Log_Pos (Exec_Master_Log_Pos)	Position of the binary log file on the source up to which SQL thread executed events.	SQL thread status

Field	Description	Subsystem
Until_Condition	Until conditions, if any.	SQL thread configuration
Source_SSL_*(Master_SSL_*)	SSL options for connecting to the source server.	IO thread configuration
Seconds_Behind_Source (Seconds_Behind_Master)	Estimated delay between source server and replica.	SQL thread status
Last_IO_Errno	Last error number of the IO thread. Cleared once resolved.	IO thread status
Last_IO_Error	Latest error on the IO thread. Cleared once resolved.	IO thread status
Last_Errno, Last_SQL_Errno	Number of the last error, received by SQL thread. Cleared once resolved.	SQL thread status
Last_Error, Last_SQL_Error	Last error of the SQL thread. Cleared once resolved.	SQL thread status
Replica_SQL_Running_State (Slave_SQL_Running_State)	Status of the SQL thread. Empty if stopped.	SQL thread status
Last_IO_Error_Timestamp	Time when last IO error happened. Cleared once resolved.	IO thread status
Last_SQL_Error_Timestamp	Time when last SQL error happened. Cleared once resolved.	SQL thread status
Retrieved_Gtid_Set	GTIDs, retrieved by the connection thread.	IO thread status
Executed_Gtid_Set	GTIDs, executed by the SQL thread.	SQL thread status
Channel_Name	Name of the replication channel.	IO and SQL thread configuration

We'll refer to this table when we discuss how to deal with specific IO and SQL threads errors.

Replication tables in the Performance Schema

An alternative diagnostic solution, tables in the Performance Schema, unlike SHOW REPLICA STATUS, do not store all the information in a single place but in separate spaces.

Information about the IO thread configuration is stored in the replication_con nection_configuration table, and information about its status is in the replica tion_connection_status table.

Information about SQL threads is stored in six tables, as shown in Table 3-3.

Table 3-3. Tables with information specific to SQL thread(s)

Table name	Description
replication_applier_configuration	SQL thread configuration
replication_applier_global_filters	Global replication filters: filters, applicable for all channels
replication_applier_filters	Replication filters, specific to particular channels
replication_applier_status	Status for the SQL thread, global

Table name	Description
replication_applier_status_by_worker	For multithreaded replica: status of each SQL thread
replication_applier_status_by_coordinator	For multithreaded replica: status of the SQL thread as seen by the coordinator

Finally, you'll find the Group Replication network configuration and status in the replication_group_members table, and statistics of the Group Replication members in the replication_group_member_stats table.

Troubleshooting an IO thread

You can determine if a replication IO thread is having issues by checking the value of the Replica_IO_Running field of SHOW REPLICA STATUS. If the value is not Yes, the connection thread is likely having issues. The reason for these issues can be found in the Last_IO_Errno and Last_IO_Error fields:

```
mysql> SHOW REPLICA STATUS\G
*************************** 1. row ***************************
...
            Replica_IO_Running: Connecting
           Replica_SQL_Running: Yes
...
                 Last_IO_Errno: 1045
                 Last_IO_Error: error connecting to master 'repl@127.0.0.1:13000' - ↵
                                retry-time: 60 retries: 1 message: ↵
                                Access denied for user 'repl'@'localhost'↵
                                (using password: NO)
...
```

In the preceding example, the replica cannot connect to the source server because access is denied for the user 'repl'@'localhost'. The IO thread is still running and will try to connect again in 60 seconds (retry-time: 60). The reason for such a failure is clear: either the user does not exist on the source server or it does not have enough privileges. You need to connect to the source server and fix the user account. Once it has been fixed, the next connection attempt will succeed.

Alternatively, you can query the replication_connection_status table in the Performance Schema:

```
mysql> SELECT SERVICE_STATE, LAST_ERROR_NUMBER,
    -> LAST_ERROR_MESSAGE, LAST_ERROR_TIMESTAMP
    -> FROM performance_schema.replication_connection_status\G
*************************** 1. row ***************************
        SERVICE_STATE: CONNECTING
    LAST_ERROR_NUMBER: 2061
   LAST_ERROR_MESSAGE: error connecting to master 'repl@127.0.0.1:13000' -↵
                       retry-time: 60 retries: 1 ↵
                       message: Authentication plugin 'caching_sha2_password' ↵
                       reported error: Authentication requires secure connection.
 LAST_ERROR_TIMESTAMP: 2020-10-17 13:23:03.663994
1 row in set (0.00 sec)
```

In this example, the LAST_ERROR_MESSAGE field contains the reason why the IO thread failed to connect: the user account on the source server uses the caching_sha2_pass word authentication plug-in, which requires a secure connection. To fix this error, you need to stop the replication, then run CHANGE REPLICATION SOURCE with either the SOURCE_SSL=1 parameter or the GET_SOURCE_PUBLIC_KEY=1 parameter. In the latter case, traffic between the replica and source server will stay insecure, and only password exchange communication will be secured. See Recipe 3.14 for details.

Troubleshooting a SQL thread

To find out why an applier thread had stopped, check the Replica_SQL_Running, Last_SQL_Errno, and Last_SQL_Error fields:

```
mysql> SHOW REPLICA STATUS\G
*************************** 1. row ***************************
...
           Replica_SQL_Running: No
...
                 Last_SQL_Errno: 1007
                 Last_SQL_Error: Error 'Can't create database 'cookbook'; ↵
                                 database exists' on query. ↵
                                 Default database: 'cookbook'. ↵
                                 Query: 'create database cookbook'
```

In the preceding listing, the error message shows that the CREATE DATABASE command failed, because the database already exists on the replica.

The same information can be found in the replication_applier_status_by_worker table in the Performance Schema:

```
mysql> SELECT SERVICE_STATE, LAST_ERROR_NUMBER,
    -> LAST_ERROR_MESSAGE, LAST_ERROR_TIMESTAMP
    -> FROM performance_schema.replication_applier_status_by_worker\G
*************************** 1. row ***************************
        SERVICE_STATE: OFF
    LAST_ERROR_NUMBER: 1007
   LAST_ERROR_MESSAGE: Error 'Can't create database 'cookbook'; ↵
                       database exists' on query. ↵
                       Default database: 'cookbook'.↵
                       Query: 'create database cookbook'
 LAST_ERROR_TIMESTAMP: 2020-10-17 13:58:12.115821
1 row in set (0.01 sec)
```

There are a few ways to resolve this issue. First, you can simply drop the database on the replica and restart the SQL thread:

```
mysql> DROP DATABASE cookbook;
Query OK, 0 rows affected (0.04 sec)

mysql> START REPLICA SQL_THREAD;
Query OK, 0 rows affected (0.01 sec)
```

Disable the binary log if it's enabled on the replica.

If you want to keep the database on the replica—for example, if it's supposed to have extra tables that don't exist on the source server—you can skip the replicated event.

If you use position-based replication, use the `sql_replica_skip_counter` (`sql_slave_skip_counter`) variable:

```
mysql> SET GLOBAL sql_replica_skip_counter=1;
Query OK, 0 rows affected (0.00 sec)

mysql> START REPLICA SQL_THREAD;
Query OK, 0 rows affected (0.01 sec)
```

In this example, we skipped one event from the binary log, then restarted replication.

For GTID-based replication, the setting `sql_replica_skip_counter` wouldn't work, because it doesn't include GTID information. Instead, you need to generate an empty transaction with the GTID of the transaction the replica could not execute. To find out which GTID failed, check the `Retrieved_Gtid_Set` and `Executed_Gtid_Set` fields of the SHOW REPLICA STATUS:

```
mysql> SHOW REPLICA STATUS\G
*************************** 1. row ***************************
  ...
            Retrieved_Gtid_Set: de7e85f9-1060-11eb-8b8f-98af65266957:1-5
             Executed_Gtid_Set: de7e85f9-1060-11eb-8b8f-98af65266957:1-4,
de8d356e-1060-11eb-a568-98af65266957:1-3
  ...
```

In this example, `Retrieved_Gtid_Set` contains transactions `de7e85f9-1060-11eb-8b8f-98af65266957:1-5`, while `Executed_Gtid_Set` contains only transactions `de7e85f9-1060-11eb-8b8f-98af65266957:1-4`. It's clear that transaction `de7e85f9-1060-11eb-8b8f-98af65266957:5` was not executed. Transactions with UUID `de8d356e-1060-11eb-a568-98af65266957` are local and are not executed by the replication applier thread.

You can also find a failing transaction by querying the `APPLYING_TRANSACTION` field of the `replication_applier_status_by_worker` table:

```
mysql> select LAST_APPLIED_TRANSACTION, APPLYING_TRANSACTION
    -> from performance_schema.replication_applier_status_by_worker\G
*************************** 1. row ***************************
LAST_APPLIED_TRANSACTION: de7e85f9-1060-11eb-8b8f-98af65266957:4
    APPLYING_TRANSACTION: de7e85f9-1060-11eb-8b8f-98af65266957:5
1 row in set (0.00 sec)
```

Once you've found the failing transaction, inject the empty transaction with the same GTID and restart the SQL thread:

```
mysql> -- set explicit GTID
mysql> SET gtid_next='de7e85f9-1060-11eb-8b8f-98af65266957:5';
Query OK, 0 rows affected (0.00 sec)

mysql> -- inject empty transaction
mysql> BEGIN;COMMIT;
```

```
Query OK, 0 rows affected (0.00 sec)

Query OK, 0 rows affected (0.00 sec)

mysql> -- revert GTID generation back to automatic
mysql> SET gtid_next='automatic';
Query OK, 0 rows affected (0.00 sec)

mysql> -- restart SQL thread
mysql> START REPLICA SQL_THREAD;
Query OK, 0 rows affected (0.01 sec)
```

 While skipping a binary log event or transaction helps to restart replication at the moment, it may cause bigger issues and lead to data inconsistency between the source and replica and, as a result, future errors. Always analyze why an error happened in the first place, and try to fix the reason, not simply skip the event.

While SHOW REPLICA STATUS and the replication_applier_status_by_worker table both store error messages, if you use a multithreaded replica, the table can offer better information about what happened. For example, the following example error message doesn't provide a full explanation of the reason for the failure:

```
mysql> SHOW REPLICA STATUS\G
*************************** 1. row ***************************
...
          Last_SQL_Errno: 1146
          Last_SQL_Error: Coordinator stopped because there were error(s) ↵
                          in the worker(s). The most recent failure being: ↵
                          Worker 8 failed executing transaction ↵
                          'de7e85f9-1060-11eb-8b8f-98af65266957:7' at ↵
                          master log binlog.000001, end_log_pos 1818. ↵
                          See error log and/or performance_schema.↵
                          replication_applier_status_by_worker table ↵
                          for more details about this failure or others, if any.
...
```

It reports that worker 8 failed but does not tell why. Querying on replication_applier_status_by_worker returns this information:

```
mysql> select SERVICE_STATE, LAST_ERROR_NUMBER, LAST_ERROR_MESSAGE, LAST_ERROR_TIMESTAMP
    -> from performance_schema.replication_applier_status_by_worker where worker_id=8\G
*************************** 1. row ***************************
       SERVICE_STATE: OFF
   LAST_ERROR_NUMBER: 1146
  LAST_ERROR_MESSAGE: Worker 8 failed executing transaction ↵
                      'de7e85f9-1060-11eb-8b8f-98af65266957:7' at master log↵
                      binlog.000001, end_log_pos 1818; Error executing row event: ↵
                      'Table 'cookbook.limbs' doesn't exist'
LAST_ERROR_TIMESTAMP: 2020-10-17 14:28:01.144521
1 row in set (0.00 sec)
```

Now it's clear that a specific table doesn't exist. You can analyze why this is the case and correct the error.

Troubleshooting Group Replication

`SHOW REPLICA STATUS` is not available for Group Replication. Therefore, you need to use the Performance Schema to troubleshoot issues with it. The Performance Schema has two special tables for Group Replication: `replication_group_members`, showing details of all members, and `replication_group_member_stats`, displaying statistics for them. However, these tables do not have information about IO and SQL thread errors. These details are available in the following `replication_connection_status` table as well as in Table 3-3.

Let's have a closer look at the Group Replication troubleshooting options.

A quick way to identify if something is wrong with Group Replication is a `replica tion_group_members` table:

```
mysql> SELECT * FROM performance_schema.replication_group_members\G
*************************** 1. row ***************************
  CHANNEL_NAME: group_replication_applier
     MEMBER_ID: de5b65cb-16ae-11eb-826c-98af65266957
   MEMBER_HOST: Delly-7390
   MEMBER_PORT: 33361
  MEMBER_STATE: ONLINE
   MEMBER_ROLE: PRIMARY
MEMBER_VERSION: 8.0.21
*************************** 2. row ***************************
  CHANNEL_NAME: group_replication_applier
     MEMBER_ID: e9514d63-16ae-11eb-8f6e-98af65266957
   MEMBER_HOST: Delly-7390
   MEMBER_PORT: 33362
  MEMBER_STATE: RECOVERING
   MEMBER_ROLE: SECONDARY
MEMBER_VERSION: 8.0.21
*************************** 3. row ***************************
  CHANNEL_NAME: group_replication_applier
     MEMBER_ID: f1e717ab-16ae-11eb-bfd2-98af65266957
   MEMBER_HOST: Delly-7390
   MEMBER_PORT: 33363
  MEMBER_STATE: RECOVERING
   MEMBER_ROLE: SECONDARY
MEMBER_VERSION: 8.0.21
3 rows in set (0.00 sec)
```

In the preceding listing, only the PRIMARY member is in MEMBER_STATE: ONLINE, meaning it is healthy. Both SECONDARY members are in RECOVERING state and are having trouble joining the group.

A failing member will stay in the RECOVERING state for some time while Group Replication tries to recover itself. If the error cannot be automatically recovered, the failing member will leave the group and stay in the ERROR state:

```
mysql> SELECT * FROM performance_schema.replication_group_members\G
*************************** 1. row ***************************
  CHANNEL_NAME: group_replication_applier
     MEMBER_ID: e9514d63-16ae-11eb-8f6e-98af65266957
```

```
       MEMBER_HOST: Delly-7390
       MEMBER_PORT: 33362
      MEMBER_STATE: ERROR
       MEMBER_ROLE:
    MEMBER_VERSION: 8.0.21
    1 row in set (0.00 sec)
```

Both listings were taken on the same secondary member of the group, but after it left the group, it reports only itself as a Group Replication member and does not display information about other members.

To determine the reason for the failure, you need to examine the `replication_con nection_status` and `replication_applier_status_by_worker` tables.

In our example, member `e9514d63-16ae-11eb-8f6e-98af65266957` stopped with a SQL error. You'll find error details in the `replication_applier_status_by_worker` table:

```
mysql> SELECT CHANNEL_NAME, LAST_ERROR_NUMBER,
    -> LAST_ERROR_MESSAGE, LAST_ERROR_TIMESTAMP,
    -> APPLYING_TRANSACTION
    -> FROM performance_schema.replication_applier_status_by_worker\G
*************************** 1. row ***************************
         CHANNEL_NAME: group_replication_recovery
    LAST_ERROR_NUMBER: 3635
   LAST_ERROR_MESSAGE: The table in transaction de5b65cb-16ae-11eb-826c-98af65266957:15 ↵
                       does not comply with the requirements by an external plugin.
 LAST_ERROR_TIMESTAMP: 2020-10-25 20:31:27.718638
 APPLYING_TRANSACTION: de5b65cb-16ae-11eb-826c-98af65266957:15
*************************** 2. row ***************************
         CHANNEL_NAME: group_replication_applier
    LAST_ERROR_NUMBER: 0
   LAST_ERROR_MESSAGE:
 LAST_ERROR_TIMESTAMP: 0000-00-00 00:00:00.000000
 APPLYING_TRANSACTION:
2 rows in set (0.00 sec)
```

The error message says that the definition of the table in the `de5b65cb-16ae-11eb-826c-98af65266957:15` transaction is not compatible with the Group Replication plug-in. To find out why, check "Group Replication Requirements and Limitations" (*https://oreil.ly/OOHfI*), identify the table used in the transaction, and fix the error.

The error message in the `replication_applier_status_by_worker` table does not give any indication which table was used in the transaction. But the error log file may. Open the error log file, search for the `LAST_ERROR_TIMESTAMP` and `LAST_ERROR_NUM BER` to identify the error, and check if the previous or next rows have more information:

```
2020-10-25T17:31:27.718600Z 71 [ERROR] [MY-011542] [Repl] Plugin group_replication↵
reported: 'Table al_winner does not have any PRIMARY KEY. This is not compatible↵
with Group Replication.'
2020-10-25T17:31:27.718644Z 71 [ERROR] [MY-010584] [Repl] Slave SQL for channel↵
'group_replication_recovery': The table in transaction↵
```

```
de5b65cb-16ae-11eb-826c-98af65266957:15 does not comply with the requirements↵
by an external plugin. Error_code: MY-003635
```

In this example, the error message on the previous row contains the table name al_winner, and the reason why it isn't compatible with Group Replication is that the table doesn't have a primary key.

To fix the error, you need to fix the table definition on the PRIMARY and failing SECONDARY node.

First, log in to the PRIMARY node, and add a surrogate primary key:

```
mysql> set sql_log_bin=0;
Query OK, 0 rows affected (0.00 sec)

mysql> alter table al_winner add id int not null auto_increment primary key;
Query OK, 0 rows affected (0.09 sec)
Records: 0  Duplicates: 0  Warnings: 0

mysql> set sql_log_bin=1;
Query OK, 0 rows affected (0.01 sec)
```

You need to disable binary logging, because otherwise this change will be replicated to the secondary members, and replication will stop with the duplicate column name error.

Then, run the same command on the secondary members to fix the table definition and restart Group Replication:

```
mysql> set global super_read_only=0;
Query OK, 0 rows affected (0.00 sec)

mysql> set sql_log_bin=0;
Query OK, 0 rows affected (0.00 sec)

mysql> alter table al_winner add id int not null auto_increment primary key;
Query OK, 0 rows affected (0.09 sec)
Records: 0  Duplicates: 0  Warnings: 0

mysql> set sql_log_bin=1;
Query OK, 0 rows affected (0.01 sec)

mysql> stop group_replication;
Query OK, 0 rows affected (1.02 sec)

mysql> start group_replication;
Query OK, 0 rows affected (3.22 sec)
```

You need to disable super_read_only first, which is set by the Group Replication plug-in if the nodes are running in single-primary mode.

Once the error is fixed, the node joins the group and reports its state as ONLINE:

```
mysql> SELECT * FROM performance_schema.replication_group_members\G
*************************** 1. row ***************************
    CHANNEL_NAME: group_replication_applier
       MEMBER_ID: d8a706aa-16ee-11eb-ba5a-98af65266957
```

```
     MEMBER_HOST: Delly-7390
     MEMBER_PORT: 33361
    MEMBER_STATE: ONLINE
     MEMBER_ROLE: PRIMARY
  MEMBER_VERSION: 8.0.21
*************************** 2. row ***************************
    CHANNEL_NAME: group_replication_applier
       MEMBER_ID: e14043d7-16ee-11eb-b77a-98af65266957
     MEMBER_HOST: Delly-7390
     MEMBER_PORT: 33362
    MEMBER_STATE: ONLINE
     MEMBER_ROLE: SECONDARY
  MEMBER_VERSION: 8.0.21
2 rows in set (0.00 sec)
```

Option --verbose

You can find what the failing transaction is doing by running the `mysqlbinlog` command with the `verbose` option:

```
$ mysqlbinlog data1/binlog.000001
> --include-gtids=de5b65cb-16ae-11eb-826c-98af65266957:15 --verbose
...
SET @@SESSION.GTID_NEXT= 'de5b65cb-16ae-11eb-826c-98af65266957:15'/*!*/;
# at 4015
#201025 13:44:34 server id 1  end_log_pos 4094 CRC32 0xad05e64e         Query ↵
thread_id=10    exec_time=0     error_code=0
SET TIMESTAMP=1603622674/*!*/;
...
### INSERT INTO `cookbook`.`al_winner`
### SET
###   @1='Mulder, Mark' /* STRING(120) meta=65144 nullable=1 is_null=0 */
###   @2=21 /* INT meta=0 nullable=1 is_null=0 */
### INSERT INTO `cookbook`.`al_winner`
### SET
###   @1='Clemens, Roger' /* STRING(120) meta=65144 nullable=1 is_null=0 */
###   @2=20 /* INT meta=0 nullable=1 is_null=0 */
### INSERT INTO `cookbook`.`al_winner`
...
### INSERT INTO `cookbook`.`al_winner`
### SET
###   @1='Sele, Aaron' /* STRING(120) meta=65144 nullable=1 is_null=0 */
###   @2=15 /* INT meta=0 nullable=1 is_null=0 */
# at 4469
#201025 13:44:34 server id 1  end_log_pos 4500 CRC32 0xddd32d63         Xid = 74
COMMIT/*!*/;
SET @@SESSION.GTID_NEXT= 'AUTOMATIC' /* added by mysqlbinlog */ /*!*/;
DELIMITER ;
# End of log file
/*!50003 SET COMPLETION_TYPE=@OLD_COMPLETION_TYPE*/;
/*!50530 SET @@SESSION.PSEUDO_SLAVE_MODE=0*/;
```

The `verbose` option required to decode row events.

We fixed the error on one node, but the third node didn't join the group. After examining the content of the `performance_schema.replication_connection_status` table, we discovered that the replication connection options were not set up correctly:

```
mysql> SELECT CHANNEL_NAME, LAST_ERROR_NUMBER, LAST_ERROR_MESSAGE, LAST_ERROR_TIMESTAMP
    -> FROM performance_schema.replication_connection_status\G
*************************** 1. row ***************************
          CHANNEL_NAME: group_replication_applier
     LAST_ERROR_NUMBER: 0
    LAST_ERROR_MESSAGE:
  LAST_ERROR_TIMESTAMP: 0000-00-00 00:00:00.000000
*************************** 2. row ***************************
          CHANNEL_NAME: group_replication_recovery
     LAST_ERROR_NUMBER: 13117
    LAST_ERROR_MESSAGE: Fatal error: Invalid (empty) username when attempting ↵
                        to connect to the master server. Connection attempt terminated.
  LAST_ERROR_TIMESTAMP: 2020-10-25 21:31:31.413876
2 rows in set (0.00 sec)
```

To fix this, we need to run the correct `CHANGE REPLICATION SOURCE` command:

```
mysql> STOP GROUP_REPLICATION;
Query OK, 0 rows affected (1.01 sec)

mysql> CHANGE REPLICATION SOURCE TO SOURCE_USER='repl', SOURCE_PASSWORD='replrepl'
    -> FOR CHANNEL 'group_replication_recovery';
Query OK, 0 rows affected, 2 warnings (0.03 sec)

mysql> START GROUP_REPLICATION;
Query OK, 0 rows affected (2.40 sec)
```

Once fixed, the node will fail with the same SQL error as the previous one and has to be fixed in the way we previously described. Finally, after the SQL error is recovered, the node will join the cluster and will be reported as `ONLINE`:

```
mysql> SELECT * FROM performance_schema.replication_group_members\G
*************************** 1. row ***************************
   CHANNEL_NAME: group_replication_applier
      MEMBER_ID: d8a706aa-16ee-11eb-ba5a-98af65266957
    MEMBER_HOST: Delly-7390
    MEMBER_PORT: 33361
   MEMBER_STATE: ONLINE
    MEMBER_ROLE: PRIMARY
 MEMBER_VERSION: 8.0.21
*************************** 2. row ***************************
   CHANNEL_NAME: group_replication_applier
      MEMBER_ID: e14043d7-16ee-11eb-b77a-98af65266957
    MEMBER_HOST: Delly-7390
    MEMBER_PORT: 33362
   MEMBER_STATE: ONLINE
    MEMBER_ROLE: SECONDARY
 MEMBER_VERSION: 8.0.21
*************************** 3. row ***************************
   CHANNEL_NAME: group_replication_applier
      MEMBER_ID: ea775284-16ee-11eb-8762-98af65266957
    MEMBER_HOST: Delly-7390
    MEMBER_PORT: 33363
   MEMBER_STATE: ONLINE
```

```
         MEMBER_ROLE: SECONDARY
      MEMBER_VERSION: 8.0.21
3 rows in set (0.00 sec)
```

To check the performance of the Group Replication query `performance_schema.rep`
`lication_group_member_stats` table, run the following:

```
mysql> SELECT * FROM performance_schema.replication_group_member_stats\G
*************************** 1. row ***************************
                          CHANNEL_NAME: group_replication_applier
                               VIEW_ID: 16036502905383892:9
                             MEMBER_ID: d8a706aa-16ee-11eb-ba5a-98af65266957
             COUNT_TRANSACTIONS_IN_QUEUE: 0
             COUNT_TRANSACTIONS_CHECKED: 10154
               COUNT_CONFLICTS_DETECTED: 0
     COUNT_TRANSACTIONS_ROWS_VALIDATING: 9247
     TRANSACTIONS_COMMITTED_ALL_MEMBERS: d8a706aa-16ee-11eb-ba5a-98af65266957:1-18,
dc527338-13d1-11eb-abf7-98af65266957:1-1588
         LAST_CONFLICT_FREE_TRANSACTION: dc527338-13d1-11eb-abf7-98af65266957:10160
COUNT_TRANSACTIONS_REMOTE_IN_APPLIER_QUEUE: 0
        COUNT_TRANSACTIONS_REMOTE_APPLIED: 5
        COUNT_TRANSACTIONS_LOCAL_PROPOSED: 10154
        COUNT_TRANSACTIONS_LOCAL_ROLLBACK: 0
*************************** 2. row ***************************
                          CHANNEL_NAME: group_replication_applier
                               VIEW_ID: 16036502905383892:9
                             MEMBER_ID: e14043d7-16ee-11eb-b77a-98af65266957
             COUNT_TRANSACTIONS_IN_QUEUE: 0
             COUNT_TRANSACTIONS_CHECKED: 10037
               COUNT_CONFLICTS_DETECTED: 0
     COUNT_TRANSACTIONS_ROWS_VALIDATING: 9218
     TRANSACTIONS_COMMITTED_ALL_MEMBERS: d8a706aa-16ee-11eb-ba5a-98af65266957:1-18,
dc527338-13d1-11eb-abf7-98af65266957:1-1588
         LAST_CONFLICT_FREE_TRANSACTION: dc527338-13d1-11eb-abf7-98af65266957:8030
COUNT_TRANSACTIONS_REMOTE_IN_APPLIER_QUEUE: 5859
        COUNT_TRANSACTIONS_REMOTE_APPLIED: 4180
        COUNT_TRANSACTIONS_LOCAL_PROPOSED: 0
        COUNT_TRANSACTIONS LOCAL_ROLLBACK: 0
*************************** 3. row ***************************
                          CHANNEL_NAME: group_replication_applier
                               VIEW_ID: 16036502905383892:9
                             MEMBER_ID: ea775284-16ee-11eb-8762-98af65266957
             COUNT_TRANSACTIONS_IN_QUEUE: 0
             COUNT_TRANSACTIONS_CHECKED: 10037
               COUNT_CONFLICTS_DETECTED: 0
     COUNT_TRANSACTIONS_ROWS_VALIDATING: 9218
     TRANSACTIONS_COMMITTED_ALL_MEMBERS: d8a706aa-16ee-11eb-ba5a-98af65266957:1-18,
dc527338-13d1-11eb-abf7-98af65266957:1-37
         LAST_CONFLICT_FREE_TRANSACTION: dc527338-13d1-11eb-abf7-98af65266957:6581
COUNT_TRANSACTIONS_REMOTE_IN_APPLIER_QUEUE: 5828
        COUNT_TRANSACTIONS_REMOTE_APPLIED: 4209
        COUNT_TRANSACTIONS_LOCAL_PROPOSED: 0
        COUNT_TRANSACTIONS_LOCAL_ROLLBACK: 0
3 rows in set (0.00 sec)
```

Important fields are `COUNT_TRANSACTIONS_REMOTE_IN_APPLIER_QUEUE`, which shows
how many transactions are waiting in the queue to be applied on the secondary
node, and `TRANSACTIONS_COMMITTED_ALL_MEMBERS`, which shows that transactions

were applied on all members. For more details, consult the User Reference Manual (*https://oreil.ly/3Gllb*).

3.16 Using Processlist to Understand Replication Performance

Problem

The replica is behind the source server, and lag is increasing. You want to understand what is going on.

Solution

Examine the status of the SQL threads using replication tables in the Performance Schema as well as regular MySQL performance instrumentation.

Discussion

The replica may fall behind the source if SQL threads are applying updates slower than the source server is. This may happen because updates on the source are running concurrently, while on the replica, fewer threads are used to process the same workload. This difference can even happen on replicas with the same or higher number of CPU cores than the source, either because you set up fewer `replica_par allel_workers` than active threads on the source server or because they're not fully used due to safety measures that prevent the replica from applying updates in the wrong order.

To understand how many parallel workers are active, you can query the `replica tion_applier_status_by_worker` table like this:

```
mysql> SELECT WORKER_ID, LAST_APPLIED_TRANSACTION, APPLYING_TRANSACTION
    -> FROM performance_schema.replication_applier_status_by_worker;
+-----------+-----------------------------------+-----------------------------------+
| WORKER_ID | LAST_APPLIED_TRANSACTION          | APPLYING_TRANSACTION              |
+-----------+-----------------------------------+-----------------------------------+
|         1 | de7e85f9-...-98af65266957:26075   | de7e85f9-...-98af65266957:26077   |
|         2 | de7e85f9-...-98af65266957:26076   | de7e85f9-...-98af65266957:26078   |
|         3 | de7e85f9-...-98af65266957:26068   | de7e85f9-...-98af65266957:26079   |
|         4 | de7e85f9-...-98af65266957:26069   |                                   |
|         5 | de7e85f9-...-98af65266957:26070   |                                   |
|         6 | de7e85f9-...-98af65266957:26071   |                                   |
|         7 | de7e85f9-...-98af65266957:25931   |                                   |
|         8 | de7e85f9-...-98af65266957:21638   |                                   |
+-----------+-----------------------------------+-----------------------------------+
8 rows in set (0.01 sec)
```

In the preceding listing, you may notice that only three threads are currently applying a transaction, while others are idle. This is not stable information, and you need to run the same query several times to find out if this is a tendency.

The threads table in the Performance Schema contains a list of all threads currently running on the MySQL server, including background ones. It has a name field, whose value is thread/sql/replica_worker (thread/sql/slave_worker) in the case of the replication SQL thread. You can query it and find more details about what each of the SQL thread workers is doing:

```
mysql> SELECT THREAD_ID AS TID, PROCESSLIST_ID AS PID,
    -> PROCESSLIST_DB, PROCESSLIST_STATE
    -> FROM performance_schema.threads WHERE NAME = 'thread/sql/replica_worker';
+-----+-----+---------------+------------------------------------+
| TID | PID | PROCESSLIST_DB | PROCESSLIST_STATE                  |
+-----+-----+---------------+------------------------------------+
|  54 |  13 | NULL          | waiting for handler commit         |
|  55 |  14 | sbtest        | Applying batch of row changes (update) |
|  56 |  15 | sbtest        | Applying batch of row changes (delete) |
|  57 |  16 | NULL          | Waiting for an event from Coordinator |
|  58 |  17 | NULL          | Waiting for an event from Coordinator |
|  59 |  18 | NULL          | Waiting for an event from Coordinator |
|  60 |  19 | NULL          | Waiting for an event from Coordinator |
|  61 |  20 | NULL          | Waiting for an event from Coordinator |
+-----+-----+---------------+------------------------------------+
8 rows in set (0.00 sec)
```

In the preceding listing, thread 54 is waiting for a transaction commit, threads 55 and 56 are applying a batch of row changes, and other threads are waiting for an event from the coordinator.

Since the source server applies changes in high numbers of threads, we may notice that the replication lag is increasing:

```
mysql> \P grep Seconds_Behind_Source
PAGER set to 'grep Seconds_Behind_Source'
mysql> SHOW REPLICA STATUS\G SELECT SLEEP(60); SHOW REPLICA STATUS\G
        Seconds_Behind_Source: 232
1 row in set (0.00 sec)

1 row in set (1 min 0.00 sec)

        Seconds_Behind_Source: 238
1 row in set (0.00 sec)
```

One of the resolutions for an issue like this is to set the binlog_transaction_depend ency_tracking option on the source server to WRITESET_SESSION or WRITESET. These options are discussed in Recipe 3.8 and allow higher parallelization on the replica. Note that changes won't take effect immediately, because the replica will have to apply binary log events, recorded with the default binlog_transaction_dependency_track ing value COMMIT_ORDER.

Still, after a while, you may notice that all SQL thread workers have become active and the replica lag has started to decrease:

```
mysql> SELECT WORKER_ID, LAST_APPLIED_TRANSACTION, APPLYING_TRANSACTION
    -> FROM performance_schema.replication_applier_status_by_worker;
+-----------+-----------------------------------+-----------------------------------+
| WORKER_ID | LAST_APPLIED_TRANSACTION          | APPLYING_TRANSACTION              |
+-----------+-----------------------------------+-----------------------------------+
|         1 | de7e85f9-...-98af65266957:170966  | de7e85f9-...-98af65266957:170976 |
|         2 | de7e85f9-...-98af65266957:170970  | de7e85f9-...-98af65266957:170973 |
|         3 | de7e85f9-...-98af65266957:170968  | de7e85f9-...-98af65266957:170975 |
|         4 | de7e85f9-...-98af65266957:170960  | de7e85f9-...-98af65266957:170967 |
|         5 | de7e85f9-...-98af65266957:170964  | de7e85f9-...-98af65266957:170972 |
|         6 | de7e85f9-...-98af65266957:170962  | de7e85f9-...-98af65266957:170969 |
|         7 | de7e85f9-...-98af65266957:170971  | de7e85f9-...-98af65266957:170977 |
|         8 | de7e85f9-...-98af65266957:170965  | de7e85f9-...-98af65266957:170974 |
+-----------+-----------------------------------+-----------------------------------+
8 rows in set (0.00 sec)

mysql> SELECT THREAD_ID, PROCESSLIST_ID, PROCESSLIST_DB, PROCESSLIST_STATE
    -> FROM performance_schema.threads WHERE NAME = 'thread/sql/replica_worker';
+-----------+----------------+----------------+------------------------------------------+
| thread_id | PROCESSLIST_ID | PROCESSLIST_DB | PROCESSLIST_STATE                        |
+-----------+----------------+----------------+------------------------------------------+
|        54 |             13 | sbtest         | Applying batch of row changes (update)   |
|        55 |             14 | NULL           | waiting for handler commit               |
|        56 |             15 | sbtest         | Applying batch of row changes (delete)   |
|        57 |             16 | sbtest         | Applying batch of row changes (delete)   |
|        58 |             17 | sbtest         | Applying batch of row changes (update)   |
|        59 |             18 | sbtest         | Applying batch of row changes (delete)   |
|        60 |             19 | sbtest         | Applying batch of row changes (update)   |
|        61 |             20 | sbtest         | Applying batch of row changes (write)    |
+-----------+----------------+----------------+------------------------------------------+
8 rows in set (0.00 sec)

mysql> \P grep Seconds_Behind_Source
PAGER set to 'grep Seconds_Behind_Source'
mysql> SHOW REPLICATION SOURCE STATUS\G SELECT SLEEP(60); SHOW REPLICA STATUS\G
        Seconds_Behind_Source: 285
1 row in set (0.00 sec)

1 row in set (1 min 0.00 sec)

        Seconds_Behind_Source: 275
1 row in set (0.00 sec)
```

Another common reason for the replication lag is a local command, affecting tables, updated by the replication. You may notice that this is the case by querying table rep lication_applier_status_by_worker and comparing the value of the field APPLY ING_TRANSACTION_START_APPLY_TIMESTAMP with the current time:

```
mysql> SELECT WORKER_ID, APPLYING_TRANSACTION, TIMEDIFF(NOW(),
    -> APPLYING_TRANSACTION_START_APPLY_TIMESTAMP) AS exec_time
    -> FROM performance_schema.replication_applier_status_by_worker;
+-----------+--------------------------------------------------+-----------------+
| WORKER_ID | APPLYING_TRANSACTION                             | exec_time       |
+-----------+--------------------------------------------------+-----------------+
|         1 | de7e85f9-1060-11eb-8b8f-98af65266957:226091      | 00:05:14.367275 |
```

```
|         2 | de7e85f9-1060-11eb-8b8f-98af65266957:226087 | 00:05:14.768701 |
|         3 | de7e85f9-1060-11eb-8b8f-98af65266957:226090 | 00:05:14.501099 |
|         4 | de7e85f9-1060-11eb-8b8f-98af65266957:226097 | 00:05:14.232062 |
|         5 | de7e85f9-1060-11eb-8b8f-98af65266957:226086 | 00:05:14.773958 |
|         6 | de7e85f9-1060-11eb-8b8f-98af65266957:226083 | 00:05:14.782274 |
|         7 | de7e85f9-1060-11eb-8b8f-98af65266957:226080 | 00:05:14.843808 |
|         8 | de7e85f9-1060-11eb-8b8f-98af65266957:226094 | 00:05:14.327028 |
+-----------+----------------------------------------------+-----------------+
8 rows in set (0.00 sec)
```

In the preceding listing, the transaction execution time is similar for all threads–around five minutes. That is ridiculously long!

To find out why transactions are executing for such a long time, query the `threads` table in the Performance Schema:

```
mysql> SELECT THREAD_ID, PROCESSLIST_ID, PROCESSLIST_DB, PROCESSLIST_STATE
    -> FROM performance_schema.threads WHERE NAME = 'thread/sql/replica_worker';
+-----------+----------------+----------------+------------------------------+
| thread_id | PROCESSLIST_ID | PROCESSLIST_DB | PROCESSLIST_STATE            |
+-----------+----------------+----------------+------------------------------+
|        54 |             13 | NULL           | Waiting for global read lock |
|        55 |             14 | NULL           | Waiting for global read lock |
|        56 |             15 | NULL           | Waiting for global read lock |
|        57 |             16 | NULL           | Waiting for global read lock |
|        58 |             17 | NULL           | Waiting for global read lock |
|        59 |             18 | NULL           | Waiting for global read lock |
|        60 |             19 | NULL           | Waiting for global read lock |
|        61 |             20 | NULL           | Waiting for global read lock |
+-----------+----------------+----------------+------------------------------+
8 rows in set (0.00 sec)
```

It's clear that the replication SQL threads aren't doing any useful job and are just waiting for a global read lock.

To find out which thread is holding a global read lock, try querying the `threads` table in the Performance Schema, but this time filter out replica threads:

```
mysql> SELECT THREAD_ID, PROCESSLIST_ID, PROCESSLIST_DB,
    -> PROCESSLIST_STATE, PROCESSLIST_INFO
    -> FROM performance_schema.threads
    -> WHERE NAME != 'thread/sql/replica_worker' AND PROCESSLIST_ID IS NOT NULL\G
*************************** 1. row ***************************
        thread_id: 46
   PROCESSLIST_ID: 7
   PROCESSLIST_DB: NULL
PROCESSLIST_STATE: Waiting on empty queue
 PROCESSLIST_INFO: NULL
*************************** 2. row ***************************
        thread_id: 50
   PROCESSLIST_ID: 9
   PROCESSLIST_DB: NULL
PROCESSLIST_STATE: Suspending
 PROCESSLIST_INFO: NULL
*************************** 3. row ***************************
        thread_id: 52
   PROCESSLIST_ID: 11
   PROCESSLIST_DB: NULL
```

```
    PROCESSLIST_STATE: Waiting for master to send event
     PROCESSLIST_INFO: NULL
*************************** 4. row ***************************
            thread_id: 53
       PROCESSLIST_ID: 12
       PROCESSLIST_DB: NULL
    PROCESSLIST_STATE: Waiting for slave workers to process their queues
     PROCESSLIST_INFO: NULL
*************************** 5. row ***************************
            thread_id: 64
       PROCESSLIST_ID: 23
       PROCESSLIST_DB: performance_schema
    PROCESSLIST_STATE: executing
     PROCESSLIST_INFO: SELECT THREAD_ID, PROCESSLIST_ID, PROCESSLIST_DB, PROCESSLIST_STATE, ↵
                       PROCESSLIST_INFO FROM performance_schema.threads WHERE ↵
                       NAME != 'thread/sql/slave_worker' AND PROCESSLIST_ID IS NOT NULL
*************************** 6. row ***************************
            thread_id: 65
       PROCESSLIST_ID: 24
       PROCESSLIST_DB: NULL
    PROCESSLIST_STATE: NULL
     PROCESSLIST_INFO: flush tables with read lock
6 rows in set (0.00 sec)
```

In our example, the offending thread is the thread executed FLUSH TABLES WITH
READ LOCK. This is a common safety lock, performed by backup programs. Since we
know the reason for the replica stall, we can either wait until this job finishes or kill
the thread. Once done, the replica will continue executing updates.

See Also

Troubleshooting performance is a long topic, and further detail is outside the scope
of this book. For additional information about troubleshooting, see *MySQL Troubleshooting* (O'Reilly) (*https://oreil.ly/BW9TL*).

3.17 Setting Up Automated Replication

Problem

You want to set up replication but do not want to configure it manually.

Solution

Use MySQL Admin API, available in MySQL Shell (Chapter 2).

Discussion

MySQL Shell provides MySQL Admin API, which allows you to automate standard
replication administrative tasks, such as creating a ReplicaSet of a source server with
one or more replicas. Or, you can create an InnoDB Cluster, using Group Replication.

InnoDB ReplicaSet

If you want to automate replication setup, use the MySQL Admin API inside MySQL Shell and InnoDB ReplicaSet. InnoDB ReplicaSet allows you to create a single-primary replication topology with as many secondary read-only servers as you wish. You can later promote one of the secondary servers to primary. Multiple-primary setups, replication filters, and automatic failovers are not supported.

First, you need to prepare the servers. Ensure that the following conditions are met:

- MySQL is version 8.0 or newer
- The GTID `gtid_mode` and `enforce_gtid_consistency` options are enabled
- The binary log format is `ROW`
- The default storage engine is InnoDB: set the option `default_stor age_engine=InnoDB`
- Parallel-replication related options are set to the following values:
  ```
  binlog_transaction_dependency_tracking=WRITESET
  replica_preserve_commit_order=ON
  replica_parallel_type=LOGICAL_CLOCK
  ```

If you're using Ubuntu and want to set up ReplicaSet on the local machine, edit the /etc/hosts file and either remove loopback address 127.0.1.1 or replace it with 127.0.0.1. Loopback addresses other than 127.0.0.1 are not supported by MySQL Shell.

Once the servers are prepared for replication, you can start configuring them with MySQL Shell:

```
 MySQL  JS > \c root@127.0.0.1:13000
Creating a session to 'root@127.0.0.1:13000'
Fetching schema names for autocompletion... Press ^C to stop.
Your MySQL connection id is 12
Server version: 8.0.28 MySQL Community Server - GPL
No default schema selected; type \use <schema> to set one.
 MySQL  127.0.0.1:13000 ssl  JS > dba.configureReplicaSetInstance(
                     -> 'root@127.0.0.1:13000', {clusterAdmin: "'repl'@'%'"})
                     ->
Please provide the password for 'root@127.0.0.1:13000':
Save password for 'root@127.0.0.1:13000'? [Y]es/[N]o/Ne[v]er (default No):
Configuring local MySQL instance listening at port 13000 for use in an InnoDB ReplicaSet...

This instance reports its own address as Delly-7390:13000
Clients and other cluster members will communicate with it through↵
this address by default. If this is not correct,  ↵
the report_host MySQL system variable should be changed.
Password for new account: ********
Confirm password: ********
```

```
applierWorkerThreads will be set to the default value of 4.

The instance 'Delly-7390:13000' is valid to be used in an InnoDB ReplicaSet.
Cluster admin user 'repl'@'%' created.
The instance 'Delly-7390:13000' is already ready to be used in an InnoDB ReplicaSet.

Successfully enabled parallel appliers.
```

The dba.configureReplicaSetInstance command takes two parameters: URI to connect to the server and configuration options. The clusterAdmin option instructs you to create a replication user. Then you can provide a password when prompted.

Repeat the configuration step for all servers in the ReplicaSet. Specify the same replication username and password.

Once all instances are configured, create a ReplicaSet:

```
MySQL  127.0.0.1:13000 ssl  JS > var rs = dba.createReplicaSet("cookbook")
A new replicaset with instance 'Delly-7390:13000' will be created.

* Checking MySQL instance at Delly-7390:13000

This instance reports its own address as Delly-7390:13000
Delly-7390:13000: Instance configuration is suitable.

* Updating metadata...

ReplicaSet object successfully created for Delly-7390:13000.
Use rs.addInstance() to add more asynchronously replicated instances to this ↵
replicaset and rs.status() to check its status.
```

The dba.createReplicaSet command creates a named ReplicaSet and returns a ReplicaSet object. Save it into a variable to perform further management.

Internally, it creates a mysql_innodb_cluster_metadata database with tables, describing ReplicaSet setup in the instance MySQL Shell connected to. At the same time, this first instance is set up as a PRIMARY ReplicaSet member. You can check it by running the rs.status() command:

```
MySQL  127.0.0.1:13000 ssl  JS > rs.status()
{
    "replicaSet": {
        "name": "cookbook",
        "primary": "Delly-7390:13000",
        "status": "AVAILABLE",
        "statusText": "All instances available.",
        "topology": {
            "Delly-7390:13000": {
                "address": "Delly-7390:13000",
                "instanceRole": "PRIMARY",
                "mode": "R/W",
                "status": "ONLINE"
            }
        },
        "type": "ASYNC"
    }
}
```

Once the PRIMARY instance is set up, you can add as many secondary instances as desired:

```
MySQL  127.0.0.1:13000 ssl  JS > rs.addInstance('root@127.0.0.1:13002')
Adding instance to the replicaset...

* Performing validation checks

This instance reports its own address as Delly-7390:13002
Delly-7390:13002: Instance configuration is suitable.

* Checking async replication topology...

* Checking transaction state of the instance...

NOTE: The target instance 'Delly-7390:13002' has not been pre-provisioned ↵
(GTID set is empty). The Shell is unable to decide whether replication can ↵
completely recover its state.
The safest and most convenient way to provision a new instance is through ↵
automatic clone provisioning, which will completely overwrite the state of ↵
'Delly-7390:13002' with a physical snapshot from an existing replicaset member. ↵
To use this method by default, set the 'recoveryMethod' option to 'clone'.

WARNING: It should be safe to rely on replication to incrementally recover ↵
the state of the new instance if you are sure all updates ever executed in ↵
the replicaset were done with GTIDs enabled, there are no purged transactions, ↵
and the new instance contains the same GTID set as the replicaset or a subset ↵
of it. To use this method by default, set the 'recoveryMethod' option to 'incremental'.


Please select a recovery method [C]lone/[I]ncremental recovery/[A]bort (default Clone):
* Updating topology
Waiting for clone process of the new member to complete. Press ^C to abort the operation.
* Waiting for clone to finish...
NOTE: Delly-7390:13002 is being cloned from delly-7390:13000
** Stage DROP DATA: Completed
** Clone Transfer
    FILE COPY  #################################################### 100%  Completed
    PAGE COPY  #################################################### 100%  Completed
    REDO COPY  #################################################### 100%  Completed

NOTE: Delly-7390:13002 is shutting down...

* Waiting for server restart... ready
* Delly-7390:13002 has restarted, waiting for clone to finish...
** Stage RESTART: Completed
* Clone process has finished: 60.00 MB transferred in about 1 second (~60.00 MB/s)

** Configuring Delly-7390:13002 to replicate from Delly-7390:13000
** Waiting for new instance to synchronize with PRIMARY...

The instance 'Delly-7390:13002' was added to the replicaset and is replicating
from Delly-7390:13000.
```

Each secondary instance performs an initial data copy from the PRIMARY member. It can copy data using either the clone plug-in or through incremental recovery from the binary logs. For the server that already has data, the clone method is preferable.

But you may need to manually restart the server to finish the installation. If you've chosen incremental recovery, ensure that no binary log containing data is purged. Otherwise, replication setup will fail.

Once all secondary members are added, ReplicaSet is ready and can be used for writes and reads. You can check its status by running the `rs.status()` command. It supports the `extended` option, controlling verbosity of the output. Still, it doesn't show all the information about replication health. If you want to have all the details, use the `SHOW REPLICA STATUS` command or query the Performance Schema.

If you want to change which server is a PRIMARY, use the `rs.setPrimaryInstance` command. Thus, `rs.setPrimaryInstance("127.0.0.1:13002")` degrades the server to secondary when listening on port 1300, and promotes the server to PRIMARY when listening on port 13002.

If you disconnected from a server participating in the ReplicaSet or destroyed a `Repli caSet` object, reconnect to one of the ReplicaSet members and run the `rs=dba.getRe plicaSet()` command to re-create the ReplicaSet object.

If you want to manage ReplicaSet with MySQL Shell, do not modify the replication setup directly by running the `CHANGE REPLICA TION SOURCE` command. All management should happen via the Admin API in MySQL Shell.

InnoDB Cluster

To automate Group Replication, create a MySQL InnoDB Cluster (*https://oreil.ly/LBvSF*). InnoDB Cluster is a complete high-availability solution that allows you to easily configure and administer a group of at least three MySQL Servers.

Before setting up an InnoDB Cluster, prepare the servers. Each of the servers in the group should meet the following conditions:

- Have a unique server ID
- Have GTID enabled
- Have the `disabled_storage_engines` option set to `"MyISAM,BLACKHOLE,FEDER ATED,ARCHIVE,MEMORY"`
- Have the `log_replica_updates` option enabled
- Have a user account with administrative privileges
- Parallel-replication related options:
  ```
  binlog_transaction_dependency_tracking=WRITESET
  replica_preserve_commit_order=ON
  replica_parallel_type=LOGICAL_CLOCK
  transaction_write_set_extraction=XXHASH64
  ```

You can set other options (Recipe 3.12) required for Group Replication, but they can also be configured by the MySQL Shell.

Once you have set up and started the MySQL instances, connect MySQL Shell to the one you want to make PRIMARY and configure them. You need to use an account (in our case, root) with administrative privileges to start the configuration process:

```
MySQL  127.0.0.1:33367 ssl  JS > dba.configureInstance('root@127.0.0.1:33367',
                            -> {clusterAdmin: "grepl",
                            -> clusterAdminPassword: "greplgrepl"})
                            ->
Please provide the password for 'root@127.0.0.1:33367':
Configuring local MySQL instance listening at port 33367 for use in an InnoDB cluster...

This instance reports its own address as Delly-7390:33367
Clients and other cluster members will communicate with it through this address by default.
If this is not correct, the report_host MySQL system variable should be changed.
Assuming full account name 'grepl'@'%' for grepl

The instance 'Delly-7390:33367' is valid to be used in an InnoDB cluster.

Cluster admin user 'grepl'@'%' created.
The instance 'Delly-7390:33367' is already ready to be used in an InnoDB cluster.
```

Repeat the configuration for other instances in the cluster.

 If an instance is manually configured for Group Replication, MySQL Shell wouldn't be able to update its options and wouldn't ensure that the Group Replication configuration persists after restart. Always run dba.configureInstance before setting up an InnoDB Cluster.

After the instances are configured, create a cluster:

```
MySQL  127.0.0.1:33367 ssl  JS > var cluster = dba.createCluster('cookbook',
                            -> {localAddress: ":34367"})
                            ->
A new InnoDB cluster will be created on instance '127.0.0.1:33367'.

Validating instance configuration at 127.0.0.1:33367...

This instance reports its own address as Delly-7390:33367

Instance configuration is suitable.
Creating InnoDB cluster 'cookbook' on 'Delly-7390:33367'...

Adding Seed Instance...
Cluster successfully created. Use Cluster.addInstance() to add MySQL instances.
At least 3 instances are needed for the cluster to be able to withstand up to
one server failure.
```

Then add instances to it: cluster.addInstance('root@127.0.0.1:33368', {local Address: ":34368"}). When MySQL Shell asks you to select a recovery method, choose "Clone." Then, depending on whether your server supports the RESTART command, either wait until it's back online or start the node manually. If it's successful, you'll see a message similar to this:

```
State recovery already finished for 'Delly-7390:33368'

The instance '127.0.0.1:33368' was successfully added to the cluster.
```

Add other instances to the cluster.

 MySQL Shell constructs a local address that Group nodes use to communicate with one another by using the `report_host` system variable for the host address and the formula `(current port of the instance) * 10 + 1` for the port number. If the auto-generated value exceeds 65535, the instance cannot be added to the cluster. Therefore, if you use nonstandard ports, specify the custom value for the `localAddress` option.

After instances are added, InnoDB Cluster is ready to use. To examine its status, use the `cluster.status()` command, which supports the `extended` key, controlling verbosity of the output. The default is 0: only basic information is printed. With option 2 and 3, you can examine which transactions are received and applied on each member. The command `cluster.describe()` gives a short overview of the cluster topology:

```
MySQL  127.0.0.1:33367 ssl  JS > cluster.describe()
{
    "clusterName": "cookbook",
    "defaultReplicaSet": {
        "name": "default",
        "topology": [
            {
                "address": "Delly-7390:33367",
                "label": "Delly-7390:33367",
                "role": "HA"
            },
            {
                "address": "Delly-7390:33368",
                "label": "Delly-7390:33368",
                "role": "HA"
            },
            {
                "address": "Delly-7390:33369",
                "label": "Delly-7390:33369",
                "role": "HA"
            }
        ],
        "topologyMode": "Single-Primary"
    }
}
```

If you destroyed the cluster object, for example, by closing the session, reconnect to one of the cluster members and re-create it by running the `cluster = dba.getClus ter()` command.

 Both InnoDB ReplicaSet and InnoDB Cluster support the software router MySQL Router (*https://oreil.ly/sbU3m*), which you can use for load balancing. We skipped this part because it's outside the scope of the book. For information on how to set up the MySQL Router together with InnoDB ReplicaSet and InnoDB Cluster, consult the User Reference Manual.

See Also

For additional information about replication automation, see the MySQL Shell Reference Manual (*https://oreil.ly/aP1DS*).

## CHAPTER 4

Writing MySQL-Based Programs

4.0 Introduction

This chapter discusses how to use MySQL from within the context of a general-purpose programming language. It covers basic application programming interface (API) operations that are fundamental to and form the basis for the programming recipes developed in later chapters. These operations include connecting to the MySQL server, executing statements, and retrieving the results.

MySQL-based client programs can be written using many languages. This book covers the languages and interfaces shown in Table 4-1 (for information on obtaining the interface software, see the Preface).

Table 4-1. Languages and interfaces covered in this book

Language	Interface
Perl	Perl DBI
Ruby	Mysql2 gem
PHP	PDO
Python	DB-API
Go	Go sql
Java	JDBC

MySQL client APIs provide the following capabilities, each covered in a section of this chapter:

Connecting to the MySQL server, selecting a database, and disconnecting from the server
    Every program that uses MySQL must first establish a connection to the server. Most programs also select a default database, and well-behaved MySQL programs close the connection to the server when they're done with it.

Checking for errors

Any database operation can fail. If you know how to find out when that occurs and why, you can take appropriate action, such as terminating the program or informing the user of the problem.

Executing SQL statements and retrieving results

The point of connecting to a database server is to execute SQL statements. Each API provides at least one way to do this, as well as methods for processing statement results.

Handling special characters and NULL *values in statements*

Data values can be embedded directly in statement strings. However, some characters such as quotes and backslashes have special meaning, and their use requires certain precautions. The same is true for NULL values. If you handle these improperly, your programs will generate SQL statements that are erroneous or yield unexpected results. If you incorporate data from external sources into queries, your program might become subject to SQL injection attacks. Most APIs enable you to avoid these problems by using placeholders, which refer to data values symbolically in a statement to be executed and supply those values separately. The API inserts data into the statement string after properly encoding any special characters or NULL values. Placeholders are also known as *parameter markers*.

Identifying NULL *values in result sets*

NULL values are special not only when you construct statements but also in the results returned from them. Each API provides a convention for recognizing and dealing with them.

No matter which programming language you use, it's necessary to know how to perform each of the fundamental database API operations just described, so this chapter shows each operation in all five languages. Seeing how each API handles a given operation should help you see the correspondences between APIs more easily and better understand the recipes shown in the following chapters, even if they're written in a language you don't use much. (Later chapters usually implement recipes using only one or two languages.)

It may seem overwhelming to see each recipe in several languages if your interest is in only one particular API. If so, we advise you to read just the introductory recipe part that provides the general background, then go directly to the section for the language in which you're interested. Skip the other languages; should you develop an interest in them later, come back and read about them then.

This chapter also discusses the following topics, which are not directly part of the MySQL APIs but help you use them more easily:

Writing library files

As you write program after program, you find that you carry out certain operations repeatedly. Library files enable encapsulating code for those operations so they can be performed easily from multiple scripts without repeating the code in each one. This reduces code duplication and makes your programs more portable. This chapter shows how to write a library file for each API that includes a routine for connecting to the server—one operation that every program that uses MySQL must perform. Later chapters develop additional library routines for other operations.

Additional techniques for obtaining connection parameters

An early section on establishing connections to the MySQL server relies on connection parameters hardwired into the code. However, there are other (and better) ways to obtain parameters, ranging from storing them in a separate file to enabling the user to specify them at runtime.

To avoid manually typing in the example programs, get a copy of the `recipes` source distribution (see the Preface). Then, when an example says something like "Create a file named *xyz* that contains the following information," you can use the corresponding file from the `recipes` distribution. Most scripts for this chapter are located under the *api* directory; library files are located in the *lib* directory.

The primary table used for examples in this chapter is named `profile`. It first appears in Recipe 4.4, which you should know in case you skip around in the chapter and wonder where it came from. See also the section at the very end of the chapter about resetting the `profile` table to a known state for use in other chapters.

 The programs discussed here can be run from the command line. For instructions on invoking programs for each language covered here, read `cmdline.pdf` in the recipes distribution.

Assumptions

To use the material in this chapter most effectively, make sure to satisfy these requirements:

- Install MySQL programming support for any languages that you plan to use (see the Preface).

- You should already have set up a MySQL user account for accessing the server and a database for executing SQL statements. As described in Recipe 1.1, the examples in this book use a MySQL account that has a username and password of `cbuser` and `cbpass`, and we'll connect to a MySQL server running on the local host to access a database named cookbook. To create the account or the database, see the instructions in that recipe.

- The discussion here shows how to use each API language to perform database operations but assumes a basic understanding of the language itself. If a recipe uses programming constructs with which you're unfamiliar, consult a general reference for the language of interest.

- Proper execution of some of the programs might require that you set certain environment variables. General syntax for doing so is covered in cmdline.pdf in the recipes distribution (see the Preface). For details about environment variables that apply specifically to library file locations, see Recipe 4.3.

MySQL Client API Architecture

Each MySQL programming interface covered in this book uses a two-level architecture:

- The upper level provides database-independent methods that implement database access in a portable way that's the same whether you use MySQL, PostgreSQL, Oracle, or whatever.

- The lower level consists of a set of drivers, each of which implements the details for a single database system.

This two-level architecture enables application programs to use an abstract interface not tied to details specific to any particular database server. This enhances portability of your programs: to use a different database system, just select a different lower-level driver. However, perfect portability is elusive:

- The interface methods provided by the upper level of the architecture are consistent regardless of the driver you use, but it's still possible to write SQL statements that use constructs supported only by a particular server. For example, MySQL has SHOW statements that provide information about database and table structure, but using SHOW with a non-MySQL server likely will produce an error.

- Lower-level drivers often extend the abstract interface to make it more convenient to access database-specific features. For example, the MySQL driver for Perl DBI makes the most recent AUTO_INCREMENT value available as a database handle attribute accessible as $dbh->{mysql_insertid}. Such features make a program easier to write but less portable. To use the program with another database system will require some rewriting.

Despite these factors that compromise portability to some extent, the general portability characteristics of the two-level architecture provide significant benefits for MySQL developers.

Another characteristic common to the APIs used in this book is that they are object oriented. Whether you write in Perl, Ruby, PHP, Python, Java, or Go, the operation that connects to the MySQL server returns an object that enables you to process statements in an object-oriented manner. For example, when you connect to the database server, you get a database connection object with which to further interact with the server. The interfaces also provide objects for statements, result sets, metadata, and so forth.

Now let's see how to use these programming interfaces to perform the most fundamental MySQL operations: connecting to and disconnecting from the server.

4.1 Connecting, Selecting a Database, and Disconnecting

Problem

You need to establish a connection to the database server and shut down the connection when you're done.

Solution

Each API provides routines for connecting and disconnecting. The connection routines require that you provide parameters specifying the host on which the MySQL server is running and the MySQL account to use. You can also select a default database.

Discussion

This section shows how to perform some fundamental operations common to most MySQL programs:

Establishing a connection to the MySQL server
> Every program that uses MySQL does this, no matter which API you use. The details on specifying connection parameters vary between APIs, and some APIs provide more flexibility than others. However, there are many common parameters, such as the host on which the server is running, and the username and password of the MySQL account to use for accessing the server.

Selecting a database
> Most MySQL programs select a default database.

Disconnecting from the server
> Each API provides a way to close an open connection. It's best to do so as soon as you're done using the server. If your program holds the connection open longer than necessary, the server cannot free up resources allocated to servicing the connection. It's also preferable to close the connection explicitly. If a program

simply terminates, the MySQL server eventually notices, but an explicit close on the user end enables the server to perform an immediate orderly close on its end.

This section includes example programs that show how to use each API to connect to the server, select the cookbook database, and disconnect. The discussion for each API also indicates how to connect without selecting any default database. This might be the case if you plan to execute a statement that doesn't require a default database, such as SHOW VARIABLES or SELECT VERSION(). Or perhaps you're writing a program that enables the user to specify the database after the connection has been made.

 The scripts shown here use localhost as the hostname. If they produce a connection error indicating that a socket file cannot be found, try changing localhost to 127.0.0.1, the TCP/IP address of the local host. This tip applies throughout the book.

Perl

To write MySQL scripts in Perl, the DBI module must be installed, as well as the MySQL-specific driver module, DBD::mysql. To obtain these modules if they're not already installed, see the Preface.

The following Perl script, *connect.pl*, connects to the MySQL server, selects cookbook as the default database, and disconnects:

```perl
#!/usr/bin/perl
# connect.pl: connect to the MySQL server

use strict;
use warnings;
use DBI;

my $dsn = "DBI:mysql:host=localhost;database=cookbook";
my $dbh = DBI->connect ($dsn, "cbuser", "cbpass")
            or die "Cannot connect to server\n";
print "Connected\n";
$dbh->disconnect ();
print "Disconnected\n";
```

To try connect.pl, locate it under the *api* directory of the recipes distribution and run it from the command line. The program should print two lines indicating that it connected and disconnected successfully:

```
$ perl connect.pl
Connected
Disconnected
```

In the rest of the section, we will walk through the code and explain how it works.

If you get an `Access Denied` error when you connect to MySQL 8.0, ensure that the version of DBD::MySQL is linked with the MySQL 8.0 client library, or use the authentication plug-in `mysql_native_password` instead of the default `caching_sha2_pass word` plug-in. We discuss authentication plug-ins in Recipe 24.2.

For background on running Perl programs, read `cmdline.pdf` in the recipes distribution (see the Preface).

The `use strict` line turns on strict variable checking and causes Perl to complain about any variables that are used without having been declared first. This precaution helps find errors that might otherwise go undetected.

The `use warnings` line turns on warning mode so that Perl produces warnings for any questionable constructs. Our example script has none, but it's a good idea to get in the habit of enabling warnings to catch problems that occur during the script development process. `use warnings` is similar to specifying the Perl `-w` command-line option but provides more control over which warnings to display. (For more information, execute a `perldoc warnings` command.)

The `use DBI` statement tells Perl to load the DBI module. It's unnecessary to load the MySQL driver module (DBD::mysql) explicitly. DBI does that itself when the script connects to the database server.

The next two lines establish the connection to MySQL by setting up a data source name (DSN) and calling the DBI `connect()` method. The arguments to `connect()` are the DSN, the MySQL username and password, and any connection attributes you want to specify. The DSN is required. The other arguments are optional, although usually it's necessary to supply a username and password.

The DSN specifies which database driver to use and other options that indicate where to connect. For MySQL programs, the DSN has the format `DBI:mysql:options`. The second colon in the DSN is required even if you specify no following options.

Use the DSN components as follows:

- The first component is always `DBI`. It's not case sensitive.
- The second component tells DBI which database driver to use, and it *is* case sensitive. For MySQL, the name must be `mysql`.
- The third component, if present, is a semicolon-separated list of *name=value* pairs that specify additional connection options, in any order. For our purposes, the two most relevant options are `host` and `database`, to specify the hostname where the MySQL server is running and the default database.

Based on that information, the DSN for connecting to the cookbook database on the local host *localhost* looks like this:

```
DBI:mysql:host=localhost;database=cookbook
```

If you omit the host option, its default value is localhost. These two DSNs are equivalent:

```
DBI:mysql:host=localhost;database=cookbook
DBI:mysql:database=cookbook
```

To select no default database, omit the database option.

The second and third arguments of the connect() call are your MySQL username and password. Following the password, you can also provide a fourth argument to specify attributes that control DBI's behavior when errors occur. With no attributes, DBI by default prints error messages when errors occur but does not terminate your script. That's why connect.pl checks whether connect() returns undef, which indicates failure:

```
my $dbh = DBI->connect ($dsn, "cbuser", "cbpass")
            or die "Cannot connect to server\n";
```

Other error-handling strategies are possible. For example, to tell DBI to terminate the script if an error occurs in any DBI call, disable the PrintError attribute and enable RaiseError instead:

```
my $dbh = DBI->connect ($dsn, "cbuser", "cbpass",
                {PrintError => 0, RaiseError => 1});
```

Then you need not check for errors yourself. The trade-off is that you also lose the ability to decide how your program recovers from errors. Recipe 4.2 discusses error handling further.

Another common attribute is AutoCommit, which sets the connection's auto-commit mode for transactions. MySQL enables this by default for new connections, but we'll set it from this point on to make the initial connection state explicit:

```
my $dbh = DBI->connect ($dsn, "cbuser", "cbpass",
                {PrintError => 0, RaiseError => 1, AutoCommit => 1});
```

As shown, the fourth argument to connect() is a reference to a hash of attribute name/value pairs. An alternative way of writing this code follows:

```
my $conn_attrs = {PrintError => 0, RaiseError => 1, AutoCommit => 1};
my $dbh = DBI->connect ($dsn, "cbuser", "cbpass", $conn_attrs);
```

Use whichever style you prefer. Scripts in this book use the $conn_attr hashref to make connect() calls simpler to read.

Assuming that connect() succeeds, it returns a database handle that contains information about the state of the connection. (In DBI parlance, references to objects are called *handles*.) Later we'll see other handles, such as statement handles, which are associated with particular statements. Perl DBI scripts in this book conventionally use $dbh and $sth to signify database and statement handles.

To specify the path to a socket file for *localhost* connections on Unix, provide a mysql_socket option in the DSN:

```
my $dsn = "DBI:mysql:host=localhost;database=cookbook"
        . ";mysql_socket=/var/tmp/mysql.sock";
```

To specify the port number for non-*localhost* (TCP/IP) connections, provide a port option:

```
my $dsn = "DBI:mysql:host=127.0.0.1;database=cookbook;port=3307";
```

Ruby

To write MySQL scripts in Ruby, the Mysql2 gem must be installed. To obtain this gem if it is not already installed, see the Preface.

The following Ruby script, *connect.rb*, connects to the MySQL server, selects cook book as the default database, and disconnects:

```
#!/usr/bin/ruby -w
# connect.rb: connect to the MySQL server

require "mysql2"

begin
  client = Mysql2::Client.new(:host => "localhost",
                              :username => "cbuser",
                              :password => "cbpass",
                              :database => "cookbook")
  puts "Connected"
rescue => e
  puts "Cannot connect to server"
  puts e.backtrace
  exit(1)
ensure
  client.close()
  puts "Disconnected"
end
```

To try connect.rb, locate it under the *api* directory of the recipes distribution and run it from the command line. The program should print two lines indicating that it connected and disconnected successfully:

```
$ ruby connect.rb
Connected
Disconnected
```

For background on running Ruby programs, read cmdline.pdf in the recipes distribution (see the Preface).

The -w option turns on warning mode so that Ruby produces warnings for any questionable constructs. Our example script has no such constructs, but it's a good idea to get in the habit of using -w to catch problems that occur during the script development process.

The require statement tells Ruby to load the Mysql2 module.

To establish the connection, create a Mysql2::Client object. Pass connection parameters as named arguments for the method new.

To select no default database, omit the database option.

Assuming that the Mysql2::Client object is successfully created, it will act as a database handle that contains information about the state of the connection. Ruby scripts in this book conventionally use client to signify a database handle object.

If the new() method fails, it raises an exception. To handle exceptions, put the statements that might fail inside a begin block, and use a rescue clause that contains the error-handling code. Exceptions that occur at the top level of a script (that is, outside of any begin block) are caught by the default exception handler, which prints a stack trace and exits. Recipe 4.2 discusses error handling further.

To specify the path to a socket file for *localhost* connections on Unix, provide a socket option for the method new:

```
client = Mysql2::Client.new(:host => "localhost",
                            :socket => "/var/tmp/mysql.sock",
                            :username => "cbuser",
                            :password => "cbpass",
                            :database => "cookbook")
```

To specify the port number for non-*localhost* (TCP/IP) connections, provide a port option:

```
client = Mysql2::Client.new(:host => "127.0.0.1",
                            :port => 3307,
                            :username => "cbuser",
                            :password => "cbpass",
                            :database => "cookbook")
```

PHP

To write PHP scripts that use MySQL, your PHP interpreter must have MySQL support compiled in. If your scripts are unable to connect to your MySQL server, check the instructions included with your PHP distribution to see how to enable MySQL support.

PHP actually has multiple extensions that enable the use of MySQL, such as mysql, the original (and now deprecated) MySQL extension; mysqli, the "MySQL improved" extension; and, more recently, the MySQL driver for the PDO (PHP Data Objects) interface. PHP scripts in this book use PDO. To obtain PHP and PDO if they're not already installed, see the Preface.

PHP scripts usually are written for use with a web server. I assume that if you use PHP that way, you can copy PHP scripts into your server's document tree, and request them from your browser, and they will execute. For example, if you run Apache as the web server on the host *localhost* and you install a PHP script named myscript.php at the top level of the Apache document tree, you should be able to access the script by requesting this URL:

```
http://localhost/myscript.php
```

This book uses the *.php* extension (suffix) for PHP script filenames, so your web server must be configured to recognize the *.php* extension. Otherwise, when you request a PHP script from your browser, the server simply sends the literal text of the script and that's what appears in your browser window. You don't want this to happen, particularly if the script contains the username and password for connecting to MySQL.

PHP scripts often are written as a mixture of HTML and PHP code, with the PHP code embedded between the special <?php and ?> tags. Here is an example:

```html
<html>
<head><title>A simple page</title></head>
<body>
<p>
<?php
  print ("I am PHP code, hear me roar!");
?>
</p>
</body>
</html>
```

For brevity in examples consisting entirely of PHP code, typically I'll omit the enclosing <?php and ?> tags. If you see no tags in a PHP example, assume that <?php and ?> surround the entire block of code that is shown. Examples that switch between HTML and PHP code do include the tags, to make it clear what is PHP code and what is not.

PHP can be configured to recognize "short" tags as well, written as <? and ?>. This book does not assume that you have short tags enabled and does not use them.

The following PHP script, *connect.php*, connects to the MySQL server, selects cook book as the default database, and disconnects:

```php
<?php
# connect.php: connect to the MySQL server

try
{
  $dsn = "mysql:host=localhost;dbname=cookbook";
  $dbh = new PDO ($dsn, "cbuser", "cbpass");
  print ("Connected\n");
}
catch (PDOException $e)
```

```
{
  die ("Cannot connect to server\n");
}
$dbh = NULL;
print ("Disconnected\n");
?>
```

To try `connect.php`, locate it under the *api* directory of the `recipes` distribution, copy it to your web server's document tree, and request it using your browser. Alternatively, if you have a standalone version of the PHP interpreter for use from the command line, execute the script directly:

```
$ php connect.php
Connected
Disconnected
```

For background on running PHP programs, read `cmdline.pdf` in the recipes distribution (see the Preface).

`$dsn` is the data source name (DSN) that indicates how to connect to the database server. It has this general syntax:

```
driver:name=value;name=value ...
```

The *driver* value is the PDO driver type. For MySQL, this is `mysql`.

Following the driver name, semicolon-separated *name=value* pairs specify connection parameters, in any order. For our purposes, the two most relevant options are `host` and `dbname`, to specify the hostname where the MySQL server is running and the default database. To select no default database, omit the `dbname` option.

To establish the connection, invoke the `new PDO()` class constructor, passing to it the appropriate arguments. The DSN is required. The other arguments are optional, although usually it's necessary to supply a username and password. If the connection attempt succeeds, `new PDO()` returns a database-handle object that is used to access other MySQL-related methods. PHP scripts in this book conventionally use `$dbh` to signify a database handle.

If the connection attempt fails, PDO raises an exception. To handle this, put the connection attempt within a `try` block and use a `catch` block that contains the error-handling code, or just let the exception terminate your script. Recipe 4.2 discusses error handling further.

To disconnect, set the database handle to `NULL`. There is no explicit disconnect call.

To specify the path to a socket file for *localhost* connections on Unix, provide a `unix_socket` option in the DSN:

```
$dsn = "mysql:host=localhost;dbname=cookbook"
       . ";unix_socket=/var/tmp/mysql.sock";
```

To specify the port number for non-*localhost* (TCP/IP) connections, provide a `port` option:

```
$dsn = "mysql:host=127.0.0.1;database=cookbook;port=3307";
```

Python

To write MySQL programs in Python, a module must be installed that provides MySQL connectivity for the Python DB API, also known as Python Database API Specification v2.0 (PEP 249). This book uses MySQL Connector/Python. To obtain it if it's not already installed, see the Preface.

To use the DB API, import the database driver module that you want to use (which is `mysql.connector` for MySQL programs that use Connector/Python). Then create a database connection object by calling the driver's `connect()` method. This object provides access to other DB API methods, such as the `close()` method that serves the connection to the database server.

The following Python script, *connect.py*, connects to the MySQL server, selects cook book as the default database, and disconnects:

```
#!/usr/bin/python3
# connect.py: connect to the MySQL server

import mysql.connector

try:
  conn = mysql.connector.connect(database="cookbook",
                                 host="localhost",
                                 user="cbuser",
                                 password="cbpass")
  print("Connected")
except:
  print("Cannot connect to server")
else:
  conn.close()
  print("Disconnected")
```

To try `connect.py`, locate it under the *api* directory of the `recipes` distribution and run it from the command line. The program should print two lines indicating that it connected and disconnected successfully:

```
$ python3 connect.py
Connected
Disconnected
```

For background on running Python programs, read `cmdline.pdf` in the recipes distribution (see the Preface).

The import line tells Python to load the mysql.connector module. Then the script attempts to establish a connection to the MySQL server by calling connect() to obtain a connection object. Python scripts in this book conventionally use conn to signify connection objects.

If the connect() method fails, Connector/Python raises an exception. To handle exceptions, put the statements that might fail inside a try statement and use an except clause that contains the error-handling code. Exceptions that occur at the top level of a script (that is, outside of any try statement) are caught by the default exception handler, which prints a stack trace and exits. Recipe 4.2 discusses error handling further.

The else clause contains statements that execute if the try clause produces no exception. It's used here to close the successfully opened connection.

Because the connect() call uses named arguments, their order does not matter. If you omit the host argument from the connect() call, its default value is 127.0.0.1. To select no default database, omit the database argument or pass a database value of "" (the empty string) or None.

Another way to connect is to specify the parameters using a Python dictionary and pass the dictionary to connect():

```
conn_params = {
  "database": "cookbook",
  "host": "localhost",
  "user": "cbuser",
  "password": "cbpass",
}
conn = mysql.connector.connect(**conn_params)
print("Connected")
```

This book generally uses that style from now on.

To specify the path to a socket file for local host connections on Unix, omit the host parameter and provide a unix_socket parameter:

```
conn_params = {
  "database": "cookbook",
  "unix_socket": "/var/tmp/mysql.sock",
  "user": "cbuser",
  "password": "cbpass",
}
conn = mysql.connector.connect(**conn_params)
print("Connected")
```

To specify the port number for TCP/IP connections, include the host parameter and provide an integer-valued port parameter:

```
conn_params = {
  "database": "cookbook",
  "host": "127.0.0.1",
```

```
    "port": 3307,
    "user": "cbuser",
    "password": "cbpass",
}
conn = mysql.connector.connect(**conn_params)
```

Go

To write MySQL programs in Go, a Go SQL Driver must be installed. This book uses Go-MySQL-Driver (*https://github.com/go-sql-driver/mysql*). To obtain it if it's not already installed, install `Git`, then issue the following command:

```
$ go get -u github.com/go-sql-driver/mysql
```

To use the Go SQL interface, import the `database/sql` package and your driver package. Then create a database connection object by calling the `sql.Open()` function. This object provides access to other `database/sql` package functions, such as the `db.Close()` that closes the connection to the database server. We also use a `defer` statement to call the `db.Close()` to make sure the function call is performed later in the program execution. You will see this usage throughout this chapter.

 The Go `database/sql` package and the Go-MySQL-Driver support context cancellation. This means that you can cancel database operations, such as running a query, if you cancel the context. To use this feature, you need to call context-aware functions of the `sql` interface. For brevity, we didn't use `Context` in our examples in this chapter. We include an example using `Context` when we discuss transaction handling in Recipe 20.9.

The following Go script, *connect.go*, connects to the MySQL server, selects `cookbook` as the default database, and disconnects:

```
// connect.go: connect to MySQL server
package main

import (
    "database/sql"
    "fmt"
    "log"

    _ "github.com/go-sql-driver/mysql"
)

func main() {

    db, err := sql.Open("mysql", "cbuser:cbpass@tcp(127.0.0.1:3306)/cookbook")

    if err != nil {
        log.Fatal(err)
    }
    defer db.Close()
```

```
    err = db.Ping()

    if err != nil {
        log.Fatal(err)
    }


    fmt.Println("Connected!")
}
```

To try `connect.go`, locate it under the *api/01_connect* directory of the `recipes` distribution and run it from the command line. The program should print a single line indicating that it connected:

```
$ go run connect.go
Connected!
```

The `import` line tells Go to load the `go-sql-driver/mysql` package. Then the script validates connection parameters and obtains a connection object by calling `sql.Open()`. *No MySQL connection established yet!*

If the `sql.Open()` method fails, `go-sql-driver/mysql` returns an error. To handle the error, store it into a variable (in our example `err`) and use an `if` block that contains the error-handling code. Recipe 4.2 discusses error handling further.

The `db.Ping()` call establishes the database connection. Only then can we say that we connected to the MySQL server successfully.

To specify the path to a socket file for local host connections on Unix, omit the `tcp` parameter in the DSN and provide a `unix` parameter:

```
// connect_socket.go : Connect MySQL server using socket
package main

import (
    "database/sql"
    "fmt"
    "log"

    _ "github.com/go-sql-driver/mysql"
)

func main() {
    db, err := sql.Open("mysql","cbuser:cbpass@unix(/tmp/mysql.sock)/cookbook")
    defer db.Close()

    if err != nil {
        log.Fatal(err)
    }


    var user string
    err = db.QueryRow("SELECT USER()").Scan(&user)

    if err != nil {
        log.Fatal(err)
```

```
        }

        fmt.Println("Connected User:", user, "via MySQL socket")
}
```

Run this program:

```
$ go run connect_socket.go
Connected User: cbuser@localhost via MySQL socket
```

To specify the port number for TCP/IP connections, include the `tcp` parameter into the DSN and provide an integer-valued `port` port number:

```go
// connect_tcpport.go : Connect MySQL server using tcp port number
package main

import (
        "database/sql"
        "fmt"
        "log"

        _ "github.com/go-sql-driver/mysql"
)

func main() {
        db, err := sql.Open("mysql",
        "cbuser:cbpass@tcp(127.0.0.1:3306)/cookbook?charset=utf8mb4")

        if err != nil {
                log.Fatal(err)
        }

        var user string
        err2 := db.QueryRow("SELECT USER()").Scan(&user)

        if err2 != nil {
                log.Fatal(err2)
        }

        fmt.Println("Connected User:", user, "via MySQL TCP/IP localhost on port 3306")
}
```

Run this program:

```
$  go run connect_tcpport.go
Connected User: cbuser@localhost via MySQL TCP/IP localhost on port 3306
```

Go accepts a DSN (Data Source Name) in this form:

```
[username[:password]@][protocol[(address)]]/dbname[?param1=value1&..&paramN=valueN]
```

Where `protocol` could be either `tcp` or `unix`.

A DSN in its fullest form is as follows:

```
username:password@protocol(address)/dbname?param=value
```

Java

Database programs in Java use the JDBC interface, together with a driver for the particular database engine you want to access. That is, the JDBC architecture provides a generic interface used in conjunction with a database-specific driver.

Java programming requires a Java Development Kit (JDK), and you must set your JAVA_HOME environment variable to the location where your JDK is installed. To write MySQL-based Java programs, you'll also need a MySQL-specific JDBC driver. Programs in this book use MySQL Connector/J. To obtain it if it's not already installed, see the Preface. For information about obtaining a JDK and setting JAVA_HOME, read cmdline.pdf in the recipes distribution (see the Preface).

The following Java program, *Connect.java*, connects to the MySQL server, selects cookbook as the default database, and disconnects:

```java
// Connect.java: connect to the MySQL server

import java.sql.*;

public class Connect {

  public static void main (String[] args) {
    Connection conn = null;
    String url = "jdbc:mysql://localhost/cookbook";
    String userName = "cbuser";
    String password = "cbpass";

    try {
      conn = DriverManager.getConnection (url, userName, password);
      System.out.println("Connected");
    } catch (Exception e) {
      System.err.println("Cannot connect to server");
      System.exit (1);
    }

    if (conn != null) {
      try {
        conn.close();
        System.out.println("Disconnected");
      } catch (Exception e) { /* ignore close errors */ }
    }
  }
}
```

To try Connect.java, locate it under the *api* directory of the recipes distribution, compile it, and execute it. The class statement indicates the program's name, which in this case is Connect. The name of the file containing the program must match this name and include a *.java* extension, so the filename for the program is *Connect.java*. Compile the program using javac:

```
$ javac Connect.java
```

If you prefer a different Java compiler, substitute its name for javac.

The Java compiler generates compiled byte code to produce a class file named *Connect.class*. Use the `java` program to run the class file (specified without the *.class* extension). The program should print two lines indicating that it connected and disconnected successfully:

```
$ java Connect
Connected
Disconnected
```

You might need to set your CLASSPATH environment variable before the example program will compile and run. The value of CLASSPATH should include at least your current directory (.) and the path to the Connector/J JDBC driver. For background on running Java programs or setting CLASSPATH, read `cmdline.pdf` in the recipes distribution (see the Preface).

 Starting from Java 11, you can skip the `javac` call for a single-file program and run it as:

```
$ java Connect.java
Connected
Disconnected
```

The `import java.sql.*` statement references the classes and interfaces that provide access to the data types used to manage different aspects of your interaction with the database server. These are required for all JDBC programs.

To connect to the server, call `DriverManager.getConnection()` to initiate the connection and obtain a `Connection` object that maintains information about the state of the connection. Java programs in this book conventionally use `conn` to signify connection objects.

`DriverManager.getConnection()` takes three arguments: a URL that describes where to connect and the database to use, the MySQL username, and the password. The URL string has this format:

```
jdbc:driver://host_name/db_name
```

This format follows the Java convention that the URL for connecting to a network resource begins with a protocol designator. For JDBC programs, the protocol is jdbc, and you'll also need a subprotocol designator that specifies the driver name (mysql, for MySQL programs). Many parts of the connection URL are optional, but the leading protocol and subprotocol designators are not. If you omit *host_name*, the default host value is `localhost`. To select no default database, omit the database name. However, you should not omit any of the slashes in any case. For example, to connect to the local host without selecting a default database, the URL is the following:

```
jdbc:mysql:///
```

In JDBC, you don't test method calls for return values that indicate an error. Instead, provide handlers to be called when exceptions are thrown. Recipe 4.2 discusses error handling further.

Some JDBC drivers (Connector/J among them) permit you to specify the username and password as parameters at the end of the URL. In this case, omit the second and third arguments of the getConnection() call. Using that URL style, write the code that establishes the connection in the example program like this:

```
// connect using username and password included in URL
Connection conn = null;
String url = "jdbc:mysql://localhost/cookbook?user=cbuser&password=cbpass";

try
{
  conn = DriverManager.getConnection (url);
  System.out.println ("Connected");
}
```

The character that separates the user and password parameters should be &, not ;.

Connector/J does not natively support Unix domain socket file connections, so even connections for which the hostname is *localhost* are made via TCP/IP. To specify an explicit port number, add :*port_num* to the hostname in the connection URL:

```
String url = "jdbc:mysql://127.0.0.1:3307/cookbook";
```

However, you can use third-party libraries that provide support for connections via a socket. See "Connecting Using Unix Domain Sockets" (*https://oreil.ly/grJEd*) in the Reference Manual for details.

4.2 Checking for Errors

Problem

Something went wrong with your program, and you don't know what.

Solution

Everyone has problems getting programs to work correctly. But if you don't anticipate problems by checking for errors, the job becomes much more difficult. Add some error-checking code so your programs can help you figure out what went wrong.

Discussion

After working through Recipe 4.1, you know how to connect to the MySQL server. It's also a good idea to know how to check for errors and how to retrieve specific error information from the API, so we cover that next. You're probably anxious to do more interesting things (such as executing statements and getting back the results), but error checking is fundamentally important. Programs sometimes fail, especially during development, and if you can't determine why failures occur, you're flying blind. Plan for failure by checking for errors so that you can take appropriate action.

When an error occurs, MySQL provides three values:

- A MySQL-specific error number
- A MySQL-specific descriptive text error message
- A five-character SQLSTATE error code defined according to the ANSI and ODBC standards

This recipe shows how to access this information. The example programs are deliberately designed to fail so that the error-handling code executes. That's why they attempt to connect using a username and password of `baduser` and `badpass`.

 A general debugging aid not specific to any API is to use the available logs. Check the MySQL server's general query log to see what statements the server is receiving. (This requires that log to be enabled; see Recipe 22.3.) The general query log might show that your program is not constructing the SQL statement string you expect. Similarly, if you run a script under a web server and it fails, check the web server's error log.

Perl

The DBI module provides two attributes that control what happens when DBI method invocations fail:

- `PrintError`, if enabled, causes DBI to print an error message using `warn()`.
- `RaiseError`, if enabled, causes DBI to print an error message using `die()`. This terminates your script.

By default, `PrintError` is enabled and `RaiseError` is disabled, so a script continues executing after printing a message if an error occurs. Either or both attributes can be specified in the `connect()` call. Setting an attribute to 1 or 0 enables or disables it, respectively. To specify either or both attributes, pass them in a hash reference as the fourth argument to the `connect()` call.

The following code sets only the `AutoCommit` attribute and uses the default settings for the error-handling attributes. If the `connect()` call fails, a warning message results, but the script continues to execute:

```
my $conn_attrs = {AutoCommit => 1};
my $dbh = DBI->connect ($dsn, "baduser", "badpass", $conn_attrs);
```

Because you really can't do much if the connection attempt fails, it's often prudent to exit instead after DBI prints a message:

```
my $conn_attrs = {AutoCommit => 1};
my $dbh = DBI->connect ($dsn, "baduser", "badpass", $conn_attrs)
            or exit;
```

To print your own error messages, leave `RaiseError` disabled and disable `PrintError` as well. Then test the results of DBI method calls yourself. When a method fails, the `$DBI::err`, `$DBI::errstr`, and `$DBI::state` variables contain the MySQL error number, a descriptive error string, and the SQLSTATE value, respectively:

```
my $conn_attrs = {PrintError => 0, AutoCommit => 1};
my $dbh = DBI->connect ($dsn, "baduser", "badpass", $conn_attrs)
            or die "Connection error: "
                . "$DBI::errstr ($DBI::err/$DBI::state)\n";
```

If no error occurs, `$DBI::err` is 0, or `undef`; `$DBI::errstr` is the empty string, or `undef`; and `$DBI::state` is empty, or `00000`.

When you check for errors, access these variables immediately after invoking the DBI method that sets them. If you invoke another method before using them, DBI resets their values.

If you print your own messages, the default settings (`PrintError` enabled, `RaiseEr ror` disabled) are not so useful. DBI prints a message automatically, then your script prints its own message. This is redundant, as well as confusing to the person using the script.

If you enable `RaiseError`, you can call DBI methods without checking for return values that indicate errors. If a method fails, DBI prints an error and terminates your script. If the method returns, you can assume it succeeded. This is the easiest approach for script writers: let DBI do all the error checking! However, if both `PrintError` and `RaiseError` are enabled, DBI may call `warn()` and `die()` in succession, resulting in error messages being printed twice. To avoid this problem, disable `PrintError` whenever you enable `RaiseError`:

```
my $conn_attrs = {PrintError => 0, RaiseError => 1, AutoCommit => 1};
my $dbh = DBI->connect ($dsn, "baduser", "badpass", $conn_attrs);
```

This book generally uses that approach. If you don't want the all-or-nothing behavior of enabling `RaiseError` for automatic error checking versus having to do all your own checking, adopt a mixed approach. Individual handles have `PrintError` and `RaiseError` attributes that can be enabled or disabled selectively. For example, you can enable `RaiseError` globally by turning it on when you call `connect()`, and then disable it selectively on a per-handle basis.

Suppose that a script reads the username and password from the command-line arguments and then loops while the user enters statements to be executed. In this case, you'd probably want DBI to die and print the error message automatically if the connection fails (you cannot proceed to the statement-execution loop in that case). After connecting, however, you wouldn't want the script to exit just because the user enters a syntactically invalid statement. Instead, print an error message and loop to get the next statement. The following code shows how to do this. The do() method used in the example executes a statement and returns undef to indicate an error:

```
my $user_name = shift (@ARGV);
my $password = shift (@ARGV);
my $conn_attrs = {PrintError => 0, RaiseError => 1, AutoCommit => 1};
my $dbh = DBI->connect ($dsn, $user_name, $password, $conn_attrs);
$dbh->{RaiseError} = 0; # disable automatic termination on error
print "Enter statements to execute, one per line; terminate with Control-D\n";
while (<>)                # read and execute queries
{
  $dbh->do ($_) or warn "Statement failed: $DBI::errstr ($DBI::err)\n";
}
```

If RaiseError is enabled, you can execute code within an eval block to trap errors without terminating your program. If an error occurs, eval returns a message in the $@ variable:

```
eval
{
  # statements that might fail go here...
};
if ($@)
{
  print "An error occurred: $@\n";
}
```

This eval technique is commonly used to perform transactions (see Recipe 20.4).

Using RaiseError in combination with eval differs from using RaiseError alone:

- Errors terminate only the eval block, not the entire script.
- Any error terminates the eval block, whereas RaiseError applies only to DBI-related errors.

When you use eval with RaiseError enabled, disable PrintError. Otherwise, in some versions of DBI, an error may simply cause warn() to be called without terminating the eval block as you expect.

In addition to using the error-handling attributes PrintError and RaiseError, lots of information about your script's execution is available using DBI's tracing mechanism. Invoke the trace() method with an argument indicating the trace level. Levels 1 to 9 enable tracing with increasingly more verbose output, and level 0 disables tracing:

```
DBI->trace (1); # enable tracing, minimal output
DBI->trace (3); # elevate trace level
DBI->trace (0); # disable tracing
```

Individual database and statement handles also have `trace()` methods, so you can localize tracing to a single handle if you want.

Trace output normally goes to your terminal (or, in the case of a web script, to the web server's error log). To write trace output to a specific file, provide a second argument that indicates the filename:

```
DBI->trace (1, "/tmp/trace.out");
```

If the trace file already exists, its contents are not cleared first; trace output is appended to the end. Beware of turning on a file trace while developing a script but forgetting to disable the trace when you put the script into production. You'll eventually find to your chagrin that the trace file has become quite large. Or worse, a filesystem will fill up, and you'll have no idea why!

Ruby

Ruby signals errors by raising exceptions, and Ruby programs handle errors by catching exceptions in a `rescue` clause of a `begin` block. Ruby Mysql2 methods raise exceptions when they fail and provide error information by means of a `Mysql2::Error` object. To get the MySQL error number, error message, and SQLSTATE value, access the `errno`, `message`, and `sql_state` methods of this object. The following example shows how to trap exceptions and access error information in a Ruby script:

```ruby
begin
  client = Mysql2::Client.new(:host => "localhost",
                              :username => "baduser",
                              :password => "badpass",
                              :database => "cookbook")
  puts "Connected"
rescue Mysql2::Error => e
  puts "Cannot connect to server"
  puts "Error code: #{e.errno}"
  puts "Error message: #{e.message}"
  puts "Error SQLSTATE: #{e.sql_state}"
  exit(1)
ensure
  client.close()s
end
```

PHP

The `new PDO()` constructor raises an exception if it fails, but other PDO methods by default indicate success or failure by their return value. To cause all PDO methods to raise exceptions for errors, use the database handle resulting from a successful connection attempt to set the error-handling mode. This enables uniform handling of all PDO errors without checking the result of every call. The following example shows how to set the error mode if the connection attempt succeeds and how to handle exceptions if it fails:

```
try
{
  $dsn = "mysql:host=localhost;dbname=cookbook";
  $dbh = new PDO ($dsn, "baduser", "badpass");
  $dbh->setAttribute (PDO::ATTR_ERRMODE, PDO::ERRMODE_EXCEPTION);
  print ("Connected\n");
}
catch (PDOException $e)
{
  print ("Cannot connect to server\n");
  print ("Error code: " . $e->getCode () . "\n");
  print ("Error message: " . $e->getMessage () . "\n");
}
```

When PDO raises an exception, the resulting PDOException object provides error information. The getCode() method returns the SQLSTATE value. The getMes sage() method returns a string containing the SQLSTATE value, MySQL error number, and error message.

Database and statement handles also provide information when an error occurs. For either type of handle, errorCode() returns the SQLSTATE value, and errorInfo() returns a three-element array containing the SQLSTATE value and a driver-specific error code and message. For MySQL, the latter two values are the error number and message string. The following example demonstrates how to get information from the exception object and the database handle:

```
try
{
  $dbh->query ("SELECT"); # malformed query
}
catch (PDOException $e)
{
  print ("Cannot execute query\n");
  print ("Error information using exception object:\n");
  print ("SQLSTATE value: " . $e->getCode () . "\n");
  print ("Error message: " . $e->getMessage () . "\n");

  print ("Error information using database handle:\n");
  print ("Error code: " . $dbh->errorCode () . "\n");
  $errorInfo = $dbh->errorInfo ();
  print ("SQLSTATE value: " . $errorInfo[0] . "\n");
  print ("Error number: " . $errorInfo[1] . "\n");
  print ("Error message: " . $errorInfo[2] . "\n");
}
```

Python

Python signals errors by raising exceptions, and Python programs handle errors by catching exceptions in the except clause of a try statement. To obtain MySQL-specific error information, name an exception class, and provide a variable to receive the information. Here's an example:

```
conn_params = {
  "database": "cookbook",
```

```
    "host": "localhost",
    "user": "baduser",
    "password": "badpass"
}

try:
  conn = mysql.connector.connect(**conn_params)
  print("Connected")
except mysql.connector.Error as e:
  print("Cannot connect to server")
  print("Error code: %s" % e.errno)
  print("Error message: %s" % e.msg)
  print("Error SQLSTATE: %s" % e.sqlstate)
```

If an exception occurs, the errno, msg, and sqlstate members of the exception object contain the error number, error message, and SQLSTATE values, respectively. Note that access to the Error class is through the driver module name.

Go

Go does not support exceptions. Instead, its multivalue returns make it easy to pass an error when needed. To handle errors in Go, store the returned value of the type Error into a variable (we use the variable name err here) and handle it accordingly. To handle errors, Go offers a defer statement and Panic() and Recover() built-in functions, shown in Table 4-2.

Table 4-2. Error handling in Go

Function or statement	Meaning
defer	Defers statement execution until the calling function returns.
Panic()	The normal execution of the calling function stops, all deferred functions are executed, then the function returns a call to panic up the stack. The process continues. Finally, the program crashes.
Recover()	Allows you to regain control in the panicking goroutine, so the program won't crash and will continue executing. This works only in the deferred functions. If called in the function that is not deferred, it does nothing and returns nil.

```
// mysql_error.go : MySQL error handling
package main

import (
    "database/sql"
    "log"
    "fmt"

    _ "github.com/go-sql-driver/mysql"
)

var actor string

func main() {

    db, err := sql.Open("mysql", "cbuser:cbpass!@tcp(127.0.0.1:3306)/cookbook")
```

```
    defer db.Close()

    if err != nil {
        log.Fatal(err)
    }

    err = db.QueryRow("SELECT actor FROM actors where actor='Dwayne Johnson'").↵
            Scan(&actor)
    if err != nil {
            if err == sql.ErrNoRows {
                    fmt.Print("There were no rows, but otherwise no error occurred")
            } else {
                    fmt.Println(err.Error())
            }
    }
    fmt.Println(actor)
}
```

If an error occurs, the function returns an object of the type error. Its Error() function returns a MySQL error code and message for the errors, raised by the Go-MySQL-Driver.

There is an exceptional case for the QueryRow() function with the subsequent Scan() call. By default, Scan() returns nil if there is no error and error if there is an error. However, if the query ran successfully but returned no rows, this function returns sql.ErrNoRows.

Java

Java programs handle errors by catching exceptions. To do the minimum amount of work, print a stack trace to inform the user where the problem lies:

```
try
{
  /* ... some database operation ... */
}
catch (Exception e)
{
  e.printStackTrace ();
}
```

The stack trace shows the location of the problem but not necessarily what the problem was. Also, it may not be meaningful except to you, the program's developer. To be more specific, print the error message and code associated with an exception:

- All Exception objects support the getMessage() method. JDBC methods may throw exceptions using SQLException objects; these are like Exception objects but also support getErrorCode() and getSQLState() methods. getErrorCode() and getMessage() return the MySQL-specific error number and message string, and getSQLState() returns a string containing the SQLSTATE value.

- Some methods generate SQLWarning objects to provide information about non-fatal warnings. SQLWarning is a subclass of SQLException, but warnings are accumulated in a list rather than thrown immediately. They don't interrupt your program, and you can print them at your leisure.

The following example program, *Error.java*, demonstrates how to access error messages by printing all the error information available to it. It attempts to connect to the MySQL server and prints exception information if the attempt fails. Then it executes a statement and prints exception and warning information if the statement fails:

```java
// Error.java: demonstrate MySQL error handling

import java.sql.*;

public class Error {
  public static void main(String[] args) {
    Connection conn = null;
    String url = "jdbc:mysql://localhost/cookbook";
    String userName = "baduser";
    String password = "badpass";

    try {
      conn = DriverManager.getConnection(url, userName, password);
      System.out.println("Connected");
      tryQuery(conn);     // issue a query
    } catch (Exception e) {
      System.err.println("Cannot connect to server");
      System.err.println(e);
      if (e instanceof SQLException)  // JDBC-specific exception?
      {
        // e must be cast from Exception to SQLException to
        // access the SQLException-specific methods
        printException((SQLException) e);
      }
    } finally {
      if (conn != null) {
        try {
          conn.close ();
          System.out.println("Disconnected");
        } catch (SQLException e) {
          printException (e);
        }
      }
    }
  }

  public static void tryQuery(Connection conn) {
    try {
      // issue a simple query
      Statement s = conn.createStatement();
      s.execute("USE cookbook");
      s.close();

      // print any accumulated warnings
      SQLWarning w = conn.getWarnings();
      while (w != null) {
```

```
            System.err.println("SQLWarning: " + w.getMessage());
            System.err.println("SQLState: " + w.getSQLState());
            System.err.println("Vendor code: " + w.getErrorCode());
            w = w.getNextWarning();
        }
    } catch (SQLException e) {
        printException(e);
    }
}

public static void printException(SQLException e) {
    // print general message, plus any database-specific message
    System.err.println("SQLException: " + e.getMessage ());
    System.err.println("SQLState: " + e.getSQLState ());
    System.err.println("Vendor code: " + e.getErrorCode ());
    }
}
```

4.3 Writing Library Files

Problem

You notice that you're repeating code to perform common operations in multiple programs.

Solution

Write routines to perform those operations, put them in a library file, and arrange for your programs to access the library. This enables you to write the code only once. You might need to set an environment variable so that your scripts can find the library.

Discussion

This section describes how to put code for common operations in library files. Encapsulation (or modularization) isn't really a "recipe" so much as a programming technique. Its principal benefit is that you need not repeat code in each program you write. Instead, simply call a routine that's in the library. For example, by putting the code for connecting to the cookbook database into a library routine, you need not write out all the parameters associated with making that connection. Simply invoke the routine from your program, and you're connected.

Connection establishment isn't the only operation you can encapsulate, of course. Later sections in this book develop other utility functions to be placed in library files. All such files, including those shown in this section, are located under the *lib* directory of the recipes distribution. As you write your own programs, be on the lookout for operations that you perform often and that are good candidates for inclusion in a library. Use the techniques in this section to write your own library files.

Library files have other benefits besides making it easier to write programs, such as promoting portability. If you write connection parameters directly into each program that connects to the MySQL server, you must change all those programs if you move them to another machine that uses different parameters. If instead you write your programs to connect to the database by calling a library routine, it's necessary only to modify the affected library routine, not all the programs that use it.

Code encapsulation can also improve security. If you make a private library file readable only to yourself, only scripts run by you can execute routines in the file. Or suppose that you have some scripts located in your web server's document tree. A properly configured server executes the scripts and sends their output to remote clients. But if the server becomes misconfigured somehow, the result can be that it sends your scripts to clients as plain text, thus displaying your MySQL username and password. If you place the code for establishing a connection to the MySQL server in a library file located outside the document tree, those parameters won't be exposed to clients.

 Be aware that if you install a library file to be readable by your web server, you don't have much security if other developers use the same server. Any of those developers can write a web script to read and display your library file because, by default, the script runs with the permissions of the web server and thus will have access to the library.

The recipes that follow demonstrate how to write, for each API, a library file that contains a routine for connecting to the cookbook database on the MySQL server. The calling program can use the error-checking techniques discussed in Recipe 4.2 to determine whether a connection attempt fails. The connection routine for each language returns a database handle or connection object when it succeeds or raises an exception if the connection cannot be established.

Libraries are of no utility in themselves, so the following discussion illustrates each one's use by a short "test harness" program (*https://oreil.ly/7MInB*). To use any of these harness programs as the basis for creating new programs, make a copy of the file and add your own code between the connect and disconnect calls.

Library-file writing involves not only the question of what to put in the file but also subsidiary issues such as where to install the file so it is accessible by your programs, and (on multiuser systems such as Unix) how to set its access privileges so its contents aren't exposed to people who shouldn't see it.

Choosing a library-file installation location

If you install a library file in a directory that a language processor searches by default, programs written in that language need do nothing special to access the library. However, if you install a library file in a directory that the language processor does not search by default, you must tell your scripts how to find it. There are two common ways to do this:

- Most languages provide a statement that can be used within a script to add directories to the language processor search path. This requires that you modify each script that needs the library.
- You can set an environment or configuration variable that changes the language processor search path. With this approach, each user who executes scripts that require the library must set the appropriate variable. Alternatively, if the language processor has a configuration file, you might be able to set a parameter in the file that affects scripts globally for all users.

We'll use the second approach. For our API languages, Table 4-3 shows the relevant variables. In each case, the variable value is a directory or list of directories.

Table 4-3. Default library paths

Language	Variable name	Variable type
Perl	PERL5LIB	Environment variable
Ruby	RUBYLIB	Environment variable
PHP	include_path	Configuration variable
Python	PYTHONPATH	Environment variable
Go	GOPATH	Environment variable
Java	CLASSPATH	Environment variable

For general information on setting environment variables, read cmdline.pdf in the recipes distribution (see the Preface). You can use those instructions to set environment variables to the values in the following discussion.

Suppose that you want to install library files in a directory that language processors do not search by default. For purposes of illustration, let's use */usr/local/lib/mcb* on Unix and *C:\lib\mcb* on Windows. (To put the files somewhere else, adjust the pathnames in the variable settings accordingly. For example, you might want to use a different directory, or you might want to put libraries for each language in separate directories.)

Under Unix, if you put Perl library files in the */usr/local/lib/mcb* directory, set the PERL5LIB environment variable appropriately. For a shell in the Bourne shell family (sh, bash, ksh), set the variable like this in the appropriate startup file:

```
export PERL5LIB=/usr/local/lib/mcb
```

For the original Bourne shell, sh, you may need to split this into two commands:

```
PERL5LIB=/usr/local/lib/mcb
export PERL5LIB
```

For a shell in the C shell family (csh, tcsh), set PERL5LIB like this in your *.login* file:

```
setenv PERL5LIB /usr/local/lib/mcb
```

Under Windows, if you put Perl library files in *C:\lib\mcb*, set PERL5LIB as follows:

```
PERL5LIB=C:\lib\mcb
```

In each case, the variable value tells Perl to look in the specified directory for library files, in addition to any other directories it searches by default. If you set PERL5LIB to name multiple directories, the separator character between directory pathnames is a colon (:) in Unix or a semicolon (;) in Windows.

Specify the other environment variables (RUBYLIB, PYTHONPATH, and CLASSPATH) using the same syntax.

Setting these environment variables as just discussed should suffice for scripts that you run from the command line. For scripts intended to be executed by a web server, you likely must configure the server as well so that it can find the library files.

For PHP, the search path is defined by the value of the include_path variable in the *php.ini* PHP initialization file. On Unix, the file's pathname is likely */usr/lib/php.ini* or */usr/local/lib/php.ini*. Under Windows, the file is likely found in the Windows directory or under the main PHP installation directory. To determine the location, run this command:

```
$ php --ini
```

Define the value of include_path in *php.ini* with a line like this:

```
include_path = "value"
```

Specify *value* using the same syntax as for environment variables that name directories. That is, it's a list of directory names, with the names separated by colons in Unix or semicolons in Windows. In Unix, if you want PHP to look for included files in the current directory and in */usr/local/lib/mcb*, set include_path like this:

```
include_path = ".:/usr/local/lib/mcb"
```

In Windows, to search the current directory and *C:\lib\mcb*, set include_path like this:

```
include_path = ".;C:\lib\mcb"
```

If PHP is running as an Apache module, restart Apache to make *php.ini* changes take effect.

Setting library-file access privileges

If you use a multiple-user system such as Unix, you must make decisions about library-file ownership and access mode:

- If a library file is private and contains code to be used only by you, place the file under your own account and make it accessible only to you. Assuming that a library file named *mylib* is already owned by you, you can make it private like this:

  ```
  $ chmod 600 mylib
  ```

- If the library file is to be used only by your web server, install it in a server library directory and make it owned by and accessible only to the server user ID. You may need to be root to do this. For example, if the web server runs as wwwusr, the following commands make the file private to that user:

  ```
  # chown wwwusr mylib
  # chmod 600 mylib
  ```

- If the library file is public, you can place it in a location that your programming language searches automatically when it looks for libraries. (Most language processors search for libraries in some default set of directories, although this set can be influenced by setting environment variables as described previously.) You may need to be root to install files in one of these directories. Then you can make the file world readable:

  ```
  # chmod 444 mylib
  ```

Now let's construct a library for each API. Each section here demonstrates how to write the library file itself and discusses how to use the library from within programs.

Perl

In Perl, library files are called *modules* and typically have an extension of *.pm* ("Perl module"). It's conventional for the basename of a module file to be the same as the identifier on the package line in the file. The following file, *Cookbook.pm*, implements a module named Cookbook:

```perl
package Cookbook;
# Cookbook.pm: library file with utility method for connecting to MySQL
# using the Perl DBI module

use strict;
use warnings;
use DBI;

my $db_name = "cookbook";
my $host_name = "localhost";
```

```perl
my $user_name = "cbuser";
my $password = "cbpass";
my $port_num = undef;
my $socket_file = undef;

# Establish a connection to the cookbook database, returning a database
# handle.  Raise an exception if the connection cannot be established.

sub connect
{
my $dsn = "DBI:mysql:host=$host_name";
my $conn_attrs = {PrintError => 0, RaiseError => 1, AutoCommit => 1};

  $dsn .= ";database=$db_name" if defined ($db_name);
  $dsn .= ";mysql_socket=$socket_file" if defined ($socket_file);
  $dsn .= ";port=$port_num" if defined ($port_num);

  return DBI->connect ($dsn, $user_name, $password, $conn_attrs);
}

1;  # return true
```

The module encapsulates the code for establishing a connection to the MySQL server into a connect() method, and the package identifier establishes a Cookbook namespace for the module. To invoke the connect() method, use the module name:

```perl
$dbh = Cookbook::connect ();
```

The final line of the module file is a statement that trivially evaluates to true. (If the module doesn't return a true value, Perl assumes that something is wrong with it and exits.)

Perl locates library files by searching the list of directories named in its @INC array. To check the default value of this variable on your system, invoke Perl as follows at the command line:

```
$ perl -V
```

The last part of the output from the command shows the directories listed in @INC. If you install a library file in one of those directories, your scripts will find it automatically. If you install the module somewhere else, tell your scripts where to find it by setting the PERL5LIB environment variable, as discussed in the introductory part of this recipe.

After installing the *Cookbook.pm* module, try it from a test harness script, har ness.pl:

```perl
#!/usr/bin/perl
# harness.pl: test harness for Cookbook.pm library

use strict;
use warnings;
use Cookbook;

my $dbh;
```

```
eval
{
  $dbh = Cookbook::connect ();
  print "Connected\n";
};
die "$@" if $@;
$dbh->disconnect ();
print "Disconnected\n";
```

harness.pl has no use DBI statement. It's unnecessary because the Cookbook module itself imports DBI; any script that uses Cookbook also gains access to DBI.

If you don't catch connection errors explicitly with eval, you can write the script body more simply:

```
my $dbh = Cookbook::connect ();
print "Connected\n";
$dbh->disconnect ();
print "Disconnected\n";
```

In this case, Perl catches any connection exception and terminates the script after printing the error message generated by the connect() method.

Ruby

The following Ruby library file, *Cookbook.rb*, defines a Cookbook class that implements a connect class method:

```
# Cookbook.rb: library file with utility method for connecting to MySQL
# using the Ruby Mysql2 module

require "mysql2"

# Establish a connection to the cookbook database, returning a database
# handle.  Raise an exception if the connection cannot be established.

class Cookbook
  @@host_name = "localhost"
  @@db_name = "cookbook"
  @@user_name = "cbuser"
  @@password = "cbpass"

  # Class method for connecting to server to access the
  # cookbook database; returns a database handle object.

  def Cookbook.connect
    return Mysql2::Client.new(:host => @@host_name,
                              :database => @@db_name,
                              :username => @@user_name,
                              :password => @@password)
  end
end
```

The connect method is defined in the library as Cookbook.connect because Ruby class methods are defined as *class_name.method_name*.

Ruby locates library files by searching the list of directories named in its $LOAD_PATH variable (also known as $:), which is an array. To check the default value of this variable on your system, use interactive Ruby to execute this statement:

```
$ irb
>> puts $LOAD_PATH
```

If you install a library file in one of those directories, your scripts will find it automatically. If you install the file somewhere else, tell your scripts where to find it by setting the RUBYLIB environment variable, as discussed in the introductory part of this recipe.

After installing the *Cookbook.rb* library file, try it from a test harness script, harness.rb:

```
#!/usr/bin/ruby -w
# harness.rb: test harness for Cookbook.rb library

require "Cookbook"

begin
  client = Cookbook.connect
  print "Connected\n"
rescue Mysql2::Error => e
  puts "Cannot connect to server"
  puts "Error code: #{e.errno}"
  puts "Error message: #{e.message}"
  exit(1)
ensure
  client.close()
  print "Disconnected\n"
end
```

harness.rb has no require statement for the Mysql2 module. It's unnecessary because the Cookbook module itself imports Mysql2; any script that imports Cookbook also gains access to Mysql2.

If you want a script to die if an error occurs without checking for an exception yourself, write the script body like this:

```
client = Cookbook.connect
print "Connected\n"
client.close
print "Disconnected\n"
```

PHP

PHP library files are written like regular PHP scripts. A *Cookbook.php* file that implements a Cookbook class with a connect() method looks like this:

```
<?php
# Cookbook.php: library file with utility method for connecting to MySQL
# using the PDO module

class Cookbook
```

```
{
  public static $host_name = "localhost";
  public static $db_name = "cookbook";
  public static $user_name = "cbuser";
  public static $password = "cbpass";

  # Establish a connection to the cookbook database, returning a database
  # handle.  Raise an exception if the connection cannot be established.
  # In addition, cause exceptions to be raised for errors.

  public static function connect ()
  {
    $dsn = "mysql:host=" . self::$host_name . ";dbname=" . self::$db_name;
    $dbh = new PDO ($dsn, self::$user_name, self::$password);
    $dbh->setAttribute (PDO::ATTR_ERRMODE, PDO::ERRMODE_EXCEPTION);
    return ($dbh);
  }

} # end Cookbook
?>
```

The connect() routine within the class is declared using the static keyword to make it a class method rather than an instance method. This designates it as directly callable without instantiating an object through which to invoke it.

The new PDO() constructor raises an exception if the connection attempt fails. Following a successful attempt, connect() sets the error-handling mode so that other PDO calls raise exceptions for failure as well. This way, individual calls need not be tested for an error return value.

Although most PHP examples throughout this book don't show the <?php and ?> tags, we've shown them as part of *Cookbook.php* here to emphasize that library files must enclose all PHP code within those tags. The PHP interpreter makes no assumptions about the contents of a library file when it begins parsing it because you might include a file that contains nothing but HTML. Therefore, you must use <?php and ?> to specify explicitly which parts of the library file should be considered as PHP code rather than as HTML, just as you do in the main script.

PHP looks for libraries by searching the directories named in the include_path variable in the PHP initialization file, as described in the introductory part of this recipe.

 PHP scripts often are placed in the document tree of your web server, and clients can request them directly. For PHP library files, we recommend that you place them somewhere outside the document tree, especially if (like *Cookbook.php*) they contain a username and password.

After installing *Cookbook.php* in one of the include_path directories, try it from a test harness script, harness.php:

```php
<?php
# harness.php: test harness for Cookbook.php library

require_once "Cookbook.php";

try
{
  $dbh = Cookbook::connect ();
  print ("Connected\n");
}
catch (PDOException $e)
{
  print ("Cannot connect to server\n");
  print ("Error code: " . $e->getCode () . "\n");
  print ("Error message: " . $e->getMessage () . "\n");
  exit (1);
}
$dbh = NULL;
print ("Disconnected\n");
?>
```

The `require_once` statement accesses the `Cookbook.php` file that is required to use the `Cookbook` class. `require_once` is one of several PHP file-inclusion statements:

- `require` and `include` instruct PHP to read the named file. They are similar, but `require` terminates the script if the file cannot be found; `include` produces only a warning.

- `require_once` and `include_once` are like `require` and `include` except that if the file has already been read, its contents are not processed again. This is useful for avoiding multiple-declaration problems that can easily occur when library files include other library files.

Python

Python libraries are written as modules and referenced from scripts using `import` statements. To create a method for connecting to MySQL, write a module file, *cookbook.py* (Python module names should be lowercase):

```python
# cookbook.py: library file with utility method for connecting to MySQL
# using the Connector/Python module

import mysql.connector

conn_params = {
  "database": "cookbook",
  "host": "localhost",
  "user": "cbuser",
  "password": "cbpass",
}

# Establish a connection to the cookbook database, returning a connection
# object.  Raise an exception if the connection cannot be established.
```

```
def connect():
    return mysql.connector.connect(**conn_params)
```

The filename basename determines the module name, so the module is called cook
book. Module methods are accessed through the module name; thus, import the
cookbook module and invoke its connect() method like this:

```
import cookbook

conn = cookbook.connect();
```

The Python interpreter searches for modules in directories named in the sys.path
variable. To check the default value of sys.path on your system, run Python interactively and enter a few commands:

```
$ python
>>> import sys
>>> sys.path
```

If you install *cookbook.py* in one of the directories named by sys.path, your scripts
will find it with no special handling. If you install *cookbook.py* somewhere else, you
must set the PYTHONPATH environment variable, as discussed in the introductory part
of this recipe.

After installing the *cookbook.py* library file, try it from a test harness script, har
ness.py:

```
#!/usr/bin/python
# harness.py: test harness for cookbook.py library

import mysql.connector
import cookbook

try:
    conn = cookbook.connect()
    print("Connected")
except mysql.connector.Error as e:
    print("Cannot connect to server")
    print("Error code: %s" % e.errno)
    print("Error message: %s" % e.msg)
else:
    conn.close()
    print("Disconnected")
```

The *cookbook.py* file imports the mysql.connector module, but a script that imports
cookbook does not thereby gain access to mysql.connector. If the script needs
Connector/Python-specific information (such as mysql.connector.Error), the script
itself must import mysql.connector.

If you want a script to die if an error occurs without checking for an exception
yourself, write the script body like this:

```
conn = cookbook.connect()
print("Connected")
```

```
conn.close()
print("Disconnected")
```

Go

Go programs are organized into packages that are a collection of the source files, located in the same directory. Packages, in their turn, are organized into modules that are collections of Go packages that are released together. Modules belong to a Go repository. A typical Go repository contains only one module, but you may have several modules in the same repository.

The Go interpreter searches for packages in directories named in the $GOPATH/src/{domain}/{project} variable. However, when using modules, Go no longer uses GOPATH. You do not need to change this variable no matter where your module is installed. We'll use modules for our examples.

To create a method for connecting to MySQL, write a package file, *cookbook.go*:

```
package cookbook

import (
  "database/sql"
  _"github.com/go-sql-driver/mysql"
)

func Connect() (*sql.DB, error) {
  db, err := sql.Open("mysql","cbuser:cbpass@tcp(127.0.0.1:3306)/cookbook")

  if err != nil {
    panic(err.Error())
  }

  err = db.Ping()

  return db, err
}
```

The filename basename does not determine the package name: Go searches through all files in the import path until it finds the one with the required package declaration. Package methods are accessed via the package name.

To test the package, you can specify a relative path to the directory where the package file is located:

```
import "../../lib"
```

This is a very easy way to quickly test your libraries, but such commands, like go install, won't work for packages imported this way. As a result, your program will be rebuilt from scratch each time you access it.

A better way to work with packages is to publish them as parts of modules. To do this, run the following in the directory where you store cookbook.go:

```
go mod init cookbook
```

This will create a file, go.mod, that will have your module name and version of Go. You can name the module as you wish.

You can publish your module on the internet and access it from the local program as you would do with any other module. However, during development, it would be useful to have the module only locally. In this case, you need to make few adjustments in the program directory that will use it.

First, create a program that will call the package, harness.go:

```go
package main

import (
  "fmt"
  "github.com/svetasmirnova/mysqlcookbook/recipes/lib"
)

func main() {
  db, err := cookbook.Connect()

  if err != nil {
    fmt.Println("Cannot connect to server")
    fmt.Printf("Error message: %s\n", err.Error())
  } else {
    fmt.Println("Connected")
  }
  defer db.Close()
}
```

Then, in the directory, after the package is installed, initialize the module:

```
go mod init harness
```

Once the module is initialized and go.mod is created, edit it with the following:

```
go mod edit -replace ↵
github.com/svetasmirnova/mysqlcookbook/recipes/lib=↵
/home/sveta/src/mysqlcookbook/recipes/lib
```

Replace the URL and the local path with the ones that are valid in your environment.

This command will tell Go to replace the remote module path with the local directory.

Once done, you can test your connection:

```
$ go run harness.go
Connected
```

Java

Java library files are similar to Java programs in most ways:

- The class line in the source file indicates a class name.

- The file should have the same name as the class (with a *.java* extension).
- Compile the *.java* file to produce a *.class* file.

Java library files also differ from Java programs in some ways:

- Unlike regular program files, Java library files have no `main()` function.
- A library file should begin with a `package` identifier that specifies the position of the class within the Java namespace.

A common convention for Java package identifiers is to use the domain of the code author as a prefix; this helps make identifiers unique and avoids conflict with classes written by other authors. Domain names proceed right to left, from more general to more specific within the domain namespace, whereas the Java class namespace proceeds left to right, from general to specific. Thus, to use a domain as the prefix for a package name within the Java class namespace, it's necessary to reverse it. For example, Paul's domain is *kitebird.com*, so if he writes a library file and places it under `mcb` within his domain's namespace, the library begins with a `package` statement like this:

```
package com.kitebird.mcb;
```

Java packages developed for this book are placed within the `com.kitebird.mcb` namespace to ensure their uniqueness in the package namespace.

The following library file, *Cookbook.java*, defines a `Cookbook` class that implements a `connect()` method for connecting to the cookbook database. `connect()` returns a `Connection` object if it succeeds and throws an exception otherwise. To help the caller deal with failures, the `Cookbook` class also defines `getErrorMessage()` and `printErrorMessage()` utility methods that return the error message as a string and print it to `System.err`, respectively:

```
// Cookbook.java: library file with utility methods for connecting to MySQL
// using MySQL Connector/J and for handling exceptions

package com.kitebird.mcb;

import java.sql.*;

public class Cookbook {
  // Establish a connection to the cookbook database, returning
  // a connection object.  Throw an exception if the connection
  // cannot be established.

  public static Connection connect() throws Exception {
    String url = "jdbc:mysql://localhost/cookbook";
    String user = "cbuser";
    String password = "cbpass";

    return (DriverManager.getConnection(url, user, password));
  }
```

```
// Return an error message as a string

public static String getErrorMessage(Exception e) {
  StringBuffer s = new StringBuffer ();
  if (e instanceof SQLException) { // JDBC-specific exception?
    // print general message, plus any database-specific message
    s.append("Error message: " + e.getMessage () + "\n");
    s.append("Error code: " + ((SQLException) e).getErrorCode() + "\n");
  } else {
    s.append (e + "\n");
  }
  return (s.toString());
}

// Get the error message and print it to System.err

public static void printErrorMessage(Exception e) {
  System.err.println(Cookbook.getErrorMessage(e));
}
}
```

The routines within the class are declared using the static keyword, which makes them class methods rather than instance methods. That is done here because the class is used directly rather than creating an object from it and invoking the methods through the object.

To use the *Cookbook.java* file, compile it to produce *Cookbook.class*, then install the class file in a directory that corresponds to the package identifier.

This means that *Cookbook.class* should be installed in a directory named *com/kitebird/mcb* (Unix) or *com\kitebird\mcb* (Windows) that is located under some directory named in your CLASSPATH setting. For example, if CLASSPATH includes */usr/local/lib/mcb* under Unix, you can install *Cookbook.class* in the */usr/local/lib/mcb/com/kitebird/mcb* directory. (For more information about the CLASSPATH variable, see the Java discussion in Recipe 4.1.)

To use the Cookbook class from within a Java program, import it and invoke the Cookbook.connect() method. The following test harness program, *Harness.java*, shows how to do this:

```
// Harness.java: test harness for Cookbook library class

import java.sql.*;
import com.kitebird.mcb.Cookbook;

public class Harness {
  public static void main(String[] args) {
    Connection conn = null;
    try {
      conn = Cookbook.connect ();
      System.out.println("Connected");
    } catch (Exception e) {
      Cookbook.printErrorMessage (e);
      System.exit (1);
```

```
      } finally {
        if (conn != null) {
          try {
            conn.close();
            System.out.println("Disconnected");
          } catch (Exception e) {
            String err = Cookbook.getErrorMessage(e);
            System.out.println(err);
          }
        }
      }
    }
  }
}
```

Harness.java also shows how to use the error message utility methods from the Cookbook class when a MySQL-related exception occurs:

- `printErrorMessage()` takes the exception object and uses it to print an error message to `System.err`.

- `getErrorMessage()` returns the error message as a string. You can display the message yourself, write it to a logfile, or whatever.

4.4 Executing Statements and Retrieving Results

Problem

You want a program to send a SQL statement to the MySQL server and retrieve its result.

Solution

Some statements return only a status code; others return a result set (a set of rows). Some APIs provide different methods for executing each type of statement. If so, use the appropriate method for the statement to be executed.

Discussion

You can execute two general categories of SQL statements. Some retrieve information from the database; others change that information or the database itself. Statements in the two categories are handled differently. In addition, some APIs provide multiple routines for executing statements, complicating matters further. Before we get to examples demonstrating how to execute statements from within each API, we'll describe the database table the examples use, and then further discuss the two statement categories and outline a general strategy for processing statements in each category.

In Chapter 1, we created a table named `limbs` to try some sample statements. In this chapter, we'll use a different table named `profile`. It's based on the idea of a "buddy list," that is, the set of people we like to keep in touch with while we're online. The table definition looks like this:

```
CREATE TABLE profile
(
    id    INT UNSIGNED NOT NULL AUTO_INCREMENT,
    name  VARCHAR(20) NOT NULL,
    birth DATE,
    color ENUM('blue','red','green','brown','black','white'),
    foods SET('lutefisk','burrito','curry','eggroll','fadge','pizza'),
    cats  INT,
    PRIMARY KEY (id)
);
```

The `profile` table indicates the things that are important to us about each buddy: name, age, favorite color, favorite foods, and number of cats. Additionally, the table uses several different data types for its columns, and these come in handy to illustrate how to solve problems that pertain to specific data types.

The table also includes an `id` column containing unique values so that we can distinguish one row from another, even if two buddies have the same name. `id` and `name` are declared as `NOT NULL` because they're each required to have a value. The other columns are implicitly permitted to be `NULL` (and that is also their default value) because we might not know the value to assign them for any given individual. That is, `NULL` signifies "unknown."

Notice that although we want to keep track of age, there is no `age` column in the table. Instead, there is a `birth` column of `DATE` type. Ages change, so if we store age values, we'd have to keep updating them. Storing birth dates is better: they don't change and can be used to calculate age any time (see Recipe 8.14). `color` is an `ENUM` column; color values can be any one of the listed values. `foods` is a `SET`, which permits the value to be any combination of the individual set members. That way we can record multiple favorite foods for any buddy.

To create the table, use the *profile.sql* script in the *tables* directory of the `recipes` distribution. Change location into that directory, then run this command:

```
$ mysql cookbook < profile.sql
```

The script also loads sample data into the table. You can experiment with the table, then restore it if you change its contents by running the script again. (See Recipe 4.9 on the importance of restoring the `profile` table after modifying it.)

The contents of the `profile` table as loaded by the *profile.sql* script look like this:

```
mysql> SELECT * FROM profile;
+----+---------+------------+-------+-----------------------+------+
| id | name    | birth      | color | foods                 | cats |
+----+---------+------------+-------+-----------------------+------+
|  1 | Sybil   | 1970-04-13 | black | lutefisk,fadge,pizza  |    0 |
|  2 | Nancy   | 1969-09-30 | white | burrito,curry,eggroll |    3 |
|  3 | Ralph   | 1973-11-02 | red   | eggroll,pizza         |    4 |
|  4 | Lothair | 1963-07-04 | blue  | burrito,curry         |    5 |
|  5 | Henry   | 1965-02-14 | red   | curry,fadge           |    1 |
|  6 | Aaron   | 1968-09-17 | green | lutefisk,fadge        |    1 |
|  7 | Joanna  | 1952-08-20 | green | lutefisk,fadge        |    0 |
|  8 | Stephen | 1960-05-01 | white | burrito,pizza         |    0 |
+----+---------+------------+-------+-----------------------+------+
```

Although most of the columns in the profile table permit NULL values, none of the rows in the sample dataset actually contain NULL yet. (We want to defer the complications of NULL value processing to Recipes 4.5 and 4.7.)

SQL statement categories

SQL statements can be grouped into two broad categories, depending on whether they return a result set (a set of rows):

INSERT, DELETE, or UPDATE
: Statements that return no result set, such as INSERT, DELETE, or UPDATE. As a general rule, statements of this type generally change the database in some way. There are some exceptions, such as USE *db_name*, which changes the default (current) database for your session without making any changes to the database itself. The example data-modifying statement used in this section is an UPDATE:

    ```
    UPDATE profile SET cats = cats+1 WHERE name = 'Sybil';
    ```

    We'll cover how to execute this statement and determine the number of rows that it affects.

SELECT, SHOW, EXPLAIN, or DESCRIBE
: Statements that return a result set, such as SELECT, SHOW, EXPLAIN, or DESCRIBE. We refer to such statements generically as SELECT statements, but you should understand that category to include any statement that returns rows. The example row-retrieval statement used in this section is a SELECT:

    ```
    SELECT id, name, cats FROM profile;
    ```

    We'll cover how to execute this statement, fetch the rows in the result set, and determine the number of rows and columns in the result set. (To get information such as the column names or data types, access the result set metadata. That's Recipe 12.2.)

The first step in processing a SQL statement is to send it to the MySQL server for execution. Some APIs (those for Perl and Java, for example) recognize a distinction between the two categories of statements and provide separate calls for executing them. Other APIs (such as the one for Python or Ruby) use a single call for all statements. However, one thing all APIs have in common is that no special character indicates the end of the statement. No terminator is necessary because the end of the statement string terminates it. This differs from executing statements in the mysql program, where you terminate statements using a semicolon (;) or \g. (It also differs from how this book usually includes semicolons in examples to make it clear where statements end.)

When you send a statement to the server, be prepared to handle errors if it did not execute successfully. If a statement fails and you proceed on the basis that it succeeded, your program won't work. For the most part, this section does not show error-checking code, but that is for brevity. Production code should always include error handling. The sample scripts in the recipes distribution from which the examples are taken do include error handling, based on the techniques illustrated in Recipe 4.2.

If a statement does execute without error, your next step depends on the statement type. If it's one that returns no result set, there's nothing else to do, unless you want to check how many rows were affected. If the statement does return a result set, fetch its rows, then close the result set. In a context where you don't know whether a statement returns a result set, Recipe 12.2 discusses how to tell.

Perl

The Perl DBI module provides two basic approaches to SQL statement execution, depending on whether you expect to get back a result set. For a statement such as INSERT or UPDATE that returns no result set, use the database handle do() method. It executes the statement and returns the number of rows affected by it, or undef if an error occurs. If Sybil gets a new cat, the following statement increments her cats count by one:

```
my $count = $dbh->do ("UPDATE profile SET cats = cats+1
                       WHERE name = 'Sybil'");
if ($count)   # print row count if no error occurred
{
  $count += 0;
  print "Number of rows updated: $count\n";
}
```

If the statement executes successfully but affects no rows, do() returns a special value, "0E0" (the value zero in scientific notation, expressed as a string). "0E0" can be used for testing the execution status of a statement because it is true in Boolean contexts (unlike undef). For successful statements, it can also be used when counting how many rows were affected because it is treated as the number zero in numeric contexts. Of course, if you print that value as is, you'll print "0E0", which might look odd to people who use your program. The preceding example makes sure that doesn't happen by adding zero to the value to coerce it to numeric form so that it displays as 0. Alternatively, use `printf` with a `%d` format specifier to cause an implicit numeric conversion:

```
if ($count)    # print row count if no error occurred
{
  printf "Number of rows updated: %d\n", $count;
}
```

If `RaiseError` is enabled, your script terminates automatically for DBI-related errors, so you need not check `$count` to find out whether `do()` failed and consequently can simplify the code:

```
my $count = $dbh->do ("UPDATE profile SET cats = cats+1
                       WHERE name = 'Sybil'");
printf "Number of rows updated: %d\n", $count;
```

To process a statement such as `SELECT` that does return a result set, use a different approach that involves these steps:

1. Specify the statement to be executed by calling `prepare()` using the database handle. `prepare()` returns a statement handle to use with all subsequent operations on the statement. (If an error occurs, the script terminates if `RaiseError` is enabled; otherwise, `prepare()` returns `undef`.)

2. Call `execute()` to execute the statement and generate the result set.

3. Loop to fetch the rows returned by the statement. DBI provides several methods for this; we cover them shortly.

4. If you don't fetch the entire result set, release resources associated with it by calling `finish()`.

The following example illustrates these steps, using `fetchrow_array()` as the row-fetching method and assuming that `RaiseError` is enabled so that errors terminate the script:

```
my $sth = $dbh->prepare ("SELECT id, name, cats FROM profile");
$sth->execute ();
my $count = 0;
while (my @val = $sth->fetchrow_array ())
{
  print "id: $val[0], name: $val[1], cats: $val[2]\n";
  ++$count;
}
$sth->finish ();
print "Number of rows returned: $count\n";
```

The row array size indicates the number of columns in the result set.

The row-fetching loop just shown is followed by a call to `finish()`, which closes the result set and tells the server to free any resources associated with it. If you fetch every row in the set, DBI notices when you reach the end and releases the resources for you. Thus, the example could omit the `finish()` call without ill effect.

As the example illustrates, to determine how many rows a result set contains, count them while fetching them. Do not use the DBI rows() method for this purpose. The DBI documentation discourages this practice because rows() is not necessarily reliable for SELECT statements—due to differences in behavior among database engines and drivers.

DBI has several methods that fetch a row at a time. The one used in the preceding example, fetchrow_array(), returns an array containing the next row, or an empty list when there are no more rows. Array elements are present in the order named in the SELECT statement. Access them as $val[0], $val[1], and so forth.

The fetchrow_array() method is most useful for statements that explicitly name the columns to select. (With SELECT *, there are no guarantees about the positions of columns within the array.)

fetchrow_arrayref() is like fetchrow_array(), except that it returns a reference to the array, or undef when there are no more rows. As with fetchrow_array(), array elements are present in the order named in the statement. Access them as $ref->[0], $ref->[1], and so forth:

```
while (my $ref = $sth->fetchrow_arrayref ())
{
  print "id: $ref->[0], name: $ref->[1], cats: $ref->[2]\n";
}
```

fetchrow_hashref() returns a reference to a hash structure, or undef when there are no more rows:

```
while (my $ref = $sth->fetchrow_hashref ())
{
  print "id: $ref->{id}, name: $ref->{name}, cats: $ref->{cats}\n";
}
```

To access the elements of the hash, use the names of the columns selected by the statement ($ref->{id}, $ref->{name}, and so forth). fetchrow_hashref() is particularly useful for SELECT * statements because you can access elements of rows without knowing anything about the order in which columns are returned. You need know only their names. On the other hand, it's more expensive to set up a hash than an array, so fetchrow_hashref() is slower than fetchrow_array() or fetchrow_arrayref(). It's also possible to "lose" row elements if they have the same name because column names must be unique. Same-name columns are not uncommon for joins between tables. For solutions to this problem, see Recipe 16.11.

In addition to the statement execution methods just described, DBI provides several high-level retrieval methods that execute a statement and return the result set in a single operation. All are database-handle methods that create and dispose of the statement handle internally before returning the result set. The methods differ in the form in which they return the result. Some return the entire result set, others return a single row or column of the set, as summarized in Table 4-4.

Table 4-4. Perl methods to retrieve results

Method	Return value
selectrow_array()	First row of result set as an array
selectrow_arrayref()	First row of result set as a reference to an array
selectrow_hashref()	First row of result set as a reference to a hash
selectcol_arrayref()	First column of result set as a reference to an array
selectall_arrayref()	Entire result set as a reference to an array of array references
selectall_hashref()	Entire result set as a reference to a hash of hash references

Most of these methods return a reference. The exception is selectrow_array(), which selects the first row of the result set and returns an array or a scalar, depending on how you call it. In array context, selectrow_array() returns the entire row as an array (or the empty list if no row was selected). This is useful for statements from which you expect to obtain only a single row. The return value can be used to determine the result set size. The column count is the number of elements in the array, and the row count is 1 or 0:

```
my @val = $dbh->selectrow_array ("SELECT name, birth, foods FROM profile
                                  WHERE id = 3");
my $ncols = @val;
my $nrows = $ncols ? 1 : 0;
```

selectrow_arrayref() and selectrow_hashref() select the first row of the result set and return a reference to it, or undef if no row was selected. To access the column values, treat the reference the same way you treat the return value from fetchrow_arrayref() or fetchrow_hashref(). The reference also provides the row and column counts:

```
my $ref = $dbh->selectrow_arrayref ($stmt);
my $ncols = defined ($ref) ? @{$ref} : 0;
my $nrows = $ncols ? 1 : 0;

my $ref = $dbh->selectrow_hashref ($stmt);
my $ncols = defined ($ref) ? keys (%{$ref}) : 0;
my $nrows = $ncols ? 1 : 0;
```

selectcol_arrayref() returns a reference to a single-column array representing the first column of the result set. Assuming a non-undef return value, access elements of the array as $ref->[i] for the value from row i. The number of rows is the number of elements in the array, and the column count is 1 or 0:

```
my $ref = $dbh->selectcol_arrayref ($stmt);
my $nrows = defined ($ref) ? @{$ref} : 0;
my $ncols = $nrows ? 1 : 0;
```

`selectall_arrayref()` returns a reference to an array containing an element for each row of the result. Each element is a reference to an array. To access row *i* of the result set, use `$ref->[i]` to get a reference to the row. Then treat the row reference the same way, as a return value from `fetchrow_arrayref()`, to access individual column values in the row. The result set row and column counts are available as follows:

```
my $ref = $dbh->selectall_arrayref ($stmt);
my $nrows = defined ($ref) ? @{$ref} : 0;
my $ncols = $nrows ? @{$ref->[0]} : 0;
```

`selectall_hashref()` returns a reference to a hash, each element of which is a hash reference to a row of the result. To call it, specify an argument that indicates which column to use for hash keys. For example, if you retrieve rows from the `profile` table, the primary key is the `id` column:

```
my $ref = $dbh->selectall_hashref ("SELECT * FROM profile", "id");
```

Access rows using the keys of the hash. For a row that has a key column value of 12, the hash reference for the row is `$ref->{12}`. That row value is keyed on column names, which you can use to access individual column elements (for example, `$ref->{12}->{name}`). The result set row and column counts are available as follows:

```
my @keys = defined ($ref) ? keys (%{$ref}) : ();
my $nrows = scalar (@keys);
my $ncols = $nrows ? keys (%{$ref->{$keys[0]}}) : 0;
```

The `selectall_XXX()` methods are useful when you need to process a result set more than once because Perl DBI provides no way to "rewind" a result set. By assigning the entire result set to a variable, you can iterate through its elements multiple times.

Take care when using the high-level methods if you have `RaiseError` disabled. In that case, a method's return value may not enable you to distinguish an error from an empty result set. For example, if you call `selectrow_array()` in scalar context to retrieve a single value, an `undef` return value is ambiguous because it may indicate any of three things: an error, an empty result set, or a result set consisting of a single NULL value. To test for an error, check the value of `$DBI::errstr`, `$DBI::err`, or `$DBI::state`.

Ruby

The Ruby Mysql2 API uses the same calls for SQL statements that do not return a result set and those that do. To process a statement in Ruby, use the `query` method. If the statement fails with an error, `query` raises an exception. Otherwise, the `affected_rows` method returns the number of rows changed for the last statement that modifies data:

```
client.query("UPDATE profile SET cats = cats+1 WHERE name = 'Sybil'")
puts "Number of rows updated: #{client.affected_rows}"
```

For statements such as SELECT that return a result set, the query method returns the result set as an instance of the Mysql2::Result class. The affected_rows method will return the number of rows in the result set for such statements. You can also obtain the number of rows in the result set by using the count method of the Mysql2::Result object:

```
result = client.query("SELECT id, name, cats FROM profile")
puts "Number of rows returned: #{client.affected_rows}"
puts "Number of rows returned: #{result.count}"
result.each do |row|
  printf "id: %s, name: %s, cats: %s\n", row["id"], row["name"], row["cats"]
end
```

result.fields contains the names of the columns in the result set.

PHP

PDO has two connection-object methods to execute SQL statements: exec() for statements that do not return a result set and query() for those that do. If you have PDO exceptions enabled, both methods raise an exception if statement execution fails. (Another approach couples the prepare() and execute() methods; see Recipe 4.5.)

To execute statements such as INSERT or UPDATE that don't return rows, use exec(). It returns a count to indicate how many rows were changed:

```
$count = $dbh->exec ("UPDATE profile SET cats = cats+1 WHERE name = 'Sybil'");
printf ("Number of rows updated: %d\n", $count);
```

For statements such as SELECT that return a result set, the query() method returns a statement handle. Generally, you use this object to call a row-fetching method in a loop, and count the rows if you need to know how many there are:

```
$sth = $dbh->query ("SELECT id, name, cats FROM profile");
$count = 0;
while ($row = $sth->fetch (PDO::FETCH_NUM))
{
  printf ("id: %s, name: %s, cats: %s\n", $row[0], $row[1], $row[2]);
  $count++;
}
printf ("Number of rows returned: %d\n", $count);
```

To determine the number of columns in the result set, call the statement handle columnCount() method.

The example demonstrates the statement handle fetch() method, which returns the next row of the result set or FALSE when there are no more. fetch() takes an optional argument that indicates what type of value it should return. As shown, with an argument of PDO::FETCH_NUM, fetch() returns an array with elements accessed using numeric subscripts, beginning with 0. The array size indicates the number of result set columns.

With a PDO::FETCH_ASSOC argument, fetch() returns an associative array containing values accessed by column name ($row["id"], $row["name"], $row["cats"]).

With a PDO::FETCH_OBJ argument, fetch() returns an object having members accessed using the column names ($row->id, $row->name, $row->cats).

fetch() uses the default fetch mode if you invoke it with no argument. Unless you've changed the mode, it's PDO::FETCH_BOTH, which is a combination of PDO::FETCH_NUM and PDO::FETCH_ASSOC. To set the default fetch mode for all statements executed within a connection, use the setAttribute database-handle method:

```
$dbh->setAttribute (PDO::ATTR_DEFAULT_FETCH_MODE, PDO::FETCH_ASSOC);
```

To set the mode for a given statement, call its setFetchMode() method after executing the statement and before fetching the results:

```
$sth->setFetchMode (PDO::FETCH_OBJ);
```

It's also possible to use a statement handle as an iterator. The handle uses the current default fetch mode:

```
$sth->setFetchMode (PDO::FETCH_NUM);
foreach ($sth as $row)
  printf ("id: %s, name: %s, cats: %s\n", $row[0], $row[1], $row[2]);
```

The fetchAll() method fetches and returns the entire result set as an array of rows. It permits an optional fetch-mode argument:

```
$rows = $sth->fetchAll (PDO::FETCH_NUM);
foreach ($rows as $row)
  printf ("id: %s, name: %s, cats: %s\n", $row[0], $row[1], $row[2]);
```

In this case, the row count is the number of elements in $rows.

Python

The Python DB API uses the same calls for SQL statements that do not return a result set and those that do. To process a statement in Python, use your database connection object to get a cursor object. Then use the cursor's execute() method to send the statement to the server. If the statement fails with an error, execute() raises an exception. Otherwise, if there is no result set, statement execution is complete, and the cursor's rowcount attribute indicates how many rows were changed:

```
cursor = conn.cursor()
cursor.execute("UPDATE profile SET cats = cats+1 WHERE name = 'Sybil'")
print("Number of rows updated: %d" % cursor.rowcount)
conn.commit()
cursor.close()
```

The Python DB API specification indicates that database connections should begin with auto-commit mode *disabled*, so Connector/Python disables auto-commit when it connects to the MySQL server. If you use transactional tables, modifications to them are rolled back when you close the connection unless you commit the changes first, which is why the preceding example invokes the `commit()` method. For more information on auto-commit mode, see Chapter 20, particularly Recipe 20.7.

If the statement returns a result set, fetch its rows, then close the cursor. The `fetch one()` method returns the next row as a sequence, or `None` when there are no more rows:

```
cursor = conn.cursor()
cursor.execute("SELECT id, name, cats FROM profile")
while True:
  row = cursor.fetchone()
  if row is None:
    break
  print("id: %s, name: %s, cats: %s" % (row[0], row[1], row[2]))
print("Number of rows returned: %d" % cursor.rowcount)
cursor.close()
```

As you can see from the preceding example, the `rowcount` attribute is useful for SELECT statements, too; it indicates the number of rows in the result set.

`len(row)` tells you the number of columns in the result set.

Alternatively, use the cursor itself as an iterator that returns each row in turn:

```
cursor = conn.cursor()
cursor.execute("SELECT id, name, cats FROM profile")
for (id, name, cats) in cursor:
  print("id: %s, name: %s, cats: %s" % (id, name, cats))
print("Number of rows returned: %d" % cursor.rowcount)
cursor.close()
```

The `fetchall()` method returns the entire result set as a list of tuples. Iterate through the list to access the rows:

```
cursor = conn.cursor()
cursor.execute("SELECT id, name, cats FROM profile")
rows = cursor.fetchall()
for row in rows:
  print("id: %s, name: %s, cats: %s" % (row[0], row[1], row[2]))
print("Number of rows returned: %d" % cursor.rowcount)
cursor.close()
```

The DB API provides no way to rewind a result set, so `fetchall()` can be convenient when you must iterate through the rows of the result set more than once or access individual values directly. For example, if `rows` holds the result set, you can access the value of the third column in the second row as `rows[1][2]` (indexes begin at 0, not 1).

Go

The Go `sql` interface has two connection-object functions to execute SQL statements: `Exec()` for statements that do not return a result set and `Query()` for the statements that do. Both return `error` if the statement fails.

To run a statement that doesn't return any row, such as INSERT, UPDATE, or DELETE, use the `Exec()` function. Its return values can have a `Result` type or an `error` type. The interface `Result` has a `RowsAffected()` function that indicates how many rows were changed:

```
sql := "UPDATE profile SET cats = cats+1 WHERE name = 'Sybil'"
res, err := db.Exec(sql)

if err != nil {
        panic(err.Error())
}

affectedRows, err := res.RowsAffected()

if err != nil {
        log.Fatal(err)
}

fmt.Printf("The statement affected %d rows\n", affectedRows)
```

For the statements that return a result set, typically SELECT, use the `Query()` function. This function returns the cursor to the object of the `Rows` type that holds the result of the query. Call the `Next()` function to iterate through the result and store returned values in the variables using the `Scan()` function. If `Next()` returns `false`, this means there is no result:

```
res, err := db.Query("SELECT id, name, cats FROM profile")

defer res.Close()

if err != nil {
        log.Fatal(err)
}

for res.Next() {

        var profile Profile
        err := res.Scan(&profile.id, &profile.name, &profile.cats)

        if err != nil {
                log.Fatal(err)
        }

        fmt.Printf("%+v\n", profile)
}
```

If `Next()` is called and returns `false`, the `Rows` are closed automatically. Otherwise, you need to close them using the `Close()` function.

For the queries that expect to return at most one row, there is a special function, QueryRow(), that returns a Row object that can be scanned immediately. QueryRow() never returns an error until Scan() is called. If the query returns no row, Scan() returns ErrNoRows:

```
row := db.QueryRow("SELECT id, name, cats FROM profile where id=3")

var profile Profile
err = row.Scan(&profile.id, &profile.name, &profile.cats)

if err == sql.ErrNoRows {
        fmt.Println("No row matched!")
} else if err != nil {
        log.Fatal(err)
} else {
        fmt.Printf("%v\n", profile)
}
```

Java

The JDBC interface provides specific object types for the various phases of SQL statement processing. Statements are executed in JDBC using Java objects of one type. The results, if any, are returned as objects of another type.

To execute a statement, first get a Statement object by calling the createStatement() method of your Connection object:

```
Statement s = conn.createStatement ();
```

Then use the Statement object to send the statement to the server. JDBC provides several methods for doing this. Choose the one that's appropriate for the type of statement: executeUpdate() for statements that don't return a result set, executeQuery() for statements that do, and execute() when you don't know. Each method raises an exception if the statement fails.

The executeUpdate() method sends a statement that generates no result set to the server and returns a count indicating the number of affected rows. When you're done with the statement object, close it:

```
Statement s = conn.createStatement ();
int count = s.executeUpdate(
            "UPDATE profile SET cats = cats+1 WHERE name = 'Sybil'");
s.close();    // close statement
System.out.println("Number of rows updated: " + count);
```

For statements that return a result set, use executeQuery(). Then get a result set object, and use it to retrieve the row values. When you're done, close the result set and statement objects:

```
Statement s = conn.createStatement ();
s.executeQuery("SELECT id, name, cats FROM profile");
ResultSet rs = s.getResultSet();
int count = 0;
```

```
while (rs.next ()) { // loop through rows of result set\
    int id = rs.getInt(1);   // extract columns 1, 2, and 3
    String name = rs.getString(2);
    int cats = rs.getInt(3);
    System.out.println("id: " + id
                        + ", name: " + name
                        + ", cats: " + cats);
    ++count;
}
rs.close ();   // close result set
s.close ();    // close statement
System.out.println ("Number of rows returned: " + count);
```

The ResultSet object returned by the getResultSet() method of your Statement object has its own methods, such as next(), to fetch rows and various getXXX() methods that access columns of the current row. Initially, the result set is positioned just before the first row of the set. Call next() to fetch each row in succession until it returns false. To determine the number of rows in a result set, count them yourself, as shown in the preceding example.

For queries that return a single result set, it isn't necessary to call getResultSet. The preceding code could be written as follows:

```
ResultSet rs = s.executeQuery("SELECT id, name, cats FROM profile");
```

A separate call is needed when your query can return multiple result sets, for example, if you call a stored routine.

To access column values, use the getInt(), getString(), getFloat(), or getDate() methods. To obtain the column value as a generic object, use getObject(). The argument to a getXXX() call can indicate either column position (beginning at 1, not 0) or column name. The previous example shows how to retrieve the id, name, and cats columns by position. To access columns by name instead, write the row-fetching loop as follows:

```
while (rs.next ()) { // loop through rows of result set
    int id = rs.getInt("id");
    String name = rs.getString("name");
    int cats = rs.getInt("cats");
    System.out.println("id: " + id
                        + ", name: " + name
                        + ", cats: " + cats);
    ++count;
}
```

To retrieve a given column value, use any getXXX() call that makes sense for the data type. For example, getString() retrieves any column value as a string:

```
String id = rs.getString("id");
String name = rs.getString("name");
String cats = rs.getString("cats");
System.out.println("id: " + id
```

```
                  + ", name: " + name
                  + ", cats: " + cats);
```

Or use `getObject()` to retrieve values as generic objects and convert the values as necessary. The following example uses `toString()` to convert object values to printable form:

```
Object id = rs.getObject("id");
Object name = rs.getObject("name");
Object cats = rs.getObject("cats");
System.out.println("id: " + id.toString()
                  + ", name: " + name.toString()
                  + ", cats: " + cats.toString());
```

To determine the number of columns in the result set, access its metadata:

```
ResultSet rs = s.getResultSet();
ResultSetMetaData md = rs.getMetaData(); // get result set metadata
int ncols = md.getColumnCount();          // get column count from metadata
```

The third JDBC statement-execution method, `execute()`, works for either type of statement. It's particularly useful when you receive a statement string from an external source and don't know whether it generates a result set or returns multiple result sets. The return value from `execute()` indicates the statement type so that you can process it appropriately: if `execute()` returns true, there is a result set, otherwise not. Typically, you'd use it something like this, where `stmtStr` represents an arbitrary SQL statement:

```
Statement s = conn.createStatement();
if (s.execute(stmtStr)) {
  // there is a result set
  ResultSet rs = s.getResultSe();

  // ... process result set here ...

  rs.close();  // close result set
} else {
  // there is no result set, just print the row count
  System.out.println("Number of rows affected: " + s.getUpdateCount ());
}
s.close();    // close statement
```

4.5 Handling Special Characters and NULL Values in Statements

Problem

You need to construct SQL statements that refer to data values containing special characters such as quotes or backslashes, or special values such as NULL. Or you are constructing statements using data obtained from external sources and want to prevent SQL injection attacks.

Solution

Use your API's placeholder mechanism or quoting function to make data safe for insertion.

Discussion

Up to this point in the chapter, our statements have used "safe" data values that require no special treatment. For example, we can easily construct the following SQL statements from within a program by writing the data values literally in the statement strings:

```
SELECT * FROM profile WHERE age > 40 AND color = 'green';

INSERT INTO profile (name,color) VALUES('Gary','blue');
```

However, some data values are not so easily handled and cause problems if you are not careful. Statements might use values that contain special characters such as quotes, backslashes, binary data, or values that are NULL. The following discussion describes the difficulties these values cause and the proper techniques for handling them.

Suppose that you want to execute this INSERT statement:

```
INSERT INTO profile (name,birth,color,foods,cats)
VALUES('Alison','1973-01-12','blue','eggroll',4);
```

There's nothing unusual about that. But if you change the name column value to something like De'Mont that contains a single quote, the statement becomes syntactically invalid:

```
INSERT INTO profile (name,birth,color,foods,cats)
VALUES('De'Mont','1973-01-12','blue','eggroll',4);
```

The problem is the single quote inside a single-quoted string. To make the statement legal by escaping the quote, precede it with either a single quote or a backslash:

```
INSERT INTO profile (name,birth,color,foods,cats)
VALUES('De''Mont','1973-01-12','blue','eggroll',4);

INSERT INTO profile (name,birth,color,foods,cats)
VALUES('De\'Mont','1973-01-12','blue','eggroll',4);
```

Alternatively, quote the name value itself within double quotes rather than within single quotes (assuming that the ANSI_QUOTES SQL mode is not enabled):

```
INSERT INTO profile (name,birth,color,foods,cats)
VALUES("De'Mont",'1973-01-12','blue','eggroll',4);
```

If you are writing a statement literally in your program, you can escape or quote the name value by hand because you know what the value is. But if the name is stored in a variable, you don't necessarily know what the variable's value is. Worse yet, a single quote isn't the only character you must be prepared to deal with; double quotes and backslashes cause problems, too. And if the database stores binary data such as images or sound clips, a value might contain anything—not only quotes or backslashes but other characters such as nulls (zero-valued bytes). The need to handle special characters properly is particularly acute in a web environment where statements are constructed using form input (for example, if you search for rows that match search terms entered by the remote user). You must be able to handle any kind of input in a general way because you can't predict in advance what kind of information a user will supply. It's not uncommon for malicious users to enter garbage values containing problematic characters in a deliberate attempt to compromise the security of your server and even execute fatal commands, such as `DROP TABLE`. That is a standard technique for exploiting insecure scripts, called *SQL injection (https://oreil.ly/5cGOT)*.

The SQL `NULL` value is not a special character, but it too requires special treatment. In SQL, `NULL` indicates "no value." This can have several meanings depending on context, such as "unknown," "missing," "out of range," and so forth. Our statements thus far have not used `NULL` values, to avoid dealing with the complications they introduce, but now it's time to address these issues. For example, if you don't know De'Mont's favorite color, you can set the `color` column to `NULL`—but not by writing the statement like this:

```
INSERT INTO profile (name,birth,color,foods,cats)
VALUES('De''Mont','1973-01-12','NULL','eggroll',4);
```

Instead, the `NULL` value must have no enclosing quotes:

```
INSERT INTO profile (name,birth,color,foods,cats)
VALUES('De''Mont','1973-01-12',NULL,'eggroll',4);
```

Were you writing the statement literally in your program, you'd simply write the word *NULL*. But if the `color` value comes from a variable, the proper action is not so obvious. You must know whether the variable's value represents `NULL` to determine whether to enclose it within quotes when you construct the statement.

You have two means at your disposal for dealing with special characters such as quotes and backslashes and with special values such as `NULL`:

- Use placeholders in the statement string to refer to data values symbolically, then bind the data values to the placeholders when you execute the statement. This is the preferred method because the API itself does all or most of the work for you of providing quotes around values as necessary, quoting or escaping special characters within the data value, and possibly interpreting a special value to map onto `NULL` without enclosing quotes.

- Use a quoting function (if your API provides one) for converting data values to a safe form that is suitable for use in statement strings.

This section shows how to use these techniques to handle special characters and NULL values for each API. One of the examples demonstrated here shows how to insert a profile table row that contains De'Mont for the name value and NULL for the color value. However, the principles shown here have general utility and handle any special characters, including those found in binary data. Also, the principles are not limited to INSERT statements. They work for other kinds of statements as well, such as SELECT. One of the other examples shown here demonstrates how to execute a SELECT statement using placeholders.

Processing of special characters and NULL values comes up in other contexts covered elsewhere:

- The placeholder and quoting techniques described here are *only* for data values and not for identifiers such as database or table names. For a discussion of identifier quoting, refer to Recipe 4.6.

- Comparisons of NULL values require different operators than non-NULL values. Recipe 5.6 discusses how to construct SQL statements that perform NULL comparisons from within programs.

- This section covers the issue of getting special characters *into* your database. A related issue is the inverse operation of transforming special characters in values returned *from* your database for display in various contexts. For example, if you generate HTML pages that include values taken from your database, you must perform output encoding to convert < and > characters in those values to the HTML entities < and > to make sure they display properly.

Using placeholders

Placeholders enable you to avoid writing data values literally in SQL statements. Using this approach, you write statements using placeholders—special markers that indicate where the values go. Two common parameter markers are ? and %s. Depending on the marker, rewrite the INSERT statement to use placeholders like this:

```
INSERT INTO profile (name,birth,color,foods,cats)
VALUES(?,?,?,?,?);
```

```
INSERT INTO profile (name,birth,color,foods,cats)
VALUES(%s,%s,%s,%s,%s);
```

Then pass the statement string to the database server and supply the data values separately. The API binds the values to the placeholders to replace them, resulting in a statement that contains the data values.

One benefit of placeholders is that parameter-binding operations automatically handle escaping of characters such as quotes and backslashes. This is especially useful for inserting binary data such as images into your database or using data values with unknown content such as input submitted by a remote user through a form in a

---

web page. Also, there is usually some special value that you bind to a placeholder to indicate that you want a SQL NULL value in the resulting statement.

A second benefit of placeholders is that you can "prepare" a statement in advance, then reuse it by binding different values to it each time it's executed. Prepared statements thus encourage statement reuse. Statements become more generic because they contain placeholders rather than specific data values. If you perform an operation over and over, you may be able to reuse a prepared statement and simply bind different data values to it each time you execute it. Some database systems (MySQL not among them) have the capability of performing some preparsing or even execution planning prior to executing a prepared statement. For a statement that is executed multiple times later, this reduces overhead because anything that can be done prior to execution need be done only once, not once per execution. For example, if a program executes a particular type of SELECT statement several times while it runs, such a database system can construct a plan for the statement and then reuse it each time, rather than rebuild the plan over and over. MySQL doesn't build query plans in advance, so you get no performance boost from using prepared statements. However, if you port a program to a database that does reuse query plans and you've written your program to use prepared statements, you can get this advantage of prepared statements automatically. You need not convert from nonprepared statements to enjoy that benefit.

A third (admittedly subjective) benefit is that code that uses placeholder-based statements can be easier to read. As you work through this section, compare the statements used here with those from Recipe 4.4 that didn't use placeholders to see which you prefer.

Using a quoting function

Some APIs provide a quoting function that takes a data value as its argument and returns a properly quoted and escaped value suitable for safe insertion into a SQL statement. This is less common than using placeholders, but it can be useful for constructing statements that you don't intend to execute immediately. However, you must have a connection open to the database server while you use such a quoting function because the API cannot select the proper quoting rules until the database driver is known. (The rules differ among database systems.)

 As we'll indicate later, some APIs quote as strings all non-NULL values, even numbers, when binding them to parameter markers. This can be an issue in contexts that *require* numbers, as described further in Recipe 5.11.

You cannot bind an array of data values to a single placeholder. Each value must be bound to a separate placeholder. To use placeholders for a list of data values that may vary in number, construct a list of placeholder characters. In Perl, the following statement creates a string consisting of *n* placeholder characters separated by commas:

```
$str = join (",", ("?") x n);
```

The x repetition operator, when applied to a list, produces *n* copies of the list, so the join() call joins these lists to produce a single string containing *n* comma-separated instances of the ? character. This is handy for binding an array of data values to a list of placeholders in a statement string because the size of the array is the number of placeholders needed:

```
$str = join (",", ("?") x @values);
```

In Ruby, use the * operator to similar effect:

```
str = (["?"] * values.size).join(",")
```

A less cryptic method is to use a loop approach, here illustrated in Python:

```
str = ""
if len(values) > 0:
    str = "?"
for i in range(1, len(values)):
    str += ",?"
```

Perl

To use placeholders with Perl DBI, put a ? in your SQL statement string at each data value location. Then bind the values to the statement by passing them to do() or execute(), or by calling a DBI method specifically intended for placeholder substitution. Use undef to bind a NULL value to a placeholder.

With do(), add the profile row for De'Mont by passing the statement string and the data values in the same call:

```
my $count = $dbh->do ("INSERT INTO profile (name,birth,color,foods,cats)
                       VALUES(?,?,?,?,?)",
                       undef,
                       "De'Mont", "1973-01-12", undef, "eggroll", 4);
```

The arguments following the statement string are undef, then one data value for each placeholder. The undef argument is a historical artifact but must be present.

Alternatively, pass the statement string to prepare() to get a statement handle, then use that handle to pass the data values to execute():

```
my $sth = $dbh->prepare ("INSERT INTO profile (name,birth,color,foods,cats)
                          VALUES(?,?,?,?,?)");
my $count = $sth->execute ("De'Mont", "1973-01-12", undef, "eggroll", 4);
```

In either case, DBI generates this statement:

```
INSERT INTO profile (name,birth,color,foods,cats)
VALUES('De\'Mont','1973-01-12',NULL,'eggroll','4');
```

The Perl DBI placeholder mechanism provides quotes around data values when they are bound to the statement string, so don't put quotes around the ? characters in the string.

Note that the placeholder mechanism adds quotes around numeric values. DBI relies on the MySQL server to perform type conversion as necessary to convert strings to numbers. If you bind undef to a placeholder, DBI puts a NULL into the statement and correctly refrains from adding enclosing quotes.

To execute the same statement over and over again, use prepare() once, then call execute() with the appropriate data values each time you run it.

You can use these methods for other types of statements as well. For example, the following SELECT statement uses a placeholder to look for rows that have a cats value larger than 2:

```
my $sth = $dbh->prepare ("SELECT * FROM profile WHERE cats > ?");
$sth->execute (2);
while (my $ref = $sth->fetchrow_hashref ())
{
  print "id: $ref->{id}, name: $ref->{name}, cats: $ref->{cats}\n";
}
```

High-level retrieval methods such as selectrow_array() and selectall_arrayref() can be used with placeholders, too. Like the do() method, the arguments are the statement string, undef, and the data values to bind to the placeholders. Here's an example:

```
my $ref = $dbh->selectall_arrayref (
  "SELECT name, birth, foods FROM profile WHERE id > ? AND color = ?",
  undef, 3, "green"
);
```

The Perl DBI quote() database-handle method is an alternative to using placeholders. Here's how to use quote() to create a statement string that inserts a new row in the profile table. Write the %s format specifiers without enclosing quotes because quote() provides them automatically as necessary. Non-undef values are inserted with quotes, and undef values are inserted as NULL without quotes:

```
my $stmt = sprintf ("INSERT INTO profile (name,birth,color,foods,cats)
                     VALUES(%s,%s,%s,%s,%s)",
                     $dbh->quote ("De'Mont"),
                     $dbh->quote ("1973-01-12"),
                     $dbh->quote (undef),
```

```
              $dbh->quote ("eggroll"),
              $dbh->quote (4));
  my $count = $dbh->do ($stmt);
```

The statement string generated by this code is the same as when you use placeholders.

Ruby

Ruby DBI uses ? as the placeholder character in SQL statements and nil as the value for binding a SQL NULL value to a placeholder.

To use the ?, pass the statement string to prepare to get a statement handle, then use that handle to invoke execute with the data values:

```
sth = client.prepare("INSERT INTO profile (name,birth,color,foods,cats)
                VALUES(?,?,?,?,?)")
sth.execute("De'Mont", "1973-01-12", nil, "eggroll", 4)
```

Mysql2 includes properly escaped quotes and a properly unquoted NULL value in the resulting statement:

```
INSERT INTO profile (name,birth,color,foods,cats)
VALUES('De\'Mont','1973-01-12',NULL,'eggroll',4);
```

The Ruby Mysql2 placeholder mechanism provides quotes around data values as necessary when they are bound to the statement string, so don't put quotes around the ? characters in the string.

PHP

To use placeholders with the PDO extension, pass a statement string to prepare() to get a statement object. The string can contain ? characters as placeholder markers. Use this object to invoke execute(), passing to it the array of data values to bind to the placeholders. Use the PHP NULL value to bind a SQL NULL value to a placeholder. The code to add the profile table row for De'Mont looks like this:

```
$sth = $dbh->prepare ("INSERT INTO profile (name,birth,color,foods,cats)
                        VALUES(?,?,?,?,?)");
$sth->execute (array ("De'Mont","1973-01-12",NULL,"eggroll",4));
```

The resulting statement includes a properly escaped quote and a properly unquoted NULL value:

```
INSERT INTO profile (name,birth,color,foods,cats)
VALUES('De\'Mont','1973-01-12',NULL,'eggroll','4');
```

The PDO placeholder mechanism provides quotes around data values when they are bound to the statement string, so don't put quotes around the ? characters in the string. (Note that even the numeric value 4 is quoted; PDO relies on MySQL to perform type conversion as necessary when the statement executes.)

Python

The Connector/Python module implements placeholders using `%s` format specifiers in the SQL statement string. (To place a literal `%` character into the statement, use `%%` in the statement string.) To use placeholders, invoke the `execute()` method with two arguments: a statement string containing format specifiers and a sequence containing the values to bind to the statement string. Use `None` to bind a `NULL` value to a placeholder. The code to add the `profile` table row for De'Mont looks like this:

```
cursor = conn.cursor()
cursor.execute('''
            INSERT INTO profile (name,birth,color,foods,cats)
            VALUES(%s,%s,%s,%s,%s)
            ''', ("De'Mont", "1973-01-12", None, "eggroll", 4))
cursor.close()
conn.commit()
```

The statement sent to the server by the preceding `execute()` call looks like this:

```
INSERT INTO profile (name,birth,color,foods,cats)
VALUES('De\'Mont','1973-01-12',NULL,'eggroll',4);
```

The Connector/Python placeholder mechanism provides quotes around data values as necessary when they are bound to the statement string, so don't put quotes around the `%s` format specifiers in the string.

If you have only a single value, *val*, to bind to a placeholder, write it as a sequence using the syntax (*val*,):

```
cursor = conn.cursor()
cursor.execute("SELECT id, name, cats FROM profile WHERE cats = %s", (2,))
for (id, name, cats) in cursor:
  print("id: %s, name: %s, cats: %s" % (id, name, cats))
cursor.close()
```

Alternatively, write the value as a list using the syntax [*val*].

Go

The Go `sql` package uses question marks (`?`) as placeholder markers. You can use placeholders with single `Exec()` or `Query()` calls, and you can also prepare the statement in advance and execute it later. The latter method is good when you need to execute the statement multiple times. The code to add the `profile` table row for De'Mont looks like this:

```
stmt := `INSERT INTO profile (name,birth,color,foods,cats)
            VALUES(?,?,?,?,?)`
_, err := db.Exec(stmt, "De'Mont", "1973-01-12", nil, "eggroll", 4)
```

The same code with the `Prepare()` call looks like this:

```
pstmt, err := db.Prepare(`INSERT INTO profile (name,birth,color,foods,cats)
                    VALUES(?,?,?,?,?)`)
if err != nil {
```

```
    log.Fatal(err)
}
defer pstmt.Close()

_, err = pstmt.Exec("De'Mont", "1973-01-12", nil, "eggroll", 4)
```

Java

JDBC provides support for placeholders if you use prepared statements. Recall that the process for executing nonprepared statements in JDBC is to create a Statement object and then pass the statement string to the executeUpdate(), executeQuery(), or execute() function. To use a prepared statement instead, create a PreparedState ment object by passing a statement string containing ? placeholder characters to your connection object's prepareStatement() method. Then bind the data values to the statement using setXXX() methods. Finally, execute the statement by calling executeUpdate(), executeQuery(), or execute() with an empty argument list.

Here is an example that uses executeUpdate() to execute an INSERT statement that adds the profile table row for De'Mont:

```
PreparedStatement s;
s = conn.prepareStatement(
            "INSERT INTO profile (name,birth,color,foods,cats)"
            + " VALUES(?,?,?,?,?)");
s.setString(1, "De'Mont");        // bind values to placeholders
s.setString(2, "1973-01-12");
s.setNull(3, java.sql.Types.CHAR);
s.setString(4, "eggroll");
s.setInt(5, 4);
s.close();   // close statement
```

The setXXX() methods that bind data values to statements take two arguments: a placeholder position (beginning with 1, not 0) and the value to bind to the place-holder. Choose each value-binding call to match the data type of the column to which the value is bound: setString() to bind a string to the name column, setInt() to bind an integer to the cats column, and so forth. (Actually, we cheated a bit by using setString() to treat the date value for birth as a string.)

One difference between JDBC and the other APIs is that you don't bind a NULL to a placeholder by specifying some special value (such as undef in Perl or nil in Ruby). Instead, invoke setNull() with a second argument that indicates the type of the column: java.sql.Types.CHAR for a string, java.sql.Types.INTEGER for an integer, and so forth.

The setXXX() calls add quotes around data values if necessary, so don't put quotes around the ? placeholder characters in the statement string.

To handle a statement that returns a result set, the process is similar, but execute the prepared statement with executeQuery() rather than executeUpdate():

```
PreparedStatement s;
s = conn.prepareStatement("SELECT * FROM profile WHERE cats > ?");
s.setInt(1, 2);  // bind 2 to first placeholder
s.executeQuery();
// ... process result set here ...
s.close();      // close statement
```

4.6 Handling Special Characters in Identifiers

Problem

You need to construct SQL statements that refer to identifiers containing special characters.

Solution

Quote each identifier so it can be inserted safely into statement strings.

Discussion

Recipe 4.5 discusses how to handle special characters in data values by using place-holders or quoting methods. Special characters can also be present in identifiers such as database, table, and column names. For example, the table name some table contains a space, which is not permitted by default:

```
mysql> CREATE TABLE some table (i INT);
ERROR 1064 (42000): You have an error in your SQL syntax near 'table (i INT)'
```

Special characters are handled differently in identifiers than in data values. To make an identifier safe for insertion into a SQL statement, quote it by enclosing it within backticks:

```
mysql> CREATE TABLE `some table` (i INT);
Query OK, 0 rows affected (0.04 sec)
```

In MySQL, backticks are always permitted for identifier quoting. The double-quote character is permitted as well, if the ANSI_QUOTES SQL mode is enabled. Thus, with ANSI_QUOTES enabled, both of these statements are equivalent:

```
CREATE TABLE `some table` (i INT);
CREATE TABLE "some table" (i INT);
```

If it's necessary to know which identifier quoting characters are permitted, execute a SELECT @@sql_mode statement to retrieve the SQL mode for your session and check whether its value includes ANSI_QUOTES.

If a quoting character appears within the identifier itself, double it when quoting the identifier. For example, quote abc`def as `abc``def`.

Be aware that although string data values in MySQL normally can be quoted using either single-quote or double-quote characters (`'abc'`, `"abc"`), that is not true when `ANSI_QUOTES` is enabled. In that case, MySQL interprets `'abc'` as a string and `"abc"` as an identifier, so you must use only single quotes for strings.

Within a program, you can use an identifier-quoting routine if your API provides one, or write one yourself if not. Perl DBI has a `quote_identifier()` method that returns a properly quoted identifier. For an API that has no such method, you can quote an identifier by enclosing it within backticks and doubling any backticks that occur within the identifier. Here's a PHP routine that does so:

```
function quote_identifier ($ident)
{
  return ('`' . str_replace('`', '``', $ident) . '`');
}
```

Portability note: if you write your own identifier-quoting routines, remember that other database management systems (DBMSs) may require different quoting conventions.

In contexts where identifiers are used as data values, handle them as such. If you select information from the `INFORMATION_SCHEMA` metadata database, it's common to indicate which rows to return by specifying database object names in the `WHERE` clause. For example, this statement retrieves the column names for the `profile` table in the `cookbook` database:

```
SELECT COLUMN_NAME FROM INFORMATION_SCHEMA.COLUMNS
WHERE TABLE_SCHEMA = 'cookbook' AND TABLE_NAME = 'profile';
```

The database and table names are used here as data values, not as identifiers. Were you to construct this statement within a program, parameterize them using placeholders, not identifier quoting. For example, in Ruby, do this:

```
sth = client.prepare("SELECT COLUMN_NAME
                      FROM INFORMATION_SCHEMA.COLUMNS
                      WHERE TABLE_SCHEMA = ? AND TABLE_NAME = ?")
names = sth.execute(db_name, tbl_name)
```

4.7 Identifying NULL Values in Result Sets

Problem

A query result includes `NULL` values, but you're not sure how to identify them.

Solution

Your API probably has some special value that represents `NULL` by convention. You just have to know what it is and how to test for it.

Discussion

Recipe 4.5 describes how to refer to NULL values when you send statements *to* the database server. In this section, we'll deal instead with the question of how to recognize and process NULL values returned *from* the database server. In general, this is a matter of knowing what special value the API maps NULL values to, or what method to call. Table 4-5 shows these values.

Table 4-5. Detected NULL values

Language	NULL-detection value or method
Perl DBI	undef value
Ruby Mysql2 gem	nil value
PHP PDO	NULL value
Python DB API	None value
Go sql interface	Go Null type implementation for the nullable data types.
Java JDBC	wasNull() method

The following sections show a very simple application of NULL value detection. The examples retrieve a result set and print all values in it, mapping NULL values onto the printable string "NULL".

To make sure that the profile table has a row that contains some NULL values, use mysql to execute the following INSERT statement, then execute the SELECT statement to verify that the resulting row has the expected values:

```
mysql> INSERT INTO profile (name) VALUES('Amabel');
mysql> SELECT * FROM profile WHERE name = 'Amabel';
+----+--------+-------+-------+-------+------+
| id | name   | birth | color | foods | cats |
+----+--------+-------+-------+-------+------+
|  9 | Amabel | NULL  | NULL  | NULL  | NULL |
+----+--------+-------+-------+-------+------+
```

The id column might contain a different number, but the other columns should appear as shown, with values of NULL.

Perl

Perl DBI represents NULL values using undef. To detect such values, use the defined() function; it's particularly important to do so if you enable warnings with the Perl -w option or by including a use warnings line in your script. Otherwise, accessing undef values causes Perl to issue Use of uninitialized value warnings.

To prevent these warnings, test column values that might be undef with defined() before using them. The following code selects a few columns from the profile table and prints "NULL" for any undefined values in each row. This makes NULL values explicit in the output without activating any warning messages:

```
my $sth = $dbh->prepare ("SELECT name, birth, foods FROM profile");
$sth->execute ();
while (my $ref = $sth->fetchrow_hashref ())
{
  printf "name: %s, birth: %s, foods: %s\n",
          defined ($ref->{name}) ? $ref->{name} : "NULL",
          defined ($ref->{birth}) ? $ref->{birth} : "NULL",
          defined ($ref->{foods}) ? $ref->{foods} : "NULL";
}
```

Unfortunately, testing multiple column values is ponderous and becomes worse the more columns there are. To avoid this, test and set undefined values using a loop or map prior to printing them. The following example uses map:

```
my $sth = $dbh->prepare ("SELECT name, birth, foods FROM profile");
$sth->execute ();
while (my $ref = $sth->fetchrow_hashref ())
{
  map { $ref->{$_} = "NULL" unless defined ($ref->{$_}); } keys (%{$ref});
  printf "name: %s, birth: %s, foods: %s\n",
          $ref->{name}, $ref->{birth}, $ref->{foods};
}
```

With this technique, the amount of code to perform the tests is constant, not proportional to the number of columns to be tested. Also, there is no reference to specific column names, so it can more easily be used in other programs or as the basis for a utility routine.

If you fetch rows into an array rather than into a hash, use map like this to convert undef values:

```
my $sth = $dbh->prepare ("SELECT name, birth, foods FROM profile");
$sth->execute ();
while (my @val = $sth->fetchrow_array ())
{
  @val = map { defined ($_) ? $_ : "NULL" } @val;
  printf "name: %s, birth: %s, foods: %s\n",
          $val[0], $val[1], $val[2];
}
```

Ruby

The Ruby Mysql2 module represents NULL values using nil, which can be identified by applying the nil? method to a value. The following example uses the nil? method and ternary operator to determine whether to print result set values as is or as the string "NULL" for NULL values:

```
result = client.query("SELECT name, birth, foods FROM profile")
result.each do |row|
  printf "name %s, birth: %s, foods: %s\n",
          row["name"].nil? ? "NULL" : row["name"],
          row["birth"].nil? ? "NULL" : row["birth"],
```

```
      row["foods"].nil? ? "NULL" : row["foods"]
end
```

PHP

PHP represents SQL NULL values in result sets as the PHP NULL value. To determine whether a value from a result set represents a NULL value, compare it to the PHP NULL value using the === "triple equal" operator:

```
if ($val === NULL)
{
  # $val is a NULL value
}
```

In PHP, the triple equal operator means "exactly equal to." The usual ==, "equal to," comparison operator is not suitable here: with ==, PHP considers the NULL value, the empty string, and 0 all equal.

The following code uses the === operator to identify NULL values in a result set and print them as the string "NULL":

```
$sth = $dbh->query ("SELECT name, birth, foods FROM profile");
while ($row = $sth->fetch (PDO::FETCH_NUM))
{
  foreach (array_keys ($row) as $key)
  {
    if ($row[$key] === NULL)
      $row[$key] = "NULL";
  }
  print ("name: $row[0], birth: $row[1], foods: $row[2]\n");
}
```

An alternative to === for NULL value tests is is_null().

Python

Python DB API programs represent NULL in result sets using None. The following example shows how to detect NULL values:

```
cursor = conn.cursor()
cursor.execute("SELECT name, birth, foods FROM profile")

for row in cursor:
  row = list(row)  # convert nonmutable tuple to mutable list

  for i, value in enumerate(row):
    if value is None:  # is the column value NULL?
      row[i] = "NULL"

  print("name: %s, birth: %s, foods: %s" % (row[0], row[1], row[2]))

cursor.close()
```

The inner loop checks for NULL column values by looking for None and converts them to the string "NULL". The example converts row to a mutable object (list) prior to the loop because `fetchall()` returns rows as sequence values, which are immutable (read only).

Go

The Go `sql` interface provides special data types to handle values in the result set that may contain NULL values. They are defined for the standard Go types. Table 4-6 contains the list of the standard data types and their nullable equivalents.

Table 4-6. Handling NULL values in Go

Standard Go type	Type that can contain NULL values
bool	NullBool
float64	NullFloat64
int32	NullInt32
int64	NullInt64
string	NullString
time.Time	NullTime

To define a variable that can take both NULL and non-NULL values when passed as an argument to the function `Scan()`, use the corresponding nullable type.

All nullable types contain two functions: `Valid()` that returns `true` if the value is not NULL and `false` if the value is NULL. The second function is the type name, started from the capital letter, for example, `String()` for `string` values and `Time()` for `time.Time` values. This method returns the actual value when it is not NULL.

The following example shows you how to handle NULL values in Go:

```go
// null-in-result.go : Selecting NULL values in Go
package main

import (
        "database/sql"
        "fmt"
        "log"

        _ "github.com/go-sql-driver/mysql"
)

type Profile struct {
    name     string
    birth    sql.NullString
    foods    sql.NullString
}

func main() {

        db, err := sql.Open("mysql", "cbuser:cbpass@tcp(127.0.0.1:3306)/cookbook")

        if err != nil {
```

```
                log.Fatal(err)
        }
        defer db.Close()

        sql := "SELECT name, birth, foods FROM profile"
        res, err := db.Query(sql)

        if err != nil {
                log.Fatal(err)
        }
        defer res.Close()

        for res.Next() {
                var profile Profile
                err = res.Scan(&profile.name, &profile.birth, &profile.foods)
                if err != nil {
                        log.Fatal(err)
                }

        if (profile.birth.Valid && profile.foods.Valid) {
          fmt.Printf("name: %s, birth: %s, foods: %s\n",
                    profile.name, profile.birth.String, profile.foods.String)
        } else if profile.birth.Valid {
          fmt.Printf("name: %s, birth: %s, foods: NULL\n",
                    profile.name, profile.birth.String)
        } else if profile.foods.Valid {
          fmt.Printf("name: %s, birth: NULL, foods: %s\n",
                    profile.name, profile.foods.String)
        } else {
          fmt.Printf("name: %s, birth: NULL, foods: NULL\n",
                    profile.name)
        }
        }
}
```

We used the `NullString` type for the `birth` column for simplicity. If you want to use the `NullTime` type, you need to add the `parse Time=true` parameter to your connection string.

Alternatively, you can use MySQL's `COALESCE()` function to convert the NULL value to a string during the query execution:

```
sql := `SELECT name,
                COALESCE(birth, '') as birthday
          FROM profile WHERE id = 9`
res, err := db.Query(sql)
defer res.Close()
```

Java

For JDBC programs, if it's possible for a column in a result set to contain NULL values, it's best to check for them explicitly. The way to do this is to fetch the value and then

---

invoke `wasNull()`, which returns true if the column is NULL and false otherwise, for example:

```
Object obj = rs.getObject (index);
if (rs.wasNull ())
{ /* the value's a NULL */ }
```

The preceding example uses `getObject()`, but the principle holds for other get*XXX*() calls as well.

Here's an example that prints each row of a result set as a comma-separated list of values, with "NULL" printed for each NULL value:

```
Statement s = conn.createStatement();
s.executeQuery("SELECT name, birth, foods FROM profile");
ResultSet rs = s.getResultSet();
ResultSetMetaData md = rs.getMetaData();
int ncols = md.getColumnCount();
while (rs.next ()) { // loop through rows of result set
  for (int i = 0; i < ncols; i++) { // loop through columns
    String val = rs.getString(i+1);
    if (i > 0)
      System.out.print(", ");
    if (rs.wasNull())
      System.out.print("NULL");
    else
      System.out.print(val);
  }
  System.out.println();
}
rs.close();  // close result set
s.close();   // close statement
```

4.8 Obtaining Connection Parameters

Problem

You need to obtain connection parameters for a script so that it can connect to a MySQL server.

Solution

There are several ways to do this. Take your pick from the alternatives described here.

Discussion

Any program that connects to MySQL specifies connection parameters such as the username, password, and hostname. The recipes shown so far have put connection parameters directly into the code that attempts to establish the connection, but that is not the only way for your programs to obtain the parameters. This discussion briefly surveys some of the available techniques:

Hardwire the parameters into the program

The parameters can be given either in the main source file or in a library file used by the program. This technique is convenient because users need not enter the values themselves, but it's also inflexible. To change parameters, you must modify your program. It is also insecure, because everyone who accesses the library would be able to read your database credentials.

Ask for the parameters interactively

In a command-line environment, you can ask the user a series of questions. In a web or GUI environment, you might do this by presenting a form or dialog. Either way, this becomes tedious for people who use the application frequently, due to the need to enter the parameters each time.

Get the parameters from the command line

You can use this method either for commands run interactively or from within a script. Like the method of obtaining parameters interactively, you must supply parameters for each command invocation. (A factor that mitigates this burden is that many shells enable you to easily recall commands from your history list for re-execution.) This method could be insecure if you provide your credentials this way.

Get the parameters from the execution environment

The most common way to do this is to set the appropriate environment variables in one of your shell's startup files (such as *.profile* for sh, bash, or ksh; or *.login* for csh or tcsh). Programs that you run during your login session then can get parameter values by examining their environment.

Get the parameters from a separate file

With this method, store information such as the username and password in a file that programs can read before connecting to the MySQL server. Reading parameters from a file that's separate from your program gives you the benefit of not having to enter them each time you use the program, without hardwiring the values into it. Also, storing the values in a file enables you to centralize parameters for use by multiple programs, and for security purposes, you can set the file access mode to keep other users from reading the file.

The MySQL client library itself supports an option file mechanism, although not all APIs provide access to it. For those that don't, workarounds may exist. (As an example, Java supports the use of properties files and supplies utility routines for reading them.)

Use a combination of methods

It's often useful to combine methods, to give users the flexibility of providing parameters different ways. For example, MySQL clients such as mysql and mysqladmin look for option files in several locations and read any that are present.

They then check the command-line arguments for further parameters. This enables users to specify connection parameters in an option file or on the command line.

These methods of obtaining connection parameters do involve security issues:

- Any method that stores connection parameters in a file may compromise your system's security unless the file is protected against access by unauthorized users. This is true whether parameters are stored in a source file, an option file, or a script that invokes a command and specifies the parameters on the command line. (Web scripts that can be read only by the web server don't qualify as secure if other users have administrative access to the server.)

- Parameters specified on the command line or in environment variables are not particularly secure. While a program is executing, its command-line arguments and environment may be visible to other users who run process status commands such as `ps -e`. In particular, storing the password in an environment variable perhaps is best limited to those situations in which you're the only user on the machine or you trust all other users.

The rest of this section discusses how to process command-line arguments to get connection parameters and how to read parameters from option files.

Getting parameters from the command line

The convention used by standard clients such as `mysql` and `mysqladmin` for command-line arguments is to permit parameters to be specified using either a short option or a long option. For example, the username `cbuser` can be specified either as `-u cbuser` (or `-ucbuser`) or `--user=cbuser`. In addition, for either of the password options (`-p` or `--password`), the password value may be omitted after the option name to cause the program to prompt for the password interactively.

The standard flags for these command options are `-h` or `--host`, `-u` or `--user`, and `-p` or `--password`. You could write your own code to iterate through the argument list, but it's much easier to use existing option-processing modules written for that purpose. Under the *api* directory of the `recipes` distribution, you'll find example programs that show how to process command arguments to obtain the hostname, username, and password for Perl, Ruby, Python, and Java. An accompanying PDF file explains how each one works.

Insofar as possible, the programs mimic option-handling behavior of the standard MySQL clients. An exception is that option-processing libraries may not permit making the password value optional, and they provide no way of prompting the user for a password interactively if a password option is specified without a password value. Consequently, the programs are written so that if you use -p or --password, you must provide the password value following the option.

Getting parameters from option files

If your API supports it, you can specify connection parameters in a MySQL option file and let the API read the parameters from the file for you. For APIs that do not support option files directly, you may be able to arrange to read other types of files in which parameters are stored or to write your own functions that read option files.

Recipe 1.4 describes the format of MySQL option files. We assume that you've read the discussion there and concentrate here on how to use option files from within programs. You can find files containing the code discussed here under the *api* directory of the `recipes` distribution.

Under Unix, user-specific options are specified by convention in *~/.my.cnf* (that is, in the *.my.cnf* file in your home directory). However, the MySQL option-file mechanism can look in several different files if they exist, although no option file is *required* to exist. (For the list of standard locations in which MySQL programs look for them, see Recipe 1.4.) If multiple option files exist and a given parameter is specified in several of them, the last value found takes precedence.

Programs you write do not use MySQL option files unless you tell them to:

- Perl DBI and Ruby Mysql2 gem provide direct API support for reading option files; simply indicate that you want to use them at the time that you connect to the server. It's possible to specify that only a particular file should be read, or that the standard search order should be used to look for multiple option files.

- PHP PDO, Connector/Python, Java, and Go do not support option files. (The PDO MySQL driver does but not if you use `mysqlnd` as the underlying library.) As a workaround for PHP, we'll write a simple option-file parsing function. For Java, we'll adopt a different approach that uses properties files. For Go, we will utilize the `INI` parsing library.

Although the conventional name under Unix for the user-specific option file is *.my.cnf* in the current user's home directory, there's no rule that your own programs must use this particular file. You can name an option file anything you like and put it wherever you want. For example, you might set up a file named *mcb.cnf* and install it in the */usr/local/lib/mcb* directory for use by scripts that access the `cookbook` database.

Under some circumstances, you might even want to create multiple option files. Then, from within any given script, select the file that's appropriate for the access privileges the script needs. For example, you might have one option file, *mcb.cnf*, that lists parameters for a full-access MySQL account, and another file, *mcb-readonly.cnf*, that lists connection parameters for an account that needs only read-only access to MySQL. Another possibility is to list multiple groups within the same option file and have your scripts select options from the appropriate group.

Perl. Perl DBI scripts can use option files. To take advantage of this, place the appropriate option specifiers in the third component of the Data Source Name (DSN) string:

- To specify an option group, use `mysql_read_default_group=`*groupname*. This tells MySQL to search the standard option files for options in the named group and in the [`client`] group. Write the *groupname* value without the surrounding square brackets. (If a group in an option file begins with a [`my_prog`] line, specify the *groupname* value as `my_prog`.) To search the standard files but look only in the [`client`] group, *groupname* should be `client`.

- To name a specific option file, use `mysql_read_default_file=`*filename* in the DSN. When you do this, MySQL looks only in that file and only for options in the [`client`] group.

- If you specify both an option file and an option group, MySQL reads only the named file but looks for options both in the named group and in the [`client`] group.

The following example tells MySQL to use the standard option-file search order to look for options in both the [`cookbook`] and [`client`] groups:

```
my $conn_attrs = {PrintError => 0, RaiseError => 1, AutoCommit => 1};
# basic DSN
my $dsn = "DBI:mysql:database=cookbook";
# look in standard option files; use [cookbook] and [client] groups
$dsn .= ";mysql_read_default_group=cookbook";
my $dbh = DBI->connect ($dsn, undef, undef, $conn_attrs);
```

The next example explicitly names the option file located in $ENV{HOME}, the home directory of the user running the script. Thus, MySQL looks only in that file and uses options from the [`client`] group:

```
my $conn_attrs = {PrintError => 0, RaiseError => 1, AutoCommit => 1};
# basic DSN
my $dsn = "DBI:mysql:database=cookbook";
# look in user-specific option file owned by the current user
$dsn .= ";mysql_read_default_file=$ENV{HOME}/.my.cnf";
my $dbh = DBI->connect ($dsn, undef, undef, $conn_attrs);
```

If you pass an empty value (undef or the empty string) for the username or password arguments of the connect() call, connect() uses whatever values are found in the option file or files. A nonempty username or password in the connect() call overrides any option-file value. Similarly, a host named in the DSN overrides any option-file value. Use this behavior to enable DBI scripts to obtain connection parameters both from option files as well as from the command line as follows:

1. Create $host_name, $user_name, and $password variables, each with a value of undef. Then parse the command-line arguments to set the variables to non-undef values if the corresponding options are present on the command line. (The cmdline.pl Perl script under the *api* directory of the recipes distribution demonstrates how to do this.)

2. After parsing the command arguments, construct the DSN string, and call connect(). Use mysql_read_default_group and mysql_read_default_file in the DSN to specify how you want option files to be used, and, if $host_name is not undef, add host=$host_name to the DSN. In addition, pass $user_name and $password as the username and password arguments to connect(). These will be undef by default; if they were set from the command-line arguments, they will have non-undef values that override any option-file values.

If a script follows this procedure, parameters given by the user on the command line are passed to connect() and take precedence over the contents of option files.

Ruby. Ruby Mysql2 scripts can read option files, specified by the default_file connection parameter. If you want to specify the default group, use the default_group option.

This example uses the standard option-file search order to look for options in both the [cookbook] and [client] groups:

```
client = Mysql2::Client.new(:default_group => "cookbook", :database => "cookbook")
```

The following example uses the *.my.cnf* file in the current user's home directory to obtain parameters from the [client] group:

```
client = Mysql2::Client.new(:default_file => "#{ENV['HOME']}/.my.cnf",↵
:database => "cookbook")
```

PHP. As mentioned earlier, the PDO MySQL driver does not necessarily support using MySQL option files (it does not if you use mysqlnd as the underlying library). To work around that limitation, use a function that reads an option file, such as the read_mysql_option_file() function shown in the following listing. It takes as arguments the name of an option file and an option group name or an array containing group names. (Group names should be written without square brackets.) It then reads any options present in the file for the named group or groups. If no option group argument is given, the function looks by default in the [client] group. The return value is an array of option name/value pairs, or FALSE if an error occurs. It is not an error for the file not to exist. (Note that quoted option values and trailing #-style comments following option values are legal in MySQL option files, but this function does not handle those constructs.):

```php
function read_mysql_option_file ($filename, $group_list = "client")
{
  if (is_string ($group_list))              # convert string to array
    $group_list = array ($group_list);
  if (!is_array ($group_list))              # hmm ... garbage argument?
    return (FALSE);
  $opt = array ();                          # option name/value array
  if (!@($fp = fopen ($filename, "r")))     # if file does not exist,
    return ($opt);                          # return an empty list
  $in_named_group = 0;  # set nonzero while processing a named group
  while ($s = fgets ($fp, 1024))
  {
    $s = trim ($s);
    if (preg_match ("/^[#;]/", $s))               # skip comments
      continue;
    if (preg_match ("/^\[([^]]+)]/", $s, $arg))   # option group line
    {
      # check whether we are in one of the desired groups
      $in_named_group = 0;
      foreach ($group_list as $group_name)
      {
        if ($arg[1] == $group_name)
        {
          $in_named_group = 1;       # we are in a desired group
          break;
        }
      }
      continue;
    }
    if (!$in_named_group)     # we are not in a desired
      continue;              # group, skip the line
    if (preg_match ("/^([^ \t=]+)[ \t]*=[ \t]*(.*)/", $s, $arg))
      $opt[$arg[1]] = $arg[2];     # name=value
    else if (preg_match ("/^([^ \t]+)/", $s, $arg))
      $opt[$arg[1]] = "";          # name only
    # else line is malformed
  }
  return ($opt);
}
```

Here are two examples showing how to use read_mysql_option_file(). The first reads a user's option file to get the [client] group parameters and uses them to connect to the server. The second reads the system-wide option file, */etc/my.cnf*, and prints the server startup parameters that are found there (that is, the parameters in the [mysqld] and [server] groups):

```php
$opt = read_mysql_option_file ("/home/paul/.my.cnf");
$dsn = "mysql:dbname=cookbook";
if (isset ($opt["host"]))
  $dsn .= ";host=" . $opt["host"];
```

```
$user = $opt["user"];
$password = $opt["password"];
try
{
  $dbh = new PDO ($dsn, $user, $password);
  print ("Connected\n");
  $dbh = NULL;
  print ("Disconnected\n");
}
catch (PDOException $e)
{
  print ("Cannot connect to server\n");
}

$opt = read_mysql_option_file ("/etc/my.cnf", array ("mysqld", "server"));
foreach ($opt as $name => $value)
  print ("$name => $value\n");
```

PHP does have a `parse_ini_file()` function that is intended for parsing *.ini* files. These have a syntax that is similar to MySQL option files, so you might find this function of use. However, there are some differences to watch out for. Suppose that you have a file written like this:

```
[client]
user=paul

[client]
host=127.0.0.1

[mysql]
no-auto-rehash
```

Standard MySQL option parsing considers both the `user` and `host` values part of the `[client]` group, whereas `parse_ini_file()` returns only the contents of the final `[client]` stanza; the `user` option is lost. Also, `parse_ini_file()` ignores options that are given without a value, so the `no-auto-rehash` option is lost.

Go. The Go-MySQL-Driver doesn't support option files. However, the INI parsing library supports reading properties files that contain lines in the *name=value* format. Here is a sample properties file:

```
# this file lists parameters for connecting to the MySQL server
[client]
user=cbuser
password=cbpass
host=localhost
```

The `MyCnf()` function shows one way to read a properties file named *~/.my.cnf* to obtain connection parameters:

```
import (
        "fmt"
        "os"
        "gopkg.in/ini.v1"
)
```

```
// Configuration Parser
func MyCnf(client string) (string, error) {
    cfg, err := ini.LoadSources(ini.LoadOptions{AllowBooleanKeys: true}, ↵
                               os.Getenv("HOME")+"/.my.cnf")
    if err != nil {
        return "", err
    }
    for _, s := range cfg.Sections() {
        if client != "" && s.Name() != client {
            continue
        }
        host := s.Key("host").String()
        port := s.Key("port").String()
        dbname := s.Key("dbname").String()
        user := s.Key("user").String()
        password := s.Key("password").String()
        return fmt.Sprintf("%s:%s@tcp(%s:%s)/%s", user, password, host, port, dbname),↵
            nil
    }
    return "", fmt.Errorf("No matching entry found in ~/.my.cnf")
}
```

The function `MyCnf()` defined in the *cookbook.go*, developed elsewhere in the chapter (see Recipe 4.3). It is used in the file *mycnf.go*, which you will find in the directory *api/06_conn_params* in the `recipes` distribution:

```
// mycnf.go : Reads ~/.my.cnf file for DSN construct
package main

import (
        "fmt"
        "github.com/svetasmirnova/mysqlcookbook/recipes/lib"
)

func main() {
    fmt.Println("Calling db.MyCnf()")
    var dsn string

    dsn, err := cookbook.MyCnf("client")
    if err != nil {
        fmt.Printf("error: %v\n", err)
    } else {
        fmt.Printf("DSN is: %s\n", dsn)
    }
}
```

The `MyCnf()` function accepts the section name as a parameter. If you want to replace the [`client`] section with any other name, change `MyCnf()` to `MyCnf("other")`, where `other` is the name of the section.

Java. The JDBC MySQL Connector/J driver doesn't support option files. However, the Java class library supports reading properties files that contain lines in the *name=value* format. This is similar but not identical to the MySQL option-file format (for example, properties files do not permit [*groupname*] lines). Here is a simple properties file:

```
# this file lists parameters for connecting to the MySQL server
user=cbuser
password=cbpass
host=localhost
```

The following program, *ReadPropsFile.java*, shows one way to read a properties file named *Cookbook.properties* to obtain connection parameters. The file must be in some directory named in your CLASSPATH variable, or you must specify it using a full pathname (the example shown here assumes that the file is in a CLASSPATH directory):

```
import java.sql.*;
import java.util.*;   // need this for properties file support

public class ReadPropsFile {
  public static void main(String[] args) {
    Connection conn = null;
    String url = null;
    String propsFile = "Cookbook.properties";
    Properties props = new Properties();

    try {
      props.load(ReadPropsFile.class.getResourceAsStream(propsFile));
    } catch (Exception e) {
      System.err.println("Cannot read properties file");
      System.exit (1);
    }
    try {
      // construct connection URL, encoding username
      // and password as parameters at the end
      url = "jdbc:mysql://"
            + props.getProperty("host")
            + "/cookbook"
            + "?user=" + props.getProperty("user")
            + "&password=" + props.getProperty("password");
      conn = DriverManager.getConnection(url);
      System.out.println("Connected");
    } catch (Exception e) {
      System.err.println("Cannot connect to server");
    } finally {
      try {
        if (conn != null) {
          conn.close();
          System.out.println("Disconnected");
        }
      } catch (SQLException e) { /* ignore close errors */ }
    }
  }
}
```

To have getProperty() return a particular default value when the named property is not found, pass that value as a second argument. For example, to use 127.0.0.1 as the default host value, call getProperty() like this:

```
String hostName = props.getProperty("host", "127.0.0.1");
```

The *Cookbook.java* library file developed elsewhere in the chapter (see Recipe 4.3) includes an extra library call in the version of the file that you'll find in the *lib* directory of the `recipes` distribution: a `propsConnect()` routine that is based on the concepts discussed here. To use it, set up the contents of the properties file, *Cookbook.properties*, and copy the file to the same location where you installed *Cookbook.class*. You can then establish a connection within a program by importing the `Cookbook` class and calling `Cookbook.propsConnect()` rather than by calling `Cookbook.connect()`.

4.9 Resetting the profile Table

Problem

While working on the examples in this chapter, you changed the original content of the `profile` table and now want it back, so you can use it while working with other recipes.

Solution

Reload the table using the `mysql` client.

Discussion

It's a good idea to reset the `profile` table used in this chapter to a known state. Change location into the *tables* directory of the `recipes` distribution, and run these commands:

```
$ mysql cookbook < profile.sql
$ mysql cookbook < profile2.sql
```

Several statements in later chapters use the `profile` table; by reinitializing it, you'll get the same results displayed in those chapters when you run the statements shown there.

This chapter discussed the basic operations provided by each of our APIs for handling various aspects of interaction with the MySQL server. These operations enable you to write programs that execute any kind of statement and retrieve the results. Up to this point, we've used simple statements because the focus is on the APIs rather than on SQL. The next chapter focuses on SQL instead, to show how to ask the database server more complex questions.

## CHAPTER 5

Selecting Data from Tables

5.0 Introduction

This chapter focuses on using the SELECT statement to retrieve information from your database. You will find the chapter helpful if your SQL background is limited or if you find out about the MySQL-specific extensions to SELECT syntax.

There are many ways to write SELECT statements; we'll look at only a few. Consult the MySQL User Reference Manual (*https://oreil.ly/cgYiU*) or a general MySQL text for more information about SELECT syntax and the functions and operators available to extract and manipulate data.

Many examples in this chapter use a table named mail that contains rows that track mail message traffic between users on a set of hosts. The following shows how that table was created:

```
CREATE TABLE mail
(
  id     INT NOT NULL AUTO_INCREMENT PRIMARY KEY,
  t      DATETIME,     # when message was sent
  srcuser VARCHAR(8),  # sender (source user and host)
  srchost VARCHAR(20),
  dstuser VARCHAR(8),  # recipient (destination user and host)
  dsthost VARCHAR(20),
  size   BIGINT,       # message size in bytes
  INDEX (t)
);
```

The mail table contents look like this:

```
mysql> SELECT t, srcuser, srchost, dstuser, dsthost, size FROM mail;
+---------------------+---------+---------+---------+---------+--------+
| t                   | srcuser | srchost | dstuser | dsthost | size   |
+---------------------+---------+---------+---------+---------+--------+
| 2014-05-11 10:15:08 | barb    | saturn  | tricia  | mars    |  58274 |
| 2014-05-12 12:48:13 | tricia  | mars    | gene    | venus   | 194925 |
```

```
| 2014-05-12 15:02:49 | phil   | mars   | phil   | saturn |    1048 |
| 2014-05-12 18:59:18 | barb   | saturn | tricia | venus  |     271 |
| 2014-05-14 09:31:37 | gene   | venus  | barb   | mars   |    2291 |
| 2014-05-14 11:52:17 | phil   | mars   | tricia | saturn |    5781 |
| 2014-05-14 14:42:21 | barb   | venus  | barb   | venus  |   98151 |
| 2014-05-14 17:03:01 | tricia | saturn | phil   | venus  | 2394482 |
| 2014-05-15 07:17:48 | gene   | mars   | gene   | saturn |    3824 |
| 2014-05-15 08:50:57 | phil   | venus  | phil   | venus  |     978 |
| 2014-05-15 10:25:52 | gene   | mars   | tricia | saturn |  998532 |
| 2014-05-15 17:35:31 | gene   | saturn | gene   | mars   |    3856 |
| 2014-05-16 09:00:28 | gene   | venus  | barb   | mars   |     613 |
| 2014-05-16 23:04:19 | phil   | venus  | barb   | venus  |   10294 |
| 2014-05-19 12:49:23 | phil   | mars   | tricia | saturn |     873 |
| 2014-05-19 22:21:51 | gene   | saturn | gene   | venus  |   23992 |
+---------------------+--------+--------+--------+--------+---------+
```

To create and load the `mail` table, change location into the *tables* directory of the recipes distribution and run this command:

```
$ mysql cookbook < mail.sql
```

This chapter also uses other tables from time to time. Some were used in previous chapters, whereas others are new. To create any of them, do so the same way as for the `mail` table, using the appropriate script in the *tables* directory. In addition, many of the other scripts and programs used in this chapter are located in the *select* directory. The files in that directory enable you to try the examples more easily.

Many of the statements shown here can be executed from within the `mysql` program, which is discussed in Chapter 1. A few examples involve issuing statements from within the context of a programming language. See Chapter 4 for information on programming techniques.

5.1 Specifying Which Columns and Rows to Select

Problem

You want to display specific columns and rows from a table.

Solution

To indicate which columns to display, name them in the output column list. To indicate which rows to display, use a `WHERE` clause that specifies conditions that rows must satisfy.

Discussion

The simplest way to display columns from a table is to use `SELECT * FROM` *tbl_name*. The * specifier is a shortcut that means "all columns":

```
mysql> SELECT t, srcuser, srchost, dstuser, dsthost, size FROM mail;
+---------------------+---------+---------+---------+---------+--------+
| t                   | srcuser | srchost | dstuser | dsthost | size   |
+---------------------+---------+---------+---------+---------+--------+
| 2014-05-11 10:15:08 | barb    | saturn  | tricia  | mars    |  58274 |
| 2014-05-12 12:48:13 | tricia  | mars    | gene    | venus   | 194925 |
| 2014-05-12 15:02:49 | phil    | mars    | phil    | saturn  |   1048 |
| 2014-05-12 18:59:18 | barb    | saturn  | tricia  | venus   |    271 |
...
```

Using * is easy, but you cannot select only certain columns or control the column display order. Naming columns explicitly enables you to select only the ones of interest, in any order. This query omits the recipient columns and displays the sender before the date and size:

```
mysql> SELECT srcuser, srchost, t, size FROM mail;
+---------+---------+---------------------+--------+
| srcuser | srchost | t                   | size   |
+---------+---------+---------------------+--------+
| barb    | saturn  | 2014-05-11 10:15:08 |  58274 |
| tricia  | mars    | 2014-05-12 12:48:13 | 194925 |
| phil    | mars    | 2014-05-12 15:02:49 |   1048 |
| barb    | saturn  | 2014-05-12 18:59:18 |    271 |
...
```

Unless you qualify or restrict a SELECT query in some way, it retrieves every row in your table. To be more precise, provide a WHERE clause that specifies one or more conditions that rows must satisfy.

Conditions can test for equality, inequality, or relative ordering. For some types of data, such as strings, you can use pattern matches. The following statements select columns from rows in the mail table containing srchost values that are exactly equal to the 'venus' string or that begin with the letter 's':

```
mysql> SELECT t, srcuser, srchost  FROM mail WHERE srchost = 'venus';
+---------------------+---------+---------+
| t                   | srcuser | srchost |
+---------------------+---------+---------+
| 2014-05-14 09:31:37 | gene    | venus   |
| 2014-05-14 14:42:21 | barb    | venus   |
| 2014-05-15 08:50:57 | phil    | venus   |
| 2014-05-16 09:00:28 | gene    | venus   |
| 2014-05-16 23:04:19 | phil    | venus   |
+---------------------+---------+---------+
mysql> SELECT t, srcuser, srchost FROM mail WHERE srchost LIKE 's%';
+---------------------+---------+---------+
| t                   | srcuser | srchost |
+---------------------+---------+---------+
| 2014-05-11 10:15:08 | barb    | saturn  |
| 2014-05-12 18:59:18 | barb    | saturn  |
| 2014-05-14 17:03:01 | tricia  | saturn  |
| 2014-05-15 17:35:31 | gene    | saturn  |
| 2014-05-19 22:21:51 | gene    | saturn  |
+---------------------+---------+---------+
```

The LIKE operator in the previous query performs a pattern match, where % acts as a wildcard that matches any string. Recipe 7.10 discusses pattern matching further.

A WHERE clause can test multiple conditions, and different conditions can test different columns. The following statement finds messages sent by barb to tricia:

```
mysql> SELECT t, srcuser, srchost, dstuser, dsthost, size FROM mail
    -> WHERE srcuser = 'barb' AND dstuser = 'tricia';
+---------------------+---------+---------+---------+---------+-------+
| t                   | srcuser | srchost | dstuser | dsthost | size  |
+---------------------+---------+---------+---------+---------+-------+
| 2014-05-11 10:15:08 | barb    | saturn  | tricia  | mars    | 58274 |
| 2014-05-12 18:59:18 | barb    | saturn  | tricia  | venus   |   271 |
+---------------------+---------+---------+---------+---------+-------+
```

Output columns can be calculated by evaluating expressions. This query combines the srcuser and srchost columns using CONCAT() to produce composite values in email address format:

```
mysql> SELECT t, CONCAT(srcuser,'@',srchost), size FROM mail;
+---------------------+-----------------------------+--------+
| t                   | CONCAT(srcuser,'@',srchost) | size   |
+---------------------+-----------------------------+--------+
| 2014-05-11 10:15:08 | barb@saturn                 |  58274 |
| 2014-05-12 12:48:13 | tricia@mars                 | 194925 |
| 2014-05-12 15:02:49 | phil@mars                   |   1048 |
| 2014-05-12 18:59:18 | barb@saturn                 |    271 |
...
```

You'll notice that the email address column label is the expression that calculates it. To provide a better label, use a column alias (see Recipe 5.2).

As of MySQL 8.0.19, you can use the TABLE statement to select all columns from the table. TABLE supports ORDER BY (see Recipe 5.3) and LIMIT (see Recipe 5.11) clauses but does not allow any other filtering of columns or rows:

```
mysql> TABLE mail ORDER BY size DESC LIMIT 3;
+----+---------------------+---------+---------+---------+---------+---------+
| id | t                   | srcuser | srchost | dstuser | dsthost | size    |
+----+---------------------+---------+---------+---------+---------+---------+
|  8 | 2014-05-14 17:03:01 | tricia  | saturn  | phil    | venus   | 2394482 |
| 11 | 2014-05-15 10:25:52 | gene    | mars    | tricia  | saturn  |  998532 |
|  2 | 2014-05-12 12:48:13 | tricia  | mars    | gene    | venus   |  194925 |
+----+---------------------+---------+---------+---------+---------+---------+
3 rows in set (0.00 sec)
```

5.2 Naming Query Result Columns

Problem

The column names in a query result are unsuitable, ugly, or difficult to work with, so you want to name them yourself.

Solution

Use aliases to choose your own column names.

Discussion

When you retrieve a result set, MySQL gives every output column a name. (That's how the mysql program gets the names you see displayed in the initial row of column headers in the result set output.) By default, MySQL assigns the column names specified in the CREATE TABLE or ALTER TABLE statement to output columns, but if these defaults are not suitable, you can use column aliases to specify your own names.

This recipe explains aliases and shows how to use them to assign column names in statements. If you're writing a program that must determine the names, see Recipe 12.2 for information about accessing column metadata.

If an output column comes directly from a table, MySQL uses the table column name for the output column name. The following statement selects four table columns, the names of which become the corresponding output column names:

```
mysql> SELECT t, srcuser, srchost, size FROM mail;
+---------------------+---------+---------+--------+
| t                   | srcuser | srchost | size   |
+---------------------+---------+---------+--------+
| 2014-05-11 10:15:08 | barb    | saturn  |  58274 |
| 2014-05-12 12:48:13 | tricia  | mars    | 194925 |
| 2014-05-12 15:02:49 | phil    | mars    |   1048 |
| 2014-05-12 18:59:18 | barb    | saturn  |    271 |
...
```

If you generate a column by evaluating an expression, the expression itself is the column name. This can produce long and unwieldy names in result sets, as illustrated by the following statement that uses one expression to reformat the dates in the t column and another to combine srcuser and srchost into email address format:

```
mysql> SELECT
    -> DATE_FORMAT(t,'%M %e, %Y'), CONCAT(srcuser,'@',srchost), size
    -> FROM mail;
+----------------------------+-----------------------------+--------+
| DATE_FORMAT(t,'%M %e, %Y') | CONCAT(srcuser,'@',srchost) | size   |
+----------------------------+-----------------------------+--------+
| May 11, 2014               | barb@saturn                 |  58274 |
| May 12, 2014               | tricia@mars                 | 194925 |
| May 12, 2014               | phil@mars                   |   1048 |
| May 12, 2014               | barb@saturn                 |    271 |
...
```

To choose your own output column name, use an AS *name* clause to specify a column alias (the keyword AS is optional). The following statement retrieves the same result as the previous one but renames the first column to date_sent and the second to sender:

```
mysql> SELECT
    -> DATE_FORMAT(t,'%M %e, %Y') AS date_sent,
    -> CONCAT(srcuser,'@',srchost) AS sender,
    -> size FROM mail;
+--------------+--------------+--------+
| date_sent    | sender       | size   |
+--------------+--------------+--------+
| May 11, 2014 | barb@saturn  |  58274 |
| May 12, 2014 | tricia@mars  | 194925 |
| May 12, 2014 | phil@mars    |   1048 |
| May 12, 2014 | barb@saturn  |    271 |
...
```

The aliases make the column names more concise, easier to read, and more meaningful. Aliases are subject to a few restrictions. For example, they must be quoted if they are SQL keywords, entirely numeric, or contain spaces or other special characters (an alias can consist of several words if you want to use a descriptive phrase). The following statement retrieves the same data values as the preceding one but uses phrases to name the output columns:

```
mysql> SELECT
    -> DATE_FORMAT(t,'%M %e, %Y') AS 'Date of message',
    -> CONCAT(srcuser,'@',srchost) AS 'Message sender',
    -> size AS 'Number of bytes' FROM mail;
+-----------------+----------------+-----------------+
| Date of message | Message sender | Number of bytes |
+-----------------+----------------+-----------------+
| May 11, 2014    | barb@saturn    |           58274 |
| May 12, 2014    | tricia@mars    |          194925 |
| May 12, 2014    | phil@mars      |            1048 |
| May 12, 2014    | barb@saturn    |             271 |
...
```

If MySQL complains about a single-word alias, the word probably is reserved. Quoting the alias should make it legal:

```
mysql> SELECT 1 AS INTEGER;
You have an error in your SQL syntax near 'INTEGER'
mysql> SELECT 1 AS 'INTEGER';
+---------+
| INTEGER |
+---------+
|       1 |
+---------+
```

Column aliases are also useful for programming purposes. If you write a program that fetches rows into an array and accesses them by numeric column indexes, the presence or absence of column aliases makes no difference because aliases don't change the positions of columns within the result set. However, aliases make a big difference if you access output columns by name because aliases change those names. Exploit this fact to give your program easier names to work with. For example, if your query displays reformatted message time values from the mail table using the expression DATE_FORMAT(t,'%M %e, %Y'), that expression is also the name you must use when referring to the output column. In a Perl hashref, for example, you'd access it as

$ref->{"DATE_FORMAT(t,'%M %e, %Y')"}. That's inconvenient. Use AS `date_sent` to give the column an alias and you can refer to it more easily as $ref->{date_sent}. Here's an example that shows how a Perl DBI script might process such values. It retrieves rows into a hash and refers to column values by name:

```
$sth = $dbh->prepare ("SELECT srcuser,
                        DATE_FORMAT(t,'%M %e, %Y') AS date_sent
                        FROM mail");
$sth->execute ();
while (my $ref = $sth->fetchrow_hashref ())
{
  printf "user: %s, date sent: %s\n", $ref->{srcuser}, $ref->{date_sent};
}
```

In Java, you'd do something like this, where the argument to `getString()` names the column to access:

```
Statement s = conn.createStatement ();
s.executeQuery ("SELECT srcuser,"
              + " DATE_FORMAT(t,'%M %e, %Y') AS date_sent"
              + " FROM mail");
ResultSet rs = s.getResultSet ();
while (rs.next ())  // loop through rows of result set
{
  String name = rs.getString ("srcuser");
  String dateSent = rs.getString ("date_sent");
  System.out.println ("user: " + name + ", date sent: " + dateSent);
}
rs.close ();
s.close ();
```

Recipe 4.4 shows for each of our programming languages how to fetch rows into data structures that permit access to column values by name. The *select* directory of the `recipes` distribution has examples that show how to do this for the `mail` table.

You cannot refer to column aliases in a WHERE clause. Thus, the following statement is illegal:

```
mysql> SELECT t, srcuser, dstuser, size/1024 AS kilobytes
    -> FROM mail WHERE kilobytes > 500;
ERROR 1054 (42S22): Unknown column 'kilobytes' in 'where clause'
```

The error occurs because an alias names an *output* column, whereas a WHERE clause operates on *input* columns to determine which rows to select for output. To make the statement legal, replace the alias in the WHERE clause with the same column or expression that the alias represents:

```
mysql> SELECT t, srcuser, dstuser, size/1024 AS kilobytes
    -> FROM mail WHERE size/1024 > 500;
+---------------------+---------+---------+-----------+
| t                   | srcuser | dstuser | kilobytes |
+---------------------+---------+---------+-----------+
| 2014-05-14 17:03:01 | tricia  | phil    | 2338.3613 |
| 2014-05-15 10:25:52 | gene    | tricia  |  975.1289 |
+---------------------+---------+---------+-----------+
```

5.3 Sorting Query Results

Problem

You want to control how your query results are sorted.

Solution

Use an ORDER BY clause to tell it how to sort result rows.

Discussion

When you select rows, the MySQL server is free to return them in any order unless you instruct it otherwise by saying how to sort the result. There are lots of ways to use sorting techniques, as Chapter 9 explores in detail. Briefly, to sort a result set, add an ORDER BY clause that names the column or columns to use for sorting. This statement names multiple columns in the ORDER BY clause to sort rows by host and by user within each host:

```
mysql> SELECT t, srcuser, srchost, dstuser, dsthost, size
    -> FROM mail WHERE dstuser = 'tricia'
    -> ORDER BY srchost, srcuser;
+---------------------+---------+---------+---------+---------+--------+
| t                   | srcuser | srchost | dstuser | dsthost | size   |
+---------------------+---------+---------+---------+---------+--------+
| 2014-05-15 10:25:52 | gene    | mars    | tricia  | saturn  | 998532 |
| 2014-05-14 11:52:17 | phil    | mars    | tricia  | saturn  |   5781 |
| 2014-05-19 12:49:23 | phil    | mars    | tricia  | saturn  |    873 |
| 2014-05-11 10:15:08 | barb    | saturn  | tricia  | mars    |  58274 |
| 2014-05-12 18:59:18 | barb    | saturn  | tricia  | venus   |    271 |
+---------------------+---------+---------+---------+---------+--------+
```

MySQL sorts rows in the ascending order by default. To sort a column in reverse (descending) order, add the keyword DESC after its name in the ORDER BY clause:

```
mysql> SELECT t, srcuser, srchost, dstuser, dsthost, size
    -> FROM mail WHERE size > 50000 ORDER BY size DESC;
+---------------------+---------+---------+---------+---------+---------+
| t                   | srcuser | srchost | dstuser | dsthost | size    |
+---------------------+---------+---------+---------+---------+---------+
| 2014-05-14 17:03:01 | tricia  | saturn  | phil    | venus   | 2394482 |
| 2014-05-15 10:25:52 | gene    | mars    | tricia  | saturn  |  998532 |
| 2014-05-12 12:48:13 | tricia  | mars    | gene    | venus   |  194925 |
| 2014-05-14 14:42:21 | barb    | venus   | barb    | venus   |   98151 |
| 2014-05-11 10:15:08 | barb    | saturn  | tricia  | mars    |   58274 |
+---------------------+---------+---------+---------+---------+---------+
```

5.4 Removing Duplicate Rows

Problem

Output from a query contains duplicate rows. You want to eliminate them.

Solution

Use DISTINCT.

Discussion

Some queries produce results containing duplicate rows. For example, to see who sent mail, query the mail table like this:

```
mysql> SELECT srcuser FROM mail;
+---------+
| srcuser |
+---------+
| barb    |
| tricia  |
| phil    |
| barb    |
| gene    |
| phil    |
| barb    |
| tricia  |
| gene    |
| phil    |
| gene    |
| gene    |
| gene    |
| phil    |
| phil    |
| gene    |
+---------+
```

That result is heavily redundant. To remove the duplicate rows and produce a set of unique values, add DISTINCT to the query:

```
mysql> SELECT DISTINCT srcuser FROM mail;
+---------+
| srcuser |
+---------+
| barb    |
| tricia  |
| phil    |
| gene    |
+---------+
```

To count the number of unique values in a column, use COUNT(DISTINCT):

```
mysql> SELECT COUNT(DISTINCT srcuser) FROM mail;
+------------------------+
| COUNT(DISTINCT srcuser) |
+------------------------+
|                      4 |
+------------------------+
```

DISTINCT works with multiple-column output, too. The following query shows which dates are represented in the mail table:

```
mysql> SELECT DISTINCT YEAR(t), MONTH(t), DAYOFMONTH(t) FROM mail;
+---------+----------+---------------+
| YEAR(t) | MONTH(t) | DAYOFMONTH(t) |
+---------+----------+---------------+
|    2014 |        5 |            11 |
|    2014 |        5 |            12 |
|    2014 |        5 |            14 |
|    2014 |        5 |            15 |
|    2014 |        5 |            16 |
|    2014 |        5 |            19 |
+---------+----------+---------------+
```

See Also

Chapter 10 revisits DISTINCT and COUNT(DISTINCT). Chapter 18 discusses duplicate removal in more detail.

5.5 Working with NULL Values

Problem

You're trying to compare column values to NULL, but it isn't working.

Solution

Use the proper comparison operators: IS NULL, IS NOT NULL, or <=>.

Discussion

Conditions that involve NULL are special because NULL means "unknown value." Consequently, comparisons such as *value* = NULL or *value* <> NULL always produce a result of NULL (not true or false) because it's impossible to tell whether they are true or false. Even NULL = NULL produces NULL because you can't determine whether one unknown value is the same as another.

To look for values that are or are not NULL, use the IS NULL or IS NOT NULL operator. Suppose that a table named expt contains experimental results for subjects who are to be given four tests each and that represents tests not yet administered using NULL:

```
+---------+------+-------+
| subject | test | score |
+---------+------+-------+
| Jane    | A    |    47 |
| Jane    | B    |    50 |
| Jane    | C    |  NULL |
| Jane    | D    |  NULL |
| Marvin  | A    |    52 |
| Marvin  | B    |    45 |
| Marvin  | C    |    53 |
| Marvin  | D    |  NULL |
+---------+------+-------+
```

You can see that = and <> fail to identify NULL values:

```
mysql> SELECT * FROM expt WHERE score = NULL;
Empty set (0.00 sec)
mysql> SELECT * FROM expt WHERE score <> NULL;
Empty set (0.00 sec)
```

Write the statements like this instead:

```
mysql> SELECT * FROM expt WHERE score IS NULL;
+---------+------+-------+
| subject | test | score |
+---------+------+-------+
| Jane    | C    |  NULL |
| Jane    | D    |  NULL |
| Marvin  | D    |  NULL |
+---------+------+-------+
mysql> SELECT * FROM expt WHERE score IS NOT NULL;
+---------+------+-------+
| subject | test | score |
+---------+------+-------+
| Jane    | A    |    47 |
| Jane    | B    |    50 |
| Marvin  | A    |    52 |
| Marvin  | B    |    45 |
| Marvin  | C    |    53 |
+---------+------+-------+
mysql> SELECT * FROM expt WHERE score <=> NULL;
+---------+------+-------+
| subject | test | score |
+---------+------+-------+
| Jane    | C    |  NULL |
| Jane    | D    |  NULL |
| Marvin  | D    |  NULL |
+---------+------+-------+
```

The MySQL-specific <=> null-safe comparison operator, unlike the = operator, is true even for two NULL values:

```
mysql> SELECT NULL = NULL, NULL <=> NULL;
+-------------+---------------+
| NULL = NULL | NULL <=> NULL |
+-------------+---------------+
|        NULL |             1 |
+-------------+---------------+
```

Sometimes it's useful to map NULL values onto some other value that has more meaning in the context of your application. For example, use IF() to map NULL onto the string Unknown:

```
mysql> SELECT subject, test, IF(score IS NULL,'Unknown', score) AS 'score'
    -> FROM expt;
+---------+------+---------+
| subject | test | score   |
+---------+------+---------+
| Jane    | A    | 47      |
| Jane    | B    | 50      |
| Jane    | C    | Unknown |
| Jane    | D    | Unknown |
| Marvin  | A    | 52      |
| Marvin  | B    | 45      |
| Marvin  | C    | 53      |
| Marvin  | D    | Unknown |
+---------+------+---------+
```

This IF()-based mapping technique works for any kind of value, but it's especially useful with NULL values because NULL tends to be given a variety of meanings: unknown, missing, not yet determined, out of range, and so forth. Choose the label that makes the most sense in a given context.

The preceding query can be written more concisely using IFNULL(), which tests its first argument and returns it if it's not NULL, or returns its second argument otherwise:

```
SELECT subject, test, IFNULL(score,'Unknown') AS 'score'
FROM expt;
```

In other words, these two tests are equivalent:

```
IF(expr1 IS NOT NULL,expr1,expr2)
IFNULL(expr1,expr2)
```

From a readability standpoint, IF() often is easier to understand than IFNULL(). From a computational perspective, IFNULL() is more efficient because *expr1* need not be evaluated twice, as happens with IF().

One more way to map NULL values is to use the COALESCE function, which returns the first not-null element from the list of parameters:

```
SELECT subject, test, COALESCE(score,'Unknown') AS 'score' FROM expt;
```

See Also

NULL values also behave differently when used by sorting and summary operations. See Recipes 9.11 and 10.9.

5.6 Writing Comparisons Involving NULL in Programs

Problem

You're writing a program that looks for rows containing a specific value, but it fails when the value is NULL.

Solution

Choose the proper comparison operator according to whether the comparison value is or is not NULL.

Discussion

Recipe 5.5 discusses the need to use different comparison operators for NULL values than for non-NULL values in SQL statements. This issue leads to a subtle danger when constructing statement strings within programs. If a value stored in a variable might represent a NULL value, you must account for that when you use the value in comparisons. For example, in Python, None represents a NULL value, so to construct a statement that finds rows in the expt table matching some arbitrary value in a score variable, you cannot do this:

```
cursor.execute("SELECT * FROM expt WHERE score = %s", (score,))
```

The statement fails when score is None because the resulting statement becomes the following:

```
SELECT * FROM expt WHERE score = NULL;
```

A comparison of score = NULL is never true, so that statement returns no rows. To take into account the possibility that score could be None, construct the statement using the appropriate comparison operator like this:

```
operator = "IS" if score is None else "="
cursor.execute("SELECT * FROM expt WHERE score {} %s".format(operator), (score,))
```

This results in statements as follows for score values of None (NULL) or 43 (not NULL):

```
SELECT * FROM expt WHERE score IS NULL
SELECT * FROM expt WHERE score = 43;
```

For inequality tests, set operator like this instead:

```
operator = "IS NOT" if score is None else "<>"
```

5.7 Using Views to Simplify Table Access

Problem

You want to refer to values calculated from expressions without writing the expressions each time you retrieve them.

Solution

Use a view defined such that its columns perform the desired calculations.

Discussion

Suppose that you retrieve several values from the `mail` table, using expressions to calculate most of them:

```
mysql> SELECT
    -> DATE_FORMAT(t,'%M %e, %Y') AS date_sent,
    -> CONCAT(srcuser,'@',srchost) AS sender,
    -> CONCAT(dstuser,'@',dsthost) AS recipient,
    -> size FROM mail;
+--------------+--------------+---------------+---------+
| date_sent    | sender       | recipient     | size    |
+--------------+--------------+---------------+---------+
| May 11, 2014 | barb@saturn  | tricia@mars   |   58274 |
| May 12, 2014 | tricia@mars  | gene@venus    |  194925 |
| May 12, 2014 | phil@mars    | phil@saturn   |    1048 |
| May 12, 2014 | barb@saturn  | tricia@venus  |     271 |
...
```

If you must issue such a statement often, it's inconvenient to keep writing the expressions. To make the statement results easier to access, use a view, which is a virtual table that contains no data. Instead, it's defined as the `SELECT` statement that retrieves the data of interest. The following view, `mail_view`, is equivalent to the `SELECT` statement just shown:

```
mysql> CREATE VIEW mail_view AS
    -> SELECT
    -> DATE_FORMAT(t,'%M %e, %Y') AS date_sent,
    -> CONCAT(srcuser,'@',srchost) AS sender,
    -> CONCAT(dstuser,'@',dsthost) AS recipient,
    -> size FROM mail;
```

To access the view contents, refer to it like any other table. You can select some or all of its columns, add a `WHERE` clause to restrict which rows to retrieve, use `ORDER BY` to sort the rows, and so forth, for example:

```
mysql> SELECT date_sent, sender, size FROM mail_view
    -> WHERE size > 100000 ORDER BY size;
+--------------+--------------+---------+
| date_sent    | sender       | size    |
+--------------+--------------+---------+
| May 12, 2014 | tricia@mars  |  194925 |
```

```
| May 15, 2014 | gene@mars    |  998532 |
| May 14, 2014 | tricia@saturn | 2394482 |
+--------------+---------------+---------+
```

Stored programs provide another way to encapsulate calculations (see Recipe 11.2).

5.8 Selecting Data from Multiple Tables

Problem

The answer to a question requires data from more than one table, so you need to select data from multiple tables.

Solution

Use a join or a subquery.

Discussion

The queries shown so far select data from a single table, but sometimes you must retrieve information from multiple tables. Two types of statements that accomplish this are joins and subqueries. A *join* matches rows in one table with rows in another and enables you to retrieve output rows that contain columns from either or both tables. A *subquery* is one query nested within another, to perform a comparison between values selected by the inner query against values selected by the outer query.

This recipe shows a couple of brief examples to illustrate the basic ideas. Other examples appear elsewhere: subqueries are used in various examples throughout the book (for example, Recipes 5.10 and 10.6). Chapter 16 discusses joins in detail, including some that select from more than two tables.

The following examples use the `profile` table introduced in Chapter 4. Recall that it lists the people on your buddy list:

```
mysql> SELECT * FROM profile;
+----+---------+------------+-------+------------------------+------+
| id | name    | birth      | color | foods                  | cats |
+----+---------+------------+-------+------------------------+------+
|  1 | Sybil   | 1970-04-13 | black | lutefisk,fadge,pizza   |    0 |
|  2 | Nancy   | 1969-09-30 | white | burrito,curry,eggroll  |    3 |
|  3 | Ralph   | 1973-11-02 | red   | eggroll,pizza          |    4 |
|  4 | Lothair | 1963-07-04 | blue  | burrito,curry          |    5 |
|  5 | Henry   | 1965-02-14 | red   | curry,fadge            |    1 |
|  6 | Aaron   | 1968-09-17 | green | lutefisk,fadge         |    1 |
|  7 | Joanna  | 1952-08-20 | green | lutefisk,fadge         |    0 |
|  8 | Stephen | 1960-05-01 | white | burrito,pizza          |    0 |
+----+---------+------------+-------+------------------------+------+
```

Let's extend the use of the `profile` table to include another table named `profile_con`
`tact`. This second table indicates how to contact people listed in the `profile` table via
various social media services and is defined like this:

```
CREATE TABLE profile_contact
(
  id           INT NOT NULL AUTO_INCREMENT PRIMARY KEY,
  profile_id   INT UNSIGNED NOT NULL, # ID from profile table
  service      VARCHAR(20) NOT NULL,  # social media service name
  contact_name VARCHAR(25) NOT NULL,  # name to use for contacting person
  INDEX (profile_id)
);
```

The table associates each row with the proper `profile` row via the `profile_id`
column. The `service` and `contact_name` columns name the media service and the
name to use for contacting the given person via that service. For the examples,
assume that the table contains these rows:

```
mysql> SELECT profile_id, service, contact_name
    -> FROM profile_contact ORDER BY profile_id, service;
+------------+----------+--------------+
| profile_id | service  | contact_name |
+------------+----------+--------------+
|          1 | Facebook | user1-fbid   |
|          1 | Twitter  | user1-twtrid |
|          2 | Facebook | user2-msnid  |
|          2 | LinkedIn | user2-lnkdid |
|          2 | Twitter  | user2-fbrid  |
|          4 | LinkedIn | user4-lnkdid |
+------------+----------+--------------+
```

A question that requires information from both tables is "For each person in the
`profile` table, show me which services I can use to get in touch and the contact
name for each service." To answer this question, use a join. Select from both tables
and match rows by comparing the `id` column from the `profile` table with the
`profile_id` column from the `profile_contact` table:

```
mysql> SELECT profile.id, name, service, contact_name
    -> FROM profile INNER JOIN profile_contact ON profile.id = profile_id;
+----+---------+----------+--------------+
| id | name    | service  | contact_name |
+----+---------+----------+--------------+
|  1 | Sybil   | Twitter  | user1-twtrid |
|  1 | Sybil   | Facebook | user1-fbid   |
|  2 | Nancy   | Twitter  | user2-fbrid  |
|  2 | Nancy   | Facebook | user2-msnid  |
|  2 | Nancy   | LinkedIn | user2-lnkdid |
|  4 | Lothair | LinkedIn | user4-lnkdid |
+----+---------+----------+--------------+
```

The `FROM` clause indicates the tables from which to select data, and the `ON` clause
tells MySQL which columns to use to find matches between the tables. In the result,
rows include the `id` and `name` columns from the `profile` table, and the `service` and
`contact_name` columns from the `profile_contact` table.

Here's another question that requires both tables to answer: "List all the `profile_con` `tact` records for Nancy." To pull the proper rows from the `profile_contact` table, you need Nancy's ID, which is stored in the `profile` table. To write the query without looking up Nancy's ID yourself, use a subquery that, given her name, looks it up for you:

```
mysql> SELECT profile_id, service, contact_name FROM profile_contact
    -> WHERE profile_id = (SELECT id FROM profile WHERE name = 'Nancy');
+------------+----------+--------------+
| profile_id | service  | contact_name |
+------------+----------+--------------+
|          2 | Twitter  | user2-fbrid  |
|          2 | Facebook | user2-msnid  |
|          2 | LinkedIn | user2-lnkdid |
+------------+----------+--------------+
```

Here the subquery appears as a nested `SELECT` statement enclosed within parentheses.

5.9 Selecting Rows from the Beginning, End, or Middle of Query Results

Problem

You want only certain rows from a result set, such as the first one, the last five, or rows 21 through 40.

Solution

Use a `LIMIT` clause, perhaps in conjunction with an `ORDER BY` clause.

Discussion

MySQL supports a `LIMIT` clause that tells the server to return only part of a result set. `LIMIT` is a MySQL-specific extension to SQL that is extremely valuable when your result set contains more rows than you want to see at a time. It enables you to retrieve an arbitrary section of a result set. Typical `LIMIT` uses include the following kinds of problems:

- Answering questions about first or last, largest or smallest, newest or oldest, least or most expensive, and so forth.

- Splitting a result set into sections so that you can process it one piece at a time. This technique is common in web applications for displaying a large search result across several pages. Showing the result in sections enables the display of smaller, easier-to-understand pages.

The following examples use the `profile` table shown in Recipe 5.8. To see the first *n* rows of a SELECT result, add LIMIT *n* to the end of the statement:

```
mysql> SELECT * FROM profile LIMIT 1;
+----+-------+------------+-------+---------------------+------+
| id | name  | birth      | color | foods               | cats |
+----+-------+------------+-------+---------------------+------+
|  1 | Sybil | 1970-04-13 | black | lutefisk,fadge,pizza |   0 |
+----+-------+------------+-------+---------------------+------+
mysql> SELECT * FROM profile LIMIT 3;
+----+-------+------------+-------+-----------------------+------+
| id | name  | birth      | color | foods                 | cats |
+----+-------+------------+-------+-----------------------+------+
|  1 | Sybil | 1970-04-13 | black | lutefisk,fadge,pizza  |    0 |
|  2 | Nancy | 1969-09-30 | white | burrito,curry,eggroll |    3 |
|  3 | Ralph | 1973-11-02 | red   | eggroll,pizza         |    4 |
+----+-------+------------+-------+-----------------------+------+
```

LIMIT *n* means "return *at most n* rows." If you specify LIMIT 10, and the result set has only four rows, the server returns four rows.

The rows in the preceding query results are returned in no particular order, so they may not be very meaningful. A more common technique uses ORDER BY to sort the result set and LIMIT to find smallest and largest values. For example, to find the row with the minimum (earliest) birth date, sort by the `birth` column, then add LIMIT 1 to retrieve the first row:

```
mysql> SELECT * FROM profile ORDER BY birth LIMIT 1;
+----+--------+------------+-------+----------------+------+
| id | name   | birth      | color | foods          | cats |
+----+--------+------------+-------+----------------+------+
|  7 | Joanna | 1952-08-20 | green | lutefisk,fadge |    0 |
+----+--------+------------+-------+----------------+------+
```

This works because MySQL processes the ORDER BY clause to sort the rows, then applies LIMIT.

To obtain rows from the end of a result set, sort them in the opposite order. The statement that finds the row with the most recent birth date is similar to the previous one, except that the sort order is descending:

```
mysql> SELECT * FROM profile ORDER BY birth DESC LIMIT 1;
+----+-------+------------+-------+---------------+------+
| id | name  | birth      | color | foods         | cats |
+----+-------+------------+-------+---------------+------+
|  3 | Ralph | 1973-11-02 | red   | eggroll,pizza |    4 |
+----+-------+------------+-------+---------------+------+
```

To find the earliest or latest birthday within the calendar year, sort by the month and day of the `birth` values:

```
mysql> SELECT name, DATE_FORMAT(birth,'%m-%d') AS birthday
    -> FROM profile ORDER BY birthday LIMIT 1;
+-------+----------+
| name  | birthday |
+-------+----------+
| Henry | 02-14    |
+-------+----------+
```

You can obtain the same information by running these statements without LIMIT and ignoring everything but the first row. The advantage of LIMIT is that the server returns only the first row, and the extra rows don't cross the network at all. This is much more efficient than retrieving an entire result set, only to discard all but one row.

To pull rows from the middle of a result set, use the two-argument form of LIMIT, which enables you to pick an arbitrary section of rows. The arguments indicate how many rows to skip and how many to return. This means that you can use LIMIT to do such things as skip two rows and return the next one, thus answering questions such as "What is the *third*-smallest or *third*-largest value?" These are questions that MIN() or MAX() are not suited for but are easy with LIMIT:

```
mysql> SELECT * FROM profile ORDER BY birth LIMIT 2,1;
+----+---------+------------+-------+---------------+------+
| id | name    | birth      | color | foods         | cats |
+----+---------+------------+-------+---------------+------+
|  4 | Lothair | 1963-07-04 | blue  | burrito,curry |    5 |
+----+---------+------------+-------+---------------+------+
mysql> SELECT * FROM profile ORDER BY birth DESC LIMIT 2,1;
+----+-------+------------+-------+-----------------------+------+
| id | name  | birth      | color | foods                 | cats |
+----+-------+------------+-------+-----------------------+------+
|  2 | Nancy | 1969-09-30 | white | burrito,curry,eggroll |    3 |
+----+-------+------------+-------+-----------------------+------+
```

The two-argument form of LIMIT also makes it possible to partition a result set into smaller sections. For example, to retrieve 20 rows at a time from a result, issue a SELECT statement repeatedly, but vary its LIMIT clause like so:

```
SELECT ... FROM ... ORDER BY ... LIMIT 0, 20;
SELECT ... FROM ... ORDER BY ... LIMIT 20, 20;
SELECT ... FROM ... ORDER BY ... LIMIT 40, 20;
...
```

 This way of using a LIMIT clause can cause performance degradations for large datasets, because it requires reading minimum OFFSET plus LIMIT rows. This means that to get the result for the LIMIT 0, 20 statement, MySQL will have to read 20 rows from the table; to get result the of LIMIT 20, 20, it will need to read 40 rows; and so on.

To determine the number of rows in a result set so that you can determine the number of sections, issue a COUNT() statement first. For example, to display profile table rows in name order, three at a time, you can find out how many there are with the following statement:

```
mysql> SELECT COUNT(*) FROM profile;
+----------+
| COUNT(*) |
+----------+
|        8 |
+----------+
```

That tells you that there are three sets of rows (the last with fewer than three rows), which you can retrieve as follows:

```
SELECT * FROM profile ORDER BY name LIMIT 0, 3;
SELECT * FROM profile ORDER BY name LIMIT 3, 3;
SELECT * FROM profile ORDER BY name LIMIT 6, 3;
```

See Also

LIMIT is useful in combination with RAND() to make random selections from a set of items. See Recipe 17.8.

You can use LIMIT to restrict the effect of a DELETE or UPDATE statement to a subset of the rows that would otherwise be deleted or updated, respectively. For more information about using LIMIT for duplicate row removal, see Recipe 18.5.

5.10 What to Do When LIMIT and the Final Result Require a Different Sort Order

Problem

LIMIT usually works best in conjunction with an ORDER BY clause that sorts rows. But sometimes that sort order differs from what you want for the final result.

Solution

Use LIMIT in a subquery to retrieve the desired rows, then use the outer query to sort them.

Discussion

If you want the last four rows of a result set, you can obtain them easily by sorting the set in reverse order and using LIMIT 4. The following statement returns the names and birth dates for the four people in the profile table who were born most recently:

```
mysql> SELECT name, birth FROM profile ORDER BY birth DESC LIMIT 4;
+-------+------------+
| name  | birth      |
+-------+------------+
| Ralph | 1973-11-02 |
| Sybil | 1970-04-13 |
| Nancy | 1969-09-30 |
| Aaron | 1968-09-17 |
+-------+------------+
```

But that requires sorting the `birth` values in descending order to place them at the head of the result set. What if you want the output rows to appear in ascending order instead? Use the `SELECT` as a subquery of an outer statement that re-sorts the rows in the desired final order:

```
mysql> SELECT * FROM
    -> (SELECT name, birth FROM profile ORDER BY birth DESC LIMIT 4) AS t
    -> ORDER BY birth;
+-------+------------+
| name  | birth      |
+-------+------------+
| Aaron | 1968-09-17 |
| Nancy | 1969-09-30 |
| Sybil | 1970-04-13 |
| Ralph | 1973-11-02 |
+-------+------------+
```

`AS t` is used here because any table referred to in the `FROM` clause must have a name, even a "derived" table produced from a subquery.

5.11 Calculating LIMIT Values from Expressions

Problem

You want to use expressions to specify the arguments for `LIMIT`.

Solution

`LIMIT` arguments must be literal integers—unless you issue the statement in a context that permits the statement string to be constructed dynamically. In that case, you can evaluate the expressions yourself and insert the resulting values into the statement string.

Discussion

Arguments to `LIMIT` must be literal integers, not expressions. Statements such as the following are illegal:

```
SELECT * FROM profile LIMIT 5+5;
SELECT * FROM profile LIMIT @skip_count, @show_count;
```

The same "no expressions permitted" principle applies if you use an expression to calculate a LIMIT value in a program that constructs a statement string. You must evaluate the expression first, and then place the resulting value in the statement. For example, if you produce a statement string in Perl or PHP as follows, an error will result when you attempt to execute the statement:

```
$str = "SELECT * FROM profile LIMIT $x + $y";
```

To avoid the problem, evaluate the expression first:

```
$z = $x + $y;
$str = "SELECT * FROM profile LIMIT $z";
```

Or do this (don't omit the parentheses or the expression won't evaluate properly):

```
$str = "SELECT * FROM profile LIMIT " . ($x + $y);
```

To construct a two-argument LIMIT clause, evaluate both expressions before placing them into the statement string.

5.12 Combining Two or More SELECT Results

Problem

You want to combine rows retrieved by two or more SELECT statements into one result set.

Solution

Use the UNION clause.

Discussion

The mail table stores user names and hosts of the email senders and recipients. But what if we want to know all the user and host combinations possible?

A naive approach would be to choose either sender or receiver pairs. But if we perform even a very basic test by comparing the number of unique user-host combinations, we'll find out that it is different for each direction:

```
mysql> SELECT COUNT(distinct srcuser, srchost) FROM mail;
+---------------------------------+
| count(distinct srcuser, srchost) |
+---------------------------------+
|                               9 |
+---------------------------------+
1 row in set (0.01 sec)

mysql> select count(distinct dstuser, dsthost) from mail;
+---------------------------------+
| count(distinct dstuser, dsthost) |
+---------------------------------+
```

```
|                           10 |
+-----------------------------+
1 row in set (0.00 sec)
```

We also don't know if our table stores emails from users who only send them and for users who receive but never send.

To get the full list, we need to select pairs for both the sender and receiver, then remove duplicates. The SQL UNION DISTINCT clause and its short form, UNION, does exactly that. It combines results of two or more SELECT queries that select the same number of columns of the same type.

By default, UNION uses the column names of the first SELECT for the full result set header, but we can also use aliases, as discussed in Recipe 5.2:

```
mysql> SELECT DISTINCT srcuser AS user, srchost AS host FROM mail
    -> UNION
    -> SELECT DISTINCT dstuser AS user, dsthost AS host FROM mail;

+--------+--------+
| user   | host   |
+--------+--------+
| barb   | saturn |
| tricia | mars   |
| phil   | mars   |
| gene   | venus  |
| barb   | venus  |
| tricia | saturn |
| gene   | mars   |
| phil   | venus  |
| gene   | saturn |
| phil   | saturn |
| tricia | venus  |
| barb   | mars   |
+--------+--------+
12 rows in set (0.00 sec)
```

You can sort an individual query, participating in UNION, as well as the whole result. If you do not want to remove duplicates from the result, use the UNION ALL clause.

To demonstrate this, let's create a query that will find four users who sent the highest number of emails and four users who received the highest number of emails, then sort the result of the union by the user name:

```
mysql> (SELECT CONCAT(srcuser, '@', srchost) AS user, COUNT(*) AS emails ❶
    -> FROM mail GROUP BY srcuser, srchost ORDER BY emails DESC LIMIT 4) ❷
    -> UNION ALL
    -> (SELECT CONCAT(dstuser, '@', dsthost) AS user, COUNT(*) AS emails
    -> FROM mail GROUP BY dstuser, dsthost ORDER BY emails DESC LIMIT 4) ❸
    -> ORDER BY user;❹
+----------------+--------+
| user           | emails |
+----------------+--------+
| barb@mars      |      2 |
| barb@saturn    |      2 |
| barb@venus     |      2 |
```

```
| gene@saturn  |    2 |
| gene@venus   |    2 | ❺
| gene@venus   |    2 |
| phil@mars    |    3 |
| tricia@saturn|    3 |
+--------------+------+
8 rows in set (0.00 sec)
```

❶ Concatenate the user and host into the email address of the user.

❷ Order the first SELECT result by the number of emails in descending order, and limit the number of retrieved rows.

❸ Order the result of the second SELECT.

❹ Order the result of UNION by the user email address.

❺ We used the UNION ALL clause instead of UNION [DISTINCT]; therefore, we have two entries for gene@venus in the result. This user is in the top list of those who send emails and also of those who receive emails.

5.13 Selecting Results of Subqueries

Problem

You want to retrieve not only table columns but also results of queries that use these columns.

Solution

Use a subquery in the column list.

Discussion

Suppose that you want to know not only how many emails were sent by a particular user but also how many emails they received. You cannot do this without accessing the mail table two times: one to count how many emails were sent and one to count how many emails were received.

One solution for this issue is to use subqueries in the column list:

```
mysql> SELECT CONCAT(srcuser, '@', srchost) AS user, COUNT(*) AS mails_sent, ❶
    -> (SELECT COUNT(*) FROM mail d WHERE d.dstuser=m.srcuser AND d.dsthost=m.srchost) ❷
    -> AS mails_received ❸
    -> FROM mail m
    -> GROUP BY  srcuser, srchost ❹
    -> ORDER BY mails_sent DESC;
+--------------+-----------+----------------+
```

```
| user          | mails_sent | mails_received |
+---------------+------------+----------------+
| phil@mars     |          3 |              0 |
| barb@saturn   |          2 |              0 |
| gene@venus    |          2 |              2 |
| gene@mars     |          2 |              1 |
| phil@venus    |          2 |              2 |
| gene@saturn   |          2 |              1 |
| tricia@mars   |          1 |              1 |
| barb@venus    |          1 |              2 |
| tricia@saturn |          1 |              3 |
+---------------+------------+----------------+
9 rows in set (0.00 sec)
```

❶ First, we retrieved a user name and a host of the sender and a count of the number of emails that they sent.

❷ To find the number of emails this user received, we're using a subquery to the same mail table. In the WHERE clause, we select only those rows where the receiver has the same credentials as the sender in the main query.

❸ A subquery in the column list must have its own alias.

❹ To display statistics per user, we use the GROUP BY clause, so the result is grouped by each user name and host. We discuss the GROUP BY clause in detail in Chapter 10.

## CHAPTER 6

Table Management

6.0 Introduction

This chapter covers topics that relate to creating and populating tables, including the following:

- Cloning a table
- Copying from one table to another
- Using temporary tables
- Generating unique table names
- Determining what storage engine a table uses or converting it from one storage engine to another

Many of the examples in this chapter use a table named `mail` containing rows that track mail message traffic between users on a set of hosts (see Recipe 5.0). To create and load this table, change location into the *tables* directory of the `recipes` distribution and run this command:

```
$ mysql cookbook < mail.sql
```

6.1 Cloning a Table

Problem

You want to create a table that has exactly the same structure as an existing table.

Solution

Use CREATE TABLE...LIKE to clone the table structure. To also copy some or all of the rows from the original table to the new one, use INSERT INTO...SELECT.

Discussion

To create a new table that is just like an existing table, use this statement:

```
CREATE TABLE new_table LIKE original_table;
```

The structure of the new table is the same as that of the original table, with a few exceptions: CREATE TABLE...LIKE does not copy foreign key definitions, and it doesn't copy any DATA DIRECTORY or INDEX DIRECTORY table options that the table might use.

The new table is empty. If you also want the contents to be the same as the original table, copy the rows using an INSERT INTO...SELECT statement:

```
INSERT INTO new_table SELECT * FROM original_table;
```

To copy only part of the table, add an appropriate WHERE clause that identifies which rows to copy. For example, these statements create a copy of the mail table named mail2, populated only with the rows for mail sent by barb:

```
CREATE TABLE mail2 LIKE mail;
INSERT INTO mail2 SELECT * FROM mail WHERE srcuser = 'barb';
```

 Selecting everything from the large table could be slow and is not recommended on the production servers. We discuss how to copy huge tables in Recipes 6.7 and 6.8.

See Also

For additional information about INSERT...SELECT, see Recipe 6.2.

6.2 Saving a Query Result in a Table

Problem

You want to save the result from a SELECT statement to a table rather than display it.

Solution

If the table exists, retrieve rows into it using INSERT INTO...SELECT. If the table does not exist, create it on the fly using CREATE TABLE...SELECT.

Discussion

The MySQL server normally returns the result of a SELECT statement to the client that executed the statement. For example, when you execute a statement from within the mysql program, the server returns the result to mysql, which in turn displays it on the screen. It's possible to save the results of a SELECT statement in a table instead, which is useful in several ways:

- You can easily create a complete or partial copy of a table. If you're developing an algorithm for your application that modifies a table, it's safer to work with a copy of a table so that you need not worry about the consequences of mistakes. If the original table is large, creating a partial copy can speed the development process because queries running against it take less time.

- For a data-loading operation based on information that might be malformed, load new rows into a test temporary table, perform some preliminary checks, and correct the rows as necessary. When you're satisfied that the new rows are okay, copy them from the temporary table to your main table.

- Some applications maintain a large repository table and a smaller working table into which rows are inserted on a regular basis, copying the working table rows to the repository periodically and clearing the working table.

- To perform summary operations on a large table more efficiently, avoid running expensive summary operations repeatedly on it. Instead, select summary information once into a second table and use that for further analysis.

This recipe shows how to retrieve a result set into a table. The table names src_tbl and dst_tbl in the examples refer to the source table from which rows are selected and the destination table into which they are stored, respectively.

If the destination table already exists, use INSERT...SELECT to copy the result set into it. For example, if dst_tbl contains an integer column i and a string column s, the following statement copies rows from src_tbl into dst_tbl, assigning column val to i and column name to s:

```
INSERT INTO dst_tbl (i, s) SELECT val, name FROM src_tbl;
```

The number of columns to be inserted must match the number of selected columns, with the correspondence between columns based on position rather than name. To copy all columns, you can shorten the statement to this form:

```
INSERT INTO dst_tbl SELECT * FROM src_tbl;
```

To copy only certain rows, add a WHERE clause that selects those rows:

```
INSERT INTO dst_tbl SELECT * FROM src_tbl
WHERE val > 100 AND name LIKE 'A%';
```

The SELECT statement can produce values from expressions, too. For example, the following statement counts the number of times each name occurs in src_tbl and stores both the counts and the names in dst_tbl:

```
INSERT INTO dst_tbl (i, s) SELECT COUNT(*), name
FROM src_tbl GROUP BY name;
```

If the destination table does not exist, create it first with a CREATE TABLE statement, then copy rows into it with INSERT...SELECT. Alternatively, use CREATE TABLE... SELECT to create the destination table directly from the result of the SELECT. For example, to create dst_tbl and copy the entire contents of src_tbl into it, do this:

```
CREATE TABLE dst_tbl SELECT * FROM src_tbl;
```

INSERT INTO...SELECT...
does not copy indexes from the source table. If you use this syntax, and the destination table should have indexes, create them after the statement completes. We discuss indexes in Recipe 21.1.

MySQL creates the columns in dst_tbl based on the name, number, and type of the columns in src_tbl. To copy only certain rows, add an appropriate WHERE clause. To create an empty table, use a WHERE clause that selects no rows:

```
CREATE TABLE dst_tbl SELECT * FROM src_tbl WHERE FALSE;
```

To copy only some of the columns, name the ones you want in the SELECT part of the statement. For example, if src_tbl contains columns a, b, c, and d, copy just b and d like this:

```
CREATE TABLE dst_tbl SELECT b, d FROM src_tbl;
```

To create columns in an order different from that in which they appear in the source table, name them in the desired order. If the source table contains columns a, b, and c that should appear in the destination table in the order c, a, b, do this:

```
CREATE TABLE dst_tbl SELECT c, a, b FROM src_tbl;
```

To create columns in the destination table in addition to those selected from the source table, provide appropriate column definitions in the CREATE TABLE part of the statement. The following statement creates id as an AUTO_INCREMENT column in dst_tbl and adds columns a, b, and c from src_tbl:

```
CREATE TABLE dst_tbl
(
  id INT NOT NULL AUTO_INCREMENT,
  PRIMARY KEY (id)
)
SELECT a, b, c FROM src_tbl;
```

The resulting table contains four columns in the order id, a, b, c. Defined columns are assigned their default values. This means that id, being an AUTO_INCREMENT column, is assigned successive sequence numbers starting from 1 (see Recipe 15.1).

If you derive a column's values from an expression, its default name is the expression itself, which can be difficult to work with later. In this case, it's prudent to give the column a better name by providing an alias (see Recipe 5.2). Suppose that src_tbl contains invoice information that lists items in each invoice. The following statement generates a summary that lists each invoice named in the table and the total cost of its items, using an alias for the expression:

```
CREATE TABLE dst_tbl
SELECT inv_no, SUM(unit_cost*quantity) AS total_cost
FROM src_tbl GROUP BY inv_no;
```

CREATE TABLE...SELECT is extremely convenient but has some limitations that arise from the fact that the information available from a result set is not as extensive as what you can specify in a CREATE TABLE statement. For example, MySQL has no idea whether a result set column should be indexed or what its default value is. If it's important to include this information in the destination table, use the following techniques:

- To make the destination table an *exact* copy of the source table, use the cloning technique described in Recipe 6.1.

- To include indexes in the destination table, specify them explicitly. For example, if src_tbl has a PRIMARY KEY on the id column, and a multiple-column index on state and city, specify them for dst_tbl as well:
  ```
  CREATE TABLE dst_tbl (PRIMARY KEY (id), INDEX(state,city))
  SELECT * FROM src_tbl;
  ```

- Column attributes such as AUTO_INCREMENT and a column's default value are not copied to the destination table. To preserve these attributes, create the table, then use ALTER TABLE to apply the appropriate modifications to the column definition. For example, if src_tbl has an id column that is not only a PRIMARY KEY but also an AUTO_INCREMENT column, copy the table and modify the copy:
  ```
  CREATE TABLE dst_tbl (PRIMARY KEY (id)) SELECT * FROM src_tbl;
  ALTER TABLE dst_tbl MODIFY id INT UNSIGNED NOT NULL AUTO_INCREMENT;
  ```

6.3 Creating Temporary Tables

Problem

You need a table only for a short time, after which you want it to disappear automatically.

Solution

Create a table using the TEMPORARY keyword, and let MySQL take care of removing it.

Discussion

Some operations require a table that exists only temporarily and that should disappear when it's no longer needed. You can, of course, execute a DROP TABLE statement explicitly to remove a table when you're done with it. Another option is to use CREATE TEMPORARY TABLE. This statement is like CREATE TABLE but creates a transient table that disappears when your session with the server ends, if you haven't already removed it yourself. This is extremely useful behavior because MySQL drops the table for you automatically; you need not remember to do it. TEMPORARY can be used with the usual table-creation methods:

- Create the table from explicit column definitions:
  ```
  CREATE TEMPORARY TABLE tbl_name (...column definitions...);
  ```
- Create the table from an existing table:
  ```
  CREATE TEMPORARY TABLE new_table LIKE original_table;
  ```
- Create the table on the fly from a result set:
  ```
  CREATE TEMPORARY TABLE tbl_name SELECT...;
  ```

Temporary tables are session-specific, so multiple clients can each create a temporary table having the same name without interfering with each other. This makes it easier to write applications that use transient tables because you need not ensure that the tables have unique names for each client. (For further discussion of table-naming issues, see Recipe 6.4.)

A temporary table can have the same name as a permanent table. In this case, the temporary table "hides" the permanent table for the duration of its existence, which can be useful for making a copy of a table that you can modify without affecting the original by mistake. The DELETE statement in the following example removes rows from a temporary mail table, leaving the original permanent table unaffected:

```
mysql> CREATE TEMPORARY TABLE mail SELECT * FROM mail;
mysql> SELECT COUNT(*) FROM mail;
+----------+
| COUNT(*) |
+----------+
|       16 |
+----------+
mysql> DELETE FROM mail;
mysql> SELECT COUNT(*) FROM mail;
+----------+
| COUNT(*) |
+----------+
|        0 |
+----------+
```

```
mysql> DROP TEMPORARY TABLE mail;
mysql> SELECT COUNT(*) FROM mail;
+----------+
| COUNT(*) |
+----------+
|       16 |
+----------+
```

Although temporary tables created with CREATE TEMPORARY TABLE have the benefits just discussed, keep the following caveats in mind:

- To reuse a temporary table within a given session, you must still drop it explicitly before re-creating it. Attempting to create a second temporary table with the same name results in an error.

- If you modify a temporary table that "hides" a permanent table with the same name, be sure to test for errors resulting from dropped connections if you use a programming interface that has reconnect capability enabled. If a client program automatically reconnects after detecting a dropped connection, modifications affect the permanent table after the reconnect, not the temporary table.

- Some APIs support persistent connections or connection pools. These prevent temporary tables from being dropped as you expect when your script ends because the connection remains open for reuse by other scripts. Your script has no control over when the connection closes. This means it can be prudent to execute the following statement prior to creating a temporary table, just in case it's still in existence from a previous execution of the script:

  ```
  DROP TEMPORARY TABLE IF EXISTS tbl_name;
  ```

The TEMPORARY keyword is useful here if the temporary table has already been dropped, to avoid dropping any permanent table that has the same name.

6.4 Generating Unique Table Names

Problem

You need to create a table with a name guaranteed not to exist.

Solution

Generate a value that is unique to your client program and incorporate it into the table name.

Discussion

MySQL is a multiple-client database server, so if a given script that creates a transient table might be invoked by several clients simultaneously, take care that multiple invocations of the script do not fight over the same table name. If the script creates tables using CREATE TEMPORARY TABLE, there is no problem because different clients can create temporary tables having the same name without clashing.

If you cannot or do not want to use a TEMPORARY table, make sure that each invocation of the script creates a uniquely named table and drops the table when it is no longer needed. To accomplish this, incorporate into the name some value guaranteed to be unique per invocation. A timestamp won't work if it's possible for two instances of a script to be invoked within the timestamp resolution. A random number may be better, but random numbers only reduce the possibility of name clashes, not eliminate it. Values, generated by the UUID function, are a better source for unique values. The UUID function returns a Universal Unique Identifier (UUID) generated according to RFC 4122, "A Universally Unique IDentifier (UUID) URN Namespace (*https://oreil.ly/rVRJ5*) and designed to produce a 128-bit string that is unique in space and time. While the value generated by this function is not necessarily unique, it's enough to generate a unique temporary table name.

It's possible to incorporate a UUID into a table name within SQL by using prepared statements. The following example illustrates this, referring to the table name in the CREATE TABLE statement and a precautionary DROP TABLE statement:

```
SET @tbl_name = CONCAT('tmp_tbl_', UUID());
SET @stmt = CONCAT('CREATE TABLE `', @tbl_name, '` (i INT)');
PREPARE stmt FROM @stmt;
EXECUTE stmt;
DEALLOCATE PREPARE stmt;
```

6.5 Checking or Changing a Table Storage Engine

Problem

You want to check which storage engine a table uses so that you can determine what engine capabilities are applicable. Or you need to change a table's storage engine because you realize that the capabilities of another engine are more suitable for the way you use the table.

Solution

To determine a table's storage engine, you can use any of several statements. To change the table's engine, use ALTER TABLE with an ENGINE clause.

Discussion

MySQL supports multiple storage engines, which have differing characteristics. For example, the InnoDB engine supports transactions, whereas Memory does not. If you need to know whether a table supports transactions, check which storage engine it uses. If the table's engine does not support transactions, you can convert the table to use a transaction-capable engine.

To determine the current engine for a table, check INFORMATION_SCHEMA or use the SHOW TABLE STATUS or SHOW CREATE TABLE statement. For the mail table, obtain engine information as follows:

```
mysql> SELECT ENGINE FROM INFORMATION_SCHEMA.TABLES
    -> WHERE TABLE_SCHEMA = 'cookbook' AND TABLE_NAME = 'mail';
+--------+
| ENGINE |
+--------+
| InnoDB |
+--------+

mysql> SHOW TABLE STATUS LIKE 'mail'\G
*************************** 1. row ***************************
          Name: mail
        Engine: InnoDB
...

mysql> SHOW CREATE TABLE mail\G
*************************** 1. row ***************************
        Table: mail
Create Table: CREATE TABLE `mail` (
... column definitions ...
) ENGINE=InnoDB DEFAULT CHARSET=utf8mb4 COLLATE=utf8mb4_0900_ai_ci
```

To change the storage engine for a table, use ALTER TABLE with an ENGINE specifier. For example, to convert the mail table to use the Memory storage engine, use this statement:

```
ALTER TABLE mail ENGINE = Memory;
```

Be aware that converting a large table to a different storage engine might take a long time and be expensive in terms of CPU and I/O activity.

To determine which storage engines your MySQL server supports, check the output from the SHOW ENGINES statement or query the INFORMATION_SCHEMA ENGINES table.

6.6 Copying a Table Using mysqldump

Problem

You want to copy a table or tables, either among the databases managed by a MySQL server or from one server to another.

Solution

Use the mysqldump program.

Discussion

The `mysqldump` program makes a backup file that can be reloaded to re-create the original table or tables:

```
$ mysqldump cookbook mail > mail.sql
```

The output file *mail.sql* consists of a CREATE TABLE statement to create the `mail` table and a set of INSERT statements to insert its rows. You can reload the file to re-create the table should the original be lost:

```
$ mysql cookbook < mail.sql
```

This method also makes it easy to deal with any triggers the table has. By default, `mysqldump` writes the triggers to the dump file, so reloading the file copies the triggers along with the table with no special handling.

By default, `mysqldump` includes the DROP TABLE IF EXISTS statement before CREATE TABLE. If you do not want to drop the table when loading the dump and prefer the operation to fail instead, run `mysqldump` with the `--skip-add-drop-table` option.

In addition to restoring tables, `mysqldump` can be used to make copies of them by reloading the output into a different database. (If the destination database does not exist, create it first.) The following examples show some useful table-copying commands.

Copying tables within a single MySQL server

- Copy a single table to a different database:
  ```
  $ mysqldump cookbook mail > mail.sql
  $ mysql other_db < mail.sql
  ```

  To dump multiple tables, name them all following the database name argument.

- Copy all tables in a database to a different database:
  ```
  $ mysqldump cookbook > cookbook.sql
  $ mysql other_db < cookbook.sql
  ```

  When you name no tables after the database name, `mysqldump` dumps them all. To also include stored routines and events, add the `--routines` and `--events` options to the `mysqldump` command. (There is also a `--triggers` option, but it's unneeded because, as mentioned previously, `mysqldump` dumps triggers with their associated tables by default.)

- Copy a table, using a different name for the copy:

  - Dump the table:
    ```
    $ mysqldump cookbook mail > mail.sql
    ```

- Reload the table into a different database that does *not* contain a table with that name:

```
$ mysql other_db < mail.sql
```

- Rename the table:

```
$ mysql other_db
mysql> RENAME mail TO mail2;
```

Or, to move the table into another database at the same time, qualify the new name with the database name:

```
$ mysql other_db
mysql> RENAME mail TO cookbook.mail2;
```

To perform a table-copying operation without an intermediary file, use a pipe to connect the mysqldump and mysql commands:

```
$ mysqldump cookbook mail | mysql other_db
$ mysqldump cookbook | mysql other_db
```

You may consider using the newer mysqlpump tool that works similarly to mysqldump but supports smarter filters and parallel processing. We discuss mysqlpump in Recipe 13.13.

Copying tables between MySQL servers

The preceding commands use mysqldump to copy tables among the databases managed by a single MySQL server. Output from mysqldump can also be used to copy tables from one server to another. Suppose that you want to copy the mail table from the cookbook database on the local host to the other_db database on the host *other-host.example.com*. One way to do this is to dump the output into a file:

```
$ mysqldump cookbook mail > mail.sql
```

Then copy *mail.sql* to *other-host.example.com*, and run the following command there to load the table into that MySQL server's other_db database:

```
$ mysql other_db < mail.sql
```

To accomplish this without an intermediary file, use a pipe to send the output of mysqldump directly over the network to the remote MySQL server. If you can connect to both servers from your local host, use this command:

```
$ mysqldump cookbook mail | mysql -h other-host.example.com other_db
```

The mysqldump half of the command connects to the local server and writes the dump output to the pipe. The mysql half of the command connects to the remote MySQL server on *other-host.example.com*. It reads the pipe for input and sends each statement to the *other-host.example.com* server.

If you cannot connect directly to the remote server using mysql from your local host, send the dump output into a pipe that uses ssh to invoke mysql remotely on *other-host.example.com*:

```
$ mysqldump cookbook mail | ssh other-host.example.com mysql other_db
```

ssh connects to *other-host.example.com* and launches mysql there. It then reads the mysqldump output from the pipe and passes it to the remote mysql process. ssh can be useful to send a dump over the network to a machine that has the MySQL port blocked by a firewall but that permits connections on the SSH port.

Regarding which table or tables to copy, similar principles apply as for local copies. To copy multiple tables over the network, name them all following the database argument of the mysqldump command. To copy an entire database, don't specify any table names after the database name; mysqldump dumps all its tables. To copy all databases that reside on your MySQL instance, specify the --all-databases option.

6.7 Copying an InnoDB Table Using Transportable Tablespaces

Problem

You want to copy an InnoDB table, but the table is too big, and dumping data from it in human-readable format takes long a time. Reload is not fast either.

Solution

Use transportable tablespaces.

Discussion

Tools like mysqldump and mysqlpump are good when you work with comparatively small tables or you want to examine the resulting SQL dump yourself before applying it to the target server. However, copying a table that occupies few gigabytes on the disk this way will take a lot of time. It will also create additional load on the server. To make things worse, protection mechanisms will affect other connections that use the same table.

To resolve this issue, binary backup and restore methods exist. These methods work on the binary table files without doing any additional data manipulations; therefore, performance is the same as if you run the cp command on Linux or copy on Windows.

As of version 8.0, MySQL stores table definitions in the data dictionary, while data is stored in the separate files. The format and name of these files depend on the storage engine. In the case of InnoDB, they are individual, general and system tablespaces. Individual tablespace files store data for each table individually and can be used for the method we describe in this section. If your tables are stored in the system or in general tablespaces, you first need to convert them to use the individual tablespace format:

```
ALTER TABLE tbl_name TABLESPACE = innodb_file_per_table;
```

To find out if your table resides in the system or in general tablespaces, query the INNODB_TABLES table in the Information Schema:

```
mysql> SELECT NAME, SPACE_TYPE FROM INFORMATION_SCHEMA.INNODB_TABLES
    -> WHERE NAME LIKE 'test/%';
+------------------------------------------+------------+
| NAME                                     | SPACE_TYPE |
+------------------------------------------+------------+
| test/residing_in_system_tablespace       | System     |
| test/residing_in_individual_tablespace   | Single     |
| test/residing_in_general_tablespace      | General    |
+------------------------------------------+------------+
```

Once you are ready to copy the tablespace, log in into the mysql client and execute:

```
FLUSH TABLES limbs FOR EXPORT;
```

This command will prepare the tablespace file for being copied and additionally create a configuration file with a .cfg extension that will contain the table metadata.

Keep the MySQL client open and in the other terminal window, copy the tablespace and configuration files into the desired location:

```
cp /var/lib/mysql/cookbook/limbs.{cfg,ibd} .
```

Once the copy finishes, unlock the table:

```
UNLOCK TABLES;
```

Now you can import the tablespace into a remote server or into a different database on the same local server.

The first step is to create a table with exactly the same definition as the original one. You can find the table definition by running the SHOW CREATE TABLE command:

```
source> SHOW CREATE TABLE limbs\G
*************************** 1. row ***************************
       Table: limbs
Create Table: CREATE TABLE `limbs` (
  `thing` varchar(20) DEFAULT NULL,
  `legs` int DEFAULT NULL,
  `arms` int DEFAULT NULL
) ENGINE=InnoDB DEFAULT CHARSET=utf8mb4 COLLATE=utf8mb4_0900_ai_ci
1 row in set (0.00 sec)
```

Once you've obtained it, connect to the destination database and create a table:

```
destination> USE cookbook_copy;
Database changed
```

```
destination> CREATE TABLE `limbs` (
       ->    `thing` varchar(20) DEFAULT NULL,
       ->    `legs` int DEFAULT NULL,
       ->    `arms` int DEFAULT NULL
       -> ) ENGINE=InnoDB DEFAULT CHARSET=utf8mb4 COLLATE=utf8mb4_0900_ai_ci;
Query OK, 0 rows affected (0.03 sec)
```

After a new empty table is created, discard its tablespace:

```
ALTER TABLE limbs DISCARD TABLESPACE;
```

 DISCARD TABLESPACE removes tablespace files. Be very careful with this command. If you make a typo and discard a tablespace for the wrong table, it can't be restored.

After tablespace is discarded, copy the table files into the new database directory:

```
$ sudo cp limbs.{cfg,ibd} /var/lib/mysql/cookbook_copy
$ sudo chown mysql:mysql /var/lib/mysql/cookbook_copy/limbs.{cfg,ibd}
```

Then import the tablespace.

```
ALTER TABLE limbs IMPORT TABLESPACE;
```

See Also

For additional information about exchanging tablespace files between MySQL databases and servers, see "Importing InnoDB Tables" (*https://oreil.ly/Jt38Q*).

6.8 Copying a MyISAM Table Using an sdi File

Problem

You want to copy a large MyISAM table on MySQL 8.0.

Solution

Use the IMPORT TABLE command.

Discussion

Tables that use the MyISAM storage engine support the importation of the raw table files with the help of the IMPORT TABLE statement. To export MyISAM tables without the risk of corrupting data during migration, open a MySQL connection first and flush the table files to the disk with a read lock:

```
FLUSH TABLES limbs_myisam WITH READ LOCK;
```

Then copy the table data, index, and metadata files into the backup location:

```
$ sudo cp /var/lib/mysql/cookbook/limbs_myisam.{MYD,MYI} .
$ sudo bash -c 'cp /var/lib/mysql/cookbook/limbs_myisam_*.sdi . '
```

Unlock the original table:

The table's metadata file with the `.sdi` extension has a random sequence of digits in its name, therefore use `sudo` to copy it to allow the shell process to expand the file glob pattern.

To copy a MyISAM table into the desired destination, put the table's metadata file with `.sdi` extension into the directory, specified by the `--secure-file-priv` option, or into any directory, readable by the target MySQL server if such an option is not set. Then copy the index and datafile into the target database directory:

```
$ sudo cp limbs_myisam.{MYD,MYI} /var/lib/mysql/cookbook_copy/
$ sudo chown mysql:mysql /var/lib/mysql/cookbook_copy/limbs_myisam.{MYD,MYI}
```

Then connect to the database and import the table:

```
IMPORT TABLE FROM '/tmp/limbs_myisam_11560.sdi';
```

If you are copying the table into a database with a different name, you need to edit the `sdi` file manually and replace the value of the `schema_ref` with the target database name.

## CHAPTER 7

Working with Strings

7.0 Introduction

Like most types of data, string values can be compared for equality or inequality or relative ordering. However, strings have additional properties to consider:

- A string can be binary or nonbinary. Binary strings are used for raw data such as images, music files, or encrypted values. Nonbinary strings are used for character data such as text and are associated with a character set and collation (sort order).

- A character set determines which characters are legal in a string. You can choose collations according to whether you need comparisons to be case sensitive or case insensitive, or to use the rules of a particular language.

- Data types for binary strings are `BINARY`, `VARBINARY`, and `BLOB`. Data types for nonbinary strings are `CHAR`, `VARCHAR`, and `TEXT`, each of which permits `CHARACTER SET` and `COLLATE` attributes.

- You can convert a binary string to a nonbinary string and vice versa, or convert a nonbinary string from one character set or collation to another.

- You can use a string in its entirety or extract substrings from it. Strings can be combined with other strings.

- You can apply pattern-matching operations to strings.

- Full-text searching is available for efficient queries on large collections of text.

This chapter discusses how to use those properties so that you can store, retrieve, and manipulate strings according to any requirements your applications have.

Scripts to create the tables used in this chapter are located in the *tables* directory of the `recipes` distribution.

7.1 String Properties

One string property is whether it is binary or nonbinary:

- A binary string is a sequence of bytes. It can contain any type of information, such as images, MP3 files, or compressed or encrypted data. A binary string is not associated with a character set, even if you store a value such as abc that looks like ordinary text. Binary strings are compared byte by byte using numeric byte values.

- A nonbinary string is a sequence of characters. It stores text that has a particular character set and collation. The character set defines which characters can be stored in the string. The collation defines the character ordering, which affects comparison and sorting operations.

To see which character sets are available for nonbinary strings, use this statement:

```
mysql> SHOW CHARACTER SET;
+----------+-----------------------------+---------------------+---------+
| Charset  | Description                 | Default collation   | Maxlen  |
+----------+-----------------------------+---------------------+---------+
| big5     | Big5 Traditional Chinese    | big5_chinese_ci     |    2    |
...
| koi8r    | KOI8-R Relcom Russian       | koi8r_general_ci    |    1    |
| latin1   | cp1252 West European        | latin1_swedish_ci   |    1    |
| latin2   | ISO 8859-2 Central European | latin2_general_ci   |    1    |
...
| utf8     | UTF-8 Unicode               | utf8_general_ci     |    3    |
| utf8mb4  | UTF-8 Unicode               | utf8mb4_0900_ai_ci  |    4    |
...
```

The default character set in MySQL 8.0 is utf8mb4 with collation of utf8mb4_0900_ai_ci. If you must store characters from several languages in a single column, consider using one of the Unicode character sets (such as utf8mb4 or utf16) because they can represent characters from multiple languages.

Some character sets contain only single-byte characters, whereas others permit multibyte characters. Some multibyte character sets contain characters of varying lengths. For others, all characters have a fixed length. For example, Unicode data can be stored using the utf8mb4 character set, in which characters take from one to four bytes, or the utf16 character set, in which all characters take two bytes.

In MySQL, to use the full set of Unicode characters, including supplemental characters that lie outside the Basic Multilingual Plane (BMP), use utf8mb4, in which characters take from one to four bytes. Other Unicode character sets that include supplemental characters are utf16, utf16le, and utf32.

To determine whether a given string contains multibyte characters, use the LENGTH( ) and CHAR_LENGTH( ) functions, which return the length of a string in bytes and characters, respectively. If LENGTH( ) is greater than CHAR_LENGTH( ) for a given string, multibyte characters are present:

- The utf8 Unicode character set has multibyte characters, but a given utf8 string might contain only single-byte characters, as in the following example:

```
mysql> SET @s = CONVERT('abc' USING utf8mb4);
mysql> SELECT LENGTH(@s), CHAR_LENGTH(@s);
+------------+-----------------+
| LENGTH(@s) | CHAR_LENGTH(@s) |
+------------+-----------------+
|          3 |               3 |
+------------+-----------------+
```

- For the utf16 Unicode character set, all characters are encoded using two bytes, even if they are single-byte characters in another character set, such as latin1. Thus, every utf16 string contains multibyte characters:

```
mysql> SET @s = CONVERT('abc' USING utf16);
mysql> SELECT LENGTH(@s), CHAR_LENGTH(@s);
+------------+-----------------+
| LENGTH(@s) | CHAR_LENGTH(@s) |
+------------+-----------------+
|          6 |               3 |
+------------+-----------------+
```

Another property of nonbinary strings is collation, which determines the sort order of characters in the character set. Use SHOW COLLATION to see all available collations; add a LIKE clause to see the collations for a particular character set:

```
mysql> SHOW COLLATION LIKE 'utf8mb4%';
+------------------------+---------+-----+---------+----------+---------+---------------+
| Collation              | Charset | Id  | Default | Compiled | Sortlen | Pad_attribute |
+------------------------+---------+-----+---------+----------+---------+---------------+
| utf8mb4_0900_ai_ci     | utf8mb4 | 255 | Yes     | Yes      |       0 | NO PAD        |
| utf8mb4_0900_as_ci     | utf8mb4 | 305 |         | Yes      |       0 | NO PAD        |
..
| utf8mb4_es_0900_ai_ci  | utf8mb4 | 263 |         | Yes      |       0 | NO PAD        |
| utf8mb4_es_0900_as_cs  | utf8mb4 | 286 |         | Yes      |       0 | NO PAD        |
| utf8mb4_es_trad_0900...| utf8mb4 | 270 |         | Yes      |       0 | NO PAD        |
| utf8mb4_es_trad_0900...| utf8mb4 | 293 |         | Yes      |       0 | NO PAD        |
..
| utf8mb4_tr_0900_ai_ci  | utf8mb4 | 265 |         | Yes      |       0 | NO PAD        |
| utf8mb4_tr_0900_as_cs  | utf8mb4 | 288 |         | Yes      |       0 | NO PAD        |
| utf8mb4_turkish_ci     | utf8mb4 | 233 |         | Yes      |       8 | PAD SPACE     |
| utf8mb4_unicode_520_ci | utf8mb4 | 246 |         | Yes      |       8 | PAD SPACE     |
```

In contexts where no collation is specified explicitly, strings in a given character set use the collation with Yes in the Default column. As shown, the default collation for utf8mb4 is utf8mb4_0900_ai_ci. (Default collations are also displayed by SHOW CHARACTER SET.)

A collation can be case sensitive (a and A are different), case insensitive (a and A are the same), or binary (two characters are the same or different based on whether their numeric values are equal). A collation name ending in _ci, _cs, or _bin is case insensitive, case sensitive, or binary, respectively.

Binary strings and binary collations both use numeric values. The difference is that binary string comparisons are always based on single-byte units, whereas a binary collation compares nonbinary strings using *character* numeric values; depending on the character set, some of these might be multibyte values.

The following example illustrates how collation affects sort order. Suppose that a table contains a utf8mb4 string column and has the following rows:

```
mysql> CREATE TABLE t (c CHAR(3) CHARACTER SET utf8mb4);
mysql> INSERT INTO t (c) VALUES('AAA'),('bbb'),('aaa'),('BBB');
mysql> SELECT c FROM t;
+------+
| c    |
+------+
| AAA  |
| bbb  |
| aaa  |
| BBB  |
+------+
```

By applying the COLLATE operator to the column, you can choose which collation to use for sorting and thus affect the order of the result:

- A case-insensitive collation sorts a and A together, placing them before b and B. However, for a given letter, it does not necessarily order one lettercase before another, as shown by the following result:
  ```
  mysql> SELECT c FROM t ORDER BY c COLLATE utf8mb4_turkish_ci;
  +------+
  | c    |
  +------+
  | AAA  |
  | aaa  |
  | bbb  |
  | BBB  |
  +------+
  ```

- A case-sensitive collation puts A and a before B and b and sorts lowercase before uppercase:
  ```
  mysql> SELECT c FROM t ORDER BY c COLLATE utf8mb4_tr_0900_as_cs;
  +------+
  | c    |
  +------+
  | aaa  |
  | AAA  |
  | bbb  |
  | BBB  |
  +------+
  ```

- A binary collation sorts characters using their numeric values. Assuming that uppercase letters have numeric values less than those of lowercase letters, a binary collation results in the following ordering:

```
mysql> SELECT c FROM t ORDER BY c COLLATE utf8mb4_bin;
+------+
| c    |
+------+
| AAA  |
| BBB  |
| aaa  |
| bbb  |
+------+
```

Note that because characters in different lettercases have different numeric values, a binary collation produces a case-sensitive ordering. However, the order differs from that for the case-sensitive collation.

If you require that comparison and sorting operations use the sorting rules of a particular language, choose a language-specific collation. For example, if you store strings using the utf8mb4 character set, the default collation (utf8mb4_0900_ai_ci) treats ch and ll as two-character strings. To use the traditional Spanish ordering that treats ch and ll as single characters that follow c and l, respectively, specify the utf8mb4_spanish2_ci collation. The two collations produce different results, as shown here:

```
mysql> CREATE TABLE t (c CHAR(2) CHARACTER SET utf8mb4);
mysql> INSERT INTO t (c) VALUES('cg'),('ch'),('ci'),('lk'),('ll'),('lm');
mysql> SELECT c FROM t ORDER BY c COLLATE utf8mb4_general_ci;
+------+
| c    |
+------+
| cg   |
| ch   |
| ci   |
| lk   |
| ll   |
| lm   |
+------+
mysql> SELECT c FROM t ORDER BY c COLLATE utf8mb4_spanish2_ci;
+------+
| c    |
+------+
| cg   |
| ci   |
| ch   |
| lk   |
| lm   |
| ll   |
+------+
```

Ideally, set the collation in the column definition in case you are not using the default collation by running the following:

```
mysql> CREATE TABLE t (c CHAR(2) CHARACTER SET utf8mb4 COLLATE utf8mb4_spanish2_ci);
```

This will make sure to avoid possible query performance degradation during sort operations by using wrong collation.

7.2 Choosing a String Data Type

Problem

You want to store string data but aren't sure which data type is the most appropriate.

Solution

Choose the data type according to the characteristics of the information to be stored and how you need to use it. Consider questions such as these:

- Are the strings binary or nonbinary?
- Does case sensitivity matter?
- What is the maximum string length?
- Do you want to store fixed- or variable-length values?
- Do you need to retain trailing spaces?
- Is there a fixed set of permitted values?

Discussion

MySQL provides several binary and nonbinary string data types. These types come in pairs, as shown in the following table. The maximum length is in bytes, whether the type is binary or nonbinary. For nonbinary types, the maximum number of *characters* is less for strings that contain multibyte characters, as we show in Table 7-1.

Table 7-1. Maximum number of characters per data type

Binary data type	Nonbinary data type	Maximum length
BINARY	CHAR	255
VARBINARY	VARCHAR	65,535
TINYBLOB	TINYTEXT	255
BLOB	TEXT	65,535
MEDIUMBLOB	MEDIUMTEXT	16,777,215
LONGBLOB	LONGTEXT	4,294,967,295

For the BINARY and CHAR data types, MySQL stores column values using a fixed width. For example, values stored in a BINARY(10) or CHAR(10) column always take 10 bytes or 10 characters, respectively. Shorter values are padded to the required length as necessary when stored. For BINARY, the pad value is 0x00 (the zero-valued byte, also known as ASCII NUL). CHAR values are padded with spaces for storage, and trailing spaces are stripped upon retrieval.

For VARBINARY, VARCHAR, and the BLOB and TEXT types, MySQL stores values using only as much storage as required, up to the maximum column length. No padding is added or stripped when values are stored or retrieved.

To preserve trailing pad values that are present in the original strings that are stored, use a data type for which no stripping occurs. For example, if you store character (nonbinary) strings that might end with spaces and want to preserve them, use VAR CHAR or one of the TEXT data types. The following statements illustrate the difference in trailing-space handling for CHAR and VARCHAR columns:

```
mysql> DROP TABLE IF EXISTS t;
mysql> CREATE TABLE t (c1 CHAR(10), c2 VARCHAR(10));
mysql> INSERT INTO t (c1,c2) VALUES('abc      ','abc      ');
mysql> SELECT c1, c2, CHAR_LENGTH(c1), CHAR_LENGTH(c2) FROM t;
+------+------------+-----------------+-----------------+
| c1   | c2         | CHAR_LENGTH(c1) | CHAR_LENGTH(c2) |
+------+------------+-----------------+-----------------+
| abc  | abc        |               3 |              10 |
+------+------------+-----------------+-----------------+
```

This shows that if you store a string that contains trailing spaces into a CHAR column, they're removed when you retrieve the value.

A table can include a mix of binary and nonbinary string columns, and its nonbinary columns can use different character sets and collations. When you declare a nonbinary string column, use the CHARACTER SET and COLLATE attributes if you require a particular character set and collation. For example, if you need to store utf8mb4 (Unicode) and sjis (Japanese) strings, you might define a table with two columns like this:

```
CREATE TABLE mytbl
(
  utf8str VARCHAR(100) CHARACTER SET utf8mb4 COLLATE utf8mb4_danish_ci,
  sjisstr VARCHAR(100) CHARACTER SET sjis COLLATE sjis_japanese_ci
);
```

The CHARACTER SET and COLLATE clauses are each optional in a column definition:

- If you specify CHARACTER SET and omit COLLATE, the default collation for the character set is used.

- If you specify COLLATE and omit CHARACTER SET, the character set implied by the collation name (the first part of the name) is used. For example, utf8mb4_dan ish_ci and sjis_japanese_ci imply utf8mb4 and sjis, respectively. This means that the CHARACTER SET attributes could have been omitted from the preceding CREATE TABLE statement.

- If you omit both CHARACTER SET and COLLATE, the column is assigned the table default character set and collation. A table definition can include those attributes following the closing parenthesis at the end of the CREATE TABLE statement. If present, they apply to columns that have no explicit character set or collation of their own. If omitted, the table defaults are taken from the database defaults. You can specify the database defaults when you create the database with the CREATE DATABASE statement. The server defaults apply to the database if they are omitted.

The server default character set and collation for MySQL 8.0 are utf8mb4 and utf8mb4_0900_ai_ci, so strings by default use the utf8mb4 character set and are not case sensitive. To change this, set the character_set_server and collation_server system variables at server startup (see Recipe 22.1).

MySQL also supports ENUM and SET string types, which are used for columns that have a fixed set of permitted values. The CHARACTER SET and COLLATE attributes apply to these data types as well.

7.3 Setting the Client Connection Character Set

Problem

You're executing SQL statements or producing query results that don't use the default character set.

Solution

Use SET NAMES or an equivalent method to set your connection to the proper character set.

Discussion

When you send information back and forth between your application and the server, you may need to tell MySQL the appropriate character set. For example, the default character set is latin1, but that may not always be the proper character set to use for connections to the server. If you have Greek data, displaying it using latin1 will result in gibberish on your screen. If you use Unicode strings in the utf8mb4 character set, latin1 might not be sufficient to represent all the characters that you might need.

To deal with this problem, configure your connection to use the appropriate character set. You have several ways to do this:

- Issue a SET NAMES statement after you connect:

  ```
  mysql> SET NAMES 'utf8mb4';
  ```

  SET NAMES permits the connection collation to be specified as well:

  ```
  mysql> SET NAMES 'utf8mb4' COLLATE 'utf8mb4_0900_ai_ci';
  ```

- If your client program supports the `--default-character-set` option, you can use it to specify the character set at program invocation time. `mysql` is one such program. Put the option in an option file so that it takes effect each time you connect to the server:

  ```
  [mysql]
  default-character-set=utf8mb4
  ```

- If you set the environment for your working environment using the `LANG` or `LC_ALL` environment variable on Unix, or the code page setting on Windows, MySQL client programs automatically detect which character set to use. For example, setting `LC_ALL` to `en_US.UTF-8` causes programs such as `mysql` to use `utf8`.

- Some programming interfaces provide their own method of setting the character set. For example, MySQL Connector/J for Java clients detects the character set used on the server side automatically when you connect, but you can specify a different set explicitly using the `characterEncoding` property in the connection URL. The property value should be the Java-style character-set name. To select `utf8mb4`, you might use a connection URL like this:

  ```
  jdbc:mysql://localhost/cookbook?characterEncoding=UTF-8
  ```

  This is preferable to SET NAMES because Connector/J performs character-set conversion on behalf of the application but is unaware of which character set applies if you use SET NAMES. Similar principles apply to programs written for other APIs. For PHP Data Objects (PDO), use a `charset` option in your data source name (DSN) string (this works in PHP 5.3.6 or later):

  ```
  $dsn = "mysql:host=localhost;dbname=cookbook;charset=utf8mb4";
  ```

  For Connector/Python, specify a `charset` connection parameter:

  ```
  conn_params = {
    "database": "cookbook",
    "host": "localhost",
    "user": "cbuser",
    "password": "cbpass",
    "charset": "utf8mb4",
  }
  ```

  For Go, specify a `charset` connection parameter:

  ```
  db, err := sql.Open("mysql",
          "cbuser:cbpass@tcp(127.0.0.1:3306)/cookbook?charset=utf8mb4")
  ```

  Some APIs may also provide a parameter to specify the collation.

Some character sets cannot be used as the connection character set: utf16, utf16le, and utf32.

You should also ensure that the character set used by your display device matches what you use for MySQL. Otherwise, even with MySQL handling the data properly, it might display as garbage. Suppose that you use the mysql program in a terminal window and that you configure MySQL to use utf8mb4 and store utf8mb4-encoded Turkish data. If you set your terminal window to use euc-tr encoding, that is also Turkish but its encoding for Turkish characters differs from utf8mb4, so the data will not display as you expect. (If you use autodetection, this should not be an issue.)

In the following example, Turkish characters inserted in a table will show up garbled in a connection made with a different character set:

```
mysql> DROP TABLE IF EXISTS t;
mysql> CREATE TABLE t (c CHAR(3) CHARACTER SET utf8mb4);
mysql> INSERT INTO t (c) VALUES('iii'),('şşş'),('ööö'),('ççç');
```

From another connection, using the Latin1 client character set will result in the following:

```
mysql> \s
--------------
mysql  Ver 8.0.27 for Linux on x86_64 (MySQL Community Server - GPL)
...
Server characterset:    utf8mb4
Db      characterset:    utf8mb4
Client characterset:    latin1
Conn.  characterset:    latin1
...
SELECT c from t;
+------+
| c    |
+------+
| iii  |
| ???  |
| ♦♦♦  |
| ♦♦♦  |
+------+
```

To verify that you're connected with the correct character set to the MySQL command-line interface, issue the following to show the status:

```
mysql> \s
--------------
mysql  Ver 8.0.27 for Linux on x86_64 (MySQL Community Server - GPL)
...
Server characterset:    utf8mb4
Db      characterset:    utf8mb4
Client characterset:    utf8mb4
Conn.  characterset:    utf8mb4
...
```

```
SELECT c from t;
+------+
| c    |
+------+
| iii  |
| $$$  |
| ööö  |
| ççç  |
+------+
```

7.4 Writing String Literals

Problem

You need to write literal strings in SQL statements.

Solution

Learn the syntax rules that govern string values.

Discussion

You can write strings several ways:

- Enclose the text of the string within single quotes or double quotes:

  ```
  'my string'
  "my string"
  ```

  When the ANSI_QUOTES SQL mode is enabled, you cannot use double quotes for quoting strings: the server interprets a double quote as the quoting character for identifiers such as table or column names and not for strings (see Recipe 4.6). If you adopt the convention of always writing quoted strings using single quotes, MySQL interprets them as strings and not as identifiers regardless of the ANSI_QUOTES setting.

- Use hexadecimal notation. Each pair of hex digits produces one byte of the string. abcd can be written using any of these formats:

  ```
  0x61626364
  X'61626364'
  x'61626364'
  ```

  MySQL treats strings written using hex notation as binary strings. Not coincidentally, it's common for applications to use hex strings when constructing SQL statements that refer to binary values:

  ```
  INSERT INTO t SET binary_col = 0xdeadbeef;
  ```

- To specify a character set for interpretation of a literal string, use an introducer consisting of a character-set name preceded by an underscore:

  ```
  _utf8mb4 'abcd'
  _utf16 'abcd'
  ```

An introducer tells the server how to interpret the string that follows it. For _utf8mb4 'abcd', the server produces a string consisting of four single-byte characters. For _ucs2 'abcd', the server produces a string consisting of two two-byte characters because ucs2 is a double-byte character set.

To ensure that a string is a binary string or that a nonbinary string has a specific character set or collation, use the instructions for string conversion given in Recipe 7.5.

A quoted string that includes the same quote character produces a syntax error if executed by an API or in the mysql batch mode:

```
mysql -e "SELECT 'I'm asleep'"
ERROR 1064 (42000) at line 1: You have an error in your SQL syntax; ↵
check the manual that corresponds to your MySQL server version ↵
for the right syntax to use near 'asleep'' at line 1
```

If executed interactively by the mysql client, it waits for the closing quote:

```
mysql> SELECT 'I'm asleep';
    '>
    '> '\c
mysql>
```

You have several ways to deal with this:

- Enclose a string containing single quotes within double quotes (assuming that ANSI_QUOTES is disabled), or enclose a string containing double quotes within single quotes:

```
mysql> SELECT "I'm asleep", 'He said, "Boo!"';
+------------+-----------------+
| I'm asleep | He said, "Boo!" |
+------------+-----------------+
| I'm asleep | He said, "Boo!" |
+------------+-----------------+
```

- To include a quote character within a string quoted by the same kind of quote, double the quote or precede it with a backslash. When MySQL reads the statement, it strips the extra quote or the backslash:

```
mysql> SELECT 'I''m asleep', 'I\'m wide awake';
+------------+----------------+
| I'm asleep | I'm wide awake |
+------------+----------------+
| I'm asleep | I'm wide awake |
+------------+----------------+
mysql> SELECT "He said, ""Boo!""", "And I said, \"Yikes!\"";
+----------------+----------------------+
| He said, "Boo!" | And I said, "Yikes!" |
+----------------+----------------------+
| He said, "Boo!" | And I said, "Yikes!" |
+----------------+----------------------+
```

A backslash turns off any special meaning of the following character, including itself. To write a literal backslash within a string, double it:

```
mysql> SELECT 'Install MySQL in C:\\mysql on Windows';
+-------------------------------------+
| Install MySQL in C:\mysql on Windows |
+-------------------------------------+
| Install MySQL in C:\mysql on Windows |
+-------------------------------------+
```

Backslash causes a temporary escape from normal string processing rules, so sequences such as \', \", and \\ are called *escape sequences*. Others recognized by MySQL are \b (backspace), \n (newline, also called *linefeed*), \r (carriage return), \t (tab), and \0 (ASCII NUL).

- Write the string as a hex value:

```
mysql> SELECT 0x49276D2061736C656570;
+------------------------+
| 0x49276D2061736C656570 |
+------------------------+
| I'm asleep             |
+------------------------+
```

 Starting from version 8.0, mysql client is running with the --binary-as-hex option by default. If you do not disable this option, you will get binary output as hex values. For example, for the preceding command, you'll see the following:

```
mysql> SELECT 0x49276D2061736C656570;
+------------------------------------------------+
| 0x49276D2061736C656570                         |
+------------------------------------------------+
| 0x49276D2061736C656570                         |
+------------------------------------------------+
1 row in set (0,00 sec)
```

To get human-readable output, start the mysql client with the --binary-as-hex=0 option.

See Also

If you execute SQL statements from within a program, you can refer to strings or binary values symbolically and let your programming interface take care of quoting: use the placeholder mechanism provided by the language's database-access API (see Recipe 4.5). Alternatively, load binary values such as images from files using the LOAD_FILE() function (see the MySQL documentation (*https://oreil.ly/ah9zM*)).

7.5 Checking or Changing a String's Character Set or Collation

Problem

You want to know the character set or collation of a string or change a string to some other character set or collation.

Solution

To check a string's character set or collation, use the CHARSET() or COLLATION() function. To change its character set, use the CONVERT() function. To change its collation, use the COLLATE operator.

Discussion

For a table created as follows, you know that values stored in the column c have a character set of utf8 and a collation of utf8_danish_ci:

```
CREATE TABLE t (c CHAR(10) CHARACTER SET utf8mb4 COLLATE utf8mb4_danish_ci);
```

But sometimes it's not so clear what character set or collation applies to a string. Server configuration can affect literal strings and some string functions, and other string functions return values in a specific character set. Symptoms that you have the wrong character set or collation are that a collation-mismatch error occurs for a comparison operation, or a lettercase conversion doesn't work properly.

To determine a string's character set or collation, use the CHARSET() or COLLATION() function. For example, did you know that the USER() function returns a Unicode string?

```
mysql> SELECT USER(), CHARSET(USER()), COLLATION(USER());
+----------------+----------------+-------------------+
| USER()         | CHARSET(USER()) | COLLATION(USER()) |
+----------------+----------------+-------------------+
| cbuser@localhost | utf8mb3       | utf8_general_ci   |
+----------------+----------------+-------------------+
```

String values that take their character set and collation from the current client configuration may change properties if the configuration changes. This is true for literal strings:

```
mysql> SET NAMES 'utf8mb4';
mysql> SELECT CHARSET('abc'), COLLATION('abc');
+----------------+-------------------+
| CHARSET('abc') | COLLATION('abc')  |
+----------------+-------------------+
| utf8mb4        | utf8mb4_0900_ai_ci|
+----------------+-------------------+
mysql> SET NAMES 'utf8mb4' COLLATE 'utf8mb4_bin';
```

```
mysql> SELECT CHARSET('abc'), COLLATION('abc');
+----------------+------------------+
| CHARSET('abc') | COLLATION('abc') |
+----------------+------------------+
| utf8mb4        | utf8mb4_bin      |
+----------------+------------------+
```

For a binary string, the CHARSET() or COLLATION() function returns a value of binary, which means that the string is compared and sorted based on numeric byte values, not character collation values.

To convert a string from one character set to another, use the CONVERT() function:

```
mysql> SET @s1 = _latin1 'my string', @s2 = CONVERT(@s1 USING utf8mb4);
mysql> SELECT CHARSET(@s1), CHARSET(@s2);
+--------------+--------------+
| CHARSET(@s1) | CHARSET(@s2) |
+--------------+--------------+
| latin1       | utf8mb4      |
+--------------+--------------+
```

To change the collation of a string, use the COLLATE operator:

```
mysql> SET @s1 = _latin1 'my string', @s2 = @s1 COLLATE latin1_spanish_ci;
mysql> SELECT COLLATION(@s1), COLLATION(@s2);
+-------------------+-------------------+
| COLLATION(@s1)    | COLLATION(@s2)    |
+-------------------+-------------------+
| latin1_swedish_ci | latin1_spanish_ci |
+-------------------+-------------------+
```

The new collation must be legal for the character set of the string. For example, you can use the utf8_general_ci collation with utf8mb3 strings but not with latin1 strings:

```
mysql> SELECT _latin1 'abc' COLLATE utf8_bin;
ERROR 1253 (42000): COLLATION 'utf8_bin' is not valid for
CHARACTER SET 'latin1'
```

To convert both the character set and collation of a string, use CONVERT() to change the character set, and apply the COLLATE operator to the result:

```
mysql> SET @s1 = _latin1 'my string';
mysql> SET @s2 = CONVERT(@s1 USING utf8mb4) COLLATE utf8mb4_spanish_ci;
mysql> SELECT CHARSET(@s1), COLLATION(@s1), CHARSET(@s2), COLLATION(@s2);
+--------------+-------------------+--------------+------------------+
| CHARSET(@s1) | COLLATION(@s1)    | CHARSET(@s2) | COLLATION(@s2)   |
+--------------+-------------------+--------------+------------------+
| latin1       | latin1_swedish_ci | utf8         | utf8_spanish_ci  |
+--------------+-------------------+--------------+------------------+
```

The CONVERT() function can also convert binary strings to nonbinary strings and vice versa. To produce a binary string, use binary; any other character-set name produces a nonbinary string:

```
mysql> SET @s1 = _latin1 'my string';
mysql> SET @s2 = CONVERT(@s1 USING binary);
```

```
mysql> SET @s3 = CONVERT(@s2 USING utf8mb4);
mysql> SELECT CHARSET(@s1), CHARSET(@s2), CHARSET(@s3);
+--------------+--------------+--------------+
| CHARSET(@s1) | CHARSET(@s2) | CHARSET(@s3) |
+--------------+--------------+--------------+
| latin1       | binary       | utf8mb4      |
+--------------+--------------+--------------+
```

Alternatively, produce binary strings using the CAST function, which is equivalent to CONVERT(*str* USING binary):

```
mysql> SELECT CHARSET(CAST(_utf8mb4 'my string' AS binary));
+-----------------------------------------------+
| CHARSET(CAST(_utf8mb4 'my string' AS binary)) |
+-----------------------------------------------+
| binary                                        |
+-----------------------------------------------+
```

See also Recipe 7.3 for more information on character sets.

7.6 Converting the Lettercase of a String

Problem

You want to convert a string to uppercase or lowercase.

Solution

Use the UPPER() or LOWER() function. If they don't work, you're probably trying to convert a binary string. Convert it to a nonbinary string that has a character set and collation and is subject to case mapping.

Discussion

The UPPER() and LOWER() functions convert the lettercase of a string:

```
mysql> SELECT thing, UPPER(thing), LOWER(thing) FROM limbs;
+--------------+--------------+--------------+
| thing        | UPPER(thing) | LOWER(thing) |
+--------------+--------------+--------------+
| human        | HUMAN        | human        |
| insect       | INSECT       | insect       |
| squid        | SQUID        | squid        |
| fish         | FISH         | fish         |
| centipede    | CENTIPEDE    | centipede    |
| table        | TABLE        | table        |
| armchair     | ARMCHAIR     | armchair     |
| phonograph   | PHONOGRAPH   | phonograph   |
| tripod       | TRIPOD       | tripod       |
| Peg Leg Pete | PEG LEG PETE | peg leg pete |
| space alien  | SPACE ALIEN  | space alien  |
+--------------+--------------+--------------+
```

But some strings are "stubborn" and resist lettercase conversion. To get human-readable output, start the mysql client with binary-as-hex=0 option:

```
mysql> CREATE TABLE t (b VARBINARY(10)) SELECT 'aBcD' AS b;
mysql> SELECT b, UPPER(b), LOWER(b) FROM t;
+------+----------+----------+
| b    | UPPER(b) | LOWER(b) |
+------+----------+----------+
| aBcD | aBcD     | aBcD     |
+------+----------+----------+
```

This problem occurs for strings that have a BINARY or BLOB data type. These are binary strings that have no character set or collation. Lettercase does not apply, and UPPER() and LOWER() do nothing.

To map a binary string to a given lettercase, convert it to a nonbinary string, choosing a character set that has uppercase and lowercase characters. The case-conversion functions then work as you expect because the collation provides case mapping:

```
mysql> SELECT b,
    -> UPPER(CONVERT(b USING utf8mb4)) AS upper,
    -> LOWER(CONVERT(b USING utf8mb4)) AS lower
    -> FROM t;
+------+-------+-------+
| b    | upper | lower |
+------+-------+-------+
| aBcD | ABCD  | abcd  |
+------+-------+-------+
```

The example uses a table column, but the same principles apply to binary string literals and string expressions.

If you're not sure whether a string expression is binary or nonbinary, use the CHAR SET() function to find out; see Recipe 7.5.

To convert the lettercase of only part of a string, break it into pieces, convert the relevant piece, and put the pieces back together. Suppose that you want to convert only the initial character of a string to uppercase. The following expression accomplishes that:

```
CONCAT(UPPER(LEFT(str,1)),MID(str,2))
```

But it's ugly to write an expression like that each time you need it. For convenience, define a stored function:

```
mysql> CREATE FUNCTION initial_cap (s VARCHAR(255))
    -> RETURNS VARCHAR(255) DETERMINISTIC
    -> RETURN CONCAT(UPPER(LEFT(s,1)),MID(s,2));
```

Then you can capitalize initial characters more easily:

```
mysql> SELECT thing, initial_cap(thing) FROM limbs;
+-------------+--------------------+
| thing       | initial_cap(thing) |
+-------------+--------------------+
| human       | Human              |
| insect      | Insect             |
| squid       | Squid              |
| fish        | Fish               |
| centipede   | Centipede          |
| table       | Table              |
| armchair    | Armchair           |
| phonograph  | Phonograph         |
| tripod      | Tripod             |
| Peg Leg Pete| Peg Leg Pete       |
| space alien | Space alien        |
+-------------+--------------------+
```

For more information about writing stored functions, see Chapter 11.

7.7 Comparing String Values

Problem

You want to know whether strings are equal or unequal or which appears first in lexical order.

Solution

Use a comparison operator. But remember that strings have properties such as case sensitivity that you must take into account. A string comparison might be case sensitive when you don't want it to be, or vice versa.

As is the case with other data types, you can compare string values for equality, inequality, or relative ordering:

```
mysql> SELECT 'cat' = 'cat', 'cat' = 'dog', 'cat' <> 'cat', 'cat' <> 'dog';
+---------------+---------------+----------------+----------------+
| 'cat' = 'cat' | 'cat' = 'dog' | 'cat' <> 'cat' | 'cat' <> 'dog' |
+---------------+---------------+----------------+----------------+
|             1 |             0 |              0 |              1 |
+---------------+---------------+----------------+----------------+
mysql> SELECT 'cat' < 'auk', 'cat' < 'dog', 'cat' BETWEEN 'auk' AND 'eel';
+---------------+---------------+-------------------------------+
| 'cat' < 'auk' | 'cat' < 'dog' | 'cat' BETWEEN 'auk' AND 'eel' |
+---------------+---------------+-------------------------------+
|             0 |             1 |                             1 |
+---------------+---------------+-------------------------------+
```

Discussion

However, comparison and sorting properties of strings are subject to complications that don't apply to other types of data. For example, sometimes you must ensure that a string comparison is case sensitive that would not otherwise be, or vice versa. This section describes how to do that.

String comparison properties depend on whether the operands are binary or nonbinary strings:

- A binary string is a sequence of bytes and is compared using numeric byte values. Lettercase has no meaning. However, because letters in different cases have different byte values, comparisons of binary strings effectively are case sensitive. (That is, a and A are unequal.) To compare binary strings such that lettercase does not matter, convert them to nonbinary strings that have a case-insensitive collation.

- A nonbinary string is a sequence of characters and is compared in character units. (Depending on the character set, some characters might have multiple bytes.) The string has a character set that defines the legal characters and a collation that defines their sort order. The collation also determines whether to consider characters in different lettercases the same in comparisons. If the collation is case sensitive, and you want a case-insensitive collation (or vice versa), convert the strings to use a collation with the desired case-comparison properties.

By default, strings have a character set of utf8mb4 and a collation of utf8mb4_0900_ai_ci unless you reconfigure the server (see Recipe 22.1). This results in case-insensitive string comparisons.

The following example shows how two binary strings that compare as unequal can be handled so that they are equal when compared as case-insensitive nonbinary strings:

```
mysql> SET @s1 = CAST('cat' AS BINARY), @s2 = CAST('CAT' AS BINARY);
mysql> SELECT @s1 = @s2;
+-----------+
| @s1 = @s2 |
+-----------+
|         0 |
+-----------+
mysql> SET @s1 = CONVERT(@s1 USING utf8mb4) COLLATE utf8mb4_0900_ai_ci;
mysql> SET @s2 = CONVERT(@s2 USING utf8mb4) COLLATE utf8mb4_0900_ai_ci;
mysql> SELECT @s1 = @s2;
+-----------+
| @s1 = @s2 |
+-----------+
|         1 |
+-----------+
```

In this case, because utf8mb4_0900_ai_ci is the default collation for utf8mb4, you can omit the COLLATE operator:

```
mysql> SET @s1 = CONVERT(@s1 USING utf8mb4);
mysql> SET @s2 = CONVERT(@s2 USING utf8mb4);
mysql> SELECT @s1 = @s2;
+-----------+
| @s1 = @s2 |
+-----------+
|         1 |
+-----------+
```

The next example shows how to compare, in case-sensitive fashion, two strings that are not case sensitive:

```
mysql> SET @s1 = _latin1 'cat', @s2 = _latin1 'CAT';
mysql> SELECT @s1 = @s2;
+-----------+
| @s1 = @s2 |
+-----------+
|         1 |
+-----------+
mysql> SELECT @s1 COLLATE latin1_general_cs = @s2 COLLATE latin1_general_cs
    ->     AS '@s1 = @s2';
+-----------+
| @s1 = @s2 |
+-----------+
|         0 |
+-----------+
```

If you compare a binary string with a nonbinary string, the comparison treats both operands as binary strings:

```
mysql> SELECT _latin1 'cat' = CAST('CAT' AS BINARY);
+---------------------------------------+
| _latin1 'cat' = CAST('CAT' AS BINARY) |
+---------------------------------------+
|                                     0 |
+---------------------------------------+
```

Thus, to compare two nonbinary strings as binary strings, cast them as the BINARY data type to either one when comparing them:

```
mysql> SET @s1 = _latin1 'cat', @s2 = _latin1 'CAT';
mysql> SELECT @s1 = @s2, CAST(@s1 AS BINARY) = @s2, @s1 = CAST(@s2 AS BINARY);
+-----------+---------------------------+---------------------------+
| @s1 = @s2 | CAST(@s1 AS BINARY) = @s2 | @s1 = CAST(@s2 AS BINARY) |
+-----------+---------------------------+---------------------------+
|         1 |                         0 |                         0 |
+-----------+---------------------------+---------------------------+
```

If you find that you've declared a column using a type not suited to the kind of comparisons for which you typically use it, use ALTER TABLE to change the type. Suppose that this table stores news articles:

```
CREATE TABLE news
(
  id      INT UNSIGNED NOT NULL AUTO_INCREMENT,
  article BLOB,
  PRIMARY KEY (id)
);
```

Here the `article` column is declared as a `BLOB`. That is a binary string type, so comparisons of text stored in the column are made without regard to character set. (In effect, they are case sensitive.) If that's not what you want, use `ALTER TABLE` to convert the column to a nonbinary type that has a case-insensitive collation:

```
ALTER TABLE news
  MODIFY article TEXT CHARACTER SET utf8mb4 COLLATE utf8mb4_0900_ai_ci;
```

7.8 Converting Between Decimal, Octal, and Hexadecimal Formats

Problem

You want to convert from one numeric base to another.

Solution

Use the `CONV()` function and SQL pattern described in this section.

Discussion

It is difficult to operate literals as text strings in some formats such as `HEX`. An alternative method is to convert them to binary values. This will produce a data type with a value of BINARY(16) that is 128 bits long. Using `BIN()`, `OCT()`, and `HEX()` functions to convert between decimal numbers to binary, octal, and hexadecimal is already possible. What if we need to do the reverse? This is where the `CONV()` function comes in handy. With the `CONV()` function, we can convert from one numeric base system to another.

The syntax to use the `CONV()` function is as follows:

```
CONV(number, from_base, to_base)
```

- A `number` is a value that we want to convert from one numeric base to another.
- A `from_base` is the original base value of the numeric base limited to a value between 2 and 36.
- A `to_base` is the target value of the numeric base. This value can be between 2 and 36 or -2 and -36:

```
mysql> SELECT CONV(8, 10, 2) AS DectoBin;
+----------+
| DectoBin |
+----------+
| 1000     |
+----------+
```

Similar to the BIN() function, we get the same result, although the BIN() function returns a string:

```
mysql> SELECT BIN(8);
+--------+
| BIN(8) |
+--------+
| 1000   |
+--------+
```

Likewise, we can convert values between one another in reverse:

```
mysql> SELECT CONV('F', 16, 10) AS Hex2Dec;
+---------+
| Hex2Dec |
+---------+
| 15      |
+---------+
```

7.9 Converting Between ASCII, BIT, and Hexadecimal Formats

Problem

You want to convert from one string format to another.

Solution

Use the MySQL CHAR(), ASCII(), and BIT_LENGTH() functions and SQL pattern described in this section.

Discussion

There are many powerful string functions to support MySQL's string operations. In different use cases, we may have to convert them to have different results. Using some of the string functions, such as ASCII(), we can convert between other formats like BIT and HEX.

The syntax to use the ASCII() function is as follows:

```
ASCII(character);
```

The ASCII() function returns only the left-most character's numeric value of the string. This is similar to MySQL's ORD() function.

```
mysql> SELECT ASCII("LARA");
+---------------+
| ASCII("LARA") |
+---------------+
|            76 |
+---------------+

mysql> SELECT ASCII("L");
+---------------+
| ASCII("L")    |
+---------------+
|            76 |
+---------------+
```

As you can see, the result is the same for both strings. The function takes only the leftmost character of the string.

In the following example, we will convert a string value to HEX format:

```
mysql> SELECT DISTINCT CONV(ASCII("LARA"),10,16) as ASCII2HEX;
+-----------+
| ASCII2HEX |
+-----------+
| 4C        |
+-----------+
```

Say we have table name and want to get all unique last_name from this table in HEX format:

```
mysql> SELECT DISTINCT CONV(ASCII(last_name),10,16) from name;
+-----------------------------+
| CONV(ASCII(last_name),10,16) |
+-----------------------------+
| 42                          |
| 47                          |
| 57                          |
+-----------------------------+
```

Bit operations before MySQL 8.0 handled unsigned 64-bit integer values. After MySQL 8.0, bit operations extended to handle binary string arguments. This allowed strings that are not integers or binary strings to be converted. A UUID (Universal Unique Identifier) specified by RFC 4122 (*https://oreil.ly/TQA22*) is a 128-bit globally unique value when complete uniqueness is required. UUIDs also come in handy for security purposes since they don't reveal any information about data. A UUID is represented in human-readable format as utf8mb4 with the string of five hexadecimal numbers. A good example is converting a UUID value to binary by using the UUID_TO_BIN function (we are running mysql with the binary-as-hex option):

```
mysql> SELECT UUID();
+--------------------------------------+
| UUID()                               |
+--------------------------------------+
| e52e0524-385b-11ec-99b1-054a662275e4 |
+--------------------------------------+

mysql> SELECT UUID_TO_BIN(UUID());
+------------------------------------------+
| UUID_TO_BIN(UUID())                      |
+------------------------------------------+
| 0xB8D11A66134E11ECB46CC15B8175C680       |
+------------------------------------------+
```

Later, we can convert this value to compare the bit count using the BIT_COUNT()
function. This function is mainly used to identify active bits in a given input:

```
mysql> select UUID_TO_BIN(UUID()) into @bin_uuid;
mysql> select BIT_COUNT(@bin_uuid);
+----------------------+
| BIT_COUNT(@bin_uuid) |
+----------------------+
|                   57 |
+----------------------+
```

The purpose of the BIT_COUNT() function is to identify active bits in a given decimal
value, for example, if we wanted to identify the active bits in number 18. Binary
conversion of 18 is 10010; hence, the active bits are only two:

```
mysql> select BIT_COUNT(18);
+---------------+
| BIT_COUNT(18) |
+---------------+
|             2 |
+---------------+
```

The BIT_COUNT() function can be combined with the BIT_OR() function to calculate
the following problem. The BIT_OR() function returns the bitwise *or* all the bits in an
expression.

Say we want to find out the number of Sundays in the month of November. We will
create a table called sundays:

```
mysql> CREATE TABLE sundays (
    year YEAR,
    month INT UNSIGNED ,
    day INT UNSIGNED
);
mysql> INSERT INTO sundays VALUES(2021,11,7),
                     (2021,11,14),
                     (2021,11,21),
                     (2021,11,28);
mysql> SELECT year, month, BIT_COUNT(BIT_OR(1 << day)) AS 'Number of Sundays'
    -> FROM sundays GROUP BY year,month;
```

```
+------+-------+-------------------+
| year | month | Number of Sundays |
+------+-------+-------------------+
| 2021 |    11 |                 4 |
+------+-------+-------------------+
```

This example can be extended to find the number of holidays in a given calendar year or date range.

Another use case is IPv6 and IPv4 network addresses that are string values by default. To return the binary value to represent it in numeric format, the INET_ATON() function can be used. This function converts the dotted-quad IPv4 address string representation to a numeric value. While use cases for this function may vary, it is widely used for storing the source and destination of IP addresses for data. Once the IPv4 address is stored in a numeric value, it can be indexed and processed faster:

```
mysql> SELECT INET_ATON('10.0.2.1');
+-----------------------+
| INET_ATON('10.0.2.1') |
+-----------------------+
|             167772673 |
+-----------------------+

mysql> SELECT HEX(INET6_ATON('10.0.2.1'));
+----------------------------+
| HEX(INET6_ATON('10.0.2.1')) |
+----------------------------+
| 0A000201                   |
+----------------------------+
```

7.10 Pattern Matching with SQL Patterns

Problem

You want to perform a pattern match, not a literal comparison.

Solution

Use the LIKE operator and a SQL pattern, described in this section. Or use a regular-expression pattern match, described in Recipe 7.11.

Discussion

Patterns are strings that contain special characters known as *metacharacters* because they stand for something other than themselves. MySQL provides two kinds of pattern matching. One is based on SQL patterns and the other on regular expressions. SQL patterns are more standard among different database systems, but regular expressions are more powerful. The two kinds of pattern match use different operators and different metacharacters. This section describes SQL patterns. Recipe 7.11 describes regular expressions.

The example here uses a table named `metal` that contains the following rows:

```
+----------+
| name     |
+----------+
| gold     |
| iron     |
| lead     |
| mercury  |
| platinum |
| tin      |
+----------+
```

SQL pattern matching uses the `LIKE` and `NOT LIKE` operators rather than = and <> to perform matching against a pattern string. Patterns may contain two special meta-characters: _ matches any single character, and % matches any sequence of characters, including the empty string. You can use these characters to create patterns that match a variety of values:

- Strings that begin with a particular substring:
  ```
  mysql> SELECT name FROM metal WHERE name LIKE 'me%';
  +----------+
  | name     |
  +----------+
  | mercury  |
  +----------+
  ```

- Strings that end with a particular substring:
  ```
  mysql> SELECT name FROM metal WHERE name LIKE '%d';
  +------+
  | name |
  +------+
  | gold |
  | lead |
  +------+
  ```

- Strings that contain a particular substring at any position:
  ```
  mysql> SELECT name FROM metal WHERE name LIKE '%in%';
  +----------+
  | name     |
  +----------+
  | platinum |
  | tin      |
  +----------+
  ```

- Strings that contain a substring at a specific position (the pattern matches only if at occurs at the third position of the `name` column):
  ```
  mysql> SELECT name FROM metal where name LIKE '__at%';
  +----------+
  | name     |
  +----------+
  | platinum |
  +----------+
  ```

A SQL pattern matches successfully only if it matches the entire comparison value. Of the following two pattern matches, only the second succeeds:

```
'abc' LIKE 'b'
'abc' LIKE '%b%'
```

To reverse the sense of a pattern match, use NOT LIKE. The following statement finds strings that contain no i characters:

```
mysql> SELECT name FROM metal WHERE name NOT LIKE '%i%';
+---------+
| name    |
+---------+
| gold    |
| lead    |
| mercury |
+---------+
```

SQL patterns do not match NULL values. This is true both for LIKE and for NOT LIKE:

```
mysql> SELECT NULL LIKE '%', NULL NOT LIKE '%';
+---------------+-------------------+
| NULL LIKE '%' | NULL NOT LIKE '%' |
+---------------+-------------------+
|          NULL |              NULL |
+---------------+-------------------+
```

In some cases, pattern matches are equivalent to substring comparisons. For example, using patterns to find strings at one end or the other of a string is like using LEFT() or RIGHT(), as shown in Table 7-2.

Table 7-2. Pattern match versus substring comparison

Pattern match	Substring comparison
str LIKE 'abc%'	LEFT(*str*,3) = 'abc'
str LIKE '%abc'	RIGHT(*str*,3) = 'abc'

If you're matching against a column that is indexed and you have a choice of using a pattern or an equivalent LEFT() expression, you'll likely find the pattern match to be faster. MySQL can use the index to narrow the search for a pattern that begins with a literal string. With LEFT(), it cannot. Also, a LIKE comparison with a % in the beginning can be slow due to the optimizer checking the entire content of the string.

Case sensitivity of a pattern match is like that of a string comparison. That is, it depends on whether the operands are binary or nonbinary strings, and for nonbinary strings, it depends on their collation. See Recipe 7.7 for a discussion of how these factors apply to comparisons.

Unlike some other database systems, MySQL permits pattern matches to be applied to nonstring values such as numbers or dates, which can sometimes be useful. Table 7-3 shows some ways to test a DATE value d using function calls that extract date parts and using the equivalent pattern matches. The pairs of expressions are true for dates occurring in the year 1975, in the month of June, or on the 21st day of the month:

Table 7-3. Pattern matching for temporal data types

Function value test	Pattern match test
YEAR(d) = 1975	d LIKE '1975-%'
MONTH(d) = 6	d LIKE '%-06-%'
DAYOFMONTH(d) = 21	d LIKE '%-21'

7.11 Pattern Matching with Regular Expressions

Problem

You want to perform a pattern match, not a literal comparison.

Solution

Use the REGEXP operator and a regular expression pattern, described in this section. Or use a SQL pattern, described in Recipe 7.10.

Discussion

SQL patterns (see Recipe 7.10) are likely to be implemented by other database systems, so they're reasonably portable beyond MySQL. On the other hand, they're somewhat limited. For example, you can easily write a SQL pattern, %abc%, to find strings that contain abc, but you cannot write a single SQL pattern to identify strings that contain any of the characters a, b, or c. Nor can you match string content based on character types such as letters or digits.

For such operations, MySQL supports another type of pattern-matching operation based on regular expressions and the REGEXP operator (or NOT REGEXP to reverse the sense of the match). REGEXP matching uses the pattern elements shown in Table 7-4.

Table 7-4. Popular regular expressions syntax

Pattern	What the pattern matches
^	Beginning of string
$	End of string
.	Any single character
[...]	Any character listed between the square brackets
[^...]	Any character not listed between the square brackets
p1|p2|p3	Alternation; matches any of the patterns p1, p2, or p3
*	Zero or more instances of preceding element
+	One or more instances of preceding element
{n}	n instances of preceding element
{m,n}	m through n instances of preceding element

You may already be familiar with these regular expression pattern characters; many of them are the same as those used by vi, grep, sed, and other Unix utilities that support regular expressions. Most of them are also used in the regular expressions understood by programming languages. (For a discussion of pattern matching in programs for data validation and transformation, see Chapter 14.)

Recipe 7.10 shows how to use SQL patterns to match substrings at the beginning or end of a string or at an arbitrary or specific position within a string. You can do the same things with regular expressions:

- Use the following for strings that begin with a particular substring:

```
mysql> SELECT name FROM metal WHERE name REGEXP '^me';
+---------+
| name    |
+---------+
| mercury |
+---------+
```

- Use the following for strings that end with a particular substring:

```
mysql> SELECT name FROM metal WHERE name REGEXP 'd$';
+------+
| name |
+------+
| gold |
| lead |
+------+
```

- Use the following for strings that contain a particular substring at any position:

```
mysql> SELECT name FROM metal WHERE name REGEXP 'in';
+----------+
| name     |
+----------+
| platinum |
| tin      |
+----------+
```

- Use the following for strings that contain a particular substring at a specific position:

```
mysql> SELECT name FROM metal WHERE name REGEXP '^..at';
+----------+
| name     |
+----------+
| platinum |
+----------+
```

In addition, regular expressions have other capabilities and can perform matches that SQL patterns cannot. For example, regular expressions can contain character classes, which match any character in the class:

- To write a character class, use square brackets and list the characters you want the class to match inside the brackets. Thus, the pattern [abc] matches a, b, or c.

- Classes can indicate ranges of characters; use a dash between the beginning and end of the range. [a-z] matches any letter, [0-9] matches digits, and [a-z0-9] matches letters or digits.

- To negate a character class ("match any character but these"), begin the list with a ^ character. For example, [^0-9] matches anything but digits.

MySQL's regular-expression capabilities also support POSIX character classes. These match specific character sets, as described in Table 7-5:

Table 7-5. POSIX regular expressions syntax

POSIX class	What the class matches
[:alnum:]	Alphabetic and numeric characters
[:alpha:]	Alphabetic characters
[:blank:]	Whitespace (space or tab characters)
[:cntrl:]	Control characters
[:digit:]	Digits
[:graph:]	Graphic (nonblank) characters
[:lower:]	Lowercase alphabetic characters
[:print:]	Graphic or space characters
[:punct:]	Punctuation characters
[:space:]	Space, tab, newline, carriage return
[:upper:]	Uppercase alphabetic characters
[:xdigit:]	Hexadecimal digits (0-9, a-f, A-F)

POSIX classes are intended for use within character classes, so use them within square brackets. The following expression matches values that contain any hexadecimal digit character:

```
mysql> SELECT name, name REGEXP '[[:xdigit:]]' FROM metal;
+----------+---------------------------+
| name     | name REGEXP '[[:xdigit:]]' |
+----------+---------------------------+
| gold     |                         1 |
| iron     |                         0 |
| lead     |                         1 |
| mercury  |                         1 |
| platinum |                         1 |
| tin      |                         0 |
+----------+---------------------------+
```

Regular expressions can specify alternations using this syntax:

```
alternative1|alternative2|...
```

An alternation is similar to a character class in the sense that it matches if any of the alternatives match. But unlike a character class, the alternatives are not limited to single characters. They can be multiple-character strings or even patterns. The following alternation matches strings that begin with a vowel or end with d:

```
mysql> SELECT name FROM metal WHERE name REGEXP '^[aeiou]|d$';
+------+
| name |
+------+
| gold |
| iron |
| lead |
+------+
```

Parentheses can be used to group alternations. For example, to match strings that consist entirely of digits or entirely of letters, you might try this pattern, using an alternation:

```
mysql> SELECT '0m' REGEXP '^[[:digit:]]+|[[:alpha:]]+$';
+------------------------------------------+
| '0m' REGEXP '^[[:digit:]]+|[[:alpha:]]+$' |
+------------------------------------------+
|                                        1 |
+------------------------------------------+
```

However, as the query result shows, the pattern doesn't work. That's because the ^ groups with the first alternative, and the $ groups with the second alternative. So the pattern actually matches strings that begin with one or more digits, or strings that end with one or more letters. If you group the alternatives within parentheses, the ^ and $ apply to both of them, and the pattern acts as you expect:

```
mysql> SELECT '0m' REGEXP '^([[:digit:]]+|[[:alpha:]]+)$';
+--------------------------------------------+
| '0m' REGEXP '^([[:digit:]]+|[[:alpha:]]+)$' |
+--------------------------------------------+
|                                          0 |
+--------------------------------------------+
```

Unlike SQL pattern matches, which are successful only if the pattern matches the entire comparison value, regular expressions are successful if the pattern matches anywhere within the value. The following two pattern matches are equivalent in the sense that each one succeeds only for strings that contain a b character, but the first is more efficient because the pattern is simpler:

```
'abc' REGEXP 'b'
'abc' REGEXP '^.*b.*$'
```

Regular expressions do not match NULL values. This is true both for REGEXP and for NOT REGEXP:

```
mysql> SELECT NULL REGEXP '.*', NULL NOT REGEXP '.*';
+------------------+----------------------+
| NULL REGEXP '.*' | NULL NOT REGEXP '.*' |
+------------------+----------------------+
|             NULL |                 NULL |
+------------------+----------------------+
```

Because a regular expression matches a string if the pattern is found anywhere in the string, you must take care not to inadvertently specify a pattern that matches the empty string. If you do, it matches any non-NULL value. For example, the pattern a* matches any number of a characters, even none. If your goal is to match only strings containing nonempty sequences of a characters, use a+ instead. The + requires one or more instances of the preceding pattern element for a match.

As with SQL pattern matches performed using LIKE, regular-expression matches performed with REGEXP sometimes are equivalent to substring comparisons. As shown in Table 7-6, the ^ and $ metacharacters serve much the same purpose as LEFT() or RIGHT(), at least if you're looking for literal strings.

Table 7-6. Regular expressions versus substring comparison functions

Pattern match	Substring comparison
str REGEXP '^abc'	LEFT(str,3) = 'abc'
str REGEXP 'abc$'	RIGHT(str,3) = 'abc'

For nonliteral patterns, it's typically not possible to construct an equivalent substring comparison. For example, to match strings that begin with any nonempty sequence of digits, use this pattern match:

```
str REGEXP '^[0-9]+'
```

That is something that LEFT() cannot do (and neither can LIKE, for that matter).

Case sensitivity of a regular-expression match is like that of a string comparison. That is, it depends on whether the operands are binary or nonbinary strings, and for nonbinary strings, it depends on their collation. See Recipe 7.7 for a discussion of how these factors apply to comparisons.

Prior to version 8.0.4, regular expressions worked only for single-byte character sets. In MySQL 8.0.4, this limitation was removed, and now you can use regular expressions with multibyte character sets such as utf8mb4 or sjis.

7.12 Reversing the String Content

Problem

You want to modify a string and find its reverse form.

Solution

Use the REVERSE() function.

Discussion

You can reverse a string or a substring by using the REVERSE() function. This function converts any string value into its reverse form by character. It's also often used in SELECT statements, like many other functions in this chapter.

The syntax to use the REVERSE() function is as follows:

```
REVERSE(expression)
```

The following examples show the basic functionality of the REVERSE() function:

```
mysql> SELECT REVERSE("sports flow");
+-----------------------+
| REVERSE("sports flow") |
+-----------------------+
| wolf strops           |
+-----------------------+

mysql> SELECT REVERSE(0123456789);
+--------------------+
| REVERSE(0123456789) |
+--------------------+
| 987654321          |
+--------------------+

mysql> SELECT REVERSE("0123456789");
+----------------------+
| REVERSE("0123456789") |
+----------------------+
| 9876543210           |
+----------------------+
```

The following example shows that when the expression is a numeric value, the zero value is omitted by the function:

```
mysql> SELECT REVERSE(001122334455);
+-----------------------+
| REVERSE(001122334455) |
+-----------------------+
| 5544332211            |
+-----------------------+
```

While we can reverse any expression, some words return exactly the same written in reverse, known as a *palindrome*. For such strings, the REVERSE function will return a string equal to the original one, for example, as follows:

```
mysql> SELECT REVERSE("STEP ON NO PETS");
+---------------------------+
| REVERSE("STEP ON NO PETS") |
+---------------------------+
| STEP ON NO PETS           |
+---------------------------+
```

The broader example uses the top_names table from the *recipes* distribution that stores the most commonly used names. Among these names, we'll find out the number of palindromic names:

```
mysql> SELECT COUNT(*) FROM top_names WHERE REVERSE(top_name) = top_name;
+----------+
| COUNT(*) |
+----------+
|      234 |
+----------+
```

Just to get a sample from this count, we can have a look at names start with *U*.

```
mysql> SELECT top_name FROM top_names
    -> WHERE REVERSE(top_name) = top_name
    -> AND top_name LIKE "U%";
+----------+
| top_name |
+----------+
| ULU      |
| UTU      |
+----------+
```

7.13 Searching for Substrings

Problem

You want to know whether a given string occurs within another string.

Solution

Use LOCATE() or a pattern match.

Discussion

The `LOCATE()` function takes two arguments representing the substring that you're looking for and the string in which to look for it. The return value is the position at which the substring occurs, or 0 if it's not present. An optional third argument may be given to indicate the position within the string at which to start looking:

```
mysql> SELECT name, LOCATE('in',name), LOCATE('in',name,3) FROM metal;
+----------+-------------------+---------------------+
| name     | LOCATE('in',name) | LOCATE('in',name,3) |
+----------+-------------------+---------------------+
| gold     |                 0 |                   0 |
| iron     |                 0 |                   0 |
| lead     |                 0 |                   0 |
| mercury  |                 0 |                   0 |
| platinum |                 5 |                   5 |
| tin      |                 2 |                   0 |
+----------+-------------------+---------------------+
```

To determine only whether the substring is present if you don't care about its position, an alternative is to use `LIKE` or `REGEXP`:

```
mysql> SELECT name, name LIKE '%in%', name REGEXP 'in' FROM metal;
+----------+------------------+------------------+
| name     | name LIKE '%in%' | name REGEXP 'in' |
+----------+------------------+------------------+
| gold     |                0 |                0 |
| iron     |                0 |                0 |
| lead     |                0 |                0 |
| mercury  |                0 |                0 |
| platinum |                1 |                1 |
| tin      |                1 |                1 |
+----------+------------------+------------------+
```

`LOCATE()`, `LIKE`, and `REGEXP` use the collation of their arguments to determine whether the search is case sensitive. Recipes 7.5 and 7.7 discuss changing the argument comparison properties if you want to change the search behavior.

7.14 Breaking Apart or Combining Strings

Problem

You want to extract a piece of a string or combine strings to form a larger string.

Solution

To obtain a piece of a string, use a substring-extraction function. To combine strings, use `CONCAT()`.

Discussion

You can break apart strings by using the appropriate substring-extraction functions. For example, `LEFT()`, `MID()`, and `RIGHT()` extract substrings from the left, middle, or right part of a string:

```
mysql> SET @date = '2015-07-21';
mysql> SELECT @date, LEFT(@date,4) AS year,
    -> MID(@date,6,2) AS month, RIGHT(@date,2) AS day;
+------------+------+-------+------+
| @date      | year | month | day  |
+------------+------+-------+------+
| 2015-07-21 | 2015 | 07    | 21   |
+------------+------+-------+------+
```

For `LEFT()` and `RIGHT()`, the second argument indicates how many characters to return from the left or right end of the string. For `MID()`, the second argument is the starting position of the substring you want (beginning from 1), and the third argument indicates how many characters to return.

The `SUBSTRING()` function takes a string and a starting position, returning everything to the right of the position. `MID()` acts the same way if you omit its third argument because `MID()` is actually a synonym for `SUBSTRING()`:

```
mysql> SET @date = '2015-07-21';
mysql> SELECT @date, SUBSTRING(@date,6), MID(@date,6);
+------------+--------------------+--------------+
| @date      | SUBSTRING(@date,6) | MID(@date,6) |
+------------+--------------------+--------------+
| 2015-07-21 | 07-21              | 07-21        |
+------------+--------------------+--------------+
```

Use `SUBSTRING_INDEX(str,c,n)` to return everything to the right or left of a given character. It searches into a string, *str*, for the *n*-th occurrence of the character *c* and returns everything to its left. If *n* is negative, the search for *c* starts from the right and returns everything to the right of the character:

```
mysql> SET @email = 'postmaster@example.com';
mysql> SELECT @email,
    -> SUBSTRING_INDEX(@email,'@',1) AS user,
    -> SUBSTRING_INDEX(@email,'@',-1) AS host;
+------------------------+------------+-------------+
| @email                 | user       | host        |
+------------------------+------------+-------------+
| postmaster@example.com | postmaster | example.com |
+------------------------+------------+-------------+
```

If there is no *n*-th occurrence of the character, `SUBSTRING_INDEX()` returns the entire string. `SUBSTRING_INDEX()` is case sensitive.

You can use substrings for purposes other than display, such as to perform comparisons. The following statement finds metal names having a first letter that lies in the last half of the alphabet:

```
mysql> SELECT name from metal WHERE LEFT(name,1) >= 'n';
+----------+
| name     |
+----------+
| platinum |
| tin      |
+----------+
```

To combine rather than pull apart strings, use the CONCAT() function. It concatenates its arguments and returns the result:

```
mysql> SELECT CONCAT(name,' ends in "d": ',IF(name LIKE '%d','YES','NO'))
    -> AS 'ends in "d"?'
    -> FROM metal;
+-------------------------+
| ends in "d"?            |
+-------------------------+
| gold ends in "d": YES   |
| iron ends in "d": NO    |
| lead ends in "d": YES   |
| mercury ends in "d": NO |
| platinum ends in "d": NO |
| tin ends in "d": NO     |
+-------------------------+
```

Concatenation can be useful for modifying column values "in place." For example, the following UPDATE statement adds a string to the end of each name value in the metal table:

```
mysql> UPDATE metal SET name = CONCAT(name,'ide');
mysql> SELECT name FROM metal;
+-------------+
| name        |
+-------------+
| goldide     |
| ironide     |
| leadide     |
| mercuryide  |
| platinumide |
| tinide      |
+-------------+
```

To undo the operation, strip the last three characters (the CHAR_LENGTH() function returns the length of a string in characters):

```
mysql> UPDATE metal SET name = LEFT(name,CHAR_LENGTH(name)-3);
mysql> SELECT name FROM metal;
+----------+
| name     |
+----------+
| gold     |
| iron     |
| lead     |
| mercury  |
| platinum |
| tin      |
+----------+
```

The concept of modifying a column in place can be applied to ENUM or SET values as well, which usually can be treated as string values even though they are stored internally as numbers. For example, to concatenate a SET element to an existing SET column, use CONCAT() to add the new value to the existing value, preceded by a comma. But remember to account for the possibility that the existing value might be NULL. In that case, set the column value equal to the new element, without the leading comma:

```
UPDATE tbl_name
SET set_col = IF(set_col IS NULL,val,CONCAT(set_col,',',val));
```

7.15 Using Full-Text Searches

Problem

You want to search long text columns.

Solution

Use a FULLTEXT index.

Discussion

Pattern matches enable you to look through any number of rows, but as the amount of text goes up, the match operation can become quite slow. It's also a common task to search for the same text in several string columns, but with pattern matching, that results in unwieldy queries:

```
SELECT * from tbl_name
WHERE col1 LIKE 'pat%' OR col2 LIKE 'pat%' OR col3 LIKE 'pat%' ...
```

A useful alternative is full-text searching, which is designed for looking through large amounts of text and can search multiple columns simultaneously. To use this capability, add a FULLTEXT index to your table, and then use the MATCH operator to look for strings in the indexed column or columns. FULLTEXT indexing can be used with MyISAM tables or InnoDB tables for nonbinary string data types (CHAR, VARCHAR, or TEXT).

Full-text searching is best illustrated with a reasonably good-sized body of text. If you don't have a sample dataset, you can find several repositories of freely available electronic text on the internet. For the examples here, the one we've chosen is the sample dump of the Amazon review data (2018), which is both available for the public to download and to scrape from Amazon Review Data (2018) (*https://oreil.ly/kZD0O*). Because of its size, this dataset is not included with the recipes distribution but is available separately as instructions at the GitHub repository. The Amazon distribution includes a file named *Appliances_5.json* that contains the product reviews for each category. This is a subset of larger datasets. As mostly text-based data are found on the internet, this data is only available in JSON data format. Some sample records look like this:

```
{
    "overall":        2.0,
    "verified":       false,
    "reviewTime":     "07 6, 2017",
    "reviewerID":     "A3LGZ8M29PBNGG",
    "asin":           "B000N6302Q",
    "style":          {"Color:": " Stainless Steel"},
    "reviewerName":   "nerenttt",
    "reviewText":     "Luved it for the few months it worked!↵
                      great little diamond ice cubes...",
    "unixReviewTime": 1499299200
}
```

What we're interested in here is the `reviewText` field, which has the large body of text we're looking to examine.

Each record contains the following fields:

overall
  Rating of the product

verified
  Purchase verification flag

reviewTime
  Date of the review

reviewerID
  ID of the reviewer(0 or N), for example, A2SUAM1J3GNN3B

asin
  ID of the product, for example, 0000013714

style
  A discretionary of the product metadata

reviewerName
  Name of the reviewer

reviewText
  Text of the review

unixReviewTime
  Time of the review (Unix time)

To import the records into MySQL, create a table named `reviews` that looks like this:

```
CREATE TABLE `reviews` (
    `id` BIGINT UNSIGNED NOT NULL AUTO_INCREMENT,
```

```
  `appliances_review` JSON NOT NULL,
    PRIMARY KEY (`id`)
);
```

To load JSON data to this table, we could have used MySQL built-in JSON functions, which is covered in Recipe 13.17. In some cases of large text, data can include escape characters, such as end of line, /n/n, which breaks the import. To overcome this, we'll use simple script to load the data, which is provided in the GitHub repository called load_amazon_reviews.py.

After loading the data, we'll convert the reviewText column as the generated column and add the FULLTEXT index to enable its use in full-text searching:

```
ALTER TABLE `reviews` ADD COLUMN `reviews_virtual` TEXT
GENERATED ALWAYS AS (`appliances_review` ->> '$.reviewText') STORED NOT NULL;
ALTER TABLE `reviews` ADD FULLTEXT idx_ft_json(reviews_virtual);
```

The table now has the FULLTEXT index to enable its use in full-text searching.

After creating the reviews table, load the *Appliances_5.json* file into it using this statement:

```
python3 load_amazon_reviews.py Appliances_5.json
```

You'll notice that the reviews table contains columns for both complete applian ces_review data and reviews_virtual to demonstrate the FULLTEXT index:

```
CREATE TABLE `reviews` (
  `id` bigint unsigned NOT NULL AUTO_INCREMENT,
  `appliances_review` json NOT NULL,
  `reviews_virtual` text GENERATED ALWAYS AS
    (json_unquote(json_extract(`appliances_review`,_utf8mb4'$.reviewText')))
  STORED NOT NULL,
  PRIMARY KEY (`id`),
  FULLTEXT KEY `idx_ft_json` (`reviews_virtual`)
) ENGINE=InnoDB AUTO_INCREMENT=2278 DEFAULT CHARSET=utf8mb4 COLLATE=utf8mb4_0900_ai_ci;
```

To perform a search using the FULLTEXT index, use MATCH() to name the indexed column and AGAINST() to specify what text to look for. For example, you might wonder, "How many times does the word *awesome* occur?" To answer that question, search the reviews_virtual column using this statement:

```
mysql> SELECT COUNT(*) from reviews WHERE MATCH(reviews_virtual) AGAINST('awesome');
+----------+
| COUNT(*) |
+----------+
|        3 |
+----------+
```

To verify that the FULLTEXT index was used, run the following:

```
mysql> EXPLAIN select reviews_virtual from reviews WHERE MATCH(reviews_virtual)
    -> AGAINST('awesome') \G
*************************** 1. row ***************************
          id: 1
  select_type: SIMPLE
```

```
           table: reviews
      partitions: NULL
            type: fulltext
   possible_keys: idx_ft_json
             key: idx_ft_json
         key_len: 0
             ref: const
            rows: 1
        filtered: 100.00
           Extra: Using where; Ft_hints: sorted
```

To find out which products had the keyword "excellent" in `reviews`, select the columns you want to see (the example here truncates the `reviews_virtual` column and uses \G so the results fit the page):

```
mysql> SELECT JSON_EXTRACT(appliances_review, "$.reviewerID") as ReviewerID,
    -> JSON_EXTRACT(appliances_review, "$.asin") as ProductID,
    -> JSON_EXTRACT(appliances_review, "$.overall") as Rating
    -> from reviews WHERE MATCH(reviews_virtual) AGAINST('excellent') \G
*************************** 1. row ***************************
ReviewerID: "A2CIEGHZ7L1WWR"
ProductID: "B00009W3PA"
    Rating: 5.0
*************************** 2. row ***************************
ReviewerID: "A1T1YSCDW0PD25"
ProductID: "B0013DN4NI"
    Rating: 5.0
*************************** 3. row ***************************
ReviewerID: "A1T1YSCDW0PD25"
ProductID: "B0013DN4NI"
    Rating: 5.0
*************************** 4. row ***************************
ReviewerID: "A26M3TN8QICJ3K"
ProductID: "B004XLDE5A"
    Rating: 5.0
*************************** 5. row ***************************
ReviewerID: "A2CIEGHZ7L1WWR"
ProductID: "B004XLDHSE"
    Rating: 5.0
```

By default, full-text searches compute a relevance ranking and use it for sorting. To make sure a search result is sorted the way you want, add an explicit ORDER BY clause:

```
SELECT reviews_virtual
FROM reviews WHERE MATCH(reviews_virtual) AGAINST('search string')
ORDER BY {column}, {column};
```

To see the relevance ranking, repeat the MATCH()...AGAINST() expression in the output column list.

To narrow the search further, include additional criteria. To provide additional fields in the search, we'll add the following virtual columns from JSON_EXTRACT:

```
ALTER TABLE `reviews`
    -> ADD COLUMN `reviews_virtual_vote` VARCHAR(10)
    -> GENERATED ALWAYS AS (`appliances_review` ->> '$.vote') STORED;
```

```
ALTER TABLE `reviews`
    -> ADD COLUMN `reviews_virtual_overall` VARCHAR(10)
    -> GENERATED ALWAYS AS (`appliances_review` ->> '$.overall') STORED;

ALTER TABLE `reviews`
    -> ADD COLUMN `reviews_virtual_verified` VARCHAR(10)
    -> GENERATED ALWAYS AS (`appliances_review` ->> '$.verified') STORED;
```

The following queries perform progressively more specific searches to determine how often each keyword occurs:

```
mysql> SELECT count(*) from reviews
    -> WHERE MATCH(reviews_virtual) AGAINST('good');
+----------+
| COUNT(*) |
+----------+
|      855 |
+----------+
mysql> SELECT count(*) from reviews
    -> WHERE MATCH(reviews_virtual) AGAINST('good')
    -> AND reviews_virtual_vote > 5;
+----------+
| COUNT(*) |
+----------+
|      620 |
+----------+
mysql> SELECT COUNT(*) from reviews
    -> WHERE MATCH(reviews_virtual) AGAINST('good')
    -> AND reviews_virtual_overall = 5;
+----------+
| COUNT(*) |
+----------+
|      646 |
+----------+
mysql> SELECT COUNT(*) from reviews
    -> WHERE MATCH(reviews_virtual) AGAINST('good')
    -> AND reviews_virtual_overall = 5 AND reviews_virtual_verified = "True";
+----------+
| COUNT(*) |
+----------+
|      645 |
+----------+
```

If you expect to frequently use search criteria that include other non-FULLTEXT columns, add regular indexes to those columns so that queries perform better. For example, to index the vote, overall rating, and verified columns, do this:

```
mysql> ALTER TABLE reviews ADD INDEX idx_vote (reviews_virtual_vote),
    -> ADD INDEX idx_overall(reviews_virtual_overall),
    -> ADD INDEX idx_verified(reviews_virtual_verified);
```

Search strings in full-text queries can include more than one word, and you might suppose that adding words would make a search more specific. But in fact that widens it because a full-text search returns rows that contain any of the words. In effect, the query performs an OR search for any of the words. The following queries illustrate this; they identify successively larger numbers of reviews as additional search words are added:

```
mysql> SELECT COUNT(*) from reviews
    -> WHERE MATCH(reviews_virtual) AGAINST('excellent');
+----------+
| COUNT(*) |
+----------+
|       11 |
+----------+
mysql> SELECT COUNT(*) from reviews
    -> WHERE MATCH(reviews_virtual) AGAINST('excellent product');
+----------+
| COUNT(*) |
+----------+
|     1480 |
+----------+
mysql> SELECT COUNT(*) from reviews
    -> WHERE MATCH(reviews_text) AGAINST('excellent product for home');
+----------+
| COUNT(*) |
+----------+
|     1486 |
+----------+
```

To perform a search for which each word in the search string must be present, see Recipe 7.17.

To use full-text searches that look through multiple columns simultaneously, name all the columns when you construct the FULLTEXT index:

```
ALTER TABLE tbl_name ADD FULLTEXT (col1, col2, col3);
```

To issue a search query that uses the index, name those same columns in the MATCH() list:

```
SELECT...FROM tbl_name
WHERE MATCH(col1, col2, col3) AGAINST('search string');
```

You need one such FULLTEXT index for each distinct combination of columns that you want to search.

See Also

For further information on FULLTEXT indexing, see Recipe 21.9.

7.16 Using a Full-Text Search with Short Words

Problem

Your full-text searches for short words return no rows.

Solution

Change the indexing engine's minimum-word-length parameter.

Discussion

In a text like the reviews, certain words have special significance, such as *ok* and *up*. You might want to check full-text index server variables first to make sure minimum length is satisfied by the engine:

```
mysql> SHOW GLOBAL VARIABLES LIKE 'innodb_ft_%';
+--------------------------------+------------+
| Variable_name                  | Value      |
+--------------------------------+------------+
| innodb_ft_aux_table            |            |
| innodb_ft_cache_size           | 8000000    |
| innodb_ft_enable_diag_print    | OFF        |
| innodb_ft_enable_stopword      | ON         |
| innodb_ft_max_token_size       | 84         |
| innodb_ft_min_token_size       | 3          |
| innodb_ft_num_word_optimize    | 2000       |
| innodb_ft_result_cache_limit   | 2000000000 |
| innodb_ft_server_stopword_table |           |
| innodb_ft_sort_pll_degree      | 2          |
| innodb_ft_total_cache_size     | 640000000  |
| innodb_ft_user_stopword_table  |            |
+--------------------------------+------------+
mysql> SELECT count(*) FROM reviews WHERE MATCH(reviews_virtual) AGAINST('ok');
+----------+
| count(*) |
+----------+
|        0 |
+----------+
SELECT count(*) FROM reviews WHERE MATCH(reviews_virtual) AGAINST('up');
+----------+
| count(*) |
+----------+
|        0 |
+----------+
```

One property of the indexing engine is that it ignores words that are "too common" (that is, words that occur in more than half the rows). This eliminates words such as *the* or *and* from the index, but that's not what is going on here. You can verify that by counting the total number of rows and by using SQL pattern matches to count the number of rows containing each word (see Recipe 10.1 regarding the use of COUNT() to produce multiple counts from the same set of values):

```
mysql> SELECT COUNT(*) AS Total_Reviews,
    -> COUNT(IF(reviews_virtual LIKE '%good%',1,NULL)) AS Good_Reviews,
    -> COUNT(IF(reviews_virtual LIKE '%great%',1,NULL)) AS Great_Reviews,
    -> COUNT(IF(reviews_virtual LIKE '%excellent%',1,NULL)) AS Excellent_Reviews
    -> FROM reviews;
+---------------+--------------+---------------+-------------------+
| Total_Reviews | Good_Reviews | Great_Reviews | Excellent_Reviews |
+---------------+--------------+---------------+-------------------+
|          2277 |          855 |          1095 |                11 |
+---------------+--------------+---------------+-------------------+
```

The InnoDB full-text indexing engine doesn't include words fewer than three characters long. The minimum word length is a configurable parameter; to change it, set the ft_min_word_len for MyISAM innodb_ft_min_token_size for the InnoDB storage engine system variable. For example, to tell the indexing engine to include words as short as two characters, add a line to the [mysqld] group of the */etc/my.cnf* file (or whatever option file you use for server settings):

```
[mysqld]
ft_min_word_len=2 ##MyISAM
innodb_ft_min_token_size=2 ##InnoDB
```

After making this change, restart the server. Next, rebuild the FULLTEXT index to take advantage of the changes. From the command line, set the innodb_optimize_full text_only parameter and run the OPTIMIZE operation:

```
mysql> SET GLOBAL innodb_optimize_fulltext_only=ON;
```

```
mysql> OPTIMIZE TABLE reviews;
```

For MyISAM, also run the REPAIR TABLE command:

```
mysql> REPAIR TABLE reviews QUICK;
```

You should also use REPAIR TABLE to rebuild the indexes for all other MyISAM tables that have FULLTEXT indexes.

Finally, try the new index to verify that it includes shorter words:

```
mysql> SELECT count(*) from reviews WHERE MATCH(reviews_virtual) AGAINST('ok');
+----------+
| count(*) |
+----------+
|       10 |
+----------+
mysql> SELECT count(*) from reviews WHERE MATCH(reviews_virtual) AGAINST('up');
+----------+
| COUNT(*) |
+----------+
|     1449 |
+----------+
```

7.17 Requiring or Prohibiting Full-Text Search Words

Problem

You want to require or prohibit specific words in a full-text search.

Solution

Use a Boolean-mode search.

Discussion

Normally, full-text searches return rows that contain any of the words in the search string, even if some of them are missing. For example, the following statement finds rows that contain either of the words *good* or *great*:

```
mysql> SELECT COUNT(*) FROM reviews
    -> WHERE MATCH(reviews_virtual) AGAINST('good great');
+----------+
| COUNT(*) |
+----------+
|     1330 |
+----------+
```

This behavior is undesirable if you want only rows that contain both words. One way to do this is to rewrite the statement to look for each word separately and join the conditions with AND:

```
mysql> SELECT COUNT(*) FROM reviews
    -> WHERE MATCH(reviews_virtual) AGAINST('good')
    -> AND MATCH(reviews_virtual) AGAINST('great');
+----------+
| COUNT(*) |
+----------+
|      620 |
+----------+
```

An easier way to require multiple words is with a Boolean-mode search. To do this, precede each word in the search string with a + character and add IN BOOLEAN MODE after the string:

```
mysql> SELECT COUNT(*) FROM reviews
    -> WHERE MATCH(reviews_virtual) AGAINST('+good +great' IN BOOLEAN MODE);
+----------+
| COUNT(*) |
+----------+
|      620 |
+----------+
```

Boolean-mode searches also permit you to exclude words by preceding each one with a - character.

The following queries select reviews rows containing the name "good" but not "great," and vice versa:

```
mysql> SELECT COUNT(*) FROM reviews
    -> WHERE MATCH(reviews_virtual) AGAINST('+good -great' IN BOOLEAN MODE);
+----------+
| COUNT(*) |
+----------+
|      235 |
+----------+
mysql> SELECT COUNT(*) FROM reviews
    -> WHERE MATCH(reviews_virtual) AGAINST('-good +great' IN BOOLEAN MODE);
+----------+
| COUNT(*) |
+----------+
|      475 |
+----------+
```

Another useful special character in Boolean searches is *; when appended to a search word, it acts as a wildcard operator. The following statement finds rows containing not only use but also words such as user, useful, and useless:

```
mysql> SELECT COUNT(*) FROM reviews
    -> WHERE MATCH(reviews_virtual) AGAINST('use*' IN BOOLEAN MODE);
+----------+
| COUNT(*) |
+----------+
|     1475 |
+----------+
```

For the complete list of Boolean full-text operators, see the MySQL Reference Manual (*https://oreil.ly/nLE94*).

7.18 Performing Full-Text Phrase Searches

Problem

You want to perform a full-text search for a phrase, that is, for words that occur adjacent to each other and in a specific order.

Solution

Use the full-text phrase-search capability.

Discussion

To find rows that contain a particular phrase, a simple full-text search doesn't work:

```
mysql> SELECT COUNT(*) FROM reviews
    -> WHERE MATCH(reviews_virtual) AGAINST('great product');
+----------+
| COUNT(*) |
+----------+
|     1725 |
+----------+
```

The query returns a result but not the one you're looking for. A full-text search computes a relevance ranking based on the presence of each word individually, no matter where it occurs within the reviews_virtual column, and the ranking is nonzero as long as any of the words are present. Consequently, that kind of statement tends to find too many rows.

Instead, use full-text Boolean mode, which supports phrase searching. Enclose the phrase in double quotes within the search string:

```
mysql> SELECT COUNT(*) FROM reviews
    -> WHERE MATCH(reviews_virtual) AGAINST('"great product"' IN BOOLEAN MODE);
+----------+
| COUNT(*) |
+----------+
|      216 |
+----------+
```

A phrase match succeeds if a column contains the same words as in the phrase, in the order specified.

## CHAPTER 8

Working with Dates and Times

8.0 Introduction

MySQL has several data types for representing dates and times, and many functions for operating on them. MySQL stores dates and times in specific formats, and it's important to understand them to avoid surprises in results from manipulating temporal data. This chapter covers the following aspects of working with date and time values in MySQL:

Choosing a temporal data type
> MySQL provides several temporal data types to choose from when you create tables. Knowing their properties enables you to choose them appropriately.

Displaying dates and times
> MySQL displays temporal values using specific formats by default. You can produce other formats by using the appropriate functions.

Changing the client time zone
> The server interprets TIMESTAMP and DATETIME values in the client's current time zone, not its own. Clients in different time zones should set their zone so that the server can properly interpret TIMESTAMP values for them.

Determining the current date and time
> MySQL provides functions that return the date and time. These are useful for applications that must know these values or need to calculate other temporal values in relation to them.

Tracking row modification times
> The TIMESTAMP and DATETIME data types have special properties that enable you to record row-creation and last-modification times automatically.

Breaking dates and times into component values and creating dates and times from component values

You can split date and time values when you need only a component, such as the month part of a date or the hour part of a time. Conversely, you can combine component values to synthesize dates and times.

Converting between dates or times and basic units

Some temporal calculations such as date arithmetic operations are more easily performed using the number of days or seconds represented by a date or time value than by using the value itself. MySQL can perform conversions between date and time values and more basic units such as days or seconds.

Date and time arithmetic

You can add or subtract temporal values to produce other temporal values or calculate intervals between values. Applications include age determination, relative date computation, and date shifting.

Selecting data based on temporal constraints

The calculations discussed in the preceding sections to produce output values can also be used in WHERE clauses to specify how to select rows using temporal conditions.

This chapter covers several MySQL functions for operating on date and time values, but there are many others. To familiarize yourself with the full set, consult the MySQL Reference Manual (*https://oreil.ly/F2eqz*). The variety of functions available to you means that it's often possible to perform a given temporal calculation more than one way. We sometimes illustrate alternative methods for achieving a given result, and many of the problems addressed in this chapter can be solved in ways other than those shown here. We invite you to experiment to find other solutions. You may find a method that's more efficient or that you find more intuitive.

Scripts that implement recipes discussed in this chapter are located in the *dates* directory of the `recipes` source distribution. Scripts that create tables used here are located in the *tables* directory.

8.1 Choosing a Temporal Data Type

Problem

You need to store temporal data but aren't sure which is the most appropriate data type.

Solution

Choose the data type according to the characteristics of the information to be stored and how you need to use it.

Discussion

To choose a temporal data type, consider questions such as these:

- Do you need times only, dates only, or combined date and time values?
- What range of values do you require?
- Do you want automatic initialization of the column to the current date and time?

MySQL provides DATE and TIME data types for representing date and time values separately, and DATETIME and TIMESTAMP types for combined date-and-time values. These values have the following characteristics:

- DATE values have *YYYY-MM-DD* format, where *YY*, *MM*, and *DD* represent the year, month, and day parts of the date. The supported range for DATE values is 1000-01-01 to 9999-12-31.

- TIME values have *hh:mm:ss* format, where *hh*, *mm*, and *ss* are the hours, minutes, and seconds parts of the time. TIME values can often be thought of as time-of-day values, but MySQL actually treats them as elapsed time. Thus, they may be greater than 23:59:59 or even negative. (The actual range of a TIME column is -838:59:59 to 838:59:59.)

- DATETIME and TIMESTAMP are combined date-and-time values in *YYYY-MM-DD hh:mm:ss* format.

  The DATETIME and TIMESTAMP data types are similar in many respects, but watch out for these differences:

  — DATETIME has a supported range of 1000-01-01 00:00:00 to 9999-12-31 23:59:59, whereas TIMESTAMP values are valid only from the year 1970 partially through 2038.

  — TIMESTAMP and DATETIME have special auto-initialization and auto-update properties (see Recipe 8.8), but for DATETIME, they are not available before MySQL 5.6.5.

  — When a client inserts a TIMESTAMP value, the server converts it from the time zone associated with the client session to UTC and stores the UTC value. When the client retrieves a TIMESTAMP value, the server performs the reverse operation to convert the UTC value back to the client session time zone. A

client in a time zone different from the server can configure its session so that
this conversion is appropriate for its own time zone (see Recipe 8.4).

- Types that include a time part can have a fractional seconds part for subsecond
resolution (see Recipe 8.2).

Many of the examples in this chapter draw on the following tables, which contain
columns representing time, date, and date-and-time values. (The `time_val` table has
two columns for use in time interval calculation examples.):

```
mysql> SELECT t1, t2 FROM time_val;
+----------+----------+
| t1       | t2       |
+----------+----------+
| 15:00:00 | 15:00:00 |
| 05:01:30 | 02:30:20 |
| 12:30:20 | 17:30:45 |
+----------+----------+
mysql> SELECT d FROM date_val;
+------------+
| d          |
+------------+
| 1864-02-28 |
| 1900-01-15 |
| 1999-12-31 |
| 2000-06-04 |
| 2017-03-16 |
+------------+
mysql> SELECT dt FROM datetime_val;
+---------------------+
| dt                  |
+---------------------+
| 1970-01-01 00:00:00 |
| 1999-12-31 09:00:00 |
| 2000-06-04 15:45:30 |
| 2017-03-16 12:30:15 |
+---------------------+
```

It is a good idea to create the `time_val`, `date_val`, and `datetime_val` tables right
now before reading further. (Use the appropriate scripts in the *tables* directory of the
`recipes` distribution.)

8.2 Using Fractional Seconds Support

Problem

Your application requires subsecond resolution of time values.

Solution

Specify fractional seconds.

Discussion

As of MySQL 5.6.4, fractional seconds are supported for temporal types that include a time part: DATETIME, TIME, and TIMESTAMP. For applications that require subsecond resolution of time values, this enables you to specify fractional seconds with precision down to the microsecond level.

The default is to have no fractional seconds part, so to include it for temporal types that support this capability, specify it explicitly in the column declaration: include (*fsp*) after the data type name in a column definition. *fsp* can be from 0 to 6 to indicate the number of fractional digits. 0 means "none" (resolution to seconds); 6 means resolution to microseconds. For example, to create a TIME column with two fractional digits (resolution to hundredths of a second), use this syntax:

```
mycol TIME(2)
```

A precision timing is crucial for specific events such as races. One of the most popular and time-sensitive events worldwide are the Formula 1 races as seen in Table 8-1. Time tracking for the fastest motorsport requires detailed timekeeping and technology. In short, the necessary time to be tracked is within ten thousandths of a second which is accomplished by using multiple transponders.

Table 8-1. Formula 1 Rolex Turkish Grand Prix 2021–Race results

Driver	Car	Time
Valtteri Bottas	MERCEDES	1:31:04.103
Max Verstappen	RED BULL RACING HONDA	1:45:58.243
Sergio Perez	RED BULL RACING HONDA	1:46:10.342

Temporal functions that return current time or date-and-time values also support fractional seconds. The default without an argument is no fractional part. Otherwise, the argument specifies the desired resolution. Permitted values are 0 to 6, the same as when declaring temporal columns:

```
mysql> SELECT CURTIME(), CURTIME(2), CURTIME(6);
+-----------+------------+-----------------+
| CURTIME() | CURTIME(2) | CURTIME(6)      |
+-----------+------------+-----------------+
| 18:07:03  | 18:07:03.24 | 18:07:03.244950 |
+-----------+------------+-----------------+
```

To better demonstrate, we'll use the Formula 1 race standings from one of the latest races held in Turkey (Table 8-1):

```
CREATE TABLE `formula1` (
    id INT AUTO_INCREMENT PRIMARY KEY,
    position INT UNSIGNED,
    no      INT UNSIGNED,
    driver  VARCHAR(25),
    car     VARCHAR(25),
```

```
    laps      SMALLINT,
    time      TIMESTAMP(3),
    points    SMALLINT
);

INSERT INTO formula1 VALUES(0,1,77,"Valtteri Bottas","MERCEDES",58,"2021-10-08
\ 1:31:04.103",26);
INSERT INTO formula1 VALUES(0,2,33,"Max Verstappen","RED BULL RACING HONDA",58,
\"2021-10-08 1:45:58.243",18);
INSERT INTO formula1 VALUES(0,3,11,"Sergio Perez","RED BULL RACING HONDA",58,
\"2021-10-08 1:46:10.342",15);

SELECT POSITION as pos,
       no,
       driver,
       car,
       laps,
       date_format(time,'%H:%i:%s:%f') as time,
       points as pts
  FROM formula1 ORDER BY time;
+------+------+----------------+-----------------------+------+-------------------+------+
| pos  | no   | driver         | car                   | laps | time              | pts  |
+------+------+----------------+-----------------------+------+-------------------+------+
|    1 |   77 | Valtteri Bottas | MERCEDES              |   58 | 01:31:04:103000   |   26 |
|    2 |   33 | Max Verstappen  | RED BULL RACING HONDA |   58 | 01:45:58:243000   |   18 |
|    3 |   11 | Sergio Perez    | RED BULL RACING HONDA |   58 | 01:46:10:342000   |   15 |
+------+------+----------------+-----------------------+------+-------------------+------+
```

To get a proper listing of the time gaps between driver performance, we will use a
CTE. We'll discuss CTEs (Common Table Expressions) further in Recipe 10.18. Here
is the solution:

```
SELECT MIN(time) from formula1 into @fastest;

WITH time_gap AS (
  SELECT
    position,
    car,
    driver,
    time,
    TIMESTAMPDIFF(SECOND, time , @fastest) AS seconds
  FROM formula1
),

DIFFERENCES AS (
  SELECT
    position as pos,
    driver,
    car,
    time,
    seconds,
    MOD(seconds, 60) AS seconds_part,
    MOD(seconds, 3600) AS minutes_part
  FROM time_gap
)

SELECT
  pos,
  driver,
  time,
```

```
CONCAT(
    FLOOR(minutes_part / 60), ' min ',
    SUBSTRING_INDEX(SUBSTRING_INDEX(seconds_part,'-',2),'-',-1),' secs'
) AS difference
FROM differences;
+------+-----------------+-------------------------+-----------------+
| pos  | driver          | time                    | difference      |
+------+-----------------+-------------------------+-----------------+
|    1 | Valtteri Bottas | 2021-10-08 01:31:04.103 | 0 min 0 secs    |
|    2 | Max Verstappen  | 2021-10-08 01:45:58.243 | -15 min 54 secs |
|    3 | Sergio Perez    | 2021-10-08 01:46:10.342 | -16 min 6 secs  |
+------+-----------------+-------------------------+-----------------+
```

8.3 Changing MySQL's Date Format

Problem

You want to change the ISO format that MySQL uses for representing date values.

Solution

You can't. However, you can rewrite non-ISO input values into ISO format when storing dates, and you can rewrite ISO values to other formats for display with the DATE_FORMAT() function.

Discussion

The *YYYY-MM-DD* format that MySQL uses for DATE values follows the ISO 8601 standard for representing dates. Because the year, month, and day parts have a fixed length and appear left to right in date strings, this format has the useful property that dates sort naturally into the proper temporal order. Recipes 9.5 and 10.15 discuss ordering and grouping techniques for date-based values.

ISO format, although common, is not used by all database systems, which can cause problems if you move data between different systems. Moreover, people commonly like to represent dates in other formats, such as *MM/DD/YY* or *DD-MM-YYYY*. This too can be a source of trouble, due to mismatches between human expectations of how dates should look and how MySQL actually represents them.

A question frequently asked by newcomers to MySQL is "How do I tell MySQL to store dates in a specific format, such as *MM/DD/YYYY*?" That's the wrong question. Instead, ask, "If I have a date in a specific format, how can I store it in MySQL's supported format, and vice versa?" MySQL always stores dates in ISO format, a fact with implications both for data entry (input) and for displaying query results (output):

- For data-entry purposes, to store values that are not in ISO format, you normally must rewrite them first. If you don't want to rewrite them, you can store them as strings (for example, in a CHAR column). But then you can't operate on them as dates.

  Chapter 13 covers the topic of date rewriting for data entry, and Chapter 14 discusses checking dates to verify that they're valid. In some cases, if your values are close to ISO format, rewriting may not be necessary. For example, MySQL interprets the string values 87-1-7 and 1987-1-7 and the numbers 870107 and 19870107 as the date 1987-01-07 when storing them into a DATE column.

- For display purposes, you can rewrite dates to non-ISO formats. The DATE_FORMAT() function provides a lot of flexibility for changing date values into other formats (see later in this section). You can also use functions such as YEAR() to extract parts of dates for display (see Recipe 8.9). For additional discussion, see Recipe 14.17.

One way to rewrite non-ISO values for date entry is to use the STR_TO_DATE() function, which takes a string representing a temporal value and a format string that specifies the "syntax" of the value. Within the formatting string, use special sequences of the form %c, where c specifies which part of the date to expect. For example, %Y, %M, and %d signify the four-digit year, the month name, and the two-digit day of the month. To insert the value May 13, 2007 into a DATE column, do this:

```
mysql> INSERT INTO t (d) VALUES(STR_TO_DATE('May 13, 2007','%M %d, %Y'));
mysql> SELECT d FROM t;
+------------+
| d          |
+------------+
| 2007-05-13 |
+------------+
```

For date display, MySQL uses ISO format (*YYYY-MM-DD*) unless you tell it otherwise. To display dates or times in other formats, use the DATE_FORMAT() or TIME_FORMAT() function to rewrite them. If you require a more specialized format those functions cannot provide, write a stored function.

The DATE_FORMAT() function takes two arguments: a DATE, DATETIME, or TIMESTAMP value and a string describing how to display the value. The format string uses the same kind of specifiers as STR_TO_DATE(). The following statement shows the values in the date_val table, both as MySQL displays them by default and as reformatted with DATE_FORMAT():

```
mysql> SELECT d, DATE_FORMAT(d,'%M %d, %Y') FROM date_val;
+------------+----------------------------+
| d          | DATE_FORMAT(d,'%M %d, %Y') |
+------------+----------------------------+
| 1864-02-28 | February 28, 1864          |
| 1900-01-15 | January 15, 1900           |
```

```
| 1999-12-31 | December 31, 1999       |
| 2000-06-04 | June 04, 2000           |
| 2017-03-16 | March 16, 2017          |
+------------+---------------------------+
```

Because DATE_FORMAT() produces long column headings, it's often useful to provide an alias (see Recipe 5.2) to make a heading more concise or meaningful:

```
mysql> SELECT d, DATE_FORMAT(d,'%M %d, %Y') AS date FROM date_val;
+------------+-------------------+
| d          | date              |
+------------+-------------------+
| 1864-02-28 | February 28, 1864 |
| 1900-01-15 | January 15, 1900  |
| 1999-12-31 | December 31, 1999 |
| 2000-06-04 | June 04, 2000     |
| 2017-03-16 | March 16, 2017    |
+------------+-------------------+
```

The MySQL Reference Manual (*https://oreil.ly/2Rwmk*) provides a complete list of format sequences to use with DATE_FORMAT(), TIME_FORMAT(), and STR_TO_DATE(). Table 8-2 shows some of them.

Table 8-2. Format sequences to use with date and time formatting functions

Sequence	Meaning
%Y	Four-digit year
%y	Two-digit year
%M	Complete month name
%b	Month name, initial three letters
%m	Two-digit month of year (01..12)
%c	Month of year (1..12)
%d	Two-digit day of month (01..31)
%e	Day of month (1..31)
%W	Weekday name (Sunday..Saturday)
%r	12-hour time with AM or PM suffix
%T	24-hour time
%H	Two-digit hour
%i	Two-digit minute
%s	Two-digit second
%f	Six-digit microsecond
%%	Literal %

The time-related format sequences shown in the table are useful only when you pass DATE_FORMAT(), a value that has both date and time parts (a DATETIME or TIMESTAMP). The following statement displays DATETIME values from the datetime_val table using formats that include the time of day:

```
mysql> SELECT dt,
    -> DATE_FORMAT(dt,'%c/%e/%y %r') AS format1,
    -> DATE_FORMAT(dt,'%M %e, %Y %T') AS format2
    -> FROM datetime_val;
+---------------------+------------------------+----------------------------+
| dt                  | format1                | format2                    |
+---------------------+------------------------+----------------------------+
| 1970-01-01 00:00:00 | 1/1/70 12:00:00 AM     | January 1, 1970 00:00:00   |
| 1999-12-31 09:00:00 | 12/31/99 09:00:00 AM   | December 31, 1999 09:00:00 |
| 2000-06-04 15:45:30 | 6/4/00 03:45:30 PM     | June 4, 2000 15:45:30      |
| 2017-03-16 12:30:15 | 3/16/17 12:30:15 PM    | March 16, 2017 12:30:15    |
+---------------------+------------------------+----------------------------+
```

TIME_FORMAT() is similar to DATE_FORMAT(). It works with TIME, DATETIME, or TIME
STAMP values but understands only time-related specifiers in the format string:

```
mysql> SELECT dt,
    -> TIME_FORMAT(dt, '%r') AS '12-hour time',
    -> TIME_FORMAT(dt, '%T') AS '24-hour time'
    -> FROM datetime_val;
+---------------------+--------------+--------------+
| dt                  | 12-hour time | 24-hour time |
+---------------------+--------------+--------------+
| 1970-01-01 00:00:00 | 12:00:00 AM  | 00:00:00     |
| 1999-12-31 09:00:00 | 09:00:00 AM  | 09:00:00     |
| 2000-06-04 15:45:30 | 03:45:30 PM  | 15:45:30     |
| 2017-03-16 12:30:15 | 12:30:15 PM  | 12:30:15     |
+---------------------+--------------+--------------+
```

If DATE_FORMAT() or TIME_FORMAT() cannot produce the results that you want, write
a stored function that does. Suppose that you want to convert 24-hour TIME values to
12-hour format but with a suffix of a.m. or p.m. rather than AM or PM. The following
function accomplishes that task. It uses TIME_FORMAT() to do most of the work, then
strips the suffix supplied by %r and replaces it with the desired suffix:

```
CREATE FUNCTION time_ampm (t TIME)
RETURNS VARCHAR(13) # mm:dd:ss {a.m.|p.m.} format
DETERMINISTIC
RETURN CONCAT(LEFT(TIME_FORMAT(t, '%r'), 9),
              IF(TIME_TO_SEC(t) < 12*60*60, 'a.m.', 'p.m.'));
```

Use the function like this:

```
mysql> SELECT t1, time_ampm(t1) FROM time_val;
+----------+---------------+
| t1       | time_ampm(t1) |
+----------+---------------+
| 15:00:00 | 03:00:00 p.m. |
| 05:01:30 | 05:01:30 a.m. |
| 12:30:20 | 12:30:20 p.m. |
+----------+---------------+
```

For more information about writing stored functions, see Chapter 11.

8.4 Setting the Client Time Zone

Problem

You have a client application that connects from a time zone different from the server. Consequently, when it stores TIMESTAMP values, they don't have the correct Coordinated Universal Time (UTC) values.

Solution

The client should set the time_zone system variable after connecting to the server.

Discussion

Time zone settings have an important effect on TIMESTAMP values:

- When the MySQL server starts, it examines its operating environment to determine its time zone. (To use a different value, start the server with the --default-time-zone option.)

- For each client that connects, the server interprets TIMESTAMP values with respect to the time zone associated with the client session. When a client inserts a TIMESTAMP value, the server converts it from the client time zone to UTC and stores the UTC value. (Internally, the server stores a TIMESTAMP value as the number of seconds since 1970-01-01 00:00:00 UTC.) When the client retrieves a TIMESTAMP value, the server performs the reverse operation to convert the UTC value back to the client time zone.

- The default session time zone for each client when it connects is the server time zone. If all clients are in the same time zone as the server, nothing special needs be done for proper TIMESTAMP time zone conversion to occur. But if a client is in a time zone different from the server and it inserts TIMESTAMP values without making the proper time zone correction, the UTC values won't be correct.

Suppose that the server and client C1 are in the same time zone, and client C1 issues these statements:

```
mysql> CREATE TABLE t (ts TIMESTAMP);
mysql> INSERT INTO t (ts) VALUES('2021-06-21 12:30:00');
mysql> SELECT ts FROM t;
+---------------------+
| ts                  |
+---------------------+
| 2021-06-21 12:30:00 |
+---------------------+
```

Here, client C1 sees the same value that it stored. A different client, C2, will also see the same value if it retrieves it, but if client C2 is in a different time zone, that value isn't correct for its zone. Conversely, if client C2 stores a value, that value when returned by client C1 won't be correct for the client C1 time zone.

To deal with this problem so that TIMESTAMP conversions use the proper time zone, a client should set its time zone explicitly by setting the session value of the time_zone system variable. Suppose that the server has a global time zone of six hours ahead of UTC. Each client initially is assigned that same value as its session time zone:

```
mysql> SELECT @@global.time_zone, @@session.time_zone;
+--------------------+---------------------+
| @@global.time_zone | @@session.time_zone |
+--------------------+---------------------+
| SYSTEM             | SYSTEM              |
+--------------------+---------------------+
```

When client C2 connects, it sees the same TIMESTAMP value as client C1:

```
mysql> SELECT ts FROM t;
+---------------------+
| ts                  |
+---------------------+
| 2021-06-21 12:30:00 |
+---------------------+
```

But that value is incorrect if client C2 is only four hours ahead of UTC. C2 should set its time zone after connecting so that retrieved TIMESTAMP values are properly adjusted for its own session:

```
mysql> SET SESSION time_zone = '+04:00';
mysql> SELECT @@global.time_zone, @@session.time_zone;
+--------------------+---------------------+
| @@global.time_zone | @@session.time_zone |
+--------------------+---------------------+
| SYSTEM             | +04:00              |
+--------------------+---------------------+
mysql> SELECT ts FROM t;
+---------------------+
| ts                  |
+---------------------+
| 2021-06-21 16:30:00 |
+---------------------+
```

To see the System Timezone, check global variables:

```
mysql> SHOW GLOBAL VARIABLES LIKE "system_time_zone";
+------------------+-------+
| Variable_name    | Value |
+------------------+-------+
| system_time_zone | UTC   |
+------------------+-------+
```

The client time zone also affects the values displayed from functions that return the current date and time (see Recipe 8.7).

See Also

To convert individual date-and-time values from one time zone to another, use the CONVERT_TZ() function (see Recipe 8.6).

8.5 Setting the Server Time Zone

Problem

You have a localized application to serve customers, but you want to have a global time zone setting.

Solution

The server should set the time_zone system variable to SYSTEM at the server. This setting should point to UTC value. Accordingly, the system_time_zone value should be set to UTC.

Discussion

The MySQL server maintains several time zone settings:

- The server system time zone. When MySQL starts, it attempts to determine the system_time_zone variable. To explicitly set the system time zone for MySQL, set the TZ environment variable before starting mysqld. Alternatively, start the mysqld_safe with its --timezone option. The values for these variables are permissible by your operating system settings.

- The server current time zone is set by the global time_zone value. It's generally set to SYSTEM on modern Linux operating systems:

```
mysql> SHOW GLOBAL VARIABLES LIKE "time_zone";
+---------------+--------+
| Variable_name | Value  |
+---------------+--------+
| time_zone     | SYSTEM |
+---------------+--------+
```

  You may choose to set the global time zone variable using SET GLOBAL. This will not change the @@session.time_zone value:

```
mysql> SET GLOBAL time_zone = "+03:00";
mysql> SELECT @@global.time_zone, @@session.time_zone;
+--------------------+---------------------+
| @@global.time_zone | @@session.time_zone |
+--------------------+---------------------+
| +03:00             | SYSTEM              |
+--------------------+---------------------+
```

The string indicating the `time_zone` value offset from UTC. Prior to MySQL 8.0.19, this value had to be in the range -12:59 to +13:00, inclusive; beginning with MySQL 8.0.19, the permitted range is -13:59 to +14:00, inclusive. Populated time zones are not permitted unless they are preloaded to MySQL tables; hence, you can't use names like UTC:

```
mysql> SET GLOBAL time_zone = "US/Eastern" ;
ERROR 1298 (HY000): Unknown or incorrect time zone: 'US/Eastern'
```

For instructions on populating the time zone tables, see the MySQL Reference Manual (*https://oreil.ly/h7SlG*).

- The `system_time_zone` variable is set when the server inherits a time zone setting from the machine defaults. Unlike the `time_zone` variable, this is not dynamic to set after the server starts. As of MySQL 8.0.26, if the server host time zone changes, such as during daylight saving time, `system_time_zone` will reflect the change. If a change happens during the execution of a query, the previous value will be cached:

```
mysql> SHOW GLOBAL VARIABLES LIKE "system_time_zone";
+---------------+------------+
| Variable_name | Value      |
+---------------+------------+
| time_zone     | US/Eastern |
+---------------+------------+
```

8.6 Shifting Temporal Values Between Time Zones

Problem

You have a date-and-time value but need to know what it would be in a different time zone. For example, you're having a teleconference with people in different parts of the world, and they need to know the meeting time in their local time zones.

Solution

Use the `CONVERT_TZ()` function.

Discussion

The `CONVERT_TZ()` function converts temporal values between time zones. It takes three arguments: a date-and-time value and two time zone indicators. The function interprets the date-and-time value as a value in the first time zone and returns the value shifted into the second time zone.

Suppose that we live in Chicago, Illinois, in the United States and that we have a meeting with people in several other parts of the world. Table 8-3 shows the location of each meeting participant and the time zone name for each:

Table 8-3. Meeting participants

Location	Time zone name
Chicago, Illinois, US	US/Central
Istanbul, Turkey	Europe/Istanbul
London, United Kingdom	Europe/London
Edmonton, Alberta, Canada	America/Edmonton
Brisbane, Australia	Australia/Brisbane

If the meeting is to take place at 8 a.m. local time for us on November 28, 2021, what time will that be for the other participants? The following statement uses CONVERT_TZ() to calculate the local times for each time zone:

```
mysql> SET @dt = '2021-11-28 08:00:00';
mysql> SELECT @dt AS Chicago,
    -> CONVERT_TZ(@dt,'US/Central','Europe/Istanbul') AS Istanbul,
    -> CONVERT_TZ(@dt,'US/Central','Europe/London') AS London,
    -> CONVERT_TZ(@dt,'US/Central','America/Edmonton') AS Edmonton,
    -> CONVERT_TZ(@dt,'US/Central','Australia/Brisbane') AS Brisbane\G
*************************** 1. row ***************************
 Chicago: 2021-11-28 08:00:00
Istanbul: 2021-11-28 17:00:00
  London: 2021-11-28 14:00:00
Edmonton: 2021-11-28 07:00:00
Brisbane: 2021-11-29 00:00:00
```

Let's hope the Brisbane participant doesn't mind being up after midnight.

The preceding example uses time zone names, so it requires that you have the time zone tables in the mysql database initialized with support for named time zones. (See the MySQL Reference Manual (*https://oreil.ly/bKUMk*) for information about setting up the time zone tables.) If you can't use named time zones, specify them in terms of their numeric relationship to UTC. (This can be a little trickier; you might need to account for daylight saving time.) The corresponding statement with numeric time zones looks like this:

```
mysql> SELECT @dt AS Chicago,
    -> CONVERT_TZ(@dt,'-06:00','+03:00') AS Istanbul,
    -> CONVERT_TZ(@dt,'-06:00','+00:00') AS London,
    -> CONVERT_TZ(@dt,'-06:00','-07:00') AS Edmonton,
    -> CONVERT_TZ(@dt,'-06:00','+10:00') AS Brisbane\G
*************************** 1. row ***************************
 Chicago: 2021-11-28 08:00:00
Istanbul: 2021-11-28 17:00:00
  London: 2021-11-28 14:00:00
Edmonton: 2021-11-28 07:00:00
Brisbane: 2021-11-29 00:00:00
```

8.7 Determining the Current Date or Time

Problem

You want to know what today's date is and/or what time it is.

Solution

Use the CURDATE(), CURTIME(), or NOW() functions to obtain values expressed in the client session time zone. Use UTC_DATE(), UTC_TIME(), or UTC_TIMESTAMP() for values in UTC time.

Discussion

Some applications must know the current date or time, such as those that write timestamped log records. This kind of information is also useful for date calculations performed in relation to the current date, such as finding the first (or last) day of the month or determining the date for Wednesday of next week.

The CURDATE() and CURTIME() functions return the current date and time separately, and NOW() returns both as a combined date-and-time value:

```
mysql> SELECT CURDATE(), CURTIME(), NOW();
+------------+-----------+---------------------+
| CURDATE()  | CURTIME() | NOW()               |
+------------+-----------+---------------------+
| 2021-11-28 | 08:42:57  | 2021-11-28 08:42:57 |
+------------+-----------+---------------------+
```

CURRENT_DATE, CURRENT_TIME, and CURRENT_TIMESTAMP are synonyms for CURDATE(), CURTIME(), and NOW(), respectively.

The preceding functions return values in the client session time zone (see Recipe 8.4). For values in UTC time, use the UTC_DATE(), UTC_TIME(), or UTC_TIMESTAMP() functions instead.

To determine the current date and time for an arbitrary time zone, pass the value of the appropriate UTC function to CONVERT_TZ() (see Recipe 8.6).

To obtain subparts of these values, such as the current day of the month or current hour of the day, use the decomposition techniques discussed in Recipe 8.9.

8.8 Using TIMESTAMP or DATETIME to Track Row-Modification Times

Problem

You want to record row-creation time or last-modification time automatically.

Solution

Use the auto-initialization and auto-update properties of the TIMESTAMP and DATE TIME data types.

Discussion

MySQL supports TIMESTAMP and DATETIME data types that store date-and-time values. Recipe 8.1 covers the range of values for these types. This recipe focuses on special column attributes that enable you to track row-creation and row-update times automatically:

- A TIMESTAMP or DATETIME column declared with the DEFAULT CURRENT_TIME STAMP attribute initializes automatically for new rows. Simply omit the column from INSERT statements and MySQL sets it to the row-creation time.

- A TIMESTAMP or DATETIME column declared with the ON UPDATE CURRENT_TIME STAMP attribute automatically updates to the current date and time when you change any other column in the row from its current value.

These special properties make the TIMESTAMP and DATETIME data types particularly suited for applications that require recording the times at which rows are inserted or updated. The following discussion shows how to take advantage of these properties using TIMESTAMP columns. With some differences to be noted later, the discussion also applies to DATETIME columns.

 The default SQL_MODE does not allow NULL values unless relaxed. Also, NO_ZERO_DATE was deprecated as of MySQL 8.0 and should be used in conjunction with STRICT MODE.

Our example table looks like this:

```
DROP TABLE IF EXISTS tsdemo;
CREATE TABLE `tsdemo` (
`val` INT UNSIGNED NOT NULL AUTO_INCREMENT PRIMARY KEY,
`ts_both` TIMESTAMP DEFAULT CURRENT_TIMESTAMP ON UPDATE CURRENT_TIMESTAMP,
`ts_create` TIMESTAMP DEFAULT CURRENT_TIMESTAMP,
```

```
`ts_update` TIMESTAMP DEFAULT CURRENT_TIMESTAMP ON UPDATE CURRENT_TIMESTAMP
) ENGINE=InnoDB ;
```

The TIMESTAMP columns have these properties:

- ts_both auto-initializes and auto-updates. This is useful for tracking the time of any change to a row, for both inserts and updates.

- ts_create auto-initializes only. This is useful when you want a column to be set to the time at which a row is created but remain constant thereafter.

- ts_update auto-updates only. It is set to the column default (or value you specify explicitly) at row-creation time, and it auto-updates for changes to the row thereafter. The use cases for this are more limited—for example, to track row-creation and last-modification times separately (using ts_update in conjunction with ts_create) rather than together in a single column like ts_both.

To see how the table works, insert some rows into the table (a few seconds apart so the timestamps differ), then select its contents:

```
mysql> INSERT INTO tsdemo (val,ts_both,ts_create,ts_update)
    -> VALUES(0,NULL,NULL,NULL);
mysql> INSERT INTO tsdemo (val) VALUES(5);
mysql> INSERT INTO tsdemo (val,ts_both,ts_create,ts_update)
    -> VALUES(10,NULL,NULL,NULL);
mysql> SELECT val, ts_both, ts_create, ts_update FROM tsdemo;
+-----+---------------------+---------------------+---------------------+
| val | ts_both             | ts_create           | ts_update           |
+-----+---------------------+---------------------+---------------------+
|   1 | 2022-03-06 14:34:17 | 2022-03-06 14:34:17 | 2022-03-06 14:34:17 |
|   5 | 2022-03-06 14:35:16 | 2022-03-06 14:35:16 | 2022-03-06 14:35:16 |
|  10 | 2022-03-06 14:35:34 | 2022-03-06 14:35:34 | 2022-03-06 14:35:34 |
+-----+---------------------+---------------------+---------------------+
```

The first two INSERT statements show that you can set the auto-initialize columns to the current date and time by omitting them from the INSERT statement entirely. The third insert shows that you can set a TIMESTAMP column to the current date and time by setting it explicitly to NULL, even one that does not auto-initialize. This NULL-assignment behavior is not specific to INSERT statements; it works for UPDATE as well. You can disable this special handling of NULL assignments, as we'll cover later in this recipe.

To see auto-updating in action, issue a statement that changes one row's val column and check its effect on the table's contents. The result shows that the auto-update columns are updated (in the modified row only):

```
mysql> UPDATE tsdemo SET val = 11 WHERE val = 10;
mysql> SELECT val, ts_both, ts_create, ts_update FROM tsdemo;
+-----+---------------------+---------------------+---------------------+
| val | ts_both             | ts_create           | ts_update           |
+-----+---------------------+---------------------+---------------------+
|   1 | 2022-03-06 14:34:17 | 2022-03-06 14:34:17 | 2022-03-06 14:34:17 |
|   5 | 2022-03-06 14:35:16 | 2022-03-06 14:35:16 | 2022-03-06 14:35:16 |
|  11 | 2022-03-06 14:38:04 | 2022-03-06 14:35:34 | 2022-03-06 14:38:04 |
+-----+---------------------+---------------------+---------------------+
```

If you modify multiple rows, updates occur for the auto-update columns in each row:

```
mysql> UPDATE tsdemo SET val = val + 1;
mysql> SELECT val, ts_both, ts_create, ts_update FROM tsdemo;
+-----+---------------------+---------------------+---------------------+
| val | ts_both             | ts_create           | ts_update           |
+-----+---------------------+---------------------+---------------------+
|   2 | 2022-03-06 14:38:45 | 2022-03-06 14:34:17 | 2022-03-06 14:38:45 |
|   6 | 2022-03-06 14:38:45 | 2022-03-06 14:35:16 | 2022-03-06 14:38:45 |
|  12 | 2022-03-06 14:38:45 | 2022-03-06 14:35:34 | 2022-03-06 14:38:45 |
+-----+---------------------+---------------------+---------------------+
```

An UPDATE statement that doesn't actually change any value in a row doesn't modify auto-update columns. To see this, set every row's val column to its current value, then review the table contents to see that auto-update columns retain their values:

```
mysql> UPDATE tsdemo SET val = val;
mysql> SELECT val, ts_both, ts_create, ts_update FROM tsdemo;
+-----+---------------------+---------------------+---------------------+
| val | ts_both             | ts_create           | ts_update           |
+-----+---------------------+---------------------+---------------------+
|   2 | 2022-03-06 14:38:45 | 2022-03-06 14:34:17 | 2022-03-06 14:38:45 |
|   6 | 2022-03-06 14:38:45 | 2022-03-06 14:35:16 | 2022-03-06 14:38:45 |
|  12 | 2022-03-06 14:38:45 | 2022-03-06 14:35:34 | 2022-03-06 14:38:45 |
+-----+---------------------+---------------------+---------------------+
```

As stated previously, automatic TIMESTAMP properties also apply to DATETIME, with some differences:

- For the first TIMESTAMP column in a table, if neither of the DEFAULT or ON UPDATE attributes are specified, the column is implicitly defined with both. For DATETIME, automatic properties never apply implicitly, only those specified explicitly.

- It is not possible to set NULL to TIMESTAMP anymore. To assign the current timestamp, set the column to CURRENT_TIMESTAMP or a synonym such as NOW().

To determine for any given TIMESTAMP column what happens when NULL is assigned to it, use SHOW CREATE TABLE to see the column definition. If the definition includes the NULL attribute, assigning NULL stores NULL. If the definition includes the NOT NULL attribute, you can specify NULL as the value to be assigned, but you cannot *store* NULL because MySQL stores the current date and time instead.

See Also

To simulate `TIMESTAMP` auto-initialization and auto-update properties for other temporal types, you can use triggers (see Chapter 11).

8.9 Extracting Parts of Dates or Times

Problem

You want to obtain just a part of a date or a time.

Solution

Invoke a function specifically intended for extracting part of a temporal value, such as `MONTH()` or `MINUTE()`. This is usually the fastest method for component extraction if you need only a single component of a value. Alternatively, use a formatting function such as `DATE_FORMAT()` or `TIME_FORMAT()` with a format string that includes a specifier for the part of the value you want to obtain.

Discussion

The following discussion shows different ways to extract parts of temporal values.

Decomposing dates or times using component-extraction functions

MySQL includes many functions for extracting date and time subparts. For example, `DATE()` and `TIME()` extract the date and time components of temporal values:

```
mysql> SELECT dt, DATE(dt), TIME(dt) FROM datetime_val;
+---------------------+------------+----------+
| dt                  | DATE(dt)   | TIME(dt) |
+---------------------+------------+----------+
| 1970-01-01 00:00:00 | 1970-01-01 | 00:00:00 |
| 1999-12-31 09:00:00 | 1999-12-31 | 09:00:00 |
| 2000-06-04 15:45:30 | 2000-06-04 | 15:45:30 |
| 2017-03-16 12:30:15 | 2017-03-16 | 12:30:15 |
+---------------------+------------+----------+
```

Table 8-4 shows several component-extraction functions; consult the MySQL Reference Manual (*https://oreil.ly/4W8oF*) for a complete list. The date-related functions work with `DATE`, `DATETIME`, or `TIMESTAMP` values. The time-related functions work with `TIME`, `DATETIME`, or `TIMESTAMP` values.

Table 8-4. Component-extraction functions

Function	Return value
YEAR()	Year of date
MONTH()	Month number (1..12)

Function	Return value
MONTHNAME()	Month name (January..December)
DAYOFMONTH()	Day of month (1..31)
DAYNAME()	Day name (Sunday..Saturday)
DAYOFWEEK()	Day of week (1..7 for Sunday..Saturday)
WEEKDAY()	Day of week (0..6 for Monday..Sunday)
DAYOFYEAR()	Day of year (1..366)
HOUR()	Hour of time (0..23)
MINUTE()	Minute of time (0..59)
SECOND()	Second of time (0..59)
MICROSECOND()	Microsecond of time (0..59)
EXTRACT()	Varies

Here's an example:

```
mysql> SELECT dt, YEAR(dt), DAYOFMONTH(dt), HOUR(dt), SECOND(dt)
    -> FROM datetime_val;
+---------------------+----------+----------------+----------+------------+
| dt                  | YEAR(dt) | DAYOFMONTH(dt) | HOUR(dt) | SECOND(dt) |
+---------------------+----------+----------------+----------+------------+
| 1970-01-01 00:00:00 |     1970 |              1 |        0 |          0 |
| 1999-12-31 09:00:00 |     1999 |             31 |        9 |          0 |
| 2000-06-04 15:45:30 |     2000 |              4 |       15 |         30 |
| 2017-03-16 12:30:15 |     2017 |             16 |       12 |         15 |
+---------------------+----------+----------------+----------+------------+

mysql> set @date_time="2021-11-24 22:11:12.000201";
    -> SELECT HOUR(@date_time) as Hour, MINUTE(@date_time)
    ->  as Minute,SECOND(@date_time) as Second, MICROSECOND(@date_time) as MicroSecond;
+------+--------+--------+-------------+
| Hour | Minute | Second | MicroSecond |
+------+--------+--------+-------------+
|   22 |     11 |     12 |         201 |
+------+--------+--------+-------------+
```

Functions such as YEAR() or DAYOFMONTH() extract values that have an obvious correspondence to a substring of the temporal value to which you apply them. Other component-extraction functions provide access to values that have no such correspondence. One is the day-of-year value:

```
mysql> SELECT d, DAYOFYEAR(d) FROM date_val;
+------------+--------------+
| d          | DAYOFYEAR(d) |
+------------+--------------+
| 1864-02-28 |           59 |
| 1900-01-15 |           15 |
| 1999-12-31 |          365 |
| 2000-06-04 |          156 |
| 2017-03-16 |           75 |
+------------+--------------+
```

Another is the day of the week, which is available by name or number:

- DAYNAME() returns the complete day name. There is a DATE_FORMAT(d, '%a') function for returning the three-character name abbreviation that you can get easily by passing the full name to DATE_FORMAT():

```
mysql> SELECT d, DAYNAME(d), DATE_FORMAT(d, '%a') FROM date_val;
+------------+------------+----------------------+
| d          | DAYNAME(d) | DATE_FORMAT(d, '%a') |
+------------+------------+----------------------+
| 1864-02-28 | Sunday     | Sun                  |
| 1900-01-15 | Monday     | Mon                  |
| 1999-12-31 | Friday     | Fri                  |
| 2000-06-04 | Sunday     | Sun                  |
| 2017-03-16 | Thursday   | Thu                  |
+------------+------------+----------------------+
```

- To get the day of the week as a number, use DAYOFWEEK() or WEEKDAY(), but pay attention to the range of values each function returns. DAYOFWEEK() returns values from 1 to 7, corresponding to Sunday through Saturday. WEEKDAY() returns values from 0 to 6, corresponding to Monday through Sunday:

```
mysql> SELECT d, DAYNAME(d), DAYOFWEEK(d), WEEKDAY(d) FROM date_val;
+------------+------------+--------------+------------+
| d          | DAYNAME(d) | DAYOFWEEK(d) | WEEKDAY(d) |
+------------+------------+--------------+------------+
| 1864-02-28 | Sunday     |            1 |          6 |
| 1900-01-15 | Monday     |            2 |          0 |
| 1999-12-31 | Friday     |            6 |          4 |
| 2000-06-04 | Sunday     |            1 |          6 |
| 2017-03-16 | Thursday   |            5 |          3 |
+------------+------------+--------------+------------+
```

EXTRACT() is another function for obtaining individual parts of temporal values:

```
mysql> SELECT dt, EXTRACT(DAY FROM dt), EXTRACT(HOUR FROM dt)
    -> FROM datetime_val;
+---------------------+----------------------+-----------------------+
| dt                  | EXTRACT(DAY FROM dt)  | EXTRACT(HOUR FROM dt)  |
+---------------------+----------------------+-----------------------+
| 1970-01-01 00:00:00 |                    1 |                     0 |
| 1999-12-31 09:00:00 |                   31 |                     9 |
| 2000-06-04 15:45:30 |                    4 |                    15 |
| 2017-03-16 12:30:15 |                   16 |                    12 |
+---------------------+----------------------+-----------------------+
```

The keyword indicating what to extract from the value should be a unit specifier such as YEAR, MONTH, DAY, HOUR, MINUTE, or SECOND. Unit specifiers are singular, not plural. (Check the MySQL Reference Manual (*https://oreil.ly/LTX6p*) for the full list.)

Decomposing dates or times using formatting functions

The DATE_FORMAT() and TIME_FORMAT() functions reformat date and time values. By specifying appropriate format strings, you can extract individual parts of temporal values:

```
mysql> SELECT dt,
    -> DATE_FORMAT(dt,'%Y') AS year,
    -> DATE_FORMAT(dt,'%d') AS day,
    -> TIME_FORMAT(dt,'%H') AS hour,
    -> TIME_FORMAT(dt,'%s') AS second
    -> TIME_FORMAT(dt,'%f') AS microsecond
    -> FROM datetime_val;
+---------------------+------+------+------+--------+-------------+
| dt                  | year | day  | hour | second | microsecond |
+---------------------+------+------+------+--------+-------------+
| 1970-01-01 00:00:00 | 1970 | 01   | 00   | 00     | 000000      |
| 1999-12-31 09:00:00 | 1999 | 31   | 09   | 00     | 000000      |
| 2000-06-04 15:45:30 | 2000 | 04   | 15   | 30     | 000000      |
| 2017-03-16 12:30:15 | 2017 | 16   | 12   | 15     | 000000      |
+---------------------+------+------+------+--------+-------------+
```

Formatting functions are advantageous when you want to extract more than one part of a value or display extracted values in a format different from the default.

For example, to extract the entire date or time from DATETIME values, do this:

```
mysql> SELECT dt,
    -> DATE_FORMAT(dt,'%Y-%m-%d') AS 'date part',
```

```
        -> TIME_FORMAT(dt,'%T') AS 'time part'
        -> FROM datetime_val;

+---------------------+------------+-----------+
| dt                  | date part  | time part |
+---------------------+------------+-----------+
| 1970-01-01 00:00:00 | 1970-01-01 | 00:00:00  |
| 1999-12-31 09:00:00 | 1999-12-31 | 09:00:00  |
| 2000-06-04 15:45:30 | 2000-06-04 | 15:45:30  |
| 2017-03-16 12:30:15 | 2017-03-16 | 12:30:15  |
+---------------------+------------+-----------+
```

To present a date in other than *YYYY-MM-DD* format or a time without the seconds part, do this:

```
mysql> SELECT dt,
    -> DATE_FORMAT(dt,'%M %e, %Y') AS 'descriptive date',
    -> TIME_FORMAT(dt,'%H:%i') AS 'hours/minutes'
    -> FROM datetime_val;
+---------------------+-------------------+---------------+
| dt                  | descriptive date  | hours/minutes |
+---------------------+-------------------+---------------+
| 1970-01-01 00:00:00 | January 1, 1970   | 00:00         |
| 1999-12-31 09:00:00 | December 31, 1999 | 09:00         |
| 2000-06-04 15:45:30 | June 4, 2000      | 15:45         |
| 2017-03-16 12:30:15 | March 16, 2017    | 12:30         |
+---------------------+-------------------+---------------+
```

8.10 Synthesizing Dates or Times from Component Values

Problem

You want to combine the parts of a date or time to produce a complete date or time value. Or you want to replace parts of a date to produce another date.

Solution

You have several options:

- Use MAKETIME() to construct a TIME value from hour, minute, and second parts.
- Use DATE_FORMAT() or TIME_FORMAT() to combine parts of the existing value with parts you want to replace.
- Pull out the parts that you need with component-extraction functions and recombine the parts with CONCAT().

Discussion

The reverse of splitting a date or time value into components is synthesizing a temporal value from its constituent parts. Techniques for date and time synthesis include using composition functions, formatting functions, and string concatenation.

The MAKETIME() function takes component hour, minute, and second values as arguments and combines them to produce a time:

```
mysql> SELECT MAKETIME(10,30,58), MAKETIME(-5,0,11);
+--------------------+-------------------+
| MAKETIME(10,30,58) | MAKETIME(-5,0,11) |
+--------------------+-------------------+
| 10:30:58           | -05:00:11         |
+--------------------+-------------------+
```

Date synthesis is often performed beginning with a given date, then keeping parts that you want to use and replacing the rest. For example, to produce the first day of the month in which a date falls, use DATE_FORMAT() to extract the year and month parts from the date, combining them with a day part of 01:

```
mysql> SELECT d, DATE_FORMAT(d,'%Y-%m-01') FROM date_val;
+------------+---------------------------+
| d          | DATE_FORMAT(d,'%Y-%m-01') |
+------------+---------------------------+
| 1864-02-28 | 1864-02-01                |
| 1900-01-15 | 1900-01-01                |
| 1999-12-31 | 1999-12-01                |
| 2000-06-04 | 2000-06-01                |
| 2017-03-16 | 2017-03-01                |
+------------+---------------------------+
```

TIME_FORMAT() can be used similarly. The following example produces time values that have the seconds part set to 00:

```
mysql> SELECT t1, TIME_FORMAT(t1,'%H:%i:00') FROM time_val;
+----------+----------------------------+
| t1       | TIME_FORMAT(t1,'%H:%i:00') |
+----------+----------------------------+
| 15:00:00 | 15:00:00                   |
| 05:01:30 | 05:01:00                   |
| 12:30:20 | 12:30:00                   |
+----------+----------------------------+
```

Another way to construct temporal values is to use date-part extraction functions in conjunction with CONCAT(). However, this method is often messier than the DATE_FOR MAT() technique just discussed, and it sometimes yields slightly different results:

```
mysql> SELECT d, CONCAT(YEAR(d),'-',MONTH(d),'-01') FROM date_val;
+------------+------------------------------------+
| d          | CONCAT(YEAR(d),'-',MONTH(d),'-01') |
+------------+------------------------------------+
| 1864-02-28 | 1864-2-01                          |
| 1900-01-15 | 1900-1-01                          |
| 1999-12-31 | 1999-12-01                         |
| 2000-06-04 | 2000-6-01                          |
| 2017-03-16 | 2017-3-01                          |
+------------+------------------------------------+
```

Note that the month values in some of these dates have only a single digit. To ensure that the month has two digits—as required for ISO format—use LPAD() to add a leading zero as necessary:

```
mysql> SELECT d, CONCAT(YEAR(d),'-',LPAD(MONTH(d),2,'0'),'-01')
    -> FROM date_val;
+------------+------------------------------------------------+
| d          | CONCAT(YEAR(d),'-',LPAD(MONTH(d),2,'0'),'-01') |
+------------+------------------------------------------------+
| 1864-02-28 | 1864-02-01                                     |
| 1900-01-15 | 1900-01-01                                     |
| 1999-12-31 | 1999-12-01                                     |
| 2000-06-04 | 2000-06-01                                     |
| 2017-03-16 | 2017-03-01                                     |
+------------+------------------------------------------------+
```

Recipe 8.18 shows other ways to solve the problem of producing ISO dates from not-quite-ISO dates.

TIME values can be produced from hours, minutes, and seconds values using methods analogous to those for creating DATE values. For example, to change a TIME value so that its seconds part is 00, extract the hour and minute parts, and then recombine them with CONCAT():

```
mysql> SELECT t1,
    -> CONCAT(LPAD(HOUR(t1),2,'0'),':',LPAD(MINUTE(t1),2,'0'),':00')
    ->   AS recombined
    -> FROM time_val;
+----------+------------+
| t1       | recombined |
+----------+------------+
| 15:00:00 | 15:00:00   |
| 05:01:30 | 05:01:00   |
| 12:30:20 | 12:30:00   |
+----------+------------+
```

To produce a combined date-and-time value from separate date and time values, simply concatenate them separated by a space:

```
mysql> SET @d = '2009-06-03', @t = '16:15:08';
mysql> SELECT @d, @t, CONCAT(@d,' ',@t);
+------------+----------+---------------------+
| @d         | @t       | CONCAT(@d,' ',@t)   |
+------------+----------+---------------------+
| 2009-06-03 | 16:15:08 | 2009-06-03 16:15:08 |
+------------+----------+---------------------+
```

8.11 Converting Between Temporal Values and Basic Units

Problem

You want to convert a temporal value such as a time or date to basic units such as seconds or days. This is often useful or necessary for performing temporal arithmetic operations (see Recipes 8.12 and 8.13).

Solution

The conversion method depends on the type of value to be converted:

- To convert between time values and seconds, use the TIME_TO_SEC() and SEC_TO_TIME() functions.

- To convert between date values and days, use the TO_DAYS() and FROM_DAYS() functions.

- To convert between date-and-time values and seconds, use the UNIX_TIME STAMP() and FROM_UNIXTIME() functions.

Discussion

The following discussion shows how to convert several types of temporal values to basic units and vice versa.

Converting between times and seconds

TIME values are specialized representations of a simpler unit (seconds). To convert from one to the other, use the TIME_TO_SEC() and SEC_TO_TIME() functions.

TIME_TO_SEC() converts a TIME value to the equivalent number of seconds, and SEC_TO_TIME() does the opposite. The following statement demonstrates a simple conversion in both directions:

```
mysql> SELECT t1,
    -> TIME_TO_SEC(t1) AS 'TIME to seconds',
    -> SEC_TO_TIME(TIME_TO_SEC(t1)) AS 'TIME to seconds to TIME'
    -> FROM time_val;
+----------+-----------------+-------------------------+
| t1       | TIME to seconds | TIME to seconds to TIME |
+----------+-----------------+-------------------------+
| 15:00:00 |           54000 | 15:00:00                |
| 05:01:30 |           18090 | 05:01:30                |
| 12:30:20 |           45020 | 12:30:20                |
+----------+-----------------+-------------------------+
```

To express time values as minutes, hours, or days, perform the appropriate divisions:

```
mysql> SELECT t1,
    -> TIME_TO_SEC(t1) AS 'seconds',
    -> TIME_TO_SEC(t1)/60 AS 'minutes',
    -> TIME_TO_SEC(t1)/(60*60) AS 'hours',
    -> TIME_TO_SEC(t1)/(24*60*60) AS 'days'
    -> FROM time_val;
+----------+---------+----------+---------+--------+
| t1       | seconds | minutes  | hours   | days   |
+----------+---------+----------+---------+--------+
| 15:00:00 |   54000 | 900.0000 | 15.0000 | 0.6250 |
| 05:01:30 |   18090 | 301.5000 |  5.0250 | 0.2094 |
| 12:30:20 |   45020 | 750.3333 | 12.5056 | 0.5211 |
+----------+---------+----------+---------+--------+
```

Use FLOOR() on the division results if you prefer integer values that have no fractional part.

If you pass TIME_TO_SEC() a date-and-time value, it extracts the time part and discards the date. This provides another means of extracting times from DATETIME (or TIMESTAMP) values, in addition to those already discussed in Recipe 8.9:

```
mysql> SELECT dt,
    -> TIME_TO_SEC(dt) AS 'time part in seconds',
    -> SEC_TO_TIME(TIME_TO_SEC(dt)) AS 'time part as TIME'
    -> FROM datetime_val;
+---------------------+----------------------+-------------------+
| dt                  | time part in seconds | time part as TIME |
+---------------------+----------------------+-------------------+
| 1970-01-01 00:00:00 |                    0 | 00:00:00          |
| 1999-12-31 09:00:00 |                32400 | 09:00:00          |
| 2000-06-04 15:45:30 |                56730 | 15:45:30          |
| 2017-03-16 12:30:15 |                45015 | 12:30:15          |
+---------------------+----------------------+-------------------+
```

Converting between dates and days

If you have a date but want a value in days, or vice versa, use the TO_DAYS() and FROM_DAYS() functions. Date-and-time values also can be converted to days if you can suffer loss of the time part since the year 0.

TO_DAYS() converts a date to the corresponding number of days, and FROM_DAYS() does the opposite:

```
mysql> SELECT d,
    -> TO_DAYS(d) AS 'DATE to days',
    -> FROM_DAYS(TO_DAYS(d)) AS 'DATE to days to DATE'
    -> FROM date_val;
+------------+--------------+----------------------+
| d          | DATE to days | DATE to days to DATE |
+------------+--------------+----------------------+
| 1864-02-28 |       680870 | 1864-02-28           |
| 1900-01-15 |       693975 | 1900-01-15           |
| 1999-12-31 |       730484 | 1999-12-31           |
| 2000-06-04 |       730640 | 2000-06-04           |
| 2017-03-16 |       736769 | 2017-03-16           |
+------------+--------------+----------------------+
```

When using TO_DAYS(), it's best to stick to the advice of the MySQL Reference Manual (*https://oreil.ly/nlUk6*) and avoid DATE values that occur before the beginning of the Gregorian calendar (1582). Changes in the lengths of calendar years and months prior to that date make it difficult to speak meaningfully of what the value of "day 0" might be. This differs from TIME_TO_SEC(), where the correspondence between a TIME value and the resulting seconds value is obvious and has a meaningful reference point of 0 seconds.

If you pass TO_DAYS() a date-and-time value, it extracts the date part and discards the time. This provides another means of extracting dates from DATETIME (or TIMESTAMP) values, in addition to those already discussed in Recipe 8.9:

```
mysql> SELECT dt,
    -> TO_DAYS(dt) AS 'date part in days',
    -> FROM_DAYS(TO_DAYS(dt)) AS 'date part as DATE'
    -> FROM datetime_val;
+---------------------+-------------------+-------------------+
| dt                  | date part in days | date part as DATE |
+---------------------+-------------------+-------------------+
| 1970-01-01 00:00:00 |            719528 | 1970-01-01        |
| 1999-12-31 09:00:00 |            730484 | 1999-12-31        |
| 2000-06-04 15:45:30 |            730640 | 2000-06-04        |
| 2017-03-16 12:30:15 |            736769 | 2017-03-16        |
+---------------------+-------------------+-------------------+
```

Converting between date-and-time values and seconds

For DATETIME or TIMESTAMP values that lie within the range of the TIMESTAMP data type (from the beginning of 1970 partially through 2038), the UNIX_TIMESTAMP() and FROM_UNIXTIME() functions convert to and from the number of seconds elapsed since the beginning of 1970. The conversion to seconds offers higher precision for date-and-time values than a conversion to days, at the cost of a more limited range of values for which the conversion may be performed (TIME_TO_SEC() is unsuitable for this because it discards the date):

```
mysql> SELECT dt,
    -> UNIX_TIMESTAMP(dt) AS seconds,
    -> FROM_UNIXTIME(UNIX_TIMESTAMP(dt)) AS timestamp
    -> FROM datetime_val;
+---------------------+------------+---------------------+
| dt                  | seconds    | timestamp           |
+---------------------+------------+---------------------+
| 1970-01-01 00:00:00 |      21600 | 1970-01-01 00:00:00 |
| 1999-12-31 09:00:00 |  946652400 | 1999-12-31 09:00:00 |
| 2000-06-04 15:45:30 |  960151530 | 2000-06-04 15:45:30 |
| 2017-03-16 12:30:15 | 1489685415 | 2017-03-16 12:30:15 |
+---------------------+------------+---------------------+
```

There is a relationship between "UNIX" in the function names and the fact that the applicable range of values begins with 1970: the "Unix epoch" begins at 1970-01-01 00:00:00 UTC. The epoch is time zero, or the reference point for measuring time in Unix systems. That being so, you may find it curious that the preceding example shows a UNIX_TIMESTAMP() value of 21600 for the first value in the datetime_val table. Why isn't it 0? The apparent discrepancy is due to the fact that the MySQL server interprets the UNIX_TIMESTAMP() argument as a value in the client's local time zone and converts it to UTC (see Recipe 8.4). Our server is in the US Central Time Zone, six hours (21,600 seconds) west of UTC. The DATETIME interpreted based on the time zone and the numbers would not change with a timestamp. Change the session time zone to `'+00:00'` for UTC time, and run the query again to observe a different result:

```
mysql> set time_zone = '+00:00';
mysql> SELECT dt,
    -> UNIX_TIMESTAMP(dt) AS seconds,
    -> FROM_UNIXTIME(UNIX_TIMESTAMP(dt)) AS timestamp
    -> FROM datetime_val;
+---------------------+------------+---------------------+
| dt                  | seconds    | timestamp           |
+---------------------+------------+---------------------+
| 1970-01-01 00:00:00 |          0 | 1970-01-01 00:00:00 |
| 1999-12-31 09:00:00 |  946630800 | 1999-12-31 09:00:00 |
| 2000-06-04 15:45:30 |  960133530 | 2000-06-04 15:45:30 |
| 2017-03-16 12:30:15 | 1489667415 | 2017-03-16 12:30:15 |
+---------------------+------------+---------------------+
```

UNIX_TIMESTAMP() can convert DATE values to seconds, too. It treats such values as having an implicit time-of-day part of `00:00:00`:

```
mysql> SELECT
    -> CURDATE(),
    -> UNIX_TIMESTAMP(CURDATE()),
    -> FROM_UNIXTIME(UNIX_TIMESTAMP(CURDATE()))\G
*************************** 1. row ***************************
                        CURDATE(): 2021-11-28
        UNIX_TIMESTAMP(CURDATE()): 1638046800
FROM_UNIXTIME(UNIX_TIMESTAMP(CURDATE())): 2021-11-28 00:00:00
```

8.12 Calculating Intervals Between Dates or Times

Problem

You want to know how long it is between two dates or times, that is, the interval between them.

Solution

To calculate an interval, use one of the temporal-difference functions, or convert your values to basic units and take the difference. The permitted functions depend on the types of the values for which you want to know the interval.

Discussion

The following discussion shows several ways to perform interval calculations.

Calculating intervals with temporal-difference functions

To calculate an interval in days between two date values, use the DATEDIFF() function:

```
mysql> SET @d1 = '2010-01-01', @d2 = '2009-12-01';
mysql> SELECT DATEDIFF(@d1,@d2) AS 'd1 - d2', DATEDIFF(@d2,@d1) AS 'd2 - d1';
+---------+---------+
| d1 - d2 | d2 - d1 |
+---------+---------+
|      31 |     -31 |
+---------+---------+
```

DATEDIFF() also works with date-and-time values but ignores the time part. This makes it suitable for producing day intervals for DATE, DATETIME, or TIMESTAMP values.

To calculate an interval between TIME values as another TIME value, use the TIME DIFF() function:

```
mysql> SET @t1 = '12:00:00', @t2 = '16:30:00';
mysql> SELECT TIMEDIFF(@t1,@t2) AS 't1 - t2', TIMEDIFF(@t2,@t1) AS 't2 - t1';
+-----------+----------+
| t1 - t2   | t2 - t1  |
+-----------+----------+
| -04:30:00 | 04:30:00 |
+-----------+----------+
```

TIMEDIFF() also works for date-and-time values. That is, it accepts either time or date-and-time values, but the types of the arguments must match.

A time interval expressed as a TIME value can be broken down into components using the techniques shown in Recipe 8.9. For example, to express a time interval in terms of its constituent hours, minutes, and seconds values, calculate time interval subparts using the HOUR(), MINUTE(), and SECOND() functions. (Don't forget that if your intervals may be negative, you must take that into account.) The following SQL statement shows how to determine the components of the interval between the t1 and t2 columns of the time_val table:

```
mysql> SELECT t1, t2,
    -> TIMEDIFF(t2,t1) AS 't2 - t1 as TIME',
    -> IF(TIMEDIFF(t2,t1) >= 0,'+','-') AS sign,
    -> HOUR(TIMEDIFF(t2,t1)) AS hour,
    -> MINUTE(TIMEDIFF(t2,t1)) AS minute,
    -> SECOND(TIMEDIFF(t2,t1)) AS second
    -> FROM time_val;
+----------+----------+-----------------+------+------+--------+--------+
| t1       | t2       | t2 - t1 as TIME | sign | hour | minute | second |
+----------+----------+-----------------+------+------+--------+--------+
| 15:00:00 | 15:00:00 | 00:00:00        | +    |    0 |      0 |      0 |
| 05:01:30 | 02:30:20 | -02:31:10       | -    |    2 |     31 |     10 |
| 12:30:20 | 17:30:45 | 05:00:25        | +    |    5 |      0 |     25 |
+----------+----------+-----------------+------+------+--------+--------+
```

If you work with date or date-and-time values, the TIMESTAMPDIFF() function provides another way to calculate intervals. It enables you to specify the units in which intervals should be expressed:

```
TIMESTAMPDIFF(unit,val1,val2)
```

unit is the interval unit, and *val1* and *val2* are the values between which to calculate the interval. With TIMESTAMPDIFF(), you can express an interval in many different ways:

```
mysql> SET @dt1 = '1900-01-01 00:00:00', @dt2 = '1910-01-01 00:00:00';
mysql> SELECT
    -> TIMESTAMPDIFF(MINUTE,@dt1,@dt2) AS minutes,
    -> TIMESTAMPDIFF(HOUR,@dt1,@dt2) AS hours,
    -> TIMESTAMPDIFF(DAY,@dt1,@dt2) AS days,
    -> TIMESTAMPDIFF(WEEK,@dt1,@dt2) AS weeks,
    -> TIMESTAMPDIFF(YEAR,@dt1,@dt2) AS years;
+---------+-------+------+-------+-------+
| minutes | hours | days | weeks | years |
+---------+-------+------+-------+-------+
| 5258880 | 87648 | 3652 |   521 |    10 |
+---------+-------+------+-------+-------+
```

Permitted *unit* specifiers are MICROSECOND, SECOND, MINUTE, HOUR, DAY, WEEK, MONTH, QUARTER, or YEAR. Note that each is singular, not plural.

Be aware of these properties of TIMESTAMPDIFF():

- Its value is negative if the first temporal value is greater than the second, which is opposite the order of the arguments for DATEDIFF() and TIMEDIFF().

- Despite the TIMESTAMP in its name, TIMESTAMPDIFF() arguments are not limited to the range of the TIMESTAMP data type.

Time interval calculation using basic units

To calculate intervals in seconds between pairs of time values, convert them to seconds with TIME_TO_SEC() and take the difference. To express the resulting interval as a TIME value, pass it to SEC_TO_TIME(). The following statement calculates the intervals between the t1 and t2 columns of the time_val table, expressing each interval both in seconds and as a TIME value:

```
mysql> SELECT t1, t2,
    -> TIME_TO_SEC(t2) - TIME_TO_SEC(t1) AS 't2 - t1 (in seconds)',
    -> SEC_TO_TIME(TIME_TO_SEC(t2) - TIME_TO_SEC(t1)) AS 't2 - t1 (as TIME)'
    -> FROM time_val;
+----------+----------+----------------------+-------------------+
| t1       | t2       | t2 - t1 (in seconds) | t2 - t1 (as TIME) |
+----------+----------+----------------------+-------------------+
| 15:00:00 | 15:00:00 |                    0 | 00:00:00          |
| 05:01:30 | 02:30:20 |                -9070 | -02:31:10         |
| 12:30:20 | 17:30:45 |                18025 | 05:00:25          |
+----------+----------+----------------------+-------------------+
```

Date or date-and-time interval calculation using basic units

When you calculate an interval between dates by converting both dates to a common unit in relation to a given reference point and take the difference, the range of your values determines which conversions are available:

- `DATE`, `DATETIME`, or `TIMESTAMP` values dating back to `1970-01-01 00:00:00` UTC —the Unix epoch—can be converted to seconds elapsed since the epoch. With dates in that range, you can calculate intervals to an accuracy of one second.

- Older dates from the beginning of the Gregorian calendar (1582) on can be converted to day values and used to compute intervals in days.

- Dates that begin earlier than either of these reference points present more of a problem. In such cases, you may find that your programming language offers computations that are not available or are difficult to perform in SQL. If so, consider processing date values directly from within your API language. For example, the Date::Calc and Date::Manip modules are available from the Comprehensive Perl Archive Network (CPAN) for use in Perl scripts.

To calculate an interval in days between date or date-and-time values, convert them to days with `TO_DAYS()` and take the difference. For an interval in weeks, do the same thing and divide the result by seven:

```
mysql> SET @days = TO_DAYS('1884-01-01') - TO_DAYS('1883-06-05');
mysql> SELECT @days AS days, @days/7 AS weeks;
+------+---------+
| days | weeks   |
+------+---------+
|  210 | 30.0000 |
+------+---------+
```

You cannot convert days to months or years by simple division because those units vary in length. To yield date intervals expressed in those units, use `TIMESTAMPDIFF()`, discussed earlier in this recipe.

For date-and-time values occurring within the `TIMESTAMP` range from 1970 partially through 2038, you can determine intervals to a resolution in seconds using the `UNIX_TIMESTAMP()` function. For intervals in other units, seconds are easily converted to minutes, hours, days, or weeks, as this expression shows for dates that lie two weeks apart:

```
mysql> SET @dt1 = '1984-01-01 09:00:00';
mysql> SET @dt2 = @dt1 + INTERVAL 14 DAY;
mysql> SET @interval = UNIX_TIMESTAMP(@dt2) - UNIX_TIMESTAMP(@dt1);
mysql> SELECT @interval AS seconds,
    -> @interval / 60 AS minutes,
    -> @interval / (60 * 60) AS hours,
    -> @interval / (24 * 60 * 60) AS days,
    -> @interval / (7 * 24 * 60 * 60) AS weeks;
+---------+------------+----------+---------+--------+
| seconds | minutes    | hours    | days    | weeks  |
+---------+------------+----------+---------+--------+
| 1209600 | 20160.0000 | 336.0000 | 14.0000 | 2.0000 |
+---------+------------+----------+---------+--------+
```

Use `FLOOR()` on the division results if you prefer integer values that have no fractional part.

For values that occur outside the `TIMESTAMP` range, this interval calculation method is more general (but messier):

1. Take the difference in days between the date parts of the values and multiply by $24 \times 60 \times 60$ to convert to seconds.

2. Adjust the result by the difference in seconds between the time parts of the values.

Here's an example, using two date-and-time values that lie slightly less than three days apart:

```
mysql> SET @dt1 = '1800-02-14 07:30:00';
mysql> SET @dt2 = '1800-02-17 06:30:00';
mysql> SET @interval =
    ->   ((TO_DAYS(@dt2) - TO_DAYS(@dt1)) * 24*60*60)
    ->   + TIME_TO_SEC(@dt2) - TIME_TO_SEC(@dt1);
mysql> SELECT @interval AS seconds, SEC_TO_TIME(@interval) AS TIME;
+---------+----------+
| seconds | TIME     |
+---------+----------+
|  255600 | 71:00:00 |
+---------+----------+
```

Do You Want an Interval or a Span?

When you take a difference between dates (or times), consider whether you want an interval or a span. Taking a difference between dates gives you the interval from one date to the next. To determine the range spanned by the two dates, you must add a unit. For example, it's a three-day interval from `2002-01-01` to `2002-01-04`, but together they span a range of four days. If you don't get the results you expect from a difference-of-values calculation, consider whether an "off-by-one" correction is needed.

8.13 Adding Date or Time Values

Problem

You want to add temporal values. For example, you want to add a given number of seconds to a time or determine what the date will be three weeks from today.

Solution

To add date or time values, you have several options:

- Use one of the temporal-addition functions.
- Use the + INTERVAL or - INTERVAL operator.
- Convert the values to basic units, and take the sum.

The applicable functions or operators depend on the types of the values.

Discussion

The following discussion shows several ways to add temporal values.

Adding temporal values using temporal-addition functions or operators

To add a time to a time or date-and-time value, use the ADDTIME() function:

```
mysql> SET @t1 = '12:00:00', @t2 = '15:30:00';
mysql> SELECT ADDTIME(@t1,@t2);
+------------------+
| ADDTIME(@t1,@t2) |
+------------------+
| 27:30:00         |
+------------------+
mysql> SET @dt = '1984-03-01 12:00:00', @t = '12:00:00';
mysql> SELECT ADDTIME(@dt,@t);
+----------------------------+
| TIMESTAMP(@d,@t)           |
+----------------------------+
| 1984-03-01 15:30:00.000000 |
+----------------------------+
```

To add a time to a date or date-and-time value, use the TIMESTAMP() function:

```
mysql> SET @d = '1984-03-01', @t = '15:30:00';
mysql> SELECT TIMESTAMP(@d,@t);
+---------------------+
| TIMESTAMP(@d,@t)    |
+---------------------+
| 1984-03-01 15:30:00 |
+---------------------+
mysql> SET @dt = '1984-03-01 12:00:00', @t = '12:00:00';
mysql> SELECT TIMESTAMP(@dt,@t);
+----------------------------+
| TIMESTAMP(@dt,@t)          |
+----------------------------+
| 1984-03-02 00:00:00.000000 |
+----------------------------+
```

MySQL also provides `DATE_ADD()` and `DATE_SUB()` functions for adding intervals to dates and subtracting intervals from dates. Each function takes a date (or date-and-time) value d and an interval, expressed using the following syntax:

```
DATE_ADD(d,INTERVAL val unit)
DATE_SUB(d,INTERVAL val unit)
```

The `+ INTERVAL` and `- INTERVAL` operators are similar:

```
d + INTERVAL val unit
d - INTERVAL val unit
```

`unit` is the interval unit, and `val` is an expression indicating the number of units. Some common unit specifiers are SECOND, MINUTE, HOUR, DAY, MONTH, and YEAR. Note that each is singular, not plural. (Check the MySQL Reference Manual (*https://oreil.ly/ubU95*) for the full list.)

Use `DATE_ADD()` or `DATE_SUB()` to perform date arithmetic operations such as these:

- Determine the date three days from today:
  ```
  mysql> SELECT CURDATE(), DATE_ADD(CURDATE(),INTERVAL 3 DAY);
  +------------+------------------------------------+
  | CURDATE()  | DATE_ADD(CURDATE(),INTERVAL 3 DAY) |
  +------------+------------------------------------+
  | 2021-11-24 | 2021-11-27                         |
  +------------+------------------------------------+
  ```

- Find the date a week ago:
  ```
  mysql> SELECT CURDATE(), DATE_SUB(CURDATE(),INTERVAL 1 WEEK);
  +------------+-------------------------------------+
  | CURDATE()  | DATE_SUB(CURDATE(),INTERVAL 1 WEEK) |
  +------------+-------------------------------------+
  | 2021-11-24 | 2021-11-17                          |
  +------------+-------------------------------------+
  ```

- For questions where you need to know both the date and the time, begin with a DATETIME or TIMESTAMP value. To answer the question "What time will it be in 60 hours?" do this:
  ```
  mysql> SELECT NOW(), DATE_ADD(NOW(),INTERVAL 60 HOUR);
  +---------------------+----------------------------------+
  | NOW()               | DATE_ADD(NOW(),INTERVAL 60 HOUR)  |
  +---------------------+----------------------------------+
  | 2021-11-24 22:44:19 | 2021-11-27 10:44:19              |
  +---------------------+----------------------------------+
  ```

- Some interval specifiers have both date and time parts. The following adds 14.5 hours to the current date and time:
  ```
  mysql> SELECT NOW(), DATE_ADD(NOW(),INTERVAL '14:30' HOUR_MINUTE);
  +---------------------+----------------------------------------------+
  | NOW()               | DATE_ADD(NOW(),INTERVAL '14:30' HOUR_MINUTE) |
  +---------------------+----------------------------------------------+
  | 2021-11-24 22:46:37 | 2021-11-25 13:16:37                          |
  +---------------------+----------------------------------------------+
  ```

Similarly, adding three days and four hours produces this result:

```
mysql> SELECT NOW(), DATE_ADD(NOW(),INTERVAL '3 4' DAY_HOUR);
+---------------------+------------------------------------------+
| NOW()               | DATE_ADD(NOW(),INTERVAL '3 4' DAY_HOUR)   |
+---------------------+------------------------------------------+
| 2021-11-24 22:47:15 | 2021-11-28 02:47:15                      |
+---------------------+------------------------------------------+
```

DATE_ADD() and DATE_SUB() are interchangeable because one is the same as the other with the sign of the interval value flipped. These two expressions are equivalent for any date value d:

```
DATE_ADD(d,INTERVAL -3 MONTH)
DATE_SUB(d,INTERVAL 3 MONTH)
```

You can also use the + INTERVAL or - INTERVAL operator to perform date interval addition or subtraction:

```
mysql> SELECT CURDATE(), CURDATE() + INTERVAL 1 YEAR;
+------------+-----------------------------+
| CURDATE()  | CURDATE() + INTERVAL 1 YEAR |
+------------+-----------------------------+
| 2021-11-24 | 2022-11-24                  |
+------------+-----------------------------+
mysql> SELECT NOW(), NOW() - INTERVAL '1 12' DAY_HOUR;
+---------------------+----------------------------------+
| NOW()               | NOW() - INTERVAL '1 12' DAY_HOUR |
+---------------------+----------------------------------+
| 2021-11-24 22:48:31 | 2021-11-23 10:48:31              |
+---------------------+----------------------------------+
```

TIMESTAMPADD() is an alternative function for adding intervals to date or date-and-time values. Its arguments are similar to those for DATE_ADD(), and the following equivalence holds:

```
TIMESTAMPADD(unit,interval,d) = DATE_ADD(d,INTERVAL interval unit)
```

Adding temporal values using basic units

Another way to add intervals to date or date-and-time values is to perform temporal "shifting" via functions that convert to and from basic units. For background information about the applicable functions, see Recipe 8.11.

Adding time values using basic units

Adding times with basic units is similar to calculating intervals between times, except that you compute a sum rather than a difference. To add an interval value in seconds to a TIME value, convert the TIME to seconds so that both values are represented in the same units, then add the values and convert the result back to a TIME. For example, two hours is 7,200 seconds ($2 \times 60 \times 60$), so the following statement adds two hours to each t1 value in the time_val table:

```
mysql> SELECT t1,
    -> SEC_TO_TIME(TIME_TO_SEC(t1) + 7200) AS 't1 plus 2 hours'
```

```
    -> FROM time_val;
+----------+----------------+
| t1       | t1 plus 2 hours |
+----------+----------------+
| 15:00:00 | 17:00:00       |
| 05:01:30 | 07:01:30       |
| 12:30:20 | 14:30:20       |
+----------+----------------+
```

If the interval itself is expressed as a TIME, it too should be converted to seconds before adding the values together. The following example calculates the sum of the two TIME values in each row of the time_val table:

```
mysql> SELECT t1, t2,
    -> TIME_TO_SEC(t1) + TIME_TO_SEC(t2)
    ->   AS 't1 + t2 (in seconds)',
    -> SEC_TO_TIME(TIME_TO_SEC(t1) + TIME_TO_SEC(t2))
    ->   AS 't1 + t2 (as TIME)'
    -> FROM time_val;
+----------+----------+----------------------+-------------------+
| t1       | t2       | t1 + t2 (in seconds) | t1 + t2 (as TIME) |
+----------+----------+----------------------+-------------------+
| 15:00:00 | 15:00:00 |               108000 | 30:00:00          |
| 05:01:30 | 02:30:20 |                27110 | 07:31:50          |
| 12:30:20 | 17:30:45 |               108065 | 30:01:05          |
+----------+----------+----------------------+-------------------+
```

It's important to recognize that MySQL TIME values represent elapsed time, not time of day, so they don't reset to 0 after reaching 24 hours. You can see this in the first and third output rows from the previous statement. To produce time-of-day values, enforce a 24-hour wraparound using a modulo operation before converting the seconds value back to a TIME value. The number of seconds in a day is $24 \times 60 \times 60$, or 86,400. To convert any seconds value s to lie within a 24-hour range, use the MOD() function or the % modulo operator like this:

```
MOD(s,86400)
s % 86400
s MOD 86400
```

The three expressions are equivalent. Applying the first of them to the time calculations from the preceding example produces the following result:

```
mysql> SELECT t1, t2,
    -> MOD(TIME_TO_SEC(t1) + TIME_TO_SEC(t2), 86400)
    ->   AS 't1 + t2 (in seconds)',
    -> SEC_TO_TIME(MOD(TIME_TO_SEC(t1) + TIME_TO_SEC(t2), 86400))
    ->   AS 't1 + t2 (as TIME)'
    -> FROM time_val;
+----------+----------+----------------------+-------------------+
| t1       | t2       | t1 + t2 (in seconds) | t1 + t2 (as TIME) |
+----------+----------+----------------------+-------------------+
| 15:00:00 | 15:00:00 |                21600 | 06:00:00          |
| 05:01:30 | 02:30:20 |                27110 | 07:31:50          |
| 12:30:20 | 17:30:45 |                21665 | 06:01:05          |
+----------+----------+----------------------+-------------------+
```

The permitted range of a TIME column is -838:59:59 to 838:59:59 (that is, -3020399 to 3020399 seconds). However, the range of TIME *expressions* can be greater, so when you add time values, you can easily produce a result that lies outside this range and cannot be stored as is into a TIME column.

Alternatively, you can use the TIMESTAMPDIFF() function to go outside of the TIME DIFF() function limits:

```
mysql> SELECT NOW(),TIMESTAMPDIFF(minute,now(), '2023-01-01 00:00:00');
+---------------------+---------------------------------------------------+
| NOW()               | TIMESTAMPDIFF(minute,now(), '2023-01-01 00:00:00') |
+---------------------+---------------------------------------------------+
| 2022-03-07 06:38:40 |                                            431601 |
+---------------------+---------------------------------------------------+

mysql> SELECT NOW(),TIMESTAMPDIFF(day,now(), '2023-01-01 00:00:00');
+---------------------+------------------------------------------------+
| NOW()               | TIMESTAMPDIFF(day,now(), '2023-01-01 00:00:00') |
+---------------------+------------------------------------------------+
| 2022-03-07 06:38:50 |                                            299 |
+---------------------+------------------------------------------------+
```

Adding to date or date-and-time values using basic units

Date or date-and-time values converted to basic units can be shifted to produce other dates. For example, to shift a date forward or backward a week (seven days), use TO_DAYS() and FROM_DAYS():

```
mysql> SET @d = '1980-01-01';
mysql> SELECT @d AS date,
    -> FROM_DAYS(TO_DAYS(@d) + 7) AS 'date + 1 week',
    -> FROM_DAYS(TO_DAYS(@d) - 7) AS 'date - 1 week';
+------------+---------------+---------------+
| date       | date + 1 week | date - 1 week |
+------------+---------------+---------------+
| 1980-01-01 | 1980-01-08    | 1979-12-25    |
+------------+---------------+---------------+
```

TO_DAYS() also can convert date-and-time values to days, if you don't mind having it chop off the time part.

To preserve the time, you can use UNIX_TIMESTAMP() and FROM_UNIXTIME() instead, if the initial and resulting values both lie in the permitted range for TIMESTAMP values (from 1970 partially through 2038). The following statement shifts a DATETIME value forward and backward by an hour (3,600 seconds):

```
mysql> SET @dt = '1980-01-01 09:00:00';
mysql> SELECT @dt AS datetime,
    -> FROM_UNIXTIME(UNIX_TIMESTAMP(@dt) + 3600) AS 'datetime + 1 hour',
    -> FROM_UNIXTIME(UNIX_TIMESTAMP(@dt) - 3600) AS 'datetime - 1 hour';
+---------------------+---------------------+---------------------+
| datetime            | datetime + 1 hour   | datetime - 1 hour   |
+---------------------+---------------------+---------------------+
| 1980-01-01 09:00:00 | 1980-01-01 10:00:00 | 1980-01-01 08:00:00 |
+---------------------+---------------------+---------------------+
```

8.14 Calculating Ages

Problem

You want to know how old someone is.

Solution

This is a date-arithmetic problem. It amounts to computing the interval between dates but with a twist. For an age in years, it's necessary to account for the relative placement of the start and end dates within the calendar year. For an age in months, it's also necessary to account for the placement of the months and the days within the month.

Discussion

Age determination is a type of date-interval calculation. However, you cannot simply compute a difference in days and divide by 365 because leap years throw off the calculation. (It is 365 days from 1995-03-01 to 1996-02-29, but that is not a year in age terms.) Dividing by 365.25 is slightly more accurate but still not correct for all dates.

To calculate ages, use the TIMESTAMPDIFF() function. Pass it a birth date, a current date, and the unit in which you want the age expressed:

```
TIMESTAMPDIFF(unit,birth,current)
```

TIMESTAMPDIFF() handles the calculations necessary to adjust for differing month and year lengths and relative positions of the dates within the calendar year. Suppose that a sibling table lists the birth dates of Ilayda and her sister Lara:

```
mysql> SELECT * FROM sibling;
+--------+------------+
| name   | birth      |
+--------+------------+
| Ilayda | 2002-12-17 |
| Lara   | 2009-06-03 |
+--------+------------+
```

Using TIMESTAMPDIFF(), you can answer questions such as these:

- How old are the Alkins' children today, in years, months, and days?

```
mysql> SELECT name,DATE_FORMAT(birth,'%Y-%m-%d') as dob,
    -> DATE_FORMAT(NOW(),'%Y-%m-%d') as today,
    -> TIMESTAMPDIFF( YEAR, birth, NOW() ) as age_years',
    -> FLOOR( TIMESTAMPDIFF( DAY, birth, now() ) % 30.4375 ) as age_days
    -> FROM sibling;
+--------+------------+------------+-----------+------------+----------+
| name   | dob        | today      | age_years | age_months | age_days |
+--------+------------+------------+-----------+------------+----------+
| Ilayda | 2002-12-17 | 2022-03-07 |        19 |          2 |       19 |
| Lara   | 2009-06-03 | 2022-03-07 |        12 |          9 |        3 |
+--------+------------+------------+-----------+------------+----------+
```

- How old was Ilayda when Lara was born, in years and months?

```
mysql> SELECT name, birth, '2009-06-03' AS 'Lara\'s birth',
    -> TIMESTAMPDIFF(YEAR,birth,'2009-06-03') AS 'age in years',
    -> TIMESTAMPDIFF( MONTH, birth,'2009-06-09' ) % 12 as age_months,
    -> FLOOR( TIMESTAMPDIFF( DAY, birth,'2009-06-09' ) % 30.4375 ) as age_days
    -> FROM sibling WHERE name <> 'Lara';
+--------+------------+-------------+-----------+------------+----------+
| name   | birth      | Lara's birth| age_years | age_months | age_days |
+--------+------------+-------------+-----------+------------+----------+
| Ilayda | 2002-12-17 | 2009-06-09  |         6 |          5 |       22 |
+--------+------------+-------------+-----------+------------+----------+
```

For further information about date calculation using these functions, consult the MySQL Reference Manual (*https://oreil.ly/pGOMr*).

8.15 Finding the First Day, Last Day, or Length of a Month

Problem

Given a date, you want to determine the date for the first or last day of the month in which the date occurs, or the first or last day for the month *n* months away. A related problem is to determine the number of days in a month.

Solution

To determine the date for the first day in a month, use date shifting (an application of date arithmetic). To determine the date for the last day, use the LAST_DAY() function. To determine the number of days in a month, find the date for its last day and use it as the argument to DAYOFMONTH().

Discussion

Sometimes you have a reference date and want to reach a target date that doesn't have a fixed relationship to the reference date. For example, the first or last days of the current month aren't a fixed number of days from the current date.

To find the first day of the month for a given date, shift the date back by one fewer days than its DAYOFMONTH() value:

```
mysql> SELECT d, DATE_SUB(d,INTERVAL DAYOFMONTH(d)-1 DAY) AS '1st of month'
    -> FROM date_val;
+------------+--------------+
| d          | 1st of month |
+------------+--------------+
| 1864-02-28 | 1864-02-01   |
| 1900-01-15 | 1900-01-01   |
| 1999-12-31 | 1999-12-01   |
| 2000-06-04 | 2000-06-01   |
| 2017-03-16 | 2017-03-01   |
+------------+--------------+
```

In the general case, to find the first of the month for any month *n* months away from a given date, calculate the first of the month for the date and shift the result by *n* months:

```
DATE_ADD(DATE_SUB(d,INTERVAL DAYOFMONTH(d)-1 DAY),INTERVAL n MONTH)
```

For example, to find the first day of the previous and following months relative to a given date, *n* is -1 and 1:

```
mysql> SELECT d,
    -> DATE_ADD(DATE_SUB(d,INTERVAL DAYOFMONTH(d)-1 DAY),INTERVAL -1 MONTH)
    ->   AS '1st of previous month',
    -> DATE_ADD(DATE_SUB(d,INTERVAL DAYOFMONTH(d)-1 DAY),INTERVAL 1 MONTH)
    ->   AS '1st of following month'
    -> FROM date_val;

+------------+-----------------------+------------------------+
| d          | 1st of previous month | 1st of following month |
+------------+-----------------------+------------------------+
| 1864-02-28 | 1864-01-01            | 1864-03-01             |
| 1900-01-15 | 1899-12-01            | 1900-02-01             |
| 1999-12-31 | 1999-11-01            | 2000-01-01             |
| 2000-06-04 | 2000-05-01            | 2000-07-01             |
| 2017-03-16 | 2017-02-01            | 2017-04-01             |
+------------+-----------------------+------------------------+
```

It's easier to find the last day of the month for a given date because there is a function for it:

```
mysql> SELECT d, LAST_DAY(d) AS 'last of month'
    -> FROM date_val;
+------------+---------------+
| d          | last of month |
+------------+---------------+
| 1864-02-28 | 1864-02-29    |
| 1900-01-15 | 1900-01-31    |
| 1999-12-31 | 1999-12-31    |
| 2000-06-04 | 2000-06-30    |
| 2017-03-16 | 2017-03-31    |
+------------+---------------+
```

For the general case, to find the last day of the month for any month *n* months away from a given date, shift the date by that many months first, then pass it to LAST_DAY():

```
LAST_DAY(DATE_ADD(d,INTERVAL n MONTH))
```

For example, to find the last day of the previous and following months relative to a given date, *n* is -1 and 1:

```
mysql> SELECT d,
    -> LAST_DAY(DATE_ADD(d,INTERVAL -1 MONTH))
    ->   AS 'last of previous month',
    -> LAST_DAY(DATE_ADD(d,INTERVAL 1 MONTH))
    ->   AS 'last of following month'
    -> FROM date_val;
+------------+------------------------+------------------------+
| d          | last of previous month | last of following month |
+------------+------------------------+------------------------+
| 1864-02-28 | 1864-01-31             | 1864-03-31             |
| 1900-01-15 | 1899-12-31             | 1900-02-28             |
| 1999-12-31 | 1999-11-30             | 2000-01-31             |
| 2000-06-04 | 2000-05-31             | 2000-07-31             |
| 2017-03-16 | 2017-02-28             | 2017-04-30             |
+------------+------------------------+------------------------+
```

To find the length of a month in days, determine the date of its last day with LAST_DAY(), then use DAYOFMONTH() to extract the day-of-month component from the result:

```
mysql> SELECT d, DAYOFMONTH(LAST_DAY(d)) AS 'days in month' FROM date_val;
+------------+---------------+
| d          | days in month |
+------------+---------------+
| 1864-02-28 |            29 |
| 1900-01-15 |            31 |
| 1999-12-31 |            31 |
| 2000-06-04 |            30 |
| 2017-03-16 |            31 |
+------------+---------------+
```

8.16 Finding the Day of the Week for a Date

Problem

You want to know the day of the week on which a date falls.

Solution

Use the DAYNAME() function.

Discussion

To determine the name of the day of the week for a given date, use DAYNAME():

```
mysql> SELECT CURDATE(), DAYNAME(CURDATE());
+------------+-------------------+
| CURDATE()  | DAYNAME(CURDATE()) |
+------------+-------------------+
| 2021-11-24 | Wednesday         |
+------------+-------------------+
```

DAYNAME() is often useful in conjunction with other date-related techniques. For example, to determine the day of the week for the first of the month, use the first-of-month expression from Recipe 8.15 as the argument to DAYNAME():

```
mysql> SET @d = CURDATE();
mysql> SET @first = DATE_SUB(@d,INTERVAL DAYOFMONTH(@d)-1 DAY);
mysql> SELECT @d AS 'starting date',
    -> @first AS '1st of month date',
    -> DAYNAME(@first) AS '1st of month day';
+---------------+-------------------+------------------+
| starting date | 1st of month date | 1st of month day |
+---------------+-------------------+------------------+
| 2021-11-24    | 2021-11-01        | Monday           |
+---------------+-------------------+------------------+
```

8.17 Finding Dates for Any Weekday of a Given Week

Problem

You want to compute the date of some weekday for the week in which a given date lies. Suppose that you want to know the date of the Tuesday that falls in the same week as 2014-07-09.

Solution

This is an application of date shifting. Figure out the number of days between the starting weekday of the given date and the desired day, and shift the date by that many days.

Discussion

This section and the next describe how to convert one date to another when the target date is specified in terms of days of the week. To solve such problems, you need to know day-of-week values. Suppose you begin with a target date of 2014-07-09. To determine the date for Tuesday of the week in which that date lies, the calculation depends on what weekday it is. If it's a Monday, you add a day to produce 2014-07-10, but if it's a Wednesday, you subtract a day to produce 2014-07-08.

MySQL provides two functions that are useful here. DAYOFWEEK() treats Sunday as the first day of the week and returns 1 through 7 for Sunday through Saturday. WEEKDAY() treats Monday as the first day of the week and returns 0 through 6 for Monday through Sunday. (The examples shown here use DAYOFWEEK().) Another

---

kind of day-of-week operation involves determining the name of the day. DAYNAME() can be used for that.

Calculations that determine one day of the week from another depend on the day you start from as well as the day you want to reach. I find it easiest to shift the reference date first to a known point relative to the beginning of the week, and then shift forward:

1. Shift the reference date back by its DAYOFWEEK() value, which always produces the date for the Saturday preceding the week.

2. Shift the Saturday date by one day to reach the Sunday date, by two days to reach the Monday date, and so forth.

In SQL, those operations can be expressed as follows for a date d, where n is 1 through 7 to produce the dates for Sunday through Saturday:

```
DATE_ADD(DATE_SUB(d,INTERVAL DAYOFWEEK(d) DAY),INTERVAL n DAY)
```

That expression splits the "shift back to Saturday" and "shift forward" phases into separate operations, but because the intervals for both DATE_SUB() and DATE_ADD() are in days, the expression can be simplified into a single DATE_ADD() call:

```
DATE_ADD(d,INTERVAL n-DAYOFWEEK(d) DAY)
```

Applying this formula to the dates in our date_val table, using an n of 1 for Sunday and 7 for Saturday to find the first and last days of the week, yields this result:

```
mysql> SELECT d, DAYNAME(d) AS day,
    -> DATE_ADD(d,INTERVAL 1-DAYOFWEEK(d) DAY) AS Sunday,
    -> DATE_ADD(d,INTERVAL 7-DAYOFWEEK(d) DAY) AS Saturday
    -> FROM date_val;
+------------+----------+------------+------------+
| d          | day      | Sunday     | Saturday   |
+------------+----------+------------+------------+
| 1864-02-28 | Sunday   | 1864-02-28 | 1864-03-05 |
| 1900-01-15 | Monday   | 1900-01-14 | 1900-01-20 |
| 1999-12-31 | Friday   | 1999-12-26 | 2000-01-01 |
| 2000-06-04 | Sunday   | 2000-06-04 | 2000-06-10 |
| 2017-03-16 | Thursday | 2017-03-12 | 2017-03-18 |
+------------+----------+------------+------------+
```

To determine the date of some weekday in a week relative to that of the target date, modify the preceding procedure a bit. First, determine the date of the desired weekday in the week containing the target date and then shift the result into the desired week.

Calculating the date for a day of the week in some other week is a problem that breaks down into a day-within-week shift (using the formula just given) plus a week shift. These operations can be done in either order because the amount of shift within the week is the same whether or not you shift the reference date into a different week first. For example, to calculate Wednesday of a week by the preceding formula, *n* is 4. To compute the date for Wednesday two weeks ago, you can perform the day-within-week shift first, like this:

```
mysql> SET @target =
    -> DATE_SUB(DATE_ADD(CURDATE(),INTERVAL 4-DAYOFWEEK(CURDATE())) DAY),
    -> INTERVAL 14 DAY);
mysql> SELECT CURDATE(), @target, DAYNAME(@target);
+------------+------------+------------------+
| CURDATE()  | @target    | DAYNAME(@target) |
+------------+------------+------------------+
| 2021-11-24 | 2021-11-10 | Wednesday        |
+------------+------------+------------------+
```

Or you can perform the week shift first:

```
mysql> SET @target =
    -> DATE_ADD(DATE_SUB(CURDATE(),INTERVAL 14 DAY),
    -> INTERVAL 4-DAYOFWEEK(CURDATE()) DAY);
mysql> SELECT CURDATE(), @target, DAYNAME(@target);

+------------+------------+------------------+
| CURDATE()  | @target    | DAYNAME(@target) |
+------------+------------+------------------+
| 2021-11-24 | 2021-11-10 | Wednesday        |
+------------+------------+------------------+
```

Some applications need to determine dates such as the *n*-th instance of particular weekdays. For example, to administer a payroll for which paydays are the second and fourth Thursdays of each month, you must know what those dates are. One way to do this for any given month is to begin with the first-of-month date and shift it forward. It's easy enough to shift the date to the Thursday in that week; the trick is to figure out how many weeks forward to shift the result to reach the second and fourth Thursdays. If the first of the month occurs on any day from Sunday through Thursday, you shift forward one week to reach the second Thursday. If the first of the month occurs on Friday or later, you shift forward by two weeks. The fourth Thursday is, of course, two weeks after that.

The following Perl code implements this logic to find all paydays in the year 2021. It runs a loop that constructs the first-of-month date for the months of the year. For each month, it issues a statement that determines the dates of the second and fourth Thursdays:

```
my $year = 2021;
print "MM/YYYY   2nd Thursday   4th Thursday\n";
foreach my $month (1..12)
{
  my $first = sprintf ("%04d-%02d-01", $year, $month);
  my ($thu2, $thu4) = $dbh->selectrow_array (qq{
                    SELECT
                      DATE_ADD(
                        DATE_ADD(?,INTERVAL 5-DAYOFWEEK(?) DAY),
                        INTERVAL IF(DAYOFWEEK(?) <= 5, 7, 14) DAY),
                      DATE_ADD(
                        DATE_ADD(?,INTERVAL 5-DAYOFWEEK(?) DAY),
                        INTERVAL IF(DAYOFWEEK(?) <= 5, 21, 28) DAY)
```

```
                    }, undef, $first, $first, $first, $first, $first, $first);
    printf "%02d/%04d   %s      %s\n", $month, $year, $thu2, $thu4;
}
```

The program produces this output:

```
MM/YYYY   2nd Thursday   4th Thursday
01/2021   2021-01-14     2021-01-28
02/2021   2021-02-11     2021-02-25
03/2021   2021-03-11     2021-03-25
04/2021   2021-04-08     2021-04-22
05/2021   2021-05-13     2021-05-27
06/2021   2021-06-10     2021-06-24
07/2021   2021-07-08     2021-07-22
08/2021   2021-08-12     2021-08-26
09/2021   2021-09-09     2021-09-23
10/2021   2021-10-14     2021-10-28
11/2021   2021-11-11     2021-11-25
12/2021   2021-12-09     2021-12-23
```

8.18 Canonizing Not-Quite-ISO Date Strings

Problem

You have a date that is in a format that's close to, but not exactly in, ISO format, and you want to convert it into an ISO-format date.

Solution

Canonize the date by passing it to a function that always returns an ISO-format date result.

Discussion

In Recipe 8.10, we ran into the problem that synthesizing dates with CONCAT() may produce values that are not quite in ISO format. For example, the following statement produces first-of-month values in which the month part may have only a single digit:

```
mysql> SELECT d, CONCAT(YEAR(d),'-',MONTH(d),'-01') FROM date_val;
+------------+------------------------------------+
| d          | CONCAT(YEAR(d),'-',MONTH(d),'-01') |
+------------+------------------------------------+
| 1864-02-28 | 1864-2-01                          |
| 1900-01-15 | 1900-1-01                          |
| 1999-12-31 | 1999-12-01                         |
| 2000-06-04 | 2000-6-01                          |
| 2017-03-16 | 2017-3-01                          |
+------------+------------------------------------+
```

Recipe 8.10 shows a technique using LPAD() for making sure the month values have two digits. Another way to standardize a close-to-ISO date is to use it in an expression that produces an ISO date result. For a date d, any of the following expressions will do:

```
DATE_ADD(d,INTERVAL 0 DAY)
d + INTERVAL 0 DAY
FROM_DAYS(TO_DAYS(d))
STR_TO_DATE(d,'%Y-%m-%d')
```

Using those expressions with the non-ISO results from the CONCAT() operation yields ISO format in several ways:

```
mysql> SELECT
    -> CONCAT(YEAR(d),'-',MONTH(d),'-01') AS 'non-ISO',
    -> DATE_ADD(CONCAT(YEAR(d),'-',MONTH(d),'-01'),INTERVAL 0 DAY) AS 'ISO 1',
    -> CONCAT(YEAR(d),'-',MONTH(d),'-01') + INTERVAL 0 DAY AS 'ISO 2',
    -> FROM_DAYS(TO_DAYS(CONCAT(YEAR(d),'-',MONTH(d),'-01'))) AS 'ISO 3',
    -> STR_TO_DATE(CONCAT(YEAR(d),'-',MONTH(d),'-01'),'%Y-%m-%d') AS 'ISO 4'
    -> FROM date_val;
+------------+------------+------------+------------+------------+
| non-ISO    | ISO 1      | ISO 2      | ISO 3      | ISO 4      |
+------------+------------+------------+------------+------------+
| 1864-2-01  | 1864-02-01 | 1864-02-01 | 1864-02-01 | 1864-02-01 |
| 1900-1-01  | 1900-01-01 | 1900-01-01 | 1900-01-01 | 1900-01-01 |
| 1999-12-01 | 1999-12-01 | 1999-12-01 | 1999-12-01 | 1999-12-01 |
| 2000-6-01  | 2000-06-01 | 2000-06-01 | 2000-06-01 | 2000-06-01 |
| 2017-3-01  | 2017-03-01 | 2017-03-01 | 2017-03-01 | 2017-03-01 |
+------------+------------+------------+------------+------------+
```

8.19 Selecting Rows Based on Temporal Characteristics

Problem

You want to select rows based on temporal conditions.

Solution

Use a date or time condition in the WHERE clause. This may be based on direct comparison of column values with known values. Or it may be necessary to apply a function to column values to convert them to a more appropriate form for testing, such as using MONTH() to test the month part of a date.

Discussion

Most of the preceding date-based techniques were illustrated by example statements that produce date or time values as output. To place date-based restrictions on the rows selected by a statement, use the same techniques in a WHERE clause. For example, you can select rows by looking for values that occur before or after a given date, within a date range, or that match particular month or day values.

Comparing dates to one another

The following statements find rows from the date_val table that occur either before 1900 or during the 1900s:

```
mysql> SELECT d FROM date_val where d < '1900-01-01';
+------------+
| d          |
+------------+
| 1864-02-28 |
+------------+
mysql> SELECT d FROM date_val where d BETWEEN '1900-01-01' AND '1999-12-31';
+------------+
| d          |
+------------+
| 1900-01-15 |
| 1999-12-31 |
+------------+
```

When you don't know the exact date needed for a comparison in a WHERE clause, you can often calculate it using an expression. For example, to perform an "on this day in history" statement to search for rows in a table named history to find events occurring exactly 50 years ago, do this:

```
SELECT * FROM history WHERE d = DATE_SUB(CURDATE(),INTERVAL 50 YEAR);
```

You see this kind of thing in newspapers that run columns showing what the news events were in times past. (In essence, the statement identifies those events that have reached their *n*-th anniversary.) To retrieve events that occurred "on this day" for any year rather than "on this date" for a specific year, the statement is a bit different. In that case, you need to find rows that match the current calendar day, ignoring the year. That topic is discussed in "Comparing dates to calendar days" on page 379.

Calculated dates are useful for range testing as well. For example, to find dates that occur later than 20 years ago, use DATE_SUB() to calculate the cutoff date:

```
mysql> SELECT d FROM date_val WHERE d >= DATE_SUB(CURDATE(),INTERVAL 20 YEAR);
+------------+
| d          |
+------------+
| 1999-12-31 |
| 2000-06-04 |
| 2017-03-16 |
+------------+
```

Note that the expression in the WHERE clause isolates the date column d on one side of the comparison operator. This is usually a good idea; if the column is indexed, placing it alone on one side of a comparison enables MySQL to process the statement more efficiently. To illustrate, the preceding WHERE clause can be written in a way that's logically equivalent but much less efficient for MySQL to execute:

```
WHERE DATE_ADD(d,INTERVAL 20 YEAR) >= CURDATE();
```

Here, the d column is used within an expression. That means *every* row must be retrieved so that the expression can be evaluated and tested, which makes any index on the column useless.

Sometimes it's not so obvious how to rewrite a comparison to isolate a date column on one side. For example, the following WHERE clause uses only part of the date column in the comparisons:

```
WHERE YEAR(d) >= 1987 AND YEAR(d) <= 1991;
```

To rewrite the first comparison, eliminate the YEAR() call, and replace its right side with a complete date:

```
WHERE d >= '1987-01-01' AND YEAR(d) <= 1991;
```

Rewriting the second comparison is a little trickier. You can eliminate the YEAR() call on the left side, just as with the first expression, but you can't just add -01-01 to the year on the right side. That produces the following result, which is incorrect:

```
WHERE d >= '1987-01-01' AND d <= '1991-01-01';
```

That fails because dates from 1991-01-02 to 1991-12-31 fail the test but should pass. To rewrite the second comparison correctly, do this:

```
WHERE d >= '1987-01-01' AND d < '1992-01-01';
```

Another use for calculated dates occurs frequently in applications that create rows that have a limited lifetime. Such applications must be able to determine which rows to delete when performing an expiration operation. You can approach this problem in a couple of ways:

- Store a date in each row indicating when it was created. (Do this by making the column a TIMESTAMP or by setting it to NOW(); see Recipe 8.8 for details.) To perform an expiration operation later, determine which rows have a creation date that is too old by comparing that date to the current date. For example, the statement to expire rows that were created more than *n* days ago might look like this:

    ```
    DELETE FROM mytbl WHERE create_date < DATE_SUB(NOW(),INTERVAL n DAY);
    ```

- Store an explicit expiration date in each row by calculating the expiration date with DATE_ADD() when the row is created. For a row that should expire in *n* days, do this:

    ```
    INSERT INTO mytbl (expire_date,...)
    VALUES(DATE_ADD(NOW(),INTERVAL n DAY),...);
    ```

To perform the expiration operation in this case, compare the expiration dates to the current date to see which have been reached:

```
DELETE FROM mytbl WHERE expire_date < NOW();
```

Comparing times to one another

Comparisons involving times are similar to those involving dates. For example, to find times in the t1 column that occurred from 9 AM to 2 PM, use an expression like one of these:

```
WHERE t1 BETWEEN '09:00:00' AND '14:00:00';
WHERE HOUR(t1) BETWEEN 9 AND 14;
```

For an indexed TIME column, the first method is more efficient. The second method has the property that it works not only for TIME columns but for DATETIME and TIMESTAMP columns as well.

Comparing dates to calendar days

To answer questions about particular days of the year, use calendar-day testing. The following examples illustrate how to do this in the context of looking for birthdays:

- Who has a birthday today? This requires matching a particular calendar day, so you extract the month and day but ignore the year when performing comparisons:
  ```
  WHERE MONTH(d) = MONTH(CURDATE()) AND DAYOFMONTH(d) = DAYOFMONTH(CURDATE());
  ```

  This kind of statement is commonly applied to biographical data to find lists of actors, politicians, musicians, and so forth who were born on a particular day of the year.

  It's tempting to use DAYOFYEAR() to solve "on this day" problems because it results in simpler statements. But DAYOFYEAR() doesn't work properly for leap years. The presence of February 29 throws off the values for days from March through December:

- Who has a birthday this month? In this case, it's necessary to check only the month:
  ```
  WHERE MONTH(d) = MONTH(CURDATE());
  ```

- Who has a birthday next month? The trick here is that you can't just add one to the current month to get the month number that qualifying dates must match. That gives you 13 for dates in December. To make sure that you get 1 (January), use either of the following techniques:
  ```
  WHERE MONTH(d) = MONTH(DATE_ADD(CURDATE(),INTERVAL 1 MONTH));
  WHERE MONTH(d) = MOD(MONTH(CURDATE()),12)+1;
  ```

## CHAPTER 9

Sorting Query Results

9.0 Introduction

This chapter covers sorting, an extremely important operation for controlling how MySQL displays results from SELECT statements. To sort a query result, add an ORDER BY clause to the query. Without such a clause, MySQL is free to return rows in any order, so sorting helps bring order to disorder and makes query results easier to examine and understand.

You can sort rows of a query result in several ways:

- Using a single column, a combination of columns, or even parts of columns or expression results
- Using ascending or descending order
- Using case-sensitive or case-insensitive string comparisons
- Using temporal ordering

Several examples in this chapter use the driver_log table, which contains columns for recording daily mileage logs for a set of truck drivers:

```
mysql> SELECT * FROM driver_log;
+--------+-------+------------+-------+
| rec_id | name  | trav_date  | miles |
+--------+-------+------------+-------+
|      1 | Ben   | 2014-07-30 |   152 |
|      2 | Suzi  | 2014-07-29 |   391 |
|      3 | Henry | 2014-07-29 |   300 |
|      4 | Henry | 2014-07-27 |    96 |
|      5 | Ben   | 2014-07-29 |   131 |
|      6 | Henry | 2014-07-26 |   115 |
|      7 | Suzi  | 2014-08-02 |   502 |
|      8 | Henry | 2014-08-01 |   197 |
```

```
|       9 | Ben   | 2014-08-02 |    79 |
|      10 | Henry | 2014-07-30 |   203 |
+---------+-------+------------+-------+
```

Many other examples use the `mail` table (used in earlier chapters):

```
mysql> SELECT t, srcuser, srchost, dstuser, dsthost, size FROM mail;
+---------------------+---------+---------+---------+---------+---------+
| t                   | srcuser | srchost | dstuser | dsthost | size    |
+---------------------+---------+---------+---------+---------+---------+
| 2014-05-11 10:15:08 | barb    | saturn  | tricia  | mars    |   58274 |
| 2014-05-12 12:48:13 | tricia  | mars    | gene    | venus   |  194925 |
| 2014-05-12 15:02:49 | phil    | mars    | phil    | saturn  |    1048 |
| 2014-05-12 18:59:18 | barb    | saturn  | tricia  | venus   |     271 |
| 2014-05-14 09:31:37 | gene    | venus   | barb    | mars    |    2291 |
| 2014-05-14 11:52:17 | phil    | mars    | tricia  | saturn  |    5781 |
| 2014-05-14 14:42:21 | barb    | venus   | barb    | venus   |   98151 |
| 2014-05-14 17:03:01 | tricia  | saturn  | phil    | venus   | 2394482 |
| 2014-05-15 07:17:48 | gene    | mars    | gene    | saturn  |    3824 |
| 2014-05-15 08:50:57 | phil    | venus   | phil    | venus   |     978 |
| 2014-05-15 10:25:52 | gene    | mars    | tricia  | saturn  |  998532 |
| 2014-05-15 17:35:31 | gene    | saturn  | gene    | mars    |    3856 |
| 2014-05-16 09:00:28 | gene    | venus   | barb    | mars    |     613 |
| 2014-05-16 23:04:19 | phil    | venus   | barb    | venus   |   10294 |
| 2014-05-19 12:49:23 | phil    | mars    | tricia  | saturn  |     873 |
| 2014-05-19 22:21:51 | gene    | saturn  | gene    | venus   |   23992 |
+---------------------+---------+---------+---------+---------+---------+
```

Other tables are used occasionally as well. To create them, use scripts found in the *tables* directory of the `recipes` distribution.

9.1 Using ORDER BY to Sort Query Results

Problem

Rows in a query result don't appear in the order you want.

Solution

Add an ORDER BY clause to the query to sort its result.

Discussion

The contents of the `driver_log` and `mail` tables shown in the chapter introduction are disorganized and difficult to make sense of. The values in the `id` and `t` columns are in order only by coincidence.

When you select rows, they're returned from the database in whatever order the server happens to use. A relational database makes no guarantee about the order in which it returns rows—unless you tell it how, by adding an ORDER BY clause to your SELECT statement. Without ORDER BY, you may find that the retrieval order changes over time as you modify the table contents. With an ORDER BY clause, MySQL always sorts rows as you indicate.

ORDER BY has the following general characteristics:

- You can sort using one or more column or expression values.
- You can sort columns independently in ascending order (the default) or descending order.
- You can refer to sort columns by name or by using an alias.

This recipe shows some basic sorting techniques, such as how to name the sort columns and specify the sort direction. Recipes later in this chapter illustrate how to perform more complex sorts. Paradoxically, you can even use ORDER BY to *disorder* a result set, which is useful for randomizing the rows or (in conjunction with LIMIT) for picking a row at random from a result set (see Recipes 17.7 and 17.8).

The following examples demonstrate how to sort on a single column or multiple columns and how to sort in ascending or descending order. The examples select the rows in the driver_log table but sort them in different orders to demonstrate the effect of the different ORDER BY clauses.

This query produces a single-column sort using the driver name:

```
mysql> SELECT * FROM driver_log ORDER BY name;
+--------+-------+------------+-------+
| rec_id | name  | trav_date  | miles |
+--------+-------+------------+-------+
|      1 | Ben   | 2014-07-30 |   152 |
|      9 | Ben   | 2014-08-02 |    79 |
|      5 | Ben   | 2014-07-29 |   131 |
|      8 | Henry | 2014-08-01 |   197 |
|      6 | Henry | 2014-07-26 |   115 |
|      4 | Henry | 2014-07-27 |    96 |
|      3 | Henry | 2014-07-29 |   300 |
|     10 | Henry | 2014-07-30 |   203 |
|      7 | Suzi  | 2014-08-02 |   502 |
|      2 | Suzi  | 2014-07-29 |   391 |
+--------+-------+------------+-------+
```

The default sort direction is ascending. To make the direction for an ascending sort explicit, add ASC after the sorted column's name:

```
SELECT * FROM driver_log ORDER BY name ASC;
```

The opposite (or reverse) of ascending order is descending order, specified by adding DESC after the sorted column's name:

```
mysql> SELECT * FROM driver_log ORDER BY name DESC;
+--------+-------+------------+-------+
| rec_id | name  | trav_date  | miles |
+--------+-------+------------+-------+
|      2 | Suzi  | 2014-07-29 |   391 |
```

```
|     7 | Suzi  | 2014-08-02 |   502 |
|    10 | Henry | 2014-07-30 |   203 |
|     8 | Henry | 2014-08-01 |   197 |
|     6 | Henry | 2014-07-26 |   115 |
|     4 | Henry | 2014-07-27 |    96 |
|     3 | Henry | 2014-07-29 |   300 |
|     5 | Ben   | 2014-07-29 |   131 |
|     9 | Ben   | 2014-08-02 |    79 |
|     1 | Ben   | 2014-07-30 |   152 |
+-------+-------+------------+-------+
```

Closely examine the output from the queries just shown and you'll notice that although rows are sorted by name, rows for any given name are in no special order. (The `trav_date` values aren't in date order for Henry or Ben, for example.) That's because MySQL doesn't sort something unless you tell it to:

- The overall order of rows returned by a query is indeterminate unless you specify an ORDER BY clause.
- Within a group of rows that sort together based on the values in a given column, the order of values in other columns is also indeterminate unless you name them in the ORDER BY clause.

To more fully control output order, specify a multiple-column sort by listing each column to use for sorting, separated by commas. The following query sorts in ascending order by `name` and by `trav_date` within the rows for each name:

```
mysql> SELECT * FROM driver_log ORDER BY name, trav_date;
+-------+-------+------------+-------+
| rec_id | name  | trav_date  | miles |
+-------+-------+------------+-------+
|     5 | Ben   | 2014-07-29 |   131 |
|     1 | Ben   | 2014-07-30 |   152 |
|     9 | Ben   | 2014-08-02 |    79 |
|     6 | Henry | 2014-07-26 |   115 |
|     4 | Henry | 2014-07-27 |    96 |
|     3 | Henry | 2014-07-29 |   300 |
|    10 | Henry | 2014-07-30 |   203 |
|     8 | Henry | 2014-08-01 |   197 |
|     2 | Suzi  | 2014-07-29 |   391 |
|     7 | Suzi  | 2014-08-02 |   502 |
+-------+-------+------------+-------+
```

Multiple-column sorts can be descending as well, but DESC must be specified after *each* column name to perform a fully descending sort.

Multiple-column ORDER BY clauses can perform mixed-order sorting where some columns are sorted in ascending order and others in descending order. The following query sorts by `name` in descending order, then by `trav_date` in ascending order for each name:

```
mysql> SELECT * FROM driver_log ORDER BY name DESC, trav_date;
+-------+-------+------------+-------+
| rec_id | name  | trav_date  | miles |
```

```
+--------+-------+------------+-------+
|      2 | Suzi  | 2014-07-29 |   391 |
|      7 | Suzi  | 2014-08-02 |   502 |
|      6 | Henry | 2014-07-26 |   115 |
|      4 | Henry | 2014-07-27 |    96 |
|      3 | Henry | 2014-07-29 |   300 |
|     10 | Henry | 2014-07-30 |   203 |
|      8 | Henry | 2014-08-01 |   197 |
|      5 | Ben   | 2014-07-29 |   131 |
|      1 | Ben   | 2014-07-30 |   152 |
|      9 | Ben   | 2014-08-02 |    79 |
+--------+-------+------------+-------+
```

The ORDER BY clauses in the queries shown thus far refer to the sorted columns by name. You can also name the columns by using aliases. That is, if an output column has an alias, you can refer to the alias in the ORDER BY clause:

```
mysql> SELECT name, trav_date, miles AS distance FROM driver_log
    -> ORDER BY distance;
+-------+------------+----------+
| name  | trav_date  | distance |
+-------+------------+----------+
| Ben   | 2014-08-02 |       79 |
| Henry | 2014-07-27 |       96 |
| Henry | 2014-07-26 |      115 |
| Ben   | 2014-07-29 |      131 |
| Ben   | 2014-07-30 |      152 |
| Henry | 2014-08-01 |      197 |
| Henry | 2014-07-30 |      203 |
| Henry | 2014-07-29 |      300 |
| Suzi  | 2014-07-29 |      391 |
| Suzi  | 2014-08-02 |      502 |
+-------+------------+----------+
```

9.2 Using Expressions for Sorting

Problem

You want to sort a query result based on values calculated from a column rather than the values actually stored in the column.

Solution

Put the expression that calculates the values in the ORDER BY clause.

Discussion

One of the mail table columns shows how large each mail message is, in bytes:

```
mysql> SELECT t, srcuser, srchost, dstuser, dsthost, size FROM mail;
+---------------------+---------+---------+---------+---------+---------+
| t                   | srcuser | srchost | dstuser | dsthost | size    |
+---------------------+---------+---------+---------+---------+---------+
| 2014-05-11 10:15:08 | barb    | saturn  | tricia  | mars    |   58274 |
```

```
| 2014-05-12 12:48:13 | tricia | mars   | gene   | venus  | 194925 |
| 2014-05-12 15:02:49 | phil   | mars   | phil   | saturn |   1048 |
| 2014-05-12 18:59:18 | barb   | saturn | tricia | venus  |    271 |
...
```

Suppose that you want to retrieve rows for "big" mail messages (defined as those larger than 50,000 bytes), but you want them to be displayed and sorted by sizes in terms of kilobytes, not bytes. In this case, the values to sort are calculated by an expression:

```
FLOOR((size+1023)/1024)
```

The +1023 in the FLOOR() expression groups size values to the nearest upper boundary of the 1,024-byte categories. Without it, the values group by lower boundaries (for example, a 2,047-byte message is reported as having a size of 1 kilobyte rather than 2). Recipe 10.13 discusses this technique in more detail.

To sort by that expression, put it directly in the ORDER BY clause:

```
mysql> SELECT t, srcuser, FLOOR((size+1023)/1024)
    -> FROM mail WHERE size > 50000
    -> ORDER BY FLOOR((size+1023)/1024);
+---------------------+---------+-------------------------+
| t                   | srcuser | FLOOR((size+1023)/1024) |
+---------------------+---------+-------------------------+
| 2014-05-11 10:15:08 | barb    |                      57 |
| 2014-05-14 14:42:21 | barb    |                      96 |
| 2014-05-12 12:48:13 | tricia  |                     191 |
| 2014-05-15 10:25:52 | gene    |                     976 |
| 2014-05-14 17:03:01 | tricia  |                    2339 |
+---------------------+---------+-------------------------+
```

Alternatively, if the sorting expression appears in the output column list, you can alias it there and refer to the alias in the ORDER BY clause:

```
mysql> SELECT t, srcuser, FLOOR((size+1023)/1024) AS kilobytes
    -> FROM mail WHERE size > 50000
    -> ORDER BY kilobytes;
+---------------------+---------+-----------+
| t                   | srcuser | kilobytes |
+---------------------+---------+-----------+
| 2014-05-11 10:15:08 | barb    |        57 |
| 2014-05-14 14:42:21 | barb    |        96 |
| 2014-05-12 12:48:13 | tricia  |       191 |
| 2014-05-15 10:25:52 | gene    |       976 |
| 2014-05-14 17:03:01 | tricia  |      2339 |
+---------------------+---------+-----------+
```

You might prefer the alias method for several reasons:

- It's easier to write the alias in the ORDER BY clause than to repeat the (cumbersome) expression.

- Without the alias, if you change the expression one place, you must change it in the other.

- The alias may be useful for display purposes, to provide a better column label. Note how the third column heading is much more meaningful in the second of the two preceding queries.

9.3 Displaying One Set of Values While Sorting by Another

Problem

You want to sort a result set using values that don't appear in the output column list.

Solution

That's not a problem. The ORDER BY clause can refer to columns you don't display.

Discussion

ORDER BY is not limited to sorting only those columns named in the output column list. It can sort using values that are "hidden" (that is, not displayed in the query output). This technique is commonly used when you have values that can be represented different ways and you want to display one type of value but sort by another. For example, you may want to display mail message sizes not in terms of bytes but as strings such as 103K for 103 kilobytes. You can convert a byte count to that kind of value using this expression:

```
CONCAT(FLOOR((size+1023)/1024),'K')
```

However, such values are strings, so they sort lexically, not numerically. If you use them for sorting, a value such as 96K sorts after 2339K, even though it represents a smaller number:

```
mysql> SELECT t, srcuser,
    -> CONCAT(FLOOR((size+1023)/1024),'K') AS size_in_K
    -> FROM mail WHERE size > 50000
    -> ORDER BY size_in_K;
+---------------------+---------+-----------+
| t                   | srcuser | size_in_K |
+---------------------+---------+-----------+
| 2014-05-12 12:48:13 | tricia  | 191K      |
| 2014-05-14 17:03:01 | tricia  | 2339K     |
| 2014-05-11 10:15:08 | barb    | 57K       |
| 2014-05-14 14:42:21 | barb    | 96K       |
| 2014-05-15 10:25:52 | gene    | 976K      |
+---------------------+---------+-----------+
```

To achieve the desired output order, display the string, but use actual numeric size for sorting:

```
mysql> SELECT t, srcuser,
    -> CONCAT(FLOOR((size+1023)/1024),'K') AS size_in_K
    -> FROM mail WHERE size > 50000
    -> ORDER BY size;
+---------------------+---------+-----------+
| t                   | srcuser | size_in_K |
+---------------------+---------+-----------+
| 2014-05-11 10:15:08 | barb    | 57K       |
| 2014-05-14 14:42:21 | barb    | 96K       |
| 2014-05-12 12:48:13 | tricia  | 191K      |
| 2014-05-15 10:25:52 | gene    | 976K      |
| 2014-05-14 17:03:01 | tricia  | 2339K     |
+---------------------+---------+-----------+
```

Displaying values as strings but sorting them as numbers helps solve some otherwise difficult problems. Members of sports teams typically are assigned a jersey number, which normally you might think should be stored using a numeric column. Not so fast! Some players like to have a jersey number of zero (0), and some like double-zero (00). If a team happens to have players with both numbers, you cannot represent them using a numeric column because both values will be treated as the same number. To solve this problem, store jersey numbers as strings:

```
CREATE TABLE roster
(
  name       CHAR(30),   # player name
  jersey_num CHAR(3),    # jersey number
  PRIMARY KEY(name)
);
```

Then the jersey numbers will display the same way you enter them, and 0 and 00 will be treated as distinct values. Unfortunately, although representing numbers as strings solves the problem of distinguishing between 0 and 00, it introduces a different problem. Suppose that a team has the following players:

```
mysql> SELECT name, jersey_num FROM roster;
+-----------+------------+
| name      | jersey_num |
+-----------+------------+
| Lynne     | 29         |
| Ella      | 0          |
| Elizabeth | 100        |
| Nancy     | 00         |
| Jean      | 8          |
| Sherry    | 47         |
+-----------+------------+
```

Now try to sort the team members by jersey number. If those numbers are stored as strings, they sort lexically, and lexical order often differs from numeric order. That's certainly true for the team in question:

```
mysql> SELECT name, jersey_num FROM roster ORDER BY jersey_num;
+-----------+------------+
| name      | jersey_num |
+-----------+------------+
| Ella      | 0          |
| Nancy     | 00         |
```

```
| Elizabeth | 100       |
| Lynne     | 29        |
| Sherry    | 47        |
| Jean      | 8         |
+-----------+-----------+
```

The values 100 and 8 are out of place, but that's easily solved: display the string values and use the numeric values for sorting. To accomplish this, add zero to the jersey_num values to force a string-to-number conversion:

```
mysql> SELECT name, jersey_num FROM roster ORDER BY jersey_num+0;
+-----------+------------+
| name      | jersey_num |
+-----------+------------+
| Ella      | 0          |
| Nancy     | 00         |
| Jean      | 8          |
| Lynne     | 29         |
| Sherry    | 47         |
| Elizabeth | 100        |
+-----------+------------+
```

 Note that because this method performs string-to-number conversion it cannot use indexes and will run slower as the table gets bigger. As an alternative solution, you can create a column that will hold the result of this calculation and use it in the ORDER BY expression.

The technique of displaying one value but sorting by another is also useful when you display values composed from multiple columns that don't sort the way you want. For example, the mail table lists message senders using separate srcuser and srchost values. To display message senders from the mail table as email addresses in srcuser@srchost format with the username first, construct those values using the following expression:

```
CONCAT(srcuser,'@',srchost)
```

However, those values are no good for sorting if you want to treat the hostname as more significant than the username. Instead, sort the results using the underlying column values rather than the displayed composite values:

```
mysql> SELECT t, CONCAT(srcuser,'@',srchost) AS sender, size
    -> FROM mail WHERE size > 50000
    -> ORDER BY srchost, srcuser;
+---------------------+---------------+---------+
| t                   | sender        | size    |
+---------------------+---------------+---------+
| 2014-05-15 10:25:52 | gene@mars     |  998532 |
| 2014-05-12 12:48:13 | tricia@mars   |  194925 |
| 2014-05-11 10:15:08 | barb@saturn   |   58274 |
| 2014-05-14 17:03:01 | tricia@saturn | 2394482 |
| 2014-05-14 14:42:21 | barb@venus    |   98151 |
+---------------------+---------------+---------+
```

The same idea commonly applies to sorting people's names. Suppose that a `names` table contains last and first names. To display rows sorted by last name first, the query is straightforward when the columns are displayed separately:

```
mysql> SELECT last_name, first_name FROM name
    -> ORDER BY last_name, first_name;
+-----------+------------+
| last_name | first_name |
+-----------+------------+
| Blue      | Vida       |
| Brown     | Kevin      |
| Gray      | Pete       |
| White     | Devon      |
| White     | Rondell    |
+-----------+------------+
```

If instead you want to display each name as a single string composed of the first name, a space, and the last name, begin the query like this:

```
SELECT CONCAT(first_name,' ',last_name) AS full_name FROM name...
```

But then how do you sort the names so they come out in last-name order? Display composite names, but refer to the constituent values in the ORDER BY clause:

```
mysql> SELECT CONCAT(first_name,' ',last_name) AS full_name
    -> FROM name
    -> ORDER BY last_name, first_name;
+---------------+
| full_name     |
+---------------+
| Vida Blue     |
| Kevin Brown   |
| Pete Gray     |
| Devon White   |
| Rondell White |
+---------------+
```

9.4 Controlling Case Sensitivity of String Sorts

Problem

String-sorting operations are case sensitive when you don't want them to be, or vice versa.

Solution

Alter the comparison characteristics of the sorted values.

Discussion

Recipe 7.1 discusses how string-comparison properties depend on whether the strings are binary or nonbinary:

- Binary strings are sequences of bytes. They are compared byte by byte using numeric byte values. Character set and lettercase have no meaning for comparisons.

- Nonbinary strings are sequences of characters. They have a character set and collation and are compared character by character using the order defined by the collation.

These properties also apply to string sorting because sorting is based on comparison. To alter the sorting properties of a string column, alter its comparison properties. (For a summary of which string data types are binary and nonbinary, see Recipe 7.2.)

The examples in this section use a table that has case-insensitive and case-sensitive nonbinary columns and a binary column:

```
CREATE TABLE str_val
(
  ci_str   CHAR(3) CHARACTER SET utf8mb4 COLLATE utf8mb4_0900_ai_ci,
  cs_str   CHAR(3) CHARACTER SET utf8mb4 COLLATE utf8mb4_0900_as_cs,
  bin_str  BINARY(3)
);
```

Suppose that the table has these contents:

```
+--------+--------+---------+
| ci_str | cs_str | bin_str |
+--------+--------+---------+
| AAA    | AAA    | AAA     |
| aaa    | aaa    | aaa     |
| bbb    | bbb    | bbb     |
| BBB    | BBB    | BBB     |
+--------+--------+---------+
```

As of MySLQ 8.0.19, `mysql` client prints binary data in hexadecimal format:

```
mysql> select * from str_val;
+--------+--------+------------------+
| ci_str | cs_str | bin_str          |
+--------+--------+------------------+
| AAA    | AAA    | 0x414141         |
| aaa    | aaa    | 0x616161         |
| bbb    | bbb    | 0x626262         |
| BBB    | BBB    | 0x424242         |
+--------+--------+------------------+
4 rows in set (0.00 sec)
```

To print values in ASCII format, start `mysql` with the `--binary-as-hex=0` option.

Each column contains the same values, but the natural sort orders for the column data types produce three different results:

- The case-insensitive collation sorts a and A together, placing them before b and B. However, for a given letter, it does not necessarily order one lettercase before another, as shown by the following result:

```
mysql> SELECT ci_str FROM str_val ORDER BY ci_str;
+--------+
| ci_str |
+--------+
| AAA    |
| aaa    |
| bbb    |
| BBB    |
+--------+
```

- The case-sensitive collation puts a and A before b and B and sorts lowercase before uppercase:

```
mysql> SELECT cs_str FROM str_val ORDER BY cs_str;
+--------+
| cs_str |
+--------+
| aaa    |
| AAA    |
| bbb    |
| BBB    |
+--------+
```

- The binary strings sort numerically. Assuming that uppercase letters have numeric values less than those of lowercase letters, a binary sort results in the following ordering:

```
mysql> SELECT bin_str FROM str_val ORDER BY bin_str;
+---------+
| bin_str |
+---------+
| AAA     |
| BBB     |
| aaa     |
| bbb     |
+---------+
```

You get the same result for a nonbinary string column that has a binary collation, as long as the column contains single-byte characters (for example, CHAR(3) CHARACTER SET latin1 COLLATE latin1_bin). For multibyte characters, a binary collation still produces a numeric sort, but the character values use multibyte numbers.

To alter the sorting properties of each column, use the techniques described in Recipe 7.7 for controlling string comparisons:

- To sort case-insensitive strings in case-sensitive fashion, order the sorted values using a case-sensitive collation:

```
mysql> SELECT ci_str FROM str_val
    -> ORDER BY ci_str COLLATE utf8mb4_0900_as_cs;
+--------+
| ci_str |
+--------+
| aaa    |
| AAA    |
| bbb    |
| BBB    |
+--------+
```

- To sort case-sensitive strings in case-insensitive fashion, order the sorted values using a case-insensitive collation:

```
mysql> SELECT cs_str FROM str_val
    -> ORDER BY cs_str COLLATE utf8mb4_0900_ai_ci;
+--------+
| cs_str |
+--------+
| AAA    |
| aaa    |
| bbb    |
| BBB    |
+--------+
```

Alternatively, sort using values that have been converted to the same lettercase, which makes lettercase irrelevant:

```
mysql> SELECT cs_str FROM str_val
    -> ORDER BY UPPER(cs_str);
+--------+
| cs_str |
+--------+
| AAA    |
| aaa    |
| bbb    |
| BBB    |
+--------+
```

- Binary strings sort using numeric byte values, so there is no concept of lettercase involved. However, because letters in different cases have different byte values, comparisons of binary strings effectively are case sensitive. (That is, a and A are unequal.) To sort binary strings using a case-insensitive ordering, convert them to nonbinary strings and apply an appropriate collation. For example, to perform a case-insensitive sort, use a statement like this:

```
mysql> SELECT bin_str FROM str_val
    -> ORDER BY CONVERT(bin_str USING utf8mb4) COLLATE utf8mb4_0900_ai_ci;
+---------+
| bin_str |
+---------+
| AAA     |
| aaa     |
| bbb     |
| BBB     |
+---------+
```

If the character-set default collation is case insensitive (as is true for utf8mb4), you can omit the COLLATE clause.

9.5 Sorting in Temporal Order

Problem

You want to sort rows in temporal order.

Solution

Sort using a date or time column. If some parts of the values are irrelevant for the sort that you want to accomplish, ignore them.

Discussion

Many database tables include date or time information, and it's very often necessary to sort results in temporal order. MySQL knows how to sort temporal data types, so there's no special trick to ordering them. The next few examples use the `mail` table, which contains a `DATETIME` column, but the same sorting principles apply to `DATE`, `TIME`, and `TIMESTAMP` columns.

Here are the messages sent by `phil`:

```
mysql> SELECT t, srcuser, srchost, dstuser, dsthost, size
    -> FROM mail WHERE srcuser = 'phil';
+---------------------+---------+---------+---------+---------+-------+
| t                   | srcuser | srchost | dstuser | dsthost | size  |
+---------------------+---------+---------+---------+---------+-------+
| 2014-05-12 15:02:49 | phil    | mars    | phil    | saturn  |  1048 |
| 2014-05-14 11:52:17 | phil    | mars    | tricia  | saturn  |  5781 |
| 2014-05-15 08:50:57 | phil    | venus   | phil    | venus   |   978 |
| 2014-05-16 23:04:19 | phil    | venus   | barb    | venus   | 10294 |
| 2014-05-19 12:49:23 | phil    | mars    | tricia  | saturn  |   873 |
+---------------------+---------+---------+---------+---------+-------+
```

To display the messages, most recently sent ones first, use ORDER BY with DESC:

```
mysql> SELECT t, srcuser, srchost, dstuser, dsthost, size
    -> FROM mail WHERE srcuser = 'phil' ORDER BY t DESC;
+---------------------+---------+---------+---------+---------+-------+
| t                   | srcuser | srchost | dstuser | dsthost | size  |
+---------------------+---------+---------+---------+---------+-------+
| 2014-05-19 12:49:23 | phil    | mars    | tricia  | saturn  |   873 |
| 2014-05-16 23:04:19 | phil    | venus   | barb    | venus   | 10294 |
| 2014-05-15 08:50:57 | phil    | venus   | phil    | venus   |   978 |
| 2014-05-14 11:52:17 | phil    | mars    | tricia  | saturn  |  5781 |
| 2014-05-12 15:02:49 | phil    | mars    | phil    | saturn  |  1048 |
+---------------------+---------+---------+---------+---------+-------+
```

Sometimes a temporal sort uses only part of a date or time column. In that case, use an expression that extracts the part or parts you need and sort the result using the expression. Some examples of this are given in the following discussion.

Sorting by time of day

You can do time-of-day sorting different ways, depending on your column type. If the values are stored in a TIME column named `timecol`, just sort them directly using ORDER BY `timecol`. To put DATETIME or TIMESTAMP values in time-of-day order, extract the time parts and sort them. For example, the `mail` table contains DATETIME values, which can be sorted by time of day like this:

```
mysql> SELECT t, srcuser, srchost, dstuser, dsthost, size FROM mail ORDER BY TIME(t);
+---------------------+---------+---------+---------+---------+--------+
| t                   | srcuser | srchost | dstuser | dsthost | size   |
+---------------------+---------+---------+---------+---------+--------+
| 2014-05-15 07:17:48 | gene    | mars    | gene    | saturn  |   3824 |
| 2014-05-15 08:50:57 | phil    | venus   | phil    | venus   |    978 |
| 2014-05-16 09:00:28 | gene    | venus   | barb    | mars    |    613 |
| 2014-05-14 09:31:37 | gene    | venus   | barb    | mars    |   2291 |
| 2014-05-11 10:15:08 | barb    | saturn  | tricia  | mars    |  58274 |
| 2014-05-15 10:25:52 | gene    | mars    | tricia  | saturn  | 998532 |
| 2014-05-14 11:52:17 | phil    | mars    | tricia  | saturn  |   5781 |
| 2014-05-12 12:48:13 | tricia  | mars    | gene    | venus   | 194925 |
...
```

Sorting by calendar day

To sort date values in calendar order, ignore the year part of the dates and use only the month and day to order values by where they fall during the calendar year. Suppose that an `occasion` table looks like this when values are ordered by date:

```
mysql> SELECT date, description FROM occasion ORDER BY date;
+------------+------------------------------------+
| date       | description                        |
+------------+------------------------------------+
| 1215-06-15 | Signing of the Magna Carta         |
| 1732-02-22 | George Washington's birthday       |
| 1776-07-14 | Bastille Day                       |
| 1789-07-04 | US Independence Day                |
| 1809-02-12 | Abraham Lincoln's birthday         |
| 1919-06-28 | Signing of the Treaty of Versailles |
| 1944-06-06 | D-Day at Normandy Beaches          |
| 1957-10-04 | Sputnik launch date                |
| 1989-11-09 | Opening of the Berlin Wall         |
+------------+------------------------------------+
```

To put these items in calendar order, sort them by month and day within month:

```
mysql> SELECT date, description FROM occasion
    -> ORDER BY MONTH(date), DAYOFMONTH(date);
+------------+------------------------------------+
| date       | description                        |
+------------+------------------------------------+
| 1809-02-12 | Abraham Lincoln's birthday         |
| 1732-02-22 | George Washington's birthday       |
| 1944-06-06 | D-Day at Normandy Beaches          |
| 1215-06-15 | Signing of the Magna Carta         |
| 1919-06-28 | Signing of the Treaty of Versailles |
| 1789-07-04 | US Independence Day                |
| 1776-07-14 | Bastille Day                       |
```

```
| 1957-10-04 | Sputnik launch date          |
| 1989-11-09 | Opening of the Berlin Wall   |
+------------+------------------------------+
```

MySQL has a DAYOFYEAR() function that you might suspect would be useful for calendar-day sorting. However, it can generate the same value for different calendar days. For example, February 29 of leap years and March 1 of nonleap years have the same day-of-year value:

```
mysql> SELECT DAYOFYEAR('1996-02-29'), DAYOFYEAR('1997-03-01');
+-------------------------+-------------------------+
| DAYOFYEAR('1996-02-29') | DAYOFYEAR('1997-03-01') |
+-------------------------+-------------------------+
|                      60 |                      60 |
+-------------------------+-------------------------+
```

This means that DAYOFYEAR() can group dates that actually occur on different calendar days.

If a table represents dates using separate year, month, and day columns, calendar sorting does not require you to extract date parts. Just sort the relevant columns directly. For large datasets, sorting using separate date-part columns can be much faster than sorts based on extracting pieces of DATE values. There's no overhead for part extraction, but more importantly, you can index the date-part columns separately—something not possible with a DATE column. The principle here is that you should design the table to make it easy to extract or sort by the values that you expect to use a lot.

Sorting by day of week

Day-of-week sorting is similar to calendar-day sorting, except that you use different functions to obtain the relevant ordering values.

You can get the day of the week using DAYNAME(), but that produces strings that sort lexically rather than in day-of-week order (Sunday, Monday, Tuesday, and so forth). Here the technique of displaying one value but sorting by another is useful (see Recipe 9.3). Display day names using DAYNAME(), but sort in day-of-week order using DAYOFWEEK(), which returns numeric values from 1 to 7 for Sunday through Saturday:

```
mysql> SELECT DAYNAME(date) AS day, date, description
    -> FROM occasion
    -> ORDER BY DAYOFWEEK(date);
+----------+------------+----------------------------------+
| day      | date       | description                      |
+----------+------------+----------------------------------+
| Sunday   | 1776-07-14 | Bastille Day                     |
| Sunday   | 1809-02-12 | Abraham Lincoln's birthday       |
| Monday   | 1215-06-15 | Signing of the Magna Carta       |
| Tuesday  | 1944-06-06 | D-Day at Normandy Beaches        |
| Thursday | 1989-11-09 | Opening of the Berlin Wall       |
| Friday   | 1957-10-04 | Sputnik launch date              |
```

```
| Friday   | 1732-02-22 | George Washington's birthday       |
| Saturday | 1789-07-04 | US Independence Day                |
| Saturday | 1919-06-28 | Signing of the Treaty of Versailles |
+----------+------------+------------------------------------+
```

To sort rows in day-of-week order but treat Monday as the first day of the week and Sunday as the last, use the modulo operation and the MOD() function to map Monday to 0, Tuesday to 1, ..., Sunday to 6:

```
mysql> SELECT DAYNAME(date), date, description
    -> FROM occasion
    -> ORDER BY MOD(DAYOFWEEK(date)+5, 7);
+---------------+------------+------------------------------------+
| DAYNAME(date) | date       | description                        |
+---------------+------------+------------------------------------+
| Monday        | 1215-06-15 | Signing of the Magna Carta         |
| Tuesday       | 1944-06-06 | D-Day at Normandy Beaches          |
| Thursday      | 1989-11-09 | Opening of the Berlin Wall         |
| Friday        | 1957-10-04 | Sputnik launch date                |
| Friday        | 1732-02-22 | George Washington's birthday       |
| Saturday      | 1789-07-04 | US Independence Day                |
| Saturday      | 1919-06-28 | Signing of the Treaty of Versailles |
| Sunday        | 1776-07-14 | Bastille Day                       |
| Sunday        | 1809-02-12 | Abraham Lincoln's birthday         |
+---------------+------------+------------------------------------+
```

Table 9-1 shows the DAYOFWEEK() expressions for putting any day of the week first in the sort order.

Table 9-1. Using modulo to properly order days of a week

Day to list first	DAYOFWEEK() expression
Sunday	DAYOFWEEK(date)
Monday	MOD(DAYOFWEEK(date)+5, 7)
Tuesday	MOD(DAYOFWEEK(date)+4, 7)
Wednesday	MOD(DAYOFWEEK(date)+3, 7)
Thursday	MOD(DAYOFWEEK(date)+2, 7)
Friday	MOD(DAYOFWEEK(date)+1, 7)
Saturday	MOD(DAYOFWEEK(date)+0, 7)

You can also use WEEKDAY() for day-of-week sorting, although it returns a different set of values (0 for Monday through 6 for Sunday).

9.6 Sorting by Substrings of Column Values

Problem

You want to sort a set of values using one or more substrings of each value.

Solution

Extract the pieces you want and sort them separately.

Discussion

This is a specific application of sorting by expression value (see Recipe 9.2). To sort rows using just a particular portion of a column's values, extract the substring you need and use it in the ORDER BY clause. This is easiest if the substrings are at a fixed position and length within the column. For substrings of variable position or length, you can still use them for sorting if you have a reliable way to identify them. The next several recipes show how to use substring extraction to produce specialized sort orders.

9.7 Sorting by Fixed-Length Substrings

Problem

You want to sort using parts of a column that occur at a given position within the column.

Solution

Pull out the parts you need with LEFT(), SUBSTRING() (MID()), or RIGHT(), and sort them.

Discussion

Suppose that a housewares table catalogs houseware furnishings, each identified by 10-character ID values consisting of three subparts: a three-character category abbreviation (such as DIN for "dining room" or KIT for "kitchen"), a five-digit serial number, and a two-character country code indicating where the part is manufactured:

```
mysql> SELECT * FROM housewares;
+------------+-----------------+
| id         | description     |
+------------+-----------------+
| DIN40672US | dining table    |
| KIT00372UK | garbage disposal |
| KIT01729JP | microwave oven  |
| BED00038SG | bedside lamp    |
| BTH00485US | shower stall    |
| BTH00415JP | lavatory        |
+------------+-----------------+
```

This is not necessarily a good way to store complex ID values, and later we'll consider how to represent them using separate columns. For now, assume that the values must be stored as shown.

To sort rows from this table based on the id values, use the entire column value:

```
mysql> SELECT * FROM housewares ORDER BY id;
+-----------+-----------------+
| id        | description     |
+-----------+-----------------+
| BED00038SG | bedside lamp    |
| BTH00415JP | lavatory        |
| BTH00485US | shower stall    |
| DIN40672US | dining table    |
| KIT00372UK | garbage disposal |
| KIT01729JP | microwave oven  |
+-----------+-----------------+
```

But you might also have a need to sort on any of the three subparts (for example, to sort by country of manufacture). For that kind of operation, functions such as LEFT(), MID(), and RIGHT() are useful to extract id value components:

```
mysql> SELECT id,
    -> LEFT(id,3) AS category,
    -> MID(id,4,5) AS serial,
    -> RIGHT(id,2) AS country
    -> FROM housewares;
+-----------+----------+--------+---------+
| id        | category | serial | country |
+-----------+----------+--------+---------+
| DIN40672US | DIN      | 40672  | US      |
| KIT00372UK | KIT      | 00372  | UK      |
| KIT01729JP | KIT      | 01729  | JP      |
| BED00038SG | BED      | 00038  | SG      |
| BTH00485US | BTH      | 00485  | US      |
| BTH00415JP | BTH      | 00415  | JP      |
+-----------+----------+--------+---------+
```

 Function MID() is a synonym of the function SUBSTRING().

Those fixed-length substrings of the id values can be used for sorting, either alone or in combination. For example, to sort by product category, extract and use the category in the ORDER BY clause:

```
mysql> SELECT * FROM housewares ORDER BY LEFT(id,3);
+-----------+-----------------+
| id        | description     |
+-----------+-----------------+
| BED00038SG | bedside lamp    |
| BTH00485US | shower stall    |
| BTH00415JP | lavatory        |
| DIN40672US | dining table    |
| KIT00372UK | garbage disposal |
| KIT01729JP | microwave oven  |
+-----------+-----------------+
```

To sort by product serial number, use MID() to extract the middle five characters from the id values, beginning with the fourth:

```
mysql> SELECT * FROM housewares ORDER BY MID(id,4,5);
+-----------+-----------------+
| id        | description     |
+-----------+-----------------+
| BED00038SG | bedside lamp    |
| KIT00372UK | garbage disposal |
| BTH00415JP | lavatory        |
| BTH00485US | shower stall    |
| KIT01729JP | microwave oven  |
| DIN40672US | dining table    |
+-----------+-----------------+
```

This appears to be a numeric sort, but it's actually a string sort because MID() returns strings. The lexical and numeric sort order are the same in this case because the "numbers" have leading zeros to make them all the same length.

To sort by country code, use the rightmost two characters of the id values (ORDER BY RIGHT(id,2)).

You can also sort using combinations of substrings, for example, by country code and serial number within country:

```
mysql> SELECT * FROM housewares ORDER BY RIGHT(id,2), MID(id,4,5);
+-----------+-----------------+
| id        | description     |
+-----------+-----------------+
| BTH00415JP | lavatory        |
| KIT01729JP | microwave oven  |
| BED00038SG | bedside lamp    |
| KIT00372UK | garbage disposal |
| BTH00485US | shower stall    |
| DIN40672US | dining table    |
+-----------+-----------------+
```

The ORDER BY clauses just shown suffice to sort by substrings of the id values, but if such operations on the table are common, it might be worth representing houseware IDs differently, for example, using separate columns for the ID components. This table, housewares2, is like housewares but uses category, serial, and country columns generated from the id column:

```
CREATE TABLE `housewares2` (
  `id` varchar(20) NOT NULL,
  `category` varchar(3) GENERATED ALWAYS AS (left(`id`,3)) STORED,
  `serial` char(5) GENERATED ALWAYS AS (substr(`id`,4,5)) STORED,
  `country` varchar(2) GENERATED ALWAYS AS (right(`id`,2)) STORED,
  `description` varchar(255) DEFAULT NULL,
  PRIMARY KEY (`id`)
);
```

In this example, we used generated columns that are generated based on the expressions, defined at the column creation time.

With the ID values split into separate parts, sorting operations are easier to specify; refer to individual columns directly rather than pulling out substrings of the original id column. You can also make operations that sort the serial and country columns more efficient by adding indexes on those columns:

```
mysql> SELECT category, serial, country, id
    -> FROM housewares2 ORDER BY category, country, serial;
+----------+--------+---------+-----------+
| category | serial | country | id        |
+----------+--------+---------+-----------+
| BED      | 00038  | SG      | BED00038SG |
| BTH      | 00415  | JP      | BTH00415JP |
| BTH      | 00485  | US      | BTH00485US |
| DIN      | 40672  | US      | DIN40672US |
| KIT      | 01729  | JP      | KIT01729JP |
| KIT      | 00372  | UK      | KIT00372UK |
+----------+--------+---------+-----------+
```

This example illustrates an important principle: you might think about values one way (id values as single strings), but you need not necessarily represent them that way in the database. If an alternative representation (separate columns) is more efficient or easier to work with, it may well be worth using—even if you must reformat the underlying columns so they appear as people expect.

9.8 Sorting by Variable-Length Substrings

Problem

You want to sort using parts of a column that do *not* occur at a given position within the column.

Solution

Determine how to identify the parts you need so that you can extract them.

Discussion

If substrings to be used for sorting vary in length, you need a reliable means of extracting just the part you want. To see how this works, let's create a housewares3 table that is like the housewares table used in Recipe 9.7, except that it has no leading zeros in the serial number part of the id values:

```
mysql> SELECT * FROM housewares3;
+-----------+------------------+
| id        | description      |
+-----------+------------------+
| DIN40672US | dining table    |
| KIT372UK  | garbage disposal |
| KIT1729JP | microwave oven   |
| BED38SG   | bedside lamp     |
```

```
| BTH485US  | shower stall     |
| BTH415JP  | lavatory         |
+-----------+------------------+
```

The category and country parts of the id values can be extracted and sorted using LEFT() and RIGHT(), just as for the housewares table. But now the numeric segments of the values have different lengths and cannot be extracted and sorted using a simple MID() call. Instead, use its full version SUBSTRING() to skip the first three characters. Of the remainder beginning with the fourth character (the first digit), take everything but the rightmost two columns. One way to do this is as follows:

```
mysql> SELECT id, LEFT(SUBSTRING(id,4),CHAR_LENGTH(SUBSTRING(id,4)-2))
    -> FROM housewares3;
+-----------+------------------------------------------------------+
| id        | LEFT(SUBSTRING(id,4),CHAR_LENGTH(SUBSTRING(id,4)-2)) |
+-----------+------------------------------------------------------+
| DIN40672US | 40672                                               |
| KIT372UK  | 372                                                  |
| KIT1729JP | 1729                                                 |
| BED38SG   | 38                                                   |
| BTH485US  | 485                                                  |
| BTH415JP  | 415                                                  |
+-----------+------------------------------------------------------+
```

But that's more complex than necessary. The SUBSTRING() function takes an optional third argument specifying a desired result length, and we know that the length of the middle part is equal to the length of the string minus five (three for the characters at the beginning and two for the characters at the end). The following query demonstrates how to get the numeric middle part by beginning with the ID and then stripping the rightmost suffix:

```
mysql> SELECT id, SUBSTRING(id,4), SUBSTRING(id,4,CHAR_LENGTH(id)-5)
    -> FROM housewares3;
+-----------+-----------------+-----------------------------------+
| id        | SUBSTRING(id,4) | SUBSTRING(id,4,CHAR_LENGTH(id)-5) |
+-----------+-----------------+-----------------------------------+
| DIN40672US | 40672US         | 40672                             |
| KIT372UK  | 372UK           | 372                               |
| KIT1729JP | 1729JP          | 1729                              |
| BED38SG   | 38SG            | 38                                |
| BTH485US  | 485US           | 485                               |
| BTH415JP  | 415JP           | 415                               |
+-----------+-----------------+-----------------------------------+
```

Unfortunately, although the final expression correctly extracts the numeric part from the IDs, the resulting values are strings. Consequently, they sort lexically rather than numerically:

```
mysql> SELECT * FROM housewares3
    -> ORDER BY SUBSTRING(id,4,CHAR_LENGTH(id)-5);
+-----------+------------------+
| id        | description      |
+-----------+------------------+
| KIT1729JP | microwave oven   |
| KIT372UK  | garbage disposal |
```

```
| BED38SG    | bedside lamp     |
| DIN40672US | dining table     |
| BTH415JP   | lavatory         |
| BTH485US   | shower stall     |
+------------+------------------+
```

How to deal with that? One way is to add zero, which tells MySQL to perform a string-to-number conversion that results in a numeric sort of the serial number values:

```
mysql> SELECT * FROM housewares3
    -> ORDER BY SUBSTRING(id,4,CHAR_LENGTH(id)-5)+0;
+------------+------------------+
| id         | description      |
+------------+------------------+
| BED38SG    | bedside lamp     |
| KIT372UK   | garbage disposal |
| BTH415JP   | lavatory         |
| BTH485US   | shower stall     |
| KIT1729JP  | microwave oven   |
| DIN40672US | dining table     |
+------------+------------------+
```

In the preceding example, the ability to extract variable-length substrings is based on the different kinds of characters in the middle of the id values, compared to the characters on the ends (that is, digits versus nondigits). In other cases, you may be able to use delimiter characters to pull apart column values. For the next examples, assume a housewares4 table with id values that look like this:

```
mysql> SELECT * FROM housewares4;
+---------------+------------------+
| id            | description      |
+---------------+------------------+
| 13-478-92-2   | dining table     |
| 873-48-649-63 | garbage disposal |
| 8-4-2-1       | microwave oven   |
| 97-681-37-66  | bedside lamp     |
| 27-48-534-2   | shower stall     |
| 5764-56-89-72 | lavatory         |
+---------------+------------------+
```

To extract segments from these values, use SUBSTRING_INDEX(*str*,*c*,*n*). It searches a string, *str*, for the *n*-th occurrence of a given character, *c*, and returns everything to the left of that character. For example, the following call returns 13-478:

```
SUBSTRING_INDEX('13-478-92-2','-',2)
```

If *n* is negative, the search for *c* proceeds from the right and returns the rightmost string. This call returns 478-92-2:

```
SUBSTRING_INDEX('13-478-92-2','-',-3)
```

By combining SUBSTRING_INDEX() calls with positive and negative indexes, it's possible to extract successive pieces from each id value: extract the first *n* segments of the value and pull off the rightmost one. By varying *n* from 1 to 4, we get the successive segments from left to right:

```
SUBSTRING_INDEX(SUBSTRING_INDEX(id,'-',1),'-',-1)
SUBSTRING_INDEX(SUBSTRING_INDEX(id,'-',2),'-',-1)
SUBSTRING_INDEX(SUBSTRING_INDEX(id,'-',3),'-',-1)
SUBSTRING_INDEX(SUBSTRING_INDEX(id,'-',4),'-',-1)
```

The first of those expressions can be optimized because the inner `SUBSTRING_INDEX()` call returns a single-segment string and is sufficient by itself to return the leftmost `id` segment:

```
SUBSTRING_INDEX(id,'-',1)
```

Another way to obtain substrings is to extract the rightmost *n* segments of the value and pull off the first one. Here we vary *n* from –4 to –1:

```
SUBSTRING_INDEX(SUBSTRING_INDEX(id,'-',-4),'-',1)
SUBSTRING_INDEX(SUBSTRING_INDEX(id,'-',-3),'-',1)
SUBSTRING_INDEX(SUBSTRING_INDEX(id,'-',-2),'-',1)
SUBSTRING_INDEX(SUBSTRING_INDEX(id,'-',-1),'-',1)
```

Again, an optimization is possible. For the fourth expression, the inner `SUBSTRING_INDEX()` call is sufficient to return the final substring:

```
SUBSTRING_INDEX(id,'-',-1)
```

These expressions can be difficult to read and understand, and experimenting with a few to see how they work may be useful. Here is an example that shows how to get the second and fourth segments from the `id` values:

```
mysql> SELECT
    -> id,
    -> SUBSTRING_INDEX(SUBSTRING_INDEX(id,'-',2),'-',-1) AS segment2,
    -> SUBSTRING_INDEX(SUBSTRING_INDEX(id,'-',4),'-',-1) AS segment4
    -> FROM housewares4;
+---------------+----------+----------+
| id            | segment2 | segment4 |
+---------------+----------+----------+
| 13-478-92-2   | 478      | 2        |
| 873-48-649-63 | 48       | 63       |
| 8-4-2-1       | 4        | 1        |
| 97-681-37-66  | 681      | 66       |
| 27-48-534-2   | 48       | 2        |
| 5764-56-89-72 | 56       | 72       |
+---------------+----------+----------+
```

To use the substrings for sorting, use the appropriate expressions in the ORDER BY clause. (Remember to force a string-to-number conversion by adding zero if you want a numeric rather than lexical sort.) The following two queries order the results based on the second `id` segment. The first sorts lexically, the second numerically:

```
mysql> SELECT * FROM housewares4
    -> ORDER BY SUBSTRING_INDEX(SUBSTRING_INDEX(id,'-',2),'-',-1);
+---------------+------------------+
| id            | description      |
```

```
+---------------+-----------------+
| 8-4-2-1       | microwave oven  |
| 13-478-92-2   | dining table    |
| 873-48-649-63 | garbage disposal|
| 27-48-534-2   | shower stall    |
| 5764-56-89-72 | lavatory        |
| 97-681-37-66  | bedside lamp    |
+---------------+-----------------+
mysql> SELECT * FROM housewares4
    -> ORDER BY SUBSTRING_INDEX(SUBSTRING_INDEX(id,'-',2),'-',-1)+0;
+---------------+-----------------+
| id            | description     |
+---------------+-----------------+
| 8-4-2-1       | microwave oven  |
| 873-48-649-63 | garbage disposal|
| 27-48-534-2   | shower stall    |
| 5764-56-89-72 | lavatory        |
| 13-478-92-2   | dining table    |
| 97-681-37-66  | bedside lamp    |
+---------------+-----------------+
```

The substring-extraction expressions here are messy, but at least the column values to which we apply the expressions have a consistent number of segments. To sort values that have varying numbers of segments, the job can be more difficult. Recipe 9.9 shows an example illustrating why that is.

9.9 Sorting Hostnames in Domain Order

Problem

You want to sort hostnames in domain order, with the rightmost parts of the names more significant than the leftmost parts.

Solution

Break apart the names, and sort the pieces from right to left.

Discussion

Hostnames are strings, and therefore their natural sort order is lexical. However, it's often desirable to sort hostnames in domain order, where the rightmost segments of the hostname values are more significant than the leftmost segments. Suppose that a hostname table contains the following names:

```
mysql> SELECT name FROM hostname ORDER BY name;
+--------------------+
| name               |
+--------------------+
| dbi.perl.org       |
| jakarta.apache.org |
| lists.mysql.com    |
| mysql.com          |
```

```
| svn.php.net        |
| www.kitebird.com   |
+--------------------+
```

The preceding query demonstrates the natural lexical sort order of the name values. That differs from domain order, as Table 9-2 shows.

Table 9-2. Lexical versus domain sort order

Lexical order	Domain order
dbi.perl.org	www.kitebird.com
jakarta.apache.org	mysql.com
lists.mysql.com	lists.mysql.com
mysql.com	svn.php.net
svn.php.net	jakarta.apache.org
www.kitebird.com	dbi.perl.org

Producing domain-ordered output is a substring-sorting problem for which it's necessary to extract each segment of the names so they can be sorted in right-to-left fashion. There is also an additional complication if your values contain different numbers of segments, as our example hostnames do. (Most of them have three segments, but mysql.com has only two.)

To extract the pieces of the hostnames, begin by using SUBSTRING_INDEX() in a manner similar to that described previously in Recipe 9.8. The hostname values have a maximum of three segments, from which the pieces can be extracted left to right like this:

```
SUBSTRING_INDEX(SUBSTRING_INDEX(name,'.',-3),'.',1)
SUBSTRING_INDEX(SUBSTRING_INDEX(name,'.',-2),'.',1)
SUBSTRING_INDEX(name,'.',-1)
```

These expressions work properly as long as all the hostnames have three components. But if a name has fewer than three, you don't get the correct result, as the following query demonstrates:

```
mysql> SELECT name,
    -> SUBSTRING_INDEX(SUBSTRING_INDEX(name,'.',-3),'.',1) AS leftmost,
    -> SUBSTRING_INDEX(SUBSTRING_INDEX(name,'.',-2),'.',1) AS middle,
    -> SUBSTRING_INDEX(name,'.',-1) AS rightmost
    -> FROM hostname;
+---------------------+----------+----------+-----------+
| name                | leftmost | middle   | rightmost |
+---------------------+----------+----------+-----------+
| svn.php.net         | svn      | php      | net       |
| dbi.perl.org        | dbi      | perl     | org       |
| lists.mysql.com     | lists    | mysql    | com       |
| mysql.com           | mysql    | mysql    | com       |
| jakarta.apache.org  | jakarta  | apache   | org       |
| www.kitebird.com    | www      | kitebird | com       |
+---------------------+----------+----------+-----------+
```

Notice the output for the mysql.com row; it has mysql for the value of the leftmost column, where it should have an empty string. The segment-extraction expressions work by pulling off the rightmost *n* segments and then returning the leftmost segment of the result. The source of the problem for mysql.com is that if there aren't *n* segments, the expression simply returns the leftmost segment of however many there are. To fix this problem, add a sufficient number of periods at the beginning of the hostname values to guarantee that they have the requisite number of segments:

```
mysql> SELECT name,
    -> SUBSTRING_INDEX(SUBSTRING_INDEX(CONCAT('..',name),'.',-3),'.',1)
    -> AS leftmost,
    -> SUBSTRING_INDEX(SUBSTRING_INDEX(CONCAT('.',name),'.',-2),'.',1)
    -> AS middle,
    -> SUBSTRING_INDEX(name,'.',-1) AS rightmost
    -> FROM hostname;
+---------------------+----------+----------+-----------+
| name                | leftmost | middle   | rightmost |
+---------------------+----------+----------+-----------+
| svn.php.net         | svn      | php      | net       |
| dbi.perl.org        | dbi      | perl     | org       |
| lists.mysql.com     | lists    | mysql    | com       |
| mysql.com           |          | mysql    | com       |
| jakarta.apache.org  | jakarta  | apache   | org       |
| www.kitebird.com    | www      | kitebird | com       |
+---------------------+----------+----------+-----------+
```

That's pretty ugly. But the expressions do serve to extract the substrings that are needed for sorting hostname values correctly in right-to-left fashion:

```
mysql> SELECT name FROM hostname
    -> ORDER BY
    -> SUBSTRING_INDEX(name,'.',-1),
    -> SUBSTRING_INDEX(SUBSTRING_INDEX(CONCAT('.',name),'.',-2),'.',1),
    -> SUBSTRING_INDEX(SUBSTRING_INDEX(CONCAT('..',name),'.',-3),'.',1);
+---------------------+
| name                |
+---------------------+
| www.kitebird.com    |
| mysql.com           |
| lists.mysql.com     |
| svn.php.net         |
| jakarta.apache.org  |
| dbi.perl.org        |
+---------------------+
```

If your hostnames have a maximum of four segments rather than three, add to the ORDER BY clause another SUBSTRING_INDEX() expression that adds three dots at the beginning of the hostname values.

9.10 Sorting Dotted-Quad IP Values in Numeric Order

Problem

You want to sort in numeric order strings that represent IP numbers.

Solution

Break apart the strings, and sort the pieces numerically. Or just use INET_ATON( ). Or consider storing the values as numbers instead.

Discussion

If a table contains IP numbers represented as strings in dotted-quad notation (192.168.1.10), they sort lexically rather than numerically. To produce a numeric ordering instead, sort them as four-part values with each part sorted numerically. Or, to be more efficient, represent the IP numbers as 32-bit unsigned integers, which take less space and can be ordered by a simple numeric sort. This section shows both methods.

To sort string-valued dotted-quad IP numbers, use a technique similar to that for sorting hostnames (see Recipe 9.9) but with the following differences:

- Dotted quads always have four segments. There's no need to add dots to the value before extracting substrings.

- Dotted quads sort left to right. The order of the substrings used in the ORDER BY clause is opposite to that used for hostname sorting.

- The segments of dotted-quad values are numbers. Add zero to each substring to force a numeric rather than lexical sort.

Suppose that a hostip table has a string-valued ip column containing IP numbers:

```
mysql> SELECT ip FROM hostip ORDER BY ip;
+-----------------+
| ip              |
+-----------------+
| 127.0.0.1       |
| 192.168.0.10    |
| 192.168.0.2     |
| 192.168.1.10    |
| 192.168.1.2     |
| 21.0.0.1        |
| 255.255.255.255 |
+-----------------+
```

The preceding query produces output sorted in lexical order. To sort the ip values numerically, extract each segment and add zero to convert it to a number like this:

```
mysql> SELECT ip FROM hostip
    -> ORDER BY
    -> SUBSTRING_INDEX(ip,'.',1)+0,
    -> SUBSTRING_INDEX(SUBSTRING_INDEX(ip,'.',-3),'.',1)+0,
    -> SUBSTRING_INDEX(SUBSTRING_INDEX(ip,'.',-2),'.',1)+0,
    -> SUBSTRING_INDEX(ip,'.',-1)+0;
+-----------------+
| ip              |
+-----------------+
| 21.0.0.1        |
| 127.0.0.1       |
| 192.168.0.2     |
| 192.168.0.10    |
| 192.168.1.2     |
| 192.168.1.10    |
| 255.255.255.255 |
+-----------------+
```

However, although that ORDER BY clause produces a correct result, it's complicated. A simpler solution uses the INET_ATON() function to convert network addresses in string form to their underlying numeric values, then sorts those numbers:

```
mysql> SELECT ip FROM hostip ORDER BY INET_ATON(ip);
+-----------------+
| ip              |
+-----------------+
| 21.0.0.1        |
| 127.0.0.1       |
| 192.168.0.2     |
| 192.168.0.10    |
| 192.168.1.2     |
| 192.168.1.10    |
| 255.255.255.255 |
+-----------------+
```

If you're tempted to sort by simply adding zero to the ip value and using ORDER BY on the result, consider the values that kind of string-to-number conversion actually produces:

```
mysql> SELECT ip, ip+0 FROM hostip;
+-----------------+---------+
| ip              | ip+0    |
+-----------------+---------+
| 127.0.0.1       |     127 |
| 192.168.0.2     | 192.168 |
| 192.168.0.10    | 192.168 |
| 192.168.1.2     | 192.168 |
| 192.168.1.10    | 192.168 |
| 255.255.255.255 | 255.255 |
| 21.0.0.1        |      21 |
+-----------------+---------+
7 rows in set, 7 warnings (0.00 sec)
```

The conversion retains only as much of each value as can be interpreted as a valid number (hence the warnings). The remainder becomes unavailable for sorting purposes, even though it's required for a correct ordering.

Use of INET_ATON() in the ORDER BY clause is more efficient than six SUB
STRING_INDEX() calls. Moreover, if you're storing IP addresses as numbers rather
than as strings, you can avoid performing any conversion at all when sorting. You
gain other benefits as well: numeric IP addresses have 32 bits, so you can use a 4-byte
INT UNSIGNED column to store them, which requires less storage than the string form.
Also, if you index the column, the query optimizer may be able to use the index
for certain queries. For cases requiring display of numeric IP values in dotted-quad
notation, convert them with the INET_NTOA() function.

9.11 Floating Values to the Head or Tail of the Sort Order

Problem

You want a column to sort the way it normally does, except for a few values that
should appear at the beginning or end of the sort order. For example, you want to sort
a list in lexical order except for certain high-priority values that should appear first no
matter where they fall in the normal sort order.

Solution

Add an initial sort column to the ORDER BY clause that places those few values where
you want them. The remaining sort columns have their usual effect for the other
values.

Discussion

To sort a result set normally *except* that you want particular values first, create an
additional sort column that is 0 for those values and 1 for everything else. This
enables you to float the values to the head of the ascending sort order. To put the
values at the tail instead, use descending sort order or store 1 for rows that you want
to be in the end of the list and 0 for others.

Suppose that a column contains NULL values:

```
mysql> SELECT val FROM t;
+------+
| val  |
+------+
|    3 |
|  100 |
| NULL |
| NULL |
|    9 |
+------+
```

Normally, sorting groups the NULL values at the beginning for an ascending sort:

```
mysql> SELECT val FROM t ORDER BY val;
+------+
| val  |
+------+
| NULL |
| NULL |
|    3 |
|    9 |
|  100 |
+------+
```

To put them at the end instead, without changing the order of other values, introduce an extra ORDER BY column that maps NULL values to a higher value than non-NULL values:

```
mysql> SELECT val FROM t ORDER BY IF(val IS NULL,1,0), val;
+------+
| val  |
+------+
|    3 |
|    9 |
|  100 |
| NULL |
| NULL |
+------+
```

The IF() expression creates a new column for the sort that is used as the primary sort value.

For descending sorts, NULL values group at the end. To put them at the beginning instead, use the same technique but reverse the second and third arguments of the IF() function to map NULL values to a lower value than non-NULL values:

```
IF(val IS NULL,0,1)
```

The same technique is useful for floating values other than NULL to either end of the sort order. Suppose that you want to sort mail table messages in sender/recipient order, but you want to put messages for a particular sender first. In the real world, the most interesting sender might be postmaster or root. Those names don't appear in the table, so let's use phil as the name of interest instead:

```
mysql> SELECT t, srcuser, dstuser, size
    -> FROM mail
    -> ORDER BY IF(srcuser='phil',0,1), srcuser, dstuser;
+---------------------+---------+---------+--------+
| t                   | srcuser | dstuser | size   |
+---------------------+---------+---------+--------+
| 2014-05-16 23:04:19 | phil    | barb    |  10294 |
| 2014-05-12 15:02:49 | phil    | phil    |   1048 |
| 2014-05-15 08:50:57 | phil    | phil    |    978 |
| 2014-05-14 11:52:17 | phil    | tricia  |   5781 |
| 2014-05-19 12:49:23 | phil    | tricia  |    873 |
| 2014-05-14 14:42:21 | barb    | barb    |  98151 |
| 2014-05-11 10:15:08 | barb    | tricia  |  58274 |
| 2014-05-12 18:59:18 | barb    | tricia  |    271 |
| 2014-05-14 09:31:37 | gene    | barb    |   2291 |
```

```
| 2014-05-16 09:00:28 | gene   | barb   |     613 |
| 2014-05-15 17:35:31 | gene   | gene   |    3856 |
| 2014-05-15 07:17:48 | gene   | gene   |    3824 |
| 2014-05-19 22:21:51 | gene   | gene   |   23992 |
| 2014-05-15 10:25:52 | gene   | tricia |  998532 |
| 2014-05-12 12:48:13 | tricia | gene   |  194925 |
| 2014-05-14 17:03:01 | tricia | phil   | 2394482 |
+---------------------+--------+--------+---------+
```

The value of the extra sort column is 0 for rows in which the srcuser value is phil, and 1 for all other rows. By making that the most significant sort column, rows for messages sent by phil float to the top of the output. (To sink them to the bottom instead, either sort the column in reverse order using DESC, or reverse the order of the second and third arguments of the IF() function.)

You can also use this technique for particular conditions, not only specific values. To put first those rows where people sent messages to themselves, do this:

```
mysql> SELECT t, srcuser, dstuser, size
    -> FROM mail
    -> ORDER BY IF(srcuser=dstuser,0,1), srcuser, dstuser;
+---------------------+---------+---------+---------+
| t                   | srcuser | dstuser | size    |
+---------------------+---------+---------+---------+
| 2014-05-14 14:42:21 | barb    | barb    |   98151 |
| 2014-05-19 22:21:51 | gene    | gene    |   23992 |
| 2014-05-15 17:35:31 | gene    | gene    |    3856 |
| 2014-05-15 07:17:48 | gene    | gene    |    3824 |
| 2014-05-12 15:02:49 | phil    | phil    |    1048 |
...
```

If you have a pretty good idea about the contents of your table, it's sometimes possible to eliminate the extra sort column. For example, srcuser is never NULL in the mail table, so the previous query can be rewritten as follows to use one fewer column in the ORDER BY clause (this relies on the property that NULL values sort ahead of all non-NULL values):

```
SELECT t, srcuser, dstuser, size
FROM mail
ORDER BY IF(srcuser=dstuser,NULL,srcuser), dstuser;
```

9.12 Defining a Custom Sort Order

Problem

You want to sort values in a nonstandard order.

Solution

Use FIELD() to map column values to a sequence that places the values in the desired order.

Discussion

Recipe 9.11 shows how to make a specific group of rows float to the head of the sort order. To impose a specific order on *all* values in a column, use the FIELD() function to map them to a list of numeric values and use the numbers for sorting. FIELD() compares its first argument to the following arguments and returns an integer indicating which one it matches. (This works best when the column contains a small number of distinct values.)

The following FIELD() call compares *value* to *str1*, *str2*, *str3*, and *str4* and returns 1, 2, 3, or 4, depending on which of them *value* is equal to:

```
FIELD(value,str1,str2,str3,str4)
```

If *value* is NULL or none of the values match, FIELD() returns 0.

You can use FIELD() to sort an arbitrary set of values into any order you please. For example, to display driver_log rows for Henry, Suzi, and Ben, in that order, do this:

```
mysql> SELECT * FROM driver_log
    -> ORDER BY FIELD(name,'Henry','Suzi','Ben');
+--------+-------+------------+-------+
| rec_id | name  | trav_date  | miles |
+--------+-------+------------+-------+
|     10 | Henry | 2014-07-30 |   203 |
|      8 | Henry | 2014-08-01 |   197 |
|      6 | Henry | 2014-07-26 |   115 |
|      4 | Henry | 2014-07-27 |    96 |
|      3 | Henry | 2014-07-29 |   300 |
|      7 | Suzi  | 2014-08-02 |   502 |
|      2 | Suzi  | 2014-07-29 |   391 |
|      5 | Ben   | 2014-07-29 |   131 |
|      9 | Ben   | 2014-08-02 |    79 |
|      1 | Ben   | 2014-07-30 |   152 |
+--------+-------+------------+-------+
```

9.13 Sorting ENUM Values

Problem

ENUM values don't sort like other string columns, and you want them to retrieve results in the order you expect.

Solution

Study how ENUM stores data, and use those properties to your advantage. You can, for example, define your own sort order for strings stored in the ENUM column.

Discussion

ENUM is a string data type, but ENUM values are actually stored numerically with values ordered the same way they are listed in the table definition. These numeric values affect how enumerations are sorted, which can be very useful. Suppose that a table named weekday contains an enumeration column named day that has weekday names as its members:

```
CREATE TABLE weekday
(
    day ENUM('Sunday','Monday','Tuesday','Wednesday',
             'Thursday','Friday','Saturday')
);
```

Internally, MySQL defines the enumeration values Sunday through Saturday in that definition to have numeric values from 1 to 7. To see this for yourself, create the table using the definition just shown, and then insert into it a row for each day of the week. To make the insertion order differ from the sorted order (so that you can see the effect of sorting), add the days in random order:

```
mysql> INSERT INTO weekday (day) VALUES('Monday'),('Friday'),
    -> ('Tuesday'), ('Sunday'), ('Thursday'), ('Saturday'), ('Wednesday');
```

Then select the values, both as strings and as the internal numeric value (obtain the latter using +0 to force a string-to-number conversion):

```
mysql> SELECT day, day+0 FROM weekday;
+-----------+-------+
| day       | day+0 |
+-----------+-------+
| Monday    |     2 |
| Friday    |     6 |
| Tuesday   |     3 |
| Sunday    |     1 |
| Thursday  |     5 |
| Saturday  |     7 |
| Wednesday |     4 |
+-----------+-------+
```

Notice that because the query includes no ORDER BY clause, the rows are returned in unsorted order. If you add an ORDER BY day clause, it becomes apparent that MySQL uses the internal numeric values for sorting:

```
mysql> SELECT day, day+0 FROM weekday ORDER BY day;
+-----------+-------+
| day       | day+0 |
+-----------+-------+
| Sunday    |     1 |
| Monday    |     2 |
| Tuesday   |     3 |
| Wednesday |     4 |
| Thursday  |     5 |
| Friday    |     6 |
| Saturday  |     7 |
+-----------+-------+
```

What about occasions when you want to sort ENUM values in lexical order? Force them to be treated as strings for sorting using the CAST() function:

```
mysql> SELECT day, day+0 FROM weekday ORDER BY CAST(day AS CHAR);
+-----------+-------+
| day       | day+0 |
+-----------+-------+
| Friday    |     6 |
| Monday    |     2 |
| Saturday  |     7 |
| Sunday    |     1 |
| Thursday  |     5 |
| Tuesday   |     3 |
| Wednesday |     4 |
+-----------+-------+
```

If you always (or nearly always) sort a non-enumeration column in a specific nonlexical order, consider changing the data type to ENUM, with its values listed in the desired sort order. To see how this works, create a color table containing a string column, and populate it with some sample rows:

```
mysql> CREATE TABLE color (name CHAR(10), PRIMARY KEY(name));
mysql> INSERT INTO color (name) VALUES ('blue'),('green'),
    -> ('indigo'),('orange'),('red'),('violet'),('yellow');
```

Sorting by the name column at this point produces lexical order because the column contains CHAR values:

```
mysql> SELECT name FROM color ORDER BY name;
+--------+
| name   |
+--------+
| blue   |
| green  |
| indigo |
| orange |
| red    |
| violet |
| yellow |
+--------+
```

Now suppose that you want to sort the column by the order in which colors occur in the rainbow. (This is "Roy G. Biv" order; successive letters of that name indicate the first letters of the corresponding color names.) One way to produce a rainbow sort is to use FIELD():

```
mysql> SELECT name FROM color
    -> ORDER BY
    -> FIELD(name,'red','orange','yellow','green','blue','indigo','violet');
+--------+
| name   |
+--------+
| red    |
| orange |
| yellow |
| green  |
```

```
| blue   |
| indigo |
| violet |
+--------+
```

To accomplish the same end without FIELD( ), use ALTER TABLE to convert the name column to an ENUM that lists the colors in the desired sort order:

```
mysql> ALTER TABLE color
    -> MODIFY name
    -> ENUM('red','orange','yellow','green','blue','indigo','violet');
```

After converting the table, sorting on the name column produces rainbow sorting naturally with no special treatment:

```
mysql> SELECT name FROM color ORDER BY name;
+--------+
| name   |
+--------+
| red    |
| orange |
| yellow |
| green  |
| blue   |
| indigo |
| violet |
+--------+
```

Note that once you switch to the ENUM data type, you will not be able to insert any value that does not belong to the list. If you need to change the ENUM definition, for example, by adding a new color, you will have to perform one more ALTER command.

## CHAPTER 10

Generating Summaries

10.0 Introduction

Database systems are useful not only for data storage and retrieval, but they can also summarize your data in more concise forms. Summaries are useful when you want the overall picture, not the details. They're more readily understood than a long list of records. They enable you to answer questions such as "How many?" or "What is the total?" or "What is the range of values?" If you run a business, you may want to know how many customers you have in each state or how much sales volume you generate each month.

The preceding examples include two common summary types: counting summaries and content summaries. The first (the number of customer records per state) is a counting summary. The content of each record is important only for purposes of placing it into the proper group or category for counting. Such summaries are essentially histograms, where you sort items into a set of bins and count the number of items in each bin. The second example (sales volume per month) is a content summary, in which sales totals are based on sales values in order of items.

Another summary type produces neither counts nor sums but simply a list of unique values. This is useful if you care *which* values are present rather than how many of each there are. To determine the states in which you have customers, you need a list of the distinct state names contained in the records, not a list consisting of the state value from every record.

The summary types available to you depend on the nature of your data. A counting summary can be generated from all kinds of values, whether they be numbers, strings, or dates. Summaries that produce sums or averages apply only to numeric values. You can count instances of customer state names to produce a demographic analysis of your customer base. And sometimes it makes sense to apply one summary technique to the result of another. For example, to determine how many states your customers live in, generate a list of unique customer states, then count them.

Summary operations in MySQL involve the following SQL constructs:

- To compute a summary value from a set of individual values, use one of the functions known as *aggregate functions*. These are so called because they operate on aggregates (groups) of values. Aggregate functions include COUNT(), which counts rows or values in a query result; MIN() and MAX(), which find smallest and largest values; and SUM() and AVG(), which produce sums and means of values. These functions can be used to compute a value for the entire result set, or with a GROUP BY clause to group rows into subsets and obtain an aggregate value for each one.

- To obtain a list of unique values, use SELECT DISTINCT rather than SELECT.

- To count unique values, use COUNT(DISTINCT) rather than COUNT().

The recipes in this chapter first illustrate basic summary techniques and then show how to perform more complex summary operations. You'll find additional examples of summary methods in later chapters, particularly those that cover joins and statistical operations. (See Chapters 16 and 17.)

Summary queries sometimes involve complex expressions. For summaries that you execute often, keep in mind that views can make queries easier to use. Recipe 5.7 demonstrates the basic technique of creating a view. Recipe 10.5 shows how it applies to summary simplification, and you'll easily see how it can be used in later sections of the chapter as well.

The primary tables used for examples in this chapter are the driver_log and mail tables. These were also used in Chapter 9, so they should look familiar. A third table used throughout the chapter is states, which has rows containing a few columns of information for each of the United States:

```
mysql> SELECT * FROM states ORDER BY name;
+---------------+--------+------------+----------+
| name          | abbrev | statehood  | pop      |
+---------------+--------+------------+----------+
| Alabama       | AL     | 1819-12-14 |  5039877 |
| Alaska        | AK     | 1959-01-03 |   732673 |
| Arizona       | AZ     | 1912-02-14 |  7276316 |
| Arkansas      | AR     | 1836-06-15 |  3025891 |
| California    | CA     | 1850-09-09 | 39237836 |
| Colorado      | CO     | 1876-08-01 |  5812069 |
| Connecticut   | CT     | 1788-01-09 |  3605597 |
...
```

The name and abbrev columns list the full state name and the corresponding abbreviation. The statehood column indicates the day on which the state entered the Union.

pop is the state population from the 2010 census, as reported by the US Census Bureau.

This chapter uses other tables occasionally as well. You can create them with scripts found in the *tables* directory of the `recipes` distribution. Recipe 7.15 describes the `reviews` table.

10.1 Summarizing with COUNT()

Problem

You want to count the number of rows in an entire table or that match particular conditions.

Solution

Use the `COUNT()` function.

Discussion

The `COUNT()` function calculates number of rows. For example, to display the rows in a table, use a `SELECT *` statement, but to count them instead, use `SELECT COUNT(*)`. Without a `WHERE` clause, the statement counts all the rows in the table, such as in the following statement that shows how many rows the `driver_log` table contains:

```
mysql> SELECT COUNT(*) FROM driver_log;
+----------+
| COUNT(*) |
+----------+
|       10 |
+----------+
```

If you don't know how many US states there are (perhaps you think there are 57?), this statement tells you:

```
mysql> SELECT COUNT(*) FROM states;
+----------+
| COUNT(*) |
+----------+
|       50 |
+----------+
```

`COUNT(*)` without a `WHERE` clause performs a full table scan unless the storage engine optimized this function. For MyISAM tables that store the exact number of rows, this is very quick. For InnoDB tables that scan all entries in the primary key to perform `COUNT(*)`, you may want to avoid using this function because it can be slow for large tables. If an approximate row count is good enough, avoid a full scan by extracting the `TABLE_ROWS` value from the `INFORMATION_SCHEMA` database:

```
SELECT TABLE_ROWS FROM INFORMATION_SCHEMA.TABLES
WHERE TABLE_SCHEMA = 'cookbook' AND TABLE_NAME = 'states';
```

To count only the number of rows that match certain conditions, include an appropriate WHERE clause in a SELECT COUNT(*) statement. The conditions can be chosen to make COUNT(*) useful for answering many kinds of questions:

- How many times did drivers travel more than 200 miles in a day?

```
mysql> SELECT COUNT(*) FROM driver_log WHERE miles > 200;
+----------+
| COUNT(*) |
+----------+
|        4 |
+----------+
```

- How many days did Suzi drive?

```
mysql> SELECT COUNT(*) FROM driver_log WHERE name = 'Suzi';
+----------+
| COUNT(*) |
+----------+
|        2 |
+----------+
```

- How many of the United States joined the Union in the 19th century?

```
mysql> SELECT COUNT(*) FROM states
    -> WHERE statehood BETWEEN '1800-01-01' AND '1899-12-31';
+----------+
| COUNT(*) |
+----------+
|       29 |
+----------+
```

The COUNT() function actually has two forms. The form we've been using, COUNT(*), counts rows. The other form, COUNT(expr), takes a column name or expression argument and counts the number of non-NULL values. The following statement shows how to produce both a row count for a table and a count of the number of non-NULL values in one of its columns:

```
SELECT COUNT(*), COUNT(mycol) FROM mytbl;
```

The fact that COUNT(expr) doesn't count NULL values is useful for producing multiple counts from the same set of rows. To count the number of Saturday and Sunday trips in the driver_log table with a single statement, do this:

```
mysql> SELECT
    -> COUNT(IF(DAYOFWEEK(trav_date)=7,1,NULL)) AS 'Saturday trips',
    -> COUNT(IF(DAYOFWEEK(trav_date)=1,1,NULL)) AS 'Sunday trips'
    -> FROM driver_log;
+----------------+--------------+
| Saturday trips | Sunday trips |
+----------------+--------------+
|              3 |            1 |
+----------------+--------------+
```

Or to count weekend versus weekday trips, do this:

```
mysql> SELECT
    -> COUNT(IF(DAYOFWEEK(trav_date) IN (1,7),1,NULL)) AS 'weekend trips',
    -> COUNT(IF(DAYOFWEEK(trav_date) IN (1,7),NULL,1)) AS 'weekday trips'
    -> FROM driver_log;
+---------------+---------------+
| weekend trips | weekday trips |
+---------------+---------------+
|             4 |             6 |
+---------------+---------------+
```

The IF() expressions determine, for each column value, whether it should be counted. If so, the expression evaluates to 1 and COUNT() counts it. If not, the expression evaluates to NULL and COUNT() ignores it. The effect is to count the number of values that satisfy the condition given as the first argument to IF().

 The COUNT() function calculates the number of elements, so you can replace 1 with any other value. The result will be the same.

See Also

For further discussion on the difference between COUNT(*) and COUNT(expr), see Recipe 10.9.

10.2 Summarizing with MIN() and MAX()

Problem

You want to find the smallest or the largest values in the dataset.

Solution

Use the MIN() and MAX() functions correspondingly.

Discussion

Finding the smallest or largest values in a dataset is somewhat akin to sorting, except that instead of producing an entire set of sorted values, you select only a single value at one end or the other of the sorted range. This operation applies to questions about smallest, largest, oldest, newest, most expensive, least expensive, and so forth. One way to find such values is to use the MIN() and MAX() functions. (Another way is to use LIMIT; see Recipe 5.9.)

Because MIN() and MAX() determine the extreme values in a set, they're useful for characterizing ranges:

- What date range is represented by the rows in the mail table? What are the smallest and largest messages sent?

```
mysql> SELECT
    -> MIN(t) AS earliest, MAX(t) AS latest,
    -> MIN(size) AS smallest, MAX(size) AS largest
    -> FROM mail;
+---------------------+---------------------+----------+---------+
| earliest            | latest              | smallest | largest |
+---------------------+---------------------+----------+---------+
| 2014-05-11 10:15:08 | 2014-05-19 22:21:51 |      271 | 2394482 |
+---------------------+---------------------+----------+---------+
```

- What are the smallest and largest US state populations?

```
mysql> SELECT MIN(pop) AS 'fewest people', MAX(pop) AS 'most people'
    -> FROM states;
+---------------+-------------+
| fewest people | most people |
+---------------+-------------+
|        578803 |    39237836 |
+---------------+-------------+
```

- What are the first and last state names, lexically speaking? What is the length of the shortest and longest names?

```
mysql> SELECT
    -> MIN(name) AS first,
    -> MAX(name) AS last,
    -> MIN(CHAR_LENGTH(name)) AS shortest,
    -> MAX(CHAR_LENGTH(name)) AS longest
    -> FROM states;
+---------+---------+----------+---------+
| first   | last    | shortest | longest |
+---------+---------+----------+---------+
| Alabama | Wyoming |        4 |      14 |
+---------+---------+----------+---------+
```

The final query illustrates that MIN() and MAX() need not be applied directly to column values; they're also useful for expressions or values derived from column values.

10.3 Summarizing with SUM() and AVG()

Problem

You want to calculate the total or average (mean) of a set of values.

Solution

Use the SUM() and AVG() functions.

Discussion

SUM() and AVG() produce the total and average (mean) of a set of values:

- What is the total amount of mail traffic in bytes and the average size of each message?

```
mysql> SELECT
    -> SUM(size) AS 'total traffic',
    -> AVG(size) AS 'average message size'
    -> FROM mail;
+---------------+----------------------+
| total traffic | average message size |
+---------------+----------------------+
|       3798185 |          237386.5625 |
+---------------+----------------------+
```

- How many miles did the drivers in the driver_log table travel? What was the average number of miles traveled per day?

```
mysql> SELECT
    -> SUM(miles) AS 'total miles',
    -> AVG(miles) AS 'average miles/day'
    -> FROM driver_log;
+-------------+-------------------+
| total miles | average miles/day |
+-------------+-------------------+
|        2166 |          216.6000 |
+-------------+-------------------+
```

- What is the total population of the United States?

```
mysql> SELECT SUM(pop) FROM states;
+-----------+
| SUM(pop)  |
+-----------+
| 331223695 |
+-----------+
```

The value represents the population reported for the 2021 census.

SUM() and AVG() are numeric functions, so they can't be used with strings or temporal values. But sometimes you can convert nonnumeric values to useful numeric forms. Suppose that a table stores TIME values that represent elapsed time:

```
mysql> SELECT t1 FROM time_val;
+----------+
| t1       |
+----------+
| 15:00:00 |
| 05:01:30 |
| 12:30:20 |
+----------+
```

To compute the total elapsed time, use TIME_TO_SEC() to convert the values to seconds before summing them. The resulting sum is also in seconds; pass it to SEC_TO_TIME() to convert it back to TIME format:

```
mysql> SELECT SUM(TIME_TO_SEC(t1)) AS 'total seconds',
    -> SEC_TO_TIME(SUM(TIME_TO_SEC(t1))) AS 'total time'
    -> FROM time_val;
+---------------+------------+
| total seconds | total time |
+---------------+------------+
|        117110 | 32:31:50   |
+---------------+------------+
```

See Also

The SUM() and AVG() functions are especially useful in statistical applications. They're explored further in Chapter 17, along with STD(), a related function that calculates standard deviations.

10.4 Using DISTINCT to Eliminate Duplicates

Problem

You want to skip duplicate values when performing calculations.

Solution

Use the keyword DISTINCT.

Discussion

A summary operation that uses no aggregate functions is determining the unique values or rows in a dataset. Do this with DISTINCT (or DISTINCTROW, a synonym). DISTINCT boils down a query result and often is combined with ORDER BY to place values in more meaningful order. This query lists in lexical order the drivers named in the driver_log table:

```
mysql> SELECT DISTINCT name FROM driver_log ORDER BY name;
+-------+
| name  |
+-------+
| Ben   |
| Henry |
| Suzi  |
+-------+
```

Without DISTINCT, the statement produces the same names but is not nearly as easy to understand, even with a small dataset:

```
mysql> SELECT name FROM driver_log ORDER BY NAME;
+-------+
| name  |
+-------+
| Ben   |
| Ben   |
```

```
| Ben   |
| Henry |
| Henry |
| Henry |
| Henry |
| Henry |
| Suzi  |
| Suzi  |
+-------+
```

To determine the number of different drivers, use COUNT(DISTINCT):

```
mysql> SELECT COUNT(DISTINCT name) FROM driver_log;
+----------------------+
| COUNT(DISTINCT name) |
+----------------------+
|                    3 |
+----------------------+
```

COUNT(DISTINCT) ignores NULL values. To count NULL as one of the values in the set if it's present, use one of the following expressions:

```
COUNT(DISTINCT val) + IF(COUNT(IF(val IS NULL,1,NULL))=0,0,1)
COUNT(DISTINCT val) + IF(SUM(ISNULL(val))=0,0,1)
COUNT(DISTINCT val) + (SUM(ISNULL(val))<>0);
```

In this example, we first calculate the number of distinct NOT NULL values, then add 1 if the sum of NULL values is greater than zero.

DISTINCT queries are often useful in conjunction with aggregate functions to more fully characterize your data. Suppose that a customer table contains a state column indicating customer location. Applying COUNT(*) to the customer table indicates how many customers you have, using DISTINCT on the state column tells you the number of states in which you have customers, and COUNT(DISTINCT) on the state column tells you how many states your customer base represents.

When used with multiple columns, DISTINCT shows the different combinations of values in the columns, and COUNT(DISTINCT) counts the number of combinations. The following statements show the different sender/recipient pairs in the mail table and the number of such pairs:

```
mysql> SELECT DISTINCT srcuser, dstuser FROM mail
    -> ORDER BY srcuser, dstuser;
+---------+---------+
| srcuser | dstuser |
+---------+---------+
| barb    | barb    |
| barb    | tricia  |
| gene    | barb    |
| gene    | gene    |
| gene    | tricia  |
| phil    | barb    |
| phil    | phil    |
| phil    | tricia  |
| tricia  | gene    |
```

```
| tricia  | phil    |
+---------+---------+
mysql> SELECT COUNT(DISTINCT srcuser, dstuser) FROM mail;
+---------------------------------+
| COUNT(DISTINCT srcuser, dstuser) |
+---------------------------------+
|                              10 |
+---------------------------------+
```

10.5 Creating a View to Simplify Using a Summary

Problem

You want to make it easier to perform a summary.

Solution

Create a view that does it for you.

Discussion

If you often need a given summary, a technique that enables you to avoid typing the summarizing expressions repeatedly is to use a view (see Recipe 5.7). For example, the following view implements the weekend versus weekday trip summary discussed in Recipe 10.1:

```
mysql> CREATE VIEW trip_summary_view AS
    -> SELECT
    -> COUNT(IF(DAYOFWEEK(trav_date) IN (1,7),1,NULL)) AS weekend_trips,
    -> COUNT(IF(DAYOFWEEK(trav_date) IN (1,7),NULL,1)) AS weekday_trips
    -> FROM driver_log;
```

Selecting from this view is much easier than selecting directly from the underlying table:

```
mysql> SELECT * FROM trip_summary_view;
+---------------+---------------+
| weekend_trips | weekday_trips |
+---------------+---------------+
|             4 |             6 |
+---------------+---------------+
```

10.6 Finding Values Associated with Minimum and Maximum Values

Problem

You want to know the values for other columns in the row that contains a minimum or maximum value.

Solution

Use two statements and a user-defined variable. Or a subquery. Or a join. Or a CTE.

Discussion

`MIN()` and `MAX()` find an endpoint of a range of values, but you may also be interested in other values from the row in which the value occurs. For example, you can find the largest state population like this:

```
mysql> SELECT MAX(pop) FROM states;
+----------+
| MAX(pop) |
+----------+
| 39237836 |
+----------+
```

But that doesn't show you which state has this population. The obvious attempt at getting that information looks like this:

```
mysql> SELECT MAX(pop), name FROM states WHERE pop = MAX(pop);
ERROR 1111 (HY000): Invalid use of group function
```

Probably everyone tries something like that sooner or later, but it doesn't work. Aggregate functions such as `MIN()` and `MAX()` cannot be used in `WHERE` clauses, which require expressions that apply to individual rows. The intent of the statement is to determine which row has the maximum population value and display the associated state name. The problem is that although you and I know perfectly well what we mean by writing such a thing, it makes no sense at all in SQL. The statement fails because SQL uses the `WHERE` clause to determine which rows to select, but the value of an aggregate function is known only *after* selecting the rows from which the function's value is determined! So, in a sense, the statement is self-contradictory. To solve this problem, save the maximum population value in a user-defined variable, then compare rows to the variable value:

```
mysql> SET @max = (SELECT MAX(pop) FROM states);
mysql> SELECT pop AS 'highest population', name FROM states WHERE pop = @max;
+--------------------+------------+
| highest population | name       |
+--------------------+------------+
|           39237836 | California |
+--------------------+------------+
```

Alternatively, for a single-statement solution, use a subquery in the `WHERE` clause that returns the maximum population value:

```
SELECT pop AS 'highest population', name FROM states
WHERE pop = (SELECT MAX(pop) FROM states);
```

This technique also works even if the minimum or maximum value itself isn't actually contained in the row but is only derived from it. To determine the length of the shortest review in the sample Amazon reviews data, do this:

```
mysql> SELECT MAX(CHAR_LENGTH(reviews_virtual)) FROM reviews;
+----------------------------------+
| MIN(CHAR_LENGTH(reviews_virtual)) |
+----------------------------------+
|                                2 |
+----------------------------------+
```

If you want to know "Which review is that?" do this instead:

```
mysql> SELECT JSON_EXTRACT(appliances_review, "$. reviewTime") as ReviewTime,
    -> JSON_EXTRACT(appliances_review, "$.reviewerID") as ReviewerID,
    -> JSON_EXTRACT(appliances_review, "$.asin") as ProductID,
    -> JSON_EXTRACT(appliances_review, "$.overall") as Rating FROM
    -> reviews WHERE CHAR_LENGTH(reviews_virtual) =
    -> (SELECT MIN(CHAR_LENGTH(reviews_virtual)) FROM reviews);
+--------------+------------------+--------------+--------+
| ReviewTime   | ReviewerID       | ProductID    | Rating |
+--------------+------------------+--------------+--------+
| "03 8, 2015" | "A3B1B4E184FSUZ" | "B000VL060M" | 5.0    |
| "03 8, 2015" | "A3B1B4E184FSUZ" | "B0015UGPWQ" | 5.0    |
| "03 8, 2015" | "A3B1B4E184FSUZ" | "B000VL060M" | 5.0    |
| "03 8, 2015" | "A3B1B4E184FSUZ" | "B0015UGPWQ" | 5.0    |
| "02 9, 2015" | "A3B1B4E184FSUZ" | "B0042U16YI" | 5.0    |
| "07 25, 2016"| "AJPRN1TD1A0SD"  | "B00BIZDI0A" | 3.0    |
+--------------+------------------+--------------+--------+
```

Yet another way to select other columns from rows containing a minimum or maximum value is to use a join. Select the value into another table, then join it to the original table to select the row that matches the value. To find the row for the state with the highest population, use a join like this:

```
mysql> CREATE TEMPORARY TABLE tmp SELECT MAX(pop) as maxpop FROM states;
mysql> SELECT states.* FROM states INNER JOIN tmp
    -> ON states.pop = tmp.maxpop;
+------------+--------+------------+----------+
| name       | abbrev | statehood  | pop      |
+------------+--------+------------+----------+
| California | CA     | 1850-09-09 | 39237836 |
+------------+--------+------------+----------+
```

As of MySQL 8.0, you can use Common Table Expressions (CTEs) to perform the same search:

```
mysql> WITH maxpop
    -> AS (SELECT MAX(pop) as maxpop FROM states)
    -> SELECT states.* FROM states
    -> JOIN maxpop ON states.pop = maxpop.maxpop;
+------------+--------+------------+----------+
| name       | abbrev | statehood  | pop      |
+------------+--------+------------+----------+
| California | CA     | 1850-09-09 | 39237836 |
+------------+--------+------------+----------+
1 row in set (0.00 sec)
```

The preceding code snippets use the same idea: create a temporary table to store the maximum population number and join it with the original table. But the latter performs this operation in the single query, so you don't need to worry about destroying the temporary table after getting the result. We discuss CTEs in detail in Recipe 10.18.

See Also

Recipe 16.7 extends the discussion here to the problem of finding rows that contain minimum or maximum values for multiple groups in a dataset.

10.7 Controlling String Case Sensitivity for MIN() and MAX()

Problem

MIN() and MAX() select strings in case-sensitive fashion when you don't want them to, or vice versa.

Solution

Use different comparison characteristics of the strings.

Discussion

Recipe 7.1 discusses how string-comparison properties depend on whether the strings are binary or nonbinary:

- Binary strings are sequences of bytes. They are compared byte by byte using numeric byte values. Character set and lettercase have no meaning for comparisons.
- Nonbinary strings are sequences of characters. They have a character set and collation and are compared character by character using the order defined by the collation.

These properties also apply to string columns used as the argument to the MIN() or MAX() function because they are based on comparison. To alter how these functions work with a string column, alter the column's comparison properties. Recipe 7.7 discusses how to control these properties, and Recipe 9.4 shows how they apply to string sorts. The same principles apply to finding minimum and maximum string values, so we'll just summarize here; read Recipe 9.4 for additional details.

- To compare case-insensitive strings in case-sensitive fashion, order the values using a case-sensitive collation:
    ```
    SELECT
    MIN(str_col COLLATE utf8mb4_0900_as_cs) AS min,
    ```

```
      MAX(str_col COLLATE utf8mb4_0900_as_cs) AS max
      FROM tbl;
```

- To compare case-sensitive strings in case-insensitive fashion, order the values using a case-insensitive collation:
```
SELECT
MIN(str_col COLLATE utf8mb4_0900_ai_ci) AS min,
MAX(str_col COLLATE utf8mb4_0900_ai_ci) AS max
FROM tbl;
```

Another possibility is to compare values that have all been converted to the same lettercase, which makes lettercase irrelevant. However, that also changes the retrieved values:
```
SELECT
MIN(UPPER(str_col)) AS min,
MAX(UPPER(str_col)) AS max
FROM tbl;
```

- Binary strings compare using numeric byte values, so there is no concept of lettercase involved. However, because letters in different cases have different byte values, comparisons of binary strings effectively are case sensitive (that is, a and A are unequal). To compare binary strings using a case-insensitive ordering, convert them to nonbinary strings and apply an appropriate collation:
```
SELECT
MIN(CONVERT(str_col USING utf8mb4) COLLATE utf8mb4_0900_ai_ci) AS min,
MAX(CONVERT(str_col USING utf8mb4) COLLATE utf8mb4_0900_ai_ci) AS max
FROM tbl;
```

If the default collation is case insensitive (as is true for utf8mb4), you can omit the COLLATE clause.

10.8 Dividing a Summary into Subgroups

Problem

You want a summary for each subgroup of a set of rows, not an overall summary value.

Solution

Use a GROUP BY clause to arrange rows into groups.

Discussion

The summary statements shown so far calculate summary values over all rows in the result set. For example, the following statement determines the number of records in the mail table, and thus the total number of mail messages sent:
```
mysql> SELECT COUNT(*) FROM mail;
+----------+
```

```
| COUNT(*) |
+----------+
|       16 |
+----------+
```

To arrange a set of rows into subgroups and summarize each group, use aggregate functions in conjunction with a GROUP BY clause. To determine the number of messages per sender, group the rows by sender name, count how many times each name occurs, and display the names with the counts:

```
mysql> SELECT srcuser, COUNT(*) FROM mail GROUP BY srcuser;
+---------+----------+
| srcuser | COUNT(*) |
+---------+----------+
| barb    |        3 |
| gene    |        6 |
| phil    |        5 |
| tricia  |        2 |
+---------+----------+
```

That query summarizes the same column that is used for grouping (srcuser), but that's not always necessary. Suppose that you want a quick characterization of the mail table, showing for each sender listed in it the total amount of traffic sent (in bytes) and the average number of bytes per message. In this case, you still use the srcuser column to group the rows but summarize the size values:

```
mysql> SELECT srcuser,
    -> SUM(size) AS 'total bytes',
    -> AVG(size) AS 'bytes per message'
    -> FROM mail GROUP BY srcuser;
+---------+-------------+-------------------+
| srcuser | total bytes | bytes per message |
+---------+-------------+-------------------+
| barb    |      156696 |        52232.0000 |
| gene    |     1033108 |       172184.6667 |
| phil    |       18974 |         3794.8000 |
| tricia  |     2589407 |      1294703.5000 |
+---------+-------------+-------------------+
```

Use as many grouping columns as necessary to achieve a grouping as fine-grained as you require. The earlier query that shows the number of messages per sender is a coarse summary. To be more specific and find out how many messages each sender sent from each host, use two grouping columns. This produces a result with nested groups (groups within groups):

```
mysql> SELECT srcuser, srchost, COUNT(srcuser) FROM mail
    -> GROUP BY srcuser, srchost;
+---------+---------+----------------+
| srcuser | srchost | COUNT(srcuser) |
+---------+---------+----------------+
| barb    | saturn  |              2 |
| barb    | venus   |              1 |
| gene    | mars    |              2 |
| gene    | saturn  |              2 |
| gene    | venus   |              2 |
| phil    | mars    |              3 |
```

```
| phil   | venus  |              2 |
| tricia | mars   |              1 |
| tricia | saturn |              1 |
+--------+--------+----------------+
```

The preceding examples in this section used COUNT(), SUM(), and AVG() for per-group summaries. You can use MIN() or MAX(), too. With a GROUP BY clause, they return the smallest or largest value per group. The following query groups mail table rows by message sender, displaying for each the size of the largest message sent and the date of the most recent message:

```
mysql> SELECT srcuser, MAX(size), MAX(t) FROM mail GROUP BY srcuser;
+---------+-----------+---------------------+
| srcuser | MAX(size) | MAX(t)              |
+---------+-----------+---------------------+
| barb    |     98151 | 2014-05-14 14:42:21 |
| gene    |    998532 | 2014-05-19 22:21:51 |
| phil    |     10294 | 2014-05-19 12:49:23 |
| tricia  |   2394482 | 2014-05-14 17:03:01 |
+---------+-----------+---------------------+
```

You can group by multiple columns and display a maximum for each combination of values in those columns. This query finds the size of the largest message sent between each pair of sender and recipient values listed in the mail table:

```
mysql> SELECT srcuser, dstuser, MAX(size) FROM mail GROUP BY srcuser, dstuser;
+---------+---------+-----------+
| srcuser | dstuser | MAX(size) |
+---------+---------+-----------+
| barb    | barb    |     98151 |
| barb    | tricia  |     58274 |
| gene    | barb    |      2291 |
| gene    | gene    |     23992 |
| gene    | tricia  |    998532 |
| phil    | barb    |     10294 |
| phil    | phil    |      1048 |
| phil    | tricia  |      5781 |
| tricia  | gene    |    194925 |
| tricia  | phil    |   2394482 |
+---------+---------+-----------+
```

When using aggregate functions to produce per-group summary values, watch out for the following trap, which involves selecting nonsummary table columns not related to the grouping columns. Suppose that you want to know the longest trip per driver in the driver_log table:

```
mysql> SELECT name, MAX(miles) AS 'longest trip'
    -> FROM driver_log GROUP BY name;
+-------+--------------+
| name  | longest trip |
+-------+--------------+
| Ben   |          152 |
| Henry |          300 |
| Suzi  |          502 |
+-------+--------------+
```

But what if you also want to show the date on which each driver's longest trip occurred? Can you just add `trav_date` to the output column list? Sorry, that doesn't work:

```
mysql> SELECT name, trav_date, MAX(miles) AS 'longest trip'
    -> FROM driver_log GROUP BY name;
+-------+------------+--------------+
| name  | trav_date  | longest trip |
+-------+------------+--------------+
| Ben   | 2014-07-30 |          152 |
| Henry | 2014-07-29 |          300 |
| Suzi  | 2014-07-29 |          502 |
+-------+------------+--------------+
```

The query does produce a result, but if you compare it to the full table (shown here), you'll see that although the dates for Ben and Henry are correct, the date for Suzi is not:

```
+--------+-------+------------+-------+
| rec_id | name  | trav_date  | miles |
+--------+-------+------------+-------+
|      1 | Ben   | 2014-07-30 |   152 |    ← Ben's longest trip
|      2 | Suzi  | 2014-07-29 |   391 |
|      3 | Henry | 2014-07-29 |   300 |    ← Henry's longest trip
|      4 | Henry | 2014-07-27 |    96 |
|      5 | Ben   | 2014-07-29 |   131 |
|      6 | Henry | 2014-07-26 |   115 |
|      7 | Suzi  | 2014-08-02 |   502 |    ← Suzi's longest trip
|      8 | Henry | 2014-08-01 |   197 |
|      9 | Ben   | 2014-08-02 |    79 |
|     10 | Henry | 2014-07-30 |   203 |
+--------+-------+------------+-------+
```

So what's going on? Why does the summary statement produce incorrect results? This happens because when you include a GROUP BY clause in a query, the only values that you can meaningfully select are the grouping columns or summary values calculated from the groups. If you display additional table columns, they're not tied to the grouped columns, and the values displayed for them are indeterminate. (For the statement just shown, it appears that MySQL may simply be picking the first date for each driver, regardless of whether it matches the driver's maximum mileage value.)

To make queries that pick indeterminate values illegal so that you won't inadvertently suppose that the `trav_date` values are correct, set the ONLY_FULL_GROUP_BY SQL mode:

```
mysql> SET sql_mode = 'ONLY_FULL_GROUP_BY';
mysql> SELECT name, trav_date, MAX(miles) AS 'longest trip'
    -> FROM driver_log GROUP BY name;
ERROR 1055 (42000): 'cookbook.driver_log.trav_date' isn't in GROUP BY
```

The ONLY_FULL_GROUP_BY SQL mode has been part of the default settings since MySQL 5.7. However, we have seen many legacy applications that disable this option.

We suggest that you always have ONLY_FULL_GROUP_BY enabled and fix queries that return an error otherwise.

The general solution to the problem of displaying contents of rows associated with minimum or maximum group values involves a join. The technique is described in Recipe 16.7. For the problem at hand, produce the required results as follows:

```
mysql> CREATE TEMPORARY TABLE t
    -> SELECT name, MAX(miles) AS miles FROM driver_log GROUP BY name;
mysql> SELECT d.name, d.trav_date, d.miles AS 'longest trip'
    -> FROM driver_log AS d INNER JOIN t USING (name, miles) ORDER BY name;
+-------+------------+--------------+
| name  | trav_date  | longest trip |
+-------+------------+--------------+
| Ben   | 2014-07-30 |          152 |
| Henry | 2014-07-29 |          300 |
| Suzi  | 2014-08-02 |          502 |
+-------+------------+--------------+
```

Or, by using a CTE:

```
mysql> WITH t AS
    -> (SELECT name, MAX(miles) AS miles FROM driver_log GROUP BY name)
    -> SELECT d.name, d.trav_date, d.miles AS 'longest trip'
    -> FROM driver_log AS d INNER JOIN t USING (name, miles) ORDER BY name;
+-------+------------+--------------+
| name  | trav_date  | longest trip |
+-------+------------+--------------+
| Ben   | 2014-07-30 |          152 |
| Henry | 2014-07-29 |          300 |
| Suzi  | 2014-08-02 |          502 |
+-------+------------+--------------+
3 rows in set (0.01 sec)
```

10.9 Handling NULL Values with Aggregate Functions

Problem

You're summarizing a set of values that may include NULL values, and you need to know how to interpret the results.

Solution

Understand how aggregate functions handle NULL values.

Discussion

Most aggregate functions ignore NULL values. COUNT() is different: COUNT(*expr*) ignores NULL instances of *expr*, but COUNT(*) counts rows, regardless of content.

Suppose that an expt table contains experimental results for subjects who are to be given four tests each and that lists the test score as NULL for tests not yet administered:

```
mysql> SELECT subject, test, score FROM expt ORDER BY subject, test;
+---------+------+-------+
| subject | test | score |
+---------+------+-------+
| Jane    | A    |    47 |
| Jane    | B    |    50 |
| Jane    | C    |  NULL |
| Jane    | D    |  NULL |
| Marvin  | A    |    52 |
| Marvin  | B    |    45 |
| Marvin  | C    |    53 |
| Marvin  | D    |  NULL |
+---------+------+-------+
```

By using a GROUP BY clause to arrange the rows by subject name, the number of tests taken by each subject, as well as the total, average, lowest, and highest scores, can be calculated like this:

```
mysql> SELECT subject,
    -> COUNT(score) AS n,
    -> SUM(score) AS total,
    -> AVG(score) AS average,
    -> MIN(score) AS lowest,
    -> MAX(score) AS highest
    -> FROM expt GROUP BY subject;
+---------+---+-------+---------+--------+---------+
| subject | n | total | average | lowest | highest |
+---------+---+-------+---------+--------+---------+
| Jane    | 2 |    97 | 48.5000 |     47 |      50 |
| Marvin  | 3 |   150 | 50.0000 |     45 |      53 |
+---------+---+-------+---------+--------+---------+
```

You can see from the results in the column labeled n (number of tests) that the query counts only five values, even though the table contains eight. Why? Because the values in that column correspond to the number of non-NULL test scores for each subject. The other summary columns display results that are calculated only from the non-NULL scores as well.

It makes a lot of sense for aggregate functions to ignore NULL values. If they followed the usual SQL arithmetic rules, adding NULL to any other value would produce a NULL result. That would make aggregate functions really difficult to use: to avoid getting a NULL result, you'd have to filter out NULL values every time you performed a summary. By ignoring NULL values, aggregate functions become a lot more convenient.

However, be aware that even though aggregate functions may ignore NULL values, some of them can still produce NULL as a result. This happens if there's nothing to summarize, which occurs if the set of values is empty or contains only NULL values. The following query is the same as the previous one, with one small difference. It selects only NULL test scores to illustrate what happens when there's nothing for the aggregate functions to operate on:

```
mysql> SELECT subject,
    -> COUNT(score) AS n,
    -> SUM(score) AS total,
    -> AVG(score) AS average,
    -> MIN(score) AS lowest,
    -> MAX(score) AS highest
    -> FROM expt WHERE score IS NULL GROUP BY subject;
+---------+---+-------+---------+--------+---------+
| subject | n | total | average | lowest | highest |
+---------+---+-------+---------+--------+---------+
| Jane    | 0 | NULL  |    NULL |   NULL |    NULL |
| Marvin  | 0 | NULL  |    NULL |   NULL |    NULL |
+---------+---+-------+---------+--------+---------+
```

For COUNT(), the number of scores per subject is zero and is reported that way. On
the other hand, SUM(), AVG(), MIN(), and MAX() return NULL when there are no values
to summarize. If you don't want an aggregate value of NULL to display as NULL, use
IFNULL() to map it appropriately:

```
mysql> SELECT subject,
    -> COUNT(score) AS n,
    -> IFNULL(SUM(score),0) AS total,
    -> IFNULL(AVG(score),0) AS average,
    -> IFNULL(MIN(score),'Unknown') AS lowest,
    -> IFNULL(MAX(score),'Unknown') AS highest
    -> FROM expt WHERE score IS NULL GROUP BY subject;
+---------+---+-------+---------+---------+---------+
| subject | n | total | average | lowest  | highest |
+---------+---+-------+---------+---------+---------+
| Jane    | 0 |     0 |  0.0000 | Unknown | Unknown |
| Marvin  | 0 |     0 |  0.0000 | Unknown | Unknown |
+---------+---+-------+---------+---------+---------+
```

COUNT() is somewhat different with regard to NULL values than the other aggregate
functions. Like other aggregate functions, COUNT(*expr*) counts only non-NULL values,
but COUNT(*) counts rows, no matter what they contain. You can see the difference
between the forms of COUNT() like this:

```
mysql> SELECT COUNT(*), COUNT(score) FROM expt;
+----------+--------------+
| COUNT(*) | COUNT(score) |
+----------+--------------+
|        8 |            5 |
+----------+--------------+
```

This tells us that there are eight rows in the expt table but that only five of them
have the score value filled in. The different forms of COUNT() can be very useful for
counting missing values. Just take the difference:

```
mysql> SELECT COUNT(*) - COUNT(score) AS missing FROM expt;
+---------+
| missing |
+---------+
|       3 |
+---------+
```

Missing and nonmissing counts can be determined for subgroups as well. The following query does so for each subject, providing an easy way to assess the extent to which the experiment has been completed:

```
mysql> SELECT subject,
    -> COUNT(*) AS total,
    -> COUNT(score) AS 'nonmissing',
    -> COUNT(*) - COUNT(score) AS missing
    -> FROM expt GROUP BY subject;
+---------+-------+------------+---------+
| subject | total | nonmissing | missing |
+---------+-------+------------+---------+
| Jane    |     4 |          2 |       2 |
| Marvin  |     4 |          3 |       1 |
+---------+-------+------------+---------+
```

10.10 Selecting Only Groups with Certain Characteristics

Problem

You want to calculate group summaries but display results only for groups that match certain criteria.

Solution

Use a HAVING clause.

Discussion

You're familiar with the use of WHERE to specify conditions that rows must satisfy to be selected by a statement. It's natural, therefore, to use WHERE to write conditions that involve summary values. The only trouble is that it doesn't work. To identify drivers in the driver_log table who drove more than three days, you might write the statement like this:

```
mysql> SELECT COUNT(*), name FROM driver_log
    -> WHERE COUNT(*) > 3
    -> GROUP BY name;
ERROR 1111 (HY000): Invalid use of group function
```

The problem is that WHERE specifies the initial constraints that determine which rows to select, but the value of COUNT() can be determined only after the rows have been selected. The solution is to put the COUNT() expression in a HAVING clause instead. HAVING is analogous to WHERE, but it applies to group characteristics rather than to single rows. That is, HAVING operates on the already-selected-and-grouped set of rows, applying additional constraints based on aggregate function results that aren't known during the initial selection process. The preceding query therefore should be written like this:

```
mysql> SELECT COUNT(*), name FROM driver_log
    -> GROUP BY name
    -> HAVING COUNT(*) > 3;
+----------+-------+
| COUNT(*) | name  |
+----------+-------+
|        5 | Henry |
+----------+-------+
```

When you use HAVING, you can still include a WHERE clause but only to select rows to be summarized, not to test already-calculated summary values.

HAVING can refer to aliases, so the previous query can be rewritten like this:

```
mysql> SELECT COUNT(*) AS count, name FROM driver_log
    -> GROUP BY name
    -> HAVING count > 3;
+-------+-------+
| count | name  |
+-------+-------+
|     5 | Henry |
+-------+-------+
```

10.11 Using Counts to Determine Whether Values Are Unique

Problem

You want to know whether values in a table are unique.

Solution

Use HAVING in conjunction with COUNT().

Discussion

DISTINCT eliminates duplicates but doesn't show which values actually were duplicated in the original data. You can use HAVING to find unique values in situations to which DISTINCT does not apply. HAVING can tell you which values were unique or nonunique.

The following statements show the days on which only one driver was active and the days on which more than one driver was active. They're based on using HAVING and COUNT() to determine which trav_date values are unique or nonunique:

```
mysql> SELECT trav_date, COUNT(trav_date) FROM driver_log
    -> GROUP BY trav_date HAVING COUNT(trav_date) = 1;
+------------+------------------+
| trav_date  | COUNT(trav_date) |
+------------+------------------+
| 2014-07-26 |                1 |
```

```
| 2014-07-27 |                  1 |
| 2014-08-01 |                  1 |
+------------+------------------+
mysql> SELECT trav_date, COUNT(trav_date) FROM driver_log
    -> GROUP BY trav_date HAVING COUNT(trav_date) > 1;
+------------+------------------+
| trav_date  | COUNT(trav_date) |
+------------+------------------+
| 2014-07-29 |                3 |
| 2014-07-30 |                2 |
| 2014-08-02 |                2 |
+------------+------------------+
```

This technique works for combinations of values, too. For example, to find message sender/recipient pairs between whom only one message was sent, look for combinations that occur only once in the mail table:

```
mysql> SELECT srcuser, dstuser FROM mail
    -> GROUP BY srcuser, dstuser HAVING COUNT(*) = 1;
+---------+---------+
| srcuser | dstuser |
+---------+---------+
| barb    | barb    |
| gene    | tricia  |
| phil    | barb    |
| tricia  | gene    |
| tricia  | phil    |
+---------+---------+
```

Note that this query doesn't print the count. The previous examples did so, to show that the counts were being used properly, but you can refer to an aggregate value in a HAVING clause without including it in the output column list.

10.12 Grouping by Expression Results

Problem

You want to group rows into subgroups based on values calculated from an expression.

Solution

In the GROUP BY clause, use an expression that categorizes values.

Discussion

GROUP BY, like ORDER BY, can refer to expressions. This means you can use calculations as the basis for grouping. As with ORDER BY, you can write the grouping expression directly in the GROUP BY clause or use an alias for the expression (if it appears in the output column list) and refer to the alias in the GROUP BY.

To find days of the year on which more than one state joined the Union, group by statehood month and day, and then use HAVING and COUNT() to find the nonunique combinations:

```
mysql> SELECT
    -> MONTHNAME(statehood) AS month,
    -> DAYOFMONTH(statehood) AS day,
    -> COUNT(*) AS count
    -> FROM states GROUP BY month, day HAVING count > 1;
+----------+------+-------+
| month    | day  | count |
+----------+------+-------+
| February |   14 |     2 |
| June     |    1 |     2 |
| March    |    1 |     2 |
| May      |   29 |     2 |
| November |    2 |     2 |
+----------+------+-------+
```

10.13 Summarizing Noncategorical Data

Problem

You want to summarize a set of values that are not naturally categorical.

Solution

Use an expression to group the values into categories.

Discussion

Recipe 10.12 shows how to group rows by expression results. One important application for this is to categorize values that are not categorical. This is useful because GROUP BY works best for columns with repetitive values. For example, you might attempt to perform a population analysis by grouping rows in the states table using values in the pop column. That doesn't work very well due to the high number of distinct values in the column. In fact, they're *all* distinct:

```
mysql> SELECT COUNT(pop), COUNT(DISTINCT pop) FROM states;
+------------+---------------------+
| COUNT(pop) | COUNT(DISTINCT pop) |
+------------+---------------------+
|         50 |                  50 |
+------------+---------------------+
```

In situations like this, in which values do not group nicely into a small number of sets, use a transformation that forces them into categories. Begin by determining the range of population values:

```
mysql> SELECT MIN(pop), MAX(pop) FROM states;
+----------+----------+
| MIN(pop) | MAX(pop) |
+----------+----------+
|   578803 | 39237836 |
+----------+----------+
```

You can see from that result that if you divide the pop values by five million, they'll group into eight categories—a reasonable number. (The category ranges will be 1 to 5,000,000, 5,000,001 to 10,000,000, and so forth.) To put each population value in the proper category, divide by five million and use the integer result:

```
mysql> SELECT FLOOR(pop/5000000) AS `max population (millions)`,
    -> COUNT(*) AS `number of states`
    -> FROM states GROUP BY `max population (millions)`
    -> ORDER BY `max population (millions)`;
+---------------------------+------------------+
| max population (millions) | number of states |
+---------------------------+------------------+
|                         0 |               26 |
|                         1 |               14 |
|                         2 |                6 |
|                         3 |                1 |
|                         4 |                1 |
|                         5 |                1 |
|                         7 |                1 |
+---------------------------+------------------+
```

Hmm. That's not quite right. The expression groups the population values into a small number of categories but doesn't report the category values properly. Let's try multiplying the FLOOR() results by five:

```
mysql> SELECT FLOOR(pop/5000000)*5 AS `max population (millions)`,
    -> COUNT(*) AS `number of states`
    -> FROM states GROUP BY `max population (millions)`
    -> ORDER BY `max population (millions)`;
+---------------------------+------------------+
| max population (millions) | number of states |
+---------------------------+------------------+
|                         0 |               26 |
|                         5 |               14 |
|                        10 |                6 |
|                        15 |                1 |
|                        20 |                1 |
|                        25 |                1 |
|                        35 |                1 |
+---------------------------+------------------+
```

That still isn't correct. The maximum state population was 35,893,799, which should go into a category for 40 million, not one for 35 million. The problem here is that the category-generating expression groups values toward the lower bound of each category. To group values toward the upper bound instead, use the following technique. For categories of size n, place a value x into the proper category using this expression:

```
FLOOR((x+(n-1))/n)
```

So the final form of our query looks like this:

```
mysql> SELECT FLOOR((pop+4999999)/5000000)*5 AS `max population (millions)`,
    -> COUNT(*) AS `number of states`
    -> FROM states GROUP BY `max population (millions)`
    -> ORDER BY `max population (millions)`;
+---------------------------+------------------+
| max population (millions) | number of states |
+---------------------------+------------------+
|                         5 |               26 |
|                        10 |               14 |
|                        15 |                6 |
|                        20 |                1 |
|                        25 |                1 |
|                        30 |                1 |
|                        40 |                1 |
+---------------------------+------------------+
```

The result shows clearly that the majority of US states have a population of five million or less.

In some instances, it may be more appropriate to categorize groups on a logarithmic scale. For example, treat the state population values that way as follows:

```
mysql> SELECT FLOOR(LOG10(pop)) AS `log10(population)`,
    -> COUNT(*) AS `number of states`
    -> FROM states GROUP BY `log10(population)`;
+-------------------+------------------+
| log10(population) | number of states |
+-------------------+------------------+
|                 5 |                5 |
|                 6 |               35 |
|                 7 |               10 |
+-------------------+------------------+
```

The query shows the number of states that have populations measured in hundreds of thousands, millions, and tens of millions, respectively.

You may have noticed that aliases in the preceding queries are written using backticks (identifier quoting) rather than single quotes (string quoting). Quoted aliases in the GROUP BY clause must use identifier quoting or the alias is treated as a constant string expression and the grouping produces the wrong result. Identifier quoting clarifies to MySQL that the alias refers to an output column. The aliases in the output column list could have been written using string quoting; we used backticks there to avoid mixing alias quoting styles within a given query.

How Repetitive Is a Set of Values?

To assess how much repetition is present in a set of values, use the ratio of COUNT(DISTINCT) and COUNT(). If all values are unique, both counts are the same and the ratio is 1. This is the case for the t values in the mail table and the pop values in the states table:

```
mysql> SELECT COUNT(DISTINCT t) / COUNT(t) FROM mail;
+-----------------------------+
| COUNT(DISTINCT t) / COUNT(t) |
+-----------------------------+
|                      1.0000 |
+-----------------------------+
mysql> SELECT COUNT(DISTINCT pop) / COUNT(pop) FROM states;
+---------------------------------+
| COUNT(DISTINCT pop) / COUNT(pop) |
+---------------------------------+
|                          1.0000 |
+---------------------------------+
```

For a more repetitive set of values, COUNT(DISTINCT) is less than COUNT(), and the ratio is smaller:

```
mysql> SELECT COUNT(DISTINCT name) / COUNT(name) FROM driver_log;
+-----------------------------------+
| COUNT(DISTINCT name) / COUNT(name) |
+-----------------------------------+
|                            0.3000 |
+-----------------------------------+
```

What's the practical use for this ratio? A result close to zero indicates a high degree of repetition, which means the values will group into a small number of categories naturally. A result of 1 or close to it indicates many unique values, with the consequence that GROUP BY won't be very efficient for grouping the values into categories. (That is, there will be a lot of categories, relative to the number of values.) This tells you that, to generate a summary, you'll probably find it necessary to impose an artificial categorization on the values, using the techniques described in this recipe.

10.14 Finding Smallest or Largest Summary Values

Problem

You want to compute per-group summary values but display only the smallest or largest of them.

Solution

Add a LIMIT clause to the statement. Or use a user-defined variable or subquery to pick the appropriate summary.

Discussion

MIN() and MAX() find the values at the endpoints of a set of values, but to find the endpoints of a set of summary values, those functions won't work. Their argument cannot be another aggregate function. For example, you can easily find per-driver mileage totals:

```
mysql> SELECT name, SUM(miles)
    -> FROM driver_log
    -> GROUP BY name;
+-------+------------+
| name  | SUM(miles) |
+-------+------------+
| Ben   |        362 |
| Henry |        911 |
| Suzi  |        893 |
+-------+------------+
```

To select only the row for the driver with the most miles, the following doesn't work:

```
mysql> SELECT name, SUM(miles)
    -> FROM driver_log
    -> GROUP BY name
    -> HAVING SUM(miles) = MAX(SUM(miles));
ERROR 1111 (HY000): Invalid use of group function
```

Instead, order the rows with the largest SUM() values first, and use LIMIT to select the first row:

```
mysql> SELECT name, SUM(miles)
    -> FROM driver_log
    -> GROUP BY name
    -> ORDER BY SUM(miles) DESC LIMIT 1;
+-------+------------+
| name  | SUM(miles) |
+-------+------------+
| Henry |        911 |
+-------+------------+
```

However, if more than one row has the given summary value, a LIMIT 1 query won't tell you that. For example, you might attempt to ascertain the most common initial letter for state names like this:

```
mysql> SELECT LEFT(name,1) AS letter, COUNT(*) FROM states
    -> GROUP BY letter ORDER BY COUNT(*) DESC LIMIT 1;
+--------+----------+
| letter | COUNT(*) |
+--------+----------+
| M      |        8 |
+--------+----------+
```

But eight state names also begin with N. To find all most-frequent values when there may be more than one, use a user-defined variable or subquery to determine the maximum count, then select those values with a count equal to the maximum:

```
mysql> SET @max = (SELECT COUNT(*) FROM states
    -> GROUP BY LEFT(name,1) ORDER BY COUNT(*) DESC LIMIT 1);
mysql> SELECT LEFT(name,1) AS letter, COUNT(*) FROM states
    -> GROUP BY letter HAVING COUNT(*) = @max;
+--------+----------+
| letter | COUNT(*) |
+--------+----------+
| M      |        8 |
| N      |        8 |
+--------+----------+
```

```
mysql> SELECT LEFT(name,1) AS letter, COUNT(*) FROM states
    -> GROUP BY letter HAVING COUNT(*) =
    ->   (SELECT COUNT(*) FROM states
    ->   GROUP BY LEFT(name,1) ORDER BY COUNT(*) DESC LIMIT 1);
+--------+----------+
| letter | COUNT(*) |
+--------+----------+
| M      |        8 |
| N      |        8 |
+--------+----------+
```

10.15 Producing Date-Based Summaries

Problem

You want to produce a summary based on date or time values.

Solution

Use GROUP BY to place temporal values into categories of the appropriate duration. Often this involves using expressions that extract the significant parts of dates or times.

Discussion

To sort rows temporally, use ORDER BY with a temporal column. To summarize rows instead, based on groupings into time intervals, determine how to categorize rows into the proper intervals, and use GROUP BY to group them accordingly.

For example, to determine how many drivers were on the road and how many miles were driven each day, group the rows in the driver_log table by date:[1]

```
mysql> SELECT trav_date,
    -> COUNT(*) AS 'number of drivers', SUM(miles) As 'miles logged'
    -> FROM driver_log GROUP BY trav_date;
+------------+-------------------+--------------+
| trav_date  | number of drivers | miles logged |
+------------+-------------------+--------------+
| 2014-07-26 |                 1 |          115 |
| 2014-07-27 |                 1 |           96 |
| 2014-07-29 |                 3 |          822 |
| 2014-07-30 |                 2 |          355 |
| 2014-08-01 |                 1 |          197 |
| 2014-08-02 |                 2 |          581 |
+------------+-------------------+--------------+
```

---

[1] The result includes an entry only for dates actually represented in the table. To generate a summary with an entry for the range of dates in the table, use a join to fill in the "missing" values. See Recipe 16.8.

However, this per-day summary grows lengthier as you add more rows to the table. Over time, the number of distinct dates will become so large that the summary fails to be useful, and you'd probably decide to increase the category size. For example, this query categorizes by month:

```
mysql> SELECT YEAR(trav_date) AS year, MONTH(trav_date) AS month,
    -> COUNT(*) AS 'number of drivers', SUM(miles) As 'miles logged'
    -> FROM driver_log GROUP BY year, month;
+------+-------+-------------------+--------------+
| year | month | number of drivers | miles logged |
+------+-------+-------------------+--------------+
| 2014 |     7 |                 7 |         1388 |
| 2014 |     8 |                 3 |          778 |
+------+-------+-------------------+--------------+
```

Now the number of summary rows grows much more slowly over time. Eventually, you could summarize based only on year to collapse rows even more.

Uses for temporal categorizations are numerous:

- To produce daily summaries from DATETIME or TIMESTAMP columns that have the potential to contain many unique values, strip the time-of-day part to collapse all values occurring within a given day to the same value. Any of the following GROUP BY clauses will do this, although the last one is likely to be slowest:

```
GROUP BY DATE(col_name)
GROUP BY FROM_DAYS(TO_DAYS(col_name))
GROUP BY YEAR(col_name), MONTH(col_name), DAYOFMONTH(col_name)
GROUP BY DATE_FORMAT(col_name,'%Y-%m-%e')
```

- To produce monthly or quarterly sales reports, group by MONTH(col_name) or QUARTER(col_name) to place dates into the correct part of the year.

10.16 Working with Per-Group and Overall Summary Values Simultaneously

Problem

You want to produce a report that requires different levels of summary detail. Or you want to compare per-group summary values to an overall summary value.

Solution

Use two statements that retrieve different levels of summary information. Or use a subquery to retrieve one summary value and refer to it in the outer query that refers to other summary values. For applications that only display multiple summary levels (rather than perform additional calculations on them), WITH ROLLUP might be sufficient.

Discussion

Some reports involve multiple levels of summary information. The following report displays the total number of miles per driver from the `driver_log` table, along with each driver's miles as a percentage of the total miles in the entire table:

```
+-------+--------------+-----------------------+
| name  | miles/driver | percent of total miles |
+-------+--------------+-----------------------+
| Ben   |          362 |                16.7128 |
| Henry |          911 |                42.0591 |
| Suzi  |          893 |                41.2281 |
+-------+--------------+-----------------------+
```

The percentages represent the ratio of each driver's miles to the total miles for all drivers. To perform the percentage calculation, you need a per-group summary to get each driver's miles and also an overall summary to get the total miles. First, run a query to get the overall mileage total:

```
mysql> SELECT @total := SUM(miles) AS 'total miles' FROM driver_log;
+-------------+
| total miles |
+-------------+
|        2166 |
+-------------+
```

Then calculate the per-group values and use the overall total to compute the percentages:

```
mysql> SELECT name,
    -> SUM(miles) AS 'miles/driver',
    -> (SUM(miles)*100)/@total AS 'percent of total miles'
    -> FROM driver_log GROUP BY name;
+-------+--------------+-----------------------+
| name  | miles/driver | percent of total miles |
+-------+--------------+-----------------------+
| Ben   |          362 |                16.7128 |
| Henry |          911 |                42.0591 |
| Suzi  |          893 |                41.2281 |
+-------+--------------+-----------------------+
```

To combine the two statements into one, use a subquery that computes the total miles:

```
SELECT name,
SUM(miles) AS 'miles/driver',
(SUM(miles)*100)/(SELECT SUM(miles) FROM driver_log)
  AS 'percent of total miles'
FROM driver_log GROUP BY name;
```

A similar problem uses multiple summary levels to compare per-group summary values with the corresponding overall summary value. Suppose that you want to display drivers who had a lower average miles per day than the group average. Calculate the overall average in a subquery, and then compare each driver's average to the overall average using a `HAVING` clause:

```
mysql> SELECT name, AVG(miles) AS driver_avg FROM driver_log
    -> GROUP BY name
    -> HAVING driver_avg < (SELECT AVG(miles) FROM driver_log);
+-------+------------+
| name  | driver_avg |
+-------+------------+
| Ben   |   120.6667 |
| Henry |   182.2000 |
+-------+------------+
```

To display different summary-level values (and not perform calculations involving one summary level against another), add WITH ROLLUP to the GROUP BY clause:

```
mysql> SELECT name, SUM(miles) AS 'miles/driver'
    -> FROM driver_log GROUP BY name WITH ROLLUP;
+-------+--------------+
| name  | miles/driver |
+-------+--------------+
| Ben   |          362 |
| Henry |          911 |
| Suzi  |          893 |
| NULL  |         2166 |
+-------+--------------+
mysql> SELECT name, AVG(miles) AS driver_avg FROM driver_log
    -> GROUP BY name WITH ROLLUP;
+-------+------------+
| name  | driver_avg |
+-------+------------+
| Ben   |   120.6667 |
| Henry |   182.2000 |
| Suzi  |   446.5000 |
| NULL  |   216.6000 |
+-------+------------+
```

In each case, the output row with NULL in the name column represents the overall sum or average calculated over all drivers.

WITH ROLLUP produces multiple summary levels if you group by more than one column. The following statement shows the number of mail messages sent between each pair of users:

```
mysql> SELECT srcuser, dstuser, COUNT(*)
    -> FROM mail GROUP BY srcuser, dstuser;
+---------+---------+----------+
| srcuser | dstuser | COUNT(*) |
+---------+---------+----------+
| barb    | barb    |        1 |
| barb    | tricia  |        2 |
| gene    | barb    |        2 |
| gene    | gene    |        3 |
| gene    | tricia  |        1 |
| phil    | barb    |        1 |
| phil    | phil    |        2 |
| phil    | tricia  |        2 |
| tricia  | gene    |        1 |
| tricia  | phil    |        1 |
+---------+---------+----------+
```

Adding WITH ROLLUP causes the output to include an intermediate count for each srcuser value (these are the lines with NULL in the dstuser column), plus an overall count at the end:

```
mysql> SELECT srcuser, dstuser, COUNT(*)
    -> FROM mail GROUP BY srcuser, dstuser WITH ROLLUP;
+---------+---------+----------+
| srcuser | dstuser | COUNT(*) |
+---------+---------+----------+
| barb    | barb    |        1 |
| barb    | tricia  |        2 |
| barb    | NULL    |        3 |
| gene    | barb    |        2 |
| gene    | gene    |        3 |
| gene    | tricia  |        1 |
| gene    | NULL    |        6 |
| phil    | barb    |        1 |
| phil    | phil    |        2 |
| phil    | tricia  |        2 |
| phil    | NULL    |        5 |
| tricia  | gene    |        1 |
| tricia  | phil    |        1 |
| tricia  | NULL    |        2 |
| NULL    | NULL    |       16 |
+---------+---------+----------+
```

10.17 Generating a Report that Includes a Summary and a List

Problem

You want to create a report that displays a summary, together with the list of rows associated with each summary value.

Solution

Use two statements that retrieve different levels of summary information. Or use a programming language to do some of the work so that you can use a single statement.

Discussion

Suppose that you want to produce a report that looks like this:

```
Name: Ben; days on road: 3; miles driven: 362
  date: 2014-07-29, trip length: 131
  date: 2014-07-30, trip length: 152
  date: 2014-08-02, trip length: 79
Name: Henry; days on road: 5; miles driven: 911
  date: 2014-07-26, trip length: 115
  date: 2014-07-27, trip length: 96
  date: 2014-07-29, trip length: 300
  date: 2014-07-30, trip length: 203
```

```
    date: 2014-08-01, trip length: 197
Name: Suzi; days on road: 2; miles driven: 893
   date: 2014-07-29, trip length: 391
   date: 2014-08-02, trip length: 502
```

For each driver in the `driver_log` table, the report shows the following information:

- A summary line showing the driver name, the number of days on the road, and the number of miles driven
- A list that details dates and mileages for the individual trips from which the summary values are calculated

This scenario is a variation on the "different levels of summary information" problem discussed in Recipe 10.16. It may not seem like it at first because one of the types of information is a list rather than a summary. But that's really just a "level zero" summary. This kind of problem appears in many other forms:

- You have a database that lists contributions to candidates in your political party. The party chair requests a printout that shows, for each candidate, the number of contributions and total amount contributed, as well as a list of contributor names and addresses.
- You want to create a handout for a company presentation that summarizes total sales per sales region with a list under each region showing the sales for each state in the region.

Such problems have multiple solutions:

- Run separate statements to get the information for each level of detail that you require. (A single query won't produce per-group summary values and a list of each group's individual rows.)
- Fetch the rows that make up the lists and perform the summary calculations yourself to eliminate the summary statement.

Let's use each approach to produce the driver report shown at the beginning of this section. The following implementation (in Python) generates the report using one query to summarize the days and miles per driver and another to fetch the individual trip rows for each driver:

```
# select total miles per driver and construct a dictionary that
# maps each driver name to days on the road and miles driven
name_map = {}
cursor = conn.cursor()
cursor.execute('''
                SELECT name, COUNT(name), SUM(miles)
                FROM driver_log GROUP BY name
                ''')
for (name, days, miles) in cursor:
  name_map[name] = (days, miles)
```

```
# select trips for each driver and print the report, displaying the
# summary entry for each driver prior to the list of trips
cursor.execute('''
                SELECT name, trav_date, miles
                FROM driver_log ORDER BY name, trav_date
                ''')
cur_name = ""
for (name, trav_date, miles) in cursor:
  if cur_name != name:  # new driver; print driver's summary info
    print("Name: %s; days on road: %d; miles driven: %d" %
          (name, name_map[name][0], name_map[name][1]))
    cur_name = name
  print("  date: %s, trip length: %d" % (trav_date, miles))
cursor.close()
```

An alternative implementation performs summary calculations within the program, which reduces the number of queries required. If you iterate through the trip list and calculate the per-driver day counts and mileage totals yourself, a single query suffices:

```
# get list of trips for the drivers
cursor = conn.cursor()
cursor.execute('''
                SELECT name, trav_date, miles FROM driver_log
                ORDER BY name, trav_date
                ''')
# fetch rows into data structure because we
# must iterate through them multiple times
rows = cursor.fetchall()
cursor.close()

# iterate through rows once to construct a dictionary that
# maps each driver name to days on the road and miles driven
# (the dictionary entries are lists rather than tuples because
# we need mutable values that can be modified in the loop)
name_map = {}
for (name, trav_date, miles) in rows:
  if name not in name_map: # initialize entry if nonexistent
    name_map[name] = [0, 0]
  name_map[name][0] += 1      # count days
  name_map[name][1] += miles # sum miles

# iterate through rows again to print the report, displaying the
# summary entry for each driver prior to the list of trips
cur_name = ""
for (name, trav_date, miles) in rows:
  if cur_name != name:  # new driver; print driver's summary info
    print("Name: %s; days on road: %d; miles driven: %d" %
          (name, name_map[name][0], name_map[name][1]))
    cur_name = name
  print("  date: %s, trip length: %d" % (trav_date, miles))
```

Should you require more levels of summary information, this type of problem gets more difficult. For example, you might want to precede the report that shows driver summaries and trip logs with a line that shows the total miles for all drivers:

```
Total miles driven by all drivers combined: 2166
```

```
Name: Ben; days on road: 3; miles driven: 362
   date: 2014-07-29, trip length: 131
   date: 2014-07-30, trip length: 152
   date: 2014-08-02, trip length: 79
Name: Henry; days on road: 5; miles driven: 911
   date: 2014-07-26, trip length: 115
   date: 2014-07-27, trip length: 96
   date: 2014-07-29, trip length: 300
   date: 2014-07-30, trip length: 203
   date: 2014-08-01, trip length: 197
Name: Suzi; days on road: 2; miles driven: 893
   date: 2014-07-29, trip length: 391
   date: 2014-08-02, trip length: 502
```

In this case, you need either another query to produce the total mileage or another calculation in your program that computes the overall total.

10.18 Generating Summaries from Temporary Result Sets

Problem

You want to generate summaries but cannot do so without using temporary result sets.

Solution

Use CTEs with the WITH clause.

Discussion

We already discussed situations when a temporary table, holding results from a query, helps to create a summary. In these cases, we referred to the temporary table from the query, generating a resulting summary. See Recipes 10.6 and 10.8 for examples.

Temporary tables are not always the best solution for such a task. They have a number of disadvantages, particularly the following:

- You need to maintain the table: delete all of the content when you're going to reuse it and drop it once you're finished working with it.

- The CREATE [TEMPORARY] TABLE...SELECT statement implicitly commits transactions, therefore it cannot be used when there is a possibility that the content of the original table will change after the data is inserted into the temporary table. You have to create the table first, then insert data into it and generate the summary in the multiple-statement transaction. For example, finding the longest trip per driver that we discussed in Recipe 10.8 may end up with the following code:

```
CREATE TEMPORARY TABLE t LIKE driver_log;
START TRANSACTION;
INSERT INTO t SELECT name, MAX(miles) AS miles FROM driver_log GROUP BY name;
SELECT d.name, d.trav_date, d.miles AS 'longest trip'
FROM driver_log AS d INNER JOIN t USING (name, miles) ORDER BY name;
COMMIT;
DROP TABLE t;
```

- The optimizer has fewer options to improve performance of the query.

CTEs allow you to create a named temporary result set inside the query. Following is the CTE syntax:

```
WITH result_name AS (SELECT ...)
SELECT ...
```

Then you can refer to the named result in the following query as if it were a regular table. You can define multiple CTEs and refer to the same named result multiple times when needed.

Thus, the example in Recipe 10.17 shows the number of trips per driver and the total mileage, together with trip details that can be resolved with a CTE:

```
mysql> WITH ❶
    -> trips AS (SELECT name, trav_date, miles FROM driver_log), ❷
    -> summaries AS (
    ->     SELECT name, COUNT(name) AS days_on_road, SUM(miles) AS miles_driven ❸
    ->     FROM driver_log GROUP BY name)
    -> SELECT trips.name, days_on_road, miles_driven, trav_date, miles ❹
    -> FROM summaries LEFT JOIN trips USING(name);
+-------+--------------+--------------+------------+-------+
| name  | days_on_road | miles_driven | trav_date  | miles |
+-------+--------------+--------------+------------+-------+
| Ben   |            3 |          362 | 2014-08-02 |    79 |  ❺
| Ben   |            3 |          362 | 2014-07-29 |   131 |
| Ben   |            3 |          362 | 2014-07-30 |   152 |
| Suzi  |            2 |          893 | 2014-08-02 |   502 |
| Suzi  |            2 |          893 | 2014-07-29 |   391 |
| Henry |            5 |          911 | 2014-07-30 |   203 |
| Henry |            5 |          911 | 2014-08-01 |   197 |
| Henry |            5 |          911 | 2014-07-26 |   115 |
| Henry |            5 |          911 | 2014-07-27 |    96 |
| Henry |            5 |          911 | 2014-07-29 |   300 |
+-------+--------------+--------------+------------+-------+
10 rows in set (0.00 sec)
```

❶ The keyword WITH starts the CTE.

❷ Assign the name trips to the SELECT statement, retrieving travel data.

❸ The second statement named SELECT, generates a summary of the number of trips and total mileage per driver.

❹ The main query refers to two named result sets and joins them using LEFT JOIN as if they were regular tables.

❺ Each resulting row contains the number of trips, the total amount of miles driven, and details of the individual trip.

## CHAPTER 11

Using Stored Routines, Triggers, and Scheduled Events

11.0 Introduction

In this book, the term *stored program* refers collectively to stored routines, triggers, and events, and *stored routine* refers collectively to stored functions and procedures.

This chapter discusses stored programs, which come in several varieties:

Stored functions and procedures

A stored function or procedure object encapsulates the code for performing an operation, enabling you to invoke the object easily by name rather than repeat all its code each time it's needed. A stored function performs a calculation and returns a value that can be used in expressions just like a built-in function such as RAND(), NOW(), or LEFT(). A stored procedure performs operations for which no return value is needed. Procedures are invoked with the CALL statement, not used in expressions. A procedure might update rows in a table or produce a result set that is sent to the client program.

Triggers

A trigger is an object that activates when a table is modified by an INSERT, UPDATE, or DELETE statement. For example, you can check values before they are inserted into a table or specify that any row deleted from a table should be logged to another table that serves as a journal of data changes. Triggers automate these actions.

Scheduled events

An event is an object that executes SQL statements at a scheduled time or times. Think of a scheduled event as something like a Unix cron job that runs within

MySQL. For example, events can help you perform administrative tasks such as deleting old table rows periodically or creating nightly summaries.

Stored programs are database objects that are user-defined but stored on the server side for later execution. This differs from sending a SQL statement from the client to the server for immediate execution. Each object also has the property in which it is defined in terms of other SQL statements to be executed when the object is invoked. The object body is a single SQL statement, but that statement can use compound-statement syntax (a BEGIN...END block) that contains multiple statements. Thus, the body can range from very simple to extremely complex. The following stored procedure is a trivial routine that does nothing but display the current MySQL version, using a body that consists of a single SELECT statement:

```
CREATE PROCEDURE show_version()
SELECT VERSION() AS 'MySQL Version';
```

More complex operations use a BEGIN...END compound statement:

```
CREATE PROCEDURE show_part_of_day()
BEGIN
  DECLARE cur_time, day_part TEXT;
  SET cur_time = CURTIME();
  IF cur_time < '12:00:00' THEN
    SET day_part = 'morning';
  ELSEIF cur_time = '12:00:00' THEN
    SET day_part = 'noon';
  ELSE
    SET day_part = 'afternoon or night';
  END IF;
  SELECT cur_time, day_part;
END;
```

Here, the BEGIN...END block contains multiple statements but is itself considered to constitute a single statement. Compound statements enable you to declare local variables and to use conditional logic and looping constructs. These capabilities provide considerably more flexibility for algorithmic expression than when you write inline expressions in noncompound statements such as SELECT or UPDATE.

Each statement within a compound statement must be terminated by a ; character. That requirement causes a problem if you use the mysql client to define an object that uses compound statements because mysql itself interprets ; to determine statement boundaries. The solution is to redefine mysql's statement delimiter while you define a compound-statement object. Recipe 11.1 covers how to do this; be sure to read that recipe before proceeding to those that follow it.

This chapter illustrates stored routines, triggers, and events by example but due to space limitations does not otherwise go into much detail about their extensive syntax. For complete syntax descriptions, see the MySQL Reference Manual (*https://oreil.ly/ smePp*).

Scripts for the examples shown in this chapter are located in the *routines*, *triggers*, and *events* directories of the `recipes` distribution. Scripts to create example tables are located in the *tables* directory.

In addition to the stored programs shown in this chapter, others can be found elsewhere in this book. See, for example, Recipes 7.6, 8.3, 16.8, and 24.2.

Stored programs used here are created and invoked under the assumption that cookbook is the default database. To invoke a program from another database, qualify its name with the database name:

```
CALL cookbook.show_version();
```

Alternatively, create a database specifically for your stored programs, create them in that database, and always invoke them qualified with that name. Remember to grant users who will use them the `EXECUTE` privilege for that database.

Privileges for Stored Programs

When you create a stored routine (function or procedure), the following privilege requirements must be satisfied or you will have problems:

- To create or execute the routine, you must have the `CREATE ROUTINE` or `EXECUTE` privilege, respectively.

- If binary logging is enabled for your MySQL server, as is the default since version 8.0, there are additional requirements for creating stored functions (but not stored procedures). These requirements are necessary to ensure that if you use the binary log for replication or for restoring backups, function invocations cause the same effect when re-executed as they do when originally executed:

  - You must have the `SUPER` or, since version 8.0, `SET_USER_ID` privilege, and you must declare either that the function is deterministic or does not modify data by using one of the `DETERMINISTIC`, `NO SQL`, or `READS SQL DATA` characteristics. (It's possible to create functions that are not deterministic or that modify data, but they might not be safe for replication or for use in backups.)

  - Alternatively, if you enable the `log_bin_trust_function_creators` system variable, the server waives both of the preceding requirements. You can do this at server startup, or at runtime if you have the `SUPER` privilege.

To create a trigger, you must have the `TRIGGER` privilege for the table associated with the trigger.

To create a scheduled event, you must have the `EVENT` privilege for the database in which the event is created.

For information about granting privileges, see Recipe 24.2.

11.1 Creating Compound-Statement Objects

Problem

You want to define a stored program, but its body contains instances of the ; statement terminator. The mysql client program uses the same terminator by default, so mysql misinterprets the definition and produces an error.

Solution

Redefine the mysql statement terminator with the delimiter command.

Discussion

Each stored program is an object with a body that must be a single SQL statement. However, these objects often perform complex operations that require several statements. To handle this, write the statements within a BEGIN...END block that forms a compound statement. That is, the block is itself a single statement but can contain multiple statements, each terminated by a ; character. The BEGIN...END block can contain statements such as SELECT or INSERT, but compound statements also permit conditional statements such as IF or CASE, looping constructs such as WHILE or REPEAT, or other BEGIN...END blocks.

Compound-statement syntax provides flexibility, but if you define compound-statement objects within the mysql client, you quickly encounter a problem: each statement within a compound statement must be terminated by a ; character, but mysql itself interprets ; to figure out where statements end so that it can send them one at a time to the server to be executed. Consequently, mysql stops reading the compound statement when it sees the first ; character, which is too early. To handle this, tell mysql to recognize a different statement delimiter so that it ignores ; characters within the object body. Terminate the object itself with the new delimiter, which mysql recognizes and then sends the entire object definition to the server. You can restore the mysql delimiter to its original value after defining the compound-statement object.

The following example uses a stored function to illustrate how to change the delimiter, but the principles apply to defining any type of stored program.

Suppose that you want to create a stored function that calculates and returns the average size in bytes of mail messages listed in the mail table. The function can be defined like this, where the body consists of a single SQL statement:

```
CREATE FUNCTION avg_mail_size()
RETURNS FLOAT READS SQL DATA
RETURN (SELECT AVG(size) FROM mail);
```

The RETURNS FLOAT clause indicates the type of the function's return value, and READS SQL DATA indicates that the function reads but does not modify data. The function body follows those clauses: a single RETURN statement that executes a subquery and returns the resulting value to the caller. (Every stored function must have at least one RETURN statement.)

In mysql, you can enter that statement as shown and there is no problem. The definition requires just the single terminator at the end and none internally, so no ambiguity arises. But suppose instead that you want the function to take an argument naming a user that it interprets as follows:

- If the argument is NULL, the function returns the average size for all messages (as before).

- If the argument is non-NULL, the function returns the average size for messages sent by that user.

To accomplish this, the function has a more complex body that uses a BEGIN...END block:

```
CREATE FUNCTION avg_mail_size(user VARCHAR(8))
RETURNS FLOAT READS SQL DATA
BEGIN
  DECLARE avg FLOAT;
  IF user IS NULL
  THEN # average message size over all users
    SET avg = (SELECT AVG(size) FROM mail);
  ELSE # average message size for given user
    SET avg = (SELECT AVG(size) FROM mail WHERE srcuser = user);
  END IF;
  RETURN avg;
END;
```

If you try to define the function within mysql by entering that definition as just shown, mysql improperly interprets the first semicolon in the function body as ending the definition. Instead, use the delimiter command to change the mysql delimiter, then restore the delimiter to its default value:

```
mysql> delimiter $$
mysql> CREATE FUNCTION avg_mail_size(user VARCHAR(8))
    -> RETURNS FLOAT READS SQL DATA
    -> BEGIN
    ->   DECLARE avg FLOAT;
    ->   IF user IS NULL
    ->   THEN # average message size over all users
    ->     SET avg = (SELECT AVG(size) FROM mail);
    ->   ELSE # average message size for given user
    ->     SET avg = (SELECT AVG(size) FROM mail WHERE srcuser = user);
    ->   END IF;
    ->   RETURN avg;
    -> END;
    -> $$
```

```
Query OK, 0 rows affected (0.02 sec)
mysql> delimiter ;
```

After defining the stored function, invoke it the same way as a built-in function:

```
mysql> SELECT avg_mail_size(NULL), avg_mail_size('barb');
+---------------------+-----------------------+
| avg_mail_size(NULL) | avg_mail_size('barb') |
+---------------------+-----------------------+
|         237386.5625 |                 52232 |
+---------------------+-----------------------+
```

11.2 Using Stored Functions to Simplify Calculations

Problem

A particular calculation to produce a value must be performed frequently by different applications, but you don't want to write the expression for it each time it's needed. Or a calculation is difficult to perform inline within an expression because it requires conditional or looping logic. Or, if a calculation logic changes, you do not want to perform changes in each application that uses it.

Solution

Use a stored function to have these details defined in a single place and make the calculation easy to perform.

Discussion

Stored functions enable you to simplify your applications. Write the code that produces a calculation result once in a function definition, then simply invoke the function whenever you need to perform the calculation. Stored functions also enable you to use more complex algorithmic constructs than are available when you write a calculation inline within an expression. This section illustrates how stored functions can be useful in these ways. (Granted, the example is not *that* complex, but the principles used here apply to writing much more elaborate functions.)

Different states in the US charge different rates for sales tax. If you sell goods to people from different states, you must charge tax using the rate appropriate for the customer's state of residence. To handle tax computations, use a table that lists the sales tax rate for each state, and a stored function that looks up the tax rate for each state.

To set up the sales_tax_rate table, use the *sales_tax_rate.sql* script in the *tables* directory of the recipes distribution. The table has two columns: state (a two-letter abbreviation) and tax_rate (a DECIMAL value rather than a FLOAT, to preserve accuracy).

Define the rate-lookup function, `sales_tax_rate()`, as follows:

```
CREATE FUNCTION sales_tax_rate(state_code CHAR(2))
RETURNS DECIMAL(3,2) READS SQL DATA
BEGIN
  DECLARE rate DECIMAL(3,2);
  DECLARE CONTINUE HANDLER FOR NOT FOUND SET rate = 0;
  SELECT tax_rate INTO rate FROM sales_tax_rate WHERE state = state_code;
  RETURN rate;
END;
```

Suppose that the tax rates for Vermont and New York are 1% and 9%, respectively. Try the function to check whether the tax rate is returned correctly:

```
mysql> SELECT sales_tax_rate('VT'), sales_tax_rate('NY');
+----------------------+----------------------+
| sales_tax_rate('VT') | sales_tax_rate('NY') |
+----------------------+----------------------+
|                 0.01 |                 0.09 |
+----------------------+----------------------+
```

If you take sales from a location not listed in the table, the function cannot determine the rate for it. In this case, the function assumes a tax rate of 0%:

```
mysql> SELECT sales_tax_rate('ZZ');
+----------------------+
| sales_tax_rate('ZZ') |
+----------------------+
|                 0.00 |
+----------------------+
```

The function handles states not listed using a CONTINUE handler for NOT FOUND, which executes if a "No Data" condition occurs: if there is no row for the given state_param value, the SELECT statement fails to find a sales tax rate, and the CONTINUE handler sets the rate to 0 and continues execution with the next statement after the SELECT. (This handler is an example of stored routine logic not available in inline expressions. "Handling Errors Within Stored Programs" on page 469 discusses handlers further.)

To compute sales tax for a purchase, multiply the purchase price by the tax rate. For example, for Vermont and New York, tax on a $150 purchase is as follows:

```
mysql> SELECT 150*sales_tax_rate('VT'), 150*sales_tax_rate('NY');
+--------------------------+--------------------------+
| 150*sales_tax_rate('VT') | 150*sales_tax_rate('NY') |
+--------------------------+--------------------------+
|                     1.50 |                    13.50 |
+--------------------------+--------------------------+
```

Or write another function that computes the tax for you:

```
CREATE FUNCTION sales_tax(state_code CHAR(2), sales_amount DECIMAL(10,2))
RETURNS DECIMAL(10,2) READS SQL DATA
RETURN sales_amount * sales_tax_rate(state_code);
```

And use it like this:

```
mysql> SELECT sales_tax('VT',150), sales_tax('NY',150);
+---------------------+---------------------+
| sales_tax('VT',150) | sales_tax('NY',150) |
+---------------------+---------------------+
|                1.50 |               13.50 |
+---------------------+---------------------+
```

11.3 Using Stored Procedures to Produce Multiple Values

Problem

You want to produce multiple values for an operation, but a stored function can only return a single value.

Solution

Use a stored procedure that has OUT or INOUT parameters, and pass user-defined variables for those parameters when you invoke the procedure. A procedure does not "return" a value the way a function does, but it can assign values to those parameters so that the user-defined variables have the desired values when the procedure returns.

Discussion

Unlike stored function parameters, which are input values only, a stored procedure parameter can be any of three types:

- An IN parameter is for input only. This is the default if you specify no type.
- An INOUT parameter is used to pass a value in and can also pass a value out.
- An OUT parameter is used to pass a value out.

Thus, to produce multiple values from an operation, you can use INOUT or OUT parameters. The following example illustrates this, using an IN parameter for input and passing back three values via OUT parameters.

Recipe 11.1 shows an avg_mail_size() function that returns the average mail message size for a given sender. The function returns a single value. To produce additional information, such as the number of messages and total message size, a function will not work. You could write three separate functions, but that is cumbersome. Instead, use a single procedure that retrieves multiple values about a given mail sender. The following procedure, mail_sender_stats(), runs a query on the mail table to retrieve mail-sending statistics about a given username, which is the input value. The procedure determines how many messages that user sent, and the total and average sizes of the messages in bytes, which it returns through three OUT parameters:

```
CREATE PROCEDURE mail_sender_stats(IN user VARCHAR(8),
                                   OUT messages INT,
                                   OUT total_size INT,
                                   OUT avg_size INT)
BEGIN
  # Use IFNULL() to return 0 for SUM() and AVG() in case there are
  # no rows for the user (those functions return NULL in that case).
  SELECT COUNT(*), IFNULL(SUM(size),0), IFNULL(AVG(size),0)
  INTO messages, total_size, avg_size
  FROM mail WHERE srcuser = user;
END;
```

To use the procedure, pass a string containing the username and three user-defined variables to receive the OUT values. After the procedure returns, access the variable values:

```
mysql> CALL mail_sender_stats('barb',@messages,@total_size,@avg_size);
mysql> SELECT @messages, @total_size, @avg_size;
+-----------+-------------+-----------+
| @messages | @total_size | @avg_size |
+-----------+-------------+-----------+
|         3 |      156696 |     52232 |
+-----------+-------------+-----------+
```

This routine passes back calculation results. It's also common to use OUT parameters for diagnostic purposes, such as status or error indicators.

If you call mail_sender_stats() from within a stored program, you can pass variables to it using routine parameters or program local variables, not just user-defined variables.

11.4 Using Triggers to Log Changes to a Table

Problem

You have a table that maintains current values of items that you track (such as auctions being bid on), but you'd also like to maintain a journal (history) of changes to the table.

Solution

Use triggers to "catch" table changes and write them to a separate log table.

Discussion

Suppose that you conduct online auctions and that you maintain information about each currently active auction in a table that looks like this:

```
CREATE TABLE auction
(
  id   INT UNSIGNED NOT NULL AUTO_INCREMENT,
  ts   TIMESTAMP DEFAULT CURRENT_TIMESTAMP ON UPDATE CURRENT_TIMESTAMP,
```

```
  item VARCHAR(30) NOT NULL,
  bid  DECIMAL(10,2) NOT NULL,
  PRIMARY KEY (id)
);
```

The `auction` table contains information about the currently active auctions (items being bid on and the current bid for each auction). When an auction begins, insert a row into the table. For each bid on an item, update its `bid` column so that as the auction proceeds, the `ts` column updates to reflect the most recent bid time. When the auction ends, the `bid` value is the final price and the row can be removed from the table.

To maintain a journal that shows all changes to auctions as they progress from creation to removal, set up another table that serves to record a history of changes to the auctions. This strategy can be implemented with triggers.

To maintain a history of how each auction progresses, use an `auction_log` table with the following columns:

```
CREATE TABLE auction_log
(
  action ENUM('create','update','delete'),
  id     INT UNSIGNED NOT NULL,
  ts     TIMESTAMP DEFAULT CURRENT_TIMESTAMP ON UPDATE CURRENT_TIMESTAMP,
  item   VARCHAR(30) NOT NULL,
  bid    DECIMAL(10,2) NOT NULL,
  INDEX (id)
);
```

The `auction_log` table differs from the `auction` table in two ways:

- It contains an `action` column to indicate for each row what kind of change was made.
- The `id` column has a nonunique index (rather than a primary key, which requires unique values). This permits multiple rows per `id` value because a given auction can generate many rows in the log table.

To ensure that changes to the `auction` table are logged to the `auction_log` table, create a set of triggers. The triggers write information to the `auction_log` table as follows:

- For inserts, log a row-creation operation showing the values in the new row.
- For updates, log a row-update operation showing the new values in the updated row.
- For deletes, log a row-removal operation showing the values in the deleted row.

For this application, AFTER triggers are used because they activate only after successful changes to the `auction` table. (BEFORE triggers might activate even if the row-change operation fails for some reason.) The trigger definitions look like this:

```
CREATE TRIGGER ai_auction AFTER INSERT ON auction
FOR EACH ROW
INSERT INTO auction_log (action,id,ts,item,bid)
VALUES('create',NEW.id,NOW(),NEW.item,NEW.bid);

CREATE TRIGGER au_auction AFTER UPDATE ON auction
FOR EACH ROW
INSERT INTO auction_log (action,id,ts,item,bid)
VALUES('update',NEW.id,NOW(),NEW.item,NEW.bid);

CREATE TRIGGER ad_auction AFTER DELETE ON auction
FOR EACH ROW
INSERT INTO auction_log (action,id,ts,item,bid)
VALUES('delete',OLD.id,OLD.ts,OLD.item,OLD.bid);
```

The INSERT and UPDATE triggers use NEW.*col_name* to access the new values being stored in rows. The DELETE trigger uses OLD.*col_name* to access the existing values from the deleted row. The INSERT and UPDATE triggers use NOW() to get the row-modification times; the ts column is initialized automatically to the current date and time, but NEW.ts will not contain that value.

Suppose that an auction is created with an initial bid of $5:

```
mysql> INSERT INTO auction (item,bid) VALUES('chintz pillows',5.00);
mysql> SELECT LAST_INSERT_ID();
+------------------+
| LAST_INSERT_ID() |
+------------------+
|              792 |
+------------------+
```

The SELECT statement fetches the auction ID value to use for subsequent actions on the auction. Then the item receives three more bids before the auction ends and is removed:

```
mysql> UPDATE auction SET bid = 7.50 WHERE id = 792;
... time passes ...
mysql> UPDATE auction SET bid = 9.00 WHERE id = 792;
... time passes ...
mysql> UPDATE auction SET bid = 10.00 WHERE id = 792;
... time passes ...
mysql> DELETE FROM auction WHERE id = 792;
```

At this point, no trace of the auction remains in the `auction` table, but the `auction_log` table contains a complete history of what occurred:

```
mysql> SELECT * FROM auction_log WHERE id = 792 ORDER BY ts;
+--------+-----+---------------------+----------------+-------+
| action | id  | ts                  | item           | bid   |
+--------+-----+---------------------+----------------+-------+
| create | 792 | 2014-01-09 14:57:41 | chintz pillows |  5.00 |
| update | 792 | 2014-01-09 14:57:50 | chintz pillows |  7.50 |
```

```
| update | 792 | 2014-01-09 14:57:57 | chintz pillows |  9.00 |
| update | 792 | 2014-01-09 14:58:03 | chintz pillows | 10.00 |
| delete | 792 | 2014-01-09 14:58:03 | chintz pillows | 10.00 |
+--------+-----+---------------------+----------------+-------+
```

With the strategy just outlined, the `auction` table remains relatively small, and you can always find information about auction histories as necessary by looking in the `auction_log` table.

11.5 Using Events to Schedule Database Actions

Problem

You want to set up a database operation that runs periodically without user intervention.

Solution

MySQL provides an event scheduler that enables you to set up database operations that run at times that you define. Create an event that executes according to a schedule.

Discussion

This section describes what you must do to use events, beginning with a simple event that writes a row to a table at regular intervals.

Begin with a table to hold the mark rows. It contains a `TIMESTAMP` column (which MySQL will initialize automatically) and a column to store a message:

```
CREATE TABLE mark_log
(
  id INT NOT NULL AUTO_INCREMENT PRIMARY KEY,
  ts      TIMESTAMP DEFAULT CURRENT_TIMESTAMP ON UPDATE CURRENT_TIMESTAMP,
  message VARCHAR(100)
);
```

Our logging event will write a string to a new row. To set it up, use a `CREATE EVENT` statement:

```
CREATE EVENT mark_insert
ON SCHEDULE EVERY 5 MINUTE
DO INSERT INTO mark_log (message) VALUES('-- MARK --');
```

The `mark_insert` event causes the message `'-- MARK --'` to be logged to the `mark_log` table every five minutes. Use a different interval for more or less frequent logging.

This event is simple, and its body contains only a single SQL statement. For an event body that executes multiple statements, use `BEGIN...END` compound-statement syntax.

In that case, if you use `mysql` to create the event, change the statement delimiter while you define the event, as discussed in Recipe 11.1.

At this point, you should wait a few minutes and then select the contents of the `mark_log` table to verify that new rows are being written on schedule. However, if this is the first event that you've set up, you might find that the table remains empty no matter how long you wait:

```
mysql> SELECT * FROM mark_log;
Empty set (0.00 sec)
```

If that's the case, very likely the event scheduler isn't running (which was its default state until version 8.0). Check the scheduler status by examining the value of the `event_scheduler` system variable:

```
mysql> SHOW VARIABLES LIKE 'event_scheduler';
+-----------------+-------+
| Variable_name   | Value |
+-----------------+-------+
| event_scheduler | OFF   |
+-----------------+-------+
```

To enable the scheduler interactively if it's not running, execute the following statement (which requires the SYSTEM_VARIABLES_ADMIN or, before version 8.0, SUPER privilege):

```
SET GLOBAL event_scheduler = 1;
```

That statement enables the scheduler but only until the server shuts down. To start the scheduler each time the server starts, enable the system variable in your *my.cnf* option file:

```
[mysqld]
event_scheduler=1
```

Or use a `SET PERSIST` statement to store the modified value of the variable:

```
SET PERSIST event_scheduler = 1;
```

When the event scheduler is enabled, the `mark_insert` event eventually creates many rows in the table. There are several ways that you can affect event execution to prevent the table from growing forever:

- Drop the event:
    ```
    DROP EVENT mark_insert;
    ```
    This is the simplest way to stop an event from occurring. But if you want it to resume later, you must re-create it.

- Disable event execution:
    ```
    ALTER EVENT mark_insert DISABLE;
    ```
    That leaves the event in place but causes it not to run until you reactivate it:
    ```
    ALTER EVENT mark_insert ENABLE;
    ```

- Let the event continue to run, but set up another event that "expires" old mark_log rows. This second event need not run so frequently (perhaps once a day). Its body should remove rows older than a given threshold. The following definition creates an event that deletes rows that are more than two days old:

```
CREATE EVENT mark_expire
ON SCHEDULE EVERY 1 DAY
DO DELETE FROM mark_log WHERE ts < NOW() - INTERVAL 2 DAY;
```

If you adopt this strategy, you have cooperating events: one event that adds rows to the mark_log table and another that removes them. They act together to maintain a log that contains recent rows but does not become too large.

11.6 Writing Helper Routines for Executing Dynamic SQL

Problem

Prepared SQL statements enable you to construct and execute SQL statements on the fly, but you want to run them in one step instead of executing three commands: PREPARE, EXECUTE and DEALLOCATE PREPARE.

Solution

Write a helper procedure that handles the drudgery.

Discussion

Using a prepared SQL statement involves three steps: preparation, execution, and deallocation. For example, if the @tbl_name and @val variables hold a table name and a value to insert into the table, you can create the table and insert the value like this:

```
SET @stmt = CONCAT('CREATE TABLE ',@tbl_name,' (i INT)');
PREPARE stmt FROM @stmt;
EXECUTE stmt;
DEALLOCATE PREPARE stmt;
SET @stmt = CONCAT('INSERT INTO ',@tbl_name,' (i) VALUES(',@val,')');
PREPARE stmt FROM @stmt;
EXECUTE stmt;
DEALLOCATE PREPARE stmt;
```

To ease the burden of going through those steps for each dynamically created statement, use a helper routine that, given a statement string, prepares, executes, and deallocates it:

```
CREATE PROCEDURE exec_stmt(stmt_str TEXT)
BEGIN
  SET @_stmt_str = stmt_str;
  PREPARE stmt FROM @_stmt_str;
  EXECUTE stmt;
  DEALLOCATE PREPARE stmt;
END;
```

The `exec_stmt()` routine enables the same statements to be executed much more simply:

```
CALL exec_stmt(CONCAT('CREATE TABLE ',@tbl_name,' (i INT)'));
CALL exec_stmt(CONCAT('INSERT INTO ',@tbl_name,' (i) VALUES(',@val,')'));
```

`exec_stmt()` uses an intermediary user-defined variable, `@_stmt_str`, because PRE PARE accepts a statement only when specified using either a literal string or a user-defined variable. A statement stored in a routine parameter does not work. (Avoid using `@_stmt_str` for your own purposes, at least if you expect its value to persist across `exec_stmt()` invocations.)

Now, how about making it safer to construct statement strings that incorporate values that might come from external sources, such as web-form input or command-line arguments? Such information cannot be trusted and should be treated as a potential SQL injection attack vector:

- The `QUOTE()` function is available for quoting data values.

- There is no corresponding function for identifiers, but it's easy to write one that doubles internal backticks and adds a backtick at the beginning and end:
  ```
  CREATE FUNCTION quote_identifier(id TEXT)
  RETURNS TEXT DETERMINISTIC
  RETURN CONCAT('`',REPLACE(id,'`','``'),'`');
  ```

Revising the preceding example to ensure the safety of data values and identifiers, we have the following:

```
SET @tbl_name = quote_identifier(@tbl_name);
SET @val = QUOTE(@val);
CALL exec_stmt(CONCAT('CREATE TABLE ',@tbl_name,' (i INT)'));
CALL exec_stmt(CONCAT('INSERT INTO ',@tbl_name,' (i) VALUES(',@val,')'));
```

A constraint on the use of `exec_stmt()` is that not all SQL statements are eligible for execution as prepared statements. See the MySQL Reference Manual (*https://oreil.ly/q6aUi*) for the limitations.

Handling Errors Within Stored Programs

Within stored programs, you can catch errors or exceptional conditions using condition handlers. A handler activates under specific circumstances, causing the code associated with it to execute. The code takes suitable action, such as performing cleanup processing or setting a variable that can be tested elsewhere in the program to determine whether the condition occurred. A handler might even ignore an error if it occurs under certain permitted conditions and you want to catch it rather than have it terminate your program.

Stored programs can also produce their own errors or warnings to signal that something has gone wrong.

Recipes 11.7, 11.8, and 11.9 illustrate these techniques. For complete lists of available condition names, SQLSTATE values, and error codes, consult the MySQL Reference Manual (*https://oreil.ly/t9UiL*).

11.7 Detecting "No More Rows" Conditions Using Condition Handlers

Problem

You want to detect "no more rows" conditions and gracefully handle them instead of interrupting the stored program execution.

Solution

One common use of condition handlers is to detect "no more rows" conditions. To process a query result one row at a time, use a cursor-based fetch loop in conjunction with a condition handler that catches the end-of-data condition. The technique has these essential elements:

- A cursor associated with a SELECT statement that reads rows. Open the cursor to start reading, and close it to stop.

- A condition handler that activates when the cursor reaches the end of the result set and raises an end-of-data condition (NOT FOUND). We used a similar handler in Recipe 11.2.

- A variable that indicates loop termination. Initialize the variable to FALSE, then set it to TRUE within the condition handler when the end-of-data condition occurs.

- A loop that uses the cursor to fetch each row and exits when the loop-termination variable becomes TRUE.

Discussion

The following example implements a fetch loop that processes the _ch states table row by row to calculate the total US population:

```
CREATE PROCEDURE us_population()
BEGIN
  DECLARE done BOOLEAN DEFAULT FALSE; ❶
  DECLARE state_pop, total_pop BIGINT DEFAULT 0;
  DECLARE cur CURSOR FOR SELECT pop FROM states; ❷
  DECLARE CONTINUE HANDLER FOR NOT FOUND SET done = TRUE; ❸

  OPEN cur;
  fetch_loop: LOOP
```

```
      FETCH cur INTO state_pop; ❹
      IF done THEN ❺
        LEAVE fetch_loop;
      END IF;
      SET total_pop = total_pop + state_pop; ❻
    END LOOP;
    CLOSE cur;
    SELECT total_pop AS 'Total U.S. Population'; ❼
  END;
```

❶ The done variable is used as a flag that checks when the procedure decides if it needs to continue executing or stop.

❷ The cursor for the query that fetches each state population.

❸ When MySQL encounters a "not found" error, it stops execution. To prevent this, we declared a CONTINUE handler that sets the value of the done variable to TRUE.

❹ We fetch each state population into the state_pop variable.

❺ If the done variable is not true, we continue the loop, otherwise leaving it.

❻ We add the value of the state_pop variable to the total_pop variable, which represents the population of the United States.

❼ After leaving the loop, we print the value of the total_pop variable.

This example is mostly for illustration, because in any real application, you'd use an aggregate function to calculate the total. But that also gives us an independent check on whether the fetch loop calculates the correct value:

```
mysql> CALL us_population();
+-----------------------+
| Total U.S. Population |
+-----------------------+
|             331223695 |
+-----------------------+
mysql> SELECT SUM(pop) AS 'Total U.S. Population' FROM states;
+-----------------------+
| Total U.S. Population |
+-----------------------+
|             331223695 |
+-----------------------+
```

NOT FOUND handlers are also useful for checking whether SELECT...INTO *var_name* statements return any results. Recipe 11.2 shows an example.

11.8 Catching and Ignoring Errors with Condition Handlers

Problem

You want to ignore benign errors or prevent errors from occurring for nonexistent users.

Solution

Use a condition handler to catch and handle the error you want to ignore.

Discussion

If you consider an error benign, you can use a handler to ignore it. For example, many DROP statements in MySQL have an IF EXISTS clause to suppress errors if objects to be dropped do not exist. But some DROP statements have no such clause and thus no way to suppress errors. DROP INDEX is one of these:

```
mysql> DROP INDEX bad_index ON limbs;
ERROR 1091 (42000): Can't DROP 'bad_index'; check that column/key exists
```

To prevent errors from occurring for nonexistent users, invoke DROP INDEX within a stored procedure that catches code 1091 and ignores it:

```
CREATE PROCEDURE drop_index(index_name VARCHAR(64), table_name VARCHAR(64))
BEGIN
  DECLARE CONTINUE HANDLER FOR 1091
    SELECT CONCAT('Unknown index: ', index_name) AS Message;
  CALL exec_stmt(CONCAT('DROP INDEX ', index_name, ' ON ', table_name));
END;
```

If the index does not exist, drop_index() writes a message within the condition handler, but no error occurs:

```
mysql> CALL drop_index('bad_index', 'limbs');
+----------------------+
| Message              |
+----------------------+
| Unknown index: bad_index |
+----------------------+
```

To ignore the error completely, write the handler using an empty BEGIN...END block:

```
DECLARE CONTINUE HANDLER FOR 1091 BEGIN END;
```

Another approach is to generate a warning, as demonstrated in the next recipe.

11.9 Raising Errors and Warnings

Problem

You want to raise an error for statements that are valid for MySQL but not valid for the application you are working on.

Solution

To produce your own errors within a stored program when you detect something awry, use the SIGNAL statement.

Discussion

This recipe shows some examples, and Recipe 11.11 demonstrates the use of SIGNAL within a trigger to reject bad data.

Suppose that an application performs a division operation for which you expect that the divisor will never be zero, and that you want to produce an error otherwise. You might expect that since version 5.7.4 ERROR_FOR_DIVISION_BY_ZERO SQL mode is enabled, by default you will get this behavior automatically. But that works only within the context of data-modification operations such as INSERT. In other contexts, division by zero produces only a warning:

```
mysql> SELECT @@sql_mode\G
*************************** 1. row ***************************
@@sql_mode: ONLY_FULL_GROUP_BY,STRICT_TRANS_TABLES,NO_ZERO_IN_DATE,NO_ZERO_DATE,↵
           ERROR_FOR_DIVISION_BY_ZERO,NO_ENGINE_SUBSTITUTION
1 row in set (0,00 sec)

mysql> SELECT 1/0;
+------+
| 1/0  |
+------+
| NULL |
+------+
1 row in set, 1 warning (0.00 sec)
mysql> SHOW WARNINGS;
+---------+------+--------------+
| Level   | Code | Message      |
+---------+------+--------------+
| Warning | 1365 | Division by 0 |
+---------+------+--------------+
```

To ensure a divide-by-zero error in any context, write a function that performs the division but checks the divisor first and uses SIGNAL to raise an error if the "can't happen" condition occurs:

```
CREATE FUNCTION divide(numerator FLOAT, divisor FLOAT)
RETURNS FLOAT DETERMINISTIC
BEGIN
```

```
  IF divisor = 0 THEN
    SIGNAL SQLSTATE '22012'
          SET MYSQL_ERRNO = 1365, MESSAGE_TEXT = 'unexpected 0 divisor';
  END IF;
  RETURN numerator / divisor;
END;
```

Test the function in a nonmodification context to verify that it produces an error:

```
mysql> SELECT divide(1,0);
ERROR 1365 (22012): unexpected 0 divisor
```

The SIGNAL statement specifies a SQLSTATE value plus an optional SET clause you can use to assign values to error attributes. MYSQL_ERRNO corresponds to the MySQL-specific error code, and MESSAGE_TEXT is a string of your choice.

SIGNAL can also raise warning conditions, not just errors. The following routine, drop_user_warn(), is similar to the drop_user() routine shown earlier, but instead of printing a message for nonexistent users, it generates a warning that can be displayed with SHOW WARNINGS. SQLSTATE value 01000 and error 1642 indicate a user-defined unhandled exception, which the routine signals along with an appropriate message:

```
CREATE PROCEDURE drop_user_warn(user TEXT, host TEXT)
BEGIN
  DECLARE account TEXT;
  DECLARE CONTINUE HANDLER FOR 1396
  BEGIN
    DECLARE msg TEXT;
    SET msg = CONCAT('Unknown user: ', account);
    SIGNAL SQLSTATE '01000' SET MYSQL_ERRNO = 1642, MESSAGE_TEXT = msg;
  END;
  SET account = CONCAT(QUOTE(user),'@',QUOTE(host));
  CALL exec_stmt(CONCAT('DROP USER ',account));
END;
```

Give it a test:

```
mysql> CALL drop_user_warn('bad-user','localhost');
Query OK, 0 rows affected, 1 warning (0.00 sec)
mysql> SHOW WARNINGS;
+---------+------+-------------------------------------+
| Level   | Code | Message                             |
+---------+------+-------------------------------------+
| Warning | 1642 | Unknown user: 'bad-user'@'localhost' |
+---------+------+-------------------------------------+
```

11.10 Logging Errors by Accessing the Diagnostic Area

Problem

You want to log all errors that your stored routine hits.

Solution

Access the diagnostic area using the GET DIAGNOSTICS statement. Then, save the error information into variables, and use them to log errors.

Discussion

You can not only gracefully handle errors inside the stored routine but also log them, so you can examine them and fix your application to prevent similar errors in the future.

The movies_actors_link table is used in Recipe 16.6 to demonstrate many-to-many relationships. It contains the id of the movies and movie actors that are stored in the movies and movies_actors tables. Both columns are defined with the NOT NULL property. Each combination of movie_id and actor_id should be unique. While Recipe 16.6 does not define foreign keys (see "Using Foreign Keys to Enforce Referential Integrity and Prevent Mismatches" on page 652), we can define them, so MySQL will reject values that do not have corresponding entries in the referenced tables:

```
ALTER TABLE movies_actors_link ADD FOREIGN KEY(movie_id) REFERENCES movies(id);
ALTER TABLE movies_actors_link ADD FOREIGN KEY(actor_id) REFERENCES actors(id);
```

Next we execute the INSERT statement from the MySQL CLI:

```
mysql> INSERT INTO movies_actors_link VALUES(7, 1);
ERROR 1452 (23000): Cannot add or update a child row: a foreign key constraint
fails (`cookbook`.`movies_actors_link`, CONSTRAINT `movies_actors_link_ibfk_1`
FOREIGN KEY (`movie_id`) REFERENCES `movies` (`id`))
```

Additionally, MySQL provides access to the diagnostic area, so you can store values from it in the user-defined variables. Use the GET DIAGNOSTICS command to access the diagnostic area:

```
mysql> GET DIAGNOSTICS CONDITION 1
    ->   @err_number = MYSQL_ERRNO,
    ->   @err_sqlstate = RETURNED_SQLSTATE,
    ->   @err_message = MESSAGE_TEXT;
Query OK, 0 rows affected (0.01 sec)
```

Clause CONDITION specifies the condition number. Our query returned only one condition; therefore, we used number 1. If a query returns multiple conditions, the diagnostic area would contain data for each of the conditions. For example, a query could produce multiple warnings.

To access data retrieved by the GET DIAGNOSTICS command, simply select the values of the user-defined variables:

```
mysql> SELECT @err_number, @err_sqlstate, @err_message\G
*************************** 1. row ***************************
  @err_number: 1452
@err_sqlstate: 23000
```

```
@err_message: Cannot add or update a child row: a foreign key constraint
             fails (`cookbook`.`movies_actors_link`,
             CONSTRAINT `movies_actors_link_ibfk_1`
             FOREIGN KEY (`movie_id`) REFERENCES `movies` (`id`))
1 row in set (0.00 sec)
```

To record all such errors that users make when inserting data into the mov ies_actors_link table, create a procedure that takes two arguments, movie_id and actor_id, and stores the error information in the log table.

First, we'll create the table that will store information about the errors:

```
CREATE TABLE `movies_actors_log` (
  `err_ts` timestamp NULL DEFAULT CURRENT_TIMESTAMP ON UPDATE CURRENT_TIMESTAMP,
  `err_number` int DEFAULT NULL,
  `err_sqlstate` char(5) DEFAULT NULL,
  `err_message` TEXT DEFAULT NULL,
  `movie_id` int unsigned DEFAULT NULL,
  `actor_id` int unsigned DEFAULT NULL
);
```

Then, define the procedure that will insert a row into the movies_actors_link table and, in case of an error, will log details into the movies_actors_log table:

```
CREATE PROCEDURE insert_movies_actors_link(movie INT, actor INT)
BEGIN
  DECLARE e_number INT; ❶
  DECLARE e_sqlstate CHAR(5);
  DECLARE e_message TEXT;

  DECLARE CONTINUE HANDLER FOR SQLEXCEPTION ❷
    BEGIN
      GET DIAGNOSTICS CONDITION 1
        e_number = MYSQL_ERRNO, ❸
        e_sqlstate = RETURNED_SQLSTATE,
        e_message = MESSAGE_TEXT;
      INSERT INTO movies_actors_log(err_number, err_sqlstate, err_message, ❹
                                    movie_id, actor_id)
        VALUES(e_number, e_sqlstate, e_message, movie, actor);
      RESIGNAL; ❺
    END;

  INSERT INTO movies_actors_link VALUES(movie, actor); ❻
END
```

❶ Declare variables that will store the error number, SQLSTATE, and the error message.

❷ Create a CONTINUE HANDLER for SQLEXCEPTION, so the procedure will first log the error, then continue executing.

❸ Store diagnostic information in the variables.

❹ Log details about the error into the movies_actors_log table.

❺ Use the `RESIGNAL` command to raise the error for the client that called the procedure.

❻ Run the `INSERT` into the `movies_actors_link` table that will either succeed or raise an error.

To test the procedure, call it few times with different parameters:

```
mysql> CALL insert_movies_actors_link(7, 11);
ERROR 1452 (23000): Cannot add or update a child row: a foreign key constraint
fails (`cookbook`.`movies_actors_link`, CONSTRAINT `movies_actors_link_ibfk_1`
FOREIGN KEY (`movie_id`) REFERENCES `movies` (`id`))
mysql> CALL insert_movies_actors_link(6, 11);
ERROR 1452 (23000): Cannot add or update a child row: a foreign key constraint
fails (`cookbook`.`movies_actors_link`, CONSTRAINT `movies_actors_link_ibfk_2`
FOREIGN KEY (`actor_id`) REFERENCES `actors` (`id`))
mysql> CALL insert_movies_actors_link(null, 10);
ERROR 1048 (23000): Column 'movie_id' cannot be null
mysql> CALL insert_movies_actors_link(6, null);
ERROR 1048 (23000): Column 'actor_id' cannot be null
mysql> CALL insert_movies_actors_link(6, 9);
ERROR 1062 (23000): Duplicate entry '6-9' for key 'movies_actors_link.movie_id'
```

As expected, because we used `RESIGNAL`, the procedure failed with errors. Still, all the errors were logged into the `movies_actors_log` table along with the values that we tried and failed to insert and a timestamp when the try happened:

```
mysql> SELECT * FROM movies_actors_log\G
*************************** 1. row ***************************
        err_ts: 2021-03-12 21:11:30
    err_number: 1452
  err_sqlstate: 23000
   err_message: Cannot add or update a child row: a foreign key constraint fails
                (`cookbook`.`movies_actors_link`,
                CONSTRAINT `movies_actors_link_ibfk_1`
                FOREIGN KEY (`movie_id`) REFERENCES `movies` (`id`))
      movie_id: 7
      actor_id: 11
*************************** 2. row ***************************
        err_ts: 2021-03-12 21:11:38
    err_number: 1452
  err_sqlstate: 23000
   err_message: Cannot add or update a child row: a foreign key constraint fails
                (`cookbook`.`movies_actors_link`,
                CONSTRAINT `movies_actors_link_ibfk_2`
                FOREIGN KEY (`actor_id`) REFERENCES `actors` (`id`))
      movie_id: 6
      actor_id: 11
*************************** 3. row ***************************
        err_ts: 2021-03-12 21:11:49
    err_number: 1048
  err_sqlstate: 23000
   err_message: Column 'movie_id' cannot be null
      movie_id: NULL
      actor_id: 10
*************************** 4. row ***************************
        err_ts: 2021-03-12 21:11:56
```

```
    err_number: 1048
  err_sqlstate: 23000
   err_message: Column 'actor_id' cannot be null
      movie_id: 6
      actor_id: NULL
*************************** 5. row ***************************
        err_ts: 2021-03-12 21:12:00
    err_number: 1062
  err_sqlstate: 23000
   err_message: Duplicate entry '6-9' for key 'movies_actors_link.movie_id'
      movie_id: 6
      actor_id: 9
5 rows in set (0.00 sec)
```

See Also

For additional information about the diagnostic area, see "GET DIAGNOSTICS Statement" (*https://oreil.ly/guhp9*).

11.11 Using Triggers to Preprocess or Reject Data

Problem

There are conditions wherein you want to check for data entered into a table, but you don't want to write the validation logic for every INSERT.

Solution

Centralize the input-testing logic into a BEFORE INSERT trigger.

Discussion

You can use triggers to perform several types of input checks:

- Reject bad data by raising a signal. This gives you access to stored program logic for more latitude in checking values than is possible with static constraints such as NOT NULL.

- Preprocess values and modify them, if you don't want to reject them outright. For example, map out-of-range values to be in range or sanitize values to put them in canonical form, if you permit entry of close variants.

Suppose that you have a table of contact information, such as name, state of residence, email address, and website URL:

```
CREATE TABLE contact_info
(
  id     INT NOT NULL AUTO_INCREMENT,
  name   VARCHAR(30),    # name of person
  state  CHAR(2),        # state of residence
```

```
  email  VARCHAR(50),   # email address
  url     VARCHAR(255),  # web address
  PRIMARY KEY (id)
);
```

If you want to enforce constraints or perform preprocessing when entering new rows, ensure the following:

- State-of-residence values are two-letter US state codes, valid only if present in the states table. (In this case, you could declare the column as an ENUM with 50 members, so it's more likely you'd use this lookup-table technique with columns for which the set of valid values is arbitrarily large or changes over time.)

- Email address values must contain an @ character to be valid.

- For website URLs, strip any leading http:// or https:// to save space.

To handle these requirements, create a BEFORE INSERT trigger:

```
CREATE TRIGGER bi_contact_info BEFORE INSERT ON contact_info
FOR EACH ROW
BEGIN
  IF (SELECT COUNT(*) FROM states WHERE abbrev = NEW.state) = 0 THEN
    SIGNAL SQLSTATE 'HY000'
          SET MYSQL_ERRNO = 1525, MESSAGE_TEXT = 'invalid state code';
  END IF;
  IF INSTR(NEW.email,'@') = 0 THEN
    SIGNAL SQLSTATE 'HY000'
          SET MYSQL_ERRNO = 1525, MESSAGE_TEXT = 'invalid email address';
  END IF;
  SET NEW.url = TRIM(LEADING 'http://' FROM NEW.url);
  SET NEW.url = TRIM(LEADING 'https://' FROM NEW.url);
END;
```

To also handle updates, define a BEFORE UPDATE trigger with the same body as bi_contact_info.

Test the trigger by executing some INSERT statements to verify that it accepts valid values, rejects bad ones, and trims URLs:

```
mysql> INSERT INTO contact_info (name,state,email,url)
    -> VALUES('Jen','NY','jen@example.com','http://www.example.com');
mysql> INSERT INTO contact_info (name,state,email,url)
    -> VALUES('Jen','XX','jen@example.com','http://www.example.com');
ERROR 1525 (HY000): invalid state code
mysql> INSERT INTO contact_info (name,state,email,url)
    -> VALUES('Jen','NY','jen','http://www.example.com');
ERROR 1525 (HY000): invalid email address
mysql> SELECT * FROM contact_info;
+----+------+-------+-----------------+-----------------+
| id | name | state | email           | url             |
+----+------+-------+-----------------+-----------------+
|  1 | Jen  | NY    | jen@example.com | www.example.com |
+----+------+-------+-----------------+-----------------+
```

## CHAPTER 12

Working with Metadata

12.0 Introduction

Most of the SQL statements we've used so far have been written to work with the data stored in the database. That is, after all, what the database is designed to hold. But sometimes you need more than just data values. You need information that characterizes or describes those values—the statement metadata. Metadata is used most often to process result sets but also applies to other aspects of your interaction with MySQL. This chapter describes how to obtain and use several types of metadata:

Information about statement results
> For statements that delete or update rows, you can determine how many rows were changed. For a SELECT statement, you can obtain the number of columns in the result set, as well as information about each column in the result set, such as the column name and its display width. For example, to format a tabular display, you can determine how wide to make each column and whether to justify values to the left or right.

Information about databases and tables
> A MySQL server can be queried to determine which databases and tables it manages. This is useful for existence tests or producing lists. For example, an application might present a display enabling the user to select one of the available databases. Table metadata can be examined to determine column definitions, for example, to determine the legal values for ENUM or SET columns to generate web form elements corresponding to the available choices.

Information about the MySQL server
> The database server provides information about itself and about the status of your current session with it. Knowing the server version can be useful for

determining whether it supports a given feature, which helps you build adaptive applications.

Metadata is closely tied to the implementation of the database system, so it tends to be database system–dependent. This means that if an application uses techniques shown in this chapter, it might need some modification if you port it to other database systems. For example, lists of tables and databases in MySQL are available by executing SHOW statements. However, SHOW is a MySQL-specific extension to SQL, so even for APIs like Perl DBI, PHP PDO, Python DB API, and JDBC that give you a database-independent way of executing statements, the SQL itself is MySQL-specific and must be changed to work with other database systems.

A more portable source of metadata is INFORMATION_SCHEMA, a database that contains information about databases, tables, columns, character sets, and so forth. INFORMATION_SCHEMA has some advantages over SHOW:

- Other database systems support INFORMATION_SCHEMA, so applications that use it are likely to be more portable than those that use SHOW statements.

- INFORMATION_SCHEMA is used with standard SELECT syntax, so it's more similar to other data-retrieval operations than SHOW statements.

Because of those advantages, recipes in this chapter use INFORMATION_SCHEMA rather than SHOW in most cases.

A disadvantage of INFORMATION_SCHEMA is that statements to access it are more verbose than the corresponding SHOW statements. That doesn't matter so much when you're writing programs, but for interactive use, SHOW statements can be more attractive because they require less typing.

 The results retrieved from INFORMATION_SCHEMA or SHOW depend on your privileges. You'll see information only for those databases or tables for which you have some privileges. Thus, an existence test for an object returns false if it exists, but you have no privileges for accessing it. You may need to use a user with administrative privileges to be able to repeat all code examples that we provide in this chapter.

Scripts that create the tables used in this chapter are located in the *tables* directory of the recipes distribution. Scripts containing code for the examples are located in the *metadata* directory. (Some of them use utility functions located in the *lib* directory.) The distribution often provides implementations in languages other than those shown.

12.1 Determining the Number of Rows Affected by a Statement

Problem

You want to know how many rows have been changed by a SQL statement.

Solution

Some APIs return the row count as a return value of the function that executes the statement. Others provide a separate function that you call after executing the statement. Use the method available in the programming language you use.

Discussion

For statements that affect rows (UPDATE, DELETE, INSERT, REPLACE), each API provides a way to determine the number of rows involved. For MySQL, the default meaning of "affected by" is "changed by," not "matched by." That is, rows not changed by a statement are not counted, even if they match the conditions specified in the statement. For example, the following UPDATE statement results in an "affected by" value of zero because it changes no columns from their current values, no matter how many rows the WHERE clause matches:

```
UPDATE profile SET cats = 0 WHERE cats = 0;
```

The MySQL server permits a client to set a connect-time flag to indicate that it wants rows-matched counts, not rows-changed counts. In this case, the row count for the preceding statement would be equal to the number of rows with a cats value of 0, even though the statement results in no net change to the table. However, not all MySQL APIs expose this flag. The following discussion indicates which APIs enable you to select the type of count you want and which use the rows-matched count by default rather than the rows-changed count.

Perl

In Perl DBI scripts, do() returns the row count for statements that modify rows:

```
my $count = $dbh->do ($stmt);
# report 0 rows if an error occurred
printf "Number of rows affected: %d\n", (defined ($count) ? $count : 0);
```

If you prepare a statement first and then execute it, execute() returns the row count:

```
my $sth = $dbh->prepare ($stmt);
my $count = $sth->execute ();
printf "Number of rows affected: %d\n", (defined ($count) ? $count : 0);
```

To tell MySQL whether to return rows-changed or rows-matched counts, specify `mysql_client_found_rows` in the options part of the Data Source Name (DSN) argument of the `connect()` call when you connect to the MySQL server. Set the option to 0 for rows-changed counts and 1 for rows-matched counts. Here's an example:

```
my $conn_attrs = {PrintError => 0, RaiseError => 1, AutoCommit => 1};
my $dsn = "DBI:mysql:cookbook:localhost;mysql_client_found_rows=1";
my $dbh = DBI->connect ($dsn, "cbuser", "cbpass", $conn_attrs);
```

`mysql_client_found_rows` changes the row-reporting behavior for the duration of the session.

Although the default behavior for MySQL itself is to return rows-changed counts, current versions of the Perl DBI driver for MySQL automatically request rows-matched counts unless you specify otherwise. For applications that depend on a particular behavior, it's best to explicitly set the `mysql_client_found_rows` option in the DSN to the appropriate value.

Ruby

In Ruby Mysql2 scripts, the `affected_rows` method returns the row count for statements that modify rows:

```
client.query(stmt)
puts "Number of rows affected: #{client.affected_rows}"
```

If you use the prepared statements `execute` method to execute a statement, use the statement handle `affected_rows` method to get the count afterward:

```
sth = client.prepare(stmt)
sth.execute()
puts "Number of rows affected: #{sth.affected_rows}"
```

The Ruby driver for MySQL returns rows-changed counts by default, but the driver supports a `Mysql2::Client::FOUND_ROWS` option that enables you to control whether the server returns rows-changed or rows-matched counts. For example, to request rows-matched counts, do this:

```
client = Mysql2::Client.new(:flags=>Mysql2::Client::FOUND_ROWS, :database=>'cookbook')
```

PHP

In PDO, the database handle `exec()` method returns the rows-affected count:

```
$count = $dbh->exec ($stmt);
printf ("Number of rows updated: %d\n", $count);
```

If you use `prepare()` plus `execute()` instead, the rows-affected count is available from the statement handle `rowCount()` method:

```
$sth = $dbh->prepare ($stmt);
$sth->execute ();
printf ("Number of rows updated: %d\n", $sth->rowCount ());
```

The PDO driver for MySQL returns rows-changed counts by default, but the driver supports a PDO::MYSQL_ATTR_FOUND_ROWS attribute that you can specify at connect time to control whether the server returns rows-changed or rows-matched counts. The new PDO class constructor takes an optional key/value array following the password argument. Pass PDO::MYSQL_ATTR_FOUND_ROWS => 1 in this array to request rows-matched counts:

```
$dsn = "mysql:host=localhost;dbname=cookbook";
$dbh = new PDO ($dsn, "cbuser", "cbpass",
                array (PDO::MYSQL_ATTR_FOUND_ROWS => 1));
```

Python

Python's DB API makes the rows-changed count available as the value of the statement cursor's rowcount attribute:

```
cursor = conn.cursor()
cursor.execute(stmt)
print("Number of rows affected: %d" % cursor.rowcount)
cursor.close()
```

To obtain rows-matched counts instead, import the Connector/Python client-flag constants and pass the FOUND_ROWS flag in the client_flags parameter of the connect() method:

```
from mysql.connector.constants import ClientFlag

conn = mysql.connector.connect(
  database="cookbook",
  host="localhost",
  user="cbuser",
  password="cbpass",
  client_flags=[ClientFlag.FOUND_ROWS]
)
```

Go

The Go SQL driver provides a RowsAffected method of the Result type that returns the number of changed rows:

```
res, err := db.Exec(sql)
// Check and handle err
affectedRows, err := res.RowsAffected()
// Check and handle err
fmt.Printf("The statement affected %d rows\n", affectedRows)
```

To retrieve the row-matched count instead, add a clientFoundRows=true parameter to the connection string:

```
db, err := ↵
sql.Open("mysql", "cbuser:cbpass@tcp(127.0.0.1:3306)/cookbook?clientFoundRows=true")
```

Java

For statements that modify rows, the Connector/J driver provides rows-matched counts rather than rows-changed counts, for conformance with the Java JDBC specification.

The JDBC interface provides row counts two different ways, depending on the method you invoke to execute the statement. If you use executeUpdate(), the row count is its return value:

```
Statement s = conn.createStatement ();
int count = s.executeUpdate (stmt);
s.close ();
System.out.println ("Number of rows affected: " + count);
```

If you use execute(), that method returns true or false to indicate whether the statement produces a result set. For statements such as UPDATE or DELETE that return no result set, execute() returns false, and the row count is available by calling the getUpdateCount() method:

```
Statement s = conn.createStatement ();
if (!s.execute (stmt))
{
  // there is no result set, print the row count
  System.out.println ("Number of rows affected: " + s.getUpdateCount ());
}
s.close ();
```

12.2 Obtaining Result Set Metadata

Problem

After retrieving the rows (see Recipe 4.4), you want to know other details *about* the result set, such as the column names and data types or how many rows and columns there are.

Solution

Use the capabilities provided by your API.

Discussion

Statements such as SELECT that generate a result set produce several types of metadata. This section discusses the information available through each API, using programs that show how to display the result-set metadata available after executing a sample statement (SELECT name, birth FROM profile). The example programs illustrate one of the simplest uses for this information: when you retrieve a row from a result set and you want to process the column values in a loop, the column count stored in the metadata serves as the upper bound on the loop iterator.

Perl

The scope of result-set metadata available from Perl DBI depends on how you process queries:

Using a statement handle
> In this case, invoke `prepare()` to get the statement handle. This handle has an `execute()` method. Invoke it to generate the result set, then fetch the rows in a loop. With this approach, access to the metadata is available while the result set is active—that is, after the call to `execute()` and until the end of the result set is reached. When the row-fetching method finds that there are no more rows, it invokes `finish()` implicitly, which causes the metadata to become unavailable. (That also happens if you explicitly call `finish()` yourself.) Thus, normally it's best to access the metadata immediately after calling `execute()`, making a copy of any values that you'll need to use beyond the end of the fetch loop.

Using a database-handle method that returns the result set in a single operation
> With this approach, any metadata generated while processing the statement will have been disposed of by the time the method returns. You can still determine the number of rows and columns from the size of the result set.

When you use a statement handle to process a query, DBI makes result-set metadata available after you invoke the handle's `execute()` method. This information is available primarily in the form of references to arrays. For each such type of metadata, the array has one element per column in the result set. Access these array references as attributes of the statement handle. For example, `$sth->{NAME}` points to the column name array, with individual column names available as elements of this array:

```
$name = $sth->{NAME}->[$i];
```

Or access the entire array like this:

```
@names = @{$sth->{NAME}};
```

Table 12-1 lists the attribute names through which you access array-based metadata and the meaning of values in each array. Names that begin with uppercase are standard DBI attributes and should be available for most database engines. Attribute names that begin with `mysql_` are MySQL-specific and nonportable.

Table 12-1. Metadata in Perl

Attribute name	Array element meaning
NAME	Column name
NAME_lc	Column name in lowercase
NAME_uc	Column name in uppercase
NULLABLE	0 or empty string = column values cannot be NULL
	1 = column values can be NULL

Attribute name	Array element meaning
	2 = unknown
PRECISION	Column width
SCALE	Number of decimal places (for numeric columns)
TYPE	Data type (numeric DBI code)
mysql_is_blob	True if column has a BLOB (or TEXT) type
mysql_is_key	True if column is part of a key
mysql_is_num	True if column has a numeric type
mysql_is_pri_key	True if column is part of a primary key
mysql_max_length	Actual maximum length of column values in result set
mysql_table	Name of table the column is part of
mysql_type	Data type (numeric internal MySQL code)
mysql_type_name	Data type name

Some types of metadata, listed in Table 12-2, are accessed as references to hashes rather than arrays. These hashes have one element per column value. The element key is the column name, and its value is the position of the column within the result set, for example:

```
$col_pos = $sth->{NAME_hash}->{col_name};
```

Table 12-2. Metadata in Perl, accessible as references to hashes

Attribute name	Hash element meaning
NAME_hash	Column name
NAME_hash_lc	Column name in lowercase
NAME_hash_uc	Column name in uppercase

The number of columns in a result set is available as a scalar value:

```
$num_cols = $sth->{NUM_OF_FIELDS};
```

This example code shows how to execute a statement and display result-set metadata:

```
my $stmt = "SELECT name, birth FROM profile";
printf "Statement: %s\n", $stmt;
my $sth = $dbh->prepare ($stmt);
$sth->execute();
# metadata information becomes available at this point ...
printf "NUM_OF_FIELDS: %d\n", $sth->{NUM_OF_FIELDS};
print "Note: statement has no result set\n" if $sth->{NUM_OF_FIELDS} == 0;
for my $i (0 .. $sth->{NUM_OF_FIELDS}-1)
{
  printf "--- Column %d (%s) ---\n", $i, $sth->{NAME}->[$i];
  printf "NAME_lc:        %s\n", $sth->{NAME_lc}->[$i];
  printf "NAME_uc:        %s\n", $sth->{NAME_uc}->[$i];
  printf "NULLABLE:       %s\n", $sth->{NULLABLE}->[$i];
  printf "PRECISION:      %d\n", $sth->{PRECISION}->[$i];
  printf "SCALE:          %d\n", $sth->{SCALE}->[$i];
  printf "TYPE:           %d\n", $sth->{TYPE}->[$i];
```

```
      printf "mysql_is_blob:    %s\n", $sth->{mysql_is_blob}->[$i];
      printf "mysql_is_key:     %s\n", $sth->{mysql_is_key}->[$i];
      printf "mysql_is_num:     %s\n", $sth->{mysql_is_num}->[$i];
      printf "mysql_is_pri_key: %s\n", $sth->{mysql_is_pri_key}->[$i];
      printf "mysql_max_length: %d\n", $sth->{mysql_max_length}->[$i];
      printf "mysql_table:      %s\n", $sth->{mysql_table}->[$i];
      printf "mysql_type:       %d\n", $sth->{mysql_type}->[$i];
      printf "mysql_type_name:  %s\n", $sth->{mysql_type_name}->[$i];
    }
    $sth->finish ();  # release result set because we didn't fetch its rows
```

The program produces this output:

```
Statement: SELECT name, birth FROM profile
NUM_OF_FIELDS: 2
--- Column 0 (name) ---
NAME_lc:          name
NAME_uc:          NAME
NULLABLE:
PRECISION:        20
SCALE:            0
TYPE:             12
mysql_is_blob:
mysql_is_key:
mysql_is_num:     0
mysql_is_pri_key:
mysql_max_length: 7
mysql_table:      profile
mysql_type:       253
mysql_type_name:  varchar
--- Column 1 (birth) ---
NAME_lc:          birth
NAME_uc:          BIRTH
NULLABLE:         1
PRECISION:        10
SCALE:            0
TYPE:             9
mysql_is_blob:
mysql_is_key:
mysql_is_num:     0
mysql_is_pri_key:
mysql_max_length: 10
mysql_table:      profile
mysql_type:       10
mysql_type_name:  date
```

To get a row count from a result set generated by calling execute(), fetch the rows and count them yourself. Using $sth->rows() to get a count for SELECT statements is expressly deprecated in the DBI documentation.

You can also obtain a result set by calling one of the DBI methods that uses a database handle rather than a statement handle, such as selectall_arrayref() or selectall_hashref(). These methods provide no access to column metadata. That information already will have been disposed of by the time the method returns, and is unavailable to your scripts. However, you can derive column and row counts by examining the result set itself. Recipe 4.4 discusses the result-set structures produced by several methods and how to use them to obtain row and column counts.

Ruby

Ruby Mysql2 gem does not provide its own methods to access result-set metadata after you execute a statement. You can get column names only by calling the `fields` method of the `Mysql2::Result` class:

```
stmt = "SELECT name, birth FROM profile"
puts "Statement: #{stmt}"
sth = client.prepare(stmt)
res = sth.execute()
# metadata information becomes available at this point ...
puts "Number of columns: #{res.fields.size}"
puts "Note: statement has no result set" if res.count == 0
puts "Columns names: #{res.fields.join(", ")}"
res.free
```

To obtain other column metadata, query the Information Schema as we suggest in Recipe 12.5

PHP

In PHP, metadata for `SELECT` statements is available from PDO after a successful call to `query()`. If you execute a statement using `prepare()` plus `execute()` instead (which can be used for `SELECT` or non-`SELECT` statements), metadata becomes available after `execute()`.

To determine metadata availability, check whether the statement handle `columnCount()` method returns a value greater than zero. If so, the handle's `getColumnMeta()` method returns an associative array containing metadata for a single column. Table 12-3 shows the elements of this array. (The format of the `flags` value might differ for other database systems.)

Table 12-3. Metadata in PHP

Name	Value
pdo_type	Column type (corresponds to a PDO::PARAM_*XXX* value)
native_type	PHP native type for the column value
name	Column name
len	Column length
precision	Column precision
flags	Array of flags describing the column attributes
table	Name of table the column is part of

This example code shows how to execute a statement and display result-set metadata:

```
$stmt = "SELECT name, birth FROM profile";
print ("Statement: $stmt\n");
$sth = $dbh->prepare ($stmt);
$sth->execute ();
# metadata information becomes available at this point ...
$ncols = $sth->columnCount ();
print ("Number of columns: $ncols\n");
if ($ncols == 0)
  print ("Note: statement has no result set\n");
for ($i = 0; $i < $ncols; $i++)
{
  $col_info = $sth->getColumnMeta ($i);
  $flags = implode (",", array_values ($col_info["flags"]));
  printf ("--- Column %d (%s) ---\n", $i, $col_info["name"]);
  printf ("pdo_type:     %d\n", $col_info["pdo_type"]);
  printf ("native_type:  %s\n", $col_info["native_type"]);
  printf ("len:          %d\n", $col_info["len"]);
  printf ("precision:    %d\n", $col_info["precision"]);
  printf ("flags:        %s\n", $flags);
  printf ("table:        %s\n", $col_info["table"]);
}
```

The program produces this output:

```
Statement: SELECT name, birth FROM profile
Number of columns: 2
--- Column 0 (name) ---
PDO type:     2
native type:  VAR_STRING
len:          20
precision:    0
flags:        not_null
table:        profile
--- Column 1 (birth) ---
PDO type:     2
native type:  DATE
len:          10
precision:    0
flags:
table:        profile
```

To get a row count from a statement that returns rows, fetch the rows and count them yourself. The rowCount() method is not guaranteed to work for result sets.

Python

For statements that produce a result set, Python's DB API makes row and column counts available, as well as a few information items about individual columns.

To get the row count for a result set, access the cursor's rowcount attribute. This requires that the cursor be buffered so that it fetches query results immediately; otherwise, you must count the rows as you fetch them. The column count is not available directly, but after calling fetchone() or fetchall(), you can determine the count as the length of any result-set row tuple. It's also possible to determine the column count without fetching any rows by using cursor.description. This is a tuple containing one element per column in the result set, so its length tells you how many columns are in the set. (If the statement generates no result set, such as for UPDATE, the value of description is None.) Each element of the description tuple is another tuple that represents the metadata for the corresponding column of the result. For Connector/Python, only a few description values are meaningful. The following code shows how to access them:

```
stmt = "SELECT name, birth FROM profile"
print("Statement: %s" % stmt)
# buffer cursor so that rowcount has usable value
cursor = conn.cursor(buffered=True)
cursor.execute(stmt)
# metadata information becomes available at this point...
print("Number of rows: %d" % cursor.rowcount)
if cursor.description is None:  # no result set
  ncols = 0
else:
  ncols = len(cursor.description)
print("Number of columns: %d" % ncols)
if ncols == 0:
  print("Note: statement has no result set")
for i, col_info in enumerate(cursor.description):
  # print name, then other information
  name, type, _, _, _, _, nullable, flags, _ = col_info
  print("--- Column %d (%s) ---" % (i, name))
  print("Type:     %d (%s)" % (type, FieldType.get_info(type)))
  print("Nullable: %d" % (nullable))
  print("Flags:    %d" % (flags))
cursor.close()
```

The code uses the FieldType class, imported as follows:

```
from mysql.connector import FieldType
```

The program produces this output:

```
Statement:  SELECT name, birth FROM profile
Number of rows: 10
Number of columns: 2
--- Column 0 (name) ---
Type:     253 (VAR_STRING)
Nullable: 0
Flags:    4097
--- Column 1 (birth) ---
Type:     10 (DATE)
Nullable: 1
Flags:    128
```

Go

Go provides column metadata as array of ColumnType values, returned by the Rows.ColumnTypes method. You can query each of the array members to obtain specific characteristic of the column.

Table 12-4 contains methods that the ColumnType supports.

Table 12-4. Metadata in Go

Method name	Description
DatabaseType Name	Database type, such as INT or VARCHAR.
DecimalSize	Scale and precision for the decimal type.
Length	Column type length for the variable length text and binary columns. Not supported by the MySQL driver.
Name	The name or the alias of the column.
Nullable	Whenever column is nullable.
ScanType	The native Go type, suitable for scanning into Rows.Scan.

You may also get the list of column names if you use the Rows.Columns method. It returns an array of strings that contain column names or aliases.

The example code demonstrates how to obtain column names and metadata in the Go application:

```
package main

import (
  "fmt"
  "log"
  "github.com/svetasmirnova/mysqlcookbook/recipes/lib/cookbook"
)

func main() {
  db := cookbook.Connect()
  defer db.Close()

  stmt := "SELECT name, birth FROM profile"
  fmt.Printf("Statement: %s\n", stmt)

  rows, err := db.Query(stmt)
  if err != nil {
    log.Fatal(err)
  }
  defer rows.Close()

  // metadata information becomes available at this point ...
  cols, err := rows.ColumnTypes()
  if err != nil {
    log.Fatal(err)
  }

  ncols := len(cols)
  fmt.Printf("Number of columns: %d\n", ncols)
  if (ncols == 0) {
    fmt.Println("Note: statement has no result set")
  }

  for i := 0; i < ncols; i++ {
    fmt.Printf("---- Column %d (%s) ----\n", i, cols[i].Name())
    fmt.Printf("DatabaseTypeName: %s\n", cols[i].DatabaseTypeName())
```

```
    collen, ok := cols[i].Length()
    if ok {
      fmt.Printf("Length: %d\n", collen)
    }

    precision, scale, ok := cols[i].DecimalSize()
    if ok {
      fmt.Printf("DecimalSize precision: %d, scale: %d\n", precision, scale)
    }

    colnull, ok := cols[i].Nullable()
    if ok {
      fmt.Printf("Nullable: %t\n", colnull)
    }

    fmt.Printf("ScanType: %s\n", cols[i].ScanType())
  }
}
```

The program produces this output:

```
Statement: SELECT name, birth FROM profile
Number of columns: 2
---- Column 0 (name) ----
DatabaseTypeName: VARCHAR
Nullable: false
ScanType: sql.RawBytes
---- Column 1 (birth) ----
DatabaseTypeName: DATE
Nullable: true
ScanType: sql.NullTime
```

Java

JDBC makes result-set metadata available through a `ResultSetMetaData` object, obtained by calling the `getMetaData()` method of your `ResultSet` object. The metadata object provides access to several kinds of information. Its `getColumnCount()` method returns the number of columns in the result set. Other types of metadata, illustrated by the following code, provide information about individual columns and take a column index as their argument. For JDBC, column indexes begin at 1 rather than 0, unlike our other APIs:

```
String stmt = "SELECT name, birth FROM profile";
System.out.println("Statement: " + stmt);
Statement s = conn.createStatement();
s.executeQuery(stmt);
ResultSet rs = s.getResultSet();
ResultSetMetaData md = rs.getMetaData();
// metadata information becomes available at this point...
int ncols = md.getColumnCount();
System.out.println("Number of columns: " + ncols);
if (ncols == 0)
  System.out.println ("Note: statement has no result set");
for (int i = 1; i <= ncols; i++) { // column index values are 1-based
  System.out.println("--- Column " + i
            + " (" + md.getColumnName (i) + ") ---");
```

```
        System.out.println("getColumnDisplaySize: " + md.getColumnDisplaySize (i));
        System.out.println("getColumnLabel:        " + md.getColumnLabel (i));
        System.out.println("getColumnType:         " + md.getColumnType (i));
        System.out.println("getColumnTypeName:     " + md.getColumnTypeName (i));
        System.out.println("getPrecision:          " + md.getPrecision (i));
        System.out.println("getScale:              " + md.getScale (i));
        System.out.println("getTableName:          " + md.getTableName (i));
        System.out.println("isAutoIncrement:       " + md.isAutoIncrement (i));
        System.out.println("isNullable:            " + md.isNullable (i));
        System.out.println("isCaseSensitive:       " + md.isCaseSensitive (i));
        System.out.println("isSigned:              " + md.isSigned (i));
    }
    rs.close();
    s.close();
```

The program produces this output:

```
Statement: SELECT name, birth FROM profile
Number of columns: 2
--- Column 1 (name) ---
getColumnDisplaySize: 20
getColumnLabel:       name
getColumnType:        12
getColumnTypeName:    VARCHAR
getPrecision:         20
getScale:             0
getTableName:         profile
isAutoIncrement:      false
isNullable:           0
isCaseSensitive:      false
isSigned:             false
--- Column 2 (birth) ---
getColumnDisplaySize: 10
getColumnLabel:       birth
getColumnType:        91
getColumnTypeName:    DATE
getPrecision:         10
getScale:             0
getTableName:         profile
isAutoIncrement:      false
isNullable:           1
isCaseSensitive:      false
isSigned:             false
```

The row count of the result set is not available directly; you must fetch the rows and count them.

JDBC has several other result-set metadata calls, but many of them provide no useful information for MySQL. To try them, consult a JDBC reference to see what the calls are, and modify the program to see what, if anything, they return.

12.3 Listing or Checking the Existence of Databases or Tables

Problem

You want to list the databases hosted by the MySQL server or the tables in a database. Or you want to check whether a particular database or table exists.

Solution

Use INFORMATION_SCHEMA to get this information. The SCHEMATA table contains a row for each database, and the TABLES table contains a row for each table or view in each database.

Discussion

To retrieve the list of databases hosted by the server, use this statement:

```
SELECT SCHEMA_NAME FROM INFORMATION_SCHEMA.SCHEMATA;
```

To sort the result, add an ORDER BY SCHEMA_NAME clause.

To check whether a specific database exists, use a WHERE clause with a condition that names the database. If you get a row back, the database exists. The following Ruby method shows how to perform an existence test for a database:

```
def database_exists(client, db_name)
  sth = client.prepare("SELECT SCHEMA_NAME
                        FROM INFORMATION_SCHEMA.SCHEMATA
                        WHERE SCHEMA_NAME = ?")
  return sth.execute(db_name).count > 0
end
```

To obtain the list of tables in a database, name the database in the WHERE clause of a statement that selects from the TABLES table:

```
SELECT TABLE_NAME FROM INFORMATION_SCHEMA.TABLES
WHERE TABLE_SCHEMA = 'cookbook';
```

To sort the result, add an ORDER BY TABLE_NAME clause.

To obtain a list of tables in the default database, use this statement instead:

```
SELECT TABLE_NAME FROM INFORMATION_SCHEMA.TABLES
WHERE TABLE_SCHEMA = DATABASE();
```

If no database has been selected, DATABASE() returns NULL and no rows match, which is the correct result.

To check whether a specific table exists, use a WHERE clause with a condition that names the table. Here's a Ruby method that performs an existence test for a table in a given database:

```
def table_exists(client, db_name, tbl_name)
  sth = client.prepare("SELECT TABLE_NAME FROM INFORMATION_SCHEMA.TABLES
                        WHERE TABLE_SCHEMA = ? AND TABLE_NAME = ?")
  return sth.execute(db_name, tbl_name).count > 0
end
```

Some APIs provide a database-independent way to get database or table lists. In Perl DBI, the database handle `tables()` method returns a list of tables in the default database:

```
@tables = $dbh->tables ();
```

For Java, there are JDBC methods designed to return lists of databases or tables. For each method, invoke your connection object's `getMetaData()` method and use the resulting `DatabaseMetaData` object to retrieve the information you want. Here's how to produce a list of databases:

```
// get list of databases
DatabaseMetaData md = conn.getMetaData ();
ResultSet rs = md.getCatalogs ();
while (rs.next ())
  System.out.println (rs.getString (1));  // column 1 = database name
rs.close ();
```

To list the tables in a database, do this:

```
// get list of tables in database named by dbName; if
// dbName is the empty string, the default database is used
DatabaseMetaData md = conn.getMetaData ();
ResultSet rs = md.getTables (dbName, "", "%", null);
while (rs.next ())
  System.out.println (rs.getString (3));  // column 3 = table name
rs.close ();
```

12.4 Listing or Checking the Existence of Views

Problem

You want to check if your database contains views.

Solution

Select only those tables from the `INFORMATION_SCHEMA.TABLES` table that have `TABLE_TYPE` equal to `VIEW`.

Discussion

The method used in the Recipe 12.3 shows both physical tables and views. If you need to distinguish them from one another, use the WHERE TABLE_TYPE='VIEW' clause to list only views:

```
mysql> SELECT TABLE_SCHEMA, TABLE_NAME, TABLE_TYPE
    -> FROM INFORMATION_SCHEMA.TABLES
    -> WHERE TABLE_TYPE='VIEW' AND TABLE_SCHEMA='cookbook';
+--------------+---------------------+------------+
| TABLE_SCHEMA | TABLE_NAME          | TABLE_TYPE |
+--------------+---------------------+------------+
| cookbook     | patients_statistics | VIEW       |
+--------------+---------------------+------------+
1 row in set (0,00 sec)
```

If you want, instead, to list only physical tables, use the TABLE_TYPE='BASE TABLE' condition:

```
mysql> SELECT TABLE_SCHEMA, TABLE_NAME, TABLE_TYPE
    -> FROM INFORMATION_SCHEMA.TABLES
    -> WHERE TABLE_TYPE='BASE TABLE' AND TABLE_SCHEMA='cookbook'
    -> AND TABLE_NAME LIKE 'trip%';
+--------------+------------+------------+
| TABLE_SCHEMA | TABLE_NAME | TABLE_TYPE |
+--------------+------------+------------+
| cookbook     | trip_leg   | BASE TABLE |
| cookbook     | trip_log   | BASE TABLE |
+--------------+------------+------------+
2 rows in set (0,00 sec)
```

12.5 Accessing Table Column Definitions

Problem

You want to find out what columns a table has and how they are defined.

Solution

There are several ways to do this. You can obtain column definitions from INFORMA TION_SCHEMA, from SHOW statements, or from mysqldump.

Discussion

Information about the structure of tables enables you to answer questions such as "What columns does a table contain and what are their types?" or "What are the legal values for an ENUM or SET column?" Here are some applications for that kind of information:

Displaying column lists

A simple use of table information is presenting a list of the table's columns. This is common in web-based or Graphical User Interface (GUI) applications that enable users to construct statements interactively by selecting a table column from a list and entering a value against which to compare column values.

Interactive record editing

Knowledge of a table's structure can be very useful for applications that modify data interactively. Suppose that an application retrieves a record from the database, displays a form containing the record's content so a user can edit it, and then updates the record in the database after the user modifies the form and submits it. You can use table structure information for validating column values, so you would not try to insert invalid values into a database. If a column is an ENUM, you can find out the valid enumeration values and check the value submitted by the user against them to determine whether it's legal. If the column is an integer type, check the submitted value to make sure that it consists entirely of digits, possibly preceded by a + or – character. If the column contains dates, look for a legal date format.

But what if the user leaves a field empty? If the field corresponds to, say, a CHAR column in the table, do you set the column value to NULL or to the empty string? This too is a question that can be answered by checking the table's structure. Determine whether the column can contain NULL values. If it can, set the column to NULL; otherwise, set it to the empty string.

Mapping column definitions onto web page elements

Some data types such as ENUM and SET correspond naturally to elements of web forms:

- An ENUM has a fixed set of values from which you choose a single value. This is analogous to a group of radio buttons, a pop-up menu, or a single-pick scrolling list.

- A SET column is similar, except that you can select multiple values; this corresponds to a group of checkboxes or a multiple-pick scrolling list.

By using table metadata to access definitions for these types of columns, you can easily determine a column's legal values and map them onto an appropriate form element. Recipe 12.6 discusses how to get definitions for these types of columns.

MySQL provides several ways to find out about a table's structure:

- Retrieve the information from INFORMATION_SCHEMA. The COLUMNS table contains the column definitions.

- Use a SHOW COLUMNS statement.

- Use the SHOW CREATE TABLE statement or the mysqldump command-line program to obtain a CREATE TABLE statement that displays the table's structure.

The following discussion shows how to ask MySQL for table information using each method. To try the examples, create an item table that lists item IDs, names, and colors in which each item is available:

```
CREATE TABLE item
(
  id      INT UNSIGNED NOT NULL AUTO_INCREMENT,
  name    CHAR(20),
  colors  ENUM('chartreuse','mauve','lime green','puce') DEFAULT 'puce',
  PRIMARY KEY (id)
);
```

Using INFORMATION_SCHEMA to get table structure information

To obtain information about a single column in a table, query the INFORMATION_SCHEMA.COLUMNS table:

```
mysql> SELECT * FROM INFORMATION_SCHEMA.COLUMNS
    -> WHERE TABLE_SCHEMA = 'cookbook' AND TABLE_NAME = 'item'
    -> AND COLUMN_NAME = 'colors'\G
*************************** 1. row ***************************
           TABLE_CATALOG: def
            TABLE_SCHEMA: cookbook
              TABLE_NAME: item
             COLUMN_NAME: colors
        ORDINAL_POSITION: 3
          COLUMN_DEFAULT: puce
             IS_NULLABLE: YES
               DATA_TYPE: enum
CHARACTER_MAXIMUM_LENGTH: 10
  CHARACTER_OCTET_LENGTH: 10
       NUMERIC_PRECISION: NULL
           NUMERIC_SCALE: NULL
        DATETIME_PRECISION: NULL
        CHARACTER_SET_NAME: utf8mb4
          COLLATION_NAME: utf8mb4_0900_ai_ci
             COLUMN_TYPE: enum('chartreuse','mauve','lime green','puce')
              COLUMN_KEY:
                   EXTRA:
              PRIVILEGES: select,insert,update,references
          COLUMN_COMMENT:
```

To obtain information about all columns, omit the COLUMN_NAME condition from the WHERE clause.

Here are some COLUMNS table columns likely to be of most use:

COLUMN_NAME
> The column name.

ORDINAL_POSITION
> The position of the column within the table definition.

COLUMN_DEFAULT

The column's default value.

IS_NULLABLE

YES or NO to indicate whether the column can contain NULL values.

DATA_TYPE, COLUMN_TYPE

Data type information. DATA_TYPE is the data-type keyword, and COLUMN_TYPE contains additional information such as type attributes.

CHARACTER_SET_NAME, COLLATION_NAME

The character set and collation for string columns. They are NULL for nonstring columns.

COLUMN_KEY

Information about whether the column is indexed.

INFORMATION_SCHEMA content is easy to use from within programs. Here's a PHP function that illustrates this process. It takes database and table name arguments, selects from INFORMATION_SCHEMA to obtain a list of the table's column names, and returns the names as an array. The ORDER BY ORDINAL_POSITION clause ensures that names in the array are returned in table-definition order:

```
function get_column_names ($dbh, $db_name, $tbl_name)
{
  $stmt = "SELECT COLUMN_NAME FROM INFORMATION_SCHEMA.COLUMNS
          WHERE TABLE_SCHEMA = ? AND TABLE_NAME = ?
          ORDER BY ORDINAL_POSITION";
  $sth = $dbh->prepare ($stmt);
  $sth->execute (array ($db_name, $tbl_name));
  return ($sth->fetchAll (PDO::FETCH_COLUMN, 0));
}
```

get_column_names() returns an array containing only column names. If you require additional column information, it's possible to write a more general get_col umn_info() routine that returns an array of column information structures. For implementations of both routines in PHP as well as other languages, check the library files in the *lib* directory of the recipes distribution.

Using SHOW COLUMNS to get table structure information

The SHOW COLUMNS statement produces one row of output for each column in the table, with each row providing various pieces of information about the corresponding column. The following example demonstrates SHOW COLUMNS output for the item table colors column:

```
mysql> SHOW COLUMNS FROM item LIKE 'colors'\G
*************************** 1. row ***************************
  Field: colors
   Type: enum('chartreuse','mauve','lime green','puce')
```

```
     Null: YES
      Key:
  Default: puce
    Extra:
```

SHOW COLUMNS displays information for all columns having a name that matches the LIKE pattern. To obtain information about all columns, omit the LIKE clause.

The values displayed by SHOW COLUMNS correspond to these columns of the INFORMA TION_SCHEMA COLUMNS table: COLUMN_NAME, COLUMN_TYPE, COLUMN_KEY, IS_NULLABLE, COLUMN_DEFAULT, EXTRA.

SHOW FULL COLUMNS displays additional Collation, Privileges, and Comment fields for each column. These correspond to the COLUMNS table COLLATION_NAME, PRIVI LEGES, and COLUMN_COMMENT columns.

SHOW interprets the pattern the same way as for the LIKE operator in the WHERE clause of a SELECT statement. (For information about pattern matching, see Recipe 7.10.) If you specify a literal column name, the string matches only that name, and SHOW COLUMNS displays information only for that column. If your column name contains SQL pattern characters (% or _) that you want to match literally, you must escape them with a backslash in the pattern string to avoid matching other names as well.

The need to escape % and _ characters to match a LIKE pattern literally also applies to other SHOW statements that permit a name pattern in the LIKE clause, such as SHOW TABLES and SHOW DATABASES.

Within a program, you can use your API language's pattern-matching capabilities to escape SQL pattern characters before putting the column name into a SHOW statement. In Perl, Ruby, and PHP, use the following expressions:

Perl:

```
$name =~ s/([%_])/\\$1/g;
```

Ruby:

```
name = name.gsub(/([%_])/, '\\\\\\1')
```

PHP:

```
$name = preg_replace ('/([%_])/', '\\\\$1', $name);
```

For Python, import the re module, and use its sub() method:

```
name = re.sub(r'([%_])', r'\\\1', name)
```

For Go, use methods from the regexp package:

```
import "regexp"
// ...
  re := regexp.MustCompile(`([_%])`)
  name = re.ReplaceAllString(name, "\\\\$1")
```

For Java, use methods from the `java.util.regex` package:

```
import java.util.regex.*;

Pattern p = Pattern.compile("([_%])");
Matcher m = p.matcher(name);
name = m.replaceAll ("\\\\$1");
```

If these expressions appear to have too many backslashes, remember that the API language processor itself interprets backslashes and strips off a level before performing the pattern match. To get a literal backslash into the result, it must be doubled in the pattern. Another level on top of that is needed if the pattern processor strips a set.

Using SHOW CREATE TABLE to get table structure information

Another way to obtain table structure information from MySQL is from the CREATE TABLE statement that defines the table. To get this information, use the SHOW CREATE TABLE statement:

```
mysql> SHOW CREATE TABLE item\G
*************************** 1. row ***************************
       Table: item
Create Table: CREATE TABLE `item` (
  `id` int(10) unsigned NOT NULL AUTO_INCREMENT,
  `name` char(20) DEFAULT NULL,
  `colors` enum('chartreuse','mauve','lime green','puce') DEFAULT 'puce',
  PRIMARY KEY (`id`)
) ENGINE=InnoDB DEFAULT CHARSET=utf8mb4 COLLATE=utf8mb4_0900_ai_ci
```

From the command line, the same CREATE TABLE information is available from `mysqldump` if you use the `--no-data` option, which tells `mysqldump` to dump only the structure of the table and not its data.

The CREATE TABLE format is highly informative and easy to read because it shows column information in a format similar to the one you used to create the table in the first place. It also shows the index structure clearly, whereas the other methods do not. However, you'll probably find this method of checking table structure more useful interactively than within programs. The information isn't provided in regular row-and-column format, so it's more difficult to parse. Also, the format is subject to change whenever the CREATE TABLE statement is enhanced, which happens from time to time as MySQL's capabilities are extended.

12.6 Getting ENUM and SET Column Information

Problem

You want to know the members of an ENUM or SET column.

Solution

This problem is a subset of getting table structure metadata. Obtain the column definition from the table metadata, then extract the member list from the definition.

Discussion

It's often useful to know the list of allowed values for an ENUM or SET column. Suppose that you want to present a web form containing a pop-up menu that has options corresponding to each legal value of an ENUM column, such as the sizes in which a garment can be ordered or the available shipping methods for delivering a package. You could hardwire the choices into the script that generates the form, but if you alter the column later (for example, to add a new enumeration value), you introduce a discrepancy between the column and the script that uses it. If instead you look up the legal values using the table metadata, the script can always produce a pop-up that contains the proper set of values. A similar approach applies to SET columns.

To determine the permitted values for an ENUM or SET column, get its definition using one of the techniques described in Recipe 12.5. For example, if you select from the INFORMATION_SCHEMA COLUMNS table, the COLUMN_TYPE value for the colors column of the item table looks like this:

```
enum('chartreuse','mauve','lime green','puce')
```

SET columns are similar, except that they say set rather than enum. For either data type, extract the permitted values by stripping the initial word and the parentheses, splitting at the commas, and removing the enclosing quotes from the individual values.

Let's write a get_enumorset_info() routine to extract these values from the data-type definition. While we're at it, we can have the routine return the column's type, its default value, and whether values can be NULL. Then the routine can be used by scripts that may need more than just the list of values. Here is a version in Ruby. Its arguments are a database handle, a database name, a table name, and a column name. It returns a hash with entries corresponding to the various aspects of the column definition (or nil if the column does not exist):

```ruby
def get_enumorset_info(client, db_name, tbl_name, col_name)
  sth = client.prepare(
        "SELECT COLUMN_NAME, COLUMN_TYPE, IS_NULLABLE, COLUMN_DEFAULT
         FROM INFORMATION_SCHEMA.COLUMNS
         WHERE TABLE_SCHEMA = ? AND TABLE_NAME = ? AND COLUMN_NAME = ?")
  res = sth.execute(db_name, tbl_name, col_name)
  return nil if res.count == 0  # no such column
  row = res.first
  info = {}
  info["name"] = row.values[0]
  return nil unless row.values[1] =~ /^(ENUM|SET)\((.*)\)$/i # not ENUM or SET
  info["type"] = $1
```

```
  # split value list on commas, trim quotes from end of each word
  info["values"] = $2.split(",").collect { |val| val.sub(/^'(.*)'$/, "\\1") }
  # determine whether column can contain NULL values
  info["nullable"] = (row.values[2].upcase == "YES")
  # get default value (nil represents NULL)
  info["default"] = row.values[3]
  return info
end
```

The routine uses case-insensitive matching when checking the data type and nullable attributes. This guards against future lettercase changes in metadata results.

The following example shows how to access and display each element of the hash returned by get_enumorset_info():

```
info = get_enumorset_info(client, db_name, tbl_name, col_name)
puts "Information for #{db_name}.#{tbl_name}.#{col_name}:"
if info.nil?
  puts "No information available (not an ENUM or SET column?)"
else
  puts "Name: " + info["name"]
  puts "Type: " + info["type"]
  puts "Legal values: " + info["values"].join(",")
  puts "Nullable: " + (info["nullable"] ? "yes" : "no")
  puts "Default value: " + (info["default"].nil? ? "NULL" : info["default"])
end
```

That code produces the following output for the profile table color column:

```
Information for cookbook.profile.color:
Name: color
Type: enum
Legal values: blue,red,green,brown,black,white
Nullable: yes
Default value: NULL
```

Equivalent routines for other APIs are similar. You can find implementations in the *lib* directory of the recipes distribution. Such routines are useful for validation of input values (see Recipe 14.11).

12.7 Getting Server Metadata

Problem

You want to get information about the MySQL server itself, such as its version, configuration, and the current status of its components.

Solution

Several SQL functions and SHOW statements return information about the server.

Discussion

MySQL has several SQL functions and statements that provide you with information about the server itself and about your current client session. Table 12-5 shows a few that you may find useful. Both SHOW statements permit a GLOBAL or SESSION keyword to select global server values or values specific to your session, and a LIKE 'pattern' clause for limiting the results to variable names matching the pattern.

Table 12-5. SQL functions and statements to obtain server metadata

Statement	Information produced by statement
SELECT VERSION()	Server version string
SELECT DATABASE()	Default database name (NULL if none)
SELECT USER()	Current user as given by client when connecting
SELECT CURRENT_USER()	User used for checking client privileges
SHOW [GLOBAL|SESSION] STATUS	Server global or session status indicators
SHOW [GLOBAL|SESSION] VARIABLES	Server global or status configuration variables

To obtain the information provided by any statement in the table, execute it and process its result set. For example, SELECT DATABASE() returns the name of the default database or NULL if no database has been selected. The following Ruby code uses the statement to present a status display containing information about the current session:

```
db = client.query("SELECT DATABASE()").first.values[0]
puts "Default database: " + (db.nil? ? "(no database selected)" : db)
```

A given API might provide alternatives to executing SQL statements to access these types of information. For example, JDBC has several database-independent methods for obtaining server metadata. Use your connection object to obtain the database metadata, then invoke the appropriate methods to get the information in which you're interested. Consult a JDBC reference for a complete list, but here are a few representative examples:

```
DatabaseMetaData md = conn.getMetaData();
// can also get this with SELECT VERSION()
System.out.println("Product version: " + md.getDatabaseProductVersion());
// this is similar to SELECT USER() but doesn't include the hostname
System.out.println("Username: " + md.getUserName());
```

See Also

For more discussion about the use of SHOW (and INFORMATION_SCHEMA) in the context of server monitoring, see Recipe 23.2.

12.8 Writing Applications That Adapt to the MySQL Server Version

Problem

You want to use a given feature that is available only in a particular version of MySQL.

Solution

Ask the server for its version number. If the server is too old to support a given feature, maybe you can fall back to a workaround, if one exists. Or ask your user to upgrade.

Discussion

With each new release of MySQL, new features are added. If you're writing an application that requires certain features, check the server version to determine whether they are present; if not, you must perform some sort of workaround (assuming there is one).

To get the server version, invoke the VERSION() function. The result is a string that looks something like 5.7.33-debug-log or 8.0.25. In other words, it returns a string consisting of major, minor, and "patch" version numbers; possibly some nondigits at the end of the "patch" version; and possibly some suffix. The version string can be used as is for presentation purposes, but for comparisons, it's simpler to work with a number—in particular, a five-digit number in Mmmtt format, in which M, mm, tt are the major, minor, and patch version numbers. Perform the conversion by splitting the string at the periods, stripping from the third piece the suffix that begins with the first nonnumeric character, and joining the pieces. For example, 5.7.33-debug-log becomes 50733, and 8.0.25 becomes 80025.

Here's a Perl DBI function that takes a database-handle argument and returns a two-element list that contains both the string and numeric forms of the server version. The code assumes that the minor and patch version parts are less than 100 and thus no more than two digits each. That should be a valid assumption because the source code for MySQL itself uses the same format:

```
sub get_server_version
{
my $dbh = shift;
my ($ver_str, $ver_num);
my ($major, $minor, $patch);

  # fetch result into scalar string
  $ver_str = $dbh->selectrow_array ("SELECT VERSION()");
  return undef unless defined ($ver_str);
```

```
    ($major, $minor, $patch) = split (/\./, $ver_str);
    $patch =~ s/\D.*$//; # strip nonnumeric suffix if present
    $ver_num = $major*10000 + $minor*100 + $patch;
    return ($ver_str, $ver_num);
}
```

To get both forms of the version information at once, call the function like this:

```
my ($ver_str, $ver_num) = get_server_version ($dbh);
```

To get just one of the values, call it as follows:

```
my $ver_str = (get_server_version ($dbh))[0]; # string form
my $ver_num = (get_server_version ($dbh))[1]; # numeric form
```

The following examples demonstrate how to use the numeric version value to check whether the server supports certain features:

```
my $ver_num = (get_server_version ($dbh))[1];
printf "Event scheduler:    %s\n", ($ver_num >= 50106 ? "yes" : "no");
printf "4-byte Unicode:     %s\n", ($ver_num >= 50503 ? "yes" : "no");
printf "Fractional seconds: %s\n", ($ver_num >= 50604 ? "yes" : "no");
printf "SHA-256 passwords:  %s\n", ($ver_num >= 50606 ? "yes" : "no");
printf "ALTER USER:         %s\n", ($ver_num >= 50607 ? "yes" : "no");
printf "INSERT DELAYED:     %s\n", ($ver_num >= 50700 ? "no" : "yes");
```

The recipes distribution *metadata* directory contains get_server_version() implementations in other API languages, and the *routines* directory contains a server_ver sion() stored function for use in SQL statements. The latter function returns only the numeric value because VERSION() already produces the string value. The following example shows how to use it to implement a stored procedure that enables password locking for *N* failed login attempts if the server is recent enough to support the ALTER USER...FAILED_LOGIN_ATTEMPTS statement (MySQL 8.0.19 or later):

```
CREATE PROCEDURE enable_failed_login_attempts(
                            user TEXT, host TEXT, failed_attempts INT)
BEGIN
  DECLARE account TEXT;
  SET account = CONCAT(QUOTE(user),'@',QUOTE(host));
  IF server_version() >= 80019 AND user <> '' THEN
    CALL exec_stmt(CONCAT('ALTER USER ',account,'
                FAILED_LOGIN_ATTEMPTS ', failed_attempts));
  END IF;
END;
```

expire_password() requires the exec_stmt() helper routine (see Recipe 11.6). Both are available in the *routines* directory. For more information about password expiration, see Recipe 24.5.

12.9 Getting Child Tables That Reference a Specific Table via Foreign Key Constraints

Problem

You want to know which other tables refer to your table as the parent via foreign key constraints.

Solution

Query the INFORMATION_SCHEMA.TABLE_CONSTRAINTS and INFORMATION_SCHEMA.KEY_COLUMN_USAGE tables.

Discussion

Foreign key constraints provide integrity checks, as we discuss in "Using Foreign Keys to Enforce Referential Integrity and Prevent Mismatches" on page 652. They do it by preventing statements that modify data, referenced by the linked table, to execute if the result of the statement can break integrity. Foreign keys help keeping the data correct, but at the same time they can raise SQL errors that are hard to troubleshoot. And while it is easy to figure out which table is a parent for the particular child, it is not easy to find which table is a child of the particular parent. Still it would be good to know if a table is referenced by a child in case you plan to modify it.

The INFORMATION_SCHEMA.TABLE_CONSTRAINTS table contains all the constraints created for your MySQL installation. To select foreign key constraints, narrow your search with the WHERE CONSTRAINT_TYPE='FOREIGN KEY' clause:

```
mysql> SELECT TABLE_SCHEMA, TABLE_NAME, CONSTRAINT_NAME
    -> FROM INFORMATION_SCHEMA.TABLE_CONSTRAINTS
    -> WHERE CONSTRAINT_TYPE='FOREIGN KEY' AND TABLE_SCHEMA='cookbook';
+--------------+--------------------+--------------------------+
| TABLE_SCHEMA | TABLE_NAME         | CONSTRAINT_NAME          |
+--------------+--------------------+--------------------------+
| cookbook     | movies_actors_link | movies_actors_link_ibfk_1 |
| cookbook     | movies_actors_link | movies_actors_link_ibfk_2 |
+--------------+--------------------+--------------------------+
2 rows in set (0,00 sec)
```

The preceding listing prints the foreign keys we created for the example in Recipe 11.10. However, this output still lists only the child table. To find out which table is the parent, we need to join INFORMATION_SCHEMA.TABLE_CONSTRAINTS with the INFORMATION_SCHEMA.KEY_COLUMN_USAGE table:

```
mysql> SELECT  ku.CONSTRAINT_NAME, ku.TABLE_NAME, ku.COLUMN_NAME,
    -> ku.REFERENCED_TABLE_NAME, ku.REFERENCED_COLUMN_NAME
    -> FROM INFORMATION_SCHEMA.TABLE_CONSTRAINTS tc
```

```
    -> JOIN INFORMATION_SCHEMA.KEY_COLUMN_USAGE ku
    -> USING (CONSTRAINT_NAME, TABLE_SCHEMA, TABLE_NAME)
    -> WHERE CONSTRAINT_TYPE='FOREIGN KEY' AND ku.TABLE_SCHEMA='cookbook'\G
*************************** 1. row ***************************
    CONSTRAINT_NAME: movies_actors_link_ibfk_1
         TABLE_NAME: movies_actors_link
        COLUMN_NAME: movie_id
 REFERENCED_TABLE_NAME: movies
REFERENCED_COLUMN_NAME: id
*************************** 2. row ***************************
    CONSTRAINT_NAME: movies_actors_link_ibfk_2
         TABLE_NAME: movies_actors_link
        COLUMN_NAME: actor_id
 REFERENCED_TABLE_NAME: actors
REFERENCED_COLUMN_NAME: id
2 rows in set (0,00 sec)
```

In the preceding listing, the TABLE_NAME and COLUMN_NAME columns refer to the child table, and the REFERENCED_TABLE_NAME and REFERENCED_COLUMN_NAME tables refer to the parent table.

For InnoDB tables, you can also query the INNODB_FOREIGN and INNODB_FOREIGN_COLS tables:

```
mysql> SELECT ID, FOR_NAME, FOR_COL_NAME, REF_NAME, REF_COL_NAME
    -> FROM INFORMATION_SCHEMA.INNODB_FOREIGN JOIN
    -> INFORMATION_SCHEMA.INNODB_FOREIGN_COLS USING(ID)
    -> WHERE ID LIKE 'cookbook%'\G
*************************** 1. row ***************************
          ID: cookbook/movies_actors_link_ibfk_1
    FOR_NAME: cookbook/movies_actors_link
FOR_COL_NAME: movie_id
    REF_NAME: cookbook/movies
REF_COL_NAME: id
*************************** 2. row ***************************
          ID: cookbook/movies_actors_link_ibfk_2
    FOR_NAME: cookbook/movies_actors_link
FOR_COL_NAME: actor_id
    REF_NAME: cookbook/actors
REF_COL_NAME: id
2 rows in set (0,01 sec)
```

Note that these tables take data from the internal InnoDB data dictionary that stores database and table names in one field. Therefore, you need to use the LIKE operator to limit results to the specific database or table.

12.10 Listing Triggers

Problem

You want to list triggers defined for your table.

Solution

Query the `INFORMATION_SCHEMA.TRIGGERS` table.

Discussion

Knowing which triggers are defined for specific tables is very useful when you tune performance, especially in the following situations:

- A simple update, affecting a couple of rows, runs much longer than you expect.
- Tables, not participating in the application load and not visible in the processlist, wait for or hold the locks.
- Disk IO is high.

For example, to list triggers created for the `auction` table, use the following query:

```
mysql> SELECT EVENT_MANIPULATION, ACTION_TIMING, TRIGGER_NAME, ACTION_STATEMENT
    -> FROM INFORMATION_SCHEMA.TRIGGERS
    -> WHERE TRIGGER_SCHEMA='cookbook' AND EVENT_OBJECT_TABLE = 'auction'\G
*************************** 1. row ***************************
EVENT_MANIPULATION: INSERT
    ACTION_TIMING: AFTER
     TRIGGER_NAME: ai_auction
 ACTION_STATEMENT: INSERT INTO auction_log (action,id,ts,item,bid)
VALUES('create',NEW.id,NOW(),NEW.item,NEW.bid)
*************************** 2. row ***************************
EVENT_MANIPULATION: UPDATE
    ACTION_TIMING: AFTER
     TRIGGER_NAME: au_auction
 ACTION_STATEMENT: INSERT INTO auction_log (action,id,ts,item,bid)
VALUES('update',NEW.id,NOW(),NEW.item,NEW.bid)
*************************** 3. row ***************************
EVENT_MANIPULATION: DELETE
    ACTION_TIMING: AFTER
     TRIGGER_NAME: ad_auction
 ACTION_STATEMENT: INSERT INTO auction_log (action,id,ts,item,bid)
VALUES('delete',OLD.id,OLD.ts,OLD.item,OLD.bid)
3 rows in set (0,01 sec)
```

This way, you can get information such as when a trigger is fired and its body definition. If there is more than one trigger, you'll see all of them.

12.11 Listing Stored Routines and Scheduled Events

Problem

You want to know which stored procedures, functions, and scheduled events are created in your database.

Solution

Query the `INFORMATION_SCHEMA.ROUTINES` and `INFORMATION_SCHEMA.EVENTS` tables.

Discussion

To list both stored functions and stored procedures, query the `INFORMA‐
TION_SCHEMA.ROUTINES` table. If you want to distinguish which kind of routine it
is, narrow your search by specifying `ROUTINE_TYPE`, either `FUNCTION` or `PROCEDURE`, by
the `WHERE` condition.

For example, to list all routines that participate in sequence generation, as we discuss
in Recipe 15.17, use the following code:

```
mysql> SELECT ROUTINE_NAME, ROUTINE_TYPE FROM INFORMATION_SCHEMA.ROUTINES
    -> WHERE ROUTINE_SCHEMA='cookbook' AND ROUTINE_NAME LIKE '%sequence%';
+---------------------+--------------+
| ROUTINE_NAME        | ROUTINE_TYPE |
+---------------------+--------------+
| sequence_next_value | FUNCTION     |
| create_sequence     | PROCEDURE    |
| delete_sequence     | PROCEDURE    |
+---------------------+--------------+
3 rows in set (0,01 sec)
```

You may additionally select the `ROUTINE_DEFINITION` column to obtain the routine
body.

To get a list of scheduled events, query the `INFORMATION_SCHEMA.EVENTS` table:

```
mysql> SELECT EVENT_NAME, EVENT_TYPE, INTERVAL_VALUE, INTERVAL_FIELD, LAST_EXECUTED,
    -> STATUS, ON_COMPLETION, EVENT_DEFINITION FROM INFORMATION_SCHEMA.EVENTS\G
*************************** 1. row ***************************
      EVENT_NAME: mark_insert
      EVENT_TYPE: RECURRING
  INTERVAL_VALUE: 5
  INTERVAL_FIELD: MINUTE
   LAST_EXECUTED: 2021-07-07 05:10:45
          STATUS: ENABLED
   ON_COMPLETION: NOT PRESERVE
EVENT_DEFINITION: INSERT INTO mark_log (message) VALUES('-- MARK --')
*************************** 2. row ***************************
      EVENT_NAME: mark_expire
      EVENT_TYPE: RECURRING
  INTERVAL_VALUE: 1
  INTERVAL_FIELD: DAY
   LAST_EXECUTED: 2021-07-07 02:56:14
          STATUS: ENABLED
   ON_COMPLETION: NOT PRESERVE
EVENT_DEFINITION: DELETE FROM mark_log WHERE ts < NOW() - INTERVAL 2 DAY
2 rows in set (0,00 sec)
```

This table holds not only event definitions but also metadata, such as when it was last
executed, its scheduled interval, and whether it is enabled or disabled.

12.12 Listing Installed Plug-Ins

Problem

You want to know which plug-ins are installed for your MySQL server.

Solution

Query the `INFORMATION_SCHEMA.PLUGINS` table.

Discussion

MySQL is a highly modular system. Many of its parts are pluggable. For example, all storage engines are also plug-ins. Therefore, it is important to know which are available on your server. To get information about installed plug-ins, query the `INFORMATION_SCHEMA.PLUGINS` table, or run the `SHOW PLUGINS` command. While the latter is convenient for interactive use, the former provides more information:

```
mysql> SELECT * FROM INFORMATION_SCHEMA.PLUGINS
    -> WHERE PLUGIN_NAME IN ('caching_sha2_password', 'InnoDB', 'Rewriter')\G
*************************** 1. row ***************************
           PLUGIN_NAME: caching_sha2_password
        PLUGIN_VERSION: 1.0
         PLUGIN_STATUS: ACTIVE
           PLUGIN_TYPE: AUTHENTICATION
   PLUGIN_TYPE_VERSION: 2.0
        PLUGIN_LIBRARY: NULL
PLUGIN_LIBRARY_VERSION: NULL
         PLUGIN_AUTHOR: Oracle Corporation
    PLUGIN_DESCRIPTION: Caching sha2 authentication
        PLUGIN_LICENSE: GPL
           LOAD_OPTION: FORCE
*************************** 2. row ***************************
           PLUGIN_NAME: InnoDB
        PLUGIN_VERSION: 8.0
         PLUGIN_STATUS: ACTIVE
           PLUGIN_TYPE: STORAGE ENGINE
   PLUGIN_TYPE_VERSION: 80025.0
        PLUGIN_LIBRARY: NULL
PLUGIN_LIBRARY_VERSION: NULL
         PLUGIN_AUTHOR: Oracle Corporation
    PLUGIN_DESCRIPTION: Supports transactions, row-level locking, and foreign keys
        PLUGIN_LICENSE: GPL
           LOAD_OPTION: FORCE
*************************** 3. row ***************************
           PLUGIN_NAME: Rewriter
        PLUGIN_VERSION: 0.2
         PLUGIN_STATUS: ACTIVE
           PLUGIN_TYPE: AUDIT
   PLUGIN_TYPE_VERSION: 4.1
        PLUGIN_LIBRARY: rewriter.so
PLUGIN_LIBRARY_VERSION: 1.10
         PLUGIN_AUTHOR: Oracle Corporation
    PLUGIN_DESCRIPTION: A query rewrite plug-in that rewrites queries using the parse tree.
```

```
        PLUGIN_LICENSE: GPL
          LOAD_OPTION: ON
3 rows in set (0,01 sec)
```

For storage engines, you can obtain even more details by querying the INFORMA
TION_SCHEMA.ENGINES table, or running the SHOW ENGINES command. Here is the
table content for the InnoDB storage engine:

```
mysql> SELECT * FROM INFORMATION_SCHEMA.ENGINES WHERE ENGINE = 'InnoDB'\G
*************************** 1. row ***************************
      ENGINE: InnoDB
     SUPPORT: DEFAULT
     COMMENT: Supports transactions, row-level locking, and foreign keys
TRANSACTIONS: YES
          XA: YES
  SAVEPOINTS: YES
1 row in set (0,00 sec)
```

12.13 Listing Character Sets and Collations

Problem

Sort order, defining which letters are equal, doesn't work for you, and you want to
determine what other options you have.

Solution

Obtain a list of characters sets, their default collation, and available collations by
querying the INFORMATION_SCHEMA.CHARACTER_SETS and INFORMATION_SCHEMA.COL
LATIONS tables.

Discussion

In Recipe 7.5, we discussed how to change or set a string's character set and collation.
But how do you choose the one that best suits your application requirements?

Fortunately, MySQL itself can help you find the answer. Inside MySQL client, select
from the INFORMATION_SCHEMA.CHARACTER_SETS table to get a list of all available
character sets, their default collations, and the maximum character length they can
store.

For example, to list all Unicode character sets, run the following query:

```
mysql> SELECT * FROM INFORMATION_SCHEMA.CHARACTER_SETS
    -> WHERE DESCRIPTION LIKE '%Unicode%' ORDER BY MAXLEN DESC;
+--------------------+----------------------+-------------------+--------+
| CHARACTER_SET_NAME | DEFAULT_COLLATE_NAME | DESCRIPTION       | MAXLEN |
+--------------------+----------------------+-------------------+--------+
| utf16              | utf16_general_ci     | UTF-16 Unicode    |      4 |
| utf16le            | utf16le_general_ci   | UTF-16LE Unicode  |      4 |
| utf32              | utf32_general_ci     | UTF-32 Unicode    |      4 |
```

```
| utf8mb4             | utf8mb4_0900_ai_ci      | UTF-8 Unicode      |     4 |
| utf8                | utf8_general_ci         | UTF-8 Unicode      |     3 |
| ucs2                | ucs2_general_ci         | UCS-2 Unicode      |     2 |
+---------------------+-------------------------+--------------------+-------+
6 rows in set (0,00 sec)
```

Each character set may have not only default collation but other collations that allow you to adjust sort order. For example, the Turkish capital letters *I* and *İ*, as well as *S* and *Ş* are considered equal by the utf8mb4 character set with the default collation. This leads to a situation in which MySQL thinks that the Turkish words *ISSIZ* ("deserted") and *İŞSİZ* ("unemployed") are the same:

```
mysql> CREATE TABLE two_words(deserted VARCHAR(100), unemployed VARCHAR(100));
Query OK, 0 rows affected (0,03 sec)

mysql> INSERT INTO two_words VALUES('ISSIZ', 'İŞSİZ');
Query OK, 1 row affected (0,00 sec)

mysql> SELECT deserted=unemployed FROM two_words;
+---------------------+
| deserted=unemployed |
+---------------------+
|                   1 |
+---------------------+
1 row in set (0,00 sec)
```

To resolve this situation, let's check the INFORMATION_SCHEMA.COLLATIONS table for the collations of the utf8mb4 character set, applicable for the Turkish language:

```
mysql> SELECT COLLATION_NAME, CHARACTER_SET_NAME
    -> FROM INFORMATION_SCHEMA.COLLATIONS
    -> WHERE CHARACTER_SET_NAME='utf8mb4' AND COLLATION_NAME LIKE '%\_tr\_%';
+----------------------+--------------------+
| COLLATION_NAME       | CHARACTER_SET_NAME |
+----------------------+--------------------+
| utf8mb4_tr_0900_ai_ci | utf8mb4           |
| utf8mb4_tr_0900_as_cs | utf8mb4           |
+----------------------+--------------------+
2 rows in set (0,00 sec)
```

If we try them, we'll receive the correct result: the words *deserted* and *unemployed* are no longer considered equal:

```
mysql> SELECT deserted=unemployed COLLATE utf8mb4_tr_0900_ai_ci FROM two_words;
+---------------------------------------------------+
| deserted=unemployed COLLATE utf8mb4_tr_0900_ai_ci |
+---------------------------------------------------+
|                                                 0 |
+---------------------------------------------------+
1 row in set (0,00 sec)

mysql> SELECT deserted=unemployed COLLATE utf8mb4_tr_0900_as_cs FROM two_words;
+---------------------------------------------------+
| deserted=unemployed COLLATE utf8mb4_tr_0900_as_cs |
+---------------------------------------------------+
|                                                 0 |
+---------------------------------------------------+
1 row in set (0,00 sec)
```

The `utf8mb4` character set is the default and works well for most setups. However, you may be in a situation where this is not the case. For example, if you store the Russian words совершенный ("perfect") and совершённый ("accomplished") in a `utf8mb4` column with default collation, MySQL will consider these two words equal:

```
mysql > CREATE TABLE `two_words` (
    -> `perfect` varchar(100) DEFAULT NULL,
    -> `accomplished` varchar(100) DEFAULT NULL
    -> ) ENGINE=InnoDB DEFAULT CHARSET=utf8mb4 COLLATE=utf8mb4_0900_ai_ci;
Query OK, 0 rows affected (0,04 sec)

mysql> INSERT INTO two_words VALUES('совершенный', 'совершённый');
Query OK, 1 row affected (0,01 sec)

mysql> SELECT perfect = accomplished FROM two_words;
+------------------------+
| perfect = accomplished |
+------------------------+
|                      1 |
+------------------------+
1 row in set (0,00 sec)
```

An intuitive way to solve this issue is to use available collations for the Russian language: `utf8mb4_ru_0900_ai_ci`. Unfortunately, this does not work:

```
mysql> SELECT perfect = accomplished COLLATE utf8mb4_ru_0900_ai_ci FROM two_words;
+-----------------------------------------------------+
| perfect = accomplished COLLATE utf8mb4_ru_0900_ai_ci |
+-----------------------------------------------------+
|                                                   1 |
+-----------------------------------------------------+
1 row in set (0,00 sec)
```

The reason for this is that the `utf8mb4_ru_0900_ai_ci` collation is accent insensitive. The case sensitive and accent sensitive `utf8mb4_ru_0900_as_cs` variation solves the issue:

```
mysql> SELECT perfect = accomplished COLLATE utf8mb4_ru_0900_as_cs FROM two_words;
+-----------------------------------------------------+
| perfect = accomplished COLLATE utf8mb4_ru_0900_as_cs |
+-----------------------------------------------------+
|                                                   0 |
+-----------------------------------------------------+
1 row in set (0,00 sec)
```

The `utf8mb4_ru_0900_ai_ci` and `utf8mb4_ru_0900_as_cs` collations were added in version 8.0. If you're still using version 5.7 and are working on the application where this difference is critical, you can also examine the `INFORMATION_SCHEMA.CHARACTER_SETS` table for a character set that supports the Cyrillic alphabet and try it:

```
mysql> SELECT * FROM INFORMATION_SCHEMA.CHARACTER_SETS
    -> WHERE DESCRIPTION LIKE '%Russian%' OR DESCRIPTION LIKE '%Cyrillic%';
+-------------------+--------------------+----------------------+--------+
| CHARACTER_SET_NAME | DEFAULT_COLLATE_NAME | DESCRIPTION          | MAXLEN |
+-------------------+--------------------+----------------------+--------+
| koi8r             | koi8r_general_ci   | KOI8-R Relcom Russian |      1 |
```

```
| cp866          | cp866_general_ci   | DOS Russian      |      1 |
| cp1251         | cp1251_general_ci  | Windows Cyrillic |      1 |
+----------------+--------------------+------------------+--------+
3 rows in set (0,00 sec)

mysql> drop table two_words;
Query OK, 0 rows affected (0,02 sec)

mysql> CREATE TABLE two_words(perfect VARCHAR(100), accomplished VARCHAR(100))
    -> CHARACTER SET cp1251;
Query OK, 0 rows affected (0,04 sec)

mysql> INSERT INTO two_words VALUES('совершенный', 'совершённый');
Query OK, 1 row affected (0,00 sec)

mysql> SELECT perfect = accomplished FROM two_words;
+------------------------+
| perfect = accomplished |
+------------------------+
|                      0 |
+------------------------+
1 row in set (0,00 sec)
```

We've chosen the cp1251 character set for our example, but all of them resolve this comparison issue.

12.14 Listing CHECK Constraints

Problem

You want to examine which CHECK constraints are defined for your database.

Solution

Query the INFORMATION_SCHEMA.CHECK_CONSTRAINTS and INFORMATION_SCHEMA.TABLE_CONSTRAINTS tables.

Discussion

The INFORMATION_SCHEMA.CHECK_CONSTRAINTS table contains a list of all constraints, the schema for which they are defined, and the CHECK_CLAUSE that is practically the constraint definition. However, the table does not store information about which table the constraint is created in. To list both constraints and tables for which they are defined, join the INFORMATION_SCHEMA.CHECK_CONSTRAINTS table with the INFORMATION_SCHEMA.TABLE_CONSTRAINTS table:

```
mysql> SELECT TABLE_SCHEMA, TABLE_NAME, CONSTRAINT_NAME, ENFORCED, CHECK_CLAUSE
    -> FROM INFORMATION_SCHEMA.CHECK_CONSTRAINTS
    -> JOIN INFORMATION_SCHEMA.TABLE_CONSTRAINTS
    -> USING(CONSTRAINT_NAME)
    -> WHERE CONSTRAINT_TYPE='CHECK' ORDER BY CONSTRAINT_NAME DESC LIMIT 2\G
*************************** 1. row ***************************
```

```
    TABLE_SCHEMA: cookbook
      TABLE_NAME: even
 CONSTRAINT_NAME: even_chk_1
        ENFORCED: YES
    CHECK_CLAUSE: ((`even_value` % 2) = 0)
*************************** 2. row ***************************
    TABLE_SCHEMA: cookbook
      TABLE_NAME: book_authors
 CONSTRAINT_NAME: book_authors_chk_1
        ENFORCED: YES
    CHECK_CLAUSE: json_schema_valid(_utf8mb4\'{"id": ↵
                  "http://www.oreilly.com/mysqlcookbook", "$schema": ↵
                  "http://json-schema.org/draft-04/schema#", "description": ↵
                  "Schema for the table book_authors", "type": "object", "properties": ↵
                  {"name": {"type": "string"}, "lastname": {"type": "string"}, ↵
                  "books": {"type": "array"}}, "required":["name", "lastname"]} \',`author`)
2 rows in set (0,01 sec)
```

## CHAPTER 13

Importing and Exporting Data

13.0 Introduction

Suppose that a file named *somedata.csv* contains 12 data columns in comma-separated values (CSV) format. From this file you want to extract only columns 2, 11, 5, and 9 and use them to create database rows in a MySQL table that contains `name`, `birth`, `height`, and `weight` columns. You must make sure that the height and weight are positive integers, and convert the birth dates from *MM/DD/YY* format to *YYYY-MM-DD* format. How can you do this?

Data transfer problems with specific requirements occur frequently when you transfer data into MySQL. Datafiles are not always formatted for being ready to load into MySQL with no preparation. As a result, it's often necessary to preprocess information to put it into a format acceptable for MySQL. The reverse also is true; data exported from MySQL may need massaging to be useful for other programs.

Although some data preparation operations require a great deal of hand checking and reformatting, in most cases you can do at least part of the job automatically. Virtually all such problems involve at least some elements of a common set of conversion issues. This chapter and the next discuss what these issues are, how to deal with them by taking advantage of the existing tools at your disposal, and how to write your own tools when necessary. The idea is not to cover all possible situations (an impossible task) but to show representative techniques and utilities. Use them as is or adapt them. (There are commercial data-handling tools, but our purpose here is to enable you to do things yourself.) With respect to the problem posed at the beginning of this Introduction, see Recipe 14.18 for the solution we arrived at.

The discussion on how to transfer data to and from MySQL begins with native MySQL facilities for importing data (the LOAD DATA statement and the mysqlim port command-line program) and for exporting data (the SELECT...INTO OUTFILE statement). For situations where the native facilities do not suffice, we move on to cover techniques for using external supporting utilities (such as sed and tr) and for writing your own. There are two broad sets of issues to consider:

- How to manipulate the *structure* of datafiles. When a file is in a format not suitable for import, you must convert it to a different format. This may involve issues such as changing the column delimiters or line-ending sequences, or removing or rearranging columns in the file. This chapter covers such techniques.

- How to manipulate the *content* of datafiles. If you don't know whether the values contained in a file are legal, you may want to preprocess it to check or reformat them. Numeric values may need verification as lying within a specific range, dates may need conversion to or from ISO format, and so forth. Chapter 14 covers those techniques.

Source code for program fragments and scripts discussed in this chapter is located in the *transfer* directory of the recipes distribution.

General Import and Export Issues

Incompatible datafile formats and differing rules for interpreting various kinds of values cause headaches when transferring data between programs. Nevertheless, certain issues recur frequently. Be aware of them and you can identify more easily what must be done to solve particular import or export problems.

In its most basic form, an input stream is just a set of bytes with no particular meaning. Successful import into MySQL requires recognizing which bytes represent structural information and which represent the data values framed by that structure. Because such recognition is key to decomposing the input into appropriate units, the most fundamental import issues are these:

- What is the record separator? Knowing this enables you to partition the input stream into records.

- What is the field delimiter? Knowing this enables you to partition each record into field values. Identifying the data values also might include stripping quotes from around the values or recognizing escape sequences within them.

The ability to break the input into records and fields is important for extracting the data values from it. If the values are still not in a form that can be used directly, you may need to consider other issues:

- Do the order and number of columns match the structure of the database table? Mismatches require rearranging or skipping columns.

- How should NULL or empty values be handled? Are they permitted? Can NULL values even be detected? (Some systems export NULL values as empty strings, making it impossible to distinguish them.)
- Do data values require validation or reformatting? If the values are in a format that matches MySQL's expectations, no further processing is necessary. Otherwise, they must be checked and possibly rewritten.

For export from MySQL, the issues are somewhat the reverse. You can assume that values stored in the database are valid, but it's necessary to add column and record delimiters to form an output stream that has a structure other programs can recognize, and values may require reformatting for use by other programs.

File Formats

Datafiles come in many formats, two of which appear frequently in this chapter:

Tab-delimited or tab-separated values (TSV) format
This is one of the simplest file structures; lines contain values separated by tab characters. A short tab-delimited file might look like this, where the whitespace between column values represents single tab characters:

```
a       b       c
a,b,c   d e     f
```

Comma-separated values (CSV) format
Files written in CSV format vary somewhat; there is apparently no formal standard describing the format. However, the general idea is that lines consist of values separated by commas, and values containing internal commas are enclosed within quotes to prevent the commas from being interpreted as value delimiters. It's also common for values containing spaces to be quoted as well. In this example, each line contains three values:

```
a,b,c
"a,b,c","d e",f
```

It's trickier to process CSV files than tab-delimited files because characters like quotes and commas have a dual meaning: they may represent file structure or be included in the content of data values.

Another important datafile characteristic is the line-ending sequence. The most common sequences are carriage return (CR), linefeed (LF) and carriage return/linefeed (CRLF) pair.

Datafiles often begin with a row of column labels. For some import operations, the row of labels must be discarded to avoid having it be loaded into your table as data. In other cases, the labels are quite useful:

- For import into existing tables, the labels help you match datafile columns with the table columns if they are not necessarily in the same order.

- The labels can be used for column names when creating a new table automatically or semiautomatically from a datafile. For example, Recipe 13.20 discusses a utility that examines a datafile and guesses the CREATE TABLE statement to use to create a table from the file. If a label row is present, the utility uses the labels for column names.

Tab-Delimited, Linefeed-Terminated Format

Although datafiles may be written in many formats, it's unwieldy to include machinery for reading multiple formats within each file-processing utility you write. For that reason, many of the utilities described in this chapter assume for simplicity that their input is in tab-delimited, linefeed-terminated format. (This is also the default format for MySQL's LOAD DATA statement.) By making this assumption, it becomes easier to write programs that read files.

On the other hand, *something* has to be able to read data in other formats. To handle that problem, we'll develop a cvt_file.pl script that can read several types of files. The script is based on the Perl Text::CSV_XS module, which despite its name is useful for much more than just CSV data. cvt_file.pl can convert between many file types, making it possible for other programs that require tab-delimited lines to be used with files not originally written in that format. In other words, you can use cvt_file.pl to convert a file to tab-delimited, linefeed-terminated format, and then any program that expects that format can process the file. The file is available in the recipes distribution.

Notes on Invoking Shell Commands

This chapter shows a number of programs that you invoke from the command line using a shell like bash or tcsh under Unix or cmd.exe ("the command prompt") under Windows. Many of the example commands for these programs use quotes around option values, and sometimes an option value is itself a quote character. Quoting conventions vary from one shell to another, but the following rules seem to work with most of them (including cmd.exe under Windows):

- For an argument that contains spaces, enclose it within double quotes to prevent the shell from interpreting it as multiple separate arguments. The shell strips the quotes and passes the argument to the command intact.

- To include a double-quote character in the argument itself, precede it with a backslash.

Some shell commands in this chapter are so long that they're shown as you would enter them using several lines, with a backslash character as the line-continuation character:

```
$ prog_name \
    argument1 \
    argument2 ...
```

That works for Unix. On Windows, the continuation character is ^ (or ` for Power-Shell). Alternatively, on any platform, enter the entire command on one line:

```
C:\> prog_name argument1 argument2 ...
```

13.1 Importing Data with LOAD DATA and mysqlimport

Problem

You want to load a datafile into a table using MySQL's built-in import capabilities.

Solution

Use the LOAD DATA statement or the mysqlimport command-line program.

Discussion

MySQL provides a LOAD DATA statement that acts as a bulk data loader. Here's an example statement that reads a file, *mytbl.txt*, from your current directory (the direc-tory from which you call mysql client) and loads it into the mytbl table in the default database:

```
mysql> LOAD DATA LOCAL INFILE 'mytbl.txt' INTO TABLE mytbl;
```

 Since MySQL 8.0, the LOCAL loading capability is disabled by default for security reasons.

To enable it on the test server, set the local_infile to ON variable:

```
SET GLOBAL local_infile = 1;
```

and start mysql client with the --local-infile option:

```
mysql -ucbuser -p --local-infile
```

Alternatively, omit LOCAL from the statement and specify the full pathname to the file, which must be readable by the server. Local versus nonlocal data loading is discussed shortly.

The MySQL utility program mysqlimport acts as a wrapper around LOAD DATA so that you can load input files directly from the command line. The mysqlimport command that is equivalent to the preceding LOAD DATA statement looks like this, assuming that mytbl is in the cookbook database:

```
$ mysqlimport --local cookbook mytbl.txt
```

For mysqlimport, as with other MySQL programs, you may need to specify connection parameter options such as --user or --host (see Recipe 1.4).

LOAD DATA provides options to address many of the import issues mentioned in the chapter introduction, such as the line-ending sequence for recognizing how to break input into records, the column value delimiter that permits records to be broken into separate values, the quoting character that may enclose column values, quoting and escaping conventions within values, and NULL value representation.

The following list describes LOAD DATA's general characteristics and capabilities; mysqlimport shares most of these behaviors. We'll note some differences as we go along, but for the most, what can be done with LOAD DATA can be done with mysqlimport as well:

- By default, LOAD DATA expects the datafile to have the same number of columns as the table into which you load it, with the columns present in the same order as in the table. If the file column number or order differ from the table, you can specify which columns are present and their order. If the datafile contains fewer columns than the table, MySQL assigns default values for the missing columns.

- LOAD DATA assumes that data values are separated by tab characters and that lines end with linefeeds (newlines). If a file doesn't conform to these conventions, you can specify its format explicitly.

- You can indicate that data values may have quotes around them that should be stripped, and you can specify the quote character.

- Several special escape sequences are recognized and converted during input processing. The default escape character is the backslash (\), but you can change it. The \N sequence is interpreted as a NULL value. The \b, \n, \r, \t, \\, and \0 sequences are interpreted as backspace, linefeed, carriage return, tab, backslash, and ASCII NUL characters. (NUL is a zero-valued byte; it differs from the SQL NULL value.)

- LOAD DATA provides diagnostic information about which input values cause problems. To display this information, execute a SHOW WARNINGS statement after the LOAD DATA statement.

This and the following eight recipes describe how to handle these issues using LOAD DATA or mysqlimport. It's lengthy because there's a lot to cover.

Specifying the datafile location

You can load files located either on the server host or on the client host from which you issue the LOAD DATA statement. Telling MySQL where to find your datafile is a matter of knowing the rules that determine where it looks for the file (particularly important for files not in your current directory).

By default, the MySQL server assumes that the datafile is located on the server host. You can load local files that are located on the client host using LOAD DATA LOCAL rather than LOAD DATA, unless LOCAL capability is disabled by default.

Many of the examples in this chapter assume that LOCAL can be used. If that's not true for your system, adapt the examples: omit LOCAL from the statement, and make sure that the file is located on the MySQL server host and readable to the server.

If the LOAD DATA statement includes no LOCAL keyword, the MySQL server looks for the file on the server host using the following rules:

- Your MySQL account must have the FILE privilege, and the file to be loaded must be either located in the data directory for the default database or world readable.

- An absolute pathname fully specifies the location of the file in the filesystem and the server reads it from the given location.

- A relative pathname is interpreted two ways, depending on whether it has a single component or multiple components. For a single-component filename such as *mytbl.txt*, the server looks for the file in the database directory for the default database. (The operation fails if you have not selected a default database.) For a multiple-component filename such as *xyz/mytbl.txt*, the server looks for the file beginning in the MySQL data directory. That is, it expects to find *mytbl.txt* in a directory named *xyz*.

- If the secure_file_priv option is set to a directory path, MySQL is able to access import and export files only in this directory. Specify absolute path if you use secure_file_priv.

Database directories are located directly under the server's data directory, so these two statements are equivalent if the default database is cookbook:

```
mysql> LOAD DATA INFILE 'mytbl.txt' INTO TABLE mytbl;
mysql> LOAD DATA INFILE 'cookbook/mytbl.txt' INTO TABLE mytbl;
```

If the LOAD DATA statement includes the LOCAL keyword, your client program reads the file on the client host and sends its contents to the server. The client interprets the pathname like this:

- An absolute pathname fully specifies the location of the file in the filesystem.
- A relative pathname specifies the file location relative to the directory from which you stated the mysql client.

If your file is located on the client host, but you forget to indicate that it's local, an error occurs:

```
mysql> LOAD DATA 'mytbl.txt' INTO TABLE mytbl;
ERROR 1045 (28000): Access denied for user: 'user_name@host_name'
(Using password: YES)
```

That `Access denied` message can be confusing: if you're able to connect to the server and issue the LOAD DATA statement, it would seem that you've already gained access to MySQL, right? The error message means the server (not the client) tried to open *mytbl.txt* on the server host and could not access it.

If your MySQL server runs on the host from which you issue the LOAD DATA statement, "remote" and "local" refer to the same host. But the rules just discussed for locating datafiles still apply. Without LOCAL, the server reads the datafile directly. With LOCAL, the client program reads the file and sends its contents to the server.

mysqlimport uses the same rules for finding files as LOAD DATA. By default, it assumes that the datafile is located on the server host. To indicate that the file is local to the client host, specify the - -local (or -L) option on the command line.

LOAD DATA assumes that the table is located in the default database. To load a file into a specific database, qualify the table name with the database name. The following statement indicates that the mytbl table is located in the other_db database:

```
mysql> LOAD DATA LOCAL 'mytbl.txt' INTO TABLE other_db.mytbl;
```

mysqlimport always requires a database argument:

```
$ mysqlimport --local cookbook mytbl.txt
```

LOAD DATA assumes no relationship between the name of the datafile and the name of the table into which you load the file's contents. mysqlimport assumes a fixed relationship between the datafile name and the table name. Specifically, it uses the last component of the filename to determine the table name. For example, mysqlimport interprets *mytbl*, *mytbl.dat*, */home/paul/mytbl.csv*, and *C:\projects\mytbl.txt* all as files containing data for the mytbl table.

> ## Naming Datafiles Under Windows
>
> Windows systems use \ as the pathname separator in filenames. That's a bit of a problem because MySQL interprets the backslash as the escape character in string values. To specify a Windows pathname, use either doubled backslashes or forward slashes. These two statements show two ways of referring to the same Windows file:
>
> ```
> mysql> LOAD DATA LOCAL INFILE 'C:\\projects\\mydata.txt' INTO mytbl;
> mysql> LOAD DATA LOCAL INFILE 'C:/projects/mydata.txt' INTO mytbl;
> ```
>
> If the NO_BACKSLASH_ESCAPES SQL mode is enabled, the backslash is not special, and you do not double it:
>
> ```
> mysql> SET sql_mode = CONCAT('NO_BACKSLASH_ESCAPES,', @@sql_mode);
> mysql> LOAD DATA LOCAL INFILE 'C:\projects\mydata.txt' INTO mytbl;
> ```

13.2 Specifying Column and Line Delimiters

Problem

Your datafile uses nonstandard column or line delimiters.

Solution

Use the FIELDS TERMINATED BY and LINES TERMINATED BY clauses for the LOAD DATA INFILE statement and the --fields-terminated-by and --lines-terminated-by options for mysqlimport.

Discussion

By default, LOAD DATA assumes that datafile lines are terminated by linefeed (newline) characters and that values within a line are separated by tab characters. To provide explicit information about datafile format, use a FIELDS clause to describe the characteristics of fields within a line, and a LINES clause to specify the line-ending sequence. The following LOAD DATA statement indicates that the input file contains data values separated by colons and lines terminated by carriage returns:

```
mysql> LOAD DATA LOCAL INFILE 'mytbl.txt' INTO TABLE mytbl
    -> FIELDS TERMINATED BY ':' LINES TERMINATED BY '\r';
```

Each clause follows the table name. If both are present, FIELDS must precede LINES. The line and field termination indicators can contain multiple characters. For example, \r\n indicates that lines are terminated by carriage return/linefeed pairs.

The LINES clause also has a STARTING BY subclause. It specifies the sequence to be stripped from each input record. (Everything *up to* the given sequence is stripped.

If you specify STARTING BY 'X' and a record begins with abcX, all four leading characters are stripped.) Like TERMINATED BY, the sequence can have multiple characters. If TERMINATED BY and STARTING BY both are present in the LINES clause, they can appear in any order.

For mysqlimport, command options provide the format specifiers. Commands that correspond to the preceding two LOAD DATA statements look like this:

```
$ mysqlimport --local cookbook mytbl.txt
$ mysqlimport --local --fields-terminated-by=":" --lines-terminated-by="\r" \
    cookbook mytbl.txt
```

Option order doesn't matter for mysqlimport.

The FIELDS and LINES clauses understand hex notation to specify arbitrary format characters, which is useful for loading datafiles that use binary format codes. Suppose that a datafile has lines with Ctrl-A between fields and Ctrl-B at the end of lines. The ASCII values for Ctrl-A and Ctrl-B are 1 and 2, so you represent them as 0x01 and 0x02:

```
FIELDS TERMINATED BY 0x01 LINES TERMINATED BY 0x02
```

mysqlimport also understands hex constants for format specifiers. You may find this capability helpful if you don't like remembering how to type escape sequences on the command line or when it's necessary to use quotes around them. Tab is 0x09, linefeed is 0x0a, and carriage return is 0x0d. This command indicates that the datafile contains tab-delimited lines terminated by CRLF pairs:

```
$ mysqlimport --local --fields-terminated-by=0x09 \
    --lines-terminated-by=0x0d0a cookbook mytbl.txt
```

When you import datafiles, don't assume that LOAD DATA (or mysqlimport) knows more than it does. Some LOAD DATA frustrations occur because people expect MySQL to know more than it possibly can. Keep in mind that LOAD DATA has no idea at all about the format of your datafile. It makes certain assumptions about the input structure, represented as the default settings for the line and field terminators, and for the quote and escape character settings. If your input differs from those assumptions, you must tell MySQL so.

The line-ending sequence used in a datafile typically is determined by the system from which the file originated. Unix files normally have lines terminated by linefeeds, which you indicate like this:

```
LINES TERMINATED BY '\n'
```

Because \n happens to be the default line terminator, you need not specify that clause in this case unless you want to indicate the line-ending sequence explicitly. If files on your system don't use the Unix default (linefeed), you must specify the line terminator explicitly. For files that have lines ending in carriage returns or carriage return/linefeed pairs, respectively, use the appropriate LINES TERMINATED BY clause:

```
LINES TERMINATED BY '\r'
LINES TERMINATED BY '\r\n'
```

For example, to load a Windows file that contains tab-delimited fields and lines ending with CRLF pairs, use this LOAD DATA statement:

```
mysql> LOAD DATA LOCAL INFILE 'mytbl.txt' INTO TABLE mytbl
    -> LINES TERMINATED BY '\r\n';
```

The corresponding mysqlimport command is:

```
$ mysqlimport --local --lines-terminated-by="\r\n" cookbook mytbl.txt
```

If the file has been transferred from one machine to another, its contents may have been changed in subtle ways of which you're not aware. For example, a file transfer protocol (FTP) transfer between machines running different operating systems typically translates line endings to those that are appropriate for the destination machine if the transfer is performed in text mode rather than in binary (image) mode.

When in doubt, check the contents of your datafile using a hex dump program or other utility that displays a visible representation of whitespace characters like tab, carriage return, and linefeed. Under Unix, programs such as od or hexdump can display file contents in a variety of formats. If you don't have these or some comparable utility, the *transfer* directory of the recipes distribution contains hex dumpers written in Perl, Ruby, and Python (hexdump.pl, hexdump.rb, and hexdump.py), as well as programs that display printable representations of all characters of a file (see.pl, see.rb, and see.py). You may find them useful for examining files to see what they really contain.

13.3 Dealing with Quotes and Special Characters

Problem

Your datafile contains quotes or special characters and therefore cannot be loaded with default options.

Solution

Use the FIELDS clause for LOAD DATA INFILE with a combination of TERMINATED BY, ENCLOSED BY and ESCAPED BY. For mysqlimport, use the --fields-enclosed-by and --fields-escaped-by options.

Discussion

If your datafile contains quoted values or escaped characters, tell LOAD DATA to be aware of them so that it doesn't load uninterpreted data values into the database.

The FIELDS clause can specify other format options besides TERMINATED BY. By default, LOAD DATA assumes that values are unquoted, and it interprets the backslash (\) as an escape character for special characters. To indicate the value-quoting character explicitly, use ENCLOSED BY; MySQL will strip that character from the ends of data values during input processing. To change the default escape character, use ESCAPED BY.

You can use the ENCLOSED BY, ESCAPED BY, and TERMINATED BY subclauses in any order. For example, these FIELDS clauses are equivalent:

```
FIELDS TERMINATED BY ',' ENCLOSED BY '"'
FIELDS ENCLOSED BY '"' TERMINATED BY ','
```

The TERMINATED BY value can consist of multiple characters. If data values are separated within input lines by *@*, sequences, indicate that like this:

```
FIELDS TERMINATED BY '*@*'
```

To disable escape processing entirely, specify an empty escape sequence:

```
FIELDS ESCAPED BY ''
```

When you specify ENCLOSED BY to indicate which quote character should be stripped from data values, it's possible to include the quote character literally within data values by doubling it or by preceding it with the escape character. For example, if the quote character is " and the escape character is \, the input value "a""b\"c" is interpreted as a"b"c.

For mysqlimport, the corresponding command options for specifying quote and escape values are --fields-enclosed-by and --fields-escaped-by. (When using mysqlimport options that include quotes or backslashes or other characters that are special to your command interpreter, you may need to quote or escape the quote or escape characters.)

13.4 Handling Duplicate Key Values

Problem

You have duplicates in your datafile, and import fails with an error.

Solution

Instruct LOAD DATA INFILE and mysqlimport to either ignore or replace duplicates.

Discussion

By default, an error occurs if an input record duplicates an existing row in the column or columns that form a PRIMARY KEY or UNIQUE index. To control this behavior, specify IGNORE or REPLACE after the filename to tell MySQL to either ignore duplicate rows or replace old rows with the new ones.

Suppose that you periodically receive meteorological data about current weather conditions from various monitoring stations and that you store various measurements from these stations in a table that looks like this:

```
CREATE TABLE weatherdata
(
  station INT UNSIGNED NOT NULL,
  type    ENUM('precip','temp','cloudiness','humidity','barometer') NOT NULL,
  value   FLOAT,
  PRIMARY KEY (station, type)
);
```

The table includes a primary key on the combination of station ID and measurement type to ensure that it contains only one row per station per type of measurement. The table is intended to hold only current conditions, so when new measurements for a given station are loaded into the table, they should kick out the station's previous measurements. To accomplish this, use the REPLACE keyword:

```
mysql> LOAD DATA LOCAL INFILE 'data.txt' REPLACE INTO TABLE weatherdata;
```

mysqlimport has --ignore and --replace options that correspond to the IGNORE and REPLACE keywords for LOAD DATA.

13.5 Obtaining Diagnostics About Bad Input Data

Problem

You found differences between the datafile and data loaded into the database and want to know why import failed for those values.

Solution

Use the SHOW WARNINGS statement.

Discussion

LOAD DATA displays an information line to indicate whether there are any problematic input values. If so, use SHOW WARNINGS to find where they are and what the problems are.

When a LOAD DATA statement finishes, it returns a line of information that tells you how many errors or data conversion problems occurred, for example:

```
Records: 134  Deleted: 0  Skipped: 2  Warnings: 13
```

These values provide general information about the import operation:

- Records indicates the number of records found in the file.
- Deleted and Skipped are related to the treatment of input records that duplicate existing table rows on unique index values. Deleted indicates how many rows were deleted from the table and replaced by input records, and Skipped indicates how many input records were ignored in favor of existing rows.
- Warnings is something of a catchall that indicates the number of problems found while loading data values into columns. Either a value stores into a column properly or it doesn't. In the latter case, the value ends up in MySQL as something different, and MySQL counts it as a warning. (Storing a string abc into a numeric column results in a stored value of 0, for example.)

What do these values tell you? The Records value normally should match the number of lines in the input file. If it doesn't, that's a sign that MySQL interprets the file as having a different format than it actually has. In this case, you'll likely also see a high Warnings value, which indicates that many values had to be converted because they didn't match the expected data type. The solution to this problem often is to specify the proper FIELDS and LINES clauses.

Assuming that your FIELDS and LINES format specifiers are correct, a nonzero Warnings count indicates the presence of bad input values. You can't tell from the numbers in the LOAD DATA information line which input records had problems or which columns were bad. To get that information, issue a SHOW WARNINGS statement.

Suppose that a table t has this structure:

```
CREATE TABLE t
(
  i INT,
  c CHAR(3),
  d DATE
);
```

And suppose that a datafile *data.txt* looks like this:

```
1          1          1
abc        abc        abc
2010-10-10 2010-10-10 2010-10-10
```

Loading the file into the table causes a number, a string, and a date to be loaded into each of the three columns. Doing so results in several data conversions and warnings, which you can see using SHOW WARNINGS immediately following LOAD DATA:

```
mysql> LOAD DATA LOCAL INFILE 'data.txt' INTO TABLE t;
Query OK, 3 rows affected, 5 warnings (0.01 sec)
Records: 3  Deleted: 0  Skipped: 0  Warnings: 5
mysql> SHOW WARNINGS;
+---------+------+-----------------------------------------------------------+
| Level   | Code | Message                                                   |
+---------+------+-----------------------------------------------------------+
| Warning | 1265 | Data truncated for column 'd' at row 1                    |
| Warning | 1366 | Incorrect integer value: 'abc' for column 'i' at row 2    |
| Warning | 1265 | Data truncated for column 'd' at row 2                    |
| Warning | 1265 | Data truncated for column 'i' at row 3                    |
| Warning | 1265 | Data truncated for column 'c' at row 3                    |
+---------+------+-----------------------------------------------------------+
5 rows in set (0.00 sec)
```

The SHOW WARNINGS output helps you determine which values were converted and why. The resulting table looks like this:

```
mysql> SELECT * FROM t;
+------+------+------------+
| i    | c    | d          |
+------+------+------------+
|    1 | 1    | 0000-00-00 |
|    0 | abc  | 0000-00-00 |
| 2010 | 201  | 2010-10-10 |
+------+------+------------+
```

13.6 Skipping Datafile Lines

Problem

You want to skip the few first lines from a datafile.

Solution

Use an IGNORE...LINES clause for LOAD DATA INFILE and the --ignore-lines option for mysqlimport.

Discussion

To skip the first *n* lines of a datafile, add an IGNORE *n* LINES clause to the LOAD DATA statement. For example, a file might include an initial line of column labels. You can skip it like this:

```
mysql> LOAD DATA LOCAL INFILE 'mytbl.txt' INTO TABLE mytbl
    -> IGNORE 1 LINES;
```

mysqlimport supports an --ignore-lines=*n* option that corresponds to IGNORE *n* LINES.

13.7 Specifying Input Column Order

Problem

Column order in the datafile and the table is different, and you need to change it for the import.

Solution

Specify the order of the columns when importing.

Discussion

LOAD DATA assumes that columns in the datafile have the same order as the columns in the table. If that's not true, specify a list to indicate the table columns into which to load the datafile columns. Suppose that your table has columns a, b, and c, but successive columns in the datafile correspond to columns b, c, and a. Load the file like this:

```
mysql> LOAD DATA LOCAL INFILE 'mytbl.txt' INTO TABLE mytbl (b,c,a);
```

mysqlimport has a corresponding --columns option to specify the column list:

```
$ mysqlimport --local --columns=b,c,a cookbook mytbl.txt
```

13.8 Preprocessing Input Values Before Inserting Them

Problem

Values in the datafile cannot be inserted into the database as is. You need to modify them before inserting.

Solution

Use a SET clause for LOAD DATA INFILE and MySQL functions to modify values.

Discussion

LOAD DATA can perform limited preprocessing of input values before inserting them, which sometimes enables you to map input data onto more appropriate values before loading them into your table. This is useful when values are not in a format suitable for loading into a table (for example, they are in the wrong units, or two input fields must be combined and inserted into a single column).

The previous section shows how to specify a column list for LOAD DATA to indicate how input fields correspond to table columns. The column list also can name user-defined variables such that for each input record, the input fields are assigned to the variables. You can then perform calculations with those variables before inserting the result into the table. Specify these calculations in a SET clause that names one or more *col_name* = *expr* assignments, separated by commas.

Suppose that a datafile has the following columns, with the first line providing column labels:

```
Date        Time      Name        Weight  State
2006-09-01  12:00:00  Bill Wills  200     Nevada
2006-09-02  09:00:00  Jeff Deft   150     Oklahoma
2006-09-04  03:00:00  Bob Hobbs   225     Utah
2006-09-07  08:00:00  Hank Banks  175     Texas
```

Suppose also that the file is to be loaded into a table that has these columns:

```
CREATE TABLE t
(
  dt         DATETIME,
  last_name  CHAR(10),
  first_name CHAR(10),
  weight_kg  FLOAT,
  st_abbrev  CHAR(2)
);
```

To import the file, you must address several mismatches between its fields and the table columns:

- The file contains separate date and time fields that must be combined into date-and-time values for insertion into the DATETIME column.

- The file contains a name field, which must be split into separate first and last name values for insertion into the first_name and last_name columns.

- The file contains a weight in pounds, which must be converted to kilograms for insertion into the weight_kg column (1 lb. equals .454 kg.).

- The file contains state names, but the table contains two-letter abbreviations. The name can be mapped to the abbreviation by performing a lookup in the states table.

To handle these conversions, skip the first line that contains the column labels, assign each input column to a user-defined variable, and write a SET clause to perform the calculations:

```
mysql> LOAD DATA LOCAL INFILE 'data.txt' INTO TABLE t
    -> IGNORE 1 LINES
    -> (@date,@time,@name,@weight_lb,@state)
    -> SET dt = CONCAT(@date,' ',@time),
    ->     first_name = SUBSTRING_INDEX(@name,' ',1),
    ->     last_name = SUBSTRING_INDEX(@name,' ',-1),
    ->     weight_kg = @weight_lb * .454,
    ->     st_abbrev = (SELECT abbrev FROM states WHERE name = @state);
```

After the import operation, the table contains these rows:

```
mysql> SELECT * FROM t;
+---------------------+-----------+------------+-----------+-----------+
| dt                  | last_name | first_name | weight_kg | st_abbrev |
+---------------------+-----------+------------+-----------+-----------+
| 2006-09-01 12:00:00 | Wills     | Bill       |      90.8  | NV        |
| 2006-09-02 09:00:00 | Deft      | Jeff       |      68.1  | OK        |
| 2006-09-04 03:00:00 | Hobbs     | Bob        |     102.15 | UT        |
| 2006-09-07 08:00:00 | Banks     | Hank       |      79.45 | TX        |
+---------------------+-----------+------------+-----------+-----------+
```

LOAD DATA can perform data value reformatting, as just shown. Other examples showing uses for this capability occur elsewhere. (For example, Recipe 13.12 uses it to map NULL values, and Recipe 14.16 rewrites non-ISO dates to ISO format during data import.) However, although LOAD DATA can map input values to other values, it cannot outright reject an input record that is found to contain unsuitable values. To do that, either preprocess the input file to remove these records or issue a DELETE statement after loading the file.

13.9 Ignoring Datafile Columns

Problem

Your datafile contains extra fields that should not be added to the database.

Solution

Specify column order when importing data. In place of the columns that need to be ignored, specify a user-defined variable.

Discussion

Extra columns at the end of input lines are easy to handle. If a line contains more columns than are in the table, LOAD DATA just ignores them (although it might produce a nonzero warning count).

Skipping columns in the middle of lines is a bit more involved. To handle this, use a column list with LOAD DATA that assigns the columns to be ignored to a dummy user-defined variable. Suppose that you want to load information from a Unix password file */etc/passwd*, which contains lines in the following format:

```
account:password:UID:GID:GECOS:directory:shell
```

Suppose also that you don't want to load the password and directory columns. A table to hold the information in the remaining columns looks like this:

```
CREATE TABLE passwd
(
  account   CHAR(8),  # login name
```

```
    uid        INT,       # user ID
    gid        INT,       # group ID
    gecos      CHAR(60),  # name, phone, office, etc.
    shell      CHAR(60),  # command interpreter
    PRIMARY KEY(account)
);
```

To load the file, specify that the column delimiter is a colon. Also, tell LOAD DATA to skip the second and sixth fields that contain the password and directory. To do this, add a column list in the statement. The list should include the name of each column to load into the table and a dummy user-defined variable for columns to be ignored (you can use the same variable for all of them). The resulting statement looks like this:

```
mysql> LOAD DATA LOCAL INFILE '/etc/passwd' INTO TABLE passwd
    -> FIELDS TERMINATED BY ':'
    -> (account,@dummy,uid,gid,gecos,@dummy,shell);
```

The corresponding mysqlimport command includes a --columns option:

```
$ mysqlimport --local \
    --columns="account,@dummy,uid,gid,gecos,@dummy,shell" \
    --fields-terminated-by=":" cookbook /etc/passwd
```

See Also

Another approach to ignoring columns is to preprocess the input file to remove columns. The yank_col.pl utility, included in the recipes distribution, can extract and display datafile columns in any order.

13.10 Importing CSV Files

Problem

You want to load a file that is in CSV format.

Solution

Use the appropriate format specifiers with LOAD DATA or mysqlimport.

Discussion

Datafiles in CSV format contain values that are delimited by commas rather than tabs and that may be quoted with double-quote characters. A CSV file, *mytbl.txt*, containing lines that end with carriage return/linefeed pairs can be loaded into mytbl using LOAD DATA:

```
mysql> LOAD DATA LOCAL INFILE 'mytbl.txt' INTO TABLE mytbl
    -> FIELDS TERMINATED BY ',' ENCLOSED BY '"'
    -> LINES TERMINATED BY '\r\n';
```

Or like this using `mysqlimport`:

```
$ mysqlimport --local --lines-terminated-by="\r\n" \
    --fields-terminated-by="," --fields-enclosed-by="\"" \
    cookbook mytbl.txt
```

13.11 Exporting Query Results from MySQL

Problem

You want to export the result of a query from MySQL into a file or another program.

Solution

Use the `SELECT...INTO OUTFILE` statement, or redirect the output of the `mysql` program.

Discussion

The `SELECT...INTO OUTFILE` statement exports a query result directly into a file on the server host. To capture the result on the client host instead, redirect the output of the `mysql` program. These methods have different strengths and weaknesses; get to know them both, and apply whichever one best suits a given situation.

Exporting using the SELECT...INTO OUTFILE statement

The syntax for the `SELECT...INTO OUTFILE` statement combines a regular `SELECT` with `INTO OUTFILE` *file_name*. The default output format is the same as for `LOAD DATA`, so the following statement exports the `passwd` table into */tmp/passwd.txt* as a tab-delimited, linefeed-terminated file:

```
mysql> SELECT * FROM passwd INTO OUTFILE '/tmp/passwd.txt';
```

To change the output format, use options similar to those used with `LOAD DATA` that indicate how to quote and delimit columns and records. For example, to export the `passwd` table (created earlier in Recipe 13.1) in CSV format with CRLF-terminated lines, use this statement:

```
mysql> SELECT * FROM passwd INTO OUTFILE '/tmp/passwd.txt'
    -> FIELDS TERMINATED BY ',' ENCLOSED BY '"'
    -> LINES TERMINATED BY '\r\n';
```

`SELECT...INTO OUTFILE` has these properties:

- The output file is created directly by the MySQL server, so the filename should indicate where to write the file on the server host. The file location is determined using the same rules as for `LOAD DATA` without `LOCAL`, as described in Recipe 13.1.

(There is no `LOCAL` version of the statement analogous to the `LOCAL` version of `LOAD DATA`.)

- You must have the MySQL `FILE` privilege to execute the `SELECT...INTO OUTFILE` statement.

- The output file must not already exist. (This prevents MySQL from overwriting files that may be important.)

- You should have a login account on the server host or some way to access files on that host. `SELECT...INTO OUTFILE` is of no value to you if you cannot retrieve the output file.

- Under Unix, before MySQL 8.0.17, the file is created world readable and is owned by the account used for running the MySQL server. This means that although you can read the file, you may not be able to delete it unless you can log in using that account. As of MySQL 8.0.17, the file is world writable.

- If the `secure_file_priv` option is set, you can only export into the specified directory.

Exporting using the mysql client program

Because `SELECT...INTO OUTFILE` writes the datafile on the server host, you cannot use it unless your MySQL account has the `FILE` privilege. To export data into a local file that you own, use another strategy. If all you require is tab-delimited output, do a "poor-man's export" by executing a `SELECT` statement with the `mysql` program and redirecting the output to a file. That way you can write query results into a file on your local host without the `FILE` privilege. Here's an example that exports the login name and command interpreter columns from the `passwd` table:

```
$ mysql -e "SELECT account, shell FROM passwd" --skip-column-names \
    cookbook > shells.txt
```

The `-e` option specifies the statement to execute (see Recipe 1.5), and `--skip-column-names` tells MySQL not to write the row of column names that normally precedes statement output (see Recipe 1.7). The `>` operator instructs `mysql` to redirect output into the file. Otherwise, the result will be printed onto the screen.

Note that MySQL writes `NULL` values as the string "NULL." Some postprocessing to convert them may be needed, depending on what you want to do with the output file. We discuss how to handle `NULL` values during export and import in Recipe 13.12.

It's possible to produce output in formats other than tab-delimited by sending the query result into a postprocessing filter that converts tabs to something else. For example, to use hash marks as delimiters, convert all tabs to # characters (*TAB* indicates where you type a tab character in the command):

```
$ mysql --skip-column-names -e "your statement here" db_name \
    | sed -e "s/TAB/#/g" > output_file
```

You can also use `tr` for this purpose, although the syntax varies for different implementations of this utility. For macOS or Linux, the command looks like this:

```
$ mysql --skip-column-names -e "your statement here" db_name \
    | tr "\t" "#" > output_file
```

The `mysql` commands just shown use `--skip-column-names` to suppress column
labels from appearing in the output. Under some circumstances, it may be useful to
include the labels (for example, if they will be useful when importing the file later). In
this respect, exporting query results with `mysql` is more flexible than `SELECT...INTO`
`OUTFILE` because the latter cannot produce output that includes column labels.

Another way to export query results to a file on the client host is to use the
`mysql_to_text.pl` utility, available in the recipes distribution. That program has
options that enable you to specify the output format explicitly. To export a query
result as an Excel spreadsheet or XML document, use `mysql_to_excel.pl` and
`mysql_to_xml.pl` utilities.

13.12 Importing and Exporting NULL Values

Problem

You need to represent `NULL` values in a datafile.

Solution

Use a value not otherwise present so that you can distinguish `NULL` from all other
legitimate non-`NULL` values. When you import the file, convert instances of that value
to `NULL`.

Discussion

There's no standard for representing `NULL` values in datafiles, which makes them
problematic for import and export operations. The difficulty arises from the fact
that `NULL` indicates the *absence* of a value, and that's not easy to represent literally
in a datafile. Using an empty column value is the most obvious thing to do, but
that's ambiguous for string-valued columns because there is no way to distinguish a
`NULL` represented that way from a true empty string. Empty values can be a problem
for other data types as well. For example, if you load an empty value with `LOAD`
`DATA` into a numeric column, it is stored as 0 rather than as `NULL` and thus becomes
indistinguishable from a true 0 in the input.

The usual solution to this problem is to represent NULL using a value not otherwise present in the data. This is how LOAD DATA and mysqlimport handle the issue: they understand the value of \N by convention to mean NULL. (\N is interpreted as NULL only when it occurs by itself, not as part of a larger value such as x\N or \Nx.) For example, if you load the following datafile with LOAD DATA, it treats the instances of \N as NULL:

```
str1    13      1997-10-14
str2    \N      2009-05-07
\N      15      \N
\N      \N      1973-07-14
```

But you might want to interpret values other than \N as signifying NULL, and you might have different conventions in different columns. Consider the following datafile:

```
str1    13 1997-10-14
str2    -1 2009-05-07
Unknown 15
Unknown -1 1973-07-15
```

The first column contains strings, and Unknown signifies NULL. The second column contains integers, and -1 signifies NULL. The third column contains dates, and an empty value signifies NULL. What to do?

To handle situations like this, use LOAD DATA's input preprocessing capability: specify a column list that assigns input values to user-defined variables, and use a SET clause that maps the special values to true NULL values. If the datafile is named *has_nulls.txt*, the following LOAD DATA statement properly interprets its contents:

```
mysql> LOAD DATA LOCAL INFILE 'has_nulls.txt'
    -> INTO TABLE t (@c1,@c2,@c3)
    -> SET c1 = IF(@c1='Unknown',NULL,@c1),
    ->     c2 = IF(@c2=-1,NULL,@c2),
    ->     c3 = IF(@c3='',NULL,@c3);
```

The resulting data after import looks like this:

```
+------+------+------------+
| c1   | c2   | c3         |
+------+------+------------+
| str1 |   13 | 1997-10-14 |
| str2 | NULL | 2009-05-07 |
| NULL |   15 | NULL       |
| NULL | NULL | 1973-07-15 |
+------+------+------------+
```

The preceding discussion pertains to interpreting NULL values for import into MySQL, but it's also necessary to think about NULL values when transferring data in the other direction—from MySQL into other programs. Here are some examples:

- `SELECT...INTO OUTFILE` writes `NULL` values as `\N`. Will another program understand that convention? If not, convert `\N` to something the program understands. For example, the `SELECT` statement can export the column using an expression like this:

  ```
  IFNULL(col_name,'Unknown')
  ```

- You can use `mysql` in batch mode as an easy way to produce tab-delimited output (see Recipe 13.11), but then `NULL` values appear in the output as instances of the word *NULL*. If that word occurs nowhere else in the output, you may be able to postprocess it to convert instances of it to something more appropriate. For example, you can use a one-line `sed` command:

  ```
  $ sed -e "s/NULL/\\N/g" data.txt > tmp
  ```

If the word *NULL* appears where it represents something other than a `NULL` value, it's ambiguous, and you should probably export your data differently. For example, use `IFNULL()` to map `NULL` values to something else.

13.13 Exporting Data in SQL Format

Problem

You want to export data in SQL format.

Solution

Use `mysqldump` or `mysqlpump`.

Discussion

SQL format is widely used for exporting and importing data. It has such advantages that it could be executed inside the MySQL clients, as we discuss in Recipes 1.6 and 13.14. SQL files can also have special information, such as replication source position (Recipe 3.3), default character set, and so on. SQL files can contain data for all tables, triggers, events, and stored routines on the server, so you can use them to copy your MySQL installation.

Since the very first versions of MySQL, MySQL distribution has contained a `mysqldump` utility that allows you to export (dump) data into a SQL file. `mysqldump` is very easy to use. For example, to dump all databases, run it with the `--all-databases` option:

```
$ mysqldump --all-databases > all-databases.sql
```

To copy all tables in the `cookbook` database, use its name as a `mysqldump` parameter:

```
$ mysqldump cookbook > cookbook.sql
```

To export just a few tables in the cookbook database, specify their names after the database name. Thus, to copy the limbs and patients tables, run the following:

```
$ mysqldump cookbook limbs patients > limbs_patients.sql
```

The shell command > redirects output of the mysqldump into a file. You can also specify a --result-file option to instruct mysqldump to store the result in the named file.

The resulting file will contain SQL instructions that allow you to re-create a database and tables in it and then fill them with data.

Normally, MySQL works in high-concurrent environments. Therefore, mysqldump supports the following options to ensure consistency of the resulting backup file:

--lock-all-tables
    Locks all tables across all databases with a read lock, preventing writes to any of the tables until the dump is finished.

--lock-tables
    Locks all tables for each dumped database separately. This protection prevents writes only into a database being exported, but it does not guarantee consistency of the resulting dump for multiple-database backups.

--single-transaction
    Starts a transaction before dumping. This option does not prevent any write and still guarantees consistency of the backup. This is the recommended option for backups of tables that use transactional storage engines.

Since ensuring consistency may affect performance of the high-concurrent writes, it is advisable to run mysqldump on the read-only replica.

mysqldump is a mature tool, but it exports data in a single thread. This may not be as performant as we expect nowadays. Therefore, since version 5.7, MySQL distribution includes one more backup tool: mysqlpump.

mysqlpump works similarly to mysqldump. You can use the same options as for mysql dump to export all databases, a single database, or just a few tables. But mysqlpump also supports parallel processing to speed up the dump process, progress indicators, smarter dumping of the user accounts, filters, and other features that mysqldump lacks.

Thus, to create a dump of the whole MySQL instance in four threads, protect the dump with the `--single-transaction` option and see the progress bar use command:

```
$ mysqlpump --default-parallelism=4 --single-transaction \
 > --watch-progress > all-databases.sql
Dump progress: 1/2 tables, 0/7 rows
Dump progress: 142/143 tables, 2574113/4076473 rows
Dump completed in 1837
```

 mysqlpump supports the `--single-transaction` option, but does not support `--lock-all-tables` and `--lock-tables`. It has the `--add-locks` option instead that surrounds each dumped table with LOCK TABLES and UNLOCK TABLES statements.

See Also

For additional information about `mysqldump`, see "mysqldump—A Database Backup Program" (*https://oreil.ly/tFK7T*), and for additional information about `mysqlpump`, see "mysqlpump—A Database Backup Program" (*https://oreil.ly/oSUHg*) in the MySQL Reference Manual.

13.14 Importing SQL Data

Problem

You have a SQL dump file and want to import it.

Solution

Process the file using `mysql` client or MySQL Shell.

Discussion

A SQL dump is just a file with SQL commands. Therefore, you can read it with `mysql` client, as we discussed in Recipe 1.6:

```
$ mysql -ucbuser -p cookbook < cookbook.sql
```

MySQL Shell supports similar functionality in SQL mode.

To load a dump from the command line, specify the `--sql` option for the `mysqlsh` client and redirect input into it:

```
$ mysqlsh cbuser:cbpass@127.0.0.1:33060/cookbook --sql < all-databases.sql
```

To load a dump while in the interactive session, switch to SQL mode and use the `\source` command, or its shortcut, `\`:

13.15 Exporting Query Results as XML

Problem

You want to export the result of a query as an XML document.

Solution

Use the `mysql` client or `mysqldump` with the `--xml` option.

Discussion

The `mysql` client can produce XML-format output from a query result (see Recipe 1.7).

Suppose that a table named `expt` contains test scores from an experiment:

```
mysql> SELECT * FROM expt;
+---------+------+-------+
| subject | test | score |
+---------+------+-------+
| Jane    | A    |    47 |
| Jane    | B    |    50 |
| Jane    | C    |  NULL |
| Jane    | D    |  NULL |
| Marvin  | A    |    52 |
| Marvin  | B    |    45 |
| Marvin  | C    |    53 |
| Marvin  | D    |  NULL |
+---------+------+-------+
```

Run `mysql` client with the `--xml` option:

```
$ mysql --xml cookbook -e "SELECT * FROM expt;" < expt.xml
```

The resulting XML document, *expt.xml*, looks like this:

```
<?xml version="1.0"?>

<resultset statement="SELECT * FROM expt"↵
xmlns:xsi="http://www.w3.org/2001/XMLSchema-instance">
  <row>
        <field name="subject">Jane</field>
        <field name="test">A</field>
        <field name="score">47</field>
  </row>
…
  <row>
        <field name="subject">Marvin</field>
        <field name="test">D</field>
        <field name="score" xsi:nil="true" />
  </row>
</resultset>
```

To produce similar output with `mysqldump`, run it with the `--xml` option. The resulting file will contain the table definition unless you specify the `--no-create-info` option:

```
$ mysqldump --xml cookbook expt
<?xml version="1.0"?>
<mysqldump xmlns:xsi="http://www.w3.org/2001/XMLSchema-instance">
SET @MYSQLDUMP_TEMP_LOG_BIN = @@SESSION.SQL_LOG_BIN;
SET @@SESSION.SQL_LOG_BIN= 0;
SET @@GLOBAL.GTID_PURGED=/*!80000 '+'*/ '910c760a-0751-11eb-9da8-0242dc638c6c:1-385,
9113f6b1-0751-11eb-9e7d-0242dc638c6c:1-385,
abf2d315-fb9a-11ea-9815-02421e8c78f1:1-52911';
<database name="cookbook">
        <table_structure name="expt">
                <field Field="subject" Type="varchar(10)"↵
                    Null="YES" Key="" Extra="" Comment="" />
                <field Field="test" Type="varchar(5)"↵
                    Null="YES" Key="" Extra="" Comment="" />
                <field Field="score" Type="int"↵
                    Null="YES" Key="" Extra="" Comment="" />
                <options Name="expt" Engine="InnoDB" Version="10" Row_format="Dynamic"↵
                    Rows="8" Avg_row_length="2048" Data_length="16384" Max_data_length="0"↵
                    Index_length="0" Data_free="0" Create_time="2022-02-06 13:06:35"↵
                    Update_time="2022-02-06 13:06:35" Collation="utf8mb4_0900_ai_ci"↵
                    Create_options="" Comment="" />
        </table_structure>
        <table_data name="expt">
        <row>
                <field name="subject">Jane</field>
                <field name="test">A</field>
                <field name="score">47</field>
        </row>
...
        <row>
                <field name="subject">Marvin</field>
                <field name="test">D</field>
                <field name="score" xsi:nil="true" />
        </row>
        </table_data>
</database>
SET @@SESSION.SQL_LOG_BIN = @MYSQLDUMP_TEMP_LOG_BIN;
```

13.16 Importing XML into MySQL

Problem

You want to import an XML document into a MySQL table.

Solution

Use the `LOAD XML` statement.

Discussion

Importing an XML document depends on being able to parse the document and extract record contents from it. How you do that depends on how the document is written. To read XML files created by the `mysql` client, use the LOAD XML statement.

To load the `expt.xml` file that we created in Recipe 13.15, run the following:

```
LOAD XML LOCAL INFILE 'expt.xml'  INTO TABLE expt;
```

The LOAD XML statement automatically recognizes three different XML formats:

Column names as attributes and column values as attribute values.

```
<row subject="Jane" test="A" score=47 />
```

Column names as tags and column values as tag values.

```
<row>
        <subject>Jane</subject>
        <test>B</test>
        <score>50</score>
    </row>
```

Column names as values of the attribute name *of the tag* field, *and column values as their values.*

```
<row>
        <field name="subject">Jane</field>
        <field name="test">C</field>
        <field name="score" xsi:nil="true" />
    </row>
```

This is the same format that `mysql`, `mysqldump`, and other MySQL utilities use.

If your XML file uses a different tag name, specify it with a ROWS IDENTIFIED BY clause. For example, if rows for the table `expt` are defined as follows:

```
<test>
    <field name="subject">Jane</field>
    <field name="test">D</field>
    <field name="score" xsi:nil="true" />
  </test>
```

Load them with the following statement:

```
LOAD XML LOCAL INFILE 'expt.xml'  INTO TABLE expt ROWS IDENTIFIED BY '<test>';
```

13.17 Importing Data in JSON Format

Problem

You have a JSON file and want to import it into a MySQL database.

Solution

Use the MySQL Shell `importJson` utility.

Discussion

JSON is a popular format for storing data so it can be application generated or directly exported from the MongoDB database.

The `importJson` utility takes the path to the JSON file and dictionary of options as arguments. You can import JSON either into a collection or into a table. In the latter case, you need to specify the `tableColumn` in which to store the document unless the default value, `doc`, works for you.

The document should contain a list of JSON objects, separated by a new line. This list should not be a member of a JSON array or another object:

```
{"arms": 2, "legs": 2, "thing": "human" }
{"arms": 0, "legs": 6, "thing": "insect" }
{"arms": 10, "legs": 0, "thing": "squid" }
{"arms": 0, "legs": 0, "thing": "fish" }
{"arms": 0, "legs": 99, "thing": "centipede" }
{"arms": 0, "legs": 4, "thing": "table" }
{"arms": 2, "legs": 4, "thing": "armchair" }
{"arms": 1, "legs": 0, "thing": "phonograph" }
{"arms": 0, "legs": 3, "thing": "tripod" }
{"arms": 2, "legs": 1, "thing": "Peg Leg Pete" }
{"arms": null, "legs": null, "thing": "space alien" }
```

You will find a JSON dump of the `CollectionLimbs` collection in the *collections/limbs.json* file of the `recipes` distribution.

To insert data from the JSON file into the `CollectionLimbs` collection, run following code:

```
MySQL  cookbook  JS > options = {❶
                    ->    schema: "cookbook",
                    ->    collection: "CollectionLimbs"
                    -> }
                    ->
{
    "collection": "CollectionLimbs",
    "schema": "cookbook"
}
 MySQL  cookbook  JS > util.importJson("limbs.json", options)❷
Importing from file "limbscol.json" to collection `cookbook`.`CollectionLimbs` ↵
in MySQL Server at 127.0.0.1:33060

.. 11.. 11
Processed 1.42 KB in 11 documents in 0.0070 sec (11.00 documents/s)
Total successfully imported documents 11 (11.00 documents/s)
```

① First, create a dictionary object with options. At the minimum, you need to specify the collection name and the schema.

② Then call `util.importJson` with the path to the JSON file and options dictionary as arguments.

You can also call the `importJson` utility from the command line without entering an interactive MySQL Shell session. To do it, use the `--import` option of the `mysqlsh` command, and specify the path to the JSON file and target collection as parameters:

```
$ mysqlsh cbuser:cbpass@127.0.0.1:33060/cookbook \
> --import limbs.json CollectionLimbs
WARNING: Using a password on the command-line interface can be insecure.
Importing from file "limbs.json" to collection `cookbook`.`CollectionLimbs` ↵
in MySQL Server at 127.0.0.1:33060

.. 11.. 11
Processed 506 bytes in 11 documents in 0.0067 sec (11.00 documents/s)
Total successfully imported documents 11 (11.00 documents/s)
```

> If no collection or a table with the specific name exists in the database, the `importJson` utility will create it for you.

13.18 Importing Data from MongoDB

Problem

You want to import data from a MongoDB collection.

Solution

Export the collection from MongoDB into a file with the help of the `mongoexport` utility, and use `importJson` with the `"convertBsonTypes": true` option to import the collection into MySQL.

Solution

`importJson` can import documents exported from MongoDB with the help of the `mongoexport` utility. Additionally, it can convert BSON data types into MySQL format. To explore this feature, put `"convertBsonTypes": true` into the options dictionary and perform the import:

```
MySQL  cookbook  JS > options = {
                -> "schema": "cookbook",
                -> "collection": "blogs",
```

```
                  ->   "convertBsonTypes": true
                  -> }
                  ->
{
    "collection": "blogs",
    "convertBsonTypes": true,
    "schema": "cookbook"
}
 MySQL  cookbook  JS > util.importJson("blogs.json", options)
Importing from file "blogs.json" to collection `cookbook`.`blogs` ↵
in MySQL Server at 127.0.0.1:33060

.. 2.. 2
Processed 240 bytes in 2 documents in 0.0070 sec (2.00 documents/s)
Total successfully imported documents 2 (2.00 documents/s)
```

The resulting `blogs` collection uses data in MySQL format. We can check it if selected all documents from the collection using MySQL Shell:

```
    MySQL  cookbook  JS > shell.getSession().
                      -> getSchema('cookbook').
                      -> getCollection('blogs').
                      -> find()
                      ->
{
    "_id": "6029abb942e2e9c45760eabc", ❶
    "author": "Ann Smith",
    "comment": "That's Awesome!",
    "date_created": "2021-02-13T23:01:13.154Z" ❷
}
{
    "_id": "6029abd842e2e9c45760eabd",
    "author": "John Doe",
    "comment": "Love it!",
    "date_created": "2021-02-14T11:20:03Z"
}
2 documents in set (0.0006 sec)
```

❶ The BSON object identification (OID) value, `"_id":{"$oid":"6029abb94 2e2e9c45760eabc"}`, converted to MySQL ID format.

❷ The BSON Date value, `"date_created":{"$date":"2021-02-13T23: 01:13.154Z"}`, converted to MySQL Date format.

You will find a JSON dump of the `blogs` collection in the *collections/blogs.json* file of the `recipes` distribution.

13.19 Exporting Data in JSON Format

Problem

You want to export a MySQL collection into a JSON file.

Solution

Use MySQL Shell to retrieve the result in the JSON format. Redirect the output into a file if needed.

Discussion

MySQL Shell allows you to retrieve data in JSON format. The following code snippet dumps the `CollectionLimbs` collection and redirects result into a file:

```
$ mysqlsh cbuser:cbpass@127.0.0.1:33060/cookbook \
> -e "limbs=shell.getSession().getSchema('cookbook').
> getCollection('CollectionLimbs'). ❶
> find().execute().fetchAll(); ❷
> println(limbs);" > limbs.json ❸
```

❶ Select the collection.

❷ Fetch all rows from the collection.

❸ Print the result and redirect command output into a file.

The resulting file will contain an array of JSON documents. This is not the same format that the MySQL Shell `importJson` utility can use. If you want to import the data back into MySQL, modify the resulting file. You can do it with help of the `jq` utility:

```
$ jq '.[]' limbs.json > limbs_fixed.json
```

jq reads the `limbs.json` file and prints each of its array elements into standard output. Then, we redirect the result into a `limbs_fixed.json` file.

See Also

For additional information about the jq utility, see the jq Manual (*https://oreil.ly/Or2KB*).

13.20 Guessing Table Structure from a Datafile

Problem

Someone gives you a datafile and says, "Here, put this into MySQL for me." But no table yet exists to hold the data. You need to create a table that will hold data from the file.

Solution

Use a utility that guesses the table structure by examining the datafile contents.

Discussion

Sometimes you must import data into MySQL for which no table has yet been set up. You can create the table yourself, based on any knowledge you have about the contents of the file. Or you might be able to avoid some of the work by using guess_table.pl, a utility located in the *transfer* directory of the recipes distribution. guess_table.pl reads the datafile to see what kind of information it contains, then attempts to produce an appropriate CREATE TABLE statement that matches the contents of the file. This script is necessarily imperfect because column contents sometimes are ambiguous. (For example, a column containing a small number of distinct strings might be a VARCHAR column or an ENUM.) Still, it may be easier to tweak the CREATE TABLE statement that guess_table.pl produces than to write the statement from scratch. This utility also has diagnostic value, although that's not its primary purpose. For example, if you believe a column contains only numbers, but guess_table.pl indicates that it should be a VARCHAR column, that tells you the column contains at least one nonnumeric value.

guess_table.pl assumes that its input is in tab-delimited, linefeed-terminated format. It also assumes valid input because any attempt to guess data types based on possibly flawed data is doomed to failure. This means, for example, that if a date column is to be recognized as such, it should be in ISO format. Otherwise, guess_table.pl may characterize it as a VARCHAR column. If a datafile doesn't satisfy these assumptions, you may be able to reformat it first using the cvt_file.pl and cvt_date.pl utilities, available in the recipes distribution.

guess_table.pl understands the following options:

--labels

Interpret the first input line as a row of column labels, and use them for table column names. Without this option, guess_table.pl uses default column names of c1, c2, and so forth.

If the file contains a row of labels and you omit this option, guess_table.pl treats the labels as data values. The likely result is that the script will characterize *all* columns as VARCHAR columns (even those that otherwise contain only numeric or temporal values), due to the presence of a nonnumeric or nontemporal value in the column.

--lower, --upper

Force column names in the CREATE TABLE statement to be lowercase or uppercase.

`--quote-names, --skip-quote-names`

Quote or do not quote table and column identifiers in the `CREATE TABLE` statement with ` characters (for example, `` `mytbl` ``). This can be useful if an identifier is a reserved word. The default is to quote identifiers.

`--report`

Generate a report rather than a `CREATE TABLE` statement. The script displays the information that it gathers about each column.

`--table=`*`tbl_name`*

Specify the table name to use in the `CREATE TABLE` statement. The default name is `t`.

Here's an example of how `guess_table.pl` works. Suppose that a file named *commodities.csv* is in CSV format and has the following contents:

```
commodity,trade_date,shares,price,change
sugar,12-14-2014,1000000,10.50,-.125
oil,12-14-2014,96000,60.25,.25
wheat,12-14-2014,2500000,8.75,0
gold,12-14-2014,13000,103.25,2.25
sugar,12-15-2014,970000,10.60,.1
oil,12-15-2014,105000,60.5,.25
wheat,12-15-2014,2370000,8.65,-.1
gold,12-15-2014,11000,101,-2.25
```

The first row indicates the column labels, and the following rows contain data records, one per line. The values in the `trade_date` column are dates, but they are in *MM-DD-YYYY* format rather than the ISO format that MySQL expects. `cvt_date.pl` can convert these dates to ISO format. However, both `cvt_date.pl` and `guess_table.pl` require input in tab-delimited, linefeed-terminated format, so first use `cvt_file.pl` to convert the input to tab-delimited, linefeed-terminated format, and `cvt_date.pl` to convert the dates:

```
$ cvt_file.pl --iformat=csv commodities.csv > tmp1.txt
$ cvt_date.pl --iformat=us tmp1.txt > tmp2.txt
```

Feed the resulting file, *tmp2.txt*, to `guess_table.pl`:

```
$ guess_table.pl --labels --table=commodities tmp2.txt > commodities.sql
```

The `CREATE TABLE` statement that `guess_table.pl` writes to *commodities.sql* looks like this:

```
CREATE TABLE `commodities`
(
  `commodity` VARCHAR(5) NOT NULL,
  `trade_date` DATE NOT NULL,
  `shares` BIGINT UNSIGNED NOT NULL,
  `price` DOUBLE UNSIGNED NOT NULL,
  `change` DOUBLE NOT NULL
);
```

`guess_table.pl` produces that statement based on heuristics such as these:

- A column that contains only numeric values is assumed to be a BIGINT if no values contain a decimal point, and DOUBLE otherwise.

- A numeric column that contains no negative values is likely to be UNSIGNED.

- If a column contains no empty values, `guess_table.pl` assumes that it's probably NOT NULL.

- Columns that cannot be classified as numbers or dates are taken to be VARCHAR columns, with a length equal to the longest value present in the column.

You might want to edit the CREATE TABLE statement that `guess_table.pl` produces, to make modifications such as using smaller integer types, increasing the size of character fields, changing VARCHAR to CHAR, adding indexes, or changing a column name that is a reserved word in MySQL.

To create the table, use the statement produced by `guess_table.pl`:

```
$ mysql cookbook < commodities.sql
```

Then load the datafile into the table (skipping the initial row of labels):

```
mysql> LOAD DATA LOCAL INFILE 'tmp2.txt' INTO TABLE commodities
    -> IGNORE 1 LINES;
```

The resulting table contents after import look like this:

```
mysql> SELECT * FROM commodities;
+-----------+------------+---------+--------+--------+
| commodity | trade_date | shares  | price  | change |
+-----------+------------+---------+--------+--------+
| sugar     | 2014-12-14 | 1000000 |   10.5 | -0.125 |
| oil       | 2014-12-14 |   96000 |  60.25 |   0.25 |
| wheat     | 2014-12-14 | 2500000 |   8.75 |      0 |
| gold      | 2014-12-14 |   13000 | 103.25 |   2.25 |
| sugar     | 2014-12-15 |  970000 |   10.6 |    0.1 |
| oil       | 2014-12-15 |  105000 |   60.5 |   0.25 |
| wheat     | 2014-12-15 | 2370000 |   8.65 |   -0.1 |
| gold      | 2014-12-15 |   11000 |    101 |  -2.25 |
+-----------+------------+---------+--------+--------+
```

## CHAPTER 14

Validating and Reformatting Data

14.0 Introduction

The previous chapter, Chapter 13, focused on methods for moving data into and out of MySQL, by reading lines and breaking them into separate columns. In this chapter, we'll focus on the content rather than structure issues. For example, if you don't know whether the values contained in a file or received via web form are legal, preprocess them to check or reformat them:

- It's often a good idea to validate data values to make sure they're legal for the data types into which you store them. For example, you can make sure that values intended for INT, DATE, and ENUM columns are integers, dates in ISO format (*YYYY-MM-DD*), and legal enumeration values, respectively.

- Data values may need reformatting. You might store credit card values as a string of digits but permit users of a web application to separate blocks of digits by spaces or dashes. These values must be rewritten before storing them. Rewriting dates from one format to another is especially common, for example, if a program writes dates in *MM-DD-YY* format to ISO format for import into MySQL. If a program understands only date and time formats and not a combined date-and-time format (such as MySQL uses for the DATETIME and TIMESTAMP data types), you must split date-and-time values into separate date and time values.

The chapter deals with formatting and validation issues primarily within the context of checking entire files, but many of the techniques discussed here can be applied to one-time validations as well. Consider a web-based application that presents a form for a user to fill in and then processes its contents to create a new row in the database. Web APIs generally make form contents available as a set of already-parsed discrete values, so the application may not need to deal with record and column delimiters.

On the other hand, validation issues remain paramount. You really have no idea what kind of values a user is sending your script, so it's important to check them.

The first three recipes introduce data validation capabilities available in MySQL. Starting from Recipe 14.4, we focus on validating and preprocessing data on the application side. We introduce techniques that allow you to process large bulks of data effectively.

Server-Side Versus Client-Side Validation

As described in Recipes 14.1, 14.2, and 14.3, you can cause data validation to be done on the server side to be restrictive about accepting bad input data. In this case, the MySQL server raises an error for values that are invalid for the data types of the columns into which you insert them.

In the next few recipes, the focus is on validation on the client side rather than on the server side. Client-side validation can be useful when you require more control over validation than simply receiving an error from the server. (For example, if you test values yourself, it's often easier to provide more informative messages to users about the exact nature of problems with the values.) Also, it might be necessary to couple validation with reformatting to transform complex values so that they are compatible with MySQL data types. You have more flexibility to do this on the client side.

Source code for program fragments and scripts discussed in this chapter is located in the *transfer* directory of the `recipes` distribution, with the exception that some utility functions are contained in library files located in the *lib* directory.

14.1 Using the SQL Mode to Reject Bad Input Values

Problem

MySQL accepts data values that are invalid, out of range, or otherwise unsuitable for the data types of the columns into which you insert them. You want the server to be more restrictive and not accept bad data.

Solution

Check the SQL mode and make sure it is not empty. There are several modes that you can use to control how strict the server is on data values. Some modes apply generally to all input values. Others apply to specific data types such as dates.

Discussion

When the SQL mode is not set or is set to an empty value, MySQL allows all input values for your table columns, even if the input data types do not match the column's data type. Consider the following table, which has integer, string, and date columns:

```
mysql> SELECT @@sql_mode;
+------------+
| @@sql_mode |
+------------+
|            |
+------------+
1 row in set (0,00 sec)
mysql> CREATE TABLE t (i INT, c CHAR(6), d DATE);
```

Inserting a row with unsuitable data values into the table causes warnings (which you can see with SHOW WARNINGS), but the server loads the values into the table after converting them to some value that fits the column:

```
mysql> INSERT INTO t (i,c,d) VALUES('-1x','too-long string!','1999-02-31');
mysql> SHOW WARNINGS;
+---------+------+-------------------------------------------+
| Level   | Code | Message                                   |
+---------+------+-------------------------------------------+
| Warning | 1265 | Data truncated for column 'i' at row 1    |
| Warning | 1265 | Data truncated for column 'c' at row 1    |
| Warning | 1264 | Out of range value for column 'd' at row 1 |
+---------+------+-------------------------------------------+
mysql> SELECT * FROM t;
+------+--------+------------+
| i    | c      | d          |
+------+--------+------------+
|   -1 | too-lo | 0000-00-00 |
+------+--------+------------+
```

One way to prevent these conversions is to check the input data on the client side to make sure that it's legal. This is a reasonable strategy in certain circumstances (see the sidebar in Recipe 14.0), but there is an alternative: let the server check data values on the server side and reject them with an error if they're invalid.

To do this, set the sql_mode system variable to enable server restrictions on input data acceptance. With the proper restrictions in place, data values that would otherwise result in conversions and warnings result in errors instead. Try the INSERT statement from the previous example again after enabling "strict" SQL mode:

```
mysql> SET sql_mode = 'STRICT_ALL_TABLES';
mysql> INSERT INTO t (i,c,d) VALUES('-1x','too-long string!','1999-02-31');
ERROR 1265 (01000): Data truncated for column 'i' at row 1
```

Here the statement doesn't even progress to the second and third data values because the first is invalid for an integer column and the server raises an error.

Without input restrictions enabled, the server checks that the month part of date values is in the range from 1 to 12 and that the day value is legal for the given month.

This means that `'2005-02-31'` generates a warning by default (with conversion to zero date `'0000-00-00'`). In strict mode, an error occurs.

MySQL still permits dates such as `'1999-11-00'` or `'1999-00-00'` that have zero parts, or the "zero" date (`'0000-00-00'`). To restrict these kinds of date values, enable the `NO_ZERO_IN_DATE` and `NO_ZERO_DATE` SQL modes to cause warnings, or errors in strict mode. For example, to prohibit dates with zero parts or "zero" dates, set the SQL mode like this:

```
mysql> SET sql_mode = 'STRICT_ALL_TABLES,NO_ZERO_IN_DATE,NO_ZERO_DATE';
```

A simpler way to enable these restrictions, and a few more besides, is to enable `TRADITIONAL` SQL mode. `TRADITIONAL` mode is actually a constellation of modes, as you can see by setting and displaying the `sql_mode` value:

```
mysql> SET sql_mode = 'TRADITIONAL';
mysql> SELECT @@sql_mode\G
*************************** 1. row ***************************
@@sql_mode: STRICT_TRANS_TABLES,STRICT_ALL_TABLES,NO_ZERO_IN_DATE,
            NO_ZERO_DATE,ERROR_FOR_DIVISION_BY_ZERO,TRADITIONAL,
            NO_ENGINE_SUBSTITUTION
```

You can read more about the various SQL modes in the MySQL Reference Manual (*https://oreil.ly/Xq6iA*).

The examples shown set the session value of the `sql_mode` system variable, so they change the SQL mode only for your current session. To set the mode globally for all clients, start the server with a `--sql_mode=`*mode_value* option. Alternatively, if you have the `SYSTEM_VARIABLES_ADMIN` or `SUPER` privilege, you can set the global mode at runtime:

```
mysql> SET GLOBAL sql_mode = 'mode_value';
```

Before MySQL 5.7, the SQL mode was forgiving by default. Newer versions are much more restrictive, and SQL mode is set to `ONLY_FULL_GROUP_BY`, `STRICT_TRANS_TABLES`, `NO_ZERO_IN_DATE`, `NO_ZERO_DATE`, `ERROR_FOR_DIVISION_BY_ZERO`, `NO_AUTO_CREATE_USER`, `NO_ENGINE_SUBSTITUTION`. Therefore, if you want to have a restrictive server, you don't need to do anything extra, unless you intentionally relaxed the SQL mode earlier.

14.2 Using CHECK Constraints to Reject Invalid Values

Problem

You want to validate data so it follows the business logic of your application and rejects values if they do not satisfy requirements.

Solution

Use CHECK constraints.

Discussion

If a value matches the MySQL data type format, it does not mean it matches the logic of the application. For example, if you want to store only even numbers, you cannot simply use a data type integer, because both odd and even numbers are valid integers.

CHECK constraints, introduced in version 8.0, allow you to set up a custom condition on the table column and reject the statement if the value does not satisfy it. Thus, to create a table that will store only even values, you would need to use CHECK to check if the number can be divided by two without a reminder:

```
mysql> CREATE TABLE even (
    -> even_value INT CHECK(even_value % 2 = 0)
    -> ) ENGINE=InnoDB;
Query OK, 0 rows affected (0.03 sec)
```

Now we can successfully insert even numbers into this table:

```
mysql> INSERT INTO even VALUES(2);
Query OK, 1 row affected (0.01 sec)
```

Odd values would be rejected:

```
mysql> INSERT INTO even VALUES(1);
ERROR 3819 (HY000): Check constraint 'even_chk_1' is violated.
```

You can also create multiple CHECK constraints for a single column. For example, to accept only even values that are less than 100, create two constraints:

```
mysql> CREATE TABLE even_100 (
    -> even_value INT CHECK(even_value % 2 = 0) CHECK(even_value < 100)
    -> ) ENGINE=InnoDB;
Query OK, 0 rows affected (0.02 sec)
```

In this case, MySQL will check the first condition, and if it is satisfied it will process the second one:

```
mysql> INSERT INTO even_100 VALUES(101);
ERROR 3819 (HY000): Check constraint 'even_100_chk_1' is violated.
mysql> INSERT INTO even_100 VALUES(102);
ERROR 3819 (HY000): Check constraint 'even_100_chk_2' is violated.
```

If you specify a CHECK constraint when defining a column, it will validate only this column. If you want to check two or more columns in the single constraint, you will need to specify it separately.

A common validation task is to check if the departure date is later than the arrival date. We can add such a check to the patients table:

```
ALTER TABLE patients ADD CONSTRAINT date_check
CHECK((date_departed IS NULL) OR (date_departed >= date_arrived));
```

Now, it will not allow you to insert records when the departure date is earlier than the arrival date:

```
mysql> INSERT INTO patients (national_id, name, surname, gender, age, diagnosis,
    -> date_arrived, date_departed)
    -> VALUES('34GD429520', 'John', 'Doe', 'M', 45, 'Data Phobia',
    -> '2020-07-20', '2020-05-31');
ERROR 3819 (HY000): Check constraint 'date_check' is violated.
```

14.3 Using Triggers to Reject Input Values

Problem

You want to validate if data to be inserted into the table follows business logic, but your logic is more complicated than CHECK constraints can handle. You may also need to rewrite the data instead of rejecting it. Or you are using an earlier version of MySQL where CHECK constraints are not available.

Solution

Use BEFORE triggers.

Discussion

CHECK constraints have certain limitations. They do not allow you to use stored or user-defined functions, subqueries, or user-defined variables. They also do not allow you to modify inserted data. If you want to format an inserted value to satisfy your business standards, you may want to explore another solution, such as validation on the application side or BEFORE triggers on the MySQL side.

To perform more complicated validation on the MySQL side, create a trigger and raise a SQL exception in it.

Let's take a look at an example. Suppose that a groceries table stores details about the products in a supermarket. In some countries, alcohol can't be sold in supermarkets between certain hours. For example, in Turkey, you wouldn't be able to buy alcohol in a supermarket between 10 p.m. and 6 a.m. If you are working with such limitations, you may want to limit times when users can place orders.

Suppose that a `groceries` table stores details about groceries in the supermarket:

```
CREATE TABLE `groceries` (
  `id` int NOT NULL,
  `name` varchar(255) DEFAULT NULL,
  `forbidden_after` time DEFAULT NULL,
  `forbidden_before` time DEFAULT NULL,
  PRIMARY KEY (`id`)
) ENGINE=InnoDB;
```

The forbidden_after and forbidden_before columns define the time range when a particular item can't be sold.

Another table, named groceries_order_items, contains information about purchases:

```
CREATE TABLE groceries_order_items
(
  order_id INT NOT NULL,
  groceries_id INT NOT NULL,
  quantity INT DEFAULT 0,
  PRIMARY KEY (order_id,groceries_id)
) ENGINE=InnoDB;
```

To disallow the purchase of items during certain times, you could create a trigger that checks the current time and if there are any restrictions to a selected product. If restrictions exist, the purchase will be rejected:

```
CREATE TRIGGER check_time
BEFORE INSERT ON groceries_order_items
FOR EACH ROW BEGIN
DECLARE forbidden_after_val TIME; ❶
DECLARE forbidden_before_val TIME;
DECLARE name_val VARCHAR(255);
DECLARE message VARCHAR(400);

SELECT forbidden_after, forbidden_before, name ❷
INTO forbidden_after_val, forbidden_before_val, name_val
FROM groceries WHERE id = NEW.groceries_id;

IF (forbidden_after_val IS NOT NULL AND TIME(NOW()) >= forbidden_after_val) ❸
  OR (forbidden_before_val IS NOT NULL AND TIME(NOW()) <= forbidden_before_val)
THEN
  SET message=CONCAT('It is forbidden to buy ', name_val,
    ' between ', forbidden_after_val, ' and ', forbidden_before_val); ❹
  SIGNAL SQLSTATE '45000' ❺
    SET MESSAGE_TEXT = message;
END IF;
END;
```

❶ Declare variables to store the time range when the purchase is forbidden, the name of the product, and an error message.

❷ Select the restricted time range and name of the product into variables.

❸ Check if the current time falls into the forbidden range for the selected product.

❹ If the time falls into the forbidden range, craft a message explaining restrictions for the product.

❺ Raise an error and reject the insert.

As a result, you can purchase cheese or water at 3 a.m., but you cannot purchase beer or wine at that time:

```
mysql> SELECT CURRENT_TIME();
+----------------+
| CURRENT_TIME() |
+----------------+
| 03:01:40       |
+----------------+
1 row in set (0.00 sec)
mysql> INSERT INTO groceries_order_items VALUES(1,3,1); -- cheese
Query OK, 1 row affected (0.03 sec)

mysql> INSERT INTO groceries_order_items VALUES(1,8,3); -- water
Query OK, 1 row affected (0.01 sec)

mysql> INSERT INTO groceries_order_items VALUES(1,7,6); -- beer
ERROR 1644 (45000): It is forbidden to buy beer between 22:00:00 and 06:00:00
mysql> INSERT INTO groceries_order_items VALUES(1,6,1); -- wine
ERROR 1644 (45000): It is forbidden to buy wine between 22:00:00 and 06:00:00
```

The purchase limitation is relaxed during the day:

```
mysql> SELECT CURRENT_TIME();
+----------------+
| CURRENT_TIME() |
+----------------+
| 14:00:35       |
+----------------+
1 row in set (0.00 sec)

mysql> INSERT INTO groceries_order_items VALUES(1,7,6); -- beer
Query OK, 1 row affected (0.01 sec)

mysql> INSERT INTO groceries_order_items VALUES(1,6,1); -- wine
Query OK, 1 row affected (0.01 sec)
```

See Also

For additional information about using triggers to reject or modify invalid values, see Recipe 11.11.

14.4 Writing an Input-Processing Loop

Problem

You want to make sure that the data values in a file are legal.

Solution

Write an input-processing loop that will check them, possibly rewriting them into a more suitable format.

Discussion

Many of the validation recipes shown in this chapter are typical of those that you perform within the context of a program that reads a file and checks individual column values. The general framework for such a file-processing utility looks like this:

```
#!/usr/bin/python3
# loop.py: Typical input-processing loop.

# Assumes tab-delimited, linefeed-terminated input lines.

import sys

for line in sys.stdin:
    line = line.rstrip()
    # split line at tabs, preserving all fields
    values = line.split("\t")
    for val in values: # iterate through fields in line
        # ... test val here ...
        pass
```

The for loop reads each input line. Within the loop, each line is broken into fields. The inner for loop iterates through the fields, enabling each to be processed in sequence. If you don't apply a given test uniformly to all the fields, replace the for loop with separate column-specific tests.

This loop assumes tab-delimited, linefeed-terminated input, an assumption shared by most of the utilities discussed throughout this chapter. To use these utilities with datafiles in other formats, you may be able to convert such files to tab-delimited format using the cvt_file.pl script, available in the recipes distribution.

14.5 Putting Common Tests in Libraries

Problem

You want to do repeated validation operations.

Solution

Package validation operations as library routines.

Discussion

It's not unusual for certain validation operations to occur repeatedly, in which case you'll probably find it useful to construct a library of functions. By packaging validation operations as library routines, it is easier to write utilities based on them, and the utilities make it easier to perform command-line operations on entire files so that you can avoid editing them yourself. This also gives the operation a name that's likely to make the meaning of it clearer than the comparison code itself. The following test in Python language performs a pattern match to check that `val` consists entirely of digits (optionally preceded by a plus sign), and then makes sure the value is greater than zero:

```python
p = re.compile('^\+?\d+$')
  s = p.search(val)
  valid = s and (s.group(0) != '0')
```

In other words, the test looks for strings that represent positive integers. To make the test easier to use and its intent clearer, package it as a function that is used like this:

```python
valid = is_positive_integer (val);
```

Define the function as follows:

```python
def is_positive_integer(val):
  p = re.compile('^\+?\d+$')
  s = p.search(val)
  return s and (s.group(0) != '0')
```

Now put the function definition into a library file so that multiple scripts can use it easily. The `cookbook_utils.py` module file in the *lib* directory of the `recipes` distribution is an example of a library file that contains a number of validation functions. Take a look through it to see which functions may be useful in your own programs (or as a model for writing your own library files). To gain access to this module from within a script, include a `use` statement like this:

```python
import cookbook_utils as cu
```

You must, of course, install the module file in a directory where Python will find it (see Recipe 4.3).

A significant benefit of putting a collection of utility routines into a library file is that you can use it for all kinds of programs. It's rare for a data manipulation problem to be completely unique. If you can pick and choose at least a few validation routines from a library, it reduces the amount of code you must write, even for highly specialized programs.

 To avoid writing your own library routines, look around to see if someone else has already written suitable routines that you can use. For example, if you check the Perl CPAN (*cpan.perl.org*), you'll find a Data::Validate module hierarchy. The modules there provide library routines that standardize a number of common validation tasks. Data::Validate::MySQL deals specifically with MySQL data types.

14.6 Using Pattern Matching to Validate Data

Problem

You want to compare a value to a set of values that is difficult to specify without writing a really ugly expression.

Solution

Use pattern matching.

Discussion

Pattern matching is a powerful validation tool that enables you to test entire classes of values with a single expression. You can also use pattern tests to break matched values into subparts for further individual testing or in substitution operations to rewrite matched values. For example, you might break a matched date into pieces to verify that the month is in the range from 1 to 12, and the day is within the number of days in the month. You might use a substitution to reorder *MM-DD-YYYY* or *DD-MM-YYYY* values into *YYYY-MM-DD* format.

The next few sections describe how to use patterns to test several types of values, but first let's review some general pattern-matching principles. The following discussion focuses on Python's regular-expression capabilities. Pattern matching in Ruby, PHP, Go, and Perl is similar, although you should consult the relevant documentation for any differences. For Java, use the `java.util.regex` package.

In Python, regular expressions are part of the module `re`. The pattern constructor is `re.compile(pat)`:

```
pattern = re.compile(pat)
```

To find if a value matches a pattern, use the `match` method:

```
it_matched = pattern.match(val)     # pattern match
```

You can construct a regular expression in the `match` method:

```
it_matched = re.match(pat, val)     # pattern match
```

Put an `re.I` flag as the second argument to the regular expression constructor to make the pattern match case insensitive:

```
it_matched = re.match(pat, val, re.I)   # case-insensitive match
```

To look for a nonmatch, replace the = operator with the combination of the = and not operators:

```
no_match = not re.match(pat, val)     # negated pattern match
```

To perform a substitution in `val` based on a pattern match, use `re.sub(`/*pat, replacement,* `val)`*replacement*/. If *pat* occurs within `val`, it's replaced by *replacement*. For a case-insensitive match, put an `re.I` flag. To conduct a substitution that replaces only a few instances of *pat* rather than all of them, add a `count` option:

```
val = re.sub(pat, replacement, val)     # substitution
val = re.sub(pat, replacement, val, flags = re.I)   # case-insensitive substitution
val = re.sub(pat, replacement, val, count = 1)   # substitution of the first match
val = re.sub(pat, replacement, val, count = 1, flags = re.I)
              # case-insensitive and the first match
```

Table 14-1 shows some of the special pattern elements available in Python regular expressions.

Table 14-1. Pattern elements in Python regular expressions

Pattern	What the pattern matches
^	Beginning of string
$	End of string
.	Any character except a newline
\s, \S	Whitespace or nonwhitespace character
\d, \D	Digit or nondigit character
\w, \W	Word (alphanumeric or underscore) or nonword character
[...]	Any character listed between the square brackets
[^...]	Any character not listed between the square brackets
p1|*p2*|*p3*	Alternation; matches any of the patterns *p1*, *p2*, or *p3*
*	Zero or more instances of preceding element
+	One or more instances of preceding element
{*n*}	*n* instances of preceding element
{*m*,*n*}	*m* through *n* instances of preceding element

Many of these pattern elements are the same as those available for MySQL's `REGEXP` regular-expression operator (see Recipe 7.11).

To match a literal instance of a character that is special within patterns, such as *, ^, or $, precede it with a backslash. Similarly, to include a character within a character class construction that is special in character classes ([,], or -), precede it with a backslash. To include a literal ^ in a character class, list it somewhere other than as the first character between the parentheses.

Many of the validation patterns shown in the following recipes are of the form ^*pat*$. Beginning and ending a pattern with ^ and $ has the effect of requiring *pat* to match the entire string that you test. This is common in data validation contexts because it's generally desirable to know that a pattern matches an entire input value, not only part of it. (To be sure that a value represents an integer, for example, it does no good to know only that it contains an integer somewhere.) This is not a hard-and-fast rule, however, and sometimes it's useful to perform a more relaxed test by omitting the ^ and $ characters as appropriate. For example, if you want to strip leading and trailing whitespace from a value, use one pattern anchored only to the beginning of the string and another anchored only to the end:

```
val = re.sub('^\s+', '', val)   # trim leading whitespace
val = re.sub('\s+$', '', val)   # trim trailing whitespace
```

That's such a common operation, in fact, that it's a good candidate for being written as a utility function. The `cookbook_utils.py` file contains a function `trim_white space()` that performs both substitutions and returns the result:

```
val = trim_whitespace (val)
```

To remember subsections of a string matched by a pattern, use parentheses around the relevant pattern parts. After a successful match, you can refer to the matched substrings using the variables \1, \2, and so forth inside the regular expression or using the match number as an argument of the method `group`:

```
match = re.match('^(\d+)(.*)$', '2021-04-25')
if match:
    first_part = match.group(1) # this is the year, 2021
    the_rest = match.group(2)   # this is the rest of the date, -04-25
```

If you want to indicate that an element within a pattern is optional, follow it with a ? character. To match values consisting of a sequence of digits, optionally beginning with a minus sign and optionally ending with a period, use this pattern:

```
^-?\d+\.?$
```

Use parentheses to group alternations within a pattern. The following pattern matches time values in *hh:mm* format, optionally followed by AM or PM:

```
^\d{1,2}:\d{2}\s*(AM|PM)?$
```

The use of parentheses in that pattern also has the side effect of remembering the optional part in \1. To suppress that side effect, use (?:*pat*) instead:

```
^\d{1,2}:\d{2}\s*(?:AM|PM)?$
```

You now have sufficient background in Python pattern matching to enable the construction of useful validation tests for several types of data values. The following recipes provide patterns that can be used to test for broad content types, numbers, temporal values, and email addresses or URLs.

The *transfer* directory of the `recipes` distribution contains a `test_pat.py` script that reads input values, matches them against several patterns, and reports which patterns each value matches. The script is easily extensible, so you can use it as a test harness to try your own patterns.

14.7 Using Patterns to Match Broad Content Types

Problem

You want to classify values into categories.

Solution

Use a pattern that uses similarly broad categories.

Discussion

To check whether values are empty or nonempty, or consist only of certain types of characters, the patterns listed in Table 14-2 may suffice.

Table 14-2. Commonly used categories of characters

Pattern	Type of value the pattern matches
^$	Empty value
.	Nonempty value
^\s*$	Whitespace, possibly empty
^\s+$	Nonempty whitespace
\S	Nonempty, and not whitespace
^\d+$	Digits only, nonempty
^[a-zA-Z]+$	Alphabetic characters only (case insensitive), nonempty
^\w+$	Alphanumeric or underscore characters only, nonempty

14.8 Using Patterns to Match Numeric Values

Problem

You want to make sure a string looks like a number.

Solution

Use a pattern that matches the type of number you're looking for.

Discussion

Patterns can be used to classify values into several types of numbers, as shown in Table 14-3.

Table 14-3. Patterns that match numbers

Pattern	Type of value the pattern matches
^\d+$	Unsigned integer
^-?\d+$	Negative or unsigned integer
^[-+]?\d+$	Signed or unsigned integer
^[-+]?(\d+(\.\d*)?|\.\d+)$	Floating-point number

The pattern ^\d+$ matches unsigned integers by requiring a nonempty value that consists only of digits from the beginning to the end of the value. If you care only that a value begins with an integer, you can match an initial numeric part and extract it. To do this, match only the initial part of the string (omit the $ that requires the pattern to match to the end of the string), and place parentheses around the \d+ part. Then refer to the matched number as group(1) after a successful match:

```
match = re.match('^(\d+)', val)
if match:
    val = match.group(1)
```

Some kinds of numeric values have a special format or other unusual constraints. Here are a few examples and how to deal with them:

ZIP codes

ZIP and ZIP+4 codes are postal codes used for mail delivery in the United States. They have values like 12345 or 12345-6789 (that is, five digits, possibly followed by a dash and four more digits). To match one form or the other, or both forms, use the patterns shown in Table 14-4.

Table 14-4. Patterns that match ZIP codes

Pattern	Type of value the pattern matches
^\d{5}$	ZIP code, five digits only
^\d{5}-\d{4}$	ZIP+4 code
^\d{5}(-\d{4})?$	ZIP or ZIP+4 code

Credit card numbers

Credit card numbers typically consist of digits, but it's common for values to be written with spaces, dashes, or other characters between groups of digits. For example, the following numbers are equivalent:

```
0123456789012345
0123 4567 8901 2345
0123-4567-8901-2345
```

To match such values, use this pattern:

```
^[- \d]+
```

(Python permits the \d digit specifier within character classes.) However, that pattern doesn't identify values of the wrong length, and it may be useful to remove extraneous characters before storing values in MySQL. To require credit card values to contain 16 digits, use a substitution that removes all nondigits, then check the length of the result:

```
val = re.sub('\D', '', val)
valid = len(val) == 16
```

14.9 Using Patterns to Match Dates or Times

Problem

You want to make sure a string looks like a date or time.

Solution

Use a pattern that matches the type of temporal value you expect. Be sure to consider issues such as how strict to be about delimiters between subparts and the lengths of the subparts.

Discussion

Dates are a validation headache because they come in so many formats. Pattern tests are extremely useful for weeding out illegal values but are often insufficient for full verification: a date might have a number where you expect a month, but the date isn't valid if the number is 13. This section introduces some patterns that match a few common date formats. Recipe 14.14 revisits this topic in more detail and discusses combining pattern tests with content verification.

To require values to be dates in ISO (*YYYY-MM-DD*) format, use this pattern:

```
^\d{4}-\d{2}-\d{2}$
```

The pattern requires the - character as the delimiter between date parts. To permit either - or / as the delimiter, use a character class between the numeric parts:

```
^\d{4}[-/]\d{2}[-/]\d{2}$
```

This pattern will match dates in the formats *YYYY-MM-DD*, *YYYY/MM/DD*, *YYYY/MM-DD*, and *YYYY-MM/DD*.

To permit any nondigit delimiter (which corresponds to how MySQL operates when it interprets strings as dates), use this pattern:

```
^\d{4}\D\d{2}\D\d{2}$
```

To permit leading zeros in values like 03 to be missing, just look for three nonempty digit sequences:

```
^\d+\D\d+\D\d+$
```

Of course, that pattern is so general that it also matches other values such as US Social Security numbers (which have the format 012-34-5678). To constrain the subpart lengths by requiring two to four digits in the year part and one or two digits in the month and day parts, use this pattern:

```
^\d{2,4}?\D\d{1,2}\D\d{1,2}$
```

For dates in other formats such as *MM-DD-YY* or *DD-MM-YY*, similar patterns apply, but the subparts are arranged in a different order. This pattern matches both of those formats:

```
^\d{2}-\d{2}-\d{2}$
```

To check the values of individual date parts, use parentheses in the pattern and extract the substrings after a successful match. If you expect dates to be in ISO format, for example, do this:

```
match = re.match('^(\d{2,4})\D(\d{1,2})\D(\d{1,2})$', val)
if match:
    (year, month, day) = (match.group(1), match.group(2), match.group(3))
```

The library file lib/cookbook_utils.py in the recipes distribution contains several of these pattern tests, packaged as function calls. If the date doesn't match the pattern, they return None. Otherwise, they return a reference to an array containing the broken-out values for the year, month, and day. This can be useful for performing further checking on the components of the date. For example, is_iso_date() looks for dates that match ISO format. It's defined as follows:

```
def is_iso_date(val):
    m = re.match('^(\d{2,4})\D(\d{1,2})\D(\d{1,2})$', val)
    return [int(m.group(1)), int(m.group(2)), int(m.group(3))] if m else None
```

The function could be used as follows:

```
ref = cu.is_iso_date(val)
if ref is not None:
    # val matched ISO format pattern;
    # check its subparts using ref[0] through ref[2]
    pass
else:
    # val didn't match ISO format pattern
    pass
```

You'll often find additional processing necessary with dates because date-matching patterns help to weed out values that are syntactically malformed but don't assess whether the individual components contain legal values. To do that, some range checking is necessary. Recipe 14.14 covers that topic.

If you're willing to skip subpart testing and just want to rewrite the pieces, use a substitution. For example, to rewrite values assumed to be in *MM-DD-YY* format into *YY-MM-DD* format, do this:

```
val = re.sub('^(\d+)\D(\d+)\D(\d+)$', r'\3-\1-\2', val)
```

Time values are somewhat more orderly than dates, usually being written with hours first and seconds last, with two digits per part:

```
^\d{2}:\d{2}:\d{2}$
```

To be more lenient, permit the hours part to have a single digit, or the seconds part to be missing:

```
^\d{1,2}:\d{2}(:\d{2})?$
```

Mark parts of the time with parentheses if you want to range-check the individual parts, or perhaps to reformat the value to include a seconds part of 00 if it happens to be missing. However, this requires some care with the parentheses and the ? characters in the pattern if the seconds part is optional. You want to permit the entire :\d{2} at the end of the pattern to be optional but not to save the : character in \3 if the third time section is present. To accomplish that, use (?:*pat*), a grouping notation that doesn't save the matched substring. Within that notation, use parentheses around the digits to save them. Then \3 is None if the seconds part is not present, and contains the seconds digits otherwise:

```
m = re.match('^(\d{1,2}):(\d{2})(?::(\d{2}))?$', val)
(hour, min, sec) = (m.group(1), m.group(2), m.group(3))
sec = '00' if sec is None else sec # seconds missing; use 00
val = hour + ':' + min + ':' + sec
```

To rewrite times from a 12-hour format with AM and PM suffixes to a 24-hour format, do this:

```
m = re.match('^(\d{1,2})\D(\d{2})\D(\d{2})(?:\s*(AM|PM))?$', val, flags = re.I)
(hour, min, sec) = (m.group(1), m.group(2), m.group(3))
# supply missing seconds
sec = '00' if sec is None else sec
if int(hour) == 12 and (m.group(4) is None or m.group(4).upper() == "AM"):
    hour = '00' # 12:xx:xx AM times are 00:xx:xx
elif int(hour) < 12 and (m.group(4) is not None) and m.group(4).upper() == "PM":
    hour = int(hour) + 12 # PM times other than 12:xx:xx
return [hour, min, sec] # return hour, minute, second
```

The time parts are placed into groups 1, 2, and 3, with 3 set to None if the seconds part is missing. The suffix goes into group 4 if it's present. If the suffix is AM or missing (None), the value is interpreted as an AM time. If the suffix is PM, the value is interpreted as a PM time.

See Also

This recipe shows just the beginning of what you can do when processing dates for data-transfer purposes. Date and time testing and conversion can be highly idiosyncratic, and the sheer number of issues to consider is mind-boggling:

- What is the basic date format? Dates come in several common styles, such as ISO (*YYYY-MM-DD*), US (*MM-DD-YY*), and British (*DD-MM-YY*) formats. And these are just some of the more standard formats. Many more are possible. For example, a datafile may contain dates written as June 17, 1959 or as 17 Jun '59.

- Are trailing times permitted on dates, or perhaps required? When times are expected, is the full time required or just the hour and minute?

- Do you permit special values like now or today?

- Are date parts required to be delimited by a particular character, such as - or /, or are other delimiters permitted?

- Are date parts required to have a specific number of digits? Or are leading zeros on month and year values permitted to be missing?

- Are months written numerically or represented as month names like January or Jan?

- How should two-digit year values be converted to have four digits? What is the transition point within the range 00 to 99 at which values change from one century to another?

- Should date parts be checked to ensure their validity? Patterns can recognize strings that look like dates or times, but while they're extremely useful for detecting malformed values, they may not be sufficient. A value like 1947-15-99 may match a pattern but isn't a legal date. Pattern testing is thus most useful in conjunction with range checks on the individual parts of the date.

The prevalence of these issues in data-transfer problems means that you'll probably end up writing some of your own validators on occasion to handle very specific date formats. Other sections of this chapter can provide additional assistance. For example, Recipe 14.13 covers conversion of two-digit year values to four-digit form, and Recipe 14.14 discusses how to perform validity checking on components of date or time values.

You might be able to save yourself some work by using existing date-checking modules for your API language. Some possibilities: the Perl Date module, the Ruby date module, the Python datetime module, the PHP DateTime class, and the Java GregorianCalendar and SimpleDateTime classes.

14.10 Using Patterns to Match Email Addresses or URLs

Problem

You want to determine if a value looks like an email address or a URL.

Solution

In your application, use a pattern tuned to the desired level of strictness on which addresses you accept and which you do not.

Discussion

The immediately preceding recipes use patterns to identify classes of values such as numbers and dates, which are fairly typical applications for regular expressions. But pattern matching has much more widespread applicability for data validation. To give some idea of a few other types of values for which pattern matching can be used, this recipe shows a few tests for email addresses and URLs.

To check values that are expected to be email addresses, the pattern should require at least an @ character with nonempty strings on either side:

```
.@.
```

Full email address specification is defined by RFC5322 (*https://oreil.ly/AcHbi*) and contains many parts. Regular expression that rejects all invalid addresses and accepts all valid addresses is pretty complicated to write. Check *http://emailregex.com* for examples in popular programming languages to have an idea.

In this recipe, we'll show you a pretty minimal test that is sufficient to help correct most innocent user errors, such as typos when they enter addresses into a web form.

It's difficult to come up with a fully general pattern that covers all the legal values and rejects all the illegal ones, but it's easy to write a pattern that's at least a little more restrictive. For example, in addition to being nonempty, the username and the domain name should consist entirely of characters other than @ characters or spaces:

```
^[^@ ]+@[^@ ]+$
```

You may also want to require that the domain name part contain at least two parts separated by a dot:

```
^[^@ ]+@[^@ .]+\.[^@ .]+
```

To look for URL values that begin with a protocol specifier of `http://`, `https://`, `ftp://`, or `mailto:`, use an alternation that matches any of them at the beginning of the string:

```
re.compile('^(https?://|ftp://|mailto:)', flags=re.I)
```

The alternatives in the pattern are grouped within parentheses because otherwise the ^ anchors only the first of them to the beginning of the string. The re.I flag follows the pattern because protocol specifiers in URLs are not case sensitive. The pattern is otherwise fairly unrestrictive because it permits anything to follow the protocol specifier. Add further restrictions as necessary.

14.11 Using Table Metadata to Validate Data

Problem

You want to check input values against the legal members of an ENUM or SET column.

Solution

Get the column definition, extract the list of members from it, and check data values against the list.

Discussion

Some forms of validation involve checking input values against information stored in a database. This includes values to be stored in an ENUM or SET column, which can be checked against the valid members stored in the column definition. Database-backed validation also applies to values that must match those listed in a lookup table to be considered legal. For example, input records that contain customer IDs can be required to match a row in a `customers` table, and state abbreviations in addresses can be verified against a table that lists each state. This recipe describes ENUM- and SET-based validation, and Recipe 14.12 discusses how to use lookup tables.

One way to check input values that correspond to the legal values of ENUM or SET columns is to get the list of legal column values into an array using the information in INFORMATION_SCHEMA, then perform an array membership test. For example, the favorite-color column `color` from the `profile` table is an ENUM defined as follows:

```
mysql> SELECT COLUMN_TYPE FROM INFORMATION_SCHEMA.COLUMNS
    -> WHERE TABLE_SCHEMA = 'cookbook' AND TABLE_NAME = 'profile'
    -> AND COLUMN_NAME = 'color';
+----------------------------------------------+
| COLUMN_TYPE                                   |
+----------------------------------------------+
| enum('blue','red','green','brown','black','white') |
+----------------------------------------------+
```

If you extract the list of enumeration members from the COLUMN_TYPE value and store them in a members list, you can perform the membership test like this:

```
valid = True ↵
if list(map(lambda v: v.upper(), members)).count(val.upper()) > 0 ↵
else False
```

We can convert the members list and val to uppercase to perform a case-insensitive comparison because the default collation is utf8mb4_0900_ai_ci, which is case insensitive. (If you have a column with a different collation, adjust accordingly. We discussed how to change column collation in Recipe 7.5.)

In Recipe 12.6, we wrote a get_enumorset_info() function that returns ENUM or SET column metadata. This includes the list of members, so it's easy to use that function to write another utility routine, check_enum_value(), that gets the legal enumeration values and performs the membership test. The routine takes four arguments: a database handle, the table name and column name for the ENUM column, and the value to check. It returns true or false to indicate whether the value is legal:

```
def check_enum_value(conn, db_name, tbl_name, col_name, val):
    valid = 0
    info = get_enumorset_info(conn, db_name, tbl_name, col_name)
    if info is not None and info['type'].upper() == 'ENUM':
        # use case-insensitive comparison because default collation
        # (utf8mb4_0900_ai_ci) is case insensitive (adjust if you use
        # a different collation)
        valid = 1 ↵
        if list(map(lambda v: v.upper(), info['values'])).count(val.upper()) > 0 ↵
        else 0
    return valid
```

For single-value testing, such as to validate a value submitted in a web form, list lookup for each value works well. However, to test a lot of values (like an entire column in a datafile), it's better to read the enumeration values into memory once, then use them repeatedly to check each data value. Furthermore, it's a lot more efficient to perform dictionary lookups than list lookups (in Python at least). To do so, retrieve the legal enumeration values and store them as keys of a dictionary. Then test each input value by checking whether it exists as a dictionary key. It's a little more effort to construct the dictionary, which is why check_enum_value() doesn't do so. But for bulk validation, the improved lookup speed more than makes up for the dictionary construction overhead. (To check for yourself the relative efficiency of list membership tests versus dictionary lookups, try the lookup_time.py script in the *transfer* directory of the recipes distribution.)

Begin by getting the metadata for the column, then convert the list of legal enumeration members to a dictionary:

```
info = get_enumorset_info(conn, db_name, tbl_name, col_name)
members={}
# convert dictionary key to consistent lettercase
```

```
for v in info['values']:
    members[v.lower()] = 1
```

The for loop makes each enumeration member exist as the key of a dictionary element. The dictionary key is what's important here; the value associated with it is irrelevant. (The example shown sets the value to 1, but you could use None, 0, or any other value.) Note that the code converts the dictionary keys to lowercase before storing them. This is done because dictionary key lookups in Python are case sensitive. That's fine if the values that you check also are case sensitive, but ENUM columns by default are not. By converting the enumeration values to a given lettercase before storing them in the dictionary, and then converting the values you want to check similarly, you perform, in effect, a case-insensitive key existence test:

```
valid = 1 if val.lower() in members else 0
```

The example converts enumeration values and input values to lowercase. You could just as well use uppercase, as long as you do so for all values consistently.

Note that the existence test may fail if the input value is the empty string. You must decide how to handle that case on a column-by-column basis. For example, if the column permits NULL values, you might interpret the empty string as equivalent to NULL and thus as being a legal value.

The validation procedure for SET values is similar to that for ENUM values, except that an input value might consist of any number of SET members, separated by commas. For the value to be legal, each element in it must be legal. In addition, because "any number of members" includes "none," the empty string is a legal value for any SET column.

For one-shot testing of individual input values, use a check_set_value() utility function that is similar to check_enum_value():

```
def check_set_value(conn, db_name, tbl_name, col_name, val):
    valid = 0
    info = get_enumorset_info(conn, db_name, tbl_name, col_name)
    if info is not None and info['type'].upper() == 'SET':
        if val == "":
            return 1 # empty string is legal element
        # use case-insensitive comparison because default collation
        # (utf8mb4_0900_ai_ci) is case insensitive (adjust if you use
        # a different collation)
        valid = 1  # assume valid until we find out otherwise
        for v in val.split(','):
            if list(map(lambda x: x.upper(), info['values'])).count(v.upper()) <= 0:
                valid = 0
                break
    return valid
```

For bulk testing, construct a dictionary from the legal SET members. The procedure is the same as shown previously for producing a dictionary from ENUM elements.

To validate a given input value against the SET member dictionary, convert it to the same lettercase as the hash keys, split it at commas to get a list of the individual elements of the value, and then check each one. If any of the elements are invalid, the entire value is invalid:

```
valid = 1 # assume valid until we find out otherwise
for v in val.split(","):
  if v.lower() not in members:
    valid = 0
    break
```

After the loop terminates, `valid` is true if the value is legal for the SET column, and false otherwise. Empty strings are always legal SET values, but this code performs no special-case test for an empty string. No such test is necessary because in that case the `split()` operation returns an empty list, the loop never executes, and `valid` remains true.

14.12 Using a Lookup Table to Validate Data

Problem

You want to check values to make sure they're listed in a lookup table.

Solution

Issue statements to check whether the values are in the table. The best way to do this depends on the number of input values and the table size. In this recipe, we will start our discussion with issuing individual statements, then create a hash from the entire lookup table, and, finally, improve our algorithm by remembering already-seen values to avoid querying the database several times for large datasets.

Discussion

To validate input values against the contents of a lookup table, the techniques are somewhat similar to those shown in Recipe 14.11 for checking ENUM and SET columns. However, whereas ENUM and SET columns usually have a small number of member values, a lookup table can have an essentially unlimited number of values. You might not want to read them all into memory.

Validation of input values against the contents of a lookup table can be done several ways, as illustrated in the following discussion. The tests shown in the examples perform comparisons against values exactly as they are stored in the lookup table. To perform case-insensitive comparisons, convert all values to a consistent lettercase. (See the discussion of case conversion in Recipe 14.11.)

Issue individual statements

For one-shot operations, test a value by checking whether it's listed in the lookup table. The following query returns true (nonzero) for a value that is present and false otherwise:

```
cursor.execute("select count(*) from tbl_name where val = %(val)s", {'val': value})
valid = cursor.fetchone()[0]
```

This kind of test may be suitable for purposes such as checking a value submitted in a web form but is inefficient for validating large datasets. It has no memory for the results of previous tests for values that have been seen before; consequently, you execute a query for every input value.

Construct a hash from the entire lookup table

To validate a large number of values, it's better to pull the lookup values into memory, save them in a data structure, and check each input value against the contents of that structure. Using an in-memory lookup avoids the overhead of executing a query for each value.

First, run a query to retrieve all the lookup table values and construct a dictionary from them:

```
members = {}  # dictionary for lookup values
cursor.execute("SELECT val FROM tbl_name");
rows = cursor.fetchall()
for row in rows:
  members[row[0]] = 1
```

Then, perform a dictionary key existence test to check a given value:

```
valid = True if val in members else False
```

This technique reduces database traffic to a single query. However, for a large lookup table, that could still be a lot of traffic, and you might not want to hold the entire table in memory.

Performing Lookups with Other Languages

The lookup example shown in this recipe uses a Python dictionary to determine whether a given value is present in a set of values.

Similar data structures exist for other languages. In Ruby, use a hash, and check input values using the has_key? method:

```
valid = members.has_key?(val)
```

In PHP, use an associative array, and perform a key lookup with isset():

```
$valid = isset ($members[$val]);
```

In Perl, use a hash, and check input values using the `exists` function:

```
$valid = exists ($members{$val});
```

For lookups in Java, use a `HashMap`, and test values with the `containsKey()` method:

```
valid = members.containsKey (val);
```

In Go, use a map, and access its keys directly:

```
valid := members[val]
```

The *transfer* directory of the `recipes` distribution contains some sample code for lookup operations in each language.

Remember already-seen values to avoid database lookups

Another lookup technique mixes individual statements with a dictionary that stores lookup value existence information. This approach can be useful if you have a very large lookup table. Begin with an empty dictionary:

```
members = {}  # dictionary for lookup values
```

Then, for each value to be tested, check whether it's present in the dictionary. If not, execute a query to check whether the value is present in the lookup table, and record the result of the query in the dictionary. The validity of the input value is determined by the value associated with the key, not by the existence of the key:

```
if val not in members: # haven't seen this value yet
    cursor.execute(f"SELECT COUNT(*) FROM {tbl_name} WHERE val = %(val)s",↵
                    {'val': val})
    count = cursor.fetchone()[0]
    # store true/false to indicate whether value was found
    members[val] = True if count > 0 else False
valid = members[val]
```

For this method, the dictionary acts as a cache so that you execute a lookup query for any given value only once, no matter how many times it occurs in the input. For datasets that have repeated values, this approach avoids issuing a separate query for every single test, while requiring an entry in the dictionary only for each unique value. It thus stands between the other two approaches in terms of the trade-off between database traffic and program memory requirements for the dictionary.

Note that the dictionary is used in a different manner for this method than for the previous method. Previously, the existence of the input value as a key in the dictionary determined the validity of the value, and the value associated with the dictionary key was irrelevant. For the dictionary-as-cache method, the meaning of key existence in the dictionary changes from "it's valid" to "it's been tested before." For each key, the value associated with it indicates whether the input value is present in the lookup table. (If you store as keys only those values that are found to be in the lookup table, you issue a query for each instance of an invalid value in the input dataset, which is inefficient.)

14.13 Converting Two-Digit Year Values to Four-Digit Form

Problem

You want to convert years in date values from two digits to four digits.

Solution

Let MySQL do this for you, or perform the operation yourself if MySQL's conversion rules aren't appropriate.

Discussion

Two-digit year values are a problem because the century is not explicit in the data values. If you know the range of years spanned by your input, you can add the century without ambiguity. Otherwise, you can only guess. For example, the date 10/2/69 would be interpreted by most people in the US as October 2, 1969. But if it represents Mahatma Gandhi's birth date, the year is actually 1869.

One way to convert years to four digits is to let MySQL do it. If you try to insert into the YEAR column a date containing a two-digit year, MySQL automatically converts it to four-digit form. MySQL uses a transition point of 1970; it interprets values from 00 to 69 as the years 2000 to 2069, and values from 70 to 99 as the years 1970 to 1999. These rules are appropriate for year values in the range from 1970 to 2069. If your values lie outside this range, add the proper century yourself before storing them into MySQL:

```
mysql> SELECT CAST(69 AS YEAR) AS `69`,
    -> CAST(70 AS YEAR) AS `70`,
    -> CAST(22 AS YEAR) AS `22`;
+------+------+------+
| 69   | 70   | 22   |
+------+------+------+
| 2069 | 1970 | 2022 |
+------+------+------+
```

To use a different transition point, convert years to four-digit form yourself. Here's a general-purpose routine that converts two-digit years to four digits and supports an arbitrary transition point:

```
def yy_to_yyyy(year, transition_point = 70):
  if year < 100:
    year += 1900 if year >= transition_point else 2000
  return year
```

The function uses MySQL's transition point (70) by default. An optional second argument may be given to provide a different transition point. yy_to_yyyy() also verifies that the year actually is less than 100 and needs converting before modifying it. That way you can pass year values regardless of whether they include the century. Some sample invocations using the default transition point have the following results:

```
val = yy_to_yyyy (60)       # returns 2060
val = yy_to_yyyy (1960)     # returns 1960 (no conversion done)
```

Suppose that you want to convert year values as follows, using a transition point of 50:

```
00 .. 49 -> 2000 .. 2049
50 .. 99 -> 1950 .. 1999
```

To do this, pass an explicit transition point argument to yy_to_yyyy():

```
val = yy_to_yyyy (60, 50)     # returns 1960
val = yy_to_yyyy (1960, 50)   # returns 1960 (no conversion done)
```

The yy_to_yyyy() function is included in the cookbook_utils.py library file of the recipes distribution.

14.14 Performing Validity Checking on Date or Time Subparts

Problem

A string passes a pattern test as a date or time, but you want to perform further validity checking.

Solution

Break the value into parts, and perform the appropriate range checking on each part.

Discussion

Pattern matching may not be sufficient for date or time checking. For example, a value like 1947-15-19 might match a date pattern, but it's not a legal date. To perform more rigorous value testing, combine pattern matching with range checking. Break out the year, month, and day values, then check whether each is within the proper range. Years should be less than 9999 (MySQL represents dates to an upper limit of 9999-12-31), month values must be in the range from 1 to 12, and days must be in the range from 1 to the number of days in the month. That last part is the trickiest: it's month-dependent, and also year-dependent for February because it changes for leap years.

Suppose that you're checking input dates in ISO format. In Recipe 14.9, we used the is_iso_date() function from the cookbook_utils.py library file to perform a pattern match on a date string and break it into component values. is_iso_date() returns None if the value doesn't satisfy a pattern that matches ISO date format. Otherwise, it returns a reference to an array containing the year, month, and day values. The cookbook_utils.py file also contains is_mmddyy_date() and is_ddmmyy_date() routines that match dates in US or British format and return None or a reference to a list of date parts. (The parts returned are always in year, month, day order, not the order in which the parts appear in the input date string.)

To perform additional checking on the result returned by any of those routines (assuming that the result is not None), pass the date parts to is_valid_date(), another library function:

```
valid = is_valid_date(ref[0], ref[1], ref[2])
```

is_valid_date() returns nonzero if the date is valid, 0 otherwise. It checks the parts of a date like this:

```
def is_valid_date(year, month, day):
  print(year, month, day)
  if year < 0: # or (month < 0) or (day < 1):
    return 0
  if year > 9999 or month > 12 or day > days_in_month(year, month):
    return 0
  return 1
```

is_valid_date() requires separate year, month, and day values, not a date string. This requires that you break candidate values into components before invoking it but makes it applicable in more contexts. For example, you can use it to check dates like 12 February 2003 by mapping the month to its numeric value before calling is_valid_date(). If is_valid_date() took a string argument assumed to be in a specific date format, it would be much less general.

is_valid_date() uses a subsidiary days_in_month() function to determine the number of days in the month represented by the date. days_in_month() requires both the year and the month as arguments because if the month is 2 (February), the number of days depends on whether the year is a leap year. This means you *must* pass a four-digit year value; two-digit years are ambiguous with respect to the century, which makes proper leap-year testing impossible. The days_in_month() and is_leap_year() functions are based on techniques taken from that recipe:

```
def is_leap_year(year):
  return ((year % 4 == 0) and ((year % 100 != 0) or (year % 400 == 0) ) )

def days_in_month(year, month):
  day_tbl = [31, 28, 31, 30, 31, 30, 31, 31, 30, 31, 30, 31]
  days = day_tbl[month - 1]

  if month == 2 and is_leap_year(year):
```

```
    days += 1
  return days
```

To perform validity checking on time values, a similar procedure applies: verify that the value matches a time pattern and break it into components, then perform range-testing on the components. For times, the ranges are 0 to 23 for the hour and 0 to 59 for the minute and second. Here is a `is_24hr_time()` function that checks for values in 24-hour format and returns the components:

```
def is_24hr_time(val):
  m = re.match('^(\d{1,2})\D(\d{2})\D(\d{2})$', val)
  if m is None:
    return None
  return[int(m.group(1)), int(m.group(2)), int(m.group(3))]
```

The following `is_ampm_time()` function is similar but looks for times in 12-hour format with an optional AM or PM suffix, converting PM times to 24-hour values:

```
def is_ampm_time(val):
  m = re.match('^(\d{1,2})\D(\d{2})\D(\d{2})(?:\s*(AM|PM))?$', val, flags = re.I)
  if m is None:
    return None
  (hour, min, sec) = (int(m.group(1)), (m.group(2)), (m.group(3)))
  # supply missing seconds
  sec = '00' if sec is None else sec
  if hour == 12 and (m.group(4) is None or m.group(4).upper() == "AM"):
    hour = '00' # 12:xx:xx AM times are 00:xx:xx
  elif int(hour) < 12 and (m.group(4) is not None) and m.group(4).upper() == "PM":
    hour = hour + 12 # PM times other than 12:xx:xx
  return [hour, min, sec] # return hour, minute, second
```

Both functions return `None` for values that don't match the pattern. Otherwise, they return a reference to a three-element array containing the hour, minute, and second values.

After you obtain the time components, pass them to `is_valid_time()`, another utility routine, to perform range checks.

14.15 Writing Date-Processing Utilities

Problem

There is a date-processing operation that you want to perform frequently.

Solution

Write a utility that performs the date-processing operation for you.

Discussion

Due to the idiosyncratic nature of dates, you might occasionally find it necessary to write date converters. This section shows some sample converters that serve various purposes:

- `isoize_date.py` reads a file looking for dates in US format (*MM-DD-YY*) and converts them to ISO format.

- `cvt_date.py` converts dates to and from ISO, US, or British formats. It is more general than `isoize_date.py` but requires that you tell it what kind of input to expect and what kind of output to produce.

- `monddyyyy_to_iso.py` looks for dates like `Feb. 6, 1788` and converts them to ISO format. It illustrates how to map dates with nonnumeric parts to a format that MySQL understands.

All three scripts are located in the *transfer* directory of the `recipes` distribution. They assume datafiles are in tab-delimited, linefeed-terminated format. To work with files that have a different format, use `cvt_file.pl`, available in the recipes distribution.

Our first date-processing utility, `isoize_date.py`, looks for dates in US format and rewrites them into ISO format. You'll recognize that it's modeled after the general input-processing loop, with some extra stuff thrown in to perform a specific type of conversion:

```python
#!/usr/bin/python3
# isoize_date.py: Read input data, look for values that match
# a date pattern, convert them to ISO format. Also converts
# 2-digit years to 4-digit years, using a transition point of 70.
# By default, this looks for dates in MM-DD-[CC]YY format.
# Does not check whether dates actually are valid (for example,
# won't complain about 13-49-1928).

# Assumes tab-delimited, linefeed-terminated input lines.

import sys
import re
import fileinput

# transition point at which 2-digit XX year values are assumed to be
# 19XX (below that, they are treated as 20XX)
transition = 70

for line in fileinput.input(sys.argv[1:]):
    val = line.split("\t", 10000);  # split, preserving all fields
    for i in range(0, len(val)):
        # look for strings in MM-DD-[CC]YY format
        m = re.match('^(\d{1,2})\D(\d{1,2})\D(\d{2,4})$', val[i])
        if not m:
            continue

        (month, day, year) = (int(m.group(1)), int(m.group(2)), int(m.group(3)))
```

```
    # to interpret dates as DD-MM-[CC]YY instead, replace preceding
    # line with the following one:
    # (day, month, year) = (int(m.group(1)), int(m.group(2)), int(m.group(3)))

    # convert 2-digit years to 4 digits, then update value in array
    if year < 100:
      year += 1900 if year >= transition else 2000
    val[i] = "%04d-%02d-%02d" % (year, month, day)
  print("\t".join (val))
```

If you feed `isoize_date.py` an input file that looks like this:

```
Sybil   04-13-70
Nancy   09-30-69
Ralph   11-02-73
Lothair 07-04-63
Henry   02-14-65
Aaron   09-17-68
Joanna  08-20-52
Stephen 05-01-60
```

It produces the following output:

```
Sybil   1970-04-13
Nancy   2069-09-30
Ralph   1973-11-02
Lothair 2063-07-04
Henry   2065-02-14
Aaron   2068-09-17
Joanna  2052-08-20
Stephen 2060-05-01
```

`isoize_date.py` serves a specific purpose: it converts only from US to ISO format. It does not perform validity checking on date subparts or permit the transition point for adding the century to be specified. A more general tool would be more useful. The next script, `cvt_date.py`, extends the capabilities of `isoize_date.py`; it recognizes input dates in ISO, US, or British formats and converts any of them to any other. It also can convert two-digit years to four digits, enable you to specify the conversion transition point, and warn about bad dates. As such, it can be used to preprocess input for loading into MySQL or postprocess data exported from MySQL for use by other programs.

`cvt_date.py` understands the following options:

`--iformat=`*format*`, --oformat=`*format*`, --format=`*format*
> Set the date format for input, output, or both. The default *format* value is `iso`; `cvt_date.py` also recognizes any string beginning with `us` or `br` as indicating US or British date format.

`--add-century`
> Convert two-digit years to four digits.

`--columns=column_list`

> Convert dates only in the named columns. By default, `cvt_date.py` looks for dates in all columns. If this option is given, `column_list` should be a list of one or more column positions or ranges separated by commas. (Ranges can be given as *m-n* to specify columns *m* through *n*.) Positions begin at 1.

`--transition=n`

> Specify the transition point for two-digit to four-digit year conversions. The default transition point is 70. This option turns on `--add-century`.

`--warn`

> Warn about bad dates. (This option can produce spurious warnings if the dates have two-digit years and you don't specify `--add-century`, because leap-year testing won't always be accurate in that case.)

We won't show the code for `cvt_date.py` here (most of it is taken up with processing command-line options), but you can examine the source for yourself if you like. As an example of how `cvt_date.py` works, suppose that you have a *newdata.txt* file with the following contents:

```
name1    01/01/99    38
name2    12/31/00    40
name3    02/28/13    42
name4    01/02/18    44
```

Running the file through `cvt_date.py` with options indicating that the dates are in US format and that the century should be added produces this result:

```
$ cvt_date.pl --iformat=us --add-century newdata.txt
name1    1999-01-01  38
name2    2000-12-31  40
name3    2013-02-28  42
name4    2018-01-02  44
```

To produce dates in British format instead with no year conversion, do this:

```
$ cvt_date.pl --iformat=us --oformat=br newdata.txt
name1    01-01-99    38
name2    31-12-00    40
name3    28-02-13    42
name4    02-01-18    44
```

`cvt_date.py` has no knowledge of the meaning of each data column, of course. If you have a nondate column with values that match the pattern, it rewrites that column, too. To deal with that, specify a `--columns` option to limit the columns that `cvt_date.py` converts.

`isoize_date.py` and `cvt_date.py` both operate on dates written in all-numeric formats. But dates in datafiles often are written differently, and it may be necessary to write a special-purpose script to process them. Suppose an input file contains dates in the following format (these represent the dates on which US states were admitted to the Union):

```
Delaware        Dec. 7, 1787
Pennsylvania    Dec 12, 1787
New Jersey      Dec. 18, 1787
Georgia         Jan. 2, 1788
Connecticut     Jan. 9, 1788
Massachusetts   Feb. 6, 1788
...
```

The dates consist of a three-character month abbreviation (possibly followed by a period), a numeric day of the month, a comma, and a numeric year. To import this file into MySQL, you must convert the dates to ISO format, resulting in a file that looks like this:

```
Delaware        1787-12-07
Pennsylvania    1787-12-12
New Jersey      1787-12-18
Georgia         1788-01-02
Connecticut     1788-01-09
Massachusetts   1788-02-06
...
```

That's a somewhat specialized kind of transformation, although this general type of problem (converting a particular date format to ISO format) is hardly uncommon. To perform the conversion, identify the dates as those values matching an appropriate pattern, map month names to the corresponding numeric values, and reformat the result. The following script, monddyyyy_to_iso.py, illustrates how:

```python
#!/usr/bin/python3
# monddyyyy_to_iso.py: Convert dates from mon[.] dd, yyyy to ISO format.

# Assumes tab-delimited, linefeed-terminated input

import re
import sys
import fileinput
import warnings

map = {"jan": 1, "feb": 2, "mar": 3, "apr": 4, "may": 5, "jun": 6,
       "jul": 7, "aug": 8, "sep": 9, "oct": 10, "nov": 11, "dec": 12
      } # map 3-char month abbreviations to numeric month

for line in fileinput.input(sys.argv[1:]):
  values = line.rstrip().split("\t", 10000)    # split, preserving all fields
  for i in range(0, len(values)):
    # reformat the value if it matches the pattern, otherwise assume
    # that it's not a date in the required format and leave it alone
    m = re.match('^([^.]+)\.? (\d+), (\d+)$', values[i])
    if m:
      # use lowercase month name
      (month, day, year) = (m.group(1).lower(), int(m.group(2)), int(m.group(3)))
#@ _CHECK_VALIDITY_
      if month in map:
#@ _CHECK_VALIDITY_
        values[i] = "%04d-%02d-%02d" % (year, map[month], day)
```

```
        else:
            # warn, but don't reformat
            warnings.warn("%s bad date?" % (values[i]))
    print("\t".join(values))
```

The script only does reformatting; it doesn't validate the dates. To do that, modify the script to use the cookbook_utils.py module by adding this statement in the beginning of the script:

```
from cookbook_utils import *
```

That gives the script access to the module's is_valid_date() routine. To use it, change this line:

```
if month in map:
```

To this:

```
if month in map and is_valid_date(year, map[month], day)):
```

14.16 Importing Non-ISO Date Values

Problem

You want to import date values, but they are not in the ISO (*YYYY-MM-DD*) format that MySQL expects.

Solution

Use an external utility to convert the dates to ISO format before importing the data into MySQL (cvt_date.py is useful here). Or use LOAD DATA's capability for preprocessing input data prior to loading it into the database.

Discussion

Suppose that a table contains three columns, name, date, and value, where date is a DATE column requiring values in ISO format (*YYYY-MM-DD*). Suppose also that you're given a *newdata.txt* datafile to be imported into the table, but its contents look like this:

```
name1   01/01/99    38
name2   12/31/00    40
name3   02/28/13    42
name4   01/02/18    44
```

The dates are in *MM/DD/YY* format and must be converted to ISO format to be stored as DATE values in MySQL. One way to do this is to run the file through the cvt_date.py script from Recipe 14.15:

```
$ cvt_date.py --iformat=us --add-century newdata.txt > tmp.txt
```

Then load the *tmp.txt* file into the table. This task also can be accomplished entirely in MySQL with no external utilities by using SQL to perform the reformatting operation. As discussed in Recipe 13.1, LOAD DATA can preprocess input values before inserting them. Applying that capability to the present problem, the date-rewriting LOAD DATA statement looks like this, using the STR_TO_DATE() function (see Recipe 8.3) to interpret the input dates:

```
mysql> LOAD DATA LOCAL INFILE 'newdata.txt'
    -> INTO TABLE t (name,@date,value)
    -> SET date = STR_TO_DATE(@date,'%m/%d/%y');
```

With the %y format specifier in STR_TO_DATE(), MySQL converts the two-digit years to four-digit years automatically, so the original *MM/DD/YY* values end up as ISO values in *YYYY-MM-DD* format. The resulting data after import looks like this:

```
+-------+------------+-------+
| name  | date       | value |
+-------+------------+-------+
| name1 | 1999-01-01 |    38 |
| name2 | 2000-12-31 |    40 |
| name3 | 2013-02-28 |    42 |
| name4 | 2018-01-02 |    44 |
+-------+------------+-------+
```

This procedure assumes that MySQL's automatic conversion of two-digit years to four digits produces the correct century values. This means that the year part of the values must correspond to years in the range from 1970 to 2069. If that's not true, you must convert the year values some other way. (For some ideas on how to do this, see Recipe 14.14.)

If the dates are not in a format that STR_TO_DATE() can interpret, perhaps you can write a stored function to handle them and return ISO date values. In that case, the LOAD DATA statement looks like this, where my_date_interp() is your stored function name:

```
mysql> LOAD DATA LOCAL INFILE 'newdata.txt'
    -> INTO TABLE t (name,@date,value)
    -> SET date = my_date_interp(@date);
```

14.17 Exporting Dates Using Non-ISO Formats

Problem

You want to export date values using a format other than MySQL's default ISO (*YYYY-MM-DD*) format. This might be a requirement when exporting dates from MySQL to applications that don't use ISO format.

Solution

Use an external utility to rewrite the dates to non-ISO format after exporting the data from MySQL (`cvt_date.py` is useful here). Or use the `DATE_FORMAT()` function to rewrite the values during the export operation.

Discussion

Suppose that you want to export data from MySQL into an application that doesn't understand ISO-format dates. One way to do this is to export the data into a file, leaving the dates in ISO format. Then run the file through a utility such as `cvt_date.py` that rewrites the dates into the required format (see Recipe 14.15).

Another approach is to export the dates directly in the required format by rewriting them with `DATE_FORMAT()`. Suppose that you have the following table:

```
CREATE TABLE datetbl
(
  i   INT,
  c   CHAR(10),
  d   DATE,
  dt  DATETIME,
  ts  TIMESTAMP,
  PRIMARY KEY(i)
);
```

Suppose also that you need to export data from this table but with the dates in any `DATE`, `DATETIME`, or `TIMESTAMP` columns rewritten in US format (*MM-DD-YYYY*). A `SELECT` statement that uses the `DATE_FORMAT()` function to rewrite the dates as required looks like this:

```
SELECT
  i,
  c,
  DATE_FORMAT(d, '%m-%d-%Y') AS d,
  DATE_FORMAT(dt, '%m-%d-%Y %T') AS dt,
  DATE_FORMAT(ts, '%m-%d-%Y %T') AS ts
FROM datetbl;
```

If `datetbl` contains the following rows:

```
3    abc    2005-12-31    2005-12-31 12:05:03    2005-12-31 12:05:03
4    xyz    2006-01-31    2006-01-31 12:05:03    2006-01-31 12:05:03
```

The statement generates output that looks like this:

```
3    abc    12-31-2005    12-31-2005 12:05:03    12-31-2005 12:05:03
4    xyz    01-31-2006    01-31-2006 12:05:03    01-31-2006 12:05:03
```

14.18 Preprocessing and Importing a File

Problem

Recall the scenario presented at the beginning of Chapter 13:

> Suppose that a file named *somedata.csv* contains 12 data columns in comma-separated values (CSV) format. From this file you want to extract only columns 2, 11, 5, and 9 and use them to create database rows in a MySQL table that contains "name,""birth,""height," and "weight" columns. You must make sure that the height and weight are positive integers, and convert the birth dates from *MM/DD/YY* format to *YYYY-MM-DD* format.

Solution

Combine techniques that we discussed in Chapter 13 and this chapter.

Discussion

Much of the work can be done using the utility programs developed in this chapter. Convert the file to tab-delimited format with `cvt_file.pl`, extract the columns in the desired order with `yank_col.pl`, and rewrite the date column to ISO format with `cvt_date.py` (see Recipe 14.15):

```
$ cvt_file.pl --iformat=csv somedata.csv \
    | yank_col.pl --columns=2,11,5,9 \
    | cvt_date.py --columns=2 --iformat=us --add-century > tmp
```

The resulting file, *tmp*, has four columns representing the `name`, `birth`, `height`, and `weight` values, in that order. It needs only to have its height and weight columns checked to make sure they contain positive integers. Using the `is_positive_inte ger()` library function from the `cookbook_utils.py` module file, that task can be achieved using a short special-purpose script that is little more than an input loop:

```
#!/usr/bin/python3
# validate_htwt.py: Height/weight validation example.

# Assumes tab-delimited, linefeed-terminated input lines.

# Input columns and the actions to perform on them are as follows:
# 1: name; echo as given
# 2: birth; echo as given
# 3: height; validate as positive integer
# 4: weight; validate as positive integer

import sys
import fileinput
import warnings
from cookbook_utils import *

line_num = 0
```

```
for line in fileinput.input(sys.argv[1:]):
    line_num += 1
    (name, birth, height, weight) = line.rstrip().split ("\t", 4)
    if not is_positive_integer(height):
        warnings.warn(f"line {line_num}:height {height} is not a positive integer")
    if not is_positive_integer(weight):
        warnings.warn(f"line {line_num}:weight {weight} is not a positive integer")
```

The `validate_htwt.py` script produces no output (except for warning messages) because it need not reformat any of the input values. If *tmp* passes validation with no errors, it can be loaded into MySQL with a simple LOAD DATA statement:

```
mysql> LOAD DATA LOCAL INFILE 'tmp' INTO TABLE tbl_name;
```

## CHAPTER 15

Generating and Using Sequences

15.0 Introduction

A sequence is a set of integers (1, 2, 3, …) generated in order on demand. Sequences see frequent use in databases because many applications require each row in a table to contain a unique value, and sequences provide an easy way to generate them. This chapter describes how to use sequences in MySQL in the following five ways:

Using AUTO_INCREMENT *columns*

The AUTO_INCREMENT column is MySQL's mechanism for generating a sequence over a set of rows. Each time you create a row in a table that contains an AUTO_INCREMENT column, MySQL automatically generates the next value in the sequence as the column's value. This value serves as a unique identifier, making sequences an easy way to create items such as customer ID numbers, shipping package waybill numbers, invoice or purchase order numbers, bug report IDs, ticket numbers, or product serial numbers.

Retrieving sequence values

For many applications, it's not enough just to create sequence values. It's also necessary to determine the sequence value for a just-inserted row. A web application may need to redisplay to a user the contents of a row created from the contents of a form just submitted by the user. The value may need to be retrieved so it can be stored in rows of a related table.

Resequencing techniques

It's possible to renumber a sequence that has holes in it due to row deletions, reuse deleted values at the top of a sequence, or add a sequence column to a table that has none.

Managing multiple simultaneous sequences

Special care is necessary when you need to keep track of multiple sequence values, such as when you create rows in multiple tables that each have an AUTO_INCREMENT column.

Using single-row sequence generators

Sequences can be used as counters. For example, to count votes in a poll, you might increment a counter each time a candidate receives a vote. The counts for a given candidate form a sequence, but because the count itself is the only value of interest, there is no need to generate a new row to record each vote. MySQL provides a solution for this problem using a mechanism that enables a sequence to be easily generated within a single table row over time. To store multiple counters in the table, use a column that identifies each counter uniquely. The same mechanism also enables creation of sequences that increase by values other than 1 or by nonuniform values.

The engines for most database systems provide sequence-generation capabilities, although the implementations tend to be engine-dependent. That's true for MySQL as well, so the material in this section is almost completely MySQL-specific, even at the SQL level. In other words, the SQL for generating sequences is itself nonportable, even if you use an API such as DBI or JDBC that provides an abstraction layer. Abstract interfaces may help you process SQL statements portably, but they don't make nonportable SQL portable.

Scripts related to the examples shown in this chapter are located in the *sequences* directory of the recipes distribution. For scripts that create the tables used here, look in the *tables* directory.

15.1 Generating a Sequence with AUTO_INCREMENT Columns

Problem

Your table includes a column that should contain only unique IDs, and you need to insert values into this column, ensuring they are part of the sequence.

Solution

Use an AUTO_INCREMENT column to generate a sequence.

Discussion

This recipe provides the essential background on using AUTO_INCREMENT columns, beginning with an example that demonstrates the sequence-generation mechanism.

The example centers around a bug-collection scenario: your eight-year-old son, Junior, is assigned the task of collecting insects for a class project at school. For each insect, Junior is to record its name ("ant," "bee," and so forth) and its date and location of collection. You have expounded the benefits of MySQL for record-keeping to Junior since his early days, so upon your arrival home from work that day, he immediately announces the necessity of completing this project and then, looking you straight in the eye, declares that it's clearly a task for which MySQL is well-suited. Who are you to argue? So the two of you get to work. Junior already collected some specimens after school while waiting for you to come home and has recorded the following information in his notebook:

Name	Date	Origin
millipede	2014-09-10	driveway
housefly	2014-09-10	kitchen
grasshopper	2014-09-10	front yard
stink bug	2014-09-10	front yard
cabbage butterfly	2014-09-10	garden
ant	2014-09-10	backyard
ant	2014-09-10	backyard
termite	2014-09-10	kitchen woodwork

Looking over Junior's notes, you're pleased to see that even at his tender age, he has learned to write dates in ISO format. However, you also notice that he's collected a millipede and a termite, neither of which actually are insects. You decide to let this pass for the moment; Junior forgot to bring home the written instructions for the project, so at this point it's unclear whether these specimens are acceptable. (You also note with some alarm Junior's discovery of termites in the house and make a mental note to call the exterminator.)

As you consider how to create a table to store this information, it's apparent that you need at least name, date, and origin columns corresponding to the types of information that Junior is required to record:

```
CREATE TABLE insect
(
  name    VARCHAR(30) NOT NULL,   # type of insect
  date    DATE NOT NULL,          # date collected
  origin  VARCHAR(30) NOT NULL    # where collected
);
```

However, those columns are insufficient to make the table easy to use. Note that the records collected thus far are not unique; both ants were collected at the same time and place. If you put the information into an insect table that has the structure just shown, neither ant row can be referred to individually because there's nothing to distinguish one from another. Unique IDs would be helpful to make the rows distinct and to provide values that make each row easy to refer to. An AUTO_INCREMENT column is good for this purpose, so a better `insect` table has a structure like this:

```
CREATE TABLE insect
(
  id      INT UNSIGNED NOT NULL AUTO_INCREMENT,
  PRIMARY KEY (id),
  name    VARCHAR(30) NOT NULL,    # type of insect
  date    DATE NOT NULL,           # date collected
  origin  VARCHAR(30) NOT NULL     # where collected
);
```

Go ahead and create the `insect` table using this second CREATE TABLE statement. (Recipe 15.2 discusses the particulars of the `id` column definition.)

Now that you have an AUTO_INCREMENT column, use it to generate new sequence values. One of the useful properties of an AUTO_INCREMENT column is that you need not assign its values yourself: MySQL does so for you. There are two ways to generate new AUTO_INCREMENT values in the `id` column. One is to explicitly set the `id` column to NULL. The following statement inserts the first four of Junior's specimens into the `insect` table that way:

```
mysql> INSERT INTO insect (id,name,date,origin) VALUES
    -> (NULL,'housefly','2014-09-10','kitchen'),
    -> (NULL,'millipede','2014-09-10','driveway'),
    -> (NULL,'grasshopper','2014-09-10','front yard'),
    -> (NULL,'stink bug','2014-09-10','front yard');
```

Alternatively, omit the `id` column from the INSERT statement entirely. MySQL permits creating rows without explicitly specifying values for columns that have a default value. MySQL assigns each missing column its default value, and the default for an AUTO_INCREMENT column is its next sequence number. Thus, this statement adds Junior's other four specimens to the `insect` table and generates sequence values without naming the `id` column at all:

```
mysql> INSERT INTO insect (name,date,origin) VALUES
    -> ('cabbage butterfly','2014-09-10','garden'),
    -> ('ant','2014-09-10','backyard'),
    -> ('ant','2014-09-10','backyard'),
    -> ('termite','2014-09-10','kitchen woodwork');
```

Whichever method you use, MySQL determines the sequence number for each row and assigns it to the `id` column, as you can verify:

```
mysql> SELECT * FROM insect ORDER BY id;
+----+-------------------+------------+------------------+
| id | name              | date       | origin           |
+----+-------------------+------------+------------------+
|  1 | housefly          | 2014-09-10 | kitchen          |
|  2 | millipede         | 2014-09-10 | driveway         |
|  3 | grasshopper       | 2014-09-10 | front yard       |
|  4 | stink bug         | 2014-09-10 | front yard       |
|  5 | cabbage butterfly | 2014-09-10 | garden           |
|  6 | ant               | 2014-09-10 | backyard         |
```

```
|  7 | ant              | 2014-09-10 | backyard         |
|  8 | termite          | 2014-09-10 | kitchen woodwork |
+----+------------------+------------+------------------+
```

As Junior collects more specimens, add more rows to the table and they'll be assigned the next values in the sequence (9, 10, …).

The concept underlying AUTO_INCREMENT columns is simple enough in principle: each time you create a new row, MySQL generates the next number in the sequence and assigns it to the row. But there are certain subtleties to know about, as well as differences in how different storage engines handle AUTO_INCREMENT sequences. Awareness of these issues enables you to use sequences more effectively and avoid surprises. For example, if you explicitly set the id column to a non-NULL value, one of two things happens:

- If the value is already present in the table, an error occurs if the column cannot contain duplicates. For the insect table, the id column is a PRIMARY KEY, which prohibits duplicates:

  ```
  mysql> INSERT INTO insect (id,name,date,origin) VALUES
      -> (3,'cricket','2014-09-11','basement');
  ERROR 1062 (23000): Duplicate entry '3' for key 'PRIMARY'
  ```

- If the value is not present in the table, MySQL inserts the row using that value. In addition, if the value is larger than the current sequence counter, the table's counter is reset to the value plus 1. The insect table at this point has sequence values 1 through 8. If you insert a new row with the id column set to 20, that becomes the new maximum value. Subsequent inserts that automatically generate id values will begin at 21. The values 9 through 19 become unused, resulting in a gap in the sequence.

The next recipe looks in more detail at how to define AUTO_INCREMENT columns and how they behave.

15.2 Choosing the Data Type for a Sequence Column

Problem

You want to choose the correct data type to define a sequence column.

Solution

Consider how many unique values your sequence should hold, and choose the data type accordingly.

Discussion

You should follow certain principles when creating AUTO_INCREMENT columns. As an illustration, consider how Recipe 15.1 declared the id column in the insect table:

```
id INT UNSIGNED NOT NULL AUTO_INCREMENT,
PRIMARY KEY (id)
```

The AUTO_INCREMENT keyword informs MySQL that it should generate successive sequence numbers for the column's values, but the other information is important, too:

- INT is the column's base data type. You need not necessarily use INT, but the column should be one of the integer types: TINYINT, SMALLINT, MEDIUMINT, INT, or BIGINT.

- UNSIGNED prohibits negative column values. This is not a required attribute for AUTO_INCREMENT columns, but sequences consist only of positive integers (normally beginning at 1), so there is no reason to permit negative values. Furthermore, *not* declaring the column to be UNSIGNED cuts the range of your sequence in half. For example, TINYINT has a range of –128 to 127. Because sequences include only positive values, the effective range of a TINYINT sequence is 1 to 127. TINYINT UNSIGNED has a range of 0 to 255, which increases the upper end of the sequence to 255. The specific integer type determines the maximum sequence value. The following table shows the maximum unsigned value of each type; use this information to choose a type big enough to hold the largest value you'll need:

Data type	Maximum unsigned value
TINYINT	255
SMALLINT	65,535
MEDIUMINT	16,777,215
INT	4,294,967,295
BIGINT	18,446,744,073,709,551,615

Sometimes people omit UNSIGNED so that they can create rows that contain negative numbers in the sequence column (using –1 to signify "has no ID," for example.) This is a bad idea. MySQL makes no guarantees about how negative numbers will be treated in an AUTO_INCREMENT column, so by using them you're playing with fire. For example, if you resequence the column, all your negative values get turned into positive sequence numbers.

- AUTO_INCREMENT columns cannot contain NULL values, so id is declared as NOT NULL. (It's true that you can specify NULL as the column value when you insert a new row, but for an AUTO_INCREMENT column, that really means "generate the next sequence value.") MySQL automatically defines AUTO_INCREMENT columns as NOT NULL if you forget.

- AUTO_INCREMENT columns must be indexed. Normally, because a sequence column exists to provide unique identifiers, you use a PRIMARY KEY or UNIQUE index to enforce uniqueness. Tables can have only one PRIMARY KEY, so if the table already has some other PRIMARY KEY column, you can declare an AUTO_INCREMENT column to have a UNIQUE index instead:

```
id INT UNSIGNED NOT NULL AUTO_INCREMENT,
UNIQUE (id)
```

When you create a table that contains an AUTO_INCREMENT column, it's also important to consider which storage engine to use (InnoDB, MyISAM, and so forth). The engine affects behaviors such as reuse of values deleted from the top of the sequence (see Recipe 15.3).

15.3 Deleting Rows Without Changing a Sequence

Problem

You want to delete a few rows from the table that contains an AUTO_INCREMENT column.

Solution

Use a regular DELETE statement. MySQL would not change the generated sequence numbers for the existing rows.

Discussion

We have thus far considered how MySQL generates sequence values in an AUTO_INCREMENT column under circumstances where rows are only added to a table. But it's unrealistic to assume that rows will never be deleted. What happens to the sequence then?

Refer again to Junior's bug-collection project, for which you currently have an insect table that looks like this:

```
mysql> SELECT * FROM insect ORDER BY id;
+----+------------------+------------+------------+
| id | name             | date       | origin     |
+----+------------------+------------+------------+
|  1 | housefly         | 2014-09-10 | kitchen    |
|  2 | millipede        | 2014-09-10 | driveway   |
|  3 | grasshopper      | 2014-09-10 | front yard |
|  4 | stink bug        | 2014-09-10 | front yard |
|  5 | cabbage butterfly| 2014-09-10 | garden     |
|  6 | ant              | 2014-09-10 | backyard   |
```

```
|  7 | ant              | 2014-09-10 | backyard        |
|  8 | termite          | 2014-09-10 | kitchen woodwork |
+----+------------------+------------+-----------------+
```

That's about to change because after Junior remembers to bring home the written instructions for the project, you read through them and discover two things that affect the table contents:

- Specimens should include only insects, not insect-like creatures such as millipedes and termites.

- The purpose of the project is to collect as many *different* specimens as possible, not just as *many* specimens as possible. This means that only one ant row is permitted.

These instructions dictate that a few rows be removed from the table—specifically those with id values 2 (millipede), 8 (termite), and 7 (duplicate ant). Thus, despite Junior's evident disappointment at the reduction in the size of his collection, you instruct him to remove those rows by issuing a DELETE statement:

```
mysql> DELETE FROM insect WHERE id IN (2,8,7);
```

This statement illustrates why it's useful to have unique ID values: they enable you to specify any row unambiguously. The ant rows are identical except for the id value. Without that column in the table, it would be more difficult to delete just one of them (though not impossible; see Recipe 18.5).

After removing the unsuitable rows, the table has these remaining:

```
mysql> SELECT * FROM insect ORDER BY id;
+----+-----------------+------------+------------+
| id | name            | date       | origin     |
+----+-----------------+------------+------------+
|  1 | housefly        | 2014-09-10 | kitchen    |
|  3 | grasshopper     | 2014-09-10 | front yard |
|  4 | stink bug       | 2014-09-10 | front yard |
|  5 | cabbage butterfly | 2014-09-10 | garden   |
|  6 | ant             | 2014-09-10 | backyard   |
+----+-----------------+------------+------------+
```

The id column sequence now has a hole (row 2 is missing), and the values 7 and 8 at the top of the sequence are no longer present. How do these deletions affect future insert operations? What sequence number will the next new row get?

Removing row 2 creates a gap in the middle of the sequence. This has no effect on subsequent inserts, because MySQL makes no attempt to fill in holes in a sequence. On the other hand, deleting rows 7 and 8 removes values at the top of the sequence. For InnoDB or MyISAM tables, values are not reused. The next sequence number is the smallest positive integer that has not previously been used. (For a sequence that stands at 8, the next row gets a value of 9 even if you delete rows 7 and 8 first.) If you require strictly monotonic sequences, you can use one of these storage engines. For other storage engines, values removed at the top of the sequence may or may not be reused. Check the properties of the engine before using it.

If a table uses an engine that differs in value-reuse behavior from the behavior you require, use ALTER TABLE to change the table to a more appropriate engine. For example, to change a table to use InnoDB (to prevent sequence values from being reused after rows are deleted), do this:

```
ALTER TABLE tbl_name ENGINE = InnoDB;
```

If you don't know what engine a table uses, consult INFORMATION_SCHEMA or use SHOW TABLE STATUS or SHOW CREATE TABLE to find out. For example, the following statement indicates that insect is an InnoDB table:

```
mysql> SELECT ENGINE FROM INFORMATION_SCHEMA.TABLES
    -> WHERE TABLE_SCHEMA = 'cookbook' AND TABLE_NAME = 'insect';
+--------+
| ENGINE |
+--------+
| InnoDB |
+--------+
```

To empty a table and reset the sequence counter (even for engines that normally do not reuse values), use TRUNCATE TABLE:

```
TRUNCATE TABLE tbl_name;
```

15.4 Retrieving Sequence Values

Problem

After creating a row that includes a new sequence number, you want to know what that number is.

Solution

Invoke the LAST_INSERT_ID() function. If you're writing a program, your MySQL API may provide a way to get the value directly without issuing a SQL statement.

Discussion

It's common for applications to need to know the AUTO_INCREMENT value of a newly created row. For example, if you write a web-based frontend for entering rows into Junior's insect table, you might have the application display each new row nicely formatted in a new page immediately after you hit the Submit button. To do this, you must know the new id value so that you can retrieve the proper row. Another situation in which the AUTO_INCREMENT value is needed occurs when you use multiple tables: after inserting a row in a main table, you need its ID to create rows in other related tables that refer to the row in the main table. (Recipe 15.11 shows how to do this.)

When you generate a new AUTO_INCREMENT value, one way to get the value from the server is to execute a statement that invokes the LAST_INSERT_ID() function. In addition, many MySQL APIs provide a client-side mechanism for making the value available without issuing another statement. This recipe discusses both methods and compares their characteristics.

Using LAST_INSERT_ID() to obtain AUTO_INCREMENT values

The obvious (but incorrect) way to determine a new row's AUTO_INCREMENT value uses the fact that when MySQL generates the value, it becomes the largest sequence number in the column. Thus, you might try using the MAX() function to retrieve it:

```
SELECT MAX(id) FROM insect;
```

This is unreliable; if another client inserts a row before you issue the SELECT statement, MAX(id) returns that client's ID, not yours. It's possible to solve this problem by grouping the INSERT and SELECT statements as a transaction or locking the table, but MySQL provides a simpler way to obtain the proper value: invoke the LAST_INSERT_ID() function. It returns the most recent AUTO_INCREMENT value generated within your session, regardless of what other clients are doing. For example, to insert a row into the insect table and retrieve its id value, do this:

```
mysql> INSERT INTO insect (name,date,origin)
    -> VALUES('cricket','2014-09-11','basement');
mysql> SELECT LAST_INSERT_ID();
+------------------+
| LAST_INSERT_ID() |
+------------------+
|                9 |
+------------------+
```

Or you can use the new value to retrieve the entire row, without even knowing what it is:

```
mysql> INSERT INTO insect (name,date,origin)
    -> VALUES('moth','2014-09-14','windowsill');
mysql> SELECT * FROM insect WHERE id = LAST_INSERT_ID();
+----+------+------------+------------+
| id | name | date       | origin     |
+----+------+------------+------------+
| 10 | moth | 2014-09-14 | windowsill |
+----+------+------------+------------+
```

The server maintains the value returned by LAST_INSERT_ID() on a session-specific basis. This property is by design, and it's important because it prevents clients from interfering with one another. When you generate an AUTO_INCREMENT value, LAST_INSERT_ID() returns that specific value, even when other clients generate new rows in the same table in the meantime.

Using API-specific methods to obtain AUTO_INCREMENT values

LAST_INSERT_ID() is a SQL function, so you can use it from within any client that can execute SQL statements. On the other hand, you do have to execute a separate statement to get its value. When you write your own programs, you may have another choice. Many MySQL interfaces include an API-specific extension that returns the AUTO_INCREMENT value without executing an additional statement. Most of our APIs have this capability:

Perl

Use the `mysql_insertid` attribute to obtain the AUTO_INCREMENT value generated by a statement. This attribute is accessed through either a database handle or a statement handle, depending on how you issue the statement. The following example references it through the database handle:

```
$dbh->do ("INSERT INTO insect (name,date,origin)
           VALUES('moth','2014-09-14','windowsill')");
my $seq = $dbh->{mysql_insertid};
```

To access `mysql_insertid` as a statement-handle attribute, use `prepare()` and `execute()`:

```
my $sth = $dbh->prepare ("INSERT INTO insect (name,date,origin)
                          VALUES('moth','2014-09-14','windowsill')");
$sth->execute ();
my $seq = $sth->{mysql_insertid};
```

Ruby

The Ruby Mysql2 gem exposes the client-side AUTO_INCREMENT value using the `last_id` method:

```
client.query("INSERT INTO insect (name,date,origin)
       VALUES('moth','2014-09-14','windowsill')")
seq = client.last_id
```

PHP

The PDO interface for MySQL has a `lastInsertId()` database-handle method that returns the most recent AUTO_INCREMENT value:

```
$dbh->exec ("INSERT INTO insect (name,date,origin)
       VALUES('moth','2014-09-14','windowsill')");
$seq = $dbh->lastInsertId ();
```

Python

The Connector/Python driver for DB API provides a `lastrowid` cursor object attribute that returns the most recent AUTO_INCREMENT value:

```
cursor = conn.cursor()
cursor.execute('''
            INSERT INTO insect (name,date,origin)
            VALUES('moth','2014-09-14','windowsill')
            ''')
seq = cursor.lastrowid
```

Java

The Connector/J JDBC driver getGeneratedKeys() method returns AUTO_INCREMENT values. It can be used with a Statement or PreparedStatement object if you supply an additional Statement.RETURN_GENERATED_KEYS argument during the statement-execution process to indicate that you want to retrieve the sequence value.

For a Statement:

```
Statement s = conn.createStatement ();
s.executeUpdate ("INSERT INTO insect (name,date,origin)"
             + " VALUES('moth','2014-09-14','windowsill')",
             Statement.RETURN_GENERATED_KEYS);
```

For a PreparedStatement:

```
PreparedStatement s = conn.prepareStatement (
             "INSERT INTO insect (name,date,origin)"
             + " VALUES('moth','2014-09-14','windowsill')",
             Statement.RETURN_GENERATED_KEYS);
s.executeUpdate ();
```

Then generate a new result set from getGeneratedKeys() to access the sequence value:

```
long seq;
ResultSet rs = s.getGeneratedKeys ();
if (rs.next ())
{
  seq = rs.getLong (1);
}
else
{
  throw new SQLException ("getGeneratedKeys() produced no value");
}
rs.close ();
s.close ();
```

Go

The Go MySQL driver provides the LastInsertId method of the Result interface that returns the latest AUTO_INCREMENT value:

```
res, err := db.Exec(`INSERT INTO insect (name,date,origin)
                    VALUES ('moth','2014-09-14','windowsill')`)
seq, err := res.LastInsertId()
```

Server-side and client-side sequence value retrieval compared

As mentioned earlier, the server maintains the value of LAST_INSERT_ID() on a session-specific basis. By contrast, the API-specific methods for accessing AUTO_INCREMENT values directly are implemented on the client side. Server-side and client-side sequence value retrieval methods have some similarities but also some differences.

All methods, both server-side and client-side, require that you access an AUTO_INCREMENT value within the same MySQL session that generated it. If you generate an AUTO_INCREMENT value, then disconnect from the server and reconnect before attempting to access the value, you'll get zero. Within a given session, the persistence of AUTO_INCREMENT values can be much longer on the server side of the session:

- After you execute a statement that generates an AUTO_INCREMENT value, the value remains available through LAST_INSERT_ID() even if you execute other statements, as long as none of those statements generate an AUTO_INCREMENT value.

- The sequence value available using client-side API methods typically is set for *every* statement, not only those that generate AUTO_INCREMENT values. If you execute an INSERT statement that generates a new value and then execute some other statement before accessing the client-side sequence value, it probably will have been set to zero. The precise behavior varies among APIs, but to be safe, you can do this: when a statement generates a sequence value that you won't use immediately, save the value in a variable that you can refer to later. Otherwise, you may find the sequence value wiped out by the time you try to access it. (For more on this topic, see Recipe 15.10.)

15.5 Renumbering an Existing Sequence

Problem

You have gaps in a sequence column, and you want to resequence it.

Solution

First, consider whether resequencing is necessary. In many cases it is not. But if you have to, resequence the AUTO_INCREMENT columns periodically.

Discussion

If you insert rows into a table that has an AUTO_INCREMENT column and never delete any of them, values in the column form an unbroken sequence. If you delete rows, the sequence begins to have holes in it. For example, Junior's insect table currently looks something like this, with gaps in the sequence (assuming that you've inserted the cricket and moth rows shown in Recipe 15.4):

```
mysql> SELECT * FROM insect ORDER BY id;
+----+------------------+------------+------------+
| id | name             | date       | origin     |
+----+------------------+------------+------------+
|  1 | housefly         | 2014-09-10 | kitchen    |
|  3 | grasshopper      | 2014-09-10 | front yard |
|  4 | stink bug        | 2014-09-10 | front yard |
|  5 | cabbage butterfly| 2014-09-10 | garden     |
|  6 | ant              | 2014-09-10 | backyard   |
|  9 | cricket          | 2014-09-11 | basement   |
| 10 | moth             | 2014-09-14 | windowsill |
+----+------------------+------------+------------+
```

MySQL won't attempt to eliminate these gaps by filling in the unused values when you insert new rows. People who dislike this behavior tend to resequence AUTO_INCREMENT columns periodically to eliminate the holes. The examples in this recipe show how to do that. It's also possible to extend the range of an existing sequence (see Recipe 15.6), force deleted values at the top of a sequence to be reused (see Recipe 15.7), number rows in a particular order (see Recipe 15.8), or add a sequence column to a table that doesn't currently have one (see Recipe 15.9).

Before you decide to resequence an AUTO_INCREMENT column, consider whether that's really necessary. It usually isn't and in some cases can cause you real problems. For example, you should *not* resequence a column containing values that are referenced by another table. Renumbering the values destroys their correspondence to values in the other table, making it impossible to properly relate rows in the two tables to one another.

Here are reasons we have seen advanced for resequencing a column:

Aesthetics
Some people prefer unbroken sequences to sequences with holes in them. If this is why you want to resequence, there's probably not much we can say to convince you otherwise. Nevertheless, it's not a particularly good reason.

Performance
The impetus for resequencing may stem from the notion that doing so "compacts" a sequence column by removing gaps and enables MySQL to run statements more quickly. This is not true. MySQL doesn't care whether there are holes, and there is no performance gain to be had by renumbering an AUTO_INCREMENT column. In fact, resequencing affects performance negatively in the sense that the table remains locked while MySQL performs the operation—which may take a nontrivial amount of time for a large table. Other clients can read from the table while this is happening, but clients trying to insert new rows are blocked until the operation is complete.

Running out of numbers
The sequence column's data type and signedness determine its upper limit (see Recipe 15.2). If an AUTO_INCREMENT sequence is approaching the upper limit

of its data type, renumbering packs the sequence and frees up more values at the top. This may be a legitimate reason to resequence a column, but it is still unnecessary in many cases. You may be able to change the column data type to increase its upper limit without changing the values stored in the column; see Recipe 15.6.

If you're still determined to resequence a column, it's easy to do: drop the column from the table, then put it back. MySQL renumbers the values in the column in an unbroken sequence. The following example shows how to renumber the id values in the insect table using this technique:

```
mysql> ALTER TABLE insect DROP id;
mysql> ALTER TABLE insect
    -> ADD id INT UNSIGNED NOT NULL AUTO_INCREMENT FIRST,
    -> ADD PRIMARY KEY (id);
```

The first ALTER TABLE statement gets rid of the id column (and as a result also drops the PRIMARY KEY, because the column to which it refers is no longer present). The second statement restores the column to the table and establishes it as the PRIMARY KEY. (The FIRST keyword places the column first in the table, which is where it was originally. Normally, ADD puts columns at the end of the table.)

When you add an AUTO_INCREMENT column to a table, MySQL automatically numbers all the rows consecutively, so the resulting contents of the insect table look like this:

```
mysql> SELECT * FROM insect ORDER BY id;
+----+------------------+------------+-----------+
| id | name             | date       | origin    |
+----+------------------+------------+-----------+
|  1 | housefly         | 2014-09-10 | kitchen   |
|  2 | grasshopper      | 2014-09-10 | front yard |
|  3 | stink bug        | 2014-09-10 | front yard |
|  4 | cabbage butterfly | 2014-09-10 | garden    |
|  5 | ant              | 2014-09-10 | backyard  |
|  6 | cricket          | 2014-09-11 | basement  |
|  7 | moth             | 2014-09-14 | windowsill |
+----+------------------+------------+-----------+
```

One problem with resequencing a column using separate ALTER TABLE statements is that the table is without that column for the interval between the two operations. This might cause difficulties for other clients that try to access the table during that time. To prevent this from happening, perform both operations with a single ALTER TABLE statement:

```
mysql> ALTER TABLE insect
    -> DROP id,
    -> ADD id INT UNSIGNED NOT NULL AUTO_INCREMENT FIRST;
```

MySQL permits multiple actions to be done with ALTER TABLE (something not true for all database systems). However, notice that this multiple-action statement is not simply a concatenation of the two single-action ALTER TABLE statements. The difference is that it is unnecessary to reestablish the PRIMARY KEY: MySQL doesn't drop it unless the indexed column is missing after all the actions specified in the ALTER TABLE statement have been performed.

15.6 Extending the Range of a Sequence Column

Problem

You want to avoid resequencing a column, but you're running out of room for new sequence numbers.

Solution

Check whether you can make the column UNSIGNED or change it to use a larger integer type.

Discussion

Resequencing an AUTO_INCREMENT column changes the contents of potentially every row in the table. It's often possible to avoid this by extending the range of the column, which changes the table's structure rather than its contents:

- If the data type is signed, make it UNSIGNED to double the range of available values. Suppose that an id column currently is defined like this:

    ```
    id MEDIUMINT NOT NULL AUTO_INCREMENT
    ```

    The upper range of a signed MEDIUMINT column is 8,388,607. To increase this to 16,777,215, make the column UNSIGNED with ALTER TABLE:

    ```
    ALTER TABLE tbl_name MODIFY id MEDIUMINT UNSIGNED NOT NULL AUTO_INCREMENT;
    ```

- If your column is already UNSIGNED and it is not already the largest integer type (BIGINT), converting it to a larger type increases its range. Use ALTER TABLE for this, too. Convert the id column in the previous example from MEDIUMINT to BIGINT like so:

    ```
    ALTER TABLE tbl_name MODIFY id BIGINT UNSIGNED NOT NULL AUTO_INCREMENT;
    ```

Recipe 15.2 shows the ranges for each integer data type, which can help you choose an appropriate type.

15.7 Reusing Values at the Top of a Sequence

Problem

You've deleted rows at the top end of your sequence, and you want to avoid resequencing the column but still reuse the values.

Solution

Use ALTER TABLE to reset the sequence counter. New sequence numbers will begin with the value one larger than the current maximum in the table.

Discussion

If you have removed rows only from the top of the sequence, those that remain are still in order with no gaps. (For example, if you have rows numbered 1 to 100 and you remove the rows with numbers 91 to 100, the remaining rows are still in unbroken sequence from 1 to 90.) In this special case, it's unnecessary to renumber the column. Instead, tell MySQL to resume the sequence beginning with the value one larger than the highest existing sequence number by executing this statement, which causes MySQL to reset the sequence counter down as far as it can for new rows:

```
ALTER TABLE tbl_name AUTO_INCREMENT = 1;
```

You can use ALTER TABLE to reset the sequence counter if a sequence column contains gaps in the middle, but doing so still reuses only values deleted from the top of the sequence. It does not eliminate the gaps. Suppose that a table contains sequence values from 1 to 10, from which you delete the rows for values 3, 4, 5, 9, and 10. The maximum remaining value is 8, so if you use ALTER TABLE to reset the sequence counter, the next row is given a value of 9, not 3. To resequence a table to eliminate the gaps, see Recipe 15.5.

15.8 Ensuring That Rows Are Renumbered in a Particular Order

Problem

You resequenced a column, but MySQL didn't number the rows the way you want.

Solution

Select the rows into another table, using an ORDER BY clause to place them in the order you want, and let MySQL number them according to the sort order as it performs the operation.

Discussion

When you resequence an AUTO_INCREMENT column, MySQL is free to pick the rows from the table in any order, so it doesn't necessarily renumber them in the order that you expect. This doesn't matter at all if your only requirement is that each row have a unique identifier. But you might have an application for which it's important that the rows be assigned sequence numbers in a particular order. For example, you may want the sequence to correspond to the order in which rows were created, as indicated by a TIMESTAMP column. To assign numbers in a particular order, use this procedure:

1. Create an empty clone of the table (see Recipe 6.1).

2. Copy rows from the original into the clone using INSERT INTO...SELECT. Copy all columns except the AUTO_INCREMENT column, using an ORDER BY clause to specify the order in which rows are copied (and thus the order in which MySQL assigns numbers to the AUTO_INCREMENT column).

3. Drop the original table, and rename the clone to have the original table's name.

4. If the table is a large MyISAM table and has multiple indexes, it is more efficient to create the new table initially with no indexes except the one on the AUTO_INCREMENT column. Then copy the original table into the new table and use ALTER TABLE to add the remaining indexes afterward.

   This applies to InnoDB as well. But InnoDB Change Buffer (*https://oreil.ly/KYIP1*) caches changes to the secondary indexes in memory and then flushes them to the disk in the background. This allows you to keep insert performance at a good speed.

An alternative procedure also works:

1. Create a new table that contains all the columns of the original table except the AUTO_INCREMENT column.

2. Use INSERT INTO...SELECT to copy the non-AUTO_INCREMENT columns from the original table into the new table.

3. Use TRUNCATE TABLE on the original table to empty it; this also resets the sequence counter to 1.

4. Copy rows from the new table back to the original table, using an ORDER BY clause to sort rows into the order in which you want sequence numbers assigned. MySQL assigns sequence values to the AUTO_INCREMENT column.

15.9 Sequencing an Unsequenced Table

Problem

You forgot to include a sequence column when you created a table. Is it too late to sequence the table rows?

Solution

No. Add an AUTO_INCREMENT column using ALTER TABLE; MySQL creates the column and numbers its rows.

Discussion

Suppose that a table contains name and age columns but no sequence column:

```
mysql> SELECT * FROM t;
+----------+------+
| name     | age  |
+----------+------+
| boris    |   47 |
| clarence |   62 |
| abner    |   53 |
+----------+------+
```

Add a sequence column named id to the table as follows:

```
mysql> ALTER TABLE t
    -> ADD id INT NOT NULL AUTO_INCREMENT,
    -> ADD PRIMARY KEY (id);
mysql> SELECT * FROM t ORDER BY id;
+----------+------+----+
| name     | age  | id |
+----------+------+----+
| boris    |   47 |  1 |
| clarence |   62 |  2 |
| abner    |   53 |  3 |
+----------+------+----+
```

MySQL numbers the rows for you; it's unnecessary to assign the values yourself. Very handy.

By default, ALTER TABLE adds new columns to the end of the table. To place a column at a specific position, use FIRST or AFTER at the end of the ADD clause. The following ALTER TABLE statements are similar to the one just shown but place the id column first in the table or after the name column, respectively:

```
ALTER TABLE t
  ADD id INT NOT NULL AUTO_INCREMENT FIRST,
  ADD PRIMARY KEY (id);

ALTER TABLE t
  ADD id INT NOT NULL AUTO_INCREMENT AFTER name,
  ADD PRIMARY KEY (id);
```

15.10 Managing Multiple Auto-Increment Values Simultaneously

Problem

You're executing multiple statements that generate AUTO_INCREMENT values, and it's necessary to keep track of them independently. For example, you're inserting rows into multiple tables, each of which has its own AUTO_INCREMENT column.

Solution

Save the sequence values in variables for later use. Alternatively, if you execute sequence-generating statements from within a program, you might be able to issue the statements using separate connection or statement objects to keep them from getting mixed up.

Discussion

As described in Recipe 15.4, the LAST_INSERT_ID() server-side sequence value function is set each time a statement generates an AUTO_INCREMENT value, whereas client-side sequence indicators may be reset for every statement. What if you issue a statement that generates an AUTO_INCREMENT value, but you don't want to refer to that value until after issuing a second statement that also generates an AUTO_INCREMENT value? In this case, the original value is no longer accessible, either through LAST_INSERT_ID() or as a client-side value. To retain access to it, save the value first before issuing the second statement. There are several ways to do this:

- At the SQL level, save the value in a user-defined variable after issuing a statement that generates an AUTO_INCREMENT value:

  ```
  INSERT INTO tbl_name (id,...) VALUES(NULL,...);
  SET @saved_id = LAST_INSERT_ID();
  ```

  Then you can issue other statements without regard to their effect on LAST_INSERT_ID(). To use the original AUTO_INCREMENT value in a subsequent statement, refer to the @saved_id variable.

- At the API level, save the AUTO_INCREMENT value in an API language variable. This can be done by saving the value returned from either LAST_INSERT_ID() or any API-specific extension that is available.

- Some APIs enable you to maintain separate client-side AUTO_INCREMENT values. For example, Perl DBI statement handles have a mysql_insertid attribute, and the attribute value for one handle is unaffected by activity on another. In Java, use separate Statement or PreparedStatement objects.

See Recipe 15.11 for application of these techniques to situations in which you must insert rows into multiple tables that each contain an AUTO_INCREMENT column.

15.11 Using Auto-Increment Values to Associate Tables

Problem

You use sequence values from one table as keys in a second table so that you can associate rows in the two tables with one another. But the associations aren't being set up properly.

Solution

You're probably not inserting rows in the proper order, or you're losing track of the sequence values. Change the insertion order, or save the sequence values so that you can refer to them when you need them.

Discussion

Be careful with an AUTO_INCREMENT value used as an ID value in a source table if you also store the value in detail table rows for the purpose of linking the detail rows to the proper source table row. Suppose that an invoice table lists invoice information for customer orders, and an inv_item table lists the individual items associated with each invoice. Here, invoice is the source table and inv_item is the detail table. To uniquely identify each order, include an AUTO_INCREMENT column, inv_id, in the invoice table. You'd also store the appropriate invoice number in each inv_item table row so that you can tell which invoice it goes with. The tables might look something like this:

```
CREATE TABLE invoice
(
  inv_id  INT UNSIGNED NOT NULL AUTO_INCREMENT,
  PRIMARY KEY (inv_id),
  date    DATE NOT NULL
  # ... other columns could go here
  # ... (customer ID, shipping address, etc.)
);
CREATE TABLE inv_item
(
  inv_id     INT UNSIGNED NOT NULL,  # invoice ID (from invoice table)
  INDEX (inv_id),
  qty        INT,                    # quantity
  description VARCHAR(40)            # description
);
```

For this kind of table relationship, it's typical to insert a row into the source table first (to generate the AUTO_INCREMENT value that identifies the row) and then insert the detail rows using LAST_INSERT_ID() to obtain the source row ID. If a customer buys a hammer, three boxes of nails, and (in anticipation of finger-bashing with the hammer) a dozen bandages, the rows pertaining to the order can be inserted into the two tables like so:

```
INSERT INTO invoice (inv_id,date)
  VALUES(NULL,CURDATE());
INSERT INTO inv_item (inv_id,qty,description)
  VALUES(LAST_INSERT_ID(),1,'hammer');
INSERT INTO inv_item (inv_id,qty,description)
  VALUES(LAST_INSERT_ID(),3,'nails, box');
INSERT INTO inv_item (inv_id,qty,description)
  VALUES(LAST_INSERT_ID(),12,'bandage');
```

The first INSERT adds a row to the invoice source table and generates a new AUTO_INCREMENT value for its inv_id column. The following INSERT statements each add a row to the inv_item detail table, using LAST_INSERT_ID() to get the invoice number. This associates the detail rows with the proper source row.

What if you have multiple invoices to process? There's a right way and a wrong way to enter the information. The right way is to insert all the information for the first invoice, then proceed to the next. The wrong way is to add all the source rows into the invoice table, then add all the detail rows to the inv_item table. If you do that, *all* the new detail rows in the inv_item table have the AUTO_INCREMENT value from the most recently entered invoice row. Thus, all items appear to be part of that invoice, and rows in the two tables don't have the proper associations.

If the detail table contains its own AUTO_INCREMENT column, you must be even more careful about how you add rows to the tables. Suppose that you want each row in the inv_item table to have a unique identifier. To do that, create the inv_item table as follows with an AUTO_INCREMENT column named item_id:

```
CREATE TABLE inv_item
(
  inv_id  INT UNSIGNED NOT NULL,  # invoice ID (from invoice table)
  item_id INT UNSIGNED NOT NULL AUTO_INCREMENT, # item ID
  PRIMARY KEY (item_id),
  qty     INT,                        # quantity
  description VARCHAR(40)              # description
);
```

The inv_id column enables each inv_item row to be associated with the proper invoice table row, just as with the original table structure. In addition, item_id uniquely identifies each item row. However, now that both tables contain an AUTO_INCREMENT column, you cannot enter information for an invoice the same way as before. If you execute the INSERT statements shown previously, they now produce a different result due to the change in the inv_item table structure. The INSERT into the invoice table works properly. So does the first INSERT into the inv_item table; LAST_INSERT_ID() returns the inv_id value from the source row in the invoice table. However, this INSERT also generates its own AUTO_INCREMENT value (for the item_id column), which changes the value of LAST_INSERT_ID() and causes the source row inv_id value to be "lost." As a result, each of the remaining inserts into the inv_item table stores the preceding row's item_id value into the inv_id column. This causes the second and following rows to have incorrect inv_id values.

To avoid this difficulty, save the sequence value generated by the insert into the source table, and use the saved value for the inserts into the detail table. To save the value, use a user-defined SQL variable or a variable maintained by your program. Recipe 15.10 describes those techniques, which apply here as follows:

Use a user-defined variable

Save the source row AUTO_INCREMENT value in a user-defined variable for use when inserting the detail rows:

```
INSERT INTO invoice (inv_id,date)
  VALUES(NULL,CURDATE());
SET @inv_id = LAST_INSERT_ID();
INSERT INTO inv_item (inv_id,qty,description)
  VALUES(@inv_id,1,'hammer');
INSERT INTO inv_item (inv_id,qty,description)
  VALUES(@inv_id,3,'nails, box');
INSERT INTO inv_item (inv_id,qty,description)
  VALUES(@inv_id,12,'bandage');
```

Use a variable maintained by your program

This method is similar to the previous one but applies only from within an API. Insert the source row, and then save the AUTO_INCREMENT value into an API variable for use when inserting detail rows. For example, in Ruby, access the AUTO_INCREMENT value using the last_id method:

```
client.query("INSERT INTO invoice (inv_id,date) VALUES(NULL,CURDATE())")
inv_id = client.last_id
sth = client.prepare("INSERT INTO inv_item (inv_id,qty,description)
                VALUES(?,?,?)")
sth.execute(inv_id, 1, "hammer")
sth.execute(inv_id, 3, "nails, box")
sth.execute(inv_id, 12, "bandage")
```

15.12 Using Sequence Generators as Counters

Problem

You're interested only in counting events, so you want to avoid having to create a new table row for each sequence value.

Solution

Increment a single row per counter.

Discussion

AUTO_INCREMENT columns are useful for generating sequences across a set of individual rows. But some applications require only a count of the number of times an event occurs, and there's no benefit from creating a separate row for each event. Instances include web page or banner ad hit counters, a count of items sold, or the number of votes in a poll. Such applications need only a single row to hold the count as it changes over time. MySQL provides a mechanism for this that enables counts to be treated like AUTO_INCREMENT values so that you can not only increment the count, but also retrieve the updated value easily.

To count a single type of event, use a trivial table with a single row and column. For example, to record copies sold of a book, create a table like this:

```
CREATE TABLE booksales (copies INT UNSIGNED);
```

However, if you're counting sales for multiple book titles, that method doesn't work well. You certainly don't want to create a separate single-row counting table per book. Instead, count them all within a single table by including a column that uniquely identifies each book. The following table does this using a title column for the book title in addition to a copies column that records the number of copies sold:

```
CREATE TABLE booksales
(
  title   VARCHAR(60) NOT NULL,      # book title
  copies  INT UNSIGNED NOT NULL,     # number of copies sold
  PRIMARY KEY (title)
);
```

To record sales for a given book, different approaches are possible:

- Initialize a row for the book with a copies value of 0:
  ```
  INSERT INTO booksales (title,copies) VALUES('The Greater Trumps',0);
  ```

  Then increment the copies value for each sale:
  ```
  UPDATE booksales SET copies = copies+1 WHERE title = 'The Greater Trumps';
  ```

  This method requires that you remember to initialize a row for each book or the UPDATE will fail.

- Use INSERT with ON DUPLICATE KEY UPDATE, which initializes the row with a count of 1 for the first sale and increments the count for subsequent sales:
  ```
  INSERT INTO booksales (title,copies)
  VALUES('The Greater Trumps',1)
  ON DUPLICATE KEY UPDATE copies = copies+1;
  ```

  This is simpler because the same statement works to initialize and update the sales count.

To retrieve the sales count (for example, to display a message to customers such as "You just purchased copy *n* of this book"), issue a SELECT query for the same book title:

```
SELECT copies FROM booksales WHERE title = 'The Greater Trumps';
```

Unfortunately, this is not quite correct. Suppose that between the times when you update and retrieve the count, some other person buys a copy of the book (and thus increments the copies value). Then the SELECT statement won't actually produce the value *you* incremented the sales count to, but rather its most recent value. In other words, other clients can affect the value before you have time to retrieve it. This is similar to the problem discussed in Recipe 15.4 that can occur if you try to retrieve the most recent AUTO_INCREMENT value from a column by invoking MAX(*col_name*) rather than LAST_INSERT_ID().

There are ways around this (such as by grouping the two statements as a transaction or by locking the table), but MySQL provides a simpler solution based on LAST_INSERT_ID(). If you call LAST_INSERT_ID() with an expression argument, MySQL treats it like an AUTO_INCREMENT value. To use this feature with the booksales table, modify the count-incrementing statement slightly:

```
INSERT INTO booksales (title,copies)
VALUES('The Greater Trumps',LAST_INSERT_ID(1))
ON DUPLICATE KEY UPDATE copies = LAST_INSERT_ID(copies+1);
```

The statement uses the LAST_INSERT_ID(*expr*) construct both to initialize and to increment the count. MySQL treats the expression argument like an AUTO_INCREMENT value so that you can invoke LAST_INSERT_ID() later with no argument to retrieve the value:

```
SELECT LAST_INSERT_ID();
```

By setting and retrieving the copies column this way, you always get back the value you set it to, even if some other client updated it in the meantime. If you issue the INSERT statement from within an API that provides a mechanism for fetching the most recent AUTO_INCREMENT value directly, you need not even issue the SELECT query. For example, using Connector/Python, update a count and get the new value using the lastrowid attribute:

```
cursor = conn.cursor()
cursor.execute('''
            INSERT INTO booksales (title,copies)
            VALUES('The Greater Trumps',LAST_INSERT_ID(1))
            ON DUPLICATE KEY UPDATE copies = LAST_INSERT_ID(copies+1)
            ''')
count = cursor.lastrowid
cursor.close()
conn.commit()
```

In Java, the operation looks like this:

```
Statement s = conn.createStatement ();
s.executeUpdate (
    "INSERT INTO booksales (title,copies)"
    + "VALUES('The Greater Trumps',LAST_INSERT_ID(1))"
    + "ON DUPLICATE KEY UPDATE copies = LAST_INSERT_ID(copies+1)",
    Statement.RETURN_GENERATED_KEYS);
long count;
ResultSet rs = s.getGeneratedKeys ();
if (rs.next ())
{
  count = rs.getLong (1);
}
else
{
  throw new SQLException ("getGeneratedKeys() produced no value");
}
rs.close ();
s.close ();
```

Use of LAST_INSERT_ID(*expr*) for sequence generation has certain other properties that differ from true AUTO_INCREMENT sequences:

- AUTO_INCREMENT values increment by one each time, whereas values generated by LAST_INSERT_ID(*expr*) can be any nonnegative value you want. For example, to produce the sequence 10, 20, 30, …, increment the count by 10 each time. You need not even increment the counter by the same value each time. If you sell a dozen copies of a book rather than a single copy, update its sales count as follows:

```
INSERT INTO booksales (title,copies)
VALUES('The Greater Trumps',LAST_INSERT_ID(12))
ON DUPLICATE KEY UPDATE copies = LAST_INSERT_ID(copies+12);
```

- To reset a counter, simply set it to the desired value. Suppose that you want to report to book buyers the sales for the current month, rather than the total sales (for example, to display messages like "You're the *n*th buyer this month"). To clear the counters to zero at the beginning of each month, use this statement:

```
UPDATE booksales SET copies = 0;
```

- One property that's not so desirable is that the value generated by LAST_INSERT_ID(*expr*) is not uniformly available via client-side retrieval methods under all circumstances. You can get it after UPDATE or INSERT statements but not for SET statements. If you generate a value as follows (in Ruby), the client-side value returned by insert_id is 0, not 48:

```
client.query("SET @x = LAST_INSERT_ID(48)")
seq = client.last_id
```

To get the value in this case, ask the server for it:

```
seq = client.query("SELECT LAST_INSERT_ID()").first.values[0]
```

15.13 Generating Repeating Sequences

Problem

You require a sequence that contains cycles.

Solution

Make cycles in the sequence with division and modulo operations.

Discussion

Some sequence-generation problems require values that go through cycles. Suppose that you manufacture items such as pharmaceutical products or automobile parts, and you must be able to track them by lot number if manufacturing problems are discovered later that require items sold within a particular lot to be recalled. Suppose also that you pack and distribute items 12 units to a box and 6 boxes to a case. In this situation, item identifiers are three-part values: the unit number (with a value from 1 to 12), the box number (with a value from 1 to 6), and a lot number (with a value from 1 to the highest current case number).

This item-tracking problem appears to require that you maintain three counters, so you might generate the next identifier value using an algorithm like this:

```
retrieve most recently used case, box, and unit numbers
unit = unit + 1      # increment unit number
if (unit > 12)       # need to start a new box?
{
  unit = 1           # go to first unit of next box
  box = box + 1
}
if (box > 6)         # need to start a new case?
{
  box = 1            # go to first box of next case
  case = case + 1
}
store new case, box, and unit numbers
```

Alternatively, it's possible simply to assign each item a sequence number identifier and derive the corresponding case, box, and unit numbers from it. The identifier can come from an AUTO_INCREMENT column or a single-row sequence generator. The formulas for determining the case, box, and unit numbers for any item from its sequence number look like this:

```
unit_num = ((seq - 1) % 12) + 1
box_num = (int ((seq - 1) / 12) % 6) + 1
case_num = int ((seq - 1)/(6 * 12)) + 1
```

The following table illustrates the relationship between some sample sequence numbers and the corresponding case, box, and unit numbers:

seq	case	box	unit
1	1	1	1
12	1	1	12
13	1	2	1
72	1	6	12
73	2	1	1
144	2	6	12

15.14 Using Custom Increment Values

Problem

You want to increment sequences not by one but by a different number.

Solution

Use the `auto_increment_increment` and `auto_increment_offset` system variables.

Discussion

By default, MySQL increases values in a column, having an `AUTO_INCREMENT` option, by one. This is not always desirable. Suppose you have a replication chain (Recipe 3.9) of three servers—Venus, Mars, Saturn—and want to distinguish from which server the inserted value is originated.

The simplest solution for this issue would be to assign a sequence of 1, 4, 7, 10, ... values to the rows inserted on Venus; a sequence of 2, 5, 8, 11, ... to the rows inserted on Mars and a sequence of 3, 6, 9, 12, ... for the rows inserted on Saturn.

To do it, set the value of the `auto_increment_increment` system variable to the number of servers: in our case 3, so MySQL will increment sequence value by three. Then set `auto_increment_offset` to 1 on Venus, to 2 on Mars and to 3 on Saturn. This will instruct MySQL to start new sequences from the specified values:

```
Venus> SET auto_increment_offset=1;
Query OK, 0 rows affected (0.00 sec)

Venus> SET auto_increment_increment=3;
Query OK, 0 rows affected (0.00 sec)

Mars> SET auto_increment_offset=2;
Query OK, 0 rows affected (0.00 sec)
```

```
Mars>  SET auto_increment_increment=3;
Query OK, 0 rows affected (0.00 sec)

Saturn> SET auto_increment_offset=3;
Query OK, 0 rows affected (0.00 sec)

Saturn> SET auto_increment_increment=3;
Query OK, 0 rows affected (0.00 sec)
```

We set session variables for our example, but if you want to affect
not only your own session, but all connections on the server, you
need to use SET GLOBAL. To preserve a configuration change after
restart, set these value in the configuration file, or, starting from
version 8.0, use the SET PERSIST command.

If you already have tables with an AUTO-INCREMENT column, specify the offset using
this statement:

```
ALTER TABLE mytable AUTO_INCREMENT = N;
```

Not all engines support the AUTO_INCREMENT option for CREATE
TABLE and ALTER TABLE. In this case, you can set the starting
value for the auto-incremented column by inserting a row with the
desired value, then removing it.

After preparations are done, MySQL will use the auto_increment_increment value
to generate the next sequence number:

```
Venus>  CREATE TABLE offset(
    -> id INT NOT NULL AUTO_INCREMENT PRIMARY KEY,
    -> host CHAR(32)
    -> );
Query OK, 0 rows affected (0.03 sec)

Venus>  INSERT INTO offset(host) VALUES(@@hostname); ❶
Query OK, 1 row affected (0.01 sec)

Venus>  INSERT INTO offset(host) VALUES(@@hostname);
Query OK, 1 row affected (0.01 sec)

Venus>  INSERT INTO offset(host) VALUES(@@hostname);
Query OK, 1 row affected (0.01 sec)

Venus>  SELECT * FROM offset; ❷
+----+-------+
| id | host  |
+----+-------+
|  1 | Venus |
|  4 | Venus |
|  7 | Venus |
+----+-------+
3 rows in set (0.00 sec)
```

```
Mars>  ALTER TABLE offset AUTO_INCREMENT=2;  ❸
Query OK, 0 rows affected (0.36 sec)
Records: 0  Duplicates: 0  Warnings: 0


Mars>  INSERT INTO offset(host) VALUES('Mars');
Query OK, 1 row affected (0.00 sec)

Mars>  INSERT INTO offset(host) VALUES('Mars');
Query OK, 1 row affected (0.01 sec)

Mars>  SELECT * FROM offset;
+----+-------+
| id | host  |
+----+-------+
|  1 | Venus |
|  4 | Venus |
|  7 | Venus |
|  8 | Mars  |  ❹
| 11 | Mars  |
+----+-------+
5 rows in set (0.00 sec)
```

❶ The hostname system variable contains the value of the MySQL host. We use it to distinguish machines.

❷ On Venus, the sequence starts from 1, and we have the expected values: 1, 4, 7.

❸ The table on Mars already existed. The ALTER TABLE command sets offset for the AUTO_INCREMENT sequence to the desired value.

❹ Since the offset table already had rows on Mars, the new AUTO_INCREMENT value started from 8 that belongs to the sequence 2, 5, 8, 11, ...

15.15 Using Window Functions to Number Rows in the Result Set

Problem

You want to enumerate the result of a SELECT query.

Solution

Use the ROW_NUMBER() window function.

Discussion

Sequences are useful not only when you store data in tables but also when you work with results of queries.

Suppose you're running a singing competition. Each singer should have a turn. To provide everyone an equal chance, the position in the queue should be defined randomly.

The singers' names are stored in the name table. To retrieve them in random order, use the RAND() function:

```
mysql> SELECT first_name, last_name FROM name ORDER BY RAND();
+------------+-----------+
| first_name | last_name |
+------------+-----------+
| Pete       | Gray      |
| Vida       | Blue      |
| Rondell    | White     |
| Kevin      | Brown     |
| Devon      | White     |
+------------+-----------+
5 rows in set (0.00 sec)
```

This query will return the list of names in different orders each time it is called.

Window functions can perform calculations per each row in the result set, and we can use them to create a new column with the order in which the singers will perform.

Window functions work over a specific window that in our case is a SELECT query. They may access multiple rows while they are executing but produce results for each row in the window:

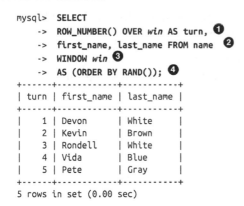

The ROW_NUMBER() function defines the position in the singing schedule.

Other columns in the name table that we want to see in the query result.

---

❸ The keyword WINDOW defines the named window over which we will use the ROW_NUMBER function.

❹ Sort the window in random order to get fair queue distribution.

Another common use of the ROW_NUMBER() function is to generate a sequence of identifiers that later could be used to join the SELECT result with another table. We discuss this approach in one of the examples in Recipe 15.16.

See Also

For additional information about window functions, see "Window Function Concepts and Syntax" (*https://oreil.ly/Kh0K5*).

15.16 Generating Series with Recursive CTEs

Problem

You want to create a custom sequence, such as a geometric progression or Fibonacci number.

Solution

Use recursive Common Table Expressions (CTEs) to create the sequence from the custom formula.

Discussion

Sequences should not always be an arithmetic progression. They could be any kind of progression and even random numbers or strings.

One way to create custom sequences is recursive CTEs. They are named temporary result sets that allow self-referencing. Basic recursive CTE syntax is as follows:

```
WITH RECURSIVE name(column[, column])
(SELECT expressin[, expression]
UNION ALL
SELECT expressin[, expression]
FROM name WHERE ...)
SELECT * FROM name;
```

Thus, to generate a geometric progression starting from 2 with a common ratio 2, use a CTE as follows:

```
mysql> WITH RECURSIVE geometric_progression(id) AS
    -> (SELECT 2 ❶
    -> UNION ALL
    -> SELECT id * 2 ❷
    -> FROM geometric_progression
```

```
  ->  LIMIT 5) ❸
  ->  SELECT * FROM geometric_progression;
+------+
| id   |
+------+
|    2 |
|    4 |
|    8 |
|   16 |
|   32 |
+------+
5 rows in set (0.00 sec)
```

❶ Starting value for the sequence.

❷ All subsequent values in the geometric progression are the previous number multiplied by the common ratio.

❸ To limit the number of the generated numbers and avoid infinite loops, use either a LIMIT clause or any valid WHERE condition.

Recursive CTEs allow you to create multiple sequences at the same time. For example, we can use them to create the following:

- An id that will use regular arithmetic progression, starting from 1 with a common difference 1

- A geometric progression, starting from 3 with a common ratio 4

- A random number between 1 and 5

To create all these in a single query, use a recursive CTE as follows:

```
mysql> WITH RECURSIVE sequences(id, geo, random) AS
    -> (SELECT 1, 3, FLOOR(1+RAND()*5)
    -> UNION ALL
    -> SELECT id + 1, geo * 4, FLOOR(1+RAND()*5)
    -> FROM sequences
    -> WHERE id < 5)
    -> SELECT * FROM sequences;
+------+------+--------+
| id   | geo  | random |
+------+------+--------+
|    1 |    3 |      4 |
|    2 |   12 |      4 |
|    3 |   48 |      2 |
|    4 |  192 |      2 |
|    5 |  768 |      3 |
+------+------+--------+
5 rows in set (0.00 sec)
```

To illustrate the use of the custom sequence, suppose that we are working on a new Data Phobia vaccine and want to start phase III trials on it. Phase III includes testing the real vaccine and a placebo. Doses are distributed randomly between volunteers.

To perform this trial, we will use a `patients` table with participants who do not already have a diagnosis of Data Phobia. We generate a sequence of two random values and assign either a real vaccine or a placebo based on that:

```
mysql> WITH RECURSIVE trial(id, dose) AS
    -> (SELECT 1, IF(1=FLOOR(1+RAND()*2), 'Vaccine', 'Placebo') ❶
    -> UNION ALL
    -> SELECT id+1, IF(1=FLOOR(1+RAND()*2), 'Vaccine', 'Placebo')
    -> FROM trial
    -> WHERE id < (SELECT COUNT(*) FROM patients
    ->                 WHERE diagnosis != 'Data Phobia' and result != 'D')), ❷
    -> volunteers AS ❸
    -> (SELECT ROW_NUMBER() OVER win AS id, ❹
    ->         national_id, name, surname
    -> FROM patients WHERE diagnosis != 'Data Phobia' and result != 'D'
    -> WINDOW win AS (ORDER BY surname))
    -> SELECT national_id, name, surname, dose ❺
    -> FROM trial JOIN volunteers USING(id);
+-------------+-----------+-----------+---------+
| national_id | name      | surname   | dose    |
+-------------+-----------+-----------+---------+
| 84DC051879  | William   | Brown     | Vaccine |
| 78FS043029  | David     | Davis     | Vaccine |
| 38BP394037  | Catherine | Hernandez | Placebo |
| 28VU492728  | Alice     | Jackson   | Vaccine |
| 71GE601633  | John      | Johnson   | Vaccine |
| 09SK434607  | Richard   | Martin    | Placebo |
| 30NC108735  | Robert    | Martinez  | Placebo |
| 02WS884704  | Sarah     | Miller    | Placebo |
| 45MY529190  | Patricia  | Rodriguez | Vaccine |
| 89AR642465  | Mary      | Smith     | Placebo |
| 99XC682639  | Emma      | Taylor    | Vaccine |
| 04WT954962  | Peter     | Wilson    | Vaccine |
+-------------+-----------+-----------+---------+
12 rows in set (0.00 sec)
```

❶ The FLOOR(1+RAND()*2) function generates two random numbers: 1 or 2. The IF function works as a ternary operator: if the first argument is true, it returns the second one; otherwise, it returns the third argument.

❷ We do not want patients who have already been diagnosed with Data Phobia to participate in our tests, and we cannot test our vaccine on patients who did not recover.

❸ While the `patients` table has an AUTO_INCREMENT column id, we cannot use it, because we couldn't exclude patients that won't participate in our tests this way. Therefore, we use a CTE to create a named result set, `volunteers`, and generate its own sequence for it.

❹ The ROW_NUMBER() function generates a new sequence for the patients who participate in the tests.

⑤ Join the generated sequence of random values for the dose and the named result set, volunteers, using a generated id without including it into the final result set.

See Also

For additional information about CTEs, see Recipe 10.18.

15.17 Creating and Storing Custom Sequences

Problem

You want to use a custom sequence as a stored id column in the table.

Solution

Create a table that will hold sequence values and a function that will update and select these values.

Discussion

Although MySQL does not support the SQL SEQUENCE object, it is pretty easy to imitate one.

First, you need to create a table that will hold sequences:

```
CREATE TABLE `sequences` (
  `sequence_name` varchar(64) NOT NULL,
  `maximum_value` bigint NOT NULL DEFAULT '9223372036854775807',
  `minimum_value` bigint NOT NULL DEFAULT '-9223372036854775808',
  `increment` bigint NOT NULL DEFAULT '1',
  `start_value` bigint NOT NULL DEFAULT '-9223372036854775808',
  `current_base_value` bigint NOT NULL DEFAULT '-9223372036854775808',
  `cycle_option` enum('yes','no') NOT NULL DEFAULT 'no',
  PRIMARY KEY (`sequence_name`)
) ENGINE=InnoDB DEFAULT CHARSET=utf8mb4 COLLATE=utf8mb4_0900_ai_ci;
```

For this recipe, we used the same table definition that the MySQL Engineering Team is planning to implement as part of WL#827: SEQUENCE object as in Oracle, Post-greSQL, and/or SQL:2003 (*https://oreil.ly/juxur*). This definition is not required for real-life sequence implementation that could be either simpler or have more options.

Columns in the sequences table all have special meanings (see Table 15-1).

Table 15-1. Columns in the sequences table

Column	Description	Comments
sequence_name	Name of the sequence.	Required field, should be unique.
maximum_value	Maximum value that the sequence can generate.	We allow negative values in our custom sequence; therefore, the maximum possible value is 9223372036854775807, which is the maximum value for the BIGINT SIGNED datatype. If you make this column BIGINT UNSIGNED, the sequence could have twice the values. This option is not critical for the sequence generation and can be skipped.
minimum_value	Minimum value for the sequence.	In our case, the default is -9223372036854775808, which is the minimum for the BIGINT SIGNED type. Depending on how you want to create custom sequences, this column could be skipped or have different types or default values.
increment	Increment for the sequence.	The SQL standard defines the sequence that uses arithmetic progression. This column contains a common difference for the progression. This is a required field. If you create custom sequence, such as geometric progression, you may have a common ratio in this field or any other value that allows you to generate the next one.
start_value	The value from which the sequence will start.	This is not an essential field for implementing sentences. In our case, it is minimum_value by default.
current_base_value	The value that the sequence needs to return when asked for the next value. Once returned, it should be replaced with the newly generated one.	This is a required field. The default is the same as start_value.
cycle_option	Does the sequence support cycles?	If enabled, the sequence will reset back to start_value when it reaches either its minimum_value or maximum_value.

Then, we need to create a stored procedure that will update the sequences table:

```
CREATE PROCEDURE create_sequence(
    sequence_name VARCHAR(64), start_value BIGINT, increment BIGINT,
    cycle_option ENUM('yes','no'), maximum_value BIGINT, minimum_value BIGINT)
BEGIN
    INSERT INTO sequences
        (sequence_name, maximum_value, minimum_value, increment, start_value,
         current_base_value, cycle_option)
        VALUES(
            sequence_name,
            COALESCE(maximum_value, 9223372036854775807),
            COALESCE(minimum_value, -9223372036854775808),
            COALESCE(increment, 1),
            COALESCE(start_value, -9223372036854775808),
            COALESCE(start_value, -9223372036854775808),
            COALESCE(cycle_option, 'no'));
END;
```

Using stored routines, rather than updating the sequences table directly, has a number of advantages:

- You don't need to worry about updating the current_base_value each time you use the sequence.

- If the cycle_option value is enabled, the sequence will reset back to start_value when it reaches either its minimum_value or maximum_value.

- You may restrict direct access to the sequences table for anyone, except the administrator, and still allow application users to use sequences. See Recipe 24.13 for details.

MySQL does not allow us to call a stored function with a variable number of arguments. The COALESCE function allows you to put defaults if NULL values are passed in place of the arguments for which you want to have default values:

```
mysql> CALL create_sequence('bar', 1, 1, 'no', 9223372036854775807, -9223372036854775808);
Query OK, 1 row affected (0.01 sec)

mysql> CALL create_sequence('baz', 1, 1, 'yes', 10, 1);
Query OK, 1 row affected (0.01 sec)

mysql> call create_sequence('foo',null,null,null, null, null);
Query OK, 1 row affected (0.00 sec)

mysql> SELECT * FROM sequences\G
*************************** 1. row ***************************
     sequence_name: bar
     maximum_value: 9223372036854775807
     minimum_value: 1
         increment: 1
       start_value: 1
current_base_value: 1
      cycle_option: no
*************************** 2. row ***************************
     sequence_name: baz
     maximum_value: 10
     minimum_value: 1
         increment: 1
       start_value: 1
current_base_value: 1
      cycle_option: yes
*************************** 3. row ***************************
     sequence_name: foo
     maximum_value: 9223372036854775807
     minimum_value: -9223372036854775808
         increment: 1
       start_value: -9223372036854775808
current_base_value: -9223372036854775808
      cycle_option: no
3 rows in set (0.00 sec)
```

In the preceding example, we first created a `bar` sequence that starts from 1, increments by 1, does not have a cycle option, and has a default `maximum_value` of 9223372036854775807. Then, we created the `baz` sequence that also starts from 1 and increments by 1 but has `cycle_option` enabled and a `maximum_value` 10, so it cycles quite fast. Finally, we created a `foo` sequence that has only custom name and all other defaults.

To get the next sequence value and update the sequence table at the same time, we will use a stored function:

```
CREATE FUNCTION sequence_next_value(name varchar(64)) RETURNS BIGINT
BEGIN
    DECLARE retval BIGINT;
    SELECT current_base_value INTO retval FROM sequences
      WHERE sequence_name=name FOR UPDATE;
    UPDATE sequences SET current_base_value=
        IF((current_base_value+increment <= maximum_value
            AND current_base_value+increment >= minimum_value),
            current_base_value+increment,
            IF('yes' = cycle_option, start_value, NULL)
        ) WHERE sequence_name=name;
    RETURN retval;
END;
```

The function first retrieves `current_base_value` of the sequence using the `SELECT...FOR UPDATE` statement, so other connections won't modify the sequence until we return the value.

Our function supports cycles. In cases where `cycle_option` is enabled, and the next sequence value exceeds the boundaries, it sets `current_base_value` to the value, defined by the `start_value`. If `cycle_option` is disabled and the next sequence value exceeds the boundaries, we insert `NULL` value into the `current_base_value` column, which MySQL will reject with an error. You may consider raising a custom exception instead.

To demonstrate how `cycle_option` option works, let's see how the `baz` sequence behaves when its boundaries are reached:

```
mysql> SELECT sequence_next_value('baz');
+----------------------------+
| sequence_next_value('baz') |
+----------------------------+
|                         10 |
+----------------------------+
1 row in set (0.00 sec)

mysql> SELECT sequence_next_value('baz');
+----------------------------+
| sequence_next_value('baz') |
+----------------------------+
|                          1 |
+----------------------------+
1 row in set (0.01 sec)
```

```
mysql> SELECT sequence_next_value('baz');
+----------------------------+
| sequence_next_value('baz') |
+----------------------------+
|                          2 |
+----------------------------+
1 row in set (0.01 sec)
```

To demonstrate function behavior when the boundaries are reached while cycle_option is not enabled, we created a sequence that has a small maximum value:

```
mysql> CALL create_sequence('boo', 1, 1, 'no', 3, 1);
Query OK, 1 row affected (0.01 sec)

mysql> SELECT sequence_next_value('boo');
+----------------------------+
| sequence_next_value('boo') |
+----------------------------+
|                          1 |
+----------------------------+
1 row in set (0.01 sec)

mysql> SELECT sequence_next_value('boo');
+----------------------------+
| sequence_next_value('boo') |
+----------------------------+
|                          2 |
+----------------------------+
1 row in set (0.01 sec)

mysql> SELECT sequence_next_value('boo');
ERROR 1048 (23000): Column 'current_base_value' cannot be null
```

To use custom sequences with tables, simply call sequence_next_value each time you need the next sequence value:

```
mysql> CREATE TABLE sequence_test(
    -> id BIGINT NOT NULL PRIMARY KEY,
    -> -- other fields
    -> );
Query OK, 0 rows affected (0.04 sec)

mysql> CALL create_sequence('sequence_test', 10, 5, 'no', null, null);
Query OK, 1 row affected (0.00 sec)

mysql> INSERT INTO sequence_test VALUES(sequence_next_value('sequence_test'));
Query OK, 1 row affected (0.01 sec)

mysql> INSERT INTO sequence_test VALUES(sequence_next_value('sequence_test'));
Query OK, 1 row affected (0.01 sec)

mysql> select * from sequence_test;
+----+
| id |
+----+
| 10 |
| 15 |
```

```
+----+
2 rows in set (0.00 sec)
```

You can automate sequence-value generation for your tables by using triggers.

```
CREATE TRIGGER sequence_test_bi BEFORE INSERT ON sequence_test
FOR EACH ROW SET NEW.id=IFNULL(NEW.id, sequence_next_value('sequence_test'));
```

In this example, we generate a new sequence value when a user tries to insert NULL into the id column of the sequence_test table. If the user, instead, decides to specify the value explicitly, the trigger would not change it:

```
mysql> INSERT INTO sequence_test VALUES();
Query OK, 1 row affected (0.01 sec)

mysql> INSERT INTO sequence_test VALUES(13);
Query OK, 1 row affected (0.00 sec)

mysql> select * from sequence_test;
+----+
| id |
+----+
| 10 |
| 13 |
| 15 |
| 20 |
+----+
4 rows in set (0.00 sec)
```

Finally, we need to define a stored procedure to delete the sequence when we don't need it:

```
CREATE PROCEDURE delete_sequence(name VARCHAR(64))
DELETE FROM sequences WHERE sequence_name=name;
```

You will find code for maintaining custom sequences in the *sequences/custom_sequences.sql* file of the recipes distribution.

## CHAPTER 16

Using Joins and Subqueries

16.0 Introduction

Most queries in earlier chapters used a single table, but for any application of even moderate complexity, you'll likely need to use multiple tables. Some questions simply cannot be answered using a single table, and the real power of a relational database comes into play when you combine the information from multiple sources:

- Combine rows from tables to obtain more comprehensive information than can be obtained from individual tables alone

- Hold intermediate results for a multiple-stage operation

- Modify rows in one table based on information from another

This chapter focuses on two types of statements that use multiple tables: joins between tables and subqueries that nest one SELECT within another. It covers the following topics:

Comparing tables to find matches or mismatches
> To solve such problems, you should know which types of joins apply. Inner joins show which rows in one table match rows in another. Outer joins show matching rows but also find rows in one table *not* matched by rows in another.

Deleting unmatched rows
> If two datasets are related, but imperfectly, you can determine which rows are unmatched and remove them as necessary.

Comparing a table to itself
> Some problems require comparing a table to itself. This is similar to performing a join between different tables, except that you must use table aliases to disambiguate table references.

Producing candidate-detail and many-to-many relationships
> Joins enable the production of lists or summaries when each item in one table can match many items in the other table, or when each item in either table can match many items in the other table.

The scripts that create the tables used in this chapter are located in the *tables* directory of the `recipes` distribution. For scripts that implement the techniques discussed here, look in the *joins* directory.

16.1 Finding Matches Between Tables

Problem

You need to perform a task that requires information from more than one table.

Solution

Use a join—that is, a query that lists multiple tables in its `FROM` clause and tells MySQL how to match information from them.

Discussion

The essential idea behind a join is that it matches rows in one table with rows in one or more other tables. Joins enable you to combine information from multiple tables when each one answers only part of the question in which you're interested.

A complete join that produces all possible row combinations is called a *Cartesian product*. For example, joining each row in a 100-row table to each row in a 200-row table produces a result containing 100 × 200 = 20,000 rows. With larger tables, or joins between more than two tables, the result set for a Cartesian product easily becomes immense, so a join normally includes an `ON` or `USING` comparison clause to produce only the desired matches between tables. (This requires that each table have one or more columns of common information that link them together logically.) You can also include a `WHERE` clause that restricts which of the joined rows to select. Each clause narrows the focus of the query.

This recipe introduces join syntax and demonstrates how joins answer specific types of questions when you are looking for matches between tables. Other sections show how to identify mismatches between tables (see Recipe 16.2) and how to compare a table to itself (see Recipe 16.4). The examples assume that you have an art collection and use the following two tables to record your acquisitions. `artist` lists those painters whose works you want to collect, and `painting` lists each painting you've actually purchased:

```
CREATE TABLE artist
(
  a_id  INT UNSIGNED NOT NULL AUTO_INCREMENT, # artist ID
  name  VARCHAR(30) NOT NULL,                 # artist name
  PRIMARY KEY (a_id),
  UNIQUE (name)
);

CREATE TABLE painting
(
  a_id  INT UNSIGNED NOT NULL,                 # artist ID
  p_id  INT UNSIGNED NOT NULL AUTO_INCREMENT,  # painting ID
  title VARCHAR(100) NOT NULL,                 # title of painting
  state VARCHAR(2) NOT NULL,                   # state where purchased
  price INT UNSIGNED,                          # purchase price (dollars)
  INDEX (a_id),
  PRIMARY KEY (p_id)
);
```

You've just begun the collection, so the tables contain only a few rows:

```
mysql> SELECT * FROM artist ORDER BY a_id;
+------+----------+
| a_id | name     |
+------+----------+
|    1 | Da Vinci |
|    2 | Monet    |
|    3 | Van Gogh |
|    4 | Renoir   |
+------+----------+
mysql> SELECT * FROM painting ORDER BY a_id, p_id;
+------+------+-------------------+-------+-------+
| a_id | p_id | title             | state | price |
+------+------+-------------------+-------+-------+
|    1 |    1 | The Last Supper   | IN    |    34 |
|    1 |    2 | Mona Lisa         | MI    |    87 |
|    3 |    3 | Starry Night      | KY    |    48 |
|    3 |    4 | The Potato Eaters | KY    |    67 |
|    4 |    5 | Les Deux Soeurs   | NE    |    64 |
+------+------+-------------------+-------+-------+
```

The low values in the price column of the painting table betray the fact that your collection actually contains only cheap imitations, not the originals. Well, that's all right: who can afford the originals?

Each table contains partial information about your collection. For example, the artist table doesn't tell you which paintings each artist produced, and the painting table lists artist IDs but not their names. To use the information in both tables, write a query that performs a join. A join names two or more tables after the FROM keyword. In the output column list, use * to select all columns from all tables (i.e., *tbl_name.**) to select all columns from a given table or name specific columns from the joined tables or expressions based on those columns.

The simplest join involves two tables and selects all columns from each. The following join between the `artist` and `painting` tables shows this (the ORDER BY clause makes the result easier to read):

```
mysql> SELECT * FROM artist INNER JOIN painting ORDER BY artist.a_id;
+------+----------+------+------+-------------------+-------+-------+
| a_id | name     | a_id | p_id | title             | state | price |
+------+----------+------+------+-------------------+-------+-------+
|    1 | Da Vinci |    1 |    1 | The Last Supper   | IN    |    34 |
|    1 | Da Vinci |    3 |    3 | Starry Night      | KY    |    48 |
|    1 | Da Vinci |    4 |    5 | Les Deux Soeurs   | NE    |    64 |
|    1 | Da Vinci |    1 |    2 | Mona Lisa         | MI    |    87 |
|    1 | Da Vinci |    3 |    4 | The Potato Eaters | KY    |    67 |
|    2 | Monet    |    1 |    2 | Mona Lisa         | MI    |    87 |
|    2 | Monet    |    3 |    4 | The Potato Eaters | KY    |    67 |
|    2 | Monet    |    1 |    1 | The Last Supper   | IN    |    34 |
|    2 | Monet    |    3 |    3 | Starry Night      | KY    |    48 |
|    2 | Monet    |    4 |    5 | Les Deux Soeurs   | NE    |    64 |
|    3 | Van Gogh |    1 |    2 | Mona Lisa         | MI    |    87 |
|    3 | Van Gogh |    3 |    4 | The Potato Eaters | KY    |    67 |
|    3 | Van Gogh |    1 |    1 | The Last Supper   | IN    |    34 |
|    3 | Van Gogh |    3 |    3 | Starry Night      | KY    |    48 |
|    3 | Van Gogh |    4 |    5 | Les Deux Soeurs   | NE    |    64 |
|    4 | Renoir   |    1 |    1 | The Last Supper   | IN    |    34 |
|    4 | Renoir   |    3 |    3 | Starry Night      | KY    |    48 |
|    4 | Renoir   |    4 |    5 | Les Deux Soeurs   | NE    |    64 |
|    4 | Renoir   |    1 |    2 | Mona Lisa         | MI    |    87 |
|    4 | Renoir   |    3 |    4 | The Potato Eaters | KY    |    67 |
+------+----------+------+------+-------------------+-------+-------+
```

An INNER JOIN produces results that combine values in one table with values in another table. The preceding query specifies no restrictions on row matching, so the join generates all row combinations (that is, the Cartesian product). This result illustrates why such a join generally is not useful: it produces a lot of unmeaningful output. Clearly, you don't maintain these tables to match every artist with every painting.

> In MySQL, JOIN, CROSS JOIN, and INNER JOIN are syntactic equivalents and can replace one another. You can use CROSS JOIN, or simply JOIN, in all places where we use INNER JOIN.

To answer questions meaningfully, produce only the relevant matches by including appropriate join conditions. For example, to produce a list of paintings together with the artist names, associate rows from the two tables using a simple WHERE clause that matches values based on the artist ID column that is common to both tables and serves to link them:

```
mysql> SELECT * FROM artist INNER JOIN painting
    -> WHERE artist.a_id = painting.a_id
    -> ORDER BY artist.a_id;
+------+----------+------+------+-------------------+-------+-------+
```

```
| a_id | name     | a_id | p_id | title            | state | price |
+------+----------+------+------+------------------+-------+-------+
|    1 | Da Vinci |    1 |    1 | The Last Supper  | IN    |    34 |
|    1 | Da Vinci |    1 |    2 | Mona Lisa        | MI    |    87 |
|    3 | Van Gogh |    3 |    3 | Starry Night     | KY    |    48 |
|    3 | Van Gogh |    3 |    4 | The Potato Eaters| KY    |    67 |
|    4 | Renoir   |    4 |    5 | Les Deux Soeurs  | NE    |    64 |
+------+----------+------+------+------------------+-------+-------+
```

The column names in the WHERE clause include table qualifiers to make it clear which a_id values to compare. The result indicates who painted each painting and, conversely, which paintings by each artist are in your collection.

Joins and Indexes

A join can easily cause MySQL to process large numbers of row combinations, so it's a good idea to index the comparison columns. Otherwise, performance drops off quickly as table sizes increase. For the artist and painting tables, joins are made by comparing the a_id columns. If you look back at the CREATE TABLE statements for those tables, you see that a_id is indexed in each table.

Another way to write the same join indicates the matching conditions with an ON clause:

```
SELECT * FROM artist INNER JOIN painting
ON artist.a_id = painting.a_id
ORDER BY artist.a_id;
```

In the special case of equality comparisons between columns with the same name in both tables, you can use an INNER JOIN with a USING clause instead. This requires no table qualifiers and names each joined column only once:

```
SELECT * FROM artist INNER JOIN painting
USING (a_id)
ORDER BY a_id;
```

For SELECT * queries, the USING form produces a result that differs from the ON form: it returns only one instance of each join column, so a_id appears once, not twice.

Any of ON, USING, or WHERE can include comparisons, so how do you know which join conditions to put in each clause? As a rule of thumb, it's conventional to use ON or USING to specify how to join the tables and the WHERE clause to restrict which of the joined rows to select. For example, to join tables based on the a_id column, but select only rows for paintings obtained in Kentucky, use an ON (or USING) clause to match the rows in the two tables, and a WHERE clause to test the state column:

```
mysql> SELECT * FROM artist INNER JOIN painting
    -> ON artist.a_id = painting.a_id
    -> WHERE painting.state = 'KY';
+------+----------+------+------+------------------+-------+-------+
```

```
| a_id | name      | a_id | p_id | title             | state | price |
+------+-----------+------+------+-------------------+-------+-------+
|    3 | Van Gogh  |    3 |    3 | Starry Night      | KY    |    48 |
|    3 | Van Gogh  |    3 |    4 | The Potato Eaters | KY    |    67 |
+------+-----------+------+------+-------------------+-------+-------+
```

The preceding queries use SELECT * to display all columns. To be more selective, name only those columns in which you're interested:

```
mysql> SELECT artist.name, painting.title, painting.state, painting.price
    -> FROM artist INNER JOIN painting
    -> ON artist.a_id = painting.a_id
    -> WHERE painting.state = 'KY';
+----------+-------------------+-------+-------+
| name     | title             | state | price |
+----------+-------------------+-------+-------+
| Van Gogh | Starry Night      | KY    |    48 |
| Van Gogh | The Potato Eaters | KY    |    67 |
+----------+-------------------+-------+-------+
```

Joins can use more than two tables. Suppose that you prefer to see complete state names rather than abbreviations in the preceding query result. The states table used in earlier chapters maps state abbreviations to names; add it to the previous query to display the name rather than the abbreviation:

```
mysql> SELECT artist.name, painting.title, states.name, painting.price
    -> FROM artist INNER JOIN painting INNER JOIN states
    -> ON artist.a_id = painting.a_id AND painting.state = states.abbrev
    -> WHERE painting.state = 'KY';
+----------+-------------------+----------+-------+
| name     | title             | name     | price |
+----------+-------------------+----------+-------+
| Van Gogh | Starry Night      | Kentucky |    48 |
| Van Gogh | The Potato Eaters | Kentucky |    67 |
+----------+-------------------+----------+-------+
```

Another common use of three-way joins is enumerating many-to-many relationships (see Recipe 16.6).

By including appropriate conditions in your joins, you can answer very specific questions:

- Which paintings did Van Gogh paint? Use the a_id value to find matching rows, add a WHERE clause to restrict output to rows that contain the artist name, and select the title from those rows:

```
mysql> SELECT painting.title
    -> FROM artist INNER JOIN painting ON artist.a_id = painting.a_id
    -> WHERE artist.name = 'Van Gogh';
+-------------------+
| title             |
+-------------------+
| Starry Night      |
| The Potato Eaters |
+-------------------+
```

- Who painted the *Mona Lisa*? Again, use the `a_id` column to join the rows, but this time use the `WHERE` clause to restrict output to rows that contain the title, and select the artist name from those rows:

```
mysql> SELECT artist.name
    -> FROM artist INNER JOIN painting ON artist.a_id = painting.a_id
    -> WHERE painting.title = 'Mona Lisa';
+----------+
| name     |
+----------+
| Da Vinci |
+----------+
```

- For which artists did you purchase paintings in Kentucky or Indiana? This is similar to the previous statement but tests a different column in the `painting` table (`state`) to restrict output to rows for KY or IN:

```
mysql> SELECT DISTINCT artist.name
    -> FROM artist INNER JOIN painting ON artist.a_id = painting.a_id
    -> WHERE painting.state IN ('KY','IN');
+----------+
| name     |
+----------+
| Da Vinci |
| Van Gogh |
+----------+
```

  The statement also uses `DISTINCT` to display each artist name just once. Try it without `DISTINCT`; Van Gogh appears twice because you obtained two Van Goghs in Kentucky.

- Joins used with aggregate functions produce summaries. This statement shows how many paintings you have per artist:

```
mysql> SELECT artist.name, COUNT(*) AS 'number of paintings'
    -> FROM artist INNER JOIN painting ON artist.a_id = painting.a_id
    -> GROUP BY artist.name;
+----------+---------------------+
| name     | number of paintings |
+----------+---------------------+
| Da Vinci |                   2 |
| Renoir   |                   1 |
| Van Gogh |                   2 |
+----------+---------------------+
```

  A more elaborate statement uses aggregates to also show how much you paid for each artist's paintings, in total and on average:

```
mysql> SELECT artist.name,
    -> COUNT(*) AS 'number of paintings',
    -> SUM(painting.price) AS 'total price',
    -> AVG(painting.price) AS 'average price'
    -> FROM artist INNER JOIN painting ON artist.a_id = painting.a_id
    -> GROUP BY artist.name;
+----------+---------------------+-------------+---------------+
| name     | number of paintings | total price | average price |
+----------+---------------------+-------------+---------------+
| Da Vinci |                   2 |         121 |       60.5000 |
| Renoir   |                   1 |          64 |       64.0000 |
```

```
| Van Gogh |                  2 |       115 |      57.5000 |
+----------+--------------------+-----------+--------------+
```

The preceding summary statements produce output only for those artists in the artist table for whom you actually have acquired paintings. (For example, Monet is listed in the artist table but is not present in the summary because you have none of his paintings yet.) To summarize all artists, including those for whom you have no paintings, you must use a different kind of join—specifically, an outer join:

- Joins written with INNER JOIN are inner joins. They produce a result only for values in one table that match values in another table.

- An outer join can produce those matches as well but also can show you which values in one table are missing from the other. Recipe 16.2 introduces outer joins.

The *tbl_name.col_name* notation that qualifies a column name with a table name is always permitted in a join but can be shortened to just *col_name* if the name appears in only one of the joined tables. In that case, MySQL can determine without ambiguity which table the column comes from, and no table name qualifier is necessary. We can't do that for the following join. Both tables have an a_id column, so the ON clause column references are ambiguous:

```
mysql> SELECT * FROM artist INNER JOIN painting ON a_id = a_id;
ERROR 1052 (23000): Column 'a_id' in on clause is ambiguous
```

By contrast, the following query is unambiguous. Each instance of a_id is qualified with the appropriate table name, only artist has a name column, and only painting has title and state columns:

```
mysql> SELECT name, title, state FROM artist INNER JOIN painting
    -> ON artist.a_id = painting.a_id
    -> ORDER BY name;
+----------+------------------+-------+
| name     | title            | state |
+----------+------------------+-------+
| Da Vinci | The Last Supper  | IN    |
| Da Vinci | Mona Lisa        | MI    |
| Renoir   | Les Deux Soeurs  | NE    |
| Van Gogh | Starry Night     | KY    |
| Van Gogh | The Potato Eaters | KY   |
+----------+------------------+-------+
```

To make the meaning of a statement clearer to human readers, it's often useful to qualify column names even when that's not strictly necessary as far as MySQL is concerned. We tend to use qualified names in join examples for that reason.

To avoid writing complete table names when qualifying column references, give each table a short alias and refer to its columns using the alias. The following two statements are equivalent:

```
SELECT artist.name, painting.title, states.name, painting.price
FROM artist INNER JOIN painting INNER JOIN states
ON artist.a_id = painting.a_id AND painting.state = states.abbrev;

SELECT a.name, p.title, s.name, p.price
FROM artist AS a INNER JOIN painting AS p INNER JOIN states AS s
ON a.a_id = p.a_id AND p.state = s.abbrev;
```

In AS *alias_name* clauses, the AS is optional.

For complicated statements that select many columns, aliases can save a lot of typing. In addition, for some types of statements, aliases are not only convenient but necessary, as will become evident when we get to the topic of self-joins (see Recipe 16.4).

Joining Tables from Different Databases

To perform a join between tables located in different databases, qualify table and column names sufficiently that MySQL knows what you're referring to. Thus far, we have used the artist and painting tables with the implicit understanding that both are in the cookbook database, so we can simply refer to the tables without specifying any database name when cookbook is the default database. For example, the following statement uses the two tables to associate artists with their paintings:

```
SELECT artist.name, painting.title
FROM artist INNER JOIN painting
ON artist.a_id = painting.a_id;
```

But suppose instead that artist is in the db1 database and painting is in the db2 database. To indicate this, qualify each table name with a prefix that specifies which database it's in. The fully qualified form of the join looks like this:

```
SELECT db1.artist.name, db2.painting.title
FROM db1.artist INNER JOIN db2.painting
ON db1.artist.a_id = db2.painting.a_id;
```

Table aliases can simplify that considerably:

```
SELECT a.name, p.title
FROM db1.artist AS a INNER JOIN db2.painting AS p
ON a.a_id = p.a_id;
```

If there is no default database, or it is neither db1 nor db2, it's necessary to fully qualify both table names. If the default database is either db1 or db2, you can dispense with the corresponding qualifiers. If the default database is db1, you can omit the db1 qualifiers. Conversely, if the default database is db2, no db2 qualifiers are necessary.

16.2 Finding Mismatches Between Tables

Problem

You want to find rows in one table that have no match in another. Or you want to produce a list on the basis of a join between tables, and you want the list to include an entry for every row in the first table, including those for which no match occurs in the second table.

Solution

Use an outer join (a LEFT JOIN or a RIGHT JOIN) or a NOT IN subquery.

Discussion

Recipe 16.1 focuses on inner joins, which find matches between two tables. However, the answers to some questions require determining which rows do *not* have a match (or, stated another way, which rows have values missing from the other table). For example, you might want to know artists in the artist table for whom you have no paintings yet. Similar questions occur in other contexts:

- You have a list of potential customers and another list of people who have placed orders. To focus sales efforts on people who are not yet actual customers, produce the set of people who are in the first list but not the second.

- You have one list of baseball players and another list of players who have hit home runs. To determine which players in the first list have *not* hit a home run, produce the set of players who are in the first list but not the second.

These types of questions require use of an outer join. Like inner joins, an outer join finds matches between tables. But unlike an inner join, an outer join also determines which rows in one table have no match in another. Two types of outer joins are LEFT JOIN and RIGHT JOIN.

To see how outer joins are useful, consider the problem of determining which artists in the artist table are missing from the painting table. At present, the tables are small, so it's easy to examine them visually and see that you have no paintings by Monet (there are no painting rows with an a_id value of 2):

```
mysql> SELECT * FROM artist ORDER BY a_id;
+------+----------+
| a_id | name     |
+------+----------+
|    1 | Da Vinci |
|    2 | Monet    |
|    3 | Van Gogh |
|    4 | Renoir   |
```

```
+------+----------+
mysql> SELECT * FROM painting ORDER BY a_id, p_id;
+------+------+------------------+-------+-------+
| a_id | p_id | title            | state | price |
+------+------+------------------+-------+-------+
|    1 |    1 | The Last Supper  | IN    |    34 |
|    1 |    2 | Mona Lisa        | MI    |    87 |
|    3 |    3 | Starry Night     | KY    |    48 |
|    3 |    4 | The Potato Eaters| KY    |    67 |
|    4 |    5 | Les Deux Soeurs  | NE    |    64 |
+------+------+------------------+-------+-------+
```

As you acquire more paintings and the tables get larger, it won't be so easy to eyeball them and answer questions by inspection. Can you answer it using SQL? Sure, although first attempts at a solution often look something like the following statement, which uses a not-equal condition to look for mismatches between the two tables:

```
mysql> SELECT * FROM artist INNER JOIN painting
    -> ON artist.a_id <> painting.a_id
    -> ORDER BY artist.a_id;
+------+----------+------+------+------------------+-------+-------+
| a_id | name     | a_id | p_id | title            | state | price |
+------+----------+------+------+------------------+-------+-------+
|    1 | Da Vinci |    4 |    5 | Les Deux Soeurs  | NE    |    64 |
|    1 | Da Vinci |    3 |    4 | The Potato Eaters| KY    |    67 |
|    1 | Da Vinci |    3 |    3 | Starry Night     | KY    |    48 |
|    2 | Monet    |    1 |    1 | The Last Supper  | IN    |    34 |
|    2 | Monet    |    4 |    5 | Les Deux Soeurs  | NE    |    64 |
|    2 | Monet    |    3 |    4 | The Potato Eaters| KY    |    67 |
|    2 | Monet    |    3 |    3 | Starry Night     | KY    |    48 |
|    2 | Monet    |    1 |    2 | Mona Lisa        | MI    |    87 |
|    3 | Van Gogh |    1 |    2 | Mona Lisa        | MI    |    87 |
|    3 | Van Gogh |    1 |    1 | The Last Supper  | IN    |    34 |
|    3 | Van Gogh |    4 |    5 | Les Deux Soeurs  | NE    |    64 |
|    4 | Renoir   |    3 |    3 | Starry Night     | KY    |    48 |
|    4 | Renoir   |    1 |    2 | Mona Lisa        | MI    |    87 |
|    4 | Renoir   |    1 |    1 | The Last Supper  | IN    |    34 |
|    4 | Renoir   |    3 |    4 | The Potato Eaters| KY    |    67 |
+------+----------+------+------+------------------+-------+-------+
```

The query may look plausible but its result obviously is not. For example, it falsely indicates that each painting was painted by several different artists. The problem is that the statement lists all combinations of values from the two tables in which the artist ID values aren't the same. What you really need is a list of values in artist that aren't present *at all* in painting, but an inner join can only produce results based on values that are present in both tables. It can't tell you anything about values that are missing from one of them.

When faced with the need to find values in one table with no match in (or missing from) another table, you should get in the habit of thinking, "Aha, that's a LEFT JOIN problem." A LEFT JOIN is one type of outer join: it's similar to an inner join in that it matches rows in the first (left) table with rows in the second (right) table. In addition, if a left table row has no match in the right table, a LEFT JOIN still produces a row—one in which all the columns from the right table are set to NULL. This means you can find values that are missing from the right table by looking for NULL. It's easier to understand how this happens by working in stages. Begin with an inner join that displays matching rows:

```
mysql> SELECT * FROM artist INNER JOIN painting
    -> ON artist.a_id = painting.a_id
    -> ORDER BY artist.a_id;
+------+-----------+------+------+------------------+-------+-------+
| a_id | name      | a_id | p_id | title            | state | price |
+------+-----------+------+------+------------------+-------+-------+
|    1 | Da Vinci  |    1 |    1 | The Last Supper  | IN    |    34 |
|    1 | Da Vinci  |    1 |    2 | Mona Lisa        | MI    |    87 |
|    3 | Van Gogh  |    3 |    3 | Starry Night     | KY    |    48 |
|    3 | Van Gogh  |    3 |    4 | The Potato Eaters| KY    |    67 |
|    4 | Renoir    |    4 |    5 | Les Deux Soeurs  | NE    |    64 |
+------+-----------+------+------+------------------+-------+-------+
```

In this output, the first `a_id` column comes from the `artist` table, and the second one comes from the `painting` table.

Now substitute LEFT for INNER to see the result you get from an outer join:

```
mysql> SELECT * FROM artist LEFT JOIN painting
    -> ON artist.a_id = painting.a_id
    -> ORDER BY artist.a_id;
+------+-----------+------+------+------------------+-------+-------+
| a_id | name      | a_id | p_id | title            | state | price |
+------+-----------+------+------+------------------+-------+-------+
|    1 | Da Vinci  |    1 |    1 | The Last Supper  | IN    |    34 |
|    1 | Da Vinci  |    1 |    2 | Mona Lisa        | MI    |    87 |
|    2 | Monet     | NULL | NULL | NULL             | NULL  | NULL  |
|    3 | Van Gogh  |    3 |    3 | Starry Night     | KY    |    48 |
|    3 | Van Gogh  |    3 |    4 | The Potato Eaters| KY    |    67 |
|    4 | Renoir    |    4 |    5 | Les Deux Soeurs  | NE    |    64 |
+------+-----------+------+------+------------------+-------+-------+
```

Compared to the inner join, the outer join produces an additional row for every `artist` row that has no `painting` table match, with all `painting` columns set to NULL.

Next, to restrict the output only to the unmatched `artist` rows, add a WHERE clause that looks for NULL values in any `painting` column that cannot otherwise contain NULL. This filters out the rows that the inner join produces, leaving those produced only by the outer join:

```
mysql> SELECT * FROM artist LEFT JOIN painting
    -> ON artist.a_id = painting.a_id
    -> WHERE painting.a_id IS NULL;
+------+-------+------+------+-------+-------+-------+
| a_id | name  | a_id | p_id | title | state | price |
+------+-------+------+------+-------+-------+-------+
|    2 | Monet | NULL | NULL | NULL  | NULL  | NULL  |
+------+-------+------+------+-------+-------+-------+
```

Finally, to show only the artist table values that are missing from the painting table, write the output column list to name only columns from the artist table. The result is that the LEFT JOIN lists those left-table rows containing a_id values not present in the right table:

```
mysql> SELECT artist.* FROM artist LEFT JOIN painting
    -> ON artist.a_id = painting.a_id
    -> WHERE painting.a_id IS NULL;
+------+-------+
| a_id | name  |
+------+-------+
|    2 | Monet |
+------+-------+
```

A similar kind of operation reports each left-table value along with an indicator as to whether it's present in the right table. To do this, perform a LEFT JOIN that counts the number of times each left-table value occurs in the right table. A count of zero indicates that the value is not present. The following statement lists each artist from the artist table and shows whether you have any paintings by the artist:

```
mysql> SELECT artist.name,
    -> IF(COUNT(painting.a_id)>0,'yes','no') AS 'in collection?'
    -> FROM artist LEFT JOIN painting ON artist.a_id = painting.a_id
    -> GROUP BY artist.name;
+----------+----------------+
| name     | in collection? |
+----------+----------------+
| Da Vinci | yes            |
| Monet    | no             |
| Renoir   | yes            |
| Van Gogh | yes            |
+----------+----------------+
```

A RIGHT JOIN is an outer join that is like LEFT JOIN but reverses the roles of the left and right tables. Semantically, RIGHT JOIN forces the matching process to produce a row from each table in the right table, even in the absence of a corresponding row in the left table. Syntactically, *tbl1* LEFT JOIN *tbl2* is equivalent to *tbl2* RIGHT JOIN *tbl1*. Therefore, references to LEFT JOIN in this book apply to RIGHT JOIN as well if you reverse the roles of the tables.

Another way to identify values present in one table but missing from another is to use a NOT IN subquery. The following example finds artists not represented in the painting table; compare it to the earlier LEFT JOIN that answers the same question:

```
mysql> SELECT * FROM artist
    -> WHERE a_id NOT IN (SELECT a_id FROM painting);

+------+-------+
| a_id | name  |
+------+-------+
|    2 | Monet |
+------+-------+
```

See Also

As shown in this section, LEFT JOIN is useful for finding values with no match in another table or for showing whether each value is matched. LEFT JOIN may also be used to produce a summary that includes all items in a list, even those for which there's nothing to summarize. This is very common for relationships between a candidate table and a detail table. For example, a LEFT JOIN can produce "total sales per customer" reports that list all customers, even those who bought nothing during the summary period. (For information about candidate-detail lists, see Recipe 16.5.)

LEFT JOIN is also useful for consistency checking when you receive two datafiles that are supposed to be related, and you want to determine whether they really are. (That is, you want to check the integrity of their relationship.) Import each file into a MySQL table, and then run a couple of LEFT JOIN statements to determine whether there are unattached rows in one table or the other—that is, rows that have no match in the other table. Recipe 16.3 discusses how to identify (and optionally delete) these unattached rows.

16.3 Identifying and Removing Mismatched or Unattached Rows

Problem

You have two datasets that are related but possibly imperfectly so. You want to determine whether there are records in either dataset that are "unattached" (not matched by any record in the other dataset) and perhaps remove them if so.

Solution

To identify unmatched values in each table, use a LEFT JOIN or a NOT IN subquery. To remove them, use DELETE with a NOT IN subquery.

Discussion

Inner joins are useful for identifying matches, and outer joins are useful for identifying mismatches. This property of outer joins is valuable when you have related datasets for which the relationship might be imperfect. Mismatches might be found, for example, when you must verify the integrity of two datafiles received from an external source.

When you have related tables with unmatched rows, you can analyze and modify them using SQL statements. Specifically, restoring their relationship is a matter of identifying the unattached rows and then deleting them:

- To identify unattached rows, use a LEFT JOIN, because this is a "find unmatched rows" problem; alternatively, use a NOT IN subquery (see Recipe 16.2).
- To delete rows that are unmatched, use DELETE with a NOT IN subquery.

It's useful to know about unmatched data because you can alert whoever gave you the data. The data collection method might have a flaw that must be corrected. For example, with sales data, a missing region might mean that some regional manager didn't report in and the omission was overlooked.

The following example shows how to identify and remove mismatched rows using two datasets that describe sales regions and volume of sales per region. One dataset contains the ID and location of each region:

```
mysql> SELECT * FROM sales_region ORDER BY region_id;
+-----------+------------------------+
| region_id | name                   |
+-----------+------------------------+
|         1 | London, United Kingdom |
|         2 | Madrid, Spain          |
|         3 | Berlin, Germany        |
|         4 | Athens, Greece         |
+-----------+------------------------+
```

The other dataset contains sales volume figures. Each row contains the amount of sales for a given quarter of a year and indicates the sales region to which the row applies:

```
mysql> SELECT region_id, year, quarter, volume
    -> FROM sales_volume ORDER BY region_id, year, quarter;
+-----------+------+---------+--------+
| region_id | year | quarter | volume |
+-----------+------+---------+--------+
|         1 | 2014 |       1 | 100400 |
|         1 | 2014 |       2 | 120000 |
|         3 | 2014 |       1 | 280000 |
|         3 | 2014 |       2 | 250000 |
|         5 | 2014 |       1 |  18000 |
|         5 | 2014 |       2 |  32000 |
+-----------+------+---------+--------+
```

A little visual inspection reveals that neither table is fully matched by the other. Sales regions 2 and 4 are not represented in the sales volume table, and the sales volume table contains rows for region 5, which is not in the sales region table. But we don't want to check the tables by inspection. We want to find unmatched rows by using SQL statements that do the work.

Mismatch identification is a matter of using outer joins. For example, to find sales regions for which there are no sales volume rows, use the following LEFT JOIN:

```
mysql> SELECT sales_region.region_id AS 'unmatched region row IDs'
    -> FROM sales_region LEFT JOIN sales_volume
    ->   ON sales_region.region_id = sales_volume.region_id
    -> WHERE sales_volume.region_id IS NULL;
+--------------------------+
| unmatched region row IDs |
+--------------------------+
|                        2 |
|                        4 |
+--------------------------+
```

Conversely, to find sales volume rows that are not associated with any known region, reverse the roles of the two tables:

```
mysql> SELECT sales_volume.region_id AS 'unmatched volume row IDs'
    -> FROM sales_volume LEFT JOIN sales_region
    ->   ON sales_volume.region_id = sales_region.region_id
    -> WHERE sales_region.region_id IS NULL;
+--------------------------+
| unmatched volume row IDs |
+--------------------------+
|                        5 |
|                        5 |
+--------------------------+
```

In this case, an ID appears more than once in the list if there are multiple volume rows for a missing region. To see each unmatched ID only once, use SELECT DISTINCT:

```
mysql> SELECT DISTINCT sales_volume.region_id AS 'unmatched volume row IDs'
    -> FROM sales_volume LEFT JOIN sales_region
    ->   ON sales_volume.region_id = sales_region.region_id
    -> WHERE sales_region.region_id IS NULL
+--------------------------+
| unmatched volume row IDs |
+--------------------------+
|                        5 |
+--------------------------+
```

You can also identify mismatches using NOT IN subqueries:

```
mysql> SELECT region_id AS 'unmatched region row IDs'
    -> FROM sales_region
    -> WHERE region_id NOT IN (SELECT region_id FROM sales_volume);
+--------------------------+
| unmatched region row IDs |
+--------------------------+
|                        2 |
|                        4 |
+--------------------------+
mysql> SELECT region_id AS 'unmatched volume row IDs'
    -> FROM sales_volume
    -> WHERE region_id NOT IN (SELECT region_id FROM sales_region);
+--------------------------+
| unmatched volume row IDs |
+--------------------------+
|                        5 |
|                        5 |
+--------------------------+
```

To get rid of unmatched rows, use a NOT IN subquery in a DELETE statement. To remove sales_region rows that match no sales_volume rows, do this:

```
DELETE FROM sales_region
WHERE region_id NOT IN (SELECT region_id FROM sales_volume);
```

To remove mismatched sales_volume rows that match no sales_region rows, the statement is similar but with the table roles reversed:

```
DELETE FROM sales_volume
WHERE region_id NOT IN (SELECT region_id FROM sales_region);
```

Using Foreign Keys to Enforce Referential Integrity and Prevent Mismatches

One feature a database system offers to help you maintain consistency between tables is the ability to define foreign key relationships. This means you can specify explicitly in the table definition that a primary key in a parent table (such as the `region_id` column of the `sales_region` table) is a parent to a key in another table (the `region_id` column in the `sales_volume` table).

By defining the ID column in the child table as a foreign key to the ID column in the parent, the database system can enforce certain constraints against illegal operations. For example, it can prevent you from creating a child row with an ID not present in the parent or from deleting parent rows without also deleting the corresponding child rows first. A foreign key implementation may also offer cascaded delete and update: if you delete or update a parent row, the database engine cascades the effect of the delete or update to any child tables and automatically deletes or updates the child rows for you. The InnoDB storage engine in MySQL supports foreign keys and cascaded deletes and updates.

16.4 Comparing a Table to Itself

Problem

You want to compare rows in a table to other rows in the same table. For example, you want to find all paintings in your collection by the artist who painted *The Potato Eaters*. Or you want to know which states listed in the `states` table joined the Union in the same year as New York. Or you want to know which states did not join the Union in the same year as any other state.

Solution

Problems that require comparing a table to itself involve an operation known as a *self-join*. It's performed much like other joins, except that you must use table aliases so that you can refer to the same table different ways within the statement.

Discussion

A special case of joining one table to another occurs when both tables are the same. This is called a self-join. This may be confusing or strange to think about at first, but it's perfectly legal. You'll likely find yourself using self-joins quite often because they are so important.

A tip-off that a self-join is required is that you want to know which pairs of rows in a table satisfy some condition. Suppose that your favorite painting is *The Potato Eaters* and you want to identify all items in your collection that were painted by the same artist. The artist ID and painting titles that we begin with look like this:

```
mysql> SELECT a_id, title FROM painting ORDER BY a_id;
+------+-------------------+
| a_id | title             |
+------+-------------------+
|    1 | The Last Supper   |
|    1 | Mona Lisa         |
|    3 | Starry Night      |
|    3 | The Potato Eaters |
|    4 | Les Deux Soeurs   |
+------+-------------------+
```

Solve the problem as follows:

1. Identify which `painting` table row contains the title *The Potato Eaters* so that you can refer to its `a_id` value.

2. Match other rows in the table that have the same `a_id` value.

3. Display the titles from those matching rows.

The trick lies in using the proper notation. First attempts at joining a table to itself often look something like this:

```
mysql> SELECT title
    -> FROM painting INNER JOIN painting
    -> ON a_id = a_id
    -> WHERE title = 'The Potato Eaters';
ERROR 1066 (42000): Not unique table/alias: 'painting'
```

The column references in that statement are ambiguous because MySQL cannot tell which instance of the `painting` table any given column name refers to. The solution is to alias at least one instance of the table so that you can distinguish column references by using different table qualifiers. The following statement shows how to do this, using the aliases `p1` and `p2` to refer to the `painting` table different ways:

```
mysql> SELECT p2.title
    -> FROM painting AS p1 INNER JOIN painting AS p2
    -> ON p1.a_id = p2.a_id
    -> WHERE p1.title = 'The Potato Eaters';
+-------------------+
| title             |
+-------------------+
| Starry Night      |
| The Potato Eaters |
+-------------------+
```

The statement output illustrates something typical of self-joins: when you begin with a reference value in one table instance (*The Potato Eaters*) to find matching rows in a second table instance (paintings by the same artist), the output includes the reference value. That makes sense: after all, the reference matches itself. To find only *other* paintings by the same artist, explicitly exclude the reference value from the output:

```
mysql> SELECT p2.title
    -> FROM painting AS p1 INNER JOIN painting AS p2
    -> ON p1.a_id = p2.a_id
    -> WHERE p1.title = 'The Potato Eaters' AND p2.title <> p1.title
+--------------+
| title        |
+--------------+
| Starry Night |
+--------------+
```

The preceding statements use ID value comparisons to match rows in the two table instances, but any kind of value can be used. For example, to use the `states` table to answer the question "Which states joined the Union in the same year as New York?" perform a temporal pairwise comparison based on the year part of the dates in the table's `statehood` column:

```
mysql> SELECT s2.name, s2.statehood
    -> FROM states AS s1 INNER JOIN states AS s2
    -> ON YEAR(s1.statehood) = YEAR(s2.statehood) AND s1.name <> s2.name
    -> WHERE s1.name = 'New York'
    -> ORDER BY s2.name;
+----------------+------------+
| name           | statehood  |
+----------------+------------+
| Connecticut    | 1788-01-09 |
| Georgia        | 1788-01-02 |
| Maryland       | 1788-04-28 |
| Massachusetts  | 1788-02-06 |
| New Hampshire  | 1788-06-21 |
| South Carolina | 1788-05-23 |
| Virginia       | 1788-06-25 |
+----------------+------------+
```

In the preceding example, we do not specify the year when New York joined the Union. Instead, we compare the value of the state hood column for the row where state name is "New York" and the same `statehood` column for other states.

Now suppose that you want to find *every* pair of states that joined the Union in the same year. In this case, the output potentially can include any pair of rows from the `states` table.

A self-join is perfect for this problem:

```
mysql> SELECT YEAR(s1.statehood) AS year,
    -> s1.name AS name1, s1.statehood AS statehood1,
    -> s2.name AS name2, s2.statehood AS statehood2
    -> FROM states AS s1 INNER JOIN states AS s2
    -> ON YEAR(s1.statehood) = YEAR(s2.statehood) AND s1.name <> s2.name
    -> ORDER BY year, name1, name2;
+------+----------------+------------+----------------+------------+
```

```
| year | name1        | statehood1 | name2        | statehood2 |
+------+--------------+------------+--------------+------------+
| 1787 | Delaware     | 1787-12-07 | New Jersey   | 1787-12-18 |
| 1787 | Delaware     | 1787-12-07 | Pennsylvania | 1787-12-12 |
| 1787 | New Jersey   | 1787-12-18 | Delaware     | 1787-12-07 |
| 1787 | New Jersey   | 1787-12-18 | Pennsylvania | 1787-12-12 |
| 1787 | Pennsylvania | 1787-12-12 | Delaware     | 1787-12-07 |
| 1787 | Pennsylvania | 1787-12-12 | New Jersey   | 1787-12-18 |
...
| 1912 | Arizona      | 1912-02-14 | New Mexico   | 1912-01-06 |
| 1912 | New Mexico   | 1912-01-06 | Arizona      | 1912-02-14 |
| 1959 | Alaska       | 1959-01-03 | Hawaii       | 1959-08-21 |
| 1959 | Hawaii       | 1959-08-21 | Alaska       | 1959-01-03 |
+------+--------------+------------+--------------+------------+
```

The condition in the ON clause that requires state pair names not to be identical eliminates the trivially duplicate rows showing that each state joined the Union in the same year as itself. But you'll notice that each remaining pair of states still appears twice. For example, there is one row that lists Delaware and New Jersey, and another that lists New Jersey and Delaware. This is often the case with self-joins: they produce pairs of rows that contain the same values but for which the values are not in the same order.

Because the values are not listed in the same order within the rows, they are not identical, and you can't get rid of these "near duplicates" by adding DISTINCT to the statement. To solve this problem, select rows in such a way that only one row from each pair ever appears in the query result. Slightly modify the ON clause, from:

```
ON YEAR(s1.statehood) = YEAR(s2.statehood) AND s1.name <> s2.name
```

to:

```
ON YEAR(s1.statehood) = YEAR(s2.statehood) AND s1.name < s2.name
```

Using < rather than <> selects only those rows in which the first state name is lexically less than the second, and eliminates rows in which the names appear in opposite order (as well as rows in which the state names are identical). The resulting query produces the desired output without duplicates:

```
mysql> SELECT YEAR(s1.statehood) AS year,
    -> s1.name AS name1, s1.statehood AS statehood1,
    -> s2.name AS name2, s2.statehood AS statehood2
    -> FROM states AS s1 INNER JOIN states AS s2
    -> ON YEAR(s1.statehood) = YEAR(s2.statehood) AND s1.name < s2.name
    -> ORDER BY year, name1, name2;
+------+--------------+------------+--------------+------------+
| year | name1        | statehood1 | name2        | statehood2 |
+------+--------------+------------+--------------+------------+
| 1787 | Delaware     | 1787-12-07 | New Jersey   | 1787-12-18 |
| 1787 | Delaware     | 1787-12-07 | Pennsylvania | 1787-12-12 |
| 1787 | New Jersey   | 1787-12-18 | Pennsylvania | 1787-12-12 |
...
| 1912 | Arizona      | 1912-02-14 | New Mexico   | 1912-01-06 |
| 1959 | Alaska       | 1959-01-03 | Hawaii       | 1959-08-21 |
+------+--------------+------------+--------------+------------+
```

For self-join problems of the "Which values are *not* matched by other rows in the table?" variety, use a LEFT JOIN rather than an INNER JOIN. An instance of this is the question "Which states did not join the Union in the same year as any other state?" In this case, the solution uses a LEFT JOIN of the states table to itself:

```
mysql> SELECT s1.name, s1.statehood
    -> FROM states AS s1 LEFT JOIN states AS s2
    -> ON YEAR(s1.statehood) = YEAR(s2.statehood) AND s1.name <> s2.name
    -> WHERE s2.name IS NULL
    -> ORDER BY s1.name;
+----------------+------------+
| name           | statehood  |
+----------------+------------+
| Alabama        | 1819-12-14 |
| Arkansas       | 1836-06-15 |
| California     | 1850-09-09 |
| Colorado       | 1876-08-01 |
| Illinois       | 1818-12-03 |
| Indiana        | 1816-12-11 |
| Iowa           | 1846-12-28 |
| Kansas         | 1861-01-29 |
| Kentucky       | 1792-06-01 |
...
| Tennessee      | 1796-06-01 |
| Utah           | 1896-01-04 |
| Vermont        | 1791-03-04 |
| West Virginia  | 1863-06-20 |
| Wisconsin      | 1848-05-29 |
+----------------+------------+
```

For each row in the states table, the statement selects rows for which the state has a statehood value in the same year, not including that state itself. For rows having no such match, the LEFT JOIN forces the output to contain a row anyway, with all the s2 columns set to NULL. Those rows identify the states with no other state that joined the Union in the same year.

16.5 Producing Candidate-Detail Lists and Summaries

Problem

Two tables have a relationship such that a row in one table, usually called the parent table with a candidate key, is referenced by one or more rows in another table, usually called the child table with a detail row. In this situation, you want to produce a list that shows each parent row with its detail rows or a list that produces a summary of the detail rows for each parent row.

Solution

This is a one-to-many relationship. The solution to this problem involves a join, but the type of join depends on the question you want answered. To produce a list containing only parent rows for which some detail row exists, use an inner join based on the primary key in the parent table. To produce a list that includes all parent rows, even those with no detail rows, use an outer join.

Discussion

To produce a list from two tables that have a candidate-detail or parent-child relationship, a given row in one table might be matched by several rows in the other. These relationships occur frequently. For example, in business contexts, one-to-many relationships involve invoices per customer or items per invoice.

This recipe suggests some candidate-detail questions that you can ask (and answer) using the `artist` and `painting` tables from earlier in the chapter.

One form of candidate-detail question for these tables is "Which paintings did each artist paint?" This is a simple inner join (see Recipe 16.1). Match each `artist` row to its corresponding `painting` rows based on the artist ID values:

```
mysql> SELECT artist.name, painting.title
    -> FROM artist INNER JOIN painting ON artist.a_id = painting.a_id
    -> ORDER BY name, title;
+----------+-------------------+
| name     | title             |
+----------+-------------------+
| Da Vinci | Mona Lisa         |
| Da Vinci | The Last Supper   |
| Renoir   | Les Deux Soeurs   |
| Van Gogh | Starry Night      |
| Van Gogh | The Potato Eaters |
+----------+-------------------+
```

To also list artists for whom you have no paintings, the join output should include rows in one table that have no match in the other. That's a form of "find the nonmatching rows" problem that requires an outer join (see Recipe 16.2). Thus, to list each `artist` row, whether or not any `painting` rows match, use a LEFT JOIN:

```
mysql> SELECT artist.name, painting.title
    -> FROM artist LEFT JOIN painting ON artist.a_id = painting.a_id
    -> ORDER BY name, title;
+----------+-------------------+
| name     | title             |
+----------+-------------------+
| Da Vinci | Mona Lisa         |
| Da Vinci | The Last Supper   |
| Monet    | NULL              |
| Renoir   | Les Deux Soeurs   |
| Van Gogh | Starry Night      |
| Van Gogh | The Potato Eaters |
+----------+-------------------+
```

Rows in the result that have NULL in the `title` column correspond to artists listed in the `artist` table for whom you have no paintings.

The same principles apply when producing summaries using candidate and detail tables. For example, to summarize your art collection by number of paintings per artist, you might ask, "How many paintings are there per artist in the `painting` table?" To find the answer based on artist ID but displaying the artist's name (from the `artist` table), count the paintings with this statement:

```
mysql> SELECT artist.name, COUNT(painting.a_id) AS paintings
    -> FROM artist INNER JOIN painting ON artist.a_id = painting.a_id
    -> GROUP BY artist.name;
+----------+-----------+
| name     | paintings |
+----------+-----------+
| Da Vinci |         2 |
| Renoir   |         1 |
| Van Gogh |         2 |
+----------+-----------+
```

On the other hand, you might ask, "How many paintings did each artist paint?" This is the same question as the previous one (and the same statement answers it), as long as every artist in the `artist` table has at least one corresponding `painting` table row. But if you have artists in the `artist` table not yet represented by any paintings in your collection, they do not appear in the statement output. To produce a summary that also includes artists with no paintings in the `painting` table, use a LEFT JOIN:

```
mysql> SELECT artist.name, COUNT(painting.a_id) AS paintings
    -> FROM artist LEFT JOIN painting ON artist.a_id = painting.a_id
    -> GROUP BY artist.name;
+----------+-----------+
| name     | paintings |
+----------+-----------+
| Da Vinci |         2 |
| Monet    |         0 |
| Renoir   |         1 |
| Van Gogh |         2 |
+----------+-----------+
```

Beware of a subtle error that is easy to make when writing that kind of statement. Suppose that you write the COUNT() function slightly differently, like so:

```
mysql> SELECT artist.name, COUNT(*) AS paintings
    -> FROM artist LEFT JOIN painting ON artist.a_id = painting.a_id
    -> GROUP BY artist.name;
+----------+-----------+
| name     | paintings |
+----------+-----------+
| Da Vinci |         2 |
| Monet    |         1 |
| Renoir   |         1 |
| Van Gogh |         2 |
+----------+-----------+
```

Now every artist appears to have at least one painting. Why the difference? The problem is the use of COUNT(*) rather than COUNT(painting.a_id). The way LEFT JOIN works for unmatched rows in the left table is that it generates a row with all the columns from the right table set to NULL. In the example, the right table is painting. The statement that uses COUNT(painting.a_id) works correctly because COUNT(*expr*) counts only non-NULL values. The statement that uses COUNT(*) is incorrect because it counts *rows*, including those containing NULL that correspond to missing artists.

LEFT JOIN is suitable for other types of summaries as well. To produce additional columns showing the total and average prices of the paintings for each artist in the artist table, use this statement:

```
mysql> SELECT artist.name,
    -> COUNT(painting.a_id) AS 'number of paintings',
    -> SUM(painting.price) AS 'total price',
    -> AVG(painting.price) AS 'average price'
    -> FROM artist LEFT JOIN painting ON artist.a_id = painting.a_id
    -> GROUP BY artist.name;
+----------+---------------------+-------------+---------------+
| name     | number of paintings | total price | average price |
+----------+---------------------+-------------+---------------+
| Da Vinci |                   2 |         121 |       60.5000 |
| Monet    |                   0 |        NULL |          NULL |
| Renoir   |                   1 |          64 |       64.0000 |
| Van Gogh |                   2 |         115 |       57.5000 |
+----------+---------------------+-------------+---------------+
```

Note that COUNT() is zero for artists that are not represented, but SUM() and AVG() are NULL. The latter two functions return NULL when applied to a set of values with no non-NULL values. To display a sum or average value of zero in that case, replace SUM(*expr*) and AVG(*expr*) with IFNULL(SUM(*expr*),0) and IFNULL(AVG(*expr*),0).

Using Subqueries in the Select List

To generate master details, you may use subqueries in the select list. For example, to answer the question "Which paintings did each artist paint?" you can use JOIN as we discussed in the beginning of this recipe, or a subquery in the SELECT list:

```
mysql> SELECT title,
    -> (SELECT name FROM artist
    ->  WHERE artist.a_id=painting.a_id) AS name
    -> FROM painting;
+------------------+----------+
| title            | name     |
+------------------+----------+
| The Last Supper  | Da Vinci |
| Mona Lisa        | Da Vinci |
| Starry Night     | Van Gogh |
| The Potato Eaters | Van Gogh |
| Les Deux Soeurs  | Renoir   |
+------------------+----------+
5 rows in set (0,00 sec)
```

You can use as many subqueries in the `SELECT` list as you wish. For example, to print the artist name and the name of the state where the painting was acquired instead of its abbreviation, use the following query:

```
SELECT title,
(SELECT name FROM artist WHERE artist.a_id=painting.a_id) AS name,
(SELECT name FROM states WHERE states.abbrev = painting.state) AS state
FROM painting;
```

This approach is useful when you join many tables that do not have referenced values that you want to use in the resulting output. At the same time, such details are stored in the separate small tables. In all other cases, using an explicit `JOIN` is more preferable for performance reasons.

16.6 Enumerating a Many-to-Many Relationship

Problem

You want to display a relationship between tables when any row in either table might be matched by multiple rows in the other.

Solution

This is a many-to-many relationship. It requires a third table for associating your two primary tables and a three-way join to produce the correspondences between them.

Discussion

The `artist` and `painting` tables used in earlier sections have a one-to-many relationship: a given artist may have produced many paintings, but each painting was created by only one artist. One-to-many relationships are relatively simple, and the two related tables can be joined using a column that is common to both.

A many-to-many relationship between tables is more complex. It occurs when a row in one table may have many matches in the other, and vice versa. An example is the relationship between movies and actors: each movie may have multiple actors, and each actor may have appeared in multiple movies. One way to represent this relationship uses a table structured as follows, with a row for each movie-actor combination:

```
mysql> SELECT * FROM movies_actors ORDER BY year, movie, actor;
+------+--------------------------+---------------+
| year | movie                    | actor         |
+------+--------------------------+---------------+
| 1997 | The Fifth Element        | Bruce Willis  |
| 1997 | The Fifth Element        | Gary Oldman   |
| 1997 | The Fifth Element        | Ian Holm      |
| 1999 | The Phantom Menace        | Ewan McGregor |
```

```
| 1999 | The Phantom Menace         | Liam Neeson   |
| 2001 | The Fellowship of the Ring | Elijah Wood   |
| 2001 | The Fellowship of the Ring | Ian Holm      |
| 2001 | The Fellowship of the Ring | Ian McKellen  |
| 2001 | The Fellowship of the Ring | Orlando Bloom |
| 2005 | Kingdom of Heaven          | Liam Neeson   |
| 2005 | Kingdom of Heaven          | Orlando Bloom |
| 2010 | Red                        | Bruce Willis  |
| 2010 | Red                        | Helen Mirren  |
| 2011 | Unknown                    | Diane Kruger  |
| 2011 | Unknown                    | Liam Neeson   |
+------+----------------------------+---------------+
```

The table captures the nature of this many-to-many relationship, but it's also in non-normal form because it unnecessarily stores repetitive information. For example, information for each movie is recorded multiple times. To better represent this many-to-many relationship, use multiple tables:

- Store each movie year and name once in a table named `movies`.

- Store each actor name once in a table named `actors`.

- Create a third table, `movies_actors_link`, that stores movie-actor associations and serves as a link, or bridge, between the two primary tables. To minimize the information stored in this table, assign unique IDs to each movie and actor within their respective tables, and store only those IDs in the `movies_actors_link` table.

The resulting `movie` and `actor` tables look like this:

```
mysql> SELECT * FROM movies ORDER BY id;
+----+------+----------------------------+
| id | year | movie                      |
+----+------+----------------------------+
|  1 | 1997 | The Fifth Element          |
|  2 | 1999 | The Phantom Menace         |
|  3 | 2001 | The Fellowship of the Ring |
|  4 | 2005 | Kingdom of Heaven          |
|  5 | 2010 | Red                        |
|  6 | 2011 | Unknown                    |
+----+------+----------------------------+
mysql> SELECT * FROM actors ORDER BY id;
+----+---------------+
| id | actor         |
+----+---------------+
|  1 | Bruce Willis  |
|  2 | Diane Kruger  |
|  3 | Elijah Wood   |
|  4 | Ewan McGregor |
|  5 | Gary Oldman   |
|  6 | Helen Mirren  |
|  7 | Ian Holm      |
|  8 | Ian McKellen  |
|  9 | Liam Neeson   |
| 10 | Orlando Bloom |
+----+---------------+
```

The `movies_actors_link` table associates movies and actors as follows:

```
mysql> SELECT * FROM movies_actors_link ORDER BY movie_id, actor_id;
+----------+----------+
| movie_id | actor_id |
+----------+----------+
|        1 |        1 |
|        1 |        5 |
|        1 |        7 |
|        2 |        4 |
|        2 |        9 |
|        3 |        3 |
|        3 |        7 |
|        3 |        8 |
|        3 |       10 |
|        4 |        9 |
|        4 |       10 |
|        5 |        1 |
|        5 |        6 |
|        6 |        2 |
|        6 |        9 |
+----------+----------+
```

You'll surely notice that the content of the `movies_actors_link` table is entirely meaningless from a human perspective. That's okay: we need never display it explicitly. Its utility derives from its ability to link the two primary tables in queries, without appearing in query output itself. The next few examples illustrate this principle. They answer questions about the movies or actors, using three-way joins that relate the two primary tables using the link table:

- List all the pairings that show each movie and who acted in it. This statement enumerates all the correspondences between the `movie` and `actor` tables and reproduces the information that was originally in the non-normal `movies_actors` table:

```
mysql> SELECT m.year, m.movie, a.actor
    -> FROM movies AS m INNER JOIN movies_actors_link AS l
    -> INNER JOIN actors AS a
    -> ON m.id = l.movie_id AND a.id = l.actor_id
    -> ORDER BY m.year, m.movie, a.actor;
+------+-----------------------------+---------------+
| year | movie                       | actor         |
+------+-----------------------------+---------------+
| 1997 | The Fifth Element           | Bruce Willis  |
| 1997 | The Fifth Element           | Gary Oldman   |
| 1997 | The Fifth Element           | Ian Holm      |
| 1999 | The Phantom Menace          | Ewan McGregor |
| 1999 | The Phantom Menace          | Liam Neeson   |
| 2001 | The Fellowship of the Ring  | Elijah Wood   |
| 2001 | The Fellowship of the Ring  | Ian Holm      |
| 2001 | The Fellowship of the Ring  | Ian McKellen  |
| 2001 | The Fellowship of the Ring  | Orlando Bloom |
| 2005 | Kingdom of Heaven           | Liam Neeson   |
| 2005 | Kingdom of Heaven           | Orlando Bloom |
| 2010 | Red                         | Bruce Willis  |
| 2010 | Red                         | Helen Mirren  |
```

```
| 2011 | Unknown                      | Diane Kruger |
| 2011 | Unknown                      | Liam Neeson  |
+------+------------------------------+--------------+
```

- List the actors in a given movie:

```
mysql> SELECT a.actor
    -> FROM movies AS m INNER JOIN movies_actors_link AS l
    -> INNER JOIN actors AS a
    -> ON m.id = l.movie_id AND a.id = l.actor_id
    -> WHERE m.movie = 'The Fellowship of the Ring'
    -> ORDER BY a.actor;
+---------------+
| actor         |
+---------------+
| Elijah Wood   |
| Ian Holm      |
| Ian McKellen  |
| Orlando Bloom |
+---------------+
```

- List the movies in which a given actor has acted:

```
mysql> SELECT m.year, m.movie
    -> FROM movies AS m INNER JOIN movies_actors_link AS l
    -> INNER JOIN actors AS a
    -> ON m.id = l.movie_id AND a.id = l.actor_id
    -> WHERE a.actor = 'Liam Neeson'
    -> ORDER BY m.year, m.movie;
+------+---------------------+
| year | movie               |
+------+---------------------+
| 1999 | The Phantom Menace  |
| 2005 | Kingdom of Heaven   |
| 2011 | Unknown             |
+------+---------------------+
```

16.7 Finding Per-Group Minimum or Maximum Values

Problem

You want to find which row within each group of rows in a table contains the maximum or minimum value for a given column. For example, you want to determine the most expensive painting in your collection for each artist.

Solution

Create a temporary table to hold the per-group maximum or minimum values, then join the temporary table with the original one to pull out the matching row for each group. If you prefer a single-query solution, use a subquery in the FROM clause rather than a temporary table.

Discussion

Many questions involve finding largest or smallest values in a particular table column, but it's also common to want to know other values in the row that contains the value. For example, using the `artist` and `painting` tables with the techniques from Recipe 10.6, it's possible to answer questions such as "What is the most expensive painting in the collection, and who painted it?" One solution is to store the highest price in a user-defined variable, then use the variable to identify the row containing the price so that you can retrieve other columns from it:

```
mysql> SET @max_price = (SELECT MAX(price) FROM painting);
mysql> SELECT artist.name, painting.title, painting.price
    -> FROM artist INNER JOIN painting
    -> ON painting.a_id = artist.a_id
    -> WHERE painting.price = @max_price;
+----------+-----------+-------+
| name     | title     | price |
+----------+-----------+-------+
| Da Vinci | Mona Lisa |    87 |
+----------+-----------+-------+
```

The same thing can be done by creating a temporary table to hold the maximum price and joining it with the other tables:

```
CREATE TABLE tmp SELECT MAX(price) AS max_price FROM painting;
SELECT artist.name, painting.title, painting.price
FROM artist INNER JOIN painting INNER JOIN tmp
ON painting.a_id = artist.a_id
AND painting.price = tmp.max_price;
```

On the face of it, using a temporary table and a join is just a more complicated way of answering the question than with a user-defined variable. Does this technique have any practical value? Yes, it does, because it leads to a more general technique for answering more difficult questions. The previous statements show information only for the single most expensive painting in the entire `painting` table. What if your question is "What is the most expensive painting *for each artist*?" You can't use a user-defined variable to answer that question because the answer requires finding one price per artist, and a variable holds only a single value. But the technique of using a temporary table works well because the table can hold multiple rows, and a join can find matches for all of them.

To answer the question, select each artist ID and the corresponding maximum painting price into a temporary table. This table contains not only the maximum painting price but the maximum within each group, where "group" is defined as "paintings by a given artist." Then use the artist IDs and prices stored in the temporary table to match rows in the `painting` table, and join the result with the `artist` table to get the artist names:

```
mysql> CREATE TABLE tmp
    -> SELECT a_id, MAX(price) AS max_price FROM painting GROUP BY a_id;
mysql> SELECT artist.name, painting.title, painting.price
```

```
-> FROM artist INNER JOIN painting INNER JOIN tmp
-> ON painting.a_id = artist.a_id
-> AND painting.a_id = tmp.a_id
-> AND painting.price = tmp.max_price;
+----------+-------------------+-------+
| name     | title             | price |
+----------+-------------------+-------+
| Da Vinci | Mona Lisa         |    87 |
| Van Gogh | The Potato Eaters |    67 |
| Renoir   | Les Deux Soeurs   |    64 |
+----------+-------------------+-------+
```

To avoid explicitly creating temporary tables and obtain the same result with a single statement, use CTEs:

```
WITH tmp AS (SELECT a_id, MAX(price) AS max_price FROM painting GROUP BY a_id)
SELECT artist.name, painting.title, painting.price
FROM artist INNER JOIN painting INNER JOIN tmp
ON painting.a_id = artist.a_id AND
painting.a_id = tmp.a_id AND painting.price = tmp.max_price;
```

We discuss CTEs in detail in Recipe 10.18.

Another way to obtain the same result with a single statement is to use a subquery in the FROM clause that retrieves the same rows contained in the temporary table:

```
SELECT artist.name, painting.title, painting.price
FROM artist INNER JOIN painting INNER JOIN
(SELECT a_id, MAX(price) AS max_price FROM painting GROUP BY a_id) AS tmp
ON painting.a_id = artist.a_id
AND painting.a_id = tmp.a_id
AND painting.price = tmp.max_price;
```

Yet another way to answer maximum-per-group questions is to use a LEFT JOIN that joins a table to itself. The following statement identifies the highest-priced painting per artist ID (use IS NULL to select all the rows from p1 for which there is *no* row in p2 with a higher price):

```
mysql> SELECT p1.a_id, p1.title, p1.price
    -> FROM painting AS p1 LEFT JOIN painting AS p2
    -> ON p1.a_id = p2.a_id AND p1.price < p2.price
    -> WHERE p2.a_id IS NULL;
+------+-------------------+-------+
| a_id | title             | price |
+------+-------------------+-------+
|    1 | Mona Lisa         |    87 |
|    3 | The Potato Eaters |    67 |
|    4 | Les Deux Soeurs   |    64 |
+------+-------------------+-------+
```

To display artist names rather than ID values, join the result of the LEFT JOIN to the artist table:

```
mysql> SELECT artist.name, p1.title, p1.price
    -> FROM painting AS p1 LEFT JOIN painting AS p2
    -> ON p1.a_id = p2.a_id AND p1.price < p2.price
    -> INNER JOIN artist ON p1.a_id = artist.a_id
```

```
-> WHERE p2.a_id IS NULL;
+----------+--------------------+-------+
| name     | title              | price |
+----------+--------------------+-------+
| Da Vinci | Mona Lisa          |    87 |
| Van Gogh | The Potato Eaters  |    67 |
| Renoir   | Les Deux Soeurs    |    64 |
+----------+--------------------+-------+
```

The self-LEFT JOIN method is perhaps less intuitive than using a temporary table, a CTE, or a subquery.

See Also

This recipe showed how to answer maximum-per-group questions by selecting summary information into a temporary table and joining that table to the original one or by using a subquery in the FROM clause. These techniques have applications in many contexts. One of them is calculating team standings, where the standings for each group of teams are determined by comparing each team in the group to the team with the best record. Recipe 17.12 discusses how to do this.

16.8 Using a Join to Fill or Identify Holes in a List

Problem

You want to produce a summary by category, but some categories are missing from the data to be summarized. Consequently, the summary has missing categories as well.

Solution

Create a reference table that lists each category, and produce the summary based on a LEFT JOIN between the list and the table containing your data. Every category in the reference table will appear in the result, even those not present in the data to be summarized.

Discussion

A summary query normally produces entries only for categories actually present in the data. Suppose that you want to summarize the driver_log table (introduced in Chapter 9), to determine how many drivers were on the road each day. The table has these rows:

```
mysql> SELECT * FROM driver_log ORDER BY rec_id;
+--------+-------+------------+-------+
| rec_id | name  | trav_date  | miles |
+--------+-------+------------+-------+
|      1 | Ben   | 2014-07-30 |   152 |
```

```
|    2 | Suzi  | 2014-07-29 |   391 |
|    3 | Henry | 2014-07-29 |   300 |
|    4 | Henry | 2014-07-27 |    96 |
|    5 | Ben   | 2014-07-29 |   131 |
|    6 | Henry | 2014-07-26 |   115 |
|    7 | Suzi  | 2014-08-02 |   502 |
|    8 | Henry | 2014-08-01 |   197 |
|    9 | Ben   | 2014-08-02 |    79 |
|   10 | Henry | 2014-07-30 |   203 |
+--------+-------+------------+-------+
```

A simple summary showing the number of active drivers per day looks like this:

```
mysql> SELECT trav_date, COUNT(trav_date) AS drivers
    -> FROM driver_log GROUP BY trav_date ORDER BY trav_date;
+------------+---------+
| trav_date  | drivers |
+------------+---------+
| 2014-07-26 |       1 |
| 2014-07-27 |       1 |
| 2014-07-29 |       3 |
| 2014-07-30 |       2 |
| 2014-08-01 |       1 |
| 2014-08-02 |       2 |
+------------+---------+
```

Here, the summary category is date, but the summary is "incomplete" in the sense that it includes entries only for dates represented in the driver_log table. To produce a summary that includes all categories (all dates within the date range represented in the table), including those for which no driver was active, create a reference table that lists each date:

```
mysql> CREATE TABLE dates (d DATE);
mysql> INSERT INTO dates (d)
    -> VALUES('2014-07-26'),('2014-07-27'),('2014-07-28'),
    -> ('2014-07-29'),('2014-07-30'),('2014-07-31'),
    -> ('2014-08-01'),('2014-08-02');
```

Then join the reference table to the driver_log table using a LEFT JOIN:

```
mysql> SELECT dates.d, COUNT(driver_log.trav_date) AS drivers
    -> FROM dates LEFT JOIN driver_log ON dates.d = driver_log.trav_date
    -> GROUP BY d ORDER BY d;
+------------+---------+
| d          | drivers |
+------------+---------+
| 2014-07-26 |       1 |
| 2014-07-27 |       1 |
| 2014-07-28 |       0 |
| 2014-07-29 |       3 |
| 2014-07-30 |       2 |
| 2014-07-31 |       0 |
| 2014-08-01 |       1 |
| 2014-08-02 |       2 |
+------------+---------+
```

Now the summary includes a row for every date in the range because the LEFT JOIN forces the output to include a row for every date in the reference table, even those missing from the driver_log table.

The example just shown uses the reference table with a LEFT JOIN to fill holes in the summary. It's also possible to use the reference table to *detect* holes in the dataset—that is, to determine which categories are not present in the data to be summarized. The following statement shows those dates on which no driver was active by looking for reference rows for which no driver_log table rows have a matching category value:

```
mysql> SELECT dates.d
    -> FROM dates LEFT JOIN driver_log ON dates.d = driver_log.trav_date
    -> WHERE driver_log.trav_date IS NULL;
+------------+
| d          |
+------------+
| 2014-07-28 |
| 2014-07-31 |
+------------+
```

Reference tables that contain a list of categories are quite useful in summary context, as just shown. But creating such tables manually is mind-numbing and error-prone. It is much easier to use a recursive CTE for this purpose:

```
WITH RECURSIVE dates (d)  AS (
  SELECT '2014-07-26'
  UNION ALL
  SELECT d + INTERVAL 1 day
  FROM dates
  WHERE d < '2014-08-02')
SELECT dates.d, COUNT(driver_log.trav_date) AS drivers
FROM dates LEFT JOIN driver_log ON dates.d = driver_log.trav_date
GROUP BY d ORDER BY d;
```

We discuss recursive CTEs in more detail in Recipe 15.16.

If you need a very long list of dates that you expect to reuse often, you may prefer to store them in a table instead of generating series each time you need them. In this case, a stored procedure that uses the endpoints of the range of category values to generate the reference table for you helps automate the process. In essence, this type of procedure acts as an iterator that generates a row for each value in the range.

The following procedure, make_date_list(), shows an example of this approach. It creates a reference table containing a row for every date in a particular date range. It also indexes the table so that it will be fast in large joins:

```
CREATE PROCEDURE make_date_list(db_name TEXT, tbl_name TEXT, col_name TEXT,
                                min_date DATE, max_date DATE)
BEGIN
  DECLARE i, days INT;
  SET i = 0, days = DATEDIFF(max_date,min_date)+1;
```

```
# Make identifiers safe for insertion into SQL statements. Use db_name
# and tbl_name to create qualified table name.
SET tbl_name = CONCAT(quote_identifier(db_name),'.',
                      quote_identifier(tbl_name));
SET col_name = quote_identifier(col_name);
CALL exec_stmt(CONCAT('DROP TABLE IF EXISTS ',tbl_name));
CALL exec_stmt(CONCAT('CREATE TABLE ',tbl_name,'(',
                      col_name,' DATE NOT NULL, PRIMARY KEY(',
                      col_name,'))'));
WHILE i < days DO
  CALL exec_stmt(CONCAT('INSERT INTO ',tbl_name,'(',col_name,') VALUES(',
                        QUOTE(min_date),' + INTERVAL ',i,' DAY)'));
  SET i = i + 1;
END WHILE;
END;
```

Use `make_date_list()` to generate the reference table, `dates`, like this:

```
CALL make_date_list('cookbook', 'dates', 'd', '2014-07-26', '2014-08-02');
```

Then use the `dates` table as shown earlier in this section to fill holes in the summary or to detect holes in the dataset.

You can find the `make_date_list()` procedure in the *joins* directory of the `recipes` distribution. It requires the `exec_stmt()` and `quote_identifier()` helper routines (see Recipe 11.6), located in the *routines* directory. The *joins* directory also contains a Perl script, `make_date_list.pl`, that implements an alternate approach; it generates date reference tables from the command line.

16.9 Using a Join to Control Query Sort Order

Problem

You want to sort a statement's output using a characteristic of the output that cannot be specified using ORDER BY. For example, you want to sort a set of rows by subgroups, putting first those groups with the most rows and last those groups with the fewest rows. But "number of rows in each group" is not a property of individual rows, so you can't use it for sorting.

Solution

Derive the ordering information and store it in an auxiliary table. Then join the original table to the auxiliary table, using the auxiliary table to control the sort order.

Discussion

Most of the time you sort a query result using an ORDER BY clause that names which column or columns to use for sorting. But sometimes the values you want to sort by aren't present in the rows to be sorted. This is the case when you want to use group characteristics to order the rows. The following example uses the `driver_log` table to illustrate this. The following query sorts the table using the ID column, which is present in the rows:

```
mysql> SELECT * FROM driver_log ORDER BY rec_id;
+--------+-------+------------+-------+
| rec_id | name  | trav_date  | miles |
+--------+-------+------------+-------+
|      1 | Ben   | 2014-07-30 |   152 |
|      2 | Suzi  | 2014-07-29 |   391 |
|      3 | Henry | 2014-07-29 |   300 |
|      4 | Henry | 2014-07-27 |    96 |
|      5 | Ben   | 2014-07-29 |   131 |
|      6 | Henry | 2014-07-26 |   115 |
|      7 | Suzi  | 2014-08-02 |   502 |
|      8 | Henry | 2014-08-01 |   197 |
|      9 | Ben   | 2014-08-02 |    79 |
|     10 | Henry | 2014-07-30 |   203 |
+--------+-------+------------+-------+
```

But what if you want to display a list and sort it on the basis of a summary value not present in the rows? That's a little trickier. Suppose that you want to show each driver's rows by date but place those drivers who drive the most miles first. You can't do this with a summary query because then you wouldn't get back the individual driver rows. But you can't do it without a summary query, either, because the summary values are required for sorting. The way out of the dilemma is to create another table containing the summary value per driver and join it to the original table. That way you can produce the individual rows and also sort them by the summary values.

To summarize the driver totals into another table, do this:

```
mysql> CREATE TABLE tmp
    -> SELECT name, SUM(miles) AS driver_miles FROM driver_log GROUP BY name;
```

That produces the values we need to put the names in the proper total-miles order:

```
mysql> SELECT * FROM tmp ORDER BY driver_miles DESC;
+-------+--------------+
| name  | driver_miles |
+-------+--------------+
| Henry |          911 |
| Suzi  |          893 |
| Ben   |          362 |
+-------+--------------+
```

Then use the `name` values to join the summary table to the `driver_log` table, and use the `driver_miles` values to sort the result:

```
mysql> SELECT tmp.driver_miles, driver_log.*
    -> FROM driver_log INNER JOIN tmp ON driver_log.name = tmp.name
    -> ORDER BY tmp.driver_miles DESC, driver_log.trav_date;
+--------------+--------+-------+------------+-------+
| driver_miles | rec_id | name  | trav_date  | miles |
+--------------+--------+-------+------------+-------+
|          911 |      6 | Henry | 2014-07-26 |   115 |
|          911 |      4 | Henry | 2014-07-27 |    96 |
```

```
|           911 |      3 | Henry | 2014-07-29 |   300 |
|           911 |     10 | Henry | 2014-07-30 |   203 |
|           911 |      8 | Henry | 2014-08-01 |   197 |
|           893 |      2 | Suzi  | 2014-07-29 |   391 |
|           893 |      7 | Suzi  | 2014-08-02 |   502 |
|           362 |      5 | Ben   | 2014-07-29 |   131 |
|           362 |      1 | Ben   | 2014-07-30 |   152 |
|           362 |      9 | Ben   | 2014-08-02 |    79 |
+---------------+--------+-------+------------+-------+
```

The preceding statement shows the mileage totals in the result. That's only to clarify how the values are being sorted. It's not actually necessary to display them; they're needed only for the ORDER BY clause.

To avoid using the temporary table, use a CTE:

```
WITH tmp AS
(SELECT name, SUM(miles) AS driver_miles FROM driver_log GROUP BY name)
SELECT tmp.driver_miles, driver_log.*
FROM driver_log INNER JOIN tmp ON driver_log.name = tmp.name
ORDER BY tmp.driver_miles DESC, driver_log.trav_date;
```

Alternatively, select the same rows using a subquery in the FROM clause:

```
SELECT tmp.driver_miles, driver_log.*
FROM driver_log INNER JOIN
(SELECT name, SUM(miles) AS driver_miles
FROM driver_log GROUP BY name) AS tmp
ON driver_log.name = tmp.name
ORDER BY tmp.driver_miles DESC, driver_log.trav_date;
```

16.10 Joining Results of Multiple Queries

Problem

You want to join results of two or more queries.

Solution

Run the queries and store results in the temporary tables, then access those temporary tables to obtain the final results. Or, use named subqueries, then join their results. Or, use our favorite method: CTEs that will help you to perform this task in the easiest and clearest manner.

Discussion

You may need to join not only tables but results of other queries. Assume you are working with the city and states tables from the recipes distribution and want to find capital names of the states that belong to the 10 states with the highest populations. At the same time, you want to include into your search results only those states where the largest city is the same as the capital.

This task is very easy to solve if you first split it into three parts:

1. Find all states where the capital and the largest city are the same. You can do it with a query:
   ```
   SELECT * FROM city WHERE capital=largest;
   ```

2. Find 10 states with the highest population:
   ```
   SELECT * FROM states ORDER BY pop DESC LIMIT 10;
   ```

3. Join the results to select rows that exist in both.

There are three ways to do this: by creating intermediate temporary tables, by joining subquery results, and by using CTEs.

Using intermediate temporary tables

Store results of the queries into temporary tables, then select from them:

```
mysql> CREATE TEMPORARY TABLE large_capitals
    -> SELECT * FROM city WHERE capital=largest;
Query OK, 17 rows affected (0,00 sec)
Records: 17  Duplicates: 0  Warnings: 0

mysql> CREATE TEMPORARY TABLE top10states
    -> SELECT * FROM states ORDER BY pop DESC LIMIT 10;
Query OK, 10 rows affected (0,00 sec)
Records: 10  Duplicates: 0  Warnings: 0

mysql> SELECT state, capital, pop FROM
    -> large_capitals JOIN top10states
    -> ON(large_capitals.state = top10states.name);
+---------+----------+----------+
| state   | capital  | pop      |
+---------+----------+----------+
| Georgia | Atlanta  | 10799566 |
| Ohio    | Columbus | 11780017 |
+---------+----------+----------+
2 rows in set (0,00 sec)
```

 The keyword TEMPORARY for the CREATE TABLE statement instructs MySQL to create a table, visible for the current session only and which will be destroyed after you close the session. See Recipe 6.3 for further details.

Using named subqueries

If you need to access the intermediate results only once, you can avoid creating temporary tables by using subqueries and joining their results.

```
mysql> SELECT state, capital, pop FROM ❶
    -> (SELECT * FROM city WHERE capital=largest) AS large_capitals, ❷
    -> (SELECT * FROM states ORDER BY pop DESC LIMIT 10) AS top10states ❸
    -> WHERE large_capitals.state = top10states.name; ❹
```

```
+---------+---------+----------+
| state   | capital | pop      |
+---------+---------+----------+
| Georgia | Atlanta | 10799566 |
| Ohio    | Columbus| 11780017 |
+---------+---------+----------+
2 rows in set (0,00 sec)
```

❶ Start the query by selecting the columns you need in the final result.

❷ Put the first subquery into brackets, and assign it a unique name.

❸ Do the same for the second subquery.

❹ Narrow the search with a WHERE clause.

Using CTEs

With CTEs, start by naming your subqueries, then join their results as if they were regular MySQL tables:

```
mysql> WITH
    -> large_capitals AS (SELECT * FROM city WHERE capital=largest),
    -> top10states AS (SELECT * FROM states ORDER BY pop DESC LIMIT 10)
    -> SELECT state, capital, pop
    -> FROM large_capitals JOIN top10states
    -> ON (large_capitals.state = top10states.name);
+---------+---------+----------+
| state   | capital | pop      |
+---------+---------+----------+
| Georgia | Atlanta | 10799566 |
| Ohio    | Columbus| 11780017 |
+---------+---------+----------+
2 rows in set (0,00 sec)
```

16.11 Referring to Join Output Column Names in Programs

Problem

You need to process the result of a join from within a program, but column names in the result set aren't unique.

Solution

Rewrite the query using column aliases so that each column has a unique name. Alternatively, refer to the columns by position.

Discussion

Joins typically retrieve columns from related tables, and it's not unusual for columns selected from different tables to have the same names. Consider the following join that shows the items in your art collection. For each painting, it displays artist name, painting title, the state in which you acquired the item, and its price:

```
mysql> SELECT artist.name, painting.title, states.name, painting.price
    -> FROM artist INNER JOIN painting INNER JOIN states
    -> ON artist.a_id = painting.a_id AND painting.state = states.abbrev;
+----------+-------------------+----------+-------+
| name     | title             | name     | price |
+----------+-------------------+----------+-------+
| Da Vinci | The Last Supper   | Indiana  |    34 |
| Da Vinci | Mona Lisa         | Michigan |    87 |
| Van Gogh | Starry Night      | Kentucky |    48 |
| Van Gogh | The Potato Eaters | Kentucky |    67 |
| Renoir   | Les Deux Soeurs   | Nebraska |    64 |
+----------+-------------------+----------+-------+
```

The statement uses table qualifiers for each output column, but MySQL doesn't include table names in the column headings, so not all column names in the output are distinct. If you process the join result from within a program and fetch rows into a data structure that references column values by name, nonunique column names cause values to become inaccessible. Suppose that you fetch rows in a Perl DBI script like this:

```
while (my $ref = $sth->fetchrow_hashref ())
{
  ... process row hash here ...
}
```

Fetching rows into the hash yields three hash elements (name, title, price); one of the name elements is lost. To solve this problem, supply aliases that make the column names unique:

```
SELECT artist.name AS painter, painting.title,
  states.name AS state, painting.price
FROM artist INNER JOIN painting INNER JOIN states
ON artist.a_id = painting.a_id AND painting.state = states.abbrev;
```

Now fetching rows into a hash yields four hash elements (painter, title, state, price).

To address the problem without column renaming, fetch the row into something other than a hash. For example, fetch the row into an array and refer to the columns by ordinal position within the array:

```
while (my @val = $sth->fetchrow_array ())
{
  print "painter: $val[0], title: $val[1], "
      . "state: $val[2], price: $val[3]\n";
}
```

## CHAPTER 17

Statistical Techniques

17.0 Introduction

This chapter covers several topics that relate to basic statistical techniques. For the most part, these recipes build on those described in earlier chapters, such as the summary techniques discussed in Chapter 10 and join techniques from Chapter 16. The examples here thus show additional ways to apply the material from those chapters. Broadly speaking, the topics discussed in this chapter include the following:

- Techniques for characterizing a dataset, such as calculating descriptive statistics, generating frequency distributions, counting missing values, and calculating least-squares regressions or correlation coefficients

- Randomization methods, such as how to generate random numbers and apply them to randomizing a set of rows or to selecting individual items randomly from the rows

- Techniques for calculating successive-observation differences, cumulative sums, and running averages

- Methods for producing rank assignments and generating team standings

Statistics covers such a large and diverse array of topics that this chapter necessarily only scratches the surface and simply illustrates a few of the potential areas in which MySQL may be applied to statistical analysis. Note that some statistical measures can be defined in different ways (for example, do you calculate standard deviation based on n degrees of freedom or $n-1$?). If the definition we use for a given term doesn't match the one you prefer, adapt the queries or algorithms shown here appropriately.

You can find scripts related to the examples discussed here in the *stats* directory of the `recipes` distribution, and scripts for creating example tables in the *tables* directory.

17.1 Calculating Descriptive Statistics

Problem

You want to characterize a dataset by computing general descriptive or summary statistics.

Solution

Many common descriptive statistics, such as mean and standard deviation, are obtained by applying aggregate functions to your data. Others, such as median or mode, are calculated based on counting queries.

Discussion

Suppose that a `testscore` table contains observations representing subject ID, age, sex, and test score:

```
mysql> SELECT subject, age, sex, score FROM testscore ORDER BY subject;
+---------+-----+-----+-------+
| subject | age | sex | score |
+---------+-----+-----+-------+
|       1 |   5 | M   |     5 |
|       2 |   5 | M   |     4 |
|       3 |   5 | F   |     6 |
|       4 |   5 | F   |     7 |
|       5 |   6 | M   |     8 |
|       6 |   6 | M   |     9 |
|       7 |   6 | F   |     4 |
|       8 |   6 | F   |     6 |
|       9 |   7 | M   |     8 |
|      10 |   7 | M   |     6 |
|      11 |   7 | F   |     9 |
|      12 |   7 | F   |     7 |
|      13 |   8 | M   |     9 |
|      14 |   8 | M   |     6 |
|      15 |   8 | F   |     7 |
|      16 |   8 | F   |    10 |
|      17 |   9 | M   |     9 |
|      18 |   9 | M   |     7 |
|      19 |   9 | F   |    10 |
|      20 |   9 | F   |     9 |
+---------+-----+-----+-------+
```

A good first step in analyzing a set of observations is to generate some descriptive statistics that summarize their general characteristics as a whole. Common statistical values of this kind include:

- The number of observations, their sum, and their range (minimum and maximum)

- Measures of central tendency, such as mean, median, and mode
- Measures of variation, such as standard deviation and variance

Aside from the median and mode, all of these can be calculated easily by invoking aggregate functions:

```
mysql> SELECT COUNT(score) AS n,
    -> SUM(score) AS sum,
    -> MIN(score) AS minimum,
    -> MAX(score) AS maximum,
    -> AVG(score) AS mean,
    -> STDDEV_SAMP(score) AS 'std. dev.',
    -> VAR_SAMP(score) AS 'variance'
    -> FROM testscore;
+----+------+---------+---------+--------+-----------+----------+
| n  | sum  | minimum | maximum | mean   | std. dev. | variance |
+----+------+---------+---------+--------+-----------+----------+
| 20 | 146  |       4 |      10 | 7.3000 |    1.8382 |   3.3789 |
+----+------+---------+---------+--------+-----------+----------+
```

The STDDEV_SAMP() and VAR_SAMP() functions produce sample measures rather than population measures. That is, for a set of *n* values, they produce a result that is based on *n*–1 degrees of freedom. For the population measures, which are based on *n* degrees of freedom, use STDDEV_POP() and VAR_POP() instead. STDDEV() and VARIANCE() are synonyms for STDDEV_POP() and VAR_POP().

Standard deviation can be used to identify outliers—values that are uncharacteristically far from the mean. For example, to select values that lie more than a standard deviation from the mean, do this:

```
SELECT AVG(score), STDDEV_SAMP(score) INTO @mean, @std FROM testscore;
SELECT score FROM testscore WHERE ABS(score-@mean) > @std;
```

MySQL has no built-in function for computing the mode or median of a set of values, but you can compute them yourself. To determine the mode (the value that occurs most frequently), count each value and see which is most common:

```
mysql> SELECT score, COUNT(score) AS frequency
    -> FROM testscore GROUP BY score ORDER BY frequency DESC;
+-------+-----------+
| score | frequency |
+-------+-----------+
|     9 |         5 |
|     6 |         4 |
|     7 |         4 |
|     4 |         2 |
|     8 |         2 |
|    10 |         2 |
|     5 |         1 |
+-------+-----------+
```

In this case, 9 is the modal score value.

The median of a set of ordered values can be calculated like this:[1]

- If the number of values is odd, the median is the middle value.
- If the number of values is even, the median is the average of the two middle values.

Based on that definition, use the following procedure to determine the median of a set of observations stored in the database:

1. Issue a query to count the number of observations. From the count, you can determine whether the median calculation requires one or two values and what their indexes are within the ordered set of observations.

2. Issue a query that includes an ORDER BY clause to sort the observations and a LIMIT clause to pull out the middle value or values.

3. If there is a single middle value, it is the median. Otherwise, take the average of the middle values.

Suppose that a table t contains a score column with 37 values (an odd number). To get the median, select a single value using a statement like this:

```
SELECT score FROM t ORDER BY score LIMIT 18,1;
```

If the column contains 38 values (an even number), select two values:

```
SELECT score FROM t ORDER BY score LIMIT 18,2;
```

Then take the values returned by the statement and compute the median from their average.

The following Perl function implements a median calculation. It takes a database handle and the names of the database, table, and column that contain the set of observations. Then it generates the statement that retrieves the relevant values and returns their average:

```
sub median
{
my ($dbh, $db_name, $tbl_name, $col_name) = @_;
my ($count, $limit);

  $db_name = $dbh->quote_identifier ($db_name);
  $tbl_name = $dbh->quote_identifier ($tbl_name);
  $col_name = $dbh->quote_identifier ($col_name);

  $count = $dbh->selectrow_array (qq{
    SELECT COUNT($col_name) FROM $db_name.$tbl_name
  });
```

---

[1] The definition of *median* given here isn't fully general; it doesn't address what to do if the middle values in the dataset are duplicated.

```
    return undef unless $count > 0;
    if ($count % 2 == 1)  # odd number of values; select middle value
    {
      $limit = sprintf ("LIMIT %d,1", ($count-1)/2);
    }
    else                  # even number of values; select middle two values
    {
      $limit = sprintf ("LIMIT %d,2", $count/2 - 1);
    }

    my $sth = $dbh->prepare (qq{
      SELECT $col_name FROM $db_name.$tbl_name ORDER BY $col_name $limit
    });
    $sth->execute ();
    my ($n, $sum) = (0, 0);
    while (my $ref = $sth->fetchrow_arrayref ())
    {
      ++$n;
      $sum += $ref->[0];
    }
    return $sum / $n;
  }
```

The preceding technique works for a set of values stored in the database. If you have already fetched an ordered set of values into an array @val, compute the median like this instead:

```
if (@val == 0)         # array is empty, median is undefined
{
  $median = undef;
}
elsif (@val % 2 == 1)   # array size is odd, median is middle number
{
  $median = $val[(@val-1)/2];
}
else                    # array size is even; median is average
{                       # of two middle numbers
  $median = ($val[@val/2 - 1] + $val[@val/2]) / 2;
}
```

The code works for arrays that have an initial subscript of 0; for languages that use 1-based array indexes, adjust the algorithm accordingly.

17.2 Calculating Descriptive Statistics for Groups

Problem

You want to produce descriptive statistics for each subgroup of a set of observations.

Solution

Use aggregate functions but employ a GROUP BY clause to arrange observations into the appropriate groups.

Discussion

Recipe 17.1 shows how to compute descriptive statistics for the entire set of scores in the `testscore` table. To be more specific, use GROUP BY to divide the observations into groups and calculate statistics for each of them. For example, the subjects in the `testscore` table are listed by age and sex, so it's possible to calculate similar statistics by age or sex (or both) by application of appropriate GROUP BY clauses.

Here's how to calculate by age:

```
mysql> SELECT age, COUNT(score) AS n,
    -> SUM(score) AS sum,
    -> MIN(score) AS minimum,
    -> MAX(score) AS maximum,
    -> AVG(score) AS mean,
    -> STDDEV_SAMP(score) AS 'std. dev.',
    -> VAR_SAMP(score) AS 'variance'
    -> FROM testscore
    -> GROUP BY age;
+-----+---+------+---------+---------+--------+-----------+----------+
| age | n | sum  | minimum | maximum | mean   | std. dev. | variance |
+-----+---+------+---------+---------+--------+-----------+----------+
|   5 | 4 |  22  |    4    |    7    | 5.5000 |   1.2910  |  1.6667  |
|   6 | 4 |  27  |    4    |    9    | 6.7500 |   2.2174  |  4.9167  |
|   7 | 4 |  30  |    6    |    9    | 7.5000 |   1.2910  |  1.6667  |
|   8 | 4 |  32  |    6    |   10    | 8.0000 |   1.8257  |  3.3333  |
|   9 | 4 |  35  |    7    |   10    | 8.7500 |   1.2583  |  1.5833  |
+-----+---+------+---------+---------+--------+-----------+----------+
```

By sex:

```
mysql> SELECT sex, COUNT(score) AS n,
    -> SUM(score) AS sum,
    -> MIN(score) AS minimum,
    -> MAX(score) AS maximum,
    -> AVG(score) AS mean,
    -> STDDEV_SAMP(score) AS 'std. dev.',
    -> VAR_SAMP(score) AS 'variance'
    -> FROM testscore
    -> GROUP BY sex;
+-----+----+------+---------+---------+--------+-----------+----------+
| sex | n  | sum  | minimum | maximum | mean   | std. dev. | variance |
+-----+----+------+---------+---------+--------+-----------+----------+
| M   | 10 |  71  |    4    |    9    | 7.1000 |   1.7920  |  3.2111  |
| F   | 10 |  75  |    4    |   10    | 7.5000 |   1.9579  |  3.8333  |
+-----+----+------+---------+---------+--------+-----------+----------+
```

By age and sex:

```
mysql> SELECT age, sex, COUNT(score) AS n,
    -> SUM(score) AS sum,
    -> MIN(score) AS minimum,
    -> MAX(score) AS maximum,
    -> AVG(score) AS mean,
    -> STDDEV_SAMP(score) AS 'std. dev.',
    -> VAR_SAMP(score) AS 'variance'
    -> FROM testscore
    -> GROUP BY age, sex;
```

```
+-----+-----+---+------+---------+---------+--------+-----------+----------+
| age | sex | n | sum  | minimum | maximum | mean   | std. dev. | variance |
+-----+-----+---+------+---------+---------+--------+-----------+----------+
|   5 | M   | 2 |   9  |    4    |    5    | 4.5000 |   0.7071  |  0.5000  |
|   5 | F   | 2 |  13  |    6    |    7    | 6.5000 |   0.7071  |  0.5000  |
|   6 | M   | 2 |  17  |    8    |    9    | 8.5000 |   0.7071  |  0.5000  |
|   6 | F   | 2 |  10  |    4    |    6    | 5.0000 |   1.4142  |  2.0000  |
|   7 | M   | 2 |  14  |    6    |    8    | 7.0000 |   1.4142  |  2.0000  |
|   7 | F   | 2 |  16  |    7    |    9    | 8.0000 |   1.4142  |  2.0000  |
|   8 | M   | 2 |  15  |    6    |    9    | 7.5000 |   2.1213  |  4.5000  |
|   8 | F   | 2 |  17  |    7    |   10    | 8.5000 |   2.1213  |  4.5000  |
|   9 | M   | 2 |  16  |    7    |    9    | 8.0000 |   1.4142  |  2.0000  |
|   9 | F   | 2 |  19  |    9    |   10    | 9.5000 |   0.7071  |  0.5000  |
+-----+-----+---+------+---------+---------+--------+-----------+----------+
```

17.3 Generating Frequency Distributions

Problem

You want to know the frequency of occurrence for each value in a table.

Solution

Derive a frequency distribution that summarizes the contents of your dataset.

Discussion

A common application for per-group summary techniques is to generate a *frequency distribution* that shows how often each value occurs. For the `testscore` table, the frequency distribution looks like this:

```
mysql> SELECT score, COUNT(score) AS counts
    -> FROM testscore GROUP BY score;
+-------+--------+
| score | counts |
+-------+--------+
|     4 |      2 |
|     5 |      1 |
|     6 |      4 |
|     7 |      4 |
|     8 |      2 |
|     9 |      5 |
|    10 |      2 |
+-------+--------+
```

Expressing the results in percentages rather than counts yields relative frequency distribution. To show each count as a percentage of the total, use one query to get the total number of observations and another to calculate the percentages for each group:

```
mysql> SET @n = (SELECT COUNT(score) FROM testscore);
mysql> SELECT score, (COUNT(score)*100)/@n AS percent
    -> FROM testscore GROUP BY score;
```

```
+-------+---------+
| score | percent |
+-------+---------+
|     4 | 10.0000 |
|     5 |  5.0000 |
|     6 | 20.0000 |
|     7 | 20.0000 |
|     8 | 10.0000 |
|     9 | 25.0000 |
|    10 | 10.0000 |
+-------+---------+
```

The distributions just shown summarize the number of values for individual scores. However, if the dataset contains a large number of distinct values and you want a distribution that shows only a small number of categories, you may want to lump values into categories and produce a count for each category. Recipe 10.13 discusses "lumping" techniques.

One typical use of frequency distributions is to export the results for use in a graphing program. But MySQL itself can generate a simple ASCII chart as a visual representation of the distribution. To display an ASCII bar chart of the test score counts, convert the counts to strings of * characters:

```
mysql> SELECT score, REPEAT('*',COUNT(score)) AS 'count histogram'
    -> FROM testscore GROUP BY score;
+-------+-----------------+
| score | count histogram |
+-------+-----------------+
|     4 | **              |
|     5 | *               |
|     6 | ****            |
|     7 | ****            |
|     8 | **              |
|     9 | *****           |
|    10 | **              |
+-------+-----------------+
```

To chart the relative frequency distribution instead, use the percentage values:

```
mysql> SET @n = (SELECT COUNT(score) FROM testscore);
mysql> SELECT score,
    -> REPEAT('*',(COUNT(score)*100)/@n) AS 'percent histogram'
    -> FROM testscore GROUP BY score;
+-------+---------------------------+
| score | percent histogram         |
+-------+---------------------------+
|     4 | *********                 |
|     5 | *****                     |
|     6 | ********************      |
|     7 | ********************      |
|     8 | *********                 |
|     9 | *************************  |
|    10 | *********                 |
+-------+---------------------------+
```

The ASCII chart method is crude, obviously, but it's a quick way to get a picture of the distribution of observations and requires no other tools.

If you generate a frequency distribution for a range of categories where some of the categories are not represented in your observations, the missing categories do not appear in the output. To force each category to be displayed, use a reference table and a LEFT JOIN (a technique discussed in Recipe 16.8). For the testscore table, the possible scores range from 0 to 10, so a reference table should contain each of those values:

```
mysql> CREATE TABLE ref (score INT);
mysql> INSERT INTO ref (score)
    -> VALUES(0),(1),(2),(3),(4),(5),(6),(7),(8),(9),(10);
```

Then join the reference table to the test scores to generate the frequency distribution. This query shows the counts as well as the histogram:

```
mysql> SELECT ref.score, COUNT(testscore.score) AS counts,
    -> REPEAT('*',COUNT(testscore.score)) AS 'count histogram'
    -> FROM ref LEFT JOIN testscore ON ref.score = testscore.score
    -> GROUP BY ref.score;
+-------+--------+-----------+
| score | counts | histogram |
+-------+--------+-----------+
|     0 |      0 |           |
|     1 |      0 |           |
|     2 |      0 |           |
|     3 |      0 |           |
|     4 |      2 | **        |
|     5 |      1 | *         |
|     6 |      4 | ****      |
|     7 |      4 | ****      |
|     8 |      2 | **        |
|     9 |      5 | *****     |
|    10 |      2 | **        |
+-------+--------+-----------+
```

This distribution includes rows for scores 0 through 3, none of which appear in the frequency distribution shown earlier.

The same principle applies to relative frequency distributions:

```
mysql> SET @n = (SELECT COUNT(score) FROM testscore);
mysql> SELECT ref.score, (COUNT(testscore.score)*100)/@n AS percent,
    -> REPEAT('*',(COUNT(testscore.score)*100)/@n) AS 'percent histogram'
    -> FROM ref LEFT JOIN testscore ON ref.score = testscore.score
    -> GROUP BY ref.score;
+-------+---------+--------------------------+
| score | percent | percent histogram        |
+-------+---------+--------------------------+
|     0 |  0.0000 |                          |
|     1 |  0.0000 |                          |
|     2 |  0.0000 |                          |
|     3 |  0.0000 |                          |
|     4 | 10.0000 | **********               |
|     5 |  5.0000 | *****                    |
```

```
|    6 | 20.0000 | ********************       |
|    7 | 20.0000 | ********************       |
|    8 | 10.0000 | **********                |
|    9 | 25.0000 | *************************  |
|   10 | 10.0000 | **********                |
+------+---------+---------------------------+
```

17.4 Counting Missing Values

Problem

A set of observations is incomplete. You want to find out how many values are missing.

Solution

Count the number of NULL values in the set.

Discussion

Values can be missing from a set of observations for any number of reasons: a test may not yet have been administered, something may have gone wrong during the test that requires invalidating the observation, and so forth. You can represent such observations in a dataset as NULL values to signify that they're missing or otherwise invalid, then use summary statements to characterize the completeness of the dataset.

If a table, testscore_withmisses, contains values to be summarized along a single dimension, a simple summary suffices to characterize the missing values. Suppose that testscore_withmisses looks like this:

```
mysql> SELECT subject, score FROM testscore_withmisses ORDER BY subject;
+---------+-------+
| subject | score |
+---------+-------+
|       1 |    38 |
|       2 |  NULL |
|       3 |    47 |
|       4 |  NULL |
|       5 |    37 |
|       6 |    45 |
|       7 |    54 |
|       8 |  NULL |
|       9 |    40 |
|      10 |    49 |
+---------+-------+
```

COUNT(*) counts the total number of rows, and COUNT(score) counts the number of nonmissing scores. The difference between the two values is the number of missing scores, and that difference in relation to the total provides the percentage of missing scores. Perform these calculations as follows:

```
mysql> SELECT COUNT(*) AS 'n (total)',
    -> COUNT(score) AS 'n (nonmissing)',
    -> COUNT(*) - COUNT(score) AS 'n (missing)',
    -> ((COUNT(*) - COUNT(score)) * 100) / COUNT(*) AS '% missing'
    -> FROM testscore_withmisses;
+-----------+----------------+-------------+-----------+
| n (total) | n (nonmissing) | n (missing) | % missing |
+-----------+----------------+-------------+-----------+
|        10 |              7 |           3 |   30.0000 |
+-----------+----------------+-------------+-----------+
```

As an alternative to counting NULL values as the difference between counts, count them directly using SUM(ISNULL(score)). The ISNULL() function returns 1 if its argument is NULL and zero otherwise:

```
mysql> SELECT COUNT(*) AS 'n (total)',
    -> COUNT(score) AS 'n (nonmissing)',
    -> SUM(ISNULL(score)) AS 'n (missing)',
    -> (SUM(ISNULL(score)) * 100) / COUNT(*) AS '% missing'
    -> FROM testscore_withmisses;
+-----------+----------------+-------------+-----------+
| n (total) | n (nonmissing) | n (missing) | % missing |
+-----------+----------------+-------------+-----------+
|        10 |              7 |           3 |   30.0000 |
+-----------+----------------+-------------+-----------+
```

If values are arranged in groups, occurrences of NULL values can be assessed on a per-group basis. Suppose that testscore_withmisses2 contains scores for subjects that are distributed among conditions for two factors, A and B, each of which has two levels:

```
mysql> SELECT subject, A, B, score FROM testscore_withmisses2 ORDER BY subject;
+---------+------+------+-------+
| subject | A    | B    | score |
+---------+------+------+-------+
|       1 |    1 |    1 |    18 |
|       2 |    1 |    1 |  NULL |
|       3 |    1 |    1 |    23 |
|       4 |    1 |    1 |    24 |
|       5 |    1 |    2 |    17 |
|       6 |    1 |    2 |    23 |
|       7 |    1 |    2 |    29 |
|       8 |    1 |    2 |    32 |
|       9 |    2 |    1 |    17 |
|      10 |    2 |    1 |  NULL |
|      11 |    2 |    1 |  NULL |
|      12 |    2 |    1 |    25 |
|      13 |    2 |    2 |  NULL |
|      14 |    2 |    2 |    33 |
|      15 |    2 |    2 |    34 |
|      16 |    2 |    2 |    37 |
+---------+------+------+-------+
```

To produce a summary for each combination of conditions, use a GROUP BY clause:

```
mysql> SELECT A, B, COUNT(*) AS 'n (total)',
    -> COUNT(score) AS 'n (nonmissing)',
    -> COUNT(*) - COUNT(score) AS 'n (missing)',
```

```
   -> ((COUNT(*) - COUNT(score)) * 100) / COUNT(*) AS '% missing'
   -> FROM testscore_withmisses2
   -> GROUP BY A, B;
+------+------+-----------+-----------------+--------------+-----------+
| A    | B    | n (total) | n (nonmissing)  | n (missing)  | % missing |
+------+------+-----------+-----------------+--------------+-----------+
|    1 |    1 |         4 |               3 |            1 |   25.0000 |
|    1 |    2 |         4 |               4 |            0 |    0.0000 |
|    2 |    1 |         4 |               2 |            2 |   50.0000 |
|    2 |    2 |         4 |               3 |            1 |   25.0000 |
+------+------+-----------+-----------------+--------------+-----------+
```

17.5 Calculating Linear Regressions or Correlation Coefficients

Problem

You want to calculate the least-squares regression line for two variables or the correlation coefficient that expresses the strength of the relationship between them.

Solution

Apply summary functions to make these calculations.

Discussion

When the data values for two variables, X and Y, are stored in a database, the least-squares regression for them can be calculated easily using aggregate functions. The same is true for the correlation coefficient. The two calculations are actually fairly similar, and many terms for performing the computations are common to the two procedures.

Suppose that you want to calculate a least-squares regression using the age and test score values for the observations in the testscore table:

```
mysql> SELECT age, score FROM testscore;
+-----+-------+
| age | score |
+-----+-------+
|   5 |     5 |
|   5 |     4 |
|   5 |     6 |
|   5 |     7 |
|   6 |     8 |
|   6 |     9 |
|   6 |     4 |
|   6 |     6 |
|   7 |     8 |
|   7 |     6 |
|   7 |     9 |
|   7 |     7 |
|   8 |     9 |
```

```
|    8 |      6 |
|    8 |      7 |
|    8 |     10 |
|    9 |      9 |
|    9 |      7 |
|    9 |     10 |
|    9 |      9 |
+------+--------+
```

The following equation expresses the regression line, where a and b are the intercept and slope of the line:

$$Y = bX + a$$

Letting age be X and score be Y, begin by computing the terms needed for the regression equation. These include the number of observations; the means, sums, and sums of squares for each variable; and the sum of the products of each variable:[2]

```
mysql> SELECT COUNT(score), AVG(age), SUM(age), SUM(age*age),
    -> AVG(score), SUM(score), SUM(score*score), SUM(age*score)
    -> INTO @n, @meanX, @sumX, @sumXX, @meanY, @sumY, @sumYY, @sumXY
    -> FROM testscore;
Query OK, 1 row affected (0,00 sec)

mysql> SELECT
    -> @n AS N,
    -> @meanX AS 'X mean',
    -> @sumX AS 'X sum',
    -> @sumXX AS 'X sum of squares',
    -> @meanY AS 'Y mean',
    -> @sumY AS 'Y sum',
    -> @sumYY AS 'Y sum of squares',
    -> @sumXY AS 'X*Y sum'
    -> FROM testscore\G
*************************** 1. row ***************************
               N: 20
          X mean: 7.000000000
           X sum: 140
X sum of squares: 1020
          Y mean: 7.300000000
           Y sum: 146
Y sum of squares: 1130
         X*Y sum: 1053
```

From those terms, calculate the regression slope and intercept as follows:

```
mysql> SET @b := (@n*@sumXY - @sumX*@sumY) / (@n*@sumXX - @sumX*@sumX);
mysql> SET @a := (@meanY - @b*@meanX);
mysql> SELECT @b AS slope, @a AS intercept;
+-------------+----------------------+
| slope       | intercept            |
+-------------+----------------------+
| 0.775000000 | 1.875000000000000000 |
+-------------+----------------------+
```

---

2 To see where these terms come from, consult any standard statistics text.

The regression equation then is:

```
mysql> SELECT CONCAT('Y = ',@b,'X + ',@a) AS 'least-squares regression';
+----------------------------------------+
| least-squares regression               |
+----------------------------------------+
| Y = 0.775000000X + 1.875000000000000000 |
+----------------------------------------+
```

To compute the correlation coefficient, use many of the same terms:

```
mysql> SELECT
    -> (@n*@sumXY - @sumX*@sumY)
    -> / SQRT((@n*@sumXX - @sumX*@sumX) * (@n*@sumYY - @sumY*@sumY))
    -> AS correlation;
+--------------------+
| correlation        |
+--------------------+
| 0.6117362044219903 |
+--------------------+
```

17.6 Generating Random Numbers

Problem

You need a source of random numbers.

Solution

Use the RAND() function.

Discussion

MySQL has a RAND() function that produces random numbers between 0 and 1:

```
mysql> SELECT RAND(), RAND(), RAND();
+---------------------+--------------------+---------------------+
| RAND()              | RAND()             | RAND()              |
+---------------------+--------------------+---------------------+
| 0.37415416573561183 | 0.9068914557871329 | 0.41199481246247405 |
+---------------------+--------------------+---------------------+
```

When invoked with an integer argument, RAND() uses that value to seed the random number generator. You can use this feature to produce a repeatable series of numbers for a column of a query result. The following example shows that RAND() without an argument produces a different column of values per query, whereas RAND(N) produces a repeatable column:

```
mysql> SELECT i, RAND(), RAND(10), RAND(20) FROM numbers;
+------+---------------------+--------------------+---------------------+
| i    | RAND()              | RAND(10)           | RAND(20)            |
+------+---------------------+--------------------+---------------------+
|    1 | 0.00708185882035816 | 0.6570515219653505 | 0.15888261251047497 |
|    2 | 0.5417692908474889  | 0.12820613023657923 | 0.6355305003333189  |
```

```
|    3 |  0.6876009085100152 |  0.6698761160204896 |  0.7010046948688149 |
|    4 |  0.8126967007412544 |  0.9647622201263553 |  0.5984320040777623 |
+------+---------------------+---------------------+---------------------+
mysql> SELECT i, RAND(), RAND(10), RAND(20) FROM numbers;
+------+----------------------+---------------------+---------------------+
| i    | RAND()               | RAND(10)            | RAND(20)            |
+------+----------------------+---------------------+---------------------+
|    1 | 0.059957268703689115 |  0.6570515219653505 | 0.15888261251047497 |
|    2 |  0.9068000166740269  | 0.12820613023657923 |  0.6355305003333189 |
|    3 |  0.35412830799271194 |  0.6698761160204896 |  0.7010046948688149 |
|    4 |  0.050241520675124156|  0.9647622201263553 |  0.5984320040777623 |
+------+----------------------+---------------------+---------------------+
```

To seed RAND() randomly, pick a seed value based on a source of entropy. Possible sources are the current timestamp or connection identifier, alone or perhaps in combination:

```
RAND(UNIX_TIMESTAMP())
RAND(CONNECTION_ID())
RAND(UNIX_TIMESTAMP()+CONNECTION_ID())
```

However, it's probably better to use other seed value sources if you have them. For example, if your system has a */dev/random* or */dev/urandom* device, read the device and use it to generate a value for seeding RAND().

How Random Is RAND()?

Does the RAND() function generate evenly distributed numbers? Check it out for yourself with the following Python script, rand_test.py, from the *stats* directory of the recipes distribution. (That directory also contains equivalent scripts in other languages.) The script uses RAND() to generate random numbers and constructs a frequency distribution from them, using 10 categories ("buckets"). This provides a means of assessing how evenly distributed the values are:

```
#!/usr/bin/python
# rand_test.pl: create a frequency distribution of RAND() values.
# This provides a test of the randomness of RAND().

# Method: Draw random numbers in the range from 0 to 1.0,
# and count how many of them occur in .1-sized intervals

import cookbook

npicks = 1000    # number of times to pick a number
bucket = [0] * 10 # buckets for counting picks in each interval

conn = cookbook.connect()
cursor = conn.cursor()

for i in range(0, npicks):
  cursor.execute("SELECT RAND()")
  (val,) = cursor.fetchone()
  slot = int(val * 10)
  if slot > 9:
    slot = 9    # put 1.0 in last slot
```

```
    bucket[slot] += 1

cursor.close()
conn.close()

# Print the resulting frequency distribution

for slot, val in enumerate(bucket):
  print("%2d  %d" % (slot+1, val))
```

17.7 Randomizing a Set of Rows

Problem

You want to randomize a set of rows or values.

Solution

Use ORDER BY RAND().

Discussion

MySQL's RAND() function can be used to randomize the order in which a query returns its rows. Somewhat paradoxically, this randomization is achieved by adding an ORDER BY clause to the query. The technique is roughly equivalent to a spreadsheet randomization method. Suppose that a spreadsheet contains this set of values:

```
Patrick
Penelope
Pertinax
Polly
```

To place these in random order, first add another column that contains randomly chosen numbers:

```
Patrick          .73
Penelope         .37
Pertinax         .16
Polly            .48
```

Then sort the rows according to the values of the random numbers:

```
Pertinax         .16
Penelope         .37
Polly            .48
Patrick          .73
```

At this point, the original values have been placed in random order; the effect of sorting the random numbers is to randomize the values associated with them. To rerandomize the values, choose another set of random numbers, and sort the rows again.

In MySQL, achieve a similar effect by associating a set of random numbers with a query result and sorting the result by those numbers. To do this, add an ORDER BY RAND() clause:

```
mysql> SELECT name FROM rand_names ORDER BY RAND();
+----------+
| name     |
+----------+
| Pertinax |
| Patrick  |
| Polly    |
| Penelope |
+----------+
mysql> SELECT name FROM rand_names ORDER BY RAND();
+----------+
| name     |
+----------+
| Polly    |
| Pertinax |
| Penelope |
| Patrick  |
+----------+
```

Applications for randomizing a set of rows include any scenario that uses selection without replacement (choosing each item from a set of items until there are no more items left). Some examples of this are the following:

- Determining the starting order for participants in an event. List the participants in a table, and select them in random order.

- Assigning starting lanes or gates to participants in a race. List the lanes in a table, and select a random lane order.

- Choosing the order in which to present a set of quiz questions.

- Shuffling a deck of cards. Represent each card by a row in a table, and shuffle the deck by selecting the rows in random order. Deal them one by one until the deck is exhausted.

To use the last example as an illustration, let's implement a card deck–shuffling algorithm. Shuffling and dealing cards is randomization plus selection without replacement: each card is dealt once before any is dealt twice; when the deck is used up, it is reshuffled to rerandomize it for a new dealing order. Within a program, this task can be performed with MySQL using a table named deck that has 52 rows, assuming a set of cards with each combination of 13 face values and 4 suits:

1. Select the entire table, and store it into an array.

2. Each time a card is needed, take the next element from the array.

3. When the array is exhausted, all the cards have been dealt. "Reshuffle" the table to generate a new card order.

Setting up the deck table is a tedious task if you insert the 52 card records by writing all the INSERT statements manually. The deck contents can be generated more easily in combinatorial fashion within a program by generating each pairing of face value with suit. Here's some PHP code that creates a deck table with face and suit columns, then populates the table using nested loops to generate the pairings for the INSERT statements:

```
$sth = $dbh->exec ("DROP TABLE IF EXISTS deck");

$sth = $dbh->exec ("
  CREATE TABLE deck
  (
    face  ENUM('A', 'K', 'Q', 'J', '10', '9', '8',
              '7', '6', '5', '4', '3', '2') NOT NULL,
    suit  ENUM('hearts', 'diamonds', 'clubs', 'spades') NOT NULL
  )
");

$face_array = array ("A", "K", "Q", "J", "10", "9", "8",
                     "7", "6", "5", "4", "3", "2");
$suit_array = array ("hearts", "diamonds", "clubs", "spades");

# insert a "card" into the deck for each combination of suit and face

$sth = $dbh->prepare ("INSERT INTO deck (face,suit) VALUES(?,?)");
foreach ($face_array as $face)
  foreach ($suit_array as $suit)
    $sth->execute (array ($face, $suit));
```

Shuffling the cards is a matter of issuing this statement:

```
SELECT face, suit FROM deck ORDER BY RAND();
```

To do that and store the results in an array within a script, write a shuffle_deck() function that issues the query and returns the resulting values in an array (again shown in PHP):

```
function shuffle_deck ($dbh)
{
  $sth = $dbh->query ("SELECT face, suit FROM deck ORDER BY RAND()");
  $sth->setFetchMode (PDO::FETCH_OBJ);
  return ($sth->fetchAll ());
}
```

Deal the cards by keeping a counter that ranges from 0 to 51 to indicate which card to select. When the counter reaches 52, the deck is exhausted and should be shuffled again.

 Use this method only for tables with small numbers of rows. Ordering by RAND() does not allow MySQL to use indexes to resolve ORDER BY; therefore, such queries will be slow on large tables.

17.8 Selecting Random Items from a Set of Rows

Problem

You want to pick an item or items randomly from a set of values.

Solution

Randomize the values, then pick the first one (or the first few, if you need more than one).

Discussion

If a set of items is stored in MySQL, choose one at random as follows:

1. Select the items in the set in random order, using ORDER BY RAND() as described in Recipe 17.7.

2. Add LIMIT 1 to the query to pick the first item.

For example, to perform a simple simulation of tossing a die, create a die table containing rows with values from 1 to 6 corresponding to the six faces of a die cube:

```
CREATE TABLE die (n INT\);
```

Then pick rows from the table at random:

```
mysql> SELECT n FROM die ORDER BY RAND() LIMIT 1;
+------+
| n    |
+------+
|    6 |
+------+
mysql> SELECT n FROM die ORDER BY RAND() LIMIT 1;
+------+
| n    |
+------+
|    4 |
+------+
mysql> SELECT n FROM die ORDER BY RAND() LIMIT 1;
+------+
| n    |
+------+
|    5 |
+------+
mysql> SELECT n FROM die ORDER BY RAND() LIMIT 1;
+------+
| n    |
+------+
|    4 |
+------+
```

As you repeat this operation, you pick a random sequence of items from the set. This is a form of selection with replacement: an item is chosen from a pool of items and then returned to the pool for the next pick. Because items are replaced, it's possible to pick the same item multiple times when making successive choices this way. Other examples of selection with replacement include:

- Selecting a banner ad to display on a web page
- Picking a row for a "quote of the day" application
- "Pick a card, any card" magic tricks that begin with a full deck of cards each time

To pick more than one item, change the LIMIT argument. For example, to draw five winning entries at random from a table named drawing that contains contest entries, use RAND() in combination with LIMIT:

```
SELECT * FROM drawing ORDER BY RAND() LIMIT 5;
```

A special case occurs when you pick a single row from a table that you know contains a column with values in the range from 1 to n in unbroken sequence. Under these circumstances, it's possible to avoid performing an ORDER BY operation on the entire table. Pick a random number in that range and select the matching row:

```
SET @id = FLOOR(RAND()*n)+1;
SELECT ... FROM tbl_name WHERE id = @id;
```

This is much quicker than ORDER BY RAND() LIMIT 1 as the table size increases.

17.9 Calculating Successive-Row Differences

Problem

A table contains successive cumulative values in its rows, and you want to compute the differences between pairs of successive rows.

Solution

Use a self-join that matches pairs of adjacent rows and calculates the differences between members of each pair.

Discussion

Self-joins are useful when you have a set of absolute (or cumulative) values that you want to convert to relative values representing the differences between successive pairs of rows. For example, if you take an automobile trip and write down the total miles traveled at each stopping point, you can compute the difference between successive points to determine the distance from one stop to the next. Here is such a table that shows the stops for a trip from San Antonio, Texas, to Madison, Wisconsin. Each row shows the total miles driven as of each stop:

```
mysql> SELECT seq, city, miles FROM trip_log ORDER BY seq;
+-----+-------------------+-------+
| seq | city              | miles |
+-----+-------------------+-------+
|   1 | San Antonio, TX   |     0 |
|   2 | Dallas, TX        |   263 |
|   3 | Benton, AR        |   566 |
|   4 | Memphis, TN       |   745 |
|   5 | Portageville, MO  |   878 |
|   6 | Champaign, IL     |  1164 |
|   7 | Madison, WI       |  1412 |
+-----+-------------------+-------+
```

A self-join can convert these cumulative values to successive differences that represent the distances from each city to the next. The following statement shows how to use the sequence numbers in the rows to match pairs of successive rows and compute the differences between each pair of mileage values:

```
mysql> SELECT t1.seq AS seq1, t2.seq AS seq2,
    -> t1.city AS city1, t2.city AS city2,
    -> t1.miles AS miles1, t2.miles AS miles2,
    -> t2.miles-t1.miles AS dist
    -> FROM trip_log AS t1 INNER JOIN trip_log AS t2
    -> ON t1.seq+1 = t2.seq
    -> ORDER BY t1.seq;
+------+------+-------------------+-------------------+--------+--------+------+
| seq1 | seq2 | city1             | city2             | miles1 | miles2 | dist |
+------+------+-------------------+-------------------+--------+--------+------+
|    1 |    2 | San Antonio, TX   | Dallas, TX        |      0 |    263 |  263 |
|    2 |    3 | Dallas, TX        | Benton, AR        |    263 |    566 |  303 |
|    3 |    4 | Benton, AR        | Memphis, TN       |    566 |    745 |  179 |
|    4 |    5 | Memphis, TN       | Portageville, MO  |    745 |    878 |  133 |
|    5 |    6 | Portageville, MO  | Champaign, IL     |    878 |   1164 |  286 |
|    6 |    7 | Champaign, IL     | Madison, WI       |   1164 |   1412 |  248 |
+------+------+-------------------+-------------------+--------+--------+------+
```

The presence of the seq column in the trip_log table is important for calculating successive difference values. It's needed for establishing which row precedes another and matching each row *n* with row *n*+1. The implication is that to perform relative-difference calculations using a table of absolute or cumulative values, it must include a sequence column that has no gaps. If the table contains a sequence column but there are gaps, renumber it (see Recipe 15.5). If the table contains no such column, add one (see Recipe 15.9).

A more complex situation occurs when you compute successive differences for more than one column and use the results in a calculation. The following table, player_stats, shows some cumulative numbers for a baseball player at the end of each month of his season. ab indicates the total at-bats, and h the total hits the player has had as of a given date. (The first row indicates the starting point of the player's season, which is why the ab and h values are zero.)

```
mysql> SELECT id, date, ab, h, TRUNCATE(IFNULL(h/ab,0),3) AS ba
    -> FROM player_stats ORDER BY id;
+----+------------+-----+----+-------+
| id | date       | ab  | h  | ba    |
+----+------------+-----+----+-------+
|  1 | 2013-04-30 |   0 |  0 | 0.000 |
|  2 | 2013-05-31 |  38 | 13 | 0.342 |
|  3 | 2013-06-30 | 109 | 31 | 0.284 |
|  4 | 2013-07-31 | 196 | 49 | 0.250 |
|  5 | 2013-08-31 | 304 | 98 | 0.322 |
+----+------------+-----+----+-------+
```

The last column of the query result also shows the player's batting average as of each date. This column is not stored in the table but is easily computed as the ratio of hits to at-bats. The result provides a general idea of how the player's hitting performance changed over the course of the season, but it provides no picture of how the player did during each individual month. To determine that, calculate relative differences between pairs of rows. This is easily done with a self-join that matches row *n* with row *n+1* to calculate differences between pairs of at-bats and hits values. These differences enable computation of batting average during each month:

```
mysql> SELECT
    -> t1.id AS id1, t2.id AS id2,
    -> t2.date,
    -> t1.ab AS ab1, t2.ab AS ab2,
    -> t1.h AS h1, t2.h AS h2,
    -> t2.ab-t1.ab AS abdiff,
    -> t2.h-t1.h AS hdiff,
    -> TRUNCATE(IFNULL((t2.h-t1.h)/(t2.ab-t1.ab),0),3) AS ba
    -> FROM player_stats AS t1 INNER JOIN player_stats AS t2
    -> ON t1.id+1 = t2.id
    -> ORDER BY t1.id;
+-----+-----+------------+-----+-----+----+----+--------+-------+-------+
| id1 | id2 | date       | ab1 | ab2 | h1 | h2 | abdiff | hdiff | ba    |
+-----+-----+------------+-----+-----+----+----+--------+-------+-------+
|   1 |   2 | 2013-05-31 |   0 |  38 |  0 | 13 |     38 |    13 | 0.342 |
|   2 |   3 | 2013-06-30 |  38 | 109 | 13 | 31 |     71 |    18 | 0.253 |
|   3 |   4 | 2013-07-31 | 109 | 196 | 31 | 49 |     87 |    18 | 0.206 |
|   4 |   5 | 2013-08-31 | 196 | 304 | 49 | 98 |    108 |    49 | 0.453 |
+-----+-----+------------+-----+-----+----+----+--------+-------+-------+
```

These results show much more clearly than the original table that the player started off well but had a slump in the middle of the season, particularly in July. They also indicate just how strong his performance was in August.

17.10 Finding Cumulative Sums and Running Averages

Problem

You have a set of observations measured over time and want to compute the cumulative sum of the observations at each measurement point. Or you want to compute a running average at each point.

Solution

Use a self-join to produce the sets of successive observations at each measurement point, then apply aggregate functions to each set of values to compute its sum or average.

Discussion

Recipe 17.9 illustrates how a self-join can produce relative values from absolute values. A self-join can do the opposite as well, producing cumulative values at each successive stage of a set of observations. The following table shows a set of rainfall measurements taken over a series of days. The values in each row show the observation date and precipitation in inches:

```
mysql> SELECT date, precip FROM rainfall ORDER BY date;
+------------+--------+
| date       | precip |
+------------+--------+
| 2014-06-01 |   1.50 |
| 2014-06-02 |   0.00 |
| 2014-06-03 |   0.50 |
| 2014-06-04 |   0.00 |
| 2014-06-05 |   1.00 |
+------------+--------+
```

To calculate cumulative rainfall for a given day, add that day's precipitation value to the values for all the previous days. For example, determine the cumulative rainfall as of 2014-06-03 like this:

```
mysql> SELECT SUM(precip) FROM rainfall WHERE date <= '2014-06-03';
+-------------+
| SUM(precip) |
+-------------+
|        2.00 |
+-------------+
```

To get the cumulative figures for all days represented in the table, it's tedious to compute the value separately for each day. A self-join can do this for all days with a single statement. Use one instance of the `rainfall` table as a reference, and determine for the date in each row the sum of the `precip` values in all rows occurring up through that date in another instance of the table. The following statement shows the daily and cumulative precipitation for each day:

```
mysql> SELECT t1.date, t1.precip AS 'daily precip',
    -> SUM(t2.precip) AS 'cum. precip'
    -> FROM rainfall AS t1 INNER JOIN rainfall AS t2
    -> ON t1.date >= t2.date
    -> GROUP BY t1.date;
+------------+--------------+-------------+
| date       | daily precip | cum. precip |
+------------+--------------+-------------+
| 2014-06-01 |         1.50 |        1.50 |
| 2014-06-02 |         0.00 |        1.50 |
```

```
| 2014-06-03 |          0.50 |       2.00 |
| 2014-06-04 |          0.00 |       2.00 |
| 2014-06-05 |          1.00 |       3.00 |
+------------+---------------+------------+
```

The self-join can be extended to display the number of days elapsed at each date, as well as the running averages for amount of precipitation each day:

```
mysql> SELECT t1.date, t1.precip AS 'daily precip',
    -> SUM(t2.precip) AS 'cum. precip',
    -> COUNT(t2.precip) AS 'days elapsed',
    -> AVG(t2.precip) AS 'avg. precip'
    -> FROM rainfall AS t1 INNER JOIN rainfall AS t2
    -> ON t1.date >= t2.date
    -> GROUP BY t1.date;
+------------+--------------+-------------+--------------+-------------+
| date       | daily precip | cum. precip | days elapsed | avg. precip |
+------------+--------------+-------------+--------------+-------------+
| 2014-06-01 |         1.50 |        1.50 |            1 |    1.500000 |
| 2014-06-02 |         0.00 |        1.50 |            2 |    0.750000 |
| 2014-06-03 |         0.50 |        2.00 |            3 |    0.666667 |
| 2014-06-04 |         0.00 |        2.00 |            4 |    0.500000 |
| 2014-06-05 |         1.00 |        3.00 |            5 |    0.600000 |
+------------+--------------+-------------+--------------+-------------+
```

In the preceding statement, the number of days elapsed and the precipitation running averages can be computed easily using COUNT() and AVG() because there are no missing days in the table. If missing days are permitted, the calculation becomes more complicated because the number of days elapsed for each calculation is no longer the same as the number of rows.

You can see this by deleting the rows for the days that had no precipitation to produce "holes" in the table:

```
mysql> DELETE FROM rainfall WHERE precip = 0;
mysql> SELECT date, precip FROM rainfall ORDER BY date;
+------------+--------+
| date       | precip |
+------------+--------+
| 2014-06-01 |   1.50 |
| 2014-06-03 |   0.50 |
| 2014-06-05 |   1.00 |
+------------+--------+
```

Deleting those rows doesn't change the cumulative sum or running average for the dates that remain, but it does change how they must be calculated. If you execute the self-join again, it yields incorrect results for the days-elapsed and average precipitation columns:

```
mysql> SELECT t1.date, t1.precip AS 'daily precip',
    -> SUM(t2.precip) AS 'cum. precip',
    -> COUNT(t2.precip) AS 'days elapsed',
    -> AVG(t2.precip) AS 'avg. precip'
    -> FROM rainfall AS t1 INNER JOIN rainfall AS t2
    -> ON t1.date >= t2.date
    -> GROUP BY t1.date;
```

```
+------------+--------------+-------------+--------------+-------------+
| date       | daily precip | cum. precip | days elapsed | avg. precip |
+------------+--------------+-------------+--------------+-------------+
| 2014-06-01 |         1.50 |        1.50 |            1 |    1.500000 |
| 2014-06-03 |         0.50 |        2.00 |            2 |    1.000000 |
| 2014-06-05 |         1.00 |        3.00 |            3 |    1.000000 |
+------------+--------------+-------------+--------------+-------------+
```

To fix the problem, determine the number of days elapsed a different way. Take the minimum and maximum date involved in each sum and calculate a days-elapsed value from them:

```
DATEDIFF(MAX(t2.date),MIN(t2.date)) + 1
```

That value must be used for the days-elapsed column and for computing the running averages. The resulting statement is as follows:

```
mysql> SELECT t1.date, t1.precip AS 'daily precip',
    -> SUM(t2.precip) AS 'cum. precip',
    -> DATEDIFF(MAX(t2.date),MIN(t2.date)) + 1 AS 'days elapsed',
    -> SUM(t2.precip) / (DATEDIFF(MAX(t2.date),MIN(t2.date)) + 1)
    -> AS 'avg. precip'
    -> FROM rainfall AS t1 INNER JOIN rainfall AS t2
    -> ON t1.date >= t2.date
    -> GROUP BY t1.date;
+------------+--------------+-------------+--------------+-------------+
| date       | daily precip | cum. precip | days elapsed | avg. precip |
+------------+--------------+-------------+--------------+-------------+
| 2014-06-01 |         1.50 |        1.50 |            1 |    1.500000 |
| 2014-06-03 |         0.50 |        2.00 |            3 |    0.666667 |
| 2014-06-05 |         1.00 |        3.00 |            5 |    0.600000 |
+------------+--------------+-------------+--------------+-------------+
```

As this example illustrates, calculation of cumulative values from relative values requires only a column that enables rows to be placed into the proper order. (For the rainfall table, that's the date column.) Values in the column need not be sequential, or even numeric. This differs from calculations that produce difference values from cumulative values (see Recipe 17.9), which require a table that has a column containing an unbroken sequence.

The running averages in the rainfall examples are based on dividing cumulative precipitation sums by number of days elapsed as of each day. When the table has no gaps, the number of days is the same as the number of values summed, making it easy to find successive averages. When rows are missing, the calculations become more complex. This demonstrates that it's necessary to consider the nature of your data and calculate averages appropriately. The next example is conceptually similar to the previous ones in that it calculates cumulative sums and running averages but performs the computations yet another way.

The following table shows a marathon runner's performance at each stage of a 26-kilometer run. The values in each row show the length of each stage in kilometers and how long the runner took to complete the stage. In other words, the values pertain to intervals within the marathon and thus are relative to the whole:

```
mysql> SELECT stage, km, t FROM marathon ORDER BY stage;
+-------+----+----------+
| stage | km | t        |
+-------+----+----------+
|     1 |  5 | 00:15:00 |
|     2 |  7 | 00:19:30 |
|     3 |  9 | 00:29:20 |
|     4 |  5 | 00:17:50 |
+-------+----+----------+
```

To calculate cumulative distance in kilometers at each stage, use a self-join like this:

```
mysql> SELECT t1.stage, t1.km, SUM(t2.km) AS 'cum. km'
    -> FROM marathon AS t1 INNER JOIN marathon AS t2
    -> ON t1.stage >= t2.stage
    -> GROUP BY t1.stage;
+-------+----+---------+
| stage | km | cum. km |
+-------+----+---------+
|     1 |  5 |       5 |
|     2 |  7 |      12 |
|     3 |  9 |      21 |
|     4 |  5 |      26 |
+-------+----+---------+
```

Cumulative distances are easy to compute because they can be summed directly. The calculation for accumulating time values is more involved: convert times to seconds, total the resulting values, and convert the sum back to a time value. To compute the runner's average speed at the end of each stage, take the ratio of cumulative distance over cumulative time. Putting all this together yields the following statement:

```
mysql> SELECT t1.stage, t1.km, t1.t,
    -> SUM(t2.km) AS 'cum. km',
    -> SEC_TO_TIME(SUM(TIME_TO_SEC(t2.t))) AS 'cum. t',
    -> SUM(t2.km)/(SUM(TIME_TO_SEC(t2.t))/(60*60)) AS 'avg. km/hour'
    -> FROM marathon AS t1 INNER JOIN marathon AS t2
    -> ON t1.stage >= t2.stage
    -> GROUP BY t1.stage;
+-------+----+----------+---------+----------+--------------+
| stage | km | t        | cum. km | cum. t   | avg. km/hour |
+-------+----+----------+---------+----------+--------------+
|     1 |  5 | 00:15:00 |       5 | 00:15:00 |      20.0000 |
|     2 |  7 | 00:19:30 |      12 | 00:34:30 |      20.8696 |
|     3 |  9 | 00:29:20 |      21 | 01:03:50 |      19.7389 |
|     4 |  5 | 00:17:50 |      26 | 01:21:40 |      19.1020 |
+-------+----+----------+---------+----------+--------------+
```

We can see from this that the runner's average pace increased a little during the second stage of the race but then decreased thereafter, presumably as a result of fatigue.

17.11 Assigning Ranks

Problem

You want to assign ranks to a set of values.

Solution

Decide on a ranking method, then put the values in the desired order and apply the method to them.

Discussion

Some kinds of statistical tests require assignment of ranks. This section describes three ranking methods and shows how each can be implemented by using window functions. The examples assume that a `ranks` table contains the following scores, which are to be ranked with the values in descending order:

```
mysql> SELECT score FROM ranks ORDER BY score DESC;
+-------+
| score |
+-------+
|     5 |
|     4 |
|     4 |
|     3 |
|     2 |
|     2 |
|     2 |
|     1 |
+-------+
```

One type of ranking simply assigns each value its row number within the ordered set of values. To produce such rankings, use the ROW_NUMBER() window function:

```
mysql> SELECT ROW_NUMBER() OVER win AS 'rank',
    -> score FROM ranks WINDOW win AS (ORDER BY score DESC);
+------+-------+
| rank | score |
+------+-------+
|    1 |     5 |
|    2 |     4 |
|    3 |     4 |
|    4 |     3 |
|    5 |     2 |
|    6 |     2 |
|    7 |     2 |
|    8 |     1 |
+------+-------+
8 rows in set (0,00 sec)
```

That kind of ranking doesn't take into account the possibility of ties (instances of values that are the same). The DENSE_RANK() window function does so by advancing the rank only when values change:

```
mysql> SELECT DENSE_RANK() OVER win AS 'rank',
    -> score FROM ranks WINDOW win AS (ORDER BY score DESC);
+------+-------+
| rank | score |
+------+-------+
|    1 |     5 |
|    2 |     4 |
|    2 |     4 |
|    3 |     3 |
|    4 |     2 |
|    4 |     2 |
|    4 |     2 |
|    5 |     1 |
+------+-------+
```

The RANK() window function is something of a combination of the other two methods. It ranks values by row number, except when ties occur. In that case, the tied values each get a rank equal to the row number of the first of the values:

```
mysql> SELECT ROW_NUMBER() OVER win AS 'row',
    -> RANK() OVER win AS 'rank',
    -> score FROM ranks WINDOW win AS (ORDER BY score DESC);
+------+------+-------+
| row  | rank | score |
+------+------+-------+
|    1 |    1 |     5 |
|    2 |    2 |     4 |
|    3 |    2 |     4 |
|    4 |    4 |     3 |
|    5 |    5 |     2 |
|    6 |    5 |     2 |
|    7 |    5 |     2 |
|    8 |    8 |     1 |
+------+------+-------+
```

Ranks are easy to assign within a program as well. For example, the following Ruby fragment ranks the scores in ranks using the third ranking method:

```ruby
res = client.query("SELECT score FROM ranks ORDER BY score DESC")
rownum = 0
rank = 0
prev_score = nil
puts "Row\tRank\tScore\n"
res.each do |row|
  score = row.values[0]
  rownum += 1
  rank = rownum if rownum == 1 || prev_score != score
  prev_score = score
  puts "#{rownum}\t#{rank}\t#{score}"
end
```

The third type of ranking is commonly used for sporting events. The following table contains the American League pitchers who won 15 or more games during the 2001 baseball season:

```
mysql> SELECT name, wins FROM al_winner ORDER BY wins DESC, name;
+-----------------+------+
| name            | wins |
+-----------------+------+
| Mulder, Mark    |   21 |
| Clemens, Roger  |   20 |
| Moyer, Jamie    |   20 |
| Garcia, Freddy  |   18 |
| Hudson, Tim     |   18 |
| Abbott, Paul    |   17 |
| Mays, Joe       |   17 |
| Mussina, Mike   |   17 |
| Sabathia, C.C.  |   17 |
| Zito, Barry     |   17 |
| Buehrle, Mark   |   16 |
| Milton, Eric    |   15 |
| Pettitte, Andy  |   15 |
| Radke, Brad     |   15 |
| Sele, Aaron     |   15 |
+-----------------+------+
```

These pitchers can be assigned ranks using the third method as follows:

```
mysql> SELECT ROW_NUMBER() OVER win AS 'row',
    -> RANK() OVER win AS 'rank',
    -> name, wins
    -> FROM al_winner WINDOW win AS (ORDER BY wins DESC);
+------+------+-----------------+------+
| row  | rank | name            | wins |
+------+------+-----------------+------+
|    1 |    1 | Mulder, Mark    |   21 |
|    2 |    2 | Clemens, Roger  |   20 |
|    3 |    2 | Moyer, Jamie    |   20 |
|    4 |    4 | Garcia, Freddy  |   18 |
|    5 |    4 | Hudson, Tim     |   18 |
|    6 |    6 | Zito, Barry     |   17 |
|    7 |    6 | Sabathia, C.C.  |   17 |
|    8 |    6 | Mussina, Mike   |   17 |
|    9 |    6 | Mays, Joe       |   17 |
|   10 |    6 | Abbott, Paul    |   17 |
|   11 |   11 | Buehrle, Mark   |   16 |
|   12 |   12 | Milton, Eric    |   15 |
|   13 |   12 | Pettitte, Andy  |   15 |
|   14 |   12 | Radke, Brad     |   15 |
|   15 |   12 | Sele, Aaron     |   15 |
+------+------+-----------------+------+
```

See Also

For additional information about window functions, see Recipe 15.15.

17.12 Computing Team Standings

Problem

You want to compute team standings from their win-loss records, including the games-behind (GB) values.

Solution

Determine which team is in first place, then join that result to the original rows.

Discussion

Standings for sports teams that compete against one another is a ranking problem, but ranks are not based on a single measure, as in Recipe 17.11. Standings are based on two values: wins and losses. Teams are ranked according to which has the best win-loss record, and teams not in first place are assigned a "games-behind" value indicating how many games out of first place they are. This section shows how to calculate those values. The first example uses a table containing a single set of team records to illustrate the logic of the calculations. The second example uses a table containing several sets of records (that is, the records for all teams in both divisions of a league, for both halves of the season). In this case, it's necessary to use a join to perform the calculations independently for each group of teams.

Consider the following table, `standings1`, which contains a single set of baseball team records representing the final standings for the Northern League in the year 1902:

```
mysql> SELECT team, wins, losses FROM standings1
    -> ORDER BY wins-losses DESC;
+-------------+------+--------+
| team        | wins | losses |
+-------------+------+--------+
| Winnipeg    |   37 |     20 |
| Crookston   |   31 |     25 |
| Fargo       |   30 |     26 |
| Grand Forks |   28 |     26 |
| Devils Lake |   19 |     31 |
| Cavalier    |   15 |     32 |
+-------------+------+--------+
```

The rows are sorted by the win-loss differential, which is how to place teams in order from first place to last place. But displays of team standings typically include each team's winning percentage and a figure indicating how many games behind the leader all the other teams are. So let's add that information to the output. Calculating the percentage is easy. It's the ratio of wins to total games played and can be determined using this expression:

```
wins / (wins + losses)
```

This expression involves division by zero when a team has not played any games yet. For simplicity, I'll assume a nonzero number of games. To handle this condition, you'd use a more general expression:

```
IF(wins=0,0,wins/(wins+losses))
```

This expression relies on the fact that no division operation is necessary unless the team has won at least one game.

Determining the games-behind value is a little trickier. It's based on the relationship of the win-loss records for two teams, calculated as the average of two values:

- How many more wins the first-place team has than the second-place team
- How many fewer losses the first-place team has than the second-place team

Suppose that two teams, A and B, have the following win-loss records:

```
+------+------+--------+
| team | wins | losses |
+------+------+--------+
| A    |   17 |     11 |
| B    |   14 |     12 |
+------+------+--------+
```

Here, team B has to win three more games, and team A has to lose one more game for the teams to be even. The average of three and one is two, thus B is two games behind A. Mathematically, the games-behind calculation for the two teams is as follows:

```
((winsA - winsB) + (lossesB - lossesA)) / 2
```

With a little rearrangement of terms, the expression becomes the following:

```
((winsA - lossesA) - (winsB - lossesB)) / 2
```

The second expression is equivalent to the first, but it has each factor written as a single team's win-loss differential, rather than as a comparison between teams. That makes it easier to work with because each factor can be determined independently from a single team record. The first factor represents the first-place team's win-loss differential, so if we calculate that value first, the other team GB values can be determined in relation to it.

The first-place team is the one with the largest win-loss differential. To find that value and save it in a variable, use this statement:

```
mysql> SET @wl_diff = (SELECT MAX(wins-losses) FROM standings1);
```

Then use the differential as follows to produce team standings that include winning percentage and GB values:

```
mysql> SELECT team, wins AS W, losses AS L,
    -> wins/(wins+losses) AS PCT,
    -> (@wl_diff - (wins-losses)) / 2 AS GB
    -> FROM standings1
```

```
    -> ORDER BY wins-losses DESC, PCT DESC;
+--------------+------+------+--------+---------+
| team         | W    | L    | PCT    | GB      |
+--------------+------+------+--------+---------+
| Winnipeg     |  37  |  20  | 0.6491 |  0.0000 |
| Crookston    |  31  |  25  | 0.5536 |  5.5000 |
| Fargo        |  30  |  26  | 0.5357 |  6.5000 |
| Grand Forks  |  28  |  26  | 0.5185 |  7.5000 |
| Devils Lake  |  19  |  31  | 0.3800 | 14.5000 |
| Cavalier     |  15  |  32  | 0.3191 | 17.0000 |
+--------------+------+------+--------+---------+
```

There are a couple of minor formatting issues to address at this point. Typically, standings list display percentages to three decimal places, and the GB value to one decimal place (except that the GB value for the first-place team is displayed as -). To display *n* decimal places, use TRUNCATE(*expr*,*n*). To display the GB value for the first-place team appropriately, use an IF() expression that maps 0 to a dash:

```
mysql> SELECT team, wins AS W, losses AS L,
    -> TRUNCATE(wins/(wins+losses),3) AS PCT,
    -> IF(@wl_diff = wins-losses,
    ->   '-',TRUNCATE((@wl_diff - (wins-losses))/2,1)) AS GB
    -> FROM standings1
    -> ORDER BY wins-losses DESC, PCT DESC;
+--------------+------+------+-------+------+
| team         | W    | L    | PCT   | GB   |
+--------------+------+------+-------+------+
| Winnipeg     |  37  |  20  | 0.649 | -    |
| Crookston    |  31  |  25  | 0.553 | 5.5  |
| Fargo        |  30  |  26  | 0.535 | 6.5  |
| Grand Forks  |  28  |  26  | 0.518 | 7.5  |
| Devils Lake  |  19  |  31  | 0.380 | 14.5 |
| Cavalier     |  15  |  32  | 0.319 | 17.0 |
+--------------+------+------+-------+------+
```

These statements order the teams by win-loss differential, using winning percentage as a tie-breaker in case there are teams with the same differential value. It's simpler to sort by percentage, of course, but then you wouldn't always get the correct ordering. It's a curious fact that a team with a lower winning percentage can actually be higher in the standings than a team with a higher percentage. (This generally occurs early in the season, when teams may have played highly disparate numbers of games, relatively speaking.) Consider the case in which two teams, A and B, have the following rows:

```
+------+------+--------+
| team | wins | losses |
+------+------+--------+
| A    |  4   |  1     |
| B    |  2   |  0     |
+------+------+--------+
```

Applying the GB and percentage calculations to these team records yields the following result, in which the first-place team actually has a lower winning percentage than the second-place team:

```
+------+------+------+-------+------+
| team | W    | L    | PCT   | GB   |
+------+------+------+-------+------+
| A    |    4 |    1 | 0.800 | -    |
| B    |    2 |    0 | 1.000 | 0.5  |
+------+------+------+-------+------+
```

The standings calculations shown thus far can be done without a join. They involve only a single set of team records, so the first-place team's win-loss differential can be stored in a variable. A more complex situation occurs when a dataset includes several sets of team records. For example, the 1997 Northern League had two divisions (Eastern and Western). In addition, separate standings were maintained for the first and second halves of the season because season-half winners in each division played one another for the right to compete in the league championship. The following table, standings2, shows what these rows look like, ordered by season half, division, and win-loss differential:

```
mysql> SELECT half, division, team, wins, losses FROM standings2
    -> ORDER BY half, division, wins-losses DESC;
+------+----------+----------------+------+--------+
| half | division | team           | wins | losses |
+------+----------+----------------+------+--------+
|    1 | Eastern  | St. Paul       |   24 |     18 |
|    1 | Eastern  | Thunder Bay    |   18 |     24 |
|    1 | Eastern  | Duluth-Superior|   17 |     24 |
|    1 | Eastern  | Madison        |   15 |     27 |
|    1 | Western  | Winnipeg       |   29 |     12 |
|    1 | Western  | Sioux City     |   28 |     14 |
|    1 | Western  | Fargo-Moorhead |   21 |     21 |
|    1 | Western  | Sioux Falls    |   15 |     27 |
|    2 | Eastern  | Duluth-Superior|   22 |     20 |
|    2 | Eastern  | St. Paul       |   21 |     21 |
|    2 | Eastern  | Madison        |   19 |     23 |
|    2 | Eastern  | Thunder Bay    |   18 |     24 |
|    2 | Western  | Fargo-Moorhead |   26 |     16 |
|    2 | Western  | Winnipeg       |   24 |     18 |
|    2 | Western  | Sioux City     |   22 |     20 |
|    2 | Western  | Sioux Falls    |   16 |     26 |
+------+----------+----------------+------+--------+
```

Generating the standings for these rows requires computing the GB values separately for each of the four combinations of season half and division. First, calculate the win-loss differential for the first-place team in each group and save the values into a separate firstplace table:

```
mysql> CREATE TEMPORARY TABLE firstplace
    -> SELECT half, division, MAX(wins-losses) AS wl_diff
    -> FROM standings2
    -> GROUP BY half, division;
```

Then join the firstplace table to the original standings, associating each team record with the proper win-loss differential to compute its GB value:

```
mysql> SELECT wl.half, wl.division, wl.team, wl.wins AS W, wl.losses AS L,
    -> TRUNCATE(wl.wins/(wl.wins+wl.losses),3) AS PCT,
```

```
    -> IF(fp.wl_diff = wl.wins-wl.losses,
    ->    '-',TRUNCATE((fp.wl_diff - (wl.wins-wl.losses)) / 2,1)) AS GB
    -> FROM standings2 AS wl INNER JOIN firstplace AS fp
    -> ON wl.half = fp.half AND wl.division = fp.division
    -> ORDER BY wl.half, wl.division, wl.wins-wl.losses DESC, PCT DESC;
+------+----------+----------------+------+------+-------+------+
| half | division | team           | W    | L    | PCT   | GB   |
+------+----------+----------------+------+------+-------+------+
|    1 | Eastern  | St. Paul       |   24 |   18 | 0.571 | -    |
|    1 | Eastern  | Thunder Bay    |   18 |   24 | 0.428 | 6.0  |
|    1 | Eastern  | Duluth-Superior|   17 |   24 | 0.414 | 6.5  |
|    1 | Eastern  | Madison        |   15 |   27 | 0.357 | 9.0  |
|    1 | Western  | Winnipeg       |   29 |   12 | 0.707 | -    |
|    1 | Western  | Sioux City     |   28 |   14 | 0.666 | 1.5  |
|    1 | Western  | Fargo-Moorhead |   21 |   21 | 0.500 | 8.5  |
|    1 | Western  | Sioux Falls    |   15 |   27 | 0.357 | 14.5 |
|    2 | Eastern  | Duluth-Superior|   22 |   20 | 0.523 | -    |
|    2 | Eastern  | St. Paul       |   21 |   21 | 0.500 | 1.0  |
|    2 | Eastern  | Madison        |   19 |   23 | 0.452 | 3.0  |
|    2 | Eastern  | Thunder Bay    |   18 |   24 | 0.428 | 4.0  |
|    2 | Western  | Fargo-Moorhead |   26 |   16 | 0.619 | -    |
|    2 | Western  | Winnipeg       |   24 |   18 | 0.571 | 2.0  |
|    2 | Western  | Sioux City     |   22 |   20 | 0.523 | 4.0  |
|    2 | Western  | Sioux Falls    |   16 |   26 | 0.380 | 10.0 |
+------+----------+----------------+------+------+-------+------+
```

That output is difficult to read, however. To make it easier to understand, you might execute the statement from within a program and reformat its results to display each set of team records separately. Here's some Perl code that does that by beginning a new output group each time it encounters a new group of standings. The code assumes that the join statement has just been executed and that its results are available through the statement handle $sth:

```perl
my ($cur_half, $cur_div) = ("", "");
while (my ($half, $div, $team, $wins, $losses, $pct, $gb)
        = $sth->fetchrow_array ())
{
  if ($cur_half ne $half || $cur_div ne $div) # new group of standings?
  {
    # print standings header and remember new half/division values
    print "\n$div Division, season half $half\n";
    printf "%-20s  %3s  %3s  %5s  %s\n", "Team", "W", "L", "PCT", "GB";
    $cur_half = $half;
    $cur_div = $div;
  }
  printf "%-20s  %3d  %3d  %5s  %s\n", $team, $wins, $losses, $pct, $gb;
}
```

The reformatted output looks like this:

```
Eastern Division, season half 1
Team                   W    L    PCT  GB
St. Paul               24   18   0.571  -
Thunder Bay            18   24   0.428  6.0
Duluth-Superior        17   24   0.414  6.5
Madison                15   27   0.357  9.0

Western Division, season half 1
```

```
Team                    W    L    PCT  GB
Winnipeg                29   12   0.707  -
Sioux City              28   14   0.666  1.5
Fargo-Moorhead          21   21   0.500  8.5
Sioux Falls             15   27   0.357  14.5

Eastern Division, season half 2
Team                    W    L    PCT  GB
Duluth-Superior         22   20   0.523  -
St. Paul                21   21   0.500  1.0
Madison                 19   23   0.452  3.0
Thunder Bay             18   24   0.428  4.0

Western Division, season half 2
Team                    W    L    PCT  GB
Fargo-Moorhead          26   16   0.619  -
Winnipeg                24   18   0.571  2.0
Sioux City              22   20   0.523  4.0
Sioux Falls             16   26   0.380  10.0
```

The code just shown comes from the `calc_standings.pl` script in the *stats* directory of the `recipes` distribution. That directory also contains a PHP script, `calc_standings.php`, that produces output in the form of HTML tables, which you might prefer for generating standings in a web environment.

## CHAPTER 18

Handling Duplicates

18.0 Introduction

Tables or result sets sometimes contain duplicate rows. In some cases, this is acceptable. For example, if you conduct a web poll that records the date and client IP number along with the votes, duplicate rows may be permitted because it's possible for large numbers of votes to appear to originate from the same IP number for an internet service that routes traffic from its customers through a single proxy host. In other cases, duplicates are unacceptable, and you'll want to take steps to avoid them. Operations involved in handling duplicate rows include the following:

- Preventing duplicates from being created in the first place. If each row in a table is intended to represent a single entity (such as a person, an item in a catalog, or a specific observation in an experiment), the occurrence of duplicates makes it impossible to refer to each row unambiguously, so it's best to make sure duplicates never occur.

- Counting the number of duplicates to determine whether they are present and to what extent.

- Identifying duplicated values (or the rows containing them) so you can see where they occur.

- Eliminating duplicates to ensure that each row is unique. This may involve removing rows from a table to leave only unique rows or selecting a result set in such a way that no duplicates appear in the output. For example, to display a list of the states in which you have customers, you probably don't want a long list of state names from all customer records. A list showing each state name only once suffices and is easier to understand.

Several tools are at your disposal for dealing with duplicate rows. Choose them according to the objective that you want to achieve:

- When you create a table, include a primary key or unique index to prevent duplicates from being added to the table. MySQL uses the index as a constraint to enforce the requirement that each row in the table contains a unique key in the indexed column or columns.

- In conjunction with a unique index, the INSERT IGNORE and REPLACE statements enable you to handle insertion of duplicate rows gracefully without generating errors. For bulk-loading operations, the same options are available in the form of the IGNORE or REPLACE modifiers for the LOAD DATA statement.

- To determine whether a table contains duplicates, use GROUP BY to categorize rows into groups and COUNT() to see how many rows are in each group. Chapter 10 describes these techniques in the context of producing summaries, but they're useful for duplicate counting and identification as well. A counting summary groups values into categories to determine how frequently each one occurs.

- SELECT DISTINCT removes duplicate rows from a result set (see Recipe 5.4 for more information). For an existing table that already contains duplicates, you can select unique rows into a second table and use it to replace the original table. Or, if you determine that there are *n* identical rows in a table, you can use DELETE...LIMIT to eliminate *n*–1 instances from that specific set of rows.

Scripts related to the examples shown in this chapter are located in the *dups* directory of the recipes distribution. For scripts that create the tables used here, look in the *tables* directory.

18.1 Preventing Duplicates from Occurring in a Table

Problem

You want to prevent a table from ever containing duplicates.

Solution

Use a PRIMARY KEY or a UNIQUE index.

Discussion

To ensure that rows in a table are unique, some column or combination of columns must be required to contain unique values in each row. When this requirement is satisfied, you can refer to any row in the table unambiguously by using its unique identifier. To make sure a table has this characteristic, include a PRIMARY KEY or

UNIQUE index in the table structure. The following table contains no such index, so it permits duplicate rows:

```
CREATE TABLE person
(
  last_name   CHAR(20),
  first_name  CHAR(20),
  address     CHAR(40)
);
```

To prevent multiple rows with the same first and last name values from being created in this table, add a PRIMARY KEY to its definition. When you do this, the indexed columns must be NOT NULL, because a PRIMARY KEY prohibits NULL values:

```
CREATE TABLE person
(
  last_name   CHAR(20) NOT NULL,
  first_name  CHAR(20) NOT NULL,
  address     CHAR(40),
  PRIMARY KEY (last_name, first_name)
);
```

The presence of a unique index in a table normally causes an error to occur if you insert a row into the table that duplicates an existing row in the column or columns that define the index. Recipe 18.3 discusses how to handle such errors or modify MySQL's duplicate-handling behavior.

Another way to enforce uniqueness is to add a UNIQUE index rather than a PRIMARY KEY to a table. The two types of indexes are similar, but a UNIQUE index can be created on columns that permit NULL values. For the person table, it's likely that you'd require both the first and last names to be filled in. If so, you still declare the columns as NOT NULL, and the following table definition is effectively equivalent to the preceding one:

```
CREATE TABLE person
(
  last_name   CHAR(20) NOT NULL,
  first_name  CHAR(20) NOT NULL,
  address     CHAR(40),
  UNIQUE (last_name, first_name)
);
```

If a UNIQUE index does happen to permit NULL values, NULL is special because it is the one value that can occur multiple times. The rationale for this is that it is not possible to know whether one unknown value is the same as another, so multiple unknown values are permitted.

Of course, you might want the person table to reflect the real world, in which people do sometimes have the same name. In this case, you cannot set up a unique index based on the name columns, because duplicate names must be permitted. Instead, each person must be assigned some sort of unique identifier, which becomes the value that distinguishes one row from another. In MySQL, it's common to accomplish this by using an AUTO_INCREMENT column:

```
CREATE TABLE person
(
    id          INT UNSIGNED NOT NULL AUTO_INCREMENT,
    last_name   CHAR(20),
    first_name  CHAR(20),
    address     CHAR(40),
    PRIMARY KEY (id)
);
```

In this case, when you create a row with an id value of NULL, MySQL assigns that column a unique ID automatically. Another possibility is to assign identifiers externally and use those IDs as unique keys. For example, citizens in a given country might have unique taxpayer ID numbers. If so, those numbers can serve as the basis for a unique index:

```
CREATE TABLE person
(
    tax_id      INT UNSIGNED NOT NULL,
    last_name   CHAR(20),
    first_name  CHAR(20),
    address     CHAR(40),
    PRIMARY KEY (tax_id)
);
```

See Also

If an existing table already contains duplicate rows that you want to remove, see Recipe 18.5. Chapter 15 further discusses AUTO_INCREMENT columns.

18.2 Having More Than One Unique Key in the Table

Problem

You need two or more column sets in the table to have unique values.

Solution

Define as many unique keys as needed.

Discussion

It may be possible that two or more column combinations need to have unique values independently from one another. For example, the person table from the last example in Recipe 18.1 has a tax_id column representing a taxpayer ID and thus needs to store unique values. You may still want to keep a unique index on (last_name, first_name). This way you can be sure that each person has their own taxpayer ID and that any taxpayer ID belongs to only one person.

Any table can have at most one primary key. Therefore, you need to choose which key will be the primary key and which will be the secondary unique key. As we describe in Recipe 21.2, primary keys for the InnoDB storage engine are included in all secondary indexes, and it is critical for performance to define them using the smallest data type possible. Therefore, it is straightforward to define a primary key for the `tax_id` column and a key on (`last_name`, `first_name`) as a secondary unique index.

The resulting table definition will look like this:

```
CREATE TABLE `person` (
  `tax_id` INT UNSIGNED NOT NULL,
  `last_name` CHAR(20) DEFAULT NULL,
  `first_name` CHAR(20) DEFAULT NULL,
  `address` CHAR(40) DEFAULT NULL,
  PRIMARY KEY (`tax_id`),
  UNIQUE KEY `last_name` (`last_name`,`first_name`)
);
```

18.3 Dealing with Duplicates When Loading Rows into a Table

Problem

You've created a table with a unique index to prevent duplicate values in the indexed column or columns. But this results in an error if you attempt to insert a duplicate row, and you want to avoid having to deal with such errors.

Solution

One approach is to just ignore the error. Another is to use an INSERT IGNORE, REPLACE, or INSERT…ON DUPLICATE KEY UPDATE statement, each of which modifies MySQL's duplicate-handling behavior. For bulk-loading operations, LOAD DATA has modifiers that enable you to specify how to handle duplicates.

Discussion

By default, MySQL generates an error when you insert a row that duplicates an existing unique key value. Suppose that the person table has the following structure, with a unique index on the last_name and first_name columns:

```
CREATE TABLE person
(
  last_name   CHAR(20) NOT NULL,
  first_name  CHAR(20) NOT NULL,
  address     CHAR(40),
  PRIMARY KEY (last_name, first_name)
);
```

An attempt to insert a row with duplicate values in the indexed columns results in an error:

```
mysql> INSERT INTO person (last_name, first_name)
    -> VALUES('Pinter', 'Marlene');
Query OK, 1 row affected (0.00 sec)
mysql> INSERT INTO person (last_name, first_name)
    -> VALUES('Pinter', 'Marlene');
ERROR 1062 (23000): Duplicate entry 'Pinter-Marlene' for key 'person.PRIMARY'
```

If you issue the statements from the `mysql` program interactively, you can simply say, "Okay, that didn't work," ignore the error, and continue. But if you write a program to insert the rows, an error may terminate the program. One way to avoid this is to modify the program's error-handling behavior to trap the error and then ignore it. See Recipe 4.2 for information about error-handling techniques.

To prevent the error from occurring in the first place, you might consider using a two-query method to solve the duplicate-row problem:

- Issue a `SELECT` to check whether the row is already present.

- Issue an `INSERT` if the row is not present.

But that doesn't really work: another client might insert the same row after the `SELECT` and before the `INSERT`, in which case the error would still occur for your `INSERT`. To make sure that doesn't happen, you could use a transaction or lock the tables, but then you've gone from two statements to four. MySQL provides three single-query solutions to the problem of handling duplicate rows. Choose from among them depending on the duplicate-handling behavior you want:

- To keep the original row when a duplicate occurs, use `INSERT IGNORE` rather than `INSERT`. If the row duplicates no existing row, MySQL inserts it as usual. If the row is a duplicate, the `IGNORE` keyword tells MySQL to discard it silently without generating an error:

  ```
  mysql> INSERT IGNORE INTO person (last_name, first_name)
      -> VALUES('Brown', 'Bartholomew');
  Query OK, 1 row affected (0.00 sec)
  mysql> INSERT IGNORE INTO person (last_name, first_name)
      -> VALUES('Brown', 'Bartholomew');
  Query OK, 0 rows affected, 1 warning (0.00 sec)
  ```

  The row count value indicates whether the row was inserted or ignored. From within a program, you can obtain this value by checking the rows-affected function provided by your API (see Recipes 4.4 and 12.1).

- To replace the original row with the new one when a duplicate occurs, use `REPLACE` rather than `INSERT`. If the row is new, it's inserted just as with `INSERT`. If it's a duplicate, the new row replaces the old one:

  ```
  mysql> REPLACE INTO person (last_name, first_name, address)
      -> VALUES('Baxter', 'Wallace', '57 3rd Ave.');
  ```

```
Query OK, 1 row affected (0.00 sec)
mysql> REPLACE INTO person (last_name, first_name, address)
    -> VALUES('Baxter', 'Wallace', '57 3rd Ave., Apt 102');
Query OK, 2 rows affected (0.00 sec)
```

The rows-affected value in the second case is 2 because the original row is deleted and the new row is inserted in its place.

- To modify columns of an existing row when a duplicate occurs, use INSERT...ON DUPLICATE KEY UPDATE. If the row is new, it's inserted. If it's a duplicate, the ON DUPLICATE KEY UPDATE clause indicates how to modify the existing row in the table. In other words, this statement can insert or update a row as necessary. The rows-affected count indicates what happened: 1 for an insert, 2 for an update.

INSERT IGNORE is more efficient than REPLACE because it doesn't actually insert duplicates. Thus, it's most applicable when you just want to make sure a copy of a given row is present in a table. REPLACE, on the other hand, is often more appropriate for tables in which other nonkey columns need to be replaced. INSERT...ON DUPLICATE KEY UPDATE is appropriate when you must insert a record if it doesn't exist but just update some of its columns if the new record is a duplicate in the indexed columns.

Suppose that you maintain a table named passtbl for a web application that contains email addresses and password hash values, and that is indexed by email address:

```
CREATE TABLE passtbl
(
  email    VARCHAR(60) NOT NULL,
  password VARBINARY(60) NOT NULL,
  PRIMARY KEY (email)
);
```

How do you create new rows for new users but change passwords of existing rows for existing users? Here's a typical algorithm for handling row maintenance:

1. Issue a SELECT to check whether a row already exists with a given email value.

2. If no such row exists, add a new one with INSERT.

3. If the row does exist, update it with UPDATE.

These steps must be performed within a transaction or with the tables locked to prevent other users from changing the tables while you're using them. In MySQL, you can use REPLACE to simplify both cases to the same single-statement operation:

```
REPLACE INTO passtbl (email,password) VALUES(address,hash_value);
```

If no row with the given email address exists, MySQL creates a new one. Otherwise, MySQL replaces it, in effect updating the password column of the row associated with the address.

INSERT IGNORE and REPLACE are useful when you know exactly what values should be stored in the table when you attempt to insert a row. That's not always the case. For example, you might want to insert a row if it doesn't exist but update only certain parts of it otherwise. This commonly occurs when you use a table for counting. Suppose that you record votes for candidates in polls, using the following table:

```
CREATE TABLE poll_vote
(
    poll_id      INT UNSIGNED NOT NULL AUTO_INCREMENT,
    candidate_id INT UNSIGNED,
    vote_count   INT UNSIGNED,
    PRIMARY KEY (poll_id, candidate_id)
);
```

The primary key is the combination of poll and candidate number. The table should be used like this:

- For the first vote received for a given poll candidate, insert a new row with a vote count of 1.

- For subsequent votes for that candidate, increment the vote count of the existing record.

Neither INSERT IGNORE nor REPLACE are appropriate here because for all votes except the first, you don't know what the vote count should be. INSERT...ON DUPLICATE KEY UPDATE works better here. The following example shows how it works, beginning with an empty table:

```
mysql> SELECT * FROM poll_vote;
Empty set (0.00 sec)
mysql> INSERT INTO poll_vote (poll_id,candidate_id,vote_count) VALUES(14,3,1)
    -> ON DUPLICATE KEY UPDATE vote_count = vote_count + 1;
Query OK, 1 row affected (0.00 sec)
mysql> SELECT * FROM poll_vote;

+---------+--------------+------------+
| poll_id | candidate_id | vote_count |
+---------+--------------+------------+
|      14 |            3 |          1 |
+---------+--------------+------------+
1 row in set (0.00 sec)
mysql> INSERT INTO poll_vote (poll_id,candidate_id,vote_count) VALUES(14,3,1)
    -> ON DUPLICATE KEY UPDATE vote_count = vote_count + 1;
Query OK, 2 rows affected (0.00 sec)
mysql> SELECT * FROM poll_vote;
+---------+--------------+------------+
| poll_id | candidate_id | vote_count |
+---------+--------------+------------+
|      14 |            3 |          2 |
+---------+--------------+------------+
1 row in set (0.00 sec)
```

For the first INSERT, no row for the candidate exists, so the row is inserted. For the second INSERT, the row exists, so MySQL just updates the vote count. With INSERT...

ON DUPLICATE KEY UPDATE, you need not check whether the row exists; MySQL does it for you. The row count indicates what action the INSERT statement performs: 1 for a new row and 2 for an update to an existing row.

The techniques just described have the benefit of eliminating overhead that might otherwise be required for a transaction. But this benefit comes at the price of portability because they all involve MySQL-specific syntax. If portability is a high priority, you might prefer to use a transactional approach, as we discuss in Chapter 20.

Using INSERT...ON DUPLICATE KEY UPDATE on a Table with Two or More Unique Keys

When a table has two or more unique keys, INSERT...ON DUPLICATE KEY UPDATE can update any row that violates the unique constraint.

Assume that the person table from Recipe 18.2 has two rows:

```
mysql> SELECT * FROM person;
+--------+-----------+------------+-------------------------+
| tax_id | last_name | first_name | address                 |
+--------+-----------+------------+-------------------------+
|  12345 | Isaacson  | Jim        | 515 Fordam St., Apt. 917 |
|  23941 | Baxter    | Wallace    | 57 3rd Ave.             |
+--------+-----------+------------+-------------------------+
2 rows in set (0,00 sec)
```

And we want to add a new row for Taylor McTavish:

```
INSERT INTO person VALUES(12345, 'McTavish', 'Taylor', '432 River Run')
ON DUPLICATE KEY UPDATE address = '432 River Run';
```

We expect that if no record for Taylor McTavish exists in the table, a new row will be inserted. Otherwise, the address will be updated. However, this is not exactly the case:

```
mysql> INSERT INTO person VALUES(12345, 'McTavish', 'Taylor',
    -> '432 River Run')
    -> ON DUPLICATE KEY UPDATE address = '432 River Run';
Query OK, 2 rows affected (0,00 sec)

mysql> SELECT * FROM person;
+--------+-----------+------------+---------------+
| tax_id | last_name | first_name | address       |
+--------+-----------+------------+---------------+
|  12345 | Isaacson  | Jim        | 432 River Run |
|  23941 | Baxter    | Wallace    | 57 3rd Ave.   |
+--------+-----------+------------+---------------+
2 rows in set (0,00 sec)
```

A new row was not inserted even though a record for Taylor McTavish does not exist in the table. Instead, the row with tax_id=12345, belonging to Jim Isaacson, was modified and now stores the address of Taylor McTavish.

MySQL does not allow you to specify if the row should be updated only if a particular unique key was violated. When the table has two or more unique keys, it is easy to

---

make a mistake and update the wrong row. We recommend that you avoid using INSERT...ON DUPLICATE KEY UPDATE for modifying tables that have more than one unique key. You may consider using stored routines instead, which we discussed in Chapter 11.

See Also

For bulk record-loading operations in which you use the LOAD DATA statement to load a set of rows from a file into a table, control duplicate-row handling using the statement's IGNORE and REPLACE modifiers. These produce behavior analogous to that of the INSERT IGNORE and REPLACE statements. For more information, see Recipe 13.1.

Recipe 15.12 further demonstrates the use of INSERT...ON DUPLICATE KEY UPDATE for initializing and updating counts.

18.4 Counting and Identifying Duplicates

Problem

You want to determine whether a table contains duplicates and to what extent they occur. Or you want to see the rows that contain the duplicated values.

Solution

Use a counting summary that displays duplicated values. To see the rows in which the duplicated values occur, join the summary to the original table to display the matching rows.

Discussion

Suppose that your website has a sign-up page that enables visitors to add themselves to your mailing list to receive periodic product catalog mailings. But you forgot to include a unique index in the table when you created it, and now you suspect that some people are signed up multiple times. Perhaps they forgot they were already on the list, or perhaps people added friends to the list who were already signed up. Either way, the result of having duplicate rows is that you mail out duplicate catalogs. This is an additional expense to you, and it annoys the recipients. This section discusses how to determine whether there are duplicate rows in a table, how prevalent they are, and how to display them. (For tables that do contain duplicates, Recipe 18.5 describes how to eliminate them.)

To determine whether duplicates occur in a table, use a counting summary (a topic covered in Chapter 10). Summary techniques can be applied to identifying and counting duplicates by grouping rows with GROUP BY and counting the rows in each group using COUNT(). For the examples here, assume that catalog recipients are listed in a table named catalog_list that has the following contents:

```
+-----------+-------------+-------------------------+
| last_name | first_name  | street                  |
+-----------+-------------+-------------------------+
| Isaacson  | Jim         | 515 Fordam St., Apt. 917 |
| Baxter    | Wallace     | 57 3rd Ave.             |
| McTavish  | Taylor      | 432 River Run           |
| Pinter    | Marlene     | 9 Sunset Trail          |
| BAXTER    | WALLACE     | 57 3rd Ave.             |
| Brown     | Bartholomew | 432 River Run           |
| Pinter    | Marlene     | 9 Sunset Trail          |
| Baxter    | Wallace     | 57 3rd Ave., Apt 102    |
+-----------+-------------+-------------------------+
```

Suppose that you define "duplicate" using the last_name and first_name columns. That is, recipients with the same name are assumed to be the same person. The following statements characterize the table and assess the existence and extent of duplicate values:

- The total number of rows in the table:

```
mysql> SELECT COUNT(*) AS rows FROM catalog_list;
+------+
| rows |
+------+
|    8 |
+------+
```

- The number of distinct names:

```
mysql> SELECT COUNT(DISTINCT last_name, first_name) AS 'distinct names'
    -> FROM catalog_list;
+----------------+
| distinct names |
+----------------+
|              5 |
+----------------+
```

- The number of rows containing duplicated names:

```
mysql> SELECT COUNT(*) - COUNT(DISTINCT last_name, first_name)
    ->    AS 'duplicate names'
    -> FROM catalog_list;
+-----------------+
| duplicate names |
+-----------------+
|               3 |
+-----------------+
```

- The fraction of the rows that contain unique or nonunique names:

```
mysql> SELECT COUNT(DISTINCT last_name, first_name) / COUNT(*)
    ->     AS 'unique',
    -> 1 - (COUNT(DISTINCT last_name, first_name) / COUNT(*))
    ->     AS 'nonunique'
    -> FROM catalog_list;
+--------+-----------+
| unique | nonunique |
+--------+-----------+
| 0.6250 |    0.3750 |
+--------+-----------+
```

Those statements help you characterize the extent of duplicates, but they don't show you which values are duplicated. To see the duplicated names in the `catalog_list` table, use a summary statement that displays the nonunique values along with the counts:

```
mysql> SELECT COUNT(*), last_name, first_name
    -> FROM catalog_list
    -> GROUP BY last_name, first_name
    -> HAVING COUNT(*) > 1;
+----------+-----------+------------+
| COUNT(*) | last_name | first_name |
+----------+-----------+------------+
|        3 | Baxter    | Wallace    |
|        2 | Pinter    | Marlene    |
+----------+-----------+------------+
```

The statement includes a `HAVING` clause that restricts the output to include only those names that occur more than once. In general, to identify sets of values that are duplicated, do the following:

1. Determine which columns contain the values that may be duplicated.

2. List those columns in the column selection list, along with `COUNT(*)`.

3. List the columns in the `GROUP BY` clause as well.

4. Add a `HAVING` clause that eliminates unique values by requiring group counts to be greater than one.

Queries constructed that way have the following form:

```
SELECT COUNT(*), column_list
FROM tbl_name
GROUP BY column_list
HAVING COUNT(*) > 1;
```

It's easy to generate duplicate-finding queries like that within a program, given database and table names and a nonempty set of column names. For example, here is a `make_dup_count_query()` Perl function that generates the proper query for finding and counting duplicated values in the specified columns:

```
sub make_dup_count_query
{
my ($db_name, $tbl_name, @col_name) = @_;

  return "SELECT COUNT(*)," . join (",", @col_name)
        . "\nFROM $db_name.$tbl_name"
        . "\nGROUP BY " . join (",", @col_name)
        . "\nHAVING COUNT(*) > 1";
}
```

make_dup_count_query() returns the query as a string. If you invoke it like this:

```
$str = make_dup_count_query ("cookbook", "catalog_list",
                             "last_name", "first_name");
```

the resulting value of $str is as follows:

```
SELECT COUNT(*),last_name,first_name
FROM cookbook.catalog_list
GROUP BY last_name,first_name
HAVING COUNT(*) > 1;
```

What you do with the query string is up to you. You can execute it from within the script that creates it, pass it to another program, or write it to a file for execution later. The *dups* directory of the `recipes` distribution contains a script named dup_count.pl that you can use to try the function (as well as some translations into other languages). Recipe 18.5 discusses the use of make_dup_count_query() to implement a duplicate-removal technique.

Summary techniques are useful for assessing the existence of duplicates, how often they occur, and displaying which values are duplicated. But if duplicates are determined using only a subset of a table's columns, a summary in itself cannot display the entire content of the rows that contain the duplicate values. (For example, the summaries shown thus far display counts of duplicated names in the `catalog_list` table or the names themselves but don't show the addresses associated with those names.) To see the original rows containing the duplicate names, join the summary information to the table from which it's generated. The following example shows how to do this to display the `catalog_list` rows that contain duplicated names. The summary is written to a temporary table, which then is joined to the `catalog_list` table to produce the rows that match those names:

```
mysql> CREATE TABLE tmp
    -> SELECT COUNT(*) AS count, last_name, first_name FROM catalog_list
    -> GROUP BY last_name, first_name HAVING count > 1;
mysql> SELECT catalog_list.*
    -> FROM tmp INNER JOIN catalog_list USING (last_name, first_name)
    -> ORDER BY last_name, first_name;

+-----------+------------+----------------------+
| last_name | first_name | street               |
+-----------+------------+----------------------+
| Baxter    | Wallace    | 57 3rd Ave.          |
| BAXTER    | WALLACE    | 57 3rd Ave.          |
```

```
| Baxter   | Wallace  | 57 3rd Ave., Apt 102 |
| Pinter   | Marlene  | 9 Sunset Trail       |
| Pinter   | Marlene  | 9 Sunset Trail       |
+----------+----------+----------------------+
```

> ## Duplicate Identification and String Case Sensitivity
>
> For strings that have a case-insensitive collation, values that differ only in lettercase are considered the same for comparison purposes. To treat them as distinct values, compare them using a case-sensitive or binary collation. Recipe 7.7 shows how to do this.

18.5 Eliminating Duplicates from a Table

Problem

You want to remove duplicate rows from a table, leaving only unique rows.

Solution

Select the unique rows from the table into a second table, then use that table to replace the original one. Or use DELETE...LIMIT *n* to remove all but one instance of a specific set of duplicate rows.

Discussion

Recipe 18.1 discusses how to prevent duplicates from being added to a table by creating it with a unique index. However, if you forget to include the index when you create a table, you may discover later that it contains duplicates and that it's necessary to apply some sort of duplicate-removal technique. The `catalog_list` table used earlier is an example of this because it contains several instances in which the same person appears multiple times:

```
mysql> SELECT * FROM catalog_list ORDER BY last_name, first_name;
+-----------+-------------+--------------------------+
| last_name | first_name  | street                   |
+-----------+-------------+--------------------------+
| Baxter    | Wallace     | 57 3rd Ave.              |
| BAXTER    | WALLACE     | 57 3rd Ave.              |
| Baxter    | Wallace     | 57 3rd Ave., Apt 102     |
| Brown     | Bartholomew | 432 River Run            |
| Isaacson  | Jim         | 515 Fordam St., Apt. 917 |
| McTavish  | Taylor      | 432 River Run            |
| Pinter    | Marlene     | 9 Sunset Trail           |
| Pinter    | Marlene     | 9 Sunset Trail           |
+-----------+-------------+--------------------------+
```

To eliminate duplicates, you can use one of these two options:

- Select the table's unique rows into another table, then use that table to replace the original one. This works when "duplicate" means "the entire row is the same as another."

- To remove duplicates for a specific set of duplicate rows, use DELETE...LIMIT *n* to remove all but one row.

This recipe discusses each duplicate-removal method. When deciding upon which method to choose for your circumstance, consider these questions:

- Does the method require the table to have a unique index?

- If the columns in which duplicate values occur may contain NULL, will the method remove duplicate NULL values?

- Does the method prevent duplicates from occurring in the future?

Removing duplicates using table replacement

If a row is considered to duplicate another only if the entire row is the same, one way to eliminate duplicates from a table is to select its unique rows into a new table that has the same structure, and then replace the original table with the new one:

1. Create a new table that has the same structure as the original one. CREATE TABLE...LIKE is useful for this (see Recipe 6.1):

   ```
   mysql> CREATE TABLE tmp LIKE catalog_list;
   ```

2. Use INSERT INTO...SELECT DISTINCT to select the unique rows from the original table into the new one:

   ```
   mysql> INSERT INTO tmp SELECT DISTINCT * FROM catalog_list;
   ```

   Select rows from the tmp table to verify that the new table contains no duplicates:

   ```
   mysql> SELECT * FROM tmp ORDER BY last_name, first_name;
   +-----------+------------+------------------------+
   | last_name | first_name | street                 |
   +-----------+------------+------------------------+
   | Baxter    | Wallace    | 57 3rd Ave.            |
   | Baxter    | Wallace    | 57 3rd Ave., Apt 102   |
   | Brown     | Bartholomew| 432 River Run          |
   | Isaacson  | Jim        | 515 Fordam St., Apt. 917 |
   | McTavish  | Taylor     | 432 River Run          |
   | Pinter    | Marlene    | 9 Sunset Trail         |
   +-----------+------------+------------------------+
   ```

3. After creating the new tmp table that contains unique rows, use it to replace the original catalog_list table:

   ```
   mysql> DROP TABLE catalog_list;
   mysql> RENAME TABLE tmp TO catalog_list;
   ```

The effective result of this procedure is that catalog_list no longer contains duplicates.

This table-replacement method works in the absence of an index (although it might be slow for large tables). For tables that contain duplicate NULL values, it removes those duplicates. It does not prevent the occurrence of duplicates in the future.

This method requires rows to be completely identical to be considered duplicates. Thus, it treats as distinct those rows for Wallace Baxter that have slightly different street values.

If duplicates are defined only with respect to a subset of the columns in the table, create a new table that has a unique index for those columns, select rows into it using INSERT IGNORE, and replace the original table with the new one:

```
mysql> CREATE TABLE tmp LIKE catalog_list;
mysql> ALTER TABLE tmp ADD PRIMARY KEY (last_name, first_name);
mysql> INSERT IGNORE INTO tmp SELECT * FROM catalog_list;
mysql> SELECT * FROM tmp ORDER BY last_name, first_name;
+-----------+-------------+-------------------------+
| last_name | first_name  | street                  |
+-----------+-------------+-------------------------+
| Baxter    | Wallace     | 57 3rd Ave.             |
| Brown     | Bartholomew | 432 River Run           |
| Isaacson  | Jim         | 515 Fordam St., Apt. 917|
| McTavish  | Taylor      | 432 River Run           |
| Pinter    | Marlene     | 9 Sunset Trail          |
+-----------+-------------+-------------------------+
mysql> DROP TABLE catalog_list;
mysql> RENAME TABLE tmp TO catalog_list;
```

The unique index prevents rows with duplicate key values from being inserted into tmp, and IGNORE tells MySQL not to stop with an error if a duplicate is found. One shortcoming of this method is that if the indexed columns can contain NULL values, you must use a UNIQUE index rather than a PRIMARY KEY, in which case the index will not remove duplicate NULL keys. (UNIQUE indexes permit multiple NULL values.) This method does prevent occurrence of duplicates in the future.

Removing duplicates of a particular row

You can use LIMIT to restrict the effect of a DELETE statement to a subset of the rows that it otherwise would delete. This makes the statement applicable to removing duplicate rows. Suppose that the original unindexed catalog_list table contains duplicates:

```
mysql> SELECT COUNT(*), last_name, first_name
    -> FROM catalog_list
    -> GROUP BY last_name, first_name
    -> HAVING COUNT(*) > 1;
+----------+-----------+------------+
| COUNT(*) | last_name | first_name |
+----------+-----------+------------+
|        3 | Baxter    | Wallace    |
|        2 | Pinter    | Marlene    |
+----------+-----------+------------+
```

To remove the extra instances of each name, do this:

```
mysql> DELETE FROM catalog_list WHERE last_name = 'Baxter'
    -> AND first_name = 'Wallace' LIMIT 2;
mysql> DELETE FROM catalog_list WHERE last_name = 'Pinter'
    -> AND first_name = 'Marlene' LIMIT 1;
mysql> SELECT * FROM catalog_list;
+-----------+-------------+-------------------------+
| last_name | first_name  | street                  |
+-----------+-------------+-------------------------+
| Isaacson  | Jim         | 515 Fordam St., Apt. 917 |
| McTavish  | Taylor      | 432 River Run           |
| Brown     | Bartholomew | 432 River Run           |
| Pinter    | Marlene     | 9 Sunset Trail          |
| Baxter    | Wallace     | 57 3rd Ave., Apt 102    |
+-----------+-------------+-------------------------+
```

This technique works in the absence of a unique index, and it eliminates duplicate NULL values. It's handy for removing duplicates only for a specific set of rows within a table. However, if there are many different sets of duplicates to remove, this is not a procedure you'd want to carry out by hand. The process can be automated by using the techniques discussed earlier in Recipe 18.4 for determining which values are duplicated. There, we wrote a make_dup_count_query() function to generate the statement needed to count the number of duplicate values in a given set of columns in a table. The result of that statement can be used to generate a set of DELETE... LIMIT *n* statements that remove duplicate rows and leave only unique rows. The *dups* directory of the recipes distribution contains code that shows how to generate these statements.

In general, using DELETE...LIMIT *n* is likely to be slower than removing duplicates by using a second table or by adding a unique index. Those methods keep the data on the server side and let the server do all the work. DELETE...LIMIT *n* involves a lot of client-server interaction because it uses a SELECT statement to retrieve information about duplicates, followed by several DELETE statements to remove instances of duplicated rows. Also, this technique does not prevent duplicates from occurring in the future.

## CHAPTER 19

Working with JSON

19.0 Introduction

Relational databases have proven to be effective for decades. They prevent duplicates and misses of data and enable fast access to stored values. However, business continually invents new scenarios in which data needs to be more flexible than the relational model allows.

For example, let's consider a record for a user who can access subscription-only digital content and leave comments. For such a user, having only basic information—their name, email address, and password—is enough to get started. However, once the users start exploring more options (for example, requiring delivery), they may need their mailing address to be stored. The mailing address could be different from the billing address. The user may want to add a social network account or a few of them.

One way of storing flexible data in the relational database is to store additional pieces of data in the referenced table that shares details for each user. We discussed this technique in Recipes 16.5 and 16.6.

However, this technique may be not the best in the following situations:

When only a few items in the main table have details in the referenced table
> If you still need to know about these details, when you query the required fields in the main table, you will need to join it with the referencing table every time. This will complicate queries and affect performance.

When most of the specific details could be missed
> Details such as a user's district or building number are necessary only for users who requested physical delivery of items. For everyone else, these fields could be

empty, but you still need to reserve space in the database for those empty fields. This adds significant cost once the database grows.

When you may not know which additional data you need in the future
You may need to add additional details to the data collections based on your needs. Appending such details in the relational model means creating new tables and columns to the existent table. This requires schema redesign and maintenance windows to implement the changes. This is not always possible or space/cost effective.

To resolve these issues, flexible data structures, such as JSON, are the best fit. MySQL allows you to store JSON values in text fields using string data types. Since version 5.7, MySQL also supports JSON data types and functions that allow you to manipulate JSON values in an effective manner. MySQL combines the advantages of both SQL and NoSQL worlds.

19.1 Choosing the Right Data Type

Problem

You want to store JSON values and don't know which data type to choose.

Solution

Use the JSON data type.

Discussion

JSON data can be stored in any text or binary column. JSON functions will work without issues, but the special JSON data type has numerous advantages, particularly the following:

Optimized performance
JSON data is converted into a format that allows quick lookup for values in the document.

Partial updates
Updates to JSON elements happen in place, without the need to rewrite a full document.

Automatic data validation
When a value is inserted into a column of JSON data type, MySQL automatically validates it and produces an error if the document is invalid JSON.

The following will create a table with a JSON author column:

```
CREATE TABLE book_authors (
  id     INT NOT NULL AUTO_INCREMENT,
  author JSON NOT NULL,
  PRIMARY KEY (id)
);
```

See Also

For additional information about the JSON data type, see "The JSON Data Type" (*https://oreil.ly/PVl8K*) in the MySQL Reference Manual.

19.2 Inserting JSON Values

Problem

You want to store JSON documents in MySQL.

Solution

Use regular INSERT statements.

Discussion

JSON is not different from other data types. Use regular INSERT statements to add your documents into the tables:

```
mysql> INSERT INTO `book_authors` VALUES
    -> (1,'{"id": 1, "name": "Paul",
    '>     "books": [
    '>       "Software Portability with imake: Practical Software Engineering",
    '>       "Mysql: The Definitive Guide to Using, Programming, ↵
              and Administering Mysql 4 (Developer\'s Library)",
    '>          "MySQL Certification Study Guide",
    '>          "MySQL (OTHER NEW RIDERS)",
    '>          "MySQL Cookbook",
    '>          "MySQL 5.0 Certification Study Guide",
    '>          "Using csh & tcsh: Type Less, Accomplish More ↵
              (Nutshell Handbooks)",
    '>          "MySQL (Developer\'s Library)"],
    '>     "lastname": "DuBois"}'),
    -> (2,'{"id": 2, "name": "Alkin",
    '>     "books": ["MySQL Cookbook"],
    '>     "lastname": "Tezuysal"}'),
    -> (3,'{"id": 3, "name": "Sveta",
    '>     "books": ["MySQL Troubleshooting", "MySQL Cookbook"],
    '>     "lastname": "Smirnova"}');
Query OK, 3 rows affected (0,01 sec)
Records: 3  Duplicates: 0  Warnings: 0
```

19.3 Validating JSON

Problem

You want to ensure that a given string is a valid JSON.

Solution

Use the JSON data type to perform automatic validation. Use the `JSON_VALID` function to validate strings. Use the JSON Schema to define the schema for the JSON documents.

Discussion

The `JSON_VALID` function checks if a given document is valid JSON:

```
mysql> SELECT JSON_VALID('"name": "Sveta"');
+------------------------------+
| JSON_VALID('"name": "Sveta"') |
+------------------------------+
|                            0 |
+------------------------------+
1 row in set (0,00 sec)

mysql> SELECT JSON_VALID('{"name": "Sveta"}');
+--------------------------------+
| JSON_VALID('{"name": "Sveta"}') |
+--------------------------------+
|                              1 |
+--------------------------------+
1 row in set (0,00 sec)
```

If a column definition is a JSON data type, MySQL will not allow you to insert invalid values. Additionally, an error message will locate the first error, so you can fix it faster:

```
mysql> INSERT INTO book_authors(author)
    -> VALUES ('{"name": "Sveta" "lastname": "Smirnova"');
ERROR 3140 (22032): Invalid JSON text: "Missing a comma or '}' after an object↵
member." at position 17 in value for column 'book_authors.author'.
```

If you want to validate a JSON document and also want it to satisfy a schema, use the `JSON_SCHEMA_VALID` function. This function supports the JSON Schema as described in Draft 4 of the JSON Schema specification (*https://oreil.ly/Qwi4k*). To use it, you need to define a schema first and compare the JSON value with it.

The `JSON_SCHEMA_VALIDATION_REPORT` function not only checks a given document against the schema but also reports which particular part of the schema is violated.

For the book_authors table, we can define a schema with name and lastname as required fields and an array of book titles as optional books element. We can use the following code for the schema:

```
{
"id": "http://www.oreilly.com/mysqlcookbook", ❶
"$schema": "http://json-schema.org/draft-04/schema#", ❷
"description": "Schema for the table book_authors", ❸
"type": "object", ❹
"properties": { ❺
  "name": {"type": "string"},
  "lastname": {"type": "string"},
  "books": {"type": "array"}
},
"required":["name", "lastname"] ❻
}
```

❶ Unique identifier of the schema.

❷ JSON schema specification. Should always be http://json-schema.org/ draft-04/schema#.

❸ Description of the schema.

❹ Type of the root element.

❺ List of properties. Each of the properties should be described. They should have a defined type and can specify other validations, such as minimum and maximum.

❻ List of required fields.

If we assign just the defined schema to a variable, say, @schema, we can check JSON data against this schema:

```
mysql> SET @schema = '{
    '> "id": "http://www.oreilly.com/mysqlcookbook",
    '> "$schema": "http://json-schema.org/draft-04/schema#",
    '> "description": "Schema for the table book_authors",
    '> "type": "object",
    '> "properties": {
    '> "name": {"type": "string"},
    '> "lastname": {"type": "string"},
    '> "books": {"type": "array"}
    '> },
    '> "required":["name", "lastname"]
    '> }';
Query OK, 0 rows affected (0,00 sec)

mysql> SELECT JSON_SCHEMA_VALIDATION_REPORT(@schema,
    -> '{"name": "Sveta"}')  AS 'Valid?'\G
*************************** 1. row ***************************
Valid?: {"valid": false, "reason": "The JSON document location '#' failed requirement ↵
'required' at JSON Schema location '#'", "schema-location": "#", ↵
```

```
"document-location": "#", "schema-failed-keyword": "required"}
1 row in set (0,00 sec)
```

In this case, validation failed, because the document contains only the name field and does not contain another required field, lastname:

```
mysql> SELECT JSON_SCHEMA_VALIDATION_REPORT(@schema,
    -> '{"name": "Sveta", "lastname": "Smirnova"}') AS 'Valid?';
+-----------------+
| Valid?          |
+-----------------+
| {"valid": true} |
+-----------------+
1 row in set (0,00 sec)
```

In this case, the document is valid, because it contains all required fields. The books field is optional and not required:

```
mysql> SELECT JSON_SCHEMA_VALIDATION_REPORT(@schema,
    -> '{"name": "Sveta", "lastname": "Smirnova",
    -> "books": "MySQL Cookbook"}') AS 'Valid?'\G
*************************** 1. row ***************************
Valid?: {"valid": false, "reason": "The JSON document location '#/books' failed ↵
requirement 'type' at JSON Schema location '#/properties/books'", ↵
"schema-location": "#/properties/books", "document-location": "#/books", ↵
"schema-failed-keyword": "type"}
1 row in set (0,00 sec)
```

In this case, the document is not valid, because the books member has a string type and not an array as defined in the schema:

```
mysql> SELECT JSON_SCHEMA_VALIDATION_REPORT(@schema,
    -> '{"name": "Sveta", "lastname": "Smirnova",
    -> "books": ["MySQL Troubleshooting", "MySQL Cookbook"]}') AS 'Valid?';
+-----------------+
| Valid?          |
+-----------------+
| {"valid": true} |
+-----------------+
1 row in set (0,00 sec)
```

This document fixes the type error for the books element and thus is valid:

```
mysql> SELECT JSON_SCHEMA_VALID(@schema, '{"name": "Sveta", "lastname": "Smirnova",
    -> "vehicles": ["Honda CRF 250L"]}') AS 'Valid 1?',
    -> JSON_SCHEMA_VALID(@schema, '{"name": "Alkin", "lastname": "Tezuysal",
    -> "vehicles": "boat"}') AS 'Valid 2?';
+----------+----------+
| Valid 1? | Valid 2? |
+----------+----------+
|        1 |        1 |
+----------+----------+
1 row in set (0,00 sec)
```

These documents are also valid, because there is no requirement for the vehicles property: it may exist or it may not exist and can be of any type.

If you want to automatically validate a JSON field in a table against a defined schema, use CHECK constraints:

```
ALTER TABLE book_authors
ADD CONSTRAINT CHECK(JSON_SCHEMA_VALID('
{"id": "http://www.oreilly.com/mysqlcookbook",
 "$schema": "http://json-schema.org/draft-04/schema#",
 "description": "Schema for the table book_authors",
 "type": "object",
 "properties": {
     "name": {"type": "string"},
     "lastname": {"type": "string"},
     "books": {"type": "array"}},
 "required":["name", "lastname"]} ',
 author));
```

19.4 Formatting JSON Values

Problem

You want to print JSON in a nice format.

Solution

Use the JSON_PRETTY function.

Discussion

By default, JSON is printed as a long string that can be hard to read. If you want MySQL to print it in human-readable format, use the JSON_PRETTY function:

```
mysql> SELECT JSON_PRETTY(author) FROM book_authors\G
*************************** 1. row ***************************
JSON_PRETTY(author): {
  "id": 1,
  "name": "Paul",
  "books": [
    "Software Portability with imake: Practical Software Engineering",
    "Mysql: The Definitive Guide to Using, Programming, ↵
     and Administering Mysql 4 (Developer's Library)",
    "MySQL Certification Study Guide",
    "MySQL (OTHER NEW RIDERS)",
    "MySQL Cookbook",
    "MySQL 5.0 Certification Study Guide",
    "Using csh & tcsh: Type Less, Accomplish More (Nutshell Handbooks)",
    "MySQL (Developer's Library)"
  ],
  "lastname": "DuBois"
}
*************************** 2. row ***************************
JSON_PRETTY(author): {
  "id": 2,
  "name": "Alkin",
  "books": [
```

```
    "MySQL Cookbook"
  ],
  "lastname": "Tezuysal"
}
*************************** 3. row ***************************
JSON_PRETTY(author): {
  "id": 3,
  "name": "Sveta",
  "books": [
    "MySQL Troubleshooting",
    "MySQL Cookbook"
  ],
  "lastname": "Smirnova"
}
3 rows in set (0,00 sec)
```

19.5 Extracting Values from JSON

Problem

You want to extract values from the JSON document.

Solution

Use the `JSON_EXTRACT` function or the operators `->` and `->>`.

Discussion

JSON by itself is no use if you cannot extract values from the documents. JSON in MySQL supports the JSON path that can be used to point to the specific element in JSON. The root element of the JSON document is represented by a $ sign. Object members are accessed by the . operator, and array members are accessed by an index, enclosed in square brackets. Indexes start from zero. You can refer to multiple array elements with the keyword `to` (e.g. `$.[3 to 5]`). The `last` keyword is a synonym of the last element in the array.

The wildcard * represents either all values of all object members if used after a dot, `.*`, or all array elements if enclosed in the square brackets, `[*]`.

The `[prefix]**suffix` expression represents all paths, beginning with the `prefix` and ending with the `suffix`. Note that while the `suffix` part is required, `prefix` is optional. In other words, a JSON path expression should not end with a double asterisk sign.

To access JSON elements, use the `JSON_EXTRACT` function.

For example, to select names of the authors, use the following SQL:

```
mysql> SELECT JSON_EXTRACT(author, '$.name') AS author FROM book_authors;
+----------+
```

```
| author  |
+---------+
| "Paul"  |
| "Alkin" |
| "Sveta" |
+---------+
3 rows in set (0,00 sec)
```

To remove quotes from the values, use the JSON_UNQUOTE function.

```
mysql> SELECT JSON_UNQUOTE(JSON_EXTRACT(author, '$.name')) AS author FROM book_authors;
+--------+
| author |
+--------+
| Paul   |
| Alkin  |
| Sveta  |
+--------+
3 rows in set (0,00 sec)
```

The -> operator is an alias of the JSON_EXTRACT function.

```
mysql> SELECT author->'$.name' AS author FROM book_authors;
+---------+
| author  |
+---------+
| "Paul"  |
| "Alkin" |
| "Sveta" |
+---------+
3 rows in set (0,00 sec)
```

The ->> operator is an alias of JSON_UNQUOTE(JSON_EXTRACT(...)):

```
mysql> SELECT author->>'$.name' AS author FROM book_authors;
+--------+
| author |
+--------+
| Paul   |
| Alkin  |
| Sveta  |
+--------+
3 rows in set (0,00 sec)
```

To extract the first and last books by the authors, use the 0 and last array indexes, respectively:

```
mysql> SELECT CONCAT(author->>'$.name', ' ', author->>'$.lastname') AS author,
    -> author->>'$.books[0]' AS `First Book`,
    -> author->>'$.books[last]' AS `Last Book` FROM book_authors\G
*************************** 1. row ***************************
    author: Paul DuBois
First Book: Software Portability with imake: Practical Software Engineering
 Last Book: MySQL (Developer's Library)
*************************** 2. row ***************************
    author: Alkin Tezuysal
First Book: MySQL Cookbook
 Last Book: MySQL Cookbook
*************************** 3. row ***************************
    author: Sveta Smirnova
```

```
 First Book: MySQL Troubleshooting
  Last Book: MySQL Cookbook
3 rows in set (0,00 sec)
```

The JSON path `$.books[*]` will return the full array of books. The same will happen if you omit a wildcard and simply refer to the books array as `$.books`. The `$.*` expression will return all elements of the JSON object as an array:

```
mysql> SELECT author->'$.*' FROM book_authors WHERE author->>'$.name' = 'Sveta';
+------------------------------------------------------------------------+
| author->'$.*'                                                          |
+------------------------------------------------------------------------+
| [3, "Sveta", ["MySQL Troubleshooting", "MySQL Cookbook"], "Smirnova"] |
+------------------------------------------------------------------------+
1 row in set (0,00 sec)
```

See Also

For additional information about JSON Path, see "JSON Path Syntax" (*https://oreil.ly/D1k9c*) in the MySQL Reference Manual.

19.6 Searching Inside JSON

Problem

You want to search for JSON documents containing particular values.

Solution

Use the `JSON_SEARCH` function.

Discussion

Accessing by key works great, but you may want to search for particular values in JSON documents. MySQL allows you to do this. For example, to find all authors of the book *MySQL Cookbook*, run the following query:

```
mysql> SELECT author->>'$.name' AS author FROM book_authors
    -> WHERE JSON_SEARCH(author, 'one', 'MySQL Cookbook');
+--------+
| author |
+--------+
| Paul   |
| Alkin  |
| Sveta  |
+--------+
3 rows in set, 1 warning (0,00 sec)
```

The `JSON_SEARCH` function takes a JSON document keyword, one or `all`, and a search string as required arguments and returns the found path of the element or elements that contain the searched value. It also supports the optional escape character and JSON path arguments.

Similarly to the operator LIKE function, JSON_SEARCH supports wildcards % and _.

Thus, to search all books with names that start with MySQL, use the following expression:

```
mysql> SELECT author->>'$.name' AS author,
    -> JSON_SEARCH(author, 'all', 'MySQL%') AS books
    -> FROM book_authors\G
*************************** 1. row ***************************
author: Paul
 books: ["$.books[2]", "$.books[3]", "$.books[4]", "$.books[5]", "$.books[7]"]
*************************** 2. row ***************************
author: Alkin
 books: "$.books[0]"
*************************** 3. row ***************************
author: Sveta
 books: ["$.books[0]", "$.books[1]"]
3 rows in set (0,00 sec)
```

When searching for a single match, you can use the return value of the JSON_SEARCH function as an argument for the JSON_EXTRACT function:

```
mysql> SELECT author->>'$.name' AS author,
    -> JSON_EXTRACT(author,
    -> JSON_UNQUOTE(JSON_SEARCH(author, 'one', 'MySQL%'))) AS book
    -> FROM book_authors;
+--------+-----------------------------------+
| author | book                              |
+--------+-----------------------------------+
| Paul   | "MySQL Certification Study Guide" |
| Alkin  | "MySQL Cookbook"                  |
| Sveta  | "MySQL Troubleshooting"           |
+--------+-----------------------------------+
3 rows in set (0,00 sec)
```

19.7 Inserting New Elements into a JSON Document

Problem

You want to insert new elements into a JSON document.

Solution

Use the JSON_INSERT, JSON_ARRAY_APPEND, and JSON_ARRAY_INSERT functions.

Discussion

You may want to not only search inside JSON values but also modify them. MySQL supports a number of functions that can modify JSON. The most wonderful thing about them is that they do not replace the JSON document as regular string functions do. Rather, they perform updates in place. This allows you to modify JSON values effectively.

MySQL functions allow you to append, remove, and replace parts of JSON as well as merge two or more documents into one. They all take the original document as an argument, a path that needs to be modified, and a new value.

To insert a new value into a JSON object, use the JSON_INSERT function. Thus, to add information about a current author's work, call the function as follows:

```
UPDATE book_authors SET author = JSON_INSERT(author, '$.work', 'Percona')
WHERE author->>'$.name' IN ('Sveta', 'Alkin');
```

To add a book into the end of the book array, use the JSON_ARRAY_APPEND function:

```
UPDATE book_authors SET author = JSON_ARRAY_APPEND(author, '$.books',
'MySQL Performance Schema in Action') WHERE author->>'$.name' = 'Sveta';
```

This will add a new book into the end of the array:

```
mysql> SELECT JSON_PRETTY(author) FROM book_authors
    -> WHERE author->>'$.name' = 'Sveta'\G
*************************** 1. row ***************************
JSON_PRETTY(author): {
  "id": 3,
  "name": "Sveta",
  "work": "Percona",
  "books": [
    "MySQL Troubleshooting",
    "MySQL Cookbook",
    "MySQL Performance Schema in Action"
  ],
  "lastname": "Smirnova"
}
1 row in set (0,00 sec)
```

To add an element into a specific place, use the JSON_ARRAY_INSERT function:

```
UPDATE book_authors SET author = JSON_ARRAY_INSERT(author, '$.books[0]',
'MySQL for Absolute Beginners') WHERE author->>'$.name' = 'Alkin';
```

This will insert a new book into the beginning of the array:

```
mysql> SELECT JSON_PRETTY(author)
    -> FROM book_authors WHERE author->>'$.name' = 'Alkin'\G
*************************** 1. row ***************************
JSON_PRETTY(author): {
  "id": 2,
  "name": "Alkin",
  "work": "Percona",
  "books": [
    "MySQL for Absolute Beginners",
    "MySQL Cookbook"
  ],
  "lastname": "Tezuysal"
}
1 row in set (0,00 sec)
```

19.8 Updating JSON

Problem

You want to update a JSON value.

Solution

Use the JSON_REPLACE and JSON_SET functions.

Discussion

While we were working on this book, Alkin changed jobs, so the content of the table needs to be updated. The JSON_REPLACE function replaces a given path with the new value:

```
UPDATE book_authors SET author = JSON_REPLACE(author, '$.work', 'PlanetScale')
WHERE author->>'$.name' = 'Alkin';
```

However, the JSON_REPLACE function will do nothing if a record that needs to be replaced does not exist in the document:

```
mysql> UPDATE book_authors SET author = JSON_REPLACE(author, '$.work', 'Oracle')
    -> WHERE author->>'$.name' = 'Paul';
Query OK, 0 rows affected (0,00 sec)
Rows matched: 1  Changed: 0  Warnings: 0

mysql> SELECT author->>'$.work' FROM book_authors WHERE author->>'$.name' = 'Paul';
+-------------------+
| author->>'$.work' |
+-------------------+
| NULL              |
+-------------------+
1 row in set (0,00 sec)
```

To resolve this problem, use the JSON_SET function to update the document if the path exists or to insert a new value if the path does not exist:

```
mysql> UPDATE book_authors SET author = JSON_SET(author, '$.work', 'MySQL')
    -> WHERE author->>'$.name' = 'Paul';
Query OK, 1 row affected (0,01 sec)
Rows matched: 1  Changed: 1  Warnings: 0

mysql> SELECT author->>'$.work' FROM book_authors WHERE author->>'$.name' = 'Paul';
+-------------------+
| author->>'$.work' |
+-------------------+
| MySQL             |
+-------------------+
1 row in set (0,00 sec)

mysql> UPDATE book_authors SET author = JSON_SET(author, '$.work', 'Oracle')
    -> WHERE author->>'$.name' = 'Paul';
Query OK, 1 row affected (0,00 sec)
```

```
Rows matched: 1  Changed: 1  Warnings: 0

mysql> SELECT author->>'$.work' FROM book_authors WHERE author->>'$.name' = 'Paul';
+-------------------+
| author->>'$.work' |
+-------------------+
| Oracle            |
+-------------------+
1 row in set (0,00 sec)
```

19.9 Removing Elements from JSON

Problem

You want to remove elements from a JSON document.

Solution

Use the JSON_REMOVE function.

Discussion

The JSON_REMOVE function removes specified elements from JSON.

For example, to remove unpublished books from the book_authors table, use the following code:

```
UPDATE book_authors SET author = JSON_REMOVE(author, '$.books[0]')
WHERE author->>'$.name' = 'Alkin';
UPDATE book_authors SET author = JSON_REMOVE(author, '$.books[last]')
WHERE author->>'$.name' = 'Sveta';
```

19.10 Merging Two or More JSON Documents into One

Problem

You want to combine two or more JSON documents into one.

Solution

Use the family of JSON_MERGE_* functions.

Discussion

Two functions, JSON_MERGE_PATCH and JSON_MERGE_PRESERVE, are available for combining multiple JSON documents into one. JSON_MERGE_PATCH removes duplicates when merging two documents, whereas JSON_MERGE_PRESERVE keeps them. Both functions take two or more arguments that should be valid JSON text.

For example, in this recipe we will store values of the `author` column in the `book_authors` table into user-defined variables: one for each author. Additionally, we will store arrays of books for Sveta in a `sveta_books` variable:

```
SELECT author INTO @paul FROM book_authors WHERE author->>'$.name'='Paul';
SELECT author INTO @sveta FROM book_authors WHERE author->>'$.name'='Sveta';
SELECT author INTO @alkin FROM book_authors WHERE author->>'$.name'='Alkin';
SELECT author->>'$.books' INTO @sveta_books FROM book_authors
  WHERE author->>'$.name'='Sveta';
```

`JSON_MERGE_PRESERVE` combines documents, provided by its arguments, into a single object. You can use this function to add new elements to your objects or arrays. Thus, to add an array of countries where the author has lived, you can just provide an object containing such an array as an argument:

```
mysql> SELECT JSON_PRETTY(JSON_MERGE_PRESERVE(@sveta,
    -> '{"places lived": ["Russia", "Turkey"]}'))\G
*************************** 1. row ***************************
JSON_PRETTY(JSON_MERGE_PRESERVE(@sveta, '{"places lived": ["Russia", "Turkey"]}')): {
  "id": 3,
  "name": "Sveta",
  "work": "Percona",
  "books": [
    "MySQL Troubleshooting",
    "MySQL Cookbook"
  ],
  "lastname": "Smirnova",
  "places lived": [
    "Russia",
    "Turkey"
  ]
}
1 row in set (0,00 sec)
```

To add a new book into the `books` array, pass it as a part of the `books` array in the object as a second argument:

```
mysql> SELECT JSON_PRETTY(JSON_MERGE_PRESERVE(@sveta,
    -> '{"books": ["MySQL Performance Schema in Action"]}'))\G
*************************** 1. row ***************************
JSON_PRETTY(JSON_MERGE_PRESERVE(@sveta, ↵
'{"books": ["MySQL Performance Schema in Action"]}')): {
  "id": 3,
  "name": "Sveta",
  "work": "Percona",
  "books": [
    "MySQL Troubleshooting",
    "MySQL Cookbook",
    "MySQL Performance Schema in Action"
  ],
  "lastname": "Smirnova"
}
1 row in set (0,00 sec)
```

The content of the `books` array in the second argument will be added to the end of the array with the same name in the first argument.

If two objects have scalar values with the same key, they will be merged into an array:

```
mysql> SELECT JSON_PRETTY(JSON_MERGE_PRESERVE(@paul, @sveta, @alkin)) AS authors\G
*************************** 1. row ***************************
authors: {
  "id": [
    1,
    3,
    2
  ],
  "name": [
    "Paul",
    "Sveta",
    "Alkin"
  ],
  "work": [
    "Oracle",
    "Percona",
    "PlanetScale"
  ],
  "books": [
    "Software Portability with imake: Practical Software Engineering",
    "Mysql: The Definitive Guide to Using, Programming, ↵
     and Administering Mysql 4 (Developer's Library)",
    "MySQL Certification Study Guide",
    "MySQL (OTHER NEW RIDERS)",
    "MySQL Cookbook",
    "MySQL 5.0 Certification Study Guide",
    "Using csh & tcsh: Type Less, Accomplish More (Nutshell Handbooks)",
    "MySQL (Developer's Library)",
    "MySQL Troubleshooting",
    "MySQL Cookbook",
    "MySQL Cookbook"
  ],
  "lastname": [
    "DuBois",
    "Smirnova",
    "Tezuysal"
  ]
}
1 row in set (0,00 sec)
```

Note that the JSON_MERGE_PRESERVE function does not try to handle duplicates, so the book title MySQL Cookbook repeats in the resulting array three times.

The JSON_MERGE_PATCH function, instead, removes duplicates in favor of its latest argument. The same combination of merging three authors will just return the one, specified as the last argument:

```
mysql> SELECT JSON_PRETTY(JSON_MERGE_PATCH(@paul, @sveta, @alkin)) AS authors\G
*************************** 1. row ***************************
authors: {
  "id": 2,
```

```
  "name": "Alkin",
  "work": "PlanetScale",
  "books": [
    "MySQL Cookbook"
  ],
  "lastname": "Tezuysal"
}
1 row in set (0,00 sec)
```

This feature could be used to remove unneeded elements from JSON. For example, if we decide that it doesn't matter which company the author works for, we can remove the work element by passing it as an object with the value null:

```
mysql> SELECT JSON_PRETTY(JSON_MERGE_PATCH(@sveta, '{"work": null}'))\G
*************************** 1. row ***************************
JSON_PRETTY(JSON_MERGE_PATCH(@sveta, '{"work": null}')): {
  "id": 3,
  "name": "Sveta",
  "books": [
    "MySQL Troubleshooting",
    "MySQL Cookbook"
  ],
  "lastname": "Smirnova"
}
1 row in set (0,00 sec)
```

When the latest document of the function is not an object, JSON_MERGE_PRESERVE will add it as the latest element of an array. For example, to add a new book to the array of books by Sveta, you can use following code:

```
mysql> SELECT JSON_PRETTY(JSON_MERGE_PRESERVE(@sveta_books,
    -> '"MySQL Performance Schema in Action"')) AS 'Books by Sveta'\G
*************************** 1. row ***************************
Books by Sveta: [
  "MySQL Troubleshooting",
  "MySQL Cookbook",
  "MySQL Performance Schema in Action"
]
1 row in set (0,00 sec)
```

JSON_MERGE_PATCH, instead, will replace the elements in the original document with the new one:

```
mysql> SELECT JSON_PRETTY(JSON_MERGE_PATCH(@sveta_books,
    -> '"MySQL Performance Schema in Action"')) AS 'Books by Sveta';
+-------------------------------------+
| Books by Sveta                      |
+-------------------------------------+
| "MySQL Performance Schema in Action" |
+-------------------------------------+
1 row in set (0,00 sec)
```

19.11 Creating JSON from Relational Data

Problem

You have relational data and want to create JSON from it.

Solution

Use the JSON_OBJECT and JSON_ARRAY functions and their aggregate variants JSON_OBJECTAGG and JSON_ARRAYAGG.

Discussion

It can be useful to create JSON out of relational data. MySQL provides the JSON_OBJECT function that combines pairs of values into a JSON object:

```
mysql> SELECT JSON_PRETTY(
    -> JSON_OBJECT("string", "Some String", "number", 42, "null", NULL)) AS my_object\G
*************************** 1. row ***************************
my_object: {
  "null": null,
  "number": 42,
  "string": "Some String"
}
1 row in set (0,00 sec)
```

The JSON_ARRAY function creates a JSON array from its arguments:

```
mysql> SELECT JSON_PRETTY(JSON_ARRAY("one", "two", "three", 4, 5)) AS my_array\G
*************************** 1. row ***************************
my_array: [
  "one",
  "two",
  "three",
  4,
  5
]
1 row in set (0,00 sec)
```

You can combine both functions to make nesting objects and arrays:

```
mysql> SELECT JSON_PRETTY(JSON_OBJECT("Example", "Nesting object and array",
    -> "Human", JSON_OBJECT("name", "Sveta", "lastname", "Smirnova"),
    -> "Numbers", JSON_ARRAY("one", "two", "three"))) AS my_object\G
*************************** 1. row ***************************
my_object: {
  "Human": {
    "name": "Sveta",
    "lastname": "Smirnova"
  },
  "Example": "Nesting object and array",
  "Numbers": [
    "one",
    "two",
    "three"
```

```
    ]
  }
1 row in set (0,00 sec)
```

The `JSON_OBJECTAGG` and `JSON_ARRAYAGG` functions are aggregate versions of `JSON_OBJECT` and `JSON_ARRAY` that allow you to create JSON objects and arrays out of data, returned by `GROUP BY` queries.

The cookbook database has a `movies_actors` table that contains a list of movies and actors that starred in them. The table has a few rows for each movie and a few others for each actor.

If you want to have a JSON object that will list a movie and all the actors who starred in that movie in an array, combine the `JSON_OBJECT` and `JSON_ARRAYAGG` functions:

```
mysql> SELECT JSON_PRETTY(JSON_OBJECT('Movie', movie,
    -> 'Starred', JSON_ARRAYAGG(actor))) AS starred
    -> FROM movies_actors GROUP BY movie\G
*************************** 1. row ***************************
starred: {
  "Movie": "Kingdom of Heaven",
  "Starred": [
    "Liam Neeson",
    "Orlando Bloom"
  ]
}
*************************** 2. row ***************************
starred: {
  "Movie": "Red",
  "Starred": [
    "Helen Mirren",
    "Bruce Willis"
  ]
}
*************************** 3. row ***************************
starred: {
  "Movie": "The Fellowship of the Ring",
  "Starred": [
    "Ian McKellen",
    "Ian Holm",
    "Orlando Bloom",
    "Elijah Wood"
  ]
}
*************************** 4. row ***************************
starred: {
  "Movie": "The Fifth Element",
  "Starred": [
    "Bruce Willis",
    "Gary Oldman",
    "Ian Holm"
  ]
}
*************************** 5. row ***************************
starred: {
  "Movie": "The Phantom Menace",
  "Starred": [
```

```
      "Ewan McGregor",
      "Liam Neeson"
   ]
}
*************************** 6. row ***************************
starred: {
  "Movie": "Unknown",
  "Starred": [
    "Diane Kruger",
    "Liam Neeson"
  ]
}
6 rows in set (0,00 sec)
```

The `JSON_OBJECTAGG` function can take table values in one column as member names and values in another column as their arguments:

```
mysql> SELECT JSON_PRETTY(JSON_OBJECTAGG(name, website)) AS websites
    -> FROM book_vendor\G
*************************** 1. row ***************************
websites: {
  "Amazon.com": "www.amazon.com",
  "Barnes & Noble": "www.barnesandnoble.com",
  "O'Reilly Media": "www.oreilly.com"
}
1 row in set (0,00 sec)
```

19.12 Converting JSON into Relational Format

Problem

You have JSON data and want to work with it the same way as you do with relational structure data.

Solution

Use the `JSON_TABLE` function.

Discussion

In the previous recipe, we converted relational data into JSON. You may need to do the opposite: convert JSON into relational format. In this case, the `JSON_TABLE` function will help.

The `JSON_TABLE` function takes a JSON document and a list of columns with paths as its arguments. It returns a table as a result.

For example, for the following document:

```
{
  "null": null,
  "number": 42,
```

```
  "string": "Some String"
}
```

JSON_TABLE can be called as follows:

```
mysql> SELECT *  ❶
    -> FROM JSON_TABLE(  ❷
    -> '{"null": null, "number": 42, "string": "Some String"}',  ❸
    -> '$'  ❹
    -> COLUMNS(  ❺
    -> number INT PATH '$.number',  ❻
    -> string VARCHAR(255) PATH '$.string' ERROR ON ERROR  ❼
    -> )) AS jt;  ❽
+--------+-------------+
| number | string      |
+--------+-------------+
|     42 | Some String |
+--------+-------------+
1 row in set (0,00 sec)
```

❶ Start the query by selecting everything from the resulting table.

❷ The JSON_TABLE function can be used only in the FROM clause.

❸ The first argument to the function is a JSON document. In this example, the function takes a string. If you want to pass a column name into another table, you need to specify this table prior to the JSON_TABLE call:

```
SELECT * FROM mytable, JSON_TABLE(mytable.mycolumn...
```

❹ A path that will be used as a document root. In this example, we're using the whole document, but you can simplify expressions for the columns if you specify the path to the part of the JSON document here.

❺ Definition of columns.

❻ The number column has a INT type and default error handling: the column is set to NULL in case an error happens. We use JSON path $.number to set a value for this column.

❼ For the column string, we decided to raise an error; therefore, we used the ERROR ON ERROR clause.

❽ Any function in the FROM clause should have an alias, so we used jt as an alias.

To call the JSON_TABLE function on an existing table, add it to the query prior to calling the function. In practice, perform a CROSS JOIN of two tables. The COLUMNS clause also supports nested paths, so you can expand arrays into multiple rows.

The `author` column in the book_authors table contains a list of books in the books array. To expand each row into its own row, use the NESTED PATH clause:

```
mysql> SELECT jt.* FROM book_authors ba,   ❶
    -> JSON_TABLE(ba.author,
    -> '$' COLUMNS (
    -> name VARCHAR(255) PATH '$.name',
    -> lastname VARCHAR(255) PATH '$.lastname',
    -> NESTED PATH '$.books[*]' COLUMNS (  ❷
    -> book VARCHAR(255) PATH '$' )  ❸
    -> )) AS jt;
+-------+----------+-------------------------------------------------------------+
| name  | lastname | book                                                        |
+-------+----------+-------------------------------------------------------------+
| Paul  | DuBois   | Software Portability with imake: Practical Software Engineering |
| Paul  | DuBois   | Mysql: The Definitive Guide to Using, Programming, ↵        |
|       |          | and Administering Mysql 4 (Developer's Library)             |
| Paul  | DuBois   | MySQL Certification Study Guide                             |
| Paul  | DuBois   | MySQL (OTHER NEW RIDERS)                                    |
| Paul  | DuBois   | MySQL Cookbook                                              |
| Paul  | DuBois   | MySQL 5.0 Certification Study Guide                         |
| Paul  | DuBois   | Using csh & tcsh: Type Less, Accomplish More ↵             |
|       |          | (Nutshell Handbooks)                                        |
| Paul  | DuBois   | MySQL (Developer's Library)                                 |
| Alkin | Tezuysal | MySQL Cookbook                                              |
| Sveta | Smirnova | MySQL Troubleshooting                                       |
| Sveta | Smirnova | MySQL Cookbook                                              |
+-------+----------+-------------------------------------------------------------+
11 rows in set (0,01 sec)
```

❶ To use a column in the existing table, put the table name before the `JSON_TABLE` call.

❷ The NESTED PATH clause expands the following path pattern into several columns. In our case, the path is $.books[*] that points to each element of the books array.

❸ Define the nested column as any other column. Note that PATH should be relative to the NESTED PATH.

See Also

For additional information about the `JSON_TABLE` function, see "JSON Table Functions" in the MySQL Reference Manual (*https://oreil.ly/sy4WB*).

19.13 Investigating JSON

Problem

You want to know details about your JSON data structure, such as how deep the value is, how many children a particular element has, and so on.

Solution

Use JSON attribute functions.

Discussion

The `JSON_LENGTH` function returns a number of elements in the JSON document or the path, if specified. For scalars, it is always 1, and for objects and arrays, it is the number of elements. You can use this function to perform such tasks as calculating the number of books written by a particular author:

```
mysql> SELECT CONCAT(author->>'$.name', ' ', author->>'$.lastname') AS 'author',
    -> JSON_LENGTH(author->>'$.books') AS 'Number of Books' FROM book_authors;
+----------------+-----------------+
| author         | Number of Books |
+----------------+-----------------+
| Paul DuBois    |               8 |
| Alkin Tezuysal |               1 |
| Sveta Smirnova |               2 |
+----------------+-----------------+
3 rows in set (0,01 sec)
```

The `JSON_DEPTH` function returns the maximum depth of the JSON document. It returns one for a scalar, empty object, or empty array. For objects and arrays with inner elements, it counts all nested levels. For the `author` column in the `book_authors` table, it returns three:

```
mysql> SELECT JSON_DEPTH(author) FROM book_authors WHERE author->>'$.name' = 'Sveta';
+--------------------+
| JSON_DEPTH(author) |
+--------------------+
|                  3 |
+--------------------+
1 row in set (0,00 sec)
```

To understand why this is, let's examine an example value in detail:

```
{ ❶
  "id": 3,
  "name": "Sveta",
  "work": "Percona", ❷
  "books": [
    "MySQL Troubleshooting", ❸
    "MySQL Cookbook"
  ],
  "lastname": "Smirnova"
}
```

❶ Level one: the object that contains all the elements.

❷ Level two: the object element.

❸ Level three: the element of the nested array.

The JSON_DEPTH function is useful when you need to understand how complex your JSON data is.

The JSON_STORAGE_SIZE function returns the number of bytes that the JSON data takes. It is useful to plan storage use for your data:

```
mysql> SELECT JSON_STORAGE_SIZE(author) FROM book_authors;
+---------------------------+
| JSON_STORAGE_SIZE(author) |
+---------------------------+
|                       475 |
|                       144 |
|                       171 |
+---------------------------+
3 rows in set (0,00 sec)
```

The JSON_TYPE function returns the type of the JSON element. Thus, for the author column in the book_authors table, the types are as shown:

```
mysql> SELECT JSON_TYPE(author), JSON_TYPE(author->'$.id'),
    -> JSON_TYPE(author->'$.name'), JSON_TYPE(author->'$.books')
    -> FROM book_authors WHERE author->>'$.name' = 'Sveta'\G
*************************** 1. row ***************************
          JSON_TYPE(author): OBJECT
  JSON_TYPE(author->'$.id'): INTEGER
JSON_TYPE(author->'$.name'): STRING
JSON_TYPE(author->'$.books'): ARRAY
1 row in set (0,00 sec)
```

Note that we used the -> operator instead of ->> to preserve quotes in scalar values.

19.14 Working with JSON in MySQL as a Document Store

Problem

You want to work with JSON in MySQL in the same way as NoSQL databases do.

Solution

Use X DevAPI. The following clients and connectors support X DevAPI and can work with JSON as a Document Store:

- MySQL Shell in JavaScript and Python mode
- Connector/C++
- Connector/J
- Connector/Node.js

- Connector/NET
- Connector/Python

Discussion

We'll use MySQL Shell for the examples in this recipe. We assume that you are connected to the MySQL server and thus have the default objects available. See Recipe 2.1 for instructions on how to connect to the MySQL server via MySQL Shell.

MySQL Document Store is a collection, stored in a table, defined as follows:

```
CREATE TABLE `MyCollection` (
  `doc` json DEFAULT NULL,
  `_id` varbinary(32) GENERATED ALWAYS AS (json_unquote(
        json_extract(`doc`,_utf8mb4'$._id'))) STORED NOT NULL,
  `_json_schema` json GENERATED ALWAYS AS (_utf8mb4'{"type":"object"}') VIRTUAL,
  PRIMARY KEY (`_id`),
  CONSTRAINT `$val_strict_2190F99D7C6BE98E2C1EFE4E110B46A3D43C9751`
  CHECK (json_schema_valid(`_json_schema`,`doc`)) /*!80016 NOT ENFORCED */
) ENGINE=InnoDB DEFAULT CHARSET=utf8mb4 COLLATE=utf8mb4_0900_ai_ci;
```

where doc is a JSON column, storing the document. _id is a unique identifier, generated by extracting the value of the _id member, and the optional _json_schema is a schema that you can enforce when creating a collection. See Recipe 2.9 for the details and an example.

X DevAPI will create such a table when you call the createCollection method:

```
MySQL  cookbook  JS > session.getDefaultSchema().createCollection('MyCollection')
<Collection:MyCollection>
```

> We use syntax that MySQL Shell in JavaScript mode understands for examples in this recipe. Syntax for different languages differs slightly. Refer to your implementation documentation for details.

Once the collection is created, you can insert documents into it and update, remove, and search them.

It is handy to store a collection object in a variable:

```
MySQL  cookbook  JS > MyCollection = session.getDefaultSchema().
                  -> getCollection('MyCollection')
<Collection:MyCollection>
```

The Collection class in X DevAPI supports four basic CRUD (Create, Read, Update, Delete) operations:

- add

- find

- modify

- remove

We already showed them in action when we discussed MySQL Shell in Recipes 2.9 and 2.10. In this recipe, we'll cover details we didn't cover there.

Adding documents to the collection

To add documents into the collection, use the `add` method, which accepts either a JSON object or an array of JSON objects, or a `mysqlx.expr` as an argument. The following code snippet demonstrates all three flavors of the syntax:

```
MySQL  cookbook  JS > MyCollection.add({"document": "one"}).
                  -> add([{"document": "two"}, {"document": "three"}]).
                  -> add(mysqlx.expr('{"document": "four"}'))
                  ->
Query OK, 4 items affected (0.0083 sec)

Records: 4  Duplicates: 0  Warnings: 0
```

Searching for documents

To search for documents, use the `find` method. If called without arguments, it will return a list of all documents in the collection:

```
MySQL  cookbook  JS > MyCollection.find()
{
    "_id": "000060d5ab750000000000000012",
    "document": "one"
}
{
    "_id": "000060d5ab750000000000000013",
    "document": "two"
}
{
    "_id": "000060d5ab750000000000000014",
    "document": "three"
}
{
    "_id": "000060d5ab750000000000000015",
    "document": "four"
}
4 documents in set (0.0007 sec)
```

Each of the documents contains an automatically generated `_id` that is also a primary key for the collection.

The `find` method narrows a result set by using search conditions, limiting the number of the documents, and grouping, sorting, and modifying the resulting values.

These are basic methods, available to modify the result of any SQL SELECT operation. However, it is not possible to join two collections like you can do with SQL tables.

To search for a particular document, pass a condition as an argument of the find method. You can use the LIKE operator and others to perform creative comparisons:

```
MySQL  cookbook  JS > MyCollection.find("document LIKE 't%'")
{
    "_id": "000060d5ab750000000000000013",
    "document": "two"
}
{
    "_id": "000060d5ab750000000000000014",
    "document": "three"
}
2 documents in set (0.0009 sec)
```

To modify the result, pass the expression to the fields method:

```
MySQL  cookbook  JS > MyCollection.find("document LIKE 't%').
                   -> fields(mysqlx.expr('{"Document": upper(document)}'))
                   ->
{
    "Document": "TWO"
}
{
    "Document": "THREE"
}
2 documents in set (0.0009 sec)
```

To group documents, use the groupBy method, and narrow the result with the having method. To illustrate how they work, we'll use the CollectionLimbs collection:

```
MySQL  cookbook  JS > limbs = session.getDefaultSchema().getCollection('CollectionLimbs')
<Collection:CollectionLimbs>

MySQL  cookbook  JS > limbs.find().fields('arms', 'COUNT(thing)').groupBy('arms')
{
    "arms": 2,
    "COUNT(thing)": 3
}
{
    "arms": 0,
    "COUNT(thing)": 5
}
{
    "arms": 10,
    "COUNT(thing)": 1
}
{
    "arms": 1,
    "COUNT(thing)": 1
}
{
    "arms": null,
    "COUNT(thing)": 1
}
5 documents in set (0.0010 sec)
```

The preceding code prints the number of things with a specific number of arms. To limit this list to only things that have both arms and legs, we can use the having method:

```
MySQL cookbook JS > limbs.find().fields('arms', 'COUNT(thing)').
                 -> groupBy('arms').having('MIN(legs) > 0')
{
    "arms": 2,
    "COUNT(thing)": 3
}
1 document in set (0.0006 sec)
```

To print the three things with the highest number of legs, use the sort method with the keywords DESC and limit:

```
MySQL cookbook JS > limbs.find().sort('legs DESC').limit(3)
{
    "_id": "000060d5ab750000000000000001a",
    "arms": 0,
    "legs": 99,
    "thing": "centipede"
}
{
    "_id": "000060d5ab7500000000000000017",
    "arms": 0,
    "legs": 6,
    "thing": "insect"
}
{
    "_id": "000060d5ab750000000000000001b",
    "arms": 0,
    "legs": 4,
    "thing": "table"
}
3 documents in set (0.0006 sec)
```

You may also bind values if you pass the parameter name after a colon sign in the find method and pass values in the bind method. You may bind as many arguments as you want:

```
MySQL cookbook JS > limbs.find('legs = :legs').bind('legs', 4)
{
    "_id": "000060d5ab750000000000000001b",
    "arms": 0,
    "legs": 4,
    "thing": "table"
}
{
    "_id": "000060d5ab750000000000000001c",
    "arms": 2,
    "legs": 4,
    "thing": "armchair"
}
2 documents in set (0.0008 sec)

MySQL cookbook JS > limbs.find('legs = :legs and arms = :arms').
                 -> bind('legs', 4).bind('arms', 2)
{
```

```
    "_id": "000060d5ab750000000000000001c",
    "arms": 2,
    "legs": 4,
    "thing": "armchair"
}
1 document in set (0.0005 sec)
```

Modifying documents

To modify documents in the collection, use the modify method. It accepts a search condition and allows you to bind parameters similarly to the find method. To modify found elements, use the set and unset methods to set or unset values of the object member. Use the arrayInsert, arrayAppend, and arrayDelete methods to modify arrays, and use the patch method to merge JSON documents.

In our examples, we'll use the MyCollection collection:

```
 MySQL  cookbook  JS > MyCollection.find('document = "one"') ❶
{
    "_id": "000060d5ab750000000000000012",
    "document": "one"
}
1 document in set (0.0005 sec)
 MySQL  cookbook  JS > MyCollection.modify('document = "one"').
                   -> set('array', [2, 3, 4])❷
Query OK, 1 item affected (0.0054 sec)

Rows matched: 1  Changed: 1  Warnings: 0
 MySQL  cookbook  JS > MyCollection.find('document = "one"')
{
    "_id": "000060d5ab750000000000000012",
    "array": [
        2,
        3,
        4
    ],
    "document": "one"
}
1 document in set (0.0005 sec)
 MySQL  cookbook  JS > MyCollection.modify('document = "one"').arrayAppend('array', 5)❸
Query OK, 1 item affected (0.0073 sec)

Rows matched: 1  Changed: 1  Warnings: 0
 MySQL  cookbook  JS > MyCollection.find('document = "one"')
{
    "_id": "000060d5ab750000000000000012",
    "array": [
        2,
        3,
        4,
        5
    ],
    "document": "one"
}
1 document in set (0.0007 sec)
 MySQL  cookbook  JS > MyCollection.modify('document = "one"').
```

```
                        -> arrayInsert('array[0]', 1)❹
 Query OK, 1 item affected (0.0072 sec)

 Rows matched: 1  Changed: 1  Warnings: 0
  MySQL  cookbook  JS > MyCollection.find('document = "one"')
 {
     "_id": "000060d5ab750000000000000012",
     "array": [
         1,
         2,
         3,
         4,
         5
     ],
     "document": "one"
 }
 1 document in set (0.0008 sec)
  MySQL  cookbook  JS > MyCollection.modify('document = "one"').arrayDelete('array[2]')❺
 Query OK, 1 item affected (0.0059 sec)

 Rows matched: 1  Changed: 1  Warnings: 0
  MySQL  cookbook  JS > MyCollection.find('document = "one"')
 {
     "_id": "000060d5ab750000000000000012",
     "array": [
         1,
         2,
         4,
         5
     ],
     "document": "one"
 }
 1 document in set (0.0009 sec)
  MySQL  cookbook  JS > MyCollection.modify('document = "one"').unset('array')❻
 Query OK, 1 item affected (0.0080 sec)

 Rows matched: 1  Changed: 1  Warnings: 0
  MySQL  cookbook  JS > MyCollection.find('document = "one"')
 {
     "_id": "000060d5ab750000000000000012",
     "document": "one"
 }
 1 document in set (0.0007 sec)

  MySQL  cookbook  JS > MyCollection.modify('document = "one"').
                        -> patch({'number': 42, 'array': [1,2,3]}).
                        -> patch({'array': [4,5]})❼
 Query OK, 1 item affected (0.0063 sec)

 Rows matched: 1  Changed: 1  Warnings: 0
  MySQL  cookbook  JS > MyCollection.find('document = "one"')
 {
     "_id": "000060d5ab750000000000000012",
     "array": [
         4,
         5
     ],
     "number": 42,
     "document": "one"
```

```
}
1 document in set (0.0007 sec)
```

❶ We'll experiment with this document from the collection.

❷ The `set` method adds or changes an element in the object.

❸ The `arrayAppend` method adds a new element to the end of the array.

❹ For the `arrayInsert` method, you can specify the position in the array where you want to add the new element.

❺ The `arrayDelete` method removes an element from the specified position.

❻ The `unset` method removes an element from the object.

❼ The `patch` method works similarly to the JSON function `JSON_MERGE_PATCH`. In our case, it first added two elements, `number` and `array`, to the original document, then replaced the content of the `array` element with the content of the element with the same name in the object, passed as a parameter to the second invocation of the `patch` method.

Removing documents and collections

To remove documents, use the `remove` method:

```
MyCollection.remove('document = :number').bind('number', 'one')
```

To drop a collection, use the `dropCollection` method in your API:

```
session.getSchema('cookbook').dropCollection('MyCollection')
```

See Also

For additional information about X DevAPI, see the X DevAPI Reference Manual (*https://oreil.ly/OJM8Z*).

CHAPTER 20
Performing Transactions

20.0 Introduction

The MySQL server can handle multiple clients at the same time because it is multi-threaded. To deal with contention among clients, the server performs any necessary locking so that two clients cannot modify the same data at once. However, as the server executes SQL statements, it's very possible that successive statements received from a given client will be interleaved with statements from other clients. If a client executes multiple statements that are dependent on one another, the fact that other clients may be updating tables in between those statements can cause difficulties.

Statement failures can be problematic, too, if a multiple-statement operation does not run to completion. Suppose that a `flight` table contains information about airline flight schedules, and you want to update the row for Flight 578 by choosing a pilot from among those available. You might do so using three statements as follows:

```
SET @p_val = (SELECT pilot_id FROM pilot WHERE available = 'yes' LIMIT 1);
UPDATE pilot SET available = 'no' WHERE pilot_id = @p_val;
UPDATE flight SET pilot_id = @p_val WHERE flight_id = 578;
```

The first statement chooses an available pilot, the second marks the pilot as unavailable, and the third assigns the pilot to the flight. That's straightforward enough in principle, but in practice there are significant difficulties:

Concurrency issues
> If two clients want to schedule pilots, it's possible for both to run the initial `SELECT` query and retrieve the same pilot ID number before either has a chance to set the pilot's status to unavailable. If that happens, the same pilot is scheduled for two flights at once.

Integrity issues

> All three statements must execute successfully as a unit. For example, if the SELECT and the first UPDATE run successfully, but the second UPDATE fails, the pilot's status is set to unavailable without the pilot being assigned a flight. The database becomes inconsistent.

To prevent concurrency and integrity problems in these types of situations, transactions are helpful. A transaction groups a set of statements and guarantees the following properties:

- No other client can update the data used in the transaction while the transaction is in progress; it's as though you have the server all to yourself. For example, other clients cannot modify the pilot or flight records while you're booking a pilot for a flight. Transactions solve concurrency problems arising from the multiple-client nature of the MySQL server. In effect, transactions serialize access to a shared resource across multiple-statement operations.

- Statements grouped within a transaction are committed (take effect) as a unit, but only if they all succeed. If an error occurs, any actions that occurred prior to the error are rolled back, leaving the relevant tables unaffected as though none of the statements had been executed. This keeps the database from becoming inconsistent. For example, if an update to the flights table fails, rollback causes the change to the pilots table to be undone, leaving the pilot still available. Rollback frees you from having to figure out how to undo a partially completed operation yourself.

This chapter shows the syntax for the SQL statements that begin and end transactions. It also describes how to implement transactional operations from within programs, using error detection to determine whether to commit or roll back.

Scripts related to the examples shown here are located in the *transactions* directory of the recipes distribution.

20.1 Choosing a Transactional Storage Engine

Problem

You want to use transactions.

Solution

To use transactions, you must use a transaction-safe engine. Check your MySQL server to determine which transactional storage engines it supports.

Discussion

MySQL supports several storage engines. Currently, the transactional engines, shipped with the standard distribution, include InnoDB and NDB. To see which your MySQL server supports, use this statement:

```
mysql> SELECT ENGINE FROM INFORMATION_SCHEMA.ENGINES
    -> WHERE SUPPORT IN ('YES','DEFAULT') AND TRANSACTIONS='YES';
+--------+
| ENGINE |
+--------+
| InnoDB |
+--------+
```

If MySQL Cluster is enabled, you'll also see a line that says ndbcluster.

Transactional engines are those that have a TRANSACTIONS value of YES; those actually usable have a SUPPORT value of YES or DEFAULT.

After determining which transactional storage engines are available, to create a table that uses a given engine, add an ENGINE = *tbl_engine* clause to your CREATE TABLE statement:

```
CREATE TABLE t (i INT) ENGINE = InnoDB;
```

If you need to modify an existing application to perform transactions, but it uses nontransactional tables, you can alter the tables to use a transactional storage engine. For example, MyISAM tables are nontransactional, and trying to use them for transactions will yield incorrect results because they do not support rollback. In this case, you can use ALTER TABLE to convert the tables to a transactional type. Suppose that t is a MyISAM table. To make it an InnoDB table, do this:

```
ALTER TABLE t ENGINE = InnoDB;
```

One thing to consider before altering a table is that changing it to use a transactional storage engine may affect its behavior in other ways. For example, the MyISAM engine provides more flexible handling of AUTO_INCREMENT columns than do other storage engines. If you rely on MyISAM-only sequence features, changing the storage engine will cause problems.

20.2 Performing Transactions Using SQL

Problem

A set of statements must succeed or fail as a unit—that is, you require a transaction.

Solution

Manipulate MySQL's auto-commit mode to enable multiple-statement transactions, and then commit or roll back the statements depending on whether they succeed or fail.

Discussion

This recipe describes the SQL statements that control transactional behavior in MySQL. The immediately following recipes discuss how to perform transactions from within programs. Some APIs require that you implement transactions by executing the SQL statements discussed in this recipe; others provide a special mechanism that enables transaction management without writing SQL directly. However, even in the latter case, the API mechanism maps program operations onto transactional SQL statements, so reading this recipe will give you a better understanding of what the API does on your behalf.

MySQL normally operates in auto-commit mode, which commits the effect of each statement as soon as it executes. (In effect, each statement is its own transaction.) To perform a transaction, you must disable auto-commit mode, execute the statements that make up the transaction, and then either commit or roll back your changes. In MySQL, you can do this two ways:

- Execute a START TRANSACTION (or BEGIN) statement to suspend auto-commit mode, then execute the statements that make up the transaction. If the statements succeed, record their effect in the database and terminate the transaction by executing a COMMIT statement:

```
mysql> CREATE TABLE t (i INT) ENGINE = InnoDB;
mysql> START TRANSACTION;
mysql> INSERT INTO t (i) VALUES(1);
mysql> INSERT INTO t (i) VALUES(2);
mysql> COMMIT;
mysql> SELECT * FROM t;
+------+
| i    |
+------+
|    1 |
|    2 |
+------+
```

If an error occurs, don't use COMMIT. Instead, cancel the transaction by executing a ROLLBACK statement. In the following example, t remains empty after the transaction because the effects of the INSERT statements are rolled back:

```
mysql> CREATE TABLE t (i INT) ENGINE = InnoDB;
mysql> START TRANSACTION;
mysql> INSERT INTO t (i) VALUES(1);
mysql> INSERT INTO t (x) VALUES(2);
ERROR 1054 (42S22): Unknown column 'x' in 'field list'
mysql> ROLLBACK;
```

```
mysql> SELECT * FROM t;
Empty set (0.00 sec)
```

- Another way to group statements is to turn off auto-commit mode explicitly by setting the autocommit session variable to 0. After that, each statement you execute becomes part of the current transaction. To end the transaction and begin the next one, execute a COMMIT or ROLLBACK statement:

```
mysql> CREATE TABLE t (i INT) ENGINE = InnoDB;
mysql> SET autocommit = 0;
mysql> INSERT INTO t (i) VALUES(1);
mysql> INSERT INTO t (i) VALUES(2);
mysql> COMMIT;
mysql> SELECT * FROM t;
+------+
| i    |
+------+
|    1 |
|    2 |
+------+
```

To turn auto-commit mode back on, use this statement:

```
mysql> SET autocommit = 1;
```

Transactions have their limits because not all statements can be part of a transaction. For example, if you execute a DROP DATABASE statement, don't expect to restore the database by executing a ROLLBACK.

20.3 Performing Transactions from Within Programs

Problem

You're writing a program that must implement transactional operations.

Solution

Use the transaction abstraction provided by your language API, if it has such a thing. If it doesn't, use the API's usual statement-execution mechanism to execute the transactional SQL statements directly.

Discussion

To perform transactional processing from within a program, use your API language to detect errors and take appropriate action. This recipe provides general background on doing this. The next recipes provide language-specific details for the MySQL APIs for Perl, Ruby, PHP, Python, Go, and Java.

Every MySQL API supports transactions, even if only in the sense that you can explicitly execute transaction-related SQL statements such as START TRANSACTION and COMMIT. However, some APIs also provide a transaction abstraction that enables control over transactional behavior without working directly with SQL. That approach hides the details and provides better portability to other database engines that have different underlying transaction SQL syntax. An API abstraction is available for each language that we use in this book.

The next few recipes each implement the same example to illustrate how to perform program-based transactions. They use a money table containing the following initial rows that show how much money two people have:

```
+------+------+
| name | amt  |
+------+------+
| Eve  |   10 |
| Ida  |    0 |
+------+------+
```

The sample transaction is a simple financial transfer that uses two UPDATE statements to give six dollars of Eve's money to Ida:

```
UPDATE money SET amt = amt - 6 WHERE name = 'Eve';
UPDATE money SET amt = amt + 6 WHERE name = 'Ida';
```

The intended result is that the table should look like this:

```
+------+------+
| name | amt  |
+------+------+
| Eve  |    4 |
| Ida  |    6 |
+------+------+
```

It's necessary to execute both statements within a transaction to ensure that both of them take effect at once. Without a transaction, Eve's money disappears without being credited to Ida if the second statement fails. By using a transaction, the table is left unchanged if statement failure occurs.

The sample programs for each language are located in the *transactions* directory of the recipes distribution. If you compare them, you'll see that they all employ a similar framework for performing transactional processing:

- The transaction statements are grouped within a control structure, along with a commit operation.
- If the status of the control structure indicates that it did not execute successfully to completion, the transaction is rolled back.

That logic can be expressed as follows, where block represents the control structure used to group statements:

```
block:
  statement 1
  statement 2
  ...
  statement n
  commit
if the block failed:
  roll back
```

If the statements in the block succeed, you reach the end of the block and perform a commit. Otherwise, occurrence of an error raises an exception that triggers execution of the error-handling code where you roll back the transaction.

The benefit of structuring your code as just described is that it minimizes the number of tests needed to determine whether to roll back. The alternative—checking the result of each statement within the transaction and rolling back on individual statement errors—quickly turns your code into an unreadable mess.

A subtle point to be aware of when rolling back within languages that raise exceptions is that it may be possible for the rollback itself to fail, causing another exception to be raised. If you don't deal with that, your program itself may terminate. To handle this, execute the rollback within another block that has an empty exception handler. The sample programs do this as necessary.

Those sample programs that disable auto-commit mode explicitly when performing a transaction enable auto-commit afterward. In applications that perform all database processing in transactional fashion, it's unnecessary to do this. Just disable auto-commit mode once after you connect to the database server, and leave it off.

Checking How API Transaction Abstractions Map onto SQL Statements

For APIs that provide a transaction abstraction, you can see how the interface maps onto the underlying SQL statements: enable the general query log for your MySQL server, then watch the log to see what statements the API executes when you run a transactional program. For instructions on enabling the log, see Recipe 22.3.

20.4 Performing Transactions in Perl Programs

Problem

You want to perform a transaction in a Perl DBI script.

Solution

Use the standard DBI transaction support mechanism.

Discussion

The Perl DBI transaction mechanism is based on explicit manipulation of auto-commit mode:

1. Turn on the `RaiseError` attribute if it's not enabled, and disable `PrintError` if it's on. You want errors to raise exceptions without printing anything, and leaving `PrintError` enabled can interfere with failure detection in some cases.

2. Disable the `AutoCommit` attribute so that a commit will be done only when you say so.

3. Execute the statements that make up the transaction within an `eval` block so that errors raise an exception and terminate the block. The last thing in the block should be a call to `commit()`, which commits the transaction if all its statements completed successfully.

4. After the `eval` executes, check the `$@` variable. If `$@` contains the empty string, the transaction succeeded. Otherwise, the `eval` will have failed due to the occurrence of some error, and `$@` will contain an error message. Invoke `rollback()` to cancel the transaction. To display an error message, print `$@` before calling `rollback()`.

5. If desired, restore the original values of the `RaiseError` and `PrintError` attributes.

Because it can be messy to change and restore the error-handling and auto-commit attributes if an application performs multiple transactions, let's put the code to begin and end a transaction into convenience functions that handle the processing that occurs before and after the `eval`:

```
sub transaction_init
{
my $dbh = shift;
my $attr_ref = {};  # create hash in which to save attributes

  $attr_ref->{RaiseError} = $dbh->{RaiseError};
  $attr_ref->{PrintError} = $dbh->{PrintError};
  $attr_ref->{AutoCommit} = $dbh->{AutoCommit};
  $dbh->{RaiseError} = 1; # raise exception if an error occurs
  $dbh->{PrintError} = 0; # don't print an error message
  $dbh->{AutoCommit} = 0; # disable auto-commit
  return $attr_ref;       # return attributes to caller
}

sub transaction_finish
{
my ($dbh, $attr_ref, $error) = @_;

  if ($error) # an error occurred
  {
    print "Transaction failed, rolling back. Error was:\n$error\n";
    # roll back within eval to prevent rollback
```

```
    # failure from terminating the script
    eval { $dbh->rollback (); };
  }
  # restore error-handling and auto-commit attributes
  $dbh->{AutoCommit} = $attr_ref->{AutoCommit};
  $dbh->{PrintError} = $attr_ref->{PrintError};
  $dbh->{RaiseError} = $attr_ref->{RaiseError};
}
```

By using those two functions, our sample transaction can be performed easily as follows:

```
$ref = transaction_init ($dbh);
eval
{
  # move some money from one person to the other
  $dbh->do ("UPDATE money SET amt = amt - 6 WHERE name = 'Eve'");
  $dbh->do ("UPDATE money SET amt = amt + 6 WHERE name = 'Ida'");
  # all statements succeeded; commit transaction
  $dbh->commit ();
};
transaction_finish ($dbh, $ref, $@);
```

In Perl DBI, an alternative to manipulating the AutoCommit attribute manually is to begin a transaction by invoking begin_work(). This method disables AutoCommit and causes it to be enabled again automatically when you invoke commit() or rollback() later.

20.5 Performing Transactions in Ruby Programs

Problem

You want to perform a transaction in a Ruby Mysql2 script.

Solution

Send transaction management statements, such as START TRANSACTIONS, BEGIN, COMMIT, and ROLLBACK, as regular queries.

Discussion

The Ruby Mysql2 module does not have built-in functions for the transaction support. Instead, it expects its users to run transaction management statements as regular queries.

To start transaction, execute client.query("START TRANSACTION"), then execute required updates, and finish the block with client.query("COMMIT").

Put your transaction into a begin...rescue block, so you can call ROLLBACK if something goes wrong:

```
begin
  client.query("START TRANSACTION")
  client.query("UPDATE money SET amt = amt - 6 WHERE name = 'Eve'")
  client.query("UPDATE money SET amt = amt + 6 WHERE name = 'Ida'")
  client.query("COMMIT")
rescue Mysql2::Error => e
  puts "Transaction failed, rolling back. Error was:"
  puts "#{e.errno}: #{e.message}"
  begin           # empty exception handler in case rollback fails
    client.query("ROLLBACK")
  rescue
  end
end
```

20.6 Performing Transactions in PHP Programs

Problem

You want to perform a transaction in a PHP script.

Solution

Use the standard PDO transaction support mechanism.

Discussion

The PDO extension supports a transaction abstraction that can be used to perform transactions. To begin a transaction, use the beginTransaction() method. Then, after executing your statements, invoke either commit() or rollback() to commit or roll back the transaction. The following code illustrates this. It uses exceptions to detect transaction failure, so it assumes that exceptions are enabled for PDO errors:

```
try
{
  $dbh->beginTransaction ();
  $dbh->exec ("UPDATE money SET amt = amt - 6 WHERE name = 'Eve'");
  $dbh->exec ("UPDATE money SET amt = amt + 6 WHERE name = 'Ida'");
  $dbh->commit ();
}
catch (Exception $e)
{
  print ("Transaction failed, rolling back. Error was:\n");
  print ($e->getMessage () . "\n");
  # empty exception handler in case rollback fails
  try
  {
    $dbh->rollback ();
  }
  catch (Exception $e2) { }
}
```

20.7 Performing Transactions in Python Programs

Problem

You want to perform a transaction in a Python DB API script.

Solution

Use the standard DB API transaction support mechanism.

Discussion

The Python DB API abstraction provides transaction processing control through connection object methods. The DB API specification indicates that database connections should begin with auto-commit mode disabled. Therefore, when you open a connection to the database server, Connector/Python disables auto-commit mode, which implicitly begins a transaction. End each transaction with either `commit()` or `rollback()`. The `commit()` call occurs within a `try` statement, and the `rollback()` occurs within the `except` clause to cancel the transaction if an error occurs:

```
try:
  cursor = conn.cursor()
  # move some money from one person to the other
  cursor.execute("UPDATE money SET amt = amt - 6 WHERE name = 'Eve'")
  cursor.execute("UPDATE money SET amt = amt + 6 WHERE name = 'Ida'")
  cursor.close()
  conn.commit()
except mysql.connector.Error as e:
  print("Transaction failed, rolling back. Error was:")
  print(e)
  try:  # empty exception handler in case rollback fails
    conn.rollback()
  except:
    pass
```

20.8 Performing Transactions in Go Programs

Problem

You want to perform a transaction in a Go program.

Solution

Use the standard transaction support mechanism, provided by the `database/sql` package.

Discussion

The Go `sql` interface supports a transaction abstraction that could be used to perform transactions. To begin a transaction, use the `DB.Begin()` function. Then, after executing your statements, invoke either `Tx.Commit()` or `Tx.Rollback()` to commit or roll back the transaction. The following code illustrates this.

```
var queries = []string{
  "UPDATE money SET amt = amt - 6 WHERE name = 'Eve'",
  "UPDATE money SET amt = amt + 6 WHERE name = 'Ida'",
}

tx, err := db.Begin()
if err != nil {
  log.Fatal(err)
}

for _, query := range queries {
  _, err := tx.Exec(query)
  if err != nil {
    fmt.Printf("Transaction failed, rolling back.\nError was: %s\n",
              err.Error())
    if txerr := tx.Rollback(); txerr != nil {
      fmt.Println("Rollback failed")
      log.Fatal(txerr)
    }
  }
}

if err := tx.Commit(); err != nil {
  log.Fatal(err)
}
```

20.9 Using Context-Aware Functions to Handle Transactions in Go

Problem

You want to roll back transactions automatically in your Go program.

Solution

The Go-MySQL-Driver supports context cancellation. This means that you can cancel database operations, such as running a query, if you cancel the context.

Discussion

To use the package context (*https://pkg.go.dev/context*) with SQL, you need to create the object of the `Context` type first, then pass it to the database function. Function names of the `sql` interface that support context are similar to ones that do not,

---

but have the prefix Context. For example, the Query() function does not support Context, whereas the QueryContext() function does.

The following example uses Context to handle database transactions. You will find code for it in the *transaction_context.go* file in the *transactions* directory of the recipes distribution:

```
// transaction_context.go: simple transaction demonstration
//                         with use of Context

// By default, this creates an InnoDB table.  If you specify a storage
// engine on the command line, that will be used instead.  Normally,
// this should be a transaction-safe engine that is supported by your
// server.  However, you can pass a nontransactional storage engine
// to verify that rollback doesn't work properly for such engines.

// The script uses a table named "money" and drops it if necessary.
// Change the name if you have a valuable table with that name. :-)
package main

import (
  "log"
  "fmt"
  "flag"
  "context" ❶
  "database/sql"
  "github.com/svetasmirnova/mysqlcookbook/recipes/lib"
)

func initTable(ctx context.Context, db *sql.DB, tblEngine string) (error) { ❷
  queries := [4]string {
    "DROP TABLE IF EXISTS money",
    "CREATE TABLE money (name CHAR(5), amt INT, PRIMARY KEY(name)) ENGINE = " + tblEngine,
    "INSERT INTO money (name, amt) VALUES('Eve', 10)",
    "INSERT INTO money (name, amt) VALUES('Ida', 0)",
  }

  for _, query := range queries {
    _, err = db.ExecContext(ctx, query) ❸
    if err != nil {
      fmt.Println("Cannot initialize test table")
      fmt.Printf("Error: %s\n", err.Error())
      return err
    }
  }

  return nil
}

func displayTable(ctx context.Context, db *sql.DB) (error) {
  rows, err := db.QueryContext(ctx, "SELECT name, amt FROM money") ❹
  if err != nil {
    return err
  }
  defer rows.Close()

  for rows.Next() {
```

```go
  var (
    name string
    amt  int32
  )
  if err := rows.Scan(&name, &amt); err != nil {
    fmt.Println("Cannot display contents of test table")
    fmt.Printf("Error: %s\n", err.Error())
    return err
  }

  fmt.Printf("%s has $%d\n", name, amt)
}

  return nil
}

func runTransaction(ctx context.Context,
                    db *sql.DB, queries []string) (error) {
  tx, err := db.BeginTx(ctx, nil) ❺
  if err != nil {
    return err
  }

  for _, query := range queries {
    _, err := tx.ExecContext(ctx, query) ❻
    if err != nil {
      fmt.Printf("Transaction failed, rolling back.\nError was: %s\n",
                 err.Error())
      if txerr := tx.Rollback(); err != nil {
        return txerr
      }
      return err
    }
  }

  if err := tx.Commit(); err != nil {
    return err
  }

  return nil
}

func main() {
  db, err := cookbook.Connect()
  if err != nil {
    log.Fatal(err)
  }
  defer db.Close()

  var tblEngine string = "InnoDB"
  flag.Parse()
  values := flag.Args()
  if len(values) > 0 {
    tblEngine = values[0]
  }
  fmt.Printf("Using storage engine %s to test transactions\n", tblEngine)

  ctx, cancel := context.WithCancel(context.Background()) ❼
  defer cancel()
```

```
    fmt.Println("----------")
    fmt.Println("This transaction should succeed.")
    fmt.Println("Table contents before transaction:")

    if err := initTable(ctx, db, tblEngine); err != nil {
      log.Fatal(err)
    }

    if err = displayTable(ctx, db); err != nil {
      log.Fatal(err)
    }

    var trx = []string{
      "UPDATE money SET amt = amt - 6 WHERE name = 'Eve'",
      "UPDATE money SET amt = amt + 6 WHERE name = 'Ida'",
    }

    if err = runTransaction(ctx, db, trx); err != nil {
      log.Fatal(err)
    }

    fmt.Println("Table contents after transaction:")
    if err = displayTable(ctx, db); err != nil {
      log.Fatal(err)
    }

    fmt.Println("----------")
    fmt.Println("This transaction should fail.")
    fmt.Println("Table contents before transaction:")

    if err := initTable(ctx, db, tblEngine); err != nil {
      log.Fatal(err)
    }

    if err = displayTable(ctx, db); err != nil {
      log.Fatal(err)
    }

    trx = []string{
      "UPDATE money SET amt = amt - 6 WHERE name = 'Eve'",
      "UPDATE money SET xamt = amt + 6 WHERE name = 'Ida'",
    }

    if err = runTransaction(ctx, db, trx); err != nil {
      log.Fatal(err)
    }

    fmt.Println("Table contents after transaction:")
    if err = displayTable(ctx, db); err != nil {
      log.Fatal(err)
    }
  }
}
```

❶ Import statement for the context support.

❷ Our user-defined functions take context.Context as a parameter.

---

③ To execute statements that do not return a result set, use the context-aware function `ExecContext()`.

④ To execute queries that do return a result set, use the context-aware function `QueryContext()`.

⑤ To start a transaction that will automatically roll back if context is canceled, use the context-aware function `BeginTx()`.

⑥ To execute a statement that could be canceled inside the transaction, use the context-aware function `Tx.ExecContext()`.

⑦ Before using context, you need to create it. In our example, we created a cancellable context. The `context.WithCancel()` function takes parent context as a parameter and returns just-created context, and a `cancel()` function. We deferred its call to the end of the `main()` function execution. You have options to call the `cancel()` function in any appropriate place in the code. You may prefer to use `context.WithDeadline()` or `context.WithTimeout()`, so your SQL execution code will be canceled if runs longer than a certain amount of time.

20.10 Performing Transactions in Java Programs

Problem

You want to perform a transaction in a JDBC application.

Solution

Use the standard JDBC transaction support mechanism.

Discussion

To perform transactions in Java, use your `Connection` object to turn off auto-commit mode. Then, after executing your statements, use the object's `commit()` method to commit the transaction or `rollback()` to cancel it. Typically, you execute the statements for the transaction in a `try` block, with `commit()` at the end of the block. To handle failures, invoke `rollback()` in the corresponding exception handler:

```
try
{
  conn.setAutoCommit (false);
  Statement s = conn.createStatement ();
  // move some money from one person to the other
  s.executeUpdate ("UPDATE money SET amt = amt - 6 WHERE name = 'Eve'");
  s.executeUpdate ("UPDATE money SET amt = amt + 6 WHERE name = 'Ida'");
```

```
    s.close ();
    conn.commit ();
    conn.setAutoCommit (true);
}
catch (SQLException e)
{
  System.err.println ("Transaction failed, rolling back. Error was:");
  Cookbook.printErrorMessage (e);
  // empty exception handler in case rollback fails
  try
  {
    conn.rollback ();
    conn.setAutoCommit (true);
  }
  catch (Exception e2) { }
}
```

## CHAPTER 21

Query Performance

21.0 Introduction

Indexes are utilized to find rows quickly if they are created and used as intended. Here are the main reasons to use indexes:

- Utilize a WHERE clause in a SELECT statement to efficiently find rows.
- Find the best query execution plan by the index's uniqueness of values stored in a given column, known as *cardinality*, and the least number of rows returned.
- Enable the join operations between different tables.

Indexes are vital to efficiently scanning and searching for values in tables. Without them, MySQL would need to read all of the rows in a given table when performing a query. Due to different table sizes, MySQL has to bring all the data read from the table to memory, and it can sort, filter, and return values only of the selected data. This operation may require additional resources to copy data to a new temporary table to perform sort operations. Indexes are crucial to query performance; hence, nonindexed tables are a considerable overhead to a database unless they are small reference tables.

For fast query performance, a primary key for each table representing one or more columns is required. While using the InnoDB storage engine, the table's data is physically ordered to do fast lookups and sorts using primary key columns. The ideal table design uses a covering index where the query results are computed using index columns. Most of the indexes used by MySQL are stored in B-trees, which allow fast data access due to reduced data access time.

If the table is big in data size and does not have any keys, creating an extra field like table_name_id as a primary key can bring a considerable benefit in setting unique pointers doing join operations. InnoDB tables always have a clustered index representing a primary key, if not already created by a user. A clustered index is a table where the data and the rows are stored in the table's order on the key values in one direction.

 If no WHERE clause is used in a query, it's a full table scan for MySQL optimizer. For example:

```
SELECT * FROM customer;
```

This does not change whether the index exists or not for the cus tomer table.

The following are some key terms you'll need to know before getting started with index strategies:

Table scan

A table scan reads all rows in the given table while performing a query. A developer should avoid full table scans as much as possible, including doing COUNT(*) operations.

Tree traversal

Tree traversal is a method that indexes use to access data in hops. The goal of the index is to make minimum hops via traversal to fetch data. The fewer the number of leaf nodes, the faster the index traversal.

Leaf nodes

Leaf nodes are part of the B-tree index structure. They maintain the changes in the index as data changes and establish a doubly linked list to connect index leaf nodes.

B-tree structure

B-tree is a self-balancing tree data structure that keeps data sorted and allows searches, sequential access, insertions, and deletions in logarithmic time. The B-tree is a generalization of a binary search tree in that a node can have more than two children.

While the B-tree index is commonly used among MySQL storage engines, different kinds of data structures are used for hash indexes. Hash indexes have different characteristics and their own use cases. Consult "Comparison of B-Tree and Hash Indexes" (*https://oreil.ly/1uHLc*) in the MySQL Reference Manual for further details.

While indexes help you retrieve rows faster, over-creating or keeping unused indexes is a burden to the database's I/O operation. Every index leaf page (the lowest level of the index where all of the keys for the index appear in sorted order) must be maintained for all UPDATE/INSERT/DELETE operations, hence creating extra overhead.

21.1 Creating Indexes

Problem

Your query is very slow to respond.

Solution

Create an index on your column to retrieve just the rows you are seeking.

Discussion

Tables without indexes are just logbook data written randomly with no reference to look up. As a result, most of the queries to such tables are slow. The exception applies only to reference tables with a limited number of rows depending on schema design.

MySQL recommends giving each table a primary key column with NOT NULL characteristic for each row.

We have a table called top_names from Names_2010Census.csv data:

```
mysql> CREATE TABLE `top_names` (
  `top_name` varchar(25) DEFAULT NULL,
  `name_rank` smallint DEFAULT NULL,
  `name_count` int DEFAULT NULL,
  `prop100k` decimal(8,2) DEFAULT NULL,
  `cum_prop100k` decimal(8,2) DEFAULT NULL,
  `pctwhite` decimal(5,2) DEFAULT NULL,
  `pctblack` decimal(5,2) DEFAULT NULL,
  `pctapi` decimal(5,2) DEFAULT NULL,
  `pctaian` decimal(5,2) DEFAULT NULL,
  `pct2prace` decimal(5,2) DEFAULT NULL,
  `pcthispanic` decimal(5,2) DEFAULT NULL
) ENGINE=InnoDB DEFAULT CHARSET=utf8mb4 COLLATE=utf8mb4_0900_ai_ci;
```

And you load the data:

```
mysql> LOAD DATA LOCAL INFILE 'Names_2010Census.csv' into table top_names
    -> FIELDS TERMINATED BY ',' ENCLOSED BY '"' LINES TERMINATED BY '\n';
Query OK, 162255 rows affected, 65535 warnings (0.93 sec)
Records: 162255  Deleted: 0  Skipped: 0  Warnings: 444813
```

Now that we have created and loaded our table, we can proceed with the following query:

```
mysql> SELECT names_id,top_name,name_rank
    -> FROM top_names WHERE top_name = "BROWN";
+----------+----------+-----------+
| names_id | top_name | name_rank |
+----------+----------+-----------+
|        5 | BROWN    |         4 |
+----------+----------+-----------+
1 row in set (0.04 sec)
```

As you can see here, MySQL has to do a full table scan to find any rows in this table outside of its PRIMARY KEY:

```
mysql> EXPLAIN SELECT names_id,top_name,name_rank
    -> FROM top_names WHERE top_name = "BROWN"\G
*************************** 1. row ***************************
           id: 1
  select_type: SIMPLE
        table: top_names
   partitions: NULL
         type: ALL
possible_keys: NULL
          key: NULL
      key_len: NULL
          ref: NULL
         rows: 161533
     filtered: 10.00
        Extra: Using where
1 row in set, 1 warning (0.01 sec)
```

Our sample query seeks a string match on the top_name field; hence, having an index on this type of data will increase query performance. First, we create an index to meet the WHERE clause of this query:

```
mysql> CREATE INDEX idx_names ON top_names(top_name);

Query OK, 0 rows affected (0.28 sec)
Records: 0  Duplicates: 0  Warnings: 0
```

We then check if the optimizer has chosen this new index for the same query:

```
mysql> EXPLAIN SELECT names_id,top_name,name_rank
-> FROM top_names WHERE top_name = "BROWN"\G
*************************** 1. row ***************************
           id: 1
  select_type: SIMPLE
        table: top_names
   partitions: NULL
         type: ref
possible_keys: idx_names
          key: idx_names
      key_len: 103
          ref: const
         rows: 1
     filtered: 100.00
        Extra: NULL
1 row in set, 1 warning (0.00 sec)
```

Dropping indexes may be required for a few reasons. After you make sure the index is no longer needed or needs to be re-created, you can drop it using the following syntax:

```
DROP INDEX index_name ON tbl_name;
```

21.2 Creating a Surrogate Primary Key

Problem

A table without a primary key is not performant enough.

Solution

Add a primary key to all InnoDB tables.

Discussion

A primary key gives you a way to uniquely identify a row in a table. In case of InnoDB, a primary key is synonymous with a *clustered index*: a special index that stores row data. When an InnoDB table is created by a user without explicitly defining a primary key, InnoDB takes the first unique index in an index where a B-Tree structure exists in the table and makes it the clustered index. A clustered index is also often referred to as a physical order of the records on disk. A clustered index is a table stored in a table, and if no unique index exists, InnoDB creates a surrogate key, called GEN_CLUST_INDEX, on an automatically generated unique 6-bytes identifier.

When InnoDB creates secondary indexes, it is useful to resolve queries because it copies primary key columns to each secondary index row. If the primary key is unnecessarily large, all secondary indexes would be large as well. Therefore, it is very important to choose a suitable column for the primary key.

In our example in Recipe 21.1, the natural primary key is top_name, which takes 26 bytes. Defining top_name as a primary key will increase the size of every row in the secondary index by 26 bytes. Therefore, we show here a technique for creating 4-byte integer surrogate keys with the AUTO_INCREMENT property, so it increases monotonically. It is also better than the surrogate key that InnoDB creates explicitly, because it's smaller, and we have full control over its values.

Our table is comparatively small, but for large tables, this difference could be critical. Besides space, larger indexes require more time to search through.

This table is missing a field with a PRIMARY KEY. The best way to include one in this table is to add an id field with AUTO INCREMENT NOT NULL properties. Ideally, you would create this in advance of loading any data to the table to order the table in the tablespace physically:

```
mysql> ALTER TABLE `top_names`
    -> ADD COLUMN `names_id` int unsigned NOT NULL
    -> AUTO_INCREMENT PRIMARY KEY FIRST;
Query OK, 0 rows affected (0.44 sec)
Records: 0  Duplicates: 0  Warnings: 0
```

Although the following is a complete index scan, it will use the new PRIMARY KEY field we have created to count the number of rows in the table:

```
mysql> SELECT COUNT(names_id) FROM top_names;
+------------------+
| count(names_id)  |
+------------------+
|          162255  |
+------------------+
1 row in set (0.04 sec)

mysql> EXPLAIN SELECT COUNT(names_id) FROM top_names\G
*************************** 1. row ***************************
           id: 1
  select_type: SIMPLE
        table: top_names
   partitions: NULL
         type: index
possible_keys: NULL
          key: idx_name_rank_count
      key_len: 8
          ref: NULL
         rows: 161533
     filtered: 100.00
        Extra: Using index
1 row in set, 1 warning (0.00 sec)
```

See Also

For additional information, see the MySQL documentation for further details on Primary Key Optimization (*https://oreil.ly/D2yzr*).

21.3 Maintaining Indexes

Problem

You want to know if existing indexes are effective for your queries and drop those that are not.

Solution

Learn basic index operations.

Discussion

To better control your data, use indexes efficiently by studying the data and access types of your schema. To continue our example from the previous recipe, we'll examine existing indexes for the `top_names` table:

```
mysql> SHOW INDEXES FROM top_names \G
*************************** 1. row ***************************
        Table: top_names
    Non_unique: 0
      Key_name: PRIMARY
  Seq_in_index: 1
   Column_name: names_id
     Collation: A
   Cardinality: 161807
      Sub_part: NULL
        Packed: NULL
          Null:
    Index_type: BTREE
       Comment:
 Index_comment:
       Visible: YES
    Expression: NULL
*************************** 2. row ***************************
        Table: top_names
    Non_unique: 1
      Key_name: idx_names
  Seq_in_index: 1
   Column_name: top_name
     Collation: A
   Cardinality: 161708
      Sub_part: NULL
        Packed: NULL
          Null: YES
    Index_type: BTREE
       Comment:
 Index_comment:
       Visible: YES
    Expression: NULL
2 rows in set (0.00 sec)
```

Here, what matters most is the `cardinality` of the index. Indexes are better utilized if the column has many different values. So, in short, indexes are inefficient on Boolean and redundant values.

In our case, the cardinality of the `idx_names` index is close to the cardinality of the primary key. This shows that the index has good selectivity. Actually, this index could also be `unique`, which we can confirm by querying the number of distinct values in this column:

```
mysql> SELECT COUNT(DISTINCT top_name), COUNT(*) FROM top_names;
+--------------------------+----------+
| count(distinct top_name) | count(*) |
+--------------------------+----------+
|                   162254 |   162254 |
```

```
+---------------------------+----------+
1 row in set (0,18 sec)
```

Since we've already created an index on the top_name column, we can drop that index, then create a new, unique one. First, to drop the index, execute the following command:

```
mysql> DROP INDEX idx_names ON top_names;
Query OK, 0 rows affected (0.02 sec)
Records: 0  Duplicates: 0  Warnings: 0
```

Alternatively, ALTER TABLE syntax can also be used:

```
ALTER TABLE tbl_name DROP INDEX name;
```

To create a unique index, specify the keyword UNIQUE for the CREATE INDEX command:

```
CREATE UNIQUE INDEX idx_names ON top_names(top_name);
```

You can rename an existing index created on the table:

```
mysql> ALTER TABLE top_names RENAME
    -> INDEX idx_names to idx_top_name, ALGORITHM=INPLACE, LOCK=NONE;
```

 Not all index operations are in place; some index operations will cause table rebuild, which may negatively impact the server's performance for large data sizes. Care must be taken before executing DDL operations. DDL (Data Definition Language) implies changing the structure of a table definition, known as the database schema. For further details, please consult the MySQL Documentation (*https://oreil.ly/j1Mkj*).

21.4 Deciding When a Query Can Use an Index

Problem

Your table has an index, but queries are still slow.

Solution

Check the query plan using EXPLAIN to make sure the right index has been used.

Discussion

Indexes are part of query plans to access data faster by using the shortest possible path. When MySQL optimizer makes a decision, it considers indexes, cardinality, number of rows, and more. Here's an example of a query where an index exists for a column but MySQL can't utilize it:

```
mysql> EXPLAIN SELECT name_rank,top_name,name_count FROM top_names
    -> WHERE name_rank < 10 ORDER BY name_count\G
    *************************** 1. row ***************************
           id: 1
  select_type: SIMPLE
        table: top_names
   partitions: NULL
         type: ALL
possible_keys: NULL
          key: NULL
      key_len: NULL
          ref: NULL
         rows: 161604
     filtered: 33.33
        Extra: Using where; Using filesort
1 row in set, 1 warning (0.00 sec)
```

From the Explain plan output, we have no index that matches the key criteria of the query. There are indexes on this table, and it looks like we'll need another index on the name_rank field:

```
mysql> CREATE INDEX idx_name_rank ON top_names(name_rank);
       Query OK, 0 rows affected (0.16 sec)
Records: 0  Duplicates: 0  Warnings: 0
```

Check the query plan again after creating the new index:

```
mysql> EXPLAIN SELECT name_rank,top_name,name_count FROM top_names
    -> WHERE name_rank < 10 ORDER BY name_count\G
    *************************** 1. row ***************************
           id: 1
  select_type: SIMPLE
        table: top_names
   partitions: NULL
         type: range
possible_keys: idx_name_rank
          key: idx_name_rank
      key_len: 3
          ref: NULL
         rows: 11
     filtered: 100.00
        Extra: Using index condition; Using filesort
1 row in set, 1 warning (0.00 sec)
```

Our query is seeking for a name_rank that is less than 10 from the top_names table. Without the newly created idx_name_rank on the name_rank column, the optimizer has to evaluate all 161,604 rows in the table to filter 11 rows in return. With the index in place, it accesses just those 11 rows.

21.5 Deciding the Order for Multiple Column Indexes

Problem

You want to speed up your multiple column query.

Solution

Use a covering index with multiple columns.

Discussion

The best query performance can be achieved if query results are computed entirely from the index pages without reading the actual table data. A *covering index* is a solution for queries referencing more than one column. This type of index contains the required data; hence, it does not need to execute additional reads on the table.

In the following example, we have a query that requires having a filter on one column (name_rank) and sort by another column (name_count):

```
mysql> SELECT name_rank,top_name,name_count FROM top_names
    -> WHERE name_rank < 10 ORDER BY name_count\G
```

We'll create an index on the columns that we think are required for the optimizer to choose the fastest path:

```
mysql> CREATE INDEX idx_name_rank_count ON top_names(name_count,name_rank);
Query OK, 0 rows affected (0.18 sec)
Records: 0  Duplicates: 0  Warnings: 0
```

In this case, MySQL cannot use the index against the following query, and it ends up needing to do a full table scan again. The reason is that despite having both columns of the query in the filter, the index is ordered in reverse:

```
mysql> EXPLAIN SELECT name_rank,top_name,name_count FROM top_names
    -> WHERE name_rank < 10 ORDER BY name_count\G
*************************** 1. row ***************************
           id: 1
  select_type: SIMPLE
        table: top_names
   partitions: NULL
         type: ALL
possible_keys: NULL
          key: NULL
      key_len: NULL
          ref: NULL
         rows: 161604
     filtered: 33.33
        Extra: Using where; Using filesort
1 row in set, 1 warning (0.00 sec)
```

To demonstrate why the order of index columns matters, let's look at the following example.

For KEY `idx_name_rank_count` (`name_rank`,`name_count`), first drop the previous index in reverse order and create a new one:

```
mysql> DROP INDEX idx_name_rank_count ON top_names;
Query OK, 0 rows affected (0.01 sec)
Records: 0  Duplicates: 0  Warnings: 0
```

```
mysql> CREATE INDEX idx_name_rank_count ON top_names(name_rank,name_count);
Query OK, 0 rows affected (0.15 sec)
Records: 0  Duplicates: 0  Warnings: 0
```

We have created a covering index for both columns our SELECT statement proposes on the *name_rank* and *name_count* filters:

```
mysql> EXPLAIN SELECT name_rank,top_name,name_count FROM top_names
    -> WHERE name_rank < 10 ORDER BY name_count\G
*************************** 1. row ***************************
           id: 1
  select_type: SIMPLE
        table: top_names
   partitions: NULL
         type: range
possible_keys: idx_name_rank_count
          key: idx_name_rank_count
      key_len: 3
          ref: NULL
         rows: 11
     filtered: 100.00
        Extra: Using index condition; Using filesort
1 row in set, 1 warning (0.00 sec)
```

As you can see from the EXPLAIN output, the optimizer chooses idx_name_rank_count for this query with a new covering index.

21.6 Using Ascending and Descending Indexes

Problem

You want to scan your data in ascending or descending order without a performance penalty.

Solution

Use ascending and descending indexes.

Discussion

MySQL can scan indexes in reverse order with a performance penalty due to index pages being physically ordered. To create a matching index for the ORDER BY clause, use DESC for descending and ASC for ascending index types.

The ideal query performance results from avoiding scanning an index backward. It's also a combination of sorting and filtering with the DESC indexes. When MySQL optimizer chooses a query plan, it evaluates if it can take advantage of these when the query needs descending order.

Remember, descending indexes are supported for the InnoDB storage engine, and there are some limitations to its use.

Also, descending indexes have the following properties:

- They are supported by all data types.
- The DISTINCT clause can use any index with a matching column.
- They can be used for MIN()/MAX() optimization when not used in conjunction with the GROUP BY clause.
- They are only limited to BTREE and HASH indexes.
- They are not supported for FULLTEXT or SPATIAL index types.

The following example starts with creating a covering index for our desired sorting for fields:

```
CREATE INDEX idx_desc_01 ON top_names(top_name, prop100k ASC, cum_prop100K DESC);

mysql> SELECT top_name,prop100k,cum_prop100k FROM top_names
    -> ORDER BY `top_name`,`prop100k`,`cum_prop100k` DESC LIMIT 10;
+----------+----------+--------------+
| top_name | prop100k | cum_prop100k |
+----------+----------+--------------+
| NULL     |     2.43 |     60231.65 |
| AAB      |     0.05 |     88770.96 |
| AABERG   |     0.16 |     82003.18 |
| AABY     |     0.07 |     86239.41 |
| AADLAND  |     0.13 |     83329.35 |
| AAFEDT   |     0.05 |     88567.34 |
| AAGAARD  |     0.10 |     84574.52 |
| AAGARD   |     0.12 |     83769.42 |
| AAGESEN  |     0.06 |     87383.27 |
| AAKER    |     0.12 |     83574.66 |
+----------+----------+--------------+
10 rows in set (0.00 sec)
```

After creating the covering index for all ORDER BY clauses, optimizer columns choose the idx_desc_01. This is particularly good for index optimization and sorting:

```
mysql> EXPLAIN SELECT top_name,prop100k,cum_prop100k FROM top_names
    -> ORDER BY `top_name`,`prop100k`,`cum_prop100k` DESC LIMIT 10\G
*************************** 1. row ***************************
           id: 1
  select_type: SIMPLE
        table: top_names
   partitions: NULL
         type: index
possible_keys: NULL
          key: idx_desc_01
      key_len: 113
          ref: NULL
         rows: 10
     filtered: 100.00
        Extra: Using index
1 row in set, 1 warning (0.00 sec)
```

When we do `SELECT * FROM top_names`, instead of specifying column order by the top_name field, it uses the previously created index, and by default, it is in ascending order:

```
mysql> EXPLAIN SELECT * FROM top_names ORDER BY top_name ASC LIMIT 10 \G
*************************** 1. row ***************************
           id: 1
  select_type: SIMPLE
        table: top_names
   partitions: NULL
         type: index
possible_keys: NULL
          key: idx_top_name
      key_len: 103
          ref: NULL
         rows: 10
     filtered: 100.00
        Extra: NULL
1 row in set, 1 warning (0.00 sec)
```

To demonstrate the use of descending indexes, we'll create a new index and use DESC to apply it:

```
mysql> CREATE INDEX idx_desc_02 ON top_names(top_name DESC, prop100k, cum_prop100K);
Query OK, 0 rows affected (0.38 sec)
Records: 0  Duplicates: 0  Warnings: 0

mysql> EXPLAIN SELECT * FROM top_names ORDER BY top_name DESC LIMIT 10\G
*************************** 1. row ***************************
           id: 1
  select_type: SIMPLE
        table: top_names
   partitions: NULL
         type: index
possible_keys: NULL
          key: idx_desc_02
      key_len: 113
          ref: NULL
         rows: 10
     filtered: 100.00
        Extra: NULL
1 row in set, 1 warning (0.00 sec)
```

Again, we'll use `top_name` with another column, `prop100k`, to illustrate the use of the DESC index on the top_name column:

```
mysql> EXPLAIN SELECT top_name FROM top_names
    -> ORDER BY top_name DESC,prop100k ASC LIMIT 10 \G
*************************** 1. row ***************************
           id: 1
  select_type: SIMPLE
        table: top_names
   partitions: NULL
         type: index
possible_keys: NULL
          key: idx_desc_02
      key_len: 113
          ref: NULL
```

```
        rows: 10
    filtered: 100.00
       Extra: Using index
1 row in set, 1 warning (0.00 sec)
```

 Order matters, as MySQL uses the leftmost order rule for the indexes compared to the ORDER BY clause. Changing the order of columns in the composite index will change the behavior of the query result. Also, be careful using SELECT * FROM when sorting by multiple fields, as * will use the column order from the table definition, which may end up with different fields than the ORDER BY clause intends.

21.7 Using Function-Based Indexes

Problem

You need to search or sort by an expression, but MySQL calculates the result of the expression for each row and therefore cannot use indexes. Performance of the query is poor.

Solution

Use functional indexes.

Discussion

Some types of information are more easily analyzed using not the original values but an expression computed from them. For example, the size column in the mail table stores size in bytes that is hard to interpret on first glance. It would be much easier to work with by using kilobytes (KB) instead. However, you may not want to lose the precision that storage in bytes provides.

You can have both precision and usability if you store data in bytes and use expressions to query the table. For example, to find messages that are larger than 100 KB, use the following query:

```
mysql> SELECT t, srcuser, srchost, size, ROUND(size/1024) AS size_KB
    -> FROM mail WHERE ROUND(size/1024) > 100;
+---------------------+---------+---------+---------+---------+
| t                   | srcuser | srchost | size    | size_KB |
+---------------------+---------+---------+---------+---------+
| 2014-05-12 12:48:13 | tricia  | mars    |  194925 |     190 |
| 2014-05-14 17:03:01 | tricia  | saturn  | 2394482 |    2338 |
| 2014-05-15 10:25:52 | gene    | mars    |  998532 |     975 |
+---------------------+---------+---------+---------+---------+
3 rows in set (0.00 sec)
```

However, MySQL won't be able to use an index on the size column to resolve this query, because it calculates an expression for each row. To resolve this issue, use function-based indexes.

The syntax of the function-based index is as follows:

```
CREATE INDEX index_name ON table_name ((expression));
```

Mind the double brackets: if you omit one pair, MySQL will think you're passing a column name instead of the expression and will return an error.

Let's create an index on ROUND(size/1024) and check if MySQL will use it to resolve the query:

```
mysql> CREATE INDEX size_KB ON mail ((ROUND(size/1024)));
Query OK, 0 rows affected (0.02 sec)
Records: 0  Duplicates: 0  Warnings: 0

mysql> EXPLAIN SELECT t, srcuser, srchost, size, ROUND(size/1024) AS size_KB
    -> FROM mail WHERE ROUND(size/1024) > 100\G
*************************** 1. row ***************************
           id: 1
  select_type: SIMPLE
        table: mail
   partitions: NULL
         type: ALL
possible_keys: NULL
          key: NULL
      key_len: NULL
          ref: NULL
         rows: 16
     filtered: 100.00
        Extra: Using where
1 row in set, 1 warning (0.00 sec)
```

The index will not be used to resolve the query because the ROUND function returns data in the NEWDECIMAL type for values that have a floating point and 100 is LONGLONG. You can examine the result if you start mysql client with the --column-type-info option:

```
$ unbuffer mysql --column-type-info -e "SELECT ROUND(10.5)" | grep Type
Type:      NEWDECIMAL
$ unbuffer mysql --column-type-info -e "SELECT 100" | grep Type
Type:      LONGLONG
```

 We need to use the unbuffer command, because mysql buffers the --column-type-info result, and it cannot be piped to grep otherwise.

To clarify, to force MySQL to use the index, you need to compare the result of the expression with a floating-point value:

```
mysql> EXPLAIN SELECT t, srcuser, srchost, size, ROUND(size/1024) AS size_KB
    -> FROM mail WHERE ROUND(size/1024) > 100.0\G
*************************** 1. row ***************************
           id: 1
  select_type: SIMPLE
        table: mail
   partitions: NULL
         type: range
possible_keys: size_KB
          key: size_KB
      key_len: 10
          ref: NULL
         rows: 3
     filtered: 100.00
        Extra: Using where
1 row in set, 1 warning (0.00 sec)
```

Alternatively, cast the result of the ROUND function to the integer value when creating the index. This also forces MySQL to use the index to resolve the query:

```
mysql> DROP INDEX size_KB ON mail;
Query OK, 0 rows affected (0.01 sec)
Records: 0  Duplicates: 0  Warnings: 0

mysql> CREATE INDEX size_KB ON mail ((CAST(ROUND(size/1024) AS SIGNED)));
Query OK, 0 rows affected (0.02 sec)
Records: 0  Duplicates: 0  Warnings: 0

mysql> EXPLAIN SELECT t, srcuser, srchost, size, ROUND(size/1024) AS size_KB
    -> FROM mail WHERE ROUND(size/1024) > 100\G
*************************** 1. row ***************************
           id: 1
  select_type: SIMPLE
        table: mail
   partitions: NULL
         type: range
possible_keys: size_KB
          key: size_KB
      key_len: 9
          ref: NULL
         rows: 3
     filtered: 100.00
        Extra: Using where
1 row in set, 1 warning (0.00 sec)
```

21.8 Using Indexes on Generated Columns with JSON Data

Problem

You want to perform a search inside JSON data, but it is slow.

Solution

Use a generated column, created from an expression that searches for a JSON value and an index on this column.

Discussion

In this recipe, we'll discuss a book_authors table:

```
CREATE TABLE `book_authors` (
  `id` int NOT NULL AUTO_INCREMENT,
  `author` json NOT NULL,
  PRIMARY KEY (`id`)
);
```

The table contains book records per author in the JSON column:

```
mysql> SELECT * FROM book_authors\G
*************************** 1. row ***************************
    id: 1
author: {"id": 1, "name": "Paul", ↵
        "books": [ ↵
          "Software Portability with imake: Practical Software Engineering", ↵
          "Mysql: The Definitive Guide to Using, Programming, ↵
          and Administering Mysql 4 (Developer's Library)", ↵
          "MYSQL Certification Study Guide", ↵
          "MySQL (OTHER NEW RIDERS)", ↵
          "MySQL Cookbook", ↵
          "MySQL 5.0 Certification Study Guide", ↵
          "Using csh & tcsh: Type Less, Accomplish More (Nutshell Handbooks)", ↵
          "MySQL (Developer's Library)"], ↵
        "lastname": "DuBois"}
lastname: "DuBois"
*************************** 2. row ***************************
    id: 2
author: {"id": 2, "name": "Alkin", "books": ["MySQL Cookbook"],↵
        "lastname": "Tezuysal"}
lastname: "Tezuysal"
*************************** 3. row ***************************
    id: 3
author: {"id": 3, "name": "Sveta", ↵
        "books": ["MySQL Troubleshooting", "MySQL Cookbook"], ↵
        "lastname": "Smirnova"}
lastname: "Smirnova"
3 rows in set (0,00 sec)
```

If you want to search for a specific author, you may consider searching by their name and last name.

The CREATE INDEX command creates an index on a column in the table. JSON data stored in a single column, therefore any index created with the simple CREATE INDEX command, would index the whole JSON document while you may need to search only part of it.

Moreover, the CREATE INDEX command will fail for the JSON column:

```
mysql> CREATE INDEX author_name ON book_authors(author);
ERROR 3152 (42000): JSON column 'author' supports indexing only ↵
via generated columns on a specified JSON path.
```

A solution for this issue would be using a generated column and creating an index on it. Values in generated columns are created using an expression defined at the time of column creation:

```
ALTER TABLE book_authors ADD COLUMN lastname VARCHAR(255)
GENERATED ALWAYS AS(JSON_UNQUOTE(JSON_EXTRACT(author, '$.lastname')));
```

In this example, we created a column, generated from the expression `JSON_EXTRACT(author, '$.lastname')`. We can also use the `->` and `->>` operators to extract the JSON value:

```
ALTER TABLE book_authors ADD COLUMN name VARCHAR(255)
GENERATED ALWAYS AS (author->>'$.name');
```

We used the `JSON_UNQUOTE` function and the `->>` operator in our expressions to remove trailing quotes in the authors' names if they exist.

Two new columns, `name` and `lastname`, do not take any space and are generated each time a query accesses the table.

 If you want to improve the performance of your `SELECT` queries at the cost of additional storage and slowness at the write time, define generated columns with the keyword `STORED`. In this case, the expression would be executed only once: when values used in the expression are inserted or modified and then physically stored on the disk.

Now we can create an index on our new generated columns:

```
CREATE INDEX author_name ON book_authors(lastname, name);
```

To access data using the newly created index, refer to the new columns as you do any other column:

```
mysql> SELECT author->'$.books' FROM book_authors
    -> WHERE name = 'Sveta' AND lastname='Smirnova';
+-------------------------------------------------+
| author->'$.books'                               |
+-------------------------------------------------+
| ["MySQL Troubleshooting", "MySQL Cookbook"]     |
+-------------------------------------------------+
1 row in set (0,00 sec)
```

EXPLAIN confirms that the new index has been used:

```
mysql> EXPLAIN SELECT author->'$.books' FROM book_authors
    -> WHERE name = 'Sveta' AND lastname='Smirnova'\G
*************************** 1. row ***************************
           id: 1
  select_type: SIMPLE
        table: book_authors
   partitions: NULL
         type: ref
possible_keys: author_name
```

```
          key: author_name
      key_len: 2046
          ref: const,const
         rows: 1
     filtered: 100.00
        Extra: NULL
1 row in set, 1 warning (0,00 sec)
```

See Also

For additional information about using JSON in MySQL, see Chapter 19.

21.9 Using Full Text Indexes

Problem

You want to take advantage of a keyword search, but queries on text fields are slow.

Solution

Use FULLTEXT indexes for full-text searches.

Discussion

MySQL supports FULLTEXT indexes on popular storage engines such as InnoDB and MyISAM. Although neither of the storage engines were originally designed to index large text operations, you can still use them to comb performance for specific queries.

FULLTEXT indexes have two other conditions:

1. They can be used only for CHAR, VARCHAR, or TEXT columns.
2. They can be used only when there is a MATCH() or AGAINST() clause in a SELECT statement.

In MySQL, the MATCH() function performs a full-text search by accepting a comma-separated list of columns, where AGAINST() takes a string to search.

> A FULLTEXT index can be used with a combination of B-tree indexes on the same column, as their purposes are different. FULL TEXT is for finding keywords versus matching values in the field.

FULLTEXT text searches also have three different modes:

- *Natural language mode* (default) is the search mode for simple phrases.
  ```
  SELECT top_name,name_rank FROM top_names WHERE MATCH(top_name)
       AGAINST("ANDREW" IN NATURAL LANGUAGE MODE) \G
  ```

- *Boolean mode* is for using Boolean operators in search mode. Recall that the strategy discussed in Recipe 7.17 makes similar use of operators here:
  ```
  SELECT top_name,name_rank FROM top_names WHERE MATCH(top_name)
       AGAINST("+ANDREW +ANDY -ANN" IN BOOLEAN MODE) \G
  ```

- *Query expansion mode* is the search mode for similar or related values in a search expression. In short, this mode will return relevant matches against a searched keyword:
  ```
  SELECT top_name,name_rank FROM top_names WHERE MATCH(top_name)
       AGAINST("ANDY"  WITH QUERY EXPANSION) \G
  ```

The InnoDB storage engine can take advantage of the following optimizations:

- Queries that return only the ID field of the search rank. *Search rank* is defined as relevance rank as a measure to show how good a match is.

- Queries that sort the matching rows in descending order.

The optimizer will not choose the fulltext index on the top_name column. For more information, see Recipe 7.10. This type of query is very efficient given the data type we have in this example with indexed unique string values in the top_name column:

```
mysql> EXPLAIN SELECT top_name,name_rank FROM top_names
    -> WHERE top_name="ANDREW" \G
*************************** 1. row ***************************
           id: 1
  select_type: SIMPLE
        table: top_names
   partitions: NULL
         type: ref
possible_keys: idx_top_name,idx_desc_01,idx_desc_02
          key: idx_top_name
      key_len: 103
          ref: const
         rows: 1
     filtered: 100.00
        Extra: NULL
1 row in set, 1 warning (0.00 sec)

mysql> CREATE FULLTEXT INDEX idx_fulltext ON top_names(top_name);
    Query OK, 0 rows affected, 1 warning (1.94 sec)
  Records: 0  Duplicates: 0  Warnings: 1

mysql> EXPLAIN SELECT top_name,name_rank FROM top_names
    -> WHERE top_name="ANDREW" \G
*************************** 1. row ***************************
           id: 1
  select_type: SIMPLE
```

```
         table: top_names
    partitions: NULL
          type: ref
 possible_keys: idx_top_name,idx_desc_01,idx_desc_02,idx_fulltext
           key: idx_top_name
       key_len: 103
           ref: const
          rows: 1
      filtered: 100.00
         Extra: NULL
1 row in set, 1 warning (0.00 sec)
```

Now, if we try a pattern match against the same column, we will be able to utilize a full text index for the given column:

```
mysql> EXPLAIN SELECT top_name,name_rank FROM top_names
    -> MATCH(top_name) AGAINST("ANDREW") \G
    *************************** 1. row ***************************
            id: 1
   select_type: SIMPLE
         table: top_names
    partitions: NULL
          type: fulltext
 possible_keys: idx_fulltext
           key: idx_fulltext
       key_len: 0
           ref: const
          rows: 1
      filtered: 100.00
         Extra: Using where; Ft_hints: sorted
1 row in set, 1 warning (0.01 sec)
```

In this case, we can see that MySQL chooses to use the FULLTEXT index. Although it's useful to have FULLTEXT index availability in MySQL, it comes with many restrictions. Please refer to the MySQL documentation for further details about Full-Text Restrictions. (*https://oreil.ly/rc0vb*)

 Despite the availability of full-text indexes in the InnoDB storage engine, there may be better alternatives in the market to take this off of MySQL's workload and put it on another optimized storage system.

21.10 Utilizing Spatial Indexes and Geographical Data

Problem

You want to store and query geographic coordinates effectively.

Solution

Use MySQL's improved Spatial Reference System.

Discussion

MySQL 8 contains all Spatial Reference System (SRS) identifications from the European Petroleum Survey Group (EPSG) agency. These SRS identifications are stored with a unique name and spatial reference identification (SRID) in informa tion_schema.

These systems represent different variations of geographic data references. You can query details of these from information_schema:

```
mysql> SELECT * FROM INFORMATION_SCHEMA.ST_SPATIAL_REFERENCE_SYSTEMS
    -> WHERE SRS_ID=4326 OR SRS_ID=3857 ORDER BY SRS_ID DESC\G
*************************** 1. row ***************************
              SRS_NAME: WGS 84
                SRS_ID: 4326
          ORGANIZATION: EPSG
ORGANIZATION_COORDSYS_ID: 4326
            DEFINITION: GEOGCS["WGS 84",DATUM["World Geodetic System 1984",
            SPHEROID["WGS 84",6378137,298.257223563,AUTHORITY["EPSG","7030"]],
            AUTHORITY["EPSG","6326"]],PRIMEM["Greenwich",0,AUTHORITY["EPSG","8901"]],
            UNIT["degree",0.017453292519943278,AUTHORITY["EPSG","9122"]],
            AXIS["Lat",NORTH],AXIS["Lon",EAST],AUTHORITY["EPSG","4326"]]
           DESCRIPTION: NULL
*************************** 2. row ***************************
              SRS_NAME: WGS 84 / Pseudo-Mercator
                SRS_ID: 3857
          ORGANIZATION: EPSG
ORGANIZATION_COORDSYS_ID: 3857
            DEFINITION: PROJCS["WGS 84 / Pseudo-Mercator",GEOGCS["WGS 84",
            DATUM["World Geodetic System 1984",SPHEROID["WGS 84",6378137,
            298.257223563,AUTHORITY["EPSG","7030"]],AUTHORITY["EPSG","6326"]],
            PRIMEM["Greenwich",0,AUTHORITY["EPSG","8901"]],UNIT["degree",
            0.017453292519943278,AUTHORITY["EPSG","9122"]],AXIS["Lat",NORTH]
            ,AXIS["Lon",EAST],AUTHORITY["EPSG","4326"]],PROJECTION["Popular
            Visualization Pseudo Mercator",AUTHORITY["EPSG","1024"]],
            PARAMETER["Latitude of natural origin",0,AUTHORITY["EPSG","8801"]],
            PARAMETER["Longitude of natural origin",0,AUTHORITY["EPSG","8802"]],
            PARAMETER["False easting",0,AUTHORITY["EPSG","8806"]],↵
            PARAMETER["False northing",
            0,AUTHORITY["EPSG","8807"]],UNIT["metre",1,AUTHORITY["EPSG","9001"]],↵
            AXIS["X",EAST],
            AXIS["Y",NORTH],AUTHORITY["EPSG","3857"]]
           DESCRIPTION: NULL
2 rows in set (0.00 sec)
```

SRS_ID 4326 represents the widespread web map projections used in Google Maps, OpenStreetMap, etc., whereas 4326 represents the GPS coordinates used for tracking locations.

Let's say we have point-of-interest data that we keep in our database. We'll create a table and load sample data to it using SRID 4326:

```
mysql> CREATE TABLE poi
    -> ( poi_id  INT UNSIGNED AUTO_INCREMENT NOT NULL  PRIMARY KEY,
    -> position POINT NOT NULL SRID 4326, name VARCHAR(200));
Query OK, 0 rows affected (0.02 sec)
```

```
mysql> INSERT INTO poi VALUES (1, ST_GeomFromText('POINT(41.0211 29.0041)', 4326),
    -> 'Maiden\'s Tower');
Query OK, 1 row affected (0.00 sec)
msyql> INSERT INTO poi VALUES (2, ST_GeomFromText('POINT(41.0256 28.9742)', 4326),
    -> 'Galata Tower');
Query OK, 1 row affected (0.00 sec)
```

Now we'll create an index on the geometry column:

```
mysql> CREATE SPATIAL INDEX position ON poi (position);
Query OK, 0 rows affected (0.01 sec)
Records: 0  Duplicates: 0  Warnings: 0
```

We'll demonstrate how to measure the distance between these two points of interest:

```
mysql> SELECT ST_AsText(position) FROM poi WHERE poi_id = 1 INTO @tower1;
Query OK, 1 row affected (0.00 sec)
mysql> SELECT ST_AsText(position) FROM poi WHERE poi_id = 2 INTO @tower2;
Query OK, 1 row affected (0.00 sec)
mysql> SELECT ST_Distance(ST_GeomFromText(@tower1, 4326),
    -> ST_GeomFromText(@tower2, 4326)) AS distance;
+--------------------+
| distance           |
+--------------------+
| 2563.9276036976544 |
+--------------------+
1 row in set (0.00 sec)
```

This is a representation of a straight line between these two points of interest. Of course, this isn't a car route–planning example; this is more like a bird's flight from point A to B in meters.

Let's check what MySQL used as query optimization:

```
mysql> EXPLAIN SELECT ST_Distance(ST_GeomFromText(@tower1, 4326),
-> ST_GeomFromText(@tower2, 4326)) AS dist \G
*************************** 1. row ***************************
           id: 1
  select_type: SIMPLE
        table: NULL
   partitions: NULL
         type: NULL
possible_keys: NULL
          key: NULL
      key_len: NULL
          ref: NULL
         rows: NULL
     filtered: NULL
        Extra: No tables used
1 row in set, 1 warning (0.00 sec)
```

Since the ST_Distance function doesn't use a table to calculate the distance between these two locations, it doesn't use a table in the query; hence, there's no index optimization allowed.

You can further improve on the distance calculation about what Earth's spherical shape should be using `ST_Distance_Sphere`, which will result in slightly different results:

```
mysql> SELECT ST_Distance_Sphere(ST_GeomFromText(@tower1, 4326),
    -> ST_GeomFromText(@tower2, 4326)) AS dist;
+---------------------+
| dist                |
+---------------------+
| 2557.7412439442496  |
+---------------------+
1 row in set (0.00 sec)
```

Let's say we have a polygon around Istanbul for covering our target search area. The required polygon coordinates can be generated via another application:

```
mysql> SET @poly := ST_GeomFromText ( 'POLYGON(( 41.104897239651905 28.876082545638166,
    -> 41.05727989444261 29.183699733138166,
    -> 40.90384226781947 29.137007838606916,
    -> 40.94119778455447 28.865096217513166,
    -> 41.104897239651905 28.876082545638166))', 4326);
```

This time we'll search points of interest using the `ST_Within` function from that polygon area. There are many functions built in to MySQL's spatial reference implementation. For details, please refer to MySQL documentation's "Spatial Analysis Functions" (*https://oreil.ly/kse0R*).

Spatial functions can be grouped into a few categories:

- Creating geometries in various formats
- Converting geometries between formats
- Accessing qualitative and quantitative properties of geometry
- Describing relations between two geometries
- Creating new geometries from existing ones

These functions allow developers to get faster access to the data and better utilize spatial analysis within MySQL.

In the following query, we're utilizing both `ST_AsText` and `ST_Within` functions at the same time:

```
mysql> SELECT  poi_id, name, ST_AsText(`position`)
    -> AS `towers` FROM poi WHERE ST_Within( `position`, @poly) ;
+--------+---------------+------------------------+
| poi_id | name          | towers                 |
+--------+---------------+------------------------+
|      1 | Maiden's Tower | POINT(41.0211 29.0041) |
|      2 | Galata Tower  | POINT(41.0256 28.9742) |
+--------+---------------+------------------------+
2 rows in set (0.00 sec)
```

Check whether the spatial index is used or not:

```
mysql> EXPLAIN  SELECT  poi_id, name,
    -> ST_AsText(`position`) AS `towers` FROM poi WHERE ST_Within( `position`, @poly) \G
*************************** 1. row ***************************
           id: 1
  select_type: SIMPLE
        table: poi
   partitions: NULL
         type: range
possible_keys: position
          key: position
      key_len: 34
          ref: NULL
         rows: 2
     filtered: 100.00
        Extra: Using where
1 row in set, 1 warning (0.00 sec)
```

21.11 Creating and Using Histograms

Problem

You want to join two or more tables, but MySQL's optimizer does not choose the right query plan.

Solution

Use optimizer histograms to aid decision making.

Discussion

Indexes are helpful for resolving query plans, but they don't always create the best query execution plan. This applies to situations when the optimizer needs to identify the order in which to join two or more tables.

Assume you have two tables. One stores product categories in a shop, and another stores sales data. The number of categories is small, but the number of sold items is huge. You may have a dozen categories and millions of sold items. When you join the two tables, MySQL has to decide which table to query first. If, however, MySQL queries the large table first, the query would be effective because it only processes a small number of sold items that satisfy the search condition. On the other hand, you may need items from the single category while the condition you used to select from the larger table returns many rows from all categories. In this case, you will have to discard all returned rows not belonging to the selected category. Such a query would run faster if you select from the small table first.

A solution to this issue is to have a combined index that takes a category ID and condition in the larger table. But this solution may not work for complicated queries when such a combined index is not applicable to the combination of the WHERE condition and JOIN clause.

Another issue with indexes is that they operate by cardinality: the number of unique values in the index. But when data distribution is not even, the optimizer can make false conclusions when it uses only cardinality. Assume you have one million items with a certain characteristic and 10 items with another characteristic. If the optimizer decides to select data that satisfy the first condition, the query would take much more time than if it first selects items that satisfy the second condition. Unfortunately it isn't possible to make the correct conclusion using information about cardinality only.

To resolve this issue, MySQL 8.0 introduces optimizer histograms. These are a lightweight data structures that store information about how many unique values exist in each data bucket.

To illustrate how optimizer histograms work, let's consider a table of six rows:

```
mysql> CREATE TABLE histograms(f1 INT);
Query OK, 0 rows affected (0,03 sec)

mysql> INSERT INTO histograms VALUES(1),(2),(2),(3),(3),(3);
Query OK, 6 rows affected (0,00 sec)
Records: 6  Duplicates: 0  Warnings: 0

mysql> SELECT f1, COUNT(f1) FROM histograms GROUP BY f1;
+------+-----------+
| f1   | COUNT(f1) |
+------+-----------+
|    1 |         1 |
|    2 |         2 |
|    3 |         3 |
+------+-----------+
3 rows in set (0,00 sec)
```

As you can see, the table contains one row with the value 1, two rows with the value 2, and three rows with the value 3.

If we run EXPLAIN on queries, selecting different rows in this table, we'll notice that the number of rows filtered from the result is the same no matter which value we're looking for:

```
mysql> \P grep filtered
PAGER set to 'grep filtered'
mysql> EXPLAIN SELECT * FROM histograms WHERE f1=1\G
       filtered: 16.67
1 row in set, 1 warning (0,00 sec)

mysql> EXPLAIN SELECT * FROM histograms WHERE f1=2\G
       filtered: 16.67
1 row in set, 1 warning (0,00 sec)

mysql> EXPLAIN SELECT * FROM histograms WHERE f1=3\G
       filtered: 16.67
1 row in set, 1 warning (0,00 sec)
```

The number of filtered rows shows how many rows would be filtered from the retrieved result. Since our table does not have indexes, MySQL first retrieves all the rows from the table, then filters those that satisfy the condition. Without any hint, the optimizer thinks that MySQL will leave only one row from the result no matter which condition we use.

Let's create a histogram and check if it changes anything:

```
mysql> ANALYZE TABLE histograms UPDATE HISTOGRAM ON f1\G
*************************** 1. row ***************************
   Table: cookbook.histograms
      Op: histogram
Msg_type: status
Msg_text: Histogram statistics created for column 'f1'.
1 row in set (0,01 sec)
```

Histograms are stored in the data dictionary `column_statistics` table and can be examined by querying the `COLUMN_STATISTICS` table in the Information Schema:

```
mysql> SELECT * FROM information_schema.column_statistics
    -> WHERE table_name='histograms'\G
*************************** 1. row ***************************
SCHEMA_NAME: cookbook
 TABLE_NAME: histograms
COLUMN_NAME: f1
  HISTOGRAM: {"buckets": [[1, 0.16666666666666666], [2, 0.5], [3, 1.0]],
              "data-type": "int",
              "null-values": 0.0,
              "collation-id": 8,
              "last-updated": "2021-05-23 17:29:46.595599",
              "sampling-rate": 1.0,
              "histogram-type": "singleton",
              "number-of-buckets-specified": 100}
1 row in set (0,00 sec)
```

Three buckets contain information about data ranges. Value 1 takes 1/6 of the table (one row out of six), values 1 and 2 both take a half (0.5) of the table, and together with value 3 they fill the table. The number of items in each bucket stored is a fraction of one. The `number-of-buckets-specified` field contains the number of buckets specified at the histogram-creation time. The default value is 100, but you're free to specify any number between 1 and 1,024. If the number of unique elements in the column exceeds the number of buckets, `histogram-type` will change from `singleton` to `equi-height`, and each bucket can contain a range of values instead of only one in case of `singleton`.

Histograms affect the value for the `filtered` field in the EXPLAIN output.

In the following example, values for the filtered rows correct and reflect the content of the table. If we search value 1, five of six table rows are predicted to be removed from the result set, which is correct. For value 2, only two rows (33.33%) would be left in the result, and in the case of value 3, half of the table will be filtered:

```
mysql> \P grep filtered
PAGER set to 'grep filtered'
mysql> EXPLAIN SELECT * FROM histograms WHERE f1=1\G
    filtered: 16.67
1 row in set, 1 warning (0,00 sec)

mysql> EXPLAIN SELECT * FROM histograms WHERE f1=2\G
    filtered: 33.33
1 row in set, 1 warning (0,00 sec)

mysql> EXPLAIN SELECT * FROM histograms WHERE f1=3\G
    filtered: 50.00
1 row in set, 1 warning (0,00 sec)
```

Histograms do not help to access data: they are statistical only, not a physical structure like indexes. They, instead, affect the query execution plan and, particularly, the order of the tables joined. For example, if we decide to join the `histograms` table with itself, the order will be different depending on the condition:

```
mysql> \P grep -B 3 table
PAGER set to 'grep -B 3 table'
mysql> EXPLAIN SELECT * FROM histograms h1 JOIN histograms h2
    -> WHERE h1.f1=1 and h2.f1=3\G
*************************** 1. row ***************************
          id: 1
 select_type: SIMPLE
       table: h1
--
*************************** 2. row ***************************
          id: 1
 select_type: SIMPLE
       table: h2
2 rows in set, 1 warning (0,00 sec)

mysql> EXPLAIN SELECT * FROM histograms h1 JOIN histograms h2
    -> WHERE h1.f1=3 and h2.f1=1\G
*************************** 1. row ***************************
          id: 1
 select_type: SIMPLE
       table: h2
--
*************************** 2. row ***************************
          id: 1
 select_type: SIMPLE
       table: h1
2 rows in set, 1 warning (0,00 sec)
```

The true power of histograms is demonstrated in large tables. The companion GitHub repository (*https://oreil.ly/56ZRl*) has data for two tables: `goods_shops` and `goods_characteristics`. They are created without histograms by default while having indexes:

```
CREATE TABLE `goods_shops` (
  `id` int NOT NULL AUTO_INCREMENT,
  `good_id` varchar(30) DEFAULT NULL,
  `location` varchar(30) DEFAULT NULL,
  `delivery_options` varchar(30) DEFAULT NULL,
```

```
  PRIMARY KEY (`id`),
  KEY `good_id` (`good_id`,`location`,`delivery_options`),
  KEY `location` (`location`,`delivery_options`)
);

CREATE TABLE `goods_characteristics` (
  `id` int NOT NULL AUTO_INCREMENT,
  `good_id` varchar(30) DEFAULT NULL,
  `size` int DEFAULT NULL,
  `manufacturer` varchar(30) DEFAULT NULL,
  PRIMARY KEY (`id`),
  KEY `good_id` (`good_id`,`size`,`manufacturer`),
  KEY `size` (`size`,`manufacturer`)
);
```

If we want to find the number of laptops with a screen size that is less than 13 inches; is manufactured by Lenovo, Dell, Toshiba, Samsung, or Acer; and is available by Premium or Urgent delivery in Moscow or Kiev, we can use the following query:

```
mysql> SELECT COUNT(*) FROM goods_shops
    -> JOIN goods_characteristics USING (good_id)
    -> WHERE size < 13 AND manufacturer
    -> IN ('Lenovo', 'Dell', 'Toshiba', 'Samsung', 'Acer')
    -> AND (location IN ('Moscow', 'Kiev')
    -> OR delivery_options IN ('Premium', 'Urgent'));
+----------+
| count(*) |
+----------+
|   816640 |
+----------+
1 row in set (6 min 31,75 sec)
```

The query took over six minutes, which is quite long for two tables of less than half a million rows. The reason for this is that the goods_shops table contains just a few rows that satisfy the condition for the shop location and delivery options, while the goods_characteristics table has many more rows that satisfy the laptop size and manufacturer conditions. In such a situation, it's better to select data from the goods_shops table first; however, the optimizer may create a different query execution plan:

```
mysql> EXPLAIN SELECT COUNT(*) FROM goods_shops JOIN goods_characteristics
    -> USING(good_id) WHERE size < 13 AND
    -> manufacturer IN ('Lenovo', 'Dell', 'Toshiba', 'Samsung', 'Acer') AND
    -> (location IN ('Moscow', 'Kiev') OR delivery_options IN ('Premium', 'Urgent'))\G
*************************** 1. row ***************************
           id: 1
  select_type: SIMPLE
        table: goods_characteristics
   partitions: NULL
         type: index
possible_keys: good_id,size
          key: good_id
      key_len: 251
          ref: NULL
         rows: 137026
     filtered: 25.00
        Extra: Using where; Using index
```

```
*************************** 2. row ***************************
           id: 1
  select_type: SIMPLE
        table: goods_shops
   partitions: NULL
         type: ref
possible_keys: good_id,location
          key: good_id
      key_len: 123
          ref: cookbook.goods_characteristics.good_id
         rows: 66422
     filtered: 36.00
        Extra: Using where; Using index
2 rows in set, 1 warning (0,00 sec)
```

Indexes would not help here, because they use cardinality that is the same for any value in the indexed column. Here is where histograms can show their power:

```
mysql> ANALYZE TABLE goods_shops UPDATE HISTOGRAM ON location, delivery_options\G
*************************** 1. row ***************************
   Table: cookbook.goods_shops
      Op: histogram
Msg_type: status
Msg_text: Histogram statistics created for column 'delivery_options'.
*************************** 2. row ***************************
   Table: cookbook.goods_shops
      Op: histogram
Msg_type: status
Msg_text: Histogram statistics created for column 'location'.
2 rows in set (0,24 sec)

mysql> SELECT COUNT(*) FROM goods_shops JOIN goods_characteristics
    -> USING(good_id) WHERE size < 13 AND
    -> manufacturer IN ('Lenovo', 'Dell', 'Toshiba', 'Samsung', 'Acer') AND
    -> (location IN ('Moscow', 'Kiev') OR delivery_options IN ('Premium', 'Urgent'));
+----------+
| COUNT(*) |
+----------+
|   816640 |
+----------+
1 row in set (1,42 sec)

mysql> EXPLAIN SELECT COUNT(*) FROM goods_shops JOIN goods_characteristics
    -> USING(good_id) WHERE size < 13 AND
    -> manufacturer IN ('Lenovo', 'Dell', 'Toshiba', 'Samsung', 'Acer') AND
    -> (location IN ('Moscow', 'Kiev') OR delivery_options IN ('Premium', 'Urgent'))\G
*************************** 1. row ***************************
           id: 1
  select_type: SIMPLE
        table: goods_shops
   partitions: NULL
         type: index
possible_keys: good_id,location
          key: good_id
      key_len: 369
          ref: NULL
         rows: 66422
     filtered: 0.09
        Extra: Using where; Using index
```

```
*************************** 2. row ***************************
           id: 1
  select_type: SIMPLE
        table: goods_characteristics
   partitions: NULL
         type: ref
possible_keys: good_id,size
          key: good_id
      key_len: 123
          ref: cookbook.goods_shops.good_id
         rows: 137026
     filtered: 25.00
        Extra: Using where; Using index
2 rows in set, 1 warning (0,00 sec)
```

Once a histogram is created, the optimizer joins tables in the effective order, and the query takes slightly more than one second instead of six minutes, as in the previous run.

See Also

For additional information about using histograms in MySQL, see "Billion Goods in Few Categories: How Histograms Save a Life?" (*https://oreil.ly/xXGdH*).

21.12 Writing Performant Queries

Problem

You want to write efficient queries.

Solution

Study how MySQL accesses data, and adjust your queries to help MySQL perform its job faster.

Discussion

As we've seen in this chapter, there are many iterations of index implementation in MySQL. While we take advantage of these index types, we also need to know how MySQL accesses data. The optimizer is a very advanced part of MySQL but still does not always make correct decisions. When it doesn't choose the right path, we'll end up with poor query performance, which may lead to degraded service or outage in our applications at production. The best way to write performant queries is to know how MySQL accesses data.

The other point here is being at scale is different than using the application in a monolith environment. As the concurrency increases with data size, the decision optimizer will choose the fastest data route that will be more complex to handle.

MySQL uses a cost-based model to estimate the cost of various operations during query execution in the following order:

1. Find the optimal method.
2. Check if the access method is useful.
3. Estimate the cost of using the access method.
4. Select the lowest-cost access method possible.

Here's the order of query execution that MySQL chooses:

1. Table scan
2. Index scan
3. Index lookup
4. Range scan
5. Index merge
6. Loose index scan

The following are some known reasons for slow index lookups for those still using an index with poor performance outcomes:

Low cardinality
When data is not diverse enough to identify a fast traversal, MySQL will end up doing a full table scan.

Large datasets
Returning large datasets often causes problems. Even if they are correctly filtered, they may be useless, as your application can't process them fast enough. Only target data that are needed in your query, and filter the rest out.

Multiple index traversal
If you have a query hitting multiple indexes, the extra I/O operation hopping through pages will lead to slow query performance.

Nonleading column lookup
If you do not use the leading column for a covering index, a covering index cannot be used.

Data type mismatch
Indexes cannot help if data types don't match when querying columns.

Character set collation mismatch
Data access should be unified around the character set and collation of the query.

Suffix lookup

Looking for a suffix will degrade performance significantly.

Index as argument

Using an indexed column as an argument will not efficiently use the index.

Stale statistics

MySQL updates statistics based on the index cardinality. This helps the optimizer to make decisions for the fastest path possible.

MySQL bug

It's rare but possible. A MySQL bug can cause slow index lookups.

Query types

When designing the application, it's useful to recognize common query patterns and when they can be applied and when they can't.

Point select

One of the fastest methods to access your data is to do a point select targeting indexed column directly. In this case, the optimizer already knows the page that your data sits on if the index exists in that column:

```
mysql> SELECT names_id,top_name,name_rank FROM top_names
    -> WHERE names_id=699 \G
*************************** 1. row ***************************
 names_id: 699
 top_name: KOCH
name_rank: 698
1 row in set (0.00 sec)
```

In this case, the names_id column is the primary key column of the table, so the access is straight to that page's path by the optimizer.

Range select

This type of SELECT is for when you need a range of rows from your dataset. MySQL can still use an index to access the data directly using the index on the same column as the WHERE clause of the query. This type of access method uses a single index or subset of values from an index or indexes. The range index is also known for using single or multipart index utilization. In the following example, the optimizer uses comparison on the name_rank field with < and > operators. Also, for all index types, AND or OR combinations will be a range condition. For MySQL, the fastest lookup is the primary key. Remember, this is also the physical order of the table:

```
mysql> EXPLAIN SELECT names_id,top_name,name_rank FROM top_names
    -> WHERE names_id>800 AND names_id < 900 \G
*************************** 1. row ***************************
           id: 1
  select_type: SIMPLE
```

```
              table: top_names
         partitions: NULL
               type: range
      possible_keys: PRIMARY
                key: PRIMARY
            key_len: 4
                ref: NULL
               rows: 99
           filtered: 100.00
              Extra: Using where
1 row in set, 1 warning (0.00 sec)
```

Covering indexes

Covering indexes are indexes that can be used to resolve the query without accessing rows' data. To make sure other supporting indexes cover your query, we can use secondary indexes. An index should be leftmost first, and each additional field should be in a composite key. A query should not access columns that do not exist in the index (see Recipe 21.5).

In the following example, the index is used to resolve the query condition without accessing that table data, but in the end, the table data is accessed, because we asked for the top_name column that doesn't exist in the index. The Using index condition statement in the Extra field of the EXPLAIN output confirms that:

```
mysql> EXPLAIN SELECT name_rank,top_name,name_count
    -> FROM top_names WHERE name_rank < 10 ORDER BY name_count\G
*************************** 1. row ***************************
                 id: 1
        select_type: SIMPLE
              table: top_names
         partitions: NULL
               type: range
      possible_keys: idx_name_rank_count
                key: idx_name_rank_count
            key_len: 3
                ref: NULL
               rows: 10
           filtered: 100.00
              Extra: Using index condition; Using filesort
1 row in set, 1 warning (0.00 sec)
```

This query uses a covering index. The Using index statement confirms that. A primary key is already part of the covering index; hence, there's no need to include names_id in the covering index:

```
mysql> EXPLAIN SELECT names_id, name_rank, name_count FROM top_names
    -> WHERE name_rank < 10 ORDER BY name_count\G
*************************** 1. row ***************************
                 id: 1
        select_type: SIMPLE
              table: top_names
         partitions: NULL
               type: range
      possible_keys: idx_name_rank_count
```

```
        key: idx_name_rank_count
    key_len: 3
        ref: NULL
       rows: 10
   filtered: 100.00
      Extra: Using where; Using index; Using filesort
1 row in set, 1 warning (0,00 sec)
```

Data type matching

Data types are also crucial for using indexes efficiently. Using numerics for numeric comparison is essential for the optimizer. The following query is an example of how MySQL doesn't like this data type conversion when it comes to names_id—an INTEGER field with a string value in it. This is the warning message we get:

```
mysql> EXPLAIN SELECT names_id,top_name,name_rank FROM
    -> top_names WHERE names_id= '123 names' \G
*************************** 1. row ***************************
            id: 1
   select_type: SIMPLE
         table: top_names
    partitions: NULL
          type: const
 possible_keys: PRIMARY
           key: PRIMARY
       key_len: 4
           ref: const
          rows: 1
      filtered: 100.00
         Extra: NULL
1 row in set, 1 warning (0,00 sec)

mysql> SHOW WARNINGS\G
*************************** 1. row ***************************
  Level: Warning
   Code: 1292
Message: Truncated incorrect DOUBLE value: '123 names'
*************************** 2. row ***************************
  Level: Note
   Code: 1003
Message: /* select#1 */ select '123' AS `names_id`,'WALLACE' AS `top_name`, ↵
         '123' AS `name_rank` from `cookbook`.`top_names` where true
2 rows in set (0,00 sec)
```

While the query may return results, MySQL has to perform a job to convert the string into a number and thus loses precision.

Negative conditions

Often, the most efficient indexes can't be used for these types of queries. The reason is that MySQL has to select all rows from the table or index, then filter those that aren't in the list.

Avoid negative clauses if possible, as they are inefficient:

- IS NOT

- IS NOT NULL

- NOT IN

- NOT LIKE

```
mysql> EXPLAIN SELECT names_id,name_rank, top_name FROM
    -> top_names WHERE top_name NOT IN ("LARA","ILAYDA","ASLIHAN") \G
*************************** 1. row ***************************
           id: 1
  select_type: SIMPLE
        table: top_names
   partitions: NULL
         type: ALL
possible_keys: idx_top_name,idx_desc_01,idx_desc_02,idx_fulltext
          key: NULL
      key_len: NULL
          ref: NULL
         rows: 161533
     filtered: 100.00
        Extra: Using where
1 row in set, 1 warning (0.00 sec)
```

ORDER BY operations

Sorting operations can be expensive as the dataset grows, especially if the query cannot use the index to resolve ORDER BY:

```
mysql> EXPLAIN SELECT names_id,name_rank, top_name FROM
    -> top_names WHERE name_rank > 15000 ORDER BY top_name \G
*************************** 1. row ***************************
           id: 1
  select_type: SIMPLE
        table: top_names
   partitions: NULL
         type: ALL
possible_keys: NULL
          key: NULL
      key_len: NULL
          ref: NULL
         rows: 161533
     filtered: 33.33
        Extra: Using where; Using filesort
1 row in set, 1 warning (0.00 sec)
```

The same applies to LIMIT operations. These type of queries usually return a small set of data with a high cost:

```
mysql> EXPLAIN SELECT names_id,name_rank, top_name FROM top_names WHERE
    -> name_rank > 15000 ORDER BY name_rank LIMIT 10\G
*************************** 1. row ***************************
           id: 1
  select_type: SIMPLE
        table: top_names
   partitions: NULL
         type: ALL
possible_keys: NULL
```

```
        key: NULL
    key_len: NULL
        ref: NULL
       rows: 161533
   filtered: 33.33
      Extra: Using where; Using filesort
1 row in set, 1 warning (0.00 sec)
```

The preceding query selects a large number of rows and then discards most of them.

JOINs

Join operations are an original way of combining or referencing data from two or more tables. While SQL joins serve a particular purpose, they can create a cartesian product on query results if not used properly. Using INNER joins to filter only the intersection of tables in the SELECT statement is highly advised versus using LEFT JOINs. Using INNER JOINs is not always possible to ensure compliance with the required business logic. In those cases, targeting indexed fields will still benefit the query execution time:

```
SELECT a.col_a, a.col_b, b.col_a FROM table_a a
INNER JOIN table_b b
ON a.key = b.key;
```

 In MySQL, JOIN is synonymous with INNER JOIN.

Help the optimizer choose the best possible path to access your data by creating correct indexes and writing efficient queries. This type of approach will improve your throughput overall. Add only the indexes you need, and don't over-index tables. Avoiding duplicate indexes is another best practice to achieve performant queries. Identify if the same indexes in your table may cause a slow-down on both reads and writes.

CHAPTER 22
Server Administration

22.0 Introduction

This chapter covers how to perform operations involved in administering a MySQL server:

- General server configuration
- The plug-in interface
- Controlling server logging
- Configuring storage engines

The chapter doesn't cover managing MySQL user accounts. That is an administrative task and is covered in Chapter 24.

 Many of the techniques shown here require administrative access, such as the ability to modify tables in the mysql system database or use statements that require the SUPER privilege. For this reason, to carry out the operations described here, you'll likely need to connect to the server as root rather than as cbuser.

22.1 Configuring the Server

Problem

You want to change the server settings and also verify that your changes took effect.

Solution

To change settings, specify them at server startup or at runtime. To verify the changes, examine the relevant system variables at runtime.

Discussion

The MySQL server places many configuration parameters under your control. For example, resources that require memory can be adjusted up or down to tailor resource usage. A heavily used server requires more memory; a lightly used one, less. You can set command options and system variables at server startup, and many system variables are settable at runtime as well. You can also examine your settings at runtime to verify that the configuration is as you intend.

Configuration control at server startup

To configure the server at startup time, specify options on the command line or in an option file. The latter is usually preferable because you can specify settings once and they'll apply at each startup. (For background on using command-line options and option files, see Recipe 1.4.)

Command option names typically use dashes, whereas system variable names use underscores. However, the server is more permissive at startup and recognizes command options and system variables written using dashes or underscores interchangeably. For example, sql_mode and sql-mode are equivalent on the command line or in an option file. This differs from runtime, when references to system variables *must* be written using underscores.

To specify server parameters in an option file, list them in the [mysqld] group of a file the server reads. To illustrate, here are some parameters you might set:

- The default character set is utf8mb4 starting from MySQL 8.0. This character set comes with utf8mb4_0900_ai_ci as the default collation.

- The default SQL mode is STRICT_TRANS_TABLES (after MySQL 5.7). To be more permissive by default, remove strict SQL mode, which is not recommended.

- The event scheduler is enabled by default after MySQL 8.0. If you plan to use scheduled events (see Recipe 11.5), you must enable it on prior releases.

- For InnoDB engine, buffer pool size defaults to 128 MB, which is not sufficient beyond development and testing. Consider increasing to a size for running the dataset in memory.

- Time zone is set to SYSTEM unless specified at startup. If you aren't intending to use SYSTEM time zone, you need to set it at startup by setting --timezone= timezone_name.

To implement these configuration ideas, write the [mysqld] group in your option file like this:

```
[mysqld]
character_set_server=utf8mb4
sql_mode=STRICT_TRANS_TABLES
event_scheduler=1
innodb_buffer_pool_size=512M
```

Those are just suggestions; adjust the server configuration for your own requirements. For information about plug-in and logging options in particular, see Recipes 22.2 and 23.0.

Configuration control and verification at runtime

After the server starts, you can make runtime adjustments by changing system variables using the SET statement:

```
SET GLOBAL var_name = value;
```

That statement sets the global value of *var_name*; that is, the value that applies to all clients by default. Changes to the global value at runtime require the SUPER privilege. Many system variables also have a session value, which is the value specific to a particular client session. The session value of a given variable is initialized from the global value when the client connects, but the client can change it thereafter. For example, the database administrator (DBA) might set the max connections at server startup:

```
[mysqld]
max_connections=1000
```

That sets the global value. A DBA with the SUPER privilege can change the global value at runtime:

```
SET GLOBAL max_connections = 1000;
```

Each client that connects subsequently has its session variable initialized to the same value but can change the value as it likes. A DBA may increase this value for troubleshooting connectivity issues:

```
SET SESSION max_connections = 1000;
```

A SET statement that includes no GLOBAL or SESSION modifier changes the session value, if there is one.

After MySQL 8.0, you can set and persist global variables. Many of the global variables are dynamic and can be set at runtime. A *PERSIST* clause will help set this value permanently even if the server is restarted without saving to the configuration file:

```
SET PERSISTS max_connections = 1000;
```

```
SET PERSISTS_ONLY max_connections = 1000;
```

```
mysql> SELECT @@GLOBAL.max_connections;
+--------------------------+
| @@GLOBAL.max_connections |
+--------------------------+
|                     1000 |
+--------------------------+
```

To reset persisted values, use the following:

```
RESET PERSIST;
```

```
RESET PERSIST max_connections;
```

There is alternative syntax for writing system variable references:

```
SET @@GLOBAL.var_name = value;
SET @@SESSION.var_name = value;
```

The @@ syntax is more flexible. It can be used in statements other than SET, enabling you to retrieve or examine individual system variables:

```
mysql> SELECT @@GLOBAL.max_connections;
+--------------------------+
| @@GLOBAL.max_connections |
+--------------------------+
|                     1000 |
+--------------------------+
```

References to system variables using @@ syntax with no GLOBAL. or SESSION. modifier access the session value if there is one, or the global value otherwise.

Other ways to access system variables include the SHOW VARIABLES statement and selecting from the INFORMATION_SCHEMA GLOBAL_VARIABLES and SESSION_VARIABLES tables.

If a setting exists only as a command option with no corresponding system variable, you cannot check its value at runtime. Fortunately, such options are rare. Nowadays, most new settings are created as system variables that can be examined at runtime.

22.2 Managing the Plug-In Interface

Problem

You want to exploit the capabilities offered by certain server plug-ins.

Solution

Learn how to control the plug-in interface.

Discussion

MySQL supports the use of plug-ins that extend server capabilities. There are plug-ins that implement storage engines, authentication methods, password policy,

PERFORMANCE_SCHEMA tables, and more. The server enables you to specify which plug-ins to use so that you can load just those you want, with no memory or processing overhead incurred for plug-ins you don't want.

This section provides the general background on controlling which plug-ins the server loads. Discussion elsewhere describes specific plug-ins and what they can do for you, including the authentication plug-ins (see Recipe 24.1) and validate_password (see Recipes 24.3 and 24.4).

The examples here refer to plug-in files using the *.so* ("shared object") filename suffix. If the suffix differs on your system, adjust the names accordingly (for example, use *.dll* on Windows). If you don't know the name of a given plug-in file, look in the directory named by the plugin_dir system variable, which is where the server expects to find plug-in files. For example:

```
mysql> SELECT @@plugin_dir;
+-----------------------------+
| @@plugin_dir                |
+-----------------------------+
| /usr/local/mysql/lib/plugin/ |
+-----------------------------+
```

To see which plug-ins are installed, use SHOW PLUGINS or query the INFORMATION_SCHEMA PLUGINS table.

> Some plug-ins are built in, need not be enabled explicitly, and cannot be disabled. The mysql_native_password and sha256_password authentication plug-ins fall into this category.

Plug-in control at server startup

To install a plug-in only for a given server invocation, use the --plugin-load-add option at server startup, naming the file that contains the plug-in. To name multiple plug-ins as the option value, separate them with semicolons. Alternatively, use the option multiple times, with each instance naming a single plug-in. That makes it easy to enable or disable individual plug-ins by using the # character to selectively comment the corresponding lines:

```
[mysqld]
plugin-load-add=caching_sha2_password.so
plugin-load-add=adt_null.so
#plugin-load-add=semisync_master.so
#plugin-load-add=semisync_slave.so
```

The --plugin-load-add option was introduced in MySQL 5.6. In MySQL 8.0, you can use a single --plugin-load option that names all the plug-ins to be loaded in a semicolon-separated list:

```
[mysqld]
plugin-load=validate_password.so;caching_sha2_password.so
```

Clearly, for dealing with more than one plug-in, `--plugin-load-add` is superior for ease of administration.

Plug-in control at runtime

To install a plug-in at runtime and make it persistent, use `INSTALL PLUGIN`. The server loads the plug-in (which becomes available immediately) and registers it in the `mysql.plugin` system table to cause it to load automatically for subsequent restarts. For example:

```
INSTALL PLUGIN caching_sha2_password SONAME 'caching_sha2_password.so';
```

The `SONAME` ("shared object name") clause specifies the file that contains the plug-in.

To disable a plug-in at runtime, use `UNINSTALL PLUGIN`. The server unloads the plug-in and removes its registration from the `mysql.plugin` table:

```
UNINSTALL PLUGIN caching_sha2_password;
```

`INSTALL PLUGIN` and `UNINSTALL PLUGIN` require the `INSERT` and `DELETE` privilege, respectively, for the `mysql.plugin` table.

22.3 Controlling Server Logging

Problem

You want to take advantage of log information the server can provide.

Solution

Learn the server options that control logging.

Discussion

The MySQL server can produce several logs:

The error log
> The error log contains information about problems or exceptional conditions the server encounters. This is useful information for debugging. In particular, if the server exits, check the error log for the reason. For example, if an exit occurs immediately after startup, it's likely that some setting in the server option file is misspelled or was set to an invalid value. The error log will contain a message to that effect.

The general query log

The general query log indicates when each client connected and disconnected and what SQL statements it executed. This tells you how much and what activity each client is engaged in.

The slow query log

The slow query log records statements that took a long time to execute (see the MySQL Reference Manual (*https://oreil.ly/u0ta9*) for the meaning of "a long time" because it can be influenced by several options). Queries that appear repeatedly in this log may be bottlenecks worth investigating to see whether they can be made more efficient.

The binary log

The binary log contains a record of data changes made by the server. To set up replication, you must enable the binary log on the source server: it serves as the storage medium for changes to be sent to replica servers. The binary log is also used, together with backup files, during data recovery operations.

Each log serves a different purpose, and most can be turned on at your discretion, enabling you to use those that suit your administrative requirements. Each log can be written to a file, and some can be written to other destinations. The error log can be sent to your terminal or to the `syslog` facility. The general and slow query logs can be written to a file, to a table in the `mysql` database, or both.

To control server logging, add lines to your server option file that specify the desired types of logging. (Some settings can also be changed at runtime.) For example, the following lines in a server option file send the error log to the *err.log* file in the data directory, enable writing the general query and slow query logs to tables in the `mysql` database, and enable writing the binary log to the */var/mysql-logs* directory using files having names beginning with *binlog*:

```
[mysqld]
log_error=err.log
log_output=TABLE
general_log=1
slow_query_log=1
log-bin=/var/mysql-logs/binlog
```

For filenames in options that produce log output to files, logfiles are written under the data directory unless specified using full pathnames. The usual reason to use full pathnames is to write logfiles to a filesystem different from the one containing the data directory, which is a useful technique for dividing disk space use and I/O activity among physical devices.

The rest of this section provides details specific to controlling individual logs. The examples show the lines to include in your server option file to produce specific logging behavior. For some ideas about using the logs for diagnostic or activity assessment purposes, see Recipe 22.6.

 For any log that you enable, see also Recipes 22.4 and 22.5 for log maintenance techniques. Logs increase in size over time, so you'll want to have a plan for managing them.

The error log

The error log cannot be disabled, but you can control where it's written. By default, on Unix, the error output goes to your terminal or to *host_name.err* in the data directory if you start the server using `mysqld_safe`. On Windows, the default is *host_name.err* in the data directory. To specify the error log filename, set the `log_error` system variable.

Examples:

- Write the error log to the *err.log* file in the data directory:
  ```
  [mysqld]
  log_error=err.log
  ```

- As of MySQL 5.7.2, you can influence the amount of error log output by setting the `log_error_verbosity` system variable. Permitted values range from 1 (errors only) to 3 (errors, warnings, notes; the default). To see errors only, do this:
  ```
  [mysqld]
  log_error=err.log
  log_error_verbosity=1
  ```

- On Unix, if you start the server using `mysqld_safe`, it's possible to redirect the error log to the `syslog` facility:
  ```
  [mysqld_safe]
  syslog
  ```

The general query and slow query logs

Several system variables control the general query and slow query logs. Each variable can be set at server startup or changed at runtime:

- `log_output` controls the log destinations. The value is `FILE` (log to files, the default), `TABLE` (log to tables), `NONE` (disable logging), or a comma-separated combination of values, in any order. `NONE` overrides any other value. If the value is `NONE`, other settings for these logs have no effect. Destination control applies to the general query and slow query logs together; you cannot write one to a file and the other to a table.

- `general_log` and `slow_query_log` enable or disable the respective logs. By default, each log is disabled. If you enable either of them, the server writes the log to the destinations specified by `log_output`, unless that variable is NONE.
- `general_log_file` and `slow_query_log_file` specify log filenames. The default names are *host_name.log* and *host_name-slow.log*; however, these settings have no effect unless `log_output` specifies FILE logging.

Examples:

- Write the general query log to the *query.log* file in the data directory:
  ```
  [mysqld]
  log_output=FILE
  general_log=1
  general_log_file=query.log
  ```
- Write the general and slow query logs to tables in the `mysql` database (the table names are `general_log` and `slow_log` and cannot be changed):
  ```
  [mysqld]
  log_output=TABLE
  general_log=1
  slow_query_log=1
  ```
- Write the general query log to a file named *query.log* and to the `general_log` table:
  ```
  [mysqld]
  log_output=FILE,TABLE
  general_log=1
  general_log_file=query.log
  ```

The binary log

Prior to MySQL 8, binary logging was disabled by default. To enable the binary log, use the `--log-bin` option, optionally specifying the logfile basename as the option value. To disable binary logging in MySQL 8.0, you can use the `--skip-log-bin` option or the `--disable-log-bin` option. The default basename is *binlog*. The value for this option is a basename because the server creates binary logfiles in numbered sequence, automatically adding to the basename suffixes of *.000001*, *.000002*, and so forth. The server advances to the next file in the sequence when it starts, when the logs are flushed, and when the current file reaches the maximum logfile size (controlled by the `max_binlog_size` system variable). In MySQL 8.0, `expire_logs_days` is deprecated and replaced with `binlog_expire_logs_seconds`. To have the server expire logfiles for you, set the `binlog_expire_logs_seconds` system variable to the age in seconds at which files become eligible for removal. The default value for *binlog_expire_logs_seconds* is 30 days (30 * 24 * 60 * 60 seconds). To disable automatic purging of binary logs, set *binlog_expire_logs_seconds* to 0.

Examples:

- Enable the binary log, writing numbered files in the data directory having names beginning with *binlog*. Additionally, expire logfiles after a week:

```
[mysqld]
max_binlog_size=4G
binlog_expire_logs_seconds=604800
```

The binary log is an essential component for the MySQL server, and the administrator needs to approach it carefully. Binary logs contain events for all data changes and hence are used for the following areas:

- Replication setup
- Point-in-time recovery
- Debugging a specific event

22.4 Rotating or Expiring Logfiles

Problem

Files used for logging grow indefinitely unless managed.

Solution

Available strategies for managing log files include rotating a logfile through a set of names and expiring files by age. But different strategies apply to different logs, so consider the log type before choosing a strategy.

Discussion

Logfile rotation is a technique that renames a logfile through a series of one or more names. This maintains the file for a certain number of rotations, at which point it reaches the end of the sequence and its contents are discarded by being overwritten. Rotation can be applied to the error log, general query log, or slow query log.

Logfile expiration removes files when they reach a certain age. This technique applies to the binary log.

Both log management methods rely on log flushing to make sure that the current logfile has been closed properly. When you flush the logs, the server closes and reopens whichever of the files it is writing. If you rename the error, general query, or slow query logfile first, the server closes the current file and reopens a new one using the original name; this is what enables rotation of the current file while the server runs. The server also closes the current binary logfile and opens a new one with the next number in the sequence.

To flush the server logs, execute a FLUSH LOGS statement or use the mysqladmin flush-logs command. (Log flushing requires the RELOAD privilege.) The following discussion shows maintenance operations as performed at the command line, so it uses mysqladmin. The examples use mv as the file renaming command, which is applicable on Unix. On Windows, use rename instead.

Rotating the error, general query, or slow query log

To maintain a single file in a log rotation, rename the current logfile and flush the logs. Suppose that the error logfile is named *err.log* in the data directory. To rotate it, change location to the data directory, then execute these commands:

```
$ mv err.log err.log.old
$ mysqladmin flush-logs
```

When you flush the logs, the server opens a new *err.log* file. You can remove *err.log.old* at your leisure. To maintain an archive copy, include it in your filesystem backups before removing it.

To maintain a set of multiple rotated files, it's convenient to use a sequence of numbered suffixes. For example, to maintain a set of three old general query logfiles, do this:

```
$ mv query.log.2 query.log.3
$ mv query.log.1 query.log.2
$ mv query.log query.log.1
$ mysqladmin flush-logs
```

The first few times you execute the command sequence, the initial commands are unneeded until the respective *query.log.N* files exist.

Successive executions of that command sequence rotate *query.log* through the names *query.log.1*, *query.log.2*, and *query.log.3*; then *query.log.3* is overwritten and its contents lost. To maintain an archive copy, include the rotated files in your filesystem backups before removing them.

Rotating the binary log

The server creates binary logfiles in numbered sequence. To expire them, you need only arrange that it removes files when they're old enough. Several factors affect how many files the server creates and maintains:

- The frequency of server restarts and log flushing operations: one new file is generated each time either of those occurs.
- The size to which files can grow: larger sizes lead to fewer files. To control this size, set the max_binlog_size system variable.
- How old files are permitted to become: longer expiration times lead to more files. To control this age, set the binlog_expire_logs_seconds system variable.

The server makes expiration checks at server startup and when it opens a new binary logfile.

The following settings enable the binary log, set the maximum file size to 4GB, and expire files after four days:

```
[mysqld]
log-bin=binlog
max_binlog_size=4G
binlog_expire_logs_seconds=4
```

You can also remove binary logfiles manually with the `PURGE BINARY LOGS` statement. For example, to remove all files up to and including the one named `binlog.001028`, do this:

```
PURGE BINARY LOGS TO 'binlog.001028';
```

If your server is a replication source, don't be too aggressive about removing binary logfiles. No file should be removed until you're certain its contents have been completely transmitted to all replicas.

Automating logfile rotation

To make it easier to perform a rotation operation, put the commands that implement it in a file to create a shell script. To perform the rotation automatically, arrange to execute the script from a job scheduler such as `cron`. The script will need to access connection parameters that enable it to connect to the server to flush the logs, using an account that has the `RELOAD` privilege. One strategy is to put the parameters in an option file and pass the file to `mysqladmin` using a `--defaults-file=file_name` option, for example:

```
#!/bin/sh
mv err.log err.log.old
mysqladmin --defaults-file=/usr/local/mysql/data/flush-opts.cnf flush-logs
```

22.5 Rotating Log Tables or Expiring Log Table Rows

Problem

Tables used for logging grow indefinitely unless managed.

Solution

Rotate the tables or expire rows within them.

Discussion

Recipe 22.4 discussed rotation and expiration of logfiles. Analogous techniques apply to log tables:

- To rotate a log table, rename it and open a new table with the original name.
- To expire log table contents, remove rows older than a certain age.

The examples here demonstrate how to implement these methods using the general query log table, `mysql.general_log`. The same methods apply to the slow query log table, `mysql.slow_log`, or to any other table containing rows that have a timestamp.

To employ log table rotation, create an empty copy of the original table to serve as the new table (see Recipe 6.1), then rename the original table and rename the new one to take its place:

```
DROP TABLE IF EXISTS mysql.general_log_old, mysql.general_log_new;
CREATE TABLE mysql.general_log_new LIKE mysql.general_log;
RENAME TABLE mysql.general_log TO mysql.general_log_old,
  mysql.general_log_new TO mysql.general_log;
```

To employ log row expiration, you can either empty the table completely or selectively:

- To empty a log table completely, truncate it:
  ```
  TRUNCATE TABLE mysql.general_log;
  ```
- To expire a table selectively, removing only rows older than a given age, you must know the name of the column that indicates row-creation time:
  ```
  DELETE FROM mysql.general_log WHERE event_time < NOW() - INTERVAL 1 WEEK;
  ```

For automatic expiration, the statements for any of the techniques just described can be executed within a scheduled event (see Recipe 11.5), for example:

```
CREATE EVENT expire_general_log
  ON SCHEDULE EVERY 1 WEEK
  DO DELETE FROM mysql.general_log
    WHERE event_time < NOW() - INTERVAL 1 WEEK;
```

22.6 Configuring Storage Engines

Problem

You want to make sure the engine of your choice is configured properly.

Solution

Understand and configure each storage engine according to its use case.

Discussion

MySQL comes with several storage engines by default, such as MyISAM and InnoDB. MySQL 8.0 and onward use InnoDB as the default database engine. Along with this

---

popular storage engine, there are some others you might want to explore. Each of these storage engine will use shared resources as well as dedicated resources from the operating system. Care must be taken not to give too many resources while mixing and matching:

InnoDB
  Supports transactions and row-level locking with full ACID (atomicity, consistency, isolation, durability) compliancy engine.

MyISAM
  Table-level locking and simple engine.

MyRocks
  LSM-based B-tree key/value storage engine.[1]

CSV
  Comma-separated values engine.

Blackhole
  All writes are sent to /dev/null no data storage engine.

Memory
  Optimized for in-memory workload storage engine.

Archive
  Write-only engine for archival data in compressed format storage engine.

 Using multiple storage engines at the same time can cause issues and may lead to data loss if used in the same transaction. Also, be careful about the compatibility of your application and tooling around it.

As each of the previously mentioned engines store data differently, we must configure them accordingly. InnoDB utilizes redo and undo log spaces for modified data. This allows both recovery and point-in-time restore with minimal data loss in the event of hardware or server failures. MyRocks is another advanced storage engine that writes to recovery log Write Ahead Log (WAL) first and supports rollback for each transaction. MyISAM and CSV-type storage engines write directly to datafiles. While it's easier to make binary backups and transport them, these engines will not support rollback operations.

---

1 The third-party storage engine via Percona and MariaDB is designed to handle write-intensive workloads with space-saving benefits.

To check the default storage engine using MySQL 8.0, do the following:

```
mysql> SELECT @@default_storage_engine;
+--------------------------+
| @@default_storage_engine |
+--------------------------+
| InnoDB                   |
+--------------------------+
```

We can see the table storage engine type by checking the schema definition:

```
mysql> SHOW CREATE TABLE limbs\G
        Table: limbs
Create Table: CREATE TABLE `limbs` (
  `thing` varchar(20) DEFAULT NULL,
  `legs` int DEFAULT NULL,
  `arms` int DEFAULT NULL,
  PRIMARY KEY(thing)
) ENGINE=InnoDB DEFAULT CHARSET=utf8mb4
COLLATE=utf8mb4_0900_ai_ci
```

If you want to change the storage engine type after you've created the table, issue an *ALTER* statement:

```
mysql> ALTER TABLE cookbook.limbs  ENGINE=MYISAM;
Query OK, 11 rows affected (0.16 sec)
Records: 11  Duplicates: 0  Warnings: 0

mysql> SHOW CREATE TABLE limbs\G
*************************** 1. row ***************************
        Table: limbs
Create Table: CREATE TABLE `limbs` (
  `thing` varchar(20) DEFAULT NULL,
  `legs` int DEFAULT NULL,
  `arms` int DEFAULT NULL,
  PRIMARY KEY(thing)
) ENGINE=MyISAM DEFAULT CHARSET=utf8mb4
COLLATE=utf8mb4_0900_ai_ci
1 row in set (0.00 sec)
```

> While you can swap between storage engines after a table has been created and data loaded, the *ALTER TABLE* operation locks for all storage engines. For large datasets, consider utilizing online schema change utilities such as pt-online-schema-change (*https://oreil.ly/pNiVP*) or gh-ost (*https://github.com/github/gh-ost*). These tools allow schema migrations to complete without creating a metadata lock, and apply changes in a controlled way.

Other storage engine settings can be checked as follows:

```
mysql> SHOW GLOBAL VARIABLES LIKE "%engine%" ;
+-------------------------------+-----------------+
| Variable_name                 | Value           |
+-------------------------------+-----------------+
| default_storage_engine        | InnoDB          |
| default_tmp_storage_engine    | InnoDB          |
| disabled_storage_engines      |                 |
| internal_tmp_mem_storage_engine | TempTable     |
| secondary_engine_cost_threshold | 100000.000000 |
+-------------------------------+-----------------+
```

CHAPTER 23

Monitoring the MySQL Server

23.0 Introduction

This chapter covers how to monitor the MySQL server using various command-line tools:

- The `mysqladmin` interface
- System variables
- Status variables
- Information and Performance Schemas
- Storage engines diagnostics
- Logfiles

This chapter doesn't cover managing administrative tasks. Instead, it focuses on the server's observability. Administrators or developers should evaluate outcomes from various command-line tools on the MySQL server carefully before taking action and modifying configuration changes listed in Chapter 22. Rather, this chapter discusses what you can find out, and how, by surveying the types of information available and how to use that information to answer questions. The purpose is not so much to consider specific monitoring problems, but to illustrate your options so you can begin to answer your questions, whatever they are. In the case of reactive monitoring on an issue, follow one of the following options:

1. Determine which of the available information sources pertain to the problem at hand.

2. Choose an approach for using the information: Are you asking a one-time question? If so, maybe a few interactive queries are sufficient. If you're trying

to solve an issue that may recur or for which you need continuous monitoring, a program-oriented approach is better. Will a script written entirely in SQL do the job, or do you need to write a program that queries the server and performs additional manipulation of the information obtained? (This is typical for operations that cannot be done in pure SQL, that have special output formatting requirements, and so forth.) If a task must run periodically, you may need to set up a scheduled event or cron job. For browser display, write a web script.

 Some of the techniques shown here require administrative access, such as accessing log files in operating system MySQL or using statements that require the SUPER privilege. For this reason, to carry out the operations described here, you'll likely need to connect to the server as root rather than as cbuser, or grant SUPER to cbuser. MySQL installation created a "root'@'localhost" superuser account that has all privileges the database user has.

23.1 Why Monitor the MySQL Server?

Problem

You want to monitor the server to capture its state, which allows you to verify or change settings explained in Chapter 22. Knowing the state of the MySQL server's wait events and status counters reveals so much information about the *server limits*. Wait events are performance indicators of the server. Monitoring can be utilized in two different areas. The most common reasons for monitoring are troubleshooting errors, crashes, and failures. The others may include better utilization of the hardware layer used for available resources such as memory, I/O subsystem, CPU utilization, and network bandwidth. Due to hardware limitations, MySQL can suffer significant degradation in performance; hence, hardware plays an important role in database operations.

Solution

To monitor the MySQL server, use the built-in functionality of MySQL client with the power of other built-in tools like mysqladmin.

Discussion

As your MySQL server runs, you want to learn if the underlying hardware is performing well for your needs.

Operating System

Before getting into MySQL-specific monitoring and troubleshooting, it's recommended that you verify Operating System (OS) vitals accordingly. Four main categories—memory, input/output (I/O), CPU, and network resources—can have a major impact on MySQL's operational behavior.

Memory utilization. The memory utilization of *mysqld* can be checked via the OS command line. It's essential to have a dedicated MySQL host for each server; hence, there's no race for OS resources, including memory. The rule of thumb is to have up to 80% of your memory allocated for a dedicated MySQL server, but you must check your workload and data size to calculate the memory needed:

```
$ sudo pmap $(pidof mysqld) |grep total
 total          1292476K
```

You can confirm this via the *sys* schema using `mysql` client:

```
mysql> USE sys
Reading table information for completion of table and column names
You can turn off this feature to get a quicker startup with -A

Database changed
mysql> SELECT * FROM memory_global_total;
+-----------------+
| total_allocated |
+-----------------+
| 476.81 MiB      |
+-----------------+
1 row in set (0.00 sec)
```

Also watch out for virtual memory utilization, and make sure your host OS is not swapping in the first place:

```
$ free -m
              total       used       free     shared  buff/cache   available
Mem:           1993        453        755          5         784        1382
Swap:           979          0        979


$ cat /proc/$(pidof mysqld)/status | grep Swap
VmSwap:           0 kB
```

The following OS configuration regarding memory utilization is crucial to MySQL's memory allocation. Make sure these have been configured accordingly:

Swappiness
> This is the concept of allowing physical memory to be moved to a swap area by the kernel. It's recommended to set this value to 1 and hence allow the kernel to perform the minimum amount of swapping:
> ```
> $ sudo sysctl vm.swappiness=1
> vm.swappiness = 1
> ```

Non-uniform memory access (NUMA)

This is the concept of balancing memory between each CPU core. MySQL 8 supports enabling NUMA interleaved mode (*https://oreil.ly/AjD80*) when multiple cores are available. This value is OFF by default. Enabling NUMA to interleave the mode operating system allows allocated memory to be balanced among the CPU cores for better utilization:

```
mysql> SHOW GLOBAL VARIABLES LIKE "innodb_numa_interleave";
+------------------------+-------+
| Variable_name          | Value |
+------------------------+-------+
| innodb_numa_interleave | ON    |
+------------------------+-------+
1 row in set (0.00 sec)
```

OOM killer

In Linux systems, MySQL generally has a concept called *out of memory killer* controlled by the kernel. This is to prevent possible runaway processes in operating systems to avoid race conditions and a server crash. Since MySQL and its optimized memory buffers are memory hogs, the operating system may often kill the mysqld process to avert a system-wide crash if not adjusted. As we mentioned earlier, we can control how much memory MySQL should allocate from the operating system. Still, if OOM kicks in, it's possible to configure on the system level or disable it altogether (not recommended):

```
$ pidof mysqld
25046
$ sudo cat /proc/25046/oom_score
34
$ sudo echo -100 > /proc/24633/oom_score_adj
$ sudo cat /proc/24633/oom_score
0
```

File system cache

Operating systems use caches for all memory operations, whereas MySQL has its own optimized caches, including the InnoDB Buffer Pool. Since there is no need to cache data twice, we opt out of using the file system cache by setting innodb_flush_method to O_DIRECT; in addition, its value needs to be changed at startup:

```
mysql> SHOW GLOBAL VARIABLES LIKE "innodb_flush_method";
+---------------------+-------+
| Variable_name       | Value |
+---------------------+-------+
| innodb_flush_method | fsync |
+---------------------+-------+
1 row in set (0.00 sec)
```

While the O_DIRECT flush method works with most installations, it does not work well with all storages subsystems. You may need to test it before setting this value.

I/O utilization. I/O performance is vital for the MySQL database. The data that is read from database (aka SELECT statements) and is written back to data (UPDATE, INSERT, DELETE statements) causes input/output operation to happen to disks (aka physical storage). Depending on the available buffers' sizes, all the data processed within buffers will eventually be flushed to a disk, which is a very costly operation in terms of data transfer. Although the data is cached, it has to be flushed to the disk regularly. Also, large datasets that don't fit in the memory will have to be read from disks. In modern hardware, Solid State Disks (SSD) offer better performance, but it's beneficial to know where the underlying bottlenecks are. You can use `iotop` to observe the I/O impact per process on the system; hence, you can drill down into each method for a specific operation.

You can use the *iotop* utility interactively to monitor I/O operations. In this example, we see disk activity for one of the MySQL threads.

```
$ sudo iotop --only
Total DISK READ : 2.93 M/s | Total DISK WRITE : 9.24 M/s
Actual DISK READ: 2.93 M/s | Actual DISK WRITE: 12.01 M/s
TID PRIO USER DISK READ DISK WRITE SWAPIN IO> COMMAND
10692 be/4 vagrant 0.00 B/s 0.00 B/s 0.00 % 56.11 % mysqld --defaults-file=/home/sandboxes
~--socket=/tmp/mysql_sandbox8021.sock --port=8021
10684 be/4 vagrant 0.00 B/s 0.00 B/s 0.00 % 53.33 % mysqld --defaults-file=/home/sandboxes
~--socket=/tmp/mysql_sandbox8021.sock --port=8021
10688 be/4 vagrant 0.00 B/s 6.96 M/s 0.00 % 30.12 % mysqld --defaults-file=/home/sandboxes
~--socket=/tmp/mysql_sandbox8021.sock --port=8021
10685 be/4 vagrant 0.00 B/s 0.00 B/s 0.00 % 26.89 % mysqld --defaults-file=/home/sandboxes
~--socket=/tmp/mysql_sandbox8021.sock --port=8021
  ...
```

In the meantime, we can check the process list from the MySQL command-line interface to see what's taking priority over other threads:

```
mysql> SELECT THREAD_OS_ID, PROCESSLIST_ID, PROCESSLIST_USER,
    -> PROCESSLIST_DB, PROCESSLIST_COMMAND
    -> FROM performance_schema.threads WHERE PROCESSLIST_COMMAND IS NOT NULL;
+--------+-----+----------+--------------------+---------+
| TOSID  | PID | PUSR     | PDB                | PCMD    |
+--------+-----+----------+--------------------+---------+
| 1964   |   5 | NULL     | NULL               | Sleep   |
| 1968   |   7 | NULL     | NULL               | Daemon  |
| 1971   |   8 | msandbox | performance_schema | Query   |
| 2003   |   9 | root     | test               | Execute |
```

```
| 2002 | 10 | root    | test                | Execute |
| 2004 | 11 | root    | test                | Execute |
| 2001 | 12 | root    | test                | Execute |
| 2000 | 13 | root    | test                | Execute |
+------+----+---------+---------------------+---------+
8 rows in set (0.00 sec)
```

We can pinpoint the process id to identify details about the query for this example:

```
mysql> EXPLAIN FOR CONNECTION 10\G
*************************** 1. row ***************************
           id: 1
  select_type: INSERT
        table: sbtest25
   partitions: NULL
         type: ALL
possible_keys: NULL
          key: NULL
      key_len: NULL
          ref: NULL
         rows: NULL
     filtered: NULL
        Extra: NULL
1 row in set (0.00 sec)
```

We can also gather further information about this thread from performance_schema by querying table_io_waits_summary_by_table, which aggregates all table I/O wait events, as generated by the wait/io/table/sql/handler instrument.

The table_io_waits_summary_by_table table has the following columns to indicate how the table aggregates events: OBJECT_TYPE, OBJECT_SCHEMA, and OBJECT_NAME. These columns have the same meaning as in the events_waits_current table. They identify the table to which the row applies. This table also contains information about the following groups:

COUNT_*
    How many times a user requested reads/writes/waits from this table.

SUM_*
    How many reads/writes in total requests from this table.

MIN_*/MAX_*/AVG_*
    Minimum, maximum, and average values for this table:

```
mysql> SELECT * FROM performance_schema.table_io_waits_summary_by_table
    -> WHERE object_schema='test' AND object_name='sbtest25'\G
*************************** 1. row ***************************
     OBJECT_TYPE: TABLE
   OBJECT_SCHEMA: test
     OBJECT_NAME: sbtest25
      COUNT_STAR: 3200367
   SUM_TIMER_WAIT: 1970633326256
   MIN_TIMER_WAIT: 1505980
   AVG_TIMER_WAIT: 615412
   MAX_TIMER_WAIT: 2759234856
```

```
    COUNT_READ: 3200367
SUM_TIMER_READ: 1970633326256
MIN_TIMER_READ: 1505980
AVG_TIMER_READ: 615412
MAX_TIMER_READ: 2759234856
   COUNT_WRITE: 0
SUM_TIMER_WRITE: 0
MIN_TIMER_WRITE: 0
AVG_TIMER_WRITE: 0
MAX_TIMER_WRITE: 0
   COUNT_FETCH: 3200367
SUM_TIMER_FETCH: 1970633326256
MIN_TIMER_FETCH: 1505980
AVG_TIMER_FETCH: 615412
MAX_TIMER_FETCH: 2759234856
  COUNT_INSERT: 0
...
```

This table is also used by the `schema_table_statistics%` views in *sys* schema. (For further reading, please refer to the documentation at "table_io_waits_summary_by_table" (*https://oreil.ly/58LW4*)):

```
mysql> SELECT * FROM sys.schema_table_statistics
    -> WHERE table_schema="test" AND table_name="sbtest23"\G
*************************** 1. row ***************************
     table_schema: test
       table_name: sbtest23
    total_latency: 14.46 s
      rows_fetched: 8389964
    fetch_latency: 14.46 s
     rows_inserted: 0
   insert_latency: 0 ps
      rows_updated: 0
   update_latency: 0 ps
      rows_deleted: 0
   delete_latency: 0 ps
 io_read_requests: 3006
          io_read: 46.97 MiB
  io_read_latency: 19.48 ms
io_write_requests: 737
         io_write: 11.61 MiB
 io_write_latency: 21.09 ms
 io_misc_requests: 284
  io_misc_latency: 1.72 s
1 row in set (0.01 sec)
```

Network utilization. The network is also a very important part of database configuration. Often, test and development systems run on local configuration, which omits network hops between the nodes. If MySQL is running on a dedicated host, all requests to the database will be coming via the application layer or proxy server. Since monitoring requires continuous data flow, it's better to utilize a tool that has at least 30 days' worth of time-series, historical data to analyze. For this, we highly recommend Percona Monitoring and Management (PMM) (*https://oreil.ly/PtQg0*) for monitoring network utilization, as shown in Figure 23-1.

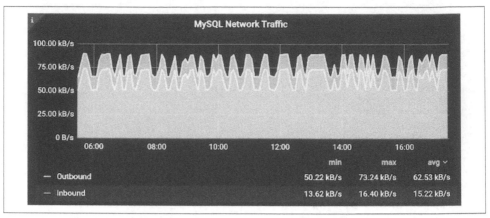

Figure 23-1. Percona Monitoring and Management—MySQL instance summary

23.2 Discovering Sources of MySQL Monitoring Information

Problem

You want to check how the server is operating with the available resources.

Solution

Let the server tell you about itself using built-in utilities.

Discussion

As your MySQL server runs, you'll have questions about aspects of its operation or performance. Or maybe it's *not* running and you want to know why.

To find out what information sources are available so that you can evaluate which are applicable and how usable they are for particular questions, here are a few built-in utilities and information resources to check:

- System variables tell you how the server is configured. (Recipe 22.1 covers how to check these values.)
- Status variables provide information about operations the server is performing, such as the number of statements executed, number of disk accesses, memory use, or cache efficiency. Status information can help indicate when configuration changes are needed, such as increasing the size of a too-small buffer to improve performance, or decreasing the size of an underused resource to reduce the server's memory footprint.

- The Performance Schema is designed for monitoring and provides a wealth of measurements, from high-level information such as which clients are connected, down to fine-grained information, such as which locks a statement holds or which files it has open. The Performance Schema is enabled by default since MySQL 5.7. To use the Performance Schema in prior versions, you must enable it. To enable it explicitly at server startup, use this configuration setting:

```
[mysqld]
performance_schema=1
```

- `Performance Schema` focuses on the performance data of the MySQL server and can be used similarly for highly specific or complex queries, including joins. It also helps to clarify everything at runtime:

```
mysql> SELECT EVENT_NAME, COUNT_STAR
    -> FROM performance_schema.events_waits_summary_global_by_event_name
    -> ORDER BY COUNT_STAR DESC LIMIT 10;
+------------------------------------------+------------+
| EVENT_NAME                               | COUNT_STAR |
+------------------------------------------+------------+
| wait/io/file/innodb/innodb_log_file      |       6439 |
| wait/io/file/innodb/innodb_data_file     |       5994 |
| idle                                     |       5309 |
| wait/io/table/sql/handler                |       3263 |
| wait/io/file/innodb/innodb_dblwr_file    |       1356 |
| wait/io/file/sql/binlog                  |        798 |
| wait/lock/table/sql/handler              |        683 |
| wait/io/file/innodb/innodb_temp_file     |        471 |
| wait/io/file/sql/io_cache                |        203 |
| wait/io/file/sql/binlog_index            |         75 |
+------------------------------------------+------------+
10 rows in set (0.16 sec)
```

- *Sys* schema is a unique schema that does not contain physical tables but contains views and stored routines over `Performance Schema` tables. `Performance Schema` provides memory instrumentation information that can be accessed much more easily by using views in *sys* schema. For memory usage, it is much easier to use *sys* schema; therefore, we recommend using five views that provide memory allocation details:

```
mysql> SHOW TABLES like "memory%";
+-----------------------------------+
| Tables_in_sys (memory%)           |
+-----------------------------------+
| memory_by_host_by_current_bytes   |
| memory_by_thread_by_current_bytes |
| memory_by_user_by_current_bytes   |
| memory_global_by_current_bytes    |
| memory_global_total               |
+-----------------------------------+
5 rows in set (0.00 sec)
```

- SHOW statements and tables in the PERFORMANCE_SCHEMA database provide information ranging from processes running in the server to active storage engines and plug-ins to system and status variables. In many cases, these two sources provide the same or similar information but in different display formats. (For example, the SHOW PLUGINS statement and the PLUGINS table are related.) Familiarity with both sources helps you choose which is more usable in a given situation:

— For interactive use, SHOW is often more convenient because it involves less typing than PERFORMANCE_SCHEMA queries. Compare these two statements, which produce the same result:

```
SHOW GLOBAL STATUS LIKE 'Threads_connected';

SELECT VARIABLE_VALUE FROM PERFORMANCE_SCHEMA.GLOBAL_STATUS
WHERE VARIABLE_NAME = 'Threads_connected';
```

— INFORMATION_SCHEMA queries use SELECT, which is more expressive than SHOW and can be used for highly specific or complex queries, including joins:

```
SELECT t.table_schema, t.table_name, c.column_name
  FROM information_schema.tables t,
       information_schema.columns c
  WHERE t.table_schema = c.table_schema
       AND t.table_name = c.table_name
       AND t.engine='InnoDB';
```

— SHOW output cannot be saved using only SQL. Should you require further processing of a PERFORMANCE_SCHEMA query result, you can use INSERT INTO... SELECT to save the results in a table for further analysis (see Recipe 6.2). To obtain an individual value, assign a scalar subquery result to a variable:

```
mysql> SET @queries =
    -> (SELECT VARIABLE_VALUE FROM PERFORMANCE_SCHEMA.GLOBAL_STATUS
    -> WHERE VARIABLE_NAME = 'Queries');
Query OK, 0 rows affected (0.00 sec)

mysql> SELECT @queries;
+----------+
| @queries |
+----------+
| 5338     |
+----------+
1 row in set (0.00 sec)
```

- Some storage engines make information available about themselves. InnoDB, for example, has its own system and status variables. It also provides its own INFORMATION_SCHEMA tables and a set of InnoDB Monitors. The INFORMATION_SCHEMA tables provide more structured information and are thus more amenable to analysis using SQL, if they contain the information you want. To see which InnoDB-related tables are available, use this statement:

```
SHOW TABLES FROM INFORMATION_SCHEMA LIKE 'innodb%';
```

The Monitors produce unstructured output. You can eyeball it, but for programmatic use, you must parse or extract the information somehow. In some cases, a simple grep command might suffice:

```
$ mysql -E -e "SHOW ENGINE INNODB STATUS" | grep "Free buffers"
Free buffers        4733
```

- Server logs provide several types of information. Here are some suggestions for using them:

  — The error log alerts you to severe problems the server encounters. It's most suited to visual inspection because messages can originate from anywhere in the server, and there is no fixed format to aid programmatic analysis. It's often only the last part of the file that's of interest anyway, because you typically check this file to find the reason for the most recent problems. These problems may include a corrupted table causing a crash or may even be related to mysql_upgrade not being run, causing further issues.

  — The general query log indicates what queries clients are running. It can aid in assessing the nature of the server's workload. It is the only log that captures everything; hence, care must be taken when enabling this log. Depending on the server's activity, it may fill up disk space quickly and cause very heavy I/O, making things worse while monitoring MySQL. A suggestion is to enable it online when needed and disable afterward.

  — The slow log contains queries that may be inefficient. It can help you find candidates for optimization.

  The server is able to write the general query and slow query logs to files, tables, or both. Log tables facilitate analysis better than the files; they are more structured and hence are subject to analysis using SQL statements. The contents are also easier to interpret. Each query row in the general_log table shows the user associated with it. With the logfile, users are named only on connection lines. To identify a user's queries, you must extract the connection ID from the connection line and look for subsequent query lines with the same ID.

  In addition, log tables are managed by the CSV storage engine, so the table datafiles are written in comma-separated values format. Look in the *mysql* directory under the server's data directory for files named *general_log.CSV* and *slow_log.CSV*. You can process them with tools that read CSV files.

  To get information from a log, it must be enabled (see Recipe 22.3 for instructions).

- The EXPLAIN statement can be useful for checking long-running queries. Although EXPLAIN is most often used to see execution plans for prospective queries, MySQL 5.7.2 and up has the capability of using EXPLAIN to examine queries currently executing in other sessions. If a query seems to be stuck, this may help you understand why. Use SHOW PROCESSLIST or the INFORMATION_SCHEMA PROCESSLIST table to determine the connection ID of the session running the problem query, then point EXPLAIN at it:

  ```
  EXPLAIN FOR CONNECTION connection_id;
  ```

EXPLAIN can produce output in tabular, tree, or JSON format. The latter can be parsed and manipulated by standard JSON modules in your programming language of choice.

23.3 Checking Server Uptime and Progress

Problem

You want to know if the server is running, and if so, how long it has been up.

Solution

Use *mysqladmin* and MySQL CLI utilities to find out if it's up.

Discussion

To tell whether the server is running, just try connecting to it. If the connection succeeds or you get an error that's from the server itself, the server is up. `mysqladmin ping` is a good choice here for interactive use or from within shell scripts. This result indicates the server is running, although you should be alerted by the monitoring system that the server is down:

```
$ mysqladmin ping
mysqld is alive
```

This connection attempt fails, but the server itself returns the second error message, so it's not down:

```
$ mysqladmin -u baduser ping
mysqladmin: connect to server at '127.0.0.1' failed
error: 'Access denied for user 'baduser'@'localhost' (using password: YES)'
```

This result indicates a complete connection failure; the server is down:

```
$ mysqladmin ping
mysqladmin: connect to server at '127.0.0.1' failed
error: 'Can't connect to MySQL server on '127.0.0.1' (61)'
```

If the server is not up, check the error log to find out why.

If the server is up, its uptime (in seconds) can be determined multiple ways:

- Use `mysqladmin status`:

  ```
  $ mysqladmin status
  Uptime: 22158655  Threads: 2  Questions: 65733141  Slow queries: 34
  Opens: 6570  Flush tables: 1  Open tables: 95  Queries per second
  avg: 2.966
  ```

  A disadvantage of this approach for programmatic use is that you must parse the output to extract the value of interest.

- Examine the `Uptime` status variable:

```
mysql> SHOW GLOBAL STATUS LIKE 'Uptime';
+---------------+----------+
| Variable_name | Value    |
+---------------+----------+
| Uptime        | 1640724  |
+---------------+----------+
1 row in set (0.00 sec)
```

Use the built-in CLI command to show the status of the current connection:

```
mysql> \status
...
Uptime:                  18 days 23 hours 45 min 43 sec
...
-------------
```

A server not running is obviously a cause for concern. But there may be issues even if it is running. If you frequently find that server uptime resets in the absence of scheduled restarts, something may be causing the server to exit, and you should investigate. Again, check the error log to see why.

As your MySQL server runs, you'll have questions about aspects of its operation or performance. Or maybe it's *not* running and you want to know why.

23.4 Troubleshooting Server Start Problems

Problem

The server quits shortly after it's started, and you want to know what caused it and what you can do about it.

Solution

Check the error log for details.

Discussion

If the server stops shortly after you start it, a likely cause is a misconfiguration in the server options file. The error log helps you here. But don't be misled by mere warnings, which do not signify that the server quit. For example, the following message means only that *innodb_ft_min_token_size* needs to be corrected to make the warning go away:

```
2022-02-17T15:05:25.482596Z 0 [Warning] [MY-013746]
        [Server] A deprecated TLS version TLSv1.1 is enabled for channel
        mysql_main 2022-02-17T15:05:25.487543Z 0 [Warning] [MY-010068]
        [Server] CA certificate ca.pem is self-signed.
```

Instead, check for [ERROR] lines, such as this:

```
2022-02-17T15:05:25.495461Z 0 [ERROR] [MY-000067]
        [Server] unknown variable 'innodb_ft_min_toke_size=2'.
```

As you can see, the server is complaining about a typo in *innodb_ft_min_token_size* that is preventing it from starting properly.

Other server start problems include the following:

- Misconfiguration of my.cnf variables
- Multiple configuration files
- Missing operating system permissions
- Incorrect path setting
- Over-allocating available memory
- Missing `mysql_upgrade` step after version upgrade

 As of version 8.0.16, `mysql_upgrade` is not needed anymore. But when upgrading to any version prior to 8.0.16, you must run this utility.

23.5 Determining the IO Utilization of the MySQL Server

Problem

You want to know the number of queries hitting the MySQL server.

Solution

Check utilization status variables for details.

Discussion

This question might be prompted by simple curiosity, or there might be a performance issue. Monitoring statement execution over time and summarizing the results can reveal patterns, such as a time of day or day of the week when activity is cumbersome. Perhaps several report generators are configured to start at the same time. Staggering them will help your server by spreading the load. It is crucial to capture baseline data to compare several reads for a given period.

In programmatic context, you might write a long-running application that probes the server periodically for the `Queries` and `Uptime` values to determine a running display of statement-execution activity. To avoid reconnecting each time you issue the statements, ask the server for its session timeout period, and probe it at intervals shorter than that value. To get the session timeout value (in seconds), use this statement:

```
SELECT @@wait_timeout;
```

The default value is 28,800 (eight hours). If it's configured to a value shorter than your desired probe interval, set it higher:

```
SET wait_timeout = seconds;
```

The preceding discussion uses Queries, which indicates the total number of statements executed. Options for more fine-grained analysis are available.

The server maintains a set of Com_xxx status variables that count executions of particular statements. For example, Com_insert and Com_update count INSERT and UPDATE statements, respectively:

```
mysql> SHOW GLOBAL STATUS LIKE "Com_select";
+---------------+-------+
| Variable_name | Value |
+---------------+-------+
| Com_select    | 100   |
+---------------+-------+
1 row in set (0.00 sec)

mysql> SHOW GLOBAL STATUS LIKE "Com_insert";
+---------------+-------+
| Variable_name | Value |
+---------------+-------+
| Com_insert    | 3922  |
+---------------+-------+
1 row in set (0.00 sec)
```

After MySQL version 5.7, some of the instruments in information_schema migrated to performance_schema; hence, querying performance_schema was advised for such monitoring.

Since the Performance Schema has comprehensive details about events, it no longer has *Com Stats* values.

```
mysql> SELECT EVENT_NAME, COUNT_STAR
    -> FROM performance_schema.events_statements_summary_global_by_event_name
    -> WHERE EVENT_NAME LIKE 'statement/sql/%';
+-------------------------------------------------+------------+
| EVENT_NAME                                      | COUNT_STAR |
+-------------------------------------------------+------------+
| statement/sql/select                            |        106 |
...
```

You also may want to calculate the InnoDB Buffer Pool Cache hit ratio to determine how many requests to InnoDB could be resolved without disk access.

To answer this question, use status variable information:

```
mysql> SHOW GLOBAL STATUS LIKE 'innodb_buffer_pool_read%s';
+-----------------------------------+----------+
| Variable_name                     | Value    |
+-----------------------------------+----------+
| Innodb_buffer_pool_read_requests  | 50350973 |
| Innodb_buffer_pool_reads          | 1622447  |
+-----------------------------------+----------+
2 rows in set (0.00 sec)
```

The `Innodb_buffer_pool_read_requests` status variable holds the value of how many times SQL queries requested data from the InnoDB Buffer Pool. This value could also be understood as a number of queries to InnoDB. The `Innodb_buffer_pool_reads` variable holds the metric on how many such queries were resolved from the InnoDB Buffer Pool without touching tablespace files on the disk.

`SHOW GLOBAL STATUS` counts the number of queries since server startup, but it's a variable value. If you wait for a certain amount of time and rerun the same query, you'll have a hit ratio:

```
mysql> SHOW GLOBAL STATUS LIKE 'innodb_buffer_pool_read%s';↵
SELECT SLEEP(60); SHOW GLOBAL STATUS LIKE 'innodb_buffer_pool_read%s';
+-----------------------------------+----------+
| Variable_name                     | Value    |
+-----------------------------------+----------+
| Innodb_buffer_pool_read_requests  | 51504330 |
| Innodb_buffer_pool_reads          | 1830647  |
+-----------------------------------+----------+
2 rows in set (0.00 sec)

+-----------+
| sleep(60) |
+-----------+
|         0 |
+-----------+
1 row in set (1 min 0.00 sec)

+-----------------------------------+----------+
| Variable_name                     | Value    |
+-----------------------------------+----------+
| Innodb_buffer_pool_read_requests  | 53626254 |
| Innodb_buffer_pool_reads          | 2214763  |
+-----------------------------------+----------+
2 rows in set (0.00 sec)
```

In this example, InnoDB received 53626254 - 51504330 = 2121924 requests for data and was able to resolve 2214763 - 1830647 = 384116 requests using the buffer only. Thus, the InnoDB Buffer Pool hit ratio is 384116 / 2121924 = 0.18. This means that the server either just started and the InnoDB Buffer Pool does not contain an active dataset yet, or it is too small and InnoDB has to purge pages from the buffer pool too often and then re-read them back. Ideally, the InnoDB Buffer Pool hit ratio should be near 1.

 If you have online transaction processing (OLTP) in-memory workload, you may have 100% of your queries in memory. The profile of the queries may change significantly, which can make hit ratio metric surrogate. It's insufficient to just monitor hit ratio for in-memory operations.

23.6 Determining MySQL Thread's CPU Utilization

Problem

You want to find the process causing high CPU utilization on your server.

Solution

Use the THREAD_OS_ID value to correlate with the Performance Schema's threads table.

Discussion

The CPU utilization of the process is somewhat problematic in finding slowness caused by an individual query. Sometimes this can be a runaway job or a running process for a large dataset. You may see this type of behavior on month-ends where a query or a job runs only once a month to process quarterly or statistical computation. The threads table contains information about each thread created after server start as well as whether the thread is historical (if instrumented, see "Pre-Filtering by Thread" (https://oreil.ly/VR68x)):

```
mysql> DESC performance_schema.threads;
+---------------------+---------------------+------+-----+---------+-------+
| Field               | Type                | Null | Key | Default | Extra |
+---------------------+---------------------+------+-----+---------+-------+
| THREAD_ID           | bigint unsigned     | NO   | PRI | NULL    |       |
| NAME                | varchar(128)        | NO   | MUL | NULL    |       |
| TYPE                | varchar(10)         | NO   |     | NULL    |       |
| PROCESSLIST_ID      | bigint unsigned     | YES  | MUL | NULL    |       |
| PROCESSLIST_USER    | varchar(32)         | YES  | MUL | NULL    |       |
| PROCESSLIST_HOST    | varchar(255)        | YES  | MUL | NULL    |       |
| PROCESSLIST_DB      | varchar(64)         | YES  |     | NULL    |       |
| PROCESSLIST_COMMAND | varchar(16)         | YES  |     | NULL    |       |
| PROCESSLIST_TIME    | bigint              | YES  |     | NULL    |       |
| PROCESSLIST_STATE   | varchar(64)         | YES  |     | NULL    |       |
| PROCESSLIST_INFO    | longtext            | YES  |     | NULL    |       |
| PARENT_THREAD_ID    | bigint unsigned     | YES  |     | NULL    |       |
| ROLE                | varchar(64)         | YES  |     | NULL    |       |
| INSTRUMENTED        | enum('YES','NO')    | NO   |     | NULL    |       |
| HISTORY             | enum('YES','NO')    | NO   |     | NULL    |       |
```

```
| CONNECTION_TYPE      | varchar(16)      | YES |     | NULL |      |      |
| THREAD_OS_ID         | bigint unsigned  | YES | MUL | NULL |      |      |
| RESOURCE_GROUP       | varchar(64)      | YES | MUL | NULL |      |      |
+----------------------+------------------+-----+-----+------+------+------+
```

On Linux systems, `THREAD_OS_ID` corresponds to the value of the `gettid()` function. This value is exposed to the `top` or `proc` file system (/proc/[pid]/task/[tid]). To help identify the related `THREAD_OS_ID`, there are a few methods outside of scraping the `proc` file system by using built-in command-line utilities. `ps -L aux` gives enough detail about the corresponding thread that is higher CPU then others. The parent ID of MySQL, `mysqld_pid`, can also be identified with `pidof mysqld`, in conjunction with the `ps` command:

```
$ ps -L aux |grep -e PID -e `pidof mysqld`
USER   PID     LWP     %CPU NLWP %MEM VSZ      RSS    TTY STAT START↵  TIME  COMMAND
mysql  740282  740282  0.0  68   20.9 1336272  209440 ?   Rsl  2021   0:05 ↵ /usr/sbin/mysqld
mysql  740282  740285  0.0  68   20.9 1336272  209440 ?   Ssl  2021   1:50 ↵ /usr/sbin/mysqld
mysql  740282  740286  0.0  68   20.9 1336272  209440 ?   Ssl  2021   1:52 ↵ /usr/sbin/mysqld
mysql  740282  740287  0.0  68   20.9 1336272  209440 ?   Ssl  2021   1:53 ↵ /usr/sbin/mysqld
mysql  740282  740288  0.0  68   20.9 1336272  209440 ?   Ssl  2021   1:50 ↵ /usr/sbin/mysqld
....
mysql  740282  1353650 0.0  48   21.0 1336272  210456 ?   Ssl  09:35  0:00 ↵ /usr/sbin/mysqld
mysql  740282  1533749 6.6  48   21.0 1336272  210456 ?   Dsl  10:11  0:18 ↵ /usr/sbin/mysqld
mysql  740282  1558301 0.8  48   21.0 1336272  210456 ?   Ssl  10:15  0:00 ↵ /usr/sbin/mysqld
mysql  740282  1558459 1.0  48   21.0 1336272  210456 ?   Ssl  10:15  0:00 ↵ /usr/sbin/mysqld
mysql  740282  1559291 0.7  48   21.0 1336272  210456 ?   Ssl  10:15  0:00 ↵ /usr/sbin/mysqld
```

This will give us the *thread_os_id* hint that we can use to figure out what it is doing:

```
mysql> SELECT * from performance_schema.threads
    -> WHERE THREAD_OS_ID = 1533749 \G
mysql> SELECT * FROM performance_schema.threads where THREAD_OS_ID = 1533749 \G
*************************** 1. row ***************************
          THREAD_ID: 213957
               NAME: thread/sql/one_connection
               TYPE: FOREGROUND
      PROCESSLIST_ID: 213905
    PROCESSLIST_USER: root
    PROCESSLIST_HOST: localhost
      PROCESSLIST_DB: mysqlslap
 PROCESSLIST_COMMAND: Query
    PROCESSLIST_TIME: 0
   PROCESSLIST_STATE: waiting for handler commit
    PROCESSLIST_INFO: INSERT INTO t1 VALUES (964445884,
    'DPh7kD1E6f4MMQk1ioopsoIIcoD83DD8Wu7689K6oHTAjD3Hts6lYGv8x9G0EL0k87q8G2ExJ
    jz2o3KhnIJBbEJYFROTpO5pNvxgyBT9nSCbNO9AiKL9QYhi0x3hL9')
    PARENT_THREAD_ID: NULL
                ROLE: NULL
         INSTRUMENTED: YES
              HISTORY: YES
      CONNECTION_TYPE: Socket
         THREAD_OS_ID: 1533749
       RESOURCE_GROUP: USR_default
```

The other alternative is using the `pidstat` command (requires `sysstat` package). First, find the process id of *mysqld* and execute the following:

```
$ pidstat -t -p 740282
         Linux 5.8.0-63-generic (localhost)    01/02/2022    _x86_64_     (1 CPU)

06:57:13 PM    UID    TGID      TID    %usr %system  %guest   %wait    %CPU   CPU
06:57:14 PM    113  740282        -   24.75   11.88    0.00    0.00   36.63     0
06:57:14 PM    113       -   740282    0.00    0.00    0.00    0.00    0.00     0
06:57:14 PM    113       -   740285    0.00    0.00    0.00    0.00    0.00     0
....
06:57:19 PM    113       -   759641    0.00    0.00    0.00    0.00    0.00     0
06:57:19 PM    113       -   839592    1.00    0.00    0.00    1.00    1.00     0
06:57:19 PM    113       -   839647   17.00    4.00    0.00   14.00   21.00     0
06:57:20 PM    113  740282        -   24.00   14.00    0.00    0.00   38.00     0
06:57:20 PM    113       -   740282    0.00    0.00    0.00    0.00    0.00     0
06:57:20 PM    113       -   740285    0.00    0.00    0.00    0.00    0.00     0
```

From this output, can see in our test run that *thread_os_id* is consuming 21% of the CPU. To co-relate this with MySQL running threads, we follow the *Performance Schema Query*:

```
mysql> SELECT * from performance_schema.threads
where THREAD_OS_ID = 839647 \G
*************************** 1. row ***************************
          THREAD_ID: 2326
               NAME: thread/sql/one_connection
               TYPE: FOREGROUND
     PROCESSLIST_ID: 2282
   PROCESSLIST_USER: root
   PROCESSLIST_HOST: localhost
     PROCESSLIST_DB: mysqlslap
PROCESSLIST_COMMAND: Query
   PROCESSLIST_TIME: 0
  PROCESSLIST_STATE: waiting for handler commit
   PROCESSLIST_INFO: INSERT INTO t1 VALUES (964445884,'DPh7kD1E6f4MMQk1ioopso
   IIcoD83DD8Wu7689K6oHTAjD3Hts6lYGv8x9G0EL0k87q8G2ExJjz2o3KhnIJBbEJYFROTpO5pN
   vxgyBT9nSCbNO9AiKL9QYhi0x3hL9')
   PARENT_THREAD_ID: NULL
               ROLE: NULL
       INSTRUMENTED: YES
            HISTORY: YES
    CONNECTION_TYPE: Socket
       THREAD_OS_ID: 839647
     RESOURCE_GROUP: USR_default
```

See Also

For additional information about the THREADS table, please refer to the threads table (*https://oreil.ly/qCivS*).

23.7 Determining if MySQL Has Reached Its Connection Limits

Problem

You want to know the limits of the MySQL server handling connections.

Solution

Check the configuration parameters.

Discussion

It's often the case that a server function is assessed using a combination of configuration settings plus current operational status. Typically, the former comes from system variables, whereas the latter comes from status variables. Connection management is an example of this concept. The `max_connections` system variable indicates the maximum number of simultaneous connections the server permits, and the `threads_connected` status variable shows how many clients are currently connected. The `threads_running` status variable shows how many clients are currently active. Furthermore, `threads_running` is a very important value for the following reasons:

- If the number of running threads increases above the number of CPU cores, they start to compete for CPU resources.
- If two threads (no matter how many threads are connected) compete for the same row, table, or other database object, the engine-level table lock set at the server level or metadata (MD) lock is in place.

Since MySQL is a single process application with multithreaded architecture, each connection creates a thread. To monitor the maximum connections reached, issue the following command:

```
mysql> SHOW GLOBAL STATUS LIKE 'Max_used_connections';
+----------------------+-------+
| Variable_name        | Value |
+----------------------+-------+
| Max_used_connections | 6     |
+----------------------+-------+
1 row in set (0.00 sec)

mysql> SHOW GLOBAL STATUS LIKE 'Max_used_connections_time';
+---------------------------+---------------------+
| Variable_name             | Value               |
+---------------------------+---------------------+
| Max_used_connections_time | 2020-12-27 17:09:59 |
+---------------------------+---------------------+
1 row in set (0.00 sec)

mysql > SHOW GLOBAL STATUS LIKE 'threads_connected';
+-------------------+-------+
| Variable_name     | Value |
+-------------------+-------+
| Threads_connected | 6     |
+-------------------+-------+
1 row in set (0.00 sec)
```

If `threads_connected` is regularly close to the value of `max_connections`, you might need to bump up the value of the latter. If there is always a wide gap, you can decrease `max_connections`. For further reading, "MySQL Connection Handling and Scaling" (*https://oreil.ly/ULZyr*) explains how MySQL handles connections and its capabilities.

One area that also impacts performance of MySQL is Mutex and metadata locks on highly concurrent environments. As seen previously, at some point running threads will start competing with one another when the same resources are requested from the database. The way InnoDB handles this is to put an exclusive lock on a particular memory resource so that the other thread will have to wait for it. While this is handled with the Mutex operation in MySQL, all Data Definition Language (DDL) as known as table structure change operations handled with metadata locks.

23.8 Verifying That the Buffer Pool Is Sized Properly

Problem

You want to know the limits of the MySQL server handling connections.

Solution

Determine storage engine memory allocation.

Discussion

The InnoDB storage engine has a data buffer. To keep physical I/O minimal, DBA should make sure to utilize server memory efficiently. InnoDB Buffer Pool cache improves index key lookups and data read operations; hence, most data access will occur in memory.

To determine the cache sizes, check the relevant system variables:

```
mysql> SELECT @@innodb_buffer_pool_size;
+---------------------------+
| @@innodb_buffer_pool_size |
+---------------------------+
|                 134217728 |
+---------------------------+
1 row in set (0.00 sec)
```

You can also use SHOW VARIABLES or the PERFORMANCE_SCHEMA GLOBAL_VARIABLES table, for example:

```
mysql> SELECT * from performance_schema.global_variables
    -> WHERE variable_name='innodb_buffer_pool_size';
+-------------------------+----------------+
| VARIABLE_NAME           | VARIABLE_VALUE |
+-------------------------+----------------+
| innodb_buffer_pool_size | 134217728      |
```

```
+-------------------------+----------------+
1 row in set (0.00 sec)
```

The efficiency measure that determines how well the read ratio is operating is its hit rate: the rate at which read requests from the InnoDB Buffer Pool are satisfied from the Buffer Pool without reading data from disk. If data is in the cache, it's a hit; if not, it's a miss. The hit ratio is a high correlation but not a guaranteed metric; hence, the OLTP rate is more important. It's also possible to verify how well the InnoDB Buffer Pool is utilized from data via the Performance Schema:

```
mysql> SELECT CONCAT(FORMAT(A.num * 100.0 / B.num,2),"%") BufferPoolFullPct FROM
    -> (SELECT variable_value num FROM performance_schema.GLOBAL_STATUS
    -> WHERE variable_name = 'Innodb_buffer_pool_pages_data') A,
    -> (SELECT variable_value num FROM performance_schema.GLOBAL_STATUS
    -> WHERE variable_name = 'Innodb_buffer_pool_pages_total') B;
+-------------------+
| BufferPoolFullPct |
+-------------------+
| 23.46%            |
+-------------------+
1 row in set (0.02 sec)
```

We can also determine memory allocation for the Buffer Pool using the *sys* schema. It's crucial to configure the Buffer Pool at startup to allocate memory resources appropriately:

```
mysql> SELECT * FROM sys.memory_global_by_current_bytes
    -> WHERE event_name like 'memory/innodb_buf_buf_pool'\G
*************************** 1. row ***************************
        event_name: memory/innodb/buf_buf_pool
     current_count: 1
     current_alloc: 131.00 MiB
 current_avg_alloc: 131.00 MiB
        high_count: 1
        high_alloc: 131.00 MiB
    high_avg_alloc: 131.00 MiB
1 row in set (0.00 sec)
```

The required information can be obtained from either SHOW STATUS or the GLOBAL_STATUS table. However, when executing queries within a program and saving the results, we must account for differences between SHOW statements and selecting from performance_schema tables. The following queries retrieve similar information, but the column headings differ in lettercase and sometimes in name, and variable names differ in lettercase:

```
mysql> SHOW GLOBAL STATUS;
+-------------------------------------------------+------------+
| Variable_name                                   | Value      |
+-------------------------------------------------+------------+
| Aborted_clients                                 | 1          |
| Aborted_connects                                | 6          |
...
...
```

To enable applications to be agnostic with respect to whether the variable information comes from SHOW or information_schema, force variable names to a consistent lettercase and use that case in expressions that reference the variables. It doesn't matter which lettercase you choose as long as you use it consistently. The following discussion uses uppercase.

Here's a simple routine (in Ruby) that takes a database handle, fetches the status variables, and returns them as a hash of values keyed by names:

```
def get_status_variables(client)
  vars = {}
  query = "SELECT VARIABLE_NAME, VARIABLE_VALUE FROM
          performance_schema.global_status"
  client.query(query).each { |row| vars[row["VARIABLE_NAME"]↵
  .upcase] = row["VARIABLE_VALUE"] }
  return vars
end
```

To get the information using a SHOW statement instead, replace the query with this one:

```
query = "SHOW GLOBAL STATUS"
```

The code applies the upcase method to the variable names. That way, no matter whether the routine uses GLOBAL_STATUS or SHOW to obtain the information, the resulting hash has elements accessed by uppercase variable names.

To calculate a hit rate, pass the variable hash and the names of the reads and requests variables to this routine:

```
def cache_hit_rate(vars,reads_name,requests_name)
  reads = vars[reads_name].to_f
  requests = vars[requests_name].to_f
  hit_rate = requests == 0 ? 0 : 1 - (reads/requests)
  printf "       Key reads: %12d (%s)\n", reads, reads_name
  printf "Key read requests: %12d (%s)\n", requests, requests_name
  printf "        Hit rate: %12.4f\n", hit_rate
end
```

Now we're all set. Call the routines that fetch status information, and calculate the hit rates like this:

```
statvars = get_status_variables(client)
cache_hit_rate(statvars,
               "INNODB_BUFFER_POOL_READS",
               "INNODB_BUFFER_POOL_READ_REQUESTS")
cache_hit_rate(statvars,
               "KEY_READS",
               "KEY_READ_REQUESTS")
```

Run the script to see your server's hit rates:

```
$ hitrate.rb
        Key reads:       6280 (INNODB_BUFFER_POOL_READS)
Key read requests:   70138276 (INNODB_BUFFER_POOL_READ_REQUESTS)
         Hit rate:     0.9999
```

```
        Key reads:          23269 (KEY_READS)
  Key read requests:      8902674 (KEY_READ_REQUESTS)
          Hit rate:          0.9974
```

For tasks involving system variables, code similar to `get_status_variables()` suffices. This implementation uses the GLOBAL_VARIABLES table:

```
def get_system_variables(client)
  vars = {}
  query = "SELECT VARIABLE_NAME, VARIABLE_VALUE FROM
          performance_schema.global_variables"
  client.query(query).each { |row| vars[row["VARIABLE_NAME"].upcase]↵
  = row["VARIABLE_VALUE"] }
  return vars
end
```

To use SHOW instead, replace the query with this one:

```
query = "SHOW GLOBAL VARIABLES"
```

23.9 Finding Information About the Storage Engine

Problem

You want to pin specific problems with MySQL's pluggable storage engine architecture.

Solution

Use MySQL's `mysql` client, and interact with the storage engine directly.

Discussion

Now we're all set. Call the SHOW ENGINE command from `mysql` client:

```
mysql> help show engine
Name: 'SHOW ENGINE'
Description:
Syntax:
SHOW ENGINE engine_name {STATUS | MUTEX}
```

SHOW ENGINE

SHOW ENGINE displays operational information about a storage engine. It requires the PROCESS privilege. The statement has these variants for InnoDB:

```
SHOW ENGINE INNODB STATUS;
SHOW ENGINE INNODB MUTEX;
```

The first command, *SHOW ENGINE INNODB STATUS*, shows extensive information about the InnoDB storage engine in sections. To digest this information, it's possible to capture the output of this command and parse it via the command line:

```
mysql> SHOW ENGINE INNODB STATUS\G
*************************** 1. row ***************************
  Type: InnoDB
  Name:
Status:
=====================================
2020-10-28 23:43:12 0x70000d0ae000 INNODB MONITOR OUTPUT
=====================================
Per second averages calculated from the last 6 seconds
-----------------
BACKGROUND THREAD
-----------------
srv_master_thread loops: 34 srv_active, 0 srv_shutdown, 768286 srv_idle
srv_master_thread log flush and writes: 0
----------
SEMAPHORES
----------
```

For example, it can reach the Buffer Pool information easily with the same command. This information is very useful when you need to acquire information fast, accurately, and without any impact to running the server:

```
----------------------
BUFFER POOL AND MEMORY
----------------------
Total large memory allocated 137363456
Dictionary memory allocated 1539651
Buffer pool size    8191
Free buffers         6250
Database pages      1924
Old database pages  725
Modified db pages   0
Pending reads       0
Pending writes: LRU 0, flush list 0, single page 0
Pages made young 131, not young 1806
0.00 youngs/s, 0.00 non-youngs/s
Pages read 913, created 1105, written 3138
0.00 reads/s, 0.00 creates/s, 0.00 writes/s
No buffer pool page gets since the last printout
Pages read ahead 0.00/s, evicted without access 0.00/s, Random read ahead 0.00/s
LRU len: 1924, unzip_LRU len: 0
I/O sum[0]:cur[0], unzip sum[0]:cur[0]
```

If you are monitoring a single event, you can set the pager and repeatedly monitor its value:

```
mysql> PAGER grep -i history
PAGER set to 'grep -i history'
mysql> SHOW ENGINE INNODB STATUS\G
History list length 0
1 row in set (0.00 sec)
```

Let's have a look at the Mutex information on the idle system. The resulting SHOW statement would be much longer if threads are competing for the resources:

```
mysql> SHOW ENGINE  INNODB MUTEX;
+--------+----------------------------+----------+
| Type   | Name                       | Status   |
+--------+----------------------------+----------+
| InnoDB | rwlock: fil0fil.cc:3206    | waits=4  |
| InnoDB | sum rwlock: buf0buf.cc:778 | waits=3  |
+--------+----------------------------+----------+
2 rows in set (0.00 sec)
```

As you can see in Figure 23-2, InnoDB consists of two types of structures: In-memory and On-disk. InnoDB utilizes the host OS memory efficiently using its internal memory management protocol. As mentioned in the introduction of this chapter, memory utilization is an important factor in MySQL monitoring.

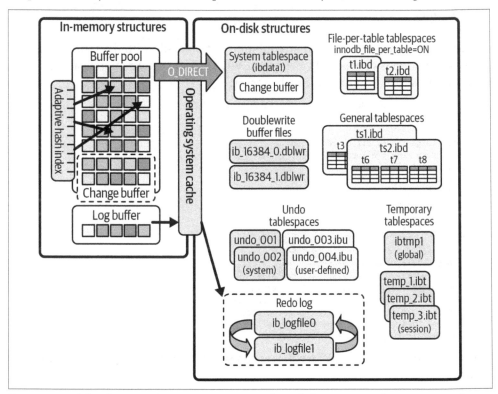

Figure 23-2. The diagram shows in-memory and on-disk structures that comprise the InnoDB storage engine architecture (adapted from © 2021, Oracle Corporation and/or its affiliates (2021); https://oreil.ly/JEzqW)

As InnoDB is by far the most complex and most adopted storage engine in the MySQL ecosystem, it also comes with *components* that can be used to debug internals of its system. Although this is an advanced topic it's good know that you can add plug-ins to the MySQL server. For additional reading, please refer to the MySQL Documentation (*https://oreil.ly/b9SBC*).

23.10 Using the Error Log File to Troubleshoot MySQL Server Crashes

Problem

The application reports, "MySQL Server has gone away" (error 2006).

Solution

There are a few possible scenarios for this very common error, including the following:

- OOM (out of memory) killer
- MySQL signals
- Crashing bug
- Various other reasons, such as server timeout, removed system files, etc.

Sometimes, while troubleshooting, information in the error log can be misleading. So we also advise that you check the system logs, such as */var/log/messages*.

Discussion

An error log is one of the most critical monitoring MySQL server statuses. From startup to shutdown, it will log all events to this file. Proactively monitoring this file will give you sufficient information about current and past events.

> The error log is tunable in MySQL 8.0 and can be fine-tuned to log and filter events by given criteria. For details, please refer to the MySQL documentation (*https://oreil.ly/RYLHT*).

Here are some pointers for monitoring and finding a solution for this error.

Server crash

The server may have disconnected while executing a large query. In this case, the client has timed out during a long running query:

```
$ ( echo -n "SELECT '" ; for i in `seq 1 110000` ; \
      do echo -n "1234567890" ; done ; echo -n "' a") | mysql | wc

ERROR 2006 (HY000) at line 1: MySQL server has gone away
      0       0       0
```

This may be one of the few reasons to check. Often, the `max_allowed_packet` size is too small for a large query like the preceding crashing *for* loop:

```
$ mysql -e "SHOW GLOBAL VARIABLES LIKE 'max_allowed_packet'"
+--------------------+---------+
| Variable_name      | Value   |
+--------------------+---------+
| max_allowed_packet | 1048576 |
+--------------------+---------+
$ mysql -e "SET GLOBAL max_allowed_packet=67108864"
$ mysql -e "SHOW GLOBAL VARIABLES LIKE 'max_allowed_packet'"
+--------------------+----------+
| Variable_name      | Value    |
+--------------------+----------+
| max_allowed_packet | 67108864 |
+--------------------+----------+
$ ( echo -n "SELECT '" ; for i in `seq 1 110000` ; do echo -n "1234567890" ; done ; \
> echo -n "' a") | mysql | wc
      2       2 1100003
```

Server timeout

The connection between the application and the results of the query returning for each request has a timeout variable. One of the most common timeout variables to monitor is `wait_timeout`:

```
$ mysql -e "SHOW GLOBAL VARIABLES LIKE 'wait_timeout'"
+---------------+-------+
| Variable_name | Value |
+---------------+-------+
| wait_timeout  | 28800 |
+---------------+-------+
```

To demonstrate this, we'll set the `wait_timeout` value to a very low four seconds and rerun the same query:

```
$ mysql -e "SET GLOBAL wait_timeout=4"
$ time ( echo -n "SELECT '" ; for i in `seq 1 1100000` ; do echo -n "1234567890" ; done ; \
> echo -n "' a") | mysql | wc
ERROR 2006 (HY000) at line 1: MySQL server has gone away
      0       0       0
real    0m8.062s
user    0m7.506s
sys     0m2.581s
$ mysql -e "SHOW GLOBAL VARIABLES LIKE 'wait_timeout'"
+---------------+-------+
| Variable_name | Value |
+---------------+-------+
| wait_timeout  | 4     |
+---------------+-------+
```

23.11 Slow Query Log File

Problem

You want to use the slow query log to identify slow queries.

Solution

Enable the slow query log and set threshold to filter queries to address them.

Discussion

MySQL can log all queries. By adjusting how slow queries are recorded, it's possible to capture all queries and digest them. The default slow query logging is set to 10 seconds, which means any query taking longer than 10 seconds is shown only in the log file.

You can control the behavior of the slow query log using a number of variables:

```
mysql> SHOW GLOBAL VARIABLES LIKE '%slow%';
+----------------------------+------------------------------------+
| Variable_name              | Value                              |
+----------------------------+------------------------------------+
| log_slow_admin_statements  | OFF                                |
| log_slow_extra             | OFF                                |
| log_slow_slave_statements  | OFF                                |
| slow_launch_time           | 2                                  |
| slow_query_log             | OFF                                |
| slow_query_log_file        | /usr/local/mysql/data/askdba-slow.log |
+----------------------------+------------------------------------+
6 rows in set (0.01 sec)
```

The most essential among them is `slow_query_log`, which enables or disables slow query logging. It is OFF by default.

The slow query log threshold is controlled with the `long_query_time` variable. You can start tuning your queries that are logged with the default threshold and then decrease it in steps. Finally, set `long_query_time` to 0 to log all the queries.

Logging all the queries

It is common practice to run a slow query log with `long_query_time` set to 0. This way you will have information about the performance of all the queries. Then you can run programs such as `pt-query-digest` or `mysqldumpslow` that can create digests of the queries.

To enable logging of all the queries, set `long_query_time` to 0:

```
mysql> SHOW GLOBAL VARIABLES LIKE 'long_query_time';
+-----------------+-----------+
| Variable_name   | Value     |
+-----------------+-----------+
| long_query_time | 10.000000 |
+-----------------+-----------+
1 row in set (0.00 sec)

mysql> SET GLOBAL LONG_QUERY_TIME=0;
Query OK, 0 rows affected (0.00 sec)

mysql> SET GLOBAL SLOW_QUERY_LOG=1;
Query OK, 0 rows affected (0.02 sec)
```

Now we're ready to test a simple query, as it will log everything by having `long_query_time` equal 0:

```
mysql> SELECT thing,legs,arms FROM limbs WHERE legs>=2;

$ sudo tail -f /usr/local/mysql/data/askdba-slow.log
# Time: 2020-11-21T15:15:12.873279Z
# User@Host: root[root] @ localhost [127.0.0.1]  Id:   326
# Query_time: 0.000239  Lock_time: 0.000098 Rows_sent: 6   Rows_examined: 11
SET timestamp=1605971712;
SELECT thing,legs,arms FROM limbs WHERE legs>=2;
```

In this example, we may see that `Query_time` is pretty small; that is expected, because the table itself is small. But the number of rows that MySQL had to examine to resolve this query (`Rows_examined`) is greater (11) than the number of rows that the query sent to the client (`Rows_sent: 6`). This means that there is a very good chance that the query needs to be optimized.

We can start optimizing the query by running EXPLAIN:

```
mysql> EXPLAIN SELECT thing,legs,arms FROM limbs WHERE legs>=2\G
*************************** 1. row ***************************
           id: 1
  select_type: SIMPLE
        table: limbs
   partitions: NULL
         type: ALL
possible_keys: NULL
          key: NULL
      key_len: NULL
          ref: NULL
         rows: 11
     filtered: 33.33
        Extra: Using where
1 row in set, 1 warning (0.00 sec)
```

Setting the value of long_query_time to 0 enables you to log every single query. You need to be careful on a busy system where your file system either can be filled or slowed down due to I/O operation.

Don't log into the table when setting long_query_time to 0, because the CSV storage engine isn't designed for working in high-concurrent environments and can affect performance.

23.12 Monitoring with the General Query Log

Problem

You want to identify what activity each client is engaged in.

Solution

Enable the general query log to investigate them.

Discussion

The MySQL general query log is proof of record for what mysqld is doing. By enabling this log, it allows the administrator to monitor how the life of the user connection interacts with mysqld.

```
mysql> SHOW GLOBAL VARIABLES LIKE 'general%';
+-----------------+-------------------------------------------------------+
| Variable_name   | Value                                                 |
+-----------------+-------------------------------------------------------+
| general_log     | OFF                                                   |
| general_log_file | /home/vagrant/sandboxes/msb_8_0_21/data/vagrant.log  |
+-----------------+-------------------------------------------------------+
2 rows in set (0.01 sec)
```

By enabling the general query log, you instruct the MySQL server to log all the queries it receives. You need to be careful on a busy system where your file system either can be filled or slowed down due to increased I/O operation.

To enable general_log in runtime, use the SET command:

```
mysql> SET GLOBAL general_log = 'ON';
Query OK, 0 rows affected (0.00 sec)

mysql> SHOW GLOBAL VARIABLES LIKE 'general_log';
+---------------+-------+
| Variable_name | Value |
+---------------+-------+
| general_log   | ON    |
```

```
+---------------+-------+
1 row in set (0.00 sec)
Query OK, 0 rows affected (0.00 sec)
```

Now we're ready to monitor everything. This value is dynamic, and we set it at runtime. If you want it to set it persistently at startup, see Recipe 22.1:

```
$ tail -f /home/vagrant/sandboxes/msb_8_0_21/data/vagrant.log
/home/vagrant/opt/mysql/8.0.21/bin/mysqld, Version: 8.0.21 (MySQL Community Server - GPL). ↵
started with:
Tcp port: 8021  Unix socket: /tmp/mysql_sandbox8021.sock
Time                  Id Command    Argument
2020-12-06T14:27:26.739541Z         8 Query     show global variables like "general_log"
2020-12-06T14:51:08.660453Z         8 Quit
```

Connect another session and run the following command while tailing the general query log file:

```
mysql> SHOW PROCESSLIST \G
*************************** 1. row ***************************
     Id: 5
   User: event_scheduler
   Host: localhost
     db: NULL
Command: Daemon
   Time: 2015
  State: Waiting on empty queue
   Info: NULL
*************************** 2. row ***************************
     Id: 10
   User: msandbox
   Host: localhost
     db: NULL
Command: Query
   Time: 0
  State: starting
   Info: show processlist
2 rows in set (0.00 sec)

$ tail -f /home/vagrant/sandboxes/msb_8_0_21/data/vagrant.log
2020-12-06T14:51:45.765019Z         10 Connect    msandbox@localhost on  using Socket
2020-12-06T14:51:45.765785Z         10 Query      select @@version_comment limit 1
2020-12-06T14:51:45.769113Z         10 Query      select USER()
2020-12-06T14:52:29.130072Z         10 Query      show processlist
```

 Unlike the MySQL slow query log, the general query log does not log query execution time. Instead, it logs an end-to-end clean record of what happens for each session in sequential order. This information may be useful for debugging MySQL crashes or figuring out what queries the application is sending.

23.13 Using the Binary Log to Identify Changes

Problem

You want to track data changes for a given period.

Solution

Enable the binary log to investigate them.

Discussion

MySQL can log all data changes to a binary log format, which has three purposes:

- Configuring primary and replica setup. By enabling this feature, we can set up MySQL-replicated topology, explained in Chapter 3.

- Point-in-time recovery after a full physical backup is performed.

- Troubleshooting or investigating an event for a specific time period.

The binary log is enabled by setting `--log-bin` at startup. Setting this value allows MySQL to track data changes to a binary log file. This logfile contains a set of sequential log files along with an index file.

To read binary logs, we must use the `--verbose` or `-v` option by using the `mysqlbin log` command.

```
$ /usr/bin/mysqlbinlog  binlog.000003 -v |more
#210208 19:39:03 server id 1  end_log_pos 517272 CRC32 0x043a9ff4 ↵
                      Write_rows: table id 112 flags: STMT_END_F
### INSERT INTO `test`.`sbtest1`
### SET
###    @1=1
###    @2=21417
###    @3='83868641912-28773972837-60736120486-75162659906-27563526494-↵
        20381887404-41576422241-93426793964-56405065102-33518432330'
###    @4='67847967377-48000963322-62604785301-91415491898-96926520291'
```

To see a statement representation of row events, use the `--verbose` (`-v`) option. To see metadata of columns, specify `--verbose` twice: `--verbose --verbose` or `-vv`. To suppress the output of row events, specify the `--base64-output=DECODE-ROWS` option.

To give a specific start time, do the following:

```
/usr/bin/mysqlbinlog --start-datetime="2020-11-29 10:50:32"
binlog.000003 -v |more
```

To filter a specific data manipulation language (DML) type, do the following:

```
$ /usr/bin/mysqlbinlog --start-datetime="2020-11-29 10:50:32"  binlog.000003 \
> -v| grep -i -e "update" -e "insert"
> -e "delete" -e "drop" -e "alter"   |cut -c1-100 | tr '[A-Z]' '[a-z]'
> | sed -e "s/\t/ /g;s/\`//g;s/(.*$//;s/ set .*$//;s/ as .*$//"
> | sed -e "s/ where .*$//" | sort | uniq -c | sort -nr

50000 ### insert into test.sbtest9
50000 ### insert into test.sbtest9
50000 ### insert into test.sbtest8
50000 ### insert into test.sbtest7
...
```

## CHAPTER 24

Security

24.0 Introduction

This chapter covers the following security-related topics:

- The `mysql.user` table that contains MySQL account information
- Statements for managing MySQL user accounts
- Password-strength checking and policy
- Password expiration
- Finding and removing anonymous accounts and accounts that permit connections from many hosts

If you like, you can skip over the initial section that describes the `mysql.user` table, but we think you'll find that reading it will help you better understand later sections, which often discuss how SQL operations map onto underlying changes in that table.

Scripts shown in this chapter are located in the *routines* directory of the `recipes` distribution.

 Whether you use the MySQL 5.7 or 8.0 release series, it's best to use a recent version within the series. Changes to the authentication system that occurred in early development versions that may produce results that differ from the descriptions here.

Many of the techniques shown here require administrative access, such as the ability to modify tables in the mysql system database or use statements that require the privileges that allow you to administer the MySQL server. For this reason, to carry out the operations described here, connect to the server as root rather than as cbuser.

24.1 Understanding the mysql.user Table

MySQL stores user account information in tables in the mysql system database. The user table is the most important because it contains account names and credentials. To see its structure, use this statement:

```
SHOW CREATE TABLE mysql.user;
```

The user table columns that concern us here specify account names and authentication information:

- The User and Host columns identify the account. MySQL account names comprise a combination of username and hostname values. For example, in the user table row for a 'cbuser'@'localhost' account, the User and Host column values are cbuser and localhost, respectively. For a 'myuser'@'myhost.example.com' account, those columns are myuser and myhost.example.com.

- The plugin and authentication_string columns store authentication credentials. MySQL does not store literal passwords in the user system table because that is insecure. Instead, the server computes a hash value from the password and stores the hash string.

  — The plugin column indicates which authentication plug-in the server uses to check credentials for clients that attempt to use the account. Different plug-ins implement password hashing methods of varying encryption strength. Table 24-1 shows the plug-ins this chapter discusses.

Table 24-1. Authentication plug-ins

Plug-in	Authentication method
mysql_native_password	Native password hashing
sha256_password	SHA-256 password hashing (from MySQL 5.6.6 to MySQL 8.0)
caching_sha2_password	SHA-256 password hashing with server-side caching (MySQL 5.7 or later)

MySQL Enterprise, the commercial version of MySQL, includes additional plug-ins for authenticating using pluggable authentication module (PAM) or Windows credentials. These enable the use of passwords external to MySQL, such as Unix login passwords or native Windows services.

— The `authentication_string` column represents a hashed password in the format required by the respective plug-in. For example, `sha256_password` uses `authentication_string` to store SHA-256 password hash values, which are cryptographically superior to native hashing, used by the `mysql_native_password` plug-in. An empty `authentication_string` value means "no password," which is insecure.

Before MySQL 5.7.2, the server permits the `plugin` value to be empty. As of MySQL 5.7.2, the `plugin` column *must* be nonempty, and the server disables any empty plug-in account until a nonempty plug-in is assigned.

24.2 Managing User Accounts

Problem

You are responsible for setting up accounts on your MySQL server.

Solution

Learn to use the account-management SQL statements.

Discussion

It's possible to modify the grant tables in the `mysql` database directly with SQL statements such as `INSERT` or `UPDATE`, but the MySQL account-management statements are more convenient. This section describes their use and covers these topics:

- Creating accounts (CREATE USER, SET PASSWORD ALTER USER)
- Assigning and checking privileges (GRANT, REVOKE, SHOW GRANTS)
- Removing and renaming accounts (DROP USER, RENAME USER)

Creating accounts

To create an account, use the `CREATE USER` statement, which creates a row in the `mysql.user` table. But before you do so, decide these three things:

- The account name, expressed in `'user_name'@'host_name'` format naming the user and the host from which the user will connect
- The account password
- The authentication plug-in the server should execute when clients attempt to use the account

Authentication plug-ins use hashing to encrypt passwords for storage and transmission. MySQL has several built-in plug-ins from which to choose:

- `mysql_native_password` implements the default password hashing method before version 8.0.

- `sha256_password` authenticates using SHA-256 password hash values, which are cryptographically more secure than hashes generated by `mysql_native_password`. This plug-in is available as of MySQL 5.6.6 and is deprecated in version 8.0 in favor of its improved version, `caching_sha2_password`. It provides security beyond that afforded by `mysql_native_password`, but additional setup is required to use it. (Clients must connect using SSL or provide an RSA certificate.)

- `caching_sha2_password` is similar to `sha256_password` but uses caching on the server side for better performance. This is the default authentication plug-in since MySQL 8.0.

The `CREATE USER` statement is commonly used in one of these forms:

```
CREATE USER 'user_name'@'host_name' IDENTIFIED BY 'password';
CREATE USER 'user_name'@'host_name' IDENTIFIED WITH 'auth_plugin' BY 'auth_string';
```

The first syntax creates the account and sets its password with a single statement. It also assigns an authentication plug-in implicitly to the plug-in named by the `--default-authentication-plugin` setting (which is `caching_sha2_password`, unless you change it at server startup).

To assign privileges to the new account, which has none initially, use the `GRANT` statement described later in this section.

`CREATE USER` fails if the account already exists.

Assigning and checking privileges

Suppose that you have just created an account named `'user1'@'localhost'`. You can assign privileges to it with `GRANT`, remove privileges from it with `REVOKE`, and check its privileges with `SHOW GRANTS`.

`GRANT` has this syntax:

```
GRANT privileges ON scope TO account;
```

Here, *account* names the account to be granted the privileges, *privileges* indicates what they are, and *scope* indicates the privilege scope, or level at which they apply. The *privileges* value can be `ALL` (or `ALL PRIVILEGES`) to specify all privileges available at the given level, or a comma-separated list of one or more privilege names such as `SELECT` or `CREATE`. (For a full discussion of available privileges and `GRANT` syntax not shown here, see the MySQL Reference Manual (*https://oreil.ly/SD8cF*).)

The following examples illustrate the syntax for granting privileges at each level:

- Granting privileges globally enables the account to perform administrative operations or operations on any database:
  ```
  GRANT FILE ON *.* TO 'user1'@'localhost';
  GRANT CREATE TEMPORARY TABLES, LOCK TABLES ON *.* TO 'user1'@'localhost';
  ```

- Granting privileges at the database level enables the account to perform operations on objects within the named database:
  ```
  GRANT ALL ON cookbook.* TO 'user1'@'localhost';
  ```

- Granting privileges at the table level enables the account to perform operations on the named table:
  ```
  GRANT SELECT ON mysql.user TO 'user1'@'localhost';
  ```

- Granting privileges at the column level enables the account to perform operations on the named table column:
  ```
  GRANT SELECT(User,Host), UPDATE(password_expired)
  ON mysql.user TO 'user1'@'localhost';
  ```

- Granting privileges at the procedure level enables the account to perform operations on the named stored procedure:
  ```
  GRANT EXECUTE ON PROCEDURE cookbook.exec_stmt TO 'user1'@'localhost';
  ```

  Use FUNCTION rather than PROCEDURE if the routine is a stored function.

To verify the privilege assignments, use SHOW GRANTS:

```
mysql> SHOW GRANTS FOR 'user1'@'localhost';
+------------------------------------------------------------------------+
| Grants for user1@localhost                                             |
+------------------------------------------------------------------------+
| GRANT FILE, CREATE TEMPORARY TABLES, LOCK TABLES                       |
| ON *.* TO 'user1'@'localhost'                                          |
| GRANT ALL PRIVILEGES ON `cookbook`.* TO 'user1'@'localhost'            |
| GRANT SELECT, SELECT (User, Host), UPDATE (password_expired)           |
| ON `mysql`.`user` TO 'user1'@'localhost'                               |
| GRANT EXECUTE ON PROCEDURE `cookbook`.`exec_stmt` TO 'user1'@'localhost' |
+------------------------------------------------------------------------+
```

To see your own privileges, omit the FOR clause.

REVOKE syntax is generally similar to GRANT but uses FROM rather than TO:

```
REVOKE privileges ON scope FROM account;
```

Thus, to remove the privileges just granted to 'user1'@'localhost', use these REVOKE statements (and SHOW GRANTS to verify that they were removed):

```
mysql> REVOKE FILE ON *.* FROM 'user1'@'localhost';
mysql> REVOKE CREATE TEMPORARY TABLES, LOCK TABLES
    -> ON *.* FROM 'user1'@'localhost';
mysql> REVOKE ALL ON cookbook.* FROM 'user1'@'localhost';
mysql> REVOKE SELECT ON mysql.user FROM 'user1'@'localhost';
mysql> REVOKE SELECT(User,Host), UPDATE(password_expired)
    -> ON mysql.user FROM 'user1'@'localhost';
```

```
mysql> REVOKE EXECUTE ON PROCEDURE cookbook.exec_stmt
    -> FROM 'user1'@'localhost';
mysql> SHOW GRANTS FOR 'user1'@'localhost';
+------------------------------------------+
| Grants for user1@localhost               |
+------------------------------------------+
| GRANT USAGE ON *.* TO 'user1'@'localhost' |
+------------------------------------------+
```

Removing accounts

To get rid of an account, use the DROP USER statement:

```
DROP USER 'user1'@'localhost';
```

The statement removes all rows associated with the account in all grant tables; you need not use REVOKE to remove its privileges first. An error occurs if the account does not exist.

Renaming accounts

To change an account name, use RENAME USER, specifying the current and new names:

```
RENAME USER 'currentuser'@'localhost' TO 'newuser'@'localhost';
```

An error occurs if the current account does not exist or the new account already exists.

24.3 Implementing a Password Policy

Problem

You want to ensure that MySQL accounts do not use weak passwords.

Solution

Use the `validate_password` plug-in to implement a password policy. New passwords must satisfy the policy, whether those chosen by the DBA for new accounts or by existing users changing their password.

Discussion

This technique requires the `validate_password` plug-in to be enabled. For plug-in installation instructions, see Recipe 22.2.

When `validate_password` is enabled, it exposes a set of system variables that enable you to configure it. These are the default values:

```
mysql> SHOW VARIABLES LIKE 'validate_password%';
+----------------------------------------+--------+
| Variable_name                          | Value  |
```

```
+-----------------------------------------+--------+
| validate_password_dictionary_file       |        |
| validate_password_length                | 8      |
| validate_password_mixed_case_count      | 1      |
| validate_password_number_count          | 1      |
| validate_password_policy                | MEDIUM |
| validate_password_special_char_count    | 1      |
+-----------------------------------------+--------+
```

Suppose that you want to implement a policy that enforces these requirements for passwords:

- At least 10 characters long

- Contains uppercase and lowercase characters

- Contains at least two digits

- Contains at least one special (nonalphanumeric) character

To put that policy in place, start the server with options that enable the plug-in, and set the values of the system variables that configure the policy requirements. For example, put these lines in your server option file:

```
[mysqld]
plugin-load-add=validate_password.so
validate_password_length=10
validate_password_mixed_case_count=1
validate_password_number_count=2
validate_password_special_char_count=1
```

After starting the server, verify the settings:

```
mysql> SHOW VARIABLES LIKE 'validate_password%';
+-----------------------------------------+--------+
| Variable_name                           | Value  |
+-----------------------------------------+--------+
| validate_password_dictionary_file       |        |
| validate_password_length                | 10     |
| validate_password_mixed_case_count      | 1      |
| validate_password_number_count          | 2      |
| validate_password_policy                | MEDIUM |
| validate_password_special_char_count    | 1      |
+-----------------------------------------+--------+
```

Now the `validate_password` plug-in prevents assigning passwords too weak for the policy:

```
mysql> SET PASSWORD = 'weak-password';
ERROR 1819 (HY000): Your password does not satisfy the current
policy requirements
mysql> SET PASSWORD = 'Str0ng-Pa33w@rd';
Query OK, 0 rows affected (0.00 sec)
```

The preceding instructions leave the `validate_password_policy` system variable set to its default value (`MEDIUM`), but you can change it to control how the server tests passwords:

- MEDIUM enables tests for password length and the number of numeric, upper-case/lowercase, and special characters.

- To be less rigorous, set the policy to LOW, which enables only the length test. To also permit shorter passwords, decrease the required length (validate_pass word_length).

- To be more rigorous, set the policy to STRONG, which is like MEDIUM but also enables you to have passwords checked against a dictionary file, to prevent use of passwords that match any word in the file. Comparisons are not case sensitive.

  To use a dictionary file, set the value of validate_password_dictionary_file to the filename at server startup. The file should contain lowercase words, one per line. MySQL distributions include a *dictionary.txt* file in the *share* directory that you can use, and Unix systems often have a */usr/share/dict/words* file.

Putting a password policy in place has no effect on existing passwords. To require users to choose a new password that satisfies the policy, expire their current password (see Recipe 24.5).

24.4 Checking Password Strength

Problem

You want to assign or change a password but verify first that it's not weak.

Solution

Use the VALIDATE_PASSWORD_STRENGTH() function.

Discussion

The validate_password plug-in not only implements policy for new passwords, but it also provides a SQL function, VALIDATE_PASSWORD_STRENGTH(), that enables strength testing of prospective passwords. Uses for this function include the following:

- An administrator wants to check passwords to be assigned to new accounts.

- An individual user wants to choose a new password but seeks assurance in advance about how strong it is.

To use VALIDATE_PASSWORD_STRENGTH(), the validate_password plug-in must be enabled. For plug-in installation instructions, see Recipe 22.2.

VALIDATE_PASSWORD_STRENGTH() returns a value from 0 (weak) to 100 (strong):

```
mysql> SELECT VALIDATE_PASSWORD_STRENGTH('abc') ;
+-----------------------------------+
| VALIDATE_PASSWORD_STRENGTH('abc') |
+-----------------------------------+
|                                 0 |
+-----------------------------------+
mysql> SELECT VALIDATE_PASSWORD_STRENGTH('weak-password');
+---------------------------------------------+
| VALIDATE_PASSWORD_STRENGTH('weak-password') |
+---------------------------------------------+
|                                          50 |
+---------------------------------------------+
mysql> SELECT VALIDATE_PASSWORD_STRENGTH('Str0ng-Pa33w@rd');
+-----------------------------------------------+
| VALIDATE_PASSWORD_STRENGTH('Str0ng-Pa33w@rd') |
+-----------------------------------------------+
|                                           100 |
+-----------------------------------------------+
```

24.5 Expiring Passwords

Problem

You want users to pick a new MySQL password.

Solution

The ALTER USER statement expires passwords.

Discussion

MySQL 5.6.7 and up provides an ALTER USER statement that enables an administrator to expire an account's password:

```
ALTER USER 'cbuser'@'localhost' PASSWORD EXPIRE;
```

Here are some uses for password expiration:

- You can implement a policy that new users must select a new password when first connecting: immediately expire the password for each new account you create.

- If you impose a stricter policy on acceptable passwords (see Recipe 24.3), you can expire all existing passwords to require each user to choose a new one that meets the more stringent requirements.

ALTER USER affects a single account. It works by setting the password_expired column to Y for the appropriate mysql.user row. To "cheat" and expire passwords for all nonanonymous accounts at once, do this (anonymous users cannot reset their password, so expiring those would have the same effect as removing these accounts from the MySQL system):

```
UPDATE mysql.user SET password_expired = 'Y' WHERE User <> '';
FLUSH PRIVILEGES;
```

Alternatively, to affect all accounts but avoid modifying the grant tables directly, use a stored procedure that loops through all accounts and executes ALTER USER for each:

```
CREATE PROCEDURE expire_all_passwords()
BEGIN
  DECLARE done BOOLEAN DEFAULT FALSE;
  DECLARE account TEXT;
  DECLARE cur CURSOR FOR
    SELECT CONCAT(QUOTE(User),'@',QUOTE(Host)) AS account
    FROM mysql.user WHERE User <> '';
  DECLARE CONTINUE HANDLER FOR NOT FOUND SET done = TRUE;

  OPEN cur;
  expire_loop: LOOP
    FETCH cur INTO account;
    IF done THEN
      LEAVE expire_loop;
    END IF;
    CALL exec_stmt(CONCAT('ALTER USER ',account,' PASSWORD EXPIRE'));
  END LOOP;
  CLOSE cur;
END;
```

The procedure requires the exec_stmt() helper routine (see Recipe 11.6). Scripts to create these routines are located in the *routines* directory of the recipes distribution.

24.6 Assigning Yourself a New Password

Problem

You want to change your password.

Solution

Use ALTER USER or SET PASSWORD statements.

Discussion

To assign yourself a new password, use the SET PASSWORD statement:

```
SET PASSWORD = 'my-new-password';
```

SET PASSWORD permits a FOR clause that enables you to specify which account gets the new password:

```
SET PASSWORD FOR 'user_name'@'host_name' = 'my-new-password';
```

This latter syntax is primarily for DBAs because it requires the UPDATE privilege for the mysql database.

Alternatively, use the ALTER USER statement:

```
ALTER USER 'user_name'@'host_name' IDENTIFIED BY 'my-new-password';
```

If you want to use the ALTER USER statement to assign yourself a password, you can check your account name first by running the CURRENT_USER function:

```
mysql> SELECT CURRENT_USER();
+----------------+
| CURRENT_USER() |
+----------------+
| cbuser@%       |
+----------------+
1 row in set (0.00 sec)
```

To check the strength of a password you're considering, use the VALIDATE_PASS WORD_STRENGTH() function (see Recipe 24.4).

24.7 Resetting an Expired Password

Problem

You cannot use MySQL because your DBA expired your password.

Solution

Assign yourself a new password.

Discussion

If the MySQL administrator has expired your password, MySQL will let you connect but not do much of anything else:

```
$ mysql --user=cbuser --password
Enter password: ******
mysql> SELECT CURRENT_USER();
ERROR 1820 (HY000): You must SET PASSWORD before executing this statement
```

If you see that message, reset your password so that you can work normally again:

```
mysql> SET PASSWORD = 'my-new-password';
Query OK, 0 rows affected (0.00 sec)

mysql> SELECT CURRENT_USER(); -- now you can work again
+------------------+
| CURRENT_USER()   |
+------------------+
| cbuser@localhost |
+------------------+
1 row in set (0.00 sec)
```

Technically, MySQL does not require a *new* password to replace an expired password, so you can assign yourself your current password to unexpire it. The exception is that if the password policy has become more restrictive and your current password no longer satisfies it, a stronger password must be chosen.

For more information about changing your password, see Recipe 24.6.

24.8 Finding and Removing Anonymous Accounts

Problem

You want to ensure that your MySQL server can be used only by accounts associated with specific usernames.

Solution

Identify and remove anonymous accounts.

Discussion

An "anonymous" account is one that has an empty user part in the account name, such as `''@'localhost'`. An empty user matches any name because the purpose of an anonymous account is to permit anyone who knows its password to connect from the named host (`localhost` in this case). This is a convenience because the DBA need not set up individual accounts for separate users. But there are security implications as well:

- Such accounts often are given no password, enabling their use with no authentication at all.

- You cannot associate database activity with specific users (for example, by checking the server query log or examining `SHOW PROCESSLIST` output), making it more difficult to tell who is doing what.

If the preceding points persuade you that anonymous accounts are not a good thing, use the following instructions to identify and remove them:

1. The `User` column is empty in the `mysql.user` rows for anonymous accounts, so you can identify them like this:

    ```
    mysql> SELECT User, Host FROM mysql.user WHERE User = '';
    +------+----------------+
    | User | Host           |
    +------+----------------+
    |      | %.example.com  |
    |      | localhost      |
    +------+----------------+
    ```

2. The `SELECT` output shows two anonymous accounts. Remove each using a `DROP USER` statement with the corresponding account name:

```
mysql> DROP USER ''@'localhost';
mysql> DROP USER ''@'%.example.com';
```

24.9 Modifying "Any Host" and "Many Host" Accounts

Problem

You want to ensure that MySQL accounts cannot be used from an overly broad set of hosts.

Solution

Find and fix accounts containing % or _ in the host part.

Discussion

The host part of MySQL account names can contain the SQL pattern characters % and _ (see Recipe 7.10). These names match client connection attempts from any host that matches the pattern. For example, the account 'user1'@'%' permits user1 to connect from any host whatsoever, and 'user2'@'%.example.com' permits user2 to connect from any host in the example.com domain.

Patterns in the host part of account names provide a convenience that enables a DBA to create an account that permits connections from multiple hosts. They correspondingly increase security risks by increasing the number of hosts from which intruders can attempt to connect. If you consider this a concern, identify the accounts and either remove them or change the host part to be more specific.

There are several ways to find accounts with % or _ in the host part. Here are two:

```
WHERE Host LIKE '%\%%' OR Host LIKE '%\_%';
WHERE Host REGEXP '[%_]';
```

The LIKE expression is more complex because we must look for each pattern character separately and escape it to search for literal instances. The REGEXP expression requires no escaping because those characters are not special in regular expressions, and a character class permits both to be found with a single pattern. So let's use that expression:

1. Identify pattern-host accounts in the mysql.user table like this:

   ```
   mysql> SELECT User, Host FROM mysql.user WHERE Host REGEXP '[%_]';
   +-------+---------------+
   | User  | Host          |
   +-------+---------------+
   | user1 | %             |
   | user2 | %.example.com |
   | user3 | _.example.com |
   +-------+---------------+
   ```

2. To remove an identified account, use DROP USER:

```
mysql> DROP USER 'user1'@'%';
mysql> DROP USER 'user3'@'_.example.com';
```

Alternatively, rename an account to make the host part more specific:

```
mysql> RENAME USER 'user2'@'%.example.com' TO 'user2'@'host17.example.com';
```

24.10 Using TLS (SSL)

Problem

You want to encrypt traffic between MySQL client and the server.

Solution

Use Transport Layer Security (TLS) protocol.

Discussion

MySQL does not use anything in addition to the standard Transmission Control Protocol (TCP) to encrypt traffic between the client and the server. Therefore, if someone wants to read data, sent in either direction, they can easily do it with help of tcpdump and similar tools. Any sensitive information, such as user passwords or stored credit card numbers, could be exposed. To prevent this, MySQL supports TLS protocol to secure communications.

 Modern versions of MySQL use TLS protocol to encrypt traffic between the client and the server. However, due to historical reasons, configuration options and the Reference Manual often refer to TLS as SSL (Secure Socket Layer) even though the latter is not used anymore, because its encryption is weak. In this book, we use the term *TLS* in the text whenever possible.

To secure traffic between the MySQL client and the server, you need the following:

On the server

- The ssl option enabled. This is the default value, and you only need to ensure that it isn't disabled in the configuration file.

- The Certificate Authority (CA) file that could be used to verify certificates. It could be a single file, specified by the ssl_ca option, or a path to a directory containing multiple such files, specified by the ssl_capath option.

- The public key certificate file, specified by the ssl_cert option. This certificate will be sent to the client to authenticate against the client's CA.

- The private key, specified by the option ssl_key.

On the client

- For the `ssl-mode` option, specify one of the following values:

  PREFERRED
  > To establish an encrypted connection if the server supports TLS and fail back to the unencrypted if it does not. This is the default value.

  REQUIRED
  > To establish an encrypted connection if the server supports TLS and fail connection attempt if it does not.

  VERIFY_CA
  > Performs the same check as REQUIRED and additionally verifies the server CA file against the configured CA certificates.

  VERIFY_IDENTITY
  > Performs the same check as VERIFY_CA and additionally performs host name verification. That said, the server certificate should have the client's host name either in the "Subject Alternative Name" or the "Common Name" fields.

  The DISABLED value disables TLS connections and should not be used if you want to encrypt client-server traffic.

- The CA file that could be used to verify certificates. It could be a single file, specified by the option `ssl_ca`, or a path to a directory containing multiple such files, specified by the `ssl_capath` option.

- The public key certificate file, specified by the `ssl_cert` option. This certificate will be sent to the server to authenticate against the server's CA.

- The private key, specified by the `ssl_key` option.

The CA, certificate, and key files should be in PEM (Privacy Enhanced Mail) format.

If the MySQL server started with the `ssl` option enabled, but with empty values for other encryption-related options, it will search for the TLS keys and certificates in the data directory. If found, they will be used. Otherwise, TLS support will be disabled.

Once you have all of these prerequisites, you can test the TLS connection:

```
$ mysql
mysql> \s
--------------
../bin/mysql  Ver 8.0.21 for Linux on x86_64 (Source distribution)
```

```
Connection id:          534
Current database:
Current user:           root@localhost
SSL:                    Cipher in use is TLS_AES_256_GCM_SHA384
...
mysql> SHOW VARIABLES LIKE 'have_ssl';
+---------------+-------+
| Variable_name | Value |
+---------------+-------+
| have_ssl      | YES   |
+---------------+-------+
1 row in set (0.01 sec)
```

MySQL supports options to further restrict TLS connections, such as `ssl-cipher`, which requires you to use only specified ciphers. Consult "Configuring MySQL to Use Encrypted Connections" (*https://oreil.ly/6gpwk*) in the MySQL Reference Manual for further details.

Creating self-signed certificates

MySQL distribution includes a `mysql_ssl_rsa_setup` command that can create self-signed keys and certificates. It invokes the `openssl` command and can be used as follows:

```
$ mysql_ssl_rsa_setup --datadir=./data
Ignoring -days; not generating a certificate
Generating a RSA private key
.........................................................................+++++
..............+++++
writing new private key to 'ca-key.pem'
-----
Ignoring -days; not generating a certificate
Generating a RSA private key
.....................................+++++
............................................+++++
writing new private key to 'server-key.pem'
-----
Ignoring -days; not generating a certificate
Generating a RSA private key
.........................................................................+++++
...................................+++++
writing new private key to 'client-key.pem'
-----
```

Upon completion, it creates in the data directory files as listed in Table 24-2.

Table 24-2. Files created by `mysql_ssl_rsa_setup`

File	Description
`ca.pem`	Self-signed CA
`ca-key.pem`	CA private key
`server-cert.pem`	Server certificate
`server-key.pem`	Server key

File	Description
client-cert.pem	Client certificate
client-key.pem	Client key
private_key.pem	RSA private key to use over unencrypted connection for accounts, authenticated by either sha256_password or caching_sha2_password plug-ins
public_key.pem	RSA public key to use over unencrypted connection for accounts, authenticated by either sha256_password or caching_sha2_password plug-ins

Keys and certificates, created by the mysql_ssl_rsa_setup, are very basic and do not contain fields such as "Common Name". If you want to add these custom values to your TLS files, you need to create them manually. We don't include instructions on how to do so in the book, because there is plenty of documentation available online, including "Creating SSL and RSA Certificates and Keys" (*https://oreil.ly/OlL70*) in the MySQL Reference Manual. Alternatively, you may perform a test run of the mysql_ssl_rsa_setup command with the --verbose option that will print the openssl commands it executes. You will only need to repeat them with custom options.

> If you simply want to test how MySQL TLS connections work and do not want to create any new keys and certificates, you can use standard keys and certificates from the MySQL Test Suite (*https://oreil.ly/eke58*), located inside the mysql-test/std_data directory of your MySQL installation.

24.11 Using Roles

Problem

You want to grant the same set of privileges to different users but do not want them to share the same user account.

Solution

Use roles.

Discussion

When MySQL installation is used by multiple people, you may need to give similar privileges to some of them. For example, application users may need access to tables in their application database, while administrators may need to execute administrative commands. When you have a single application user or single database administrator, you can simply create two user accounts. But when your organization and MySQL usage grows, you may need to allow different people to perform the same tasks.

You may resolve such a problem by sharing a single user account between different people. But this is insecure for various reasons, including when a user leaves the company and should lose access to the database. Or, if someone from the group leaks their access credentials, all the database users are compromised.

Another solution is to duplicate privilege lists for individual user accounts. While it is more secure, it becomes error-prone when you need to add or remove a privilege. Doing it manually for dozens of users may easily lead to mistakes.

To resolve these drawbacks, MySQL 8.0 introduced roles that are, practically, the named collections of privileges.

You can create a role like any other user account. You just do not need to specify access credentials for it:

```
mysql> CREATE ROLE cookbook, admin;
Query OK, 0 rows affected (0.00 sec)
```

In the preceding listing, we created a role cookbook that will have access to the cookbook database and an admin role that will be used for the database administration.

The next step is to assign privileges to our new roles:

```
mysql> GRANT SELECT, INSERT, UPDATE, DELETE, EXECUTE ON cookbook.* TO 'cookbook';
Query OK, 0 rows affected (0.00 sec)

mysql> GRANT GROUP_REPLICATION_ADMIN, PERSIST_RO_VARIABLES_ADMIN,
    -> REPLICATION_SLAVE_ADMIN, RESOURCE_GROUP_ADMIN,
    -> ROLE_ADMIN, SYSTEM_VARIABLES_ADMIN, SYSTEM_USER,
    -> RELOAD, SHUTDOWN ON *.* to 'admin';
Query OK, 0 rows affected (0.01 sec)
```

Once roles are set up, we can assign them to different users. For example, to give access to the cookbook database to users cbuser, sveta, and alkin, use these commands:

```
mysql> GRANT cookbook TO cbuser;
Query OK, 0 rows affected (0.01 sec)

mysql> GRANT cookbook TO sveta;
Query OK, 0 rows affected (0.00 sec)

mysql> GRANT cookbook TO alkin;
Query OK, 0 rows affected (0.00 sec)
```

To grant administrator access to users paul and amelia, use the commands:

```
mysql> GRANT admin TO paul;
Query OK, 0 rows affected (0.00 sec)

mysql> GRANT admin TO amelia;
Query OK, 0 rows affected (0.01 sec)
```

Revoking role access is as easy as granting it:

```
mysql> REVOKE cookbook FROM sveta;
Query OK, 0 rows affected (0.01 sec)
```

See Also

MySQL supports other operations with roles, such as setting the default role for the newly added users or activating and deactivating roles. For additional information about roles in MySQL, see Using Roles in the MySQL Reference Manual (*https://oreil.ly/RrtZC*).

24.12 Using Views to Secure Data Access

Problem

You want to give users access only to certain query results but do not want them to see the actual data stored in the tables.

Solution

Use views.

Discussion

You may want certain users to be able to get access to the query results but want to cover real data stored in the tables. For example, the statistical department may want to know the number of patients in the hospital, their gender and age distribution, and how this data correlates to the recovery rate, but the department shouldn't have access to actual patient data, such as their names or ID numbers, or be able to correlate their identity and diagnosis.

To achieve this goal, you can create a view querying for certain data and grant specific users access only to this view.

Consider a `patients` table:

```
mysql> SHOW CREATE TABLE patients\G
*************************** 1. row ***************************
       Table: patients
Create Table: CREATE TABLE `patients` (
  `id` int NOT NULL AUTO_INCREMENT,
  `national_id` char(32) DEFAULT NULL,
  `name` varchar(255) DEFAULT NULL,
  `surname` varchar(255) DEFAULT NULL,
  `gender` enum('F','M') DEFAULT NULL,
  `age` tinyint unsigned DEFAULT NULL,
  `additional_data` json DEFAULT NULL,
  `diagnosis` varchar(255) DEFAULT NULL,
```

```
 `result` enum('R','N','D') DEFAULT NULL ↵
   COMMENT 'R=Recovered, N=Not Recovered, D=Dead',
 `date_arrived` date NOT NULL,
 `date_departed` date DEFAULT NULL,
 PRIMARY KEY (`id`)
) ENGINE=InnoDB AUTO_INCREMENT=21 DEFAULT CHARSET=utf8mb4 COLLATE=utf8mb4_0900_ai_ci
1 row in set (0.00 sec)
```

If you want to give the statistical department access to this data, you may want to give access to the gender, age, diagnosis, and result columns but restrict access to national_id, name, surname, and additional_data. You also may want to let them know how many days a patient spent in the hospital and in which month and year they arrived but do not want to let them explore actual arriving and departing dates. In other words, you want to restrict access to date_arrived and date_departed but still provide data that could be calculated based on the values stored in these columns.

You can do this by creating a view:

```
mysql> CREATE VIEW patients_statistics AS
    ->    SELECT age, gender, diagnosis, result,
    ->           datediff(date_departed, date_arrived) as recovered_time,
    ->           MONTH(date_arrived) AS month_arrived,
    ->           YEAR(date_arrived) AS year_arrived
    ->    FROM patients;
Query OK, 0 rows affected (0.03 sec)
```

Then create a user for the statistics department that has read-only access to this view and does not have access to the underlying table:

```
mysql> CREATE USER statistics;
Query OK, 0 rows affected (0.03 sec)

mysql> GRANT SELECT ON cookbook.patients_statistics TO statistics;
Query OK, 0 rows affected (0.02 sec)
```

Now the statistics department can log in and run analytical queries, such as finding the most frequent diagnosis, or how many patients with such a diagnosis arrived per month:

```
# mysql cookbook -A -ustatistics
Welcome to the MySQL monitor.  Commands end with ; or \g.
Your MySQL connection id is 17
...
mysql> SELECT diagnosis, AVG(recovered_time) AS recovered_time_avg, COUNT(*) AS cases
    -> FROM patients_statistics WHERE year_arrived='2020'
    -> GROUP BY diagnosis ORDER BY cases DESC;
+---------------+--------------------+-------+
| diagnosis     | recovered_time_avg | cases |
+---------------+--------------------+-------+
| Data Phobia   |            24.8333 |     6 |
| Diabetes      |            10.0000 |     4 |
| Asthma        |            10.3333 |     3 |
| Arthritis     |            22.0000 |     3 |
| Appendicitis  |             5.5000 |     2 |
| Breast Cancer |            75.0000 |     2 |
+---------------+--------------------+-------+
```

```
6 rows in set (0.00 sec)

mysql> SELECT diagnosis, month_arrived, COUNT(*) AS month_cases
    -> FROM patients_statistics WHERE diagnosis='Data Phobia' AND year_arrived='2020'
    -> GROUP BY diagnosis, month_arrived ORDER BY month_arrived;
+--------------+---------------+-------------+
| diagnosis    | month_arrived | month_cases |
+--------------+---------------+-------------+
| Data Phobia  |             4 |           1 |
| Data Phobia  |             9 |           2 |
| Data Phobia  |            10 |           2 |
| Data Phobia  |            11 |           1 |
+--------------+---------------+-------------+
4 rows in set (0.00 sec)
```

But they would not be able to access the table data directly:

```
mysql> SELECT * FROM patients;
ERROR 1142 (42000): SELECT command denied to user 'statistics'@'localhost' ↵
                                        for table 'patients'

mysql> SELECT diagnosis, result, date_arrived FROM patients;
ERROR 1142 (42000): SELECT command denied to user 'statistics'@'localhost' ↵
                                        for table 'patients'
```

> Views support the SQL SECURITY clause, allowing you to specify
> security context when executing a view. This clause is discussed in
> detail in Recipe 24.13.

See Also

For additional information about using views, see Recipe 5.7.

24.13 Using Stored Routines to Secure Data Modifications

Problem

You want to let users modify their personal data but want to prevent them from
accessing similar data for others.

Solution

Use stored routines.

Discussion

You may want to let users view and change their own personal information. For
example, patients may marry and change their surnames or decide to add new
additional information about themselves, such as address, weight, and so on. But

---

you do not want them to see similar information for other patients. In this case, restricting access only on the column level wouldn't work.

Stored routines support the SQL SECURITY clause that allows you to specify if you want to execute the routine with access privileges for the DEFINER, the user that created the procedure, or the INVOKER, the user that is currently executing the procedure.

In our case, we do not want to grant the INVOKER any privilege that allows them to access data stored in the sensitive columns. Therefore, we need to grant such privileges to the DEFINER of the procedure and specify the argument SQL SECURITY DEFINER.

 The default value for SQL SECURITY is DEFINER; therefore, this clause could be omitted.

To illustrate this, let's take the patients table from the previous recipe. But now we'll access only columns containing sensitive data:

```
mysql> SHOW CREATE TABLE patients\G
*************************** 1. row ***************************
       Table: patients
Create Table: CREATE TABLE `patients` (
  ...
  `national_id` char(32) DEFAULT NULL,
  `name` varchar(255) DEFAULT NULL,
  `surname` varchar(255) DEFAULT NULL,
  ...
  `additional_data` json DEFAULT NULL,
  ...
```

First, let's prepare a user that will be a DEFINER for our procedure. We do not want this account to be used by anyone except the stored routine, so first let's install the mysql_no_login authentication plug-in:

```
mysql> INSTALL PLUGIN mysql_no_login SONAME 'mysql_no_login.so';
Query OK, 0 rows affected (0.01 sec)
```

Then let's create the user account and grant it access to the patients table:

```
mysql> CREATE USER sp_access IDENTIFIED WITH mysql_no_login;
Query OK, 0 rows affected (0.00 sec)

mysql> GRANT SELECT, UPDATE ON cookbook.patients TO sp_access;
Query OK, 0 rows affected (0.01 sec)
```

Now let's create a procedure that will return sensitive data for a patient, identified by national_id:

```
mysql> delimiter $$
mysql> CREATE DEFINER='sp_access'@'%' PROCEDURE get_patient_data(IN nat_id CHAR(32))
```

```
    ->   SQL SECURITY DEFINER
    ->   BEGIN
    ->     SELECT name, surname, gender, age, additional_data
    ->     FROM patients WHERE national_id=nat_id;
    ->   END
    -> $$
Query OK, 0 rows affected (0.01 sec)

mysql> delimiter ;
```

And a procedure that will update the record:

```
mysql> delimiter $$
mysql> CREATE DEFINER='sp_access'@'%' PROCEDURE update_patient_data(
    ->                                 IN nat_id CHAR(32),
    ->                                 IN new_name varchar(255),
    ->                                 IN new_surname varchar(255),
    ->                                 IN new_additional_data JSON)
    ->   SQL SECURITY DEFINER
    ->   BEGIN
    ->     UPDATE patients
    ->       SET name=COALESCE(new_name, name),
    ->           surname=COALESCE(new_surname, surname),
    ->           additional_data=JSON_MERGE_PATCH(COALESCE(additional_data, '{}'),
    ->                                 COALESCE(new_additional_data, '{}'))
    ->       WHERE national_id=nat_id;
    ->   END
    -> $$
Query OK, 0 rows affected (0.01 sec)

mysql> delimiter ;
```

Then, add privileges to execute these procedures to our DEFINER:

```
mysql> GRANT EXECUTE ON PROCEDURE cookbook.get_patient_data TO sp_access;
Query OK, 0 rows affected (0.01 sec)

mysql> GRANT EXECUTE ON PROCEDURE cookbook.update_patient_data TO sp_access;
Query OK, 0 rows affected (0.00 sec)
```

Finally, let's create a user that will use these procedures without any additional privileges:

```
mysql> CREATE USER patient;
Query OK, 0 rows affected (0.01 sec)

mysql> GRANT EXECUTE ON PROCEDURE cookbook.get_patient_data TO patient;
Query OK, 0 rows affected (0.02 sec)

mysql> GRANT EXECUTE ON PROCEDURE cookbook.update_patient_data TO patient;
Query OK, 0 rows affected (0.01 sec)
```

Now let's log in as this user and check how our procedures work:

```
mysql> SHOW GRANTS;
+-----------------------------------------------------------------------+
| Grants for patient@%                                                  |
+-----------------------------------------------------------------------+
| GRANT USAGE ON *.* TO `patient`@`%`                                   |
| GRANT EXECUTE ON PROCEDURE `cookbook`.`get_patient_data` TO `patient`@`%` |
```

```
| GRANT EXECUTE ON PROCEDURE `cookbook`.`update_patient_data` TO `patient`@`%` |
+-----------------------------------------------------------------------------+
3 rows in set (0.00 sec)

mysql> CALL update_patient_data('89AR642465', NULL, 'Johnson',
    -> ' {"Height": 165, "Weight": 55, "Hair color": "Blonde"}');
Query OK, 1 row affected (0.00 sec)

mysql> CALL get_patient_data('89AR642465')\G
*************************** 1. row ***************************
          name: Mary
       surname: Johnson
        gender: F
           age: 24
additional_data: {"Height": 165, "Weight": 55, "Hair color": "Blonde"}
1 row in set (0.00 sec)

Query OK, 0 rows affected (0.00 sec)
```

As you can see, we can change details for the specific patient, identifying them by a national ID, while having no access to the data of other patients.

See Also

For additional information about stored routines, see Chapter 11.

Index

Symbols

" (double quote)
  escaping in command line arguments, 523
  escaping in data values, 211
  identifier quoting if ANSI_QUOTES, 220, 291
  importing data, 529
  shell command arguments, 522
  writing string literals, 291

$ (dollar sign)
  JSON root element, 736
  prompt, 4
  regexp end of string, 308, 566

% (percent)
  formatting for date and time values, 337
  hostname containing, 879
  matching sequence of characters, 103, 306

' (single quote)
  escaping in data values, 211
  exporting data, 538
  importing CSV files, 537
  writing string literals, 291

( ) parentheses
  function-based indexes, 793
  regexp pattern matches, 567

* (asterisk)
  COUNT rows including NULLs, 420, 436
  JSON all values, 736
  regexp pattern matching, 308, 566
    matching empty string, 312
  SELECT all columns, 240

+ (plus) regexp pattern matching, 308, 566
  avoiding empty string match, 312

- (dash)

  option file underscores and, 12, 818
  single versus double, 9

-> (JSON_EXTRACT()), 736
->> (JSON_UNQUOTE()), 737

. (dot)
  JSON object members, 736
  regexp matching single character, 308, 566

/ (slash) pathname separator, 13
/dev/null, 31
  Blackhole "storage" engine, 830
/dev/random for seed, 689
/var/log/messages system log, 859

:= as variable assignment operator, 25

; (semicolon)
  end of SQL statement, 14, 17
    multiple SQL statements executed, 16
    none in API SQL statements, 199
    \G for vertical output, 15, 17
    \g synonym, 14, 17
  redefining mysql terminator for
    BEGIN...END, 458

< (left angle bracket) to redirect input, 16, 17
<=> for NULL comparison, 248

= (equal sign)
  spaces around, 12
  variable assignment operator, 25
    := synonym, 25

> (right angle bracket) redirecting output, 539
? (question mark) optional regexp element, 567

@ (at sign)
  account names, 3, 869
    anonymous accounts, 878
    hostnames with pattern characters, 879
  variable assignment, 23

@@ (double at sign)
  examples of use
    buffer pool size, 853
    data directory, 28
    global variable read, 819
    GTID, 95
    mysqlx_socket value, 35
    plugin_dir system variable, 821
    Ruby, 187
    session and global specified, 340, 341
    showing default storage engine, 831
  sql_mode, 473, 527, 556
  writing or reading system variables, 820
    no GLOBAL. or SESSION. modifier, 820
[ ] (square brackets)
  regexp pattern matching, 308, 310, 566, 568
    JSON array members, 736
    POSIX character classes, 310
    [^] not version, 308, 566
\ (backslash)
  escape sequences, 293
    LOAD DATA escape sequences, 524
  escaping double quotes, 523
  escaping identifier quoted strings, 292
  escaping in data values, 211
  line-continuation character in Unix, 523
  literal matches of characters, 502, 566
  option file pathnames, 13
  Windows pathname separator, 527
    LOAD DATA pathnames, 527
\! for system command, 28
\. for source command, 18
\0 for ASCII NUL, 293, 524
\1, \2, ... in regexp pattern matches, 567
\b for backspace, 293
\c for \connect command, 35-37
\d for regexp digit character, 566, 568
\D for regexp nondigit character, 566
\g at end of SQL statement, 14, 17
\G for vertical output, 15, 17
\n for linefeed or newline, 293
  line-ending sequence in files, 521, 528
\n for nopager to reset pager, 31
\r for carriage return, 293
  line-ending sequence in files, 521, 528
\R to customize mysql prompt, 26
\S for regexp nonwhitespace character, 566, 568
\s for regexp whitespace character, 566, 568
\t for tab, 293

\W for regexp nonword character, 566
\w for regexp word character, 566, 568
^ (caret)
  line-continuation in Windows, 523
  regexp beginning of string, 308, 566
  regexp empty and nonempty values, 568
_ (underscore)
  character set for string literal, 291
  hostname containing, 879
  option file dashes interchangeable, 12, 818
  pattern matching single character, 103, 306
` (backtick)
  around identifier in SQL statement, 220
  GROUP BY identifier quoting, 442
  line-continuation in PowerShell, 523
  SQL injection attack prevention, 469
{ } (curly braces)
  multiline code, 54
  regexp pattern matching, 308, 566
| (pipe) output as input, 18, 19
| (vertical bar) regexp pattern matching, 308, 311, 566

A

access denied error
  built-in report privileges, 61
  importing data, 526
  invoking mysql, 8
access privileges (see privileges)
access to option files by other users, 14
accounts (see user account for MySQL)
add() to Python mode collections, 55
add_or_replace_one() in Python mode collections, 55
adjacent words in specific order, 327
Admin API, 67
  automated replication setup, 144
administration of server (see server administration)
administrative privileges
  CREATE USER and GRANT, 4
  mysqladmin, 9
  security, 868
  server administration, 817
  server monitoring, 834
  server shutdown, 9
  SUPER privileges, 819
AGAINST(), 318
age calculations, 368

aggregate functions
   descriptive statistics calculations, 676
   JSON object and array functions, 746
   NULL values ignored, 435
   query result rows numbered, 624
   summary values via, 418
      (see also summaries)
      caution: nonsummary columns, 432
   WHERE clause not allowing, 427
aliases for tables, 643
aliasing column names in results, 242
   benefits for programming, 244
   DATE_FORMAT() results, 337
   expressions for sorting, 386
   GROUP BY referring to, 439
      identifier quoting in backticks, 442
   HAVING referring to, 438
   join output column names, 673
   restrictions on, 244
   saving query results to a table, 269
   UNION using, 261
ALTER EVENT to disable or enable, 467
ALTER TABLE
   adding AUTO_INCREMENT column, 612
   changing storage engine, 272, 603, 831
   column names in results, 243
   dropping column to renumber sequence, 609
   foreign keys added, 475
   general tablespaces to individual, 276
   index renamed, 786
   query results saved as a table, 269
   resetting sequence counter, 610
   tablespace discarded, 278
ALTER USER
   changing your password, 876
   expiring passwords, 875
Amazon review data for download, xxvii, 318
   script to load data, 320
anonymous account management, 878
ANSI_QUOTES, 220, 291
APIs
   about book use, xxiii
      recipes distribution, xxvii, 155
   about object orientation, 157
   architecture of, 156
      portability of SQL code, 156
   AUTO_INCREMENT values via, 605
   character set for client connections, 289

connecting to MySQL server, 153, 157-172
   disconnecting from, 157
   obtaining connection parameters, 227-237
creating tables via scripts
   about recipes distribution, xxvii, 2
   recipes distribution script files, 17
date calculations, 361
error handling by scripts, 154, 172-180
   Go connection script, 168, 192
   Java connection script, 172, 196
   Perl connection script, 160, 185
   PHP connection script, 164, 188
   Python connection script, 166, 191
   Ruby connection script, 162, 188
executing SQL, 154, 196-210
   categories of SQL statements, 196, 198
   error handling, 199
   no SQL statement terminators, 199
languages supported by MySQL, xxiii, 153
   MySQL Shell, 2
   recipes distribution on GitHub, xxvii, 155
library file writing, 155, 181-196
   data validation tests, 563
   Go, 192
   location of library file, 182
   Perl, 185
   PHP, 188
   Python, 190
   recipes distribution lib directory, 155, 181
   Ruby, 187
   test harness, 182
metadata
   listing databases or tables, 497
   matched versus changed, 483
   number of rows changed by SQL, 483
   result set metadata obtained, 486
   server and database metadata, 506
   server version, 507
NULL data values, 154, 210-219
   identifying in result sets, 221-227
persistent connections and temporary tables, 271
resetting the profile table, 237
special character handling, 154
special characters in data values, 210-219
special characters in identifiers, 220

quoted string with same quote character, 292
test data via Python, 73-82
transactions, 765
  APIs mapped onto SQL, 767
architecture of APIs, 156
  portability of SQL code, 156
architecture of InnoDB storage engine, 857
Archive storage engine, 830
arrays
  card deck–shuffling algorithm, 691
  JSON array from relational data, 746
  JSON array members accessed, 736
  JSON new array members, 739
  PHP associative arrays, 579
  result-set metadata
    Go, 492
    Perl, 487
AS to specify column name alias, 243
  alias benefits in programming, 244
ASCII NUL (\0), 293, 524
ASCII() to convert string format, 302
asterisk (*)
  COUNT rows including NULLs, 420, 436
  JSON all values, 736
  regexp pattern matching, 308, 566
    matching empty string, 312
  SELECT all columns, 240
asynchronous API of X protocol, 34
at sign (@)
  account names, 3, 869
    anonymous accounts, 878
    hostnames with pattern characters, 879
  variable assignment, 23
authentication
  caching_sha2_password plug-in, 90
  database access, 3
    (see also privileges)
  mysql.user table, 868
    anonymous accounts, 878
  replication user, 90
auto-commit mode of MySQL, 764
auto-vertical-output, 15
autocommit session variable, 765
AUTO_INCREMENT column
  counting with, 617
  custom increment values, 622
  data type for, 599
    extending range of sequence, 610

deleting rows, 601
  renumbering an existing sequence, 607
  reusing values at top of sequence, 610
duplicate rows prevented, 713
extending range of, 610
id column, 268, 596
LAST_INSERT_ID() value, 24, 604
managing multiple simultaneously, 614
renumbering an existing, 607
  particular order, 611
retrieving values, 603
  APIs, 605
  server-side versus client-side, 606
sequences via, 596
  emptying table, resetting counter, 603
  repeating sequences, 621
  sequencing an unsequenced table, 612
storage engines and, 601, 602
tables associated via, 615
AVG(), 422

B

B (batch) option for output, 20
B-tree indexes, 780
  FULLTEXT index on same column, 797
  hash indexes versus, 780
backslash (\)
  escape sequences, 293
    LOAD DATA escape sequences, 524
  escaping double quotes, 523
  escaping identifier quoted strings, 292
  escaping in data values, 211
  line-continuation character in Unix, 523
  literal matches of characters, 502, 566
  option file pathnames, 13
  Windows pathname separator, 527
    LOAD DATA pathnames, 527
  \! for system command, 28
  \. for source command, 18
  \0 for ASCII NUL, 293, 524
  \1, \2, ... in regexp pattern matches, 567
  \b for backspace, 293
  \g at end of SQL statement, 14, 17
  \G for vertical output, 15, 17
  \n for linefeed or newline, 293
    line-ending sequence in files, 521, 528
  \n for nopager to reset pager, 31
  \P for pager command, 30
  \r for carriage return, 293

line-ending sequence in files, 521, 528
\R to customize mysql prompt, 26
\t for tab, 293
backspace (\b), 293
backtick (`)
    around identifier in SQL statement, 220
    GROUP BY identifier quoting, 442
    line-continuation in PowerShell, 523
    SQL injection attack prevention, 469
backups
    backup server via replication, 87
    binary versus logical, 94
    cp for binary backups, 94
    MySQL backup tools, 94
    mysqldump for, 18
        backing up server for replication, 93
        mysql client to load dump, 18, 94
        renaming database, 106
    replication server, 93
        multisource replication, 112
    table copying via, 273
Basic Multilingual Plane (BMP), 282
batch (B) option for output, 20
batch mode in mysql
    about mysql, 1
        (see also scripts)
    creating tables
        about recipes distribution, xxvii, 2
        recipes distribution script files, 17
    distributing SQL via script files, 17
    executing SQL from file, 16
    output format default, 17, 19
BEGIN...END block, 456
    redefining mysql ; terminator, 458
BIN() for binary format conversion, 301
binary collations, 284
    comparisons, 284
binary log files
    configuring, 825
    configuring format, 98
        format of replica binary log, 99
    enabling, 865
    GTIDs, 89, 97
    point-in-time recovery, 102, 865
    position via SHOW MASTER STATUS, 91
        stopping writes for in-use future source, 93
    reading, 137, 865
    record of data changes, 823, 865

recording prevented by filters, 100
rotating, 827
source replication server, 88, 823
binary output as hexadecimal notation, 293
BINARY string data type, 286
binary strings, 282, 286
    bit operations, 303
    comparisons, 284, 298, 391, 429
        case sensitivity controlled, 429
        sorting of binary strings, 391
    hexadecimal notation treated as, 291
    UUID converted to binary, 303
binlog-do-db configuration option, 100
    binlog-ignore-db, 102
binlog_rows_query_log_events, 88
binlog_transaction_dependency_tracking, 108, 141
bit operations, 303
BIT_COUNT(), 304
BIT_LENGTH() to convert string format, 302
BIT_OR(), 304
Blackhole "storage" engine, 830
BLOB string data type, 286
book GitHub repository, xxvi
    email address for problems with code examples, xxx
    web page for errata, examples, and information, xxxi
Boolean-mode full-text searches, 325

C

ca-key.pem, 882
ca.pem, 882
caching_sha2_password plug-in, 90
calendar operations
    date values (see date values)
    number of holidays, 305
    number of Sundays, 304
    sorting by calendar day, 395
    time values (see time values)
CALL to invoke stored programs, 457, 469
Camel-case syntax, 66
candidate keys, 656
candidate-detail lists and summaries, 656
card deck–shuffling algorithm, 691
cardinality of index, 785, 804
caret (^)
    line-continuation in Windows, 523
    regexp beginning of string, 308, 566

regexp empty and nonempty values, 568
carriage return (\r), 293
   line-ending sequence in files, 521, 528
Cartesian products, 636
case conversion for strings, 296
case sensitivity
   collation name ending, 284
   duplicate identification, 724
   keywords, 7
   regular expressions, 312
   sorting strings, 390
   user variable names, 25
central tendency, 676
certificates
   Certificate Authority (CA) file, 880
   creating self-signed, 882
   public key certificate file, 880
CHANGE MASTER, 124
CHANGE REPLICATION FILTER, 106
CHANGE REPLICATION SOURCE, 91
   replication user credential security, 123
   TLS for replication security, 124
   two or more source servers, 111
changing your password, 876
CHAR string data type, 286
CHAR() to convert string format, 302
character classes in regexp, 310
   POSIX character classes, 310
character sets for nonbinary strings, 282
   changing, 294
   checking, 294
   client connection, 288
     some cannot be used as connection
       character sets, 290
   default (MySQL 8), 282
   listing character sets and collations, 514
   multibyte characters determination, 283
   table columns, 287
   Unicode, 282
CHARSET(), 294
charting frequency distributions, 682
CHAR_LENGTH(), 283
CHECK constraints, 558
   listing defined CHECK constraints, 517
checking if server is up, 844
   "MySQL Server has gone away", 859
chmod command
   library file access privileges, 185
   protecting option files, 14

Classic MySQL protocol, 34
   import_table requiring, 65
CLASSPATH environment variable, 183, 195
clear screen via cls parameter
   nocls to not clear screen, 63
client for MySQL, xxviii, 1
   timeout of client, 859
client-cert.pem, 882
client-key.pem, 882
client-server architecture of MySQL, 1
cloning a table, 265
Cluster (InnoDB) managed by Admin API, 67
   automating Group Replication, 148
clustered index, 783
cmdline.pdf
   environment variables, 183
   running programs, 155, 159, 161, 165, 171
cmdline.pl, 232
COALESCE(), 250
COLLATE to change collation, 294
collation of strings
   changing, 294
   checking, 294
   COLLATE example, 284
   comparisons, 284
   duplicate identification and case sensitivity,
     724
   listing character sets and collations, 514
   sort order affected by, 283
     listing character sets and collations, 514
   table columns, 287
   _ci, _cs, _bin for case sensitivity and binary,
     283
COLLATION(), 294
collections
   about, 51
     schema validation, 52
   CookbookCollection object, 69-72
   JavaScript mode Document Store, 51
   Python mode Document Store, 54
column definitions accessed, 498
column headings suppressed in output, 21
column names aliased in results, 242
   alias restrictions, 244
   benefits for programming, 244
   DATE_FORMAT() results, 337
   expression for original name, 269
   expressions for sorting, 386

GROUP BY identifier quoting in backticks, 442
GROUP BY referring to aliases, 439
HAVING referring to aliases, 438
join output column names, 673
UNION using, 261
columns specified in SELECT, 240
 column order, 792
columns with date and timestamps, 345
comma-separated values (see CSV)
command line
 cmdline.pdf, 155
 dba global object, 68
 executing SQL statements directly, 15
  reading from script file, 17
 invoking commands overview, 522
  line-continuation characters, 523
 invoking mysql
  command not found, 7
  specifying command options, 8
 json/array for passing data, 58
 mixing option file parameters and, 13
 MySQL Shell client, 2
 parameters in short or long form, 229
 process list, 837
 processing arguments to obtain parameters, 229
 running MySQL Shell utilities, 66
 security issues, 229
 server configuration, 818
 "Executing Programs from the Command Line" document
  GitHub repository, xxvii
  PATH variable, 8
command not found, 7
command options
 default values, 9
 invoking mysql, 8
 MySQL Shell output formatting, 57
 mysqldump, 9
 single versus double dash, 9
 vertical output for session, 15
comments in option files, 13
COMMIT, 764
commit()
 Perl transactions, 768
 Python mode table modifications, 50
Common Table Expressions (CTEs)
 data from MIN or MAX rows, 428

Formula 1 fractional seconds example, 333
 query results joined, 673
 recursive CTEs, 626
 sequence generation, 626
 summaries from temporary result sets, 452
comparison operators
 binary string comparisons, 284, 298, 391, 429
  case sensitivity controlled, 429
  sorting of binary strings, 391
 date values, 376
  dates to calendar days, 379
 NULL values
  <=>, 249
  IFNULL(), 250, 436
  IS NULL or IS NOT NULL, 248
  ISNULL(), 685
  programming, 251
 string values, 298
  regexp patterns equivalent to substring comparisons, 312
  SQL patterns equivalent to substring comparisons, 307
 time values, 379
CONCAT(), 317
 date and time values synthesized, 352
  ISO date format, 375
 email address format produced, 242
concurrency in transactions, 761
condition handlers
 about error handling, 469
 benign errors ignored, 472
 No More Rows conditions, 470
 sales tax example, 461
configuration files
 global configuration file mysqlshrc, 83
 library file installation location, 183
 option files (see option files)
 personal configuration file, 83
 replication
  binary log enabled, 90
  GTID-based replication, 94, 96
  server_id, 90
\connect command (\c), 35-37
connect.go, 167
Connect.java, 170
connect.php, 163
connect.pl, 158
connect.py, 165

connect.rb, 161
connection limits of MySQL server, 851
    buffer pool sizing, 853
connection objects (conn)
    Java, 171
    Python, 166
connection parameters
    character set, 288
    command line, 9
    Go connection script, 167
    Java connection script, 170
    obtaining via script, 227-237
        parameters from command line, 229
        security issues, 229
    option file, 10
        mysql_config_editor for credential secu-
        rity, 11
    Perl connection script, 158
    PHP connection script, 163
    Python connection script, 165
    Ruby connection script, 161
context cancellation support of Go, 167
CONTINUE handler for NOT FOUND, 461
CONV() to convert between numeric bases,
    301
CONVERT() to change character set, 294
CONVERT_TZ() for time zones, 342
cookbook database, 2
    creating, 5, 5
        PRIMARY KEY clause, 6
        rows inserted, 5
        tables created, 5
    user account privileges, 3-5
cookbook.py module, 85
CookbookCollection object, 69-72
CookbookCollectionModule.js, 84
cookbook_utils.py library module file, 564
    regexp date patterns, 571, 583
    regexp time patterns, 584
    trim_whitespace(), 567
    year from two digits to four, 582
copying database to another MySQL server, 18
correlation coefficients, 686, 688
COUNT()
    displaying results in groups, 258
    DISTINCT for unique values, 248, 418
        repetitiveness of a set of values, 442
    missing values counted, 684
    non-NULL values versus rows, 420, 436

    summarizing with, 419
covering index, 787
cp for binary backups, 94
CPU monitoring
    high-utilization process on server, 849
        thread-filtering documentation, 849
    monitoring the operating system, 835
    non-uniform memory access (NUMA), 836
CREATE DATABASE, 5
    renaming database, 106
CREATE EVENT, 466
    about events, 455
        (see also events)
    log maintenance, 829
CREATE FUNCTION, 458
    about stored functions, 455
        (see also stored functions)
    READS clause, 458
    RETURN statement, 458
    RETURNS clause, 458
CREATE INDEX, 794
CREATE PROCEDURE
    about stored procedures, 455
        (see also stored procedures)
    about stored programs, 456
        BEGIN...END compound statement, 456
        redefining mysql ; terminator, 458
    IN parameters, 462
    INOUT parameters, 462
    OUT parameters, 462
CREATE TABLE, 5
    column names in results, 243
    CREATE TEMPORARY TABLE, 269
        caveats, 271
        same name hides permanent, 270
        same table names do not clash, 271
        summary results via, 428, 434, 452
    LIKE to clone existing structure, 265
    LIKE to clone existing table structure, 725
    mysqldump output file containing, 274
    saving results of query to a table, 266
    scripts in recipes distribution, xxvii, 2, 17,
        197, 240
    transaction engine specified, 763
        (see also transactions)
CREATE TEMPORARY TABLE, 269
    caveats, 271
    same name hides permanent, 270
    same table names do not clash, 271

summary results via, 428, 434, 452
CREATE USER, 3-5, 869
  administrative privileges needed, 4
  GRANT, 3-5
    replication user, 90
  replication user, 90
CREATE VIEW
  summaries simplified, 426
  table access simplified, 252
createCollection, 51
credit card number regexp patterns, 569
cron jobs in batch mode
  batch mode in mysql, 1
CSV (comma separated values) files
  about file format, 521
  exporting, 22, 538
  importing, 537
  MySQL Shell utility, 64
  read_csv() (pandas), 76
CSV storage engine, 830
  log table management, 843
CTEs (see Common Table Expressions)
Ctrl-C to terminate running query, 63
Ctrl-D (Unix) to terminate mysql session, 4
cumulative sums, 696
cumulative values to relative values, 694
CURDATE(), 344
  extracting components, 351
curly braces ({ })
  multiline code, 54
  regexp pattern matching, 308, 566
current date and time, 344
  extracting components, 351
CURRENT_USER(), 877
CURTIME(), 344
  extracting components, 351
custom_sequences.sql, 634
cvt_date.py, 585
cvt_file.pl utility, 22, 522, 552, 563

D

dash (-)
  option file underscores and, 12, 818
  single versus double, 9
data
  access security via stored routines, 887
  access security via views, 885
  incomplete
    counting missing values, 684

frequency distribution range of cate-
    gories, 683
JSON data type, 730
  (see also JSON data format)
reformatting (see reformatting data)
special characters, 210-219
test data via Python data science modules,
  73-82
tracking changes, 865
transferring to and from MySQL, 519
  exporting data (see exporting data)
  importing data (see importing data)
  source code in recipes distribution, 520
  validating (see validating data)
data dictionary holding table definitions, 276
data source name (DSN) in Perl connection
  script, 159
database handles
  Perl ($dbh), 160, 487, 507
  PHP ($dbh), 164
  Python connection objects (conn), 166
  Ruby (client), 162
databases
  APIs selecting, 157-172
    Go connection script, 167
    Java connection script, 170
    Perl connection script, 158
    PHP connection script, 163
    Python connection script, 165
    Ruby connection script, 161
  automated operations via events, 466
  backing up via mysqldump, 18
  CHECK constraints, 558
    listing defined CHECK constraints, 517
  checking if database exists, 496
  cookbook database, 2
  copying to another MySQL server, 18
  creating, 5
    PRIMARY KEY clause, 6
    rows inserted, 5
    table data from program output, 18
    tables created, 5
    tables created via scripts, 17
  foreign keys preventing mismatches, 652
  JSON data structure versus, 729
    (see also JSON data format)
  listing databases hosted by server, 496
  listing tables in a database, 496
  metadata, 481

default database name, 506
prompt showing current default, 27
renaming databases, 106
user account privileges, 3-5
views listed or checked for existence, 497
DATE data type, 331
(see also date values)
date showing in prompt, 27
date values
about capabilities, 329
about scripts in recipes distribution, 330
age calculations, 368
combining components, 352
converting basic units (days, seconds), 354
current date determined, 344
extracting components, 351
data type to use, 330
date of any given weekday, 372
date processing utility, 584
day of week for a date, 371
extracting part of, 348
format of date, 335
date processing utility, 584
ISO to non-ISO, 590
non-ISO to ISO, 589
year from two digits to four, 581
interval calculations, 358
interval or span, 362
ISO format for, 375
exporting to non-ISO, 590
reformatting to, 589
patterns with nonstring values, 308
regexp patterns for, 570, 573
row insertion and last modification timestamps, 345
NULL values not allowed, 345, 347
selecting rows based on, 376
calendar days, 379
sorting by, 394
calendar day, 395
day of week, 396
sum of, 362
summaries grouped by date, 445
synthesizing a date value, 352
ISO format for, 375
validity checking of subparts, 582
DATE() extracting date component, 348
DATEDIFF(), 358
DATETIME data type, 331

daily summaries, 446
DEFAULT CURRENT_TIME STAMP, 345
fractional seconds, 332
ON UPDATE CURRENT_TIME STAMP,
345
row creation and last modification timestamps, 345
DATE_FORMAT(), 335
combining components, 352
exporting dates to non-ISO formats, 591
extracting part of a date value, 351
day of week for a date, 371
day of week sorted on, 396
DAYNAME(), 348, 371
DAYOFMONTH()
extracting component from date value, 348
number of days in a month, 369
pattern matching with nonstring values, 308
DAYOFWEEK(), 348
Sunday as first day, 372
DAYOFYEAR(), 348
dba global object of DBA class, 67
command line, 68
DDL (Data Definition Language) operations
caution, 786
documentation online, 786
debugging InnoDB storage engine, 858
decimal values converted between octal and
hexadecimal, 301
delayed copying to replica, 88
DELETE
about SQL statement categories, 198
duplicate rows eliminated, 724
rows with AUTO_INCREMENT column,
601
renumbering an existing sequence, 607
reusing values at top of sequence, 610
"unattached" rows removed, 649
delete()
JavaScript mode table queries, 48
Python mode table queries, 51
delimiter command, 41
redefining mysql ; terminator for
BEGIN...END, 458
delimiter for output columns, 21
DENSE_RANK(), 702
deploying a sandbox instance, 67
stopping instance, 68
DESCRIBE, 198

descriptive statistics calculations, 676
/dev/null, 31
    Blackhole "storage" engine, 830
/dev/random for seed, 689
dictionaries
    data validation lookup table into, 579, 580
    Python connection script, 166
DISTINCT for unique values, 418, 424
    HAVING instead, 438
    remove duplicate rows, 247
distributing SQL via script files, 17
division by zero error, 473
Document Store
    JavaScript mode collections, 51
    JSON and X DevAPI, 752
    Python mode collections, 54
documentation online for MySQL
    B-tree versus hash indexes, 780
    Boolean full-text operators, 327
    date and time value component extraction,
        348, 350
    date and time values, 330, 337
    DDL operations, 786
    encryption, 882
    error log configuration, 859
    full-text index restrictions, 799
    I/O utilization, 839
    JSON data type, 731
    JSON Path syntax, 738
    memory usage, 29
    mysql prompt customization, 27
    prepared SQL statements, 469
    roles, 885
    SELECT statements, 239
    server plug-ins, 858
    sql_mode, 558
    stored program error handling, 470
    stored routines, triggers, and events, 456
    time zones, 343
    TO_DAYS() and Gregorian calendar, 356
    window functions, 626
dollar sign ($)
    JSON root element, 736
    prompt, 4
    regexp end of string, 308, 566
domain socket file (Unix), 10
domain-order sort of hostnames, 405
dot (.)
    JSON object members, 736

regexp matching single character, 308, 566
dotted quad IP values (see IP addresses)
double at sign (@@)
    examples of use
        buffer pool size, 853
        data directory, 28
        global variable read, 819
        GTID, 95
        mysqlx_socket value, 35
        plugin_dir system variable, 821
        Ruby, 187
        session and global specified, 340, 341
        showing default storage engine, 831
    sql_mode, 473, 527, 556
    writing or reading system variables, 820
        no GLOBAL. or SESSION. modifier, 820
double quote (")
    escaping in command line arguments, 523
    escaping in data values, 211
    identifier quoting if ANSI_QUOTES, 220,
        291
    importing data, 529
    shell command arguments, 522
    writing string literals, 291
DROP a column to renumber sequence, 609
DROP EVENT to stop, 467
DROP INDEX, 783
    benign errors ignored, 472
    unused indexes should be dropped, 781
DROP TABLE
    mysqldump output file containing, 274
    scripts for creating tables containing, 17
    SQL injection, 212
DROP USER, 872
    anonymous accounts, 878
    hostnames containing pattern characters,
        880
duplicates handled
    about, 711
    counting duplicates, 720
    duplicate key values on import, 530
    duplicate rows in results removed, 247
    eliminating from table, 724
    identifying duplicates, 720
    loading rows into table, 715
    more than one unique key in table, 714
        ON DUPLICATE KEY UPDATE, 719
    NULL values occurring multiple times, 713
    preventing duplicates from occurring, 712

strings with case-insensitive collation, 724
UNION clause
   ALL to not remove duplicates, 261
   DISTINCT default removing duplicates, 261
unique identifiers via UUID(), 272
dup_count.pl, 723
dynamic variables
   binlog_transaction_dependency_tracking, 108
   server_id, 90
   SET PERSIST since MySQL v8, 90

E

e (execute) option, 15
E (vertical) option, 15
email address validity
   regexp pattern matching, 574
      patterns online, 574
   specification in RFC, 574
   trigger for, 479
encrypted replication setup, 124
encryption of network traffic, 880
ENUM values
   CONCAT(), 318
   data validation using table metadata, 575
      for loop, 577
   ENUM column members determined, 503
   sorting, 413
   US state codes, 479
environment variables
   CLASSPATH for Java scripting, 171, 195
   CLASSPATH for library location, 183
   GOPATH for library location, 183, 192
   JAVA_HOME, 170
   library file installation location, 183
   MYSQL_PS1 to customize prompt, 26
   PATH, 7
   PERL5LIB, 183, 186
   PYTHONPATH for library location, 183, 191
   RUBYLIB for library location, 183, 188
   security issues, 229
   setting environment variables link, xxvii
   setting for programming examples, 156
equal sign (=)
   spaces around, 12
   variable assignment operator, 25
      := synonym, 25

errors
   access denied
      built-in report privileges, 61
      importing data, 526
      invoking mysql, 8
   API script connection error, 158
   API scripts handling, 154, 172-180, 199
      Go connection script, 168, 192
      Java connection script, 172, 196
      Perl connection script, 160, 185
      PHP connection script, 164, 188
      Python connection script, 166, 191
      Ruby connection script, 162, 188
      SQL statements, 199
   command not found, 7
   condition handlers for stored programs, 469
      (see also condition handlers)
   CREATE USER on existing account, 870
   division by zero, 473
   dropping a user that does not exist, 872
   duplicate row in table, 715
   ERROR 2006 "MySQL Server has gone away", 859
   error log, 822, 824
      configuration documentation, 859
      monitoring the server, 843
      rotating, 827
      server crash troubleshooting, 859
      server startup problems, 845
   foreign key constraint, 475
   importing data
      access denied, 526
      data file and loaded database differ, 531
      duplicate key values, 530
   import_table requiring Classic protocol, 65
   invalid use of group function, 427
   invoking mysql
      access denied, 8
      command not found, 7
   local_infile error, 65
   "MySQL Server has gone away", 859
   No Data condition of stored function, 461
   password expired, 877
   Perl
      access denied, 159
      RaiseError, 200
      use warnings, 159
   raising own errors, 473
   renaming user accounts, 872

result consisted of more than one row, 24

semisynchronous replication failing back to asynchronous, 117

SHOW WARNINGS command, 24

stored routine GET DIAGNOSTICS, 474

Unknown column, 245

unknown option, 12

escaping special characters, 210-219

  escape sequences, 293

    hex constants, 528

  LOAD DATA escape sequences, 524

  quoted strings, 293

events

  about, 455

  ALTER EVENT to disable or enable, 467

  checking status of scheduler, 467

    enabling scheduler, 467

  DROP EVENT to stop, 467

  listing, 511

  log maintenance, 829

  privileges

    enabling scheduler, 467

    EVENT privilege, 457

  scheduling automatic database operations, 466

    cooperating events, 468

execute (e) option, 15

execute()

  Java SQL statement execution, 208, 219

    result-set-produced Boolean, 486

  not needed interactively, 48

  Perl SQL statement execution, 200, 215

    result-set metadata available, 487

    row count returned, 483

  PHP SQL statement execution, 204, 217

    result-set metadata available, 490

    row count returned, 484

  Python SQL statement execution, 205, 218

  Ruby returning row counts, 484

  sql() or runSQL() methods, 43

"Executing Programs from the Command Line" document

  GitHub repository, xxvii

  PATH variable, 8

executing SQL statements

  directly from command line, 15

  interactively, 14

    output format default, 17, 19

  read from a file or program, 16-18

scripting, 154, 196-210

exit command to terminate mysql session, 4

EXPLAIN

  about SQL statement categories, 198

  checking long-running queries, 843

  connection ID via SHOW PROCESSLIST, 843

  query plan for index suitability, 786

  verify FULLTEXT index used, 320

exporting data, 538

  about, 519

    file formats, 521

    general issues, 520

    source code in recipes distribution, 520

  CSV format, 538

  dates to non-ISO format, 590

  file location, 538

  FILE privilege to write outfile, 539, 539

  JSON file format, 550

  mysql_to_text.pl utility, 540

  NULL as string "NULL", 539, 541

  postprocessing filter, 539

  SQL format, 542

  tab-delimited, linefeed-terminated default, 538

  XML format, 545

exportTable() utility, 64

external programs from mysql prompt, 28

EXTRACT() date and time components, 348

F

FIELD() for custom sort orders, 412

FILE privilege

  exporting, 539, 539

  importing, 525

file system cache, 836

files

  batch mode in mysql, 1

    (see also scripts)

  executing SQL from a file, 16-18

  html output to web browser, 20

  mysqldump output redirected, 18

  saving output to (see redirecting output)

filtering and processing output, 29

  postprocessing filter of export, 539

filters preventing binary log file recording, 100

find()

  JavaScript mode collections, 54

  Python mode collections, 55

finish() making metadata unavailable, 487
FLOOR() for integers, 356, 361
FLUSH TABLES
    copying via sdi file, 278
    copying via transportable tablespaces, 277
flushing log files, 826
for loops
    data file check, 562
    enumeration members, 577
    execute() method, 44, 48
foreign keys
    adding to table, 475
    constraints providing integrity checks, 509
    error handling with GET DIAGNOSTICS,
        475
    identifying table as parent, 509
    referential integrity preventing mismatches,
        652
Formula 1 fractional seconds example, 333
fractional seconds in time values, 332
    Formula 1 example, 333
frequency distributions, 681
    charting, 682
    randomness of RAND(), 689
FROM_DAYS(), 355
FROM_UNIXTIME(), 355
full-text searches
    Amazon review data for download, xxvii,
        318
        script to load data, 320
    EXPLAIN to verify, 320
    FULLTEXT index, 318, 797
        B-tree index on same column, 797
    modes
        Boolean mode, 798
        natural language mode, 798
        query expansion mode, 798
    non-FULLTEXT column regular indexes,
        322
    phrase searches, 327
    requiring or prohibiting specific words, 325
    short words return no rows, 323

G

games-behind in team standings, 704
general query log, 823, 824
    enabling, 863
    log table rotation, 829
    monitoring client activity, 863
    monitoring the server, 843
    rotating, 827
generated column index, 794
generate_patients_data JavaScript code, 80
geographic data and spatial indexes, 799
GET DIAGNOSTICS to log all stored routine
    errors, 474
getCurrentSchema() (JavaScript), 51
getDefaultSchema()
    JavaScript mode table querying, 47
getTable() (JavaScript), 46
get_collection() (Python), 55
get_current_schema() (Python), 55
get_schema() (Python), 49
get_table() (Python), 49
GitHub repository for MySQL
    Amazon review data for download, xxvii,
        318
        script to load data, 320
    appendices from previous editions, xxvii
    "Executing Programs from the Command
        Line" document, xxvii
    large tables for histograms, 806
    recipes distribution, xxvi
    (see also recipes distribution)
global objects, 66
    dba object of DBA class, 67
        command line, 68
    util object of MySQL Shell, 63
global transaction identifiers (GTIDs)
    about, 89, 94
    replica set up using, 94
        configuration options, 94, 96
        SHOW MASTER STATUS for GTIDs, 95
        source replication server binary log files, 89,
            97
global variables
    server_uuid, 95
    time_zone, 339, 341
Go-MySQL-Driver API support, xxiii, 153
    about scripting requirements, 167
    AUTO_INCREMENT value, 606
    character set for client connections, 289
    context cancellation support, 167
    download links, xxx
    error handling, 168, 172, 178, 192
    library file writing, 192
        library path, 183, 192
    map to check input values, 580

metadata
    result set metadata retrieved, 492
    row count of matched versus changed, 485
    NULL values identified in result sets, 221, 225
    option files for connection parameters, 230, 234
    scripts
        connecting to server, 157, 167
        executing SQL statements, 196-199, 207
    special characters and NULL in data values, 210-215, 218
    special characters in identifiers, 220
    transactions, 771
        context-aware functions, 772
GOPATH environment variable, 183, 192
GRANT, 3-5, 870
    replication user, 90
    roles, 883
Gregorian calendar and TO_DAYS(), 356, 361
GROUP BY clause
    date categories, 445
    descriptive statistics per subgroups, 679
    expression results for groupings, 439
    summary for each subgroup, 430
    time categories, 445
    WITH ROLLUP, 448
Group Communication Engine, 118
Group Replication plug-in, 118
    existent data, 122
    writing on multiple nodes, 122
GTIDs (see global transaction identifiers)
gtid_executed variable, 95
guess_table.pl, 551

H

H (html) option for output, 20
Handler_* session status variable, 31
handles
    Java connection objects (conn), 171
    Perl
        database handles ($dbh), 160, 487, 507
        statement handles ($sth), 160, 487
    PHP database handles ($dbh), 164
    Python connection objects (conn), 166
    Ruby database handles (client), 162
hashes
    B-tree versus hash indexes, 780

lookup table for data validation, 579
    Perl result-set metadata, 488
HAVING clause, 437
    COUNT() determining if values unique, 438
help command (mysql), 9
    permitted option-file locations, 10
help options for all MySQL Shell commands, 62
HEX() for hexadecimal format conversion, 301
hexadecimal notation
    binary output as, 293
    converting between ASCII and BIT, 302
    converting between decimal and octal, 301
    format specifiers, 528
    treated as binary strings, 291
    writing string literals, 291
histograms for optimizing, 803
    large table data for, 806
host as URI parameter, 34
hostname
    % (percent) character within, 879
    _ (underscore) character within, 879
    command options for invoking mysql, 8
    granting database privileges, 3
    localhost, 10
        API connection scripts, 158
        database privileges, 3
        default host, 9, 160
        IP address, 10, 158
    prompt showing hostname, 27
    sorting in domain order, 405
hot standby, 87
HOUR(), 348
how old someone is, 368
html (H) option for output, 20
HTML output, 20
    web browser opened to read, 20

I

id column in table, 197
    AUTO_INCREMENT, 268, 596
        (see also AUTO_INCREMENT column)
    custom sequence as, 629
    duplicate rows prevented, 713
    multiple tables in query, 254
    retrieving column values, 603
    saving query results to a table, 268
identifiers containing special characters, 220
IFNULL(), 250, 436

importing data, 523
  about, 519
    file formats, 521
    general issues, 520
    source code in recipes distribution, 520
  column input order specified, 534
  converting imported data via cvt_file.pl, 522
  CSV files, 537
  datafile and loaded database differ, 531
  datafile columns skipped deliberately, 536
  datafile lines skipped deliberately, 533
  datafile location, 525
  date values from non-ISO to ISO, 589
  delimiters for columns and lines specified,
    527
  duplicate key values, 530
  errors
    access denied, 526
    data file and loaded database differ, 531
    duplicate key values, 530
  FILE privilege for datafile, 525
  JSON documents, 547
    extracting values, 736
  JSON format, 547
  LOCAL data loading disabled by default,
    523, 525
  MongoDB, 549
  NULL values, 540
  preprocessing values before inserting, 534
  quotes and special characters, 529
  SQL data, 544
  tab-delimited, linefeed-terminated default,
    522, 524, 527
    delimiters specified, 527
  XML format, 546
importJson utility
  JSON format, 547
  MongoDB format, 549
import_table() utility, 65
indexes
  about, 779
    not too many, 781
  ascending and descending, 789
  AUTO_INCREMENT columns, 601
  cardinality of index, 785, 804
  clustered index, 783
  covering index, 787
  dropping, 783
  duplicate key values handled, 530
  duplicate rows prevented, 712
  FULLTEXT index, 318, 797
    B-tree index on same column, 797
    Boolean mode, 798
    natural language mode, 798
    non-FULLTEXT column regular
      indexes, 322
    query expansion mode, 798
    short words return no rows, 323
  function-based, 792
  generated columns, 794
  INSERT INTO...SELECT does not copy, 268
  joins and, 639
  JSON data, 794
  maintaining, 784
    not too many, 781
    renaming, 786
  more than one unique key in table, 714
  multiple column queries, 787
  NULLs permitted, 713
  optimizer histograms, 803
  primary key created for slow queries, 781
    primary key optimization, 783
  query plans, 786
  query results saved as a table, 269
  query slow with index, 786
  spatial indexes and geographic data, 799
  WHERE clause indexed column, 377
INET_ATON(), 305, 408
INFORMATION_SCHEMA
  character sets and their collations listed, 514
  listing databases or tables in database, 496
  metadata source for portability, 482
  plug-ins installed, 513, 821
  results depend on privileges, 482
  stored routines listed, 511
  table CHECK constraints listed, 517
  table column definitions, 498
  table engines, 273, 603
  table identified as parent via foreign key,
    509
  table in system or general tablespaces, 277
  transaction storage engine support, 763
  triggers listed, 510
  views listed or checked for existence, 497
inner joins, 635, 638
InnoDB buffer pool, 836
InnoDB Buffer Pool
  architecture of storage engine, 857

SHOW ENGINE INNODB STATUS, 857
  sizing properly, 853
InnoDB Cluster managed by Admin API, 67
  automating Group Replication, 148
InnoDB ReplicaSet managed by Admin API, 67
  automating replication setup, 144
InnoDB storage engine
  about, 830
    query performance, 779
  about primary keys, 783
  architecture, 857
  auto-generated primary key, 99
  buffer pool sizing, 853
  configuration, 829
  copying tables via transportable tablespaces,
    276
  debugging with plug-in Components, 858
  full-text searches, 318, 324, 797
  Group Replication plug-in, 119
  identifying table as parent via foreign key,
    510
  monitoring, 842
  primary keys, 715
  SHOW ENGINE
    INNODB MUTEX, 856
    INNODB STATUS, 31, 856
  transaction support, 272
input redirected to execute SQL, 16-18
input-testing logic into BEFORE INSERT trigger, 478
input/output monitoring (see I/O (input/out-
  put) monitoring)
INSERT INTO
  about SQL statement categories, 198
  adding table rows, 5
  copying rows from existing table, 266
    duplicates removed, 725
  duplicate rows prevented, 712, 715
    (see also duplicates handled)
  IGNORE, 715
  JSON data, 731
  ON DUPLICATE KEY UPDATE, 715
    two or more unique keys, 719
  saving results of query to a table, 266
    indexes not copied from source table,
      268
  tables created via scripts, 17
  timestamping row creation, 345
  user-defined variables, 23

insert()
  JavaScript mode table queries, 48
  Python mode table queries, 50
INSTALL PLUGIN, 822
integrity in transactions, 761
interactively executing SQL statements, 14
  directly from command line, 15
  mysqlsh -i option, 58
  output format default, 17, 19
INTERVAL, 361, 363
intervals calculated for dates and times, 358
  age calculations, 368
  interval or span, 362
  summing date and time values, 362
introducers for character sets, 291
I/O (input/output) monitoring, 837
  connection limits, 851
    buffer pool sizing, 853
  iotop utility, 837
  monitoring the operating system, 835
  number of queries hitting server, 846
iotop utility, 837
IP addresses
  localhost, 10, 158
  sorted numerically, 408
  strings, 305
    INET_ATON() to numeric, 305, 408
IPv6 and IPv4 network addresses as strings, 305
IS NULL comparison operator, 248
ISNULL(), 685
ISO format for date values, 335, 375, 570
  reformatting to, 589
isoize_date.py, 585

J

Java Development Kit (JDK), xxx, 170
Java MySQL Connector/J API support, xxiii,
  153
  about scripting requirements, 170
  AUTO_INCREMENT value, 606
  character set for client connections, 289
  CLASSPATH environment variable, 171,
    183
  download links, xxx
  error handling, 172, 179, 196
  HashMap to check input values, 580
  Java Development Kit, xxx, 170
  javac compiler, 170
  JAVA_HOME environment variable, 170

library file writing, 193
    library path, 183
metadata
    listing databases or tables, 497
    result set metadata retrieved, 494
    row count of matched versus changed, 486
    server and database metadata, 506
namespaces, 194
    book packages, 194
NULL values identified in result sets, 221, 226
option files for connection parameters, 230, 235
regular expressions package, 565
running Java programs link, xxvii
scripts
    connecting to server, 157, 170
    executing SQL statements, 196-199, 208
special characters and NULL in data values, 210-215, 219
special characters in identifiers, 220
transactions, 776
JavaScript mode of MySQL Shell, 40
    about inheritance support, 69
    collections, 51
    curly braces for multiline code, 54
    deploySandboxInstance, 67
    objects, 69-72
        exporting to preload, 84
    \source command, 82
        scripts executed at startup, 83
    SQL session, 42
    table querying, 46
    util object, 63
JDBC interface support, xxiii, 153, 170
    download links, xxx
JDK (Java Development Kit), xxx, 170
JOIN
    about joins, 253, 635, 636
        scripts in recipes distribution, 636
    aliases for tables, 643
    candidate-detail lists and summaries, 656
    Cartesian products, 636
    comparing table to itself, 652
    finding matches between tables, 636-643
    finding mismatches between tables, 644
        "unattached" rows removed, 649

frequency distribution range of categories, 683
holes in list filled or identified, 666
indexes and joins, 639
inner joins, 635, 638
many-to-many relationships, 660
multiple tables in query, 253
one-to-many relationships, 656
optimizer histograms, 803
outer joins, 635, 642
    LEFT JOIN, 645, 683
    mismatches between tables, 644
    other ways to write, 648
    RIGHT JOIN, 647
output column names referred to, 673
parent rows with child detail rows, 656
per-group minimum or maximum values, 663
Python mode table queries, 50
query sort order control, 669
results of multiple queries joined, 671
self-joins, 652
    cumulative sums, 696
    running averages, 696
    successive-row differences, 694
successive-row differences calculated, 694
summary results via, 428, 434
table aliases, 643
tables from different databases, 643
json command-line parameter, 57
    diagnostic information printed, 59
JSON data format
    about, 729
    Amazon review data, 319
    attribute functions, 750
    data structure details, 750
    Document Store, 752
    EXPLAIN output, 844
    exporting, 550
    extracting values from, 736
    formatting JSON values, 735
    importing, 547
    indexes for query performance, 794
    inserting into MySQL, 731
    inserting new elements into document, 739
    JSON data type, 730
    JSON Schema, 732
    merging two or more documents into one, 742

relational data from JSON, 748
relational data to JSON, 746
removing elements, 742
searching inside, 738
updating a JSON value, 741
validating, 732
JSON Schema, 732
JSON_ARRAY(), 746
JSON_ARRAY_APPEND(), 739
JSON_ARRAY_INSERT(), 739
JSON_DEPTH(), 750
JSON_EXTRACT() (->), 736
JSON_INSERT(), 739
JSON_LENGTH(), 750
JSON_MERGE functions, 742
JSON_OBJECT(), 746
JSON_PRETTY(), 735
JSON_REMOVE(), 742
JSON_REPLACE(), 741
JSON_SCHEMA_VALID(), 732
JSON_SCHEMA_VALIDATION_REPORT(),
    732
JSON_SEARCH(), 738
JSON_SET(), 741
JSON_STORAGE_SIZE(), 750
JSON_TABLE(), 748
JSON_TYPE(), 750
JSON_UNQUOTE() (->>), 737
JSON_VALID(), 732

K

Kebab-case syntax, 66
keyword case insensitivity, 7

L

languages supported by MySQL, xxiii, 153
    APIs (see APIs)
    error handling, 172-180
    MySQL Shell, 2
    recipes distribution on GitHub, xxvii, 155
    scripting (see scripts)
LAST_DAY(), 369
LAST_INSERT_ID()
    AUTO_INCREMENT values via, 604
        server-side versus client-side retrieval,
        606
    managing multiple sequences simultane-
        ously, 614
    saving value of, 24

leaf nodes, 780
least-squares regression line, 686
left angle bracket (<) to redirect input, 16, 17
LEFT JOIN, 645
    frequency distribution range of categories,
        683
    other ways to write, 648
LEFT(), 316
    pattern matches similar to, 307, 312
    sorting on substrings, 398
LENGTH(), 283
less utility as pager, 30
library file writing, 155, 181-196
    access privileges, 185
    data validation tests, 563
    Go, 192
    Java, 193
    location of library file, 182
    Perl, 185
    PHP, 188
    Python, 190
    recipes distribution lib directory, 155, 181
    Ruby, 187
    test harness, 182
LIKE
    SQL pattern matching, 305
    table cloned, 265
    WHERE clause using, 242
LIMIT clause, 255
    ORDER BY clause with, 255
        results in different sort order, 258
    smallest or largest summary values, 443
    value from expression, 259
line-ending sequence in files, 521, 528
    tab-delimited, linefeed-terminated, 522, 524
    terminators and delimiters specified, 527
linear regressions, 686
linefeed (\n), 293
    line-ending sequence in files, 521, 528
literal strings, 291
LOAD DATA, 523
    column input order specified, 534
    CSV files, 537
    datafile and loaded database differ, 531
    datafile columns skipped deliberately, 536
    datafile lines skipped deliberately, 533
    datafile location, 525
    date values from non-ISO to ISO, 589

delimiters for columns and lines specified, 527
duplicate key values, 530
FIELDS clause, 527, 529
LINES clause, 527
name of datafile and name of table, 526
NULL values, 540
preprocessing values before inserting, 534
quotes and special characters, 529
tab-delimited, linefeed-terminated default, 522, 524, 527
LOAD XML, 546
localhost, 10
API connection scripts, 158
database privileges, 3
default host, 9
Perl connection script, 160
IP address, 10, 158
local_infile for data loading, 523
LOCATE() string function, 314
log files
digests of query logs, 861
InnoDB storage engine architecture, 857
replica server relay log files, 88
server log files, 822
binary log, 823, 825
error log, 822, 824, 843, 845, 859
expiring log files, 826
flushing log files, 826
general query log, 823, 824, 843, 863
log maintenance needed, 824, 826
monitoring the server, 843
rotating log files, 826
rotation automated, 828
slow query log, 823, 824, 843, 861
source replication server binary log files, 88
enabling via log-bin option, 90
global transaction identifiers (GTIDs), 97
GTIDs, 89
triggers logging table changes, 463
/var/log/messages system log, 859
log tables
CSV storage engine managing, 843
expiring rows within, 828
rotating, 828
log-bin option to enable binary log, 90
logarithmic scale in summary results, 442
login account versus user account for MySQL, 5

log_output, 824
LONGBLOB string data type, 286
LONGTEXT string data type, 286
lookup table to validate data, 578
lookup_time.py, 576
LOWER() to convert string to lowercase, 296
LPAD() for leading zeros, 353

M

mail table for chapter examples, 239, 265
MAKETIME(), 352
make_date_list(), 668
make_date_list.pl, 669
many-to-many relationships, 660
master and slave terminology, 88
MASTER_DELAY option, 88
master_info_repository variable, 89, 112
MATCH() for FULLTEXT index, 318, 320, 797
MAX(), 421
case sensitivity controlled, 429
per-group maximum values, 663
range of values, 676
unreliable method for last ID, 604
value from another column, 426
max_binlog_size, 88
mean, 676
median, 676
MEDIUMBLOB string data type, 286
MEDIUMTEXT string data type, 286
Memory storage engine, 830
changing to, 273
memory usage
file system cache, 836
InnoDB storage engine architecture, 857
monitoring usage of mysqld, 835
non-uniform memory access (NUMA), 836
OOM killer (out of memory killer), 836
Performance Schema to monitor, 29
server configuration, 818
swappiness, 835
virtual memory, 835
metacharacters
filtering on replica, 103
regular expression pattern matching, 308
SQL pattern matching, 305
metadata
about, 481
scripts for code in recipes distribution, 482, 508

checking if database exists, 496
checking if table exists, 496
data validation using table metadata, 575
ENUM column members, 503
finish() making unavailable in Perl program, 487
identifying table as parent via foreign key, 509
listing databases hosted by server, 496
listing tables in a database, 496
number of rows affected by a statement, 483
result set metadata retrieved, 486
   Go, 492
   Java, 494
   Perl, 487
   PHP, 490
   Python, 491
   Ruby, 490
server metadata obtained, 505
   version-specific applications, 507
SET column members, 503
table column definitions, 498
views listed or existence checked for, 497
MICROSECOND(), 348
MID(), 316
   sorting on substrings, 398
MIN(), 421
   case sensitivity controlled, 429
   per-group minimum values, 663
   range of values, 676
   value from another column, 426
MINUTE() to extract part of time value, 348
mode, 676
modify() Python mode collections, 55
monddyyy_to_iso.py, 585
MongoDB
   importing data, 549
   mongoexport utility, 549
monitoring MySQL server
   about, 833
      reactive monitoring, 833
   binary log, 865
   buffer pool sizing, 853
   checking if server is up, 844
   client activity, 863
   connection limits of MySQL server, 851
      buffer pool sizing, 853
   CPU monitoring
      finding high-utilization process, 849

thread-filtering documentation, 849
   error log for troubleshooting, 859
   general query log, 863
   number of queries hitting server, 846
   operating system, 835
      I/O (input/output) monitoring, 837
      memory utilization, 835
      network resource monitoring, 839
   server startup problems, 845
   slow query log, 861
   sources of monitoring information, 840
   storage engine operational information, 856
   tracking data changes, 865
   why monitor, 834
month first day, last day, length, 369
MONTH()
   extracting part of a date value, 348
   monthly summaries, 446
   pattern matching with nonstring values, 308
MONTHNAME(), 348
more utility as pager, 30
multiline code via curly braces, 54
multiple replication applier threads, 107
my.cnf or my.ini personal option file, 10
   event scheduler enabled, 467
MyISAM storage engine
   about, 830
   configuration, 829
   copying via sdi file, 278
   full-text searches, 797
   FULLTEXT indexing, 318
      full-text indexing engine, 324
      REPAIR TABLE command, 325
mylogin.cnf file, 11
MyRocks storage engine, 830
MySQL
   about, xvii
      companion GitHub repository, xxvi
      distributions, xxviii
      obtaining MySQL, xxvii
      platforms supported, xxiv
      versions used in book, xxiv
   backups, 94
      binary versus logical, 94
      mysqldump for, 18, 93
      server for replication, 93
   case insensitivity of keywords, 7
   client software, xxviii, 1
      timeout of client, 859

client-server architecture, 1
  assumptions made in book, 2
languages supported, xxiii, 153
  APIs (see APIs)
  error handling, 172-180
  MySQL Shell modes, 2
  recipes distribution on GitHub, xxvii,
    155
  scripting (see scripts)
master and slave terminology, 88
memory usage via Performance Schema, 29
  (see also memory usage)
option files, 10-14
plug-ins, 820
  (see also plug-ins)
Spatial Reference System, 799
user account, 2, 4
  default values, 3
  setting up, 2, 869
User Reference Manual link (see documentation online for MySQL)
writing efficient queries, 809
  (see also query performance)
mysql client program
  about, 1
  alternatives to, 2
  Ctrl-D (Unix) to terminate session, 4
  distributions, xxviii
  error when invoking mysql, 4, 7
  executing SQL statements
    directly from command line, 15
    interactively, 14
    output format defaults, 17, 19
    read from file or program, 16-18
    scripting, 154, 196-210
  exit to terminate session, 4
  exporting data (see exporting data)
  help command, 9
    option-file permitted locations, 10
  importing data (see importing data)
  invoking, 8
    error when invoking, 4, 7
    option files, 10-14
    specifying command options, 8
  mysql> prompt, 4, 14
    customizing, 26
    external programs from, 28
    resetting to default value, 26
    user account in prompt, 27

option-file permitted locations, 10
print-defaults parameter, 13
program variables, 12
quit to terminate session, 4
semicolon terminator redefined for
  BEGIN...END, 458
timeout of client, 859
user account default values, 3
User Reference Manual link, 27
verbosity level, 23
MySQL Enterprise Backup, 94
MySQL server
  about, xxviii, 1
    assumed to be running locally, 2
  administration, 817
    (see also server administration)
  APIs connecting to, 153, 157-172
    disconnecting from, 157
    obtaining connection parameters script,
      227-237
  character set for client connection, 288
  checking if database exists, 496
  checking if server is up, 844
    "MySQL Server has gone away", 859
  connecting MySQL Shell, 34
    selecting protocol, 37
  connection limits, 851
    buffer pool sizing, 853
  connection parameters when invoking
    mysql, 8
  copying database to, 18
  copying tables
    between servers, 273, 275
    within a single server, 273
  data validity via sql_mode, 557
  executing SQL statements
    directly from command line, 15
    interactively, 14
    output format defaults, 17, 19
    read from file or program, 16-18
    scripting, 154, 196-210
  listing databases hosted by server, 496
  logging, 822
    (see also log files)
  metadata, 481
    obtaining, 505
    version-specific applications, 507
  monitoring, 833
    (see also monitoring MySQL server)

multithreaded, 107
plug-ins
    about, 820
    listing installed plug-ins, 513
    plug-in interface, 820
    plugin_dir system variable, 821
    runtime installation, 822
    server startup, 821
server startup problems, 845
shutting down requiring privileges, 9
storage engine support determination, 273
timeout of server, 860
    timeout of client, 859
transactions, 761
    (see also transactions)
uptime, 844
user account for MySQL
    about, 2, 4
    default values, 3
    login account versus, 5
    mysql.user table, 868
        (see also user account for MySQL)
    setting up, 2, 869
validation, server- versus client-side, 556
    (see also validating data)
MySQL Shell
about, 2, 33
connecting to MySQL server, 34
    selecting protocol, 37
downloading, 33
exit or quit session, 35
    history lost, 42
exporting to JSON format, 550
help options for all commands, 62
import JSON format, 547
import MongoDB format, 549
interactive -i option, 58
JavaScript mode default, 40
    collections, 51
    curly braces for multiline code, 54
    objects, 69-72
    \source command, 82
    SQL session, 42
    table querying, 46
    util object, 63
mysqlsh command, 34
output format control, 56
pandas module, 74
prompt customization, 39

protocols
    Classic MySQL protocol, 34
    X protocol, 34
Python mode, 40
    collections, 54
    \source command, 82
    SQL session, 44
    table querying, 49
    util object, 63
reports, 60
    thread report on all threads, 61
sandbox deployment, 67
shell.status() command, 39
SQL mode, 40
    \source command, 82
    SQL session, 41
transactions, 47
    (see also transactions)
utilities, 63
    \? for utilities supported, 64
    CSV export from table, 64
MySQL Workbench graphical interface, 2
mysql.user table, 868
    anonymous accounts, 878
mysqladmin
    checking if server is up, 844
    option file [client] group, 12
    server uptime, 844
mysqladmin for administrative privileges, 9
mysqlbinlog verbose option, 137, 865
mysqld
    about, 1
    data directory, 28
    general query log to monitor, 863
    monitoring memory usage, 835
    program variables, 12
mysqldump
    backing up databases, 18
        backing up server for replication, 93
        mysql client to load dump, 18, 94
    command options, 9
    CREATE TABLE information, 503
    exporting data in SQL format, 542
        importing SQL format, 544
    exporting data in XML format, 545
        importing XML format, 546
my_print_defaults utility, 13
option file [client] group, 12
redirecting output, 18

renaming database, 106
table copying, 273
   between MySQL servers, 275
   dropping table if exists, 274
   triggers copied, 274
mysqld_safe and error log, 824
mysqlimport command-line program, 523
   datafile location, 526
   delimiters for columns and lines specified, 528
   importing CSV files, 537
   name of datafile and name of table, 526
   quotes and special characters, 529
mysqlpump to export with parallel processing, 542
mysqlsh, 34
   about MySQL Shell, 2, 33
      downloading, 33
   connecting to MySQL server, 34
      selecting protocol, 37
   exit or quit session, 35
      history, 42
   exporting to JSON format, 550
   help options for all commands, 62
   import JSON format, 547
   import MongoDB format, 549
   interactive -i option, 58
   JavaScript mode default, 40
      collections, 51
      curly braces for multiline code, 54
      objects, 69-72
      \source command, 82
      SQL session, 42
      table querying, 46
      util object, 63
   output format control, 56
   pandas module, 74
   prompt customization, 39
   Python mode, 40
      collections, 54
      \source command, 82
      SQL session, 44
      table querying, 49
      util object, 63
   reports, 60
      thread report on all threads, 61
   sandbox deployment, 67
   shell.status() command, 39
   SQL mode, 40

\source command, 82
   SQL session, 41
transactions, 47
   (see also transactions)
utilities, 63
   \? for utilities supported, 64
   CSV export from table, 64
mysqlshrc.js for scripts executed at startup, 83
mysqlshrc.py for scripts executed at startup, 83
MYSQLSH_HOME variable, 83
mysqlx URI scheme, 34
mysql_config_editor for credential security, 11
MYSQL_PS1 to customize prompt, 26
mysql_to_excel.pl utility, 540
mysql_to_text.pl utility, 540
mysql_to_xml.pl utility, 540
my_print_defaults utility, 13

N
name generator for tables, 271
name test data via Python, 73-82
naming files under Windows, 527
network resource monitoring, 839
   connection limits, 851
      buffer pool sizing, 853
   monitoring the operating system, 835
network traffic encryption, 880
newline (\n), 293, 293
nocls parameter to not clear screen, 63
non-uniform memory access (NUMA), 836
nonbinary strings, 282, 286
   character sets, 282
   comparisons, 298, 391
noncategorical data summaries, 440
nopager (\n) to reset pager, 31
NoSQL
   collections queried, 51
      table queries (see SQL)
   JavaScript mode Document Store, 51
   MySQL Shell, 2, 33
   Python mode Document Store, 54
   X protocol for, 34
not
   CONTINUE handler for NOT FOUND, 461
   NOT LIKE, 305
   NOT REGEXP, 308
      NULL not matched, 312
   [^] regexp pattern matching, 308, 566

\D for regexp nondigit character, 566
\S for regexp nonwhitespace character, 566, 568
\W for regexp nonword character, 566
NOW(), 344
NUL (ASCII; \0), 293, 524
NULL
    about, 212
    aggregate functions ignoring NULL values, 435
    APIs handling, 154
    AUTO_INCREMENT columns cannot contain, 600
    COALESCE(), 250
    comparison operators
        <=>, 249
        IFNULL(), 250, 436
        IS NULL or IS NOT NULL, 248
        ISNULL(), 685
        programming, 251
    COUNT of non-NULL values versus rows, 420, 436
    counting missing values, 684
    date and timestamp columns not allowing, 345, 347
    /dev/null, 31
        Blackhole "storage" engine, 830
    exporting data to file, 541
        string "NULL", 539, 542
    forced sorting to end of sort, 410
    identifying in result sets, 221-227
    importing data, 540
    LOAD DATA \N sequence, 524
    NOT NULL declaration, 197
    NULL data values, 210-219
    PRIMARY KEY versus UNIQUE index, 713
    regular expressions not matching, 312
    UNIQUE indexes allowing multiple, 713
    unknown value, 197, 248
        mapping to string "Unknown", 249, 436
        user-defined variables, 24
NUMA (non-uniform memory access), 836
numeric data
    AUTO_INCREMENT column data types, 599
    converting between decimal, octal, and hexadecimal, 301
    FLOOR() for integers, 356, 361
    maximum unsigned values, 600

patterns with nonstring values, 308
random number generator, 688
regexp patterns for strings of numbers, 568
REVERSE() dropping leading zero, 313

O

objects in JavaScript mode of MySQL Shell, 69-72
    exporting to preload, 84
observability of server, 833
    (see also monitoring MySQL server)
OCT() for octal format conversion, 301
octal values converted between decimal and hexadecimal, 301
one-to-many relationships, 656
online backup tools, 94
online resources (see resources online)
OOM killer (out of memory killer), 836
    "MySQL Server has gone away", 859
openssl system tool, 28
operating system
    monitoring, 835
    physical resource usage, 29
    tools from mysql prompt, 28
optimizer histograms, 803
    large table data for, 806
option as URI parameter, 34
\option command, 57
option files
    comments, 13
    customizing mysql prompt, 26
    format of, 11-13
    invoking mysql, 10
        connection parameters, 10
        localhost, 10
    mixing command line parameters and, 13
    pathname separator character, 13
    personal option file, 10
    program variables, 12
    protecting from other users, 14
    scripts reading for connection parameters, 230
    server configuration, 818
        log files, 823
        [mysqld] group, 818
    unknown option error, 12
options member of Shell class, 57
Oracle Java site, xxx
ORDER BY clause to sort results, 246, 382-385

case sensitivity issues, 390
custom sort order defined, 412
date information, 394
displaying values, sorting on another, 387
ENUM values, 413
expressions for sorting, 385
INET_ATON() for IP addresses, 305, 408
joins to control sort order, 669
LIMIT clause with, 255
   results in different sort order, 258
RAND(), 690, 693
special values to head or tail of sort, 410
time information, 394
out of memory killer (OOM killer), 836
   "MySQL Server has gone away", 859
outer joins, 635, 642
   LEFT JOIN, 645, 683
   mismatches between tables, 644
      "unattached" rows removed, 649
   other ways to write, 648
   RIGHT JOIN, 647
output
   binary output as hexadecimal notation, 293
   filtering and processing, 29
   format control, 19-23
      about, 18
      column headings suppressed, 21
      comma-separated values (CSV), 22
      HTML or XML, 20
      JSON values, 735
      MySQL Shell, 56
      output column delimiter changed, 21
      tabular or tab-delimited, 19
   I/O monitoring (see I/O (input/output) monitoring)
   interactive versus batch mode, 17, 19
   pager command (\P), 30
      sending output nowhere, 31
   redirecting, 18
      exporting to a file, 539
      exporting to JSON file, 550
      exporting to XML format, 545
      mysqldump, 18
      pager with redirection, 32
      pipe from program, 18
      sending output nowhere, 31
   screen as default, 19
   verbosity level of mysql, 23
   vertical in MySQL Shell JavaScript mode, 57

vertical via \G, 15
   all statements within session, 15

P

\P (pager command), 32
pager command (\P), 30
   nopager (\n) to reset, 31
   sending output nowhere, 31
   sending output to a file, 32
   set to grep Running, 92
   SHOW ENGINE INNODB STATUS, 31, 857
pager option, 30
pandas
   about, 74
      installing in MySQL Shell, 74
   read_csv method, 76
parallelization
   multiple replication applier threads, 107
   replication performance, 140
parameters for mysql command, 8
   single versus double dash before, 9
parent tables and child tables, 656
   candidate keys, 656
parentheses ( )
   function-based indexes, 793
   regexp pattern matches, 567
password
   anonymous accounts without, 878
   changing your password, 876
   command line option, 9
      no default value, 9
   connection parameters from command line, 229
   default for user account, 2
   expiring, 875
      resetting an expired, 877
   policy via validate_password plug-in, 872
   pwgen system tool, 28
   replication user credential security, 123
   resetting an expired, 877
   security
      command line option, 9
      option file plain text format, 11
      PHP library files, 189
      strength check, 874
   setting up user account, 3
      database privileges, 3
URI parameter, 34

PATH environment variable
  error when invoking mysql, 4
    solution, 7
  library file location, 183
  option file separator character, 13
patient test data via Python, 73-82
pattern matching
  about, 305
  data validation via, 565
    Python regexp overview, 565
    script for testing patterns, 567
  full-text searching, 318
    short words return no rows, 323
  hostnames with % or _ within, 879
  nonstring values, 308
  regular expressions (see regular expres-
    sions)
  SQL patterns, 305-307
  substrings within strings, 314
Paxos algorithm, 118
pem files for TLS, 882
percent (%)
  formatting for date and time values, 337
  hostname containing, 879
  matching sequence of characters, 103, 306
Percona Monitoring and Management (PMM),
  839
Percona XtraBackup, 94
Performance Schema
  built-in reports, 61
  I/O utilization, 838
  memory usage, 29
  monitoring the server, 841
  replication performance, 140
  replication troubleshooting, 126, 129-140
  sys schema for information, 841
  threads table, 141, 849
performance tuning
  indexes, 781
  query performance (see query performance)
  triggers listed, 511
period (.)
  JSON object members, 736
  regexp matching single character, 308, 566
Perl DBI module API support, xxiii, 153
  "0E0" return value, 199
  about scripting requirements, 158
  AUTO_INCREMENT value, 605
  date calculations, 361

error handling, 160, 172-176, 185, 200
  access denied, 159
handles
  database handles ($dbh), 160, 487, 507
  statement handles ($sth), 160, 487
hash to check input values, 580
@INC array, 186
library file writing, 185
  library path, 183, 186
metadata
  listing tables, 497
  result set metadata retrieved, 487
  row count of matched versus changed,
    483
  server version, 507
NULL values identified in result sets,
  221-223
option files for connection parameters, 230
running Perl programs link, xxvii
scripts
  connecting to server, 157-161
  cvt_file.pl for converting imported data,
    22, 522
  executing SQL statements, 196-203
  export utilities, 540
  Perl CPAN site for, 564
special characters and NULL in data values,
  210-217
special characters in identifiers, 220
transactions, 767
use strict, 159
use warnings, 159
PERL5LIB environment variable, 183, 186
PHP PDO API support, xxiii, 153
  about PHP scripting, 163
    scripting requirements, 162
  AUTO_INCREMENT value, 605
  character set for client connections, 289
  download links, xxix
  error handling, 164, 172, 176, 188
  input values checked via associative array,
    579
  library file writing, 188
    library path, 183, 189
  metadata
    result set metadata retrieved, 490
    row count of matched versus changed,
      484

NULL values identified in result sets, 221, 224

option files for connection parameters, 230, 232

running PHP programs link, xxvii

scripts
    connecting to server, 157, 162
    executing SQL statements, 196-199, 204

special characters and NULL in data values, 210-215, 217

special characters in identifiers, 220

transactions, 770

phpMyAdmin, 2

phrase searches in full-text, 327

pipe (|)
    output as input, 18, 19
    regexp pattern matching, 308, 311, 566

placeholders in data values, 212
    generating a list of, 215

platforms supported by MySQL, xxiv

plug-ins
    authentication, 868
    built in, 821
    debugging InnoDB storage engine, 858
    filename suffix on plug-ins, 821
    listing installed plug-ins in server, 513
    plug-in interface, 820
    runtime installation, 822
    server startup, 821

plugin_dir system variable, 821

plus (+) regexp pattern matching, 308, 566
    avoiding empty string match, 312

point-in-time recovery (PITR) via binary log files, 102, 823, 865

port numbers
    default 3306 for TCP/IP, 10
        X protocol, 34
    URI parameter, 34

portability
    date format, 335
    metadata, 482
    regular expression syntax, 309
    sequences, 596
    SHOW versus INFORMATION_SCHEMA, 482
    SQL code and APIs, 156
    SQL patterns, 308
    user-defined variables, 23

POSIX character classes of regexp, 310

postprocessing filter of export, 539

prepare() for statement handle
    Go, 218
    Perl, 200, 215, 487
    PHP, 217

prepared SQL statements
    about, 468
    helper routines to simplify, 468
    MySQL Reference Manual link, 469

preprocessing data, 534, 592
    converting imported data via cvt_file.pl, 522, 592
    importing data
        about, 519
        about file formats, 521
        about general issues, 520
        source code in recipes distribution, 520
    triggers for, 478

PRIMARY KEY clause, 6, 781
    about primary keys, 783
    about query performance, 779
    cardinality of index, 785
    creating, 781
        primary key optimization, 783
    duplicate rows prevented, 712
    handling duplicate key values, 530
    if already assigned, UNIQUE index, 601
    maintaining indexes, 784
    more than one unique key in table, 714
    NULLs not permitted, 713
    primary key optimization, 783

print-defaults parameter to mysql, 13

printing (see output)

private key for TLS, 880

private_key.pem, 882

privileges
    built-in reports, 61
    database access, 3
    events, 457, 467
    FILE privilege
        exporting, 539, 539
        importing, 525
    INFORMATION_SCHEMA results, 482
    library files, 185
    PROCESS privilege, 3
    roles, 883
    security, 868
        account management, 870

SELECT CURRENT_USER() for client privileges, 506
server administration, 817
   runtime changes to global values, 819
server monitoring, 834
server shutdown, 9
SHOW ENGINE, 856
SHOW GRANTS, 871
stored programs, 457
stored routine access privileges, 185
   security via, 888
SUPER privileges, 819
triggers for tables, 457
process list displayed, 837
PROCESS privilege, 3
PROCESSLIST versus thread report, 61
profile table for chapter examples, 155
   resetting the profile table, 237
profile.sql, 197
program variables, 12
programs (see APIs; scripts)
prompt command, 26
   resetting prompt to default value, 26
   user account in prompt, 27
prompt option, 26
prompt.json file, 39
prompts
   commands shown in text, 4
   customizing mysql prompt, 26
      resetting prompt to default value, 26
      user account in prompt, 27
   external programs from, 28
   interactively executing SQL, 14
      directly from command line, 15
      semicolon (;) at end, 14
   MySQL Shell customization, 39
protocol=tcp to force TCP/IP, 10
protocols
   Classic MySQL protocol, 34
      import_table requiring, 65
   MySQL Shell connected to MySQL server, 37
   URI scheme, 34
   X protocol, 34
public key certificate file, 880
public_key.pem, 882
pwgen system tool, 28
Python DB API support, xxiii, 153
   about, 74

about scripting requirements, 165
   connection objects, 166
   database connections with auto-commit disabled, 206
AUTO_INCREMENT value, 605
character set for client connections, 289
dictionaries, 166
   data validation lookup table into, 579, 580
download links, xxix
error handling, 166, 172, 177, 191
library file writing, 190
   data validation tests, 563
   library path, 183, 191
metadata
   result set metadata retrieved, 491
   row count of matched versus changed, 485
NULL values identified in result sets, 221, 224
Python mode (see Python mode of MySQL Shell)
regular expressions overview, 565
   table of pattern elements, 566
   validating data, 567
running Python programs link, xxvii
scripts
   Amazon review data load, 320
   connecting to server, 157, 165
   executing SQL statements, 196-199, 205
   library file of data validation tests, 564
   regular expression pattern tester, 567
special characters and NULL in data values, 210-215, 218
special characters in identifiers, 220
test data via data science modules, 73-82
transactions, 771
Python mode of MySQL Shell, 40
collections, 54
deploy_sandbox_instance, 67
\source command, 82
   scripts executed at startup, 83
SQL session, 44
table queries, 49
util object, 63
PYTHONPATH environment variable, 183, 191

Q

QUARTER() for quarterly sales reports, 446

query logs, 823, 824
  digests of query logs, 861
  log table rotation, 829
  monitoring client activity, 863
  monitoring the server, 843
  rotating, 827
  troubleshooting with slow query log, 861
query performance
  about, 779
    terms to know, 780
  full-text indexes, 797
  function-based indexes, 792
  geographic data and spatial indexes, 799
  JSON data, 794
  long-running queries
    EXPLAIN checking, 843
    server crash, 859
  maintaining indexes, 784
  multiple column queries, 787
  number of queries hitting server, 846
  optimizer histograms, 803
  primary key created for slow queries, 781
    primary key optimization, 783
  query slow with index, 786
  scanning data in ascending and descending order, 789
  stuck queries, 843
  trouble shooting with slow query log, 861
  writing efficient queries, 809
query plans
  about, 786
  EXPLAIN statement, 843
  optimizer histograms, 803
  prepared statements and, 214
  right index used, 786
query report, 60
query result rows numbered, 624
query results joined, 671
query results sorted, 246
  joins to control sort order, 669
  randomized, 690
question mark (?) optional regexp element, 567
quit command to terminate mysql session, 4
quote mark, double (")
  escaping in command line arguments, 523
  escaping in data values, 211
  identifier quoting if ANSI_QUOTES, 220, 291
  importing data, 529

  shell command arguments, 522
  writing string literals, 291
quote mark, single (')
  escaping in data values, 211
  exporting data, 538
  importing CSV files, 537
  writing string literals, 291
QUOTE() for SQL injection attack prevention, 469
quoting functions converting data values, 212, 214

R

RAND() for random numbers, 688
  card deck–shuffling algorithm, 691
  how random is RAND(), 689
  return result rows randomized, 690
  seed value sources, 689
  selecting randomly from set of values, 693
rand_test.py, 689
range of values, 676
RANK(), 702
ranks assigned to set of values, 701
read scale, 87
read_csv() (pandas), 76
recipes distribution from GitHub, xxvi
  additional languages, xxvii, 155
  batch files, xxvii
  cmdline.pdf, 155, 159, 161, 165, 171
    environment variables, 183
  CookbookCollection code, 72
  cookbook_utils.py library module file, 564, 567
  lib directory for library files, 155, 181
    column information structures, 501, 505
  patient name test data generator code, 82
    datasets for, 75
  scripts
    APIs, 155
    connecting to MySQL server, 158, 161, 163, 165, 167, 170
    connection parameters, 229, 230
    converting imported data, 22, 522, 563, 585, 592
    datafile columns in any order, 537, 592
    date processing utilities, 584, 589, 591, 592
    date values, 330
    duplicates counted, 723

events, 457
exporting query results, 540
guess table structure from datafile, 552
hex dumpers, 529
importing and exporting, 520
joins, 636
metadata, 482, 508
mysql, 2
parsing command-line arguments, 232
printable representations of file characters, 529
randomness of RAND(), 689
regular expression pattern tester, 567
routines, 457
security, 867
sequences, 596
statistical techniques, 675
strings, 281
table lookup for data validation, 580
tables created, xxvii, 2, 17, 197, 240
time values, 330
transactions, 762, 766
triggers, 457
validating data, 556
redirecting input to execute SQL from file or program, 16-18
redirecting output, 18
exporting to a file, 539
JSON format, 550
XML format, 545
mysqldump, 18
pager with redirection, 32
pipe from program, 18
sending output nowhere, 31
reformatting data
about, 555
date processing utility, 584
non-ISO date values, 589
source code in recipes distribution, 556
year values from two digits to four, 581
REGEXP(), 308-313
regular expressions (regexp)
data validation via, 565
Python regexp overview, 565
Python validating data, 567
script for testing patterns, 567
pattern matching, 308-313
overview, 565
broad content types matched, 568

case sensitivity, 312
date strings, 570, 573
email address validity, 574
multibyte character sets, 313
NULL values not matched, 312
numeric values matched, 568
POSIX character classes, 310
script for testing patterns, 567
table of pattern elements, 308, 566, 568
time strings, 572
URL validity, 574
rejecting bad data via BEFORE INSERT trigger, 478
relative values from cumulative values, 694
relay log files of replica server, 88
relay_log_info_repository, 112
remove() from collection (Python), 56
removing duplicate rows in results, 247
RENAME USER, 872
renaming database, 106
ReplicaSet automation via Admin API, 67
automating replication setup, 144
replicate-do-db configuration option, 102
replicate-ignore-db, 102
replication
about, 87
asynchronous, 115
master and slave terminology, 88
source and replica terminology, 88
automated replication setup, 144
binary log format configuration, 98
circular via chain of servers, 109
credential security, 123
data transfer security via TLS, 124
Group Replication plug-in, 118
existent data, 122
troubleshooting, 134
writing on multiple nodes, 122
IO and SQL threads, 127
troubleshooting IO thread, 130
troubleshooting SQL thread, 131
metadata repositories
relay log status, 112
replication credential security, 123
source server information, 112
multithreaded replica, 107
one source, one replica, 89
about position-based replication, 94
in-use position-based configuration, 92

new position-based configuration, 91
    replica via global transaction identifiers,
      94
performance tools, 140
replica server, 88
    check if running, 92
    replication filters, 100, 102
    start the replica, 92
    start the replica with secure credentials,
      123
    STOP REPLICA on parameter change,
      104
    update before COMMIT declared suc-
      cess, 115
replication filters, 100
    replica database with different name, 105
semisynchronous replication plug-in, 115
    failing back to asynchronous, 117
    variables that control behavior, 116
source server, 88
    metadata repositories, 112
    replication filters, 100
troubleshooting, 126-140
    Group Replication, 134
    IO thread, 130
    Performance Schema, 129-140
    SHOW REPLICA STATUS, 127-129
    SQL thread, 131
tuning for safety and performance, 90
two or more source servers, 111
replication-rewrite-db replication filter, 105
replication_applier_status_by_worker table,
    140
replica_parallel_type variable, 108
replica_parallel_workers variable, 107, 140
reports, 60
    built-in reports, 60
    \show, 60
      thread built-in report, 60
    \watch, 62
resetting profile table, 237
RESIGNAL command to raise error, 476
resources online
    book web page for errata and information,
      xxxi
    companion GitHub repository, xxvi
    email address regexp patterns, 574
    email address specifications, 574
    MySQL distributions, xxviii

MySQL Shell download page, 33
MySQL User Reference Manual link
    B-tree versus hash indexes, 780
    Boolean full-text operators, 327
    date and time value component extrac-
      tion, 348, 350
    date and time values, 330, 337
    DDL operations, 786
    encryption, 882
    error log configuration, 859
    full-text index restrictions, 799
    I/O utilization, 839
    JSON data type, 731
    JSON Path syntax, 738
    memory usage, 29
    mysql prompt customization, 27
    prepared SQL statements, 469
    roles, 885
    SELECT statements, 239
    server plug-ins, 858
    sql_mode, 558
    stored program error handling, 470
    stored routines, triggers, and events, 456
    time zones, 343
    window functions, 626
Perl CPAN site, 564
User Reference Manual link
    TO_DAYS() and Gregorian calendar,
      356
X DevAPI reference manual, 759
Result consisted of more than one row error, 24
result set duplicate data, 711
    (see also duplicates handled)
result set metadata, 481
    number of rows changed by SQL, 483
      matched versus changed, 483
    retrieving, 486
result set row numbering, 624
result-format command-line parameter, 57
resultFormat configuration option, 57
REVERSE(), 313
REVOKE, 871
right angle bracket (>) redirecting output, 539
RIGHT JOIN, 647
    other ways to write, 648
RIGHT(), 316
    pattern matches similar to, 307, 312
    sorting on substrings, 398
roles for user accounts, 883

ROLLBACK, 764
rollback() (JavaScript), 48
rolling back transactions, 47
root account
  CREATE USER and GRANT, 4
  mysqladmin, 9
  security, 868
  server administration, 817
rows inserted into tables, 5
  duplicates prevented, 712, 715
    (see also duplicates handled)
  tables created via scripts, 17
  timestamping row creation, 345
rows specified in SELECT, 240
  COUNT() for count summary, 419
  date condition in WHERE clause, 376
  metadata
    how many rows changed by SQL, 483
    matched versus changed, 483
    result set metadata, 486
  multiple SELECTs via subqueries, 262
  portion of results, 255
  removing duplicate rows, 247
  sorting the query results, 246
  subgroup summaries for sets of rows, 430
  time condition in WHERE clause, 379
  two or more SELECTs combined, 260
ROW_NUMBER(), 624
  ranks assigned to set of values, 701
Ruby Mysql2 API support, xxiii, 153
  about scripting requirements, 161
  AUTO_INCREMENT value, 605
  download links, xxix
  error handling, 162, 172, 176, 188
  hash for checking input values, 579
  library file writing, 187
    library path, 183, 188
  metadata
    current session status display, 506
    result set metadata retrieved, 490
    row count of matched versus changed,
      484
  NULL values identified in result sets, 221,
    223
  option files for connection parameters, 230,
    232
  running Ruby programs link, xxvii
  scripts
    connecting to server, 157, 161

  executing SQL statements, 196-199, 203
  special characters and NULL in data values,
    210-215, 217
  special characters in identifiers, 220
  transactions, 769
Ruby Mysql2 gem, xxix
  required for running scripts, 161
RUBYLIB environment variable, 183, 188
running averages, 696
runSQL() (JavaScript), 42
run_SQL() (Python), 44
Russian word sort order, 516

S

s (silent) option, 23
  suppressing column headings, 21
sales tax computation via stored function, 460
sandbox instance via Admin API, 67
  stopping instance, 68
save() (JavaScript), 69
scheduled events (see events)
schema
  getDefaultSchema() (JavaScript), 47
  URI parameter, 34
  validation supported by collections, 52
Schema class
  createCollection (JavaScript), 51
  get_collection (Python), 55
scheme as URI parameter, 34
screen output as default, 19
scripts
  about object orientation, 157
  Amazon reviews data script, 320
  API architecture, 156
    (see also APIs)
  api directory in recipes distribution, 155
  batch mode in mysql, 1
  column aliases, 244
  connecting to MySQL server, 153, 157-172
    disconnecting from, 157
    obtaining connection parameters,
      227-237
  converting imported data via cvt_file.pl, 22,
    522, 563
    guess_table.pl to guess structure, 551
  distributing SQL, 17
  error handling, 154, 172-180
    SQL statements, 199
  executed at startup, 83

executing code from a file, 16
  source command for mysql, 18
  \source command for mysqlsh, 82
executing SQL, 154
  categories of SQL statements, 196, 198
  error handling, 199
  no SQL statement terminators, 199
executing SQL statements and retrieving
  results, 196-210
languages supported by MySQL, xxiii, 153
  MySQL Shell, 2
  recipes distribution on GitHub, xxvii,
  155
library file writing, 155, 181-196
  access privileges, 185
  data validation tests, 563
  Go, 192
  location of library file, 182
  Perl, 185
  PHP, 188
  Python, 190
  recipes distribution lib directory, 155,
  181
  Ruby, 187
  test harness, 182
metadata directory of recipes distribution,
  482
NULL data values, 154, 210-219
  comparisons involving NULL, 251
  identifying in result sets, 221-227
persistent connections and temporary
  tables, 271
recipes distribution (see recipes distribution
  from GitHub)
resetting the profile table, 237
special character handling, 154
  data values, 210-219
  identifiers, 220, 292
  quoted string with same quote character,
  292
tables created via recipes distribution
  scripts, xxvii, 197, 240, 281, 419
test data via Python, 73-82
sdi file for copying MyISAM table, 278
searching in JSON documents, 738
searching in strings
  Boolean-mode searches, 325
  full-text searches, 318

Amazon review data for download,
  xxvii, 318
phrase searches, 327
requiring or prohibiting words, 325
script to load Amazon data, 320
short words return no rows, 323
substrings searched for, 314
SECOND(), 348
secondary indexes created, 783
seconds resolution in time values, 332
Seconds_Behind_Source inaccuracy, 96
Secure Socket Layer (SSL), 880
security
  about administrative access required, 868
  about MySQL version, 867
  about scripts in recipes distribution, 867
  certificates
    Certificate Authority (CA) file, 880
    creating self-signed, 882
    public key certificate file, 880
  connection parameters via script, 229
  encryption of network traffic, 880
  LOCAL data loading disabled, 523
  option files protected from other users, 14
  passwords
    changing your password, 876
    command line option, 9
    expiring, 875
    option file plain text format, 11
    PHP library files, 189
    policy for passwords, 872
    resetting an expired, 877
    strength check, 874
  replication credential security, 123
  roles, 883
  SQL injection attack prevention, 210-219
    about SQL injection, 212
    prepared SQL in stored procedures, 469
  stored routines for data security, 887
  user account management
    anonymous accounts, 878
    creating user account, 869
    mysql.user table, 868
    privileges, 870
    removing accounts, 872
    renaming accounts, 872
  views to secure data access, 885
SEC_TO_TIME(), 355
sed utility to change column delimiters, 21

SELECT
  about, 239
    documentation online, 239
  about SQL statement categories, 198
  column names in results, 242
    alias benefits in programming, 244
    alias restrictions, 244
    choosing own names, 243
  columns specified, 240
    all columns via asterisk (*), 240
    all columns via TABLE, 242
  creating database and setting up tables, 7
  CURRENT_USER() for client privileges, 506
  DATABASE() for default database name, 506
  DISTINCT for unique values, 418, 424
  ENGINE for storage engines, 763
  INTO OUTFILE to export to file, 538
    NULL as \N, 542
  mail table for chapter examples, 239
  multiple result sets via subqueries, 262
  multiple tables, 253
  result set metadata, 481
    matched versus changed, 483
    number of rows changed by SQL, 483
    retrieving, 486
  results assigned to variable, 23, 25
  results by default returned to client, 267
  rows from multiple SELECTs combined, 260
  rows from multiple SELECTs via subqueries, 262
  rows from portion of results, 255
    LIMIT value from expression, 259
    results in different sort order, 258
  rows specified, 240
    date and time conditions, 376
    removing duplicate rows, 247
  saving query results in a table, 266
    columns in different order from source, 268
  sorting query results, 246
  @@sql_mode
    ANSI_QUOTES, 220
  table storage engine identification, 273
  USER() for current user, 506
  VERSION() for server version string, 506
  VIEW simplifying table access, 252

select()
  JavaScript mode table queries, 47
  Python mode table queries, 49
self-joins, 652
  cumulative sums, 696
  running averages, 696
  successive-row differences, 694
semicolon (;)
  end of SQL statement, 14, 17
    BEGIN...END blocks, 456
    multiple SQL statements executed, 16
    none in API SQL statements, 199
    \G for vertical output, 15, 17
    \g synonym, 14, 17
  redefining mysql terminator for BEGIN...END, 458
semisynchronous replication plug-in, 115
  failing back to asynchronous, 117
  variables that control behavior, 116
sequences
  about, 595
    portability, 596
    scripts in recipes distribution, 596
  AUTO_INCREMENT columns, 596
    emptying table, resetting counter, 603
  counting with, 617
  custom increment values, 622
  custom sequence as id column, 629
  data type for, 599
    extending range of sequence, 610
  deleting rows without changing, 601
    renumbering an existing sequence, 607
    reusing values at top of, 610
  duplicate rows prevented, 713
  extending range of, 610
  managing multiple simultaneously, 614
  recursive Common Table Expressions, 626
  renumbering an existing, 607
    particular order, 611
  repeating sequences generated, 621
  result set row numbering, 624
  retrieving values, 603
    APIs, 605
    server-side versus client-side, 606
  sequencing an unsequenced table, 612
  successive-row differences calculated, 694
  tables associated via, 615
server administration
  about, 817

administrative access, 817
  SUPER access, 819
checking if server is up, 844
  "MySQL Server has gone away", 859
configuring server, 817
  runtime, 819
  server startup, 818
error log for troubleshooting, 859
log files, 822
  binary log, 823, 825
  error log, 822, 824, 843, 845, 859
  expiring log files, 826
  flushing log files, 826
  general query log, 823, 824, 843
  log maintenance needed, 824, 826
  monitoring the server, 843
  rotating log files, 826
  rotation automated, 828
  slow query log, 823, 824, 843
log tables
  expiring rows within, 828
  rotating, 828
monitoring the server, 833
  (see also monitoring MySQL server)
plug-in interface, 820
  built-in plug-ins, 821
  filename suffix on plug-ins, 821
  plugin_dir system variable, 821
  runtime installation, 822
  server startup, 821
server startup problems, 845
storage engine configuration, 829
server-cert.pem, 882
server-key.pem, 882
server_id for replication servers, 90
server_uuid global variable, 95
Session class sql() and runSQL()
  JavaScript mode, 42, 43
  Python mode, 44
session status Handler_* variable, 31
SET
  assigning values for SIGNAL statement, 474
  GLOBAL
    event scheduler enabled, 467
    general query log enabled, 863
    global time zone, 341
    LOCAL data loading, 523
    server administration system variables, 819

NAMES for connection character set, 288
  no GLOBAL or SESSION modifier, 819
  PASSWORD, 876
  PERSIST
    event scheduler, 467
    RESET PERSIST, 820
    server administration at runtime, 819
    since MySQL v8, 90
  preprocessing LOAD DATA input, 534
  SESSION versus GLOBAL, 819
  variable assignments, 25
SET columns
  concatenating element to existing, 318
  data validation using table metadata, 577
  members determined, 503
set() (JavaScript), 57
Shell class (JavaScript), 57
shell commands (see command line)
shell.status() command, 39
shortcuts (Windows), 8
SHOW
  about SQL statement categories, 198
  CHARACTER SET, 282
    default collations, 283
  COLUMNS for column definitions, 498
  CREATE TABLE for table definition, 277,
    498, 831
    mysql.user, 868
    NULL values for timestamp columns,
      347
    table engine used, 603
  ENGINE, 856
    INNODB MUTEX, 856
    INNODB STATUS, 31, 856
  GLOBAL STATUS, 506
    Buffer Pool allocation, 854
    connection limit, 852
    monitoring the server, 842
  GLOBAL VARIABLES
    Buffer Pool allocation, 856
    indexing engine minimum word length,
      324
    server global configuration variables,
      506
    slow query log settings, 861
    storage engine settings, 832
    time_zone, 341
  GRANTS, 871
  INDEXES for maintaining, 785

INFORMATION_SCHEMA instead, 482
MASTER STATUS
    binary log filters, 102
    binary log position, 91
    CHANGE REPLICATION SOURCE, 91
    File and Position values, 96
    GTIDs, 95
    Seconds_Behind_Source inaccuracy, 96
    stopping writes for in-use source, 93
PLUGINS, 821
portability of command, 482
PROCESSLIST for connection ID, 843
REPLICA STATUS
    replica filters, 104
    to troubleshoot, 126-129
SESSION STATUS, 506
SESSION VARIABLES, 506
TABLE STATUS, 273
VARIABLES
    event_scheduler, 467
    system variables, 820
WARNINGS, 24
    LOAD DATA diagnostic information,
      524, 531
\show for report, 60
    thread built-in report, 60
    help for options, 62
shutdown command requiring administrative
    privileges, 9
SIGNAL statement to raise own errors, 473
    warning conditions, 474
silent (s) option, 23
    suppressing column headings, 21
single quote (')
    escaping in data values, 211
    exporting data, 538
    importing CSV files, 537
    writing string literals, 291
skip-column-names option, 21
slash (/) pathname separator, 13
slave and master terminology, 88
slow query log, 823, 824
    enabling, 861
    log table rotation, 829
    monitoring queries, 861
    monitoring the server, 843
    rotating, 827
Snake-case syntax, 66
socket parameter, 10

URI parameter, 34
sorting query results
    about, 381
    as comparison, 391
    case sensitivity issues, 390
    collation affecting sort order, 283
      listing character sets and collations, 514
    custom sort order defined, 412
    date information, 394
      calendar day, 395
      day of week, 396
    displaying values, sorting on another, 387
    ENUM values, 413
    expressions for sorting, 385
    hostnames in domain order, 405
    IP addresses in numeric order, 408
    joins to control sort order, 669
    ORDER BY, 246, 382-385
    randomizing, 690
    special values to head or tail, 410
    substrings from values, 397
      given position within string, 398
      not given position in string, 401
    time information, 394
      time of day, 395
source and replica terminology, 88
source command (\.) for mysql, 18
    importing SQL data, 544
\source command for mysqlsh, 82
    importing SQL data, 544
SOURCE_DELAY option, 88
span of time versus interval, 362
spatial indexes and geographic data, 799
Spatial Reference System (SRS) of MySQL, 799
special characters
    APIs handling, 154
    data values containing, 210-219
    identifiers containing, 220
      quoted string with same quote character,
        292
    importing data, 529
    NULL data values, 210-219
SQL
    case insensitivity of keywords, 7
    distributing via script files, 17
    executing statements and retrieving results
      script, 196-210
    categories of SQL statements, 196, 198
    error handling, 199

exporting data in SQL format, 542
injection attack prevention, 210-219
  about SQL injection, 212
  prepared SQL in stored procedures, 469
NULL data values, 210-219
script for executing statements and retrieving results, 154
special characters in data values, 210-219
statement categories, 196, 198
statement terminators, 14, 17
  BEGIN...END blocks, 456
  multiple SQL statements executed, 16
  none in API SQL statements, 199
  redefining terminator for BEGIN...END,
    458
  \G for vertical output, 15, 17
table queries, 51
  collections (see NoSQL)
transactions, 763
writing efficient queries, 809
  (see also query performance)
X protocol, 34
\sql command
  JavaScript mode, 42
  Python mode, 44
SQL injection attack prevention, 210-219
  about SQL injection, 212
  prepared SQL in stored procedures, 469
SQL mode (see SQL mode of MySQL Shell;
  sql_mode)
SQL mode of MySQL Shell, 40
  escaping backslashes in pathnames, 527
  \source command, 82
  SQL session, 41
sql()
  JavaScript mode table queries, 42
  Python mode table queries, 44, 50
sql_mode
  --sql_mode, 558
  \G, 473
  data validity, 556
  SET GLOBAL at runtime, 558
  setting backslash escape mode, 527
  sql-mode equivalent at server startup, 818
square brackets ([ ])
  regexp pattern matching, 308, 310, 566, 568
    JSON array members, 736
    POSIX character classes, 310
    [^] not version, 308, 566

ssh for copying tables, 276
SSL (Secure Socket Layer), 880
standard deviation, 676
START REPLICA, 92
  replication credential security, 123
START TRANSACTION, 764
startup execution of scripts, 83
statement handles in Perl ($sth), 160
  result set metadata retrieved, 487
statistical techniques
  correlation coefficients, 686, 688
  counting missing values, 684
  cumulative sums, 696
  descriptive statistics calculations, 676
    sample versus population functions, 677
    subgroups of observations, 679
  frequency distributions, 681
    randomness of RAND(), 689
  linear regressions, 686
  random number generation, 688
    card deck–shuffling algorithm, 691
    how random is RAND(), 689
    seed value sources, 689
    selecting randomly from set of values,
      693
    set of rows randomized, 690
  ranks assigned, 701
  running averages, 696
  scripts in recipes distribution, 675
  successive-row differences calculated, 694
  team standings including games-behind,
    704
status variables
  monitoring the server, 840
  session status Handler_*, 31
STDDEV_POP(), 677
STDDEV_SAMP(), 677
storage engines for tables
  AUTO_INCREMENT columns and, 601,
    602
  available storage engines, 830
  buffer pool sizing, 853
  changing, 272, 603, 831
  configuring, 829
  identifying, 272
  InnoDB architecture, 857
  multiple in use, 830
  operational information, 856
  plug-ins installed listed, 513

showing default, 831
stored functions
  about, 455
  about stored programs, 456
    BEGIN...END compound statement, 456
    redefining mysql ; terminator, 458
  data security, 887
  error handling, 469
    benign errors ignored, 472
    GET DIAGNOSTICS to log all, 474
    No Data condition, 461
    No More Rows conditions, 470
    raising own errors, 473
    sales tax example, 461
  invoking, 460
  listing, 511
  READS clause, 458
  RETURN statement, 458
    returning only a single value, 462
  RETURNS clause, 458
  sales tax computation example, 460
  simplifying calculations with, 460
stored procedures
  about, 455
  about stored programs, 456
    BEGIN...END compound statement, 456
    redefining mysql ; terminator, 458
  data security, 887
  error handling, 469
    benign errors ignored, 472
    GET DIAGNOSTICS to log all, 474
    No More Rows conditions, 470
    raising own errors, 473
  IN parameters, 462
  INOUT parameters, 462
  invoking, 469
  listing, 511
  OUT parameters, 462
  prepared SQL helper function, 468
    MySQL Reference Manual link, 469
  "returning" multiple values, 462
stored programs
  about, 455
    database objects, 456
    default database, 457
  CALL to invoke, 457
  error handling, 469
    benign errors ignored, 472
    No More Rows conditions, 470

    raising own errors, 473
    sales tax example, 461
  privileges, 457
  redefining mysql ; terminator, 458
  stored functions (see stored functions)
stored routines defined, 455
  (see also stored functions; stored procedures)
strings
  about, 281
  APIs quoting all non-NULL values as, 214
  Boolean-mode full-text searches, 325
  character sets (see character sets)
  collation (see collation of strings)
  combining strings into one, 315
  comparisons
    binary strings versus binary collations, 284
    string values compared, 298
  CONCAT(), 242
    generating a unique table name, 272
  converting between ASCII, BIT, and hexadecimal, 302
  converting lettercase, 296
  converting to dates, 336
    ISO format for, 375
  data types, 281
    choosing which to use, 286
  extracting a substring, 315
  full-text searches, 318, 797
    Amazon review data for download, xxvii, 318
    phrase searches, 327
    requiring or prohibiting words, 325
    script to load Amazon data, 320
    short words return no rows, 323
  IP addresses as, 305
    INET_ATON() to numeric, 305
  length in bytes or characters, 283
    multibyte characters determination, 283
  LIMIT value from expression, 259
  NULL values mapped to "Unknown", 249
  pattern matching (see pattern matching)
  properties, 281
    binary or nonbinary, 282, 286
    collation, 283
  regexp patterns that match numbers, 568
  reversing, 313
  scripts in recipes distribution, 281

searching for substrings, 314
searching long text, 318
   Amazon review data for download,
      xxvii, 318
   phrase searches, 327
   requiring or prohibiting words, 325
   script to load Amazon data, 320
   short words return no rows, 323
server version, 507
sorting
   case sensitivity and, 390
   collation affecting order, 283
   IP addresses in numeric order, 408
   numeric order, 387
   substrings given position in string, 398
   substrings of values, 397, 401
special characters in data values, 210-219
special characters in identifiers, 292
writing string literals, 291
STR_TO_DATE(), 336
subqueries
   about, 253, 635
   LIMIT with results in different sort order,
      258
   multiple tables in query, 253
   query results joined, 672
   SELECT list subqueries, 659
SUBSTRING(), 316
   sorting on substrings, 397
      given position in string, 398
      not given position in string, 401
substrings located within strings, 314
substrings of values sorted on, 397, 401
   given position within string, 398
SUBSTRING_INDEX(), 316
   hostname component extraction, 406
SUM(), 422
summaries
   about, 417
   AVG(), 422
   candidate-detail lists and summaries, 656
   COUNT(), 419
      (see also COUNT())
      whether values unique, 438
   date-based or time-based, 445
   frequency distributions, 681
      (see also statistical techniques)
   grouping by expression results, 439
      logarithmic scale, 442

   noncategorical data summaries, 440
   holes in list filled or identified, 666
   MAX(), 421
      case sensitivity controlled, 429
      value from another column, 426
   MIN(), 421
      case sensitivity controlled, 429
      value from another column, 426
   noncategorical data, 440
   only groups with certain characteristics, 437
   per-group and overall together, 446
   query log digests, 861
   repetitiveness of a set of values, 442
   report with summary and list, 449
   smallest or largest of per-group summary
      values, 443
   subgroup summaries for sets of rows, 430
   SUM(), 422
   temporary result sets for, 452
   views simplifying, 426
SUPER privileges, 819
swappiness, 835
sys schema
   Buffer Pool allocation, 854
   built-in reports, 61
   memory usage, 29, 835
   monitoring the server, 841
system command (\!), 28
system variables
   about how server configured, 840
   local_infile error, 65
   local_infile for data loading, 523
   time_zone, 339, 341
system_time_zone variable, 341

T

t (table) option for output, 20
tab (\t), 293
tab character column delimiter changed, 21
tab-delimited or tab-separated (TSV) file format, 521
   converting imported data via cvt_file.pl,
      522, 563
   export tab-delimited, linefeed-terminated,
      538
   import tab-delimited, linefeed-terminated,
      522, 524, 527
      delimiters for specified, 527
tabbed command-line parameter, 57

table (t) option for output, 20
Table class
    JavaScript mode queries, 46
    Python mode queries, 49
table command-line parameter, 57
table scan, 780
TABLE to select all columns, 242
tables
    aliases, 643
    AUTO_INCREMENT column
        associating tables, 615
        emptying table, resetting counter, 603
        LAST_INSERT_ID() value, 24, 604
        retrieving values, 603
            (see also AUTO_INCREMENT col-
            umn)
    changes logged via triggers, 463
    CHECK constraints, 558
        listing defined CHECK constraints, 517
    checking if a table exists, 496
    column names in results, 242
        (see also column names aliased)
    Common Table Expressions
        data from MIN or MAX rows, 428
        Formula 1 fractional seconds, 333
        query results joined, 673
        recursive CTEs, 626
        sequence generation, 626
        summaries from temporary result sets,
        452
    copying a MyISAM table via sdi file, 278
    copying an InnoDB table via transportable
        tablespaces, 276
    copying via mysqldump, 273
        dropping table if exists, 274
        triggers copied, 274
    creating, 5
        guessing structure from data file, 551
        PRIMARY KEY clause, 6
        rows inserted, 5
        same structure as existing table, 265
        scripts in recipes distribution, xxvii, 2,
        17, 240
        temporary tables, 269
        transaction engine specified, 763
            (see also transactions)
    data from program via pipe, 18
    data from Python data science modules,
    73-82

data imported (see importing data)
DDL operations caution, 786
definitions
    data dictionary holding, 276
    DDL operations caution, 786
    SHOW CREATE TABLE, 277
    SHOW CREATE TABLE to show, 498,
    831
duplicate rows prevented, 712, 715
    (see also duplicates handled)
foreign keys
    adding to table, 475
    error handling with GET DIAGNOS-
        TICS, 475
generating unique names, 271
guessing structure from datafile, 551
id column, 197
    AUTO_INCREMENT, 268, 596
        (see also AUTO_INCREMENT col-
        umn)
    custom sequence as, 629
    multiple tables in query, 254
    retrieving values, 603
    saving query results to a table, 268
indexes for query performance, 781
JavaScript mode queries, 46
joins
    Cartesian products, 636
    comparing table to itself, 652
    finding matches between tables, 636-643
    finding mismatches between tables, 644
    indexes and, 639
    inner joins, 635, 638
    many-to-many relationships, 660
    multiple tables in query, 253
    one-to-many relationships, 656
    outer joins, 635, 642, 644
    Python mode table queries, 50
    self-joins, 652
    tables from different databases, 643
    "unattached" rows removed, 649
JSON data to relational structure, 748
listing tables in a database, 496
mail table for chapter examples, 239
metadata, 481
    column definitions, 498
    data validation using, 575
    identifying as parent via foreign key, 509
multiple tables in query, 253

names as variables, 25
NULL data values, 210-219
parent tables and child tables, 656
profile table for chapter examples, 155
    resetting the profile table, 237
Python mode queries, 49
saving query results in a table, 266
special character data values, 210-219
special characters in identifiers, 220
storage engine
    available storage engines, 830
    buffer pool sizing, 853
    changing, 272, 603, 831
    configuring, 829
    identifying, 272
    InnoDB architecture, 857
    multiple in use, 830
    operational information, 856
string columns
    binary and nonbinary, 287
    CHARACTER SET and COLLATE, 287
temporary tables created, 269
    caveats, 271
    query results joined, 671
    same name hides permanent, 270
    summary results via, 428, 434
timestamping last modification, 345
triggers (see triggers for tables)
VIEW simplifying access, 252
tablespace
    converting general to individual, 276
    discarding, 278
    FLUSH TABLES, 277
    importing, 278
    Information Schema query, 276
    InnoDB storage engine architecture, 857
    InnoDB tables copied via, 276
tabular or tab-delimited output, 19
TCP/IP
    default 3306 port number, 10
    forcing a TCP/IP connection to local server,
        10
team standings including games-behind, 704
temporal values (see date values; time values)
temporary tables created, 269
    caveats, 271
    query results joined, 671
    same name hides permanent, 270
    summary results via, 428, 434

terminators and delimiters to datafile lines, 521,
    527
    tab-delimited, linefeed-terminated, 522, 524
    terminators and delimiters specified, 527
terminators to SQL statements, 14, 17
    BEGIN...END blocks, 456
        redefining mysql terminator, 458
test data via Python data science modules,
    73-82
test harness, 182
test_pat.py, 567
TEXT string data type, 286
thread built-in report, 60
    help for options, 62
threads table in Performance Schema, 141, 849
TIME data type, 331
    (see also time values)
    fractional seconds, 332
time showing in prompt, 27
time values, 336
    about capabilities, 329
    about scripts in recipes distribution, 330
    age calculations, 368
    combining components, 352
    converting 24-hour to 12-hour format, 338
    converting basic units (days, seconds), 354
    current time determined, 344
        extracting components, 351
    data type to use, 330
    extracting part of, 348, 356
    fractional seconds, 332
        Formula 1 example, 333
    interval calculations, 358
        interval or span, 362
    pattern matching for temporal data types,
        308
    regexp patterns for, 572
    row creation and last modification time-
        stamps, 345
    row insertion and last modification time-
        stamps
        NULL values not allowed, 345, 347
    selecting rows based on, 379
    sorting by, 394
        time of day, 395
    sum of, 362
    summaries grouped by time, 445
    synthesizing a time value, 352
    time zones

client, 339
    converting from one to another, 342
    current date and time functions, 344
    server, 341
  validity checking of subparts, 584
time zones
    client time zone, 339
    converting from one to another, 342
    current date and time functions, 344
    server time zone, 341
TIME() component extracted, 348
TIMEDIFF(), 359
timeouts
    client timing out, 859
    server timing out, 860
TIMESTAMP data type, 331
    1970 through 2038 validity, 331, 357
    daily summaries, 446
    DEFAULT CURRENT_TIME STAMP, 345
    fractional seconds, 332
    ON UPDATE CURRENT_TIME STAMP, 345
    renumbering sequence according to, 612
    row creation and last modification time-stamps, 345
    time zone for client, 339
    UTC_TIMESTAMP(), 344
TIMESTAMPDIFF(), 359
    age calculations, 368
TIME_FORMAT(), 336
    combining components, 352
    extracting part of a time value, 351
TIME_TO_SEC(), 355
    interval calculation, 360
time_zone global variable, 339, 341
TINYBLOB string data type, 286
TINYTEXT string data type, 286
TLS (Transport Layer Security), 880
    replication data transfer security, 124
      checking if enabled, 125
    TLS connection for caching_sha2_pass-word, 90
TO_DAYS(), 355
    Gregorian calendar and later, 356
    only dates after Gregorian calendar, 361
tr utility
    postprocessing then redirecting to file, 540
    tab column delimiters changed, 21
transactions

about, 761
    scripts in recipes distribution, 762, 766
  commit synchronization between storage engine and filesystem, 112
  concurrency, 761
  global transaction identifiers, 89, 94
    replica set up using, 94
  integrity, 762
  JavaScript mode, 47
  mysqlbinlog verbose option, 137
  performing
    API overview, 765
    APIs mapped onto SQL, 767
    Go, 771
    Go context-aware functions, 772
    Java, 776
    Perl programs, 767
    PHP programs, 770
    Python programs, 771
    Ruby programs, 769
    SQL, 763
  Python mode applying to both tables or none, 50
  replica update before COMMIT success, 115
  storage engines
    choosing, 762
    InnoDB supporting transactions, 272
  table altered specifying engine, 763
  table created specifying engine, 763
  thread built-in report, 61
  transaction dependency, 108
Transport Layer Security (TLS), 880
transportable tablespaces to copy InnoDB tables, 276
tree traversal, 780
triggers for tables
  about, 455
  AFTER triggers, 465
  BEFORE triggers, 465, 560
  input-testing logic into BEFORE INSERT, 478
  listing defined triggers, 510
  logging changes to a table, 463
  mysqldump copying to dump file, 274
  TRIGGER privilege, 457
trim_whitespace() utility, 567
TRUNCATE TABLE, 603
Turkish word sort order, 515

U

underscore (_)
  character set for string literal, 291
  hostname containing, 879
  option file dashes interchangeable, 12, 818
  pattern matching single character, 103, 306
Unicode character sets, 282
  some cannot be used as connection charac-
    ter sets, 290
  USER() returning Unicode string, 294
UNION clause, 260
  ALL to not remove duplicates, 261
  column name aliases work, 261
  DISTINCT default removing duplicates, 261
unique identifiers via UUID(), 272
  (see also duplicates handled)
Unix
  1970 as start of Unix epoch, 357
  backslash as line-continuation character,
    523
  Ctrl-D to terminate mysql session, 4
  domain socket file, 10
  output column delimiter via postprocessing,
    21
  user-specific options in .my.cnf file, 230
UNIX_TIMESTAMP(), 355
unknown option error, 12
UPDATE
  about SQL statement categories, 198
  timestamping modifications, 345
update()
  JavaScript mode table queries, 48
  Python mode table queries, 50
updating replica with delay, 88
UPPER() to convert string to uppercase, 296
uptime of server, 844
URI for connection options, 34
  protocol selection, 37
URLs
  preprocessing via trigger, 479
  validity check via regexp pattern, 574
user account for MySQL
  about, 2, 4
  anonymous account management, 878
  connection parameters from command line,
    229
  creating, 2, 869
  mysql.user table, 868
    anonymous accounts, 878

privileges to create and modify database, 3-5
prompt showing user account, 27
removing accounts, 872
renaming accounts, 872
replication user, 90
  credential security, 123
roles, 883
security, 869
SELECT USER() for current user, 506
user as URI parameter, 34
User Reference Manual link (see documentation online for MySQL)
USER() returning Unicode string, 294
user-defined variables, 23
  case insensitivity of names, 25
  error if more than one row assigned, 24
  GET DIAGNOSTICS error information,
    475
  NULL before assignment, 24
  permitted where expressions permitted, 25
  SELECT results assigned to, 25
  SET statement, 25
username in user account, 3
UTC value for TIMESTAMP, 331
  client time zone, 339
  UNIX_TIMESTAMP and time zone, 357
UTC_DATE(), 344
UTC_TIME(), 344
UTC_TIMESTAMP(), 344
utf8mb4 default character set
  SET NAMES, 288
  utf8mb4_0900_ai_ci collation, 282
util object of MySQL Shell, 63
  \? for utilities supported, 64
utilities in MySQL Shell, 63
  \? for help, 64
UUID()
  returning Universal Unique Identifier, 272
  unique table name generator, 272
  UUID in human-readable format, 303
UUID_TO_BIN(), 303

V

v (verbose) option for mysql, 23
validate_password plug-in, 872
VALIDATE_PASSWORD_STRENGTH(), 874
validating data
  about, 555
    source code in recipes distribution, 556

CHECK constraints, 558
   listing defined CHECK constraints, 517
datafile checked via input-processing loop, 562
date subparts, 582
JSON data, 732
libraries of common tests, 563
   cookbook_utils.py module in distribution, 564, 567, 571
   Perl CPAN site, 564
lookup table for, 578
pattern matching for, 565
   broad content types, 568
   credit card numbers, 569
   date values, 570
   email addresses, 574
   numeric values, 568
   time values, 572
   URLs, 574
   ZIP codes, 569
server side versus client side, 556
sql_mode, 556
table metadata for, 575
time subparts, 584
triggers, 560
   (see also triggers)
values()
   JavaScript mode table queries, 48
   Python mode table queries, 50
VARBINARY string data type, 286
VARCHAR string data type, 286
variables
   autocommit session variable, 765
   case insensitivity of names, 25
   data types for strings, 281
   dynamic
      binlog_transaction_dependency_tracking, 108
      server_id for replication servers, 90
      SET PERSIST since MySQL v8, 90
   Handler_* session status variable, 31
   local_infile
      data loading, 523
      enabling, 65
      error, 65
   master_info_repository variable, 89, 112
   MYSQLSH_HOME variable, 83
   NULL before assignment, 24
   plugin_dir system variable, 821

relay_log_info_repository, 112
replica_parallel_type variable, 108
replica_parallel_workers variable, 107, 140
SELECT results assigned to, 25
semisynchronous replication plug-in behavior, 116
server administration, 817
server_uuid, 95
SET statement, 25
slow query log settings, 861
sql_mode
   data validity, 556
   setting backslash escape mode, 527
   \G, 473
status variable Handler_*, 31
time_zone, 339, 341
user-defined variables, 23
variance, 676
/var/log/messages system log, 859
VAR_POP(), 677
VAR_SAMP(), 677
verbose (v) option for mysql, 23
verbosity level of mysql, 23
VERSION() for server version, 507
version-specific applications for server, 507
vertical (E) option, 15
vertical bar (|) regexp pattern matching, 308, 311, 566
vertical command-line parameter, 57
vertical output
   MySQL Shell JavaScript mode, 57
   \G, 15
      all statements within session, 15
VIEW
   data access security via, 885
   listed or checked for existence, 497
   summaries simplified with, 426
   table access simplified with, 252
virtual memory utilization, 835

W

warnings shown, 24
\watch for repeated reports, 60, 62
web browsers
   opened to read HTML output file, 20
   phpMyAdmin interface, 2
   special characters in form input, 212
WEEKDAY(), 348
   Monday as first day, 372

WHERE clause
    aggregate functions not allowed, 427
    checking whether database exists, 496
    column aliases illegal, 245
    date and time conditions, 376
    listing tables in a database, 496
    rows specified in SELECT, 240
    user-defined variables, 23
wildcard syntax
    Boolean-mode searches, 327
    hostnames with % or _ within, 879
    JSON searches, 739
    JSON value extraction, 736
    replication filters on replica, 103
    SQL pattern matching, 306
window functions
    DENSE_RANK(), 702
    RANK(), 702
    ROW_NUMBER()
        query result rows numbered, 624
        ranks assigned to set of values, 701
    WINDOW keyword, 625
Windows
    backslash as pathname separator, 527
        LOAD DATA pathnames, 527
    caret (^) line continuation character, 523
    naming files, 527

writing library file (see library file writing)

X

X (xml) option for output, 20
X DevAPI, 67
    JSON as Document Store, 752
    reference manual online, 759
X protocol, 34
    mysqlx for, 34
xml (X) option for output, 20
XML format
    exporting data, 545
    importing data, 546
    output, 20

Y

yank_col.pl utility, 537
year values from two digits to four, 581
    MySQL automatically from 1970 to 2069,
        581
YEAR()
    extracting component from date value, 348
    pattern matching with nonstring values, 308

Z

ZIP code regexp pattern matching, 569

About the Authors

Sveta Smirnova is principal support escalation specialist at Percona. Her main professional interests include problem-solving, working with tricky issues, and teaching others how to effectively deal with MySQL problems, bugs, and gotchas. She's the author of *MySQL Troubleshooting* and has spoken at many events, including Fosdem, Percona Live, and Oracle Open World.

Alkin Tezuysal is executive vice president of global services at ChistaDATA, Inc. He has extensive experience in open source relational databases, working in various sectors, and large functions. With over 25 years of industry experience, he has led global operations teams for MySQL customers and users. He's a known speaker at worldwide open source database events.

Colophon

The animal on the cover of *MySQL Cookbook, Fourth Edition* is a green anole *(Anolis carolinensis)*. These common lizards can be found in the southeastern United States, the Caribbean, and South America. Green anoles dwell in moist, shady environments, such as inside trees and shrubs. They subsist on small insects like crickets, roaches, moths, grubs, and spiders.

Green anoles are slight in build, with narrow heads and long, slender tails that can be twice as long as their bodies. The special padding on their feet enables them to climb, cling to, and run on any surface. They range in size from six to eight inches long. Though, as their name implies, green anoles are usually bright green, their color can change to match their surroundings, varying among gray-brown, brown, and green. Male anoles have pink dewlaps that they extend when courting or protecting their territory.

Many of the animals on O'Reilly covers are endangered; all of them are important to the world.

The cover illustration is by Karen Montgomery, based on an antique line engraving from *Dover Pictorial Archive*. The cover fonts are Gilroy Semibold and Guardian Sans. The text font is Adobe Minion Pro; the heading font is Adobe Myriad Condensed; and the code font is Dalton Maag's Ubuntu Mono.

Lightning Source UK Ltd.
Milton Keynes UK
UKHW031155080922
408497UK00010B/23